Fodor's
ITALY

Fodor's Features

6

8

MAPS

Chapter 1

EXPERIENCE ITALY

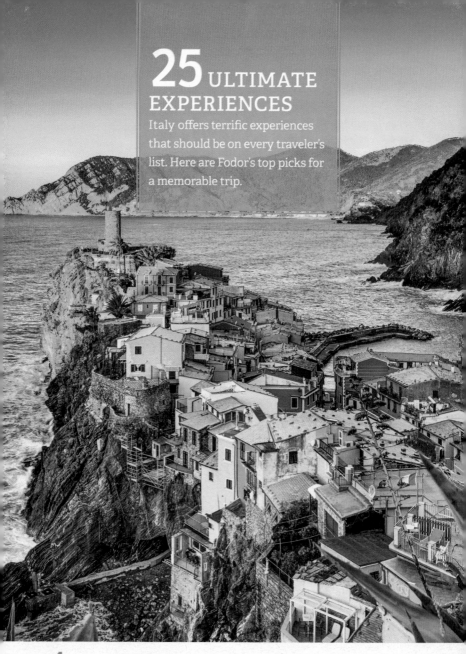

25 ULTIMATE EXPERIENCES

Italy offers terrific experiences that should be on every traveler's list. Here are Fodor's top picks for a memorable trip.

1 Hike the Cinque Terre

Walk the scenic footpaths that connect the five former fishing villages that make up the Cinque Terre; each one appears to hang off the cliffs, allowing for absolutely stunning views of the vineyards above and blue waters below. (Ch. 10)

2 People-Watch in Venice

Venice's Piazza San Marco (St. Mark's Square), flanked by the gorgeous Basilica di San Marco, is certainly one of the world's loveliest squares for people-watching. (Ch. 5)

3 Shop in Milan

In Italy's fashion capital of Milan, you'll find the highest of high-end designers in the Quadrilatero della Moda district, north of the Duomo. (Ch. 8)

4 See Assisi's Frescoes

The peaceful medieval town of Assisi is home to enormous Basilica di San Francesco, which includes 28 frescoes showing the life of St. Francis. (Ch. 14)

5 Sail Away to Capri

This fabled island off the coast of Naples has long stood for glitz and glamour. It's a lovely place to escape to. (Ch. 15)

6 Ponder *The Last Supper*

Restoration work has returned *The Last Supper* to its original glory, so the painting is amazingly clear and luminous. (Ch. 8)

7 Roam a Medieval City

Perhaps Italy's best-preserved medieval city, Siena's narrow streets are fun to explore. The Piazza del Campo is one of the most beautiful squares in the country. (Ch. 13)

8 Discover Ravello

Wander the Amalfi Coast's refined mountaintop village and discover lush, hidden gardens, medieval fountains, and sweeping Mediterranean views. (Ch. 15)

9 Rent a Villa in Tuscany

One of the supreme pleasures of a visit to the countryside of Tuscany is the chance to stay in a villa—preferably one with a swimming pool and vineyard views. (Ch. 13)

10 Admire the Architecture

The city of Lecce is a jewel of Baroque architecture, but that is by no means its only style. Stand in Piazza Sant'Oronzo to best see and appreciate the blend. (Ch. 16)

11 Marvel at Mosaics

Some of the greatest Byzantine mosaics can be found in the unassuming city of Ravenna. You can view the most elaborate ones in the 5th-century Mausoleo di Galla Placidia. (Ch. 11)

12 Go Wine Tasting

The Barolo region produces excellent wine and is filled with hill towns and vistas. Make an appointment for a tour and tasting at one of the many wineries. (Ch. 9)

13 Explore Lava Fields

The largest and highest volcano in Europe, Sicily's Mt. Etna, has moon-like dunes that you can walk across, or view from the comfort of a cable car (the Funivia dell'Etna). (Ch. 17)

14 Enjoy Magical Views

Nowhere inspires as many oohs and aahs as the magnificent town of Positano, with its pastel-colored houses seemingly spilling off the mountainside. (Ch. 15)

15 See Great Art

Florence's Galleria deglia Uffizi contains the collection of art from the Medicis, including Botticelli's *Birth of Venus*, Michelangelo's *Doni Tondo*, and Caravaggio's *Bacchus*. (Ch. 12)

16 Relax by the Sea

The lovely village of Portofino hugs the coast of the Italian Riviera, with the Santa Margherita cliffs on one side and the Ligurian Sea on the other. (Ch. 10)

17 Feel Romantic

Set on the shores of beautiful Lake Como, Bellagio is often considered one of the loveliest towns in Italy. Its steep streets, lined with cobblestones, are supremely romantic. (Ch. 8)

18 Visit a Volcanic Island

Just a ferry away from Sicily's northeast coast sit the Aeolian Islands, seven volcanic islands offering dramatic scenery and wonderful snorkeling and scuba diving. (Ch. 17)

19 Hit the Slopes

The gorgeous craggy peaks of the Dolomites make the perfect place for an unforgettable ski holiday in the winter or a rejuvenating hike in the spring and summer. (Ch. 7)

20 Toss a Coin in Trevi Fountain

The can't-miss Trevi Fountain, in Rome, is a Baroque fantasy of sea beasts, seashells, and mermaids in front of a triumphal arch. (Ch. 3)

21 Step Back in Time

The best-preserved excavated site in the world, the commercial center of Pompeii was frozen in time when Vesuvius erupted in AD 79. (Ch. 15)

22 Explore a Hill Town

Wander the narrow winding streets of the walled city of San Gimignano, which is filled with 14 soaring medieval towers (originally there were more than 70). (Ch. 13)

23 Enjoy the Coastline

In Italy's southern-most region of Puglia, around the heel of the boot, is a wonderfully dramatic coastline, with sandstone cliffs crashing into the ocean. (Ch. 16)

24 Lounge on a Beach

Sardinia is justly famed for its white sand beaches. Spend the day soaking up the sun on these beautiful strands. (Ch. 18)

25 Stand in Awe

Dominating Florence's skyline, the magnificent Duomo is an architectural marvel that took almost 600 years to complete. (Ch. 12)

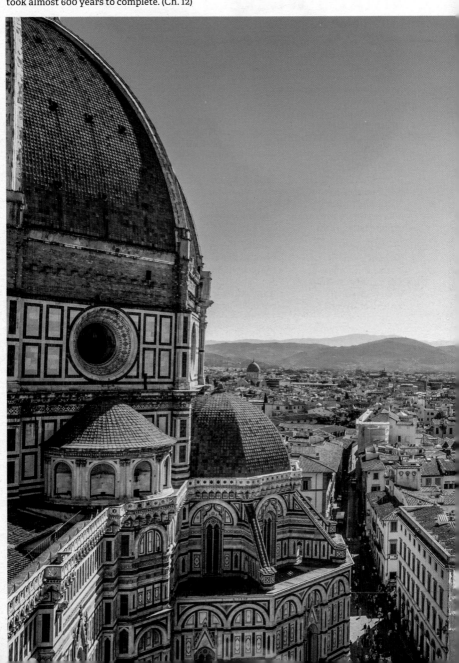

WHAT'S WHERE

1 Rome. Italy's capital is one of the greatest cities in Europe. It's a busy, modern metropolis where you'll encounter powerful evocations of its storied and spectacular past, from the Colosseum to St. Peter's.

2 Side Trips from Rome. The Eternal City is surrounded by intriguing towns and villages where you can explore without the crowds.

3 Venice. One of the world's most unusual—and beautiful—cities, Venice has canals instead of streets, along with an atmosphere of faded splendor.

4 The Veneto and Friuli–Venezia Giulia. The green plains stretching west of Venice hold three of northern Italy's most artistically significant midsize cities: Padua, Vicenza, and Verona. Farther north and east, Alpine foothills are dotted with welcoming villages and some of Italy's finest vineyards.

5 The Dolomites. Along Italy's northeast border, the Dolomites are the country's finest mountain playground, with gorgeous cliffs, curiously shaped peaks, lush meadows, and crystalline lakes.

6 Milan, Lombardy, and the Lakes. The lakes of Lombardy have been attracting vacationers since the days of ancient Rome. At the center of Lombardy is Milan, Italy's second-largest city and its business capital. It's also the hub of Italian fashion and design.

7 Piedmont and Valle d'Aosta. Here you'll find great Alpine peaks, one of the most highly esteemed food-and-wine cultures in Italy, and an elegant regional capital in Turin.

8 The Italian Riviera. Northern Italy's most attractive coastline runs along the Italian Riviera in the region of Liguria. The best beaches and temperate winter climate are west of Genoa, but the main appeal lies to the east, where fishing villages dot the seaside cliffs and coves.

9 Emilia-Romagna. Many of Italy's signature foods come from the Emilia-Romagna region. Bologna is a significant cultural center, and the mosaics of Ravenna are glittering Byzantine treasures.

WHAT'S WHERE

10 Florence. The hub of the 15th century Renaissance, Florence is awash with artistic treasures, exceptional restaurants, and first-rate shopping, as well as a never-ending stream of tourists.

11 Tuscany. Nature outdid herself in Tuscany. The central Italian region has Florence as its principal city and many other interesting midsize towns, but the region's greatest appeal lies in the smaller towns, often perched on hilltops and not significantly altered since the Middle Ages.

12 Umbria and the Marches. A number of the smaller towns, particularly Assisi, Perugia, Spoleto, and Orvieto, are fun to explore, and Umbria's Roman past is everywhere—expect to see Roman villas, aqueducts, and temples. Urbino's Ducal Palace reveals more about the Renaissance than a shelf of art history books.

13 Naples and Campania. Campania is the gateway to southern Italy. Dream away two magical weeks on the pint-size islands of Capri and Ischia and at the fabled resorts of the Amalfi Coast. Or explore the past at the archaeological ruins of Pompeii, Herculaneum, and Paestum. Naples is a fun, chaotic metropolis.

14 Puglia, Basilicata, and Calabria. The southernmost regions of the peninsula—Puglia, Basilicata, and Calabria—are known for their laid-back medieval villages, shimmering seas, and varied landscapes. The coastline of Puglia, along the heel of Italy's boot, is popular with beachgoers, but for the most part you're off the beaten path here.

15 Sicily. The breezes are sultry and everyday life is without pretense, as witnessed in the workaday stalls of the fish markets in ports all along the Tyrrhenian and Ionian coasts, bursting with tuna, swordfish, and sardines.

16 Sardinia. The beaches here rank among the Mediterranean's finest, and ancient sites, including the Carthaginian and Roman settlements of Nora and Tharros, add to the island's distinctive character.

Italy Today

ENDURING CUISINE

The old joke goes that three-quarters of the food and wine served in Italy is good—and the rest is amazing. In some sense, that's still true, and the "good" 75% has gotten even better. Those pundits would claim that ingredients that in the past were available only to the wealthy can now be found even in the remotest parts of the country at reasonable prices. Dishes originally conceived to make the most of inferior cuts of meat or the least flavorful part of vegetables are now made with the best.

But many Italians would say that the food in Italy is getting worse. There's a proliferation of fast-food establishments, and increasing tourism has allowed many restaurants to lower their standards while raising their prices. This is true not only in Rome, but in most other tourist centers as well. The good news is Italy is home to one of the world's greatest cuisines, and its traditional favorites still put meat on bones and smiles on faces. Italian restaurateurs seem determined to make the most of the country's reputation for good food. Although quaint, family-run trattorias with checkered tablecloths, traditional dishes, and an informal atmosphere are still common if on the decline, nearly every town has a newer eatery with matching flatware, a proper wine list, and an innovative menu.

This also holds for Italian wine. Today, through investment and experimentation, Italy's winemakers are figuring out how to get the most from their gorgeous vineyards. It's fair to say that Italy now produces more types of high-quality wine from more different grape varieties than any other country in the world.

SOCCER RULES

Soccer (or, as the Italians say, *calcio*—which means "kick") stands without rival as the national sport of Italy, though some complain that big-money influence and loose financial regulations are polluting the beautiful game. That aside, Italy did win its fourth World Cup in 2006 giving the country more world titles than any other this side of Brazil. More recently, Italy won the prestigious UEFA Euro 2020 championship (though due to COVID-19 it was played in 2021). Although the game is still played at a high level, its teams have not fared as well in European club competitions recently. More games in the schedule and a dwindling fan base mean fewer people are seen at the stadium. Still, fans can't stop watching the game on television.

AN AGING POPULATION

Italy's population is the oldest in Europe (as percentage of population)—the result of its low birth rate and one of the highest life-expectancy rates in the world. The median age of an Italian in 2015 was 45.9; projections for 2021 are 47.3. Chronic underfunding of the public healthcare system has left older Italians particularly vulnerable to COVID-19.

Italy's famously stable population is now aging and set to contract according to recent estimates, putting a strain on the country's pension system and on families because elderly family members are likely to live with their children or grandchildren in a country where retirement homes are rare.

The trend also has an impact in other areas, including politics (where older politicians are eager to promote policies aimed at older voters), the popular culture (where everything from fashion to television programming takes older consumers into consideration), and a kind of far-reaching nostalgia. Thanks to a long collective memory, it's common to hear even younger Italians celebrate or rue something that happened 50 or 60 years earlier as if it had just taken place.

THE BLACK-MARKET ECONOMY

Nobody knows how big Italy's black-market economy is, though experts all agree it's massive. The presence of the black market isn't obvious to the casual observer, but whenever a customer isn't given a printed receipt in a store or restaurant, tobacco without a tax seal is bought from a street seller, or a product or service is exchanged for another product or service, that means the transaction goes unrecorded, unreported, and untaxed. But that's all penny-ante stuff compared to what many professionals evade by neglecting to declare all they earn.

Austerity measures imposed in 2012 have led to much disgruntlement among the population; now most shopkeepers insist that you take a receipt. If you don't, you could be fined, as could the shopkeeper. These measures remain in place, but the country still struggles to meet the 3% limit to its budget deficit as mandated by European Union (EU) agreements, and it is pretty certain that Italy will continue to struggle to meet it in coming years.

A GROWING PARKS SYSTEM

Italy has 25 national parks covering a total of around 1½ million hectares (5,800 square miles), or about 6% of the entire surface area of the country—more than twice as much as 25 years ago.

Part of the reason for the expansion has been a growing environmental movement in Italy, which has lobbied the government to annex undeveloped land for parks, thus protecting against development. But the trend is a boon for visitors and nature lovers, who can enjoy huge expanses of unspoiled territory.

STAYING HOME IN AUGUST

Italy used to be the best example of Europe's famous August exodus, when city dwellers would spend most of the month at the seaside or in the mountains, leaving the cities nearly deserted. Today the phenomenon is less prevalent, as economic pressures have forced companies to keep operating through August. As a result, vacations are more staggered and more modest.

The loss of shared vacation time for Italian workers means good things for visitors: in August there's a little more room on beaches and mountains; in addition, cities promote events for nonvacationing natives. Summers in Italy now offer a plethora of outdoor concerts and theatrical events, extended museum hours, and local festivals.

MUSEI DIFFUSI

In recent years the idea of promoting tourism away from Italy's increasingly clogged destinations has spurred the idea of Musei Diffusi or "Scattered Museums." COVID regulations and social-distancing measures have only accelerated the need to support local communities and encourage visitors to seek out art and linger in sleepy, overlooked hilltop *borghi* instead of queuing for hours to glimpse Botticelli's *Venus*. The trend has evolved from Strade dei Vini (Wine Roads) and themed itineraries: now grand collections like the Uffizi are launching curator-led online exhibition tours and dusting off artworks in storage destined for display in municipal collections.

Best Hilltop Villages in Tuscany and Umbria

MONTEFOLLONICO, SIENA

Montefollonico's name alludes to textile workers, likely honoring the wool-working monks who settled the village in the Middle Ages, though the area has been inhabited for at least 60,000 years, from the time Neanderthals left behind artifacts that have been more recently uncovered.

ASSISI, UMBRIA

Assisi claims history as ancient as 1000 BC and is probably best known for its most famous resident, St. Francis, whose 13th-century basilica is now a UNESCO World Heritage Site. In fact, the entire village itself is, too. Plenty of other impressive churches, Roman ruins, and not one but two castles top the extensive list of architectural offerings of this ancient town. From ceramics to medieval weaponry, Assisi's artisan history remains strong. Cured meats and chocolate are popular here, so grab a snack between sword fights, and refuel on the Assisi ribbon-type pasta *stringozzi*, often served with Norcia black truffles, asparagus, or *piccante* (spicy) tomato sauce.

ORVIETO, UMBRIA

A quintessential medieval Italian village so evocative that dozens of Italian TV shows and movies have been filmed there, Orvieto is also a foodie's dream. Famous for both white and red wines, Orvieto's culinary classics run the gamut from boar and dove to pastas and pastries that will keep you eating around the clock. Above all, olive oil reigns supreme in this Umbrian village, which is probably the reason why Orvieto's culinary specialty seems to be . . . everything. While architectural wonders adorn the village (including the massive 13th-century Duomo), what's underground may be even more fascinating: a series of more than 1,000 tunnels forms a labyrinth under Orvieto, and much of it is now open to the public for exploration.

PITIGLIANO, TUSCANY

While most Italian villages are overflowing with impressive churches, Pitigliano may be most famous for its synagogue, drawing attention to its rich history of Jewish settlement and giving the old town its nickname of Little Jerusalem. Of course, countless churches dot the rest of this Tuscan village, as do a smattering of museums and other historic gems like the Palazzo Orsini, a Renaissance palace built on the ruins of medieval fortresses and containing both art and archaeological museums of its own.

SAN GIMIGNANO, TUSCANY

While most medieval towers have given way to war and erosion through the centuries, San Gimignano retains so many that it has been dubbed the Town of Fine Towers and its historic center is a UNESCO World Heritage Site. While packed with immaculate examples of medieval architecture, this village is among the more tourist-minded, with contemporary events like music festivals and art exhibitions, and plenty of modern conveniences and services for travelers. San Gimignano even has its own app.

SORANO, TUSCANY

Ham it up in Sorano, where the local ham is so revered they hold a festival for it every August. If you don't eat pork, don't worry; there are plenty of other local specialties highlighted in this festival, particularly dairy products including sheep's milk ricotta cheese and fruits, such as oranges—not to mention the ever-popular Italian liqueur, limoncello. Don't miss the Masso Leopoldina (sometimes called the Rocca Vecchia), which was once central to the defense of the town but is now a fabulous terrace for panoramic views of Tuscany (and a great place to swig another limoncello).

VOLTERRA, UMBRIA

Twelve miles from the better-known village of San Gimignano is the less visited (less crowded) Volterra. While there are some serious medieval remnants in this village, especially its narrow streets in the town center, it's much more famous for the historical periods before and after. Some of its ancient Etruscan fortification walls still surround Roman ruins, including an impressive amphitheater worth exploring (there are also remains of ancient Roman baths and a forum). The Florentine influence of the Medici family left behind some dazzling Renaissance art and architecture throughout the once bustling mercantile village. The alabaster trade remains strong today and provides beautiful souvenirs from this Tuscan treasure.

TODI, UMBRIA

Compact and ancient Todi is a hilltop citadel town with a strong whiff of a real-life fairytale medieval castle complex. Todi's beautiful patchwork architecture interweaves three sturdy walls, begun by the 3rd-century Etruscans followed by Romans and medieval dynasties. Starting at the café-community hub Piazza del Popolo, with an imposing 12th-century Romanesque-Gothic Duomo built upon a Roman temple, a maze of cobbled lanes and steep staircases fan out, inviting leisurely exploration. For grandstand views over roofs and the Umbrian hills beyond, climb the campanile of San Fortunato, and leafy walks abound in the Parco della Rocca, the city-wall park.

Best Beaches in Italy

TORRE GUACETO, PUGLIA
The color palate at Torre Guaceto is classic and calming: blue waters lapping chalky sands near the so-called Città Bianca (White City) of Ostuni. The beach is part of a marine reserve that extends 12 miles along the coast and 4 miles inland.

CALA GOLORITZÉ, SARDINIA
The beach's gleaming-white limestone pebbles, limpid waters, and dramatic geological formations make it a paradisiacal summer playground. The pinnacle towering over the cove is often dotted with climbers; dozens of nearby marine caves have wonderful natural light effects; and the surrounding mountainous national park is laced with challenging trails.

BAIA DEL SILENZIO, LIGURIA
Line a curvy bay with a sandy beach and warm-hued buildings, and you have Baia del Silenzio, one of Liguria's most captivating seaside amphitheaters. This very popular spot in the resort town of Sestri Levante is a fabulous place to people-watch.

CALA DEL GESSO, TUSCANY
Gorgeous Cala del Gesso is nestled in a relatively sheltered nook on southern Tuscany's Monte Argentario peninsula. Stake out a spot early in high season: the beach's shiny limestone pebbles and crystal-clear turquoise waters draw sun-worshippers and snorkelers aplenty.

ROCA VECCHIA, PUGLIA

A big draw at Roca Vecchia is the Grotta della Poesia (Cave of Poetry)—a natural ovoid sinkhole-pool set into limestone along the stunning Salento Coast. Swimmers like to dive in (a 16-foot drop), and scuba divers like to swim in (via an underwater sea cave).

TONNARA DI SCOPELLO, SICILY

Rustic houses, a church, medieval towers on craggy cliffs, and sea-stack rock formations make Tonnara di Scopello on the Golfo del Castellammare one of Sicily's most picturesque beaches.

SPIAGGIA NERA–CALA JANNITA, BASILICATA

Maratea is one of the Tyrrhenian coast's most alluring towns, where the fabulous Spiaggia Nera (Black Beach) has limpid waters and dramatic scenery. Spread your towel out on the dark volcanic gravel, and float amid igneous boulders.

Spiaggia di Fegina

SPIAGGIA DELLA MARINELLA, CAMPANIA

Near the town of Palinuro on the oft-overlooked Cilento Coast, stunning Spiaggia della Marinella mixes pebbles and volcanic sand against a backdrop of otherworldly rock formations.

MARASUSA, CALABRIA

The area around the lovely town of Tropea has some of Calabria's most recognizable seascapes, including those on Marasusa, where the water is a remarkable greenish-blue, the sand light-hued and ultra-fine, and buildings seem to grow from the rock atop sheer cliffs.

SPIAGGIA DI FEGINA, LIGURIA

Hikers tackling the famous Cinque Terre often take a breather on the beautiful, pebbly Spiaggia di Fegina. If you're feeling sprightly, clamber over *faraglioni* (sea stacks) amid the waves or trek down to one end of the beach to see the 46-foot Statua del Gigante (Giant Statue) hewn into the rock.

Best Vineyard and Wine Tasting Experiences in Tuscany

Castiglion del Bosco

ANTINORI

Antinori produces one of the best-known Super Tuscans, called Tignorello, a blend of Sangiovese with Cabernet Sauvignon and Cabernet Franc. They offer several options for touring the winery and cellars, always followed by a tasting. If you're inspired to purchase a bottle (or two), the wineshop is well stocked.

AVIGNONESI

The 16th-century manor house surrounded by vineyards makes a wonderful setting for tastings, and visitors can also see the vin santo aging cellar, the drying room, and the barrel tunnel while learning about the biodynamic wine-making process. Opt for special offerings like cooking classes and hot-air balloon rides.

BADIA A COLTIBUONO

Guests can choose from a number of tour and tasting options, including visiting the former crypt to see Chianti Classico aging in oak barrels or taking a walking tour of the vineyards, about a 20-minute drive from the abbey. In addition to its wine, the estate also produces olive oil.

BARONE RICASOLI

Not only is it the oldest winery in Italy, but Bettino Ricasoli, known as the "Iron Baron," is said to have come up with the original formula for Chianti wine in 1872. Pop by the wineshop for a tasting, or make an appointment for a winery tour.

CAPEZZANA

Visits, by reservation only, include a tour of their cellars, olive oil mill, and vin santo aging cellar, followed by a tasting of wine and olive oil. Cooking classes are also available. There's even a charming *agriturismo* with eight rooms where you can spend the night.

CASTELLARE DI CASTELLINA

Besides offering panoramic views, the winery is particularly known for its I Sodi di S. Niccolò Super Tuscan and Chianti Classico, along with vin santo dessert wine, all produced using sustainable agriculture. Make an appointment for an hour-long tour of the cellars followed by a tasting.

CASTELLO DI AMA

Ninety-minute visits (which must be booked in advance) include a tour of the cellars, the 18th-century villas and gardens on the property, and the artwork, and end with a tasting of Castello di Ama wines. If you can't get enough, spend the night in one of the five suites located in the Villa Ricucci.

CASTIGLION DEL BOSCO

Castiglion del Bosco is part of a full-fledged resort including the luxury Rosewood Castiglion del Hotel. Private tours, by appointment only, include visits to the cellars and vineyards plus tastings ranging from several wines to full vertical flights.

FONTODI

Tours, offered by appointment only, take visitors through the winery, cellars (some of their wines are being aged in terra-cotta pots), and bottling process, and end with a tasting. If you've come with a group, look into staying at one of their three villas nestled in the vineyards.

SALCHETO

Overlooking the hill town of Montepulciano, Salcheto is a biodynamic winery using fully sustainable practices, including energy from renewable sources such as solar, recycled materials in the winery building, and purified and recycled wastewaters.

Best Ancient Sites in Rome

COLOSSEUM

Perhaps the monument most symbolic of ancient Rome, the Colosseum is one of the city's most fascinating—and popular—tourist attractions. It officially opened in AD 80 with 100 days of games, including wild-animal fights and gladiatorial combat.

FORO DI TRAIANO

Trajan's Forum was the last of imperial Rome's forums—and the grandest. Comprising a basilica, two libraries, and a colonnade surrounding a piazza, it's connected to a market that once bustled with commercial activity.

PANTHEON

Built as a pagan temple to the gods, the Pantheon is Rome's best-preserved ancient site, perhaps because it was later consecrated as a church. Step inside and you'll be amazed at its perfect proportions and the sunlight streaming in from the 30-foot-wide oculus. It's truly a wonder of ancient engineering.

ROMAN FORUM

One of the Eternal City's most emblematic sites, the Roman Forum stretches out between the Capitoline and Palatine Hills. This vast area filled with crumbling columns and the ruins of temples, palaces, and shops was once the hub of the ancient world and the center of political, commercial, and religious life in the city.

CIRCUS MAXIMUS

It might be hard to imagine now, but the grassy area between the Palatine and Aventine Hills was once the site of the largest hippodrome in the Roman Empire. The huge oval course was rebuilt under Julius Caesar and later enlarged by subsequent emperors. During its heyday, it hosted epic chariot races and competitions that sometimes lasted as long as 15 days.

BOCCA DELLA VERITÀ

Legend has it the mouth in this ancient stone face will bite off the hand of a liar, and tourists line up to stick their hand inside the mouth and put it to the test. (Gregory Peck's character tricks Audrey Hepburn's Princess Ann into thinking he lost a hand inside it in a scene from *Roman Holiday*.) You'll find the enigmatic face in the portico of the Church of Santa Maria in Cosmedin, near the Circus Maximus.

TEATRO MARCELLO

It may look a bit like a smaller version of the Colosseum, but the Teatro Marcello was once ancient Rome's largest and most important theater. Julius Caesar ordered the land for the theater to be cleared, but he was murdered before it was built. It was inaugurated in AD 12 by Augustus and hosted performances of drama and song. It's kept that purpose even today, at least during the summer, when it hosts concerts.

APPIA ANTICA

Head to the southeastern edge of the city to Appia Antica Park and you can walk on the same stones that ancient Roman soldiers and citizens once trod—which are incredibly well-preserved. This ancient thoroughfare once stretched all the way to Brindisi, some 300 miles away on the Adriatic Coast. Today, the first 10 miles are part of a regional park, and it's a perfect spot for bike rides and picnics in the grass under the shadow of Rome's emblematic umbrella pines.

ARA PACIS AUGUSTAE

Now housed in a modern glass-and-travertine building designed by renowned American architect Richard Meier, the Ara Pacis Augustae has some of the most incredible reliefs you'll see on any ancient monument. It was commissioned to celebrate the Emperor Augustus's victories in battle and the Pax Romana, a peaceful period that followed. It's centrally located on the Tiber River and definitely worth a visit.

BATHS OF CARACALLA

A testament to ancient Rome's bathing culture, this site was essentially a massive spa, with saunas, baths, what would be an Olympic-size pool, and two gymnasiums for boxing, weightlifting, and wrestling.

Best Places to Discover Italy's Volcanoes

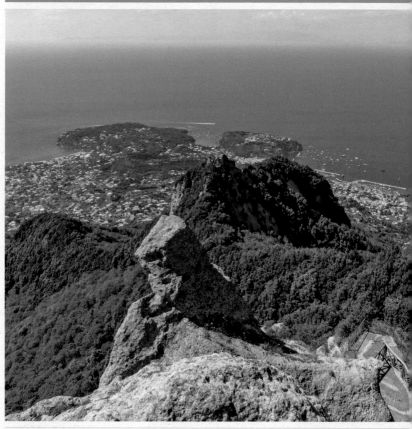

Ischia

CRATER RIM OF VESUVIUS

Peering over the edge into the 650-foot-deep crater you glimpse steamy fumaroles and may even feel the odd, unnerving earth tremor. Up here the views of the bay and the surrounding area—Pompeii, Herculaneum, Oplontis—hint at its immense eruptive might.

POMPEII'S PLASTER-CAST FIGURES

To get an idea of the merciless nature of Vesuvius, visit Pompeii to see the plaster-cast ghosts of some of its AD 79 victims. It's a chilling reminder of how the earth's awesome natural power can take lives in an instant.

CAMPI FLEGREI

The Campi Flegrei, or Fiery Fields, is a complex caldera volcano that some scientists now deem to be Europe's largest supervolcano.

FUMAROLES AND THERMAL SPRINGS OF ISCHIA

The island of Ischia sits within the Campi Flegrei caldera, whose gargantuan magma chambers fuel the

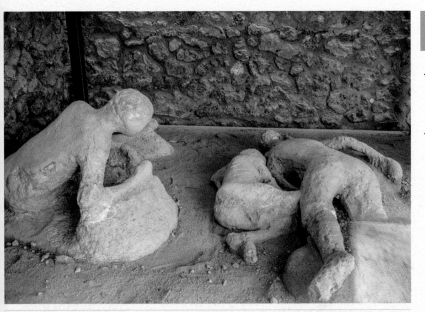

hydrothermal springs and fumaroles that soothe and heal thousands of spa-goers each day.

VILLA ROMANA
Although the Amalfi Coast is a limestone spur of the Apennines, without a fumarole or lava flow in sight, the communities some 13 miles from Vesuvius have been shaped by volcanology. By descending into the Villa Romana ruins by the beach at Positano, you are traveling through the volcanic debris spewed by the eruption of AD 79.

SOLFATARA CRATER
In this land scarred by constant tectonic activity, there is one steamy, fumarole-fizzing, and mud-bubbling 4,000-year-old crater that has become an emblem for volcanism in this part of the world. Solfatara was a bathing curiosity

on the Grand Tour and has appeared in numerous movies and music videos, including Rossellini's *Journey to Italy* and Pink Floyd's *Live at Pompeii.*

BAIA
Down at the shoreline of Baia, the sea has swallowed part of the town, and at nearby Pozzuoli, marine mollusk bore-holes 20 feet up the Roman columns indicate that the sea was once much higher. These two towns attest to the shifting water levels—the rise and fall of the land surface caused by the constant emptying and filling of the magma chambers below.

HERCULANEUM
Walking down the sloping path into the Herculaneum archaeological site, you are struck by the enormity of the eruption that buried

Pompeii. Scientists believe that Herculaneum was seared by a 900°F pyroclastic surge that roared down the mountain at 250 mph.

SAN SEBASTIANO
In 1944, liquid lava enveloped buildings and took off the church cupola, while walls of cooler lava crushed buildings. Today the curious can walk on those lava flows and enter modern buildings built in the 1950s and 1960s atop the lava and half-destroyed main street, Via Roma.

OSSERVATORIO VESUVIANO
Vesuvius remains the most closely monitored volcano on the planet; the research here started the science of volcanology.

Fantastic Cooking Classes in Italy

TASTE BOLOGNA (BOLOGNA, EMILIA-ROMAGNA)
Any cook worth his or her *sale* (salt) should spend time in Italy's foodie capital, and Taste Bologna provides a fulsome introduction to its riches. Combine their Classic Bologna Tour with the Cooking Class to get a feel for life in the market and in the kitchen.

MONTESE COOKING EXPERIENCE (SAN GIMIGNANO, TUSCANY)
Situated just outside San Gimignano, the well-loved Montese Cooking Experience is blessed with fabulous facilities, chefs, and views. The intensive four-hour Pasta Fatta in Casa session highlights not only long pastas, but also stuffed varieties.

TASTING SARDINIA: THE CENTENARIANS MEAL (CAGLIARI, SARDINIA)
The enlightening Centenarians Meal session, one of many offerings from Tasting Sardinia, takes its premise—that cooking with fresh ingredients is essential to living long and well—straight from the island's centenarians.

BUCA DI BACCO (POSITANO, CAMPANIA)
The venerable Hotel Buca di Bacco opened in the 1950s, but tucked within is the even older, eponymous restaurant, established in 1916, which hosts Buca di Bacco cooking classes. You'll learn about pizza- and pasta-making, as well as the restaurant's signature antipasto: *gamberetti alla Clark*. The dish was created for U.S. General Clark, who was stationed here at the end of World War II. When he requested a prawn cocktail, the chef combined shrimp, lettuce, and a sauce to create a version that reflected the local climate and wartime larder.

COOKING TAORMINA (TAORMINA, SICILY)
In addition to helping you hone your cooking skills, the animated young chef at Cooking Taormina explains the many exotic influences that shaped *la cucina sicili-ana*. The first part of the lesson stimulates the senses on a visit to Taormina's produce and fish market. Afterward, you'll use your fresh ingredients in classic Sicilian specialties.

MAMMA ISA'S COOKING SCHOOL (PADUA, VENETO)
In Padua, a 30-minute drive inland from Venice, Mamma Isa and family offer a tempting array of courses—from half-day introductory lessons to six-day extravaganzas—covering many of the Veneto region's culinary traditions. There are weeks' worth of classes, including bread- and pasta-making, vegan

and vegetarian cooking, and dessert and pastry creation—even how to prepare the perfect risotto.

BARI WALKING TOUR WITH PASTA-MAKING (BARI, PUGLIA)

Deep in Bari's atmospheric *centro storico*, you'll learn about the art of making orecchiette, which is still practiced on the city's streets. The two-hour Bari Walking Tour with Pasta-Making starts with a tour of the city and its food market before heading to the chef's house to get fiddly with the dough. By the end of the session, you will have created hundreds of edible "little ears" to enjoy with a few bottles of Puglia's red Primitivo wine during the all-important tasting lunch.

COOK WITH US IN ROME (ROMA, LAZIO)

The enthusiasm of the two Roman chefs who conduct the Cook with Us in Rome classes is contagious, making it truly fun to learn about the city's food in a morning or afternoon session.

ITALIANNA COOKING CLASS (ALBA, PIEDMONT)

Renowned for its rich tradition of food and wine, greatly influenced by nearby France, Piedmont is a fine destination for a foodie adventure. ItaliAnna's beginner pasta-making class, for example, is fun, flour-filled, and interactive—and just one of their offerings.

SLOW COOKING CLASS (PACIANO, UMBRIA)

The family-run Country Slow Living is based in an organic olive press, Il Fontanaro. Its most popular offering involves a tour of the mill, a rummage around the verdant market garden to select ingredients, and then a chance to get messy: mixing and kneading dough, shaping pasta, and creating the accompanying *sugo* (sauce) from scratch.

Architectural Wonders in Venice

PONTE DI RIALTO

The iconic Ponte di Rialto was completed in 1591. Its generous arch, central portal, and Renaissance arcade make it appear so beautifully balanced that Palladio himself would surely have approved.

SAN FRANCESCO DELLA VIGNA

The harmonious combination of architectural designs by two Renaissance maestri and the tranquil neighborhood setting make this church a wonderful place to escape the crowds.

MOLINO STUCKY

This behemoth, neo-Gothic warehouse-like building, formerly a flour mill and pasta factory, on the western end of the Giudecca certainly stands out on the Venetian skyline.

SANTA MARIA DELLA SALUTE

One of the city's most beloved and iconic churches, La Salute was built to mark the end of the 1630 plague that took almost 50,000 Venetian lives.

PUNTA DELLA DOGANA

There has been a Punta della Dogana (Sea Customs House) situated between the Grand and Giudecca Canals since the 15th century, although the building you see today was designed in the 1860s. Above the entrance tower, two Atlases lift a bronze sphere topped by the figure of Fortune.

ARSENALE

For centuries, the colossal Arsenale complex of shipyards, warehouses, and armories was Europe's largest military-industrial compound. Although many areas are still cordoned off as military zones, the southern side is open to the public during the Biennale di Arte.

JEWISH GHETTO

Originally the site of a foundry (*geto* in the local dialect), both the atmosphere and the architecture set the Jewish Ghetto apart: *palazzi* and *case* are taller here than elsewhere, with story upon story piled on high in an effort to make the best use of limited space.

PALAZZO DUCALE
Adorned with a series of soaring Gothic arches topped by an ornately columned arcade, the labyrinthine Palazzo Ducale has a wedding-cake-like delicacy when viewed from the Piazza San Marco or the waterside Bacino di San Marco.

MADONNA DELL'ORTO
An alluring, redbrick Gothic church with ornate marble decoration, it was dedicated to St. Christopher, the patron saint of travelers, until a Madonna statue was found in a nearby *orto* (kitchen vegetable garden).

CA' DA MOSTO
As you drift along the Grand Canal, you'll see palazzi far more eye-catching than the Ca' da Mosto, but none more enduring—the crumbling Byzantine-style palace has been here since the 13th century. The ground and first floors are an example of a *casa-fondaco*.

What to Watch and Read

ITALIAN FOLKTALES
BY ITALO CALVINO

In 1956 the celebrated, Cuban-born and Liguria-raised, magical realist published this fabulous collection of some 200 traditional folktales from across the archipelago. The prose in the 800-page *Fiabe italiane* tome is simple yet evocative, and the stories appeal to young and old alike. They're largely fantastical morality tales involving love, loss, revenge, and adventure on the part of kings, princesses, saints, and peasants. The book is a fabulous bedtime or beach read.

AMARCORD, DIRECTED
BY FEDERICO FELLINI

Amarcord ("I remember," in the Romagnol dialect) is filled with comic archetypes and dreamlike excursions inspired by Fellini's 1930s adolescence in Rimini. The rosy-cheeked protagonist, Titta, and his pals have humorous encounters with authority figures—pompous schoolteachers, frustrated fathers, cruel Fascist officials—as well as with the buxom hairdresser, Gradisca. The 1973 movie, which won the Oscar for Best Foreign Language Film, offers poignant, entertaining, and often bonkers insight into the Italian psyche, family dynamics, and interwar society. Nino Rota's wistful soundtrack adds to the feeling of nostalgia.

THE ITALIANS BY JOHN HOOPER

In this 2015 book, longtime Rome correspondent John Hooper addresses the complexities of contemporary Italy, attempting to reveal "what makes the Italian tick." Here you'll learn the lexicon needed to negotiate and understand Italian culture. Of course, food, sex, and the weather—among other things—are heartily embraced in everyday life, but there is also an *amaro* (bitter) side. Hooper illustrates how the power of the *famiglia* (family) and the *chiesa* (church) has produced a society in which *furbizia* (cunning) is rewarded and meritocracy is replaced with *raccomandazioni* (favors) to get ahead in the world.

THE LEOPARD
BY GIUSEPPE TOMASI
DI LAMPEDUSA

Il gattopardo, an Italian literary classic, chronicles the tumultuous, revolutionary years of the Risorgimento (1860s–early 20th century). Lampedusa was the last in a line of minor princes, and the novel, borne of a lengthy depression, was published in 1958, a year after his death. Set in Sicily, the epic story of decay amid a changing society centers on the ebbing influence and power of Don Fabrizio, Prince of Salina, and his family, and hints at the emergence of the Mafia. One particularly insightful quote in the book—spoken by the prince's young nephew, Tancredi—sheds light on how Italy adapts to shifting political forces and class struggle: "For everything to stay the same, everything must change."

COSA NOSTRA BY JOHN DICKIE

Journalist and academic John Dickie packs a lot of gruesome detail into this fast-paced history of the Mafia. He traces the Cosa Nostra's origins during the Risorgimento years, its infiltration and corruption of the First Republic, and the curious and notorious role of the town of Corleone in its development. Dickie also recounts the organization's birth and rise in America, the Mafia Wars, and the recent crises and tragedies connected to Italy's corrupt political system.

THE CONFORMIST, DIRECTED BY BERNARDO BERTOLUCCI

Il conformista, Bertolucci's stylish psychological thriller set in 1930s Fascist Italy, is considered a postwar cinematic classic. As its name suggests, the 1970 film tackles the issue of conformity through the lens of the cruel, febrile political atmosphere created by Mussolini and his followers. Despite its dark themes, the movie is beautifully lit and shot, filled with vibrant colors, exquisite costuming, and atmospheric locations. It has inspired many directors of the American New Wave and beyond, including Martin Scorsese, Francis Ford Coppola, and the Coen brothers.

DELIZIA! BY JOHN DICKIE

If you think you know all there is to know about Italian food, you'll think again after reading this book. Dickie's gastronomic journey across the regions of Italy through the ages covers everything from *pastasciutta* in 12th-century Palermo to today's Slow Food movement in Turin. Carry this book with you as you travel, so you can compare your menu to, say, that for a 1529 Ferrara banquet, which featured "105 soused sea bream" and "15 large salted eels" for starters, followed by "104 roasted capon livers" and "sweet pastry tarts deep-filled with the spleens of sea bass, trout, pike and other fish." *Che delizia!*

THE GREAT BEAUTY, DIRECTED BY PAOLO SORRENTINO

Although directed by a Neapolitan, this Oscar-winning 2013 film is set in Rome and serves as a kind of contemporary *La Dolce Vita*. The lead character in *La grande bellezza*, Jep Gambardella (Toni Servillo), is an aging hedonistic journalist, who, while pining for his glory days, comes to realize the superficiality of his bourgeois lifestyle. Beset by Roman ennui after his raucous rooftop 65th-birthday bash, Jep goes in search of beauty beyond the vanity of his milieu.

THE NEAPOLITAN NOVELS

Elena Ferrante's novels (2012–15) and the HBO TV series bring multilayered postwar Naples to life, going beyond postcard beauty to portray the grim, savage reality of growing up in a rough *rione* (district). The four books explore the complexities of friendship and Italian society. With vivid depictions—mixing the palatial and the squalid—the pseudonymous author details the lifetime bond and inner lives of Elena and Lila and their interactions with a cast of characters across Italy as well as in Naples.

1992, 1993, AND 1994

The ten-episode television series *1992* and its follow-ups, *1993* and *1994*, (originally aired in 2015, 2017, and 2019, respectively) are political dramas that follow the intertwined lives of six people amid the tumult of early-1990s Italy. Massive cracks appear in the postwar political compromise, with the *Mani Pulite* (Clean Hands) investigation led by prosecutor Antonio Di Pietro initiating the fall of the First Republic. As the country is rocked by the so-called *Tangentopoli* (Bribesville) scandal, marketing man Stefano Accorsi sees an opportunity for an outside figure to seize power. And so up steps media tycoon Silvio Berlusconi and his populist Forza Italia party. Sound familiar?

Making the Most of Your Euros

TRANSPORTATION

Italy's state-sponsored train system has been given a run for its money by a private company. Sadly, the competitor (Italo) only operates major, high-speed connections (such as Rome to Naples, Florence to Venice, Milan to Bologna) and not local routes. Because of the competition, Trenitalia and Italo engage in price wars, which only plays to the consumer's advantage; depending on time of day and how far in advance you purchase the tickets, great bargains can be had.

No such good news exists for the *regionali* trains. These are trains connecting cities, highly frequented by commuters and used often by visitors who want to get to less visible towns. These trains are habitually late and almost always crowded. Patience is a virtue, and much-needed when taking them, particularly during high season.

FOOD AND DRINK

Always remember, when you enter a bar, that there is almost always a two-tier pricing system: one if you stand, and one if you sit. It's always cheaper to stand, but sometimes sitting is not only necessary, but fun: you can relax and watch the world go by.

Italians love a good sandwich for lunch. Seek out popular sandwich shops (long lines signify that the place is worth visiting) or go to a *salumeria* (delicatessen) and have them make a sandwich for you. It will be simple—cheese and/or cold cuts with bread, no trimmings—but it will be made while you wait, fresh, delicious, and inexpensive.

SIGHTS

There are plenty of free wonderful things to see. Visit the Musei Vaticani, the Uffizi, and the Accademia in Florence (book ahead whenever possible), but don't forget that many artistic gems are found in churches, most of which can be visited with no charge (some of Caravaggio's best work can be found in various churches in Rome). Also consider renting audio guides if you want direction to any specific place; if you find the idea of joining an organized tour daunting, most museums sell official guidebooks that can help you target what to see. Walking in *centri storici* (historic centers) is also a joy, and free. Seek out piazzas, climb towers, and look for views.

LODGING

High season in Italy runs from Easter to mid-October. If you want to have Florence practically to yourself, come in November or February (most Italian cities are very crowded during the Christmas holidays, which begin around Christmas and finish on January 6). Many hotels in cities offer bargain rates in July and August because most people are off to the beach or the mountains. Remember to factor in great heat and massive crowds, along with the money you'll save. If you decide to travel then, ensure that you have access to a pool and/or air-conditioning.

A great budget-conscious way to travel is via Airbnb (www.airbnb.com). You can sleep on someone's couch, rent a private room in an apartment (sometimes with en suite bathroom), or spread out in an entire apartment or house. One of the best things about Airbnb is that many of these accommodations come with refrigerators and kitchens, which means you don't have to spend all your money eating out.

In general, whatever your lodging choice, book sooner rather than later. You'll often find better deals that way.

Chapter 2

TRAVEL SMART

Updated by
Fergal Kavanaugh

★ **CAPITAL:**
Rome

👥 **POPULATION:**
60,396,434

💬 **LANGUAGE:**
Italian

$ **CURRENCY:**
Euro

☎ **COUNTRY CODE:**
39

⚠ **EMERGENCIES:**
112

🚗 **DRIVING:**
On the right

⚡ **ELECTRICITY:**
220v/50 cycles; electrical
plugs have two round prongs

🕐 **TIME:**
6 hours ahead of New York

🌐 **WEB RESOURCES:**
www.italia.it
www.beniculturali.it

ITALY

★ Rome

SARDINIA

SICILY

Mediterranean Sea

Know Before You Go

A TALE OF TWO COUNTRIES

Italy as we know it is just over 160 years old, united by Giuseppe Garibaldi in 1861, and traditions and customs die hard. Differences and rivalries between the wealthier north and the more relaxed south abound, but you will need to spend time in both for the full Italian experience.

DRINK YOUR FILL

Bottled water is available everywhere but often at an inflated price. Carry a refillable bottle and fill up for free at the strategically placed water fountains in cities. In restaurants you can ask for tap water (*acqua del rubinetto*), although you may have to insist.

GO FOOTBALL CRAZY

Soccer—*calcio*—is taken very seriously in Italy, with rivalries running deep. A little knowledge of a local team's performance makes for great conversation. Just avoid wearing your Juventus shirt in Naples if you want to make new friends.

BOOK IN ADVANCE

Avoid waiting in line for hours by buying museum tickets online before your visit. Also, the earlier you buy train tickets, the less expensive they're likely to be. Trenitalia and Italo offer substantial first-come, first-served discounts on high-speed services; check their websites, and prepare to be flexible with your travel times. Discounts aren't offered on regional trains, and neither is seat reservation. Unless bought online, tickets for regional trains must be stamped before boarding.

TAKE THE BACK ROADS

So you've rented a car. Why stick to the highways? Much of Italy's beauty is along winding mountain roads or coastal secondary routes, so take your time and wander a little. Not only will you save on tolls, but you'll save on fuel, too, as gas prices are generally lower than on the *autostradas*. Also, if you're renting a car between November 15 and April 15, remember to ask for snow chains (obligatory on many roads).

EAT FOR (NEARLY) NOTHING

The *aperitivo* is a staple of many areas of the north, where, for little more than the price of a drink, you can partake of a vast buffet to substitute for your evening meal. Bars vie with each other to provide the best array of pasta dishes, *pizzette*, and panini, so check out a few of them before sitting down.

PLAN YOUR DAY

Although breakfast (*la colazione*) is generally served from 7 to 10:30, other mealtimes vary by region. In the north, lunch (*il pranzo*) is noon to 2, whereas restaurants in the south often serve it until 3. You may have difficulty finding dinner (*la cena*) in the north after 9 pm, when most southerners are just sitting down to eat (restaurants there tend not to open until 7:30). And shoppers take note: many stores close from 1 to 4:30.

LACE UP YOUR WALKING SHOES

The best—and often the only—way to see a city is on foot. Public transport works well (albeit generally better in the north), and in recent years many city and town centers have been pedestrianized. Parking costs can add up, so when possible don your most comfortable shoes and prepare to pound the pavement. Fall in with a weekend afternoon *passeggiata* in smaller towns, where Italians stroll up and down the main street dressed in their Sunday best.

DRINK LOCAL

Italy offers a vast array of fine wines, with each region boasting its own appellation. While you may see Chianti on a wine list in Catania, it will probably be no different to what you find at home; for a more authentic taste of the area, try a local Sicilian wine instead.

YOU GET A COFFEE IN A BAR

Coffee culture is different here. Italians take their single-shot espresso standing at a bar—where snacks and alcoholic drinks are also served, and which usually closes in the evening. Pay the cashier, then set your receipt on the counter and place your order. If you choose to sit, there is usually a surcharge, whether there is table service or not. Also, if you order a latte you'll get a glass of milk.

NEVER PASS A RESTROOM

Public restrooms in train stations usually cost €1, and bars frown on the use of theirs without making a purchase, so before you leave the hotel, restaurant, or museum, use the facilities.

DAY TRIPPER

Lodging in tourist hot spots is at a premium during high season, but deals can be found a little farther from the action. Consider booking outside town and taking a local train or bus to see the sights—you might miss the evening atmosphere, but you'll have more to spend on lunch.

TAKE YOUR TIME

The Italian experience differs from region to region. Try to plan an itinerary that leaves time to explore each destination at leisure. Sure, quick in-and-out visits to cities will allow you to see the major sights, but rushing things means missing out on each area's unique atmosphere.

BE ITALIAN

Food is one of Italy's defining features, and locals continue to be horrified by the idea of pineapple on pizza or (heaven forbid!) ketchup on pasta. You don't need a knife to eat spaghetti (although using a spoon to help wind the pasta around a fork is allowed), and it's fine to pick your pizza up. Most restaurants set a per-person fee for *pane e coperto* (bread and cover charge), although waiters also appreciate a tip—which is standard (around 10%) in the south.

BEWARE OF SCAMS

Larger train stations are notorious for porters insisting on carrying your bags, then charging a fee, so be firm if you're not interested. Also, be careful where you store your wallet and valuables and avoid purchasing from illegal street vendors.

LOOK INTO SIGHT PASSES

Many cities and towns sell multiday passes for access to different museums and sites. These offer great savings if you plan to visit several attractions; some include deals on public transport.

LEARN THE LINGO

Most Italians have some command of English, although this isn't a fail-safe rule, particularly in the south. You can get by on hand gestures and pointing, but a *grazie* or *buongiorno* here and there can't hurt.

Getting Here and Around

Air

Most nonstop flights between North America and Italy serve Rome's Aeroporto Internazionale Leonardo da Vinci (FCO), better known as Fiumicino, and Milan's Aeroporto Malpensa (MXP), though the airports in Venice, Pisa, and Naples also accommodate nonstop flights from the United States. Flying time to Milan or Rome is approximately 8–8½ hours from New York, 10–11 hours from Chicago, and 11½ hours from Los Angeles.

Alitalia has direct flights from London to Milan and Rome, while British Airways and smaller budget carriers provide services between Great Britain and other locations in Italy. EasyJet connects London's Gatwick and Stansted Airports with 15 Italian destinations. Ryanair flies from Stansted to 21 airports. Since tickets are frequently sold at discounted prices, investigate the cost of flights within Italy (even one-way) as an alternative to train travel.

You can take the Ferrovie dello Stato Italiane (FS) airport train or bus to Rome's Termini station or to Cadorna or Centrale in Milan; from the latter you can then catch a train to any other location in Italy. It will take about 40 minutes to get from Fiumicino to Roma Termini, less than an hour from Malpensa to Milano Centrale.

A helpful website for information (location, phone numbers, local transportation, etc.) about all of the airports in Italy is www.italianairportguide.com.

Bus

Italy's far-reaching regional bus network, often operated by private companies, isn't as attractive an option as in other European countries, partly due to convenient train travel. Schedules are often drawn up with commuters and students in mind and can be sketchy on weekends. But, car travel aside, regional bus companies often provide the only means of getting to out-of-the-way places. Even when this isn't the case, buses can be faster and more direct than local trains, so it's worth taking time to compare bus and train schedules. Busitalia–Sita Nord covers Tuscany and the Veneto. Sita Sud caters to travelers in Puglia, Basilicata, and Campania. FlixBus offers a low-cost long-distance service.

All buses, even those on long-distance routes, offer a single class of service. Cleanliness and comfort levels are high on private motor coaches, which have plenty of legroom, sizable seats, luggage storage, and usually toilets. Smoking isn't permitted on buses. Private lines usually have a ticket office in town or allow you to pay when you board.

Major Italian cities have inexpensive urban bus service. Although some city buses have ticket machines on board, generally you buy tickets from newsstands or tobacconists and have them validated on board. Buses can get packed during busy travel periods and rush hours.

Car

Italy has an extensive network of *auto-stradas* (toll highways), complemented by equally well-maintained but free *super-stradas* (expressways). You'll need your autostrada ticket from entry to pay the toll when you exit; on some shorter auto-stradas, you pay the toll when you enter. The condition of provincial roads varies, but maintenance is generally good.

Most gas stations have self-service options. Those on autostradas are open 24 hours; others are generally open Monday through Saturday 7–7, with a break at lunchtime. Automobile Club Italiano offers 24-hour road service. To call the police in an emergency, dial 112.

PARKING

Curbside spaces are marked by blue lines; pay at a nearby *parcometro* machine, and leave the printed ticket on your dashboard. Fines for violations are high, and towing is common. You often need a permit to enter historic centers with a vehicle—violating this strictly enforced rule can also result in hefty fines. It's best to park in designated (preferably attended) lots; even small towns often have them just outside their historic centers.

RULES OF THE ROAD

You can rent a car with a U.S. driver's license, but Italy also requires non-Europeans to carry an International Driver's Permit (IDP), available for a nominal fee via the AAA website (www.aaa.com). Speed limits are generally 130 kph (80 mph) on autostradas, 90 kph (55 mph) on state roads, and 50 kph (30 mph) in towns; this can drop to 10 kph (6 mph) in congested areas. Exceed the speed limit by more than 60 kph (37 mph), and your license could be confiscated.

Right turns on red lights are forbidden. Headlights must be kept on outside municipalities, and you must wear seat belts. Fines for using mobile phones while driving can exceed €1,000. The blood alcohol limit is 0.05% (stricter than in the United States).

Train

The fastest trains on the Ferrovie dello Stato Italiane (FS), or Italian State Railways, are the *Frecciarossa*. Their privately owned competitor, Nuovo Trasporto Viaggiatori (NTV), or Italo, also runs high-speed service between all major northern cities and as far as Salerno in the south. Seat reservations are mandatory for these bullet trains, just as they are for the Eurostar and slower Intercity (IC) trains; tickets for the latter are about half the price of those for the faster trains.

You can buy your tickets at machines in the station or on www.trenitalia.com—consider downloading the Trenitalia app. Reservations are not available on *Regionale* and *Espresso* trains, which are slower, make more stops, and are less expensive. For these trains, you must validate your ticket before boarding by punching it at a wall- or pillar-mounted yellow or green box—if you forget to do this, find a conductor immediately. Fines for attempting to ride a train without a ticket are €200.

TRAIN PASSES

A rail pass can save you money on train travel, but it's good to compare the cost with actual fares to make sure. Generally, the more often you plan to travel long distances on high-speed trains, the more sense a rail pass makes. Keep in mind that even with a rail pass you still need to reserve seats on the trains that require them.

Travel Times
by Train and Ferry

TO AUSTRIA & EAST EUROPE
TARVISIO

TO SLOVENIA
& CROATIA

Trieste

TO AUSTRIA & GERMANY
BRENNERO

Udine

Belluno

Treviso
< 40mn >

< 1hr 45mn >

Venezia

VENEZIA - POLA, CROATIA 3HRS

TO GREECE

ANCONA - ZADAR, CROATIA 4HRS

ANCONA - SPLIT, CROATIA 8HRS

PESCARA - SPLIT, CROATIA 5HRS

TO GREECE

Ancona

< 1hr 20mn >

Pescara

Bolzano/Bozen

Trento

< 2hrs >

Vicenza

< 2hr >

Padova

Ferrara

< 1hr 45mn >

Forlì

Rimini

Bologna

< 1hr >

< 45mn >

Ascoli

Teramo

Perugia

< 15mn >

< 3hrs >

L'Aquila

Sondrio

Bergamo

Brescia

< 1hr >

< 1hr 30mn >

Verona

< 30mn >

Mantova

Modena

Lucca

Pistoia

< 1hr >

Firenze

Arezzo

< 1hr 45mn >

Siena

Terni

Viterbo

Lecco

Piacenza

< 1hr 40mn >

Parma

< 1hr >

Livorno

< 3hrs >

< 20mn >

Grosseto

< 5HRS >

Milano

< 1hr 20mn >

Pavia

< 1hr 30mn >

Novara

Vercelli

Asti

Alessandria

Genova

< 30mn >

La Spezia

< 2hrs >

Pisa

GENOVA - PALERMO 20HRS

TO SWITZERLAND
DOMODOSSOLA

Aosta

Torino

Cuneo

Savona

Imperia

MODANE
TO FRANCE

CHIASSO

GENOVA - PORTO TORRES 13HRS

VENTIMIGLIA
TO FRANCE &
CÔTE D'AZUR

10 HRS

TO GREECE

Essentials

Hotels

Many Italian lodgings, some quite luxurious, are in palazzi, villas, monasteries, and smaller historic buildings that have been restored to blend modern comforts with original atmosphere. Another option is renting a vacation property—although, in addition to budget, you should keep in mind location (street noise and neighborhood ambience in cities and towns, degree of isolation in the countryside), the availability of an elevator or the number of stairs, the utility costs, and what's supplied (furnishings, including pots and linens, as well as sundries like dish detergent).

If you're intrigued by the "locavore" movement, ask local tourism offices about *agriturismo* accommodations. Rural farm-stay properties range from luxury villas to farmhouses with basic facilities.

The lodgings we list are the cream of the crop in each price category. Properties are assigned price categories based on the rate for two people sharing a standard double room in high season, including tax and service.

🍴 Restaurants

Italian cuisine is still largely regional, so try spaghetti *alla carbonara* (with bacon and egg) in Rome, pizza in Naples, *cinghiale* (wild boar) in Tuscany, or truffles in Piedmont. Nowadays, vegetarian and gluten-free options are widely available. Still, if you have dietary restrictions, ask about ingredients; not everything is listed in menu descriptions.

The restaurants we list are the finest in each price category. Unless otherwise noted, they're open for lunch and dinner, closing one or two days a week.

MEALS

Although the distinction has blurred, *ristoranti* tend to be more elegant and expensive than trattorias or *osterie,* which serve traditional, home-style fare. Meals generally consist of an *antipasto* (starter) followed by a *primo* (first course), a *secondo* (main course) or *contorno* (vegetable side dish), and *dolce* (dessert). You can, of course, eat less (perhaps just a primo or secondo and a dolce). Single dishes are more the norm at an enoteca or pizzeria, and you can grab affordable snacks at bars, cafés, and spots for pizza *al taglio* (by the slice).

WINES, BEER, AND SPIRITS

The grape has been cultivated here since the time of the Etruscans, with Tuscany, Piedmont, the Veneto, Puglia, Calabria, Sicily, Le Marche, and Umbria among the renowned areas. Beer is readily available, and Italy has some excellent microbreweries, so ask about local brews. In addition, Italians are imaginative with their cocktails, so consider trying the *aperitivo della casa* (house aperitif). The minimum drinking age in Italy is 16.

➕ Health/Safety

EMERGENCIES

No matter where you are in Italy, dial 112 for all emergencies. Key words to remember for emergency situations are *aiuto* for "help" (pronounced "aye-*you*-toh") and *pronto soccorso,* which means "first aid." When confronted with a health emergency, head straight for the Pronto Soccorso department of the nearest hospital or dial 118. To call a Red Cross *ambulanza* (ambulance), dial 800/065510. If you just need a doctor, ask for *un medico.* Ask the physician for *una fattura* (an invoice) to present to your insurance company for reimbursement.

HEALTH

Smoking is banned inside all public places, so sit indoors (where there's also often air-conditioning) if the smoke in outdoor seating areas bothers you.

It's always best to travel with your own trusted medications. Should you need prescription medication while in Italy, speak with a physician to ensure it's the proper kind. Aspirin (*l'aspirina*) can be purchased at any pharmacy, as can over-the-counter medicines, such as ibuprofen or acetaminophen.

COVID-19

COVID-19 brought travel to a virtual standstill for most of 2020 and into 2021, but vaccinations have made travel possible and more safe. However, each destination (and each business with-in that destination) may have its own requirements and regulations. Travelers may expect to continue to wear a mask in some places and obey any other rules (and non-vaccinated travelers may face certain restrictions). Given how abruptly travel was curtailed at the onset of the pandemic, it is wise to consider protect-ing yourself by purchasing a travel insur-ance policy that will reimburse you for cancellation costs related to COVID-19. Not all travel insurance policies protect against pandemic-related cancellations, so always read the fine print.

$ Money

Of Italy's major cities—where, as in other countries, prices are higher than in the countryside—Milan is by far the most expensive. Resort areas like Capri, Portofino, and Cortina d'Ampezzo cater to wealthy vacationers and also charge top prices. Good value can be found in

Item	Average Cost
Cup of Coffee	€0.90–€1.50
Soft Drink (glass/can/bottle)	€2–€3
Glass of Beer	€3–€6
Sandwich	€3–€5.50
2-km (1-mile) Taxi Ride in Rome	€9

the scenic Trentino–Alto Adige region of the Dolomites and in Umbria and Le Marche. With a few exceptions, southern Italy and Sicily also offer bargains for those who do their homework before they leave home.

$ Tipping

In restaurants a service charge of 10%–15% may appear on your check, but it's not a given that your server will receive this; consider leaving a tip of 5%–10% (in cash) for good service. At a hotel bar, tip €1 and up for a round or two of drinks. Taxi drivers also appreciate a euro or two, particularly if they help with luggage.

In hotels, give the *portiere* (concierge) about 10% of the bill for services or €3–€5 for help with dinner reservations and such. In moderately priced hotels, leave chambermaids about €1 per day, and tip a minimum of €1 for valet or room service. In expensive hotels, double these amounts. Sightseeing guides should receive €1.50 per person for a half-day group tour, more if the tour is longer and/or they're especially knowledgeable.

Helpful Italian Phrases

BASICS

English	Italian	Pronunciation
Yes/no	Sí/No	see/no
Please	Per favore	pear fa-**vo**-ray
Thank you	Grazie	**grah**-tsee-ay
You're welcome	Prego	**pray**-go
I'm sorry (apology)	Mi dispiace	mee dis-pee-**atch**-ay
Excuse me, sorry	Scusi	**skoo**-zee
Good morning/ afternoon	Buongiorno	bwohn-**jor**-no
Good evening	Buona sera	**bwoh**-na **say**-ra
Good-bye	Arrivederci	a-ree-vah-**dare**-chee
Mr. (Sir)	Signore	see-**nyo**-ray
Mrs. (Ma'am)	Signora	see-**nyo**-ra
Miss	Signorina	see-nyo-**ree**-na
Pleased to meet you	Piacere	pee-ah-**chair**-ray
How are you?	Come sta?	**ko**-may-**stah**
Hello (phone)	Pronto?	**proan**-to

NUMBERS

English	Italian	Pronunciation
one-half	mezzo	**mets**-zoh
one	uno	**oo**-no
two	due	**doo**-ay
three	tre	Tray
four	quattro	**kwah**-tro
five	cinque	**cheen**-kway
six	sei	Say
seven	sette	**set**-ay
eight	otto	**oh**-to
nine	nove	**no**-vay
ten	dieci	dee-**eh**-chee
eleven	undici	**oon**-dee-chee
twelve	dodici	**doh**-dee-chee
thirteen	tredici	**trey**-dee-chee
fourteen	quattordici	kwah-**tor**-dee-chee
fifteen	quindici	**kwin**-dee-chee
sixteen	sedici	**say**-dee-chee
seventeen	dicissette	dee-chah-**set**-ay
eighteen	diciotto	dee-chee-**oh**-to
nineteen	diciannove	dee-chee-ahn-**no**-vay
twenty	venti	**vain**-tee
twenty-one	ventuno	**vent**-oo-no
thirty	trenta	**train**-ta
forty	quaranta	kwa-**rahn**-ta
fifty	cinquanta	cheen-**kwahn**-ta
sixty	sessanta	seh-**sahn**-ta
seventy	settanta	seh-**tahn**-ta
eighty	ottanta	o-**tahn**-ta
ninety	novanta	no-**vahn**-ta
one hundred	cento	**chen**-to
one thousand	mille	**mee**-lay
one million	un milione	oon **mill**-oo-nay

COLORS

black	Nero	**nair**-ro
blue	Blu	bloo
brown	Marrone	ma-**rohn**-nay
green	Verde	**ver**-day
orange	Arancione	ah-rahn-**cho**-nay
red	Rosso	**rose**-so
white	Bianco	bee-**ahn**-koh
yellow	Giallo	**jaw**-low

DAYS OF THE WEEK

English	Italian	Pronunciation
Sunday	Domenica	do-**meh**-nee-ka
Monday	Lunedi	loo-ne-**dee**
Tuesday	Martedi	mar-te-**dee**
Wednesday	Mercoledi	**mer**-ko-le-**dee**
Thursday	Giovedi	jo-ve-**dee**
Friday	Venerdì	ve-ner-**dee**
Saturday	Sabato	**sa**-ba-toh

MONTHS

English	Italian	Pronunciation
January	Gennaio	jen-**ay**-o
February	Febbraio	feb-**rah**-yo
March	Marzo	**mart**-so
April	Aprile	a-**pril**-ay
May	Maggio	**mahd**-joe
June	Giugno	**joon**-yo
July	Luglio	**lool**-yo
August	Agosto	a-**gus**-to
September	Settembre	se-**tem**-bre
October	Ottobre	o-**toh**-bre
November	Novembre	no-**vem**-bre
December	Dicembre	di-**chem**-bre

USEFUL WORDS AND PHRASES

English	Italian	Pronunciation
Do you speak English?	Parla Inglese?	**par**-la een-**glay**-zay
I don't speak Italian	Non parlo italiano	non **par**-lo ee-tal-**yah**-no
I don't understand	Non capisco	non ka-**peess**-ko
I don't know	Non lo so	non lo **so**
I understand	Capisco	ka-**peess**-ko
I'm American	Sono Americano(a)	**so**-no a-may-ree-**kah**-no(a)
I'm British	Sono inglese	so-no een-**glay**-zay
What's your name?	Come si chiama?	**ko**-may see kee-**ah**-ma
My name is …	Mi Chiamo…	mee kee-**ah**-mo
What time is it?	Che ore sono?	kay **o**-ray **so**-no
How?	Come?	**ko**-may
When?	Quando?	**kwan**-doe
Yesterday/today/ tomorrow	Ieri/oggi/domani	**yer**-ee/ **o**-jee/ do-**mah**-nee

This morning	Stamattina/Oggi	sta-ma-**tee**-na/ **o**-jee
Afternoon	Pomeriggio	po-mer-**ee**-jo
Tonight	Stasera	sta-**ser**-a
What?	Che cosa?	kay **ko**-za
What is it?	Che cos'è?	kay ko-**zey**
Why?	Perchè?	pear-**kay**
Who?	Chi?	**Kee**
Where is ...	Dov'è...	doe-**veh**
the train station?	la stazione?	la sta-tsee-**oh**-nay
the subway?	la metropolitana?	la may-tro-po-lee-**tah**-na
the bus stop?	la fermata dell'autobus?	la fer-**mah**-ta del-ow-tor-**booss**
the airport	l'aeroporto	la-er-roh-**por**-toh
the post office?	l'ufficio postale	loo-**fee**-cho po-**stah**-lay
the bank?	la banca?	la **bahn**-ka
the hotel?	l'hotel...?	lo-**tel**
the museum?	Il museo	eel moo-**zay**-o
the hospital?	l'ospedale?	lo-spay-**dah**-lay
the elevator?	l'ascensore	la-shen-**so**-ray
the restrooms?	il bango?	eel **bahn**-yo
Here/there	Qui/là	kwee/la
Left/right	A sinistra/a destra	a see-**neess**-tra/a **des**-tra
Is it near/far?	È vicino/lontano?	ay vee-**chee**-no/ lon-**tah**-no
I'd like ...	Vorrei...	vo-**ray**
a room	una camera	**oo**-na **kah**-may-ra
the key	la chiave	la kee-**ah**-vay
a newspaper	un giornale	oon jore-**nah**-vay
a stamp	un francobollo	oon frahn-ko-**bo**-lo
I'd like to buy ...	Vorrei comprare...	vo-**ray** kom-**prah**-ray
a city map	una mappa della città	**oo**-na **mah**-pa **day**-la chee-**tah**
a road map	una carta stradale	**oo**-na **car**-tah stra-**dahl**-lay
a magazine	una revista	**oo**-na ray-**vees**-tah
envelopes	buste	**boos**-tay
writing paper	carta de lettera	**car**-tah dah **leyt**-ter-rah
a postcard	una cartolina	**oo**-na car-tog-**leen**-ah
a ticket	un biglietto	oon bee-**yet**-toh
How much is it?	Quanto costa?	**kwahn**-toe **coast**-a
It's expensive/ cheap	È caro/ economico	ay **car**-o/ ay-ko-**no**-mee-ko
A little/a lot	Poco/tanto	**po**-ko/**tahn**-to
More/less	Più/meno	pee-**oo**/**may**-no
Enough/too (much)	Abbastanza/ troppo	a-bas-**tahn**-sa/tro-po
I am sick	Sto male	sto **mah**-lay
Call a doctor	Chiama un dottore	kee-**ah**-mah-oondoe-**toe**-ray

Help!	Aituo!	a-**yoo**-to
Stop!	Alt!	ahlt

DINING OUT

A bottle of ...	Una bottiglia di...	**oo**-na bo-**tee**-lee-ah dee
A cup of ...	Una tazza di...	**oo**-na **tah**-tsa dee
A glass of ...	Un bicchiere di...	oon bee-key-**air**-ay dee
Beer	La birra	la **beer**-rah
Bill/check	Il conto	eel **cone**-toe
Bread	Il pane	eel **pah**-nay
Breakfast	La prima colazione	la **pree**-ma ko-la-**tsee**-oh-nay
Butter	Il burro	eel **boor**-roh
Cocktail/aperitif	L'aperitivo	la-pay-ree-**tee**-vo
Dinner	La cena	la **chen**-a
Fixed-price menu	Menù a prezzo fisso	may-**noo** a **pret**-so **fee**-so
Fork	La forchetta	la for-**ket**-a
I am vegetarian	Sono vegetariano(a)	**so**-no vay-jay-ta-ree-**ah**-no/a
I cannot eat ...	Non posso mangiare	non **pose**-so mahn-gee-**are**-ay
I'd like to order	Vorrei ordinare	vo-**ray** or-dee-**nah**-ray
Is service included?	Il servizio è incluso?	eel ser-**vee**-tzee-o ay een-**kloo**-zo
I'm hungry/ thirsty	Ho fame/sede	oh **fah**-meh/**sehd**-ed
It's good/bad	E buono/cattivo	ay **bwo**-bo/ka-**tee**-vo
It's hot/cold	E caldo/freddo	ay **kahl**-doe/**fred**-o
Knife	Il coltello	eel kol-**tel**-o
Lunch	Il pranzo	eel **prahnt**-so
Menu	Il menu	eel may-**noo**
Napkin	Il tovagliolo	eel toe-va-lee-**oh**-lo
Pepper	Il pepe	eel **pep**-peh
Plate	Il piatto	eel pee-**aht**-toe
Please give me ...	Mi dia...	mee **dee**-a
Salt	Il sale	eel **sah**-lay
Spoon	Il cucchiaio	eel koo-kee-ah-yo
Tea	tè	tay
Water	acqua	**awk**-wah
Wine	vino	**vee**-noh

Essentials

⊕ Passports

A U.S. passport is relatively simple to obtain and is valid for 10 years. You must apply in person if you're getting a passport for the first time; if your previous passport was lost, stolen, or damaged; or if it has expired and was issued more than 15 years ago or when you were under 16. The cost of a new passport is $145 for adults, $115 for children under 16; renewals are $110 for adults, $115 for children under 16. Allow four to six weeks for processing.

■ TIP→ **Before your trip, make two copies of your passport's data page (one for someone at home and another for you to carry separately). Alternatively, scan the page and email it to someone at home and/or yourself.**

⊕ Visa

When staying for 90 days or less, U.S. citizens aren't required to obtain a visa prior to traveling to Italy. A recent law requires that you fill in a declaration of presence within eight days of your arrival—the stamp from passport control at the airport substitutes for this. If you plan to travel or live in Italy or the European Union for longer than 90 days, you must acquire a valid visa from the Italian consulate serving your state *before you leave the United States*. The process of obtaining a visa will take at least 30 days, and the Italian government doesn't accept applications submitted by visa expediters.

⊕ U.S. Embassy/Consulate

In addition to the embassy in Rome, the United States has consulates general in Florence, Milan, and Naples. (Note: you aren't allowed to bring laptops into any of these facilities.) If you're arrested or detained, ask Italian officials to notify the embassy or nearest consulate immediately. Consider participating in the U.S. Department of State's Smart Traveler Enrollment Program (STEP, step.state. gov) to receive alerts and make it easier to locate you in an emergency.

⊞ When to Go

High Season: June through September is expensive and busy. In August, most Italians take their own summer holidays; cities are less crowded, but many shops and restaurants close. July and August can be uncomfortably hot.

Low Season: Unless you're skiing, winter offers the least appealing weather, although it's the best time for airfare and hotel deals and to escape the crowds. Temperatures in the south can be mild.

Value Season: By late September, temperate weather, saner airfares, and more cultural events can make for a happier trip. October is also great, but November is often rainy. March and early April weather is changeable. From late April to early May, the masses have not yet arrived.

Contacts

Air

AIRLINE SECURITY ISSUES Transportation Security Administration. *(TSA).* ☎ *866/289–9673* ⊕ *www.tsa.gov.*

AIRPORT INFORMATION Aeroporto di Bologna. *(BLQ, aka Guglielmo Marconi).* ✉ *6 km (4 miles) northwest of Bologna* ☎ *051/6479615* ⊕ *www.bologna-airport.it.* **Aeroporto di Cagliari.** *(CAG, aka Elmas).* ✉ *7 km (4½ miles) from Cagliari, Via dei Trasvolatori, Elmas, Cagliari* ☎ *070/211211* ⊕ *www.sogaer.it.* **Aeroporto di Catania.** *(CTA, aka Fontanarossa).* ✉ *7 km (4½ miles) south-west of Catania* ☎ *095/7239111* ⊕ *www.aeroporto. catania.it.* **Aeroporto di Firenze.** *(FLR, aka Amerigo Vespucci or Peretola).* ✉ *6 km (4 miles) northwest of Florence* ☎ *055/3061830* ⊕ *www.aeroporto.firenze. it.* **Aeroporto di Milan Linate.** *(LIN).* ✉ *8 km (5 miles) southeast of Milan* ☎ *02/232323* ⊕ *www. milanolinate-airport.com.* **Aeroporto di Pisa.** *(PSA, aka Aeroporto Galileo Galilei).* ✉ *2 km (1 mile) south of Pisa, 80 km (50 miles) west of Florence* ☎ *050/849111* ⊕ *www. pisa-airport.com.* **Aeroporto di Roma Ciampino.**

(CIA). ✉ *15 km (9 miles) southwest of Rome* ☎ *06/65951* ⊕ *www.adr.it.* **Aeroporto di Venezia.** *(VCE, aka Marco Polo).* ✉ *6 km (4 miles) north of Venice* ☎ *041/2609260* ⊕ *www. veneziaairport.com.* **Aeroporto di Roma Fiumicino.** *(FCO, aka Leonardo da Vinci).* ✉ *35 km (20 miles) southwest of Rome* ☎ *06/65951* ⊕ *www.adr. it.* **Aeroporto Internazionale di Napoli.** *(NAP, aka Capodichino).* ✉ *5 km (3 miles) northeast of Naples* ☎ *081/7896111 weekdays 8–4* ⊕ *www.aeroporto-dinapoli.it.* **Aeroporto di Milano Malpensa.** *(MXP).* ✉ *45 km (28 miles) north of Milan* ☎ *02/232323* ⊕ *www.milanomalpen-sa-airport.com.* **Aeroporto Orio al Serio (BGY).** ✉ *Via Orio al Serio 49/51* ☎ *035/326323* ⊕ *www. milanbergamoairport.it.*

Bus

ACTV. ☎ *041/2424* ⊕ *actv. avmspa.it.* **ANM.** ✉ *Via G. Marino 1, Naples* ☎ *800/639525 toll-free in Italy* ⊕ *www.anm. it.* **ATAC.** ☎ *06/0606* ⊕ *www.atac.roma.it.* **ATAF.** ✉ *Stazione Centrale di Santa Maria Novella, Florence* ☎ *800/424500, 199/104245 from mobile phone (toll)* ⊕ *www.ataf.*

net. **ATM.** ☎ *02/48607607* ⊕ *www.atm.it.* **Busita-lia-Sita Nord.** ✉ *Viale dei Cadorna, 105, Florence* ☎ *80075/373760 toll free* ⊕ *www.fsbusitalia.it.* **Dolomiti Bus.** ✉ *Via Col da Ren 14,* ☎ *0437/217111* ⊕ *www.dolomitibus.it.* **FlixBus.** ☎ *02/94759208* ⊕ *www.flixbus.com.* **Mari-no Bus.** ☎ *080/3112335* ⊕ *www.marinobus.it.* **Sita Sud.** ✉ *Via S. Francesco d'Assisi 1,* ☎ *080/5790111* ⊕ *www.sitasudtraspor-ti.it.* **Trasporti Toscani.** ✉ *Via Bellatalla,1, Pisa* ☎ *050/884111* ⊕ *www. cttnord.it.*

Train

TRAIN INFORMATION FS-Trenita-lia. ☎ *06/68475475 from outside Italy (English),* 892021 in Italy ⊕ *www. trenitalia.com.* **NTV Italo.** ☎ *06/0708* ⊕ *www. italotreno.it.*

CONTACTS Eurail. ⊕ *www. eurail.com.* **Italia Rail.** ☎ *877/375–7245 in U.S., 06/9763 2451 in Italy* ⊕ *www.italiarail.com.* **Rail Europe.** ⊕ *www. raileurope.com.* **RailPass.** ☎ *877/3757245 toll-free from US* ⊕ *www.railpass. com.*

Great Itineraries

Northern Italy

Northern Italy is a region with high fashion, big wines, and beautiful lakes.

DAY 1: MILAN

Start off in **Milan,** Italy's capital of art, fashion, and design. Explore elegant shops around the **Duomo** and **Via Montenapoleone.** Some of Europe's great art treasures are housed in the **Brera Gallery.** The elegant **Basilica di Santa Maria presso San Satiro** is about a 20-minute walk from **Santa Maria delle Grazie,** where Leonardo's stunning *Last Supper* is housed. Spend a night at the opera in **La Scala,** Italy's most illustrious opera house.

Logistics: Central Milan is compact, with excellent public transportation.

DAY 2: BELLAGIO

Lake Como combines some of Italy's most beautiful scenery with elegant historic villas and gardens, making it truly worthy of a full-day excursion. **Bellagio** is a pretty village from which you can ferry to other points along the lake, take walking tours, hike, or just sit on a terrace watching the light play on the sapphire water and the snowcapped mountains.

Logistics: Como's San Giovanni station is just one hour by train from Milan, and Bus C10 leaves hourly from here for the 70-minute lakeside journey to Bellagio. In Bellagio you won't need a car, since most of your touring will be on foot, by ferry, or by bus.

DAYS 3 TO 5: VERONA/ MANTUA/VICENZA

Take an early train to **Verona** (90 minutes from Milan) and settle into your hotel. Start your exploration of northern Italy's three most important art cities with Verona's ancient Roman arena, theater, and city gates; its brooding medieval palaces and castle; and its graceful bridge spanning the Adige.

The next day, make the 30- to 45-minute train trip to **Mantua,** arriving in time for lunch featuring a local specialty: *tortelli di zucca* (pumpkin-filled ravioli) served with sage butter and Parmesan cheese. Check out the Mantegna frescoes in the **Palazzo Ducale,** or visit Giulio Romano's **Palazzo Te,** a 16th-century pleasure palace. Take the train back to Verona in time for dinner and, perhaps, an opera in the Roman amphitheater.

On Day 3, head to **Vicenza** (30 minutes by train) to see the palaces, villas, and public buildings of the lion of late-16th-century architecture, Andrea Palladio. Don't miss his **Teatro Olimpico** and his famous villa, **La Rotonda,** slightly out of town. If time allows, try to see the frescoes by Gianbattista and Giandomenico Tiepolo in the **Villa Valmarana ai Nani,** near La Rotonda. For lunch, try *baccalà alla vicentina,* the local salt-cod dish.

DAY 6: PADUA

Most people visit this important art and university center on a day trip out of Venice, but then they miss one of **Padua**'s main attractions: the nightlife that goes on in the city's wine bars and cafés from evening until quite late. See the Giotto frescoes in the **Cappella degli Scrovegni** and the **Basilica di Sant'Antonio** before lunch, then spend a relaxing afternoon at the **Villa Pisani,** enjoying its gardens and important Tiepolo fresco.

Logistics: Trains run frequently to Padua from Verona (1 hour) and Vicenza (30 minutes); you don't really have to schedule ahead.

DAY 7: VENICE

The first things you'll probably want to do in **Venice** are to take a vaporetto ride down the **Grand Canal** and see **Piazza San Marco.** After that, move on to the adjacent **Palazzo Ducale** and Sansovino's **Biblioteca Marciana,** across the piazzetta.

For lunch, take Vaporetto No. 1 to Ca'
Rezzonico, and have a sandwich and a
spritz in **Campo Santa Margherita.** From
here, make your way to the **Galleria
dell'Accademia** and spend a few hours
taking in its wonderful collection of
Venetian paintings. In the evening, walk
up the Zattere and have a drink at one
of the cafés overlooking the **Canale della
Giudecca.**

Logistics: Seeing the Grand Canal and
Piazza San Marco in relative tranquility
will be your reward for getting up at the
crack of dawn (arrive at the vaporetto
before 8:30 to avoid the rush) and doing
a little extra planning.

DAY 8: VENICE

If the Galleria dell'Accademia has whet-
ted your appetite for Venetian painting,
start the day by visiting churches and
institutions where you can see more.
If your taste runs to modern art, head
to the **Peggy Guggenheim Collection** and,
down the street, the Pinault Collection in
the refashioned **Punta della Dogana.**

In the afternoon, head for the Fondamenta Nuova station to catch a vaporetto to
the outer islands: **Murano,** where you can
shop for Venetian glass and visit a glass

museum and workshops; **Burano,** known
for lace-making and colorful houses; and
Torcello, Venice's first inhabited island
and home to a beautiful cathedral.

DAY 9: VENICE

Pay a visit to the **Rialto,** one of Europe's
largest and most varied fish markets,
where Venetians also buy their fruit and
vegetables as well as, of course, their
fish. Note that the Rialto Market is closed
on Sunday and Monday; since there is no
fishing on Sunday, there can be no fresh
fish available on Monday.

Have lunch in one of the excellent mar-
ket-area restaurants. Then, on your last
afternoon in Venice, leave time to sit with
a coffee or spritz in a lively square or in a
café along the **Fondamenta della Misericordia** in Cannaregio. Alternatively, visit Tullio
Lombardo's lyrical **Miracoli,** a short walk
from the San Marco end of the Rialto
Bridge, or Palladio's masterpiece, the
Redentore church on **Giudecca.**

DAY 10: VENICE/DEPARTURE

Take one last vaporetto trip up the Grand
Canal to **Piazzale Roma** and, after saying
good-bye to Venice, catch Bus No. 5 or
an ATVO (private line) bus to the airport.

Great Itineraries

Central Italy

Visit central Italy for the great art, sumptuous countryside, and outstanding food and wine.

DAY 1: FLORENCE

If you're coming in on an international flight, you'll probably settle in Florence in time for an afternoon stroll or siesta (depending on your jet-lag strategy) before dinner.

Logistics: Begin anticipating the first dinner of your trip. Look for a place near your hotel, and when you arrive, reserve a table (or have your concierge do it for you). Making a meal the focus of your first day is a great way to ease into Italian life.

DAY 2: FLORENCE

Begin at the **Uffizi Gallery,** whose extensive collection will occupy much of your morning. Next, take in the neighboring **Piazza della Signoria,** then head a few blocks north to the **Duomo** to check out Ghiberti's famous bronze doors on the **Battistero** (actually high-quality copies; the originals are in the **Museo dell'Opera del Duomo**). Climb up Brunelleschi's cathedral dome to the cupola. Spend the afternoon wandering Florence's medieval streets; or head out to **Fiesole** to see the ancient amphitheater.

Logistics: It's a good idea to reserve Uffizi tickets online ahead of your visit; climbs up Brunelleschi's dome must be reserved in advance.

DAY 3: FLORENCE

Spend your morning seeing Michelangelo's *David* at the **Galleria dell'Accademia,** the **Medici Chapels,** the **Palazzo Pitti** and **Boboli Gardens,** and the churches of **Santa Maria Novella** and **Santa Croce.** If it's a clear day, spend the afternoon making your way up to **Piazzale Michelangelo** for sweeping views of the idyllic Florentine countryside. Recharge with a dinner featuring *bistecca alla fiorentina* (a grilled, very rare T-bone steak).

Logistics: You can reach Piazzale Michelangelo by taxi or by taking Bus No. 12 or 13 from the Lungarno. Otherwise, do your best to get around on foot; Florence is a brilliant city for walking.

DAY 4: SAN GIMIGNANO

After breakfast, pick up your car and make the lazy drive from Florence to **San Gimignano.** Upon arriving in town, you'll no doubt be awed by its towers—medieval skyscrapers that provided security and served as symbols of wealth and power. After finding your way to a hotel in the old town, set out on foot to check out the city's turrets and alleyways, then enjoy a leisurely dinner.

Logistics: San Gimignano is only 57 km (35 miles) to the southwest. Consider taking a detour on the SS222 (Strada Chiantigiana) to a winery in one of the Chianti wine towns.

DAY 5: SIENA

In the morning, set out for nearby **Siena,** which is known worldwide for its Palio, a horse race involving the city's 17 *contrade* (medieval neighborhoods). You will be blown away by the precious medieval streets and memorable fan-shape **Piazza del Campo.** Don't miss the spectacular **Duomo,** the **Battistero,** and the **Spedale di Santa Maria della Scala,** an old hospital and hostel that now contains an underground archaeological museum.

Logistics: Parking can be a challenge. Look for the *stadio* (soccer stadium), where there's a parking lot that often has space.

DAY 6: AREZZO/CORTONA

From Siena you'll first head to **Arezzo,** home to the **Basilica di San Francesco,** which contains important frescoes by Piero della Francesca. Check out the **Piazza Grande** along with its beautiful Romanesque church of **Santa Maria della Pieve.** Try to do all of this before lunch, after which you'll head straight to **Cortona.** Cortona is a town for walking and relaxing, not sightseeing, so enjoy yourself as you wander through the **Piazza della Repubblica** and **Piazza Signorelli,** perhaps doing a bit of shopping.

Logistics: Siena to Arezzo is 70 km (43.5 miles) on the SS715 and A1 autostrada. From Arezzo to Cortona, it's just 30 km (18 miles)—take SR71.

DAY 7: ASSISI

Cross over into Umbria and see **Assisi,** the home of St. Francis that today hosts many religious pilgrims. After arrival and check-in, head straight for the **Basilica di San Francesco,** which displays the tomb of St. Francis and some unbelievable frescoes. From here, take Via San Francesco to **Piazza del Comune** and see the **Tempio di Minerva.** Break for lunch and then see **San Rufino,** the cathedral, before returning through the piazza to Corso Mazzini and **Santa Chiara.**

Logistics: From Cortona, take the SR71 to the A1 autostrada toward Perugia. After about 40 km (24 miles), take the Assisi exit (E45), and it's another 14 km (8 miles) to Assisi.

DAY 8: SPOLETO

This morning will take you to the walled city of **Spoleto,** home to a world-renowned summer arts festival. Its **Duomo** is wonderful; its fortress, **La Rocca,** is impressive; and the **Ponte delle Torri,** a 14th-century bridge that separates Spoleto from Monteluco, is a marvelous sight. Save your appetite for a serious last dinner in Italy. Do your best to sample black truffles, a proud product of the region.

Logistics: The trip from Assisi to Spoleto is a pretty 47-km (29-mile) drive (SS75 to SS3) that should take less than an hour.

DAY 9: SPOLETO/DEPARTURE

It's a fair distance from Spoleto to the Florence airport, your point of departure; depending on your comfort level with Italian driving, allow at least 2½ hours to get there.

One alternative would be to fly out of the tiny airport in Perugia. Otherwise, just get an early start and drive to Florence along the A1 autostrada.

Great Itineraries

Southern Italy

Come for the archaeological wonders, azure sea, and excellent Neapolitan fare.

DAY 1: NAPLES

Fly into Naples's **Aeroporto Capodichino,** a scant 5 km (3 miles) from the city. Naples is classic Italy, and many visitors end up falling in love with its alluring palazzi and spectacular pizza.

Recharge with a nap and, after that, a good caffè—Naples has some of the world's best. You should be back on your feet in time for an evening stroll down the city's bustling shopping street, Via Toledo, to Piazza Plebiscito, before dinner and bed.

DAY 2: NAPLES

Start the day at the **Museo Archeologico Nazionale,** budgeting at least two hours for its collection, before stopping for coffee at a café in Piazza Bellini. From here, head down Via dei Tribunali, crossing Via Duomo to see Caravaggio's *The Seven Works of Mercy* at **Pio Monte della Misericordia.** Make your way back along Spaccanapoli with a brief stop at the **Cappella Sansevero** for a look at the pinnacle of Masonic sculpture. Continue on to the port and the **Castel Nuovo** and then past the **Teatro San Carlo** to the enormous **Palazzo Reale** in **Piazza Plebiscito.** Just beyond this is the **Santa Lucia** waterfront area, with the **Castel dell'Ovo.** Return to your hotel for a short rest before dinner and perhaps a night out at one of Naples's lively bars or clubs.

Logistics: This entire day is easily done on foot.

DAY 3: POMPEII/SORRENTO

After breakfast, pack your luggage, and head from Naples to **Pompeii,** one of Europe's true archaeological gems. If it's summer, be prepared for sweltering heat as you make your way through the incredible preserved ruins of a city that was devastated by the whims of **Mt. Vesuvius** nearly 2,000 years ago. You'll see the houses of noblemen and merchants, brothels, political graffiti, and more. **Sorrento,** the beginning of the fabled Amalfi Coast, is touristy, but it may well be the Italian city of your imagination: cliffhanging, cobblestone-paved, and graced with an infinite variety of fishing ports and coastal views. Stop here for a relaxing dinner of fish and white wine.

Logistics: Rather than rent a car, take the Circumvesuviana, a twice-hourly train to Sorrento that stops near the ruins at Pompeii's Villa dei Misteri.

DAY 4: POSITANO/RAVELLO

Positano, your next stop, is one of Italy's most visited towns for good reason: its blue-green seas, stairs "as steep as ladders," and white Moorish-style houses are all memorable. Walk, gaze, and eat (lunch), before heading on to the less visited, yet even loftier town of **Ravello.** This aerie "closer to the sky than it is to the sea" is an Amalfi Coast dream come true. Don't miss the **Duomo, Villa Rufolo,** and **Villa Cimbrone** before settling in for dinner in the sky.

Logistics: Sorrento to Positano is a slow 15-km (9.5-mile) jaunt, and then Ravello is another 26 km (16 miles) to the east, with the winding roads drawing it out for the better part of an hour. The SITA bus is your best option. Motorists should be prepared to use low gears if driving a stick shift.

DAY 5: MATERA

Those with a car will have a bit of a drive from the Amalfi Coast; leaving Campania and entering Basilicata is generally a lonely experience. Little-traveled roads, wild hills, and distant farms are the hallmarks of this province, which has perfected the art of peasant food and the deep, dark *aglianico* wines to go with it. The lengthy journey to **Matera** is worthwhile, however, to see this beautiful ancient city full of Paleolithic **Sassi** (cave-like dwellings hewn out of rock). Spend the afternoon exploring them, then enjoy a relaxing dinner at one of Matera's excellent restaurants.

Logistics: It's a long haul from Ravello to Matera—if using public transportation you may find it easier to return first to Naples—but the effort is worth it, as Basilicata's landscape is so pretty.

DAY 6: LECCE

Get an early start for your journey to the Baroque city of **Lecce,** which will mark your introduction to Puglia, the heel of Italy's boot. It's one of the country's best-kept secrets, as you'll soon find out upon checking out the spectacular church of **Santa Croce,** the ornate **Duomo,** and the harmonious **Piazza Sant'Oronzo.**

The shopping, the food, and the evening passeggiata are all great.

Logistics: It's not far from Matera to Lecce as the crow flies, but the 2½-hour trip is more involved than you might think; patience is required. Those without a car should head to Bari, then take the train south. The best driving route is via Taranto, *not* up through Bari.

DAY 7: BARI

It is a 2-hour drive from Lecce to **Bari,** and many make a pit stop halfway at the beautiful hilltop town of **Ostuni.** Spend the day wandering through Bari's historic center and finish with a good fish dinner.

Logistics: Take a direct train or the coastal SS16 for 154 km (95 miles) until you hit Bari.

DAY 8: BARI/DEPARTURE

Bari's Aeroporto Palese is small but quite serviceable, with frequent connections through Rome and Milan.

Logistics: Bari hotels offer easy airport transfers; take advantage of them.

Great Itineraries

Venice, Florence, Rome, and Highlights in Between

Think of this itinerary as a rough draft for you to revise according to your interests and time constraints.

DAY 1: VENICE

Arrive in Venice's Marco Polo Airport, and hop on the bus to the city's main bus station. Check into your hotel, get out, and get lost along the canals for a couple of hours before dinner.

Logistics: At the main bus station, you can immediately transfer to the most delightful "bus" in the world: the vaporetto. Enjoy your first ride up the Grand Canal, and make sure you're paying attention to the *fermata* (stop) where you need to get off.

DAY 2: VENICE

Have coffee at a real Italian coffee shop before taking in the top sights, including the **Basilica di San Marco, Palazzo Ducale,** and **Galleria dell'Accademia.** Don't forget **Piazza San Marco**: the intense anticipation as you near the giant square climaxes in a stunning view of the piazza. Stop for lunch, sampling the traditional Venetian specialty *sarde in saor* (sardines in a mouthwatering sweet-and-sour preparation with onions and raisins), and check out the fish market at the foot of the **Rialto Bridge**; then see the sunset at the **Zattere** before dinner. Later, stop at a bar on the **Campo San Luca** or **Campo Santa Margherita,** where you can toast to being free of automobiles.

Logistics: Venice is best seen on foot, with the occasional vaporetto ride. Always carry a city map: it's very easy to get totally lost here.

Tips

■ The itinerary can also be completed by car on the autostradas. Obviously, it's best to pick up your car on Day 3, when you leave Venice.

■ The sights along this route can be crowded; you'll have a better time if you make the trip outside the busy months of June, July, and August.

DAY 3: FERRARA/BOLOGNA

The ride to **Ferrara,** your first stop in Emilia-Romagna, is about 90 minutes. Visit the **Castello Estense** and **Duomo** before grabbing lunch. Wander Ferrara's cobblestone streets, then hop on the train to **Bologna** (less than an hour away). Check into your hotel, and walk around **Piazza Maggiore** before dinner. Later check out some of Italy's best nightlife.

Logistics: The train station lies a bit outside the center of Ferrara, so you may want to take a taxi or a less expensive city bus into town.

DAY 4: BOLOGNA/FLORENCE

After breakfast, visit some of Bologna's churches and piazzas, and climb the leaning **Torre degli Asinelli** for a red-rooftop-studded panorama. After lunch, take the short train ride to **Florence.** You'll arrive in time for an afternoon siesta and an evening passeggiata.

DAY 5: FLORENCE

Start with the **Uffizi Gallery,** where you'll see Botticelli's *Primavera* and *Birth of Venus,* among other works. Next, walk to **Piazza del Duomo,** site of Brunelleschi's spectacular dome, which you can climb for an equally spectacular view. After a simple trattoria lunch, either devote the afternoon to art or hike up to **Piazzale**

Michelangelo, which overlooks the city. Finish the evening in style with a traditional *bistecca alla fiorentina* (grilled T-bone steak with olive oil).

Logistics: It's best to reserve Uffizi Gallery tickets in advance; you *must* reserve in advance to climb Brunelleschi's dome.

DAY 6: LUCCA/PISA
After breakfast, board a train for a 90-minute ride to the walled medieval city of **Lucca.** Don't miss the Romanesque **Duomo** or a walk along the city's ramparts. Have lunch at a trattoria before continuing on to **Pisa** (30 minutes away) and its **Campo dei Miracoli,** where you'll spend an afternoon seeing the **Leaning Tower,** along with the **Duomo** and **Battistero.** Walk down to the banks of the Arno River and dine at one of the inexpensive local restaurants in the real city center.

Logistics: Lucca's train station is conveniently situated just outside the walled city. Although across town from the Leaning Tower, Pisa's train station isn't far from the city center.

DAY 7: ROME
Take a high-speed train bound for **Rome,** a 90-minute trip from Florence, or 3 hours from Pisa. Although the Eternal City took millennia to build, on this whirlwind trip you'll have just two days to tour it. Make your way to your hotel and relax for a bit before heading to the **Piazza Navona, Campo de' Fiori,** and **Trevi Fountain**—it's best in the evening—and have a stand-up *aperitivo* (Campari and soda is a classic) at an unpretentious local bar. For dinner, you can't go wrong at any of Rome's popular local pizzerias.

DAY 8: ROME
In the morning, head to the **Vatican Museums** to see Michelangelo's glorious frescoes at the **Sistine Chapel.** Visit **St. Peter's Basilica and Square** before heading for lunch near the Pantheon. Next, visit the magnificent **Pantheon,** and then the **Colosseum,** stopping along Via dei Fori Imperiali to check out the **Roman Forum** from above. From the Colosseum, walk or take a taxi to **Piazza di Spagna,** a good place to shop at stylish boutiques.

Logistics: Avoid lines and waits by buying tickets online.

DAY 9: ROME/DEPARTURE
Head by taxi to Termini station and catch the train to Fiumicino airport.

Logistics: For most people, the train from Termini station is preferable to a taxi ride.

Great Itineraries

Rome in 3 Days

Rome wasn't built in a day—so don't try to see it all in a day. Three days is a doable, if jam-packed, amount of time to visit the ancient city's major attractions.

Logistics: Much of the city shuts down on Sunday (including the Vatican Museums, except for the last Sunday of the month), and many restaurants and state museums are closed on Monday. To skip lines and better enjoy your experiences, reservations are a good idea at the Colosseum and the Vatican Museums; they're required for the Galleria Borghese.

DAY 1: ANCIENT ROME
Spend your first day in Rome exploring the likes of the **Roman Forum**, **Musei Capitolini**, and the **Colosseum**. This area is pretty compact, but you can easily spend a full morning and afternoon exploring its treasures. It's best to try and beat the crowds at the Colosseum by getting there right when it opens at 8:30 am (advance tickets help, too). A guided tour of the Forum is also a good way to make the most out of your afternoon. After your day of sightseeing, stop for a classic Roman dinner in nearby Monti.

DAY 2: THE VATICAN AND PIAZZA NAVONA
Another full day of sightseeing awaits when you make your way to the city-state known as the **Vatican**. You'll once again want to try and avoid the biggest crowds here, especially for a glimpse of the Sistine Chapel (the best way to do this is to make online reservations for an extra €4 ahead of time). Booking a tour of the **Vatican Museums** is a good way to take full advantage of the site; most tours last two hours. Be sure to stop in and marvel at **St. Peter's Basilica**, too. Stop for lunch in nearby Prati, but after you're done with the Vatican, cross the river to **Piazza Navona**. Spend some time exploring this glorious piazza and its sculptures, but make sure to stop by the **Pantheon** before heading to Campo de' Fiori for dinner at an outdoor restaurant. Afterward, there are plenty of nearby bars to keep you occupied.

DAY 3: PIAZZA DI SPAGNA, VILLA BORGHESE, AND TRASTEVERE
Start your morning with breakfast near the **Trevi Fountain**, before doing some window-shopping up Via Condotti and along the many surrounding backstreets as you make your way to the **Spanish Steps**. Pose for some postcard-worthy photos there before heading to nearby **Villa Borghese**. If you're sick of museums, feel free to explore Rome's main park and enjoy the great views; if you're up for some more art, the **Galleria Borghese** is one of the city's best art museums. Afterwards, head to trendy Trastevere for dinner, and soak in the cobblestone streets and charming medieval houses as you barhop your last night in town.

IF YOU HAVE MORE TIME
If you want to make the most of your time in the city itself, take your time exploring the many churches and cathedrals, like **Sant'Ignazio** or **San Clemente**. You can also stop by to explore gorgeous palaces, like the **Palazzo Doria Pamphilij**, and check out lesser known but just as impressive museums, like the MAXXI or the MACRO. Visiting the ancient Roman road known as the Via Appia Antica and its spooky yet mesmerizing catacombs is another great way to spend an afternoon immersed in Roman history.

On the Calendar

Winter

Festa di Santa Lucia. The feast of Siracusa's patron, Santa Lucia, is held from December 13 to 20 at the Church of Santa Lucia alla Badia. A splendid silver statue of the saint is carried from the church to the Duomo: a torchlight procession and band music accompany the bearers, while local families watch from their balconies. ⊕ *www.basilicasantalucia.com.*

Sagra del Mandorlo in Fiore. In late February and early March, when most of the almond trees are in blossom, Agrigento hosts the Sagra del Mandorlo in Fiore, with international folk dances, a costumed parade, and the sale of marzipan and other sweet treats made from almonds. ⊕ *www.mandorloinfiore.online.*

Sant'Orso Fair. On the last weekend of January, the streets of Aosta are brightened by an arts-and-crafts market that brings artisans from all over the Valle d'Aosta. All the traditional techniques are featured: wood carving and sculpture, soapstone work, wrought iron, leather, wool, lace, and household items of all kinds. Food and wine are sold at outdoor stands and wandering minstrels enliven the whole event. ⊕ *www.fieradisantorso.it.*

Spring

Carnevale. Venice earned its international reputation as the "city of Carnevale" in the 18th century, when partying would begin several months before Lent and the city seemed to be one continuous masquerade. The celebration was revived for good in the 1970s, and each year over the 15- to 17-day Carnevale period (ending on the Tuesday before Ash Wednesday), more than a half-million people attend concerts, theater and street performances, masquerade balls, historical processions, fashion shows, and contests.

If you're not planning on joining in the revelry, you'd be wise to choose another time to visit Venice. Crowds throng the streets (which become one-way, with police directing foot traffic), bridges are designated "no-stopping" zones to avoid gridlock, and prices skyrocket. ⊕ *www.carnevale.venezia.it.*

Carnevale di Acireale. With fantastical floats and entertaining parades, Acireale's carnival celebrations are known as being the best in Sicily. The exact dates depend on Easter, but events are held over the course of three weekends before the start of Lent (Ash Wednesday), when thousands of revelers pack the streets of the coastal town. ⊕ *carnevaleacireale.eu.*

Festa della Madonna a Cavallo. In Scicli, southern Italy, the last Saturday in May brings the festival of the town's savior, Madonna delle Milizie (Virgin Mary of Militias), celebrating the supposed moment in the 11th century when the Virgin Mary descended on horseback to rescue the Norman-ruled town from a Saracen invasion. The weekend festival includes parading a statue of the Madonna on horseback through the main piazza to intervene in a mock battle before reveling in salvation by indulging in a sweet pastry towering with whipped cream, known as a *testa di turco.*

Festa di Sant'Efisio. On May 1, thousands of costumed villagers parade through town during Sardinia's greatest annual festival, the Festa di Sant'Efisio, named after the martyred saint who saved the city from the plague in the 17th century. The saint's statue is carried aloft through Cagliari's flower-lined streets, part of a four-day procession from Cagliari to Nora and back again (64 km [40 miles]

On the Calendar

round-trip), and is accompanied by colorful costumed groups from throughout the island in an enthusiastic celebration of traditional culture. Ask at Cagliari's tourist office about viewing the grand spectacle along the main route in Cagliari. From April on, you can find tickets at ⊕ *www.boxofficesardegna.it.*

Sagra del Pesce. The highlight of the festival of San Fortunato is held on the second Sunday of May each year. It's a crowded, colorful, and free-to-the-public feast of freshly caught fish, cooked outside at the port in a 12-foot frying pan. ⊕ *www.camogliturismo.it.*

Scoppio del Carro (Explosion of the Cart). On Easter Sunday, Florentines and foreigners alike flock to the Piazza del Duomo to watch as the Scoppio del Carro, a monstrosity of a carriage pulled by two huge oxen decorated for the occasion, makes its way through the city center and ends up in the piazza. Through an elaborate wiring system, an object representing a dove is sent from inside the cathedral to the baptistery across the way. The dove sets off an explosion of fireworks that come streaming from the carriage. You have to see it to believe it.

Vinitaly. This widely attended international wine and spirits event takes place for a few days in April. Recent gatherings have attracted more than 4,000 exhibitors from two dozen countries. The festivities kick off with Opera Wine, a showcase for the top 100 Italian wines as chosen by *Wine Spectator* magazine, which takes place in the Palazzo della Gran Guardia, in Piazza Bra. ⊕ *www.vinitaly.com.*

Summer

Arena di Verona Opera Festival. Milan's La Scala and Naples' San Carlo offer performances more likely to attract serious opera fans, but neither offers a greater spectacle than the Arena di Verona. During the venue's summer season (June to August), as many as 16,000 attendees sit on the original stone terraces or in modern cushioned stalls. Most of the operas presented are big and splashy, like *Aida* or *Turandot*, demanding huge choruses, lots of color and movement, and, if possible, camels, horses, or elephants. Order tickets by phone or through the arena website: if you book a spot on the cheaper terraces, be sure to take or rent a cushion—four hours on a 2,000-year-old stone bench can be an ordeal (from €27 for general admission). ⊕ *www.arena.it.*

Estate Fiesolana. From June through August, Estate Fiesolana, a festival of theater, music, dance, and film, takes place in Fiesole's churches and in the Roman amphitheater—demonstrating that the ancient Romans knew a thing or two about acoustics. ⊕ *www.estate-fiesolana.it.*

Festa del Redentore. On the third Sunday in July, crowds cross the Canale della Giudecca by means of a pontoon bridge, built every year to commemorate the doge's annual visit to Palladio's Chiesa del Santissimo Redentore to offer thanks for the end of a 16th-century plague. The evening before, Venetians—accompanied each year by an increasing number of tourists—set up tables and chairs along the canals. As evening falls, practically the whole city takes to the streets and tables, and thousands more take to the water. Boats decorated with colored lanterns (and well provisioned with traditional Redentore meals) jockey for position to watch the grand event. Half an hour before midnight, Venice kicks off a fireworks display over the Bacino, with brilliant reflections on its waters. You'll find good viewing anywhere along the Riva degli Schiavoni; you could also try Zattere, as close to Punta Dogana as you can get, or on the Zitelle end of the Giudecca. After the fireworks, join the young folks and stay out all night, greeting the sunrise on the Lido beach, or rest up and make the procession to mass on Sunday morning. If you're on a boat, allow a couple of hours to dislodge yourself from the nautical traffic jam when the festivities break up. ⊕ www.redentorevenezia.it.

Festa di San Giovanni (Feast of St. John the Baptist). On June 24 Florence mostly grinds to a halt to celebrate the Festa di San Giovanni in honor of its patron saint. Many shops and bars close, and at night a fireworks display lights up the Arno and attracts thousands.

Festival dei Due Mondi. Each summer Umbria hosts one of Italy's biggest arts festivals: Spoleto's Festival of the Two Worlds. Starting out as a classical music festival, it has now evolved into one of Italy's brightest gatherings of arts aficionados. Running from late June through mid-July, it features modern and classical music, theater, dance, and opera. Increasingly there are also a number of small cinema producers and their films. ⊕ www.festivaldispoleto.com.

Luminaria. Pisa is at its best during the Luminaria feast day, on June 16. The day honors St. Ranieri, the city's patron saint. Palaces along the Arno are lit with white lights, and there are plenty of fireworks.

Ravenna Festival. Orchestras from all over the world perform in city churches and theaters during this renowned music festival, which takes place in June and July, as well as during a few days at the beginning of November. ⊕ www.ravennafestival.org.

Taormina Film Festival. Sicily's famous festival takes place in late June and early July. ⊕ www.taorminafilmfest.it.

Umbria Jazz Festival. Perugia is hopping for 10 days in July, when more than a million people flock to see famous names in contemporary music perform at the Umbria Jazz Festival. In recent years the stars have included Wynton Marsalis, Sting, Eric Clapton, Lady Gaga, Tony Bennett, and Elton John. There's also a shorter Umbria Jazz Winter Festival from late December to early January. ⊕ www.umbriajazz.com.

Fall

Douja d'Or National Wine Festival. For 10 days in mid-September, Asti is host to a popular wine festival—an opportunity to see Asti and celebrate the product that made it famous. ⊕ www.doujador.it.

Eurochocolate Festival. If you've got a sweet tooth and are visiting in fall, book early and head to Perugia for the Eurochocolate Festival. This is one of the biggest chocolate festivals in the world, with a million visitors, and is held over a week in late October. ⊕ www.eurochocolate.com.

On the Calendar

Fiera Internazionale del Tartufo Bianco (International White Truffle Fair). From early October to early December, Alba hosts an internationally famous truffle fair. Merchants, chefs, and other aficionados of this pungent yet delicious fungus come from all over the world to buy and taste white truffles at the height of their season. The fourth Sunday of September sees the **Palio degli Asini**, a hilarious donkey race, a lampoon of Asti's eminently serious horse race. Tickets to watch this competition between Alba's districts, with riders dressed in medieval garb astride their stubborn beasts, can be hard to get. ■TIP→ **Hotel and restaurant reservations for October and November should be made well in advance.** ⊕ *www.fieradeltartufo.org.*

Palio di Asti. September is a month of fairs and celebrations in Asti, and this horse race that runs through the streets of town is the highlight. First mentioned in 1275, this annual event has been going strong ever since. After an elaborate procession in period costumes, nine horses and jockeys representing different sections of town vie for the honor of claiming the *palio*, a symbolic flag of victory. The race happens on a Sunday at the beginning of September each year. ⊕ *www.paliodiasti.com.*

Sagra Musicale Umbra. Held mid-September, the Sagra Musicale Umbra celebrates sacred music in Perugia and in several towns throughout the region. ⊕ *www.perugiamusicaclassica.com.*

Chapter 3

ROME

Updated by
Laura Itzkowitz

3

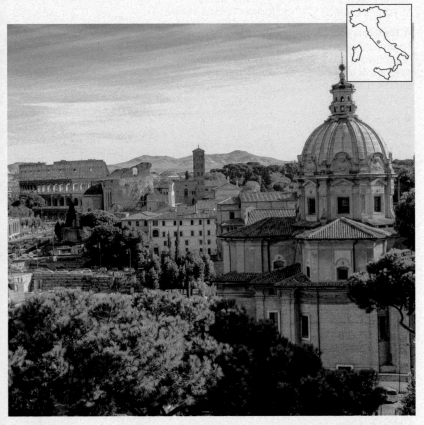

👁 Sights	🍴 Restaurants	🛏 Hotels	🛍 Shopping	🍸 Nightlife
★★★★★	★★★☆☆	★★★★★	★★★★☆	★★★★☆

WELCOME TO ROME

TOP REASONS TO GO

★ **The Vatican:** Although its population numbers only in the hundreds, the Vatican makes up for it with the millions who visit each year. Marvel at Michelangelo's Sistine Chapel and St. Peter's Basilica.

★ **The Colosseum:** The largest amphitheater of the Roman world was begun by Emperor Vespasian and inaugurated by his son Titus in AD 80.

★ **Piazza Navona:** You couldn't concoct a more Roman street scene: crowded café tables at street level, wrought-iron balconies above, and, at the center, Bernini's Fountain of the Four Rivers and Borromini's Sant'Agnese.

★ **Roman Forum:** This fabled labyrinth of ruins variously served as a political playground, a center of commerce, and a place where justice was dispensed during the Roman Republic and Empire.

★ **Trastevere:** This neighborhood is a maze of jumbled alleyways, traditional Roman trattorias, cobblestone streets, and medieval houses.

1 Ancient Rome with Monti and Celio. The Forum and Palatine Hill were once the hub of Western civilization.

2 The Vatican with Borgo and Prati. St. Peter's Basilica and the Sistine Chapel draw millions.

3 Piazza Navona, Campo de' Fiori, and the Jewish Ghetto. This is the heart of the historic quarter. The Ghetto still preserves the flavor of Old Rome.

4 Piazza di Spagna. Travel back to the days of the Grand Tour in this area.

5 Repubblica and the Quirinale. These areas house government offices, churches, and sights.

6 Villa Borghese and Around. Rome's most famous park is home to the Galleria Borghese.

7 Trastevere. Rome's left bank has kept its authentic roots.

8 Aventino and Testaccio. Aventino is a posh residential area, and Testaccio is more working class.

9 Esquilino and Via Appia Antica. These neighborhoods have plenty of ancient sights and churches.

FLAMINIO

Viale delle Belle Arti

Villa Giulia

Viale delle Belle Arti

Giardino Zoologico

Giardino D.Lago

Parco D.Daini

Galleria Borghese ◆

Villa Strohl Fern

6 VILLA BORGHESE

Villa Borghese

Via Flaminia

Via L. di Savoia

PIAZZA DEL POPOLO

Villa Medici

Corso d'Italia

Viale del Muro Torto

Via Vitt. Veneto

Via Boncompagni

Via Piave

PIAZZA DI SPAGNA

4

Via Ludovisi

Via Sistina

Via Vitt. Veneto

Via L. Bissolati

Via Barberini

Via del Corso

Via del Tritone

Via d. Quattro Fontane

REPUBBLICA

QUIRINALE

5

Via del Quirinale

ESQUILINO

9

PIAZZA NAVONA

3

Piazza Navona ◆

Corso del Rinascimento

Via del Corso

Via Nazionale

MONTI

Vittorio Emanuele II

V.d. Plebiscito

Via G. Lanza

CAMPO DE'FIORI

V. delle Botteghe Oscure

Via Cavour

JEWISH GHETTO

Roman Forum

1

ANCIENT ROME

◆ Palatine Hill

Colosseum ●

CELIO

TRASTEVERE

7

Via del Circo Massimo

Villa Celimontana

AVENTINO & TESTACCIO

8

Parco di Porta Capena

EAT LIKE A LOCAL IN ROME

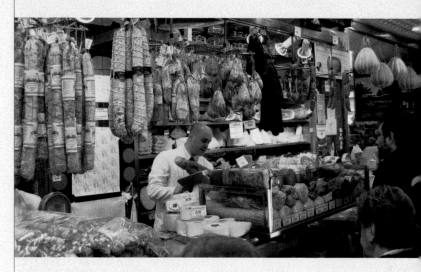

In Rome, tradition is the dominant feature of the cuisine, with a focus on freshness and simplicity, so when Romans continue ordering the standbys, it's easy to understand why. That said, Rome is the capital of Italy, and the influx of residents from other regions of the country has yielded many variations on the staples.

ARTICHOKES

There are two well-known preparations of *carciofo,* or artichoke, in Rome. Carciofi *alla romana* are stuffed with wild mint, garlic, and pecorino, then braised in olive oil, white wine, and water. Carciofi *alla giudia* (Jewish-style) are whole artichokes, deep-fried twice, so that they open like a flower, the outer leaves crisp and golden brown, while the heart remains tender. When artichokes are in season—late winter through the spring—they're served everywhere.

BUCATINI ALL'AMATRICIANA

It might look like spaghetti with red sauce, but there's much more to *bucatini all'amatriciana*. It's a spicy, rich, and complex dish that owes its flavor to *guanciale,* or cured pork jowl, as well as tomatoes and crushed red pepper flakes. It's often served over *bucatini,* a hollow, spaghetti-like pasta, and topped with grated pecorino Romano.

CODA ALLA VACCINARA

Rome's largest slaughterhouse in the 1800s was in the Testaccio neighborhood, and that's where you'll find dishes like *coda alla vaccinara*, or "oxtail

in the style of the cattle butcher."
This dish is made from ox or veal tails
stewed with tomatoes, carrots, celery,
and wine, and it's usually seasoned
with cinnamon. It's simmered for hours
and then finished with raisins and pine
nuts or bittersweet chocolate.

GELATO

Its consistency is often said to be a
cross between regular American ice
cream and soft-serve. The best versions
of gelato are extremely flavorful, and
almost always made fresh daily. When
choosing a *gelateria*, watch for signs
that say *gelato artigianale* (artisan- or
homemade); otherwise, keep an eye
out for the real deal by avoiding gelato
that looks too bright or fluffy.

PIZZA

There are two kinds of Roman pizza:
al taglio (by the slice) and *tonda* (round
pizza). The former has a thicker, focac-
cia-like crust and is cut into squares;
these are sold by weight and generally
available all day. The typical Roman
pizza tonda has a very thin crust and
is served almost charred. Because
they're so hot, the ovens are usually
fired up only in the evening, which is
why Roman *pizzerie* tend to open for
dinner only.

CACIO E PEPE

The name means "cheese and pepper,"
and this is a simple pasta dish from
the *cucina povera*, or rustic cooking,
tradition. It's a favorite Roman primo,
usually made with *tonnarelli* (fresh egg
pasta a bit thicker than spaghetti), which
is coated with a pecorino-cheese sauce
and lots of freshly ground black pepper.
Some restaurants serve the dish in an
edible bowl of paper-thin baked cheese.

FRITTI

The classic Roman starter in a trattoria
and especially at the pizzeria, is *fritti*:
an assortment of fried treats, usually
crumbed or in batter. Often, before
selecting a pizza, locals will order their
fritti: *filetti di baccalà* (salt cod in batter),
fiori di zucca (zucchini flowers, usually
stuffed with anchovy and mozzarella),
supplì (rice balls stuffed with mozzarella
and other ingredients), or *olive ascolane*
(stuffed olives).

LA GRICIA

This dish is often referred to as a "white
amatriciana" because it's precisely that:
pasta (usually spaghetti or rigatoni)
served with pecorino cheese and guanciale—thus amatriciana without the
tomato sauce. It's a lighter alternative
to *carbonara* in that it doesn't contain
egg, and its origins date back further
than the amatriciana.

The timeless city to which all roads lead, Mamma Roma enthralls visitors today as she has since time immemorial. Here the ancient Romans made us heirs-in-law to what we call Western Civilization; where centuries later Michelangelo painted the Sistine Chapel; and where Gian Lorenzo Bernini's Baroque nymphs and naiads still dance in their marble fountains.

Today the city remains a veritable Grand Canyon of culture. Ancient Rome rubs shoulders with the medieval, the modern runs into the Renaissance, and the result is like nothing so much as an open-air museum.

But always remember: "*Quando a Roma vai, fai come vedrai*" (When in Rome, do as the Romans do). Don't feel intimidated by the press of art and culture. Instead, contemplate the grandeur from a table at a sun-drenched café on Piazza della Rotonda; let Rome's colorful life flow around you without feeling guilty because you haven't seen everything. It can't be done, anyway. There's just so much here that you'll have to come back, so be sure to throw a coin in the Trevi Fountain.

Planning

When to Go

Spring and fall are the best times to visit, with mild temperatures and many sunny days. Summers are often sweltering, so come in July and August if you like, but we advise doing as the Romans do—get up and out early, seek refuge from the afternoon heat, resume activities in early evening, and stay up late to enjoy the nighttime breeze.

Most attractions are closed on major holidays. Come August, many shops and restaurants shutter as locals head out for vacation. Remember that air-conditioning is still a relatively rare phenomenon in this city, so carrying a small paper fan in your bag can work wonders. Roman winters are relatively mild, with persistent rainy spells.

Getting Around

The Metro is the easiest and fastest way to get around Rome. There are stops near most of the main tourist attractions; street entrances are marked with red "M" signs. The Metro has three lines: A and B, which intersect at Termini station, and also C. Linea A (red) runs from the eastern part of the city, with stops at San Giovanni in Laterano, Piazza Barberini, Piazza di Spagna, Piazzale Flaminio (Piazza del Popolo), and Ottaviano/San Pietro, near the Basilica di San Pietro and the Musei Vaticani. Linea B (blue) has stops near the Colosseum, the Circus Maximus, the Pyramid (Ostiense station and trains for Ostia Antica), and the Basilica di San Paolo fuori le Mura. Linea C runs from the eastern outskirts of the city through Pigneto. The Metro opens at 5:30 am, and the last trains leave the last station at either end at 11:30 pm (on Friday and Saturday nights the last trains on the A and B lines leave at 1:30 am).

Although not as fast as the Metro, bus and tram travel is more scenic. With reserved bus lanes and numerous tram lines, surface transportation is surprisingly efficient, given the volume of Roman traffic. At peak times, however, buses can be very crowded. If the distance you have to travel is not too great, walking can be a more comfortable alternative. ATAC city buses are orange, gray-and-red, or blue-and-orange; trams are orange or green. Remember to board at the rear and to exit at the middle: some bus drivers may refuse to let you out the front door, leaving you to scramble through the crowd to exit the middle or rear doors. Don't forget that you must buy your ticket before boarding, and be sure to stamp it in a machine as soon as you enter. The ticket is good for a transfer and one Metro trip within the next 100 minutes. Buses and trams run 5:30 am–midnight, after which time there's an extensive network of night buses with service throughout the city.

The bus system is a bit complicated to navigate due to the number of lines, but ATAC has a website (www.atac.roma.it/en/home) that will help you calculate the number of stops and bus route needed, and even give you a map directing you to the appropriate stops.

Rome's integrated transportation system includes buses and trams (ATAC), the Metropolitana (the subway, or Metro), suburban trains and buses (COTRAL), and commuter rail run by the state railway (Trenitalia). A ticket (BIT), valid for 100 minutes on any combination of buses and trams and one entrance to the Metro, costs €1.50. Tickets are sold at ATAC ticket booths, tobacco shops, newsstands, some coffee bars, and some bus stops, as well as in automatic ticket machines in Metro stations and on some buses. You can purchase individual tickets or buy in quantity. It's always a good idea to have a few tickets handy so you don't have to hunt for a vendor when you need one. All tickets must be validated by time-stamping in the yellow meter boxes aboard buses and in underground stations, immediately prior to boarding. Failure to validate your ticket will result in a fine of €54.90.

A Roma24H ticket, or *biglietto integrato giornaliero* (integrated daily ticket), is valid for 24 hours (from the moment you stamp it) on all public transit and costs €7. You can also purchase a Roma48H (€12.50), a Roma72H (€18), and a CIS (Carta Integrata Settimanale), which is valid for one week (€24). Each option gives unlimited travel on ATAC buses, COTRAL urban bus services, trains for the Lido and Viterbo, and the Metro. There's an ATAC kiosk at the bus terminal in front of Termini station. If you're going farther afield, or planning to spend more than a week in Rome, think about getting a BIRG (daily regional ticket) or a CIRS (weekly regional ticket) from the railway station. These give you unlimited travel on all state transport throughout the region of Lazio. This can take you as far as the Etruscan city of Tarquinia or medieval Viterbo.

Making the Most of Your Time

There's so much to do in Rome that it's hard to fit it all in, no matter how much time you have. If you're a first-time visitor, the Vatican Museums and the remains of ancient Rome are must-sees, but both require at least half a day, so if you only have one day, you're best off picking one or the other. Save time and skip lines by purchasing tickets for the Vatican Museums and the Colosseum (with the Roman Forum and Palatine Hill) online beforehand. If you have more than one day, do one on one morning and the other on the next. If you're planning to visit the Galleria Borghese, tickets can sell out days (or weeks) in advance during high season, so make sure to book early.

Addresses in Rome

In the *centro storico* (old town/historic center), most street names are posted on ceramic-like plaques on the sides of buildings, which can make them hard to see. Addresses are fairly straightforward: the street name is followed by the street number, but it's worth noting that Roman street numbering, even in the newer outskirts of town, can be erratic. Usually numbers are even on one side of the street and odd on the other, but sometimes numbers are in ascending consecutive order on one side of the street and descending order on the other side.

Etiquette

Although you may find Rome much more informal then many other European cities, Romans will nevertheless appreciate attempts to abide by local etiquette. When entering an establishment, the key words to know are: *buongiorno* (good morning), *buona sera* (good evening), and *buon pomeriggio* (good afternoon). These words can also double as a goodbye upon exit. Italians greet friends with a kiss, usually first on the right cheek, and then on the left. When you meet a new person, shake hands and say *piacere* (*pee*-ah-*chair*-ay).

How to Save Money

In addition to single- and multiday transit passes, a three-day Roma Pass (🖃 *€52*) covers unlimited use of buses, trams, and the Metro, plus free admission to two museums or archaeological sites of your choice and discounted entrance to others. A two-day pass is €32 and includes one museum.

Hop-On, Hop-Off

Some might consider them kitsch, but guided bus tours can prove a blissfully easy way to enjoy a quick introduction to the city's top sights—if you don't feel like being on your feet all day. Sitting in a bus, with friendly tour-guide commentary (and even friendlier fellow sightseers from every country under the sun), can make for a fun experience—so give one a whirl even if you're an old Rome hand. Of course, you'll want to savor these incredible sights at your own leisure later on.

The least expensive organized sightseeing tour of Rome is the one run by **CitySightseeing Roma**. Double-decker buses leave from Via Marsala, beside Termini station, but you can pick them up at any of their nine stopping points. A day ticket costs €24 and allows you to get off and on as often as you like. The price includes an audio guide system in six languages. The total tour takes about two hours and covers the Colosseum, Piazza Navona, St. Peter's, the Trevi Fountain, and Via Veneto. Tickets can be bought on board. Two- and three-day tickets are also available. Tours leave from Termini station every 20 minutes 9–7:30.

All operators can provide a luxury car for up to three people, a limousine for up to seven, or a minibus for up to nine, all with an English-speaking driver, but guide service is extra. Almost all operators offer "Rome by Night" tours, with or without dinner and entertainment. You can book tours through travel agents.

Roman Hours

In Italy, almost nothing starts on time except for (sometimes) a theater, opera, or movie showing. Italians even joke about a "15-minute window" before actually being late somewhere. In addition, the day starts a little later than normal here, with many shops not opening until 10 am, lunch never happens before 1 pm, and dinner rarely starts before 8 pm. On Sunday, Rome virtually shuts down, and on Monday, most state museums and exhibition halls, plus many restaurants, are closed. Daily food shop hours generally run 10 am–1 pm and 4 pm–7:30 pm or 8 pm; but other stores in the center usually observe continuous opening hours. Pharmacies tend to close for a lunch break and keep night hours (*ora rio notturno*) in rotation. As for churches, most open at 8 or 9 in the morning, close noon–3 or 4, then reopen until 6:30 or 7. St. Peter's, however, has continuous hours 7 am–7 pm (until 6 pm in the fall and winter); and the Vatican Museums are open Monday but closed Sunday (except for the last Sunday of the month).

Restaurants

In Rome, the Eternal(ly culinarily conservative) City, simple yet traditional cuisine reigns supreme. Most chefs prefer to follow the mantra of freshness over fuss and simplicity of flavor and preparation over complex cooking techniques.

Rome has been known since antiquity for its grand feasts and banquets, and dining out has always been a favorite Roman pastime. Until recently, the city's *buongustai* (gourmands) would have been the first to tell you that Rome is distinguished more by its enthusiasm for eating out than for a multitude of world-class restaurants—but this is changing. There is an ever-growing promotion of Slow Food practices, a focus on sustainably and locally sourced produce. Economic crisis has forced the food industry in Rome to adopt innovative ways to maintain a clientele who are increasingly looking to dine out but want to spend less. The result has been the rise of "street food" restaurants, selling everything from inexpensive and novel takes on classic *supplì* (Roman fried-rice balls) to sandwich shops that use a variety of organic ingredients.

Generally speaking, Romans like Roman food, and that's what you'll find in many of the city's trattorias and wine bars. For the most part, today's chefs cling to the traditional and excel at what has taken hundreds, sometimes thousands, of years to perfect. This is why the basic trattoria menu is more or less the same wherever you go. And it's why even the top Roman chefs feature their versions of simple trattoria classics like carbonara, and why those who attempt to offer it in a "deconstructed" or slightly varied style will often come under criticism. To a great extent, Rome is still a town where the Italian equivalent of "What are you in the mood for?" still gets the answer, "Pizza or pasta."

Hotels

It's the click of your heels on inlaid marble, the whisper of 600-thread-count Frette sheets, the murmured *buongiorno* of a coat-tailed porter bowing low as you pass. It's a rustic attic room with a wood-beam ceiling, a white umbrella on a roof terrace, a 400-year-old palazzo. Maybe it's birdsong pouring into your room as you swing open French windows to a sun-kissed view of the Colosseum, a timeworn piazza, or a flower-filled marketplace.

When it comes to accommodations, Rome offers a wide selection of high-end hotels, bed-and-breakfasts, designer boutique hotels—options that run the gamut from whimsical to luxurious. Whether you want a simple place to rest your head or a complete cache of exclusive amenities, you have plenty to choose from.

Restaurant and hotel reviews have been shortened. For full information, visit Fodors.com.

WHAT IT COSTS in Euros

	$	$$	$$$	$$$$
RESTAURANTS				
	under €15	€15–€24	€25–€35	over €35
HOTELS				
	under €125	€125–€200	€201–€300	over €300

Visitor Information

The Department of Tourism in Rome, called Roma Capitale, staffs green information kiosks (with multilingual personnel) near important sights, as well as at Termini station and Leonardo da Vinci Airport.

Ancient Rome with Monti and Celio

Time has reduced ancient Rome to fields of silent ruins, but the powerful impact of what happened here, of the genius and power that made Rome the center of the Western world, echoes across the millennia. In this one compact area of the city, you can step back into the Rome of Cicero, Julius Caesar, and Virgil. You can walk along the streets they knew, cool off in the shade of the Colosseum that loomed over the city, and see the sculptures poised over their piazzas. Today, this part of Rome, more than any other, is a perfect example of the layering of historic eras, the overlapping of ages, of religions, of a past that is very much a part of the present.

Outside the actual ancient sites, you'll find neighborhoods like Monti and Celio, *riones* that are just as much part of Rome's history as its ruins. These are the city's oldest neighborhoods, and today they are a charming mix of the city's past and present. Once you're done exploring ancient Rome, these are the easiest places to head for a bite to eat or some shopping.

GETTING HERE AND AROUND
The Colosseo Metro station is right across from the Colosseum and a short walk from both the Roman and the Imperial Forums, as well as the Palatine Hill. Walking from the very heart of the historic center will take about 20 minutes, much of it along the wide Via dei Fori Imperiali. The little electric Bus No. 117 from the center or No. 85 from Termini will also deliver you to the Colosseum's doorstep. Any of the following buses will take you to or near the Roman Forum: Nos. 60, 75, 85, and 170.

⊙ Sights

Arco di Costantino (*Arch of Constantino*)
RUINS | This majestic arch was erected in AD 315 to commemorate Constantine's victory over Maxentius at the Milvian Bridge. It was just before this battle, in AD 312, that Constantine—the emperor who converted Rome to Christianity—legendarily had a vision of a cross and heard the words, "In this sign thou shalt conquer." Many of the costly marble decorations for the arch were scavenged from earlier monuments, both saving money and placing Constantine in line with the great emperors of the past. It is easy to picture ranks of Roman centurions marching under the great barrel vault. ⊠ *Piazza del Colosseo, Monti* Ⓜ *Colosseo.*

★ The Campidoglio
PLAZA/SQUARE | Spectacularly transformed by Michelangelo's late-Renaissance designs, the Campidoglio was once the epicenter of the Roman Empire, the place where the city's first shrines stood, including its most sacred, the Temple of Jupiter. The Capitoline Hill originally

consisted of two peaks: the Capitolium and the Arx (where Santa Maria in Aracoeli now stands). The hollow between them was known as the Asylum. Here, prospective settlers once came to seek the protection of Romulus, legendary first king of Rome—hence the term "asylum." Later, during the Republic, in 78 BC, the Tabularium, or Hall of Records, was erected here. By the Middle Ages, however, the Capitoline had become an unkempt hill strewn with ancient rubble. In preparation for the impending visit of Charles V in 1536, triumphant after the empire's victory over the Moors, his host, Pope Paul III Farnese, decided that the Holy Roman Emperor should follow the route of the emperors, finishing triumphantly at the Campidoglio. The pope was embarrassed by the decrepit goat pasture the hill had become and so commissioned Michelangelo to restore the site to glory. The resulting design added a third palace along with Renaissance-style facades and a grand paved piazza. Newly excavated ancient sculptures, designed to impress the visiting emperor, were installed in the palaces, and the piazza was ornamented with the giant stone figures of the Dioscuri and the ancient Roman equestrian statue of Emperor Marcus Aurelius. A copy of this extraordinary statue is still the piazza's centerpiece (the 2nd-century original has been housed in the neighbouring Musei Capitolini since 1999). While there are great views of the Roman Forum from the terrace balconies to either side of the Palazzo Senatorio, the best view is from the 1st century BC Tabularium, now part of the Musei Capitolini. The museum café is on the Terrazza Caffarelli, with a magical view toward Trastevere and St. Peter's, and is accessible without a museum ticket. ⊠ *Piazza del Campidoglio, including the Palazzo Senatorio and the Musei Capitolini, the Palazzo Nuovo, and the Palazzo dei Conservatori, Piazza Venezia* Ⓜ *Colosseo.*

Circo Massimo (*Circus Maximus*)

RUINS | From the belvedere of the Domus Flavia on the Palatine Hill, you can see the Circus Maximus; there's also a great free view from Piazzale Ugo La Malfa on the Aventine Hill side. The giant space where once 300,000 spectators watched chariot races while the emperor looked on is ancient Rome's oldest and largest racetrack; it lies in a natural hollow between the two hills. The oval course stretches about 650 yards from end to end; on certain occasions, there were as many as 24 chariot races a day and competitions could last for 15 days. The charioteers could amass fortunes rather like the sports stars of today. (The Portuguese Diocles is said to have totted up winnings of 35 million sestertii.) The noise and the excitement of the crowd must have reached astonishing levels as the charioteers competed in teams, each with their own colors—the Reds, the Blues, etc. Betting also provided Rome's majority of unemployed with a potentially lucrative occupation. The central ridge was the site of two Egyptian obelisks (now in Piazza del Popolo and Piazza San Giovanni in Laterano). Picture the great chariot race scene from MGM's *Ben-Hur* and you have an inkling of what this all looked like. ⊠ *Between Palatine and Aventine Hills, Aventino* Ⓜ *Circo Massimo.*

★ The Colosseum

RUINS | The most spectacular extant edifice of ancient Rome, the Colosseum has a history that is half gore, half glory. Once able to house 50,000 spectators, it was built to impress Romans with its spectacles involving wild animals and fearsome gladiators from the farthest reaches of the Empire. Senators had marble seats up front and the vestal virgins took the ringside position, while the plebs sat in wooden tiers at the back, then the masses above on the top tier. Looming over all was the amazing velarium, an ingenious system of sail-like awnings rigged on ropes and maneuvered by sailors from the imperial fleet, who would unfurl them to protect the arena's occupants from sun or rain. From the second floor, you can get a bird's-eye view of the hypogeum: the subterranean passageways that were the architectural engine rooms that made the slaughter above proceed like clockwork. In a scene prefiguring something from Dante's *Inferno*, hundreds of beasts would wait to be eventually launched via a series of slave-powered hoists and lifts into the bloodthirsty sand of the arena above. Designed by order of the emperor Vespasian in AD 72, and completed by his son Titus in AD 80, the arena has a circumference of 573 yards, and its external walls were built with travertine from nearby Tivoli. Its construction was a remarkable feat of engineering, for it stands on marshy terrain reclaimed by draining an artificial lake that formed part of the vast palace of Nero. Originally known as the Flavian amphitheater (Vespasian's and Titus's family name was Flavius), it came to be known as the Colosseum thanks to a colossal gilded bronze statue which once stood nearby. The legend made famous by the Venerable Bede says that as long as the Colosseum stands, Rome will stand; and when Rome falls, so will the world … not that the prophecy deterred medieval and Renaissance princes and popes from using the Colosseum as a quarry. In the 19th century, poets came to view the arena by moonlight; today, mellow golden spotlights make the arena a spectacular sight at night, and evening visits are possible with guided tours from May through October. One way to beat the notoriously long ticket lines is to buy a Roma Pass ticket, which includes the Colosseum. You can also book a timed ticket in advance online for a €2 surcharge. Aim for early or late slots to minimize lines, as even the preferential lanes get busy in the middle of the day. Alternatively you can book a tour online with a company (do your research to make sure it's reputable) that lets you skip the line.

Avoid the tours sold on-the-spot around the Colosseum; although you can skip the lines, the tour guides tend to be dry, the tour groups huge, and the tour itself rushed. ⊠ *Piazza del Colosseo, Monti* ☎ *06/39967700* ⊕ *www.coopculture.it* 🎟 *€16 (combined ticket with the Roman Forum and Palatine Hill, 1 entry for either site if used within 2 days)* Ⓜ *Colosseo.*

Domus Aurea (*Golden House of Nero*)
RUINS | Legend has it that Nero famously fiddled while Rome burned. Fancying himself a great actor and poet, he played, as it turns out, his harp to accompany his recital of "The Destruction of Troy" while gazing at the flames of Rome's catastrophic fire of AD 64. Anti-Neronian historians propagandized that Nero, in fact, had set the Great Fire to clear out a vast tract of the city center to build his new palace. Today's historians discount this as historical folderol (going so far as to point to the fact that there was a full moon on the evening of July 19, hardly the propitious occasion to commit arson). But legend or not, Nero did get to build his new palace, the extravagant Domus Aurea (Golden House)—a vast "suburban villa" that was inspired by the emperor's pleasure palace at Baia on the Bay of Naples. His new digs were huge and sumptuous, with a facade of pure gold; seawater piped into the baths; decorations of mother-of-pearl, fretted ivory, and other precious materials; and vast gardens. It was said that after completing this gigantic house, Nero exclaimed, "Now I can live like a human being!" Note that access to the site is currently only on weekends and exclusively via guided tours that use virtual reality headsets for part of the presentation. Booking ahead is essential. ⊠ *Viale della Domus Aurea 1, Monti* ☎ *06/39967700 booking information* ⊕ *www.coopculture.it* 🎟 *€16 including booking fee and guided visit* ⊘ *Closed weekdays* Ⓜ *Colosseo.*

Rome Metro and Suburban Railway

Tickets

A ticket (BIT) valid for 100 minutes on any combination of buses and trams and one entrance to the metro costs €1.50. Tickets are sold at newsstands, some coffee bars, ticket machines in metro stations, and ATAC and COTRAL ticket booths. Time-stamp your ticket when boarding the first vehicle, and stamp it again when boarding for the last time within 75 minutes. You stamp the ticket at Metro sliding electronic doors, and in the little yellow machines on buses and trams.

Fare fees	Price
Single fare	€1.50
Biglietto integrato giornaliero (Integrated Daily Ticket) BIG	€6
Biglietto turistico integrato (Three-Day Pass) BTI	€16.50
Weekly pass	€24
Monthly unlimited pass	€35

Foro di Traiano (*Forum of Trajan*)

RUINS | Of all the Fori Imperiali, Trajan's was the grandest and most imposing, a veritable city unto itself. Designed by architect Apollodorus of Damascus, it comprised a vast basilica, two libraries, and a colonnade laid out around the square—all at one time covered with rich marble ornamentation. Adjoining the forum were the Mercati di Traiano (Trajan's Markets), a huge, multilevel brick complex of shops, taverns, walkways, and terraces, as well as administrative offices involved in the mammoth task of feeding the city. The Museo dei Fori Imperiali (Imperial Forums Museum) takes advantage of the Forum's soaring vaulted spaces to showcase archaeological fragments and sculptures while presenting a video re-creation of the original complex. In addition, the series of terraced rooms offers an impressive overview of the entire forum. A pedestrian walkway, the Via Alessandrina, also allows for an excellent (and free) view of Trajan's Forum. To build a complex of this magnitude, Apollodorus and his patrons clearly had great confidence, not to mention almost unlimited means and cheap labor at their disposal (readily provided by slaves captured in Trajan's Dacian Wars). The complex also contained two semicircular lecture halls, one at either end, which are thought to have been associated with the libraries in Trajan's Forum. The markets' architectural centerpiece is the enormous curved wall, or *exedra*, that shores up the side of the Quirinal Hill excavated by Apollodorus's gangs of laborers. Covered galleries and streets were constructed at various levels, following the exedra's curves and giving the complex a strikingly modern appearance. As you enter the markets, a large, vaulted hall stands in front of you. Two stories of shops and offices rise up on either side. Head for the flight of steps at the far end that leads down to Via Biberatica. (*Bibere* is Latin for "to drink," and the shops that open onto the street are believed to

have been taverns.) Then head back to the three retail and administrative tiers that line the upper levels of the great exedra and look out over the remains of the Forum. Empty and bare today, the cubicles were once ancient Rome's busiest market stalls. Though it seems to be part of the market, the Torre delle Milizie (Tower of the Militia), the tall brick tower that is a prominent feature of Rome's skyline, was actually built in the early 1200s. ✉ *Via IV Novembre 94, Monti* ☎ *06/0608* ⊕ *www.mercatiditraiano.it* 💶 *€11.50* Ⓜ *Cavour.*

Fori Imperiali

RUINS | A compound of five grandly conceived complexes flanked with colonnades, the Fori Imperiali contain monuments of triumph, law courts, and temples. The complexes were tacked on to the Roman Forum, from the time of Julius Caesar in the 1st century BC until Trajan in the very early 2nd century AD, to accommodate the ever-growing need for administrative buildings as well as grand monuments. From Piazza del Colosseo, head northwest on Via dei Fori Imperiali toward Piazza Venezia. Now that the road has been closed to private traffic, it's more pleasant for pedestrians (it's closed to all traffic on Sunday). On the walls to your left, maps in marble and bronze, put up by Benito Mussolini, show the extent of the Roman Republic and Empire (at the time of writing, these were partially obstructed by work on Rome's new subway line, Metro C). The dictator's own dreams of empire led him to construct this avenue, cutting brutally through the Fori Imperiali and the medieval and Renaissance buildings that had grown upon the ruins, so that he would have a suitable venue for parades celebrating his expected military triumphs. Among the Fori Imperiali along the avenue, you can see the Foro di Cesare (Forum of Caesar) and the Foro di Augusto (Forum of Augustus). The grandest was the Foro di Traiano (Forum of Trajan), with its huge semicircular Mercati di Traiano and the

Colonna Traiana (Trajan's Column). You can walk through part of Trajan's Markets on the Via Alessandrina and visit the Museo dei Fori Imperiali, which presents the Imperial Forums and shows how they would have been used through ancient fragments, artifacts, and modern multimedia. ⊠ *Via dei Fori Imperiali, Monti* ☎ *06/0608* ⊕ *www.mercatiditraiano.it* ▣ *Museum €11.50* Ⓜ *Colosseo.*

★ Musei Capitolini

RUINS | Surpassed in size and richness only by the Musei Vaticani, this immense collection was the world's first public museum. A greatest-hits of Roman art through the ages, from the ancients to the Baroque, it's housed in the Palazzo dei Conservatori and the Palazzo Nuovo, which mirror one another across Michelangelo's famous piazza. The collection was begun by Pope Sixtus IV (the man who built the Sistine Chapel) in 1473, when he donated a room of ancient statuary to the people of the city. This core of the collection includes the She Wolf, which is the symbol of Rome, and the piercing gaze of the Capitoline Brutus. Buy your ticket and enter the Palazzo dei Conservatori where, in the first courtyard, you'll see the giant head, foot, elbow, and imperially raised finger of the fabled seated statue of Constantine, which once dominated the Basilica of Maxentius in the Forum. Upstairs is the resplendent Sala degli Orazi e Curiazi (Hall of the Horatii and Curatii), decorated with a magnificent gilt ceiling, carved wooden doors, and 16th-century frescoes depicting the history of Rome's legendary origins. At each end of the hall are statues of two of the most important popes of the Baroque era, Urban VIII and Innocent X. The heart of the museum is the modern Exedra of Marcus Aurelius (Esedra di Marco Aurelio), which displays the spectacular original bronze statue of the Roman emperor whose copy dominates the piazza outside. To the right, the room segues into the area of the Temple of Jupiter, with the ruins of

part of its vast base rising organically into the museum space. A reconstruction of the temple and the Capitoline Hill from the Bronze Age to the present day makes for a fascinating glimpse through the ages. On the top floor, the museum's *pinacoteca*, or painting gallery, has some noted Baroque masterpieces, including Caravaggio's *The Fortune Teller* and *St. John the Baptist.* To get to the Palazzo Nuovo section of the museum, take the stairs or elevator to the basement of the Palazzo dei Conservatori, where the corridor uniting the two contains the Epigraphic Collection, a poignant assembly of ancient gravestones. Just over halfway along the corridor, and before going up into the Palazzo Nuovo, be sure to take the staircase to the right to the Tabularium gallery and its unparalleled view over the Forum. On the stairs inside the Palazzo Nuovo, you'll be immediately dwarfed by Mars in full military rig and lion-topped sandals. Upstairs is the noted Sala degli Imperatori, lined with busts of Roman emperors, and the Sala dei Filosofi, where busts of philosophers sit in judgment—a fascinating who's who of the ancient world. Within these serried ranks are 48 Roman emperors, ranging from Augustus to Theodosius. Nearby are rooms filled with sculptural masterpieces, including the famed *Dying Gaul*, the *Red Faun* from Hadrian's Villa, and a *Cupid and Psyche.* ⊠ *Piazza del Campidoglio 1, Piazza Venezia* ☎ *06/0608* ⊕ *www.museicapitolini.org* ▣ *€11.50 (€15 with exhibitions); €13.50 with access to Centrale Montemartini; audio guide €7* Ⓜ *Colosseo.*

★ Palatine Hill

RUINS | Just beyond the Arco di Tito, the Clivus Palatinus—the road connecting the Forum and the Palatine Hill—gently rises to the heights of the **Colle Palatino** (Palatine Hill), the oldest inhabited site in Rome. Now charmingly bucolic, with pines and olive trees providing shade in summer, this is where Romulus is said to have founded the city that bears his

Sights ▼

Restaurants ▼

Quick Bites ▼

Hotels ▼

name, and despite its location overlooking the Forum's traffic and attendant noise, the Palatine was the most coveted address for ancient Rome's rich and famous. During the Roman Republic it was home to wealthy patrician families—Cicero, Catiline, Crassus, and Agrippa all had homes here—and when Augustus (who had himself been born on the hill) came to power, declaring himself to be the new Romulus, it would thereafter become the home of emperors. The Houses of Livia and Augustus (which you can visit with the S.U.P.E.R. ticket, for the same price as the Roman Forum admission) are today the hill's best-preserved structures, replete with fabulous frescoes. If you only have time for one, the House of Augustus is the more spectacular of the two. After Augustus's relatively modest residence, Tiberius extended the palace and other structures followed, notably the gigantic extravaganza constructed for Emperor Domitian which makes up much of what we see today. ⊠ *Entrances at Piazza del Colosseo and Via di San Gregorio 30, Monti* ☎ *06/39967700* ⊕ *www.coopculture.it* ✉ *€16 combined ticket, includes single entry to Palatine Hill–Forum site and single entry to Colosseum (if used within 24 hours); S.U.P.E.R. ticket €22 (€24 with online reservation) includes access to the Houses of Augustus and Livia, the Palatine Museum, Aula Isiaca, Santa Maria Antiqua, and Temple of Romulus* Ⓜ *Colosseo.*

★ **The Roman Forum**

RUINS | Whether it's from the main entrance on Via dei Fori Imperali or by the entrance at the Arch of Titus, descend into the extraordinary archaeological complex that is the Foro Romano and the Palatine Hill, once the very heart of the Roman world. The Forum began life as a marshy valley between the Capitoline and Palatine Hills—a valley crossed by a mud track and used as a cemetery by Iron Age settlers. Over the years, a market center and some huts

were established here, and after the land was drained in the 6th century BC, the site eventually became a political, religious, and commercial center: the Forum. Hundreds of years of plunder reduced the Forum to its current desolate state. But this enormous area was once Rome's pulsating hub, filled with stately and extravagant temples, palaces, and shops and crowded with people from all corners of the empire. Adding to today's confusion is the fact that the Forum developed over many centuries; what you see today are not the ruins from just one period but from a span of almost 900 years, from about 500 BC to AD 400. Nonetheless, the enduring romance of the place, with its lonely columns and great broken fragments of sculpted marble and stone, makes for a quintessential Roman experience. There is always a line at the Colosseum ticket office for the combined Colosseum/Palatine/Forum ticket, but in high season, lines sometimes also form at the Forum and Palatine entrances. Those who don't want to risk waiting in line can book their tickets online in advance, for a €2 surcharge. Choose the print-at-home option (a PDF on a smartphone works, too) and avoid the line to pick up tickets. Your ticket is valid for one entrance to the Roman Forum and the Palatine Hill, which are part of a single continuous complex. Certain sites within the Forum require a S.U.P.E.R. ticket. ⊠ *Entrance at Via dei Fori Imperiali, Monti* ☎ *06/39967700* ⊕ *www.coopculture.it* ✉ *€16 (combined ticket with the Colosseum and Palatine Hill, if used within 24 hours); audio guide €5* Ⓜ *Colosseo.*

★ **San Clemente**

CHURCH | One of the most impressive archaeological sites in Rome, San Clemente is a historical triple-decker. A 12th-century church was built on top of a 4th-century church, which had been built over a 2nd-century pagan temple to the god Mithras and 1st-century Roman apartments. The layers were uncovered in 1857, when a curious prior, Friar Joseph Mullooly, started excavations beneath the present basilica. Today, you can descend to explore all three. The upper church (at street level) is a gem in its own right. In the apse, a glittering 12th-century mosaic shows Jesus on a cross that turns into a living tree. Green acanthus leaves swirl and teem with small scenes of everyday life. Early Christian symbols, including doves, vines, and fish, decorate the 4th-century marble choir screens. In the left nave, the Castiglioni chapel holds frescoes painted around 1400 by the Florentine artist Masolino da Panicale (1383–1440), a key figure in the introduction of realism and one-point perspective into Renaissance painting. Note the large Crucifixion and scenes from the lives of Saints Catherine, Ambrose, and Christopher, plus the Annunciation (over the entrance). To the right of the sacristy (and bookshop), descend the stairs to the 4th-century church, used until 1084, when it was damaged beyond repair during a siege of the area by the Norman prince Robert Guiscard. Still intact are some vibrant 11th-century frescoes depicting stories from the life of St. Clement. Don't miss the last fresco on the left, in what used to be the central nave. It includes a particularly colorful quote—including "Go on, you sons of harlots, pull!"—that's not only unusual for a religious painting, but also one of the earliest examples of written vernacular Italian. Descend an additional set of stairs to the Mithraeum, a shrine dedicated to the god Mithras. His cult spread from Persia and gained a foothold in Rome during the 2nd and 3rd centuries AD. Mithras was believed to have been born in a cave and was thus worshipped in cavernous, underground chambers, where initiates into the all-male cult would share a meal while reclining on stone couches, some visible here along with the altar block. Most such pagan shrines in Rome were destroyed by Christians, who often built churches over their remains, as happened here. ✉ *Via San Giovanni in Laterano 108, Celio* ☎ *06/7740021* ⊕ *www.basilicasanclemente.com* ✉ *Archaeological area €10* Ⓜ *Colosseo*.

Santa Maria di Aracoeli

CHURCH | Sitting atop 124 steps, Santa Maria di Aracoeli perches on the north slope of the Capitoline Hill. The church rests on the site of the temple of Juno Moneta (Admonishing Juno), which also housed the Roman mint (hence the origin of the word "money"). According to legend, it was here that the Sibyl, a prophetess, predicted to Augustus the coming of a Redeemer. He in turn responded by erecting an altar, the Ara Coeli (Altar of Heaven). This was eventually replaced by a Benedictine monastery, and then a church, which was passed in 1250 to the Franciscans, who restored and enlarged it in Romanesque-Gothic style. Today, the Aracoeli is best known for the Santo Bambino, a much-revered olivewood figure of the Christ Child (today a copy of the 15th-century original that was stolen in 1994). At Christmas, everyone pays homage to the "Bambinello" as children recite poems from a miniature pulpit. In true Roman style, the church interior is a historical hodgepodge, with classical columns and large marble fragments from pagan buildings, as well as a 13th-century Cosmatesque pavement. The richly gilded Renaissance ceiling commemorates the naval victory at Lepanto in 1571 over the Turks. The first chapel on the right is noteworthy for Pinturicchio's frescoes of St. Bernardino of Siena (1486). ✉ *Via del Teatro di Marcello, at top of long, steep stairway, Piazza Venezia* ☎ *06/69763839* Ⓜ *Colosseo*.

★ Santa Maria Maggiore

CHURCH | Despite its florid 18th-century facade, Santa Maria Maggiore is one of the oldest churches in Rome, built around 440 by Pope Sixtus III. One of the four great pilgrimage churches of Rome, it's also the city center's best example of an Early Christian basilica—one of the immense, hall-like structures derived from ancient Roman civic buildings and divided into thirds by two great rows of columns marching up the nave. The other three major basilicas in Rome (San Giovanni in Laterano, St. Peter's, and St. Paul Outside the Walls) have been largely rebuilt. Paradoxically, the major reason why this church is such a striking example of Early Christian design is that the same man who built the undulating exteriors circa 1740, Ferdinando Fuga, also conscientiously restored the interior, throwing out later additions and, crucially, replacing a number of the great columns. Precious 5th-century mosaics high on the nave walls and on the triumphal arch in front of the main altar bear splendid testimony to the basilica's venerable age. Those along the nave show 36 scenes from the Old Testament (unfortunately, tough to see clearly without binoculars), and those on the arch illustrate the Annunciation and the Youth of Christ. The resplendent carved-wood ceiling dates to the early 16th century; it's supposed to have been gilded with the first gold brought from the New World. The inlaid marble pavement (called Cosmatesque, after the family of master artisans who developed the technique) in the central nave is even older, dating to the 12th century. The Cappella Sistina (Sistine Chapel), in the right-hand transept, was created by architect Domenico Fontana for Pope Sixtus V in 1585. Elaborately decorated with precious marbles "liberated" from the monuments of ancient Rome, the chapel includes a lower-level museum in which some 13th-century sculptures by Arnolfo da Cambio are all that's left of what was the once richly endowed chapel of the *presepio* (Christmas crèche), looted during the Sack of Rome in 1527. Directly opposite, on the church's other side, stands the Cappella Paolina (Pauline Chapel), a rich Baroque setting for the tombs of the Borghese popes Paul V—who commissioned the chapel in 1611 with the declared intention of outdoing Sixtus's chapel across the nave—and Clement VIII. The Cappella Sforza (Sforza Chapel) next door was designed by Michelangelo and completed by Della Porta. Just right of the altar, next to his father, lies Gian Lorenzo Bernini; his monument is an engraved slab, as humble as the tombs of his patrons are grand. Above the loggia, the outside mosaic of Christ raising his hand in blessing is one of Rome's most beautiful sights, especially when lighted at night. The loggia mosaics can be seen close-up by following a 30-minute guided tour (€5). Tours run roughly every hour, though have no fixed timetable. For information or to join either tour, go through the souvenir shop inside the church on the right and down the stairs to the right to the museum entrance. ✉ *Piazza di Santa Maria Maggiore, Monti* ☎ *06/69886802* ✉ *Museum tour €4, loggia mosaics tour €5* Ⓜ *Termini.*

🍴 Restaurants

★ Urbana 47

$$$ | MODERN ITALIAN | This restaurant serving breakfast through dinner embodies the *kilometro zero* concept, highlighting hyper-local food from the surrounding Lazio region. The local boho crowd comes in the morning for a continental or "American" breakfast (with free Wi-Fi); lunch means tasty "fast slow-food" options like grain salads and healthy panini, as well as a few more substantial dishes, with a more extensive menu for dinner. **Known for:** hyper-local produce; healthy lunch options; aperitivo and tapas. Ⓢ *Average main: €30* ✉ *Via Urbana 47, Monti* ☎ *06/47884006* ⊕ *www.urbana47.it* ⊘ *Closed Tuesday* Ⓜ *Cavour.*

☕ Coffee and Quick Bites

★ Fatamorgana

$ | ICE CREAM | The emphasis is on all-natural ingredients at this woman-owned gelateria, which has several locations in Rome. Flavors change often, but might include favorites like stracciatella and hazelnut as well as more unusual flavors like matcha. **Known for:** gluten-free with many vegan options; all natural ingredients; unusual flavors. $ *Average main: €3* ✉ *Piazza degli Zingari 5, Monti* ☎ *06/48906955* ⊕ *www.gelateriafatamorgana.com* Ⓜ *Cavour.*

▼ Nightlife

★ Ai Tre Scalini

WINE BARS | An ivy-covered wine bar in the center of Monti, Rome's trendiest 'hood, Ai Tre Scalini has a warm and cozy menu of delicious antipasti and light entrées to go along with its enticing wine list. After about 8 pm, if you haven't booked, be prepared to wait—this is one extremely popular spot with locals. ✉ *Via Panisperna 251, Monti* ☎ *06/48907495* ⊕ *www.aitrescalini.org* Ⓜ *Cavour.*

★ The Court

COCKTAIL LOUNGES | For a winning combination of creative cocktails and incredible views of the Colosseum, this bar in Palazzo Manfredi can't be beat. Bar manager Matteo "Zed" Zamberlan cut his teeth in New York's top bars and here his creativity is on full display. The cocktails are pricey, but they come with a bounty of snacks from the hotel's acclaimed restaurant. ✉ *Via Labicana 125, Colosseo* ☎ *06/77591380* ⊕ *www.palazzomanfredi.com* Ⓜ *Colosseo.*

👜 Shopping

★ Sacripante

WOMEN'S CLOTHING | This tiny Monti art gallery/boutique/bar houses some of the most sophisticated retro-inspired fashion garments around Rome. Its owner, Wilma Silvestri, cleverly combines ethnic and contemporary fabrics for her label Le Gallinelle, evolving them into stylish clothing with a modern edge made for everyday wear. ✉ *Via Panisperna 59, Monti* ☎ *06/48903495* ⊕ *www.sagripantegallery.com* Ⓜ *Cavour.*

The Vatican with Borgo and Prati

Climbing the steps to St. Peter's Basilica feels monumental, like a journey that has reached its climactic end. Suddenly, all is cool and dark … and you are dwarfed by the gargantuan nave and its magnificence. Above is a ceiling so high it must lead to heaven itself. Great, shining marble figures of saints frozen mid-whirl loom from niches and corners. And at the end, a throne for an unseen king whose greatness, it is implied, must mirror the greatness of his palace. For this basilica is a palace, the dazzling center of power for a king and a place of supplication for his subjects. Whether his kingdom is earthly or otherwise may lie in the eye of the beholder.

For good Catholics and sinners alike, the Vatican is an exercise in spirituality, requiring patience but delivering joy. Some come here for a transcendent glimpse of a heavenly Michelangelo fresco; others come in search of a direct connection with the divine. But what all visitors share, for a few hours, is an awe-inspiring landscape that offers a famous sight for every taste: rooms

The Vatican with Borgo and Prati

VATICAN

BORG

Museo Pio Clementino

Cortile della Pigna

Giardino Quadrato

Giardini Vaticani

Cortile del Belvedere

Piazza de Risorgimento

decorated by Raphael, antique sculptures like the Apollo Belvedere, famous paintings by Giotto and Bellini, and, perhaps most of all, the Sistine Chapel—for the lover of beauty, few places are as historically important as this epitome of faith and grandeur.

The Borgo and Prati are the neighborhoods immediately surrounding the Vatican, and it's worth noting that, while the Vatican may well be a priority, these neighborhoods are not the best places to choose a hotel, as they're quite far from other top sights in the city.

GETTING HERE AND AROUND

Metro stop Cipro or Ottaviano will get you within about a 10-minute walk of the entrance to the Musei Vaticani. Or, from Termini station, Bus No. 40 Express or the famously crowded No. 64 will take you to Piazza San Pietro. Both routes swing past Largo Argentina, where you can also get Bus No. 46.

A leisurely meander from the centro storico, across the exquisite Ponte Sant'Angelo, will take about a half hour.

 Sights

★ Basilica di San Pietro

CHURCH | The world's largest church, built over the tomb of St. Peter, is the most imposing and breathtaking architectural achievement of the Renaissance (although much of the lavish interior dates to the Baroque). No fewer than five of Italy's greatest artists—Bramante, Raphael, Peruzzi, Antonio da Sangallo the Younger, and Michelangelo—died while striving to erect this new St. Peter's. The history of the original St. Peter's goes back to AD 326, when the emperor Constantine completed a basilica over the site of the tomb of Saint Peter, the Church's first pope. The original church stood for more than 1,000 years, undergoing a number of restorations and alterations, until, toward the middle of the 15th century, it was on the verge of

collapse. In 1452, a reconstruction job began but was abandoned for lack of money. In 1503, Pope Julius II instructed the architect Bramante to raze all the existing buildings and build a new basilica, one that would surpass even Constantine's for grandeur. It wasn't until 1626 that the new basilica was completed and consecrated. Highlights include the Loggia delle Benedizioni (Benediction Loggia), the balcony where newly elected popes are proclaimed; Michelangelo's *Pietà*; and Bernini's great bronze baldacchino, a huge, spiral-columned canopy—at 100,000 pounds, perhaps the largest bronze object in the world—as well as many other Bernini masterpieces. There's also the collection of Vatican treasures in the Museo Storico-Artistico e Tesoro, and the Grotte Vaticane crypt. For views of both the dome above and the piazza below, take the elevator or stairs to the roof; those with more stamina (and without claustrophobia) can then head up more stairs to the apex of the dome. ■ TIP→ **The basilica is free to visit, but a security check at the entrance can create very long lines. Arrive before 8:30 or after 5:30 to minimize the wait and avoid the crowds.** ✉ *Piazza San Pietro, Vatican* ⊕ *www.vaticanstate.va* ⊙ *Closed during Papal Audience (Wed. until 1 pm) and during other ceremonies in piazza* Ⓜ *Ottaviano.*

★ Cappella Sistina (*Sistine Chapel*)

ART MUSEUM | In 1508, the redoubtable Pope Julius II commissioned Michelangelo to fresco the more than 10,000 square feet of the Sistine Chapel's ceiling. (*Sistine,* by the way, is simply the adjective form of *Sixtus,* in reference to Pope Sixtus IV, who commissioned the chapel itself.) The task took four years, and it's said that, for many years afterward, Michelangelo couldn't read anything without holding it over his head. The result, however, was the greatest artwork of the Renaissance. A pair of binoculars helps greatly, as does a small mirror—hold it facing the ceiling and look down to study the reflection. More than 20 years after his work on the ceiling, Michelangelo was called on again, this time by Pope Paul III, to add to the chapel's decoration by painting the Last Judgment on the wall over the altar. By way of signature on this, his last great fresco, Michelangelo painted his own face on the flayed-off human skin in St. Bartholomew's hand. ■TIP➜ **The chapel is entered through the Musei Vaticani, and lines are much shorter after 2:30 (reservations are always advisable)—except free Sundays, which are extremely busy and when admissions close at 12:30.** ✉ *Musei Vaticani, Vatican* ⊕ *www. museivaticani.va* ✉ *€17 (part of the Vatican Museums)* ⊗ *Closed Sun.* ⚓ *Reservations required* Ⓜ *Ottaviano.*

Castel Sant'Angelo

CASTLE/PALACE | FAMILY | Standing between the Tiber and the Vatican, this circular castle has long been one of Rome's most distinctive landmarks. Opera lovers know it well as the setting for the final scene of Puccini's *Tosca*. Started in AD 135, the structure began as a mausoleum for the emperor Hadrian and was completed by his successor, Antoninus Pius. From the mid-6th century the building became a fortress, a place of refuge for popes during wars and sieges. Its name dates to AD 590, when Pope Gregory the Great, during a procession to plead for the end of a plague, saw an angel standing on the summit of the castle, sheathing his sword. Taking this as a sign that the plague was at an end, the pope built a small chapel at the top, placing a statue next to it to celebrate his vision—thus the name, Castel Sant'Angelo. In the rooms off the Cortile dell'Angelo, look for the Cappella di Papa Leone X (Chapel of Pope Leo X), with a facade by Michelangelo. In the Pope Alexander VI courtyard, a wellhead bears the Borgia coat of arms. The stairs at the far end of the courtyard lead to the open terrace for a view of the Passetto, the fortified corridor connecting Castel Sant'Angelo with the Vatican. In the

appartamento papale (papal apartment), the Sala Paolina (Pauline Room) was decorated in the 16th century by Perino del Vaga and assistants with lavish frescoes of scenes from the Old Testament and the lives of Saint Paul and Alexander the Great. ✉ *Lungotevere Castello 50, Prati* ☎ *06/6819111 central line, 06/6896003 tickets* ⊕ *castelsantangelo.beniculturali.it* ✉ *€15* ⊗ *Closed Mon.* ⚓ *Online reservations recommended* Ⓜ *Lepanto.*

★ **Musei Vaticani** (*Vatican Museums*) ART MUSEUM | Other than the pope and his papal court, the occupants of the Vatican are some of the most famous artworks in the world. The Vatican Palace, residence of the popes since 1377, consists of an estimated 1,400 rooms, chapels, and galleries. The pope and his household occupy only a small part; most of the rest is given over to the Vatican Library and Museums. Beyond the glories of the Sistine Chapel, the collection is extraordinarily rich: highlights include the great antique sculptures (including the celebrated Apollo Belvedere in the Octagonal Courtyard and the Belvedere Torso in the Hall of the Muses); the Stanze di Raffaello (Raphael Rooms), with their famous gorgeous frescoes; and the Old Master paintings, such as Leonardo da Vinci's beautiful (though unfinished) *St. Jerome in the Wilderness*, some of Raphael's greatest creations, and Caravaggio's gigantic *Deposition in the Pinacoteca* (*Picture Gallery*). For those interested in guided visits to the Vatican Museums, tours start at €34, including entrance tickets, and can also be booked online. Other offerings include a regular two-hour guided tour of the Vatican gardens; call or check online to confirm. For more information, call 06/69884676 or go to museivaticani.va. For information on tours, call 06/69883145 or 06/69884676; visually impaired visitors can arrange tactile tours by calling 06/69884947. ✉ *Viale Vaticano, near intersection with*

Continued on page 104

HEAVENS ABOVE:
THE SISTINE CEILING

Forming lines that are probably longer than those waiting to pass through the Pearly Gates, hordes of visitors arrive at the Sistine Chapel daily to view what may be the world's most sublime example of artistry.

Michelangelo: *The Creation of Adam,* Sistine Chapel, The Vatican, circa 1511.

Michelangelo's Sistine Ceiling. To paint this 12,000-square-foot barrel vault, it took four years, 343 frescoed figures, and a titanic battle of wits between the artist and Pope Julius II. While in its typical fashion, Hollywood focused on the element of agony, not ecstasy, involved in the saga of creation, a recently completed restoration of the ceiling has revolutionized our appreciation of

MICHELANGELO'S
MISSION IMPOSSIBLE

Designed to match the proportions of Solomon's Temple described in the Old Testament, the Sistine Chapel is named after Pope Sixtus VI, who commissioned it as a place of worship for himself and as the venue where new popes could be elected. Before Michelangelo, the barrel-vaulted ceiling was an expanse of azure fretted with golden stars. Then, in 1504, an ugly crack appeared. Bramante, the architect, managed do some patchwork using iron rods, but when signs of a fissure remained, the new Pope Julius II summoned Michelangelo to cover it with a fresco 135 feet long and 44 feet wide.

Taking in the entire span of the ceiling, the theme connecting the various participants in this painted universe could be said to be mankind's anguished waiting. The majestic panel depicting the Creation of Adam leads, through the stages of the Fall and the expulsion from Eden, to the tragedy of Noah found naked and mocked by his own sons; throughout all runs the underlying need for man's redemption. Witnessing all from the side and end walls, a chorus of ancient Prophets and Sibyls peer anxiously forward, awaiting the Redeemer who will come to save both the Jews and the Gentiles.

APOCALYPSE NOW

The sweetness and pathos of his *Pietà*, carved by Michelangelo only ten years earlier, have been left behind. The new work foretells an apocalypse, its congregation of doomed sinners facing the wrath of heaven through hanging, beheading, crucifixion, flood, and plague. Michelangelo, by nature a misanthrope, was already filled with visions of doom thanks to the fiery orations of Savonarola, whose thunderous preachments he had heard before leaving his hometown of Florence. Vasari, the 16th-century art historian, coined the word "terrabilità" to describe Michelangelo's tension-ridden style, a rare case of a single word being worth a thousand pictures.

Michelangelo wound up using a Reader's Digest condensed version of the stories from Genesis, with the dramatis personae overseen by a punitive and terrifying God. In real life, poor Michelangelo answered to a flesh-and-blood taskmaster who was almost as vengeful: Pope Julius II. Less vicar of Christ than latter-day Caesar, he was intent on uniting Italy under the power of the Vatican, and was eager to do so by any means, including riding into pitched battle. Yet this "warrior pope" considered his most formidable adversary to be Michelangelo. Applying a form of blackmail, Julius threatened to wage war on Michelangelo's Florence, to which the artist had fled after Julius canceled a commission for a grand papal tomb unless Michelangelo agreed to return to Rome and take up the task of painting the Sistine Chapel ceiling.

MICHELANGELO, SCULPTOR

A sculptor first and foremost, however, Michelangelo considered painting an inferior genre—"for rascals and sissies" as he put it. Second, there was the sheer scope of the task, leading Michelangelo to suspect he'd been set up by a rival, Bramante, chief architect of the new St. Peter's Basilica. As Michelangelo was also a master architect, he regarded this fresco commission as a Renaissance mission-impossible. Pope Julius's powerful will prevailed—and six years later the work of the Sistine Ceiling was complete. Irving Stone's famous novel *The Agony and the Ecstasy*—and the granitic 1965 film that followed—chart this epic battle between artist and pope.

THINGS ARE LOOKING UP

To enhance your viewing of the ceiling, bring along opera-glasses, binoculars, or just a mirror (to prevent your neck from becoming bent like Michelangelo's). Note that no photos are permitted. Insiders know the only time to get the chapel to yourself is during the papal blessings and public audiences held in St. Peter's Square. Failing that, get there during lunch hour. Admission and entry to the Sistine Chapel is only through the Musei Vaticani (Vatican Museums).

SCHEMATIC OF THE SISTINE CEILING

PAINTING THE BIBLE

The ceiling's biblical symbols were ideated by three Vatican theologians, Cardinal Alidosi, Egidio da Viterbo, and Giovanni Rafanelli, along with Michelangelo. As for the ceiling's painted "framework," this quadratura alludes to Roman triumphal arches because Pope Julius II was fond of mounting "triumphal entries" into his conquered cities (in imitation of Christ's procession into Jerusalem on Palm Sunday).

THE CENTER PANELS
Prophet turned art-critic or, perhaps doubling as ourselves, the ideal viewer, Jonah the prophet (painted at the altar end) gazes up at the Creation, or Michelangelo's version of it.

1 The first of three scenes taken from the Book of Genesis: God separates Light from Darkness.

2 God creates the sun and a craterless pre-Galilean moon while the panel's other half offers an unprecedented rear view of the Almighty creating the vegetable world.

3 In the panel showing God separating the Waters from the Heavens, the Creator tumbles towards us as in a self-made whirlwind.

4 Pausing for breath, next admire probably Western Art's most famous image—God giving life to Adam.

5 The Creation of Eve from Adam's rib leads to the sixth panel.

6 In a sort of diptych divided by the trunk of the Tree of Knowledge of Good and Evil, Michelangelo retells the Temptation and the Fall.

7 Illustrating Man's fallen nature, the last three panels narrate, in un-chronological order, the Flood. In the first Noah offers a pre-Flood sacrifice of thanks.

8 Damaged by an explosion in 1794, next comes Michelangelo's version of Flood itself.

9 Finally, above the monumental Jonah, you can just make out the small, wretched figure of Noah, lying drunk—in pose, the shrunken anti-type of the majestic Adam five panels down the wall.

THE CREATION OF ADAM

Michelangelo's Adam was partly inspired by the Creation scenes Michelangelo had studied in the sculpted doors of Jacopo della Quercia in Bologna and Lorenzo Ghiberti's Doors of Paradise in Florence. Yet in Michelangelo's version Adam's hand hangs limp, waiting God's touch to impart the spark of life. Facing his Creation, the Creator—looking a bit like the pagan god Jupiter—is for the first time ever depicted as horizontal, mirroring the Biblical "in his own likeness." Decades after its completion, a crack began to appear, amputating Adam's fingertips. Believe it or not, the most famous fingers in Western art are the handiwork, at least in part, of one Domenico Carnevale.

Via Leone IV, Vatican ☎ *06/69883145* ⊕ *www.museivaticani.va* ⊘ *Closed Sun. and church holidays* ⚲ *Reservations required* ✉ *€17 with online reservations* Ⓜ *Cipro–Musei Vaticani or Ottaviano–San Pietro; Bus 64 or 40.*

Necropoli Vaticana (*Vatican Necropolis*)
CEMETERY | With advance notice you can take a 1½-hour guided tour in English of the Vatican Necropolis, under the Basilica di San Pietro, which gives a rare glimpse of Early Christian Roman burial customs and a closer look at the tomb of St. Peter. Apply via the contact form online, by fax, or in person (the entrance to the office is on the left of the Bernini colonnade), specifying the number of people in the group (all must be age 15 or older), preferred language, preferred time, available dates, and your contact information in Rome. Each group will have about 12 participants. Visits are not recommended for those with mobility issues or who are claustrophobic. ✉ *Ufficio Scavi, Vatican* ☎ *06/69885318, 06/69873017 reservations* ⊕ *www.scavi.va* ✉ *€13* ⊘ *Closed Sun. and Roman Catholic holidays* ⚲ *Reservations required* Ⓜ *Ottaviano.*

★ **Piazza di San Pietro**
PLAZA/SQUARE | Mostly enclosed within high walls that recall the papacy's stormy history, the Vatican opens the spectacular arms of Bernini's colonnade to embrace the world only at St. Peter's Square, scene of the pope's public appearances. One of Bernini's most spectacular masterpieces, the elliptical Piazza di San Pietro was completed in 1667 after only 11 years' work and holds about 100,000 people. Surrounded by a pair of quadruple colonnades, it is gloriously studded with 140 statues of saints and martyrs. At the piazza's center, the 85-foot-high Egyptian obelisk was brought to Rome by Caligula in AD 37 and moved here in 1586 by Pope Sixtus V. The Vatican post offices can be found on both sides of St. Peter's Square and inside the Vatican Museums complex and are open to the public. ■ TIP→ **The main information office is just left of the basilica as you face it.** ✉ *Piazza di San Pietro, Vatican* ⊕ *www. vaticanstate.va* Ⓜ *Ottaviano.*

 Restaurants

★ **Del Frate**
$$ | MODERN ITALIAN | This impressive wine bar matches sleek, modern decor with creative cuisine and three dozen wines available by the glass. The house specialty is marinated meat and fish, but you can also get cheeses, smoked meats, and composed salads. **Known for:** wide selection of after-dinner drinks, including mezcal (smoky agave liquor) and amari (bitter cordial); daily aperitivo with a nice selection of wines by the glass; adjacent to one of Rome's noted wine shops. ⑤ *Average main: €23* ✉ *Via degli Scipioni 118, Prati* ☎ *06/3236437* ⊕ *www.enotecadelfrate.it* ⊘ *Closed Aug.* Ⓜ *Ottaviano.*

Sant'Isidoro Pizza & Bolle
$ | PIZZA | Taking the traditional pairing of pizza and beer up a notch, this modern pizzeria on a quiet street pairs its pies with an extensive selection of sparkling wines. More upscale than a typical pizzeria but casual enough for a weeknight, this place serves classic flavor combinations as well as some creative options, like a pizza topped with stracciatella, raw shrimp, lemon peel, and mint. **Known for:** chic modern design; wide selection of sparkling wines; creative pizzas. ⑤ *Average main: €12* ✉ *Via Oslavia 41, Prati* ☎ *06/89822607* ⊕ *www.pizzaebolle. it* Ⓜ *Lepanto.*

Taverna Angelica
$$ | MODERN ITALIAN | The Borgo area near St. Peter's Basilica hasn't been known for culinary excellence, but this is starting to change, and Taverna Angelica was one of the first refined restaurants in this part of town. The dining room is small, which allows the chef to create a menu that's inventive without being pretentious. **Known for:** tiramisu with amaretti biscuits;

eclectic Italian dishes; elegant surroundings. $ *Average main: €22* ⊠ *Piazza Amerigo Capponi 6, Borgo* ☎ *06/6874514* ⊕ *www.tavernaangelica.com* ⊗ *Closed Mon.* Ⓜ *Ottaviano.*

Coffee and Quick Bites

Al Settimo Gelo

$ | **ICE CREAM** | The unusual flavors of gelato scooped up here include cinnamon and ginger and fig with cardamom and walnut, but the classics also get rave reviews. Ask for a taste of the *passito* flavor, if it's available; it's inspired by the popular sweet Italian dessert wine. **Known for:** completely gluten-free shop; organic Sicilian lemon sorbetto; homemade whipped cream. $ *Average main: €5* ⊠ *Via Vodice 21/a, Prati* ☎ *06/3725567* ⊕ *www.alsettimogelo.it* ⊗ *Closed Mon., and 1 wk in Aug.* Ⓜ *Lepanto.*

Bonci Pizzarium

$ | **PIZZA** | This tiny storefront by famed pizzaiolo Gabriele Bonci is the city's most famous place for pizza *al taglio*. It serves more than a dozen flavors, from the standard margherita to slices piled high with prosciutto and other tasty ingredients. **Known for:** long lines; Rome's best pizza *al taglio*; over a dozen flavors. $ *Average main: €5* ⊠ *Via della Meloria 43, Prati* ☎ *06/39745416* ⊕ *www.bonci. it* Ⓜ *Cipro.*

🛏 Hotels

Hotel al San Pietrino

$ | **HOTEL** | This simple budget hotel on the third floor of a 19th-century palazzo offers rock-bottom rates at a five-minute walk from the Vatican. **Pros:** air-conditioning and Wi-Fi; free parking; heavenly rates near the Vatican. **Cons:** no bar; flat pillows and basic bedding; a couple of Metro stops from the centro storico. $ *Rooms from: €65* ⊠ *Via Giovanni Bettolo 43, Prati* ☎ *06/3700132* ⊕ *www.sanpietrino.it* ⊷ *12 rooms* ⊖| *No Meals* Ⓜ *Ottaviano.*

Residenza Paolo VI

$$ | **HOTEL** | Set in a former monastery—still an extraterritorial part of the Vatican—magnificently abutting Bernini's colonnade of St. Peter's Square, the Paolo VI (pronounced "Sesto," a reference to Pope Paul VI) is unbeatably close to St. Peter's, with comfortable and amazingly quiet guest rooms. **Pros:** direct views of St. Peter's from the rooftop terrace; lovely staff and service; quiet rooms. **Cons:** some rooms are really small; bathrooms are a tight space; far away from Rome's historical attractions. $ *Rooms from: €143* ⊠ *Via Paolo VI 29, Borgo* ☎ *06/684870* ⊕ *www.residenzapaolovi. com* ⊷ *35 rooms* ⊖| *Free Breakfast* Ⓜ *Ottaviano.*

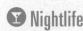 Nightlife

Bukowski's Bar

COCKTAIL LOUNGES | This cozy spot outside the Vatican is furnished like a familiar living room with a giant velvet sofa and armchairs, making it easy to meet the people sitting next to you. In addition to a strong cocktail and wine menu, the owners regularly host art, theater, and shopping events. Aperitivo is served every evening, with a selection of drinks and the option of adding a small plate for €5. ⊠ *Via Degli Ombrellari 25, Borgo* ☎ *06/64760105* Ⓜ *Ottaviano.*

Emerald's Bar

COCKTAIL LOUNGES | This classy cocktail bar a few blocks from the Vatican makes you feel transported to a cozy salon in New York or London. The bartenders shake up reliably good classics, including an excellent Dirty Martini, and also some original creations. ⊠ *Via Crescenzio 91C, Prati* ☎ *06/88654275* ⊕ *www.emeraldsbar. com* ⊗ *Closed Mon.* Ⓜ *Ottaviano.*

Shopping

★ **Castroni**

FOOD | Opening its flagship shop near the Vatican in 1932, this gastronomic paradise has long been Rome's port-of-call for decadent delicacies from around the globe; there are now 13 locations throughout the city. Jonesing expats and study-abroad students pop in for local sweets, Twinings teas, and even some good old-fashioned Kraft Macaroni & Cheese. If you're just doing a little window-shopping, be sure to try their in-house roasted espresso, some of the best coffee in Rome. ✉ *Via Cola di Rienzo 196/198, Prati* ☎ *06/6874383* ⊕ *www.castronicoladirienzo.com* Ⓜ *Lepanto, Ottaviano.*

Savelli Arte e Tradizione

CRAFTS | Here you'll find a fully stocked selection of religious gifts: everything from rosaries and crosses to religious artwork and Pope Francis memorabilia. Founded in 1898, this family business provides a place for pilgrims to pick up a souvenir from the Holy See and also specializes in mosaics. The store has another location at Il Colonnato Self Service Restaurant in Piazza del Sant'Uffizio. ✉ *Via Paolo VI 27–29, Borgo* ☎ *06/68307017* ⊕ *www.savellireligious.com* Ⓜ *Ottaviano.*

Piazza Navona, Campo de' Fiori, and the Jewish Ghetto

Set between Via del Corso and the Tiber bend, these time-burnished districts are some of the city's most beautiful. They're filled with airy piazzas, half-hidden courtyards, and narrow streets bearing curious names. Some of Rome's most coveted residential addresses are nestled here. So, too, are the ancient Pantheon and the Renaissance square of Campo de' Fiori, but the spectacular, over-the-top

Baroque monuments of the 16th and 17th centuries predominate.

The hub of the district is the queen of squares, Piazza Navona—a cityscape adorned with the most jaw-dropping fountain by Gian Lorenzo Bernini, father of the Baroque. Streets running off the square lead to many historic must-sees, including noble churches by Borromini and Caravaggio's greatest paintings at San Luigi dei Francesi. This district has been an integral part of the city since ancient times, and its position between the Vatican and Lateran palaces, both seats of papal rule, put it in the mainstream of Rome's development from the Middle Ages onward. Craftsmen, shopkeepers, and famed artists toiled in the shadow of the huge palaces built to consolidate the power of leading figures in the papal court. Artisans and artists still live here, but their numbers are diminishing as the district becomes increasingly posh and—so critics say—"Disneyfied." But three of the liveliest piazzas in Rome—Piazza Navona, Piazza della Rotonda (home to the Pantheon), and Campo de' Fiori—are lodestars in a constellation of some of the city's finest cafés, stores, and wine bars.

Although today most of Rome's Jews live outside the Ghetto, the area remains the spiritual and cultural home of Jewish Rome, and that heritage permeates its small commercial area of Judaica shops, kosher bakeries, and restaurants. The Jewish Ghetto was established by papal decree in the 16th century. It was by definition a closed community, where Roman Jews lived under lock and key until Italian unification in 1870. In 1943–44, the already small Jewish population there was decimated by deportations. Today there are a few Judaica shops and kosher groceries, bakeries, and restaurants (especially on Via di Portico d'Ottavia), but the neighborhood mansions are now being renovated and much coveted by rich and stylish expats.

GETTING HERE AND AROUND

The Piazza Navona and Campo de' Fiori are an easy walk from the Vatican or Trastevere, or a half-hour stroll from the Spanish Steps. From Termini or the Vatican, take Bus No. 40 Express or the No. 64 to Largo Torre Argentina; then walk 10 minutes to either piazza. Bus No. 62 winds from Piazza Barberini past the Trevi Fountain to Campo de' Fiori.

From the Vatican or the Spanish Steps, it's a 30-minute walk to the Jewish Ghetto, or take the No. 40 Express or the No. 64 bus from Termini station to Largo Torre Argentina.

Sights

Campo de' Fiori

MARKET | A bustling marketplace in the morning (Monday through Saturday from 8 to 2) and a trendy meeting place the rest of the day and night, this piazza has plenty of down-to-earth charm. Just after lunchtime, all the fruit and vegetable vendors disappear, and this so-called *piazza trasformista* takes on another identity, becoming a circus of bars particularly favored by study-abroad students, tourists, and young expats. Brooding over the piazza is a hooded statue of the philosopher Giordano Bruno, who was burned at the stake here in 1600 for heresy, one of many victims of the Roman Inquisition. ⊠ *Intersection of Via dei Baullari, Via Giubbonari, Via del Pellegrino, and Piazza della Cancelleria, Campo de' Fiori.*

★ Crypta Balbi

RUINS | The fourth component of the magnificent collections of the Museo Nazionale Romano, this museum is unusual because it represents several periods of Roman history. The crypt is part of the Balbus Theater complex (13 BC), and other parts of the complex are from the medieval period, up through the 20th century. The written explanations accompanying the well-lit exhibits are excellent, and this museum is a popular field trip for teachers and school groups. ⊠ *Via delle Botteghe Oscure 31, Jewish Ghetto* ☎ *06/39967701* ⊕ *www.coopculture. it* ⊠ *€8 Crypta Balbi only; €10 includes 3 other Museo Nazionale Romano sites over a 1-week period (Palazzo Altemps, Palazzo Massimo, Museo Diocleziano)* Ⓜ *Bus Nos. 64 and 40, Tram No. 8.*

Fontana delle Tartarughe

FOUNTAIN | Designed by Giacomo della Porta in 1581 and sculpted by Taddeo Landini, this fountain, set in pretty Piazza Mattei, is one of Rome's most charming. The focus of the fountain is four bronze boys, each grasping a dolphin spouting water into a marble shell. Bronze turtles held in the boys' hands drink from the upper basin. The turtles were added in the 17th century by Bernini. ⊠ *Piazza Mattei, Jewish Ghetto.*

Il Gesù

CHURCH | The mother church of the Jesuits in Rome is the prototype of all Counter-Reformation churches, and its spectacular interior tells a great deal about an era of religious triumph and turmoil. Its architecture influenced ecclesiastical buildings in Rome for more than a century (the overall design was by Vignola, the facade by della Porta) and was exported by the Jesuits throughout the rest of Europe. Though consecrated in 1584, the interior of the church wasn't fully decorated for another 100 years. It was originally intended that the interior be left plain to the point of austerity—but, when it was finally embellished, the mood had changed and no expense was spared. Its interior drips with gold and lapis lazuli, gold and precious marbles, gold and more gold, all covered by a fantastically painted ceiling. Unfortunately, the church is also one of Rome's most crepuscular, so its visual magnificence is considerably dulled by lack of light. The architectural significance of Il Gesù extends far beyond the splendid interior. As the first of the great Counter-Reformation churches, it was put up

Piazza Navona, Campo de' Fiori, and the Jewish Ghetto

Sights ▼

1 Campo de' Fiori E7
2 Crypta Balbi H7
3 Fontana delle Tartarughe H8
4 Il Gesù................................ I7
5 Palazzo Altemps E3
6 Palazzo Spada E8
7 Pantheon G5
8 Piazza Navona E5
9 Portico d'Ottavia H9
10 San Luigi dei Francesi............. F4
11 Santa Maria sopra Minerva H5
12 Sant'Andrea della Valle........... F7
13 Sant' Ignazio I5
14 Sant'Ivo alla Sapienza F5
15 Sinagoga............................ H9
16 Via Giulia............................ C7

Restaurants ▼

1 Armando al Pantheon............. G5
2 Ba' Ghetto J3
3 Bar del Fico......................... D4
4 Bellacarne.......................... H9
5 Cul de Sac E6
6 Ditirambo E6
7 Emma G7
8 Enoteca Corsi H6
9 Etablì D4
10 Filetti di Baccalà F8
11 Il Convivio Troiani................. E3
12 Il Sanlorenzo F7
13 La Ciambella G6
14 L'Angolo Divino..................... E8
15 Osteria dell'Ingegno............... I4
16 Pesci Fritti F7
17 Pianostrada E9
18 Pierluigi C6
19 Salumeria Roscioli................. F8

Quick Bites ▼

1 Gelateria Del Teatro D4
2 Giolitti H3
3 Pasticceria Boccione H8
4 Sant'Eustachio il Caffè........... G5

Hotels ▼

1 Albergo Santa Chiara G6
2 Casa di Santa Brigida D7
3 Chapter Roma...................... G9
4 D.O.M. Hotel Roma B6
5 Hotel de' Ricci...................... C7
6 Hotel Genio E4
7 Hotel Ponte Sisto E4
8 Pantheon Iconic Hotel G5

after the Council of Trent (1545–63) had signaled the determination of the Roman Catholic Church to fight back against the Reformed Protestant heretics of northern Europe. The church decided to do so through the use of overwhelming pomp and majesty, in an effort to woo believers. As a harbinger of ecclesiastical spectacle, Il Gesù spawned imitations throughout Italy and the other Catholic countries of Europe as well as the Americas. The most striking element is the ceiling, which is covered with frescoes that swirl down from on high to merge with painted stucco figures at the base, the illusion of space in the two-dimensional painting becoming the reality of three dimensions in the sculpted figures. Baciccia, their painter, achieved extraordinary effects in these frescoes, especially in the *Triumph of the Holy Name of Jesus*, over the nave. Here, the figures representing evil are cast out of heaven and seem to be hurtling down onto the observer. To appreciate in detail, the spectacle is best viewed through a specially tilted mirror in the nave. The founder of the Jesuit order himself is buried in the Chapel of St. Ignatius, in the left-hand transept. This is surely the most sumptuous Baroque altar in Rome; as is typical, the enormous globe of lapis lazuli that crowns it is really only a shell of lapis over a stucco base—after all, Baroque decoration prides itself on achieving stunning effects and illusions. The heavy, bronze altar rail by architect Carlo Fontana is in keeping with the surrounding opulence. ⊠ *Via degli Astalli 16, Campo de' Fiori* ☎ *06/697001* ⊕ *www.chiesadelgesu.org.*

★ **Palazzo Altemps**

CASTLE/PALACE | Containing some of the finest ancient Roman statues in the world, Palazzo Altemps is part of the Museo Nazionale Romano. The palace's sober exterior belies a magnificence that appears as soon as you walk into the majestic courtyard, studded with statues and covered in part by a retractable awning. The restored interior hints at the Roman lifestyle of the 16th–18th centuries while showcasing the most illustrious pieces from the Museo Nazionale, including the collection of the Ludovisi noble family. In the frescoed salons you can see the *Galata Suicida,* a poignant sculptural work portraying a barbarian warrior who chooses death for himself and his wife, rather than humiliation by the enemy. Another highlight is the large Ludovisi sarcophagus, magnificently carved from marble. In a place of honor is the *Ludovisi Throne*, which shows a goddess emerging from the sea and being helped by her acolytes. For centuries this was heralded as one of the most sublime Greek sculptures, but, today, at least one authoritative art historian considers it a colossally overrated fake. Look for the framed explanations of the exhibits that detail (in English) how and exactly where Renaissance sculptors, Bernini among them, added missing pieces to the classical works. In the lavishly frescoed Loggia stand busts of the Caesars. In the wing once occupied by early-20th-century poet Gabriele d'Annunzio (who married into the Altemps family), three rooms host the museum's Egyptian collection. ⊠ *Piazza di Sant'Apollinare 46, Piazza Navona* ☎ *06/39967701* ⊕ *www.coopculture.it* ⊠ *€8, or €10 including 3 other Museo Nazionale Romano sites over 1 week (Crypta Balbi, Palazzo Massimo alle Terme, Museo delle Terme di Diocleziano); €11, or €13 (including 3 other sites) if a special exhibit is on.*

Palazzo Spada

CASTLE/PALACE | In this neighborhood of huge, austere palaces, Palazzo Spada strikes an almost frivolous note, with its pretty ornament-encrusted courtyard and its upper stories covered with stuccoes and statues. While the palazzo houses an impressive collection of Old Master paintings, it's most famous for its trompe-l'oeil garden gallery, a delightful example of the sort of architectural games rich Romans of the 17th century found irresistible. Even if you don't go into the gallery, step into the courtyard and look through the glass window of the library to the colonnaded corridor in the adjacent courtyard. See—or seem to see—a 26-foot-long gallery quadrupled in depth, a sort of optical telescope taking the Renaissance's art of perspective to another level, as it stretches out for a great distance with a large statue at the end. In fact the distance is an illusion: the corridor grows progressively narrower and the columns progressively smaller as they near the statue, which is just 2 feet tall. The Baroque period is known for special effects, and this is rightly one of the most famous. It was long thought that Borromini was responsible for this ruse; it's now known that it was designed by an Augustinian priest, Giovanni Maria da Bitonto. Upstairs is a seignorial picture gallery with the paintings shown as they would have been, piled on top of each other clear to the ceiling. Outstanding works include Brueghel's *Landscape with Windmills,* Titian's *Musician,* and Andrea del Sarto's *Visitation.* Look for the fact-sheets that have descriptive notes about the objects in each room. ✉ *Piazza Capo di Ferro 13, Campo de' Fiori* ☎ *06/6874896* ⊕ *www.galleriaspada. beniculturali.it* ✍ *€5* ⊙ *Closed Tues.*

★ **Pantheon**

RELIGIOUS BUILDING | The best preserved ancient building in the city, this former Roman temple is a marvel of architectural harmony and proportion. It was entirely rebuilt by the emperor Hadrian around AD 120 on the site of an earlier Pantheon (from the Greek: *pan,* all, and *theon,* gods) erected in 27 BC by Augustus's right-hand man and son-in-law, Agrippa. The most striking thing about the Pantheon is not its size, immense though it is, nor even the phenomenal technical difficulties posed by so massive a construction; rather, it's the remarkable unity of the building. The diameter described by the dome is exactly equal to its height. It's the use of such simple mathematical balance that gives

classical architecture its characteristic sense of proportion and its nobility. The opening at the apex of the dome, the *oculus,* is nearly 30 feet in diameter and was intended to symbolize the "all-seeing eye of the heavens." On a practical note, this means when it rains, it rains inside: look out for the drainage holes in the floor. Although little is known for sure about the Pantheon's origins or purpose, it's worth noting that the five levels of trapezoidal coffers (sunken panels in the ceiling) represent the course of the five then-known planets and their concentric spheres. Ruling over them is the sun, represented symbolically and literally by the 30-foot-wide eye at the top. The heavenly symmetry is further paralleled by the coffers: 28 to each row, the number of lunar cycles. In the center of each would have shone a small bronze star. Down below, the seven large niches were occupied not by saints, but, it's thought, by statues of Mars, Venus, the deified Caesar, and the other "astral deities," including the moon and sun, the "sol invictus." (Academics still argue, however, about which gods were most probably worshipped here.) One of the reasons the Pantheon is so well preserved is the result of it being consecrated as a church in AD 608. (It's still a working church today.) No building, church or not, though, escaped some degree of plundering through the turbulent centuries of Rome's history after the fall of the empire. In 655, for example, the gilded bronze covering the dome was stripped. The Pantheon is also one of the city's important burial places. Its most famous tomb is that of Raphael (between the second and third chapels on the left as you enter). Mass takes place on Sunday and on religious holidays at 10:30; it's open to the public, but you are expected to arrive before the beginning and stay until the end. General access usually resumes at about 11:30. ✉ *Piazza della Rotonda, Piazza Navona* ☎ *06/68300230* ⊕ *www.pantheonroma.com* ✍ *Free; audio guide €7.*

★ Piazza Navona

PLAZA/SQUARE | Always camera-ready, the beautiful Baroque plaza known as Piazza Navona has Bernini sculptures, three gorgeous fountains, a magnificently Baroque church (Sant'Agnese in Agone), and under it all the remains of a Roman athletics track. Pieces of the arena are still visible near the adjacent Piazza Sant'Apollinare, and the ancient spirit of entertainment lives on in the buskers and mimes who populate the piazza today. The piazza took on its current look during the 17th century, after Pope Innocent X of the Pamphilj family decided to make over his family palace (now the Brazilian embassy and an ultra-luxe hotel) and the rest of the piazza. Center stage is the Fontana dei Quattro Fiumi, created for Innocent by Bernini in 1651. Bernini's powerful figures of the four rivers represent the longest rivers of the four known continents at the time: the Nile (his head covered because the source was unknown); the Ganges; the Danube; and the Plata (the length of the Amazon was then unknown). Popular legend has it that the figure of the Plata—the figure closest to Sant'Agnese in Agone—raises his hand before his eyes because he can't bear to look upon the church's "inferior" facade designed by Francesco Borromini, Bernini's rival. If you want a café with one of the most beautiful, if pricey, views in Rome, grab a seat at Piazza Navona. Just be aware that all the restaurants here are heavily geared toward tourists, so while it's a beautiful place for a coffee, you can find cheaper, more authentic, and far better meals elsewhere. ⊠ *Piazza Navona.*

Portico d'Ottavia

RUINS | Looming over the Jewish Ghetto, this huge portico, with a few surviving columns, is one of the area's most picturesque set pieces, with the church of Sant'Angelo in Pescheria built right into its ruins. Named by Augustus in honor of his sister Octavia, it was originally 390 feet wide and 433 feet long, encompassed two temples, a meeting hall, and a library, and served as a kind of grandiose entrance foyer for the adjacent Teatro di Marcello. The ruins of the portico became Rome's *pescheria* (fish market) during the Middle Ages. A stone plaque on a pillar (a copy; the original is in the Musei Capitolini) states in Latin that the head of any fish surpassing the length of the plaque was to be cut off "up to the first fin" and given to the city fathers, or else the vendor was to pay a fine of 10 gold florins. The heads were used to make fish soup and were considered a great delicacy. ⊠ *Via Portico d'Ottavia 29, Jewish Ghetto.*

★ San Luigi dei Francesi

CHURCH | A pilgrimage spot for art lovers, San Luigi's Contarelli Chapel (the fifth and last chapel on the left, toward the main altar) is adorned with three stunningly dramatic works by Caravaggio (1571–1610), the Baroque master of the heightened approach to light and dark. They were commissioned for the tomb of Mattheiu Cointerel in one of Rome's French churches (San Luigi is St. Louis, patron saint of France). The inevitable coin machine will light up his *Calling of Saint Matthew, Saint Matthew and the Angel,* and *Martyrdom of Saint Matthew* (seen from left to right), and Caravaggio's mastery of light takes it from there. When painted, they caused considerable consternation among the clergy of San Luigi, who thought the artist's dramatically realistic approach was scandalously disrespectful. A first version of the altarpiece was rejected; the priests were not particularly happy with the other two, either. Time has fully vindicated Caravaggio's patron, Cardinal Francesco del Monte, who secured the commission for these works and stoutly defended them. ⊠ *Piazza di San Luigi dei Francesi, Piazza Navona* ☎ *06/688271* ⊕ *www.saintlouis-rome.net.*

★ Santa Maria sopra Minerva

CHURCH | The name of the church reveals that it was built *sopra* (over) the ruins of a temple of Minerva, the ancient goddess of wisdom. Erected in 1280 by Dominicans along severe Italian Gothic lines, it has undergone a number of more or less happy restorations to the interior. Certainly, as the city's major Gothic church, it provides a refreshing contrast to Baroque flamboyance. Have a €1 coin handy to illuminate the Cappella Carafa in the right transept, where Filippino Lippi's (1457–1504) glowing frescoes are well worth the small investment, opening up the deepest azure expanse of sky where musical angels hover around the Virgin. Under the main altar is the tomb of St. Catherine of Siena, one of Italy's patron saints. Left of the altar you'll find Michelangelo's *Risen Christ* and the tomb of the gentle artist Fra Angelico. Bernini's unusual and little-known monument to the Blessed Maria Raggi is on the fifth pier of the left-hand aisle. In front of the church, Bernini's *Elephant and Obelisk* is perhaps the city's most charming sculpture. An inscription on the base references the church's ancient patroness, reading something to the effect that it takes a strong mind to sustain solid wisdom. ⊠ *Piazza della Minerva, Piazza Navona* ☏ *06/792257* ⊕ *www.santamariasopraminerva.it.*

Sant'Andrea della Valle

CHURCH | Topped by the highest dome in Rome after St. Peter's (designed by Maderno), this huge and imposing 17th-century church is remarkably balanced in design. Fortunately, its facade, which had turned a sooty gray from pollution, has been cleaned to a near-sparkling white. Use one of the handy mirrors to examine the early-17th-century frescoes by Domenichino in the choir vault and those by Lanfranco in the dome. One of the earliest ceilings done in full Baroque style, its upward vortex was influenced by Correggio's dome in Parma, of which Lanfranco was also a citizen. (Bring a few coins to light the paintings, which can be very dim.) The three massive paintings of Saint Andrew's martyrdom are by Mattia Preti (1650–51). Richly marbled and decorated chapels flank the nave, and in such a space, Puccini set the first act of *Tosca.* ⊠ *Piazza Vidoni 6, Corso Vittorio Emanuele II, Campo de' Fiori* ☏ *06/6861339* ⊕ *www.santandrea.teatinos.org.*

★ Sant'Ignazio

CHURCH | Rome's second Jesuit church, this 17th-century landmark set on a rococo piazza harbors some of the city's most magnificent trompe l'oeils. To get the full effect of the marvelous illusionistic ceiling by priest-artist Andrea Pozzo, stand on the small yellow disk set into the floor of the nave. The heavenly vision above you, seemingly extending upward almost indefinitely, represents the *Allegory of the Missionary Work of the Jesuits* and is part of Pozzo's cycle of works in this church exalting the early history of the Jesuit Order, whose founder was the reformer Ignatius of Loyola. The saint soars heavenward, supported by a cast of thousands, creating a jaw-dropping effect that was fully intended to rival the glorious ceiling produced by Baciccia in the nearby mother church of Il Gesù. Be sure to have coins handy for the machine that switches on the lights so you can marvel at the false dome, which is actually a flat canvas—a trompe l'oeil trick Pozzo used when the architectural budget drained dry. The dazzling church hardly stops there: scattered around the nave are several awe-inspiring altars; their soaring columns, gold-on-gold decoration, and gilded statues are pure splendor. The church is often host to concerts of sacred music performed by choirs from all over the world. Look for posters by the main doors or check the website for more information. ⊠ *Via del Caravita 8A, Piazza Navona* ☏ *06/6794406* ⊕ *www. chiesasantignazio.it.*

Sant'Ivo alla Sapienza

CHURCH | The main facade of this eccentric Baroque church, probably Borromini's best, is on the stately courtyard of an austere building that once housed Rome's university. Sant'Ivo has what must surely be one of the most delightful "domes" in all of Rome—a dizzying spiral said to have been inspired by a bee's stinger. The apian symbol is a reminder that Borromini built the church on commission from the Barberini pope Urban VIII (a swarm of bees figure on the Barberini family crest), although it was completed by Alexander VII. The interior, open only for three hours on Sunday morning, is worth a look, especially if you share Borromini's taste for complex mathematical architectural idiosyncrasies. "I didn't take up architecture solely to be a copyist," he once said. Sant'Ivo is certainly the proof. ⊠ *Corso del Rinascimento 40, Piazza Navona* ☎ *06/6864987* ⊘ *Closed Aug., and Mon.–Sat.*

Sinagoga

RELIGIOUS BUILDING | This synagogue has been the city's largest Jewish temple, and a Roman landmark with its aluminum dome, since its construction in 1904. The building also houses the Jewish Museum, with its precious ritual objects and other exhibits, which document the uninterrupted presence of a Jewish community in the city for nearly 22 centuries. Until the 16th century, Jews were esteemed citizens of Rome. Among them were bankers and physicians to the popes, who had themselves given permission for the construction of synagogues. But in 1555, during the Counter-Reformation, Pope Paul IV decreed the building of the walls of the Ghetto, confining the Jews to this small area and imposing a series of restrictions, some of which continued to be enforced until 1870. For security reasons, entrance is via guided visit only, and tours in English start every hour at about 10 minutes past the hour; entrance to the synagogue is through the museum located in Via Catalana (*Largo 16 Ottobre 1943*). ⊠ *Lungotevere de' Cenci 15, Jewish Ghetto* ☎ *06/68400661* ⊕ *www.museoebraico.roma.it* ⊠ *€11* ⊘ *Museum closed Sat. and Jewish holidays.*

★ Via Giulia

STREET | Still a Renaissance-era diorama and one of Rome's most exclusive addresses, Via Giulia was the first street in Rome since ancient times to be deliberately planned. Straight as a die, it was named for Pope Julius II (of Sistine Chapel fame), who commissioned it in the early 1500s as part of a scheme to open up a grandiose approach to St. Peter's Basilica, and it is flanked with elegant churches and palaces. Although the pope's plans to change the face of the city were only partially completed, Via Giulia became an important thoroughfare in Renaissance Rome. Today, after more than four centuries, it remains the "salon of Rome," address of choice for Roman aristocrats, although controversy has arisen about a recent change—the decision to add a large parking lot along one side of the street—that meant steamrolling through ancient and medieval ruins underneath. A stroll will reveal elegant palaces and churches (one, San Eligio, on the little side street Via di Sant'Eligio, was designed by Raphael himself). The area around Via Giulia is wonderful to wander through and get the feel of daily life as carried on in a centuries-old setting. Among the buildings that merit your attention are Palazzo Sacchetti (Via Giulia 66), with an imposing stone portal (inside are some of Rome's grandest staterooms, still, after 300 years, the private quarters of the Marchesi Sacchetti), and the forbidding brick building that housed the Carceri Nuove (New Prison; Via Giulia 52), Rome's prison for more than two centuries and now the offices of Direzione Nazionale Antimafia. Near the bridge that arches over the southern end of Via Giulia is the church of Santa Maria dell'Orazione e Morte (Holy Mary of Prayer and Death), with stone skulls on its door. These are a symbol of a confraternity that was charged with burying the bodies of the unidentified dead found in the city streets. Home since 1927 to the Hungarian Academy, the Palazzo Falconieri (Via Giulia 06/6889671) was designed by Borromini—note the architect's rooftop belvedere adorned with statues of the family "falcons," best viewed from around the block along the Tiber embankment. (The Borromini-designed salons and loggia are sporadically open as part of a guided tour; call the Hungarian Academy for information.) Remnant of a master plan by Michelangelo, the arch over the street was meant to link massive Palazzo Farnese, on the east side of Via Giulia, with the building across the street and a bridge to the Villa Farnesina, directly across the river. Finally, on the right and rather green with age, dribbles that star of many a postcard, the Fontana del Mascherone. ⊠ *Via Giulia, between Piazza dell'Oro and Piazza San Vincenzo Palloti, Campo de' Fiori.*

🍴 Restaurants

Armando al Pantheon

$$ | **ROMAN** | In the shadow of the Pantheon, this small family-run trattoria, open since 1961, delights tourists and locals alike. There's an air of authenticity to the Roman staples here, and the quality of the ingredients and the cooking mean booking ahead is a must. **Known for:** good wine list; traditional Roman cooking beautifully executed; spaghetti *cacio e pepe.* ⑤ *Average main: €16* ⊠ *Salita dei Crescenzi 31, Piazza Navona* 🖷 *06/68803034* ⊕ *www.armandoalpantheon.it* ⊙ *Closed Sun., and Dec.–Jan. 6. No dinner Sat.*

⭐ Ba' Ghetto

$$ | **ITALIAN** | **FAMILY** | This hot spot on the main promenade in the Jewish Ghetto has been going strong for years, with pleasant indoor and outdoor seating. The kitchen is kosher (many places featuring Roman Jewish fare are not) and serves meat dishes (so no dairy) from the Roman Jewish tradition as well as from elsewhere in the Mediterranean; down the street is Ba'Ghetto Milky (Via del Portico d'Ottavia 2/a), the kosher dairy version of the original. **Known for:** outside tables on the pedestrianized street; *carciofi alla giudia* (deep-fried artichokes) and other Roman Jewish specialities; casual family atmosphere. ⑤ *Average main: €22* ⊠ *Via del Portico d'Ottavia 57, Jewish Ghetto* 🖷 *06/68892868* ⊕ *www.baghetto.com* ⊙ *Dinner Fri. and lunch Sat. are strictly for those who observe Shabbat with advance payment.*

Bar del Fico

$ | **ITALIAN** | **FAMILY** | Everyone in Rome knows Bar del Fico, located right behind Piazza Navona, so if you're looking to hang out with the locals, this is the place to come for a drink or something to eat at any time of day or night. Just about every evening of the year, it's packed with people sipping cocktails in the square. **Known for:** buzzy atmosphere; outside tables in a pretty square; Italian-style brunch. ⑤ *Average main: €10* ⊠ *Piazza de Fico 26, Piazza Navona* 🖷 *06/68891373* ⊕ *www.bardelfico.com.*

Bellacarne

$$ | **ROMAN** | *Bellacarne* means "beautiful meat," and that's the focus of the menu here, though the double entendre is that it's also what a Jewish Italian grandmother might say while pinching her grandchild's cheek. The kosher kitchen makes its own pastrami, though the setting is definitely more fine-dining than deli. **Known for:** deep-fried artichokes; outside seating; house-made pastrami. ⑤ *Average main: €17* ⊠ *Via Portico d'Ottavia 51, Jewish Ghetto* 🖷 *06/6833104* ⊕ *www.bellacarne.it* ⊙ *No dinner Fri. No lunch Sat.*

⭐ Cul de Sac

$ | **WINE BAR** | This popular wine bar near Piazza Navona is among the city's oldest and offers a book-length selection of wines from Italy, France, the Americas, and elsewhere. Offering great value and pleasant service a stone's throw from Piazza Navona, it's open all afternoon, making it a great spot for a late lunch or an early dinner when most restaurants aren't open yet. **Known for:** relaxed atmosphere and outside tables; great wine list (and wine bottle–lined interior); eclectic Italian and Mediterranean fare. $ *Average main: €14* ⊠ *Piazza di Pasquino 73, Piazza Navona* ☎ *06/68801094* ⊕ *www. enotecaculdesacroma.it.*

Ditirambo

$$ | **ITALIAN** | Don't let the country-kitchen ambience fool you: at this little spot off Campo de' Fiori, the constantly changing selection of offbeat takes on Italian classics makes this a step beyond the ordinary. There are several good options for vegetarians. **Known for:** good vegetarian options; hearty meat and pasta dishes; cozy and casual atmosphere. $ *Average main: €16* ⊠ *Piazza della Cancelleria 74, Campo de' Fiori* ☎ *06/6871626* ⊕ *www. ristoranteditirambo.it* ⊙ *Closed Aug.*

★ Emma

$$$ | **ROMAN** | **FAMILY** | With dough by Rome's renowned family of bakers, the Rosciolis, this large, sleek, modern pizzeria is smack in the middle of the city, with the freshest produce right outside the door. The wine list features many local Lazio options. **Known for:** tasty *fritti* (classic fried Roman pizzeria appetizers); light and airy, casual atmosphere; thin-crust Roman pizza. $ *Average main: €25* ⊠ *Via Monte della Farina 28–29, Campo de' Fiori* ☎ *06/64760475* ⊕ *www. emmapizzeria.com.*

Enoteca Corsi

$ | **ITALIAN** | Very convenient for a good-value lunch in the centro storico, this trattoria is undeniably old-school—renovations were done a few years back, but you wouldn't know it—and that's all part of the charm. It's packed at lunch with a mix of civil servants from the nearby government offices, construction workers, and in-the-know tourists, when a few specials—classic pastas, a

delicious octopus salad, and some secondi like roast veal with peas—are offered. **Known for:** brusque but friendly service; casual atmosphere; Roman specialities. $ *Average main: €12* ⊠ *Via del Gesù 88, Piazza Navona* ☎ *06/6790821* ⊕ *www. enotecacorsi.com* ⊙ *Closed Sun., and 3 wks in Aug. No dinner Sat.*

★ Etablì

$ | **MEDITERRANEAN** | On a narrow *vicolo* (alley) off lovely cobblestone Piazza del Fico, this multifunctional restaurant and lounge space is decorated according to what could be called a modern Italian farmhouse-chic aesthetic, with vaulted wood-beam ceilings, wrought-iron touches, plush leather sofas, and chandeliers. The food is Mediterranean, with touches of international flavors. **Known for:** great location by Piazza Navona; popular after-dinner spot for sipping; casually romantic boho-chic atmosphere. $ *Average main: €12* ⊠ *Vicolo delle Vacche 9/a, Piazza Navona* ☎ *06/97616694* ⊕ *www. etabli.it.*

Filetti di Baccalà

$ | **ITALIAN** | The window reads "Filetti di Baccalà," but the official name of this small restaurant that specializes in one thing—deliciously battered and deep-fried fillets of salt cod—is Dar Filettaro a Santa Barbara. The location, down the street from Campo de' Fiori in a little piazza in front of the beautiful Santa Barbara church, practically begs you to eat at one of the outdoor tables, where service is brusque. **Known for:** tables outside on the pretty square; *filetti di baccalà*; functional "hole-in-the-wall" interior. $ *Average main: €6* ⊠ *Largo dei Librari 88, Campo de' Fiori* ☎ *06/6864018* ⊙ *Closed Mon., and Aug.*

★ Il Convivio Troiani

$$$$ | **MODERN ITALIAN** | In a tiny, nondescript alley north of Piazza Navona, the three Troiani brothers—Angelo in the kitchen, and brothers Giuseppe and Massimo presiding over the dining room and wine cellar—have been quietly

redefining the experience of Italian *alta cucina* (haute cuisine) since 1990 at this well-regarded establishment. Service is attentive without being overbearing, and the wine list is exceptional. **Known for:** amazing wine cellar and a great sommelier; fine dining in elegant surroundings; inventive modern Italian cooking with exotic touches. $ *Average main: €38* ✉ *Vicolo dei Soldati 31, Piazza Navona* ☎ *06/6869432* ⊕ *www.ilconviviotroiani. it* ⊘ *Closed Sun., and 1 wk in Aug. No lunch.*

Il Sanlorenzo

$$$$ | SEAFOOD | This gorgeous space, with its chandeliers and soaring original brickwork ceilings, houses one of the best seafood restaurants in the Eternal City. Order à la carte, or if you're hungry, the eight-course tasting menu is extremely tempting—it might include the likes of cuttlefish-ink tagliatelle with mint, artichokes, and roe, or shrimp from the island of Ponza with rosemary, bitter herbs, and porcini mushrooms—and, given the quality of the fish, a relative bargain at €90. **Known for:** elegant surroundings; top-quality fish and seafood; spaghetti *con ricci* (sea urchins). $ *Average main: €36* ✉ *Via dei Chiavari 4/5, Campo de' Fiori* ☎ *06/6865097* ⊕ *www. ilsanlorenzo.it* ⊘ *Closed Sun., and 2 wks in Aug. No lunch Sat. and Mon.*

La Ciambella

$$ | ITALIAN | The sprawling space is styled after American restaurants, with a lively bar in front, but the structure itself is all Roman, with brick archways, high ceilings, and a skylight in one of the dining rooms that allows guests to gaze at the fantastic Roman sky. The emphasis here is on high-quality ingredients and classic Italian culinary traditions. **Known for:** great location near the Pantheon; elegant setting; sophisticated classic Italian cuisine. $ *Average main: €17* ✉ *Via dell'Arco della Ciambella 20, Piazza Navona* ☎ *06/6832930* ⊕ *www.la-ciambella.it* ⊘ *Closed Mon.*

L'Angolo Divino

$$ | WINE BAR | There's something about this cozy wine bar that feels as if it's in a small university town instead of a bustling metropolis. Serene blue-green walls lined with wooden shelves of wines from around the Italian peninsula add to the warm atmosphere, and the kitchen stays open until the wee hours on weekends. **Known for:** late-night snacks; excellent wine selection and advice; cozy atmosphere. $ *Average main: €13* ✉ *Via dei Balestrari 12, Campo de' Fiori* ☎ *06/6864413* ⊕ *www.angolodivino.it* ⊘ *Closed 2 wks in Aug.*

Osteria dell'Ingegno

$$ | MODERN ITALIAN | This casual, trendy place is a great spot to enjoy a glass of wine or a gourmet meal in an ancient piazza in the city center, but the modern interior—vibrant with colorful paintings by local artists—brings you back to the present day. The simple but innovative menu includes dishes like Roman artichokes with *baccalà*, beef *tagliata* (sliced grilled steak) with a red-wine reduction, and a perfectly cooked duck breast with red fruit sauce. **Known for:** outdoor seating with views of ancient ruins; a great spot both for aperitifs and/or a meal; beautiful location on a pedestrian square. $ *Average main: €22* ✉ *Piazza di Pietra 45, Piazza Navona* ☎ *06/6780662* ⊕ *www.osteriadellingegno.com.*

Pesci Fritti

$$ | SOUTHERN ITALIAN | This cute jewel box of a restaurant sits on the seating of the ancient Theatre of Pompey just behind Campo de' Fiori (note the curve of the street). Step inside, and the whitewashed walls with touches of pale sea blue will make you feel like you've escaped to the Mediterranean for seafood favorites. **Known for:** cozy setting; fried fish and seafood choices; spaghetti with clams. $ *Average main: €18* ✉ *Via di Grottapinta 8, Campo de' Fiori* ☎ *06/68806170* ⊕ *www.pescifritti.it* ⊘ *Closed Mon. and Aug.*

★ Pianostrada

$$ | MODERN ITALIAN | This gourmet restaurant has an open kitchen, where you can watch the talented women owners cook up a storm of inventive delights—this is a "kitchen *lab*," after all, where top local ingredients are whipped into delicious plates. The spaghetti with tomato sauce, smoked ricotta, parmigiano, basil, and lemon peel is one of the signature dishes, and the amped up traditional recipe is a delicious indication of how interesting the food can get. **Known for:** homey atmosphere; freshly baked focaccia with various toppings; creative burgers and salads. ⑤ *Average main: €20* ✉ *Via delle Zoccolette 22, Campo de' Fiori* ☎ *06/89572296.*

★ Pierluigi

$$$ | ITALIAN | This popular seafood restaurant is a fun spot on balmy summer evenings, with tables out on the pretty Piazza de' Ricci. As at most Italian restaurants, fresh fish is sold per hectogram (100 grams, or about 3.5 ounces), so you may want to double-check the cost after it's been weighed. **Known for:** elegant atmosphere with great service; tables on the pretty pedestrianized piazza; top-quality fish and seafood. ⑤ *Average main: €30* ✉ *Piazza de' Ricci 144, Campo de' Fiori* ☎ *06/6861302* ⊕ *www.pierluigi.it.*

★ Salumeria Roscioli

$$ | WINE BAR | The shop in front of this wine bar will beckon you in with top-quality comestibles like hand-sliced cured ham from Italy and Spain, more than 300 cheeses, and a dizzying array of wines—but venture farther inside to try an extensive selection of unusual dishes and interesting takes on the classics. There are tables in the cozy wine cellar downstairs, but try and bag a table at the back on the ground floor (reserve well ahead; Roscioli is very popular). **Known for:** best prosciutto in town; extensive wine list; arguably Rome's best spaghetti alla carbonara. ⑤ *Average main: €22* ✉ *Via dei Giubbonari 21, Campo de' Fiori* ☎ *06/6875287* ⊕ *www.salumeriaroscioli. com* ☉ *Closed Sun. and 1 wk in Aug.*

☕ Coffee and Quick Bites

★ Gelateria Del Teatro

$ | ICE CREAM | FAMILY | In a window next to the entrance of this renowned gelateria, you can see the fresh fruit being used in the laboratory to create the flavors of the day, which highlight the best of Italy, from Amalfi lemons to hazelnuts from Alba. In addition to traditional flavors, they serve a few interesting combinations, like raspberry and sage or white chocolate with basil. **Known for:** charming location on a cobblestone street; seasonal, all natural ingredients; sublime gelato. ⑤ *Average main: €3* ✉ *Via dei Coronari 65/66, Piazza Navona* ☎ *06/45474880* ⊕ *www.gelateriadelteatro.it.*

★ Giolitti

$ | ITALIAN | FAMILY | Open since 1900, Giolitti near the Pantheon is Rome's old-school gelateria par excellence. Pay in advance at the register by the door and take your receipt to the counter, where you can choose from dozens of flavors, including chocolate, cinnamon, and pistachio. **Known for:** wide selection of flavors; excellent gelato; old-school ambiance. ⑤ *Average main: €3* ✉ *Via degli Uffici del Vicario 40, Piazza Navona* ☎ *06/6991243* ⊕ *www.giolitti.it.*

Pasticceria Boccione

$ | BAKERY | This tiny, old-school bakery is an institution in the Ghetto area and is famed for its Roman Jewish sweet specialties. Service is brusque, choices are few, what's available depends on the season, and when it's sold out, it's sold out. **Known for:** old-school bakery, so no frills and no seats; pizza ebraica ("Jewish pizza," a dense baked sweet rich in nuts and raisins); ricotta and cherry tarts. ⑤ *Average main: €4* ✉ *Via del Portico d'Ottavia 1, Jewish Ghetto* ☎ *06/6878637* ☉ *Closed Sat.*

Sant'Eustachio il Caffè

$ | CAFÉ | Frequented by tourists and government officials from the nearby Senate alike, this café is considered by many to make Rome's best coffee. Take it at the counter Roman-style: servers are hidden behind a huge espresso machine, where they vigorously mix the sugar and coffee to protect their "secret method" for the perfectly prepared cup (if you want your caffè without sugar here, ask for it *senza zucchero*). **Known for:** '30s interior; *gran caffè* (large sugared espresso); old-school Roman coffee bar vibe. **⑤** *Average main: €2 ⊠ Piazza Sant'Eustachio 82, Piazza Navona ☎ 06/68802048 ⊕ www.santeus-tachioilcaffe.it.*

 ## Hotels

Albergo Santa Chiara

$$$ | HOTEL | If you're looking for a good location and top-notch service at great rates—not to mention comfortable beds and a quiet stay—look no further than this historic hotel, run by the same family for some 200 years. **Pros:** lovely sitting area in front, overlooking the piazza; great location near the Pantheon; free Wi-Fi. **Cons:** street-side rooms can be noisy; some rooms are on the small side and need updating; Wi-Fi can be slow. **⑤** *Rooms from: €210 ⊠ Via Santa Chiara 21, Piazza Navona ☎ 06/6872979 ⊕ www.albergosantachiara.com ⌲ 96 rooms ⦿ Free Breakfast.*

Casa di Santa Brigida

$ | B&B/INN | The friendly sisters of Santa Brigida oversee simple, straightforward, and centrally located accommodations in one of Rome's loveliest convents, with a rooftop terrace overlooking Palazzo Farnese. **Pros:** free Wi-Fi; large library and sunroof; insider papal tickets. **Cons:** no TVs in the rooms (though there is a common TV room); weak air-conditioning; far from a Metro stop. **⑤** *Rooms from: €50 ⊠ Piazza Farnese 96, entrance around the corner at Via Monserrato 54, Campo de' Fiori ☎ 06/68892596 ⊕ www.brigidine.org ⌲ 20 rooms ⦿ Free Breakfast.*

Chapter Roma

$$$ | HOTEL | This hip new member of Design Hotels has an edgy, of-the-moment design that juxtaposes plush midcentury Italian furnishings with street art murals and industrial touches. **Pros:** healthy food options at the Market café; trendy design; coworking space available. **Cons:** no spa; no gym; service can be a bit spotty. **⑤** *Rooms from: €230 ⊠ Via di Santa Maria de' Calderari 47, Jewish Ghetto ☎ 06/89935351 ⊕ www.chapter-roma.com ⌲ 47 ⦿ Free Breakfast.*

D.O.M Hotel Roma

$$$$ | HOTEL | In an old convent on Via Giulia, one of Rome's romantic ivy-covered streets, the D.O.M (Deo Optimo Maximo) is an ultrachic luxury hotel that resembles an aristocratic *casa nobile*. **Pros:** hip decor; complimentary Acqua di Parma toiletries; heated towel racks. **Cons:** delicious but expensive cocktails; an armed guard at the anti-terrorism headquarters opposite the hotel may be off-putting for some; standard rooms are small for a five-star hotel. **⑤** *Rooms from: €320 ⊠ Via Giulia 131, Campo de' Fiori ☎ 06/6832144 ⊕ www.domhotelroma.com ⌲ 18 rooms ⦿ Free Breakfast.*

Hotel de' Ricci

$$$$ | HOTEL | This intimate boutique hotel from the team behind Pierluigi is a top spot for wine lovers. **Pros:** perks include complimentary aperitivo and priority reservations at Pierluigi; excellent wine cellar and wine tastings; great location on a quiet street. **Cons:** the bar is only open to hotel guests; there's a charge of 50 euros per day to bring pets; there's no spa or gym. **⑤** *Rooms from: €350 ⊠ Via della Barchetta 14, Campo de' Fiori ☎ 06/6874775 ⊕ www.hoteldericci.com ⌲ 8 rooms ⦿ No Meals.*

Hotel Genio

$$ | **HOTEL** | Just off one of Rome's most beautiful piazzas—Piazza Navona—this pleasant hotel has a lovely rooftop terrace perfect for enjoying a cappuccino or a glass of wine while taking in the view. **Pros:** spacious, elegant bathrooms; free Wi-Fi; breakfast buffet is abundant. **Cons:** spotty Internet; rooms facing the street can be noisy; beds can be too firm for some. ⑤ *Rooms from: €160* ✉ *Via Giuseppe Zanardelli 28, Piazza Navona* ☎ *06/6833781* ⊕ *www.hotelgenioroma.it* ⇥ *60 rooms* ⦿❘ *Free Breakfast* Ⓜ *Spagna.*

Hotel Ponte Sisto

$$$ | **HOTEL** | Situated in a remodeled Renaissance palazzo with one of the prettiest patio-courtyards in Rome, this hotel is a relaxing retreat close to Trastevere and Campo de' Fiori. **Pros:** luxury bathrooms; beautiful courtyard garden; rooms with views (and some with balconies and terraces). **Cons:** carpets starting to show signs of wear; some upgraded rooms are small and not worth the price difference; street-side rooms can be a bit noisy. ⑤ *Rooms from: €250* ✉ *Via dei Pettinari 64, Campo de' Fiori* ☎ *06/6863100* ⊕ *www.hotelpontesisto.it* ⇥ *106 rooms* ⦿❘ *Free Breakfast.*

Pantheon Iconic Hotel

$$$ | **HOTEL** | A member of Marriott's Autograph Collection, this boutique hotel is a sleek retreat in the center of the action. **Pros:** Marriott Bonvoy members can use and redeem points; restaurant by one of the city's best chefs; modern design and amenities. **Cons:** no spa or gym; some rooms lack external views; design might be considered a bit cold and corporate. ⑤ *Rooms from: €250* ✉ *Via di Santa Chiara 4A, Piazza Navona* ☎ *06/87807070* ⊕ *www.thepantheonhotel.com* ⇥ *79 rooms* ⦿❘ *No Meals.*

Nightlife

★ Bar del Fico

CAFÉS | Bar del Fico looks a lot different from the days of yore when raucous outdoor chess matches accompanied cocktails at the once-bare-bones local hangout. Though the chess tables are still sitting in the shade of the historic fig tree, Bar del Fico is now a happening bar, restaurant, evening cocktail spot, and late-night hangout. ✉ *Piazza del Fico 26, Piazza Navona* ☎ *06/68891373* ⊕ *www. bardelfico.com/en/bar.*

Etablì

WINE BARS | If you set up a wine bar in your living room, it'd feel a lot like Etablì. This is the perfect spot for meeting friends before a night out on the town. ✉ *Vicolo delle Vacche 9, Piazza Navona* ☎ *06/97616694* ⊕ *www.etabli.it.*

Jerry Thomas Project

COCKTAIL LOUNGES | One of just a handful of hidden bars in Rome, this intimate bar looks like a Prohibition-era haunt and serves the kind of classic cocktails you find in New York speakeasies. It's seating room only, so reservations must be made in advance. Upon booking, you'll receive a password via email. ✉ *Vicolo Cellini 30, Piazza Navona* ☎ *370/1146287* ⊕ *www. thejerrythomasproject.it.*

L'Angolo Divino

WINE BARS | Nestled on a quiet side street around the corner from the ever-vivacious Campo de' Fiori, this wood-paneled enoteca is a hidden treasure of wines. Its extensive selection lists more than 1,000 labels to go along quite nicely with its quaint menu of delicious homemade pastas and local antipasti. And because it's open every night until 1:30 am, it's the ideal place for a late-night tipple. ✉ *Via dei Balestrari 12, Campo de' Fiori* ☎ *06/6864413* ⊕ *www.angolodivino.it.*

★ **Roof Garden Bar at Grand Hotel de la Minerve**

COCKTAIL LOUNGES | During warm months, this lofty perch offers perhaps the most inspiring view in Rome—directly over the Pantheon's dome. The Roof Garden has an equally impressive cocktail menu. Take advantage of summer sunsets and park yourself in a front-row seat as the dome glows. Even if you're just going for a drink, it's a good idea to book a table, especially on weekends. ⊠ *Grand Hotel de la Minerve, Piazza della Minerve 69, Piazza Navona* ☎ *06/695201* ⊕ *www. minervaroofgarden.it.*

Vinoteca Novecento

WINE BARS | A lovely, tiny enoteca with a very old-fashioned vibe, Vinoteca Novecento has a seemingly unlimited selection of wines, proseccos, vini santi, and grappe, along with salami-and-cheese tasting menus. Inside is standing-room only; in good weather, sit outside on one of the oak barriques. ⊠ *Piazza delle Coppelle 47, Piazza Navona* ☎ *06/6833078.*

🎭 Performing Arts

★ Teatro Argentina

THEATER | A gorgeous 18th-century theater, the Teatro Argentina evokes glamour and sophistication with its velvet upholstery, large crystal chandeliers, and beautifully dressed theatergoers, who come to see international productions of stage and dance performances. ⊠ *Largo di Torre Argentina 52, Campo de' Fiori* ☎ *06/684000314* ⊕ *www.teatrodiroma.net.*

🛍 Shopping

CERAMICS AND DECORATIVE ARTS

★ **IN.OR. dal 1952**

CRAFTS | For more than 50 years, IN.OR. dal 1952 has served as a trusty friend for Romans in desperate need of an exclusive wedding gift or those oh-so-perfect china place settings for a

fancy Sunday dinner. Entrance is via a secluded 15th-century courtyard and up a flight of stairs. The store specializes in work handcrafted by the silversmiths of Pampaloni and Bastianelli in Florence. ⊠ *Via della Stelletta 23, Piazza Navona* ☎ *06/6878579.*

CLOTHING

★ L'Archivio di Monserrato

WOMEN'S CLOTHING | This airy, spacious boutique curated by Soledad Twombly (daughter-in-law of painter Cy Twombly) showcases her original designs as well as a sophisticated mix of antique Turkish and Indian textiles, jewelry, shoes, and small homewares picked up on her travels. Tailored jackets trimmed with exotic fabrics, dresses in eclectic prints and bold colors, and smart linen suits are some of Twombly's signatures. ⊠ *Via di Monserrato 150, Campo de' Fiori* ☎ *06/6868168* ⊕ *www. soledadtwombly.com.*

Le Tartarughe

WOMEN'S CLOTHING | A familiar face on the catwalks of Rome's fashion shows, designer Susanna Liso, a Rome native, adds suggestive elements of playful experimentation to her haute couture and ready-to-wear lines, which are much loved by Rome's aristocracy and intelligentsia. With intense, enveloping designs, she mixes raw silks or cashmere and fine merino wool together to form captivating garments that combine seduction and linear form. ⊠ *Via Piè di Marmo 17, Piazza Navona* ☎ *06/6792240* ⊕ *www.letartarughe.eu.*

Vestiti Usati Cinzia

MIXED CLOTHING | Vintage-clothes hunters, costume designers, and stylists alike love browsing through the racks at Vestiti Usati Cinzia. The shop is fun and very inviting and stocked with wall-to-wall funky 1960s and '70s apparel and loads of goofy sunglasses. There's definitely no shortage of flower-power bell-bottoms and hippie shirts, embroidered tops, trippy and psychedelic boots, and other awesome accessories that will take you back to the days of peace and love. ✉ *Via del Governo Vecchio 45, Piazza Navona* ☎ *06/6832945.*

FOOD AND WINE
Moriondo e Gariglio

CANDY | Not exactly Willy Wonka (but in the same vein), Moriondo e Gariglio is a chocolate lover's paradise, churning out some of the finest chocolate delicacies in town. The shop dates back to 1850 and adheres strictly to family recipes passed on from generation to generation. Whether you favor marrons glacés or dark-chocolate truffles, you'll delight in choosing from more than 80 delicacies. ✉ *Via Piè di Marmo 21, Piazza Navona* ☎ *06/6990856.*

JEWELRY
MMM—Massimo Maria Melis

JEWELRY & WATCHES | Drawing heavily on ancient Roman and Etruscan designs, Massimo Maria Melis jewelry will carry you back in time. Working with 21-carat gold, he often incorporates antique coins in many of his exquisite bracelets and necklaces. Some of his pieces are done with an ancient technique, much-loved by the Etruscans, in which tiny gold droplets are fused together to create intricately patterned designs. ✉ *Via dell'Orso 57, Piazza Navona* ☎ *06/6869188* ⊕ *www. massimomariamelis.com.*

Quattrocolo

JEWELRY & WATCHES | This historic shop dating to 1938 showcases exquisite antique micro-mosaic jewelry painstakingly crafted in the style perfected by the masters at the Vatican mosaic studio. You'll also find 18th- and 19th-century cameos and beautiful engraved stones as well as contemporary jewelry handmade in the studio. The small works were beloved by cosmopolitan clientele of the Grand Tour age and offer modern-day shoppers a taste of yesteryear's grandeur. ✉ *Via della Scrofa 48, Piazza Navona* ☎ *06/68801367* ⊕ *www.quattrocolo.com.*

SHOES AND ACCESSORIES
★ Chez Dede

OTHER SPECIALTY STORE | Husband-and-wife duo Andrea Ferolla and Daria Reina (he's a fashion illustrator, she's a photographer) curate an edited selection of clothes, bags, vintage jewelry, books, home decor, and anything else you might need in this cult favorite lifestyle-concept shop. Their signature bags are designed to go from the plane straight to the beach, and they regularly release collectible items featuring Ferolla's whimsical illustrations. ✉ *Via di Monserrato 35, Campo de' Fiori* ☎ *06/83772934* ⊕ *www. chezdede.com.*

Ibiz

LEATHER GOODS | In business since 1972, this family team creates colorful, stylish leather handbags, belts, and sandals near Piazza Campo de' Fiori. Choose from the premade collection or order something in the color of your choice; their workshop is visible in the boutique. ✉ *Via dei Chiavari 39, Campo de' Fiori* ☎ *06/68307297* ⊕ *www.ibizroma.it.*

★ Maison Halaby

HANDBAGS | Lebanese designer and artist Gilbert Halaby was featured in fashion magazines like *Vogue* and created jewelry for Lady Gaga before giving up the rat race and opening his own shop, where the ethos is all about slow fashion. He designs boldly colored leather handbags incorporating suede, python, fringe, raffia, or jeweled handles, as well as silk scarves printed with his original watercolors, which he sells in this small boutique that feels like an extension of his home, with a velvet sofa, plenty of books and plants, and his own paintings on the walls. The shop is mainly open by appointment, but if Gilbert is there when you pass by, ring the bell and he'll invite you in for coffee or Campari. ✉ *Via di Monserrato 21, Campo de' Fiori* ☎ *06/96521585* ⊕ *www.maisonhalaby. com* ☺ *Open by appointment.*

STATIONERY

⭐ Cartoleria Pantheon dal 1910

STATIONERY | Instead of sending a post-card home, head to the simply sumptu-ous Cartoleria Pantheon dal 1910 for fine handmade paper to write that special letter. In addition to simple, stock paper and artisanal sheets of handcrafted Amal-fi paper, there are hand-bound leather journals in an extraordinary array of colors and sizes. The store has two locations in the neighborhood. ✉ *Via della Madd-alena 41, Piazza Navona* ☎ *06/6795633* ⊕ *www.cartoleriapantheon.it.*

TOYS

Al Sogno

TOYS | **FAMILY** | If you're looking for quality toys that encourage imaginative play and learning, look no further than Al Sogno. With an emphasis on the artistic as well as the multisensory, the shop has a selection of toys that are both discerning and individual, making them perfect for children of all ages. Carrying an exquisite collection of fanciful puppets, collectible dolls, masks, stuffed animals, and illus-trated books, this Navona jewel, around since 1945, is crammed top-to-bottom with beautiful, well-crafted playthings. If you believe that children's toys don't have to be high-tech, you will adore reliving some of your best childhood memories here. ✉ *Piazza Navona 53, corner of Via Agonale, Piazza Navona* ☎ *06/6864198* ⊕ *www.alsogno.com.*

⭐ Bartolucci

TOYS | **FAMILY** | This shop opened in the '90s, but the Bartolucci family has been making whimsical, handmade curiosities out of pine, including clocks, bookends, bedside lamps, and wall hangings, since 1936. You can even buy a child-size motorbike entirely made of wood (wheels, too). Don't miss the life-size Pinocchio pedaling furiously on a wooden bike. ✉ *Via dei Pastini 98, Piazza Navona* ☎ *06/69190894* ⊕ *www.bartolucci.com.*

Piazza di Spagna

In spirit (and in fact) this section of the city is its most grandiose. The overblown Vittoriano monument, the labyrinthine treasure-chest palaces of Rome's surviv-ing aristocracy, even the diamond-draped denizens of Via Condotti's shops—all embody the exuberant ego of a city at the center of its own universe. Here's where you'll see ladies in furs gobbling pastries at café tables and walk through a thousand snapshots as you climb the famous Spanish Steps, admired by gen-erations from Byron to Versace. Cultural treasures abound around here: gilded 17th-century churches, glittering palazzi, and the greatest example of portraiture in Rome, Velázquez's incomparable *Innocent X* at the Galleria Doria Pamphilj. Have your camera ready—along with a coin or two—for that most beloved of Rome's landmarks, the Trevi Fountain.

GETTING HERE AND AROUND

Piazza di Spagna is a short walk from Piazza del Popolo, the Pantheon, and the Trevi Fountain. One of Rome's handiest subway stations, Spagna, is tucked just left of the steps. Buses No. 117 (from the Colosseum) and No. 119 (from Piazza del Popolo) hum through the area; the latter tootles up Via del Babuino, famed for its shopping.

Sights

⭐ Ara Pacis Augustae

(*Altar of Augustan Peace*)

MONUMENT | In a city better known for its terra-cotta–colored palazzi, this pristine monument sits inside one of Rome's newer architectural landmarks: a gleaming, rectangular glass-and-trav-ertine structure designed by American architect Richard Meier. Overlooking the Tiber on one side and the ruins of the marble-clad Mausoleo di Augusto (Mau-soleum of Augustus) on the other, the result is a serene, luminous oasis right in the center of Rome. The altar itself dates back to 13 BC; it was commissioned to celebrate the Pax Romana, the era of peace ushered in by Augustus's military victories. Like all ancient Roman monuments of this kind, you have to imagine its spectacular and moving relief sculptures painted in vibrant colors, now long gone. The reliefs on the short sides portray myths associated with Rome's founding and glory; the long sides display a procession of the imperial family. It's fun to try to play "who's who"—although half of his body is missing, Augustus is identifiable as the first full figure at the procession's head on the south-side frieze—but academics still argue over exact identifications of most of the figures. This one splendid altar is the star of the small museum downstairs, which hosts rotating exhibits on Italian culture, with themes ranging from design to film. ✉ *Lungotevere in Augusta, at the corner of Via Tomacelli, Piazza di Spagna* ☎ *06/0608* ⊕ *www.arapacis.it* 💰 *€10.50, €17 when there's an exhibit* Ⓜ *Flaminio.*

Keats-Shelley Memorial House

HISTORIC HOME | Sent to Rome in a last-ditch attempt to treat his consumptive condition, English Romantic poet John Keats lived—and died—in this house at the foot of the Spanish Steps. At the time, this was the heart of the colorful bohemian quarter of Rome that was especially favored by English expats. He took his last breath here on February 23, 1821, and is now buried in the Non-Catholic Cemetery in Testaccio. Even before his death, Keats was celebrated for such poems as "Ode to a Nightingale" and "Endymion." In this "Casina di Keats," you can visit his final home and see his death mask, though all his furnishings were burned after his death as a sanitary measure by the local authorities. You'll also find a rather quaint collection of memorabilia of English literary figures of the period—Lord Byron, Percy Bysshe Shelley, Joseph Severn, and Leigh Hunt, as well as Keats—and

an exhaustive library of works on the Romantics. ✉ *Piazza di Spagna 26, Piazza di Spagna* ☎ *06/6784235* ⊕ *www.keats-shelley-house.org* 💰 *€6* 🕐 *Closed Sun.* Ⓜ *Spagna.*

Mausoleo di Augusto

TOMB | The largest circular tomb in the world, the mausoleum certainly made a statement about the glory of Augustus, Julius Caesar's successor. He was only 35 years old when he commissioned it following his victory over Marc Anthony and Cleopatra. Though the ruins we see now are brick and stone, it was originally covered in marble and travertine, with evergreen trees planted on top, a colossal statue of the emperor at the summit, and a pair of bronze pillars inscribed with his achievements at the entrance. The mausoleum's innermost sepulchral chamber housed the ashes of several members of the Augustan dynasty, but it was subsequently raided and the urns were never found. Between the 13th and 20th centuries, it lived several other lives as a garden, an amphitheater that hosted jousting tournaments, and a concert hall, which Mussolini tore down in 1936 in a bid to restore the monument to its imperial glory. His plans were interrupted by World War II, after which the mausoleum was all but abandoned until a recent restoration reopened it to the public. A new public piazza is currently being constructed around it. ✉ *Piazza Augusto Imperatore, Piazza di Spagna* ☎ *06/0608* ⊕ *www.mausoleodiaugusto.it* 💰 *€4* Ⓜ *Spagna.*

Monumento a Vittorio Emanuele II, or Altare della Patria (*Victor Emmanuel II Monument, or Altar of the Nation*)

MONUMENT | The huge white mass known as the "Vittoriano" is an inescapable landmark that has been likened to a huge wedding cake or an immense typewriter. Present-day Romans joke that you can only avoid looking at it if you are standing on it, but it was the source of great civic pride at the time of its construction at the turn of the 20th century. To create this elaborate marble monster and the vast piazza on which it stands, its architects blithely destroyed many ancient and medieval buildings and altered the slope of the Campidoglio (Capitoline Hill), which abuts it. Built to honor the unification of Italy and the nation's first king, Victor Emmanuel II, it also shelters the eternal flame at the tomb of Italy's Unknown Soldier, killed during World War I. You can't miss the Monumento, so enjoy neo-imperial grandiosity at its most bombastic. The underwhelming exhibit inside the building tells the history of the country's unification, but the truly enticing feature of the Vittoriano is its rooftop terrace, which offers some of the best panoramic views of Rome. The only way up is by elevator (the entrance is located several flights of stairs up on the right as you face the monument). ✉ *Entrances on Piazza Venezia, Piazza del Campidoglio, and Via di San Pietro in Carcere, Piazza di Spagna* 🕾 *06/0608* ⊕ *vittoriano.beniculturali.it* 💳 *€10* Ⓜ *Colosseo.*

⭐ **Palazzo Colonna**

HISTORIC HOME | Rome's grandest family built themselves Rome's grandest private palace, a fusion of 17th- and 18th-century buildings that has been occupied by the Colonna family for more than 20 generations. The immense palatial residence faces Piazza dei Santi Apostoli on one side and the Quirinale (Quirinal Hill) on the other (with a little bridge over Via della Pilotta linking to the gardens on the hill). The palazzo is still home to some Colonna patricians, but it also holds an exquisite art gallery, which is open to the public on Saturday mornings. The gallery is itself a setting of aristocratic grandeur; you might recognize the Sala Grande as the site where Audrey Hepburn meets the press in *Roman Holiday.* An ancient red marble column (*colonna* in Italian), which is the family's emblem, looms at one end, but the most spectacular feature is the ceiling fresco of the Battle of Lepanto painted by Giovanni Coli

and Filippo Gherardi beginning in 1675. Adding to the opulence are works by Poussin, Tintoretto, and Veronese, and a number of portraits of illustrious members of the family, such as Vittoria Colonna, Michelangelo's muse and longtime friend. There is a guided tour in English at noon that is included in the entrance fee and can help you to navigate through the array of madonnas, saints, goddesses, popes, and cardinals to see Annibale Carracci's lonely *Beaneater,* spoon at the ready and front teeth missing. The gallery also has a café with a pleasant terrace. ✉ *Via della Pilotta 17, Piazza di Spagna* 🕾 *06/6784350* ⊕ *www.galleriacolonna.it* 💳 *€12* 🕒 *Closed Sun.–Fri.* Ⓜ *Barberini.*

⭐ **Palazzo Doria Pamphilj**

HISTORIC HOME | Along with the Palazzo Colonna and the Galleria Borghese, this dazzling family palace provides the best glimpse of aristocratic Rome. The main attractions in the gilded galleries are the legendary Old Master paintings, including treasures by Velázquez and Caravaggio; the splendor of the halls themselves; and a unique suite of private family apartments. The understated beauty of the graceful facade, designed by Gabriele Valvassori in 1730, is best admired by crossing to the opposite side of the street for a good view, but it barely hints at the opulence that awaits inside. The palace passed through several hands before becoming the property of the Pamphilj family, who married into the famous seafaring Doria family of Genoa in the 18th century. The family still lives in part of the palace. The gallery contains 550 paintings, including three by Caravaggio—a young *St. John the Baptist, Mary Magdalene,* and the breathtaking *Rest on the Flight to Egypt.* Off the eye-popping **Galleria degli Specchi** (Gallery of Mirrors)—a smaller version of the one at Versailles—are the famous Velázquez *Pope Innocent X,* considered by some historians to be the greatest portrait ever painted, and the Bernini bust of the same Pamphilj pope. The delightful

Sights ▼

1 Ara Pacis Augustae **B3**
2 Keats-Shelley Memorial House... **E3**
3 Mausoleo di Augusto **C3**
4 Monumento a Vittorio
  Emanuele II, or Altare
  della Patria **E9**
5 Palazzo Colonna **F7**
6 Palazzo Doria Pamphilj............**E8**
7 The Spanish Steps.................**E3**
8 Trevi Fountain **F5**

Restaurants ▼

1 Il Marchese **B4**
2 Mirabelle **G2**
3 Moma **I3**
4 Ristorante Nino **E3**
5 Settimo.............................. **G2**

Quick Bites ▼

1 Antico Caffè Greco **E3**

Hotels ▼

1 Aleph Rome Hotel **H3**
2 Babuino 181 .... **C1**
3 Baglioni Hotel Regina **H2**
4 The Hassler........................ **F3**
5 Hotel de la Ville **F3**
6 Hotel d'Inghilterra **D3**
7 Hotel Eden......................... **G2**
8 Hotel Vilòn.......................... **C4**
9 Il Palazzetto **E2**
10 Margutta 19 .... **D2**
11 Scalinata di Spagna...............**F3**

audio guide is included in the ticket price and narrated by the current heir, Prince Jonathan Doria Pamphilj, who divulges an intimate family history. ⊠ *Via del Corso 305, Piazza di Spagna* ☎ *06/6797323* ⊕ *www.doriapamphilj.it* ⊙ *Closed Mon.–Thurs.* ⚑ *reservations required* ⛳ *€14* Ⓜ *Barberini.*

★ **The Spanish Steps**

NOTABLE BUILDING | FAMILY | The iconic Spanish Steps (often called simply *la scalinata,* or "the staircase," by Italians) and the Piazza di Spagna from which they ascend both get their names from the Spanish Embassy to the Vatican on the piazza—even though the staircase was built with French funds by an Italian in 1723. In honor of a diplomatic visit by the King of Spain, the hillside was transformed by architect Francesco de Sanctis with a spectacular piece of urban planning to link the church of Trinità dei Monti at the top with the Via Condotti below. In an allusion to the church, the staircase is divided by three landings (beautifully lined by potted azaleas mid-April–mid-May). Bookending the bottom of the steps are two beloved holdovers from the 18th century, when the area was known as the "English Ghetto": to the right, the Keats-Shelley House, and to the left, Babington's Tea Rooms—both beautifully redolent of the era of the Grand Tour. For weary sightseers who find the 135 steps too daunting, there is an elevator at Vicolo del Bottino 8, next to the Metro entrance. (Those with mobility problems should be aware that there is still a small flight of stairs after, however, and that the elevator is sporadically closed for repair.) At the bottom of the steps, Bernini's splendid "Barcaccia" (sinking ship) fountain dates to the early 17th century and still spouts drinking water from the ancient Aqua Vergine aqueduct. ⊠ *Piazza di Spagna* Ⓜ *Spagna*

★ **Trevi Fountain**

FOUNTAIN | Alive with rushing waters commanded by an imperious sculpture of Oceanus, the Fontana di Trevi has been all about theatrical effects from the start; it is an aquatic marvel in a city filled with them. The fountain's unique drama is largely due to its location: its vast basin is squeezed into the tight confluence of three little streets (the *tre vie,* which may give the fountain its name), with cascades emerging as if from the wall of Palazzo Poli. The dream of a fountain emerging full-force from a palace was first envisioned by Bernini and Pietro da Cortona from Pope Urban VIII's plan to rebuild an older fountain, which had earlier marked the end-point of the ancient Acqua Vergine aqueduct, created in 18 BC by Agrippa. Three popes later, under Pope Clement XIII, Nicola Salvi finally broke ground with his winning design. Unfortunately, Salvi did not live to see his masterpiece of sculpted seashells, roaring sea beasts, and diva-like mermaids completed; he caught a cold and died while working in the culverts of the aqueduct 11 years before the fountain was finally finished in 1762. Everyone knows the famous legend that if you throw a coin into the Trevi Fountain you will ensure a return trip to the Eternal City, but not everyone knows how to do it the right way. You must toss a coin with your right hand over your left shoulder, with your back to the fountain. One coin means you'll return to Rome; two, you'll return *and* fall in love; three, you'll return, find love, and marry. The fountain grosses some €600,000 a year, with every cent going to the Italian Red Cross, which is why Fendi was willing to foot the bill and fully funded the Trevi's marvelous recent restoration. ⊠ *Piazza di Trevi, Piazza di Spagna* Ⓜ *Barberini.*

🍴 Restaurants

⭐ Il Marchese

$$ | **ITALIAN** | This rustic-meets-glamorous bistro attracts locals for its flawless execution of Roman classics (many served photogenically in metal cooking pans) as well as original dishes. Its bar is known among amaro connoisseurs for having the largest selection in Rome, and the bitter liquors are the stars of the expertly crafted cocktail menu. **Known for:** extensive selection of amaros and great cocktails; well-executed classics; beautiful design. ⑤ *Average main: €18* ✉ *Via di Ripetta 162, Piazza di Spagna* ☎ *06/90218872* ⊕ *www.ilmarcheseroma.it* Ⓜ *Spagna.*

Mirabelle

$$$$ | **MODERN ITALIAN** | Old World elegance is the name of the game here—think white-jacketed waiters who attend to your every need, classic decor, and impeccable dishes, which are the most modern thing about this restaurant on the seventh floor of the Hotel Splendide Royal. Be sure to request a table on the terrace, which boasts panoramic views of leafy Villa Borghese and the center of Rome. **Known for:** top-notch food and service; romantic atmosphere; panoramic terrace. ⑤ *Average main: €54* ✉ *Hotel Splendide Royal, Via di Porta Pinciana 14, Piazza di Spagna* ☎ *06/42168838* ⊕ *www. robertonaldicollection.com/ristorante-mirabelle* 🎩 *business casual* Ⓜ *Spagna, Barberini.*

⭐ Moma

$$$ | **MODERN ITALIAN** | In front of the American embassy, a favorite of the design *trendoisie*, modern, Michelin-starred Moma attracts well-heeled businessmen at lunch but turns into a more intimate affair for dinner. The kitchen turns out hits as it creates *alta cucina* (haute cuisine) made using Italian ingredients sourced from small producers. **Known for:** affordable fine dining; creative presentation; pasta with a twist.

⑤ *Average main: €25* ✉ *Via San Basilio 42/43, Piazza di Spagna* ☎ *06/42011798* ⊕ *www.ristorantemoma.it* ⊙ *Closed Sun.* Ⓜ *Barberini.*

Ristorante Nino

$$$ | **ITALIAN** | Almost more of a landmark than an eatery, Nino has been a favorite among international journalists and the rich and famous since the 1930s and does not seem to have changed at all over the decades. The interior is country rustic *alla toscana,* and the menu accordingly sticks to the Tuscan classics. **Known for:** *ribollita* (Tuscan bean soup); warm crostini spread with pâté; upscale old-school Italian vibe. ⑤ *Average main: €26* ✉ *Via Borgognona 11, Piazza di Spagna* ☎ *06/6786752* ⊕ *www.ristorantenino.it* ⊙ *Closed Sun. and Aug.* Ⓜ *Spagna.*

Settimo

$$$ | **ITALIAN** | Crowning the Sofitel Rome Villa Borghese hotel, this chic restaurant serves fancified takes on Rome's *cucina povera* (peasant cooking) in a chic space with graphic punches of color. The terrace offers fantastic views that stretch from Villa Borghese to the dome of St. Peter's, but the interior dining room, with its floor-to-ceiling windows and terrazzo-inspired floors, is lovely too. **Known for:** terrace with great views; amped up version of classic Roman recipes; colorful, modern design. ⑤ *Average main: €26* ✉ *Sofitel Rome Villa Borghese, Via Lombardia 47, Piazza di Spagna* ☎ *06/478021* ⊕ *www.settimoristorante.it* Ⓜ *Barberini.*

☕ Coffee and Quick Bites

Antico Caffè Greco

$ | **CAFÉ** | Pricey Antico Caffè Greco is a national landmark and Rome's oldest café; its red-velvet chairs, marble tables, and marble busts have seen the likes of Byron, Shelley, Keats, Goethe, and Casanova. Add to this the fact that it's in the middle of the shopping madness on the upscale Via dei Condotti, and you won't be surprised that the place is often filled with tourists. **Known for:** crystal goblets and high prices to match; perfect espresso; lavish historic design. $ *Average main: €12* ✉ *Via dei Condotti 86, Piazza di Spagna* ☎ *06/6791700* ⊕ *www.caffegreco.shop* Ⓜ *Spagna.*

 ## Hotels

Aleph Rome Hotel

$$$$ | **HOTEL** | Fashionable couples tend to favor the Aleph, a former bank–turned–luxury Rome hotel, where the motto seems to be "more marble, everywhere." Now part of Hilton's Curio Collection, the hotel has ample facilities that include two pools (one in the spa and one on the roof), a cigar lounge, a cocktail bar, and two restaurants, one on the ground floor and one on the rooftop. **Pros:** terrace with pool; free access to the spa for hotel guests; award-winning design. **Cons:** rooftop views don't showcase Rome's most flattering side; rooms are too petite for the price; buffet breakfast not included. $ *Rooms from: €380* ✉ *Via San Basilio 15, Piazza di Spagna* ☎ *06/4229001* ⊕ *alephrome.com* ⬿ *88 rooms* ❗❙ *No Meals* Ⓜ *Barberini.*

Babuino 181

$$$ | **HOTEL** | On chic Via del Babuino, known for its high-end boutiques, jewelry stores, and antiques shops, this discreet and stylish hotel is an ideal Roman pied à terre that has spacious rooms spread over two historic buildings. **Pros:** iPhone docks and other handy in-room amenities; spacious suites; luxury Frette linens. **Cons:** breakfast is nothing special; rooms can be a bit noisy; annex rooms feel removed from service staff. $ *Rooms from: €250* ✉ *Via del Babuino 181, Piazza di Spagna* ☎ *06/32295295* ⊕ *www.rome-luxurysuites.com/babuino* ⬿ *24 rooms* ❗❙ *Free Breakfast* Ⓜ *Flaminio, Spagna.*

Baglioni Hotel Regina

$$$$ | **HOTEL** | The former home of Queen Margherita of Savoy, the Baglioni Hotel Regina, which enjoys a prime spot on the Via Veneto, is still a favorite among today's international jet-setters. **Pros:** excellent on-site restaurant and bar; nice decor; luxury on-site spa. **Cons:** service is hit-or-miss; some rooms are noisy; location isn't as prestigious as it once was. $ *Rooms from: €319* ✉ *Via Veneto 72, Piazza di Spagna* ☎ *06/421111* ⊕ *www.baglionihotels.com/rome* ⬿ *114 rooms* ❗❙ *No Meals* Ⓜ *Barberini.*

★ The Hassler

$$$$ | **HOTEL** | When it comes to million-dollar views, the best place to stay in the whole city is the Hassler, so it's no surprise many rich and famous (Tom Cruise, Jennifer Lopez, and the Beckhams among them), are willing to pay top dollar for a room at this exclusive hotel atop the Spanish Steps. **Pros:** sauna access included with each reservation; prime location and panoramic views; private rooftop with bar service upon request. **Cons:** breakfast not included (continental option is €29 plus 10% V.A.T. per person); VIP rates (10% V.A.T. not included); rooms are updated on a rolling basis, leaving some feeling dated. $ *Rooms from: €600* ✉ *Piazza Trinità dei Monti 6, Piazza di Spagna* ☎ *06/699340, 800/223–6800 in U.S.* ⊕ *www.hotelhasslerroma.com* ⬿ *87 rooms* ❗❙ *No Meals* Ⓜ *Spagna.*

★ Hotel de la Ville

$$$$ | **HOTEL** | Occupying a prime position at the top of the Spanish Steps, the sister property to the beloved Hotel de Russie is the most glamorous new hotel in town. **Pros:** must-visit rooftop bar with panoramic views; pampering spa uses signature made-in-Italy organic products; prestigious location atop the Spanish Steps. **Cons:** some rooms are a bit small; service can be a bit slow at the bar; no pets allowed. $ *Rooms from: €594* ✉ *Via Sistina 69, Piazza di Spagna* ☎ *06/977931* ⊕ *www.roccofortehotels.com/hotels-and-resorts/hotel-de-la-ville* ⬿ *104 rooms* ❗❙ *No Meals* Ⓜ *Spagna.*

Hotel d'Inghilterra

$$$ | HOTEL | Situated in a stately 16th-century building and founded in 1845, Hotel d'Inghilterra has a long, storied history: it has been used as a guesthouse for aristocratic travelers visiting a noble family who once lived across the cobblestone street and has been the home away from home for various monarchs and movie stars, like Elizabeth Taylor, not to mention some of the greatest writers of all time—Lord Byron, John Keats, Mark Twain, and Ernest Hemingway among them. **Pros:** excellent in-house restaurant; distinct character and opulence; turndown service (with chocolates). **Cons:** the location, despite soundproofing, is still noisy; elevator is small; some rooms badly in need of renovations and maintenance. ⑤ *Rooms from: €280* ✉ *Via Bocca di Leone 14, Piazza di Spagna* ☎ *06/699811* ⊕ *www.starhotelscollezione.com/en/ our-hotels/hotel-d-inghilterra-rome* ⇥ *84 rooms* ⦿ *Free Breakfast* Ⓜ *Spagna.*

★ Hotel Eden

$$$$ | HOTEL | Once a favorite haunt of Ingrid Bergman, Ginger Rogers, and Fellini, this superlative hotel combines dashing elegance, exquisitely lush decor, and stunning vistas of Rome with true Italian hospitality to create one of the city's top luxury lodgings. **Pros:** 24-hour room service; gorgeous rooftop terrace restaurant; tranquil spa facilities. **Cons:** gym is standard but small; breakfast not included (and very expensive, at €45); some rooms overlook an unremarkable courtyard. ⑤ *Rooms from: €780* ✉ *Via Ludovisi 49, Piazza di Spagna* ☎ *06/478121* ⊕ *www.dorchestercollection.com/en/rome/hotel-eden* ⇥ *98 rooms* ⦿ *No Meals* Ⓜ *Spagna.*

★ Hotel Vilòn

$$$$ | HOTEL | This intimate hotel in the 16th-century mansion annexed to Palazzo Borghese might be Rome's best-kept secret. **Pros:** fantastic location; gorgeous design; attentive staff. **Cons:** some rooms are a bit small; no spa or gym; not much outdoor space. ⑤ *Rooms from: €460* ✉ *Via dell'Arancio 69, Piazza di Spagna* ☎ *06/878187* ⊕ *www.hotelvilon.com* ⇥ *18 rooms* ⦿ *Free Breakfast* Ⓜ *Spagna.*

Il Palazzetto

$$$ | B&B/INN | Once a retreat for one of Rome's richest noble families, this 15th-century house is one of the most intimate and luxurious hotels in Rome, with gorgeous terraces and a rooftop bar where you can watch the never-ending theater of the Spanish Steps. **Pros:** guests have full access to the Hassler's services; location and view; free Wi-Fi. **Cons:** bedrooms do not access communal terraces; restaurant often rented out for crowded special events; often books up far in advance, particularly in high season. ⑤ *Rooms from: €250* ✉ *Vicolo del Bottino 8, Piazza di Spagna* ☎ *06/69934560* ⊕ *www. ilpalazzettoroma.com* ⇥ *4 rooms* ⦿ *No Meals* Ⓜ *Spagna.*

Margutta 19

$$$$ | HOTEL | Tucked away on a quiet, leafy street known for its art galleries, this 22-suite property is like your very own hip, New York–style loft in the center of old-world Rome, with top-drawer amenities, contemporary design, and a restaurant with a verdant terrace. **Pros:** deluxe furnishings; studio-loft feel in center of town; complete privacy. **Cons:** no elevator in the annex to reach rooms on higher floors; no spa or gym; entry-level rooms lack views. ⑤ *Rooms from: €400* ✉ *Via Margutta 19, Piazza di Spagna* ☎ *06/97797979* ⊕ *www.romeluxurysuites.com/margutta* ⇥ *22 suites* ⦿ *Free Breakfast* Ⓜ *Spagna.*

Scalinata di Spagna

$ | B&B/INN | Perched atop the Spanish Steps, this charming boutique hotel makes guests fall in love over and over again—so popular, in fact, it's often booked far in advance. **Pros:** friendly and helpful concierge; free Wi-Fi throughout; fresh fruit in guest rooms. **Cons:** no porter and no elevator; small rooms; hike up the hill to the hotel. $ *Rooms from: €116* ✉ *Piazza Trinità dei Monti 17, Piazza di Spagna* ☎ *06/45686150* ⊕ *www. hotelscalinata.com* ⌁ *30 rooms* ◯ *Free Breakfast* Ⓜ *Spagna.*

 Nightlife

Wine Bar at the Palazzetto

COCKTAIL LOUNGES | The prize for perfect aperitivo spot goes to the Palazzetto, with excellent drinks and appetizers, as well as a breathtaking view of Rome's domes and rooftops—all from its fifth-floor rooftop overlooking Piazza di Spagna. Reach it by climbing the Spanish Steps or getting a lift from the elevator inside the Spagna Metro station. Just keep an eye on the sky, as any chance for a rainy day will close the terrace (as do special events). ✉ *Vicolo del Bottino 8, Piazza di Spagna* ⊹ *The main entrance is a small gate at the top of the Spanish Steps* ☎ *06/69934560* ⊕ *www.ilpalazzettoroma.com* Ⓜ *Spagna.*

 Shopping

ACCESSORIES

Furla

HANDBAGS | Furla very well might be the best deal in Italian leather, selling high-end quality handbags and purses at affordable prices. There are multiple locations throughout the Eternal City (including one at Fiumicino Airport), but its flagship store can be found in the heart of Piazza di Spagna. Be prepared to fight your way through crowds of passionate handbag lovers, all anxious to possess one of the delectable bags, wallets, or whimsical key chains in trendy sherbet hues or timeless bold color combos. ✉ *Piazza di Spagna 22, Piazza di Spagna* ☎ *06/6797159* ⊕ *www.furla.com* Ⓜ *Spagna.*

CLOTHING

★ Brioni

MEN'S CLOTHING | Founded in 1945, Brioni is hailed for its impeccable craftsmanship in creating made-to-measure menswear. The classic brand hires the best men's tailors in Italy, who design bespoke suits to exacting standards, measured to the millimeter and completely personalized from a selection of more than 5,000 spectacular fabrics. A single made-to-measure wool suit will take a minimum of 32 hours to create. Their prêt-à-porter line is also praised for peerless cutting and stitching. Past and present clients include Clark Gable, Barack Obama, and, of course, James Bond. ✉ *Via Condotti 21A, Piazza di Spagna* ☎ *06/6783428* ⊕ *www.brioni.com* ⊙ *Closed Sun.* Ⓜ *Spagna.*

Dolce & Gabbana

MIXED CLOTHING | Dolce and Gabbana met in 1980 when both were assistants at a Milan fashion atelier, and they opened their first store in 1982. With a modern aesthetic that screams sex appeal, the brand has always thrived on excess and is known for its bold, creative designs. The Rome store has a glass ceiling above a sparkling chandelier to allow natural light to spill in, illuminating the marble floors, antique brass accents, and (of course) the latest lines for men, women, and even children, plus an expansive accessories area. ✉ *Via Condotti 49–51, Piazza di Spagna* ☎ *06/69924999* ⊕ *www.dolcegabbana.com* Ⓜ *Spagna.*

Elena Mirò

WOMEN'S CLOTHING | Elena Mirò is a high-end brand that specializes in sophisticated, beautifully feminine clothes for curvy, European-styled women size 46 (U.S. size 12, U.K. size 14) and up. There are several locations in Rome, including one on Via Nazionale. ✉ *Via Frattina 11, Piazza di Spagna* ☎ *06/6784367* ⊕ *www. elenamiro.com* Ⓜ *Spagna.*

Fendi

MIXED CLOTHING | Fendi has been a fixture of the Roman fashion landscape since "Mamma" Fendi first opened shop with her husband in 1925. With an eye for crazy genius, she hired Karl Lagerfeld, who began working with the group at the start of his career. His furs and runway antics made him one of the most influential designers of the 20th century and brought international acclaim to Fendi along the way. The atelier, now owned by the Louis Vuitton group, continues to symbolize Italian glamour at its finest, though the difference in ownership is noticeable. It's also gotten new life in the Italian press for its "Fendi for Fountains" campaign, which included funding the restoration of Rome's Trevi Fountain, and for moving its global headquarters to a striking Mussolini-era building known as the "square Colosseum" in the city's EUR neighborhood. The flagship store in Rome can be found on the ground floor of Palazzo Fendi. The upper floors are home to the brand's seven private suites (the first ever Fendi hotel), and the rooftop hosts Zuma, a modern Japanese restaurant with an oh-so-cool bar that has sweeping views across Rome. ⌧ *Largo Carlo Goldoni 420, Piazza di Spagna* ☎ *06/33450896* ⊕ *www.fendi.com* Ⓜ *Spagna.*

Giorgio Armani

MIXED CLOTHING | One of the most influential designers of Italian haute couture, Giorgio Armani creates fluid silhouettes and dazzling evening gowns with sexy peek-a-boo cutouts; his signature cuts are made with the clever-handedness and flawless technique achievable only by working with tracing paper and Italy's finest fabrics over the course of a lifetime. His menswear collection uses traditional textiles like wide-ribbed corduroy and stretch jersey in nontraditional ways while staying true to a clean, masculine aesthetic. The iconic Italian brand has an Emporio Armani shop on Via del Babuino, but the flagship store is the best place to find pieces that range from exotic runway-worthy masterpieces to more wearable collections emphasizing casual Italian elegance with just the right touch of whimsy and sexiness. ⌧ *Via dei Condotti 77, Piazza di Spagna* ☎ *06/6991460* ⊕ *www.armani.com* Ⓜ *Spagna.*

Gucci

MIXED CLOTHING | Guccio Gucci opened his first leather shop selling luggage in Florence in 1921, and as the glamorous fashion label celebrates its centennial, the success of the double-G trademark is unquestionable. Tom Ford joined as creative director in 1994, helping the fashion house move into a new era that continues today, maintaining the label's trendiness while bringing in a breath of fresh air, thanks to old-school favorites like reinterpreted horsebit styles and Jackie Kennedy scarves. Now helmed by Alessandro Michele, Gucci remains a fashion must for virtually every A-list celebrity, and their designs have moved from heart-stopping sexy rock star to something classically subdued and retrospectively feminine, making the handbags and accessories more covetable than ever. ⌧ *Via Condotti 6–8, Piazza di Spagna* ☎ *06/6790405* ⊕ *www.gucci.com* Ⓜ *Spagna.*

★ Laura Biagiotti

WOMEN'S CLOTHING | Until her death in 2017, Laura Biagiotti was a worldwide ambassador of Italian fashion. Considered the Queen of Cashmere, her soft-as-velvet pullovers have been worn by Sophia Loren, and her snow-white cardigans were said to be a favorite of the late pope John Paul II. Princess Diana even sported one of Biagiotti's cashmere maternity dresses. In addition to stocking the luxe clothing line, the flagship store has a bold red lounge where shoppers can indulge in sampling her line of his-and-her perfumes or sip a Campari cocktail while purchases are customized with Swarovski crystals. ⌧ *Via Belsiana 57, Piazza di Spagna* ☎ *06/6791205* ⊕ *www.laurabiagiotti.it* Ⓜ *Spagna.*

★ Patrizia Pepe

WOMEN'S CLOTHING | One of Florence's best-kept secrets for up-and-coming designs, Patrizia Pepe first emerged on the scene in 1993 with an aesthetic that's both minimalist and bold, combining classic styles with low-slung jeans and jackets with oversize lapels that are bound to draw attention. Her line of shoes is hot-hot-hot for those who can walk on stilts. As a relative newcomer to the crowded Italian fashion scene, the brand's stand-alone fame is still under the radar, but take a look at this shop before the line becomes the next fast-tracked craze. ⊠ *Via Frattina 44, Piazza di Spagna* ☎ *06/6781851* ⊕ *www.patrizia-pepe.com* Ⓜ *Spagna.*

Prada

MIXED CLOTHING | Besides the devil, plenty of serious shoppers wear Prada season after season, especially those willing to sell their souls for one of their ubiquitous handbags. If you are looking for that blend of old-world luxury with a touch of fashion-forward finesse, you'll hit it big here. Mario Prada first founded the Italian luggage brand in 1913, but it has been his granddaughter, Miuccia, who updated the designs into the timeless investment pieces of today. You'll find the Rome store more service-oriented than the New York City branches—a roomy elevator delivers you to a series of thickly carpeted salons where a flock of discreet assistants will help you pick out dresses, shoes, lingerie, and fashion accessories. The men's store is located at Via dei Condotti 88/90, while the women's is down the street at 92/95. ⊠ *Via dei Condotti 88/90 and 92/95, Piazza di Spagna* ☎ *06/6790897* ⊕ *www.prada.com* Ⓜ *Spagna.*

Schostal

MIXED CLOTHING | A Piazza di Spagna fixture since 1870, the shop was once the go-to place for women looking to stock up on corsets, bonnets, stockings, and petticoats. Today, it's the place to stop for those essential basics that are increasingly difficult to find, like fine-quality shirts, underwear, and handkerchiefs made of wool and pure cashmere at affordable prices. ⊠ *Via della Fontanella di Borghese 29, Piazza di Spagna* ☎ *06/6791240* ⊕ *www.schostalroma1870.com* ◔ *Closed Sun.* Ⓜ *Spagna.*

Valentino

MIXED CLOTHING | Since taking the Valentino reins, creative director Pierpaolo Piccioli has faced numerous challenges, the most basic of which is keeping Valentino true to Valentino after the designer's retirement in 2008. He served as accessories designer under Valentino for more than a decade and understands exactly how to make the next generation of Hollywood stars swoon. Valentino has taken over most of Piazza di Spagna, where he lived for decades in a lovely palazzo next to one of the multiple boutiques showcasing his eponymous designs with a romantic edginess; think studded heels or a showstopping prêt-à-porter evening gown worthy of the Oscars. Rock stars and other music lovers can also have their Valentino guitar straps personalized when they buy one at this enormous boutique. ⊠ *Piazza di Spagna 38, Piazza di Spagna* ☎ *06/94515710* ⊕ *www.valentino.com* Ⓜ *Spagna.*

Versace

MIXED CLOTHING | Versace's Rome flagship is a gem of architecture and design, with Byzantine-inspired mosaic floors and futuristic interiors with transparent walls, not to mention, of course, fashion: here shoppers will find apparel, jewelry, watches, fragrances, cosmetics, and home furnishings in designs every bit as flamboyant as Donatella and Allegra (Gianni's niece), drawing heavily on the sexy rocker gothic underground vibe. ⊠ *Piazza di Spagna 12, Piazza di Spagna* ☎ *06/6784600* ⊕ *www.versace.com* Ⓜ *Spagna.*

DEPARTMENT STORES

★ La Rinascente

DEPARTMENT STORE | Italy's best-known department store is located in a dazzling space that has seven stories packed with the best luxury goods the world has to offer. Here, one can find oodles of cosmetics on the ground floor, as well as a phalanx of ready-to-wear designer sportswear and blockbuster handbags and accessories, and kitchen and homeware in the basement. Even if you're not planning on buying anything, the basement excavations of a Roman aqueduct and the roof terrace bar with its splendid view are well worth a visit. There's also a location at Piazza Fiume. ✉ *Via del Tritone 61, Piazza di Spagna* ☎ *06/879161* ⊕ *www.rinascente.it* Ⓜ *Barberini.*

JEWELRY

Bulgari

JEWELRY & WATCHES | Every capital city has its famous jeweler, and Bulgari is to Rome what Tiffany is to New York and Cartier to Paris. The jewelry giant has developed a reputation for meticulous craftsmanship melding noble metals with precious gems. In the middle of the 19th century, the great-grandfather of the current Bulgari brothers began working as a silver jeweler in his native Greece and is said to have moved to Rome with less than 1,000 lire in his pocket. The recent makeover of the store's temple-inspired interior pays homage to the brand's ties to both places. Today the mega-brand emphasizes colorful and playful jewelry as the principal cornerstone of its aesthetic. Popular collections include Bulgari-Bulgari and B.zero1. ✉ *Via dei Condotti 10, Piazza di Spagna* ☎ *06/696261* ⊕ *www.bulgari.com* Ⓜ *Spagna.*

SHOES

A. Testoni

SHOES | Amedeo Testoni, the brand's founder and original designer, was born in 1905 in Bologna, the heart of Italy's shoe-making territory. In 1929, he opened his first shop and began producing shoes as artistic as the Cubist and Art Deco artwork of the period. His shoes have adorned the feet of Fred Astaire, proving that lightweight footwear can be comfortable and luxurious and still turn heads. Today the Testoni brand includes a line of enviable handbags and classically cool leather jackets—all found at this Roman boutique, exclusively dedicated to the women's collection. For gentlemen there are dreamy calfskin sneakers and matching messenger bags. ✉ *Via Borgognona 21, Piazza di Spagna* ☎ *06/6787718* ⊕ *www.testoni.com* Ⓜ *Spagna.*

★ Braccialini

HANDBAGS | Founded in 1954 by Florentine stylist Carla Braccialini and her husband, Robert, Braccialini—currently managed by their sons—makes bags that are authentic works of art in bright colors and delightful shapes, such as London black cabs or mountain chalets. The adorably quirky tote bags have picture-postcard scenes of luxury destinations made of brightly colored appliquéd leather. Be sure to check out their eccentric Temi (Theme) creature bags; the snail-shape handbag made out of python skin makes an unforgettable fashion statement. ✉ *Galleria Alberto Sordi 20/21, Piazza Colonna, Piazza di Spagna* ☎ *06/6784339* ⊕ *www.braccialini.it* Ⓜ *Spagna.*

Fausto Santini

SHOES | Shoe lovers with a passion for minimalist design flock to Fausto Santini to get their hands on his nerdy-chic shoes with their statement-making lines. Santini has been in business since 1970 and caters to a sophisticated, avant-garde clientele looking for elegant, classic shoes with a kick and a rainbow color palette. An outlet at Via Cavour 106, named for Fausto's father, Giacomo, sells last season's shoes at a big discount. ✉ *Via Frattina 120, Piazza di Spagna* ☎ *06/6784114* ⊕ *www.faustosantini.com* Ⓜ *Spagna.*

3

Rome PIAZZA DI SPAGNA

Repubblica and the Quirinale

★ Tod's

SHOES | First founded in the 1920s, Tod's has grown from a small family brand into a global powerhouse so wealthy that its owner, Diego Della Valle, donated €20 million to the Colosseum restoration project. The shoe baron's trademark is his simple, classic, understated designs and butter-soft leather. Sure to please are his light and flexible slip-on Gommino driving shoes with rubber-bottomed soles for extra driving-pedal grip. There is also a location on Via dei Condotti. ⊠ *Via della Fontanella di Borghese 56a–57, Piazza di Spagna* ☎ *06/68210066* ⊕ *www.tods. com* Ⓜ *Spagna.*

HEALTH & BEAUTY

Modàfferi Barber Shop

OTHER HEALTH & BEAUTY | Run by two friendly brothers, who took over the business from their father, this barbershop is preferred by actors performing at the nearby Teatro Sistina. It was founded in the 1970s and still has charmingly retro decor. They offer haircuts, beard care, manicures, pedicures, facials, and massages and have their own line of products. For extra privacy, you can request the private room. ⊠ *Via dei Cappuccini 11, Piazza di Spagna* ☎ *06/4817077* ⊕ *www.modafferibarbershop.it* ☉ *Closed Sun. & Mon.* Ⓜ *Barberini.*

Repubblica and the Quirinale

This sector of Rome stretches down from the 19th-century district built up around the Piazza della Repubblica—originally laid out to serve as a monumental foyer between the Termini train station and the rest of the city—and over the rest of the Quirinale. The highest of ancient Rome's famed seven hills, the Quirinale is crowned by the massive Palazzo Quirinale, home to the popes until 1870 and now Italy's presidential palace. Along the way, you can see ancient Roman sculptures, early Christian churches, and highlights from the 16th and 17th centuries, when Rome was conquered by the Baroque—and by Bernini.

Although Bernini's work feels omnipresent in much of the city center, the Renaissance-man range of his creations is particularly notable here. The artist as architect considered the church of Sant'Andrea al Quirinale one of his best; Bernini the urban designer and water worker is responsible for the muscle-bound sea god who blows his conch so provocatively in the fountain at the center of whirling Piazza Barberini. And Bernini the master gives religious passion a joltingly corporeal treatment in what is perhaps his greatest work, the *Ecstasy of St. Teresa,* in the church of Santa Maria della Vittoria.

GETTING HERE AND AROUND

Located between Termini station and the Spanish Steps, this area is about a 15-minute walk from either. Bus No. 40 will get you from Termini to the Quirinale in two stops; from the Vatican take Bus No. 64. The very central Repubblica Metro stop is on the piazza of the same name.

Sights

★ Capuchin Museum

RELIGIOUS BUILDING | Devoted to teaching visitors about the Capuchin order, this museum is mainly notable for a crypt visitable at the end of the museum circuit. Not for the easily spooked, the crypt under the church of Santa Maria della Concezione holds the bones of some 4,000 dead Capuchin monks. With bones arranged in odd decorative designs around the shriveled and decayed remains of their kinsmen, a macabre reminder of the impermanence of earthly life, the crypt is strangely touching and beautiful. As one sign proclaims: "What you are, we once were. What we are, you someday will be." Upstairs in the church, the first chapel on the right contains Guido Reni's mid-17th-century *Archangel St. Michael Trampling the Devil.* The painting caused great scandal after an astute contemporary observer remarked that the face of the devil bore a surprising resemblance to Pope Innocent X, archenemy of Reni's Barberini patrons. Compare the devil with the bust of the pope that you saw in the Palazzo Doria Pamphilj and judge for yourself. ⊠ *Via Veneto 27, Quirinale* ☎ *06/88803695* ⊕ *www.cappucciniviaveneto.it* 🖃 *€8.50* Ⓜ *Barberini.*

Fontana delle Api (*Fountain of the Bees*) **FOUNTAIN** | Decorated with the famous heraldic bees of the Barberini family, the upper shell and the inscription are from a fountain that Bernini designed for Pope Urban VIII; the rest was lost when the fountain was moved to make way for a new street. The inscription was the cause of a considerable uproar when the fountain was first built in 1644. It said that the fountain had been erected in the 22nd year of the pontiff's reign, although in fact the 21st anniversary of Urban's election to the papacy was still some weeks away. The last numeral was hurriedly erased, but to no avail—Urban died eight days before the beginning of his 22nd year as pope. The superstitious Romans, who had immediately recognized the inscription as a foolhardy tempting of fate, were vindicated. ⊠ *Piazza Barberini, Quirinale* Ⓜ *Barberini.*

MACRO
ART MUSEUM | Formerly known as Rome's Modern and Contemporary Art Gallery, and before that as the Peroni beer factory, this redesigned industrial space has brought new life to the gallery and museum scene of a city hitherto hailed for its "then," not its "now." The collection here covers Italian contemporary artists from the 1960s through today. The goal is to bring current art to the public in innovative spaces and, not incidentally, to give support and bring recognition

to Rome's contemporary art scene, which labors in the shadow of the city's artistic heritage. After a few days—or millennia—of dusty marble, it's a breath of fresh air. ■TIP→ **Check the website for occasional late-night openings and events.** ⊠ *Via Nizza 138, Repubblica* ☎ *06/696271* ⊕ *www.museomacro.it* 🖃 *Free* ☉ *Closed Mon.* Ⓜ *Castro Pretorio.*

★**Palazzo Barberini/Galleria Nazionale d'Arte Antica**
CASTLE/PALACE | One of Rome's most splendid 17th-century buildings, the Palazzo Barberini is a landmark of the Roman Baroque style. The grand facade was designed by Carlo Maderno (aided by his nephew, Francesco Borromini), but when Maderno died, Borromini was passed over in favor of his great rival, Gian Lorenzo Bernini. Now home to the Galleria Nazionale d'Arte Antica, the palazzo holds a splendid collection that includes Raphael's *La Fornarina,* a luminous portrait of the artist's lover (a resident of Trastevere, she was reputedly a baker's daughter). Also noteworthy are Guido Reni's portrait of the doomed *Beatrice Cenci* (beheaded in Rome for patricide in 1599)—Hawthorne called it "the saddest picture ever painted" in his Rome-based novel, *The Marble Faun*—and Caravaggio's dramatic *Judith Beheading Holofernes.* The showstopper here is the palace's Gran Salone, a vast ballroom with a ceiling painted in 1630 by the third (and too-often-neglected) master of the Roman Baroque, Pietro da Cortona. It depicts the *Glorification of Urban VIII's Reign* and has the spectacular conceit of glorifying Urban VIII as the agent of Divine Providence, escorted by a "bomber squadron" (to quote art historian Sir Michael Levey) of huge Barberini bees, the heraldic symbol of the family. ⊠ *Via delle Quattro Fontane 13, Quirinale* ☎ *06/4814591* ⊕ *www.barberinicorsini. org* ☉ *Closed Mon.* 🖃 *€10, includes Galleria Corsini* Ⓜ *Barberini.*

★ Palazzo Massimo alle Terme

ART MUSEUM | Come here to get a real feel for ancient Roman art—the collection rivals even the Vatican's. The Museo Nazionale Romano, with a collection ranging from striking classical Roman paintings to marble bric-a-brac, has four locations: Palazzo Altemps, Crypta Balbi, the Museo delle Terme di Diocleziano, and this, the Palazzo Massimo alle Terme. This vast structure holds the great ancient treasures of the archaeological collection and also the coin collection. Highlights include the *Dying Niobid*, the famous bronze *Boxer at Rest*, and the *Discobolus Lancellotti*. But the best part of the museum are the ancient frescoes on view on the top floor, stunningly set up to "re-create" the look of the homes they once decorated. These include stuccoes and wall paintings found in the area of the Villa Farnesina (in Trastevere) and the legendary frescoes from Empress Livia's villa at Prima Porta, delightful depictions of a garden in bloom and an orchard alive with birds. Their colors are remarkably well preserved. These delicate decorations covered the walls of cool, sunken rooms in Livia's summerhouse outside the city. ⊠ *Largo di Villa Peretti 2, Repubblica* ☎ *06/39967700* ⊕ *www.museonazionaleromano.beniculturali.it* ⧉ *€10, or €12 for a combined ticket including access to Crypta Balbi, Museo delle Terme di Diocleziano, and Palazzo Altemps (valid for 3 days)* ⊘ *Closed Mon.* ⬢ *Reservations required* Ⓜ *Repubblica, Termini.*

Piazza del Quirinale

PLAZA/SQUARE | This strategic location atop the Quirinale has long been of great importance. It served as home of the Sabines in the 7th century BC—at that time, deadly enemies of the Romans, who lived on the Campidoglio and Palatino (all of 1 km [½ mile] away). Today, it's the foreground for the presidential residence, **Palazzo del Quirinale**, and home to the **Palazzo della Consulta,** where Italy's Constitutional Court sits. The open side of the piazza has an impressive vista over the rooftops and domes of central Rome and St. Peter's. The **Fontana di Montecavallo,** or Fontana dei Dioscuri, comprises a huge Roman statuary group and an obelisk from the tomb of the emperor Augustus. The group of the Dioscuri trying to tame two massive marble steeds was found in the Baths of Constantine, which occupied part of the summit of the Quirinale. Unlike just about every other ancient statue in Rome, this group survived the Dark Ages intact and accordingly became one of the city's great sights, especially during the Middle Ages. Next to the figures, the ancient obelisk from the Mausoleo di Augusto (Tomb of Augustus) was put here by Pope Pius VI at the end of the 18th century. ⊠ *Piazza del Quirinale, Quirinale* Ⓜ *Barberini.*

Piazza della Repubblica

PLAZA/SQUARE | Often the first view that spells "Rome" to weary travelers walking from Termini station, this round piazza was laid out in the late 1800s and follows the line of the caldarium of the vast ancient public baths, the Terme di Diocleziano. At its center, the exuberant Fontana delle Naiadi (Fountain of the Naiads) teems with voluptuous bronze ladies happily wrestling with marine monsters. The nudes weren't there when the pope unveiled the fountain in 1888—sparing him any embarrassment—but when the figures were added in 1901, they caused a scandal. It's said that the sculptor, Mario Rutelli (grandfather of Francesco Rutelli, former mayor of Rome), modeled them on the ample figures of two musical-comedy stars of the day. The colonnades now house the luxe hotel Palazzo Naiadi and various shops and cafés. Ⓜ *Repubblica.*

San Carlo alle Quattro Fontane

CHURCH | Sometimes known as San Carlino because of its tiny size, this is one of Borromini's masterpieces. In a space no larger than the base of one of the piers of St. Peter's Basilica, he created a church that is an intricate exercise in geometric perfection, with a coffered dome that seems to float above the curves of the walls. Borromini's work is often bizarre, definitely intellectual, and intensely concerned with pure form. In San Carlo, he invented an original treatment of space that creates an effect of rippling movement, especially evident in the double-S curves of the facade. Characteristically, the interior decoration is subdued, in white stucco with no more than a few touches of gilding, so as not to distract from the form. Don't miss the cloister: a tiny, understated Baroque jewel, with a graceful portico and loggia above, echoing the lines of the church. ⊠ *Via del Quirinale 23, Quirinale* ☎ *06/4883261* ⊕ *www.sancarlino.eu* Ⓜ *Barberini.*

★ **Santa Maria della Vittoria**

CHURCH | Designed by Carlo Maderno, this church is best known for Bernini's sumptuous Baroque decoration of the Cappella Cornaro (Cornaro Chapel, the last on the left as you face the altar), which houses his interpretation of divine love, the *Ecstasy of St. Teresa.* Bernini's masterly fusion of sculpture, light, architecture, painting, and relief is a multimedia extravaganza, with the chapel modeled as a theater, and one of the key examples of the Roman high Baroque. The members of the Cornaro family meditate on the communal vision of the great moment of divine love before them: the swooning saint's robes appear to be on fire, quivering with life, and the white marble group seems suspended in the heavens as golden rays illuminate the scene. An angel assists at the moment of Teresa's vision as the saint abandons herself to the joys of heavenly love. Bernini represented this mystical experience in what, to modern eyes, may seem very earthly terms. Or, as the visiting French dignitary Charles de Brosses put it in the 18th century, "If this is divine love, I know all about it." ⊠ *Via XX Settembre 17, Largo Santa Susanna, Repubblica* ☎ *06/42740571* Ⓜ *Repubblica.*

★ **Sant'Andrea al Quirinale**

CHURCH | Designed by Bernini, this small church is one of the triumphs of the Roman Baroque period. His son wrote that Bernini considered it his best work and that he used to come here occasionally, just to sit and contemplate. Bernini's simple oval plan, a classic form in Baroque architecture, is given drama and movement by the church's decoration, which carries the story of St. Andrew's martyrdom and ascension into heaven, starting with the painting over the high altar, up past the figure of the saint above, to the angels at the base of the lantern and the dove of the Holy Spirit that awaits on high. ⊠ *Via del Quirinale 30, Quirinale* ☎ *06/4819399* ⊕ *santandrea.gesuiti.it* ⊗ *Closed Mon.* Ⓜ *Barberini.*

🍽 Restaurants

Trimani Il Winebar

$$ | WINE BAR | This wine bar is run by the Trimani family of wine merchants, whose shop next door has been in business for nearly two centuries. Hot food is served at lunch and dinner in the minimalist interior, and it is also perfect for an aperitif or an early supper (it opens for evening service at 5:30). **Known for:** 6,000 wines on sale from around the world; candlelit second floor for sipping; *torte salate* (savory tarts). ⑤ *Average main: €18* ⊠ *Via Cernaia 37, Repubblica* ☎ *06/4469630* ⊕ *www.trimani.com* ⊗ *Closed Sun. and Aug.* Ⓜ *Castro Pretorio.*

☕ Coffee and Quick Bites

Dagnino

$ | SICILIAN | Hidden inside a covered arcade, this Sicilian pasticceria, which opened in 1955 and proudly wears its mid-century modern design, boasts pastry cases filled with sweets like cannoli, cassata, cakes, and marzipan. Go for breakfast and try the cornetto filled with ricotta and chocolate chips—this is one of the few places in Rome where you can find it. **Known for:** Sicilian desserts; mid-century modern design; cornetti filled with ricotta and chocolate chips. $ *Average main: €3* ✉ *Via Vittorio Emanuele Orlando 75, Repubblica* ☎ *06/4818660* ⊕ *www.pasticceriadagnino.com* Ⓜ *Repubblica.*

La Romana dal 1947

$ | ICE CREAM | In summertime, the line at this gelateria stretches out the door and around the corner. Though it's a franchise that originated in Rimini, La Romana is loved by Romans for its rich, creamy gelato made with organic milk, fresh fruit, nuts, and chocolate. **Known for:** modern decor; big portions; reasonably priced. $ *Average main: €3* ✉ *Via Venti Settembre 60, Repubblica* ☎ *06/42020828* ⊕ *www.gelateriaromana. com* Ⓜ *Repubblica.*

Pinsere

$ | PIZZA | FAMILY | In Rome, you'll usually find either pizza *tonda* or pizza *al taglio,* but there's also pizza *pinsa:* it's an oval-shape individual pie, and a little thicker than the classic Roman pizza. Pinsere is mostly a take-out shop, with people eating on the street for their lunch break, so it's the perfect quick meal. **Known for:** mortadella and pistachio pizzas; budget-friendly options; seasonal toppings. $ *Average main: €6* ✉ *Via Flavia 98, Repubblica* ☎ *06/42020924* ⊕ *www. facebook.com/Pinsere* ⊘ *Closed weekends and Aug.* Ⓜ *Castro Pretorio.*

 Hotels

The St. Regis Rome

$$$$ | HOTEL | Originally opened by César Ritz in 1894, this grand dame is looking fabulous thanks to a $40 million renovation completed in 2018. **Pros:** fresh off a complete renovation; the library lounge serves a lovely afternoon tea; every room comes with butler service. **Cons:** the restaurant feels more like a lounge than a proper restaurant; breakfast is not included; no pets allowed. $ *Rooms*

from: €650 ✉ *Via Vittorio E. Orlando 3, Repubblica* ☎ *06/47091* ⊕ *www.stregisrome.com* ⇆ *161 rooms* ⍟ *No Meals* Ⓜ *Repubblica.*

Yes Hotel

$ | HOTEL | This chic hotel may fool you into thinking the digs are expensive, but the contemporary coolness of Yes Hotel, located around the corner from Termini station, actually comes at a bargain. **Pros:** a great value without the budget feel; around the corner from Termini station; discount if you pay in cash. **Cons:** not near many top sights; small rooms; neighborhood can be noisy at night. $ *Rooms from: €80* ✉ *Via Magenta 15, Repubblica* ☎ *06/44363836* ⊕ *www.yeshotelrome. com* ⇆ *42 rooms* ⍟ *Free Breakfast* Ⓜ *Termini, Castro Pretorio.*

 Performing Arts

★ Teatro dell'Opera

OPERA | Long considered a far younger sibling of La Scala in Milan and La Fenice in Venice, the company commands an audience during its mid-November–May season. In the hot summer months, they move to the Terme di Caracalla for its outdoor opera series. As can be expected, the oft-preferred performance is *Aida,* for its spectacle, which once included real elephants. The company has lately taken a new direction, using projections atop the ancient ruins to create cutting-edge sets. ✉ *Piazza Beniamino Gigli 1, Repubblica* ☎ *06/481601, 06/4817003 tickets* ⊕ *www.operaroma.it* Ⓜ *Repubblica.*

Villa Borghese and Around

Touring Rome's artistic masterpieces while staying clear of its hustle and bustle can be, quite literally, a walk in the park. Some of the city's finest sights are tucked away in or next to green lawns and pedestrian piazzas, offering a breath of fresh air for weary sightseers, especially in the Villa Borghese park. One of Rome's largest, this park can alleviate gallery gout by offering an oasis in which to cool off under the ilex, oak, and umbrella pine trees. If you feel like a picnic, have an *alimentari* (food shop) make you some panini before you go; food carts within the park are overpriced.

GETTING HERE AND AROUND

The Metro stop for Piazza del Popolo is Flaminio on Line A. The Villa Giulia, the Galleria Nazionale d'Arte Moderna e Contemporanea, and the Bioparco in Villa Borghese are accessible from Via Flaminia, 1 km (½ mile) from Piazza del Popolo. Tram No. 19 and Bus No. 3 stop at each. Bus No. 160 and No. 628 connect Piazza del Popolo to Piazza Venezia. Bus No. 116 goes into Villa Borghese.

◉ Sights

★ Galleria Borghese

ART MUSEUM | It's a real toss-up as to which is more magnificent: the museum built for Cardinal Scipione Borghese in 1612 or the art that lies within it. The luxury-loving cardinal had the museum custom built as a showcase for his fabulous collection of both antiquities and more "modern" works, including those he commissioned from the masters Caravaggio and Bernini. Today, it's a monument to Roman interior decoration at its most extravagant. One of the most famous works in the collection is Canova's neoclassical sculpture *Pauline Borghese as Venus Victorious.* The next three rooms hold three key early Baroque sculptures: Bernini's *David, Apollo and Daphne,* and *The Rape of Persephone.* All were done when the artist was in his twenties, and all illustrate Bernini's extraordinary skill. *Apollo and Daphne* shows the moment when, to aid her escape from the pursuing Apollo, Daphne is turned into a laurel tree. Leaves and twigs sprout from her fingertips as she stretches agonizingly away from Apollo.

In *The Rape of Persephone,* Pluto has just plucked Persephone (or Proserpina) from her flower-picking, or perhaps he's returning to Hades with his prize. (Don't miss the realistic way his grip causes dimples in Persephone's flesh.) This is the stuff that makes the Baroque exciting—and moving. Other Berninis on view in the collection include a large, unfinished figure called *Verità,* or Truth. Room 8 contains six paintings by Caravaggio, the hotheaded genius who died at age 37. All of his paintings, even the charming *Boy with a Basket of Fruit,* seethe with an undercurrent of darkness. The disquieting *Sick Bacchus* is a self-portrait of the artist who, like the god, had a fondness for wine. *David and Goliath,* painted in the last year of Caravaggio's life—while he was on the run, murder charges hanging over his head—includes his self-portrait in the head of Goliath. Upstairs, the Pinacoteca (Picture Gallery) boasts paintings by Raphael (including his moving *Deposition*), Pinturicchio, Perugino, Bellini, and Rubens. Probably the gallery's most famous painting is Titian's allegorical *Sacred and Profane Love,* a mysterious and yet-unsolved image with two female figures, one nude, one clothed. ■**TIP→ Admission to the Galleria is by reservation only. Visitors are admitted in two-hour shifts 9–5. Prime-time slots can sell out days in advance, so reserve directly through the Borghese's website.** ⊠ *Piazzale Scipione Borghese 5, off Via Pinciana, Villa Borghese* ☎ *06/32810 reservations, 06/8413979 info* ⊕ *www.galleriaborghese.it* ⊠ *€15, including €2 reservation fee; increased fee during temporary exhibitions* ⊙ *Closed Mon.* ⚐ *Reservations required.*

MAXXI—Museo Nazionale delle Arti del XXI Secolo (*National Museum of 21st-Century Arts*)

ART MUSEUM | Designed by the late Iraqi-British starchitect Zaha Hadid, this modern building plays with lots of natural light, curving and angular lines, and big open spaces, all meant to question the

Sights ▼

1 Galleria Borghese **I4**

2 MAXXI—Museo Nazionale
delle Arti del
XXI Secolo **B1**

3 Piazza del Popolo **C6**

4 Santa Maria del
Popolo **C5**

5 Villa Borghese **G5**

Restaurants ▼

1 Acquolina **C7**

2 Al Ceppo **I1**

3 La Pergola **A2**

Quick Bites ▼

1 Canova **D6**

Hotels ▼

1 The First Roma Arte **C7**

2 Hotel de Russie **D6**

3 The Hoxton Rome **J2**

4 Rome Cavalieri,
A Waldorf
Astoria Hotel **A2**

Villa Borghese and Around

division between "within" and "without" (think glass ceilings and steel staircases that twist through the air). The MAXXI hosts temporary exhibitions of art, architecture, film, and more. The permanent collection, exhibited on a rotating basis, boasts more than 350 works from modern and contemporary artists, including Andy Warhol, Francesco Clemente, and Gerhard Richter. ⊠ *Via Guido Reni 4/A, Flaminio* ☎ *06/3201954* ⊕ *www.maxxi.art* 🎫 *€12* ⊙ *Closed Mon.* Ⓜ *Flaminio, then Tram No. 2 to Apollodoro.*

★ Piazza del Popolo

PLAZA/SQUARE | With its obelisk and twin churches, this immense square is a famed Rome landmark. It marks what was for centuries the northern entrance to the city, where all roads from the north converge and where visitors, many of them pilgrims, would get their first impression of the Eternal City. The desire to make this entrance to Rome something special had been a pet project of popes and their architects for more than three centuries. The piazza, crowded with fashionable carriages and carnival revelers in the past, is a pedestrian zone today. At election time, it's the scene of huge political rallies, and on New Year's Eve, Rome stages a mammoth alfresco party here. ⊠ *Piazza del Popolo* Ⓜ *Flaminio*

★ Santa Maria del Popolo

CHURCH | Standing inconspicuously in a corner of the vast Piazza del Popolo, this church often goes unnoticed, but the treasures inside make it a must for art lovers. Bramante enlarged the apse, which was rebuilt in the 15th century on the site of a much older place of worship. Inside, in the first chapel on the right, you'll see some frescoes by Pinturicchio from the mid-15th century; the adjacent Cybo Chapel is a 17th-century exercise in decorative marble. Raphael designed the famous Chigi Chapel, the second on the left, with vault mosaics—showing God the Father in benediction—as well as statues of Jonah and Elijah. More than

a century later, Bernini added the oval medallions on the tombs and the statues of Daniel and Habakkuk. Finally, the Cerasi Chapel, to the left of the high altar, holds two Caravaggios: *The Crucifixion of St. Peter* and *The Conversion of St. Paul.* Exuding drama and realism, both are key early Baroque works that show how "modern" 17th-century art can appear. Compare their style with the much more restrained and classically "pure" *Assumption of the Virgin* by Annibale Carracci, which hangs over the altar of the chapel. ⊠ *Piazza del Popolo 12, near Porta Pinciana, Piazza del Popolo* ☎ *3923612243* ⊕ *www.smariadel-popolo.com/it* ⊙ *Closed Sun.* Ⓜ *Flaminio.*

★ Villa Borghese

CITY PARK | **FAMILY** | Rome's Central Park, the Villa Borghese was originally laid out as a recreational garden in the early 17th century by Cardinal Scipione Borghese. The word "villa" was used to mean suburban estate, of the type developed by the ancient Romans and adopted by Renaissance nobles. Today's gardens cover a much smaller area—by 1630, the perimeter wall was almost 5 km (3 miles) long. At the end of the 18th century, Scottish painter Jacob More remodeled the gardens into the English style popular at the time. In addition to the gloriously restored Galleria Borghese, the highlights of the park are Piazza di Siena, a graceful amphitheater, and the botanical garden on Via Canonica, where there is a pretty little lake as well as the neoclassical faux–Temple of Aesculapius, the Biopark zoo, Rome's own replica of London's Globe Theatre, and the Villa Giulia museum. The Carlo Bilotti Museum (www.museo-carlobilotti.it) is particularly attractive for Giorgio de Chirico fans, and there is more modern art in the nearby Galleria Nazionale d'Arte Moderna e Contemporanea. The 63-seat children's movie theater, Cinema dei Piccoli, shows films for adults in the evening. There's also Casa del Cinema, where film buffs can screen films or sit at the sleek, cherry-red, indoor-outdoor caffè (you can find a schedule of events at www.casadelcinema.it). ✉ *Main entrances at Porta Pinciana, the Pincio, Piazzale Flaminio (Piazza del Popolo), Viale delle Belle Arti, and Via Mercadante, Villa Borghese* Ⓜ *Flaminio.*

Restaurants

Acquolina

$$$$ | **MODERN ITALIAN** | This Michelin-starred restaurant turns out delicious and high-quality seafood dishes that incorporate top-of-the-line ingredients like truffles and caviar. Tortelli are served with butter, anchovies, and black truffle, and all the dishes are artfully presented. **Known for:** sophisticated desserts; elaborate tasting menus; linguine with clams. Ⓢ *Average main: €40* ✉ *The First Roma Arte, Via del Vantaggio 14, Piazza del Popolo* ☎ *06/3201590* ⊕ *www.acquolinaristorante.it* ☾ *Closed Sun. and 10 days in Aug. No lunch* Ⓜ *Flaminio.*

Al Ceppo

$$$ | **ITALIAN** | The well-heeled, the business-minded, and those of refined palates frequent this outpost of tranquility. The owners hail from Le Marche, the region northeast of Rome that encompasses inland mountains and the Adriatic coastline, and these ladies dote on their customers as you'd wish a sophisticated Italian mamma would. **Known for:** authentic Le Marche cuisine; excellent wine list; grilled meat and fish. Ⓢ *Average main: €30* ✉ *Via Panama 2, Villa Borghese* ☎ *06/8419696* ⊕ *www.ristorantealceppo.it* ☾ *Closed 3 wks in Aug.*

★ La Pergola

$$$$ | **MODERN ITALIAN** | Dinner here is a truly spectacular and romantic event, with incomparable views across the city matched by a stellar dining experience that includes top-notch service as well as sublimely inventive fare. The difficulty comes in choosing from among Michelin-starred chef Heinz Beck's alta cucina specialties. **Known for:** weekend reservations that book up three months

in advance; fagotelli La Pergola stuffed with pecorino, eggs, and cream with guanciale and zucchini; award-winning wine list. Ⓢ *Average main: €65* ✉ *Rome Cavalieri, A Waldorf Astoria Resort, Via Alberto Cadlolo 101, Monte Mario* ☎ *06/35092152* ⊕ *www.romecavalieri.com/lapergola.php* ☾ *Closed Sun. and Mon., 3 wks in Aug., and Jan. No lunch* ⌂ *Jacket and tie.*

Coffee and Quick Bites

Canova

$$ | **ITALIAN** | Esteemed director Federico Fellini, who lived around the corner on Via Margutta, used to come here all the time and even had an office in the back. His drawings and black-and-white stills from his films remain on display in the hallway that leads to the interior dining room, but the best place to sit for people-watching with a coffee, light lunch, or aperitivo is on the terrace out front. **Known for:** Fellini's old hangout; great people-watching on Piazza del Popolo; sandwiches and other light fare. Ⓢ *Average main: €15* ✉ *Piazza del Popolo 16, Piazza del Popolo* ☎ *06/3612231* ⊕ *www.canovapiazzadelpopolo.it* Ⓜ *Flaminio.*

🛏 Hotels

The First Roma Arte

$$$$ | **HOTEL** | Set in a 19th-century neoclassical palace, this cozy boutique hotel was remodeled to feature high-tech, elegant guest rooms while keeping the core structure, including unique windows and tall ceilings, intact. **Pros:** more than 200 works of art on display from Galleria Mucciaccia; fitness room with Technogym equipment; incredible staff that is eager to please. **Cons:** many rates don't include breakfast; some rooms can be a bit dark; not a lot of in-room storage for luggage. Ⓢ *Rooms from: €450* ✉ *Via del Vantaggio 14, Piazza del Popolo* ☎ *06/45617070* ⊕ *www.thefirsthotel.com/arte* ⤳ *29 rooms* ⁝◯⁝ *No Meals* Ⓜ *Flaminio.*

★ Hotel de Russie

$$$$ | **HOTEL** | Occupying a 19th-century hotel that once hosted royalty, Picasso, and Cocteau, the Hotel de Russie is now the first choice in Rome for government bigwigs and Hollywood high rollers seeking ultimate luxury in a secluded retreat. **Pros:** excellent Stravinskij cocktail bar also has tables in the garden; big potential for celebrity sightings; well-equipped gym and world-class spa with hydropool Jacuzzi, steam room, and sauna. **Cons:** expensive; faster Internet comes at a fee; breakfast not included. $ *Rooms from: €700* ✉ *Via del Babuino 9, Piazza del Popolo* ☎ *06/328881* ⊕ *www.roccofortehotels. com/hotels-and-resorts/hotel-de-russie* ⮌ *120 rooms* ⦿ *No Meals* Ⓜ *Flaminio.*

The Hoxton Rome

$$ | **HOTEL** | British brand The Hoxton's first foray into Italy is a design lover's dream filled with 1970s-inspired bespoke furniture, art tomes, and plants that transform the large lobby into intimate seating nooks perfect for socializing and co-working. **Pros:** great food and drinks; stylish design; friendly staff. **Cons:** rooms have little storage space for clothes; location far from tourist sites, with no metro nearby; no gym or spa. $ *Rooms from: €189* ✉ *Largo Benedetto Marcello 220, Parioli* ☎ *06/94502700* ⊕ *www.thehoxton.com/rome* ⮌ *192 rooms* ⦿ *No Meals.*

Rome Cavalieri, A Waldorf Astoria Hotel

$$$$ | **RESORT** | A hilltop oasis far from the noise of the centro storico, the Rome Cavalieri comes with magnificent views, three outdoor pools, one indoor pool, and a palatial spa perched atop the Monte Mario amid 15 acres of lush Mediterranean parkland. **Pros:** impressive on-site restaurant; famed art collection, including a Tiepolo triptych from 1725; complimentary shuttle to city center. **Cons:** outside the city center; you definitely pay for the luxury of staying here—everything is expensive; not all rooms have great views. $ *Rooms from:*

€370 ✉ *Via Alberto Cadlolo 101, Monte Mario* ☎ *06/35091* ⊕ *www.romecavalieri. com* ⮌ *370 rooms* ⦿ *No Meals.*

Nightlife

★ Stravinskij Bar at the Hotel de Russie

COCKTAIL LOUNGES | The Stravinskij Bar, in the Hotel de Russie's gorgeous garden, is the best place to catch a glimpse of la dolce vita. Celebrities, blue bloods, and VIPs hang out in the private courtyard garden where mixed drinks and cocktails are well above par. There are also healthy smoothies and bites if you need to refuel. ✉ *Hotel de Russie, Via del Babuino 9, Piazza del Popolo* ☎ *06/328881* ⊕ *www. roccofortehotels.com/hotels-and-resorts/ hotel-de-russie/restaurant-and-bar/stravin-skij-bar* Ⓜ *Flaminio.*

Performing Arts

★ Auditorium Parco della Musica

CONCERTS | Architect Renzo Piano conceived and constructed the Auditorium Parco della Musica, a futuristic complex made up of three enormous, pod-shaped concert halls, which have hosted some of the world's greatest music acts. The Sala Santa Cecilia is a massive hall for grand orchestra and choral concerts; the Sala Sinopoli is more intimately scaled for smaller troupes; and the Sala Petrassi was designed for alternative events. All three are arrayed around the Cavea (amphitheater), a vast outdoor Greco-Roman-style theater. The Auditorium also hosts seasonal festivals, including the Rome Film Fest, a Christmas market, and a gardening festival in May. ✉ *Viale Pietro de Coubertin 30, Flaminio* ☎ *06/80241281* ⊕ *www.auditorium.com* Ⓜ *Flaminio, then Tram No. 2 to Ankara/Tiziano.*

Teatro Olimpico

THEATER | Part of Rome's theater circuit, the 1930s-era Teatro Olimpico is one of the main venues for cabaret, contemporary dance companies, visiting international ballet companies, and touring Broadway shows. ✉ *Piazza Gentile da Fabriano 17, Flaminio* ☎ *06/32659916* ⊕ *www.teatroolimpico.it* Ⓜ *Flaminio, then Tram 2.*

Shopping

★ **Il Marmoraro**

ANTIQUES & COLLECTIBLES | This tiny shop is a holdout of Via Margutta's days as a street full of artists and artisans. Sandro Fiorentino's father opened the shop in 1969 (he carved plaques like the one that marks Federico Fellini's house up the street) and Sandro still engraves the marble by hand. The shop is packed full of plaques, many with clever phrases, which make a great souvenir. Sandro will also engrave a message of your choice upon request. ✉ *Via Margutta 53B, Piazza del Popolo* ☎ *06/3207660* ⊘ *Closed Sun.* Ⓜ *Spagna.*

★ **Saddlers Union**

HANDBAGS | Saddlers Union first launched in 1957 and quickly gained a cult following among those who valued Italian artistry and a traditional aesthetic. If you're searching for a sinfully fabulous handbag in a graceful, classic shape or that "I have arrived" attorney's briefcase, these preppy creations will always hit the mark. Prices are a bit steep, but the quality is definitely worth it. ✉ *Via Paolo Frisi 50, Parioli* ☎ *06/32120237* ⊕ *www.saddlersunion.com.*

Trastevere

Across the Tiber from the Jewish Ghetto is Trastevere (literally "across the Tiber"), long cherished as Rome's Greenwich Village and now subject to rampant gentrification. In spite of this, Trastevere remains about the most tightly knit community in the city, the Trasteverini proudly proclaiming their descent from the ancient Romans. Ancient bridges—the Ponte Fabricio and the Ponte Cestio—link Trastevere and the Ghetto to Isola Tiberina (Tiber Island), a diminutive sandbar and one of Rome's most picturesque sights.

GETTING HERE AND AROUND
From the Vatican or Spanish Steps, expect a 30- to 40-minute walk to reach Trastevere. From Termini station, take Bus No. 40 Express or No. 64 to Largo di Torre Argentina, where you can switch to Tram No. 8 to get to Trastevere. If you don't feel like climbing the steep Gianicolo, take Bus No. 115 from Largo dei Fiorentini, then enjoy the walk down to the northern reaches of Trastevere or explore the leafy residential area of Monteverde Vecchio on the other side of the hill.

Sights

Isola Tiberina (*Tiber Island*)
ISLAND | It's easy to overlook this tiny island in the Tiber, but you shouldn't. In terms of history and sheer loveliness, charming Isola Tiberina—shaped like a boat about to set sail—gets high marks. Cross onto the island via Ponte Fabricio, Rome's oldest remaining bridge, constructed in 62 BC; on the north side of the island crumbles the romantic ruin of the Ponte Rotto (Broken Bridge), which dates back to 179 BC. Descend the steps to the lovely river embankment to see a Roman relief of the intertwined-snakes symbol of Aesculapius, the great god of healing. In imperial times, Romans sheathed the entire island with marble to make it look like Aesculapius's ship, replete with a towering obelisk as a mast. Amazingly, a fragment of the ancient sculpted ship's prow still exists. You can marvel at it on the downstream end of the embankment. Today, medicine still reigns here. The island is home to the hospital of Fatebenefratelli (literally, "Do good, brothers"). Nearby is San Bartolomeo, built at the end of the 10th century by the Holy Roman Emperor Otto III and restored in the 18th century. ✉ *Trastevere* ✥ *Isola Tiberina can be accessed by Ponte Fabricio or Ponte Cestio.*

Palazzo Corsini
GARDEN | A brooding example of Baroque style, the palace (once home to Queen Christina of Sweden) is across the road

Trastevere

F   **G**   **H**   **I**   **J**

CAMPO
DE' FIORI

Piazza d.
Monte di
Pietà

Via dei Funari

Via dei Giubbonari

Via Arenula

Via D.
Reginella

Via d. Progresso

V. del Portico d'Ottavia

Via Tempio

V. Catalana

JEWISH
GHETTO

Via del Teatro di Marcello

1

V. Pattinari

Piazzale
Cenci

Pte. Sisto

Lgt. dei Vallati

V. delle Zoccolette

Lgt. dei Cenci

2

Lgt. Raff. Sanzio

V. d'Mora

V. Renella

Ponte Garibaldi

ISOLA
TIBERINA

1

Pte.
Fabricio

Lgt. d. Pierleoni

3

Lgt. d. Anguillara

Pte.
Cestio

Piazza
Santa Maria
in Trastevere

Via del
Arco di S. Calisto

Pza S.
Sonnino

Via della Lungaretta

Piazza in
Piscinula

Pte. Palatino

4

V. di S. Cosimato

Via S. Francesco a Ripa

Via d. S.Gallicano

Via della Luce

Via dei Salumi

Via dei Genovesi

1

1 **3**

Lgt. Ripa

Via delle Fratte
di Trastevere

4

1

3

Via S. Maria in Cappella

5

N. del Grande

2

Piazza
Mastai

Via della Luce

Via Anicia

Fiume Tevere

Viale di Trastevere

Via di S. Michele

Porto di Ripa

Lgt. Aventino

Via di Porta Portese

6

V.le delle Mura Portuensi

Piazza di
Porta
Portese

0   500 feet

Via M. Carcani

Via Portuense

Ponte
Sublicio

0   150 m

7

KEY	
1	*Sights*
1	*Restaurants*
1	*Quick Bites*
1	*Hotels*

from the Villa Farnesina and houses part of the 16th- and 17th-century sections of the collection of the Galleria Nazionale d'Arte Antica. Among the star paintings in this manageably sized collection are Rubens's *St. Sebastian Healed by Angels* and Caravaggio's *St. John the Baptist.* Stop in if only to climb the 17th-century stone staircase, itself a drama of architectural shadows and sculptural voids. Behind, but separate from, the palazzo is the University of Rome's Orto Botanico, home to 3,500 species of plants, with various greenhouses around a stairway/fountain with 11 jets. ⊠ *Via della Lungara 10, Trastevere* ☎ *06/68802323 Galleria Corsini, 06/32810 Galleria Corsini tickets, 06/49917107 Orto Botanico* ⊕ *www.barberinicorsini.org* ⊠ *Galleria Corsini €12, including entrance to Palazzo Barberini; Orto Botanico* ⊠ *€8* ⊙ *Closed Tues.*

★ **Santa Cecilia in Trastevere**

CHURCH | This basilica commemorates the aristocratic St. Cecilia, patron saint of musicians. One of ancient Rome's most celebrated Early Christian martyrs, she was most likely put to a supernaturally long death by the Emperor Diocletian just before the year AD 300. After an abortive attempt to suffocate her in the baths of her own house (a favorite means of quietly disposing of aristocrats in Roman days), she was brought before the executioner. But not even three blows of the executioner's sword could dispatch the young girl. She lingered for several days, converting others to the Christian cause, before finally dying. In 1595, her body was exhumed—it was said to look as fresh as if she still breathed—and the heart-wrenching sculpture by eyewitness Stefano Maderno that lies below the main altar was, the sculptor insisted, exactly how she looked. Time your visit to enter the cloistered convent to see what remains of Pietro Cavallini's *Last Judgment,* dating to 1293. It's the only major fresco in existence known to have been painted by Cavallini, a contemporary of Giotto. To visit the frescoes, ring the bell of the convent to the left of the church entrance. ⊠ *Piazza di Santa Cecilia 22, Trastevere* ☎ *06/5899289* ⊕ *www.benedettinesantacecilia.it/htm/Basilica.html* ⊠ *Frescoes €2.50, underground €2.50* ⊙ *Access to frescoes closed in the afternoon.*

★ **Santa Maria in Trastevere**

CHURCH | Originally built during the 4th century and rebuilt in the 12th century, this is one of Rome's oldest and grandest churches. It is also the earliest foundation of any Roman church to be dedicated to the Virgin Mary. With a nave framed by a processional of two rows of gigantic columns (22 in total) taken from the ancient Baths of Caracalla, and an apse studded with gilded mosaics, the interior conjures the splendor of ancient Rome better than any other in the city. Overhead is Domenichino's gilded ceiling (1617). The 18th-century portico draws attention to the facade's 800-year-old mosaics, which represent the parable of the Wise and Foolish Virgins. They enhance the whole piazza, especially at night, when the church front and bell tower are illuminated. The church's most important mosaics, Pietro Cavallini's six panels of the *Life of the Virgin,* cover the semicircular apse. Note the building labeled "Taberna Meritoria" just under the figure of the Virgin in the Nativity scene, with a stream of oil flowing from it; it recalls the legend that a fountain of oil appeared on this spot, prophesying the birth of Christ. Off the piazza's northern side is a street called Via delle Fonte dell'Olio in honor of this miracle. ⊠ *Piazza Santa Maria in Trastevere, Trastevere* ☎ *06/5814802.*

★ **Villa Farnesina**

CASTLE/PALACE | Money was no object to the extravagant Agostino Chigi, a banker from Siena who financed many papal projects. His munificence is evident in this elegant villa, built for him about 1511. He was especially proud of the decorative frescoes in the airy loggias, some painted by Raphael himself, notably a luminous *Triumph of Galatea*. Agostino entertained the popes and princes of 16th-century Rome, impressing his guests at riverside suppers by having his servants clear the table by casting the precious silver and gold dinnerware into the Tiber (indeed, nets were unfurled a foot or two beneath the water's surface to retrieve the valuable ware). In the magnificent Loggia of Psyche on the ground floor, Giulio Romano and others worked from Raphael's designs. Raphael's lovely *Galatea* is in the adjacent room. On the floor above you can see the trompe-l'oeil effects in the aptly named Hall of Perspectives by Peruzzi. Agostino Chigi's bedroom, next door, was frescoed by Il Sodoma with the *Wedding of Alexander and Roxanne*, which is considered to be the artist's best work. The palace also houses the Gabinetto Nazionale delle Stampe, a treasure trove of old prints and drawings. ⊠ *Via della Lungara 230, Trastevere* 🕾 *06/68027268 info, 06/68027397 tour reservations* ⊕ *www.villafarnesina.it* 🎫 *€10* ⊗ *Closed Sun.*

🍴 Restaurants

Ai Marmi

$ | PIZZA | FAMILY | This place is about as lively as it gets—indeed, it's packed pretty much every night, with diners munching on crisp pizzas that come out of the wood-burning ovens at top speed. It's best not to go during peak dining hours, so go early or late if you don't want to wait. **Known for:** open until midnight for a late-night bite; excellent wood-oven pizzas; fried starters, such as *suppli* (breaded fried rice balls). ⑤ *Average main: €12* ⊠ *Viale Trastevere 53, Trastevere* 🕾 *06/5800919* ⊗ *Closed Wed. and 3 wks in Aug. Lunch only on Sun.*

★ Antico Arco

$$$ | MODERN ITALIAN | Founded by three friends with a passion for wine and fine food, Antico Arco attracts foodies from Rome and beyond with its refined culinary inventiveness. The location on top of the Janiculum Hill makes for a charming setting, and inside, the dining rooms are plush, modern spaces, with whitewashed brick walls, dark floors, and black velvet chairs. **Known for:** open noon until midnight daily; changing seasonal menu; molten chocolate soufflé cake. ⑤ *Average main: €29* ⊠ *Piazzale Aurelio 7, Trastevere* 🕾 *06/5815274* ⊕ *www.anticoarco.it* ⊗ *Closed Tues.*

★ Da Enzo

$$ | ROMAN | In the quieter part of Trastevere, the family-run Da Enzo is everything you would imagine a classic Roman trattoria to be. There are just a few tables, but diners from around the world line up to eat here—a testament to the quality of the food. **Known for:** small space with long waits; *cacio e pepe*, carbonara, and other Roman classics; boisterous, authentic atmosphere. ⑤ *Average main: €14* ⊠ *Via dei Vascellari 29, Trastevere* 🕾 *06/5812260* ⊕ *www.daenzoal29.com* ⊗ *Closed Sun. and 2 wks in Aug.*

Da Lucia

$$ | ROMAN | There's no shortage of old-school trattorias in Trastevere, but Da Lucia has a strong following among them. Both locals and expats enjoy the brusque but "authentic" service and the hearty Roman fare; snag a table outside in warm weather for the true Roman experience of cobblestone-terrace dining. **Known for:** beef rolls *(involtini)*; *bombolotti* (a tubular pasta) *all'amatriciana*; spaghetti *cacio e pepe*. ⑤ *Average main: €14* ⊠ *Vicolo del Mattonato 2, Trastevere* 🕾 *06/5803601* ⊗ *Closed Mon.–Wed. and Aug.*

☕ Coffee and Quick Bites

Biscottificio Innocenti

$ | ITALIAN | FAMILY | The scent of cookies wafts out into the street as you approach this family-run bakery, where a small team of bakers makes sweet treats the old-school way in an oven bought in the

1960s. There are dozens of varieties of baked goods, mostly sweet but some savory. **Known for:** dozens of varieties of baked goods; brutti ma buoni cookies; old-school family-run bakery. $ *Average main: €3 ⊠ Via della Luce 21, Trastevere* ☎ *06/5803926* ⊘ *Closed 2 wks in Aug.*

Supplì

$ | **ROMAN** | Trastevere's best *supplì* have been served at this hole-in-the-wall take-out spot since 1979. At lunchtime, the line spills out onto the street with locals who've come for the namesake treats, as well as fried baccalà fillets and stuffed zucchini flowers. **Known for:** pistachio and salmon pasta; old-fashioned baked pizza with zucchini and straciatella cheese; gnocchi on Thursday (the traditional day for it in Rome). $ *Average main: €5 ⊠ Via di San Francesco a Ripa 137, Trastevere* ☎ *06/5897110* ⊕ *www.suppliroma.it* ⊘ *Closed Sun. and 2 wks in Aug.*

 ## Hotels

Casa di Santa Francesca Romana a Ponte Rotto

$ | **HOTEL** | In the heart of Trastevere but tucked away from the hustle and bustle of the medieval quarter, this cheap, clean, comfortable hotel in a former monastery is centered on a lovely green courtyard. **Pros:** excellent restaurants nearby; away from rowdy tourist side of Trastevere; rates can't be beat. **Cons:** spotty Wi-Fi; few amenities besides TV room and reading room; a bit far from Metro, but there are tram and bus stops nearby. $ *Rooms from: €98 ⊠ Via dei Vascellari 61, Trastevere* ☎ *06/5812125* ⊕ *www.sfromana.it* ⊏ *37 rooms* ⦿ *Free Breakfast.*

Hotel Santa Maria

$ | **HOTEL** | A Trastevere treasure with a pedigree going back four centuries, this ivy-covered, mansard-roof, rosy-brick-red, erstwhile Renaissance-era convent—just steps away from the glorious Santa Maria in Trastevere church and a few blocks from the Tiber—has sweet and simple guest rooms: a mix of brick walls, "cotto" tile floors, oak furniture, and matching bedspreads and curtains. **Pros:** a quaint and pretty oasis in a central location; lovely rooftop terrace; free bicycles to use during your stay. **Cons:** some rooms can be noisy; not the best value for money; tricky to find. $ *Rooms from: €120 ⊠ Vicolo del Piede 2, Trastevere* ☎ *06/5894626* ⊕ *www.hotelsantamariatrastevere.it* ⊏ *20 rooms* ⦿ *Free Breakfast.*

Hotel Trastevere

$$ | **HOTEL** | This hotel captures the villagelike charm of the Trastevere district and offers basic, clean, comfortable rooms. **Pros:** friendly staff; convenient to tram and bus; good rates for location. **Cons:** few amenities; rooms are a little worn on the edges; standard rooms are quite small. $ *Rooms from: €130 ⊠ Via Luciano Manara 24/a, Trastevere* ☎ *06/5814713* ⊕ *www.hoteltrastevere. net* ⊏ *14 rooms* ⦿ *Free Breakfast.*

Relais Le Clarisse

$ | **B&B/INN** | Set within the former cloister grounds of the Santa Chiara order, with beautiful gardens, Le Clarisse makes you feel like a personal guest at a friend's villa, thanks to the comfortable size of the guest rooms and personalized service. **Pros:** complimentary high-speed Wi-Fi; spacious rooms with comfy beds; high-tech showers/tubs with good water pressure. **Cons:** check when booking as you may be put in neighboring building; this part of Trastevere can be noisy at night; no restaurant or bar. $ *Rooms from: €70 ⊠ Via Cardinale Merry del Val 20, Trastevere* ☎ *06/58334437* ⊕ *www. leclarissetrastevere.com* ⊏ *17 rooms* ⦿ *Free Breakfast.*

Nightlife

★ Freni e Frizioni

CAFÉS | This hipster hangout has a cute artist vibe, and is great for an afternoon coffee, tea, or aperitivo, or for late-night socializing. Though the vibe is laid-back, the bartenders take their cocktails seriously—and have the awards to prove it. In warmer weather, the crowd overflows into the large terrazzo overlooking the Tiber and the side streets of Trastevere. ⊠ *Via del Politeama 4, Trastevere* ☎ *06/45497499* ⊕ *www.freniefrizioni.com.*

Shopping

BOOKSTORES

Almost Corner Bookshop

BOOKS | Bursting at the seams, with not an ounce of space left on its shelves, this tiny little bookshop is a favorite meeting point for English speakers in Trastevere. Irish owner Dermot O'Connell goes out of his way to find what you're looking for, and if he doesn't have it in stock he'll make a special order for you. The shop carries everything from popular best sellers to translated Italian classics, as well as lots of good books about Rome. ⊠ *Via del Moro 45, Trastevere* ☎ *06/5836942.*

FLEA MARKETS

Porta Portese

MARKET | One of the biggest flea markets in Italy, Porta Portese welcomes visitors in droves every Sunday from 7 am to 2 pm. Treasure seekers and bargain hunters love scrounging around tents for new and used clothing, antique furniture, used books, accessories, and other odds 'n' ends. Bring your haggling skills, and cash (preferably small bills—it'll work in your favor when driving a bargain); many stallholders don't accept credit cards, and the nearest ATM is a hike. ⊠ *Via Portuense and adjacent streets between Porta Portese and Via Ettore Rolli, Trastevere.*

SHOES

Joseph Debach

SHOES | With his shoe boutique in Rome that is open only in the evenings (or by appointment), Joseph Debach has made eccentric creations that are more art than footwear. Entirely handmade from wood, metal, and leather in his small and chaotic studio, his abacus wedge is worthy of a museum. The sometimes outrageous styles earn a "wow" and are occasionally finished with hand-painted strings, odd bits of comic books, newspapers, and other unexpected baubles. ⊠ *Piazza de' Renzi 21, Trastevere* ☎ *3460255265* ⊕ *www.josephdebach.it.*

Aventino and Testaccio

The **Aventino** district is somewhat rarefied, where some houses still have their own bell towers and private gardens are called "parks," without exaggeration. Like the emperors of old on the Palatine, the fortunate residents here look out over the Circus Maximus and the river, winding its way far below. **Testaccio** is perhaps the world's only district built on broken pots: the hill of the same name was born from discarded pottery used to store oil, wine, and other goods loaded from nearby Ripa, when Rome had a port and the Tiber was once a mighty river to an empire. It's quiet during the day, but on Saturday buzzes with the loud music from rows of discos and clubs.

Sights

★ Centrale Montemartini

ART MUSEUM | A decommissioned power plant (Rome's first electricity plant) was reopened as a permanent exhibition space in 2005 and today houses the overflow of ancient art from the Musei Capitolini collection. After strolling Rome's medieval lanes, the Centrale Montemartini's early-20th-century style can feel positively modern. A 15-minute walk from the heart of Testaccio in one direction will lead you past walls covered in street art to the urban district of Ostiense. Head southwest and saunter under the train tracks to admire buildings bedecked with four-story-high murals until you reach the Centrale Montemartini. With Roman sculptures and mosaics

Aventino and Testaccio

A   **B**   **C**   **D**   **E**   **F**

Lgt. dei Cenci
ISOLA TIBERINA
Ponte Garibaldi
Lgt. d. Anguillara
Via della Lungaretta
Via di Scala
Via G. Medici
Garibaldi
Via
Via L. Manara
Via E. Vlamei
Via N. Fabrizi
Via N. del Grande
Via Morosini
Piazza in Piscinula
Via dei Genovesi
Pte. Palatino
Lgt. d. Pierleoni
Piazza Bocca d. Verità
Piazza Mastai
Via Amicia
TRASTEVERE
Lgt. Ripa
Villa Sciarra
Viale Glorioso
Viale G. Trastevere
Via di S. Michele
Porto di Ripa
Parco di S. Alessio
Giardino degli Aranci
Piazza Porta Portese
Via M. Carcani
Ponte Sublicio
Lgt. Aventino
Via di S. Sabina
Via di S. Domenico
Piazza Tempio Diana
Piaz. S. Prís
AVENTINO
Via Felice Cavallotti
Via Giacinto Carini
Via Alessandro Poerio
Via Aurelio Saffi
Via U. Bassi
Via Francesco dell' Ongaro
Via B. Musolino
Via Portuense
Lgt. Portuense
Via Testaccio
Via Cressi
Via Bianchi
Via Rubattino
Via Florio
Via B. Franklin
Fiume Tevere
Via Torelli
Via Giovanni Branca
Via G. B. Bodoni
Via N. Giorgio
Via Aldo Manunzio
Via Marmorata
Piazza dei Servilli
Via di S. Melania
Via S. Anselmo
Via S. Alessio
Via Marc.
Via M. Gelsomini
Piazzale Ostiense
V. Baccon
Viale di Trastevere
Via T. Nievo
Via F. Denaglia
Via V. Bargoni
Via I. Parboni
TESTACCIO
Via Galvani
Via Galvani
Via Nicola Zabaglia
Via Galvani
Parco della Resistenza dell' 8 Settembre
Piazza Porta S. Paolo
Piazzale Ostiense
M Piram.
Stazione Roma-Ostia
Via d. Piramide C.
Viale Cave Ardeatine
Via A. Traversari
Via G. Parrasio
Via Ettore Rolli
Ponte Testaccio
Lgt. degli Artigiani
Lgt. Testaccio
Piazza O. Giustiniani
Monte Testaccio
Piazza
Monte
Via C. Cestio
Via del Campo Boario
Viale del Campo Boario
Circonvallazione Gianicolense
Via P. Castaldi
Via A. Bellani
Baccio Baldini
Ponte dell'Industria
Via G. da Empoli
Porto Fluviale
Via Magazzini Generali
Via Matteucci
Via G. Volpato
Via G. Ricci Curbastro
Via A. Pacinotti
Via Portuense
Via di Pietra
Piazza della Radio
Via Papareschi
Riva Ostiense
Commercio
Via F. Negri
Via Quirino Majorana
Via Biatchini Luigi
Viale Guglielmo Marconi
Via Odericit da Gubbio
Via Pietro Blaserna
Via Vittorio Gassman
Garbatella M
Via Ostiense
Via B. Bossi
Via F. Ferraris

Piazza Bocca d. Verità ❸

❷ ❶ AVENTINO

Testaccio ❶ ❷ Monte

❸ ❹

❶

0   1,000 feet
0   300 m

Sights ▼

Restaurants ▼

Quick Bites ▼

Hotels ▼

set against industrial machinery and pipes, nowhere else in Rome is the contrast between old and new more apparent or enjoyable. A pleasure, too, is the fact that you're likely to be one of the few visitors here, making it the perfect stop for those feeling claustrophobic from Rome's crowds. Unusually, the collection is organized by the area in which the ancient pieces were found. Highlights include the former boiler room filled with ancient marble statues that once decorated Rome's private villas, such as the beautiful *Esquiline Venus*, as well as a large mosaic of a hunting scene. ⊠ *Via Ostiense 106, Testaccio* ☎ *06/0608* ⊕ *www.centralemontemartini.org* ⊠ *€10* ⊘ *Closed Mon.* Ⓜ *Garbatella.*

★ **Piazza dei Cavalieri di Malta**

PLAZA/SQUARE | Peek through the keyhole of the Priorato di Malta, the walled compound of the Knights of Malta, and you'll get a surprising eyeful: a picture-perfect view of the dome of St. Peter's Basilica, far across the city. The top of the church is flawlessly framed by trimmed hedges that lie beyond a nondescript, locked green door. The square and the priory within the walls are the work of Giovanni Battista Piranesi, an 18th-century engraver who is more famous for etching Roman views than for orchestrating them, but he fancied himself a bit of an architect and did not disappoint. As for the Order of the Knights of Malta, it is the world's oldest and most exclusive order of chivalry, founded in the Holy Land during the Crusades. Though nominally ministering to the sick in those early days—a role that has since become the order's raison d'être—the knights amassed huge tracts of land in the Middle East. From 1530 they were based on the Mediterranean island of Malta, but in 1798 Napoléon expelled them, and, in 1834, they established themselves in Rome. Tours are sometimes available if you would like to go inside; call for more information. ⊠ *Via Santa Sabina and Via Porta Lavernale,*

Aventino ☎ *06/5779193 tour reservations* Ⓜ *Circo Massimo; Tram No. 3.*

★ **Santa Maria in Cosmedin**

CHURCH | FAMILY | Although this is one of Rome's oldest churches, with a haunting interior, it plays second fiddle to the renowned artifact installed out in the portico. The **Bocca della Verità** (Mouth of Truth) is in reality nothing more than an ancient drain cover, unearthed during the Middle Ages. Legend has it, however, that the teeth will clamp down on a liar's hand if they dare to tell a fib while holding their fingers up to the fearsome mouth. Hordes of tourists line up to take the test every day (kids especially get a kick out of it), but there is never a wait to enter the church itself, which was built in the 6th century. Head inside to stand before the flower-crowned skull of St. Valentine, who is celebrated every February 14th, but go ahead and pass on the trip down to the tiny, empty crypt. Heavily restored at the end of the 19th century, the church stands across from the **Piazza della Bocca della Verità,** originally the location of the Forum Boarium, ancient Rome's cattle market, and later the site of public executions. ⊠ *Piazza della Bocca della Verità 18, Aventino* ☎ *06/6787759* ⊕ *www.cosmedin.org* Ⓜ *Circo Massimo.*

Terme di Caracalla (*Baths of Caracalla*)

RUINS | FAMILY | The Terme di Caracalla are some of Rome's most massive—yet least visited—ruins. Begun in AD 206 by the emperor Septimius Severus and completed by his son, Caracalla, the 28-acre complex could accommodate 1,600 bathers at a time. Along with an Olympic-size swimming pool and baths, the complex also had two gyms, a library, and gardens. The impressive baths depended on slave labor, particularly the unseen stokers who toiled in subterranean rooms to keep the fires roaring in order to heat the water. Rather than a simple dip in a tub, Romans turned "bathing" into one of the most lavish leisure activities imaginable. A bath began in the sudatoria, a series of small rooms resembling saunas, which then led to the caldarium, a circular room that was humid rather than simply hot. Here a strigil, or scraper, was used to get the dirt off the skin. Next stop: the warm(-ish) tepidarium, which helped start the cool-down process. Finally, it ended with a splash around the frigidarium, a chilly swimming pool. Today, the complex is a shell of its former self. Some black-and-white mosaic fragments remain, but most of the opulent mosaics, frescoes, and sculptures have found their way into Rome's museums. However, the towering walls and sheer size of the ruins give one of the best glimpses into ancient Rome's ambitions. If you're here in summer, don't miss the chance to catch an open-air opera or ballet in the baths, put on by the **Teatro dell'Opera di Roma**. ⊠ *Viale delle Terme di Caracalla 52, Aventino* ☎ *06/39967702* ⊕ *www.coopculture.it* 🎫 *€8 (includes Villa dei Quintili and Tomba di Cecilia Metella)* Ⓜ *Circo Massimo.*

🍽 Restaurants

Checchino dal 1887

$$ | ROMAN | Literally carved into the side of a hill made up of ancient shards of amphorae, Checchino is an example of a classic, upscale, family-run Roman establishment, with one of the best wine cellars in the region. One of the first restaurants to open near Testaccio's (now long closed) slaughterhouse, they still serve classic offal dishes (though the white-jacketed waiters can also suggest other options). **Known for:** *coda alla vaccinara* (Roman-style oxtail); old-school Roman cooking; old-school Roman waiters. ⑤ *Average main: €23* ⊠ *Via di Monte Testaccio 30, Testaccio* ☎ *06/5743816* ⊕ *www.checchino-dal-1887. com* 🕐 *Closed Mon., Aug., and 1 wk at Christmas* Ⓜ *Piramide.*

★ Flavio al Velavevodetto

$$ | ROMAN | It's everything you're looking for in a true Roman eating experience: authentic, in a historic setting, and filled with Italians eating good food at good prices. In this very *romani di Roma* (Rome

of the Romans) neighborhood, surrounded by discos and bars sharing Monte Testaccio, you can enjoy a meal of classic local dishes, from vegetable antipasto to cacio e pepe (said to be the best version in the city) and lamb chops. **Known for:** *polpette di bollito* (fried breaded meatballs); authentic Roman atmosphere and food; outdoor covered terrace in summer. ⑤ *Average main: €16* ⊠ *Via di Monte Testaccio 97, Testaccio* ☎ *06/5744194* ⊕ *www. ristorantevelavevodetto.it* Ⓜ *Piramide.*

Marigold

$ | SCANDINAVIAN | Run by a husband-and-wife team (she's Danish, he's Italian), this hip restaurant blends the best of both their cultures with a Scandinavian-meets-Italian design and menu. It draws a young, international crowd who come for the sourdough, cinnamon buns, and veggie-forward dishes. **Known for:** minimalist design; Danish breads and baked goods; weekend brunch. ⑤ *Average main: €13* ⊠ *Via Giovanni da Empoli 37, Testaccio* ☎ *06/87725679* ⊕ *www. marigoldroma.com* 🕐 *Closed Mon., Dinner Fri. and Sat. only* Ⓜ *Ostiense.*

Porto Fluviale

$ | ITALIAN | This massive structure takes up the better part of a block on a street that's gone from gritty clubland to popular nightspot, thanks largely to Porto Fluviale. The place pulls double duty as a bar, café, pizzeria, lunch buffet, and lively evening restaurant. **Known for:** *cicchetti* (Venetian-style tapas); good cocktails; pizza from wood-burning oven. ⑤ *Average main: €13* ⊠ *Via del Porto Fluviale 22, Testaccio* ☎ *06/5743199* ⊕ *www. portofluviale.com* Ⓜ *Piramide.*

☕ Coffee and Quick Bites

Trapizzino

$ | ROMAN | FAMILY | Stefano Callegari is one of Rome's most famous pizza makers, but at Trapizzino he's doing something a bit different. The name of the restaurant is derived from the Italian words for sandwich (*tramezzino*) and pizza, and the result is something like an upscale pizza pocket, stuffed on the spot with local specialties like chicken alla cacciatore, or trippa, or roast pumpkin, pecorino, and almonds. **Known for:** Italian craft beer; casual setting, with seating available next door; eggplant parmigiana and meatball sandwiches. $ *Average main: €4* ⊠ *Via Giovanni Branca 88, Testaccio* ☎ *06/43419624* ⊕ *www.trapizzino. it* ⊘ *Closed 1 wk in Aug.* Ⓜ *Piramide.*

 Hotels

Hotel San Anselmo

$ | **HOTEL** | This refurbished 19th-century villa is a romantic retreat from the city, set in a *molto* charming garden atop the Aventine Hill. **Pros:** historic building with artful interior; garden where you can enjoy breakfast; free Wi-Fi. **Cons:** no full restaurant; limited public transportation; some rooms are quite small. $ *Rooms from: €80* ⊠ *Piazza San Anselmo 2, Aventino* ☎ *06/570057* ⊕ *www.aventinohotels.com* ⇆ *34 rooms* ⓘ *Free Breakfast* Ⓜ *Circo Massimo.*

Esquilino and Via Appia Antica

Esquilino, covering Rome's most sprawling hill—the Esquiline—lies at the edge of the tourist maps, near the Termini station. Today, culturally diverse inhabitants of different nationalities live and work in the area. It's not the cobblestone-street atmosphere that most think of when they think of Rome. Far south lies catacomb country—the haunts of the fabled underground graves of Rome's earliest Christians, arrayed to either side of the Queen of Roads, the Via Appia Antica (Appian Way). Strewn with classical ruins and dotted with grazing sheep, the road stirs images of chariots and legionnaires returning from imperial conquests. It was completed in 312 BC by Appius Claudius,

who laid it out to connect Rome with settlements in the south, in the direction of Naples. Though time and vandals have taken their toll on the ancient relics along the road, the catacombs remain to cast their spirit-warm spell. Today, the dark, gloomy catacombs contrast strongly with the Appia Antica's fresh air, verdant meadows, and evocative classical ruins.

GETTING HERE AND AROUND
The Esquiline Hill can be reached via the Vittorio Emanuele subway station, one stop from Termini station. Bus No. 150F runs from Piazza del Popolo to Esquilino.

The initial stretch of the Via Appia Antica is not pedestrian-friendly—there is fast, heavy traffic and no sidewalk all the way from Porta San Sebastiano to the Catacombe di San Callisto. To reach the catacombs, take Bus No. 218 from San Giovanni in Laterano. Alternatively, take Metro Line A to Colli Albani and then Bus No. 660 to the Tomba di Cecilia Metella.

 Sights

Catacombe di San Callisto

(*Catacombs of St. Calixtus*)
CEMETERY | Burial place of several very early popes, this is Rome's oldest and best-preserved underground cemetery. One of the (English-speaking) friars who act as custodians of the catacomb will guide you through its crypts and galleries, some adorned with Early Christian frescoes. Watch out for wrong turns: this catacomb is five stories deep! ■**TIP**➔ **The large parking area means this is favored by large groups; it can get busy.** ⊠ *Via Appia Antica 110, Via Appia Antica* ☎ *06/5130151* ⊕ *www.catacombe.roma.it* 🎟 *€8* ⊘ *Closed Wed. and mid-Jan.–Feb.*

★ Catacombe di San Sebastiano

(*Catacombs of St. Sebastian*)
CEMETERY | The 4th-century church was named after the saint who was buried in the catacomb, which burrows underground on four different levels. This was the only Early Christian cemetery

Esquilino and Via Appia Antica

to remain accessible during the Middle Ages, and it was from here that the term *catacomb* is derived—it's in a spot where the road dips into a hollow, known to the Romans as *catacumba* (Greek for "near the hollow"). ✉ *Via Appia Antica 136, Via Appia Antica* ☎ *06/7850350* ⊕ *www. catacombe.org* 🎟 *€8* ⊘ *Closed Sun.*

Parco degli Acquedotti

CITY PARK | FAMILY | This massive park was named for the six remaining aqueducts that formed part of the famously elaborate system that carried water to ancient Rome. It's technically part of the Parco dell'Appia Antica and you can indeed walk on a piece of an ancient Roman road that once went all the way to Benevento, a city near Naples. The park has some serious film cred: it was featured in the opening scene of *La Dolce Vita* and in a rather memorable scene depicting some avant-garde

performance art in *La Grande Bellezza*. On weekends, it's a popular place for locals to picnic, exercise, and bring their kids or dogs. ✉ *Via Lemonia 221, Via Appia Antica* ⊕ *www.parcodegliacquedotti.it* Ⓜ *Giulio Agricola, Subaugusta.*

Porta Maggiore (*Great Gate*)

RUINS | The massive 1st-century-AD arch was built as part of the original Aqua Claudia and then incorporated into the walls hurriedly erected in the late 3rd century as Rome's fortunes began to decline; the great arch of the aqueduct subsequently became a *porta* (city gate). It gives an idea of the grand scale of ancient Roman public works. On the Piazzale Labicano side, to the east, is the curious **Baker's Tomb,** erected in the 1st century BC by a prosperous baker (predating both the aqueduct and the city walls); it's shaped like an oven to signal the deceased's trade. The site is now in the middle of a public transport node, and is close to Rome's first tram depot (going back to 1889). ⊠ *Piazza di Porta Maggiore, Esquilino* Ⓜ *Tram No. 3, 5, 14, or 19.*

Tomba di Cecilia Metella

CEMETERY | For centuries, sightseers have flocked to this famous landmark, one of the most complete surviving tombs of ancient Rome. One of the many round mausoleums that once lined the Appian Way, this tomb is a smaller version of the Mausoleum of Augustus, but impressive nonetheless. It was the burial place of a Roman noblewoman: the wife of the son of Crassus, who was one of Julius Caesar's rivals and known as the richest man in the Roman Empire (infamously entering the English language as "crass"). The original decoration includes a frieze of bulls' skulls near the top. The travertine stone walls were made higher and the medieval-style crenellations were added when the tomb was transformed into a fortress by the Caetani family in the 14th century. An adjacent chamber houses a small museum of the area's geological phases. Entrance to this site also includes access to the splendid Villa dei Quintili, but you can get a super view without going in. ⊠ *Via Appia Antica 161, Via Appia Antica* ☎ *06/7886254* ⊕ *www. parcoarcheologicoappiaantica.it* 🎫 *€10, includes all the sites in the Parco dell'Appia Antica (Villa dei Quintili, Antiquarium di Lucrezia Romana, Complesso di Capo di Bove, Tombe della Via Latina, and the Villa dei Setti Bassi)* ⊗ *Closed Mon.*

🍴 Restaurants

L'Archeologia

$$ | ITALIAN | In this farmhouse just beyond the catacombs, founded around 1890, you can dine indoors beside the fireplace in cool weather or in the garden under age-old vines in summer. Specialties include *mezze maniche all'amatriciana*, lamb with smoked potatoes and artichokes, and fresh seafood. **Known for:**

romantic setting; ancient wine cellar La Cantina; hand-painted frescoes. $ *Average main: €24* ⊠ *Via Appia Antica 139, Via Appia Antica* ☎ *06/7880494* ⊕ *www. larcheologia.it* ⊗ *Closed Tues.*

Li Rioni

$ | PIZZA | FAMILY | This busy pizzeria conveniently close to the Colosseum has been serving real-deal Roman-style pizza—super thin and cooked to a crisp—since the mid-1980s. The magic might be due to the fact that they let their pizza dough rise 24–48 hours before baking to guarantee an extra-light pizza, said to be more easily digested than others. **Known for:** homemade tiramisu; olive *ascolane* (fried, breaded olives stuffed with sausage); pizza margherita. $ *Average main: €12* ⊠ *Via dei Santi Quattro 24, Esquilino* ☎ *06/70450605* ⊕ *www.lirioni.it* ⊗ *Closed 2 wks in Aug. No lunch* Ⓜ *Colosseo.*

☕ Coffee and Quick Bites

Panella

$ | BAKERY | Opened in 1929, this nearly century-old spot is one of Rome's best bakeries and sells both sweet and savory baked goods, including over 70 types of bread. Line up for the pizza al taglio at lunchtime or sit down at one of the outdoor tables for a cappuccino and cornetto or an aperitivo replete with mini sandwiches made on homemade buns. **Known for:** over 70 types of bread; crostata, tartlettes, and other sweet treats; one of Rome's best bakeries. $ *Average main: €5* ⊠ *Via Merulana 54, Esquilino* ☎ *06/4872435* ⊕ *www.panellaroma.com* ⊗ *Closed Sun.* Ⓜ *Vittorio Emanuele.*

Chapter 4

SIDE TRIPS FROM ROME

4

Updated by
Laura Itzkowitz

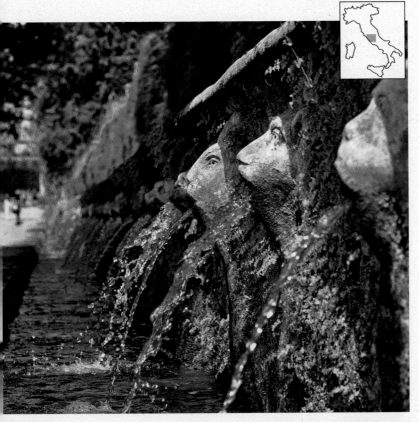

⦿ **Sights**
★★★★☆

🍴 **Restaurants**
★★☆☆☆

🛏 **Hotels**
★☆☆☆☆

🛍 **Shopping**
★☆☆☆☆

🍸 **Nightlife**
★★★☆☆

WELCOME TO
SIDE TRIPS FROM ROME

TOP REASONS TO GO

★ **Ostia Antica:** This excavated port city of ancient Rome is brimming with ruins, mosaics, and structures, which convey a picture of everyday life in the empire.

★ **Tivoli's Villa d'Este:** Hundreds of fountains cascading and shooting skyward (one even plays music on organ pipes) will delight you at this spectacular garden.

★ **Castelli Romani:** Be a Roman for a day and enjoy an escape to the ancient hilltop wine towns on the city's doorstep.

★ **Viterbo:** This town may be modern, but it has a Gothic papal palace, a Romanesque cathedral, and the magical medieval quarter of San Pellegrino. It's also the gateway to the *terme* (hot springs) closest to Rome.

★ **Bizarre and beautiful gardens:** The 16th-century proto-Disneyland Parco dei Mostri (Monster Park) is famed for its fantastic sculptures; the stately Villa Lante, a few miles away, is a postcard-perfect Renaissance garden of swirling, manicured hedges.

1 Viterbo. The capital of Tuscia and a 13th-century time capsule with papal connections.

2 Bagnaia. The site of a 16th-century cardinal's summer home.

3 Caprarola. A quiet village that is also home to the huge Palazzo Farnese.

4 Bomarzo. The town with the eccentric Monster Park garden.

5 Ostia Antica. An ancient Roman port, now an archaeological site.

6 Tivoli. A fitting setting for the regal Villa Adriana and the unforgettable Villa d'Este, a park filled with gorgeous fountains.

7 Palestrina. Originally an ancient pagan sanctuary and home to the father of musical counterpoint.

8 Frascati. A historic getaway amid the Alban Hills and famed for its wine.

9 Castel Gandolfo. A little town otherwise known as the pope's summer retreat.

10 Ariccia. Home to the grand Palazzo Chigi.

11 Nemi. A pretty hamlet, with an eagle's-nest perch above a volcanic lake.

Less well known than neighboring Tuscany, Lazio, the region that encompasses Rome, is often bypassed by foreign visitors. This is a pity, since the area, which stretches from the Apennine mountain range to the Mediterranean coast, holds dozens of fascinating towns and villages, as well as scenic lakes, enchanting gardens, national parks, and forests.

A trip outside Rome introduces you to a more intimate aspect of Italy, where local customs and feast days are still enthusiastically observed and local gastronomic specialties take precedence on restaurant menus.

Despite these small towns' proximity to the capital and the increased commuter traffic congestion of today, they still each manage to preserve their individual character. Ostia Antica, ancient Rome's seaport, is one of the region's top attractions—it rivals Pompeii in the quality of its preservation, and it easily outshines the Roman Forum thanks to its beautiful setting and expansive, inspiring view on the past. Emperors, cardinals, and popes have long escaped to verdant retreats in nearby Tivoli, Viterbo, and the Alban Hills, and their amazing villas, palaces, and gardens add to nature's allure. So if the nonstop Vespa traffic and long lines at the Colosseum start to wear on you, do as the Romans do: get out of town. There's plenty to see and do.

MAJOR REGIONS

Tuscia. Tuscia (the modern name for the Etruscan domain of Etruria) is a region of dramatic beauty punctuated by deep, rocky gorges and thickly forested hills, with dappled light falling on wooded paths. This has been a preferred locale for the retreats of wealthy Romans for ages, a place where they could build grand villas and indulge their sometimes-eccentric gardening tastes.

The provincial capital, Viterbo, which overshadowed Rome as a center of papal power for a time during the Middle Ages, lies in the heart of Tuscia. The farmland east of Viterbo conceals small quarries of the dark, volcanic *peperino* stone, which shows up in the walls of many buildings here. Lake Bolsena lies in an extinct volcano, and the sulfur springs still bubbling up in the modern spas were once used by the ancient Romans. Bagnaia and Caprarola are home to palaces and gardens; the garden statuary at Bomarzo is in a league of its own—somewhere between the beautiful and the bizarre. The ideal way to explore this region is by car. From Rome you can reach Viterbo by train and then get to Bagnaia by local bus. If you're traveling by train or bus, check schedules carefully; you may have to allow for an overnight if you want to do a round of the region's sights.

Tivoli and Palestrina. Tivoli is a five-star draw, its main attractions being its two villas. There's an ancient one in which Hadrian reproduced the most beautiful monuments in the then-known world, and a Renaissance one, in which Cardinal Ippolito d'Este created a water-filled wonderland. Unfortunately, the Via Tiburtina from Rome to Tivoli passes through miles of industrial areas with chaotic traffic, so whether you are driving or taking the bus, take the A24 motorway to avoid it. Or take the train, which offers a slightly more scenic journey. Whichever way you decide to go, persevere and it'll be worth it for the small but charming city center, expansive park, and Tivoli's two gems that are rightly world famous. You'll know you're close to Tivoli when you see vast quarries of travertine marble and smell the sulfurous vapors of the little spa, Bagni di Tivoli. Both sites in Tivoli are outdoors and entail walking. With a car, you can continue your loop through the mountains east of Rome, taking in the ancient pagan sanctuary at Palestrina, spectacularly set on the slopes of Mt. Ginestro.

The Castelli Romani. These *castelli* aren't really castles, as their name would seem to imply. Rather, they're little towns that are scattered on the slopes of the Alban Hills just to the southeast of Rome. And the Alban Hills aren't really hills, but extinct volcanoes. There were castles here in the Middle Ages, however, when each of these towns, fiefs of rival Roman lords, had its own fortress to defend it. Some centuries later, the area was given over to villas and retreats, notably the pope's summer residence at Castel Gandolfo and the 17th- and 18th-century villas that transformed Frascati into the Beverly Hills of Rome. Arrayed around the rim of an extinct volcano that encloses two crater lakes, the string of picturesque towns of the Castelli Romani are surrounded by vineyards, olive groves, and chestnut woods—no wonder overheated Romans have always loved to escape here.

In addition to their lovely natural settings, the Castelli have also been renowned for their wine since the ancient Roman times. In the narrow, medieval alleyways of the oldest parts of the various villages, you can still find old-fashioned taverns where the locals sit on wooden benches, quaffing the golden nectar straight from the barrel. Traveling around the countryside, you can also pop into some of the local vineyards, where they will be happy to give you a tasting of their wines. Exclusive local gastronomic specialties include the bread of Genzano, baked in traditional wood-fired ovens, the *porchetta* (roast suckling pig) of Ariccia, and the *pupazza* biscuits of Frascati, shaped like women or mermaids with three or more breasts (an allusion to ancient fertility goddesses). Each town has its own feasts and saints' days, celebrated with costumed processions and colorful events. Some are quite spectacular, like Marino's annual Wine Festival in October, where the town's fountains flow with wine; or the Flower Festival of Genzano in June, when an entire street is carpeted with millions of flower petals, arranged in elaborate patterns.

Planning

Making the Most of Your Time

Ostia Antica is in many ways an ideal day trip from Rome: it's fascinating, it's not far from the city, it's reachable by public transit, and it takes about half a day to do. Villa d'Este and Villa Adriana in Tivoli

Ostia Antica
see detail map

also make for a manageable, though fuller, day trip. There's so much to see at these two sights alone, but also be sure to visit Tivoli's picturesque gorge, which is strikingly crowned by an ancient Roman temple to Vesta (which is now a part of the incomparable outdoor terrace at the famed Sibilla restaurant). Other destinations can be visited in a day, but you'll get more out of them if you stay the night.

One classic five-day itinerary that takes in the area's grand villas, ancient ruins, and pretty villages begins with Ostia Antica, the excavated port town of ancient Rome. You can then head north to explore Viterbo's medieval streets on Day 2. On Day 3, take in the hot springs or the gardens of Bomarzo, Bagnaia, and Caprarola. For Day 4, head to Tivoli's delights. Then on Day 5 take a relaxing trip to the Castelli Romani, where Frascati wine is produced. Admire the sparkling volcanic lakes, find a spot at a family-style local restaurant, and explore the narrow streets of these small hill towns.

Getting Here and Around

There's reliable public transit from Rome to Ostia Antica, Frascati, Tivoli, and Viterbo. COTRAL is the regional bus company. For other destinations, having a car is a big advantage—going by bus or Trenitalia can add hours to your trip, and the routes and schedules are often puzzling.

CONTACTS COTRAL. ✉ *Via Bernardino Alimena 105* ☎ *800/174471* ⊕ *www.cotralspa.it.* **Trenitalia.** (*Italian National Railway System*) ☎ *199/892021, 06/68475475* ⊕ *www.trenitalia.com.*

Restaurants

You certainly won't go hungry when you're exploring the Roman countryside. Whether you choose a five-star establishment or a simple eatery, you can be sure of a fresh, clean tablecloth and friendly, attentive service. Odds are that the ingredients will come from down the road and the owner will be in the kitchen, personally preparing the time-honored dishes that have made Italian cuisine so famous.

Hotels

Former aristocratic houses with frescoed ceilings, *agriturismi* farmhouses, luxury spas, and cozy bed-and-breakfasts in the village center are just a few of the lodging options here. You won't find much in the way of big chain hotels, though.

Restaurant and hotel reviews have been shortened. For full information, visit Fodors.com.

WHAT IT COSTS in Euros			
$	$$	$$$	$$$$
RESTAURANTS			
under €15	€15–€24	€25–€35	over €35
HOTELS			
under €125	€125–€200	€201–€300	over €300

Visitor Information

Tourist information kiosks, which are scattered around Rome's main squares and tourist sights, can give you information about the Castelli Romani, Ostia Antica, and Tivoli. The Tuscia area is served by the central tourist office in Viterbo.

CONTACT Visit Lazio. ⊕ *www.visitlazio.com.*

Viterbo

104 km (64 miles) northwest of Rome.

Viterbo's moment of glory was in the 13th century, when it became the seat of the papal court. The medieval core of the city still sits within 12th-century walls. Its old buildings, with windows bright with geraniums, are made of dark peperino, the local stone that colors the medieval part of Viterbo a dark gray, contrasted here and there with the golden tufa rock of walls and towers. Peperino is also used in the characteristic and typically medieval exterior staircases that you see throughout the old town.

Viterbo has blossomed into a regional commercial center, and much of the modern city is loud and industrial. However, in Viterbo's San Pellegrino district you'll get the feel of the Middle Ages—artisan shops and bottegas still operate in a setting that has remained practically unchanged over the centuries. The Papal Palace and the cathedral, which sit at the heart of the oldest part of the city, enhance the effect. The city has remained a renowned spa center for its natural hot springs just outside town, which have been frequented by popes and mere mortals alike since medieval times.

GETTING HERE AND AROUND

Viterbo is well served by public transport from Rome. Direct train service from Stazione Trastevere takes 1 hour and 40 minutes, making frequent stops in the capital's more rural suburbs. Try to avoid peak hours, as many commuters live in towns along the line. By road, take either the old Roman consular road, the Via Cassia, which passes near Caprarola, or, if you are in a hurry, the A1 toll highway to the Orte exit and then the 204 highway, with a detour to Bomarzo. The trip can take a couple of hours or even more, depending on traffic.

VISITOR INFORMATION
CONTACT Viterbo Tourism Office.
✉ *Piazza Martiri D'Ungheria, Viterbo*
☎ *0761/226427* ⊕ *www.promotuscia.it.*

◉ Sights

Cattedrale di San Lorenzo
CHURCH | Viterbo's Romanesque cathedral was built over the ruins of the ancient Roman Temple of Hercules. During World War II, the roof and the vault of the central nave were destroyed, and you can still see the mark the shrapnel left on the columns closest to the pulpit. Subsequently, the church was rebuilt to its original medieval design, but it still has many original details, including a beautiful Cosmati floor that dates back to the 13th century. Three popes are buried here, including Pope Alexander IV (1254–61), whose body was hidden so well by the canons, out of fear that it would be desecrated, that it has never been found. The adjoining Museo del Colle del Duomo has a collection of 18th-century reliquaries, Etruscan sarcophagi, and a painting of the Crucifixion that has been attributed to Michelangelo. The ticket to the museum also grants you entrance to the Palazzo Papale, located on the same square. ✉ *Piazza San Lorenzo, Viterbo* ☎ *320/7911328* ⊕ *www.archeoares.it* 🎫 *€9, includes tour of Cattedrale di San Lorenzo, Palazzo dei Papi, and Museo del Colle del Duomo.*

Palazzo dei Papi *(Papal Palace)*
CASTLE/PALACE | This Gothic palace was built in the 13th century as a residence for popes looking to get away from the city. At the time, Rome was notoriously ridden with malaria and the plague, not to mention rampaging factions of rival barons. In 1271 the palace was the scene of a novel type of rebellion. A conclave held that year to elect a new pope dragged on for months. The people of Viterbo were exasperated by the delay, especially as custom decreed that they had to provide for the cardinals' board and lodging for the duration of the conclave. To speed up the deliberations, the townspeople tore the roof off the great hall where the cardinals were meeting, and put them on bread and water. A new pope—Gregory X—was elected in short order. Today, you can visit the great hall, step out on the pretty loggia, and admire the original frescoes in the small adjoining room. ■TIP➔ **An audio guided tour is free with the purchase of a ticket and lasts 45 minutes, starting from Museo del Colle del Duomo.** ✉ *Piazza San Lorenzo, Viterbo* ☎ *320/7911328* ⊕ *www.archeoares.it* 🎫 *€9, includes tour of Cattedrale di San Lorenzo, Palazzo dei Papi, and Museo del Colle del Duomo.*

San Pellegrino
HISTORIC DISTRICT | One of the best preserved medieval districts in Italy, San Pellegrino has charming vistas of arches, vaults, towers, exterior staircases, worn wooden doors on great iron hinges, and tiny hanging gardens. You pass many antiques shops and craft workshops, as well as numerous restaurants, as you explore the little squares and byways. The **Fontana Grande** in the piazza of the same name is the largest and most extravagant of Viterbo's Gothic fountains. ✉ *Via San Pellegrino, near Palazzo dei Papi and Cattedrale di San Lorenzo, Viterbo* ⊕ *www.promotuscia.it.*

★ Terme dei Papi
HOT SPRING | Viterbo has been a spa town for centuries, and this excellent spa not far removed continues the tradition, providing the usual health and beauty treatments with an Etruscan twist: try a facial with local volcanic mud, or a steam bath in an ancient cave, where scalding hot mineral water direct from the spring splashes down a waterfall to a pool beneath your feet. The Terme dei Papi's main draw, however, comes from the *terme* (baths) themselves: a 21,000-square-foot outdoor limestone pool, into the shallow end of which Viterbo's famous hot water pours at

59°C (138°F)—and gives a jolt with its sulfurous odor. Floats and deck chairs are for rent, but bring your own bathrobe and towel unless you're staying at the hotel. There are moonlight swims on Saturday night, when the pool is open late (9 pm–1 am). ■TIP→ **Shuttle buses operate between Rome's Piazza del Popolo and the Terme. Round-trip tickets cost €8; call or check website for travel times.** ⊠ *Strada Bagni 12, 5 km (3 miles) west of town center, Viterbo* ☎ *0761/3501* ⊕ *www. termedeipapi.it* 🍽 *Pool €12 weekdays, €18 weekends* 🕐 *Closed Tues.*

🍴 Restaurants

★ Osteria del Vecchio Orologio

$ | **ITALIAN** | Tucked away in a side street off the medieval Piazza delle Erbe, the Osteria del Vecchio Orologio offers top-quality Tuscia specialties in a warm and informal atmosphere. They're a member of the Slow Food movement, with a menu that changes according to the season. **Known for:** extensive wine list; cute, cupboard-lined walls; local ingredients. 💲 *Average main: €14* ⊠ *Via Orologio Vecchio 25, Viterbo* ☎ *335/337754* ⊕ *www.alvecchioorologio. it* 🕐 *No lunch Mon. and Tues.*

Taverna Etrusca

$$ | **ITALIAN** | **FAMILY** | Located between the heart of San Pellegrino and Porta Romana, this friendly trattoria is known for its excellent home cooking and pizza. Be sure to admire the Etruscan-inspired decorations and check out the dessert—all the excellent gelato is made on-site. **Known for:** excellent gelato; homemade pasta alla viterbese (spicy red sauce with fennel); tagliolini with lemon. 💲 *Average main: €15* ⊠ *Via Annio 8, Viterbo* ☎ *0761/226694* ⊕ *www.tavernaetrusca.it* 🕐 *Closed Sun.*

Tre Re

$$ | **ITALIAN** | Viterbo's oldest restaurant—and one of the most ancient in Italy—has been operating in the *centro storico*

(historic center) since 1622. The small, wood-paneled dining room, chummily packed with tables, was a favorite haunt of movie director Federico Fellini and, before that, of British and American soldiers during World War II. **Known for:** locals touch the Tre Re (Three Kings) sign outside for luck; roasted suckling pig; traditional local dishes. 💲 *Average main: €15* ⊠ *Via Macel Gattesco 3, Viterbo* ☎ *0761/304619* ⊕ *www.ristorantetrere. com* 🕐 *Closed Thurs.*

Bagnaia

5 km (3 miles) east of Viterbo.

The quiet village of Bagnaia is the site of the 16th-century cardinal Alessandro Montalto's summer retreat, which is quite an extravaganza.

GETTING HERE AND AROUND

Local buses from Viterbo are one way to get here. By local train, it's 10 minutes beyond the Viterbo stop—few local trains actually do stop, though, so be sure to check beforehand. If you prefer to drive, take the A1 to the exit for Orte and follow signs for Bagnaia. There is free parking across the bridge from the main square.

Sights

Villa Lante

CASTLE/PALACE | The main draw in this otherwise sweet but underwhelming village is the hillside garden and park that surround the two small, identical residences built by different owners in the 16th century, more than 30 years apart. The first belonged to Cardinal Gianfrancesco Gambara, but it was Cardinal Alessandro Montalto who built the second and soon commissioned the creation of a stunning garden filled with grottoes, fountains, and immaculately manicured hedges. The garden and the park were designed by the virtuoso architect Giacomo Barozzi (circa 1507–73), known as Vignola, who later worked with Michelangelo on St. Peter's. On the lowest terrace a delightful Italian garden has a centerpiece fountain fed by water channeled down the hillside. On another terrace, a stream of water runs through a groove carved in a long stone table where the cardinal entertained his friends alfresco, chilling wine in the running water. That's only one of the most evident of the whimsical water games that were devised for the cardinal. The symmetry of the formal gardens contrasts with the wild, untamed park adjacent to it, reflecting the paradoxes of nature and artifice that are the theme of this pleasure garden. ⊠ *Via Jacopo Barozzi 71, Bagnaia* ☎ *0761/288008* ⊕ *www.polomuseale-lazio.beniculturali.it/index.php?it/243/villa-lante* ⊠ *€5* ⊗ *Closed Mon.*

Caprarola

21 km (13 miles) southeast of Bagnaia, 19 km (12 miles) southeast of Viterbo.

The wealthy and powerful Farnese family took over this sleepy village in the 1500s and had the architect Vignola design a huge palace and gardens to rival the great residences of Rome. He also rearranged the little town of Caprarola to enhance the palazzo's setting.

GETTING HERE AND AROUND
Caprarola is served by COTRAL bus, leaving from Rome's Saxa Rubra station on the Roma Nord suburban railway line.

Sights

★ Palazzo Farnese
CASTLE/PALACE | When Cardinal Alessandro Farnese, Pope Paul III's grandson, retired to Caprarola, he intended to build a residence that would reflect the family's grandeur. In 1559, he entrusted the task to the leading architect Giacomo Barozzi da Vignola, who came up with some innovative ideas. A magnificent

spiral staircase, lavishly decorated with allegorical figures, mythical landscapes, and grotesques by Antonio Tempesta, connected the main entrance with the cardinal's apartments on the main floor. The staircase was gently inclined, with very deep but low steps, so that the cardinal could ride his horse right up to his bedchamber. A tour of the five-sided palatial villa includes the Hall of Farnese Triumphs, the Hercules Room, and the Antechamber of the Council of Trent, all painted by the Zuccari brothers. Of special interest is the Hall of the Maps, with the ceiling depicting the zodiac and the walls frescoed with maps of the world as known to 16th-century cartographers. The palace is surrounded by a formal Renaissance garden. ⊠ *Piazza Farnese 1, Caprarola* ☎ *0761/646052* ⊕ *www.caprarola.com* ⊠ *€5, includes garden* ⊗ *Closed Mon.*

Restaurants

Antica Trattoria del Borgo
$$ | ROMAN | FAMILY | Visitors to Caprarola's landmark Palazzo Farnese often round out the experience with a hearty meal at this celebrated trattoria. There's a cozy, familial atmosphere inside, and when the weather permits, a pleasant seating area outside. **Known for:** homemade desserts; local salumi and grilled meat; expansive wine cellar. ⑤ *Average main: €20* ⊠ *Via Borgo Vecchio 107, Caprarola* ☎ *0761/645252* ⊕ *www.antic-atrattoriadelborgo.it* ⊗ *Closed Mon. No dinner Sun.–Wed.*

Bomarzo

15 km (9 miles) northeast of Viterbo.

Once a fief of the powerful Orsini family, Bomarzo is home to the Parco dei Mostri, the town's main attraction, which was created to amuse and astound the Orsinis' guests. The 16th-century Palazzo Orsini is now the seat of the town council.

Inside, there is a princely hall, frescoed by Pietro da Cortona, the famous Italian Baroque fresco painter and architect.

GETTING HERE AND AROUND
Bomarzo is easily reached by car from the A1 autostrada. If you want to go there directly, carry on to the Attigliano exit. Parco dei Monstri is some 6 km (4 miles) from that point. Alternatively, come out at Orte and branch off at Casalone on the Viterbo road. A COTRAL bus also goes here, from Viterbo.

 Sights

Parco dei Mostri (*Monster Park*)
GARDEN | FAMILY | This eerie fantasy, originally known as the Village of Marvels, or the Sacred Wood, was created in 1552 by Prince Vicino Orsini, with the aid of the famous artist Pirro Ligorio. The surreal park is populated with weird and fantastic sculptures of mythical creatures intended to astonish illustrious guests. The sculptures, carved in outcroppings of mossy stone in shady groves and woodland, include giant tortoises and griffins and an ogre's head with an enormous gaping mouth and a table with chairs set inside. Children love it, and there are photo ops galore. The park has a self-service café (open Sunday only, in winter) and a gift shop. ⊠ *Localita Giardino, 1½ km (1 mile) west of Bomarzo,* ☎ *0761/924029* ⊕ *www.sacrobosco.it* ⊠ *€11.*

Ostia Antica

30 km (19 miles) southwest of Rome.

Founded around the 4th century BC, Ostia served as Rome's port city for several centuries until the Tiber changed course, leaving the town high and dry. What has been excavated here is a remarkably intact Roman town. To get the most out of a visit, fair weather and good walking shoes are essential. To avoid the worst extremes of hot days, be here when the gates open or go late in the afternoon. A visit to the excavations takes two to three hours, including 20 minutes for the museum. Inside the site, there's a snack bar and a bookshop, but the best idea is to plan to have lunch in the town's nearby medieval quarter.

GETTING HERE AND AROUND
The best way to get to Ostia Antica is by train. The Ostia Lido train leaves every 15 minutes from the Porta San Paolo station adjacent to Rome's Piramide Line B Metro station, stopping off at Ostia Antica en route; the trip takes 35 minutes. By car, take the Via del Mare that leads off from Rome's EUR district. Be prepared for heavy traffic, especially at peak hours, on weekends, and in summer.

 Sights

Castello di Giulio II
CASTLE/PALACE | The distinctive castle, easily spotted as you come off the footbridge from the train station and part of the medieval *borgo* (town), was built in 1483 by the future Pope Julius II when he was the cardinal bishop of Ostia. The structure's triangular form is unusual for military architecture. The castle is occasionally (and unpredictably) open to visitors, but only if you have booked ahead (updated days and times for available visits are listed on the official website). Even if you can't get inside, its towers and walls add to the atmosphere of the charming old town. ⊠ *Piazza della Rocca 13, Ostia Antica* ⊕ *www.ostiaantica.beniculturali.it* ⊠ *Free.*

★ **Scavi di Ostia Antica**
(*Ostia Antica Excavations*)
RUINS | Today some of Rome's most impressive ruins, the ancient port town was covered by tidal mud and windblown sand and lay buried until the 19th century, when it was extensively excavated. The massive archaeological site can be explored on foot and is brimming with curious corners, mosaic floors, fallen

Ostia Antica

Castello di Giulio II

Via G. Patroni

TO ROME

Stazione

Via d. Stazione

Stazione Ostia Antica

Via Capo Due Rami

Viale dei Romagnoli

Via del Mare

Via del Mare

Viale degli Scavi

Porta Romana

Via Ostiense

Decumanus Maximus

Via Gherardo

Fire Dept. Barracks

Terme di Nettuno

Tempio di Cerere

Piazzale delle Corporazioni

Teatro

Decumanus Maximus

Scavi di Ostia Antica

Mithraeum

Domus di Apuleio

Domus della Fortuna Annonaria

Molino

V. dei Molini

Thermopolium

Decumanus Maximus

Porta Laurentina

Ostiense Museum

V. dei Dipinti

Forum

Via do lor Boacciana

Cardine Massimo

Fiume Tevere

V. Epagathiana

V. Diana

Bivio del Castrum

Domus di Amore e Psiche

Horrea

V. della foce

Termi dei Sette Sapienti

Via degli Aurighi

Decumanus Maximus

Casa di Serapide

Porta Marina

Sinagoga

200 yards

200 meters

0   200 meters

columns, and a huge Roman amphitheater. At its peak, it was home to a cosmopolitan population of rich businessmen, wily merchants, sailors, slaves, and their respective families. Great warehouses were built here in the 2nd century AD to handle goods that passed through the town, notably huge shipments of grain from Africa; the port did so much business that it necessitated the construction of *insulae* (apartment buildings) to provide housing for the city's growing population. The increasing importance of nearby Portus and the inexorable decline of the Roman Empire eventually led to the port's abandonment. Over the last two millennia the coastline has retreated, and a 16th-century flood diverted the course of the Tiber, so only a glimpse of the river (near the café) can be seen today. The on-site Museo Ostiense displays sculptures, mosaics, and objects of daily use found here. There's a cafeteria on-site. ■TIP→ **The recently excavated ports of Tiberius and Claudius are nearby and also well worth visiting.** ⊠ *Viale dei Romagnoli 717, Ostia Antica* ☎ *06/56358099* ⊕ *www.ostiaantica.beniculturali.it* ✉ *€12, includes Museo Ostiense (small increase if there is an exhibition); free 1st Sun. of month* ⊗ *Closed Mon.*

ⓧ Restaurants

Arianna al Borghetto

$$ | ROMAN | FAMILY | This cozy trattoria is tucked away in the charming walled medieval *borgo* (old town) of Ostia Antica next to the Castello di Giulio II. A short walk from the excavations, it's an ideal spot to restore your energy with some seasonal dishes and Roman specialties. **Known for:** charming outdoor seating; traditional Roman food; homemade pastas. ⑤ *Average main: €15* ⊠ *Via del Forno 11, Ostia Antica* ☎ *06/56352956* ⊗ *Closed Mon. No dinner Sun.*

Tivoli

36 km (22 miles) northeast of Rome.

In ancient times, just about anybody who was anybody had a villa in Tivoli, including Crassus, Trajan, Hadrian, Horace, and Catullus. Tivoli fell into obscurity in the medieval era until the Renaissance, when popes and cardinals came back to the town and built villas showy enough to rival those of their extravagant predecessors.

Nowadays Tivoli is small but vibrant, with winding streets and views over the surrounding countryside. The deep Aniene River gorge runs through the center of town and comes replete with a romantically sited bridge, cascading waterfalls, and two jewels of ancient Roman architecture that crown its cliffs—the round Temple of Vesta (or the Sybil, the prophetess credited with predicting the birth of Christ) and the ruins of the rectangular temple of the hero-god Tibur, the mythical founder of the city. These can be picturesquely viewed across the gorge from the Villa Gregoriana Park, named for Pope Gregory XVI, who saved Tivoli from chronic river damage by diverting the river through a tunnel, weakening its flow. An unexpected side effect was the creation of the Grande Cascata (Grand Cascade), a waterfall formed by the huge jet of water that shoots into the valley below. You may also want to set your sights on the Antico Ristorante Sibilla, set up against the Temple of Vesta. From its dining terrace you can take in one of the most memorably romantic landscape views in Italy.

GETTING HERE AND AROUND

Unless you have nerves of steel, it's best to skip the drive to Tivoli. Hundreds of businesses line the Via Tiburtina from Rome and bottleneck traffic is nearly constant. You can avoid some, but not all, of the congestion by taking the Roma–L'Aquila toll road. Luckily, there's abundant public transport (although leaving your own car behind does make it slightly more inconvenient to visit Hadrian's Villa). Buses leave every 15 minutes from the Ponte Mammolo stop on Metro Line B; the ride takes an hour. Regional Trenitalia trains connect from both Termini and Tiburtina stations and will have you in Tivoli in under an hour, or 30 minutes if you plan to take one of the few express trains each day. Villa d'Este is in the town center, and there is bus service from Tivoli's main square to Hadrian's Villa.

VISITOR INFORMATION

CONTACT PIT (Punto Informativo Turistico). (*Tivoli Tourist Office*) ⊠ *Piazzale Nazioni Unite, Tivoli* ☎ *0774/313536* ⊕ *www. visittivoli.eu.*

 Sights

★ Villa Adriana (*Hadrian's Villa*)

RUINS | An emperor's theme park, this astonishingly grand 2nd-century villa was an exclusive retreat below the ancient settlement of Tibur, where the marvels of the classical world were reproduced for a ruler's pleasure. Hadrian, who succeeded Trajan as emperor in AD 117, was a man of genius and intellectual curiosity, fascinated by the accomplishments of the Hellenistic world. From AD 125 to 134, architects, laborers, and artists worked on his dreamy villa, re-creating some of the monuments and sights that the emperor had seen on his travels in Egypt, Asia Minor, and Greece. During the Middle Ages, the site was sacked by barbarians and Romans alike, and many of the statues and architectural features ended up in the Vatican Museums. Nonetheless, the colossal remains are impressive: the ruins rise in a garden setting of green lawns framed with oleanders, pines, and cypresses. Not surprisingly, Villa Adriana is a UNESCO World Heritage site, and it's one that has not yielded up all its secrets. Archaeologists recently discovered the site of the Temple of Isis, complete with several

sculptures, including one of the falcon-headed god Horus. ■TIP→ **A visit to the villa, which sits outside of town, takes at least two hours (carry water on hot days); maps dispensed at the ticket office will help you get your bearings.** ⊠ *Largo Margherite Yourcenar 1, Tivoli* ☎ *0774/382733* ⊕ *www.levillae.com/en* ⊠ *€10; free 1st Sun. of month.*

★ Villa d'Este

GARDEN | One of Italy's UNESCO World Heritage sites, Villa d'Este was created by Cardinal Ippolito d'Este in the 16th century. This villa in the center of Tivoli was the most amazing pleasure garden of its day, and it still stuns modern visitors with its beauty. Cardinal d'Este (1509–72), a devotee of the Renaissance celebration of human ingenuity over nature, was inspired by the excavation of nearby Villa Adriana. He paid architect Pirro Ligorrio an astronomical sum to create an extraordinary garden filled with nymphs and grottoes. However, water is the true artistic centerpiece here, and the Aniene River had to be diverted to water the garden and feed the several hundred fountains that cascade, shoot skyward, imitate birdsong, and simulate rain. The musical Fontana dell'Organo has been restored to working order: the water dances to an organ tune every two hours starting at 10:30 am. Romantics will love the night tour of the gardens and floodlit fountains that takes place on Friday and Saturday in summer. ■TIP→ **Allow at least an hour for a visit, which involves steep inclines and many stairs. There are vending machines for refreshments by the bookshop.** ⊠ *Piazza Trento 5, Tivoli* ☎ *0774/332920* ⊕ *www.levillae.com/en* ⊠ *€10; free 1st Sun. of month.*

 Restaurants

★ Antico Ristorante Sibilla

$$ | **ITALIAN** | Founded as a hotel and restaurant in 1720 beside the striking Roman Temple of Vesta and the Sanctuary of the Sybil, the idyllic wisteria-draped

errace has a spectacular view over the deep gorge of the Aniene River, with the thundering waters of the waterfall in the background. Standards are high, and the trip to Tivoli is worth it even if you do nothing more than order a lunch of upscale versions of local dishes in this unforgettable setting. **Known for:** homemade pasta with seasonal ingredients; beautiful terrace with a super view; special take on fried zucchini blossoms. $ *Average main: €20* ⊠ *Via della Sibilla 50, Tivoli* ☎ *0774/335281* ⊕ *www.ristoranatesibilla.com* ⊘ *Closed Mon.*

 ## Hotels

Torre Sant'Antonio

$ | B&B/INN | Set inside a tower that dates back to the 1300s, this small but cozy hotel offers two private rooms on the edge of the historic center. **Pros:** easy walk to most major sites; historic setting; modern interior design. **Cons:** old window panes let in some street noise; limited parking nearby; no 24-hour front desk. $ *Rooms from: €80* ⊠ *Vicolo Sant'Antonio 35, Tivoli* ☎ *347/8037983* ⊕ *www. torresantantoniotivoli.it* ⇲ *2 rooms* ⊙ *No Meals.*

Palestrina

27 km (17 miles) southeast of Tivoli, 37 km (23 miles) east of Rome.

Except to students of ancient history and music lovers, Palestrina is little known outside Italy. Set on a steep hillside, Romans flock to the small town of sherbet-colored houses in summer, when its cool country breezes offer a refreshing break from the hot city. In addition to the relatively cooler weather, the town is best known for its most famous native son, Giovanni Pierluigi da Palestrina, born here in 1525, and considered the master of counterpoint and polyphony. He composed 105 Masses, as well as madrigals, Magnificats, and motets. There is a small

museum dedicated to his life and work in the town center.

Ancient Praeneste (modern Palestrina) flourished much earlier than Rome. It was the site of the Temple of Fortuna Primigenia, which dates from the 2nd century BC. This was one of the largest, richest, most frequented temple complexes in all antiquity—people came from far and wide to consult its famous oracle. In modern times no one had any idea of the extent of the complex until World War II bombings exposed ancient foundations occupying huge artificial terraces, which stretch from the upper part of the town as far downhill as its central Duomo.

GETTING HERE AND AROUND
COTRAL buses leave from the Anagnina terminal on Rome's Metro Line A and from the Tiburtina railway station. Alternatively, you can take a train to Zagarolo, where a COTRAL bus takes you on to Palestrina. The total trip takes 40 minutes. By car, take the A1 (Autostrada del Sole) to the San Cesareo exit and follow the signs to Palestrina. Expect it to take about an hour.

 ## Sights

Palazzo Barberini

RUINS | A bomb blast during World War II exposed the remains of the immense Temple of Fortune that covered the entire hillside under the present town. Large arches and terraces are now visible and you can walk or take a local bus up to the imposing Palazzo Barberini, which crowns the highest point. The palace was built in the 17th century along the semicircular lines of the original Roman temple. It now contains the Museo Nazionale Archeologico di Palestrina, with material found on the site that dates from throughout the classical period. There is a well-labeled collection of Etruscan bronzes, pottery, and terra-cotta statuary as well as Roman artifacts, but all of these take a distant second place to the main event, a massive 1st-century BC mosaic depicting a buzzing scene on the Nile River, complete with ancient Egyptian boats, waving palm trees, and intricately crafted African animals. This highly colorful and detailed work is worth the trip to Palestrina by itself. But there's more: a model of the temple as it was in ancient times helps you appreciate the immensity of the original construction. ⊠ *Piazza della Cortina 1, Palestrina* ☎ *06/9538100* ⊕ *www.polomusealelazio. beniculturali.it* ⊠ *€5.*

🍴 Restaurants

Il Piscarello

$$ | ITALIAN | FAMILY | Tucked away at the bottom of a steep side road, this elegant dining room immersed in a garden comes as a bit of a surprise. Specialties of the house include meat carpaccio and fish, seafood, and meat dishes with white and black truffles, and the pasta can even be made gluten-free if you call at least one day ahead of time. **Known for:** outdoor seating in summer; truffle-topped dishes; fresh seafood. ⑤ *Average main: €20* ⊠ *Via delle Pratarine 2, Palestrina* ☎ *06/9574326* ⊕ *www. ristoranteilpiscarello.it* ⊘ *Closed Mon. No lunch Tues.–Thurs. No dinner Sun.*

Frascati

20 km (12 miles) south of Rome.

Frascati is one of the easiest villages of the Castelli Romani to get to from Rome, as well as one of the most enjoyable to navigate. After climbing the stairs from the train station or driving up hill to the entrance of the town, it's worth taking a stroll through Frascati's lively old center. Via Battisti, leading away from the looming presence of Villa Aldobrandini, takes you into Piazza San Pietro with its imposing gray-and-white cathedral. Inside is the cenotaph of Prince Charles Edward, last of the Scottish Stuart dynasty, who

tried unsuccessfully to regain the British Crown and died an exile in Rome in 1788. A little arcade beside the monumental fountain at the back of the piazza leads into Market Square, where the smell of fresh baking will entice you into the Purificato family bakery to see the traditional honey-flavored pupazza biscuits, modeled on old pagan fertility symbols.

Take your pick from the cafés and trattorias fronting the central Piazzale Marconi, or do as the locals do: buy fruit from the market gallery at Piazza del Mercato, then get a huge slice of porchetta from one of the stalls, a hunk of *casareccio* bread, and a few *ciambelline frascatane* (ring-shape cookies made with wine), and take your picnic to any one of the nearby *cantine* (homey wine bars) to settle in for some sips of tasty, inexpensive vino. Or continue on to nearby Grottaferrata to take in its one-of-a-kind abbey.

GETTING HERE AND AROUND

An hourly train service along a single-track line through vineyards and olive groves takes you to Frascati from Termini station. The trip takes 45 minutes. By car, take the Via Tuscolano, which branches off the Appia Nuova road just after St. John Lateran in Rome, and drive straight up.

VISITOR INFORMATION

CONTACT Frascati Point (Tourism Office). ⊠ *Piazza G. Marconi 5, Frascati* ☎ *06/94184406* ⊕ *www.comune.frascati. rm.it.*

Sights

Abbey of San Nilo Grottaferrata

CHURCH | In Grottaferrata, a busy village a couple of miles from Frascati, the main attraction is a walled citadel founded by St. Nilo, who brought his group of Basilian monks here in 1004, when he was 90. The order is unique in that it's Roman Catholic but observes Greek Orthodox rites. It is the last surviving Byzantine-Greek monastery in Italy, and has a distinctive blend of art and architecture. The fortified abbey with its soaring bell tower, considered a masterpiece of martial architecture, was restructured in the 15th century by Antonio da Sangallo for the future Pope Julius II. The abbey church, inside the second courtyard, is a jewel of Oriental opulence, with glittering Byzantine mosaics and a revered icon of Mary with child set into a marble tabernacle designed by Bernini. The Farnese chapel, leading from the right nave, contains a series of frescoes by Domenichino. If you make arrangements in advance you can visit the library, which is one of the oldest in Italy. The abbey also has a famous laboratory for the restoration of antique books and manuscripts, where Leonardo's *Codex Atlanticus* was restored in 1962 and more than a thousand precious volumes were saved after the disastrous Florence flood in 1966. ⊠ *Corso del Popolo 128, Grottaferrata* ☎ *06/9459309* ⊕ *www. abbaziagreca.it* ⊠ *Free.*

★ Poggio Le Volpi

WINERY | Lazio's wines may not be as famous as those of Tuscany or Piedmont, but this award-winning family-run winery is leading the way for the region. The family's wine-making roots stretch back to 1920, but it was third-generation wine-maker Felice Mergè who turned the winery into a destination with two restaurants: the casual Epos bistro and the fine-dining Barrique, where a tasting menu is served in the barrel aging room. Tours of the winery are available by appointment only, but the best way to experience this place is to book a table at one of the restaurants and request a tour. ⊠ *Via Fontana Candida 3/C, Bomarzo* ☎ *06/9426980* ⊕ *www.poggiolevolpi. com* ⊠ *Tours available by appointment* ⊘ *Closed Mon.*

🍴 Restaurants

Antica Fontana

$$ | **ROMAN** | Across the road from the Abbey of San Nilo, this is one of Grottaferrata's most esteemed restaurants, and it tends to be slightly higher priced than other nearby eateries. Run by the Consoli family since 1989, the decor is rustic but stylish, with plants hanging from the ceiling and rows of polished antique copper pans and molds decorating the walls. **Known for:** pleasant outdoor terrace; homemade pizza with excellent dough; fettuccine with porcini. ⑤ *Average main: €22* ⊠ *Via Domenichino 24, Grottaferrata* ☎ *06/9413687* ⊘ *Closed Mon.*

★ Cacciani

$$ | **ITALIAN** | The Cacciani family has been running this stylish restaurant in the heart of Frascati old town since 1922, when it was a popular hangout for the likes of Clark Gable and Gina Lollobrigida. Perched high on a rise overlooking the town and the Roman plain, there are spectacular views from the Cacciani terrace, but you can also keep an eye on the gorgeous food being prepared in the open kitchen. **Known for:** welcoming, family-run vibe; tonnarelli cacio e pepe prepared at the table; great views. ⑤ *Average main: €18* ⊠ *Via Armando Diaz 13, Frascati* ☎ *06/9420378* ⊕ *www.cacciani.it* ⊘ *Closed Mon. No dinner Sun.*

Il Grottino Frascati

$$ | **ITALIAN** | This former wine cellar just beyond Frascati's market square is now an old-fashioned and cheerful trattoria serving traditional Roman dishes and pizza. In summer you can sit under an awning outside and enjoy the sweeping view over the plain toward Rome. **Known for:** extensive wine list; pasta alla gricia; casual atmosphere. ⑤ *Average main: €15* ⊠ *Viale Regina Margherita 41–43, Frascati* ☎ *06/94289772.*

★ Osteria del Fico Vecchio

$$ | **ITALIAN** | Only a couple of miles outside Frascati, this 16th-century coaching inn has a tastefully renovated dining room and an old fig tree (its namesake) that shades the restaurant's charming garden filled with outdoor tables. Long known for its excellent cooking, the classic restaurant still prepares typical Roman dishes, among them *pollo al diavolo* (spicy braised chicken) and *abbacchio allo scottadito* (sizzling grilled lamb). **Known for:** typical Roman dishes; classic cacio e pepe; pretty garden for outdoor dining. ⑤ *Average main: €20* ⊠ *Via Anagnina 257, Grottaferrata* ☎ *06/9459261* ⊕ *www.alfico.it* ☉ *No lunch Thurs.*

Hotels

★ Park Hotel Villa Grazioli

$ | **HOTEL** | One of the region's most famous residences, this patrician villa halfway between Frascati and Grottaferrata is now a first-class hotel, though the standard-issue guest rooms are a bit of a letdown amid the impressive frescoed salons of the main building. **Pros:** wonderful views of the countryside; incredible frescoes in the main building; elegant atmosphere. **Cons:** not all rooms are in the main building; situated at the end of a long, narrow lane; Wi-Fi connection can be poor. ⑤ *Rooms from: €120* ⊠ *Via Umberto Pavoni, 19, Grottaferrata* ⊹ *Narrow turnoff from the SP216 road going from Grottaferrata roundabout to Frascati* ☎ *06/945400* ⊕ *www.villa-grazioli.it* ⇋ *62 rooms* ⁍⊙⁌ *Free Breakfast.*

Castel Gandolfo

8 km (5 miles) southwest of Frascati, 25 km (15 miles) south of Rome.

This scenic little town has been the preferred summer retreat of popes for centuries. It was the Barberini Pope Urban VIII who first headed here, eager to escape the malarial miasmas that afflicted summertime Rome; before long, the city's princely families also set up country estates around here.

The 17th-century Villa Pontificia has a superb position overlooking Lake Albano and is set in one of the most gorgeous gardens in Italy. Fortunately, these treasures are now open to the public as papal audiences are no longer held at Castel Gandolfo. On the little square in front of the palace there's a fountain by Bernini, who also designed the nearby Church of San Tommaso da Villanova, which has works by Pietro da Cortona.

The village has a number of interesting craft workshops and food purveyors, in addition to the souvenir shops on the square. On the horizon, the silver astronomical dome belonging to the Specola Vaticana observatory—one of the first in Europe—where the scientific Pope Gregory XIII indulged his interest in stargazing, is visible for miles around.

GETTING HERE AND AROUND

There's an hourly train service for Castel Gandolfo from Termini station (Rome–Albano line). Otherwise, buses leave frequently from the Anagnina terminal of Metro Line A. The trip takes about 40 minutes, and the village is reachable by a 10-minute walk from the station. By car, take the Appian Way from San Giovanni in Rome and follow it straight to Albano, where you branch off for Castel Gandolfo (about an hour, depending on traffic).

VISITOR INFORMATION

CONTACT PIT Tourist Office Castel Gandolfo. ⊠ *Via Massimo D'Azeglio, Castel Gandolfo* ⊹ *A green kiosk on your right as you walk up the road, just outside the town walls* ⊕ *www.comune.castelgandolfo.rm.it.*

Sights

Lakeside Lido

BEACH | FAMILY | This waterside promenade below the pretty town is lined with restaurants, ice cream parlors, and cafés and is a favorite spot for Roman families to relax on summer days. No motorized craft are allowed on the lake, but you can ent paddleboats and kayaks. In summer, you can also take a short guided boat trip to learn about the geology and history of the lake, which lies at the bottom of an extinct volcanic crater. The deep sapphire waters are full of swans, herons, and other birds, and there is a nature trail along the wooded end of the shore for those who want to get away from the crowds. Deck chairs are available for rent; you might also want to stop for a plate of freshly prepared pasta or a gigantic Roman sandwich at one of the little snack bars under the oak and alder trees. There's also a small permanent fairground for children, and local vendors often set up temporary shops selling crafts, toys, and snacks on the warmer weekends. ⊠ *Lake Albano, Castel Gandolfo* 🖼 *Free.*

Palazzo Apostolico di Castel Gandolfo
CASTLE/PALACE | For centuries the Apostolic Palace of Castel Gandolfo was the summer retreat of popes, who kept the papal villa and extensive grounds completely private. Luckily for tourists, Pope Francis decided that he was too busy to use it and had it opened to the public. Inside you can view the Gallery of Pontifical Portraits, ceremonial garments, and the imposing papal throne in the Sala degli Svizzeri. The private area of the palace with the pope's bedchamber, his library, study, and offices—all strictly off-limits before 2016—are also open to visitors. ⊠ *Piazza della Libertà, Castel Gandolfo* 🕾 *06/69883145* ⊕ *www.museivaticani.va* 🖼 *€11* 🕙 *Closed Sun. and on Catholic holidays.*

⭐ **Pontifical Gardens Villa Barberini**
GARDEN | In 2016, Pope Francis opened the 136-acre Pontificial estate and its glorious gardens to the public. Once rarely accessible, the Pontifical gardens of Villa Barberini can now be visited in a 60-minute tour by an ecologically friendly electric vehicle. The tour takes in the landscaped gardens as well as the archaeological remains of the palace of the Roman Emperor Domitian (dating back to the 1st century AD) and the home farm, which supplies the Vatican with fresh dairy products and eggs. Multilingual audio guides are included in the price. ⊠ *Via Massimo D'Azeglio (entrance gate), Castel Gandolfo* ⊕ *www.museivaticani.va/content/museivaticani/en.html* 🖼 *Villa Barberini gardens with minibus tour €20; Gardens only €12; Gardens and Apostolic Palace €19* 🕙 *Closed Mon.–Fri.* 🖼 *Reservations required.*

🍴 Restaurants

Antico Ristorante Pagnanelli
$$$ | ITALIAN | One of the most refined restaurants in the Castelli Romani has been in the same family since 1882. Its dining-room windows open onto a breathtaking view across Lake Albano to the conical peak of Monte Cavo. **Known for:** famous wine cellar and wine museum in basement; homemade gnocchetti with clams and black truffles; elegant and cozy interior with an open fire in winter. 🖼 *Average main: €30* ⊠ *Via Gramsci 4, Castel Gandolfo* 🕾 *06/9360004* ⊕ *www. pagnanelli.it.*

🛏 Hotels

Hotel Castelgandolfo
$ | HOTEL | Overlooking the volcanic crater of Lake Albano and a minute's walk from the Apostolic Palace, this intimate hotel in the heart of Castel Gandolfo makes an ideal retreat for romantics. **Pros:** ideal for romantics; convenient location; intimate. **Cons:** balconies are small and narrow; some rooms have street views; stunning terrace sometimes closed for private events. 🖼 *Rooms from: €120* ⊠ *Via De' Zecchini 27, Castel Gandolfo* 🕾 *06/9360521* ⊕ *www.hotelcastelgandolfo.com* 🛏 *18 rooms* 🍴 *Free Breakfast.*

The Monumental Bridge connects Ariccia to Albano and offers beautiful views of Palazzo Chigi and Santa Maria Assunta.

Ariccia

8 km (5 miles) southwest of Castel Gandolfo, 26 km (17 miles) south of Rome.

Ariccia is a gem of Baroque town planning. When Fabio Chigi, scion of the superwealthy banking family, became Pope Alexander VII, he commissioned Gian Lorenzo Bernini to redesign his country estate to make it worthy of his new station. Bernini restructured not only the existing 16th-century palace, but also the town gates, the main square, with its loggias and graceful twin fountains, and the round church of Santa Maria dell'Assunzione (the dome is said to be modeled on the Pantheon). The rest of the village was coiled around the apse of the church down into the valley below.

Ariccia's splendid heritage was largely forgotten in the 20th century, and yet it was once one of the highlights of every artist's and writer's Grand Tour. Corot, Ibsen, Turner, Longfellow, and Hans Christian Andersen all came to stay here.

GETTING HERE AND AROUND

For Ariccia, take the COTRAL bus from the Anagnina terminal of Metro Line A. Buses on the Albano–Genzano–Velletri line stop under the monumental bridge that spans the Ariccia Valley, where an elevator whisks you up to the main town square. If you take a train to Albano Laziale, you can proceed by bus to Ariccia or go on foot (it's just under 1½ km [1 mile]). If you're driving, follow the Via Appia Nuova to Albano and carry on to Ariccia.

Sights

★ Palazzo Chigi

CASTLE/PALACE | This is a true rarity: a Baroque residence whose original furniture, paintings, drapes, and decorations are largely intact. The Italian film director Luchino Visconti used the villa, which sits just at the end of Ariccia's famous bridge, for most of the interior scenes in his 1963 film *The Leopard*. The rooms of the piano nobile (main floor)—which, unlike Rome's Palazzo Chigi, does open o the public, but only on guided tours—contain intricately carved pieces of 7th-century furniture, as well as textiles and costumes from the 16th to the 20th century. The Room of Beauties is lined with paintings of the loveliest ladies of the day, and the Nuns' Room showcases portraits of 10 Chigi sisters, all of whom took the veil. You can get a close look at Le Stanze del Cardinale (Cardinal's Rooms), the suites occupied by the pleasure-loving Cardinal Flavio Chigi, with a guide on most days. The upper floors contain the Museo del Barocco (Baroque Museum), with an important collection of 17th-century paintings with largely religious themes. The expansive park stretching behind the palace is the last remnant of the ancient Latium forest, where herds of deer still graze under the trees. Be sure to check the website for the hours when various rooms are open to the public and plan to book ahead to secure a tour in English. ⊠ *Piazza di Corte 14, Ariccia* ☎ *06/9330053* ⊕ *www. palazzochigiariccia.com* 🖾 *€19 full villa tour (when possible), €8 piano nobile, €6 Cardinal's Rooms, €6 Baroque Museum, €6 park* ⊙ *Palazzo closed Mon. Park closed Oct.–Mar.*

Santa Maria Assunta in Cielo (Church of the Assumption)

CHURCH | Directly across from Palazzo Chigi is the Church of the Assumption, with its distinctive blue dome and round shape designed by none other than Gian Lorenzo Bernini. The artistic architect had his best students execute most of the work of building and decorating the Pantheon-inspired church, creating porticoes outside and an intricately plastered cupola inside, which steals the show in the otherwise simple interior. ⊠ *Piazza di Corte, Ariccia* ⊕ *www.chiesediariccia.it.*

🍴 Restaurants

A visit to Ariccia isn't complete without tasting the local gastronomic specialty: *porchetta*, a delicious roast whole pig

stuffed with herbs, that is best with a side of local Romanella wine. The shops on the Piazza di Corte will make up a sandwich for you, or you can do what the Romans do: head for one of the *fraschetta* wine cellars, which also serve cheese, cold cuts, pickles, olives, and sometimes a plate of pasta. Pass Palazzo Chigi and turn left under the arch to find several in a long row on the other side of the street. Take your pick and ask for a seat on a wooden bench at a trestle table covered with simple white paper; be ready to make friends and maybe join in a sing-along.

L'Aricciarola

$ | ITALIAN | FAMILY | This fraschetta around the corner from Palazzo Chigi is great for people-watching, which you can do while enjoying a platter of cold cuts and mixed cheeses, washed down with a carafe of local Castelli wine. Order your own appetizers and slices of porchetta at the counter near the door, snag a table on the patio, flag down a waiter if you want to order pasta, and then settle into the rustic setting surrounded by Roman families who've come to enjoy the local food. **Known for:** very casual and friendly atmosphere; classic porchetta; local cold cuts. ⑤ *Average main: €12* ⊠ *Via Borgo S. Rocco 9, Ariccia* ☎ *06/9334103* ⊕ *osteri-alaricciarola.it* ⊙ *Closed Mon. and 2 wks in Jan.*

Nemi

8 km (5 miles) east of Ariccia, 34 km (21 miles) south of Rome.

A bronze statue of Diana the Huntress greets you at the entrance to Nemi, the smallest and prettiest village of the Castelli Romani. It's perched on a spur of rock 600 feet above the little oval-shape lake of the same name, which is formed from a volcanic crater. Nemi has an eagle's-nest view over the rolling Roman countryside as far as the coast, some 18 km (11 miles) away. The one main street, Corso Vittorio Emanuele, takes you to the baronial Castello Ruspoli (not open to the public), where there's an 11th-century watchtower, and the quaint Piazza Umberto I, lined with outdoor cafés serving the town's famous tiny wild strawberries harvested from the woodlands that line the crater bowl.

GETTING HERE AND AROUND

Nemi is difficult to get to unless you come by car. Buses from the Anagnina station on Metro Line A go to the town of Genzano, where a local bus travels to Nemi every two hours. If the times aren't convenient, you can take a taxi or walk the 5 km (3 miles) around Lake Nemi. By car, take the panoramic route known as the Via dei Laghi (Road of the Lakes). Follow the Appia Nuova from St. John Lateran and branch off on the well-signposted route after Ciampino airport. Follow the Via dei Laghi toward Velletri until you see signs for Nemi.

Sights

Museo delle Navi Romane (*Roman Ship Museum*)

HISTORY MUSEUM | In the 1930s, the Italian government drained Nemi's lake to recover two magnificent ceremonial ships, loaded with sculptures, bronzes, and art treasures, that were submerged for 2,000 years. The Museo delle Navi Romane, on the lakeshore, was built to house the ships, but they were burned during World War II. Inside are scale models and finds from the Bronze Age Diana sanctuary and the area nearby. There's also a colossal statue of the infamous and extravagant Roman emperor Caligula, who had the massive barges built on the pretty lake. Italian police once snatched the marble sculpture back from tomb robbers just as they were about to smuggle it out of the country. ⊠ *Via del Tempio di Diana 13, Nemi* ☎ *06/9398040* ⊕ *www.beniculturali.it* ⊠ *€4* ☉ *Closed Mon.*

Restaurants

★ **La Fiocina**

$$ | ITALIAN | With its privileged position on the tranquil shores of Lake Nemi next to the Roman Ship Museum, La Fiocina has been serving local specialties, including lake fish and homemade gnocchi with wild boar sauce, for more than 50 years. The dining room is elegant and welcoming, and there's a terrace on which you can dine alfresco, overlooking the small lakeside garden. **Known for:** tiny wild Nemi strawberries; coregone lake fish; garden terrace with lake views. ⓢ *Average main: €15* ⊠ *Via delle Navi di Tiberio 9, Nemi* ☎ *06/9391120* ☉ *Closed Mon. and Tues.*

Chapter 5

VENICE

Updated by
Liz Humphreys

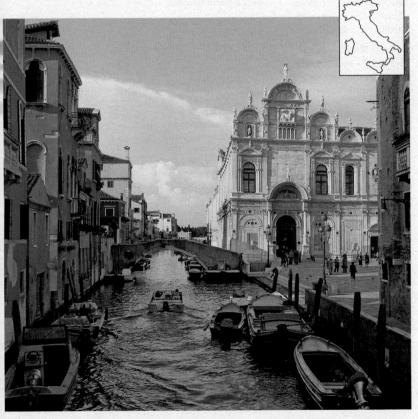

◉ Sights	🍴 Restaurants	🛏 Hotels	🛍 Shopping	🍸 Nightlife
★★★★★	★★★★☆	★★★★★	★★★☆☆	★★☆☆☆

WELCOME TO VENICE

TOP REASONS TO GO

★ **Cruising the Grand Canal:** The beauty of its palaces, enhanced by the play of light on the water, make a trip down Venice's "Main Street" unforgettable.

★ **Basilica di San Marco:** Don't miss the gorgeous mosaics inside—they're worth standing in line for.

★ **Santa Maria Gloriosa dei Frari:** Its austere, cavernous interior houses Titian's *Assumption*—one of the world's most beautiful altarpieces—plus several other spectacular art treasures.

★ **Gallerie dell'Accademia:** Legendary masterpieces of Venetian painting will overwhelm you in this fabled museum.

★ **Sipping wine and snacking at a bacaro:** For a sample of tasty local snacks and excellent Veneto wines in a uniquely Venetian setting, head for one of the city's many wine bars.

1 San Marco. The neighborhood at the center of Venice is filled with fashion boutiques, art galleries, and grand hotels.

2 Dorsoduro. This graceful residential area is home to renowned art galleries; the Campo Santa Margherita is a lively student hangout.

3 San Polo and Santa Croce. These bustling *sestieri* (districts) have all sorts of shops, several major churches, and the Rialto fish and produce markets.

4 Cannaregio. This sestiere has some of the sunniest open-air canalside walks in town; the Jewish Ghetto has a fascinating history.

5 Castello. With its gardens, park, and narrow, winding walkways, it's the sestiere least influenced by Venice's tourist culture.

6 San Giorgio Maggiore and the Giudecca. San Giorgio is graced with its magnificent namesake church, and the Giudecca has wonderful views of Venice.

7 Islands of the Lagoon. Each island in Venice's northern lagoon has its own allure.

LAGUNA
VENETA

EATING AND DRINKING WELL IN VENICE

The catchword in Venetian restaurants is "fish." How do you learn about the catch of the day? A visit to the Rialto's *pescheria* (fish market) is more instructive than any book, and when you're dining at a well-regarded restaurant, ask for a recommendation.

Traditionally, fish is served with a bit of salt, maybe some chopped parsley, and a drizzle of olive oil—no lemon; lemon masks the flavor. Ask for an entire wild-caught fish; it's much more expensive than its farmed cousin, but certainly worth it. Antipasto may be prosciutto *di San Daniele* (from the Veneto region) or *sarde in saor* (fresh panfried sardines marinated with onions, raisins, and pine nuts). Risotto, cooked with shellfish or veggies, is a great first course. Pasta? Enjoy it with seafood: this is *not* the place to order spaghetti with tomato sauce. Other pillars of regional cooking include *pasta e fagioli* (thick bean soup with pasta); polenta, often with *fegato alla veneziana* (liver with onion); and that dessert invented in the Veneto, tiramisu.

GOING BACARO

You can sample regional wines and scrumptious *cicheti* (small snacks) in *bacari* (wine bars), a great Venetian tradition. Crostini and *polpette* (meat, fish, or vegetable croquettes) are popular cicheti, as are small sandwiches, seafood salads, *baccalà mantecato* (creamy, whipped salt cod), and toothpick-speared items like roasted peppers, marinated artichokes, and mozzarella balls.

SEAFOOD

Granseola (crab), *moeche* (tiny, locally caught soft-shell crabs), sweet *canoce* (mantis shrimp), *capelunghe* (razor clams), calamari, and *seppie* or *seppioline* (cuttlefish) are all prominently featured, as well as *rombo* (turbot), *branzino* (sea bass), *San Pietro* (John Dory), *sogliola* (sole), *orate* (gilthead bream), and *triglia* (mullet). Trademark dishes include sarde in saor, *frittura mista* (tempura-like fried fish and vegetables), and *baccalà mantecato*.

RISOTTO, PASTA, POLENTA

As a first course, Venetians favor the creamy rice dish risotto *all'onda* ("undulating," as opposed to firm), prepared with vegetables or shellfish. When pasta is served, it's generally accompanied by seafood sauces, too: *pasticcio di pesce* is lasagna-type pasta baked with fish, and *bigoli* is a strictly local whole-wheat pasta shaped like thick spaghetti, usually served *in salsa* (an anchovy-onion sauce with a dash of cinnamon), or with *nero di seppia* (cuttlefish-ink sauce). *Pasta e fagioli* is another classic first course, and polenta is a staple—served creamy or fried in wedges, generally as an accompaniment to stews or *seppie in nero* (cuttlefish in black ink).

VEGETABLES

The larger islands of the lagoon are known for their legendary vegetables, such as the Sant'Erasmo *castraure*, sinfully expensive but heavenly tiny white artichokes that appear for a few days in spring. Spring treats include the fat white asparagus from neighboring Bassano or Verona, and artichoke bottoms (*fondi*), usually sautéed with olive oil, parsley, and garlic. From December to March the prized local radicchio *di Treviso* is grilled and frequently served with a bit of melted Taleggio cheese from Lombardy. Fall brings small wild mushrooms called *chiodini* and *zucca di Mantova,* a yellow squash with a gray-green rind used in soups, puddings, and ravioli stuffing.

SWEETS

Tiramisu lovers will have ample opportunity to sample this creamy delight made from ladyfingers soaked in espresso and rum or brandy and covered with mascarpone cream and cinnamon. Gelato, *sgroppino* (prosecco, vodka, and lemon sorbet), and *semifreddo* (soft homemade ice cream) are other sweets frequently seen on Venetian menus, as are almond cakes and dry cookies served with dessert wine. Try *focaccia veneziana,* a sweet raised cake made in the late fall and winter.

Venice is often called La Serenissima, or "the most serene," a reference to the majesty, wisdom, and power of this city that was for centuries a leader in trade between Europe and Asia and a major center of European culture. Built on water by people who saw the sea as defender and ally, and who constantly invested in its splendor with magnificent architectural projects, Venice is a city unlike any other.

No matter how often you've seen it in photos and films, the real thing is more dreamlike than you could ever imagine. Its most notable landmarks, the Basilica di San Marco and the Palazzo Ducale, are exotic mixes of Byzantine, Romanesque, Gothic, and Renaissance styles, reflecting Venice's ties with the rest of Italy and with Constantinople to the east. Shimmering sunlight and silvery mist soften every perspective here; it's easy to understand how the city became renowned in the Renaissance for its artists' use of color. It's full of secrets, inexpressibly romantic, and frequently given over to pure, sensuous enjoyment.

You'll see Venetians going about their daily affairs in vaporetti, in the *campi* (squares), and along the *calli* (narrow streets). Despite their many challenges (including more frequent flooding and overcrowding), they are proud of their city and its history and are still quite helpful to those who show proper respect for Venice and its way of life.

Planning

Making the Most of Your Time

The hordes of tourists here are legendary, especially in spring and fall but during other seasons too—there's really no "off-season" in Venice. Unfortunately, tales of impassable tourist-packed streets and endless queues to get into the Basilica di San Marco are not exaggerated. A little bit of planning, however, will help you avoid the worst of the crowds.

Most tourists do little more than take the vaporetto down the Grand Canal to Piazza San Marco, see the piazza and the basilica, and walk up to the Rialto and back to the station. You'll want to visit these areas, too, but do so in the early morning, before most tourists have finished their breakfast cappuccinos.

Because many tourists are other Italians who come for a weekend outing, you can further decrease your competition for Venice's pleasures by choosing to visit the city on weekdays.

Away from San Marco and the Rialto, the streets and quays of Venice's beautiful medieval and Renaissance residential districts receive only a moderate amount of traffic. Besides the Grand Canal and the Piazza San Marco, and perhaps Torcello, the other historically and artistically important sites are seldom overcrowded. Even on weekends you probably won't have to queue up for the Gallerie dell'Accademia.

Getting Oriented

Venice proper is quite compact, and you should be able to walk across it in a couple of hours, even counting a few minutes for getting lost. Vaporetti will save wear and tear on tired feet, but won't always save you much time.

Venice is divided into six sestieri: Cannaregio, Castello, Dorsoduro, San Polo, and Santa Croce. More sedate outer islands float around them—San Giorgio Maggiore and the Giudecca just to the south; beyond them the Lido, the barrier island; and to the north, Murano, Burano, and Torcello.

Getting Here and Around

AIR

Aeroporto Marco Polo. ☎ *041/2609260* ⊕ *www.veniceairport.it.*
LAND TRANSFERS
ATVO. ☎ *0421/594672* ⊕ *www.atvo.it.*
WATER TRANSFERS
From Marco Polo terminal, it's a mostly covered seven-minute walk to the dock where boats depart for Venice's historic center. The ride is in a closed boat so you won't get much of a view; plus, it's more expensive and generally slower than the

bus to Piazzale Roma (unless your hotel is near a boat station).

Alilaguna. ☎ *041/2401701* ⊕ *www.alilaguna.it.*
CAR
Venice is at the end of the SR11, just off the east–west A4 autostrada. There are no cars in Venice; if possible, return your rental when you arrive.

A warning: don't be waylaid by illegal touts, often wearing fake uniforms, who try to flag you down and offer to arrange parking and hotels. Use one of the established garages and consider reserving a space in advance. The **Autorimessa Comunale** (041/2727307, avm.avmspa.it) costs €26–€29 for 24 hours (slight discounts if you book online). The **Garage San Marco** (041/5232213, www.garagesanmarco.it) costs €35 for 24 hours, with slight discounts for prepaid online reservations. On its own island, **Tronchetto** (041/5207555, www.tronchettoparking.it) charges €21 for 24 hours. Watch for signs coming over the bridge—you turn right just before Piazzale Roma. Many hotels and the casino have guest discounts with San Marco or Tronchetto garages. Another alternative is to park in Mestre, on the mainland, and take a train (10 minutes, €1) or bus into Venice. The garage across from the station and the Bus No. 2 stop costs €8 per day.

PUBLIC TRANSPORTATION
WATER BUSES
ACTV. ☎ *041/041 041* ⊕ *www.actv.it.*
WATER TAXIS
A *motoscafo* isn't cheap: you'll spend about €70 for a short trip in town, €90 to the Lido, and €100 or more per hour to visit the outer islands. It is strongly suggested to book through the **Consorzio Motoscafi Venezia** (041/5222303, www.motoscafivenezia.com) to avoid an argument with your driver over prices. A water taxi can carry up to 10 passengers, with an additional charge of €10 per person for more than 5 people, so if you're

traveling in a group, it may not be that much more expensive than a vaporetto.

TRAIN

Venice has rail connections with many major cities in Italy and Europe. Note that Venice's train station is **Venezia Santa Lucia,** not to be confused with Venezia Mestre, which is the mainland stop prior to arriving in the historic center. Some trains don't continue beyond the Mestre station; in such cases you can catch the next Venice-bound train. Get a ticket on the Trenitalia app or a paper ticket from the kiosk on the platform and validate it (in the yellow time-stamp machine) to avoid a fine.

Restaurants

Dining options in Venice range from ultra-high-end establishments, where jackets are required, to very casual eateries. Once staunchly traditional, many restaurants have revamped their dining rooms and their menus, creating dishes that blend classic elements with ingredients and methods less common to the region. Mid- and upper-range restaurants often offer innovative options as well as mainstays like sarde in saor and *fegato alla veneziana.*

Unfortunately, Venice also has its share of overpriced, mediocre eateries. Restaurants catering to tourists have little motivation to maintain quality since most diners are one-time patrons. You are better off at a restaurant frequented by locals, who are interested in the food, not the views. Avoid places with cajoling waiters outside, as well as those that don't display their prices or have showy tourist menus translated into a dozen languages. For the same €15–€20 you'd spend at such places, you could do better at a *bacaro* making a meal of *cicheti.*

Restaurant listings have been shortened. For full information, visit Fodors.com.

WHAT IT COSTS in Euros

	$	$$	$$$	$$$$
AT DINNER				
	under €15	€15–€24	€25–€35	over €35

Hotels

Venetian magic lingers when you retire for the night, whether you're staying in a grand hotel or budget *locanda* (inn). Hotels usually occupy very old buildings, often without elevators or lounge areas. It's not at all unusual for each room to be different, even on the same floor: windows overlooking charming canals and bleak alleyways are both common. Venice is one of the most popular destinations on Earth—so book your lodging as far in advance as possible.

In terms of location, the area in and around San Marco is the most crowded and expensive. Still convenient but more tranquil areas include Dorsoduro, Santa Croce, and Cannaregio (though the area around the train station can be hectic), or even Castello in the area beyond the Pietà church. Also take into consideration the proximity of a vaporetto stop, especially if you have heavy baggage. Regardless of where you stay, it's essential that you have detailed directions to your hotel: note not only its street address but also its sestiere as well as a nearby landmark or two. Even if you arrive by water taxi, you may still have a bit of a walk.

Hotel reviews have been shortened. For full information, visit Fodors.com.

WHAT IT COSTS in Euros

	$	$$	$$$	$$$$
LODGING FOR TWO				
	under €125	€125–€200	€201–€300	over €300

Nightlife

Nightlife offerings in Venice are, even by rather sedate standards, fairly tame. Most bars must close by midnight, especially those that offer outdoor seating. Piazza San Marco is a popular meeting place in nice weather, when the cafés stay open relatively late and all seem to compete to offer the best live music. The younger crowd, Venetians and visitors alike, tend to gravitate toward the area around the Ponte di Rialto, with Campi San Bartolomeo and San Luca on one side and Campo Rialto Nuovo on the other. Especially popular with university students and young people from the mainland are the bars around Campo Santa Margherita. Visit 2night.it/venezia for nightlife listings and reviews.

Performing Arts

Visit www.agendavenezia.org for a preview of musical, artistic, and sporting events. *Venezia News* (*VENews*), available at newsstands, has similar information but also includes in-depth articles about noteworthy events. The tourist office publishes a handy, free quarterly *Calendar* in Italian and English, listing daily events and current museum and venue hours. *Venezia da Vivere* (www.veneziadavivere. com) is a seasonal guide listing cool cultural happenings and places. And don't ignore the posters you see plastered on the walls as you walk—often they contain the most up-to-date information you can find.

TIP→ For more information on festivals in Venice, see On the Calendar in Travel Smart.

CARNEVALE

Although Carnevale has traditionally been associated with the time leading up to the Roman Catholic period of Lent, it originally started out as a principally secular annual period of partying and feasting to celebrate Venice's victory over Ulrich II, Patriarch of Aquileia, in 1162. To commemorate the annual tribute Ulrich was forced to pay, a bull and 12 pigs were slaughtered in Piazza San Marco each year on the day before Lent. Since then, the city has marked the days preceding *Quaresima* (Lent) with abundant feasting and wild celebrations. The word *carnevale* is derived from the words *carne* (meat) and *levare* (to remove), as eating meat was restricted during Lent. The use of masks for Carnevale was first mentioned in 1268, and its direct association with Lent was not made until the end of the 13th century.

Venice earned its international reputation as the "city of Carnevale" in the 18th century, when partying would begin several months before Lent and the city seemed to be one continuous masquerade. During this time, income from tourists became a major source of funds in La Serenissima's coffers. With the Republic's fall in 1797, Carnevale was prohibited by the French and the Austrians. From Italian reunification in 1866 until the fall of Fascism in the 1940s, the event was alternately allowed or banned, depending on the government's stance.

It was revived for good in the 1970s, when residents began taking to the calli and campi in their own impromptu celebrations. It didn't take long for the tourist industry to embrace Carnevale as a means to stimulate business in low season. And their faith is well placed: each year over the 10- to 12-day Carnevale period (ending on the Tuesday before Ash Wednesday), more than a half-million people attend concerts, theater and street performances, masquerade balls, historical processions, fashion shows, and contests. Since 2008 Carnevale has been organized by **Venezia Marketing & Eventi** (www.carnevale.venezia. it). *A Guest in Venice* is also a complete guide to public and private Carnevale festivities. Stop by the **tourist office** (*041/2424 www.veneziaunica.it*) or the Venice Pavilion for information, but be aware they can be mobbed. If you're not planning on joining in the revelry, you'd be wise to choose another time to visit Venice. Crowds throng the streets (which become one-way, with police directing foot traffic), bridges are designated "no-stopping" zones to avoid gridlock, and prices skyrocket.

Shopping

Alluring shops abound in Venice. You'll find countless vendors of such trademark wares as glass, lace, and high-end textiles. The authenticity of some goods can be suspect, but they're often pleasing to the eye, regardless of origin. You will also find interesting craft and art studios with high-quality, one-of-a-kind articles. Antiques, especially antique Venetian glass, are almost invariably cheaper outside of Venice, because Venetians are ready to pay high prices for their own heritage.

The San Marco area is full of shops and couture boutiques, such as Armani, Missoni, Valentino, Fendi, and Versace. Leading from Piazza San Marco, you'll find some of Venice's busiest shopping streets—Le Mercerie, the Frezzeria, Calle dei Fabbri, and Calle Larga XXII Marzo. Other good shopping areas surround Calle del Teatro and Campi San Salvador, Manin, San Fantin, and San Bartolomeo. You can find somewhat less expensive, more varied, and more imaginative shops between the Ponte di Rialto and San Polo and in Santa Croce, and art galleries in Dorsoduro from the Salute to the Accademia. Regular store hours are usually 9 to 12:30 and 3:30 or 4 to 7:30; some stores close Saturday afternoon or Monday morning.

Passes and Discounts

Avoid lines and hassle with the online **Venezia Unica City Pass** (www.veneziaunica.it). This all-in-one pass can be used for public transportation and entry to museums, churches, and other attractions; you only pay for the services you wish to add. You'll receive an email with the pass, which you can show for entry at sights, though you'll still need to physically collect your transportation pass at an ACTV automatic ticket machine or ticket point located around the city.

Fifteen of Venice's most significant churches covered by the Venezia Unica City Pass are part of the **Chorus Foundation** umbrella group (*041/2750462,* www. chorusvenezia.org), which coordinates their administration, hours, and admission fees. Churches in this group are open to visitors all day except Sunday morning. Single church entry costs €3; you have a year to visit all 15 with the €12 Chorus Pass, which you can get at any participating church or online.

The Museum Pass (€35) from **Musei Civici** (*041/2405211,* www.visitmuve.it/en/ tickets) includes single entry to 12 Venice city museums for six months.

Tours

Venice has a variety of tours with expert guides; just be sure to choose a guide that's authorized if you book a private tour. Some excursions also include a boat tour as a portion of a longer walking tour.

PRIVATE TOURS
A Guide in Venice
GUIDED TOURS | This popular company offers a wide variety of innovative, entertaining, and informative themed tours—including master artisan, art, and architecture tours—for groups of up to eight people. Individual tours are also available and generally last two to three hours. The guide fee is €75 per hour, which does not include admissions or transportation fees. Small group tours running May–October are also available at €62.50 per person. ☎ *0347/7876846 Sabrina Scaglianti* ⊕ *www.aguideinvenice.com.*

Continued on page 202

CRUISING THE GRAND CANAL

THE BEST INTRODUCTION TO VENICE IS A TRIP DOWN MAIN STREET

Venice's Grand Canal is one of the world's great thoroughfares. It winds its way from Piazzale Roma to Piazza San Marco, passing 200 palazzi built from the 13th to the 18th centuries by Venice's richest and most powerful families. There's a theatrical quality to a boat ride on the canal: it's as if each pink- or gold-tinted facade is trying to steal your attention from its rival across the way.

In medieval and Renaissance cities, wars and sieges required defense to be an element of design; but in rich, impregnable Venice, you could safely show off what you had. But more than being simply an item of conspicuous consumption, a Venetian's palazzo was an embodiment of his person—not only his wealth, but also his erudition and taste.

The easiest and cheapest way to see the Grand Canal is to take the Line 1 vaporetto (water bus) from Piazalle Roma to San Marco. The ride takes about 35 minutes. Invest in a day ticket and you can spend the better part of a day hopping on and off at the vaporetto's many stops, visiting the sights along the banks. Keep your eyes open for the highlights listed here; some have fuller descriptions later in this chapter.

FROM PIAZZALE ROMA TO RIALTO

Palazzo Labia
Tiepolo's masterpiece, the cycle of Antony and Cleopatra, graces the grand ballroom in this palazzo. The Labia family, infamous for their ostentation, commissioned the frescos to celebrate a marriage and had Tiepolo use the face of the family matriarch, Maria Labia, for that of Cleopatra. Luckily, Maria Labia was known not only for her money, but also for her intelligence and her beauty.

Santa Maria di Nazareth

Ponte di Scalzi

R. Di BIAS

Stazione Ferrovia Santa Lucia

FERROVIA

SANTA CROCE

Ponte di Calatrava

After you pass the Ferrovia, the baroque church immediately to your left is the Baroque **Santa Maria di Nazareth**, called the Chiesa degli Scalzi (Church of the Barefoot).

After passing beneath the Ponte di Scalzi, ahead to the left, where the Canale di Cannaregio meets the Grand Canal, you'll spy **Palazzo Labia**, an elaborate 18th-century palace built for the social-climbing Labia family.

Known for their ostentation even in this city where modesty was seldom a virtue, the Labias chose a location that required three facades instead of the usual one.

A bit farther down, across the canal, is the 13th-century **Fondaco dei Turchi**, an elegant residence that served as a combination commercial center and ghetto for the Turkish community. Try not to see the side towers and the crenellations; they were

added during a 19th-century restoration.

Beyond it is the obelisk-topped **Ca' Belloni-Battagia**, designed for the Belloni family by star architect Longhena. Look for the family crest he added prominently on the facade.

On the opposite bank is architect Mauro Codussi's magnificent **Palazzo Vendramin-Calergi**, designed just before 1500. Codussi ingeniously married the fortress-like Renaissance style of the Florentine Alberti's Palazzo Rucellai to the lacy delicacy of the Venetian Gothic, creating the prototype of the Venetian Renaissance palazzo. The palazzo is now Venice's casino.

Palazzo Vendramin-Calergi
Venice's first Renaissance palazzo. Immediately recognized as a masterpiece, it was so highly regarded that later, when its subsequent owners, the Calergi, were convicted of murder and their palace was to be torn down as punishment, the main building was spared.

Ca' d'Oro
Inspired by stories of Nero's Domus Aurea (Golden House) in Rome, the first owner had parts of the façade gilded with 20,000 sheets of gold leaf. The gold has long worn away, but the Ca' D'Oro is still Venice's most beautiful Gothic palazzo.

Ca' da Mosto
Venice's oldest surviving palazzo gives you an idea of Marco Polo's Venice. More than any other Byzantine palazzo in town, it maintains its original 13th-century appearance.

Ca' Belloni-Battagia

S. MARCUOLA

S. STAE

Ca' Pesaro

ondaco dei Turchi

Depositi del Megio

San Stae Church

SAN POLO

Ca' Corner della Regina

CA' D'ORO

Rialto Mercato

Pescheria
Stop by in the morning to see the incredible variety of fish for sale. Produce stalls fill the adjacent fondamenta. Butchers and cheesemongers occupy the surrounding shops.

Fondaco dei Tedeschi

Ca' dei Camerlenghi

RIALTO

SAN MARCO

The whimsically Baroque church of **San Stae** on the right bank is distinguished by a host of marble saints on its facade.

Farther along the bank is one of Longhena's Baroque masterpieces, **Ca' Pesaro**. It is now the Museum of Modern Art.

Next up on the left is **Ca' d'Oro** (1421-1438), the canal's most spendid example of Venetian Gothic domestic design. Across from this palazzo is the loggia of the neo-Gothic **pescheria**, Venice's fish market.

Slightly farther down, on the bank opposite from the vegetable market, is the early 13th-century **Ca' da Mosto**, the oldest building on the Grand Canal. The upper two floors are later additions, but the ground floor and piano nobile give you a good idea of a rich merchant's house during the time of Marco Polo.

As you approach the Rialto Bridge, to the left, just before the bridge, is the **Fondaco dei Tedeschi**. German merchants kept warehouses, offices, and residences here; its facade was originally frescoed by Titian and Giorgione.

FROM RIALTO TO THE PONTE DELL' ACCADEMIA

Ca' Foscari
The canal's most imposing Gothic masterpiece, Ca' Foscari was built to blot out the memory of a traitor to the Republic.

SAN POLO

Ponte di Rialto

RIA

Palazzo Barzizza

Ca' Loredan

S. SILVESTRO

Ca' Farsetti

Palazzo Pisani Moretta

Ca' Grimani

S. ANGELO

TOMA

Ca' Garzoni

Ca' Balbi

Palazzo Grassi

Ca' Rezzonico

REZZONICO

SAN MARCO

ACCADEMIA

Gallerie dell'Accademia

DORSODURO

The shop-lined **Ponte di Rialto** was built in stone after former wooden bridges had burned or collapsed. As you pass under the bridge, on your left stands star architect Sansovino's Palazzo Dolfin Manin. The white stone–clad Renaissance palace was built at huge expense and over the objections of its conservative neighbors.

A bit farther down stand **Ca' Loredan** and **Ca' Farsetti**, 13th-century Byzantine palaces that today make up Venice's city hall.

Along the same side is the **Ca' Grimani**, by the Veronese architect Sanmichele. Legend has it that the palazzo's oversized windows were demanded by the young Grimani's fiancée,

who insisted that he build her a palazzo on the Canale Grande with windows larger than the portal of her own house.

At the Sant'Angelo landing, the vaporetto passes close to Codussi's **Ca' Corner-Spinelli**. Back on the right bank, in a lovely salmon color, is the graceful **Palazzo Pisani Moretta**, built in the mid-15th century and typical of the Venetian Gothic palazzo of the generation after the Ca' D'Oro.

A bit farther down the right bank, crowned by obelisks, is **Ca' Balbi**. Niccolò Balbi built this elegant palazzo in order to upstage his former landlord, who had insulted him in public.

Farther down the right bank, where the Canale makes a sharp turn, is the imposing

Ca' Foscari. Doge Francesco Foscari tore down an earlier palazzo on this spot and built this splendid palazzo to erase memory of the traitorous former owner. It is now the seat of the University of Venice.

Continuing down the right bank you'll find Longhena's **Ca' Rezzonico**, a magnificent baroque palace. Opposite stands the Grand Canal's youngest palace, Giorgio Massari's **Palazzo Grassi**, commissioned in 1749. It houses part of the François Pinot contemporary art collection.

Near the canal's fourth bridge, is the former church and monastery complex that houses the world-renowned **Gallerie dell'Accademia**, the world's largest and most distinguished collection of Venetian art.

ARCHITECTURAL STYLES ALONG THE GRAND CANAL

BYZANTINE: 13th century
Distinguishing characteristics: high, rounded arches, relief panels, multicolored marble.
Examples: Fondaco dei Turchi, Ca' Loredan, Ca' Farsetti, Ca' da Mosto

GOTHIC: 14th and 15th centuries
Distinguishing characteristics: pointed arches, high ceilings, and many windows.
Examples: Ca' d'Oro, Ca' Foscari, Palazzo Pisani Moretta, Ca' Barbaro (and, off the canal, Palazzo Ducale)

RENAISSANCE: 16th century
Distinguishing characteristics: classically influenced emphasis on harmony and motifs taken from classical antiquity.

Examples: Palazzo Vendramin-Calergi, Ca' Grimani, Ca' Corner-Spinelli, Ca' dei Camerlenghi, Ca' Balbi, Palazzo Corner della Ca' Granda, Palazzo Dolfin Manin, and, off the canal, Libreria, Sansoviniana on Piazza San Marco

BAROQUE: 17th century
Distinguishing characteristics: Renaissance order wedded with a more dynamic style, achieved through curving lines and complex decoration.

Examples: churches of Santa Maria di Nazareth, San Stae, and Santa Maris della Salute; Ca' Belloni Battaglia, Ca' Pesaro, Ca' Rezzonico

FROM THE PONTE DELL'ACCADEMIA TO SAN ZACCARIA

Ca' Barbaro
John Singer Sargent, Henry James, and Cole Porter are among the guests who have stayed at Ca' Barbaro. It was a center for elegant British and American society during the turn of the 20th century.

Santa Maria Della Salute
Baldessare Longhena was only 26 when he designed this church, which was to become one of Venice's major landmar. Its rotunda form and dynamic Baroque decoration predate iconic Baroque churches in other Italian cities.

SAN MARCO

Ponte dell' Accademia

ACCADEMIA

Ca' Pisani-Gritti

Palazzo Corner della Ca' Granda

DORSODURO

Casetta Rossa

S. M. DEL GIGLIO

Ca' Barbarigo

SALUTE

Palazzo Salviati

Palazzo Venier dei Leoni
Eccentric art dealer Peggy Guggenheim's personal collection of modern art is here. At the Grand Canal entrance to the palazzo stands Marino Marini's sexually explicit equestrian sculpture, the Angel of the Citadel. Numerous entertaining stories have been spun around the statue and Ms. Guggenheim's overtly libertine ways.

S. Maria della Salute

Ca' Dario
Graceful and elegant Ca' Dario is reputed to carry a curse. Almost all its owners since the 15th century have met violent deaths or committed suicide. It was, nevertheless, a center for elegant French society at the turn of the 20th century.

Down from the Accademia bridge, on the left bank next door to the fake Gothic Ca' Franchetti, is the beautiful **Ca' Barbaro**, designed by Giovanni Bon, who was also at work about that time on the Ca' D'Oro.

Farther along on the left bank Sansovino's first work in Venice, the **Palazzo Corner della Ca' Granda**, begun in 1533, still shows the influence of his Roman Renaissance contemporaries, Bramante and Giulio Romano. It faces the uncompleted **Palazzo Venier dei Leoni**, which holds the Peggy Guggenheim Collection, a good cross-section of the visual arts from 1940 to 1960.

Ca' Dario a bit farther down, was originally a Gothic palazzo, but in 1487 it was given an early Renaissance multi-colored marble facade.

At this point on the canal the cupola of **Santa Maria della Salute** dominates the scene. The commission for the design of the church to celebrate the Virgin's rescuing Venice from the disastrous plague of 1630, was given to the 26-year-old Longhena. The young architect stressed the new and inventive aspects of his design, likening the rotunda shape to a crown for the Virgin.

Basilica di S. Marco

Palazzo Ducale

PIAZZA
SAN MARCO

S. ZACCARIA

VALLARESSO

Palazzo
Dandolo
a San Moise

Punta della Dogana

The Grand Canal is 2½ miles
long, has an average depth
of 9 feet, and is 76 yards wide
at its broadest point and 40
yards at its narrowest.

SAN GIORGIO
MAGGIORE

Across from the Salute,
enjoying the magnificent
view across the canal, are
a string of luxury hotels
whose historic facades
have either been radically
modified or are modern
neo-Gothic fantasies. The
main interest here is the
rather unimposing Hotel
Monaco e Gran Canal, the
former Palazzo Dandolo a
San Moise, which contains
Europe's first casino, the
famous ridotto, founded
in 1638. It was a stomping
ground of Casanova, and
was closed by the Republic
in 1774 because too much
money was being lost to
foreigners.

At the **Punta della Dogana**
on the tip of Dorsoduro, Japanese architect Tadao Ando,
using Zen-inspired concepts
of space, has transformed
a 17th–century customs
house into a museum for
contemporary art. It is a fitting coda to the theme of
Venice as living center for
international artistic creativ-
ity, as set by Calatrava's
bridge at the beginning of
the Grand Canal.

At the Vallaresso vaporetto
stop you've left the Grand
Canal, but stay on board
for a view of the **Palazzo
Ducale**, with **Basilica di
San Marco** behind it, then
disembark at San Zaccaria.

See Venice

GUIDED TOURS | Luisella Romeo is a delightful guide capable of bringing to life even the most convoluted aspects of Venice's art and history. She can customize tours depending on guests' areas of interest, including Murano and glass art, music in Venice, and photography tours. ☎ 0349/0848303 ⊕ www.seevenice.it.

Walks Inside Venice

GUIDED TOURS | For a host of particularly creative group and private tours—from history to art to gastronomy—check out Walks Inside Venice. The maximum group size is 6, and tour guides include people with advanced university degrees and published authors. ☎ 041/5241706, 041/2750687 ⊕ www.walksinsidevenice. com.

Visitor Information

The multilingual staff of the **Venice tourism office** (041/2424, www.veneziaunica.it) can provide directions and up-to-the-minute information. Branches can be found at Marco Polo Airport; the Venezia Santa Lucia train station; Garage Comunale, on Piazzale Roma; and at Piazza San Marco near Museo Correr at the southwest corner. The train station branch is open daily 7–9; other branches have similar hours.

San Marco

Extending from Piazza San Marco (St. Mark's Square) to the Ponte di Rialto, this sestiere is the historical and commercial heart of Venice. Restaurants in its eponymous square—the only one in Venice given full stature as a "piazza" and, hence, often referred to simply as "the Piazza"—heave with tourists, but enjoying an aperitivo here is an unforgettable experience.

This sestiere is also graced with some of Venice's loveliest churches, best-endowed museums, and finest hotels (often with Grand Canal views). In addition, it's the city's main shopping district. Some of the famous Venetian glass producers from Murano have boutiques in San Marco, as do many Italian designers. Its mazes of streets are also lined with shops that sell elegantly wrought jewelry among other items.

TIMING

You can easily spend several days seeing the historical and artistic monuments in and around Piazza San Marco alone, but at a bare minimum, plan on at least an hour for the basilica and its wonderful mosaics. Add on another half hour if you want to see its Pala d'Oro, Galleria, and Museo di San Marco. You'll want at least an hour to appreciate the Palazzo Ducale. Leave another hour for the Museo Correr, through which you also enter the archaeological museum and the Libreria Sansoviniana. If you choose to simply take in the piazza itself from a café table at an establishment with an orchestra, keep in mind there will be an additional charge for the music.

 Sights

⭐ **Basilica di San Marco**

CHURCH | The Basilica di San Marco is not only the religious center of a great city, but also an expression of the political, intellectual, and economic aspiration and accomplishments of a place that, for centuries, was at the forefront of European culture. It is a monument not just to the glory of God, but also to the glory of Venice. The basilica was the doges' personal chapel, linking its religious function to the political life of the city, and was endowed with all the riches the Republic's admirals and merchants could carry off from the Orient (as the Byzantine Empire was then known), earning it the nickname "Chiesa D'Oro," (Golden Church). When the present church was begun in the 11th century, rare colored marbles and gold leaf mosaics were used in its decoration. The 12th and 13th centuries were a period of intense military expansion, and by the early 13th century, the facades began to bear testimony to Venice's conquests, including gilt-bronze ancient Roman horses taken from Constantinople in 1204. The low lighting, the single massive Byzantine chandelier, the giant iconostasis (altar screen), the matroneum (women's gallery) high above the naves—even the Greek-cross ground plan—give San Marco an exotic aspect quite unlike that of most Western Christian churches. The effect is remarkable. Here the pomp and mystery of Oriental magnificence are wedded to Christian belief, creating an intensely awesome impression. The glory of the basilica is, of course, its medieval mosaic work; about 30% of the mosaics survive in something close to their original form. The earliest date from the late 12th century, but the great majority date from the 13th century. The taking of Constantinople in 1204 was a deciding moment for the mosaic decoration of the basilica. Large amounts of mosaic material were brought in, and a Venetian school of mosaic decoration began to develop. Moreover, a 4th- or 5th-century treasure—the Cotton Genesis, the earliest illustrated Bible—was brought from Constantinople and supplied the designs for the exquisite mosaics of the Creation and the stories of Abraham, Joseph, and Moses that adorn the narthex (entrance hall). They are among the most beautiful and best preserved in all the basilica. In the Sanctuary, the main altar is built over the tomb of St. Mark, its green marble canopy lifted high on 6th-century carved alabaster columns—again, pillaged art. The Pala d'Oro, a dazzling gilt-silver, gem-encrusted screen containing 255 enameled panels, was commissioned in 976 in Constantinople by the Venetian doge Pietro I Orseolo and enlarged over the subsequent four centuries. Remember that this is a sacred place: guards may deny admission to people in shorts, sleeveless dresses, and tank tops. ✉ Piazza San Marco, San Marco 328, San

Marco ☎ 041/2708311 ⊕ www.basilicasanmarco.it ✎ Basilica €3, treasury €3, sanctuary and Pala d'Oro €5, museum €7 Ⓜ Vallaresso/San Zaccaria.

Campanile

VIEWPOINT | Construction of Venice's famous brick bell tower (325 feet tall, plus the angel) began in the 9th century; it took on its present form in 1514. During the 15th century, the tower was used as a place of punishment: immoral clerics were suspended in wooden cages from the tower, some forced to subsist on bread and water for as long as a year; others were left to starve. In 1902, the tower unexpectedly collapsed, taking with it Jacopo Sansovino's marble loggia (1537–49) at its base. The largest original bell, called the Marangona, survived. The crushed loggia was promptly reconstructed, and the new tower, rebuilt to the old plan, reopened in 1912. Today, on a clear day the stunning view includes the Lido, the lagoon, and the mainland as far as the Alps, but strangely enough, none of the myriad canals that snake through the city. ✉ Piazza San Marco ☎ 041/2708311 ⊕ www.basilicasanmarco.it ✎ €10 Ⓜ Vaporetto: Vallaresso, San Zaccaria.

★ Museo Correr

HISTORY MUSEUM | This museum of Venetian art and history contains an important sculpture collection by Antonio Canova and important paintings by Giovanni Bellini, Vittore Carpaccio (Carpaccio's famous painting of the Venetian courtesans is here), and other major local painters. There are nine sumptuously decorated Imperial Rooms, where the Empress of Austria once stayed, and several rooms convey the city's proud naval history through highly descriptive paintings and numerous maritime objects, including ships' cannons and some surprisingly large iron mast-top navigation lights. The museum also houses curiosities like the absurdly high-soled shoes worn by 16th-century Venetian ladies (who walked with the aid of a servant) and has

Piazza San Marco

A   **B**   **C**   **D**   **E**

Riva del Ferro

Calle Larga

R. Barizza

Campo S. Sa...

Grand Canal

C. Bembo

Cor. d'
Appello

Cor. del
Teatro

C. d. Carbon

C. dei Cavalli

C. Loredan

C. S. Antonio

Saliz
S. Luca

C. d.
Teatro Ovo

C. d.
Forno

C. S.
Luca

C. della Vida

R. di S. Luca

della Locanda

Campo
S. Luca

C. d.
Magazer

C. S. Andrea

C. Ilo
S. Luca

Campo
Manin

C. Carlo Goldoni

Saliz del Teatro

C. S. Paternian

C. del
Magazen

C. d. Cortesia

C. d. Mandola

R. Terrà degli Assassini

R. d.
Madonna

C. d.
Madonna

C. del
Caffettier

**Palazzo Contarini
del Bovolo** ◆

R.d. Fuseri

R. d.
Fuseri

Calle dei Fuseri

Calle Colonna

Rio della Verona

C. Venier

C. d. Fruttarol Frezzeria

C. Venier

C. Brentana

C. di Piscina

Campo
Sant'Angelo

C. della
Verona

C. Minelli

Rio del Bacaroli

C. d. Carro

C. Bognolo

Calle del Pestrin

Campo San Barnaba

5 ◀

1

Santa Stefano ◆

Campo
S. Fantin

C. dietro
la Chiesa

R.d. Veste

S

MA

R. 1ª Conta

Campo
Santo
Stefano

Calle della Spezier

Rio dietro
la Fenice

C. d. Fenice

R. d. Fenice

Piscine
S. Moisè

C. d.
Cristo

C. del
Squero

Campo
S. Moisè

1

Calle Dose da Ponte

Calle Zaguri

C. Piovan
Gritti

Cor.
Michiel

Sol. de
la Vicenza

C. Veste

Via 22 Marzo

**Santa Maria
del Giglio** ◆

C. d. Ostreghe

Campo
S. Maria
Zobenigo

2 ↓

Fond.
Ostreghe

C. d. Pestrin

C. Bergamaschi

C. del Teatro

C. Pedrocchi

3

C. Barozzi

Rio di S. Moisè

4

5

Cor.
Barozzi

---

a significant collection of antique gems. It's also the main repository of Venetian drawings and prints, which, unfortunately, can be seen only by special arrangement, or during special exhibitions. The Correr exhibition rooms lead directly into the **Museo Archeologico,** which houses the Grimani collection—an important 16th- and 17th-century collection of Greek and Roman art, still impressive even after the transfer of many objects to Paris and Vienna during the Napoleonic and Austrian occupations—and the Stanza del Sansovino, the only part of the **Biblioteca Nazionale Marciana** open to visitors. ⊠ *Piazza San Marco, Ala Napoleonica, opposite basilica, Piazza San Marco* ☎ *041/2405211* ⊕ *correr.visitmuve.it* ↻ *The tour is currently limited to the first floor only, including the Procuratie Nuove and Imperial Apartments.* ⌷ *Museums of San Marco Pass €25, includes Museo Correr, Museo Archeologico, Biblioteca Nazionale Marciana, and Palazzo Ducale. Museum Pass €36, includes all four museums plus eight civic museums* Ⓜ *Vaporetto: Vallaresso, San Zaccaria.*

★ **Palazzo Ducale** (*Doge's Palace*)
HISTORY MUSEUM | Rising grandly above the Piazzetta San Marco, this Gothic fantasia of pink-and-white marble is a majestic expression of Venetian prosperity and power. Although the site was the doges' residence from the 10th century, the building began to take its present form around 1340; what you see now is essentially a product of the first half of the 15th century. It served not only as a residence, but also as the central administrative center of the Venetian Republic. Unlike other medieval seats of authority, the Palazzo Ducale is free of any military defenses—a sign of the Republic's self-confidence. The position of the loggias below instead of above the retaining wall, and the use of pink marble to emphasize the decorative function of that wall, gave the palazzo a light and airy aspect, one that could impress visitors—and even intimidate them,

through opulence and grace rather than fortresslike bulk. You'll find yourself in an immense courtyard that holds some of the first evidence of Renaissance architecture in Venice, such as Antonio Rizzo's Scala dei Giganti (Stairway of the Giants), erected between 1483 and 1491, directly ahead, guarded by Sansovino's huge statues of Mars and Neptune, added in 1567. Though ordinary mortals must use the central interior staircase, its upper flight is the lavishly gilded Scala d'Oro (Golden Staircase), also designed by Sansovino, in 1555. The palace's sumptuous chambers have walls and ceilings covered with works by Venice's greatest artists. Visit the Anticollegio, a waiting room outside the Collegio's chamber, where you can see the *Rape of Europa* by Veronese and Tintoretto's *Bacchus, Ariadne,* and *Venus.* The ceiling of the Sala del Senato (Senate Chamber), featuring *The Triumph of Venice* by Tintoretto, is magnificent, but it's dwarfed by his masterpiece, *Paradise,* in the Sala del Maggiore Consiglio (Great Council Hall). A vast work commissioned for a vast hall, this dark, dynamic piece is the world's largest oil painting (23 feet by 75 feet). The room's carved gilt ceiling is breathtaking, especially with Veronese's majestic *Apotheosis of Venice* filling one of the center panels. A narrow canal separates the palace's east side from the cramped cell blocks of the Prigioni Nuove (New Prisons). High above the water arches the enclosed marble Ponte dei Sospiri (Bridge of Sighs), which earned its name in the 19th century, from Lord Byron's *Childe Harold's Pilgrimage.* Reserve your spot for the palazzo's popular Secret Itineraries tour well in advance. You'll visit the doge's private apartments, through hidden passageways to the interrogation (torture) chambers, and into the rooftop *piombi* (lead) prison, named for its lead roofing. Venetian-born writer and libertine Giacomo Casanova (1725–98), along with an accomplice, managed to escape from the piombi in 1756; they were the only men ever to do so.

Let's Get Lost

Getting around Venice presents some unusual problems: the city's layout has few straight lines; house numbering seems nonsensical; and the six sestieri of San Marco, Cannaregio, Castello, Dorsoduro, Santa Croce, and San Polo all duplicate each other's street names. What's more, addresses in Venice are given by sestiere rather than street, making them of limited help in getting around. Venetians commonly give directions by pinpointing a major landmark, such as a church, and telling you where to go from there.

The numerous vaporetto lines can be bewildering, too, and often the only option for getting where you want to go is to walk. Yellow signs, posted on many busy corners, point toward the major landmarks—San Marco, Rialto, Accademia, and so forth—but don't count on finding such markers once you're deep into residential neighborhoods. Even buying a good map at a newsstand—the kind showing all street names and vaporetto routes—won't necessarily keep you from getting lost. To make matters worse, map apps on smart phones, for some reason, give frequently erroneous results for Venice.

Fortunately, as long as you maintain your patience, getting lost in Venice can be a pleasure. For one thing, being lost is a sign that you've escaped the tourist throngs. And although you might not find the Titian masterpiece you'd set out to see, you could wind up coming across an ageless *bacaro* (a traditional wine bar) or a quirky shop that turns out to be the highlight of your afternoon. Opportunities for such serendipity abound. Keep in mind that the city is self-contained: sooner or later, perhaps with the help of a patient native, you can rest assured you'll regain your bearings.

⊠ *Piazzetta San Marco, Piazza San Marco* ☎ *041/42730892 tickets, 848/082000 outside Italy* ⊕ *palazzoducale.visitmuve. it* 🎫 *Museums of San Marco Pass €25, includes Palazzo Ducale, Museo Correr, Museo Archeologico, and Biblioteca Nazionale Marciana. Museum Pass €36, includes all four museums plus eight civic museums. Secret Itineraries tour €29* Ⓜ *Vaporetto: San Zaccaria, Vallaresso.*

Palazzo Grassi
ART MUSEUM | Built between 1748 and 1772 by Giorgio Massari for a Bolognese family, this palace is one of the last of the great noble residences on the Grand Canal. Once owned by auto magnate Gianni Agnelli, it was bought by French businessman François Pinault in 2005 to showcase his highly esteemed collection of modern and contemporary art (which has now grown so large that Pinault rented the Punta della Dogana, at the entryway to the Grand Canal, for his newest acquisitions). Pinault brought in Japanese architect Tadao Ando to remodel the Grassi's interior. Check online for a schedule of temporary art exhibitions. ⊠ *Campo San Samuele 3231, San Marco* ☎ *041/2001057* ⊕ *www.palazzograssi.it* 🎫 *€15* Ⓜ *Vaporetto: Sant'Angelo (Line 1).*

★ Piazza San Marco
PLAZA/SQUARE | **FAMILY** | One of the world's most beautiful squares, Piazza San Marco (St. Mark's Square) is the spiritual and artistic heart of Venice, a vast open space bordered by an orderly procession of arcades marching toward the fairy-tale cupolas and marble

lacework of the Basilica di San Marco. From midmorning on, it is generally packed with tourists. (If Venetians have business in the piazza, they try to conduct it in the early morning, before the crowds swell.) At night the piazza can be magical, especially in winter, when mists swirl around the lampposts and the campanile. Facing the basilica, on your left, the long, arcaded building is the Procuratie Vecchie, renovated to its present form in 1514 as offices and residences for the powerful procurators, or magistrates. On your right is the Procuratie Nuove, built half a century later in a more imposing, classical style. It was originally planned by Venice's great Renaissance architect Jacopo Sansovino (1486–1570), to carry on the look of his Libreria Sansoviniana (Sansovinian Library), but he died before construction on the Nuove had begun. Vincenzo Scamozzi (circa 1552–1616), a pupil of Andrea Palladio (1508–80), completed the design and construction. Still later, the Procuratie Nuove was modified by architect Baldassare Longhena (1598–1682), one of Venice's Baroque masters. When Napoléon (1769–1821) entered Venice with his troops in 1797, he expressed his admiration for the piazza and promptly gave orders to alter it. His architects demolished a church with a Sansovino facade in order to build the Ala Napoleonica (Napoleonic Wing), or Fabbrica Nuova (New Building), which linked the two 16th-century procuratie and effectively enclosed the piazza. Piazzetta San Marco is the "little square" leading from Piazza San Marco to the waters of Bacino San Marco (St. Mark's Basin); its *molo* (landing) once served as the grand entrance to the Republic. Two imposing columns tower above the waterfront. One is topped by the winged lion, a traditional emblem of St. Mark that became the symbol of Venice itself; the other supports St. Theodore, the city's first patron, along with his dragon. (A third column fell off its barge and ended up in the bacino before it could be placed alongside the others.) Although the columns are a glorious vision today, the Republic traditionally executed convicts here—and some superstitious Venetians still avoid walking between them. ⊠ *San Marco* Ⓜ *Vaporetto: Calle Valaresso, Giardinetti, or San Zaccaria*

★ **Ponte di Rialto** (*Rialto Bridge*)
BRIDGE | FAMILY | The competition to design a stone bridge across the Grand Canal attracted the best architects of the late 16th century, including Michelangelo, Palladio, and Sansovino, but the job went to the less famous (if appropriately named) Antonio da Ponte (1512–95). His pragmatic design, completed in 1591, featured shop space and was high enough for galleys to pass beneath. Putting practicality and economy over aesthetic considerations—unlike the classical plans proposed by his more famous contemporaries—da Ponte's bridge essentially followed the design of its wooden predecessor. But it kept decoration and cost to a minimum at a time when the Republic's coffers were low, due to continual wars against the Turks and competition brought about by the Spanish and Portuguese opening of oceanic trade routes. Along the railing you'll enjoy one of the city's most famous views: the Grand Canal vibrant with boat traffic. ⊠ *San Marco* Ⓜ *Vaporetto: Rialto.*

🍴 Restaurants

Enoteca al Volto
$$ | VENETIAN | A short walk from the Ponte di Rialto, this bar has been around since 1936, and the satisfying cicheti and primi have a lot to do with its staying power. Grab one of the tables out front, or take refuge in two small, dark rooms with a ceiling plastered with wine labels

that provide a classic backdrop for simple fare, including a delicious risotto that is served daily from noon, plus a solid wine list of both Italian and foreign vintages. **Known for:** fantastic main courses, including risotto and pasta with seafood; great local and international wine selection; tasty and inexpensive cicheti. $ *Average main: €17* ⊠ *Calle Cavalli, San Marco 4081, San Marco* ☎ *041/5228945* ⊕ *enotecaalvolto.com* Ⓜ *Vaporetto: Rialto.*

⭐ **Harry's Bar**

$$$$ | **VENETIAN** | For those who can afford it, lunch or dinner at Harry's Bar is as much a part of a visit to Venice as a walk across the Piazza San Marco or a vaporetto ride down the Grand Canal. Inside, the suave, subdued beige-on-white decor is unchanged from the 1930s, and the classic Venetian fare is carefully and excellently prepared. **Known for:** signature crepes flambées and famous Cipriani chocolate cake; being the birthplace of the Bellini cocktail; see-and-be-seen atmosphere. $ *Average main: €58* ⊠ *Calle Vallaresso, San Marco 1323, San Marco* ☎ *041/5285777* ⊕ *www.cipriani. com* 🍸 *Jacket required* Ⓜ *Vaporetto: San Marco (Calle Vallaresso).*

⭐ **Ristorante Quadri**

$$$$ | **VENETIAN** | Although the lavish interior has been updated by designer Philippe Starck, this restaurant above the famed café of the same name is still steeped in Venetian ambience and history (it was where Turkish coffee was introduced to the city in the 1700s). When the Alajmo family (of the celebrated Le Calandre near Padua) took over, they put their accomplished sous-chef from Padua in charge of the kitchen, resulting in the addition of dishes—best sampled with a tasting menu—that are complex and sophisticated, with a wonderful wine list to match. **Known for:** revitalized designer decor; seasonal tasting menus; sophisticated and modern Italian cuisine. $ *Average main: €60* ⊠ *Piazza San Marco 121, San Marco* ☎ *041/5222105* ⊕ *alajmo.it*

🕐 *Closed Mon. and Tues. No lunch Wed.– Fri.* Ⓜ *Vaporetto: San Marco.*

🍴 Coffee and Quick Bites

Bar all'Angolo

$ | **CAFÉ** | This corner of Campo Santo Stefano is a pleasant place to sit and watch the Venetian world go by. The café staff are in constant motion, so you'll receive your coffee, spritz, panino, or *tramezzino* (sandwich on untoasted white bread, usually with a mayonnaise-based filling) in short order; consume it at your leisure at one of the outdoor tables, at the bar, or at the tables in the back. **Known for:** good people-watching; simple yet satisfying fare, like tramezzini and panini; tasty homemade desserts, including tiramisu and cakes. $ *Average main: €10* ⊠ *Campo Santo Stefano, San Marco 3464, just in front of Santo Stefano church, San Marco* ☎ *041/5220710* 🕐 *Closed Sun. and Jan.* Ⓜ *Vaporetto: Sant'Angelo.*

⭐ Caffè Florian

$$ | **CAFÉ** | Florian is not only Italy's first café (1720), but also one of its most beautiful, with glittering, neo-Baroque decor and 19th-century wall panels depicting Venetian heroes. The coffee, drinks, and snacks are good, but most people—including Venetians from time to time—come for the atmosphere and history: this was the only café to serve women during the 18th century (hence Casanova's patronage); it was frequented by artistic notables like Wagner, Goethe, Goldoni, Lord Byron, Marcel Proust, and Charles Dickens; and it was the birthplace of the international art exhibition that became the Venice Biennale. **Known for:** hot chocolate, coffee, and quick nibbles; prime location on St. Mark's Square; beautiful, historic interior. $ *Average main: €16* ⊠ *Piazza San Marco, San Marco 56, San Marco* ☎ *041/5205641* ⊕ *www.caffeflorian.com* 🕐 *Closed early Jan.* Ⓜ *Vaporetto: San Marco.*

★ Gran Caffè Quadri

$$ | **CAFÉ** | Come for breakfast, a pre-dinner aperitivo, or anything in between at this always lively historic coffeehouse—opened in 1775 and taken over by the famous culinary Alajmo family in 2011—in the center of the action on Piazza San Marco. Choose from a wide selection of pastries at breakfast (though the cappuccino and brioche combo is always a classic), pizzas at lunch, and *tramezzini* all day long, including one with lobster. **Known for:** prime people-watching; extensive (though pricey) aperitivo; celebrity owners. ⑤ *Average main: €17* ✉ *Piazza San Marco, San Marco 121, San Marco* ☎ *041/5222105* ⊕ *www.alajmo.it* Ⓜ *Vaporetto: San Marco.*

 ## Hotels

Bauer Palazzo

$$$$ | **HOTEL** | This palazzo with an ornate 1930s neo-Gothic facade facing the Grand Canal has large (by Venetian standards), lavishly decorated guest rooms with high ceilings, tufted walls of Bevilacqua and Rubelli fabrics, Murano glass, marble bathrooms, damask drapes, and reproduction antique furniture. **Pros:** pampering service; Venice's highest rooftop terrace; high-end luxury. **Cons:** decor could be a bit dark and old-fashioned for some; furnishings are, as is the facade, an imitation; no spa on-site. ⑤ *Rooms from: €406* ✉ *Campo San Moisè, San Marco 1413/D, San Marco* ☎ *041/5207022* ⊕ *www.bauervenezia. com* ⦿ *No Meals* ⇲ *191 rooms* Ⓜ *Vaporetto: Vallaresso.*

★ The Gritti Palace

$$$$ | **HOTEL** | With handblown chandeliers, sumptuous textiles, and sweeping canal views, this grande dame (whose history dates from 1525, when it was built as the residence of the prominent Gritti family) represents aristocratic Venetian living at its best. **Pros:** classic Venetian experience; truly historical property; Grand Canal location. **Cons:** food served at the hotel gets mixed reviews; major

splurge; few spa amenities. ⑤ *Rooms from: €1000* ✉ *Campo Santa Maria del Giglio, San Marco 2467, San Marco* ☎ *041/794611* ⊕ *www.thegrittipalace. com* ⇲ *82 rooms* ⦿ *No Meals* Ⓜ *Vaporetto: Santa Maria del Giglio.*

Hotel Flora

$$ | **HOTEL** | The elegant and refined facade announces a charming, and reasonably priced, place to stay; the hospitable staff, the tastefully decorated rooms, and the lovely garden, where guests can breakfast or drink, do not disappoint. **Pros:** central location; excellent breakfast; peaceful hidden garden. **Cons:** old-fashioned lobby doesn't invite hanging out; no water views; some rooms can be on the small side. ⑤ *Rooms from: €160* ✉ *Calle Bergamaschi, San Marco 2283/A, just off Calle Larga XXII Marzo, San Marco* ☎ *041/5205844* ⊕ *www.hotelflora.it* ⇲ *40 rooms* ⦿ *Free Breakfast* Ⓜ *Vaporetto: San Marco (Vallaresso).*

★ Novecento

$$ | **HOTEL** | A stylish yet intimate retreat tucked away on a quiet calle midway between Piazza San Marco and the Accademia Bridge offers exquisite rooms tastefully decorated with original furnishings and tapestries from the Mediterranean and Far East. **Pros:** complimentary afternoon tea; unique design sensibility; intimate, romantic atmosphere. **Cons:** most rooms only have showers, not tubs; some rooms can be noisy; no elevator. ⑤ *Rooms from: €170* ✉ *Calle del Dose, San Marco 2683/84, off Campo San Maurizio, San Marco* ☎ *041/2413765* ⊕ *www. novecento.biz* ⇲ *9 rooms* ⦿ *Free Breakfast* Ⓜ *Vaporetto: Santa Maria del Giglio.*

★ The St. Regis Venice

$$$$ | **HOTEL** | Whimsical design details evoking the Venetian landscape abound in this elegant, contemporary hotel (the former Westin Europa & Regina) constructed from five historic palazzi with phenomenal views onto the Grand Canal. **Pros:** terraces with unbeatable views; St. Regis butler service for all guests;

wonderful central location. **Cons:** few spa amenities (no pool or saunas); standard rooms on the small side; sleek modern style not for fans of Venetian opulence. ⧉ *Rooms from: €627* ⊠ *San Marco 2159, San Marco* ☎ *041/2400001* ⊕ *www.marriott.com/hotels/travel/vcexr-the-st-regis-venice* ⧉ *Free Breakfast* ⤳ *169 rooms* ⧉ *Vaporetto: Vallaresso.*

▼ Nightlife

B Bar Lounge

BARS | This gold mosaic-lined bar in the Bauer Venezia hosts live jazz bands Wednesday to Sunday nights, plus a late-night DJ on Friday and Saturday. ⊠ *Bauer Palazzo, Campo San Moisè, San Marco 1459, San Marco* ☎ *041/5207022* ⊕ *www.bbarvenezia.com* Ⓜ *Vaporetto: Vallaresso.*

Bacaro Jazz

BARS | This Venetian-style dive bar has strong cocktails, a jazz soundtrack, and hundreds of bras hanging from the ceiling. The lively daily happy hour is a great time to visit. ⊠ *San Marco 5546, San Marco* ☎ *041/5285249* ⊕ *bacarojazz. it* Ⓜ *Vaporetto: Rialto.*

★ Bar Longhi

BARS | The Gritti Palace is home to one of the most exclusive watering holes in town (though thankfully open to the public), lined with 18th-century paintings and Murano chandeliers. You can also enjoy your cocktail on the patio with prime views onto the Grand Canal. ⊠ *The Gritti Palace, Campo Santa Maria del Giglio, San Marco 2467, San Marco* ☎ *041/794611* ⊕ *www.thegrittipalace. com* Ⓜ *Vaporetto: Giglio.*

🛍 Shopping

Arnoldo/Battois

WOMEN'S CLOTHING | Venetian designers Silvano Arnoldo and Massimiliano Battois create beautifully crafted handbags, accessories, and women's clothing in rich

colors using luxurious materials. There's a second store in San Marco at Calle dei Fuseri. ⊠ *Campo San Maurizio, San Marco 2671, San Marco* ☎ *0348/4123797* ⊕ *www.arnoldoebattois.com* Ⓜ *Vaporetto: Giglio.*

★ Atelier Segalin di Daniela Ghezzo

SHOES | This artist turned master shoemaker produces one-of-a-kind creations from exotic leathers. Though the shoes start at €650 and usually take at least six weeks to finish, you'll truly feel like you're wearing a masterpiece. ⊠ *Calle dei Fuseri, San Marco 4365, San Marco* ☎ *041/5222115* ⊕ *www.danielaghezzo.it* Ⓜ *Vaporetto: Rialto.*

★ Bevilacqua

FABRICS | This renowned studio has kept the weaving tradition alive in Venice since 1875, using 18th-century hand looms for its most precious creations. Its repertoire of 3,500 different patterns and designs yields a ready-to-sell selection of hundreds of brocades, Gobelins, damasks, velvets, taffetas, and satins. You'll also find tapestry, cushions, and braiding. Fabrics made by this prestigious firm have been used to decorate the Vatican, the Royal Palace of Stockholm, and the White House. There is another location behind the San Marco Basilica. If you're interested in seeing the actual 18th-century looms in action making the most precious fabrics, request an appointment at the Luigi Bevilacqua production center in Santa Croce. ⊠ *Campo di Santa Maria del Giglio, San Marco 2520, San Marco* ☎ *041/2410662 main retail outlet, 041/5287581 retail outlet behind Basilica, 041/721566 Santa Croce production center* ⊕ *www.bevilacquatessuti.com* Ⓜ *Vaporetto: Giglio.*

★ Dittura Massimo

SHOES | Run by a second-generation shoemaker, this shop is one of the only places left in the city still producing Venice's iconic *friulane* slippers, invented in the 19th century and handstitched from velvet and rubber. The shoes are still worn by gondoliers today. ✉ *Calle Fiubera, San Marco 943, San Marco* ☎ *041/5231163* ⊕ *ditturamassimo.it* Ⓜ *Vaporetto: San Marco.*

Fondaco dei Tedeschi

HATS & GLOVES | This 15th-century Renaissance commercial center served as Venice's main post office for many years, but was remodeled and returned to its historical roots as a luxury department store. Here you can find a large assortment of high-end jewelry, clothing, and other luxury items, plus fabulous views from the rooftop terrace; book online for a free 15-minute visit. ✉ *Calle Fondaco dei Tedeschi, near San Marco end of Ponte di Rialto, San Marco* ☎ *041/3142000* ⊕ *www.dfs.com/en/venice/stores/t-fondaco-dei-tedeschi-by-dfs* Ⓜ *Vaporetto: Rialto.*

Giuliana Longo

SOUVENIRS | A hat shop that's been around since 1901 offers an assortment of Venetian and gondolier straw hats, Panama hats from Ecuador, caps and berets, and some select scarves of silk and fine wool; there's even a special corner dedicated to accessories for antique cars. ✉ *Calle del Lovo, San Marco 4813, San Marco* ☎ *041/5226454* ⊕ *www.giulianalongo.com* Ⓜ *Vaporetto: San Marco.*

★ Jesurum

FABRICS | A great deal of so-called Burano Venetian lace is now machine-made in China—and there really is a difference. Unless you have some experience, you're best off going to a trusted place. Jesurum has been the major producer of handmade Venetian lace since 1870. Its lace is, of course, all modern production, but if you want an antique piece, the people at Jesurum can point you in the right direction. ✉ *Calle Veste, San Marco 2024, San Marco* ☎ *041/5238969*

⊕ *www.jesurum.it* Ⓜ *Vaporetto: San Marco (Vallaresso).*

★ Venini

GLASSWARE | When connoisseurs of Venetian glass think of the firms who have restored Venice to its place as the epicenter of artistic glass production, Venini is, without any major discussion, the firm that immediately comes to mind. Since the beginning of the 20th century, Venini has found craftsmen and designers that have made their trademark synonymous with the highest quality both in traditional and in creative glass design. A piece of Venini glass, even one of modest price and proportions, will be considered not only a charming decorative object, but also a work of art that will maintain its value for years to come. While Venini's more exciting and innovative pieces may cost thousands of dollars, the Venini showrooms in the Piazza San Marco and on Fondamenta Vetrai in Murano also have small, more conventional designs for prices as low as €100. ✉ *Piazzetta Leoncini, San Marco 314, San Marco* ☎ *041/5224045 San Marco, 041/273721 Murano* ⊕ *www.venini.com* Ⓜ *Vaporetto. San Marco (San Zaccaria).*

Dorsoduro

The sestiere Dorsoduro (named for its "hard back" solid clay foundation) is across the Grand Canal to the south of San Marco. It is a place of meandering canals, the city's finest art museums, monumental churches, and *scuole* (Renaissance civic institutions) filled with works by Titian, Veronese, and Tiepolo, and a promenade called the Zattere, where on sunny days you'll swear half the city is out for *passeggiata* (a stroll). The eastern tip of the peninsula, the

Venetian Art Glass

The glass of Murano is Venice's number-one product, and you'll be confronted by mind-boggling displays of traditional and contemporary glassware—much of it kitsch and not made in Venice. Traditional Venetian glass is hot blown glass, not lead crystal; it comes in myriad forms that range from the classic ornate goblets and chandeliers, to beads, vases, sculpture, and more. Beware of paying "Venetian" prices for glass made elsewhere. A piece claiming to be made in Murano may guarantee its origin, but not its value or quality; the prestigious Venetian glassmakers—like Venini, Seguso, Salviati, and others—sign their pieces, but never use a "made in Murano" label. To make a smart purchase, take your time and be selective. You can learn a great deal without sales pressure at the Museo del Vetro (museovetro.visitmuve. it) on Murano; unfortunately, you'll likely find the least attractive glass where public demonstrations are offered. Although prices in Venice and on Murano are comparable, shops in Venice with wares from various glassworks may charge slightly less.

■ TIP→ A "free" taxi to Murano always comes with sales pressure. Take the vaporetto included in your transit pass, and, if you prefer, a private guide who specializes in the subject but has no affinity to any specific furnace.

Punta della Dogana, is capped by the dome of Santa Maria della Salute and was once the city's customs point; the old customs house is now a museum of contemporary art.

Dorsoduro is home to the Gallerie dell'Accademia, with an unparalleled collection of Venetian painting, and the gloriously restored Ca' Rezzonico, which houses the Museo del Settecento Veneziano. Another of its landmark sites, the Peggy Guggenheim Collection, has a fine selection of 20th-century art. Add to this some wonderful restaurants, charming places to stay, and inviting bars for an early-evening spritz, and you've got a sestiere well worth exploring,

TIMING

You can easily spend a full day in the neighborhood. Devote at least a half hour to admiring the Titians in the imposing and monumental Santa Maria della Salute, and another half hour for the wonderful Veroneses in the peaceful, serene church of San Sebastiano. The Gallerie dell'Accademia demands a few hours, but if time is short an audio guide can help you cover the highlights in about an hour. Ca' Rezzonico deserves at least an hour, as does the Peggy Guggenheim Collection.

◉ Sights

★ Ca' Rezzonico

HISTORY MUSEUM | Designed by Baldassare Longhena in the 17th century, this gigantic palace was completed nearly 100 years later by Giorgio Massari and became the last home of English poet Robert Browning (1812–89). Stand on the bridge by the Grand Canal entrance to spot the plaque with Browning's poetic excerpt, "Open my heart and you will see graved inside of it, Italy…" on the left side of the palace. The spectacular centerpiece is the eye-popping Grand

Venice's Scuola Days

An institution you'll inevitably encounter from Venice's glory days is the *scuola*. These weren't schools, as the word today translates, but important fraternal institutions. The smaller ones (*scuole piccole*) were established by different social groups—enclaves of foreigners, tradesmen, followers of a particular saint, and parishioners. The *scuole grandi*, however, were open to all citizens and included people of different occupations and ethnicities. They formed a more democratic power base than the Venetian governmental Grand Council, which was limited to nobles.

For the most part secular, despite their devotional activities, the scuole concentrated on charitable work, either helping their own membership or assisting the city's neediest citizens. The tradesmen's and servants' scuole formed social-security nets for elderly and disabled members. Wealthier scuole assisted orphans or provided dowries so poor girls could marry. By 1500 there were more than 200 minor scuole in Venice, but only six scuole grandi, some of which contributed substantially to the arts. The Republic encouraged their existence—the scuole kept strict records of the names and professions of contributors to the brotherhood, which helped when it came time to collect taxes.

Ballroom, which has hosted some of the grandest parties in the city's history, from its 18th-century heyday to the 1969 Bal Fantastica (a Save Venice charity event that attracted every notable of the day, from Elizabeth Taylor to Aristotle Onassis). Today the upper floors of the Ca' Rezzonico are home to the especially delightful **Museo del Settecento** (Museum of Venice in the 1700s). Its main floor successfully retains the appearance of a magnificent Venetian palazzo, decorated with period furniture and tapestries in gilded salons, as well as Gianbattista Tiepolo ceiling frescoes and oil paintings. Upper floors contain a fine collection of paintings by 18th-century Venetian artists, including the famous Pulcinella frescoes by Tiepolo's son, Giandomenico, moved here from the Villa di Zianigo. There's even a restored apothecary, complete with powders and potions. ⊠ *Fondamenta Rezzonico, Dorsoduro 3136, Dorsoduro* ☎ *041/2410100* ⊕ *carezzonico. visitmuve.it* 🎟 *€10 (free with Museum Pass)* 🕒 *Closed Tues.* Ⓜ *Vaporetto: Ca' Rezzonico.*

Campo Santa Margherita
PLAZA/SQUARE | Lined with cafés and restaurants generally filled with students from the nearby university, Campo Santa Margherita also has produce vendors and benches where you can sit and take in the bustling local life of the campo. Also close to the Ca' Rezzonico and the Scuola Grande dei Carmini, and only a 10-minute walk from the Gallerie dell'Accademia, the square is the center of Dorsoduro social life. It takes its name from the church to one side, closed since the early 19th century and now used as an auditorium. On weekend evenings it sometimes attracts hordes of high school students from the mainland. ⊠ *Campo Santa Margherita, Dorsoduro* Ⓜ *Vaporetto: San Basilio.*

★ Gallerie dell'Accademia
ART MUSEUM | The greatest collection of Venetian paintings in the world

hangs in these galleries founded by Napoléon back in 1807 on the site of a religious complex he had suppressed. The galleries were carefully and subtly restructured between 1945 and 1959 by the renowned architect Carlo Scarpa. Jacopo Bellini is considered the father of the Venetian Renaissance, and in Room 2 you can compare his *Madonna and Child with Saints* with such later works as *Madonna of the Orange Tree* by Cima da Conegliano (circa 1459–1517) and *Ten Thousand Martyrs of Mt. Ararat* by Vittore Carpaccio (circa 1455–1525). Jacopo's more accomplished son Giovanni (circa 1430–1516) attracts your eye not only with his subject matter but also with his rich color. Rooms 4 and 5 have a good selection of his madonnas. Room 5 contains *The Tempest* by Giorgione (1477–1510), a revolutionary work that has intrigued viewers and critics for centuries. It is unified not only by physical design elements, as was usual, but more importantly by a mysterious, somewhat threatening atmosphere. In Room 10, *Feast in the House of Levi,* commissioned as a Last Supper, got Veronese summoned to the Inquisition over its depiction of dogs, jesters, and other extraneous figures. The artist responded with the famous retort, *"Noi pittori ci prendiamo le stesse libertà dei poeti e dei pazzi"* (We painters permit ourselves the same liberties as poets and madmen). He resolved the problem by simply changing the title, so that the painting represented a different, less solemn biblical feast. Don't miss the views of 15th- and 16th-century Venice by Carpaccio and Gentile Bellini, Giovanni's brother—you'll see how little the city has changed. Booking tickets in advance isn't essential but helps during busy seasons and costs only an additional €1.50. A free map notes art and artists, and the bookshop sells a more informative English-language booklet. In the main galleries a €4 audio guide saves reading but adds little to each room's excellent annotation.

✉ *Dorsoduro 1050, Campo della Carità just off Accademia Bridge, Dorsoduro* ☎ *041/5222247, 041/5200345 reservations* ⊕ *www.gallerieaccademia.it/en* 🎟 *€12, subject to increases for special exhibitions* Ⓜ *Vaporetto: Accademia.*

Gesuati (*Church of Santa Maria del Rosario*)
CHURCH | When the Dominicans took over the church of Santa Maria della Visitazione from the suppressed order of Gesuati laymen in 1668, Giorgio Massari, the last of the great Venetian Baroque architects, was commissioned to build this structure between 1726 and 1735. It has an important Gianbattista Tiepolo (1696–1770) illusionistic ceiling and several other of his works, plus those of his contemporaries, Giambattista Piazzetta (1683–1754) and Sebastiano Ricci (1659–1734). ✉ *Zattere, Dorsoduro* ☎ *041/2750462* ⊕ *www.chorusvenezia. org* ☉ *Closed Sun.* 🎟 *€3 (free with Chorus Pass)* Ⓜ *Vaporetto: Zattere.*

Peggy Guggenheim Collection
ART MUSEUM | **FAMILY** | Housed in the incomplete but nevertheless charming Palazzo Venier dei Leoni, this choice selection of 20th-century painting and sculpture represents the taste and extraordinary style of the late heiress Peggy Guggenheim. Through wealth, social connections, and a sharp eye for artistic trends, Guggenheim (1898–1979) became an important art dealer and collector from the 1930s through the 1950s, and her personal collection here includes works by Picasso, Kandinsky, Pollock, Motherwell, and Ernst (her onetime husband). The museum serves beverages, snacks, and light meals in its refreshingly shady and artistically sophisticated garden. ✉ *Fondamenta Venier dei Leoni, Dorsoduro 701, Dorsoduro* ☎ *041/2405411* ⊕ *www.guggenheim-venice.it* 🎟 *€15* ☉ *Closed Tues.* ☞ *Timed tickets must be purchased online in advance. Weekend tickets*

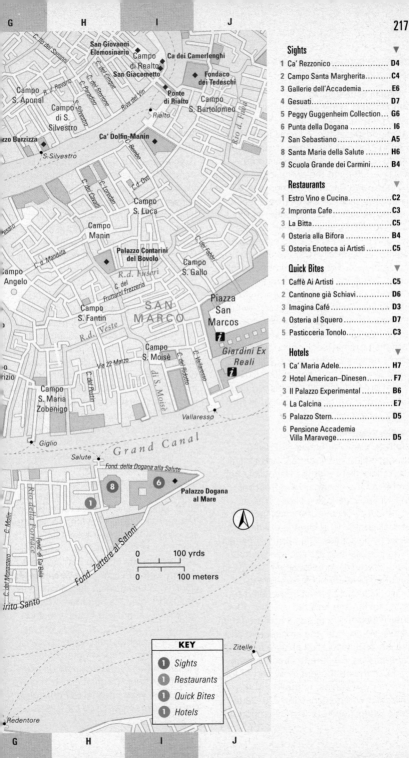

must be booked at least one day ahead Ⓜ *Vaporetto: Accademia.*

★ Punta della Dogana

ART MUSEUM | Funded by the billionaire who owns a major share in Christie's Auction House, the François Pinault Foundation had Japanese architect Tadao Ando redesign this fabled customs house—sitting at the *punta,* or very head, of the Grand Canal—now home to a changing roster of works from Pinault's renowned collection of contemporary art. The streaming light, polished surfaces, and clean lines of Ando's design contrast beautifully with the massive columns, sturdy beams, and brick of the original Dogana. Even if you aren't into contemporary art, a visit is worthwhile just to see Ando's amazing architectural transformation. Be sure to walk down to the punta for a magnificent view of the Venetian basin. Check online for a schedule of temporary exhibitions. ✉ *Punta della Dogana, Dorsoduro* ☎ *041/2001057* ⊕ *www.palazzograssi.it* ☉ *Closed Tues.* ▣ *€15; €20 with Palazzo Grassi* Ⓜ *Vaporetto: Salute.*

★ San Sebastiano

CHURCH | Paolo Veronese (1528–88), though still in his twenties, was already the official painter of the Republic when he began the oil panels and frescoes at San Sebastiano, his parish church, in 1555. For decades he continued to embellish the church with very beautiful illusionistic scenes. The cycles of panels in San Sebastiano are considered to be his supreme accomplishment. Veronese is buried beneath his bust near the organ. The church itself, remodeled by Scarpagnino and finished in 1548, offers a rare opportunity to see a monument in Venice where both the architecture and the pictorial decoration all date from the same period. Be sure to check out the portal of the ex-convent, now part of the University of Venice, to the left of the church; it was designed in 1976–78 by Carlo Scarpa, one of the most important Italian architects of the 20th century. ✉ *Campo San Sebastiano, Dorsoduro* ☎ *041/2750462* ⊕ *www.chorusvene- zia.org* ▣ *€3 (free with Chorus Pass)* ☉ *Closed Sun.* Ⓜ *Vaporetto: San Basilio.*

★ Santa Maria della Salute

CHURCH | The most iconic landmark of the Grand Canal, La Salute (as this church is commonly called) is most unforgettably viewed from the Riva degli Schiavoni at sunset, or from the Accademia Bridge by moonlight. En route to becoming Venice's most important Baroque architect, 32-year-old Baldassare Longhena won a competition in 1631 to design a shrine honoring the Virgin Mary for saving Venice from a plague that in the space of two years (1629–30) killed 47,000 residents, or one-third of the city's population. It was not completed, however, until 1687—five years after Longhena's death. Outside, this ornate white Istrian stone octagon is topped by a colossal cupola with snail-like ornamental buttresses—in truth, piers encircled by finely carved "ropes," an allusion to the sail-making industry of the city (or so say today's art historians). Inside, a white-and-gray color scheme is complemented by a polychrome marble floor and the six chapels. The Byzantine icon above the main altar has been venerated as the Madonna della Salute (Madonna of Health) since 1670, when Francesco Morosini brought it here from Crete. Above it is a sculpture showing Venice on her knees before the Madonna as she drives the wretched plague from the city. Do not leave the church without visiting the **Sacrestia Maggiore,** which contains a dozen works by Titian, including his *San Marco Enthroned with Saints* altarpiece. You'll also see Tintoretto's *Wedding at Cana.* For the Festa della Salute, held November 21, a votive bridge is constructed across the Grand Canal, and Venetians make a pilgrimage here to light candles in prayer for another year's health. ✉ *Punta della Dogana, Dorsoduro* ☎ *041/2743928*

⊕ *basilicasalutevenezia.it* ✉ *Church free, sacristy €4* Ⓜ *Vaporetto: Salute.*

Scuola Grande dei Carmini

HISTORIC SIGHT | When the order of Santa Maria del Carmelo commissioned Baldassare Longhena to finish the work on the Scuola Grande dei Carmini in the 1670s, their brotherhood of 75,000 members was the largest in Venice and one of the wealthiest. Little expense was spared in the stuccoed ceilings and carved ebony paneling, and the artwork is remarkable. The paintings by Gianbattista Tiepolo that adorn the Baroque ceiling of the **Sala Capitolare** (Chapter House) are particularly alluring. In what many consider his best work, the artist's nine canvases vividly transform some rather conventional religious themes into dynamic displays of color and movement. ✉ *Campo dei Carmini, Dorsoduro 2617, Dorsoduro* ☎ *041/5289420* ⊕ *www.scuolagrande-carmini.it* ✆ *Closed Mon.–Wed.* 🎫 *€7* Ⓜ *Vaporetto: Ca' Rezzonico.*

🍴 Restaurants

⭐ Estro Vino e Cucina

$$$ | MODERN ITALIAN | Wine lovers shouldn't miss this cozy and compact eatery run by the Spezzamonte brothers, which offers a fantastic selection of natural wines along with modern takes on classic Venetian dishes, such as scampi in saor and local grilled amberjack. If you can't choose, let the helpful servers suggest the perfect vino from their list of more than 700 bottles to pair with your à la carte dishes or tasting menu. **Known for:** vibrant atmosphere; extensive natural wine list; ambitious local cuisine. Ⓢ *Average main: €28* ✉ *Calle San Pantalon, Dorsoduro 3778, Dorsoduro* ☎ *041/4764914* ⊕ *www.estrovenezia.com* ✆ *Closed Tues. No lunch Wed.* Ⓜ *Vaporetto: San Tomà.*

Impronta Cafe

$$ | VENETIAN | This sleek café is a favorite lunchtime haunt for professors from the nearby university and local businesspeople, when you can easily have a beautifully prepared primo or secondo, plus a glass of wine, for a reasonable price; there's also a good selection of sandwiches and salads. Unlike most local eateries, this spot is open from breakfast through late dinner, and you can dine well and economically in the evening on classic pasta, seafood, and meat dishes. **Known for:** all-day dining; contemporary decor; well-prepared classic Venetian dishes. Ⓢ *Average main: €20* ✉ *Intersection of Calle Crosera and Calle San Pantalon, Dorsoduro 3815, Dorsoduro* ☎ *041/2750386* ⊕ *www.improntacafe-venice.com* ✆ *Closed Sun. and 2 wks in Aug.* Ⓜ *Vaporetto: San Tomà.*

⭐ La Bitta

$$ | NORTHERN ITALIAN | For a break from all the fish and seafood options in Venice, this is your place; the meat-and veggie-focused menu (inspired by the cuisine of the Venetian terra firma) presents a new temptation at every course, and market availability keeps the dishes changing almost every day. The homemade desserts are all luscious (it's been said that La Bitta serves the best *panna cotta* in town), and you can trust the owner's selections from her excellent wine and grappa lists. **Known for:** friendly and efficient service; meat dishes (no seafood); seasonally inspired menus. Ⓢ *Average main: €18* ✉ *Calle Lunga San Barnaba, Dorsoduro 2753/A, Dorsoduro* ☎ *041/5230531* ✆ *Closed Sun. No lunch* Ⓜ *Vaporetto: Ca' Rezzonico.*

⭐ Osteria alla Bifora

$$ | VENETIAN | A beautiful and atmospheric bacaro, Alla Bifora has such ample, satisfying fare that most Venetians consider it a full-fledged restaurant. Offerings include overflowing trays of cold, sliced meats and cheeses; various preparations of baccalà; and Venetian classics, such as polpette, sarde in saor, and marinated anchovies. **Known for:** warm and friendly owners; *seppie in nero con polenta* (cuttlefish in ink with polenta); good

selection of regional wines by the glass. $ *Average main: €18* ✉ *Campo Santa Margherita, Dorsoduro 2930, Dorsoduro* ☎ *041/5236119* ⊗ *Closed Jan. and Aug.* Ⓜ *Vaporetto: Ca' Rezzonico.*

★ Osteria Enoteca ai Artisti

$$$ | VENETIAN | Pop into this canalside restaurant at lunch for a satisfying primo or come for dinner to sample fine and fresh offerings; the candle-lighted tables that line the *fondamenta* suggest romance, and the service is friendly and welcoming. The posted menu—with choices like tagliatelle with porcini mushrooms and tiger prawns, or a filleted John Dory with tomatoes and pine nuts—changes daily (spot the date at the top) and seasonally. **Known for:** truly helpful service; delicious pasta and seafood offerings; superlative tiramisu. $ *Average main: €25* ✉ *Fondamenta della Toletta, Dorsoduro 1169a, Dorsoduro* ☎ *041/5238944* ⊕ *www.enotecaartisti. com* ⊗ *Closed Sun. and Mon.*

☕ Coffee and Quick Bites

Caffè Ai Artisti

$ | CAFÉ | Caffè Ai Artisti gives locals, students, and travelers alike good reason to pause and refuel. The location is central, pleasant, and sunny—perfect for people-watching and taking a break before the next destination—and the hours are long. **Known for:** chilling with the locals; relaxing with a coffee; evening Aperol spritz or wine. $ *Average main: €8* ✉ *Dorsoduro 2771, Dorsoduro* ☎ *393/9680135* Ⓜ *Vaporetto: Ca' Rezzonico.*

★ Cantine del Vino già Schiavi

$ | WINE BAR | A mainstay for anyone living or working in the area, this beautiful, family-run, 19th-century bacaro across from the *squero* (gondola boatyard) of San Trovaso has original furnishings and one of the city's best wine cellars, and the walls are covered floor-to-ceiling with bottles for purchase. The cicheti

here are some of the most inventive—and freshest—in Venice (feel free to compliment the Signora, who makes them up to twice a day); everything's eaten standing up, as there's no seating. **Known for:** boisterous local atmosphere; excellent quality cicheti; plenty of wine choices. $ *Average main: €8* ✉ *Fondamenta Nani, Dorsoduro 992, Dorsoduro* ☎ *041/5230034* ⊕ *www.cantinaschiavi. com* ⊗ *Closed Sun. and 3 wks in Aug.* Ⓜ *Vaporetto: Zattere, Accademia.*

Imagina Cafè

$ | ITALIAN | This friendly café and art gallery, located between Campo Santa Margherita and Campo San Barnaba, is a great place to stop for a spritz, or even for a light lunch or dinner. The highlights are the freshly made salads, but their panini and tramezzini are also among the best in the area. **Known for:** pleasant outdoor seating; tasty sandwiches and salads; good wines and cocktails. $ *Average main: €10* ✉ *Rio Terà Canal, Dorsoduro 3126, Dorsoduro* ☎ *041/2410625* ⊕ *www.imaginacafe.it/english.html* Ⓜ *Vaporetto: Ca' Rezonnico.*

Osteria al Squero

$$ | ITALIAN | It wasn't long after this lovely little wine bar (not, as its name implies, a restaurant) appeared across from the Squero San Trovaso that it became a neighborhood—and citywide—favorite. The Venetian owner has created a personal vision of what a good bar should offer: a variety of sumptuous cicheti, panini, and cheeses to be accompanied by just the right regional wines (ask for his recommendation). **Known for:** tasty cicheti; good veggie options; pretty canal views. $ *Average main: €20* ✉ *Fondamenta Nani, Dorsoduro 943/944, Dorsoduro* ☎ *335/6007513* ⊕ *osteriaalsquero. wordpress.com* ⊗ *Closed Sun.* Ⓜ *Vaporetto: Accademia, Zattere.*

Pasticceria Tonolo

$ | BAKERY | Venice's premier confectionery has been in operation since 1886. During Carnevale it's still one of the best places in town for *frittelle,* or fried doughnuts (traditional raisin, or cream-filled), and at Christmas and Easter, this is where Venetians order their *focaccia veneziana,* the traditional raised cake—well in advance. **Known for:** can't-miss doughnuts; arguably the best pastries in Venice; excellent coffee. Ⓢ *Average main: €5* ✉ *Calle San Pantalon, Dorsoduro 3764, Dorsoduro* ☎ *041/5237209* ⊕ *pasticceria-tonolo-venezia.business. site* ⊗ *Closed Sun. afternoon and Mon.* Ⓜ *Vaporetto: San Tomà.*

Hotels

★ Ca' Maria Adele

$$$$ | HOTEL | One of the city's most intimate and elegant getaways blends terrazzo floors, dramatic Murano chandeliers, and antique-style furnishings with contemporary touches, particularly in the African-wood reception area and breakfast room. **Pros:** quiet and romantic; tranquil yet convenient spot near Santa Maria della Salute; imaginative decor. **Cons:** no restaurant (just breakfast room); bathrooms on the small side; no elevator and lots of stairs. Ⓢ *Rooms from: €462* ✉ *Campo Santa Maria della Salute, Dorsoduro 111, Dorsoduro* ☎ *041/5203078* ⊕ *www.camariaadele.it* ⊗ *Closed 3 wks in Jan.* ↩ *14 rooms* Ⓞ *Free Breakfast* Ⓜ *Vaporetto: Salute.*

Hotel American–Dinesen

$$ | HOTEL | If you're in Venice to see art, you can't beat the location of this hotel, where all the spacious rooms have brocade fabrics and Venetian-style lacquered furniture. **Pros:** on a bright, quiet, exceptionally picturesque canal; some rooms have canal-view terraces; wonderfully located near Gallerie dell'Accademia, Peggy Guggenheim Collection, and Punta della Dogana. **Cons:** bathrooms can feel cramped; style could be too understated for those expecting Venetian opulence;

canal-view rooms are more expensive. Ⓢ *Rooms from: €171* ✉ *San Vio, Dorsoduro 628, Dorsoduro* ☎ *041/5204733* ⊕ *www.hotelamerican.it* ↩ *34 rooms* Ⓞ *No Meals* Ⓜ *Vaporetto: Accademia, Salute, and Zattere.*

Il Palazzo Experimental

$$$ | HOTEL | Of-the-moment Parisian designer Dorothée Meilichzon composed the striped pastel color palette at this hip boutique hotel— the first Experimental Group property in Italy—hidden inside a Renaissance palazzo across from the Giudecca Canal. **Pros:** quiet location away from the Venice crowds; trendy cocktail bar on-site; fun, whimsical decor. **Cons:** no gym; little storage space in bathrooms; not all rooms have water views. Ⓢ *Rooms from: €270* ✉ *Fondamenta Zattere Al Ponte Lungo, Dorsoduro 1411, Dorsoduro* ☎ *041/0980200* ⊕ *www.palazzoexperimental.com* ↩ *32 rooms* Ⓞ *No Meals* Ⓜ *Vaporetto: Zattere, San Basilio.*

La Calcina

$$ | HOTEL | Many notables (including Victorian-era art critic John Ruskin) have stayed at this hotel, which has an enviable location along the sunny Zattere, as well as comfy rooms and apartments with parquet floors, original 19th-century furniture, and firm beds. **Pros:** well-regarded restaurant with terrace over the Giudecca Canal; panoramic views from some rooms; quiet, peaceful atmosphere. **Cons:** no elevator; not for travelers who prefer ultramodern surroundings; most rooms on the small side. Ⓢ *Rooms from: €130* ✉ *Zattere, Dorsoduro 780, Dorsoduro* ☎ *041/5206466* ⊕ *www.lacalcina.com* ↩ *25 rooms* Ⓞ *Free Breakfast* Ⓜ *Vaporetto: Zattere.*

★ Palazzo Stern

$$ | HOTEL | This opulently refurbished neo-Gothic palazzo features marble-column arches, terrazzo floors, frescoed ceilings, mosaics, and a majestic carved

staircase, and some rooms have tufted walls and parquet flooring, but the gracious terrace that overlooks the Grand Canal is almost reason alone to stay here. **Pros:** modern renovation retains historic ambience; lovely views from many rooms; excellent hotel service. **Cons:** standard rooms don't have views; no restaurant, gym, or spa; Grand Canal–facing rooms can be a bit noisy. $ *Rooms from: €192* ⊠ *Calle del Traghetto, Dorsoduro 2792, Dorsoduro* ☎ *041/2770869* ⊕ *www.palazzostern.com* ❤️ *Free Breakfast* ↳ *24 rooms* Ⓜ *Vaporetto: Ca' Rezzonico.*

Pensione Accademia Villa Maravege

$$ | **HOTEL** | Behind iron gates in one of the most densely packed parts of the city, you'll find yourself in front of a large and elegant garden and Gothic-style villa where accommodations are charmingly decorated with Venetian-style antique reproductions and fine tapestry. **Pros:** a unique villa in the heart of Venice; complimentary drinks and snacks at the bar; two gardens where guests can breakfast, drink, and relax. **Cons:** no guest rooms have Grand Canal views; bathrooms can be on the small side; no restaurant. $ *Rooms from: €128* ⊠ *Fondamenta Bollani, Dorsoduro 1058, Dorsoduro* ☎ *041/5210188* ⊕ *www.pensioneacca-demia.it* ↳ *27 rooms* ❤️ *Free Breakfast* Ⓜ *Vaporetto: Accademia.*

 Nightlife

Al Chioschetto

BARS | Although this popular place consists only of a kiosk set up to serve some outdoor tables, it is located on the Zattere, and thus provides panoramic views. It's a handy meet-up for locals and a stop-off for tourists in nice weather for a spritz, a panino, or a sunny read as the Venetian world eases by. But go for the view and the sunshine; the food and drink, while acceptable, are not exceptional. ⊠ *Near Ponte Lungo, Dorsoduro*

1406/A, Dorsoduro ☎ *348/3968466* Ⓜ *Vaporetto: Zattere.*

★ **Il Caffè** (*Bar Rosso*)

BARS | Commonly called "Bar Rosso" for its bright-red exterior, Il Caffè has far more tables outside than inside. A favorite with students and faculty from the nearby university, it's a good place to enjoy a spritz—the preferred Venetian aperitif of white wine, Campari or Aperol, soda water, an olive, and a slice of orange. It has excellent tramezzini (among the best in town) and panini, and a hip, helpful staff. It's been recently frequented by high-school students from the mainland on weekend nights, so it can be more enjoyable around lunchtime or in the early evening. ⊠ *Campo Santa Margherita, Dorsoduro 2963, Dorsoduro* ☎ *041/5287998* Ⓜ *Vaporetto: Ca' Rezzonico.*

Orange

BARS | Modern, hip, and complemented by an internal garden, this welcoming bar anchors the south end of Campo Santa Margherita, the liveliest campo in Venice. You can have *piadine* sandwiches, salads, and drinks while watching soccer games on a massive screen inside, or sit at the tables in the campo. Despite being close to the university, Orange is frequented primarily by young working people from the mainland and tourists. ⊠ *Campo Santa Margherita, Dorsoduro 3054/A, Dorsoduro* ☎ *041/5234740* Ⓜ *Vaporetto: Ca' Rezzonico.*

Venice Jazz Club

LIVE MUSIC | Owner Federico and his band play live jazz, in styles including classic, modern, Latin jazz, and bossa nova, at this intimate venue. Concerts usually start at 9 pm every night except Thursday and Sunday, and dinner is available beforehand for an extra charge. ⊠ *Ponte dei Pugni, Dorsoduro 3102, Dorsoduro* ☎ *041/5232056* ⊕ *venicejazzclub.weebly.com* Ⓜ *Vaporetto: Ca' Rezzonico.*

Shopping

Grifone

HANDBAGS | Of Venice's few remaining artisan leather shops, Il Grifone is the standout with respect to quality, tradition, and the guarantee of an exquisite product. For more than 30 years, Antonio Peressin has been making bags, purses, belts, and smaller leather items that have a wide following because of his precision and attention to detail. His goods remain reasonably and accessibly priced. ⊠ *Fondamenta del Gaffaro, Dorsoduro 3516, Dorsoduro* ☎ *041/5229452* ⊕ *www.ilgrifonevenezia.it* Ⓜ *Vaporetto: Piazzale Roma.*

Marina and Susanna Sent

JEWELRY & WATCHES | The beautiful and elegant glass jewelry of Marina and Susanna Sent has been featured in *Vogue.* Look also for vases and other exceptional design pieces. Other locations are on the Fondamenta Serenella on Murano and in the Sottoportico de Rialto in San Polo. ⊠ *Campo San Vio, Dorsoduro·669, Dorsoduro* ☎ *041/5208136 for Dorsoduro, 041/5210016 for San Polo, 041/5274665 for Murano* ⊕ *www. marinaesusannasent.com* Ⓜ *Vaporetto: Accademia, Zattere, Giglio, Murano Serenella.*

San Polo and Santa Croce

The two smallest of Venice's six sestieri, San Polo and Santa Croce, were named after their main churches, although the Chiesa di Santa Croce was demolished in 1810. The city's most famous bridge, the Ponte di Rialto, unites San Marco (east) with San Polo (west). The Rialto takes its name from Rivoaltus, the high ground on which it was built. You'll find some of Venice's most lauded restaurants here, and shops abound in the area surrounding the Ponte di Rialto. On the San Marco side you'll find fashion, on the San Polo side, food.

TIMING

To do the area justice requires at least half a day. If you want to take part in the food shopping, come early to beat the crowds. Campo San Giacomo dell'Orio, west of the main thoroughfare that takes you from the Ponte di Rialto to Santa Maria Gloriosa dei Frari, is a peaceful place for a drink and a rest. The museums of Ca' Pesaro are a time commitment—you'll want at least two hours to see them both.

Sights

Ca' Pesaro

ART MUSEUM | Baldassare Longhena's grand Baroque palace, begun in 1676, is the beautifully restored home of two impressive collections. The Galleria Internazionale d'Arte Moderna has works by 19th- and 20th-century artists, such as Klimt, Kandinsky, Matisse, and Miró. It also has a collection of representative works from the Venice Biennale that amounts to a panorama of 20th-century art. The pride of the Museo Orientale is its collection of Japanese art—and especially armor and weapons—of the Edo period (1603–1868). It also has a small but striking collection of Chinese and Indonesian porcelains and musical instruments. ⊠ *Santa Croce 2076, Santa Croce* ☎ *041/721127 Galleria, 041/5241173 Museo Orientale* ⊕ *capesaro.visitmuve. it* 🎫 *€10, includes both museums (free with Museum Pass)* 🕐 *Closed Mon.* Ⓜ *Vaporetto: San Stae.*

Campo San Polo

PLAZA/SQUARE | Only Piazza San Marco is larger than this square, and the echo of children's voices bouncing off the surrounding palaces makes the space seem even bigger. Campo San Polo once hosted bull races, fairs, military parades, and packed markets, and now comes especially alive on summer nights, when

San Polo and Santa Croce

F **G** **H** **I** **J**

1 2 3 4 5 6 7

GIO

Campo d. Maddalena

Campo di S. Fosca

Campo Marcuola

S. Marcuola

co chi

Depositi del Megio

Ca' Belloni-Battaglia

S.Stae

C. del Megio

R. di Ca' Tron

C. dell'Orto

Strada Nova

Rio di Noale

Fond. di S.Felice

C. della Rachetta

C. Forno

C. Zotti

C. Corrente

C. delle Vere

C. del Forno

5

1

1

6

Palazzo Mocenigo

Ca' Corner della Regina

C. della Rosa

Ca' d'Oro

Rio Terra di Barba Frutarol

Campo dei SS. Apostoli

San Cassiano

1

Pescheria

Campo della Pescaria

Rialto Mercato

C. dei Botteri

Campo delle Beccarie

2

4

Campo Cesare Battisti

2

4

San Giovanni Elemosinario

Palazzo Muti Baglioni

C.llo dei Sansoni

C.S. Mattio

C. del Lume

Campo di Realto

Ca dei Camerlenghi

San Giacometto

Ponte di Rialto

5

o di ostin

7

Rio di S.Polo

SAN POLO

5

C. del Storione

Campo S. Aponal

R. d. Ravano

C. del Paradiso

Campo di S. Polo

2

San Polo

C. del Lume

3

Riva del Vin

C. Paradiso

C. Sturione

Campo di S. Silvestro

S. Silvestro

2

Rialto

Campo S. Bartolomeo

Rio d. Fava

Palazzo Barzizza

S. Silvestro

Palazzo Bernardo

Palazzo Querini

alazzo Barbarigo dell'Terrazza

Palazzo isani Moretta

San Angelo

Grand Canal

C. dei Cavalli

C. Loredan

C. d. Ovo

C. Bembo

Campo S. Luca

Campo de la Guerra

Palazzo Pisani Moretta

Ca' Mocenigo

C. del Pestrin

SAN MARCO

Campo Manin

Palazzo Contarini del Bovolo

C. dei Fabbri

Torre dell'Orologio

Procuratie Vecchie

Campo S. Angelo

C. d. Mandola

R. d. Fuseri

C. del Fruttarol Frezzeria

Campo S. Gallo

Piazza San Marco

Santo Stefano

Campo S. Fantin

it's home to the city's outdoor cinema. The **Chiesa di San Polo** has been restored so many times that little remains of the original 9th-century church, and the 19th-century alterations were so costly that, sadly, the friars sold off many great paintings to pay bills. Although Gianbattista Tiepolo is represented here, his work is outdone by 16 paintings by his son Giandomenico (1727–1804), including the *Stations of the Cross* in the oratory to the left of the entrance. The younger Tiepolo also created a series of expressive and theatrical renderings of the saints. Look for altarpieces by Tintoretto and Veronese that managed to escape auction. San Polo's bell tower (begun 1362) remained unchanged over the centuries—don't miss the two lions, playing with a disembodied human head and a serpent, that guard it. Tradition has it that the head refers to that of Marino Faliero, the doge executed for treason in 1355. ⊠ *Campo San Polo, San Polo* ☎ *041/2750462 Chorus Foundation* ⊕ *www.chorusvenezia. org* ⊘ *Closed Sun.* ☒ *Chiesa di San Polo €3 (free with Chorus Pass)* Ⓜ *Vaporetto: San Silvestro, San Tomà.*

San Giacomo dell'Orio

PLAZA/SQUARE | This lovely square was named after a laurel tree (*orio*), and today trees lend it shade and character. Add benches and a fountain (with a drinking bowl for dogs), and the pleasant, oddly shaped campo becomes a welcoming place for friendly conversation and neighborhood kids at play. Legend has it the **Chiesa di San Giacomo dell'Orio** was founded in the 9th century on an island still populated by wolves. The current church dates from 1225; its short, unmatched Byzantine columns survived renovation during the Renaissance, and the church never lost the feel of an ancient temple sheltering beneath its 14th-century ship's-keel roof. In the sanctuary, large marble crosses are surrounded by a group of small medieval Madonnas. The altarpiece is *Madonna with Child and Saints* (1546) by Lorenzo

Lotto (1480–1556), and the sacristies contain 12 works by Palma il Giovane (circa 1544–1628). ⊠ *Campo San Giacomo dell'Orio, Santa Croce* ☎ *041/2750462 Chorus Foundation* ⊕ *www.chorusvenezia.org* ☒ *Church €3 (free with Chorus Pass)* ⊘ *Church closed Sun.* Ⓜ *Vaporetto: San Stae.*

San Giovanni Elemosinario

CHURCH | Storefronts make up the facade, and market guilds—poulterers, messengers, and fodder merchants—built the altars at this church intimately bound to the Rialto Market. The original church was completely destroyed by a fire in 1514 and rebuilt in 1531 by Scarpagnino, who had also worked on the Scuola di San Rocco. During a more recent restoration, workers stumbled upon a frescoed cupola by Pordenone (1484–1539) that had been painted over centuries earlier. Don't miss Titian's *St. John the Almsgiver* and Pordenone's *Sts. Catherine, Sebastian, and Roch.* ⊠ *Rialto Ruga Vecchia San Giovanni, Santa Croce* ☎ *041/2750462 Chorus Foundation* ⊕ *www.chorusvenezia.org* ☒ *€3 (free with Chorus Pass)* ⊘ *Closed Mon.–Sat. after 1:15 and Sun.* Ⓜ *Vaporetto: San Silvestro, Rialto.*

San Stae

CHURCH | The church of San Stae—the Venetian name for Sant'Eustachio (St. Eustace)—was reconstructed in 1687 by Giovanni Grassi and given a new facade in 1707 by Domenico Rossi. Renowned Venetian painters and sculptors of the early 18th century decorated this church around 1717 with the legacy left by Doge Alvise II Mocenigo, who's buried in the center aisle. San Stae affords a good opportunity to see the early works of Gianbattista Tiepolo, Sebastiano Ricci, and Piazzetta, as well as those of the previous generation of Venetian painters, with whom they had studied. ⊠ *Campo San Stae, Santa Croce* ☎ *041/2750462 Chorus Foundation*

⊕ *www.chorusvenezia.org* ⊗ *Closed Sun.* ⊠ *€3 (free with Chorus Pass)* Ⓜ *Vaporetto: San Stae.*

★ Santa Maria Gloriosa dei Frari

CHURCH | Completed in 1442, this immense Gothic church of russet-color brick, known locally as "I Frari," is famous worldwide for its array of spectacular Venetian paintings. Visit the sacristy first, to see Giovanni Bellini's 1488 triptych *Madonna and Child with Saints* in all its mellow luminosity, painted for precisely this spot. The Corner Chapel on the other side of the chancel is graced by Bartolomeo Vivarini's (1415–84) 1474 altarpiece *St. Mark Enthroned and Saints John the Baptist, Jerome, Peter, and Nicholas*, which is much more conservative, displaying an attention to detail generally associated with late medieval painting. In the first south chapel of the chorus, there is a fine sculpture of St. John the Baptist by Donatello, dated 1438 (perhaps created before the artist came to Venice), which conveys a psychological intensity rare for early Renaissance sculpture. You can see the rapid development of Venetian Renaissance painting by contrasting Bellini with the heroic energy of Titian's *Assumption,* over the main altar, painted only 30 years later. Unveiled in 1518, it was the artist's first public commission and, after causing a bit of controversy, did much to establish his reputation. Upon viewing this painting at the far end of the nave, you'll first think it has been specially spotlit: up close, however, you'll discover this impression is due to the painter's unrivaled use of light and color. Titian's beautiful *Madonna di Ca' Pesaro* is in the left aisle. The painting took seven years to complete (finished in 1526), and in it Titian disregarded the conventions of his time by moving the Virgin out of center and making the saints active participants. The composition, built on diagonals, anticipates structural principals of Baroque painting in the following century. The Frari also holds a Sansovino sculpture of St. John

the Baptist and Longhena's impressive Baroque tomb designed for Doge Giovanni Pesaro. ⊠ *Campo dei Frari, San Polo* ☎ *041/2728618, 041/2750462 Chorus Foundation* ⊕ *www.basilicadeifrari.it* ⊠ *€3 (free with Chorus Pass)* Ⓜ *Vaporetto: San Tomà.*

★ Scuola Grande di San Rocco

HISTORY MUSEUM | This elegant example of Venetian Renaissance architecture was built between 1517 and 1560 for the essentially secular charitable confraternity bearing the saint's name. The Venetian "scuole" were organizations that sometimes had loose religious affiliations, through which the artisan class could exercise some influence upon civic life. Although San Rocco is bold and dramatic outside, its contents are even more stunning—a series of more than 60 paintings by Tintoretto. In 1564, Tintoretto edged out competition for a commission to decorate a ceiling by submitting not a sketch, but a finished work, which he moreover offered free of charge. *Moses Striking Water from the Rock, The Brazen Serpent,* and *The Fall of Manna* represent three afflictions—thirst, disease, and hunger—that San Rocco, and later his brotherhood, sought to relieve. ⊠ *Campo San Rocco, San Polo 3052, San Polo* ☎ *041/5234864* ⊕ *www.scuolagrandesanrocco.it* ⊠ *€10* Ⓜ *Vaporetto: San Tomà.*

🍴 Restaurants

Al Nono Risorto

$$ | VENETIAN | FAMILY | Although in the Santa Croce neighborhood, this friendly trattoria popular with the locals is really only a short walk from the Rialto Market. The pizza—not a Venetian specialty, generally speaking—is pretty good here, but the star attractions are the generous appetizers and excellent shellfish pastas, and in good weather you can enjoy your meal in the pergola-covered courtyard (do reserve if you want to snag a table there). **Known for:** pretty outdoor garden seating; traditional starters and pastas; quite tasty pizzas. $ *Average main: €19* ✉ *Ramo Quinto Gallion O del Pezzetto 2338, Santa Croce* ☎ *041/5241169* ⊕ *alnono-risortovenezia.com* ⊗ *Closed Wed. and Jan.* Ⓜ *Vaporetto: Rialto Mercato.*

★ Al Paradiso

$$$ | MODERN ITALIAN | In a small dining room made warm and cozy by its pleasing and unpretentious decor, proprietor Giordano makes all diners feel like honored guests. Unlike many elegant restaurants, Al Paradiso serves generous portions, and many of the delicious antipasti and primi are quite satisfying; you may want to follow the traditional Italian way of ordering and wait until you've finished your antipasto or your primo before you order your secondo. **Known for:** central location near the Ponte di Rialto; large appetizer and pasta portions; tasty meat and fish mains. $ *Average main: €26* ✉ *Calle del Scaleter 767, San Polo* ☎ *041/5234910* ⊕ *fantecchiathos.wixsite.com/ristorantealparadiso* ⊗ *Closed 3 wks Jan.–Feb.* Ⓜ *Vaporetto: San Silvestro.*

Alla Madonna

$ | VENETIAN | "The Madonna" used to be world-famous as "the" classic Venetian trattoria, but in recent decades has settled into middle age. Owned and operated by the Rado family since 1954, this Venetian institution looks like one, with wood beams, stained-glass windows, and a panoply of paintings on white walls; folks still head here to savor the classic Venetian repertoire, with a strong focus on seafood. **Known for:** old-time atmosphere; traditional Venetian cuisine; freshly prepared seafood. $ *Average main: €14* ✉ *Calle della Madonna, San Polo 594, San Polo* ☎ *041/5223824* ⊕ *www.ristoranteallamadonna.com* ⊗ *Closed Wed. and Jan.* Ⓜ *Vaporetto: San Silvestro.*

Antica Besseta

$$ | VENETIAN | Tucked away in a quiet corner of Santa Croce, with a few tables under an ivy shelter, the Antica Besseta dates from the 19th century, and it retains some of its old feel. The menu focuses on vegetables and fish, according to what's at the market, with some pasta and meat dishes, too. **Known for:** charming old-fashioned feel; classic Italian pastas, like spaghetti con vongole (with clams); simple menu of fish and meat choices. $ *Average main: €22* ✉ *Salizzada de Ca' Zusto, Santa Croce 1395, Santa Croce* ☎ *041/721687* ⊕ *www.anticabesseta.it* Ⓜ *Vaporetto: Riva di Biasio.*

★ Antiche Carampane

$$$ | SEAFOOD | Judging by its rather modest and unremarkable appearance, you wouldn't guess that Piera Bortoluzzi Librai's trattoria is among the finest fish restaurants in the city both because of the quality of the ingredients and because of the chef's creative magic. You can choose from a selection of classic dishes with a modern and creative touch. **Known for:** popular with visitors and locals (so book ahead); superlative fish and seafood; modernized Venetian dishes. $ *Average main: €25* ✉ *Rio Terà delle Carampane, San Polo 1911, San Polo* ☎ *041/5240165* ⊕ *www.antichecarampane.com* ⊗ *Closed Sun. and Mon., 10 days in Jan., and 3 wks July–Aug.* Ⓜ *Vaporetto: San Silvestro.*

La Zucca

$$ | NORTHERN ITALIAN | Simple place settings, wood lattice walls, and a mélange of languages make La Zucca (The Pumpkin) feel much like a typical, somewhat sophisticated vegetarian restaurant that you could find in any European city. What makes La Zucca special is the use of fresh, local ingredients—many of which, like the particularly sweet zucca itself, aren't normally found outside northern Italy—and simply great cooking. **Known for:** flan di zucca, a luscious pumpkin pudding topped with aged ricotta cheese; seasonal vegetarian-focused dishes; home-style Italian cooking. $ *Average main: €21* ✉ *Calle del Tintor, at Ponte del Megio, Santa Croce 1762, Santa*

Croce ☎ *041/5241570* ⊕ *www.lazucca.it* ⊗ *Closed Sun.* Ⓜ *Vaporetto: San Stae.*

★ Osteria Da Fiore

$$$$ | VENETIAN | The understated atmosphere, simple decor, and quiet elegance featured alongside Da Fiore's modern take on traditional Venetian cuisine certainly merit its international reputation. With such beautifully prepared cuisine, you would expect the kitchen to be run by a chef with a household name; however, the kitchen is headed by owner Maurizio Martin's wife, Mara, who learned to cook from her grandmother. **Known for:** reservations required in advance; sophisticated traditional Venetian dishes; delicious tasting menus. ⑤ *Average main: €40* ⊠ *Calle del Scaleter, San Polo 2002, San Polo* ☎ *041/721308* ⊕ *www.dafiore.net* ⊗ *Closed 3 wks in Jan.* Ⓜ *Vaporetto San Tomà.*

Coffee and Quick Bites

Al Prosecco

$$ | WINE BAR | Locals drop into this friendly bacaro to explore wines from this region and elsewhere in Italy. They accompany a carefully chosen selection of meats, cheeses, and other food from small, artisanal producers, used in tasty panini like the *porchetta romane verdure* (roasted pork with greens) and in elegant cold platters. **Known for:** outdoor seating on the lively campo; great selection of biodynamic wines, including prosecco; lovely meat and cheese platters. ⑤ *Average main: €20* ⊠ *Campo San Giacomo da l'Orio 1503, Santa Croce* ☎ *041/5240222* ⊕ *www.alprosecco.com* ⊗ *Closed Sun.* Ⓜ *Vaporetto: San Stae.*

All'Arco

$ | WINE BAR | Just because it's noon and you only have enough time between sights for a sandwich doesn't mean that it can't be a satisfying, even awe-inspiring, one. There's no menu at All'Arco, but a scan of what's behind the glass counter is all you need; order what entices you, or have Roberto or Matteo (father and son) suggest a cicheto or panino. **Known for:** friendly and helpful service; top-notch cicheti; platters of meats and cheeses. ⑤ *Average main: €8* ⊠ *Calle Arco, San Polo 436, San Polo* ☎ *041/5205666* ⊗ *Closed Sun, 2 wks in Feb., and Aug. No dinner* Ⓜ *Vaporetto: San Silvestro.*

Caffè dei Frari

$ | CAFÉ | Just over the bridge in front of the Frari church is this old-fashioned place where you'll find an assortment of sandwiches and snacks, but it is the atmosphere, and not the food, that is the main attraction. Established in 1870, it's one of the last Venetian tearooms with its original decor, and while prices are a bit higher than in cafés in nearby Campo Santa Margherita, the vibe and the friendly "retro" atmosphere make the added cost worthwhile. **Known for:** quality *cicheti* (finger food); lovely historic setting; well-made cocktails. ⑤ *Average main: €8* ⊠ *Fondamenta dei Frari, San Polo 2564, San Polo* ☎ *347/8293158* ⊗ *Closed Sun and Mon. No dinner* Ⓜ *Vaporetto: San Tomà.*

Cantina Do Mori

$ | WINE BAR | This is the original bacaro, in business continually since 1462; cramped but warm and cozy under hanging antique copper pots, it has served generations of workers from the Rialto Market. In addition to young local whites and reds, the well-stocked cellar offers reserve labels, many available by the glass; between sips you can choose to munch the myriad cicheti on offer, or a few tiny well-stuffed tramezzini, appropriately called *francobolli* (postage stamps). **Known for:** delicious baccalà mantecato, with or without garlic and parsley; good choice of wines by the glass; fine selection of cicheti and sandwiches. ⑤ *Average main: €8* ⊠ *Calle dei Do Mori, San Polo 429, San Polo* ☎ *041/5225401*

🕐 *Closed Sun.* Ⓜ *Vaporetto: Rialto Mercato.*

 Hotels

★ Hotel al Ponte Mocenigo

$ | **HOTEL** | At this hotel—once home to the Santa Croce branch of the Mocenigo family, which counts a few doges in its lineage—a columned courtyard welcomes you, and guest room decor nods to the building's history, with canopied beds, striped damask fabrics, lustrous terrazzo flooring, and gilt-accented furnishings. **Pros:** enchanting courtyard (the perfect spot for an aperitivo); fantastic value; friendly and helpful staff. **Cons:** standard rooms are small; beds are on the hard side; rooms in the annex can be noisy. $ *Rooms from: €110* ✉ *Fondamento de Rimpeto a Ca' Mocenigo, Santa Croce 2063, Santa Croce* ☎ *041/5244797* ⊕ *www.alpontemocenigo.com* 🛏 *11 rooms* ❍ *Free Breakfast* Ⓜ *Vaporetto: San Stae.*

La Villeggiatura

$ | **HOTEL** | If eclectic Venetian charm is what you seek, this luminous residence near the Rialto has it: each of the individually decorated guest rooms has its own theater-themed wall painting by a local artist. **Pros:** relaxed atmosphere and friendly, personalized service; well located near markets, artistic monuments, and restaurants; meticulously maintained. **Cons:** no restaurant (though breakfast is served); no view to speak of, despite the climb; no elevator and lots of stairs. $ *Rooms from: €104* ✉ *Calle dei Botteri, San Polo 1569, San Polo* ☎ *041/5244673* ⊕ *www.lavilleggiatura.it* 🛏 *6 rooms* ❍ *Free Breakfast* Ⓜ *Vaporetto: Rialto Mercato.*

★ Oltre il Giardino

$$$ | **HOTEL** | Behind a brick wall, just over the bridge from the Frari church, this palazzo is hard to find but well worth the effort: a sheltered location, large garden, and individually decorated guest rooms make it feel like a country house. **Pros:** friendly owners happy to share their Venice tips; peaceful, gracious, and convenient setting; glorious walled garden. **Cons:** rooms book up quickly; a beautiful, but not particularly Venetian, ambience; no in-house restaurant (though breakfast served). $ *Rooms from: €218* ✉ *Fondamenta Contarini, San Polo 2542, San Polo* ☎ *041/2750015* ⊕ *www.oltreil-giardino-venezia.com* 🕐 *Closed Jan.* 🛏 *6 rooms* ❍ *Free Breakfast* Ⓜ *Vaporetto: San Tomà.*

 Nightlife

★ Il Mercante

COCKTAIL LOUNGES | When the clock strikes 6 pm, historic Caffè dei Frari transforms into this lively craft cocktail bar. Relax on a velvet sofa while enjoying your inventive drink, which is sure to have an intricate story behind it. There's also a good selection of small bites on offer. ✉ *Fondamenta dei Frari, San Polo 2564, San Polo* ☎ *041/4767305* ⊕ *www.ilmercantevenezia.com* Ⓜ *Vaporetto: San Tomà.*

Naranzaria

BARS | At the friendliest of the several bar-restaurants that line the Erbaria, near the Rialto Market, enjoy a cocktail outside, along the Canal Grande, or at a cozy table inside the renovated 16th-century warehouse. Although the food is acceptable, the ambience is really the main attraction. After the kitchen closes at 10:30, light snacks are served until midnight, and there is live music (usually jazz, Latin, or rock) occasionally on Sunday evening. ✉ *L'Erbaria, San Polo 130, along Grand Canal, San Polo* ☎ *041/7241035* ⊕ *www.naranzaria.it* Ⓜ *Vaporetto: Rialto Mercato.*

Shopping

Gilberto Penzo

ANTIQUES & COLLECTIBLES | FAMILY | Find amazingly detailed handmade wooden models of all types of Venetian ships and boats, as well as affordable kits for kids to create their own boats at home. ⊠ *Calle Seconda dei Saoneri, San Polo 2681, San Polo* ☎ *041/5246139* ⊕ *www. veniceboats.com* Ⓜ *Vaporetto: San Tomà.*

★ Il Tabarro San Marco di Monica Daniele

OTHER SPECIALTY STORE | This petite shop is the best place in town to find traditional Venetian wool capes, known as *tabarro*, and classic hats, such as the Ezra Pound (curved hat with a brim), the *tricorno* (three-cornered hat), and the *cilindro* (top hat). ⊠ *Calle del Scaleter, San Polo 2235, San Polo* ☎ *041/5246242* ⊕ *www. monicadaniele.com* Ⓜ *Vaporetto: San Stae, San Silvestro.*

Laberintho

JEWELRY & WATCHES | A tiny bottega near Campo San Polo is run by a team of young goldsmiths and jewelry designers specializing in inlaid stones. The work on display in their shop is exceptional, and they also create customized pieces. ⊠ *Calle del Scaleter, San Polo 2236, San Polo* ☎ *041/710017* ⊕ *www.laberintho.com* Ⓜ *Vaporetto: San Stae, San Silvestro.*

Cannaregio

Seen from above, this part of town seems like a wide field plowed by several long, straight canals linked by perpendicular streets—not typical of Venice, where the shape of the islands usually defines the shape of the canals. Cannaregio's main thoroughfare, the Strada Nova (New Street, as it was converted from a canal in 1871), is the longest street in Venice; it runs parallel to the Grand Canal. Today the Strada Nova serves as a pedestrian walkway from the train station almost to the Rialto. Cannaregio, first settled in the 14th century, is one of the more "modern" of Venice's neighborhoods, with *fondamente* (walkways) along the major canals north of the Strada Nova, making it ideal for canalside strolls with views of spectacular Gothic and Baroque facades. There are also some fine eateries and pretty palazzo hotels—all of them away from the San Marco crowds.

TIMING

Although it's more residential and less sight-rich than other Venice neighborhoods, you'll still need several hours here to explore the Ca' d'Oro palace and Madonna dell'Orto and Santa Maria dei Miracoli churches, and to wander the Jewish Ghetto. Cannaregio is a great place to spend a morning before taking the vaporetto to Murano and Burano, which departs from the Fondamente Nove stop.

Sights

★ Ca' d'Oro

HISTORY MUSEUM | One of the classic postcard sights of Venice, this exquisite Venetian Gothic palace was once literally a "Golden House," when its marble tracery and ornaments were embellished with gold. It was created by Giovanni and Bartolomeo Bon between 1428 and 1430 for the patrician Marino Contarini, who had read about the Roman emperor Nero's golden house in Rome, the Domus Aurea, and wished to imitate it as a present to his wife. Her family owned the land and the Byzantine *fondaco* (palace-trading house) previously standing on it; you can still see the round Byzantine arches incorporated into the Gothic building's entry porch. The last proprietor, Baron Giorgio Franchetti, left Ca' d'Oro to the city after having it carefully restored and furnished with antiquities, sculptures, and paintings that today make up the Galleria Franchetti. Besides Andrea Mantegna's *St. Sebastian* and other Venetian works, the Galleria Franchetti contains the type of fresco that

Cannaregio

once adorned the exteriors of Venetian buildings (commissioned by those who could not afford a marble facade). One such detached fresco displayed here was made by the young Titian for the facade of the Fondaco dei Tedeschi near the Rialto. ✉ *Calle Ca' d'Oro, Cannaregio 3933, Cannaregio* ☎ *041/5200345* ⊕ *www. cadoro.org* 🎫 *€6* Ⓜ *Vaporetto: Ca' d'Oro.*

★ **Gesuiti** (*Chiesa di Santa Maria Assunta*)

CHURCH | The interior walls of this early-18th-century church (1715–30) resemble brocade drapery, and only touching them will convince skeptics that rather than embroidered cloth, the green-and-white walls are inlaid marble. This trompe-l'oeil decor is typical of the late Baroque's fascination with optical illusion. Toward the end of his life, Titian tended to paint scenes of suffering and sorrow in a nocturnal ambience. A dramatic example of this is on display above the first altar to the left: Titian's daring *Martyrdom of St. Lawrence* (1578), taken from an earlier church that stood on this site. To the left of the church is the Oratory of the Crociferi, which features some of Palma Giovane's best work, painted between 1583 and 1591. ✉ *Campo dei Gesuiti, Cannaregio* ☎ *041/5286579* 🎫 *Gesuiti €1; oratory €3* 🕐 *Oratory closed Mon.–Wed., Jan.–mid-Feb., and Sept.–Oct.* Ⓜ *Vaporetto: Fondamente Nove.*

★ **Jewish Ghetto**

HISTORIC DISTRICT | The neighborhood that gave the world the word *ghetto* is today a quiet area surrounding a large campo. It is home to Jewish institutions, several kosher restaurants, a rabbinical school, and five synagogues. Present-day Venetian Jews live all over the city, and the contemporary Jewish life of the ghetto, with the exception of the Jewish Museum and the synagogues, is an enterprise conducted almost exclusively by American Hasidic Jews of eastern European descent and tradition. Although Jews may have arrived earlier, the first synagogues weren't built and a cemetery (on the Lido) wasn't founded until the Ashkenazi, or eastern European Jews, came in the late 1300s. Dwindling coffers may have prompted the Republic to sell temporary visas to Jews, who were over the centuries alternately tolerated and expelled. The Rialto commercial district, as mentioned in Shakespeare's *The Merchant of Venice,* depended on Jewish moneylenders for trade and to help cover ever-increasing war expenses. In 1516, relentless local opposition forced the Senate to confine Jews to an island in Cannaregio, then on the outer reaches of the city, named for its *geto* (foundry). The term "ghetto" also may come from the Hebrew "ghet," meaning separation or divorce. Gates at the entrance were locked at night, and boats patrolled the surrounding canals. Jews were allowed only to lend money at low interest, operate pawnshops controlled by the government, trade in textiles, or practice medicine. Jewish doctors were highly respected and could leave the ghetto at any hour when on duty. Though ostracized, Jews were nonetheless safe in Venice, and in the 16th century, the community grew considerably—primarily with refugees from the Inquisition, which persecuted Jews in Spain, Portugal, and southern and central Italy. The ghetto was allowed to expand twice, but it still had the city's densest population and consequently ended up with the city's tallest buildings. Although the gates were pulled down after Napoléon's 1797 arrival, the ghetto was reinstated during the Austrian occupation. The Jews realized full freedom only in 1866 with the founding of the Italian state. Many Jews fled Italy as a result of Mussolini's 1938 racial laws, so that on the eve of World War II, there were about 1,500 Jews left in the ghetto. Jews continued to flee, and the remaining 247 were deported by the Nazis; only eight returned. The area has Europe's highest density of Renaissance-era synagogues, and visiting them is interesting not only culturally, but also aesthetically. Though each is marked by the tastes of its individual builders, Venetian influence is evident throughout. Women's galleries resemble those of theaters from the same era, and some synagogues were decorated by artists who were simultaneously active in local churches; Longhena, the architect of Santa Maria della Salute, renovated the Spanish synagogue in 1635. ⊠ *Campo del Ghetto Nuovo, Cannaregio.*

★ Madonna dell'Orto

CHURCH | Though built toward the middle of the 14th century, this church takes its character from its beautiful late-Gothic facade, added between 1460 and 1464; it's one of the most beautiful Gothic churches in Venice. Tintoretto lived nearby, and this, his parish church, contains some of his most powerful work. Lining the chancel are two huge (45 feet by 20 feet) canvases, *Adoration of the Golden Calf* and *Last Judgment.* In glowing contrast to this awesome spectacle is Tintoretto's *Presentation of the Virgin at the Temple* and the simple chapel where he and his children, Marietta and Domenico, are buried. Paintings by Domenico, Cima da Conegliano, Palma il Giovane, Palma il Vecchio, and Titian also hang in the church. A chapel displays a photographic reproduction of a precious *Madonna with Child* by Giovanni Bellini. The original was stolen one night in 1993. Don't miss the beautifully austere, late-Gothic cloister (1460), which you enter through the small door to the right of the church; it is frequently used for exhibitions but may be open at other times as well. ⊠ *Campo della Madonna dell'Orto, Cannaregio* ☎ *041/795991* 🎫 *€3* Ⓜ *Vaporetto: Orto.*

Museo Ebraico (*Jewish Museum*)

SYNAGOGUE | The small but well-arranged museum highlights centuries of Venetian Jewish culture with splendid silver Hanukkah lamps and Torahs, and beautifully decorated wedding contracts handwritten in Hebrew. Tours of the ghetto and its five synagogues in Italian and English leave from the museum hourly (on the half hour). ⊠ *Campo del Ghetto Nuovo, Cannaregio 2902/B, Cannaregio* ☎ *041/715359* ⊕ *www.museoebraico. it* 🎫 *€10* 🕑 *Closed Sat.* Ⓜ *Vaporetto: San Marcuola, Guglie.*

Palazzo Vendramin-Calergi

CASINO | Hallowed as the site of Richard Wagner's death and today Venice's most glamorous casino, this magnficent edifice found its fame centuries earlier: Venetian star architect Mauro Codussi (1440–1504) essentially invented Venetian Renaissance architecture with this design. Built for the Loredan family around 1500, Codussi's palace married the fortresslike design of the Florentine Alberti's Palazzo Rucellai with the lightness and delicacy of Venetian Gothic. Note how Codussi beautifully exploits the flickering light of Venetian waterways to play across the building's facade and to pour in through the generous windows. Venice has always prized the beauty of this palace. In 1652 its owners were convicted of a rather gruesome murder, and the punishment would have involved, as was customary, the demolition of their palace. The murderers were banned from the Republic, but the palace, in view of its beauty and historical importance, was spared. Only a newly added wing was torn down. ⊠ *Cannaregio 2040, Cannaregio* ☎ *041/5297111* ⊕ *www.casinovenezia.it* 🎫 *Casino €5–€10; free for visitors staying at a Venice hotel* Ⓜ *Vaporetto: San Marcuola.*

★ Santa Maria dei Miracoli

CHURCH | Tiny yet harmoniously proportioned, this Renaissance gem, built between 1481 and 1489, is sheathed in marble and decorated inside with exquisite marble reliefs. Architect Pietro Lombardo (circa 1435–1515) miraculously compressed the building to fit its lot, then created the illusion of greater size by varying the color of the exterior, adding extra pilasters on the building's canal side and offsetting the arcade windows to make the arches appear deeper. The church was built to house *I Miracoli*, an image of the Virgin Mary by Niccolò di Pietro (1394–1440) that is said to have performed miracles—look for it on the high altar. ✉ *Campo Santa Maria Nova, Cannaregio* ☎ *041/2750462 Chorus Foundation* ⊕ *www.chorusvenezia.org* ▣ *€3 (free with Chorus Pass)* ⊙ *Closed Sun.* Ⓜ *Vaporetto: Rialto.*

🍴 Restaurants

Algiubagiò
$$$ | **ITALIAN** | Algiubagiò has a dual personality: at lunch it serves big salads (a better bet than the pizza) and other light fare; at dinner, you'll find heartier primi like their classic guinea fowl ravioli followed by secondi like Angus fillets with rosemary. The young, friendly staff also serve ice cream, drinks, and sandwiches all day. **Known for:** lovely waterfront seating with views of the Dolomites; airy respite for lunch or a snack; romantic spot for dinner. ⑤ *Average main: €30* ✉ *Fondamente Nove, Cannaregio 5039, Cannaregio* ☎ *041/5236084* ⊕ *www.algiubagio.net* Ⓜ *Vaporetto: Fondamente Nove.*

★ Dalla Marisa
$$ | **ITALIAN** | This is the most famous workingman's restaurant in Venice; if you can get a table for lunch, you'll eat, without any choice, what Marisa prepares for her blue-collar clientele—generally, enormous portions of excellent pasta, followed by a hearty roast meat course (frequently game, more infrequently fish) for an unbelievably inexpensive fixed price. Dinner is a bit more expensive, and you may have some choice, but not much; for the authentic "Marisa experience," go for lunch. **Known for:** very reasonable prices; authentic, well-prepared Venetian food; limited menu choices. ⑤ *Average main: €15* ✉ *Fondamenta di San Giobbe 652b,*

Cannaregio ☎ *041/720211* ⊙ *Closed 1 wk. in Aug. No dinner Sun.–Mon. and Wed.*

Enoteca Do Colonne
$ | **WINE BAR** | Venetians from this working-class neighborhood frequent this friendly bacaro, not just for a glass of very drinkable wine, but also because of its excellent selection of traditional Venetian cicheti for lunch. There's a large assortment of sandwiches and panini, as well as luscious tidbits like grilled vegetables, breaded and fried sardines and shrimp, and a superb version of baccalà mantecato, along with Venetian working-class specialties, such as *musetto* (a sausage made from pigs' snouts served warm with polenta) and *nervetti* (veal tendons with lemon and parsley). **Known for:** the best *musetto* (sausage with polenta) in town; a cozy place for locals to hang out; classic cicheti and sandwiches. ⑤ *Average main: €8* ✉ *Rio Terà Cristo, Cannaregio 1814, Cannaregio* ☎ *041/5240453* ⊕ *www.docolonne.it* Ⓜ *Vaporetto: San Marcuola.*

Osteria Ca' d'Oro (alla Vedova)
$ | **VENETIAN** |"The best polpette in town," you'll hear fans of the venerable Vedova say, and that explains why it's an obligatory stop on any *giro d'ombra* (bacaro tour); the polpette are always hot and crunchy—and also gluten-free, as they're made with polenta. Ca' d'Oro is a full-fledged trattoria as well, but make sure to reserve ahead: it's no secret to those seeking traditional Venetian fare at reasonable prices, locals and travelers alike. **Known for:** house wine served in tiny traditional glasses; famous polpette (meatballs); classic Venetian cuisine. ⑤ *Average main: €12* ✉ *Calle del Pistor, Cannaregio 3912, off Strada Nova, Cannaregio* ☎ *041/5285324* ⊙ *Closed Aug. No lunch Sun.* Ⓜ *Vaporetto: Ca' d'Oro.*

Osteria La Bottega ai Promessi Sposi
$$ | **VENETIAN** | Join locals at the *banco* (counter) premeal for an *ombra* (small glass of wine) and cicheti like polpette or violet eggplant rounds, or reserve a table for a full meal in the dining room or the

intimate courtyard. A varied, seasonal menu includes local standards like calf's liver or grilled *canestrelli* (tiny Venetian scallops), along with creative variations on classic Venetian fare, such as home-made ravioli stuffed with radicchio di Treviso or orecchiette with a scrumptious minced-duck sauce. **Known for:** friendly, helpful service; creative cicheti and wine; regularly changing menu with both traditional and modern choices. $ *Average main: €18* ⊠ *Calle de l'Oca, just off Campo Santi Apostoli, Cannaregio 4367, Cannaregio* ☎ *041/2412747* ⊘ *No lunch Mon.* Ⓜ *Vaporetto: Ca' d'Oro.*

Osteria Orto dei Mori

$$$ | ITALIAN | This small, popular neighborhood osteria—located canalside, just under the nose of the campo's famous corner statue—specializes in creative versions of classic Italian (but not necessarily Venetian) dishes; don't skip dessert, as their tiramisu wins raves. When the weather's nice, dining outside in the square can be a truly memorable experience. **Known for:** buzzing atmosphere with locals and tourists alike; traditional Italian dishes with modern accents; choice local wine selection. $ *Average main: €26* ⊠ *Campo dei Mori, Fondamenta dei Mori, Cannaregio 3386, Cannaregio* ☎ *041/5243677* ⊕ *www.osteriaortodeimori.com* ⊘ *Closed Tues. and Wed.* Ⓜ *Vaporetto: Orto, Ca' d'Oro, San Marcuola.*

Tiziano

$ | ITALIAN | A fine variety of excellent tramezzini lines the display cases at this *tavola calda* (roughly the Italian equivalent of a cafeteria) on the main thoroughfare from the Rialto to Santi Apostoli; inexpensive salad plates and daily pasta specials are also served. This is a great place for a light meal or snack before a performance at the nearby Teatro Malibran. **Known for:** efficient (if occasionally grumpy) service; quick meals or snacks, especially tramezzini; modest prices. $ *Average*

main: €8 ⊠ *Salizada San Giovanni Crisostomo, Cannaregio 5747, Cannaregio* ☎ *041/5235544* Ⓜ *Vaporetto: Rialto.*

★ Vini da Gigio

$$ | VENETIAN | A brother-sister team run this refined trattoria, where you're made to feel as if you've been personally invited to lunch or dinner. Indulge, perhaps, in rigatoni with duck sauce or arugula-stuffed ravioli, seafood risotto made to order, or sesame-encrusted tuna. Just note, though, that it's the meat dishes that steal the show: the steak with red-pepper sauce and the *tagliata di agnello* (sautéed lamb fillet with a light, crusty coating) are both superb, and you'll never enjoy a better *fegato alla veneziana* (Venetian-style liver with onions). **Known for:** superb meat dishes like *fegato alla veneziana* (Venetian-style liver with onions); helpful and professional service; one of the city's best wine cellars. $ *Average main: €24* ⊠ *Fondamenta San Felice, Cannaregio 3628/A, Cannaregio* ☎ *041/5285140* ⊕ *www.vinidagigio.com* ⊘ *Closed Mon. and Tues. and 2 wks in Aug.* Ⓜ *Vaporetto: Ca' d'Oro.*

☕ Coffee and Quick Bites

★ Vino Vero

$ | WINE BAR | Swing by this pint-sized wine bar for cicheti and crostini that's just a bit different and fresher than what you'll find elsewhere, along with a fine selection of natural wines. Though there's not much space inside, try to snag one of the coveted seats by the canal. **Known for:** pretty canalside seating; large selection of both Italian and international natural wines; delectable small bites. $ *Average main: €10* ⊠ *Fondamenta de la Misericordia, Cannaregio 2497, Cannaregio* ☎ *041/2750044* ⊕ *vinovero.wine* ⊘ *No lunch Mon.* Ⓜ *Vaporetto: Madonna dell'Orto, Ca' d'Oro.*

Hotels

Al Palazzetto

$$ | B&B/INN | FAMILY | Understated Venetian decor, original exposed-beam ceilings and terrazzo flooring, and large rooms suitable for families or small groups are hallmarks of this intimate, family-owned guesthouse. **Pros:** good value for money; authentic 18th-century palace; clean and quiet. **Cons:** not many amenities; old-fashioned decor; a bit rough around the edges. $ *Rooms from: €149* ✉ *Calle delle Vele, Cannaregio 4057, Cannaregio* ☎ *041/2750897* ⊕ *www.guesthouse.it* ⌁ *5 rooms* |◎| *Free Breakfast* Ⓜ *Vaporetto: Ca' d'Oro.*

★ Al Ponte Antico

$$$$ | HOTEL | This hospitable 16th-century palace inn has lined its Gothic windows with tiny white lights, creating an inviting glow that's emblematic of the luxurious, distinctively Venetian warmth inside. **Pros:** upper-level terrace overlooks Grand Canal; superior service; family run. **Cons:** books up quickly; beds a little hard for some; in one of the busiest areas of the city (although not particularly noisy). $ *Rooms from: €330* ✉ *Calle dell'Aseo, Cannaregio 5768, Cannaregio* ☎ *041/2411944* ⊕ *www.alponteantico. com* ⌁ *9 rooms* |◎| *Free Breakfast* Ⓜ *Vaporetto: Rialto.*

★ Ca' Sagredo Hotel

$$$ | HOTEL | This expansive palace has been the Sagredo family residence since the mid-1600s and has the decor to prove it: a massive staircase has Longhi wall panels soaring above it; large common areas are adorned with original art by Tiepolo, Longhi, and Ricci; and a traditional Venetian style dominates guest rooms, many of which have canal views and some of which have original art and architectural elements. **Pros:** rooftop terrace and indoor bar; excellent location; some of the city's best preserved interiors. **Cons:** heat in rooms controlled by front desk; more opulent than intimate; no coffee- or tea-making facilities in rooms. $ *Rooms from: €280* ✉ *Campo Santa Sofia, Cannaregio 4198/99, Cannaregio* ☎ *041/2413111* ⊕ *www.casagredohotel.com* ⌁ *42 rooms* |◎| *No Meals* Ⓜ *Vaporetto: Ca' d'Oro.*

Hotel Antico Doge

$$ | HOTEL | Once the home of Marino Faliero, a 14th-century doge who was executed for treason, this palazzo has been attentively "modernized" in elegant 18th-century Venetian style: all rooms are adorned with brocades, damask-tufted walls, gilt mirrors, and parquet floors—even the breakfast room has a stuccoed ceiling and Murano chandelier. **Pros:** some rooms have whirlpool tubs; convenient to the Rialto and beyond; romantic, atmospheric decor. **Cons:** no elevator; no outdoor garden or terrace; area outside hotel can get very busy. $ *Rooms from: €200* ✉ *Campo Santi Apostoli, Cannaregio 5643, Cannaregio* ☎ *041/2411570* ⊕ *www.anticodoge.com* ⌁ *20 rooms* |◎| *Free Breakfast* Ⓜ *Vaporetto: Ca' d'Oro, Rialto.*

Locanda Ca' Amadi

$$ | HOTEL | A historic 13th-century palazzo near the Rialto Market is a welcome retreat on a tranquil *corte,* and individually decorated rooms have tufted walls and views of a lively canal or a quiet courtyard. **Pros:** handy for sightseeing; classic Venetian style; some canal-view rooms. **Cons:** no restaurant (simple continental breakfast served, though); rooms vary a lot in size and quality; reception staff not always helpful or available. $ *Rooms from: €138* ✉ *Corte Amadi, Cannaregio 5815, Cannaregio* ☎ *041/5285210* ⊕ *www.caamadi.it* ⌁ *6 rooms* |◎| *Free Breakfast* Ⓜ *Vaporetto: Rialto.*

★ Palazzo Abadessa

$$ | HOTEL | At this late-16th-century palazzo, you can experience gracious hospitality, a luxurious atmosphere, a lush private garden, and unusually spacious guest rooms well appointed with antique-style furniture, frescoed or stuccoed ceilings, and silk fabrics. **Pros:** superb guest service; enormous walled garden, a rare and delightful treat in crowded Venice; unique and richly decorated guest rooms. **Cons:** no restaurant (buffet breakfast served); some bathrooms are small and plain; Wi-Fi can be iffy. $ *Rooms from: €170* ✉ *Calle Priuli, Cannaregio 4011, off Strada Nova, Cannaregio* ☎ *041/2413784* ⊕ *www. abadessa.com* ⊗ *Closed last 2 wks in Jan.* ➭ *15 rooms* ◯| *Free Breakfast* Ⓜ *Vaporetto: Ca' d'Oro.*

3749 Ponte Chiodo

$ | **B&B/INN** | Spending time at this charming guesthouse near the Ca' d'Oro vaporetto stop is like staying with a friend: service is warm and helpful, with lots of suggestions for dining and sightseeing. **Pros:** highly attentive service; pretty private garden; relaxed atmosphere. **Cons:** not for those looking for large-hotel amenities (no spa or gym); no restaurant, though breakfast is served in the garden; some bathrooms are smallish. $ *Rooms from: €98* ✉ *Calle Racheta, Cannaregio 3749, Cannaregio* ☎ *041/2413935* ⊕ *www.pontechiodo.it* ➭ *6 rooms* ◯| *Free Breakfast* Ⓜ *Vaporetto: Ca' d'Oro.*

🍸 Nightlife

El Sbarlefo

WINE BARS | The odd name is Venetian for "smirk," although you'll be hard-pressed to find one at this cheery, familiar bacaro with a wine selection as ample as the cicheti on offer. The spread of delectables ranges from classic polpette of meat and tuna to tomino cheese rounds to speck and robiola rolls, and the selection of wines is equally intriguing. There's often live jazz and blues on Friday and Saturday nights. El Sbarlefo has a second location in Dorsoduro, in the calle just behind the

church of San Pantalon. ✉ *Salizada del Pistor, off Campo Santi Apostoli, Cannaregio 4556/C, Cannaregio* ☎ *041/5246650* ⊕ *www.elsbarlefo.it* Ⓜ *Vaporetto: Ca' d'Oro.*

Time Social Bar

COCKTAIL LOUNGES | The seasonal cocktails at this charming mixology bar, many of which use fruit and homemade bitters, win rave reviews from visitors and locals alike. There are also small nibbles on offer if hunger strikes. ✉ *Rio Terà Farsetti, Cannaregio 1414, Cannaregio* ☎ *0338/3636951* Ⓜ *Vaporetto: San Marcuola Casino.*

Un Mondo di Vino

WINE BARS | Recharge with some wine or a cicheto or two—meat, fish, and vegetarian choices are on offer—at this cozy, friendly spot near the Miracoli church. Numerous wines are available by the glass, and the helpful servers are often happy to crack open a bottle for sampling if there's something you fancy. ✉ *Salizzada San Cancian, Cannaregio* ☎ *041/5211093* ⊕ *www.bacarounmondodivino.it* Ⓜ *Vaporetto: Rialto, Ca' d'Oro.*

🛍 Shopping

★ Gianni Basso Stampatore

STATIONERY | This traditional printer creates handmade business cards, stationery, and invitations using vintage letterpress machinery. You can choose from the selection on offer, or have your own custom designed and shipped to you at home. ✉ *Calle del Fumo, Cannaregio 5306, Cannaregio* ☎ *041/5234681* Ⓜ *Vaporetto: Fondamente Nove.*

Vittorio Constantini

ANTIQUES & COLLECTIBLES | **FAMILY** | This glass artist's workshop features unusual, intricate pieces inspired by nature—birds, butterflies, beetles, and other insects—appreciated by adults and children alike. ✉ *Calle del Fumo, Cannaregio 5311, Cannaregio* ☎ *041/5222265* ⊕ *www.*

vittoriocostantini.com *Vaporetto: Fondamente Nove.*

Castello

Castello, Venice's largest sestiere, includes all of the land from east of Piazza San Marco to the city's easternmost tip. Its name probably comes from a fortress that once stood on one of the eastern islands. Not every well-off Venetian family could find a spot or afford to build a palazzo on the Grand Canal. Many who couldn't instead settled in western Castello, taking advantage of its proximity to the Rialto and San Marco, and built the noble palazzi that today distinguish this area from the fisher's enclave in the more easterly streets of the sestiere. During the days of the Republic, eastern Castello was the primary neighborhood for workers in the shipbuilding Arsenale located in its midst and now home to the Venice Biennale. Foodies flock here for some of the city's most creative modern Italian cuisine.

TIMING

Unless you're here during the Biennale—in which case, you'll be spending at least a full day or two at the Arsenale—you can check out the neighborhood's three gorgeous churches (San Francesco della Vigna, Santi Giovanni e Paolo, and San Zaccaria), as well as the lovely rooms in the Scuola di San Giorgio degli Schiavoni (if it's open, which it isn't always), in half a day.

👁 Sights

Arsenale

MILITARY SIGHT | Visible from the street, the Porta Magna (1460), an impressive Renaissance gateway designed by Antonio Gambello, was the first classical structure to be built in Venice. It is guarded by four lions—war booty of Francesco Morosini, who took the Peloponnese from the Turks in 1687. The 10-foot-tall lion on the left stood sentinel more

than 2,000 years ago near Athens, and experts say its mysterious inscription is runic "graffiti" left by Viking mercenaries hired to suppress 11th-century revolts in Piraeus. If you look at the winged lion above the doorway, you'll notice that the Gospel at his paws is open but lacks the customary *Pax* inscription; praying for peace perhaps seemed inappropriate above a factory that manufactured weapons. The interior is not regularly open to the public, since it belongs to the Italian Navy, but it opens for the Biennale di Arte and for Venice's festival of traditional boats, Mare Maggio, held every May. If you're here at those times, don't miss the chance to look inside; you can enter from the back via a northern-side walkway leading from the Ospedale vaporetto stop. The Arsenale is said to have been founded in 1104 on twin islands. The immense facility that evolved—it was the largest industrial complex in Europe built prior to the Industrial Revolution—was given the old Venetian dialect name *arzanà*, borrowed from the Arabic *darsina'a,* meaning "workshop." At the height of its activity, in the early 16th century, it employed as many as 16,000 *arsenalotti,* workers who were among the most respected shipbuilders in the world. The Arsenale developed a type of pre–Industrial Revolution assembly line, which allowed it to build ships with astounding speed and efficiency. (This innovation existed even in Dante's time, and he immortalized these toiling workers armed with boiling tar in his *Inferno,* canto 21.) The Arsenale's efficiency was confirmed time and again—whether building 100 ships in 60 days to battle the Turks in Cyprus (1597) or completing one perfectly armed warship, start to finish, while King Henry III of France attended a banquet. ✉ *Campo de la Tana 2169, Castello* Ⓜ *Vaporetto: Arsenale.*

⭐ San Francesco della Vigna

CHURCH | Although this church contains some interesting and beautiful paintings and sculptures, it's the architecture that makes it worth the hike through a lively, middle-class residential neighborhood. The Franciscan church was enlarged and rebuilt by Jacopo Sansovino in 1534, giving it the first Renaissance interior in Venice; its proportions are said to reflect the mystic significance of the numbers three and seven dictated by Renaissance neo-Platonic numerology. The soaring but harmonious facade was added in 1562 by Palladio. The church represents a unique combination of the work of the two great stars of 16th-century Veneto architecture. As you enter, a late Giovanni Bellini *Madonna with Saints* is down some steps to the left, inside the Cappella Santa. In the Giustinian chapel to the left is Veronese's first work in Venice, an altarpiece depicting the Virgin and child with saints. In another, larger chapel on the left are bas-reliefs by Pietro and his son Tullio Lombardo. Be sure to ask to see the attached cloisters, which are usually open to visitors and quite lovely. ✉ *Campo di San Francesco della Vigna, Castello* ☎ *041/5206102* ✆ *Free* ⊘ *Closed weekends* Ⓜ *Vaporetto: Celestia.*

★ San Zaccaria

CHURCH | More a museum than a church, San Zaccaria has a striking Renaissance facade, with central and upper portions representing some of Mauro Codussi's best work. The lower portion of the facade and the interior were designed by Antonio Gambello. The original structure of the church was 14th-century Gothic, with its facade completed in 1515, some years after Codussi's death in 1504, and it retains the proportions of the rest of the essentially Gothic structure. Inside is one of the great treasures of Venice, Giovanni Bellini's celebrated altarpiece, *La Sacra Conversazione*, easily recognizable in the left nave. Completed in 1505, when the artist was 75, it shows Bellini's ability to incorporate the aesthetics of the High Renaissance into his work. It bears a closer resemblance to the contemporary works of Leonardo (it dates from approximately the same time

as the *Mona Lisa*) than it does to much of Bellini's early work. The Cappella di San Tarasio displays frescoes by Tuscan Renaissance artists Andrea del Castagno (1423–57) and Francesco da Faenza (circa 1400–51). Castagno's frescoes (1442) are considered the earliest examples of Renaissance painting in Venice. The three outstanding Gothic polyptychs attributed to Antonio Vivarini earned it the nickname "Golden Chapel." ✉ *Campo San Zaccaria, 4693 Castello, Castello* ☎ *041/5221257* ✆ *Church free, chapels and crypt €1.50* ⊘ *Closed Sun. morning* Ⓜ *Vaporetto: San Zaccaria.*

★ Santi Giovanni e Paolo

CHURCH | A venerated jewel, this gorgeous church looms over one of the most picturesque squares in Venice: the Campo Giovanni e Paolo, centered on the magnificent 15th-century equestrian statue of Bartolomeo Colleoni by the Florentine Andrea del Verrocchio. Also note the beautiful facade of the Scuola Grande di San Marco (now the municipal hospital), begun by Pietro Lombardo and completed after the turn of the 16th century by Mauro Codussi. The massive Italian Gothic church itself is of the Dominican order and was consecrated in 1430. Bartolomeo Bon's portal, combining Gothic and classical elements, was added between 1458 and 1462, using columns salvaged from Torcello. The 15th-century stained-glass window near the side entrance is breathtaking for its brilliant colors and beautiful figures; it was made in Murano from drawings by Bartolomeo Vivarini and Girolamo Mocetto (circa 1458–1531). The second official church of the Republic after San Marco, San Zanipolo is the Venetian equivalent of London's Westminster Abbey, with a great number of important people, including 25 doges, buried here. Artistic highlights include an early (1465) polyptych by Giovanni Bellini (right aisle, second altar) where the influence of Mantegna is still very evident, Alvise Vivarini's *Christ Carrying the Cross*

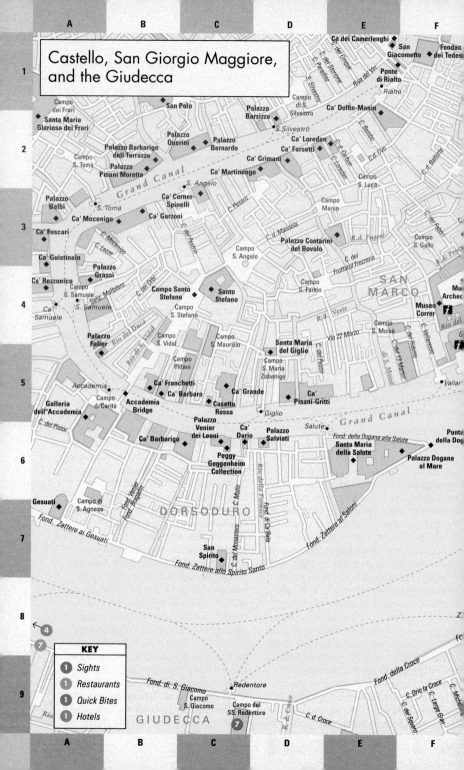

Castello, San Giorgio Maggiore, and the Giudecca

A **B** **C** **D** **E** **F**

1

Ca dei Camerlenghi • San Giacometto • Fondac dei Tedes

C. del Cinto
S. Paradiso
C. del Sterlino
Riva del Vin
Ponte di Rialto
Rialto

S. Silvestro
Campo di S. Silvestro
Ca' Dolfin-Manin

2

Santa Maria Gloriosa dei Frari •

San Polo •

Palazzo Barzizza
S. Silvestro

Palazzo Querini •
Palazzo Bernardo •

Ca' Loredan •
Ca' Farsetti •

C.d. Dio

Campo S. Tomà

Palazzo Barbarigo dell'Terrazza •
Palazzo Pisani Moretta •

Ca' Grimani •

C.d. Cabán
C. Loredan
Campo S. Luca

C.d. Ballotte

Grand Canal
Ca' Martinengo •

S. Angelo
C. Pesaro

C. Bembo

Campo Manin

C.d. Fuseri

3

Palazzo Balbi •

Ca' Corner-Spinelli •
Ca' Garzoni •

C.d. Mandola
Palazzo Contarini del Bovolo •

R.d. Fuseri
Campo S. Gallo

Ca' Mocenigo •
Ca' Foscari •

C. Mocenigo
C. Tezze
C. del Pestrin

Campo S. Angelo

C. del Fruttarol Frezzeria

R.d. Proc

Ca' Guistinain •

Palazzo Grassi •

Campo S. Angelo

SAN MARCO

4

Ca' Rezzonico •

Campo S. Samuele
S. Samuele
Saliz. Malipiero

Campo Santo Stefano •
Santo Stefano •

Campo S. Fantin

Museo Archeo

Ca' Samuele

S. Samuele

Campo S. Stefano

R.d. Veste

Museo Correr

Via 22 Marzo
Campo S. Moisè

Rio del

Rio del Duca

5

Palazzo Falier •

Campo S. Vidal
Rio di S. Vidal

Campo S. Maurizio

Santa Maria del Giglio •

C. del Pestrin
C. del Ridotto
C. del 13 Martiri
di S. Moisè

Vallar

Galleria dell'Accademia •

Accademia
Campo d. Carità

Campo Pidani

Campo S. Maria Zobenigo

Campo S. Moisè

Ca' Franchetti •
Ca' Barbaro •

Ca' Grande •

Ca' Pisani-Gritti •

Grand Canal

C. del Pistor

Accademia Bridge

Casetta Rossa •

Giglio

Salute

Fond. della Dogana alla Salute
Punta della Do

6

Ca' Barbarigo •

Palazzo Venier dei Leoni •

Ca' Dario •

Palazzo Salviati •

Santa Maria della Salute •
Palazzo Dogana al Mare •

Fond. Venier
Fond. Brazzetti

Peggy Guggenheim Collection •

Rio della Fornace
Rio di Ca' Bala

7

Gesuati •

Campo di S. Agnese

DORSODURO

Fond. Zattere ai Gesuati

San Spirito •

C. del Monastero

Fond. Zattere allo Spirito Santo

Fond. Zattere ai Saloni

8

← ④
⑦

Z

Fo

9

KEY
① *Sights*
① *Restaurants*
① *Quick Bites*
① *Hotels*

Fond. di S. Giacomo

Campo S. Giacomo

Redentore

Campo del SS. Redentore
⑦

GIUDECCA

Fond. di S. Giacomo

R.d. Croce
C.d. Croce

Fond. della Croce

C. Drio la Croce
C. Larga Gen
C. del Squero
C. Michelo

A **B** **C** **D** **E** **F**

Sights ▼
1 Arsenale J4
2 Fondazione Giorgio Cini I7
3 San Francesco della Vigna J1
4 San Giorgio Maggiore I6
5 San Zaccaria I3
6 Santi Giovanni e Paolo H1
7 Santissimo Redentore C9
8 Scuola di San Giorgio
   degli Schiavoni J2

Restaurants ▼
1 Al Covo J4
2 Alle Testiere H2
3 Cip's Club H8
4 Corte Sconta J3
5 CoVino J3
6 Il Ridotto H3
7 La Palanca A8
8 Local J2
9 Osteria di Santa Marina G1

Quick Bites ▼
1 Aciugheta H3
2 El Rèfolo J4
3 Wine Bar 5000 .... I2

Hotels ▼
1 Belmond Hotel Cipriani H8
2 Ca' dei Dogi H3
3 Ca' di Dio J4
4 Hilton Molino Stucky Venice A8
5 Hotel Danieli H4
6 Hotel La Residenza J3
7 Metropole J4
8 Ruzzini Palace Hotel H1

(sacristy), and Lorenzo Lotto's *Charity of St. Antonino* (right transept). Don't miss the Cappella del Rosario (Rosary Chapel), off the left transept, built in the 16th century to commemorate the 1571 victory of Lepanto in western Greece, when Venice led a combined European fleet to defeat the Turkish Navy. The chapel was devastated by a fire in 1867 and restored in the early years of the 20th century with works from other churches, among them the sumptuous Veronese ceiling paintings. However quick your visit, don't miss the Pietro Mocenigo tomb to the right of the main entrance, by Pietro Lombardo and his sons. Note also Tullio Lombardo's tomb of Andrea Vendramin, the original home of Tullio's *Adam*, which has recently been restored in New York City's Metropolitan Museum of Art. ⊠ *Campo dei Santi Giovanni e Paolo, Castello* ☎ *041/5235913* ⊕ *www.santigiovanniepaolo.it* ☒ *€3.50* ⊗ *Closed weekends* Ⓜ *Vaporetto: Fondamente Nove, Rialto.*

⭐ **Scuola di San Giorgio degli Schiavoni**
HISTORIC HOME | Founded in 1451 by the Dalmatian community, this small *scuola,* or confraternity, was, and still is, a social and cultural center for migrants from what is now Croatia. It contains one of Italy's most beautiful rooms, harmoniously decorated between 1502 and 1507 by Vittore Carpaccio. Although Carpaccio generally painted legendary and religious figures against backgrounds of contemporary Venetian architecture, here is perhaps one of the first instances of "Orientalism" in Western painting. Note the turbans and exotic dress of those being baptized and converted, and even the imagined, arid Middle Eastern or North African landscape in the background of several of the paintings. In this scuola for immigrants, Carpaccio focuses on "foreign" saints especially venerated in Dalmatia: Sts. George, Tryphone, and Jerome. He combined keen empirical observation with fantasy, a sense of warm color, and late medieval realism.

(Look for the priests fleeing St. Jerome's lion, or the body parts in the dragon's lair.) ■ **TIP→ Opening hours are quite flexible. Since this is a must-see site, check in advance so you won't be disappointed.** ⊠ *Calle dei Furlani, Castello 3259/A, Castello* ☎ *041/5228828* ⊕ *www.scuoladalmatavenezia.com* ☒ *€5* ⊗ *Closed Tues. and Wed.* Ⓜ *Vaporetto: Arsenale, San Zaccaria.*

🍴 Restaurants

Al Covo
$$$ | VENETIAN | For years, Diane and Cesare Binelli's Al Covo has set the standard of excellence for traditional, refined Venetian cuisine; the Binellis are dedicated to providing their guests with the freshest, highest-quality fish from the Adriatic, and vegetables, when at all possible, from the islands of the Venetian lagoon and the fields of the adjacent Veneto region. Although their cuisine could be correctly termed "classic Venetian," it always offers surprises, like the juicy crispness of their legendary fritto misto—reliant upon a nonconventional secret ingredient in the batter—or the heady aroma of their fresh anchovies marinated in wild fennel, an herb somewhat foreign to Veneto. **Known for:** Diane's chocolate cake for dessert; sophisticated Venetian flavors; top-notch local ingredients. ⑤ *Average main: €29* ⊠ *Campiello Pescaria, Castello 3968, Castello* ☎ *041/5223812* ⊕ *www.ristorantealcovo.com* ⊗ *Closed Wed.–Thurs., 3 wks. in Jan., and 10 days in Aug.* Ⓜ *Vaporetto: Arsenale.*

⭐ Alle Testiere
$$$ | VENETIAN | The name is a reference to the old headboards that adorn the walls of this tiny, informal restaurant, but the food (not the decor) is undoubtedly the focus. Local foodies consider this one of the most refined eateries in the city thanks to chef Bruno Cavagni's gently creative take on classic Venetian fish dishes; the chef's artistry seldom draws

attention to itself, but simply reveals new dimensions to familiar fare, creating dishes that stand out for their lightness and balance. **Known for:** wonderful wine selection; daily changing fish offerings, based on what's fresh at the market; excellent pasta with seafood. ⑤ *Average main: €29* ✉ *Castello 5801, Castello* ☎ *041/5227220* ⊕ *www.osterialletestiere.it* ⊘ *Closed Sun. and Mon., 3 wks in Jan.–Feb., and 4 wks in July–Aug.*

★ Corte Sconta
$$$ | **SEAFOOD** | The heaping seafood antipasti alone is reason enough to visit this classic seafood-focused eatery close to the Biennale—think tuna and swordfish carpaccio, spider crab, clams, crab paté, and a variety of fish. But you'll also want to stay for the excellent mains, particularly soft-shell crab, mixed grilled fish, and spaghetti vongole, plus the lovely courtyard setting. **Known for:** service with a sense of humor; charming atmosphere with outdoor seating; some of the best seafood in town. ⑤ *Average main: €25* ✉ *Calle del Pestrin, Castello 3886, Castello* ☎ *041/5227024* ⊕ *www. cortescontavenezia.com* ⊘ *Closed Sun. and Mon.* Ⓜ *Vaporetto: Arsenale.*

★ CoVino
$$ | **MODERN ITALIAN** | You'll feel like a part of the action in this miniscule natural wine–focused eatery, where the seasonal, organic dishes are prepared right in front of you in the open kitchen. The wine list includes more than 100 labels available by the bottle, or ask for their expert advice on pairing terroir-driven wines with your Slow Food meal. **Known for:** friendly atmosphere; focus on local ingredients; fixed-price menus (2–3 courses for lunch and 3 courses for dinner). ⑤ *Average main: €22* ✉ *Calle del Pestrin, Castello 3829, Castello* ☎ *041/2412705* ⊕ *www. covinovenezia.com* ⊘ *Closed Tues. and Wed.* Ⓜ *Vaporetto: Arsenale.*

★ Il Ridotto
$$$$ | **MODERN ITALIAN** | Longtime restaurateur Gianni Bonaccorsi (proprietor of the popular Aciugheta nearby) has established an eatery where he can pamper a limited number of lucky patrons with his imaginative cuisine and impeccable taste in wine. *Ridotto* means "small, private place," which this very much is, evoking an atmosphere of secrecy and intimacy; the innovative menus tend toward lighter but wonderfully tasty versions of classic dishes. Ask them to recommend a wine from the excellent cantina. **Known for:** extensive wine recommendations; some of the most creative cuisine in Venice; excellent five-, seven-, or nine-course tasting menus. ⑤ *Average main: €40* ✉ *Campo SS. Filippo e Giacomo, Castello 4509, Castello* ☎ *041/5208280* ⊕ *www. ilridotto.com* ⊘ *Closed Tues. and Wed.* Ⓜ *Vaporetto: San Zaccaria.*

★ Local
$$$$ | **VENETIAN** | In a simple yet charming setting with beamed ceilings and terrazzo floors, a sister and brother team oversee their "New Venetian Cuisine," where local ingredients are used to prepare reinvented traditional dishes, often with Japanese influences. Menus are tasting-menu only, ranging from three to 12 courses (with a less expensive three-course option at weekday lunch), and wine pairings from their extensive list are a recommended treat. **Known for:** highly attentive staff; ingredients from Italian producers; risotto with *gò* (goby fish), nori seaweed, and *katsuobushi* (dried smoked tuna). ⑤ *Average main: €95* ✉ *Salizzada dei Greci, Castello 3303, Castello* ☎ *041/2411128* ⊕ *www.ristorantelocal.com* ⊘ *Closed Tues. and Wed.* Ⓜ *Vaporetto: San Zaccaria.*

★ Osteria di Santa Marina
$$$ | **VENETIAN** | The candlelit tables on this romantic campo are inviting enough, but it's the intimate restaurant's imaginative kitchen that's likely to win you over; you can order consistently excellent pasta, fish, or meat dishes à la carte or opt for one of the rewarding tasting menus. The wine list is ample and well thought

out, and service is gracious, warm, and professional. **Known for:** charming and romantic setting; innovative and artfully presented modern Venetian food; wonderful wine pairings. $ *Average main: €28* ⌂ *Campo Santa Marina, Castello 5911, Castello* ☎ *041/5285239* ⊕ *www. osteriadisantamarina.com* ◷ *Closed Sun. and 2 wks in Aug. No lunch Mon.* Ⓜ *Vaporetto: Rialto.*

☕ Coffee and Quick Bites

Aciugheta
$$ | **WINE BAR** | Almost an institution, the "Tiny Anchovy" (as the name translates) doubles as a pizzeria-trattoria, but the real reason for coming is the bar's tasty cicheti, like the eponymous anchovy minipizzas, the *arancioni* rice balls, and the polpette. Wines by the glass change daily, but there is always a good selection of local wines on hand, as well as some Tuscan and Piedmontese choices thrown in for good measure. **Known for:** good selection of Italian wines by the glass; *pizzetta con l'acciuga* (minipizza with anchovy); mix of traditional and more modern cicheti. $ *Average main: €15* ⌂ *Campo SS. Filippo e Giacomo, Castello 4357, Castello* ☎ *041/5224292* ⊕ *www. aciugheta.com* ◷ *Closed Mon.* Ⓜ *Vaporetto: San Zaccaria.*

El Rèfolo
$$ | **WINE BAR** | At this contemporary cantina and hip hangout in a very Venetian neighborhood, the owner pairs enthusiastically chosen wines and artisanal beers with select meat, savory cheese, and seasonal vegetable combos. With outside-only seating (not particularly comfortable), it's more appropriate for an aperitivo and a light meal. **Known for:** boisterous atmosphere outside in nice weather; good selection of wine and beer; filling meat and cheese plates. $ *Average main: €15* ⌂ *Via Garibaldi,*

Castello 1580, Castello ☎ *344/1636759* ⊕ *www.elrefolo.it* ◷ *Closed Mon.* Ⓜ *Vaporetto: Arsenale.*

Wine Bar 5000
$ | **WINE BAR** | Nibble on a selection of cicheti or a cheese or meat plate at this cozy wine bar on Campo San Severo, near the Basilica dei Frari. You can either dine inside the brick-walled, Murano glass-chandeliered space, or watch the gondolas sail by at a table outdoors next to the quiet adjacent Severno canal. **Known for:** small but well-prepared choice of cicheti; lovely outdoor seating area; large wine list, including biodynamic options. $ *Average main: €10* ⌂ *Campo San Severo, Castello 5000, Castello* ☎ *041/5201557* ⊕ *www.lunasentada.it/ winebar5000* ◷ *Closed Tues. and Wed.* Ⓜ *Vaporetto: San Zaccaria.*

🛏 Hotels

★ Ca' dei Dogi
$ | **HOTEL** | A quiet courtyard secluded from the San Marco melee offers an island of calm in six guest rooms and two apartments (some with private terraces overlooking the Doge's Palace, one with a Jacuzzi), which are individually decorated with contemporary furnishings and accessories. **Pros:** traditional Italian restaurant on-site; amazing location close to Doge's Palace and Piazza San Marco; balconies with wonderful views. **Cons:** no elevator and lots of stairs; rooms are on the small side; bathrooms can feel cramped. $ *Rooms from: €116* ⌂ *Corte Santa Scolastica, Castello 4242, Castello* ☎ *041/2413751* ⊕ *www.cadeidogi. it* ◷ *Closed 3 wks. in Dec.* ⇆ *6 rooms* ⦿ *Free Breakfast* Ⓜ *Vaporetto: San Zaccaria.*

Ca' di Dio
$$$$ | **HOTEL** | Housed in a palace dating from 1272, with interiors updated by of-the-moment architect Patricia

Urquiola, this deluxe hotel offers rooms with views of San Giorgio Maggiore island, two restaurants, and two internal courtyards, all within striking distance of the Venice Biennale grounds. **Pros:** convenient to the Biennale; most guest rooms are suites; on-site gym and spa. **Cons:** not for fans of traditional design; quite expensive; a walk from traditional Venetian sights. $ *Rooms from: €500* ⊠ *Riva Ca' di Dio, Castello 5866, Castello* ⊕ *vretreats.com/en/ca-di-dio* ⦿ *Free Breakfast* Ⓜ *Vaporetto: Arsenale.*

★ Hotel Danieli

$$$$ | HOTEL | One of the city's most famous lodgings—built in the 14th century and run as a hotel since 1822—lives up to its reputation: the chance to explore the wonderful, highly detailed lobby is itself a reason to book an overnight stay, plus the views along the lagoon are fantastic, the rooms gorgeous, and the food fabulous. **Pros:** historical and inviting lobby; tasty cocktails at Bar Dandolo; amazing rooftop views. **Cons:** service can be indifferent; some rooms feel dated; lots of American tourists. $ *Rooms from: €500* ⊠ *Riva degli Schiavoni, Castello 4196, Castello* ☎ *041/5226480* ⊕ *www. marriott.com/hotels/travel/vcelc-hotel-danieli-a-luxury-collection-hotel-venice* ⦿ *210 rooms* ⦿ *No Meals* Ⓜ *Vaporetto: San Zaccaria.*

Hotel La Residenza

$ | HOTEL | Set in a quiet campo, this renovated 15th-century Gothic-Byzantine palazzo has simple but spacious rooms and lovely public spaces filled with chandeliers, 18th-century paintings, and period reproduction furnishings. **Pros:** affordable rates; lavish salon and breakfast room; quiet residential area, steps from Riva degli Schiavoni and 10 minutes from Piazza San Marco. **Cons:** basic guest rooms; no elevator; sparse breakfast. $ *Rooms from: €80* ⊠ *Campo Bandiera e Moro (or Bragora), Castello 3608, Castello* ☎ *041/5285315* ⊕ *www.*

venicelaresidenza.com ⦿ *15 rooms* ⦿ *No Meals* Ⓜ *Vaporetto: Arsenale.*

★ Metropole

$$$ | HOTEL | Atmosphere prevails in this labyrinth of opulent, intimate spaces featuring classic Venetian decor combined with exotic Eastern influences: the owner—a lifelong collector of unusual objects—has filled the common areas and sumptuously appointed guest rooms with an assortment of antiques and curiosities. **Pros:** great restaurant and bar; hotel harkens back to the gracious Venice of a bygone era; suites have private roof terraces with water views. **Cons:** rooms with views are considerably more expensive; one of the most densely touristed locations in the city; quirky, eccentric collections on display not for everyone. $ *Rooms from: €216* ⊠ *Riva degli Schiavoni, Castello 4149, Castello* ☎ *041/5205044* ⊕ *www.hotelmetropole. com* ⦿ *67 rooms* ⦿ *Free Breakfast* Ⓜ *Vaporetto: San Zaccaria.*

Ruzzini Palace Hotel

$$ | HOTEL | Renaissance- and Baroque-style common areas are soaring spaces with Venetian terrazzo flooring, frescoed and exposed beam ceilings, and Murano chandeliers; guest rooms tastefully mix historical style with contemporary furnishings and appointments. **Pros:** great buffet breakfast (not included in all rates); a luminous, aristocratic ambience; located on a lively Venetian campo not frequented by tourists. **Cons:** relatively far from a vaporetto stop; plain bathrooms; no restaurant on-site. $ *Rooms from: €192* ⊠ *Campo Santa Maria Formosa, Castello 5866, Castello* ☎ *041/2410447* ⊕ *www.ruzzinipalace.com* ⦿ *28 rooms* ⦿ *No Meals* Ⓜ *Vaporetto: San Zaccaria, Rialto.*

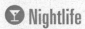 Nightlife

Bar Dandolo

COCKTAIL LOUNGES | Even if you're not staying at Hotel Danieli, it's worth a stop to marvel at its bar's over-the-top decor inside a 14th-century palace. Though pricey, it's a highly atmospheric place to sample their signature Vesper martini (gin, vodka, martini dry, and Angostura bitters), or another cocktail of your choice, usually accompanied by live piano music. ✉ *Hotel Danieli, Riva degli Schiavoni, Castello 4196, Castello* ☎ *041/5226480* ⊕ *www.marriott.com* Ⓜ *Vaporetto: San Zaccaria.*

Zanzibar

CAFÉS | This kiosk bar is very popular on warm summer evenings with Venetians-in-the-know and tourists. Although there's food, it's mostly limited to conventional Venetian sandwiches and commercial ice cream. The most interesting thing about the place is its location with a view of the church of Santa Maria Formosa, which makes it a pleasant place for a drink and a good place for people-watching. ✉ *Campo Santa Maria Formosa, Castello 5840, Castello* ☎ *345/9423998* Ⓜ *Vaporetto: San Zaccaria.*

 ## Shopping

★ Banco Lotto No. 10

WOMEN'S CLOTHING | All of the one-of-a-kind clothes and bags on sale at this vintage-inspired boutique were designed and created by residents of the women's prison on Giudecca Island. ✉ *Salizada Sant'Antonin, Castello 3478/A, Castello* ☎ *041/5221439* Ⓜ *Vaporetto: San Zaccaria.*

★ Papier Mache–Laboratorio di Artigianato Artistico

OTHER SPECIALTY STORE | **FAMILY** | If you're looking for an authentic Venetian mask, this is the place to come. Owner Stefano and his talented team of artists create exquisite handmade masks that can be custom ordered if you don't see what you want, as well as shipped worldwide. ✉ *Calle Lunga Santa Maria Formosa, Castello 5174/B, Castello* ☎ *041/5229995*

⊕ *www.papiermache.it* Ⓜ *Vaporetto: Ospedale.*

San Giorgio Maggiore and the Giudecca

Beckoning travelers across St. Mark's Basin is the island of San Giorgio Maggiore, separated by a small channel from the Giudecca. A tall brick campanile on that distant bank nicely complements the Campanile of San Marco. Beneath it looms the stately dome of one of Venice's greatest churches, San Giorgio Maggiore, the creation of Andrea Palladio. To the west, on the Giudecca, is Palladio's other masterpiece, the church of the Santissimo Redentore.

You can reach San Giorgio Maggiore via Vaporetto Line 2 from San Zaccaria. The next three stops on the line take you to the Giudecca. The island's past may be shrouded in mystery, but despite recent gentrification by artists and well-to-do bohemians, it's still down-to-earth and one of the city's few remaining primarily working-class neighborhoods. Interestingly, you find that most Venetians don't even consider the Giudecchini Venetians at all.

TIMING

A half day should be plenty of time to visit the area. Allow about a half hour to see each of the churches and an hour or two to look around the Giudecca.

 ## Sights

★ Fondazione Giorgio Cini

(*Cini Foundation*)

OTHER MUSEUM | Adjacent to San Giorgio Maggiore is a complex that now houses the Cini Foundation; it contains a very beautiful cloister designed by Palladio in 1560, his refectory, and a library designed by Longhena, as well as 10 "Vatican Chapels" created for the 2018

Did You Know?

The nobility in Venice used to be extremely competitive about their gondolas, decorating them in flamboyant colors and over-the-top ornaments. A law in the 16th century put an end to that. Today, all gondolas in Venice must be painted boring black, though they are allowed three flourishes: a curly tail, a pair of seahorses, and a multi-pronged prow.

Architecture Biennale by renowned architects, including Norman Foster, now on permanent display. Guided tours are given from 11 am to 2:30 pm daily (except Wednesday) from November through mid-March and from 10 am to 6 pm daily from mid-March through October; reservations are required. ⊠ *Isola di San Giorgio Maggiore, San Giorgio Maggiore* ☎ *041/2710237* ⊕ *www.cini.it* ⌛ *Reservations required* ⛴ *€14 for guided tour of either the Foundation buildings or the Vatican Chapels; €18 for guided tour of both the Foundation buildings and the Vatican Chapels* ⊗ *Closed Wed. Nov.– mid-Mar.* Ⓜ *Vaporetto: San Giorgio.*

★ **San Giorgio Maggiore**

CHURCH | There's been a church on this island since the 8th century, with the addition of a Benedictine monastery in the 10th. Today's refreshingly airy and simply decorated church of brick and white marble was begun in 1566 by Palladio and displays his architectural hallmarks of mathematical harmony and classical influence. *The Last Supper* and the *Gathering of Manna,* two of Tintoretto's later works, line the chancel. To the right of the entrance hangs *The Adoration of the Shepherds* by Jacopo Bassano (1517–92); affection for his home in the foothills, Bassano del Grappa, is evident in the bucolic subjects and terra-firma colors he chooses. If they have time, monks are happy to show Carpaccio's *St. George and the Dragon,* which hangs in a private room. The campanile dates from 1791, the previous structures having collapsed twice. ⊠ *Isola di San Giorgio Maggiore, San Giorgio Maggiore* ☎ *041/5227827 San Giorgio Maggiore* ⊕ *www.abbaziasan-giorgio.it* ⛴ *Church free, campanile €6* Ⓜ *Vaporetto: San Giorgio.*

Santissimo Redentore

CHURCH | After a plague in 1576 claimed some 50,000 people—nearly one-third of the city's population (including Titian)— Andrea Palladio was asked to design a commemorative church. The Giudecca's

Capuchin friars offered land and their services, provided the building's design was in keeping with the simplicity of their hermitage. Consecrated in 1592, after Palladio's death, the Redentore (considered Palladio's supreme achievement in ecclesiastical design) is dominated by a dome and a pair of slim, almost minaretlike bell towers. Its deceptively simple, stately facade leads to a bright, airy interior. There aren't any paintings or sculptures of note, but the harmony and elegance of the interior makes a visit worthwhile. For hundreds of years, on the third weekend in July, it was tradition for the doge to make a pilgrimage here and give thanks to the Redeemer for ending the 16th-century plague. The event has become the Festa del Redentore, a favorite Venetian festival featuring boats, fireworks, and outdoor feasting. It's the one time of the year when you can walk to the Giudecca—across a temporary pontoon bridge connecting Redentore with the Zattere. ⊠ *Fondamenta San Giacomo, Giudecca* ☎ *041/5231415, 041/2750462 Chorus Foundation* ⊕ *www.chorusvenezia. org* ⛴ *€3 (free with Chorus Pass)* ⊗ *Closed Sun.* Ⓜ *Vaporetto: Redentore.*

🍴 Restaurants

Cip's Club

$$$$ | VENETIAN | Though it's all about the views at the Belmond Cipriani's indoor/outdoor restaurant—on the water's edge, looking out at the Venice skyline—the well-prepared renditions of Venetian classics and extensive wine list certainly don't play second fiddle. Taking the complimentary 10-minute boat ride to and from San Marco also adds to the thoroughly romantic feel. **Known for:** relaxing lunch destination; sophisticated service; sublime Venice vistas. ⓢ *Average main: €48* ⊠ *Belmond Hotel Cipriani, Giudecca 10, Giudecca* ☎ *041/240801* ⊕ *www.belmond.com/hotels/europe/italy/venice/belmond-hotel-cipriani/dining* Ⓜ *Vaporetto: Zitelle.*

La Palanca

$$ | ITALIAN | It's all about the views at this classic wine bar–restaurant, where tables perched on the water's edge are often filled with both locals and visitors, particularly at lunchtime. The homemade pasta and fish dishes are highly recommended, and although they don't really serve dinner, a filling selection of cicheti is offered in the evening. **Known for:** superlative views; sea bass ravioli; good wine list. $ *Average main: €15* ✉ *Isola della Giudecca 448, Giudecca* ☎ *041/5287719* ⊘ *Closed Sun.* Ⓜ *Vaporetto: Palanca.*

 ## Hotels

★ Belmond Hotel Cipriani

$$$$ | HOTEL | With amazing service, wonderful rooms, fab restaurants, and a large pool and spa—all just a five-minute boat ride from Piazza San Marco (the hotel water shuttle leaves every 15 minutes, 24 hours a day)—the Cipriani is Venetian luxe at its best. **Pros:** old-world charm; Michelin-starred restaurant; Olympic-size saltwater pool. **Cons:** amazingly expensive; some rooms not quite up to par; gym not open 24 hours. $ *Rooms from: €1406* ✉ *Giudecca 10, Giudecca* ☎ *041/240801* ⊕ *www.belmond.com/hotels/europe/italy/venice/belmond-hotel-cipriani* ⊘ *Closed mid-Nov.–late Mar.* ➟ *96 rooms* ⧖ *Free Breakfast* Ⓜ *Vaporetto: Zitelle.*

Hilton Molino Stucky Venice

$$ | HOTEL | FAMILY | Wooden beams and iron columns are some of the original details still visible in this redbrick — former flour mill turned hotel— which also features sublime views across the lagoon to Venice, particularly from the lively rooftop bar. **Pros:** extremely helpful staff; ample breakfast buffet; convenient boat shuttle to Venice proper. **Cons:** can hear noise from other rooms; hotel itself a bit confusing to navigate; food offerings on the pricey side. $ *Rooms from: €192* ✉ *Giudecca 810, Giudecca* ☎ *041/2723311* ⊕ *www3.hilton.com/en/hotels/italy/hilton-molino-stucky-venice-VCEHIHI/index.html* ⧖ *No Meals* ➟ *379 rooms* Ⓜ *Vaporetto: Palanca.*

 ## Nightlife

★ Skyline Rooftop Bar

COCKTAIL LOUNGES | For arguably the best views of Venice anywhere, visit this buzzy eighth-floor hotel cocktail bar. There are regular DJ and live music events during the summer months. ✉ *Hilton Molino Stucky Venice, Giudecca 810, Giudecca* ☎ *041/2723316* ⊕ *www.skylinebarvenice.it* Ⓜ *Vaporetto: Palanca.*

 ## Shopping

★ Fortuny Showroom and Factory

FABRICS | While you can't visit the factory where exquisite Fortuny fabrics have been produced since 1921, the showroom is open to the public on weekdays year-round, and fabric is available for purchase. ✉ *Fondamenta San Biagio, Giudecca 805, Giudecca* ☎ *0393/8257651* showroom ⊕ *fortuny.com/venice* Ⓜ *Vaporetto: Palanca.*

Islands of the Lagoon

The perfect vacation from your Venetian vacation is an escape to Murano, Burano, and sleepy Torcello, the islands of the northern lagoon, or to the Lido, Venice's barrier island that forms the southern border of the Venetian Lagoon. Torcello is legendary for its beauty and breathing room, and makes a wonderful destination for a picnic (be sure to pack a lunch). Burano, which has a long history of lace production, is an island of fishing traditions and houses painted in a riot of colors—blue, yellow, pink, ocher, and dark red. Murano is renowned for its glass, and you can tour a glass factory here, but be warned that you

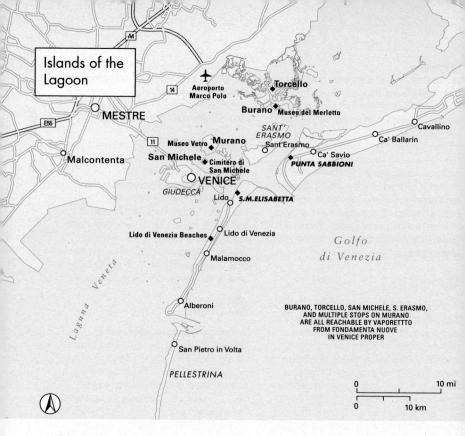

Islands of the Lagoon

A4

14 ✈ Aeroporto
Marco Polo

● Torcello

MESTRE

Burano ●   Museo del Merletto

E55

SANT'
ERASMO

11   Museo Vetro ◆ **Murano** ● Sant'Erasmo

Cavallino ●

Ca' Ballarin ●

San Michele ◆ Cimitero di
San Michele

● Ca' Savio

PUNTA SABBIONI

Malcontenta

○ **VENICE**

GIUDECCA   Lido ○ ◆ **S.M.ELISABETTA**

Lido di Venezia Beaches ◆ Lido di Venezia

*Golfo
di Venezia*

◆ Malamocco

Laguna Veneta

○ Alberoni

BURANO, TORCELLO, SAN MICHELE, S. ERASMO,
AND MULTIPLE STOPS ON MURANO
ARE ALL REACHABLE BY VAPORETTTO
FROM FONDAMENTA NUOVE
IN VENICE PROPER

● San Pietro in Volta

PELLESTRINA

0   10 mi

0   10 km

will be pressured to buy. San Michele, a vaporetto stop on the way to Murano, is the cemetery island of Venice, the resting place of many international artists who have chosen to spend eternity in this beautiful city. Finally, the Lido, which protects Venice from the waters of the Adriatic, forms the beach of Venice, and is home to a series of elegant bathing establishments.

TIMING

Hitting all the sights on all the islands takes a busy, full day. If you limit yourself to Murano and San Michele, you can easily explore for an ample half day; the same goes for Burano and Torcello. In summer the express Vaporetto Line 7 will take you to Murano from San Zaccaria (the Jolanda landing) in 25 minutes; Line 3 will take you from Piazzale Roma to Murano via the Canale di Cannaregio

in 21 minutes; otherwise, local Line 4.1 makes a 45-minute trip from San Zaccaria every 20 minutes, circling the east end of Venice, stopping at Fondamente Nove and San Michele island cemetery on the way. To see glassblowing, get off at Colonna; the Museo stop will put you near the Museo del Vetro.

Line 12 goes from Fondamente Nove direct to Murano and Burano every 30 minutes (from there, Torcello is a 5-minute ferry ride on Line 9); the full trip takes 45 minutes each way. To get to Burano and Torcello from Murano, pick up Line 12 at the Faro stop (Murano's lighthouse). Line 1 runs from San Marco to the Lido in about 15 minutes.

Sights

Cimitero di San Michele (San Michele Cemetery)

CEMETERY | It's no surprise that serenity prevails on San Michele in Venice's northern lagoon. The city's island cemetery is surrounded by ocher brick walls and laced with cypress-lined pathways amid plots filled with thousands of graves; there's also a modern extension completed by British architect David Chipperfield in 2017. Among those who have made this distinctive island their final resting place are such international arts and sciences luminaries as Igor Stravinsky, Sergei Diaghilev, Ezra Pound, and the Austrian mathematician Christian Doppler (of the Doppler effect). You're welcome to explore the grounds if you dress respectfully and adhere to a solemn code of conduct. Photography and picnicking are not permitted. ⊠ *Isola di San Michele, San Michele* ☎ *041/7292841* ⊠ *Free* Ⓜ *Vaporetto: San Michele.*

Lido di Venezia Beaches

BEACH | FAMILY | Venice's legendary beachfront, the Lido, still retains elements of Belle Époque grandeur. Most hotels here have access to charming beach clubs with cabanas, striped umbrellas, and chaise longues—all of which are often available for nonguests to use for a fee. On either end of the long barrier island, the public beaches offer a more rustic but still delightful setting for nature lovers to dig their toes in the sand. **Amenities:** food and drink; lifeguards; showers; toilets. **Best for:** swimming; walking. ⊠ *Lido di Venezia, Lido* Ⓜ *Vaporetto: Lido.*

Museo del Merletto (Lace Museum)

OTHER MUSEUM | FAMILY | Home to the Burano Lace School from 1872 to 1970, the palace of Podestà of Torcello now houses a museum dedicated to the craft for which this island is known. Detailed explanations of the manufacturing process and Burano's distinctive history as a lace-making capital provide insight into displays that showcase everything from black Venetian Carnival capes to fingerless, elbow-length "mitten gloves" fashionable in 17th-century France. Portraits of Venice's aristocracy as well as embroidered silk and brocade gowns with lace embellishments provide greater societal context on the historical use of lace in European fashion. You can also watch interesting lace-making demonstrations. ⊠ *Piazza Galuppi 187, Burano* ☎ *041/730034* ⊕ *museomerletto. visitmuve.it/en* ⊗ *Closed Mon.* ⊠ *€5* Ⓜ *Vaporetto: Burano.*

★ Museo Vetro (Glass Museum)

ART MUSEUM | FAMILY | This compact yet informative museum displays glass items dating from the 3rd century AD to today. You'll learn all about techniques introduced through the ages (many of which are still in use), including 15th-century gold-leaf decoration, 16th-century filigree work that incorporated thin bands of white or colored glass into the crystal, and the 18th-century origins of Murano's iconic chandeliers. A visit here will help you to understand the provenance of the glass you'll see for sale—and may be tempted to buy—in shops around the island. ⊠ *Fondamenta Marco Giustinian 8, Murano* ☎ *041/739586* ⊕ *museovetro. visitmuve.it/en/home* ⊠ *€10* Ⓜ *Vaporetto: Museo Murano.*

🍴 Restaurants

Acquastanca

$$ | VENETIAN | Grab a seat among locals at this charming, intimate eatery—the perfect place to pop in for a lunchtime primo or to embark on a romantic evening. The name, referring to the tranquillity of the lagoon at the turn of the tide, reflects this restaurant's approach to food and service, and you'll find such tempting seafood-based dishes as gnocchi with scallops and zucchini and curried scampi with black *venere* rice. **Known for:** relaxing atmosphere; light and fresh traditional food; focus on seafood

dishes. $ *Average main: €20* ✉ *Fonda- menta Manin 48, Murano* ☎ *041/3195125* ⊕ *www.acquastanca.it* ⊗ *Closed Sun. No dinner Tues.–Thurs. and Sat.* Ⓜ *Vaporetto: Murano Colonna, Murano Faro.*

Al Gatto Nero da Ruggero

$$ | SEAFOOD | Around since 1965, Al Gat- to Nero da Ruggero offers the best fish on Burano. No matter what you order, though, you'll savor the pride the owner and his family have in their lagoon, their island, and the quality of their cucina (maybe even more so when enjoying it on the picturesque fondamenta). **Known for:** the freshest fish and seafood around; tagliolini with spider crab; risotto Burano-style, using local ghiozzi fish. $ *Average main: €22* ✉ *Fondamenta della Giudecca 88, Burano* ☎ *041/730120* ⊕ *www.gattonero.com* ⊗ *Closed Mon., 1 wk in July, and 3 wks in Nov. No dinner Sun.* Ⓜ *Vaporetto: Burano.*

Busa alla Torre da Lele

$$ | VENETIAN | If you're shopping for glass on Murano and want to sample some first-rate home cooking for lunch, you can't do better than stopping in this unpretentious trattoria in the island's central square. Friendly waiters will bring you ample portions of pasta, with freshly made seafood-based sauces, and a substantial variety of carefully grilled or baked fish. **Known for:** outdoor dining on a square; tasty local fish and seafood; reliable lunch stop in Murano. $ *Aver- age main: €20* ✉ *Campo Santo Stefano 3, Murano* ☎ *041/739662* ⊗ *No dinner* Ⓜ *Vaporetto: Murano Colonna.*

Locanda Cipriani Restaurant

$$$ | VENETIAN | A nearly legendary res- taurant—Hemingway came here often to eat, drink, and brood under the green veranda—established by a nephew of Giuseppe Cipriani (the founder of Harry's Bar), this inn profits from its idyllic loca- tion on the island of Torcello. The food is not exceptional, especially considering

the high prices, but dining here is more about getting lost in Venetian magic. **Known for:** a peaceful lunch choice when you want to get away from Venice; wonderful historic atmosphere; tradi- tional Venetian cuisine, with a focus on seafood. $ *Average main: €34* ✉ *Piazza Santa Fosca 29, Torcello* ☎ *041/730150* ⊕ *www.locandacipriani.com* ⊗ *Closed Tues. and Jan.–early Feb. No dinner Sun.–Mon. and Wed.–Thurs.* Ⓜ *Vaporetto: Torcello.*

★ Venissa

$$$$ | MODERN ITALIAN | Stroll across the bridge from Burano to the islet of Mazzorbo to see some of the Venetian islands' only working vineyards, amid which sits this charming restaurant where seasonal dishes incorporate veg- etables, herbs, and flowers from its own gardens and fish fresh from the lagoon. To accompany your meal, pick out a local wine like the Venissa Vino Bianco, made with the island's native Dorona grape. **Known for:** perfect wine pairings; creative, sometimes avant-garde dishes; relaxed setting with tables overlooking the vines. $ *Average main: €53* ✉ *Fondamenta Santa Caterina 3, Burano* ☎ *041/5272281* ⊕ *www.venissa.it/en/restaurant* ⊗ *Closed Tues. and Nov.–Mar.* Ⓜ *Vaporetto: Mazzorbo.*

 Hotels

Hotel Excelsior Venice Lido Resort

$$$$ | HOTEL | FAMILY | Built in 1908, this grand hotel with Moorish decor has old-fashioned charm and loads of amenities—from a private beach with white cabanas and a seasonal bar and restaurant to a swimming pool, gym, and tennis courts (though, oddly, no spa). **Pros:** convenient water shuttle every 30 mins to and from Venice proper; friendly, welcoming staff; lovely beachfront loca- tion. **Cons:** can get very busy in summer and around the Venice Film Festival;

could do with a refresh; restaurant on the expensive side. $ *Rooms from: €515* ⊠ *Lungomare Marconi 41, Lido* ☎ *041/5260201* ⊕ *www.hotelexcelsiorvenezia.com* ⇴ *196* ⦿ *No Meals* Ⓜ *Vaporetto: Lido.*

Hyatt Centric Murano Venice

$$ | HOTEL | Befitting its location on Murano, this well-situated hotel is in a former glass-making factory and has vitreous works of art throughout; it also has spacious, contemporary guest rooms with dark-wood floors, brown-and-cream color schemes, and good-size bathrooms with rain showers. **Pros:** vaporetto stop right outside the hotel, free airport transfers; easy walk to restaurants and shops; excellent breakfast buffet. **Cons:** most rooms have no views; gym is basic; extra charge for using wellness center. $ *Rooms from: €190* ⊠ *Riva Longa 49, Murano* ☎ *041/2731234* ⊕ *www.hyatt. com* ⇴ *119 rooms* ⦿ *No Meals* Ⓜ *Vaporetto: Museo Murano.*

JW Marriott Venice Resort & Spa

$$$$ | RESORT | Once you get a taste of the resort's lush gardens, fabulous spa, and fantastic pools—all set on an exclusive island called Isole Delle Rose, a 20-minute boat ride from Venice—you may find yourself quickly settling in to *la dolce vita* (the sweet life). **Pros:** loads of amenties not found at hotels in Venice proper; relaxed vibe far from the Venice crowds; spacious rooms. **Cons:** not much Venetian style in rooms; getting to and from Venice can feel like a hassle; extra charge for spa. $ *Rooms from: €450* ⊠ *Isola delle Rose, Laguna di San Marco, Venezia Succursale 12, Venice* ☎ *041/8521300* ⊕ *www.jwvenice.com* ⊙ *Closed midNov.–Feb.* ⇴ *266 rooms* ⦿ *No Meals.*

🛍 Shopping

Davide Penso

JEWELRY & WATCHES | This Venice-born, Murano-based artist makes gorgeous glass necklaces, earrings, and bracelets using the lampwork technique, where he shapes colored glass rods over a flame. ⊠ *Fondamenta Riva Longa 48, Murano* ☎ *041/5274634* ⊕ *www.davidepenso. com* Ⓜ *Vaporetto: Museo Murano.*

★ Emilia Burano

FABRICS | This is not your grandmother's lace—these fourth-generation lace makers have updated their designs to produce exquisite bed linens, lampshades, sleepwear, and other items with lace trims and insets. There's also a small museum of antique lace and wedding garments from the 16th and 17th centuries. ⊠ *Piazza Galuppi 205, Burano* ☎ *041/735245* ⊕ *www.emiliaburano.it* Ⓜ *Vaporetto: Burano.*

★ Mama Salvadore Murano

GLASSWARE | To see more of glassmaking's artistic side, visit this gallery/shop that highlights works from international contemporary glass artists, including renowned 11th-generation Venice glassworker Davide Salvadore. ⊠ *Fondamenta dei Vetrai 113, Corte del Fabbro 120, Murano* ☎ *0331/6224359* ⊕ *www.mamamurano.com* Ⓜ *Vaporetto: Murano.*

★ Salviati

GLASSWARE | One of the oldest and most prestigious Italian glassmakers (founded in 1859), Salviati partners with renowned international designers, including Tom Dixon, to create beautiful contemporary pieces. ⊠ *Fondamenta Radi 16, Murano* ☎ *041/5274085* ⊕ *www.salviati.com* Ⓜ *Vaporetto: Murano Museo, Murano Navagero.*

★ Simone Cenedese

GLASSWARE | This talented second-generation glass master produces intricately designed and often whimsical glass chandeliers and sculptures. ✉ *Calle Bertolini, 6, Murano* ☎ *041/5274455* ⊕ *www. simonecenedese.it* Ⓜ *Vaporetto: Murano Faro, Murano Colonna.*

Chapter 6

THE VENETO AND FRIULI–VENEZIA GIULIA

6

Updated by
Nick Bruno

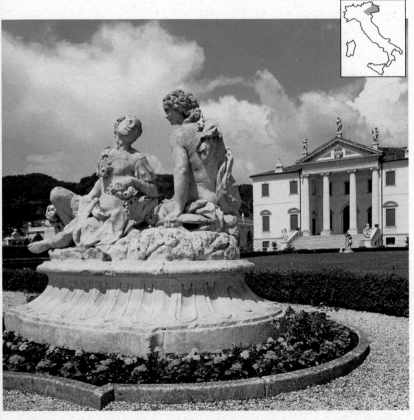

⊙ Sights   🍴 Restaurants   🛏 Hotels   🛍 Shopping   🍸 Nightlife
★★★☆☆   ★★★★★   ★★★★☆   ★★☆☆☆   ★☆☆☆☆

WELCOME TO THE VENETO AND FRIULI–VENEZIA GIULIA

TOP REASONS TO GO

★ **Giotto's frescoes in the Cappella degli Scrovegni:** In this Padua chapel, Giotto's expressive and innovative frescoes foreshadowed the Renaissance.

★ **Villa Barbaro in Maser:** Master architect Palladio's graceful creation meets Veronese's splendid frescoes in a one-time-only collaboration.

★ **Opera in Verona's ancient arena:** The performances may not be top-notch, but even serious opera fans can't resist the spectacle of these shows.

★ **Roman and early-Christian ruins at Aquileia:** Aquileia's beautiful ruins offer a glimpse of the transition from pagan to Christian Rome and are almost entirely free of tourists.

★ **The wine roads north of Treviso:** A series of routes takes you through beautiful hillsides to some of Italy's finest wines.

1 **Padua.** A city of both high-rises and history, Padua is most noted for Giotto's frescoes in the Cappella degli Scrovegni.

2 **Verona.** One of the best preserved and most beautiful cities in Italy.

3 **Vicenza.** This elegant art city bears the signature of the great 16th-century architect Andrea Palladio.

4 **Marostica.** A small hilltop-citadel town with a medieval heart and renowned for a biennial human-scale chess game.

5 **Asolo.** The "City of a Hundred Horizons" is in the wine-producing hills.

6 **Treviso.** This town with beguiling canals has more than a touch of Venetian style.

7 **Udine.** Compact and charming, this city has medieval and Renaissance splendors, including works by Tiepolo.

8 **Cividale del Friuli.** The Natisone River and ravine and the Julian Alps provide a ravishing backdrop to this town.

9 **Aquileia.** This was a pivotal port town in Augustus's Rome.

10 **Trieste.** This port city has Belle Époque cafés and palaces.

EATING AND DRINKING WELL IN THE VENETO AND FRIULI–VENEZIA GIULIA

With the decisive seasonal changes of the Venetian Arc, it's little wonder that many restaurants shun printed menus. Elements from field and forest define much of the region's cuisine, including white asparagus, herbs, chestnuts, radicchio, and wild mushrooms.

Restaurants of the Venetian Arc tend to cling to tradition, not only in the food they serve, but also when they serve it. From 2:30 in the afternoon until about 7:30 in the evening most places are closed (though you can pick up a snack at a bar during these hours), and on Sunday afternoon restaurants are packed with Italian families and friends indulging in the weekly ritual of lunching out.

Meals are still sacred for most Italians, so don't be surprised if you get disapproving looks as you gobble down a sandwich or a slice of pizza while seated on the church steps or a park bench. (In many places it's actually illegal to do so.)

THE BEST IN BEANS

Pasta e fagioli (a thick bean soup with pasta, served slightly warm or at room temperature) is made all over Italy. Folks in the Veneto, though, take special pride in their version, made from particularly fine beans grown around the village of Lamon, near Belluno. *Il fagiolo di Lamon* derives from the *Borlotto di Vigevano* bean and was first introduced by a monk in the 1500s via the Spanish court's colonial links to Mexico and Guatemela.

FISH

The catch of the day is always a good bet, whether it's sweet and succulent Adriatic shellfish, sea bream, bass, or John Dory, or freshwater fish from Lake Garda, near Verona. A staple in the Veneto is *baccalà*: this is dried salt cod, which, alongside *stoccafisso*, air-dried cod, was introduced to Italy during the Renaissance by northern European traders. Dried cod is soaked in water or milk and then prepared in a different way in each city. In Vicenza, baccalà *alla vicentina* confusingly uses stoccafisso, which is cooked with onions, milk, and cheese, and is generally served with polenta.

MEAT

In the Veneto, traditional dishes feature offal as much as the prime cuts. Beef (including veal), pork, rabbit, horse, and donkey meat are standard, while goose, duck, and guinea fowl are common poultry options. In Friuli–Venezia Giulia, menus show the influence of Austria-Hungary: you may find deer and hare on the menu, as well as Eastern European–style goulash. One unusual treat served throughout the Veneto is *nervetti*—cubes of gelatin from a calf's knee prepared with onions, parsley, olive oil, and lemon.

PASTA, RISOTTO, POLENTA

For *primi* (first courses), the Veneto dines on *bigoli* (thick whole-wheat pasta), generally served with an anchovy-onion sauce delicately flavored with cinnamon, or creamy risotto flavored with vegetables or shellfish. Polenta is everywhere, whether it's a stiff porridge topped with Gorgonzola, or a stew, or a patty grilled and served alongside meat or fish.

RADICCHIO DI TREVISO

In fall and winter be sure to try the radicchio di Treviso, a red endive grown near that town but popular all over the region. Cultivation is very labor-intensive, so it can be expensive. It's best in a veal or chicken stew, in a risotto, or just grilled or baked with a drizzle of olive oil and perhaps a little Taleggio cheese from neighboring Lombardy.

WINE

The Veneto produces more D.O.C. (Denominazione di Origine Controllata) wines than any other region in Italy. Amarone, the region's crowning achievement, is a robust, full-bodied red. The best of the whites are Soave, prosecco, and *pinot bianco* (pinot blanc). In Friuli–Venezia Giulia, local wines include *friulano*, a dry, lively white made from the sauvignon vert grape, and *picolit*, a dessert wine.

The arc around Venice—stretching from Verona to Trieste, encompassing the Veneto and Friuli–Venezia Giulia regions—is indisputably one of the most culturally rich areas in Italy, an intellectual and spiritual feast of architecture, painting, and sculpture. Since the 16th century, the art, architecture, and way of life here have all reflected Venetian splendor. Whether on the coast or inland, the emblem of Venice, St. Mark's winged lion, is emblazoned on palazzi and poised on pedestals.

It wasn't always this way. Back in the Middle Ages, Padua and Verona were independent cities that developed substantial cultural traditions of their own, leaving behind many artistic treasures. And even while it was under Venice's political domination, 16th-century Vicenza contributed more to the cultural heritage of La Serenissima than it took from her—in large part because of its master architect, Andrea Palladio.

This region is primarily flat, green farmland. As you move inland, though, you encounter low hills, which swell and rise in a succession of plateaus and high meadows, culminating in the snowcapped Dolomite Alps. Much of the pleasure of exploring here comes from discovering the variations on the Venetian theme that give a unique character to each of the towns. Some, such as Verona, Treviso, and Udine, have a solid

medieval look at their heart. Padua, with its narrow arcaded streets and tree-lined canals, is romantic. Vicenza, ennobled by the architecture of Palladio, is more elegant. Udine, in Friuli–Venezia Giulia, is a genteel, intricately sculpted city that's home to the first important frescoes by Gianbattista Tiepolo. In Trieste, once the main port of the Austro-Hungarian Empire, you can find survivors of those days in its Viennese-inspired coffeehouses and *buffets*—hole-in-the-wall eateries serving sausages and other pork dishes.

Unlike the western regions of northern Italy, the Veneto and Friuli–Venezia Giulia were slow to move from an agricultural to an industrial economy, and even now the region depends upon small and medium-size businesses, many of which are still family-run. The area, therefore, has attracted far fewer migrants from elsewhere in Italy and thus maintained its cultural identity; local dialects, for example, may have all but died out in places like Milan and Turin, but they still thrive in the Veneto and Friuli–Venezia Giulia. Even when residents speak standard Italian, it is frequently laced with local words and pronounced with a distinctive nasal-sounding musicality.

MAJOR REGIONS

The **Veneto,** for centuries influenced by the city of Venice on the marshy Adriatic coast, is a prosperous region dotted by fortified cities with captivating history and undulating vineyards. Padua's alluring architecture, art, and canal network may reflect the Venetian influence as the closest terra firma dominion, but its ancient, pioneering university—famed for its humanist alumni—creates a beguiling buzz of cycling students, food markets, and commerce. With the cooling Dolomite Alpine waters of the Adige River snaking through its medieval, Roman, and Venetian heart, Verona combines splendor with intimacy. Perfectly formed and wealthy Vicenza is where the peerless Palladio put his harmonious architectural plans into bricks, mortar, and gleaming marble. Heading north toward the snowcapped Dolomites, Marostica draws visitors moved by commanding views and an annual human-scale game of chess on a colossal board. Set amid verdant hills, Asolo dines out on its 19th-century heyday as an idyllic village muse for artists and poets. Moated and medieval Treviso retains a thriving and tranquil air in arcaded streets and leafy canals.

Heading northeast of the Veneto, the atmosphere of the **Friuli–Venezia Giulia** region derives from its fascinating mix of Italian, Slavic, and Central European influences. Sitting atop foothills below the Carnic Alps, the university city of Udine mixes semirural provincial charms with the grandeur of Venetian architecture and the rococo riches of 18th-century artist Gianbattista Tiepolo. A short hop east and set amid scenic wooded valleys, Cividale del Friuli brims with Roman, Celtic, and Lombard archaeological artifacts. Following the Natisone River down to tranquil Aquileia, you'll hear echoes of ancient Rome in this erstwhile port and spot signs of early Christianity in its mosaics. Bordering Slovenia, the strategic Adriatic port city of Trieste mixes Eastern, Central, and Western European cultures, giving it a liminal atmosphere of nostalgia and intrigue, beloved by writers and artists.

Planning

When to Go

The towns and services of the Veneto and Friuli–Venezia Giulia are generally busy all year, with all but a few attractions accessible to visitors. Summer months are generally very humid but dry and hot. The most precipitation and fog fall between November and March, although these months can be rewarding for city sightseeing and immersion in local culture and seasonal food. Toward the foothills of the Dolomites, there are cooler summers and snowfall in winter, while the northeast Adriatic corner around the Gulf of Trieste can have year-round breezy days from eastern winds.

Planning Your Time

Lined up in a row west of Venice are Padua, Vicenza, and Verona—three prosperous small cities that are worth at least one day each on a northern Italy itinerary. Verona has the most grandeur and most varied attractions, as well as the widest selection of hotels and restaurants. It's probably the best choice for a base in the area, even though it also draws the most tourists. The hills north of Venice make for good driving, with appealing villages set in a visitor-friendly wine country.

East of the Veneto, the region of Friuli–Venezia Giulia is off the main tourist circuit. You probably won't go here on a first trip to Italy, but by your second or third visit you may be drawn by its caves and castles, its battle-worn hills, and its mix of Italian and Central European culture. The port city of Trieste, famous for its elegant cafés, has a quiet character that some people find dull but others find alluring.

Note that several of the most interesting and important sights in the Venetian Arc require reservations or are open only at limited times, so plan ahead. For instance, reservations are required to see the Giotto frescoes in Padua's Cappella degli Scrovegni (if there's space, however, you can still "reserve" on the spot). On the outskirts of Vicenza, the Villa della Rotonda, one of Palladio's masterpieces, is not open in winter and has very limited hours when it is open. Another important Palladian conception, Villa Barbaro near Maser, also has limited hours.

Getting Here and Around

BUS

There are interurban and interregional connections throughout the Veneto and Friuli–Venezia Giulia, handled by nearly a dozen private bus lines. To figure out which line will get you where, the best strategy is to seek assistance from local tourist offices.

CAR

Padua, Vicenza, and Verona are on the highway (and train line) between Venice and Milan. Seeing them without a car isn't a problem; in fact, having a car can even complicate matters. The cities sometimes limit automobile access, permitting cars only with plates ending in an even number on even days, odd on odd, or prohibiting them altogether on weekends. There's no central source for information about these sporadic traffic restrictions; the best strategy is to check with your hotel before arrival for

an update. You will need a car to get the most out of the hill country that makes up much of the Venetian Arc, and it will be particularly useful for visiting Aquileia, a rather interesting archaeological site with limited public transportation.

The two main access roads to the Venetian Arc from southern Italy are both linked to the A1 (Autostrada del Sole), which connects Bologna, Florence, and Rome. They are the A13, which ends in Padua, and the A22, which passes through Verona running north–south. Linking the region from east to west is the A4, the primary route from Milan to Trieste, skirting Verona, Padua, and Venice along the way. The distance from Verona to Trieste via the A4 is 263 km (163 miles; 2½ hours), with one break in the autostrada near Venice/Mestre. Branches link the A4 with Treviso (A27) and Udine (A23).

TRAIN

Trains on the main routes from the south stop twice hourly in Verona, Padua, and Venice. From northern Italy and the rest of Europe, trains usually enter via Milan or through Porta Nuova in Verona. Treviso and Udine both lie on the main line from Venice to Tarvisio. Unfortunately, there are no daytime express trains between Venice and Tarvisio, only the slower interregional and regional service. There is now a regional through-train service between Trieste and the neighboring Slovenian capital Ljubljana (Lubiana in Italian). To the west of Venice, the main line running across the north of Italy stops at Padua (30 minutes from Venice), Vicenza (1 hour), and Verona (1½ hours); to the east is Trieste (2 hours). Local trains link Vicenza to Treviso (1 hour) and Udine to Trieste (1 hour).

Be sure to take Regionale Veloce (fast regional) trains whenever possible; a local "milk run" or Regionale that stops in every village along the way can take considerably longer. The fastest trains are the Frecce, but reservations are mandatory and fares are much higher than on regional services.

TRAIN CONTACT Trenitalia. ☎ 892021 ⊕ www.trenitalia.com.

Restaurants

Although the Veneto is not considered one of Italy's major culinary destinations, the region offers many opportunities for exciting gastronomic adventures. The fish offerings are among the most varied and freshest in Italy (and possibly Europe), and the vegetables from the islands in the Venetian lagoon are considered a national treasure. Take a break from pasta and try the area's wonderful, creamy risottos and hearty polenta.

Restaurant reviews have been shortened. For full information, visit Fodors. com.

Hotels

Rates tend to be higher in Padua and Verona; in Verona especially, seasonal rates vary widely and soar during trade fairs and the opera season. There are fewer good lodging choices in Vicenza, perhaps because overnighters are drawn to the better restaurant scenes in Verona and Padua. *Agriturismo* (farm stay) information is available at tourist offices and sometimes on their websites. Ask about weekend discounts, often available at hotels catering to business clients. Substantial savings can sometimes be had by booking through reservation services on the Internet.

Hotel reviews have been shortened. For full information, visit Fodors.com.

WHAT IT COSTS in Euros			
$	$$	$$$	$$$$
RESTAURANTS			
under €15	€15–€24	€25–€35	over €35
HOTELS			
under €125	€125–€200	€201–€300	over €300

Padua

A romantic warren of arcaded streets, Padua is a major cultural center in northern Italy. It has first-rate artistic monuments and, along with Bologna, is one of the few cities in the country where you can catch a glimpse of student life.

Its university, founded in 1222 and Italy's second oldest, attracted such cultural icons as Dante (1265–1321), Petrarch (1304–74), and Galileo (1564–1642), thus earning the city the sobriquet *"la Dotta"* (the Learned). Padua's Basilica di Sant'Antonio, begun around 1238, attracts droves of pilgrims, especially on his feast day, June 13. Three great artists—Giotto (1266–1337), Donatello (circa 1386–1466), and Mantegna (1431–1506)—left significant works in Padua. Giotto's Capella degli Scrovegni here is one of the best-known and most meticulously preserved works of art in the country. Today, a bicycle-happy student body—some 60,000 strong—influences every aspect of local culture; don't be surprised if you spot a *laurea* (graduation) ceremony marked by laurel leaves, mocking lullabies, and X-rated caricatures.

GETTING HERE AND AROUND
Many people visit Padua from Venice: the train trip between the cities is short, and regular bus service originates from Venice's Piazzale Roma. By car from Milan or Venice, Padua is on the Autostrada Torino–Trieste (A4/E70). Take the

San Carlo exit and follow Via Guido Reni to Via Tiziano Aspetti into town. From the south, take the Autostrada Bologna–Padova (A13). Regular bus service connects Venice's Marco Polo airport with downtown Padua.

Padua is a walker's city—parking is difficult, and cars are prohibited in much of the city center. If you arrive by car, leave your vehicle at your hotel or in one of the parking lots on the outskirts. Unlimited bus service is included with the PadovaCard (€18 or €24, valid for 48 or 72 hours), which allows entry to all the city's principal sights (€1 extra for a Capella degli Scrovegni reservation). It's available at tourist information offices and at some museums.

VISITOR INFORMATION

CONTACTS PadovaCard. ⊠ *Padua* ☏ *049/2010020 for Cappella degli Scrovegni reservations* ⊕ *www. cappelladegliscrovegni.it.* **Padua Tourism Office.** ⊠ *Padova Railway Station, Piazzale Stazione, Padua* ☏ *049/5207415* ⊕ *www. turismopadova.it.*

Sights

Abano Terme

TOWN | A very popular hot-springs spa town about 12 km (7 miles) southwest of Padua, Abano Terme lies at the foot of the Euganean Hills among hand-tilled vineyards. If a bit of pampering sounds better than traipsing through yet another church or castle, indulge yourself with a soak, a massage, stone therapy, a skin peel, or a series of mud treatments, which are especially recommended for joint aches. A good-value day pass (€35) is available at the central and well-equipped Hotel Antiche Terme Ariston Molino Buja (www.aristonmolino.it). For a longer stay check out the latest offers on the Abano spa hotel hub website (www.abano.it). The nearest railway stop on the Bologna–Padua line is Terme

Euganee–Montegrotto. Alternatively, you can board a train on the Milan–Venice line, disembark at Padua, and board an Abano-bound bus in front of the train station. The trip takes about half an hour. ⊠ *Abano Terme* ✛ *Take the Padua West exit off A4, or the Terme Euganee exit off A13* ⊕ *www.abano.it; www.aristonmolino.it.*

★ Basilica di Sant'Antonio
(*Basilica del Santo*)

CHURCH | Thousands of faithful make the pilgrimage here each year to pray at the tomb of St. Anthony, while others come to admire works by the 15th-century Florentine master Donatello. His equestrian statue (1453) of the condottiere Erasmo da Narni, known as Gattamelata, in front of the church is one of the great masterpieces of Italian Renaissance sculpture. It was inspired by the ancient statue of Marcus Aurelius in Rome's Campidoglio. Donatello also sculpted the series of bronze reliefs in the imposing interior illustrating the miracles of St. Anthony, as well as the bronze statues of the Madonna and saints on the high altar. The huge church, which combines elements of Byzantine, Romanesque, and Gothic styles, was probably begun around 1238, seven years after the death of the Portuguese-born saint. It underwent structural modifications into the mid-15th century. Masses are held in the basilica almost constantly, which makes it difficult to see these artworks. More accessible is the restored Cappella del Santo (housing the tomb of the saint), dating from the 16th century. Its walls are covered with impressive reliefs by important Renaissance sculptors. The Museo Antoniano part of the basilica complex contains a Mantegna fresco and works by Tiepolo, Carpaccio, and Piazzetta. ⊠ *Piazza del Santo, Padua* ☏ *049/8225652* ⊕ *www. basilicadelsanto.it* ⊟ *Basilica free, museum complex €7* ⊗ *Museum complex closed Mon.*

Burchiello Excursion, Brenta Canal

BODY OF WATER | During the 16th century the Brenta was transformed into a main-land version of Venice's Grand Canal with the building of nearly 50 waterside villas. Back then, boating parties viewed them in *burchielli*—beautiful boats. Today the Burchiello excursion boat makes full- and half-day tours along the Brenta in season, departing from Padua and Venice; tickets can also be bought at travel agencies. You visit three houses, including the Villas Pisani and Foscari, with a lunch-time break in Oriago (€23 or €30 extra). Note that most houses are on the left side coming from Venice, or the right from Padua. ⊠ *Via Porciglia 34, Padua* ☎ *049/8760233* ⊕ *www.ilburchiello.it* ✉ *€70 for half day, €99 for full day; lunch extra* ⊗ *Closed Mon. and Nov.–Feb.*

★ Cappella degli Scrovegni

(The Arena Chapel)

CHURCH | The spatial depth, emotional intensity, and naturalism of the frescoes illustrating the lives of Mary and Jesus in this world-famous chapel broke new ground in Western art. Enrico Scrovegni commissioned these frescoes to atone for the sins of his deceased father, Reginaldo, the usurer condemned to the Seventh Circle of the Inferno in Dante's *Divine Comedy*. Giotto and his assistants worked on the frescoes from 1303 to 1305, arranging them in tiers to be read from left to right. Opposite the altar is a *Last Judgment*, most likely designed and painted by Giotto's assistants. ◼ **TIP→ Mandatory timed-entry reservations (nonrefundable) should be made in advance at the ticket office, online, or by phone. Payments online or by phone by credit card must be made one day in advance. Reservations are necessary even if you have a PadovaCard.** To preserve the artwork, doors are opened only every 15 minutes. A maximum of 25 visitors must spend 15 minutes in an acclimatization room before making a 15-minute chapel visit (20 minutes in certain months). Tickets should be picked up at least one hour before your reservation. It's sometimes possible to buy admission on the spot. A good place to get some background before visiting the chapel is the multimedia room. ⊠ *Piazza Eremitani 8, Padua* ☎ *049/2010020 reservations* ⊕ *www.cappelladegliscrovegni.it* ✉ *€14, includes Musei Civici and Palazzo Zuckermann.*

Chiesa degli Eremitani

CHURCH | This 13th-century church houses substantial fragments of Andrea Mantegna's frescoes (1448–50), which were damaged by Allied bombing in World War II. Despite their fragmentary condition, Mantegna's still beautiful and historically important depictions of the martyrdom of St. James and St. Christopher show the young artist's mastery of extremely complex problems of perspective. ⊠ *Piazza Eremitani, Padua* ☎ *049/8756410.*

Montegrotto Terme

TOWN | At this spa town about 13 km (8 miles) southwest of Padua, you can luxuriate in thermal mineral pools. Montegrotto Terme has several hotels whose treatments vary from simple massage and thermal and mud baths to hydrokinetic therapy. Scuba enthusiasts head here for the world's deepest indoor pool, Y-40 Deep Joy. The nearest railway stop, on the Bologna–Padua line, is Terme Euganee–Montegrotto. Taxis are available outside the station. ⊠ *Montegrotto Terme* ✛ *Terme Euganee exit off A13* ⊕ *www.visitabanomontegrotto.com.*

★ Musei Civici degli Eremitani

(Civic Museum)

OTHER MUSEUM | Usually visited along with the neighboring Cappella degli Scrovegni, this former monastery houses a rich array of exhibits and has wonderful cloister gardens with a mix of ancient architectural fragments and modern sculpture. The Pinacoteca displays works of medieval and modern masters, including some by Tintoretto, Veronese, and Tiepolo. Standouts are the Giotto Crucifix, which once hung in the Cappella degli Scrovegni, and the *Portrait of a Young Senator,*

Padua

KEY

1 Sights

1 Restaurants

1 Quick Bites

1 Hotels

Sights	▼	Restaurants	▼	Quick Bites	▼	Hotels	▼
1 Abano Terme	**A5**	1 Enoteca dei Tadi	**B2**	1 Bar Romeo	**C2**	1 Al Fagiano	**D5**
2 Basilica di Sant'Antonio	**E5**	2 L'Anfora	**C3**			2 Albergo Verdi	**B2**
3 Burchiello Excusion, Brenta Canal	**E1**	3 Le Calandre	**A1**			3 Methis Hotel & Spa	**A5**
4 Cappella degli Scrovegni	**D1**	4 Osteria Dal Capo	**C3**				
5 Chiesa degli Eremitani	**D2**						
6 Montegrotto Terme	**A5**						
7 Musei Civici degli Eremitani	**D2**						
8 Orto Botanico	**D5**						
9 Palazzo del Bo	**D3**						
10 Palazzo della Ragione	**C2**						
11 Piazza dei Signori	**C2**						
12 Villa Pisani	**D5**						

The Venetian Arc, Past and Present

Long before Venetians made their presence felt on the mainland in the 15th century, Ezzelino III da Romano (1194–1259) laid claim to Verona, Padua, and the surrounding lands and towns. He was the first of a series of brutal and aggressive rulers who dominated the cities of the region until the rise of Venetian rule.

After Ezzelino was ousted, powerful families, such as Padua's Carrara and Verona's Della Scala (Scaligeri), vied throughout the 14th century to dominate these territories. With the rise of Venetian rule came a time of relative peace, when noble families from the lagoon and the mainland commissioned Palladio and other accomplished architects to design their palazzi and villas. This rich classical legacy, superimposed upon medieval castles and fortifications, is central to the identities of present-day Padua, Vicenza, and Verona.

The region remained under Venetian control until the Napoleonic invasion and the fall of the Venetian Republic in 1797. The Council of Vienna ceded it, along with Lombardy, to Austria in 1815. The region revolted against Austrian rule and joined the Italian Republic in 1866.

Friuli–Venezia Giulia's complicated history is reflected in its architecture, language, and cuisine. It's been marched through, fought over, hymned by patriots, and romanticized by writers who include James Joyce, Rainer Maria Rilke, Ernest Hemingway, Pier Paolo Pasolini, Italo Svevo, and Jan Morris. The region has seen Fascists and Communists, Romans, Hapsburgs, and Huns. It survived by forging sheltering alliances—Udine beneath the wings of San Marco (1420), Trieste choosing Duke Leopold of Austria (1382) over Venetian domination.

Some of World War I's fiercest fighting took place in Friuli–Venezia Giulia, where memorials and cemeteries commemorate the hundreds of thousands who died before the arrival of Italian troops in 1918 finally liberated Trieste from Austrian rule. Trieste, along with the whole of Venezia Giulia, was annexed to Italy in 1920. During World War II, Germany occupied the area and placed Trieste in an administrative zone along with parts of Slovenia. The only Nazi extermination camp on Italian soil, the Risiera di San Sabba, was in a suburb of Trieste. After the war, during a period of Cold War dispute, Trieste was governed by an Allied military administration; it was officially re-annexed to Italy in 1954, when Italy ceded the Istrian peninsula to the south to Yugoslavia. These arrangements were not finally ratified by Italy and Yugoslavia until 1975.

by Giovanni Bellini (1430–1516). Among the archaeological finds is an intriguing Egyptian section, while the *Gabinetto Fotografico* is an important collection of photographs. Set aside at least 60–90 minutes to appreciate the scope of this fabulous museum complex. ✉ *Piazza Eremitani 8, Padua* ☎ *049/8204551* 💶 *€10, €14 with Scrovegni Chapel and Palazzo Zuckermann; free with PadovaCard* ⊗ *Closed Mon.*

Orto Botanico (*Botanical Garden*)

GARDEN | The Venetian Republic ordered the creation of Padua's botanical garden in 1545 to supply the university with medicinal plants, and it retains its original layout. You can stroll the arboretum—still part of the university—and wander through hothouses and beds of plants that were introduced to Italy in this late-Renaissance garden. A St. Peter's palm, planted in 1585, inspired Goethe to write his 1790 essay, "The Metamorphosis of Plants." ✉ *Via Orto Botanico 15, Padua* ☎ *049/8273939* ⊕ *www.ortobotanicopd.it* ☎ *€10 (€5 with PadovaCard)* ⊘ *Closed Mon. May–Mar.*

Palazzo del Bo

COLLEGE | The University of Padua, founded in 1222, centers around this predominantly 16th-century palazzo with an 18th-century facade. It's named after the Osteria del Bo (*bo* means "ox"), an inn that once stood on the site. It's worth a visit to see the perfectly proportioned anatomy theater (1594), the beautiful Old Courtyard, and a hall with a lectern used by Galileo. You can enter only as part of a guided tour; most guides speak English, but it is worth checking ahead by phone. ✉ *Via 8 Febbraio, Padua* ☎ *049/8275111 university switchboard, 049/8273939* ⊕ *www.unipd.it* ☎ *€7* ⊘ *Closed Sat. and Sun.*

Palazzo della Ragione

CASTLE/PALACE | Also known as Il Salone, the spectacular arcaded reception hall in Padua's original law courts is as notable for its grandeur—it's 85 feet high—as for its colorful setting, surrounded by shops, cafés, and open-air fruit and vegetable markets. Nicolò Miretto and Stefano da Ferrara, working from 1425 to 1440, painted the frescoes after Giotto's plan, which was destroyed by a fire in 1420. The stunning space hosts art shows, and an enormous wooden horse, crafted for a public tournament in 1466, commands pride of place. It is patterned after the famous equestrian statue by Donatello in front of the Basilica di Sant'Antonio, and may, in fact, have been designed by Donatello himself in the last year of his life. ✉ *Piazza della Ragione, Padua* ☎ *049/8205006* ⊘ *Closed Sat. and Sun.* ☎ *€7 (free with PadovaCard).*

Piazza dei Signori

PLAZA/SQUARE | Some fine examples of 15th- and 16th-century buildings line this square. On the west side, the **Palazzo del Capitanio** (facade constructed 1598–1605) has an impressive **Torre dell'Orologio,** with an astronomical clock dating from 1344 and a portal made by Falconetto in 1532 in the form of a Roman triumphal arch. The 12th-century **Battistero del Duomo** (Cathedral Baptistry), with frescoes by Giusto de' Menabuoi (1374–78), is a few steps away. ✉ *Piazza dei Signori, Padua* ☎ *049/656914* ☎ *Battistero €4 (free with PadovaCard).*

Villa Pisani

CASTLE/PALACE | FAMILY | Extensive grounds with rare trees, ornamental fountains, and garden follies surround this extraordinary palace in Stra, 13 km (8 miles) southeast of Padua. Built in 1721 for the Venetian doge Alvise Pisani, it recalls Versailles more than a Veneto villa. This was one of the last and grandest of many stately residences constructed along the Brenta River from the 16th to 18th century by wealthy Venetians for their villeggiatura escape from midsummer humidity. Gianbattista Tiepolo's (1696–1770) spectacular fresco on the ballroom ceiling, *The Apotheosis of the Pisani Family* (1761), alone is worth the visit. For a relaxing afternoon, explore the gorgeous park and maze. To get here from Padua, take the SITA bus, or from Venice or Padua, take ACTV Bus No. 53E. The villa is a five-minute walk from the bus stop in Stra. ■TIP➔ **Mussolini invited Hitler here for their first meeting, but they stayed only one night because of the mosquitoes, which remain. If visiting on a late afternoon in summer, carry bug repellent.** ✉ *Via Doge Pisani 7, Stra* ☎ *049/502074* ⊕ *www.villapisani.beniculturali.it* ☎ *€7.50, €4.50 park only* ⊘ *Closed Mon.*

Restaurants

Enoteca dei Tadi

$$ | ITALIAN | In this cozy and atmospheric cross between a wine bar and a restaurant you can put together a fabulous, inexpensive dinner from various classic dishes from all over Italy. Portions are small, but prices are reasonable—just follow the local custom and order a selection, perhaps starting with fresh *burrata* (mozzarella's creamier cousin) with tomatoes, or a selection of prosciutti or salami. **Known for:** bountiful wine and grappa list; several kinds of lasagna; intimate and rustic setting. $ *Average main: €21* ✉ *Via dei Tadi 16, Padua* ☎ *049/8364099, 388/4083434 mobile* ⊕ *www.enotecadeitadi.it* ⊘ *Closed Mon., 2 wks in Jan., and 2 wks late June–July. No lunch.*

L'Anfora

$$ | WINE BAR | This mix between a traditional *bacaro* (wine bar) and an osteria is a local institution, opened in 1922. Stand at the bar with a cross section of Padovano society, from construction workers to professors, and peruse the reasonably priced menu of simple *casalinga* (home-cooked dishes), plus salads and a selection of cheeses. **Known for:** very busy at lunchtime; no-nonsense traditional Veneto food; atmospheric art-filled osteria with wood interior. $ *Average main: €19* ✉ *Via Soncin 13, Padua* ☎ *049/656629* ⊘ *Closed Sun. (except in Dec.), 1 wk in Jan., and 1 wk in Aug.*

Le Calandre

$$$$ | MODERN ITALIAN | Traditional Veneto recipes are given a highly sophisticated and creative treatment here, and the whole theatrical tasting-menu experience and gorgeous table settings can seem by turns revelatory or overblown at this high-profile place. Owner-chef Massimiliano Alajmo's creative, miniscule-portion dishes, passion for design (bespoke lighting, carved wooden tables, and quirky plates), and first-class wine list make this an option for a pricey celebratory meal. **Known for:** reservations essential; theatrical, sensory dining experience; playful (or to some pretentious) touches. $ *Average main: €175* ✉ *Via Liguria 1, Sarmeola* ⊕ *7 km (4 miles) west of Padua* ☎ *049/630303* ⊕ *www.calandre.com* ⊘ *Closed Sun., Mon., and Jan. 1–22. No lunch Tues.*

Osteria Dal Capo

$$ | VENETIAN | Located in the heart of what used to be Padua's Jewish ghetto, this friendly trattoria serves almost exclusively traditional Veneto dishes, and it does so with refinement and care. Everything from the well-crafted dishes to the unfussy ship's dining cabin–like decor and elegant plates reflect decades of Padovano hospitality. **Known for:** limited tables mean reservations essential; liver and onions with grilled polenta; intimate and understated dining at decent prices. $ *Average main: €21* ✉ *Via degli Obizzi 2, Padua* ☎ *049/663105* ⊕ *www.osteriadal-capo.it* ⊘ *Closed Sun. No lunch Mon.*

Cocktail Hour on Padua's Piazzas

A great Padua tradition is the outdoor consumption of *aperitivi*—a *spritz* (a mix of Aperol or Campari, soda water, and wine), prosecco, or wine—in the Piazza delle Erbe and Piazza delle Frutta. Several bars there provide drinks in plastic cups so you can take them outside and mingle among the crowds. The ritual begins at 6 or so, and may be accompanied with tasty cocktail stick–pierced appetizers known to the Padovani as *spunciotti*. Bars generally close shortly after midnight.

Coffee and Quick Bites

Bar Romeo

$ | NORTHERN ITALIAN | Deep in the atmospheric Sotto Salone market, this busy bar does a fab selection of filled *tramezzini* (triangular sandwiches), panini, and other snacks. It's a great place to hear the local dialect and mingle with the market workers and shoppers any time of day; grab a breakfast caffè and brioche, a cheeky glass of Falanghina, or a bit later—after 11 am perhaps—an apertivo with snacks. **Known for:** superb selection of wine by the glass; good value sandwiches; friendly staff and Padovano vibe. $ *Average main: €5* ⊠ *26 Sotto Salone, Padua* ☎ *340/556 0611.*

🛏 Hotels

Al Fagiano

$ | HOTEL | The refreshingly funky surroundings in this self-styled art hotel include sponge-painted walls, brush-painted chandeliers, and views of the spires and cupolas of the Basilica di Sant'Antonio. **Pros:** convenient location; relaxed, quirky, homey atmosphere; great for art lovers or those after a unique atmosphere. **Cons:** some find the way-out-there (some risqué) art a bit much; not all rooms have views; lots of stairs. $ *Rooms from: €90* ⊠ *Via Locatelli 45, Padua* ☎ *049/8750073* ⊕ *www.alfagiano. com* ⇋ *40 rooms* ⦿ *No Meals.*

Albergo Verdi

$ | HOTEL | One of the best-situated hotels in the city provides understated modern rooms and public areas that tend toward the minimalist without being severe, while the intimate breakfast room with stylish Eames Eiffel chairs and adjoining terrace is a tranquil place to start the day. **Pros:** excellent location close to the Piazza dei Signori; 24-hour bar service; attentive staff. **Cons:** steep stairs and small elevator; few views; student noise in piazza-facing rooms. $ *Rooms from:*

€100 ⊠ *Via Dondi dell'Orologio 7, Padua* ☎ *049/8364163* ⊕ *www.albergoverdipadova.it* ⇋ *14 rooms* ⦿ *Free Breakfast.*

Methis Hotel & Spa

$$ | HOTEL | Four floors of sleekly designed guest rooms reflect the elements at this modern spa hotel: there are gentle earth tones and fiery red in the Classic rooms; watery, cool blues in Superior rooms; and airy white in the top-floor suites. **Pros:** gym, sauna, Turkish bath, and spa treatments; superb canal walks nearby; better views of canal across road from front rooms. **Cons:** public spaces lack some character; 15-minute walk from major sights and restaurants; some maintenance issues. $ *Rooms from: €130* ⊠ *Riviera Paleocapa 70, Padua* ☎ *049/8725555* ⊕ *www.methishotel.com* ⇋ *59 rooms* ⦿ *Free Breakfast.*

Nightlife

⭐ Caffè Pedrocchi

CAFÉS | No visit to Padua is complete without taking time to sit in this historic café and iconic Padovano venue, patronized by luminaries like the French novelist Stendhal in 1831. Nearly 200 years later, it remains central to the city's social life. The café was built in the Egyptian Revival style, and it's now famed for its innovative aperitivi and signature mint coffee. The accomplished, innovative restaurant serves breakfast, lunch, and dinner. The grand salons and terrace provide a backdrop for the occasional jazz, swing, and cover bands. ⊠ *Piazzetta Pedrocchi, Padua* ☎ *049/8781231* ⊕ *www.caffepedrocchi.it.*

🛍 Shopping

⭐ Mercato Sotto il Salone

FOOD | Under the Salone there's an impressive food market where shops sell choice salami and cured meats, local cheeses, wines, coffee, and tea. With the adjacent Piazza delle Erbe fruit and vegetable market, you can pick up all the makings of a fine picnic. On weekends and public holidays, the piazza is often filled with fabulous street food, as well as wine and beer stalls. ⊠ *Piazza della Ragione, Padua* ⊕ *mercatosottoilsalone.it.*

Zotti Antiquariato

ANTIQUES & COLLECTIBLES | Owned by antiques dealer Pietro Maria Zotti—who has worked for more than 40 years in the trade—this always-changing shop has fascinating finds from Venetian artworks to stylish midcentury furniture, plus lots of smaller, more affordable items including books, prints, jewelry, militaria, and coins. ⊠ *Selciato San Nicolò 5, Padua* ☎ *338/2930830* ⊕ *www.zottiantiquariato.it.*

Verona

On the banks of the fast-flowing River Adige and 60 km (37 miles) west of Vicenza, enchanting Verona has timeless monuments, a picturesque town center, fascinating museums, and a romantic reputation as the setting of Shakespeare's *Romeo and Juliet*. Verona grew to power and prosperity within the Roman Empire as a result of its key commercial and military position in northern Italy. With its Roman arena, theater, and city gates, it has the most significant monuments of Roman antiquity north of the Eternal City itself. After the fall of the empire, the city continued to flourish under the guidance of barbarian kings, such as Theodoric, Alboin, Pepin, and Berengar I. It reached its cultural and artistic peak in the 13th and 14th centuries under the Della Scala (Scaligeri) dynasty. (Look for the *scala,* or ladder, emblem all over town.) In 1404 Verona traded its independence for security and placed itself under the control of Venice. (The other recurring architectural motif is the lion of St. Mark, a symbol of Venetian rule.)

With its well-heeled yet lively Veneto atmosphere and proximity to Lake Garda, Verona attracts many tourists, especially Germans and Austrians. Tourism peaks during summer's renowned season of open-air opera in the arena and during spring's Vinitaly, one of the world's most important wine and spirits expos.

If you're going to visit more than one or two sights, it's worth purchasing a VeronaCard, available at museums, churches, and tobacconists for €20 (for 24 hours) or €25 (48 hours). It buys single admission to most of the city's significant museums and churches, and allows you to ride for free on city buses. If you're mostly interested in churches, a €6 cumulative ticket is sold at Verona's major houses of worship and gains you entry to the Duomo, San Fermo Maggiore, San Zeno Maggiore, and Sant'Anastasia (all covered by the VeronaCard as well). Verona's churches enforce a dress code: no shorts, short skirts, or sleeveless shirts.

GETTING HERE AND AROUND

Verona is midway between Venice and Milan. Its small Aeroporto Valerio Catullo accommodates domestic and European flights, though many travelers fly into Venice or Milan and drive or take the train to Verona. Several trains per hour depart from points along the Milan–Venice line. By car, from the east or west, take the Autostrada Trieste–Torino (A4/E70) to the SS12 and follow it north into town. From the north or south, take the Autostrada del Brennero (A22/E45) to the SR11 East (initially called the Strada Bresciana) directly into town.

VISITOR INFORMATION

CONTACTS Verona Tourism Office (IAT Verona). ⊠ *Via degli Alpini 9, Verona* ☎ *045/8068680* ⊕ *www.veronatouristoffice.it/en.* **VeronaCard.** ⊠ *Verona* ⊕ *www.turismoverona.eu.*

Sights

In addition to ancient Verona's famous Roman theater and arena, two of its city gates (Porta dei Leoni and Porta dei Borsari) and a beautiful triumphal arch (Arco dei Gavi) have survived. These graceful and elegant portals provide an idea of the high aesthetic standards of their time. Look, too, beyond the main sights of the Città Antica (historic center): take time to wander the streets, and be sure not to miss out on the many leafy stretches of the riverside Lungadige. Away from the crowds there's a wealth of varied architecture from ancient Rome to the Fascist era to the contemporary, as well as tranquil spots for feeding the ducks.

Arche Scaligere

TOMB | On a little square off the Piazza dei Signori are the fantastically sculpted Gothic tombs of the Della Scala family, who ruled Verona during the late Middle Ages. The 19th-century English traveler and critic John Ruskin described the tombs as graceful places where people who have fallen asleep live. The tomb of Cangrande I (1291–1329) hangs over the portal of the adjacent church and is the work of the Maestro di Sant'Anastasia. The tomb of Mastino II, begun in 1345, has an elaborate baldachin, originally painted and gilded, and is surrounded by an iron grillwork fence and topped by an equestrian statue. The latest and most elaborate tomb is that of Cansignorio (1375), the work principally of Bonino da Campione. The major tombs are all visible from the street. ⊠ *Via Arche Scaligere, Verona.*

★ Arco dei Gavi

RUINS | This stunning structure is simpler and less imposing, but also more graceful, than the triumphal arches in Rome. Built in the 1st century AD by the architect Lucius Vitruvius Cerdo to celebrate the accomplishments of the patrician Gavia family, it was highly esteemed by several Renaissance architects, including Palladio. ⊠ *Corso Cavour, Verona.*

Arena di Verona

RUINS | FAMILY | Only Rome's Colosseum and Capua's arena would dwarf this amphitheater, built for gymnastic competitions, choreographed sacrificial rites, and games involving hunts, fights, battles, and wild animals. Although four arches are all that remain of the arena's outer arcade, the main structure is complete and dates from AD 30. In summer, you can join up to 16,000 (3,000 during COVID-19 restrictions) for spectacular opera productions and pop or rock concerts (extra costs for these events). ■ TIP→ **The opera's the main thing here: when there is no opera performance, you can still enter the interior, but the arena is less impressive inside than the Colosseum or other Roman amphitheaters.** ⊠ *Piazza Bra 5, Verona* ☎ *045/8003204* ⊕ *www. arena.it* ☎ *€10 (free with VeronaCard); €11 includes entrance to nearby Museo Lapidario Maffeiano* ⊗ *Closed Mon. Oct.–May.*

★ Castelvecchio

CASTLE/PALACE | This crenellated, russet brick building with massive walls, towers, turrets, and a vast courtyard was built for Cangrande II della Scala in 1354 and presides over a street lined with attractive old buildings and palaces of the nobility. Only by going inside the **Museo di Castelvecchio** can you really appreciate this massive castle complex with its vaulted halls. You also get a look at a significant collection of Venetian and Veneto art, medieval weapons, and jewelry. The interior of the castle was restored and redesigned as a museum between 1958 and 1975 by Carlo Scarpa, one of Italy's most accomplished architects. Behind the castle is the Ponte Scaligero (1355), which spans the River Adige. ⊠ *Corso Castelvecchio 2, Verona* ☎ *045/8062611* ⊕ *museodicastelvecchio.comune.verona.it* ☎ *€4.50 (free with VeronaCard).*

Verona

275

KEY

- ● Sights
- ● Restaurants
- ● Quick Bites
- ● Hotels

Sights ▶

1	Arche Scaligere	G2
2	Arco dei Gavi	D3
3	Arena di Verona	E3
4	Castelvecchio	D3
5	Duomo	F1
6	Funicular of Castel San Pietro	G1
7	Loggia del Consiglio	F2
8	Museo Archeologico and Teatro Romano	G1
9	Palazzo degli Scaligeri	F2
10	Palazzo della Ragione and Torre dei Lamberti	F2
11	Piazza delle Erbe	F2
12	Porta dei Borsari	F2
13	Porta Leoni	F3
14	San Zeno Maggiore	B2
15	Sant'Anastasia	G1

Restaurants ▶

1	Antica Osteria al Duomo	F1
2	Il Desco	G2
3	Ristorante 12 Apostoli	F2

Quick Bites ▶

| 1 | Caffè Borsari | F2 |

Hotels ▶

1	Best Western Hotel Armando	F3
2	Escalus Luxury Suites	E3
3	Gabbio d'Oro	F2
4	Hotel Accademia	F3
5	L'Ospite Appartamenti	H3

Duomo

CHURCH | The present church was begun in the 12th century in the Romanesque style; its later additions are mostly Gothic. On pilasters guarding the main entrance are 12th-century carvings thought to represent Oliver and Roland, two of Charlemagne's knights and heroes of several medieval epic poems. Inside, Titian's *Assumption* (1532) graces the first chapel on the left. ⊠ *Via Duomo, Verona* ☎ *045/592813* ⊕ *www.chieseverona.it* 🎫 *€3 (free with Church Cumulative Ticket or VeronaCard).*

★ Funicular of Castel San Pietro

VIEWPOINT | Opened in 2017, this funicular ride ascends 500 feet from near Teatro Romano up to a panoramic terrace in just 90 seconds, affording fabulous Veronese views. For the adventurous, there's scope for long walks around the parkland paths and quiet lanes crisscrossing the elevated city walls. ⊠ *Via Fontanelle S. Stefano, Verona* ☎ *342/8966695* ⊕ *www. funicolarediverona.it* 🎫 *€2.50 round-trip, €1.50 one way.*

Loggia del Consiglio

GOVERNMENT BUILDING | This graceful structure on the north flank of the Piazza dei Signori was finished in 1492 and built to house city council meetings. Although the city was already under Venetian rule, Verona still had a certain degree of autonomy, which was expressed by the splendor of the loggia. Very strangely for a Renaissance building of this quality, its architect remains unknown, but it's the finest surviving example of late-15th-century architecture in Verona. The building is not open to the public, but the exterior is worth a visit. ⊠ *Piazza dei Signori, Verona.*

Museo Archeologico and Teatro Romano

HISTORY MUSEUM | The archaeological holdings of this museum in a 15th-century former monastery consist largely of the donated collections of Veronese citizens proud of their city's classical past. You'll find few blockbusters here, but there are some noteworthy pieces (especially among the bronzes), and it is interesting to see what cultured Veronese collected between the 17th and 19th century. The museum complex includes the Teatro Romano, Verona's 1st-century-AD theater, which is open to visitors. ⊠ *Rigaste del Redentore 2, Verona* ☎ *045/8000360* ⊕ *museoarcheologico.comune.verona.it* 🎫 *€4.50 (free with VeronaCard).*

Palazzo degli Scaligeri (*Palazzo di Cangrande*)

CASTLE/PALACE | The Della Scala family ruled Verona from this stronghold built (over Roman ruins) at the end of the 13th century and then inhabited by Cangrande I. At that time Verona controlled the mainland Veneto from Treviso and Lombardy to Mantua and Brescia, hence the building's alternative name as a seat of Domini di Terraferma (Venetian administration): Palazzo del Podestà. The portal facing the Piazza dei Signori was added in 1533 by the accomplished Renaissance architect Michele Sanmicheli. You have to admire the palazzo from the outside, as it's not open to the public. ⊠ *Piazza dei Signori, Verona.*

★ Palazzo della Ragione and Torre dei Lamberti

VIEWPOINT | An elegant 15th-century pink marble staircase leads up from the *mercato vecchio* (old market) courtyard to the magistrates' chambers in this 12th-century palace, built at the intersection of the main streets of the ancient Roman city. The interior now houses exhibitions of art from the **Galleria d'Arte Moderna Achille Forti.** You can get the highest view in town from atop the attached 270-foot-high Romanesque Torre dei Lamberti. About 50 years after a lightning strike in 1403 knocked its top off, it was rebuilt and extended to its current height. ⊠ *Piazza dei Signori, Verona* ☎ *045/9273027* ⊕ *torredeilamberti.it* 🎫 *Gallery and tower €8 (free with VeronaCard); tower €5 on Mon.* ⊙ *Gallery closed Mon.*

Piazza delle Erbe

PLAZA/SQUARE | Frescoed buildings surround this medieval square, where a busy Roman forum once stood; during the week it's still bustling, as vendors sell produce and trinkets, much as they have been doing for generations. Eyes are drawn to the often sun-sparkling Madonna Verona fountain (1368) and its Roman statue (the body is from AD 380, with medieval additions). ⊠ *Verona.*

★ Porta dei Borsari

RUINS | As its elegant decoration suggests, this is the main entrance to ancient Verona—dating, in its present state, from the 1st century AD. It's at the beginning of the narrow, pedestrianized Corso Porta Borsari, now a smart shopping street leading to Piazza delle Erbe. ⊠ *Corso Porta Borsari, Verona.*

Porta Leoni

RUINS | The oldest of Verona's elegant and graceful Roman portals, the Porta Leoni (on Via Leoni, just a short walk from Piazza delle Erbe) dates from the 1st century BC, but its original earth-and-brick structure was sheathed in local marble during the early imperial era. It has become the focus of a campaign against violence—there are often flowers and messages by the monument—in memory of the murder of a young Veronese here in 2009. ⊠ *Via Leoni, Verona.*

★ San Zeno Maggiore

CHURCH | One of Italy's finest Romanesque churches is filled with treasures, including a rose window by the 13th-century sculptor Brioloto that represents a wheel of fortune, with six of the spokes formed by statues depicting the rising and falling fortunes of mankind. The 12th-century porch is the work of Maestro Niccolò; it's flanked by marble reliefs by Niccolò and Maestro Guglielmo depicting scenes from the Old and New Testaments and from the legend of Theodoric. The bronze doors date from the 11th and 12th centuries; some were probably imported from Saxony, and some are from Veronese workshops. They combine allegorical representations with scenes from the lives of saints. Inside, look for the 12th-century statue of San Zeno to the left of the main altar. In modern times it has been dubbed the "Laughing San Zeno" because of a misinterpretation of its conventional Romanesque grin. A famous *Madonna and Saints* triptych by Andrea Mantegna (1431–1506) hangs over the main altar, and a peaceful cloister (1120–38) lies to the left of the nave. The detached bell tower was finished in 1173. ⊠ *Piazza San Zeno, Verona* ☎ *045/592813* ⊕ *www. chieseverona.it* 🎟 *€3 (free with Church Cumulative Ticket or VeronaCard).*

Sant'Anastasia

CHURCH | Verona's largest church, begun in 1290 but only consecrated in 1471, is a fine example of Gothic brickwork and has a grand doorway with elaborately carved biblical scenes. The main reason for visiting this church, however, is *St. George and the Princess* (dated 1434, but perhaps earlier) by Pisanello (1377–1455). It's above the Pellegrini Chapel off the main altar. As you come in, look also for the *gobbi* (hunchbacks) supporting the holy-water basins. ⊠ *Piazza Sant'Anastasia, Verona* ☎ *045/592813* ⊕ *www. chieseverona.it* 🎟 *€3 (free with Church Cumulative Ticket or VeronaCard).*

 Restaurants

★ Antica Osteria al Duomo

$$ | NORTHERN ITALIAN | This side-street eatery, lined with old wood paneling and decked out with musical instruments, serves traditional Veronese classics, like *bigoli* (thick whole-wheat spaghetti) with donkey ragù and *pastissada con polenta* (horsemeat stew with polenta). Don't be deterred by the unconventional meats—they're tender and delicious, and this is probably the best place in town to sample them. **Known for:** popular and busy; blackboard menu, bar, and wooden interiors; occasional live music.

⑤ *Average main: €19* ✉ *Via Duomo 7/A, Verona* ☎ *045/8004505* ⊘ *Closed Sun. except in Dec. and during wine fair.*

★ Il Desco

$$$$ | MODERN ITALIAN | Opened in 1981 by Elia Rizzo, the nationally renowned fine-dining Desco cuisine is now crafted by talented son Matteo. True to Italian and Rizzo culinary traditions, he preserves natural flavors through careful ingredient selection, adding daring combinations inspired by stints in kitchens around the world. **Known for:** pricey tasting menus; inventive, colorful plates of food; elegant, arty surroundings fit for a modern opera. ⑤ *Average main: €50* ✉ *Via Dietro San Sebastiano 7, Verona* ☎ *045/595358* ⊕ *www.ristoranteildesco. it* ⊘ *Closed Sun. and Mon. (open for dinner Mon. in July, Aug., and Dec.).*

Ristorante 12 Apostoli

$$$$ | NORTHERN ITALIAN | Run by the Gioco family for over a century, 12 Apostoli offers a fine-dining experience amid gorgeous frescoes and dramatically lit place settings. Near Piazza delle Erbe, this historic palazzo setting stands on the foundations of a Roman temple: you can view architectural fragments and a model in the wine cellar. **Known for:** innovative tasting menus; elegant, atmospheric rooms and cantina; slow and sumptuous dining. ⑤ *Average main: €40* ✉ *Vicolo Corticella San Marco 3, Verona* ☎ *045/596999* ⊕ *www.12apostoli. com* ⊘ *Closed Sun. and Mon. No lunch weekdays.*

☕ Coffee and Quick Bites

★ Caffè Borsari

$ | NORTHERN ITALIAN | This bustling caffè-bar is famed for its excellent creamy coffee and freshly made brioche—pre-Covid it was cheek-by-jowl *al banco* (at the bar), but for now the Veronese patrons must spill outside. The narrow space on the charming Corso Borsari cobbles is packed with coffee- and tea-making pots and cups, as are its walls with colorful gifts and oddities according to the time of year. **Known for:** fab staff may decorate your *schiuma* (froth); indulgent hot chocolate; selection of coffee, tea, candies, and chocolates to take away. ⑤ *Average main: €4* ✉ *Corso Portoni Borsari 15, Verona* ☎ *045/8031313.*

Hotels

Book hotels far in advance if you'll be in town during Vinitaly (usually mid-April) and for opera season. Verona hotels are also very busy during the January, May, and September gold fairs in neighboring Vicenza. Hotels jack up prices considerably at all these times.

Best Western Hotel Armando

$$ | HOTEL | In a residential area a few minutes' walk from the Arena, this contemporary Best Western hotel offers respite from the busy city as well as easier parking. **Pros:** free Wi-Fi; good breakfast; large rooms for Italy. **Cons:** simple room decor; no parking valet; noise from neighboring restaurant. ⑤ *Rooms from: €167* ✉ *Via Dietro Pallone 1, Verona* ☎ *045/8000206* ⊕ *www.hotelarmando. it* ⦿⦙ *Free Breakfast* ⊘ *Closed 2 wks late Dec.–early Jan.* ⤶ *28 rooms.*

Escalus Luxury Suites

$$$ | HOTEL | FAMILY | Near the Arena and Verona's marble-paved main shopping street, Via Mazzini, these suites and mini-apartments offer contemporary minimalist style in muted colors; the larger ones have handy kitchenettes, and all have swank bathrooms. **Pros:** large showers; chic location near sights and shopping; family-friendly Glamour Deluxe Suite with balcony. **Cons:** constant *passeggiata* hum from Via Mazzini; checkout is before 11 am; minimalist decor not to everyone's taste. ⑤ *Rooms from: €250* ✉ *Vicolo Tre Marchetti 12, Verona* ☎ *045/8036754* ⊕ *www. escalusverona.com* ⤶ *6 suites* ⦿⦙ *Free Breakfast.*

Gabbia d'Oro

$$$$ | HOTEL | Occupying a historic building off Piazza delle Erbe in the ancient heart of Verona, this hotel is a romantic fantasia of ornamentation, rich fabrics, and period-style furniture. **Pros:** great breakfast; central location; romantic atmosphere. **Cons:** some guests may find the decor overly ornate, even stuffy; some very small rooms, especially considering the price; small bathrooms. ⑤ *Rooms from: €350* ✉ *Corso Porta Borsari 4/a, Verona* ☎ *045/8003060* ⊕ *www. hotelgabbiadoro.it* ⦿ *Free Breakfast* ⇌ *27 rooms.*

Hotel Accademia

$$$ | HOTEL | The Palladian facade of columns and arches here hint at the well-proportioned interior layout: expect an elegant contemporary take on art deco in public spaces and immaculate if impersonal traditional-style decor in guest rooms. **Pros:** rooftop solarium; central location; good fitness room. **Cons:** rates increase greatly during summer opera season and trade fairs; expensive parking; service can be patchy. ⑤ *Rooms from: €292* ✉ *Via Scala 12, Verona* ☎ *045/596222* ⊕ *www.accademiavr.it* ⇌ *96 rooms* ⦿ *Free Breakfast.*

L'Ospite Appartamenti

$ | HOTEL | Friendly and energetic Federica has transformed this three-story property, owned by her family (of De Rossi pasticceria fame), into some of the most stylish contemporary apartments—and one of the best values—in Verona, complete with kitchenettes. **Pros:** immaculately clean; great location in the Veronetta near the university and the Adige River; helpful host offers tips and some cooking courses. **Cons:** on a busy road; narrow pavement outside; books up early. ⑤ *Rooms from: €105* ✉ *Via Venti Settembre 3, Verona* ☎ *045/8036994, 329/4262524 (mobile)* ⊕ *www.lospite. com* ⊗ *Closed early Jan.* ⇌ *6 apartments* ⦿ *No Meals.*

Vicenza

A visit to Vicenza is a must for any student or fan of architecture. This elegant, prosperous city bears the distinctive signature of the architect Andrea Palladio (1508–80), whose name has been given to the Palladian style of architecture.

Palladio emphasized the principles of order and harmony using the classical style of architecture established by Renaissance architects such as Brunelleschi, Alberti, and Sansovino. He used these principles and classical motifs not only for public buildings but also for private dwellings. His elegant villas and palaces were influential in propagating classical architecture in Europe, especially Britain, and later in America—most notably at Thomas Jefferson's Monticello.

In the mid-16th century Palladio was commissioned to rebuild much of Vicenza, which had been greatly damaged during wars waged against Venice by the League of Cambrai (1505), an alliance of the papacy, France, the Holy Roman Empire, and several neighboring city-states. He made his name with the renovation of Palazzo della Ragione, begun in 1549 in the heart of Vicenza, and then embarked on a series of noble buildings, all of which adhere to the same principles of classicism and harmony.

GETTING HERE AND AROUND

Vicenza is midway between Padua and Verona, and several trains leave from both cities every hour. By car, take the Autostrada Brescia–Padova/Torino–Trieste (A4/E70) to SP247 North directly into Vicenza.

CONTACT Vicenza Tourism Office. ✉ *Piazza Giacomo Matteotti 12, Vicenza* ☎ *0444/320854* ⊕ *www.vicenzae.org.*

Sights

Palazzo Barbaran da Porto (Palladio Museum)

CASTLE/PALACE | Palladio executed this beautiful city palace for the Vicentine noble Montano Barbarano between 1570 and 1575. The noble patron, however, did not make things easy for Palladio; the architect had to incorporate at least two preexisting medieval houses, with irregularly shaped rooms, into his classical, harmonious plan. It also had to support the great hall of the *piano mobile* (moving floor) above the fragile walls of the original medieval structure. The wonder of it is that this palazzo is one of Palladio's most harmonious constructions; the viewer has little indication that this is actually a transformation of a medieval structure. The palazzo also contains a museum dedicated to Palladio and is the seat of a center for Palladian studies. ⊠ *Contrà Porti 11, Vicenza* ☎ *0444/323014* ⊕ *www.palladiomuseum.org* ⊠ *€8; €20 Vicenza Card, includes Palazzo Chiericati and Teatro Olimpico, plus others* ⊗ *Closed Mon.*

Palazzo Chiericati

CASTLE/PALACE | This imposing Palladian palazzo (1550) would be worthy of a visit even if it didn't house Vicenza's **Museo Civico.** Because of the ample space surrounding the building, Palladio combined elements of an urban palazzo with those he used in his country villas. The museum's important Venetian holdings include significant paintings by Cima, Tiepolo, Piazzetta, and Tintoretto, but its main attraction is an extensive collection of rarely found works by painters from the Vicenza area, among them Jacopo Bassano (1515–92) and the eccentric and innovative Francesco Maffei (1605–60), whose work foreshadowed important currents of Venetian painting of subsequent generations. ⊠ *Piazza Matteotti, Vicenza* ☎ *0444/222811* ⊕ *www.musei-civicivicenza.it* ⊠ *€7; €20 Vicenza Card,*

includes Palazzo Barbaran da Porto and Teatro Olimpico, plus others.

Piazza dei Signori

PLAZA/SQUARE | At the heart of Vicenza, this square contains the **Palazzo della Ragione** (1549), the project with which Palladio made his name by successfully modernizing a medieval building, grafting a graceful two-story exterior loggia onto the existing Gothic structure. Commonly known as Palladio's basilica, the palazzo served as a courthouse and public meeting hall (the original Roman meaning of the term *basilica*) and is now open only when it houses exhibits. The main point of interest, though, the loggia, is visible from the piazza. Take a look also at the **Loggia del Capitaniato,** opposite, which Palladio designed but never completed. ⊠ *Vicenza.*

Santa Corona

CHURCH | An exceptionally fine *Baptism of Christ* (1502), a work of Giovanni Bellini's maturity, hangs over the altar on the left, just in front of the transept of this church. Santa Corona also houses the elegantly simple Valmarana chapel, designed by Palladio. ⊠ *Contrà S. Corona, Vicenza* ☎ *0444/320854* ⊠ *€3 (free with Vicenza Card)* ⊗ *Closed Mon.*

★ Teatro Olimpico

PERFORMANCE VENUE | Palladio's last, perhaps most spectacular work was begun in 1580 and completed in 1585, after his death, by Vincenzo Scamozzi (1552–1616). Based closely on the model of ancient Roman theaters, it represents an important development in theater and stage design and is noteworthy for its acoustics and the cunning use of perspective in Scamozzi's permanent backdrop. The anterooms are frescoed with images of important figures in Venetian history. One of the few Renaissance theaters still standing, it can be visited (with guided tours) during the day and is used for concerts, operas, and other performances. ⊠ *Ticket office, Piazza Matteotti 12, Vicenza* ☎ *0444/964380*

KEY

- 1 Sights
- 1 Restaurants
- 1 Quick Bites
- 1 Hotels

⊕ www.teatrolimpicovicenza.it ⊠ €11; €20 Vicenza Card, includes Palazzo Barbaran da Porto and Palazzo Chiericati, plus others ⊘ Closed Mon.

★ **Villa della Rotonda**
(Villa Almerico Capra)

HISTORIC HOME | Commissioned in 1556 as a suburban residence for Paolo Almerico, this beautiful Palladian villa is the purest expression of Palladio's architectural theory and aesthetic. More a villa-temple than a residence, it contradicts the rational utilitarianism of Renaissance architecture and demonstrates the priority Palladio gave to the architectural symbolism of celestial harmony over practical considerations. A visit to view the interior can be difficult to schedule—the villa remains privately owned, and visiting hours are limited and constantly change—but this is a worthwhile stop,

if only to see how Palladio's harmonious arrangement of smallish interconnected rooms around a central domed space paid little attention to the practicalities of living. The interior decoration, mainly later Baroque stuccowork, contains some allegorical frescoes in the cupola by Palladio's contemporary, Alessandro Maganza. Even without a peek inside, experiencing the exterior and the grounds is a must for any visit to Vicenza. The villa is a 20-minute walk from town or a cab (€10) or bus ride (#8) from Vicenza's Piazza Roma. Private tours are by appointment; see their website for the latest visiting details. ⊠ Via della Rotonda, Vicenza ☎ 0444/321793 ⊕ www.villalarotonda. it ⊠ €10 villa and grounds, €5 grounds only ⊘ Interior closed weekdays early Apr.–early Dec.

★ **Villa Valmarana ai Nani**

HISTORIC HOME | Inside this 17th- to 18th-century country house, named for the statues of dwarfs adorning the garden, is a series of frescoes executed in 1757 by Gianbattista Tiepolo depicting scenes from classical mythology, *The Iliad,* Tasso's *Jerusalem Delivered,* and Ariosto's *Orlando furioso* (*The Frenzy of Orlando*). They include his *Sacrifice of Iphigenia,* a major masterpiece of 18th-century painting. The neighboring *foresteria* (guesthouse) is also part of the museum; it contains frescoes showing 18th-century life at its most charming, and scenes of chinoiserie popular in the 18th century, by Tiepolo's son Giandomenico (1727–1804). The garden dwarfs are probably taken from designs by Giandomenico. You can reach the villa on foot by following the same path that leads to Palladio's Villa della Rotonda. ⊠ *Via dei Nani 2/8, Vicenza* ☎ *0444/321803* ⊕ *www.villavalmarana. com* 🎟 *€11.*

 Restaurants

Da Vittorio

$ | **PIZZA | FAMILY** | You'll find little in the way of atmosphere or style at this tiny, casual place, but Vicentini flock here for what may be the best pizza north of Naples. There's an incredible array of toppings, from the traditional to the exotic (think mango), but the pizzas taste so authentic you may feel transported to the Bay of Naples. **Known for:** tightly packed tables create a warm atmosphere; authentic wood-fired Neapolitan pizza convenient to Palladio villas; cheery naive artworks. ⑤ *Average main: €12* ⊠ *Borgo Berga 52, Vicenza* ☎ *0444/525059* ⊗ *Closed Tues., No lunch Sat. and Sun.*

Ponte delle Bele

$$ | **NORTHERN ITALIAN** | Many of Vicenza's wealthier residents spend at least part of the summer in the Alps to escape the heat, and the dishes of this popular and friendly trattoria reflect the hearty

Alpine influences on local cuisine. The house specialty, *stinco di maiale al forno* (roast pork shank), is wonderfully fragrant, with herbs and aromatic vegetables. **Known for:** mountain cheeses and cold cuts; hearty Vicentina classics including baccalà served with polenta; unfussy, relaxed atmosphere and kitschy Alpine decor. ⑤ *Average main: €15* ⊠ *Contrà Ponte delle Bele 5, Vicenza* ☎ *0444/320647* ⊕ *www.pontedellebele. com* ⊗ *Closed Sun. and 2 wks in Aug.*

Righetti

$ | **ITALIAN** | Vicentini of all generations gravitate to this popular cafeteria for classic dishes that don't put a dent in your wallet. Expect hearty helpings of fare such as *orzo e fagioli* (barley and bean soup) and baccalà *alla vicentina* (stockfish Vicenza style). **Known for:** entertaining local atmosphere; classic dishes; very popular, especially for lunch. ⑤ *Average main: €12* ⊠ *Piazza Duomo 3, Vicenza* ☎ *0444/543135* ⊗ *Closed weekends and 1 wk in Jan. and Aug.*

☕ **Coffee and Quick Bites**

Magazzino Del Caffè

$ | **NORTHERN ITALIAN** | Il Magazzino is a great spot to grab a snack any time of day, as this well-run, modern place covers all the bases from caffè and brioche breakfast fixes, to brunch panini and plates of pasta or risotto with a glass of wine later. Check out their fab selection of brioche pastries with novel fruit and nutty fillings, as well as heaped salads. **Known for:** tempting biscuits and gelato; aperitivi with stuzzichini snacks; friendly, youthful staff. ⑤ *Average main: €8* ⊠ *Corso Palladio 152, Vicenza* ☎ *335/573 9054.*

🛏 **Hotels**

During annual gold fairs in January, May, and September, it may be quite difficult to find lodging. If you're coming then, be sure to reserve well in advance and expect to pay higher rates.

★ Due Mori

$ | **HOTEL** | The public areas and guest rooms at one of the oldest (1883) hotels in the city, just off the Piazza dei Signori, are filled with turn-of-the-20th-century antiques, and regulars favor the place because the high ceilings in the main building make it feel light and airy. **Pros:** free Wi-Fi; comfortable, tastefully furnished rooms in central location; rate same year-round. **Cons:** no help with luggage; no AC, although ceiling fans minimize the need for it; no TVs in rooms. **$** *Rooms from: €100* ✉ *Contrà Do Rode 24, Vicenza* ☎ *0444/321886* ⊕ *www.hotelduemori.com* ☉ *Closed 2 wks in early Aug. and 2 wks in late Dec.* ⇨ *30 rooms* ⊚| *No Meals.*

Hotel Campo Marzio

$$ | **HOTEL** | Rooms at this comfortable full-service hotel—a five-minute walk from the train station and right in front of the city walls—are ample in size, with a mix of contemporary and traditional accents. **Pros:** set back from the street, so it's quiet and bright; free Wi-Fi in rooms; free bike hire. **Cons:** breakfast room a tad uninspiring; no in-room tea- or coffee-making facilities; businesslike exterior. **$** *Rooms from: €125* ✉ *Viale Roma 21, Vicenza* ☎ *0444/5457000* ⊕ *www.hotelcampomarzio.com* ⇨ *36 rooms* ⊚| *Free Breakfast.*

Marostica

26 km (16 miles) northeast of Vicenza, 93 km (58 miles) northwest of Venice.

From the 14th-century Castello Inferiore, where the town council still meets, an ancient stone wall snakes up the hill to enclose the Castello Superiore, which has commanding views. Marostica's most celebrated feature is the checkerboard-like square made with colored stone, Piazza Castello. The big annual event here, held in September in even-number years, is the Partita a Scacchi, a human-scale chess game.

GETTING HERE AND AROUND

There's no train station in Marostica. The closest rail connection is Bassano del Grappa, about 8 km (5 miles) away. There are regular bus connections from Vicenza's main station on FTV Bus No. 5; the trip takes about 45 minutes. By car, take the SS248 northeast from Vicenza, or southwest from Bassano.

VISITOR INFORMATION

CONTACT Marostica Tourism Office. ✉ *Piazza Castello 1, Marostica* ☎ *0424/72127* ⊕ *www.marosticascacchi.it.*

◉ Sights

Partita a Scacchi

THEATER | **FAMILY** | A human-scale chess game known as the Partita a Scacchi is acted out by players in medieval costume on the second weekend in September in even-number years. The game dates from 1454 and originated as a peaceful way of settling a love dispute for the hand of the daughter of the lord of Marostica Castle. The orders are still given in the local Veneto dialect. A game is presented on Friday, Saturday, and Sunday evenings as well as Sunday afternoon. If you book an evening show and do not have a hotel reservation in Marostica, be sure you have a way of getting back afterward. Buses do not run late in the evening, and taxis, if you can find one, may hike up their rates. Tickets go on sale in February; the tourist office can help with bookings. ✉ *Piazza Castello 1, Marostica* ☎ *0424/72127* ⊕ *www.marosticascacchi. it* ⊠ *€25–€100.*

Palladio's Architecture

Wealthy 16th-century patrons commissioned Andrea Palladio to design villas that would reflect their sense of cultivation and status. Using a classical vocabulary of columns, arches, and domes, he gave them a series of masterpieces in the towns and hills of the Veneto that exemplify the neo-Platonic ideals of harmony and proportion. Palladio's creations are the perfect expression of how a learned 16th-century man saw himself and his world, and as you stroll through them today, their serene beauty is as powerful as ever. Listen closely and you might even hear that celestial harmony, the music of the spheres, that so moved Palladio and his patrons.

Town and Country

Although the *villa*, or country residence, was still a relatively new phenomenon in the 16th century, it quickly became all the rage once the great lords of Venice turned their eyes from the sea toward the fertile plains of the Veneto. They were forced to do this once their trade routes had faltered when Ottoman Turks conquered Constantinople in 1456 and Columbus opened a path for Spain to the riches of America in 1492. In no time, canals were built, farms were laid out, and the fashion for villeggiatura became a favored lifestyle. As a means of escaping an overheated Rome, villas had been the original brainchild of the ancient emperors, and it was no accident that the Venetian lords wished to emulate this palatial style of country residence. Palladio's method of evaluating the standards, and standbys, of ancient Roman life through the eye of the Italian Renaissance, combined with his innate sense of proportion and symmetry, became the lasting foundation of his art. In turn, Palladio threw out the mélange of styles prevalent in Venetian architecture—Byzantine, Gothic, and Renaissance—for the pure, noble lines found in the buildings of the Caesars.

Andrea Palladio (1508–80)

"Face dark, eyes fiery. Dress rich. His appearance that of a genius." So was Palladio described by his wealthy mentor, Count Trissino. Trissino encouraged the young student to trade in his birth name, Andrea di Pietro della Gondola, for the elegant Palladio. He did, and it proved a wise move indeed. Born in Padua in 1508, Andrea moved to nearby Vicenza in 1524 and was quickly taken up by the city's power elite. He experienced a profound revelation on his first trip, in 1541, to Rome, where he sensed the harmony of the ancient ruins and saw the elements of classicism that were working their way into contemporary architecture. This experience led to his spectacular conversion of Vicenza's Palazzo della Ragione into a Roman basilica, recalling the great meeting halls of antiquity. In years to come, after relocating to Venice, he created some memorable churches, such as San Giorgio Maggiore (1564). Despite these varied projects, Palladio's unassailable position as one of the world's greatest architects is tied to the countryside villas, which he spread across the Veneto plains like a firmament of stars. Nothing else in the Veneto illuminates more clearly the idyllic beauty of the region than these elegant residences, their stonework now nicely mellowed and suntanned after five centuries.

Vicenza

To see Palladio's pageant of palaces, head for Vicenza. His Palazzo della Ragione marks the city's heart, the Piazza dei Signori. This building rocketed young Palladio from an unknown to an architectural star. Across the way is his redbrick Loggia del Capitaniato. One block past the loggia is Vicenza's main street, appropriately named Corso Andrea Palladio. Just off this street is the Contrà Porti, where you'll find the Palazzo Barbaran da Porto (1570) at No. 11, with its fabulously rich facade erupting with Ionic and Corinthian pillars. Today, this is the Centro Internazionale di Studi di Architettura Andrea Palladio (www.palladiomuseum.org), a study center that mounts impressive temporary exhibitions. A few steps away, on the Contrà San Gaetano Thiene, is the Palazzo Thiene (1542–58), designed by Giulio Romano and completed by Palladio. Doubling back to Contrà Porti 21, you find the Palazzo Iseppo da Porto (1544), the first palazzo where you can see the neoclassical effects of young Palladio's trip to Rome. Following the Contrà Riale, you come to Corso Fogazzaro 16 and the Palazzo Valmarana Braga (1565). Its gigantic pilasters were a first for domestic architecture. Returning to the Corso Palladio, head left to the opposite end of the Corso, about five blocks, to the Piazza Matteotti and Palazzo Chiericati (1550). This was practically a suburban area in the 16th century, and for the palazzo Palladio combined elements of urban and rural design. The pedestal raising the building and the steps leading to the entrance—unknown in urban palaces—were to protect from floods and to keep cows from wandering in the front door. Across the Corso Palladio is Palladio's last and one of his most spectacular works, the Teatro Olimpico (1580). By careful study of ancient ruins and architectural texts, he reconstructed a Roman theater with archaeological precision. Palladio died before it was completed, but he left clear plans for the project. Although it's on the outskirts of town, the Villa Almerico Capra, better known as La Rotonda or Villa della Rotonda (1566), is an indispensable part of any visit to Vicenza. It's the iconic Palladian building, the purest expression of his aesthetic.

Palladio Country

At the Villa Barbaro (1554) near the town of Maser in the province of Treviso, 48 km (30 miles) northeast of Vicenza, you can see the results of a onetime collaboration between two of the greatest artists of their age. Palladio was the architect, and Paolo Veronese decorated the interior with an amazing cycle of trompe-l'oeil frescoes—walls dissolve into landscapes, and illusions of courtiers and servants enter rooms and smile down from balustrades. Legend has it a feud developed between Palladio and Veronese, with Palladio feeling the illusionistic frescoes detracted from his architecture; but there is practically nothing to support the idea of such a rift. It's also noteworthy that Palladio for the first time connected the two lateral granaries to the main villa. This was a working farm, and Palladio thus created an architectural unity by connecting the working parts of the estate to the living quarters with graceful arcades, bringing together the Renaissance dichotomy of the active and the contemplative.

Restaurants

Osteria Madonnetta

$ | VENETIAN | Opened in 1904, this ever-re-liable osteria serves hearty traditional *cucina veneta* in wonderfully homey, rustic surroundings. Take a seat under the dark wooden beams or in the leafy courtyard, and let the friendly staff guide you through a menu, dominated by meat dishes and seasonal soups, that has barely changed in decades. **Known for:** quirky, history-filled decor including a chess-themed fireplace; sweet, grappa-infused zaeti biscuits; baccalà alla vicentina. $ *Average main: €12* ✉ *Via Vajenti 21, Marostica* ☎ *0424/75859* ⊕ *www.osteriamadonnetta.it* ⊘ *Closed Thurs.*

Hotels

Due Mori

$ | B&B/INN | Although this inn dates from the 18th century, the interior is minimalist and clean-lined—Rooms 7, 8, 11, and 12 redress the balance with picture-perfect views of the town's upper castle, while other windows look out onto the city walls or olive-tree-filled terraces. **Pros:** great views of castle from some rooms; only hotel within the city walls; train station transfers available. **Cons:** noise from Corso Mazzini–facing rooms; limited breakfast choice; bland decoration. $ *Rooms from: €120* ✉ *Corso Mazzini 73, Marostica* ☎ *0424/471777* ⊕ *www.duemori.com* ⊋ *12 rooms* ⦿ *Free Breakfast.*

Asolo

27 km (17 miles) east of Marostica.

Once considered the most romantic and charming of Veneto towns, the hamlet of Asolo has unfortunately lost much of its appeal, now that it's given over completely to tourism and vacation houses, with almost no local population. It does still make a nice stop for lunch after a visit to the Palladian villa at Maser, but try to avoid it on weekends and holidays, when the crowds pour in.

Through the centuries, Veneto aristocrats built elegant villas on the hillside, and in the 19th century Asolo became the idyllic haunt of musicians, poets, and painters. Back then it was one of Italy's most perfectly situated villages, with views across miles of hilly countryside; now it bears some of the scars of modern development.

Asolo hosts a modest antiques market on the second Sunday of every month.

GETTING HERE AND AROUND
There's no train station in Asolo; the closest one is in Montebelluna, 12 km (7½ miles) away. Bus connections are infrequent, and buses are not coordinated with trains, making it about a 2½-hour trip from Venice via public transportation. The best option is to drive.

By car from Treviso, take Via Feltrina and continue onto Via Padre Agostino Gemelli (SR348). Follow SR348 about 16 km (10 miles), then turn left on SP667, which you follow for almost 4 km (2½ miles). At the roundabout, take the first exit, Via Monte Grappa (SP248), and follow it for 6½ km (4 miles) to Via Loredan, where you turn right and then left onto Via Biordo Vecchio. Asolo is less than 7 km (4½ miles) away from the Palladian Villa Barbaro at Maser.

VISITOR INFORMATION
CONTACT Asolo Tourism Office. ✉ *Piazza Maggiore (aka Piazza Garibaldi), Asolo* ☎ *0423/529046* ⊕ *www.asolo.it.*

Sights

Brion Family Tomb

MONUMENT | One of the major monuments of contemporary Italian architecture, the Brion family tomb was designed and built by the architect Carlo Scarpa (1906–78) between 1970 and 1972. Combining Western rationalism with Eastern spirituality, Scarpa avoids the gloom and bombast of conventional commemorative monuments, creating, in his words, a secluded Eden. ⊠ SP6 (Via Castellana), about 7 km (4½ miles) south of Asolo, near village of San Vito 🔁 Free.

★ **Museo Canova** (Gypsoteca)

ART MUSEUM | The most significant cultural monument in the Asolo area is this museum dedicated to the work of the Italian neoclassical sculptor Antonio Canova (1757–1822), whose sculptures are featured in many major European and North American cultural institutions. Set up shortly after the sculptor's death in his hometown, the village of Possagno, the museum houses most of the original plaster casts, models, and drawings made by the artist in preparation for his marble sculptures. In 1957 the Museo Canova was extended by the Italian architect Carlo Scarpa. ⊠ Via Canova 74, 13½ km (8¼ miles) northwest of Asolo, Possagno 🕾 0423/544323 ⊕ www.museocanova.it 🔁 €10 🕙 Closed Mon.

Museo Civico, Torre Civica, and La Rocca

HISTORY MUSEUM | In the Piazza Maggiore, the frescoed 15th-century Loggia del Capitano contains the Museo Civico, which displays a collection of eccentric memorabilia—the Italian actress Eleonora Duse's correspondence, the poet Robert Browning's spinet, and portraits of the noble Caterina Cornaro (1454–1510). There is also access to the nearby medieval tower, Torre Civica, partially rebuilt after an earthquake in 1685. It affords great views just above its handsome 18th-century clock, designed by Bartolomeo Ferracina, the genius engineer behind clocks in Venice's Piazza San Marco and Sant'Antonio da Padova. Temporary exhibitions are also staged in the tower, along with guided tours. Those after a woodland stroll should head up to the 1000-foot Monte Ricco medieval-hilltop fortress La Rocca—the views are fabulous but the structure itself is sometimes off limits. ⊠ Piazza Maggiore, Asolo

🕾 0423/952313 ⊕ www.museoasolo.it 🕙 Closed weekdays 🔁 €5 Museo Civico; €2 Torre Civica; €1 La Rocca.

Piazza Maggiore

PLAZA/SQUARE | Also known as Piazza Giuseppe Garibaldi, this graceful square is surrounded by Renaissance palaces, historical cafés, and the mosiac-adorned cathedral. The Fontana Maggiore is fed by the remains of a Roman aqueduct; the fountain's latest form combines 16th-century marble with a lion added in 1918, attesting to centuries of Venetian rule here. ⊠ Asolo.

★ **Tempio Canoviano**

MONUMENT | One of the most impressive and historically significant neoclassical buildings in Italy, the Tempio Canoviano, a church, was designed by Canova in 1819 and finished in 1830, incorporating motifs from the rotunda of the Roman Pantheon and the pronaos of the Parthenon. The church contains several works by Canova, including his tomb, along with paintings by Luca Giordano, Palma il Giovane, and Il Pordenone. ⊠ Piazza Canova, Possagno ✛ 16 km (10 miles) north of Asolo 🕾 0423/544323 ⊕ www.tempiocanoviano.it 🔁 Free.

🍴 Restaurants

Al Bacaro

$$ | **ITALIAN** | At this rustic, wood-rich family-style osteria, it's worth giving the robust local specialties, such as tripe, snails, or stewed game, a go—many of them served with polenta. Less adventurous diners can go for other homey options, such as goulash, polenta with cheese and mushrooms, or one of Bacaro's open-face sandwiches, generously topped with fresh salami, speck, or other cold cuts. **Known for:** seasonal vegetables and meat; good, meaty country fare; jolly osteria crammed with local artifacts and patrons' hand-scribbled witticisms. ⑤ Average main: €17 ⊠ Via Browning

165, Asolo ☎ 0423/55150 ⏱ No dinner Sat. and Sun.

★ Locanda Baggio

$$ | ITALIAN | A fabulous garden setting and warm yet unfussy country-style dining rooms elevate this family-run restaurant, renowned for Nino Baggio's elegant creative take on traditional cuisine. This is the finest restaurant in Asolo, and the prix-fixe menu (you can also order à la carte) delivers one of the best-value top-quality dining options in the Veneto. **Known for:** warm hospitality; inventive, tasty food; white truffles and other seasonal specialties. ⑤ *Average main: €23* ✉ *Via Bassane 1, Asolo* ☎ *0423/529648* ⊕ *www.locandabaggio.it* ⏱ *Closed Mon.*

 ## Hotels

Albergo Al Sole

$$ | HOTEL | This elegant pink-washed hotel in a 16th-century building overlooks the main square and has wide views over picturesque Asolo or its leafy hinterland. **Pros:** shuttle service to the surrounding area; central location with beautiful views; free bike hire. **Cons:** standard rooms have less interesting views than more expensive ones; huge rate increase in the high season; expensive drinks and hidden extras. ⑤ *Rooms from: €180* ✉ *Via Collegio 33, Asolo* ☎ *0423/951332* ⊕ *www.albergoalsole.com* ⏱ *Generally closed early Jan.–mid-Feb.* 🛏 *23 rooms* ⑪ *Free Breakfast.*

Hotel Duse

$$ | HOTEL | A spiral staircase winds its way up this narrow, centrally located building—filled with traditional furnishings like gilded chairs—to rooms with grandstand-like views of the main square. **Pros:** bike rental and tours available; simple but tasteful good-value rooms; central location. **Cons:** not as much of a bargain when you add the cost of breakfast and parking; some street noise; dated, garish decor in some rooms. ⑤ *Rooms from: €130* ✉ *Via Browning 190, Asolo*

☎ *0423/55241* ⊕ *www.hotelduse.com* 🛏 *14 rooms* ⑪ *No Meals* ⏱ *Closed 3 wks in Jan. and Feb.*

Villa Cipriani

$$$ | HOTEL | From its 19th-century furnishings to a 21st-century spa and a romantic garden, this luxurious 16th-century villa turned hotel strives for opulence. **Pros:** spa services and outdoor panoramic pool; incomparable views, including from the terrace; truly elegant grounds. **Cons:** exorbitant parking fees; small bathrooms; rooms in the annex are very small. ⑤ *Rooms from: €235* ✉ *Via Canova 298, Asolo* ☎ *0423/523411* ⊕ *www.villaciprianiasolo.com* 🛏 *29 rooms* ⑪ *Free Breakfast.*

Treviso

37 km (23 miles) southeast of Asolo, 30 km (19 miles) north of Venice.

Treviso has been dubbed "Little Venice" because of its meandering, moss-bank canals. They can't really compare with Venice's spectacular waterways, but Treviso's historic center, with its medieval arcaded streets, does have a great deal of charm. Treviso is a fine place to stop for a few hours on the way from Venice to the wine country in the north or to the Palladian villas in the hinterland.

Allied bombing on Good Friday in 1944 destroyed half the city—it was bombed by mistake after a report that Hitler would be in Tarvisio, on the Austrian border, was misread. Despite this, Treviso managed to preserve what remained of its old town's narrow streets while introducing modernity far more gently than in many other parts of Italy. These days it's one of the wealthiest small cities in the country, with fashionable shops and boutiques at every turn in the busy city center.

Treviso and
the Hillside Towns

GETTING HERE AND AROUND

Treviso is 30 minutes by train from Venice; there are frequent daily departures. By car from Venice, pick up the SS13 (Via Terraglio) in Mestre and follow it all the way to Treviso; the trip takes about 45 minutes.

VISITOR INFORMATION

CONTACT Treviso Tourism Office (IAT Treviso). ✉ *Via Fiumicelli 30, Treviso* ☎ *0422/547632* ⊕ *www.visittreviso.it.*

⊚ Sights

Conegliano

TOWN | This attractive town, with Venetian-style villas and arcaded streets, lies 23 km (14 miles) north of Treviso in wine-producing country and is known for its sparkling white wine, prosecco. Its other claim to fame is its connection with Gianbattista Cima—called Cima di Conegliano. Along with Giovanni Bellini, Cima is one of the greatest painters of the early Venetian Renaissance, and the town's elegant 14th-century Duomo houses an altarpiece he painted in 1492. The front of the Duomo is formed by the frescoed late-medieval facade and Gothic arcade of the Scuola dei Battuti. If you stop in town, be sure to taste the prosecco, sold in local wine bars and shops. There is regular train service from Treviso. ✉ *Conegliano.*

Duomo

CHURCH | *The Cattedrale San Pietro Apostolo,* or Duomo, was given a 19th century neo-classical makeover but retains the Renaissance splendor of the Malchiostro Chapel, with an *Annunciation* by Titian (1520) and Pordenone's (1484–1539) *Adoration of the Magi* frescoes. The crypt

Traveling the Wine Roads

You'd be hard-pressed to find a more stimulating and varied wine region than northeastern Italy. From the Valpolicella, Bardolino, and Soave produced near Verona to the superlative whites of the Collio Goriziano region, wines from the Veneto and Friuli–Venezia Giulia earn more Denominazione di Origine Controllata (DOC) seals for uniqueness and quality than those of any other area of Italy.

You can travel on foot, by car, or by bicycle over hillsides covered with *cantine* (vineyards), each field nurturing subtly different grape varieties. Be advised that Italy has become more stringent about its driving regulations; designated drivers can help avoid the risk of fines, embarrassment, or worse.

In the stretch of country north of Treviso, you can follow designated wine roads—tours that blend a beautiful rural setting with the delights of the grape. Authorized wineshops, where you can stop and sample, are marked with a sign showing a triangular arrangement of red and yellow grapes. There are three routes to choose from, and you can do them all comfortably over the course of a day or two.

Montello and Asolo Hills

This route provides a good balance of vineyards and nonwine sights. It winds from Nervesa della Battaglia, 18 km (10 miles) north of Treviso, past two prime destinations in the area, the village of Asolo and the Villa Barbaro at Maser. Asolo produces good prosecco, while Montello, a hill near Nervesa, favors merlot and cabernet. Both areas also yield pinot noir and chardonnay.

Piave River

The circular route follows the Piave River and runs through orchards, woods, and hills. Among the area's gems are the dessert wines Torchiato di Fregona and Refrontolo Passito, both made according to traditional methods.

Raboso del Piave, renowned since Roman times, ages well and complements local dishes such as beans and pasta or goose stuffed with chestnuts. Other reds include merlot and cabernet sauvignon.

Prosecco

La Strada del Prosecco (Prosecco Road) runs for 47 km (29 miles) between Valdobbiadene and Conegliano, home of Italy's first wine institute, winding between knobby hills covered in grapevines. These hang in festoons on row after row of pergolas to create a thick mantle of green.

Turn off the main route to explore the narrower country lanes. They meander past numerous family wineries where you can taste and buy the wines. It's well worth setting aside time to explore the most scenic southern stretches: between Renfrontolo and Col San Martino there's the ancient San Vigilio church and the celebrated Follador winery; while the Cartizze hills afford breathtaking views. Spring is an excellent time to visit, with no fewer than 15 local wine festivals held between March and early June.

has 12th-century columns. Bring a handful of coins for the coin-operated lights that illuminate the artwork. To the left of the Duomo is the Romanesque Battistero di San Giovanni (11th-12th centuries), which is probably quite similar in style to the medieval Duomo; it's open only for special exhibitions. ✉ *Piazza del Duomo, Treviso* ☎ *0422/545720.*

Piazza dei Signori

PLAZA/SQUARE | The center of medieval Treviso, this piazza remains the town's social hub, with outdoor cafés and some impressive public buildings. The most important of these, the Palazzo dei Trecento (1185–1268), was the seat of the city government, composed of the Council of 300, during the Middle Ages. Behind it is a small alley that leads to *pescheria* (fish market), on an island in one of the small canals that flow through town. ✉ *Treviso.*

Quartiere Latino

HISTORIC DISTRICT | While strolling the city, take in this restored district between Riviera Garibaldi and Piazza Santa Maria Battuti. It's the site of university buildings, upscale apartments, and bustling restaurants and shops. ✉ *Treviso.*

San Nicolò

CHURCH | The most important church in Treviso, this huge Venetian Gothic structure from the early 14th century has an ornate vaulted ceiling and frescoes (circa 1350) of saints by Tommaso da Modena (circa 1325–79) on the columns. The depiction of St. Agnes on the north side is particularly interesting, combining the naturalism initiated a few decades earlier by Giotto with the grace and elegance of Gothic abstraction. Also worth examining are Tommaso's realistic portraits of 40 Dominican friars, found in the Sala del Capitolo of the seminary next door. They include the earliest known painting of a subject wearing eyeglasses, an Italian invention (circa 1280–1300). ✉ *Seminario Vescovile, Via San Nicolò, Treviso*

☎ *0422/548626* ⊕ *www.sannicolotreviso. it* ♥ *Closed Sun. except to worshippers.*

★ Villa Barbaro (Villa di Maser)

NOTABLE BUILDING | At the Villa Barbaro (1554) near the town of Maser, you can see the exquisite results of a onetime collaboration between two of the greatest artists of their age: Palladio was the architect, and Paolo Veronese did the interiors. You can easily spend a couple of hours here, so set aside time for lingering in the gorgeous grounds, admiring the honey-hue exterior and ornate statuary, including the dreamlike nymphaeum and pool. A visit is particularly immersive because the superb condition of the grounds and interior creates an uncanny atmosphere: nowhere else in the Veneto do you get such a vivid feeling for the combination of grandeur and leisure with a tangible whiff of a working farm. Villa Barbaro, a short drive from Asolo, is most accessible by private car; the closest train station is Montebelluna. Buses leave for Maser from the bus station at Treviso, Montebelluna, or Bassano di Grappa. The bus will leave you at a stop about 1½ km (1 mile) from Maser. Hours can vary, so check the website. ✉ *Via Cornuda 7, Maser, Treviso* ☎ *0432/923004* ⊕ *www.villadimaser.it* ♥ *Closed Mon. Apr.–Oct. and weekdays Nov.–Mar., except for rare events* 🎫 *€9.*

🍴 Restaurants

All'Antico Portico

$$ | ITALIAN | FAMILY | This little old brick trattoria on a beguiling piazza with views of the Santa Maria Maggiore church is a favorite among locals and tourists, who flock to its cozy wood-trimmed interior. The menu changes daily but always features well-executed versions of simple local dishes, from risottos and pastas to a variety of seafood and meat dishes. **Known for:** mamma's baccalà alla veneziana recipe; homemade pasta and white truffle; set under the 15th-century porticoes. $ *Average main: €18*

✉ *Piazza Santa Maria Maggiore 18, Treviso* ☎ *0422/545259* ⊕ *www.anticoportico. it* ☉ *Closed Tues. No dinner Mon.*

Beccherie

$$$ | ITALIAN | Adventurous foodies should book a table in this stylish blue-and-wood-accented dining room, located behind Treviso's Palazzo dei Trecento old meat market, for an experience that marries Trevigiano culinary traditions with contemporary elegance. The owner's mother, Alba di Pillo Campeol, invented the famous dessert tiramisu in the 1960s, and the Beccherie, opened in 1939, still makes it to the original, feather-light recipe. **Known for:** reservations recommended for dinner; inventive food and special tiramisu; contemporary design above the canal. ⑤ *Average main: €27* ✉ *Piazza Ancilotto 10, Treviso* ☎ *0422/540871* ⊕ *www.lebeccherie.it* ☉ *Closed Tues.*

Il Basilisco

$$ | ITALIAN | Gastronomically adventurous diners who visit this quirky restaurant filled with stylish midcentury furnishings will find *cucina povera* (peasant food) given an inventive twist. The chef is a passionate Slow Food champion, so expect local and seasonal meat and vegetables, as well as excellent seafood and an extensive wine list from Italy and farther afield. **Known for:** homemade pasta, cured meats, and antipasti; inventive use of *quinto quarto* (offal); vibrant contemporary decor and design. ⑤ *Average main: €19* ✉ *Via Bison, Treviso 34,* ☎ *0422/541822* ⊕ *www.ristorante-basilisco.com* ☉ *No lunch Mon.–Sat., no dinner Tues.–Sun.*

Toni del Spin

$$ | ITALIAN | Wood-paneled and with a 1930s-style interior, this bustling trattoria has a wholesome menu based on local Veneto cooking. The *spin* in the restaurant's name refers to the spine of the baccalà, one of several justly famous specialties (served without the titular spine); also try the *sopa coada,* a

pigeon-and-bread soup. ■TIP→ **Reservations are essential, even for lunch, since the word is out that this is the best value in town. Known for:** reservations essential at lunch and dinner; Veneto specialties and great wine choices; idiosyncratic, sometimes brusque service. ⑤ *Average main: €19* ✉ *Via Inferiore 7, Treviso* ☎ *393/986 3597* ⊕ *www.ristorantetonidelspin.com* ☉ *Closed 3 wks in July and Aug. No lunch Mon.*

☕ Coffee and Quick Bites

Caffetteria Broli

$ | NORTHERN ITALIAN | This central coffee bar serves lots of different *espressi* and *cappuccini*—topped with chocolate and cream and other enhancements—as well as a cornucopia of great-value *tramezzini* sandwiches, *piadine* (Italian flat-bread wraps), and panini. Pop in most times of the day (closes at 7:30 pm) for a selection of classic pasta primi and secondi, as well as healthy juices and vegan options. **Known for:** vegan selection; brioche and other pastries topped with fruit; *insalatoni* (heaped salads). ⑤ *Average main: €6* ✉ *Vicolo Broli 8/10, Treviso* ☎ *0422/582225.*

🛏 Hotels

Hotel San Nicolò

$$ | HOTEL | Comfort combines with warm hospitality and distinctive decor—public areas are elegant with choice antiques, while each guest room is themed after a global city—at this well-run central hotel in a handsome palazzo near Chiesa di San Nicolò. **Pros:** only a dozen steps up to rooms; individual character in each guest room; warm, family-run customer service. **Cons:** some rooms on the small size; road noise in some rooms; no elevator. ⑤ *Rooms from: €160* ✉ *Via Risorgimento 54, Treviso* ☎ *0422/590114* ⊕ *www.relais-sannicolo.com* ⇥ *10 rooms* ⊚l *Free Breakfast.*

Udine

*94 km (58 miles) northeast of Treviso,
127 km (79 miles) northeast of Venice.*

The main reason for devoting some time
to Udine is to see works by Gianbattista
Tiepolo (1696–1770), one of the greatest
European painters of the 18th century. Distributed in several palaces and
churches around town, this is the largest
assembly of his art outside Venice. In
fact, Udine calls itself "la città di Tiepolo."

The largest city on the Friuli side of Friuli–
Venezia Giulia, Udine has a provincial,
genteel atmosphere and lots of charm.
The city sometimes seems completely
unaffected by tourism, and things are still
done the way they were decades ago. In
the medieval and Renaissance historical center of town, you'll find unevenly
spaced streets with appealing wine bars
and open-air cafés. Friulani are proud of
their culture, with many restaurants featuring local cuisine and street signs and
announcements written in both Italian
and Friulano (Furlan). Although Friulano
is sometimes classified as a dialect, it's
really a separate language from Italian.

Commanding a view from the Alpine
foothills to the Adriatic Sea, Udine
stands on a mound that, according to
legend, was erected so Attila the Hun
could watch the burning of Aquileia, an
important Roman center to the south.
Although the legend is unlikely (Attila
burned Aquileia about 500 years before
the first historical mention of Udine), the
view from Udine's castle across the allu-
vial plane down to the sea is impressive.
In the Middle Ages Udine flourished,
thanks to its favorable trade location and
the right granted by the local patriarch to
hold regular markets.

GETTING HERE AND AROUND

There's frequent train service from both
Venice and Trieste; the trip takes about
two hours from Venice, and a little over
an hour from Trieste. By car from Venice,
take the SR11 to the E55 and head east.
Follow the E55 (it eventually becomes
the A23 Autostrada Alpe–Adria) to SS13
(Viale Venezia) east into Udine. Driving
from Trieste, take the SS202 to the E70,
which becomes the A4. Turn north onto
the E55 (the same road you take coming
from Venice). Driving times are 1½ hours
from Venice and one hour from Trieste.

VISITOR INFORMATION

The tourist office sells the FVG (Friuli
Venezia Giulia) Card, which includes
admission to most museums in Udine
and other important sites in the region.
Its price ranges from €25 (for 48 hours)
up to €39 (for one week).

CONTACT Udine Tourism Office. ⊠ *Piazza I
Maggio 7, Udine* ☎ *0432/295972* ⊕ *www.
turismofvg.it.*

Sights

★ Castello and Musei Civici

CASTLE/PALACE | The hilltop castle (con-
struction began in 1517) has panoramic
views extending to Monte Nero (7,360
feet) in neighboring Slovenia, but head
inside to see Udine's civic museums
of art and archaeology, with myriad
collections that can detain you for hours.
On the ground floor are the Museo del
Risorgimento (tracing the history of Italian unification) and Museo Archeologico;
the third floor is the Museo della Fotogra-
fia, with fascinating 19th- and 20th-cen-
tury images of the Friuli. Particularly
worthwhile is the national and regional
art collection in the Galleria d'Arte Antica,
which has canvases by Venetians Vittore
Carpaccio (circa 1460–1525) and Gianbattista Tiepolo, the recently restored (2020)
*Il San Francesco Riceve le Stimmate
(Saint Francis Receiving the Stigmata)* by
Caravaggio, and carefully selected works
by lesser known but still interesting Veneto and Friuli artists. ■**TIP→ The museum's
small collection of drawings includes
several by Tiepolo; some find his drawings even more moving than his paintings.**

Duomo

CHURCH | A few steps from the Piazza
della Libertà is Udine's 1335 Duomo, with some significant works by
Tiepolo. Its Cappella del Santissimo has
important early frescoes by Tiepolo, and
the Cappella della Trinità has a Tiepolo
altarpiece. There is also a beautiful
late Tiepolo *Resurrection* (1751) in an
altar by the sculptor Giuseppe Toretti.
Ask the Duomo's attendant to let you
into the adjacent **Chiesa della Purità** to
see more important late paintings by
Tiepolo. ✉ *Piazza del Duomo 1, Udine*
☎ *0432/505302* ⊕ *www.cattedraleu-
dine.it* ✉ *Free.*

★ Museo d'Arte Moderna e Contempora-
nea–Casa Cavazzini

ART GALLERY | Udine's fine civic collec-
tion of modern and contemporary art is
housed in the handsome and part-mod-
ernized 16th-century Casa Cavazzini,
which retains some ornate apartment
interiors. The first and second floors
display the permanent collection: first-
floor highlights include bold sculptural
works by the three Udinese brothers
Dino, Mirko, and Afro Basaldella, with
a backdrop of 14th-century frescoes
discovered during the 2012 refurbishing.
There are also fine works by Giorgio
Morandi, Renato Guttuso, and Carlo
Carrà. Up a floor is the Collezione
Astaldi, spanning the 1920s through the
1960s, and Collezione FRIAM, with '60s
and '70s works. Worth seeking out are
Giorgio de Chirico's *I Gladiatori* (1931)
and pieces by 20th-century American

icons Willem de Kooning, Roy Lichtenstein, and Sol LeWitt. ⊠ *Via Cavour 14, Udine* ☎ *0432/1273772* ⊕ *www. civicimuseiudine.it* ⊠ *€5, €10 Unico ticket also includes Castello and Museo Etnografico del Friuli (free with FVG Card)* ⊗ *Closed Mon.*

★ Museo Diocesano e Gallerie del Tiepolo

CASTLE/PALACE | The handsome Palazzo Patriarcale o Arcivescovile contains several rooms of frescoes by the young Gianbattista Tiepolo, painted from 1726 to 1732, which comprise the most important collection of early works by Italy's most brilliant 18th-century painter. The Galleria del Tiepolo (1727) contains superlative Tiepolo frescoes depicting the stories of Abraham, Isaac, and Jacob. *The Judgment of Solomon* (1729) graces the Pink Room. There are also beautiful and important Tiepolo frescoes in the staircase, throne room, and palatine chapel of this palazzo. Even in these early works we can see the Venetian master's skill in creating an illusion of depth, not only through linear perspective, but also through subtle gradations in the intensity of the colors, with the stronger colors coming forward and the paler ones receding into space. Tiepolo was one of the first artists to use this method of representing space and depth, which reflected the scientific discoveries of perception and optics in the 17th century. The Museo Diocesano here features sculptures from Friuli churches from the 13th through 18th century; and don't miss the magnificent library, the *Biblioteca Arcivescovile Delfiniana.* ⊠ *Piazza Patriarcato 1, Udine* ☎ *0432/25003* ⊕ *www.musdioc-tiepolo.it* ⊠ *€8, includes Museo Diocesano (free with FVG Card)* ⊗ *Closed Tues.*

Piazza della Libertà

PLAZA/SQUARE | Udine was conquered by the Venetians in 1420, so there is a distinctly Venetian stamp on the architecture of the historic center, most noticeably here, in the large main square.

The Loggia del Leonello, begun in 1428, dominates the square and houses the municipal government. Its similarity to the facade of Venice's Palazzo Ducale (finished in 1424) is clear, but there is no evidence that it is an imitation of that palace. It's more likely a product of the same architectural fashion. Opposite stands the Renaissance Porticato di San Giovanni (1533–35) and the Torre dell'Orologio, a 1527 clock tower with naked *mori* (Moors), who strike the hours on the top. ⊠ *Udine.*

🍴 Restaurants

★ Hostaria alla Tavernetta

$$$ | FRIULIAN | The trusty Hostaria (open since 1954) has rustic fireside dining downstairs and more elegantly decorated rooms upstairs, where there's also an intimate terrace under the Duomo. It's a great place for sampling regional specialties such as *orzotto* (barley prepared like risotto), delicious *cjalzòns* (ravioli from the Carnia), and seasonal meat dishes, accompanied by a fabulous wine list. **Known for:** superb local Collio wine, grappa, and regional selections; rustic yet sophisticated atmosphere; Friulian ingredients and traditions. ⑤ *Average main: €25* ⊠ *Via di Prampero 2, Udine* ☎ *0432/501066* ⊕ *www.allatavernetta.com* ⊗ *Closed Sun. and Mon. No lunch Sat.*

★ Vitello d'Oro

$$ | ITALIAN | Udine's very chic landmark restaurant is the one reserved most by locals for special occasions, and the menu features the freshest meat and fish in sophisticated dishes served with moodily lit culinary stagecraft. You might start with an antipasto of assorted raw shellfish, including the impossibly sweet Adriatic scampi, followed by the fresh fish of the day. **Known for:** multicourse tasting menu; seafood served raw and cooked; large terrace popular in summer. ⑤ *Average main: €24* ⊠ *Via Valvason 4, Udine* ☎ *0432/508982* ⊕ *www.vitello-doro.com* ⊗ *Closed Sun. No lunch Mon.*

Coffee and Quick Bites

★ **Grosmi Caffè**

$ | **NORTHERN ITALIAN** | Under the porticoes of gorgeous Piazza Matteoti, with its vibrant student and dialect-speaking locals, Grosmi is a reliable choice for excellent coffee, pastries, and people watching. Although the brioche filled with chocolate, custard, or fruit jam are staples, some opt for a cheeky small cake or macaroon to accompany their caffeine fix. **Known for:** brioche, pastries and cakes; selection of imported blends; tables on the piazza. $ *Average main: €5* ⊠ *Piazza Giacomo Matteotti 9, Udine* ☎ *0432/506411* ⊕ *biquadrocaffe.it.*

🛏 Hotels

Hotel Clocchiatti Next

$ | **HOTEL** | You have two smart and contrasting choices here: the 19th-century villa, with canopy beds and Alpine-style wood ceilings and paneling; and the "Next Wing," with rich colors and spare furnishings in starkly angular rooms. **Pros:** a tranquil Zen-garden haven; stylish, individually decorated rooms; excellent breakfast. **Cons:** small bathrooms; 10-minute drive from town center; no restaurant. $ *Rooms from: €110* ⊠ *Via Cividale 29, Udine* ☎ *0432/505047* ⊕ *www.hotelclocchiatti.it* ⇘ *27 rooms* ⍵ *Free Breakfast.*

Hotel Ristorante Allegria

$$ | **HOTEL** | Renovation of this 15th-century building took a decidedly minimalist approach: the breakfast room, lounges, and guest rooms feature plenty of light wood, mood lighting, and sleek, angular design. **Pros:** easy walking distance to the center; well-appointed, neutral-hue rooms; discounted weekend rates. **Cons:** fee for parking; rooms may be too minimalist for some; AC can be unreliable. $ *Rooms from: €150* ⊠ *Via Grazzano 18, Udine* ☎ *0432/201116* ⊕ *www.hotelallegria.it* ⇘ *21 rooms* ⍵ *Free Breakfast.*

Cividale del Friuli

17 km (11 miles) east of Udine, 144 km (89 miles) northeast of Venice.

Cividale is the most important place for taking in the impressive and beautiful art of the Lombards, a Germanic people who entered Italy in 568 and who ruled parts of Italy until the late 8th century. The city was founded in AD 53 by Julius Caesar, then commander of Roman legions in the area. Here you can also find Celtic, Roman, and medieval Jewish ruins alongside Venetian Gothic buildings, including the Palazzo Comunale. Strolling through the part of the city that now occupies the former Gastaldia, the Lombard ducal palace, gives you spectacular views of the medieval city and the river.

GETTING HERE AND AROUND

There's half-hourly train service from Udine. Since the Udine–Cividale train line isn't part of the Italian national rail system, you have to buy the tickets from the electronic machines, the MPL tobacconist, or the newsstand Edicola 103 within the Udine station. You can't buy a ticket through to Cividale from another city.

By car from Udine, take Via Cividale, which turns into SS54; follow SS54 into Cividale.

VISITOR INFORMATION

CONTACT Informacittà office. ⊠ *Piazza Paolo Diacono 10, Cividale del Friuli* ☎ *0432/710460* ⊕ *www.cividale.com.*

Sights

Duomo

CHURCH | Cividale's Renaissance Duomo is largely the work of Pietro Lombardo, principal architect of Venice's famous Santa Maria dei Miracoli. The interior was restructured in the 18th century by another prominent Venetian architect, Giorgio Massari. The church contains a magnificent 12th-century silver gilt altarpiece. ⊠ *Piazza Duomo, Cividale del Friuli* ☎ *0432/731144* ⊕ *www.duomo-cividale.it.*

Museo Archeologico

HISTORY MUSEUM | Trace the area's history here and learn about the importance of Cividale and Udine in the period following the collapse of the Roman Empire. The collection includes weapons and exquisite jewelry from 6th-century Lombard warriors, who swept through much of what is now Italy. ⊠ *Piazza Duomo 13, Cividale del Friuli* ☎ *0432/700700* ⊕ *www.museoarcheologicocividale. beniculturali.it* ⌨ *€4; €9 combined ticket, includes Museo Archeologico and Museo Cristiano e Tesoro del Duomo (free with FVG Card).*

Museo Cristiano e Tesoro del Duomo

OTHER MUSEUM | Entered via a courtyard to the right of the Duomo, this museum contains two interesting, important, and surprisingly beautiful monuments of Lombard art: the Altar of Duke Ratchis (737–744) and the Baptistry of Patriarch Callisto (731–776). Both were found under the floor of the present Duomo in the early 20th century. The museum also has two fine paintings by Veronese, one by Il Pordenone, and a small collection of medieval and Renaissance vestments. ⊠ *Via Candotti 1, Cividale del Friuli* ☎ *0432/730403* ⊗ *Closed Mon. and Tues.* ⌨ *€4; €9 combined ticket, includes Museo Archeologico and Museo Cristiano e Tesoro del Duomo (free with FVG Card).*

★ Tempietto Longobardo
(*Lombard Church*)

CHURCH | Seeing the beautiful and historically important Tempietto Longobardo from the 8th century is more than enough reason to visit Cividale. Now inside the 16th-century Monastery of Santa Maria in Valle, the Tempietto was originally the chapel of the ducal palace, known as the Gastaldia. The west wall is the best-preserved example of the art and architecture of the Lombards, a

Germanic people who entered Italy in 568. It has an archway with an exquisitely rendered vine motif, guarded by an 8th-century procession of female figures, showing the Lombard interpretation of classical forms that resembles the style of the much earlier Byzantine mosaics in Ravenna, a town that had passed briefly to Lombard rule in 737. The post-Lombard frescoes decorating the vaults and the east wall date from the 13th and 14th centuries, and the fine carved wooden stalls also date from the 14th century. ⊠ *Via Monastero Maggiore, Cividale del Friuli* ☎ *0432/700867* ⊕ *www.tempietto-longobardo.it* ⌨ *€4; €9 combined ticket, includes Museo Archeologico and Museo Cristiano e Tesoro del Duomo (free with FVG Card).*

Palazzo de Nordis: Galleria d'arte De Martiis

ART GALLERY | Opened in 2020 and housed in a magnificent historic palazzo, originally dating from the 15th century, the Gallery showcases the De Martiis family's exquisite collection of 20th century art. Among the figurative works is a saucy Toulouse-Lautrec, and there are eye-popping impressionist masterpieces by Karel Appel and Victor Vasarely. ■TIP➔ **For tourist info visit the ground floor Sportello Informacittà.** ⊠ *Piazza Duomo 5, Cividale del Friuli* ⊕ *palazzodenordis.it* ⌨ *€10; Free with FVG Card.*

 Hotels

B&B dai Toscans

$ | B&B/INN | In a central location, this 15th-century palazzo, once home to the dukes of Tuscany, is now a charming and romantic bed-and-breakfast with parquet flooring throughout, a pleasant if unremarkable breakfast room, and large guest rooms furnished in antique style. **Pros:** no- or low-fee nearby parking; large, well-appointed rooms; triples for families. **Cons:** quirky decor not to everyone's taste; some noise from the street and the cathedral bells; can be a struggle hauling luggage in this pedestrianized area. $\boxed{S}$ *Rooms from: €75* ✉ *Corso Mazzini 15/1, Cividale del Friuli* ☎ *3490/765288 (mobile)* ⊕ *daitoscans.it* ⇆ *5 rooms* ❢⭕❢ *Free Breakfast.*

Aquileia

44 km (27 miles) south of Cividale del Friuli, 77 km (48 miles) northwest of Trieste, 163 km (101 miles) east of Venice.

This sleepy little town is refreshingly free of the tourists that you might expect at such a culturally historic place. In the time of Emperor Augustus, it was Italy's fourth-most-important city (after Rome, Milan, and Capua), as well as the principal northern Adriatic port of Italy and the beginning of Roman routes north. Aquileia's Roman and early-Christian remains convey an image of the transition from pagan to Christian Rome.

GETTING HERE AND AROUND

Getting to Aquileia by public transportation is difficult but not impossible. There's frequent train service from Venice and Trieste to Cervignano di Friuli (Cervignano-Aquileia-Grado station), which is 8 km (5 miles) from Aquileia by taxi (about €25), and infrequent bus service. (Ask the newsstand attendant or the railroad ticket agent for assistance.) By car from Venice or Trieste, take the A4 (Venezia–Trieste) to the Palmanova exit and continue 17 km (11 miles) to Aquileia. From Udine, take the A23 to the Palmanova exit.

VISITOR INFORMATION

CONTACT Aquileia Infopoint. ✉ *Via Giulia Augusta 11, Aquileia* ☎ *0431/919491* ⊕ *www.turismofvg.it.*

 Sights

Aquileia Archaeological Site

RUINS | Roman remains of the forum, houses, cemetery, and port are surrounded by cypresses here, and the little stream was once an important waterway extending to Grado. Unfortunately, many of the excavations of Roman Aquileia could not be left exposed, because of the extremely high water table under the site, and had to be reburied after archaeological studies had been conducted; nevertheless, what remains above ground, along with the monuments in the archaeological museum, gives an idea of the grandeur of this ancient city. The area is well signposted. ✉ *Near basilica, Aquileia* 🎫 *Free.*

★ Basilica

CHURCH | The highlight here is the spectacular 3rd- to 4th-century mosaic covering the entire floor of the basilica and the adjacent crypt, which make up one of the most important early-Christian monuments. Theodore, the basilica's first bishop, built two parallel basilicas (now the north and the south halls) on the site of a Gnostic chapel in the 4th century. These were joined by a third hall, forming a "U." The complex later accumulated the Romanesque portico and Gothic bell tower. The mosaic floor of the basilica is the remains of the floor of Theodore's south hall. In his north hall, Theodore retained much of the floor of the earlier Gnostic chapel, whose mosaics represent the ascent of the soul, through the realm of the planets and constellations, to God, who is represented as a ram. (The ram, at the head of the zodiac, is the Gnostic generative force.) This integration of Gnosticism into a Christian church is interesting, since Gnosticism had been branded a heresy by early church fathers. The 4th-century mosaics of the south hall (the present-day nave) represent the story of Jonah as prefiguring the salvation offered by the Church. Down a flight of steps, the Cripta degli Affreschi contains 12th-century frescoes. ✉ *Piazza Capitolo 1, Aquileia* ☎ *0431/919719* ⊕ *www. fondazioneaquileia.it* 🎫 *€3 basilica and Cripta degli Affreschi, €5 with Cripta degli Scavi; €2 campanile; €10 whole complex; all sites free with FGV Card* ☉ *Campanile closed Oct.–Mar.*

Museo Archeologico

OTHER MUSEUM | The museum's wealth of material from the Roman era includes portrait busts from the Republican era, semiprecious gems, amber—including preserved flies—and goldwork, and a fine glass collection. Beautiful pre-Christian mosaics are from the floors of Roman houses and palaces. ⊠ *Via Roma 1, Aquileia* ☎ *0431/91035* ⊕ *www.museoarcheologicoaquileia.beniculturali.it* ✏ *€7 (free with FGV card)* ⊘ *Closed Mon.*

Trieste

53 km (33 miles) southeast of Aquileia, 163 km (101 miles) east of Venice.

Trieste is Italy's only truly cosmopolitan city. In a country—perhaps even in a continent—where the amalgamation of cultures has frequently proved difficult, Trieste stands out as one of the few authentic melting pots. Not only do Italian, Slavic, and Central European cultures meet here, they actually merge to create a unique Triestino culture. To discover this culture, visiting Trieste's coffeehouses, local eateries, and piazzas is probably more important than visiting its churches and museums, interesting though they are.

Trieste is built along a fringe of coastline where the rugged Karst Plateau tumbles abruptly into the beautiful Adriatic. It was the only port of the Austro-Hungarian Empire and, therefore, a major industrial and financial center. In the early years of the 20th century, Trieste and its surroundings also became famous by their association with some of the most important names of Italian literature, such as Italo Svevo, and Irish and German writers. James Joyce drew inspiration from the city's multiethnic population, and Rainer Maria Rilke was inspired by the coast to the west.

The city has lost its importance as a port and a center of finance, but perhaps because of its multicultural nature, at the juncture of Latin, Slavic, and Germanic Europe, it's never fully lost its role as an intellectual center. In recent years the city has become a center for science and technology. The streets hold a mix of monumental Neoclassical and Art Nouveau architecture, built by the Austrians during Trieste's days of glory, granting an air of melancholy stateliness to a city that lives as much in the past as the present.

Italian revolutionaries of the 1800s rallied their battle cry around Trieste, because of what they believed was foreign occupation of their motherland. After World War II the sliver of land including Trieste and a small part of Istria became an independent, neutral state that was officially recognized in a 1947 peace treaty. Although it was actually occupied by British and American troops for its nine years of existence, the Free Territory of Trieste issued its own currency and stamps. In 1954 a Memorandum of Understanding was signed in London, giving civil administration of Trieste to Italy.

GETTING HERE AND AROUND

Trains to Trieste depart regularly from Venice, Udine, and other major Italian cities. By car, it's the eastern terminus of the Autostrada Torino–Trieste (E70). The city is served by Trieste–Friuli Venezia Giulia Airport, which receives flights from major Italian airports and some European cities. The airport is 33 km (20½ miles) from the city; transfers into Trieste are by taxi or APT coach No. 51.

VISITOR INFORMATION

CONTACT Trieste Infopoint. ⊠ *Via dell'Orologio 1, Piazza Unità d'Italia, Trieste* ☎ *040/3478312* ⊕ *www.turismofvg.it.*

Sights

Castello di Duino

CASTLE/PALACE | This 14th-century castle, the property of the Princes of Thurn and Taxis, contains a collection of antique furnishings and an amazing Palladian circular staircase, but the main attractions are the surrounding gardens and the spectacular views. In 1912 Rainer Maria Rilke wrote his masterpiece, the *Duino Elegies,* here. The easy path along the seacoast from the castle toward Trieste has gorgeous views that rival those of the Amalfi Coast and the Cinque Terre. ✉ *Frazione Duino 32, 12 km (7½ miles) from Trieste ⊕ Take Bus No. 44 or 51 from the Trieste train station to Duino* ☎ *040/208120* ⊕ *www.castellodiduino.it* 🎫 *€8* ⊙ *Closed Tues.; closed weekdays Jan.–mid-Mar., Nov., and Dec.*

Castello di San Giusto

CASTLE/PALACE | This hilltop castle, built between 1470 and 1630, was constructed on the ruins of the Roman town of Tergeste. Given the excellent view, it's no surprise that 15th-century Venetians turned the castle into a shipping observation point; the structure was further enlarged by Trieste's subsequent rulers, the Habsburgs. The castle also contains the Civic Museum, which has a collection of furnishings, tapestries, and weaponry, as well as Roman artifacts in the atmospheric Lapidario Tergestino. ✉ *Piazza della Cattedrale 3, Trieste* ☎ *040/309362* ⊕ *www.castellodisangiustotrieste.it* 🎫 *€5 includes all complex museums* ⊙ *Closed Mon. during winter months.*

Cattedrale di San Giusto

CHURCH | Dating from the 14th century and occupying the site of an ancient Roman forum, the cathedral contains remnants of at least three previous buildings, the earliest a hall dating from the 5th century. A section of the original floor mosaic still remains, incorporated into the floor of the present church. In the 9th and 11th centuries two adjacent churches were built—the Church of the Assumption and the Church of San Giusto. The beautiful apse mosaics of these churches, done in the 12th and 13th centuries by a Venetian artist, still remain in the apses of the side aisles of the present church. The mosaics in the main apse date from 1932. In the 14th century the two churches were joined and a Romanesque-Gothic facade was attached, ornamented with fragments of Roman monuments taken from the forum. The jambs of the main doorway are the most conspicuous Roman element. ✉ *Piazza della Cattedrale 2, Trieste* ☎ *040/3224575* ⊕ *www.sangiustomartire.it.*

★ Miramar

CASTLE/PALACE | FAMILY | A 19th-century castle on the Gulf of Trieste, this is nothing less than a major expression of the culture of the decaying Austrian Hapsburg monarchy: nowhere else—not even in Vienna—can you savor the decadent opulence of the last years of the empire. Maximilian of Hapsburg, brother of Emperor Franz Josef and the retired commander of the Austrian Navy, built the seafront extravaganza between 1856 and 1860, complete with a throne room under a wooden ceiling shaped like a ship's keel. The rooms are generally furnished with copies of medieval, Renaissance, and French period furniture, and the walls are covered in red damask. In 1864 Maximilian became emperor of Mexico at the initiative of Napoléon III. He was executed three years later by a Mexican firing squad. During the last years of the Hapsburg reign, Miramar became one of the favorite residences of Franz Josef's wife, the Empress Elizabeth (Sissi). The castle was later owned by Duke Amedeo of Aosta. Changing exhibitions in the revamped *Sala Progetti* showcase the impressive museum archive. Tours in English are available by reservation. Surrounding the castle is a 54-acre park. To get here from central Trieste, take Bus No. 36 from Piazza Oberdan; it runs every half hour. ✉ *Viale*

Miramare, off SS14, Trieste ✦ 7 km (4½ miles) NW of Trieste ☎ 040/224143 ⊕ www.castello-miramare.it ✉ €10.

★ Museo Revoltella–Galleria d'Arte Moderna

ART MUSEUM | Housed in three magnificent buildings and partly remodelled by influential Italian architect Carlo Scarpa, the Revoltella provides a stimulating survey of 19th and 20th century art and decoration. Building on the bequeathment of the grand palazzo and art of Triestino collector-industrialist Pasquale Revoltella (1795–1869), the institution has continued to add important artworks from the Venice Biennale by the likes of Carrà, Mascherini, Morandi, de Chirico, Manzù, Fontana, and Burri. In contrast, a gorgeous cochlear staircase connects the three floors of the museum: its history and 1850–60 cityscapes are on the ground floor; 19th-century classical statuary, portraits, and historic scenes take up the first; while the third preserves opulent saloni. ⊠ *Via Diaz 27, Trieste* ☎ *040/6754350* ⊕ *museorevoltella.it* ✉ *Free* ⏱ *Closed Tues.*

Piazza della Borsa

PLAZA/SQUARE | A statue of Hapsburg emperor Leopold I looks out over this square, which contains Trieste's original stock exchange, the Borsa Vecchia (1805), an attractive neoclassical building now serving as the chamber of commerce. It sits at the end of the Canal Grande, dug in the 18th century by the Austrian empress Maria Theresa as a first step in the expansion of what was then a small fishing village of 7,000 into the port of her empire. ⊠ *Trieste.*

Piazza Unità d'Italia

PLAZA/SQUARE | The imposing square, ringed by grandiose facades, was set out as a plaza open to the sea, like Venice's Piazza San Marco, in the late Middle Ages. It underwent countless changes through the centuries, and its present size and architecture are essentially products of late-19th- and early-20th-century Austria. It was given its current name in 1955, when Trieste was finally given to Italy. On the inland side of the piazza, note the facade of the **Palazzo Comunale** (Town Hall), designed by the Triestino architect Giuseppe Bruni in 1875. It was from this building's balcony in 1938 that Mussolini proclaimed the infamous racial laws, depriving Italian Jews of most of their rights. The sidewalk cafés on this vast seaside piazza are popular meeting places in the summer months. ⊠ *Trieste.*

Risiera di San Sabba

HISTORIC SIGHT | In September 1943 the Nazi occupation established Italy's only concentration camp in this rice-processing factory outside Trieste. In April 1944 a crematorium was put into operation. The Nazis destroyed much of the evidence of their atrocities before their retreat, but a good deal of the horror of the place is still perceivable in the reconstructed museum (1975). The site, an Italian national monument since 1965, receives more than 100,000 visitors per year. ⊠ *Via Giovanni Palatucci 5, Trieste* ✦ *Take municipal Bus No. 8 or 10; off the Autostrada A4, take exit Valmaura/Stadio/Cimitero* ☎ *040/826202* ⊕ *www.risierasansabba.it* ✉ *Free.*

San Silvestro

CHURCH | This small Romanesque gem, dating from the 9th to the 12th century, is the oldest church in Trieste that's still in use and in approximately its original form. Its interior walls have some fragmentary remains of Romanesque frescoes. The church was deconsecrated under the secularizing reforms of the Austrian emperor Josef II in 1785 and was later sold to the Swiss Evangelical community; it then became, and is still, the Reformed Evangelical and Waldesian Church of Trieste. ⊠ *Piazza San Silvestro 1, Trieste* ☎ *040/632770* ⊕ *triestevangelica.org.*

Teatro Romano

RUINS | The ruins of this 1st-century-AD amphitheater, near the Via Giuseppe Mazzini opposite the city's *questura* (police station), were discovered during 1938 demolition work. Its statues are now displayed at the Museo Civico, and the space is used for summer plays and concerts. ⊠ *Via del Teatro Romano, Trieste.*

🍴 Restaurants

Al Bagatto

$$$ | SEAFOOD | At this warm and sophisticated seafood place, going strong since 1966 near the Piazza Unità d'Italia, you'll find exquisite dishes that honor the family tradition of the Mancussi family. The ethos follows Roberto Mancussi's culinary approach: integrating nouvelle ingredients without overshadowing the freshness of whatever local fish he bought in the market that morning. **Known for:** decades of family experience; more than 300 wine labels and spirits; freshest seafood beautifully prepared. ⑤ *Average main: €25* ⊠ *Via Luigi Cadorna 7, Trieste* ☎ *040/301771* ⊕ *www.albagatto.it* ⊘ *Closed Sun. No lunch Mon.*

Buffet da Siora Rosa

$$ | NORTHERN ITALIAN | FAMILY | Serving delicious and generous portions of traditional Triestino buffet fare, such as boiled pork and sausages with savory sauerkraut, Siora Rosa is a bit more comfortable than many buffets. In addition to ample seating in the simple dining room, there are tables outside for when the weather is good. **Known for:** meat dishes galore; well-loved Trieste institution (opened 1921); chatty locals speaking in dialect. ⑤ *Average main: €19* ⊠ *Piazza Hortis 3, Trieste* ☎ *040/301460* ⊘ *Closed Sun. and Mon.*

Mare alla Voliga

$ | SEAFOOD | Hidden halfway up the hill to the Castello di San Giusto, in what the Triestini call *Zità Vecia* (Old City),

this informal little restaurant specializes in simply prepared seafood. Amid whitewashed wooden walls and nautical ephemera, you can sample the freshest catches—bluefish, sardines, mackerel, mussels, and squid—accompanied by salad, potatoes, polenta, and house wine. **Known for:** beach-hut decor and atmosphere; locals packed in like sarde; tasty fish and seafood. ⑤ *Average main: €14* ⊠ *Via della Fornace 1, Trieste* ☎ *040/309606 mobile* ⊕ *www.allavoliga.it* ⊘ *Closed Mon. and Tues.*

★ Suban

$$ | NORTHERN ITALIAN | An easy trip just outside town, this landmark trattoria—serving Triestino food with Slovene, Hungarian, and Austrian accents—has been in business since 1865. Sit by the dining room fire or relax on a huge terrace with a pergola, watching the sun set as you tuck into rich soups and roasts spiced with rosemary, thyme, and sweet paprika. ■TIP→ **Portions tend to be small, so if you're hungry, order both a first and second course, as well as an antipasto. Known for:** smallish portions; warm hospitality; jota carsolina (a rich soup of cabbage, potatoes, and beans). ⑤ *Average main: €24* ⊠ *Via Comici 2, Trieste* ⊹ *Take Bus No. 35 from Piazza Oberdan* ☎ *040/54368* ⊕ *www.suban.it* ⊘ *Closed Tues. and 2 wks in early Jan.*

☕ Coffee and Quick Bites

★ Da Pepi

$ | NORTHERN ITALIAN | A Triestino institution, this is the oldest and most esteemed of the many "buffet" restaurants serving pork and sausages around town, with a wood-paneled interior and seating outside. It specializes in *bollito di maiale*, a dish of boiled pork and pork sausages accompanied by delicately flavored sauerkraut, mustard, and grated horseradish. **Known for:** good for a snack on the hoof; porky platter La Caldaia Da Pepi; panino porzina with mustard and kren (horseradish). ⑤ *Average main:*

€13 ⊠ Via Cassa di Risparmio 3, Trieste
☏ 040/366858 ⊕ www.buffetdapepi.it
🕑 Closed Sun. and last 2 wks in July.

🛏 Hotels

★ Duchi d'Aosta

$$$ | HOTEL | Bang smack in the regal
Piazza Unità d'Italia, this *grande dama o
duco* of a hotel is beautifully furnished in
Venetian Renaissance style, with dark-
wood antiques, rich carpets, and plush
fabrics. **Pros:** sumptuous breakfast; lots
of charm paired with modern conveni-
ence; outstanding indoor pool and spa on
grand scale. **Cons:** restaurant overpriced;
rooms overlooking the piazza can be very
expensive; expensive and inconvenient
parking. Ⓢ *Rooms from: €261* ⊠ *Piazza
Unità d'Italia 2/1, Trieste* ☏ *040/7600011*
⊕ *www.grandhotelduchidaosta.com*
↵ 55 rooms ❦ Free Breakfast.

Hotel Riviera & Maximilian's

$$$ | HOTEL | Set on gorgeous, verdant
grounds with stunning sea views, this
clifftop hotel—a villa with a modern
annex—offers a mix of traditional and
minimalist rooms, many with private balconies. **Pros:** spa facilities; superb views
of the Golfo di Trieste; area for swimming
in sea. **Cons:** some areas need a revamp;
far from town; small spa. Ⓢ *Rooms
from: €250* ⊠ *Strada Costiera 22, Trieste*
☏ *040/224551* ⊕ *www.hotelrivierae-
maximilian.com* ↵ 67 rooms ❦ *Free
Breakfast.*

★ L'Albero Nascosto Hotel Residence

$$ | B&B/INN | There's plenty of architec-
tural character mixed with contemporary,
artsy warmth in the guest rooms of this
central 18th-century building, while the
nearby annex offers five spacious apartments. **Pros:** great tea and coffee; very
central; spacious and simple but tasteful
rooms. **Cons:** street noise can be a problem (if noise sensitive, ask for a room
in the back); no elevator; tricky parking
nearby. Ⓢ *Rooms from: €155* ⊠ *Via
Felice Venezian 18, Trieste* ☏ *040/300188*

⊕ *www.alberonascosto.it* ↵ 10 rooms
❦ *Free Breakfast.*

Victoria Hotel Letterario

$$ | HOTEL | The former home of James
Joyce is a real gem of a hotel—with
stylish, unfussy traditional decor and a
just-out-of-town location that's convenient for both local sightseeing and trips
into the Karst mountains. **Pros:** wellness
center and spa; large, pleasant, light-
filled rooms; excellent two-bedroom
apartments for longer stays. **Cons:** a bit
removed and a stroll into town; parking
fee; some rooms suffer from traffic
noise. Ⓢ *Rooms from: €130* ⊠ *Alfredo
Oriani 2, Trieste* ☏ *040/362415* ⊕ *www.
hotelvictoriatrieste.com* ↵ 44 rooms
❦ *No Meals.*

🍸 Nightlife

Antico Caffè San Marco

CAFÉS | Few cafés in Italy can rival Antico
Caffè San Marco for its historic and
cultured atmosphere. Founded in 1914, it
was largely destroyed in World War I and
rebuilt in the 1920s, then restored several more times, but some of the original
art nouveau interior remains. It became a
meeting place for local intellectuals and
was the haunt of the Triestino writers
Italo Svevo and Umberto Saba. It remains
open until midnight on Friday and
Saturday, and light meals are available.
⊠ *Via Battisti 18, Trieste* ☏ *040/0641724*
⊕ *www.caffesanmarco.com.*

Caffè Degli Specchi

CAFÉS | For a great view of the great
piazza, you can't do better than this café,
whose many mirrors make for engaging
people-watching. Originally opened in
1839, it was taken over by the British
Navy after World War II, and Triestini were
not allowed in unless accompanied by
someone British. Because of its location,
the café—which stays open late—is
heavily frequented by tourists. It's now
owned by the Segafredo Zanetti coffee
company, and some feel it has lost its

local character. ✉ *Piazza Unità d'Italia 7, Trieste* ☎ *040/368033* ⊕ *www.caffespec-chi.it.*

Caffè Tommaseo

CAFÉS | Founded in 1830, this classic café is a comfortable place to linger, especially on weekend evenings and at lunchtime (11–1:30) on Sunday, when there's live music. Although you can still have just a coffee, Tommaseo has evolved into a restaurant, with an extensive menu. It's open nightly until 10. ✉ *Piazza Tommaseo 4/C, Trieste* ☎ *040/362666* ⊕ *www. caffetommaseo.it.*

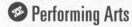 Performing Arts

Teatro Verdi

OPERA | Trieste's main opera house, built under Austrian rule in 1801, is of interest to aficionados of fine architecture as well as music lovers. Gian Antonio Selva, the architect of Venice's Teatro La Fenice, designed the interior, and Matteo Pertsch, responsible for Milan's Teatro alla Scala, designed the facade. You'll have to attend a performance to view Teatro Verdi's interior; guided tours aren't conducted for individuals. ■**TIP**→ **Opera season runs from October through May, with a brief operetta festival in July and August.** ✉ *Piazza Verdi 1, Trieste* ☎ *040/6722111* ⊕ *www.teatroverdi-trieste.com.*

🛍 Shopping

Trieste has some 60 local dealers in jewelry, antiques, and antique wannabes; the city's old center hosts an antiques and collectibles market on the third Sunday (Largo Granatieri) and fourth Saturday (Piazza Vittorio Veneto) of each month, and there's a large antiques fair, **Trieste Antiqua,** at the end of November. Trieste's busy shopping street, **Corso Italia,** is off the Piazza della Borsa.

Chapter 7

THE DOLOMITES

Updated by
Liz Humphreys

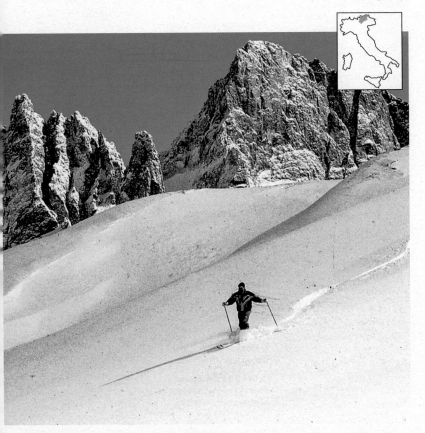

👁 Sights	🍴 Restaurants	🛏 Hotels	🛍 Shopping	🍸 Nightlife
★★★★☆	★★★★☆	★★★★☆	★☆☆☆☆	★★☆☆☆

WELCOME TO THE DOLOMITES

TOP REASONS TO GO

★ **Driving in the Dolomites:** Your Fiat rental will think it's a Ferrari on a gorgeous drive through the heart of the Dolomites.

★ **Hiking:** No matter your fitness level, there's an unforgettable walk in store for you here.

★ **Skiing:** The Dolomites are renowned as one of Europe's top locations for winter sports.

★ **Museo Archeologico dell'Alto Adige, Bolzano:** The impossibly well-preserved body of the iceman Ötzi, the star attraction at this museum, provokes countless questions about what life was like 5,000 years ago.

★ **Trento:** A graceful fusion of Austrian and Italian styles, this breezy frescoed town is famed for its imposing castle.

1 Trento. Piazza del Duomo is a highlight.

2 Rovereto. Enjoy the medieval center.

3 Madonna di Campiglio. A favorite for skiers and hikers.

4 Bolzano (Bozen). High-gabled houses are hallmarks.

5 Bormio. History, ski trails, and spa treatments.

6 Merano (Meran). Come here to take a cure.

7 Naturno (Naturns). Known for its hiking trails and castle museum.

8 Caldaro (Kaltern). The Strada del Vino runs through this wine town.

9 Bressanone (Brixen). A castle is a big draw.

10 Brunico (Bruneck). Don't miss the medieval quarter.

11 Misurina. The Three Peaks views are lovely.

12 Canazei. Come for the hiking and skiing.

13 Ortisei (St. Ulrich). Woodcarving workshops dot this town.

14 Corvara. Hiking, skiing, and fine hotels.

15 Cortina d'Ampezzo. This ski resort has lots of summer activities.

EATING AND DRINKING WELL IN THE DOLOMITES

Everything in Alto Adige (and, to a lesser extent, Trentino) has more than a tinge of the Teutonic—and food is no exception. The rich and creamy cuisine here, including fondue, polenta, and barley soup, reflects the Alpine climate and Austrian and Swiss influences.

The quintessential restaurant is the wood-paneled Tyrolean *stube* (pub) serving hearty meat-and-dumpling fare, and there's also a profusion of pastry shops and lively beer halls.

Although the early dining schedule you'll find in Germany or Austria is somewhat tempered here, your options for late-night meals are more limited than they are in places farther south, where *la dolce vita* has a firmer grip.

Thankfully, the coffee is every bit as good as in parts south—just expect to hear "*danke, grazie*" when paying for your cappuccino.

BEST OF THE WURST

Not to be missed are the outdoor wurst carts. After placing your order you'll get a sheet of wax paper, followed by a dollop of mustard, a kaiser roll, and your chosen sausage. You can sometimes make your selection by pointing to whatever picture is most appealing; if not, pass on the familiar-sounding *Frankfurter* and try the local *Meraner*. Carts can reliably be found in Bolzano (try Piazza delle Erbe, or in front of the archaeological museum) and Merano (Piazza del Grano, or along the river).

POLENTA AND DUMPLINGS

Polenta is a staple in the region, in both creamy and firm renditions, often topped with cheese or mushrooms (or both). Dumplings also appear on many menus; the most distinctive to the region are *canederli* (also known as *Knödel*), *(pictured at right)* made from seasoned bread in many variations, and served either in broth or with a sauce. Other dumplings to look for are the dense *strangolapreti* (literally, "priest-chokers") and *gnocchi di ricotta alla zucca* (ricotta and pumpkin dumplings).

CHEESE

Every isolated mountain valley in Trentino–Alto Adige seems to make its own variety of cheese, and the local specialty is often simply called *nostrano* (ours). The best known of them are the mild Asiago and *fontal,* as well as the more pungent *puzzone di Moena* (literally, "stinkpot"). Also try the *schiz*: fresh cheese that's sliced and fried in butter.

PASTRIES AND BAKED GOODS

Bakeries turn out a wide selection of crusty dark rolls and caraway-studded rye breads—maybe not typical Italian bread, but full of flavor. Pastries here are reminiscent of what you'd find in Vienna. Apple strudel is everywhere, and for good reason: the best apples

in Italy are grown here. There are other exceptional fruits as well, including pears, plums, and grapes, which make their way into baked goods.

ALIMENTARI

If you're planning a picnic or getting provisions for a hike, you'll be well served by the fine *alimentari* (food shops) of Trentino and Alto Adige. They stock a bounty of regional specialties, including cheeses, pickles, salami, and smoked meats. These are good places to pick up a sample of *speck tirolese*, the salt-cured, cold-smoked deboned ham hock usually cut in paper-thin slices like prosciutto (though proud speck producers often bristle at the comparison).

WINE

Although Trentino and Alto Adige aren't as esteemed for their wines as many other Italian regions, they produce a wide variety of crisp, dry, and aromatic whites—*Kerner, Müller-Thurgau,* and *Traminer,* to name a few—not surprisingly, more like what you'd expect from German vineyards than Italian. Among the reds, look for *lagrein* and the native *teroldego,* a fruity, spicy variety produced only in the tiny valley north of Trento. The Trento D.O.C. appellation yields a marvelous sparkling wine in a class with Champagne.

The Dolomites, those inimitable craggy peaks Le Corbusier called "the most beautiful work of architecture ever seen," are never so arresting as at dusk, when the last rays of sun create a pink hue that languishes into purple—a magnificent transformation locals call the *enrosadira*. You can certainly enjoy this glow from a distance, but the Dolomites are such an appealing year-round destination precisely because of the many ways to get into the mountains themselves. And once there, in short order your perspective—like the peaks around you—will take on a rosy hue.

The Dolomites are strange, rocky pinnacles that jut straight up like chimneys; they are, in fact, the otherworldly pinnacles that Leonardo depicted in the background of his *Mona Lisa*. In spite of this incredible beauty, the vast mountainous domain of northeastern Italy has remained relatively undeveloped. Below the peaks, rivers meander through valleys dotted with peaceful villages, while pristine lakes are protected by picture-book castles. In the most secluded Dolomite vales, unique cultures have flourished: the Ladin language, an offshoot of Latin still spoken in the Val Gardena and Val di Fassa, owes its unlikely survival to centuries of topographic isolation.

The more accessible parts of Trentino–Alto Adige, on the other hand, have a history of near-constant intermingling of cultures. The region's Adige and Isarco Valleys make up the main access route between Italy and Central Europe, and as a result, the language, cuisine, and architecture are a blend of north and south. The province of Trentino is largely Italian-speaking, but Alto Adige is predominantly Germanic: until World War I the area was Austria's Südtirol. As you move north toward the famed Brenner Pass—through the prosperous valley towns of Rovereto, Trento, and Bolzano—the Teutonic influence is increasingly dominant; by the time you reach Bressanone, it's hard to believe you're in Italy at all.

MAJOR REGIONS

Trentino. Until the end of World War I, the Trentino–Alto Adige/Südtirol region was part of Austria-Hungary. Although today the province of Trentino remains unmistakably Italian, Germanic influences are palpable in its architecture, cuisine, culture, and language. Visitors are drawn by the historical sites and cosmopolitan nature of Trento, while numerous year-round mountain resorts, like the fashionable Madonna di Campiglio, can be found in the wings of this butterfly-shape region. Culture-hounds will want to visit Rovereto, a town just south of Trento known for its fine contemporary art museum.

Bolzano. With castles and steeples topping the landscape, this quiet city at the confluence of the Isarco (Eisack) and Talvera Rivers has retained its provincial appeal. Proximity to fabulous skiing and mountain climbing—not to mention the world's oldest preserved human body—make it a very worthwhile destination. And its streets are immaculate: after Milan, residents here have the highest per capita earnings of any city in Italy.

The Western Dolomites. The Parco Nazionale dello Stelvio extends through western Trentino and the Altoatesino area of Alto Adige and beyond into eastern Lombardy. It's named for the famed Stelvio, Europe's highest road pass and site of the highest battle fought during World War I. Even if you don't want to ski its trails or indulge in one of its renowned spa treatments, the well-preserved town of Bormio still merits a visit for its history and character.

Alto Adige. In the province of Alto Adige (Südtirol/South Tyrol), Germanic and Italian culture balance harmoniously, as do medieval and modern influences, with ancient castles regularly hosting contemporary art exhibitions. Prosperous valley towns, such as the famed spa center of Merano, the medieval town of Bressanone, and the wine village of Caldaro, entice those seeking both relaxation and the finer pleasures.

The Heart of the Dolomites. This area between Bolzano and the mountain resort Cortina d'Ampezzo is dominated by two major valleys, Val di Fassa and Val Gardena. Both share the spectacular panorama of the Sella mountain range. Along the scenic Grande Strada delle Dolomiti (Great Dolomites Road), you'll find Canazei, Ortisei, and Corvara, resort towns with skiing and hiking galore. The Tre Cime (Three Peaks), the best-known symbol of the Dolomites, are visible from the lakeside town of Misurina and worth a gander if not a hike.

Planning

Making the Most of Your Time

For a brief stay, your best choice for a base is vibrant Bolzano, where you can get a sense of the region's contrasts—Italian and German, medieval and modern. After a day or two in town, venture an hour south to history-laden Trento, north to the lovely spa town of Merano, or southwest to Caldaro and its Strada di Vino; all are viable day trips from Bolzano, and Trento and Merano make good places to spend the night as well.

If you have more time, you'll want to get up into the mountains, which are the region's main attraction. The trip on the Grande Strada delle Dolomiti through the Heart of the Dolomites from Bolzano to Cortina d'Ampezzo is one of Italy's most spectacular drives. Summer or winter, this is a great destination for mountain sports, with scores of trails for world-class hiking and skiing.

Be sure to look into the Südtirol Museumobil Card when planning your visit. Besides entry to more than 90 museums, the card allows you free use of the regional train system from Brennero to Trento, and the use of all public buses in Alto Adige (Südtirol/South Tyrol). The card is available for three days (€30) or seven days (€34). The Museumobil Card can be purchased at train stations, tourist offices, some museums, and hotels (www.mobilcard.info). The Brixen Card (free with paid lodging in Bressanone) offers free transportation throughout Trentino and Alto Adige (Südtirol/South Tyrol) and entrance to nearly 90 museums, plus free guided tours and discounts at partner venues. See www.brixen.org for a list of participating hotels and bed-and-breakfasts.

As of April 26, 2021, all visitors over the age of six require a CoronaPass South Tyrol to visit museums, thermal baths, and gyms, spas, and swimming pools at hotels. This is a QR code that shows you have been fully vaccinated against Covid, have tested negative within 72 hours of your visit, or have a medical certificate showing recovery from Covid within the past six months. Check the latest rules at www.suedtirol.info/en/information/coronavirus/coronaPass-south-tyrol and get your CoronaPass at coronapass.civis.bz.it. Free nose swab tests are available to visitors throughout the region (see www.provinz.bz.it/sicherheit-zivilschutz/zivilschutz/coronavirus-suedtirol-testet.asp for locations).

Detailed information about Vie Ferrate in the eastern Dolomites can be found at www.dolomiti.org. Capable tour organizers include the **Scuola di Alpinismo** (Mountaineering School) in Madonna di Campiglio (*0465/442634*, www.guidealpinecampiglio.it) and Cortina d'Ampezzo (*0436/868505*, www.guidecortina.com).

Getting Here and Around

BUS

Regular bus service connects larger cities to the south (Verona, Venice, and Milan) with valley towns in Trentino–Alto Adige (Rovereto, Trento, Bolzano, and Merano). You'll need to change to less frequent local buses to reach resorts and smaller villages in the mountains beyond. At the time of this writing, masks must be worn on all buses.

If you're equipped with current schedules and don't mind adapting your schedules to theirs, it's possible to visit even the remotest villages by bus. ATVO provides year-round service to Cortina from Venice's Piazzale Roma bus park (daily in high season, weekends only in low season), while CortinaExpress has a fast winter bus connection to Venice airport and the nearby Mestre train station. DolomitiBus covers the eastern Dolomites, including a number of small towns. SAD provides service from Bolzano and Bressanone, as does the seasonal Val Gardena Ski Express. Südtirolmobil provides further information on local services.

BUS CONTACTS ATVO. ☎ *0421/5944* ⊕ *www.atvo.it*. **CortinaExpress.** ☎ *0436/867350* ⊕ *www.cortinaexpress.it*. **DolomitiBus.** ☎ *0437/217111* ⊕ *www.dolomitibus.it*. **SAD.** ✉ *Bolzano* ☎ *0471/450111* ⊕ *www.sad.it*. **südtirolmobil.** ☎ *0471/220880* ⊕ *www.suedtirolmobil.info*. **Trentino Trasporti.** ☎ *0461/821000* ⊕ *www.ttesercizio.it*.

CAR

Driving is easily the most convenient way to travel in the Dolomites; it can be difficult to reach the ski areas (or any town outside of Rovereto, Trento, Bolzano, or Merano) without a car. Driving is also the most exhilarating way to get around, as you rise from broad valleys into mountains with narrow, winding roads straight out of a sports-car ad. The most important route in the region is the

A22 autostrada, the main north–south highway linking Italy with Central Europe by way of the Brenner Pass. It connects Innsbruck with Bressanone, Bolzano, Trento, and Rovereto, and near Verona joins the A4, which runs east–west across northern Italy, from Trieste to Turin. By car, Trento is 3 hours from Milan and 2½ hours from Venice. Bolzano is another 45-minute drive to the north, with Munich 4 hours farther on.

Caution is essential (tap your horn in advance of hairpin turns), as are chains in winter, when roads are often covered in snow. Sudden closures are common, especially on high mountain passes, and can occur as early as September and as late as May. Even under the best conditions, expect to negotiate mountain roads at speeds no greater than 50 kph (30 mph).

TRAIN

The rail line following the course of the Isarco and Adige Valleys—from Munich and Innsbruck, through the Brenner Pass, and southward past Bressanone, Bolzano, Trento, and Rovereto en route to Verona—is well trafficked, making trains a viable option for travel between these towns. Eurocity trains on the Dortmund–Venice and Munich–Innsbruck–Rome routes stop at these stations, and you can connect with other Italian lines at Verona. Although branch lines from Trento and Bolzano do extend into some of the smaller valleys (including hourly service between Bolzano and Merano), most mountain attractions are beyond the reach of trains. At the time of this writing, masks must be worn on all trains.

TRAIN CONTACT Trenitalia. ☏ *892021 within Italy* ⊕ *www.trenitalia.com.*

Restaurants

When dining out in the Dolomites, it's evident you are in a part of Italy that was once part of Austria-Hungary. Although you can still find traditional Italian pasta and pizza, in this region there's a considerable amount of Austro-Germanic flair. Sausages, spaetzle, meats, cheeses, and polenta—foods that will sustain the body through a long day of skiing or hiking—can be found on nearly every menu, although you'll also find more contemporary restaurants using seasonal ingredients in a lighter style. Many restaurants either raise their own crops and livestock or have a direct relationship with their farmers and providers.

Restaurant reviews have been shortened. For full information, visit Fodors. com.

Hotels

Classic Dolomite lodging includes restored castles, chalets, and stately 19th-century hotels. The small villages that pepper the Dolomites often have scores of flower-bedecked inns, many of them inexpensive. Hotel information offices at train stations and tourist offices can help if you've arrived without reservations. The Bolzano train station has a 24-hour hotel service, and tourist offices will give you a list of all the hotels in the area, arranged by location, stars, and price. Hotels at ski resorts cater to longer stays at full or half board. Many Italians come to the Dolomites every winter for their Settimana Bianca (White Week), and if you care to join them you should book ski vacations as packages well in advance. Most rural accommodations close from early November to mid- or late December, as well as for two months or so after Easter. The majority of *rifugi* (mountain huts) on hiking trails are operated by the **Club Alpino Italiano** (www.cai. it). Contact information for both CAI-run and private rifugi is available from local tourist offices; most useful are those in Madonna di Campiglio (www.campiglio.com), Cortina d'Ampezzo (www.dolomiti.org), Val di Fassa (www.fassa.com), and Val Gardena (www.val-gardena.com).

Hotel reviews have been shortened. For full information, visit Fodors.com.

WHAT IT COSTS in Euros

	$	$$	$$$	$$$$
RESTAURANTS				
	under €15	€15–€24	€25–€35	over €35
HOTELS				
	under €125	€125–€200	€201–€300	over €300

Trento

58 km (36 miles) south of Bolzano.

Trento is a prosperous, cosmopolitan university town that retains an architectural charm befitting its historical importance. It was here, from 1545 to 1563, that the structure of the Catholic Church was redefined at the Council of Trent, the starting point of the Counter-Reformation, which brought half of Europe back to Catholicism. Today, the word *consiglio* (council) appears everywhere in Trento—in hotel, restaurant, and street names, and even on wine labels. The Piazza del Duomo remains splendid, and its enormous medieval palazzo dominates the city landscape in virtually its original form.

The 24-hour Trentino Card (www.visittrentino.info) is given free to hotel guests, and grants free or discounted admission to museums as well as all public transportation. Non–hotel guests can make use of the 48-hour Museum Pass (€22), which allows unlimited access to all museums and castles in Trento and Rovereto as well as free public transportation in Trentino. It can be bought online

(www.visittrentino.info/en/experience/museum-pass), at tourist offices, or at participating museums, and can even be converted into a three-month card for no extra charge.

GETTING HERE AND AROUND

The A22 autostrada is the main highway to Trento. From the north, take the Trento Nord exit; from the south, take the Trento Sud exit. There are signs directing you to the city center. Trento is easily accessible from Venice (2½ hours) and Verona (just over an hour), and is only 4½ hours from Munich. The city center is pedestrian-friendly, or you can use the transit options in conjunction with the Trentino Card for discounts on the city buses.

TOURS

Guided Tours of Trento

VISITOR CENTER | Guided tours of Trento depart from the tourist office on Saturday at 3 pm. Private two-hour (€150), three-hour (€160), and six-hour (€230) tours can be arranged for groups of up to 50 people. ■**TIP**→ **Tours are not always offered in English; to guarantee an English-speaking guide, call for reservations.** ✉ *Piazza Dante 24, Trento* ☎ *0461/216000* ⊕ *www.discovertrento.it/en/citta-di-trento/visite-guidate* ✆ *€6.*

VISITOR INFORMATION

CONTACT Trento Tourism Office. ✉ *Piazza Dante 24, Trento* ☎ *0461/216000* ⊕ *www.discovertrento.it.*

Sights

Belvedere di Sardagna

VIEWPOINT | **FAMILY** | Take the Funivia Trento–Sardagna cable car up to the Belvedere di Sardagna, a lookout point 1,200 feet above medieval Trento. ■**TIP**→ **This is open year-round, but can close due to inclement weather.** ✉ *Via Monte Grappa 1, Trento* ☎ *0461/232154* ⊕ *www.trentinotrasporti.it/viaggia-con-noi/funivia* ✆ *€5 round-trip.*

Trentino and the
Western Dolomites

0   10 mi
0   10 km

★ Castello del Buonconsiglio
(Castle of Good Counsel)

CASTLE/PALACE | FAMILY | The position and size of this stronghold of the prince-bishops made it easier to defend than the Palazzo Pretorio. Look for the evolution of architectural styles: the medieval fortifications of the Castelvecchio section (on the far left) were built in the 13th century; the fancier Renaissance Magno Palazzo section (on the far right) wasn't completed until 300 years later. The 13th-century **Torre dell'Aquila** (Eagle's Tower) is home to the castle's artistic highlight, a 15th-century *ciclo dei mesi* (cycle of the months). The four-wall fresco is full of charming and detailed scenes of medieval life in both court and countryside. ☒ *Via Bernardo Clesio 5, Trento* ☎ *0461/233770* ⊕ *www. buonconsiglio.it* ☞ *€10; Torre Aquila €2.50* ☉ *Closed Mon.* ⚲ *Timed visits must be booked online in advance.*

Duomo

CHURCH | This massive Romanesque church, also known as the Cathedral of San Vigilio (St. Vigilius), forms the southern edge of the Piazza del Duomo. Locals refer to this square as the city's *salotto* (sitting room), as in fine weather it's always filled with students and residents drinking coffee, sipping an aperitif, or reading the newspaper. The Baroque Fontana del Nettuno presides over it all. When skies are clear, pause here to savor the view of the mountaintops enveloping the city. Within the Duomo, unusual arcaded stone stairways border the austere nave. Ahead is the *baldacchino* (altar canopy), a copy of Bernini's masterpiece in St. Peter's in Rome. To the left of the altar is a mournful 16th-century crucifixion, flanked by the Virgin Mary and John the Apostle. This crucifix, by German artist Sisto Frey, was a focal point of the Council of Trent: each decree agreed on during the two decades of deliberations was solemnly read out in front of it. Stairs on the left side of the altar lead down to the 4th-century Paleo-Christian burial vault. Outside, check out the bronze scale-model of the city on the south side of the cathedral, then walk around to the back to see an exquisite display of 14th-century stonemason artistry, from the small porch to the intriguing knotted columns on the graceful apse. ⊠ *Piazza del Duomo, Trento* ☎ *0461/231293* ⊕ *www.cattedralesanvigilio.it* ⊘ *Burial vault closed Sun. morning and Tues.* ⊜ *Burial vault €2.*

Museo Diocesano Tridentino

HISTORY MUSEUM | Located inside the **Palazzo Pretorio,** the Museo Diocesano Tridentino is where you can see paintings and other objects that come from the treasury of the adjoining Cathedral of San Vigilio. This includes many carved wood altars and statues; an 11th-century sacramentary, or book of services; the seating plan of the prelates during the Council of Trent; and early-16th-century tapestries by Pieter van Aelst (1502–56), the Belgian artist who carried out Raphael's 15th-century designs for the Vatican tapestries. The palazzo itself was built in the 13th century and designed to seem like a wing of the Duomo; it became the fortified residence of the prince-bishops, who enjoyed considerable power and autonomy within the medieval hierarchy. The remarkable palazzo has lost none of its original splendor. Accessible through the museum, a subterranean archaeological area beneath the adjacent cathedral reveals remnants of the Early Christian Basilica of San Vigilio. ⊠ *Piazza del Duomo 18, Trento* ☎ *0461/234419* ⊕ *www. museodiocesanotridentino.it* ⊜ *€7, includes entrance to Duomo burial vault (free 1st Sun. of month)* ⊘ *Closed Tues.* ⊘ *Recommended to purchase tickets online in advance.*

Santa Maria Maggiore

CHURCH | Many sessions of the Council of Trent met in this Renaissance church. Limited light enters through the simple rose window over the main door, so you have to strain to see the magnificent ceiling, an intricate combination of frescoes and stuccowork. The church is off the northwest side of the Piazza del Duomo, about 200 yards down Via Cavour. ⊠ *Vicolo Orsoline 1, Trento* ☎ *0461/230037* ⊜ *Free.*

Tridentum

RUINS | The ancient Roman city of Tridentum lies beneath much of Trento's city center. Centuries of Adige River flooding buried ruins that only recently have been unearthed on public and private land. Beneath this piazza lies the largest of the archaeological sites, which reveals some marvels of Roman technology, such as underfloor heating and subterranean sewers complete with manhole covers. The Romans also used lead pipes for four centuries before recognizing it was hazardous to health. ⊠ *Piazza Cesare Battisti, Trento* ☎ *0461/230171* ⊜ *€2.50* ⊘ *Closed Mon.*

Via Belenzani

STREET | Locals refer to this street as Trento's outdoor gallery because of the frescoed facades of the hallmark Renaissance palazzi. It's an easy 50-yard walk up the lane behind the church of Santa Maria Maggiore. ⊠ *Trento.*

🍴 Restaurants

Al Vò

$ | NORTHERN ITALIAN | Trento's oldest trattoria (it's the descendant of a 14th-century tavern) remains one of its most popular lunch spots. Locals crowd into a simple, modern dining room to enjoy regional specialties like gnocchi with vegetables and *baccalà* (salt cod). **Known for:** fine selection of wines; Trento's oldest eatery; knowledgeable, welcoming staff. ⑤ *Average main: €11* ⊠ *Vicolo del Vò 11,*

Trento ☎ 0461/985374 ⊕ www.risto-rantealvo.it ⊙ Closed Sun. No dinner.

Osteria a Le Due Spade

$$$$ | **NORTHERN ITALIAN** | What started out as a Tyrolean tavern around the time of the Council of Trent is today an intimate restaurant that adeptly serves superb traditional and more innovative dishes. The menu changes throughout the year and is divided into mountain and seafood specialties, such as *mezzelune di patate* (potato ravioli with cheese and black truffles) or *salmarino in fiore di zucchine* (Arctic char in zucchini blossoms). **Known for:** cozy wood-paneled interior; fine dining; knowledgeable, welcoming personnel. ⑤ *Average main: €50* ⊠ *Via Rizzi 11, Trento* ☎ *0461/234343* ⊕ *www. leduespade.com* ⊙ *Closed Sun. No lunch Mon.*

Ristorante Pizzeria Orso Grigio

$$ | **NORTHERN ITALIAN** | Located on a nondescript side street, this friendly family-run trattoria serves tasty region-al dishes like *rufioi* (homemade ravioli stuffed with savoy cabbage) along with a fine selection of pizza. The wine list is also dominated by regional selections, which pair well with items on the menu. **Known for:** dining in a shady vine-covered courtyard when the weather is nice; gen-erations of culinary expertise; congenial atmosphere. ⑤ *Average main: €17* ⊠ *Via degli Orti 19, Trento* ☎ *0461/984400* ⊕ *www.orso-grigio.it.*

Scrigno del Duomo

$$ | **NORTHERN ITALIAN** | More than 30 wines by the glass, accompanied by an excellent selection of local cheeses, are served in this chic eatery, which has outside seating in the piazza. Salads and regional specialties are prepared in the open kitchen by gourmet chefs; they also bake their own bread daily. **Known for:** local art and history; traditional food and local wine; fine views of the cathedral. ⑤ *Average main: €22* ⊠ *Piazza del Duo-mo 29, Trento* ☎ *0461/220030* ⊕ *www. scrignodelduomo.com.*

☕ Coffee and Quick Bites

Antica Birreria Pedavena

$ | **NORTHERN ITALIAN** | **FAMILY** | Come for the beer: several varieties are brewed in-house and served in this charismatic beer hall. Meals include wursts, meat and cheese platters, pizzas, and huge salads. **Known for:** enormous beer hall; fine selection of brewed-in-house beers; typical Bavarian meats. ⑤ *Average main: €10* ⊠ *Piazza di Fiera 13, Trento* ☎ *0461/986255* ⊕ *www.birreriapedave-na.com.*

Hotels

Accademia

$ | **HOTEL** | Stylish, contemporary bedrooms with comfortable beds and handsome lithographs occupy an ancient, character-filled house close to the railway station and Piazza del Duomo. **Pros:** central location; gluten-free breakfast; beautiful courtyard. **Cons:** very basic decor; guests have complained about flies; some rooms are small. ⑤ *Rooms from: €102* ⊠ *Vicolo Colico 4, Trento* ☎ *0461/233600* ⊕ *www.accademiahotel. it* ⊙ *Closed 1 wk at Christmas* ⇱ *40 rooms* ⑩ *Free Breakfast.*

Buonconsiglio

$ | **HOTEL** | Public areas in this hotel near the train station are decorated with con-temporary paintings by the hotel's owner, and the well-kept guest rooms have sound-resistant windows. **Pros:** spacious rooms; good-size modern bathrooms; efficient service. **Cons:** some signs of wear; basic breakfast; outside the town center. ⑤ *Rooms from: €92* ⊠ *Via Romagnosi 16, Trento* ☎ *0461/272888* ⊕ *www.hotelbuonconsiglio.com* ⇱ *47 rooms* ⑩ *Free Breakfast.*

★ Castel Pergine

$$$ | **B&B/INN** | The stone and brick cham-bers, prison cells, and chapels in this labyrinthine 13th-century castle (occu-pied by Trento's prince-bishops in the

16th century) today contain spare, rustic guest rooms with carved-wood trim, lace curtains, and heavy wooden beds—some of them canopied. **Pros:** romantic setting; authentic castle experience; great restaurant. **Cons:** bathrooms are very small; need a car to get around; simple accommodations. $ *Rooms from: €220* ✉ *Via al Castello 10, 11 km (7 miles) east of Trento, Pergine Valsugana* ☎ *0461/531158* ⊕ *www.castelpergine.it* ☯ *Closed Nov.–Mar.* 🛏 *20 rooms* ⊙ *Free Breakfast.*

Grand Hotel Trento

$$ | HOTEL | This contemporary, rounded facade stands out among the ancient palazzi nearby, but inside you'll find a handsome marble-paved lobby, rich drapery in the restaurant, and ample rooms with clubby wood-trimmed furniture. **Pros:** professional service; wellness center; near train station. **Cons:** basic bathroom amenities; dated decor; busy neighborhood. $ *Rooms from: €127* ✉ *Piazza Dante 20, Trento* ☎ *0461/271000* ⊕ *www.grandhoteltrento.com* 🛏 *136 rooms* ⊙ *No Meals.*

Hotel Garni Aquila d'Oro

$$ | HOTEL | Each room has its own contemporary design, some have saunas with hot tubs and stunning views, and all enjoy a prime location near Piazza del Duomo. **Pros:** excellent location; comfortable beds; friendly service. **Cons:** common areas rather cramped; furniture is a bit dated; no on-site parking. $ *Rooms from: €126* ✉ *Via Belenzani 76, Trento* ☎ *0461/986282* ⊕ *www.aquiladoro.it* 🛏 *16 rooms* ⊙ *Free Breakfast.*

Hotel Garni Venezia

$ | B&B/INN | For reasonably priced accommodations, it's hard to beat this *garni* (bed-and-breakfast) right on Piazza Duomo, where six of the simple rooms have wonderful views. **Pros:** great location; won't break the bank; friendly environs. **Cons:** piazza can be noisy; not all rooms have private baths; guest rooms could use a refresh. $ *Rooms from: €87* ✉ *Via Belenzani 70, Piazza Duomo 45, Trento*

☎ *0461/234559* ⊕ *www.hotelveneziatn.it* 🛏 *43 rooms* ⊙ *Free Breakfast.*

Imperial Grand Hotel Terme

$$ | RESORT | If you're in the mood for some pampering, choose a grand room with a frescoed ceiling in the graciously restored golden-yellow palace in the nearby spa town of Levico Terme. **Pros:** interesting history; pleasant indoor pool; beautiful park setting. **Cons:** no A/C in some rooms; use of thermal baths costs extra; standard rooms are small. $ *Rooms from: €125* ✉ *Via Silva Domini 1, 20 km (12 miles) east of Trento, Levico Terme* ☎ *0461/700512* ⊕ *www.hotel-imperial-levico.com* 🛏 *81 rooms* ⊙ *Free Breakfast.*

Performing Arts

I Suoni delle Dolomiti (*The Sounds of the Dolomites*)

FESTIVALS | FAMILY | Held from June through September high in the hills of Trentino, this series of free concerts offers the chance to enjoy chamber music performances amid grassy meadows. ✉ *Trento* ☎ *0461/219300* ⊕ *www.isuonidelledolomiti.it* 🎫 *Free, except for certain concerts.*

Shopping

Enoteca di Corso

FOOD | A bit outside the town center, this atmospheric shop is laden with wines, sweets, and other local products. ✉ *Corso 3 Novembre 64, Trento* ☎ *0461/916424* ⊕ *www.enotecadelcorsotrento.it.*

La Salumeria Lunelli

FOOD | This specialty food shop boasts an impressive array of sauces, as well as wines, grappas, and liqueurs. A picnic can be handily assembled from a huge assortment of local salamis and cheeses. ✉ *Via Mazzini 46, Trento* ☎ *0461/238053* ⊕ *www.lunelli.it.*

Panificio Pulin

FOOD | Whole-grain breads and delicate pastries are on offer in this fragrant bakery. There's a second location on Via Suffragio. ⊠ *Via Cavour 23, Trento* ☎ *0461/234544.*

Piazza Alessandro Vittoria

MARKET | You can pick up meats, cheeses, produce, local truffles, and porcini mushrooms at the small morning market in the square. ⊠ *Trento.*

Rovereto

24 km (15 miles) south of Trento, 75 km (47 miles) south of Bolzano.

A 15th-century Venetian castle dominates Rovereto's compact medieval *centro storico* (historic center), with one of Italy's finest contemporary art museums just steps away. ■**TIP**→ **The Trento Museum Pass also includes entry to sites here in Rovereto.**

VISITOR INFORMATION

CONTACT Rovereto Tourism Office. ⊠ *Corso Rosmini 21, Rovereto* ☎ *0464/430363* ⊕ *www.visitrovereto.it.*

 Sights

Museo di Arte Moderna e Contemporanea di Trento e Rovereto (MART)

ART MUSEUM | Most of the more than 25,000 works of contemporary and modern art in this collection are from the 20th century. Rotating exhibitions and special events throughout the year highlight still more contemporary art. ⊠ *Corso Bettini 43, Rovereto* ☎ *0464/438887* ⊕ *www. mart.tn.it* ⊠ *€11* ⊙ *Closed Mon.* ⚐ *Reservations required on weekends.*

Museo Storico Italiano della Guerra

(*Italian Historical War Museum*)
HISTORY MUSEUM | This museum was founded after World War I to commemorate the conflict—and to warn against repeating its atrocities. An authoritative exhibition of military artifacts is displayed in the medieval castle perched above Rovereto; the views alone warrant a visit. From May through October you can also see a collection of artillery from the Great War housed in a former air-raid shelter. ⊠ *Via Castelbarco 7, Rovereto* ☎ *0464/438100* ⊕ *www.museodellaguerra.it* ⊠ *€9* ⊙ *Closed Mon.* ⚐ *Reservations required at least one day before Sat. and Sun. visits.*

 Hotels

Hotel Rovereto

$ | **HOTEL** | The Zani family runs this modern, centrally located hotel, which has welcoming public spaces, warm-color guest rooms, and one of the city's most appealing restaurants. **Pros:** distinctive decor; excellent restaurant; unbeatable location. **Cons:** small parking area; some rooms are on the small side; restaurant not open every night. **⑤** *Rooms from: €77* ⊠ *Corso Rosmini 82/D, Rovereto* ☎ *0464/435222* ⊕ *www.hotelrovereto. it* ⊙ *Restaurant closed Sun. No lunch Mon.–Thurs.* ⇆ *49 rooms* ⦿❘ *No Meals.*

Madonna di Campiglio

80 km (50 miles) northwest of Trento, 100 km (62 miles) southwest of Bolzano.

The winter resort of Madonna di Campiglio vies with Cortina d'Ampezzo as the most fashionable place for Italians to ski and be seen in the Dolomites. Madonna's popularity is well deserved, with 62 lifts connecting more than 150 km (93 miles) of well-groomed ski runs and equally good lodging and trekking facilities. The resort itself is a modest 5,000 feet above sea level, but the downhill runs, summer hiking paths, and mountain-biking trails venture high up into the surrounding peaks (including Pietra Grande at 9,700 feet).

GETTING HERE AND AROUND

By car from Trento, take the SS45 toward Vezzano. After Vezzano, continue to the SS237 until Ragoli, and turn onto the SP34. Follow the SP34 for 6 km (4 miles), and turn onto the SS239 for another 23 km (15 miles) until you arrive at Madonna di Campiglio. The more convenient railway station is at Trento; then you can ride the Trentini Trasporti bus for two and a half hours from Trento for €5.10.

VISITOR INFORMATION

CONTACT Madonna di Campiglio Tourism Office. ⊠ *Via Pradalago 4, Madonna di Campiglio* ☎ *0465/447501* ⊕ *www.campigliodolomiti.it.*

Sights

Campo Carlo Magno

VIEWPOINT | The stunning pass at Campo Carlo Magno (5,500 feet) is 3 km (2 miles) north of Madonna di Campiglio. This is where Charlemagne is said to have stopped in AD 800 on his way to Rome to be crowned emperor. You, too, can stop here to gaze upon the whole of northern Italy. If you continue north, take the descent with caution—in the space of a mile or so, hairpin turns and switchbacks deliver you down more than 2,000 feet. ⊠ *Madonna di Campiglio.*

Restaurants

Cascina Zeledria

$$ | NORTHERN ITALIAN | Although most of Madonna's visitors dine at resort hotels, Italians consider an on-mountain meal in a remote, rustic refuge like this one to be an indispensable part of a proper ski week. In winter, you'll be collected by a Sno-Cat and ferried up the slopes (you hike up in warmer months), where, after the 10-minute ride, you'll sit down to grill your own meats and vegetables over stone griddles. ■TIP→ **You must call in advance to reserve a table and arrange transportation. Known for:** local wine; authentic experience in a rural mountain setting; house specialty mushrooms and polenta. $ *Average main: €18* ⊠ *Località Zeledria, Madonna di Campiglio* ☎ *0465/440303* ⊕ *www.hotelcampigliobellavista.it/gourmet/ristorante-cascina-zeledria* ⊗ *Closed Apr.–May and Oct.–Nov.*

Ferrari Spazio Bollicine Nabucco

$$$ | WINE BAR | Although it has a stylish black-and-white color scheme, this restaurant nevertheless has the feel of a rustic, intimate chalet. Settle into pleasant surroundings for an après-ski aperitif or a light meal made with local ingredients and paired with the sparkling wines of Ferrari, a well-known Trentino vintner. **Known for:** central location; predinner cocktails; intimate atmosphere. $ *Average main: €30* ⊠ *Piazza Righi B3, Madonna di Campiglio* ☎ *0465/440756* ⊕ *www.ferraritrento.com/en/places/ferrari-spazio-bollicine/nabucco* ⊗ *Closed May–Nov.*

Hotels

Hotel Casa del Campo

$$ | HOTEL | Just yards from both the downhill slopes and the *ski-fondo* (cross-country skiing) paths, this charming, Tyrolean-style hotel has an on-site restaurant as well as spacious guest rooms, complete with orthopedic mattresses, soaking tubs, regional wood-and-fabric decor, and tremendous views. **Pros:** sheltered parking; good-size rooms; great location for outdoor activities year-round. **Cons:** thin pillows; some months have seven-night minimum stay; small TVs. $ *Rooms from: €178* ⊠ *Passo Campo Carlo Magno, Madonna di Campiglio* ☎ *0465/443130* ⊕ *www.casadelcampo.it* ⇆ *15 rooms* ⦿| *Free Breakfast.*

★ Savoia Palace Hotel

$$ | HOTEL | At Madonna's most traditional lodging, guest rooms and lounges are full of carved-wood and mountain-style furnishings, and two fireplaces blaze away in the bar, where you can relax while recalling the day's exploits on the ski slopes. **Pros:** central location in town; nice spa; warm atmosphere. **Cons:** can be noisy; faces a busy street; breakfast is nothing special. $ *Rooms from: €187* ✉ *Viale Dolomiti di Brenta 18, Madonna di Campiglio* ☎ *0465/441004* ⊕ *www. savoiapalace.it* ⊗ *Closed mid-Apr.–late June and mid-Sept.–Nov.* ⇌ *60 rooms* ◯✦ *Free Breakfast.*

Style Hotel Grifone
▸ | **HOTEL** | At this comfortable lodge with a distinctive wooden facade, flower-bedecked balconies catch the sun, and contemporary guest rooms and suites have views of the forested slopes. **Pros:** complimentary afternoon snack; charming decor; convenient location. **Cons:** mattresses can be uncomfortable; a bit out of town (but the Spinale cable car is nearby); lacks A/C. $ *Rooms from: €100* ✉ *Via Vallesinella 7, Madonna di Campiglio* ☎ *0465/442002* ⊕ *www.style-hotelgrifone.it* ⊗ *Closed mid-Apr.–June and Sept.–Nov.* ⇌ *40 rooms* ◯✦ *Free Breakfast.*

TH Madonna di Campiglio Golf Hotel
$$ | **HOTEL** | You need to make your way north to the Campo Carlo Magno Pass to reach this grand hotel, the former summer residence of Habsburg emperor Franz Josef, replete with verandas, Persian rugs, and bay windows. **Pros:** kids' club for children and teens; elegant rooms; attractive indoor pool. **Cons:** rooms can be noisy; food not up to par; long walk into town. $ *Rooms from: €190* ✉ *Via Cima Tosa 3, Madonna di Campiglio* ☎ *0465/441003, 049/2956411 for reservations* ⊕ *www. thcampiglio.it* ⇌ *109 rooms* ◯✦ *Free Breakfast* ⊗ *Closed late Apr.–June and Sept.–early Dec.*

🏃 Activities

GOLF
Campo Carlo Magno
GOLF | The 9-hole Campo Carlo Magno course is one of the highest in Europe, at 5,400 feet. It's only open mid-June through mid-September. ✉ *Via Cima Tosa 16, near Golf Hotel, Madonna di Campiglio* ☎ *0465/440622* ⊕ *www. golfcampocarlomagno.it* ⊗ *Closed mid-Sept.–mid-June* ⏣ *€40; €70 late July–late Aug.* ⅓ *9 holes, 6090 yards, par 70.*

HIKING AND CLIMBING
The Madonna di Campiglio tourism office has maps of a dozen trails leading to waterfalls, lakes, and stupefying views.

Monte Spinale (*Spinale Peak*)
HIKING & WALKING | **FAMILY** | The cable car to 6,900-foot-high Monte Spinale offers skiers magnificent views of the Brenta Dolomites in winter. It also runs during peak summer season. ✉ *Off Via Monte Spinale, Madonna di Campiglio* ☎ *0465/447744* ⊕ *www.ski.it/en/madonna-di-campiglio-trentino* ⏣ *€14 round-trip.*

SKIING
Funivie Madonna di Campiglio
SKIING & SNOWBOARDING | **FAMILY** | Miles of interconnecting ski runs—some of the best in the Dolomites—are linked by the cable cars and lifts of Funivie Madonna di Campiglio. Advanced skiers will like the extremely difficult terrain found on certain mountain faces, and intermediate and beginner skiers will find many runs at their levels, all accessible from town. There are also plenty of off-piste opportunities. Passes can be purchased at the main *funivia* (cable car) in town, and multiday passes are available. ✉ *Via Presanella 12, Madonna di Campiglio* ☎ *0465/447744* ⊕ *www.ski.it/en/madonna-di-campiglio-trentino* ⏣ *Passes €36–€56 per day.*

Bolzano (Bozen)

32 km (19 miles) south of Merano, 50 km (31 miles) north of Trento.

Bolzano (Bozen), capital of the autonomous province of Alto Adige, is tucked among craggy peaks in a Dolomite valley 77 km (48 miles) from the Brenner Pass and Austria. Tyrolean culture dominates Bolzano's language, food, architecture, and people. It may be hard to remember that you're in Italy when walking the city's colorful cobblestone streets and visiting its lantern-lighted cafés, where you may enjoy sauerkraut and a beer among a lively crowd of blue-eyed German speakers. That said, the fine Italian espresso and the boutiques will help to remind you where you are. The long, narrow arcades of Via dei Portici house shops that specialize in Tyrolean crafts and clothing, as well as many Italian designers.

The Bolzano-Bozen Card, free of charge at participating accommodations, grants free entry to 90 museums in Bolzano and Alto Adige, as well as free transport throughout the region, guided tours, and discounts on bike rentals.

GETTING HERE AND AROUND

By car from Trento, take the A22 for 60 km (37 miles) to Bolzano Sud. The train station is just steps away from Piazza Walther and has regular service from Italy and Munich (four hours). The SASA bus can help you connect between Bolzano and other parts of the region. There is an airport in Bolzano, but its connections are not as convenient as the larger airports serving Venice, Verona, and Munich.

VISITOR INFORMATION

CONTACT Bolzano Tourism Office. ⊠ *Via Alto Adige 60, Bolzano* ☎ *0471/307000* ⊕ *www.bolzano-bozen.it.*

Sights

Castel Roncolo (*Schloss Runkelstein*)
CASTLE/PALACE | Green hills and farmhouses north of town surround this meticulously kept castle with a tiled roof. It was built in 1237, destroyed half a century later, and then rebuilt soon thereafter. The world's largest cycle of secular medieval frescoes, beautifully preserved, is inside. A tavern in the courtyard serves excellent local food and wines. To get here from Piazza Walther, take Bus No. 12 or 14. It's a 45-minute walk from Piazza delle Erbe: head north along Via Francescani, continue through Piazza Madonna, connecting to Via Castel Roncolo. ⊠ *Via San Antonio 15, Bolzano* ☎ *0471/329808 castle, 0471/324073 tavern* ⊕ *www.roncolo.info* 🎫 *€8* ⏱ *Closed Mon.*

Chiesa dei Domenicani

CHURCH | The 13th-century Dominican Church is renowned for its Cappella di San Giovanni, where frescoes from the Giotto school show the birth of a pre-Renaissance sense of depth and individuality. ⊠ *Piazza Domenicani, Bolzano* ☎ *0471/982027* 🎫 *Free.*

Duomo

CHURCH | A lacy spire looks down on the mosaic-like roof tiles of the city's Gothic cathedral, built between the 12th and 14th centuries. Inside are 14th- and 15th-century frescoes and an intricately carved stone pulpit dating from 1514. Outside, don't miss the Porta del Vino (Wine Gate) on the northeast side; decorative carvings of grapes and harvest workers attest to the long-standing importance of wine to this region. ⊠ *Piazza della Parrocchia 27, Bolzano* ☎ *0471/978676* 🎫 *Free.*

★ **Messner Mountain Museum Firmian**
ART MUSEUM | Perched on a peak overlooking Bolzano, the 10th-century Castle Sigmundskron is home to one of six mountain museums established by Reinhold Messner—the first climber to conquer Everest solo and the first to reach

ts summit without oxygen. The Tibetan tradition of *kora,* a circular pilgrimage around a sacred site, is an inspiration for the museum, where visitors contemplate the relationship between man and mountain, guided by images and objects Messner collected during his adventures. The museum is 3 km (2 miles) southwest of Bolzano, just off the Appiano exit on the highway to Merano. ☒ *Sigmundskron Castle 53, Sigmundskronerstrasse, Bolzano* ☎ *0471/631264* ⊕ *www.messner-mountain-museum.it* ⊘ *Closed Thurs. and mid-Nov.–mid-Mar.* ☐ *€12.*

★ **Museo Archeologico dell'Alto Adige**
HISTORY MUSEUM | FAMILY | This museum has gained international fame for Ötzi, its 5,300-year-old iceman, discovered in 1991 and the world's oldest naturally preserved body. In 1998 Italy acquired it from Austria after it was determined that the body lay 100 yards inside Italian territory. The iceman's leathery remains are displayed in a freezer vault, preserved along with his longbow, ax, and clothing. The rest of the museum relies on models and artifacts from nearby archaeological sites, and exhibitions change regularly. An English audio guide leads you not only through Ötzi's Copper Age, but also into the preceding Mesolithic and Neolithic eras, and the Bronze and Iron Ages that followed. In July and August, the museum's supervised play area keeps young children entertained while adults experience the museum. ☒ *Via Museo 43, Bolzano* ☎ *0471/320100* ⊕ *www.iceman. it* ☐ *€9* ⊘ *Closed Mon.* ☐ *Advance online reservations recommended.*

Passeggiata del Guncina
PROMENADE | An 8-km (5-mile) botanical promenade dating from 1892 ends with a panoramic view of Bolzano. Recent updates include signposting for various species of plants and trees, as well as benches and picnic tables. You can choose to return to town along the same path, or you can walk along the River Fago and end up back in the center of Bolzano. ☒ *Entrance near Vecchia Parrocchiale di Gries, across river and up Corsa Libertà, Bolzano.*

Piazza delle Erbe
PLAZA/SQUARE | A bronze statue of Neptune, which dates from 1745, presides over this square's bountiful fruit and vegetable market. Stalls spill over with colorful displays of local produce; bakeries and grocery stores showcase hot breads, pastries, cheeses, and delicatessen meats—a complete picnic. Try the speck tirolese and the apple strudel. ☒ *Bolzano.*

Piazza Walther
PLAZA/SQUARE | This pedestrians-only square is Bolzano's heart; in warmer weather it serves as an open-air living room where locals and tourists can be found at all hours sipping a drink (such as a glass of chilled Riesling). The piazza's namesake was the 12th-century German wandering minstrel Walther von der Vogelweide, whose songs lampooned the papacy and praised the Holy Roman Emperor. In the center of the piazza stands Heinrich Natter's white-marble, neo-Romanesque *Monument to Walther,* built in 1889. ☒ *Piazza Walther, Bolzano.*

Renon (Ritten) Plateau
NATURE SIGHT | FAMILY | The earth pyramids of Renon Plateau are a bizarre geological formation where erosion has left a forest of tall, thin, needlelike spires of rock, each topped with a boulder. To get here, take the Soprabolzano cable car from Via Renon, about 300 yards left of the Bolzano train station. At the top, switch to the electric train that takes you to the plateau, which is in Collalbo, just above Bolzano. The two rides cost €16 round-trip and take about 12 minutes total. The final 30-minute hike along gentle Trail No. 24 is free. ☒ *Via Renon, Collalbo* ☎ *0471/356100* ⊕ *www.ritten.com* ☐ *€16 round-trip.*

Bolzano (Bozen)

Vecchia Parrocchiale di Gries
(*Old Parish Church*)

CHURCH | Visit this church, said to have been built in 1141, to see two medieval treasures: an 11th-century Romanesque crucifix and an elaborate 15th-century wooden altar, carved by Michael Pacher and a masterpiece of the Gothic style. ✉ *Via Martin Knoller, in Gries, Bolzano* ☎ *0471/283089* 🎫 *Free* ⊗ *Closed weekends.*

Restaurants

Batzen Brau
$ | ECLECTIC | Locals hold animated conversations over glasses of regional wine in this modern take on a traditional stube. Tasty South Tyrolean specialties include speck tirolese and *mezzelune casarecce ripiene* (homemade stuffed half-moons of pasta). **Known for:** late dining; convivial atmosphere; large portions. ⑤ *Average main: €14* ✉ *Via Andreas Hofer 30, Bolzano* ☎ *0471/050950* ⊕ *www.batzen.it.*

Cavallino Bianco Weisses Rossl
$$ | NORTHERN ITALIAN | A spacious, comfortable dining room near Via dei Portici is a dependable favorite with locals and visitors alike. A wide selection of Italian and German dishes are served to large tables of families enjoying their meals together. **Known for:** local dishes; generations of cooking; crowded, friendly atmosphere. ⑤ *Average main: €16* ✉ *Via Bottai 6, Bolzano* ☎ *0471/973267* ⊕ *www.weissesroessl.org* ⊗ *Closed Sun. No dinner Sat.*

Hopfen & Co.
$ | NORTHERN ITALIAN | Fried white *Würstel* (sausage), sauerkraut, and grilled ribs complement the excellent home-brewed Austrian-style pilsner and wheat beer at this bustling pub-restaurant, which attracts Bolzano's students and young professionals. **Known for:** traditional pub environment; bustling atmosphere; home-brewed beer. ⑤ *Average main: €12*

✉ *Piazza delle Erbe, Obstplatz 17, Bolzano* ☎ *0471/300788* ⊕ *www.boznerbier.it.*

Wirtshaus Vögele
$$ | NORTHERN ITALIAN | Ask locals where they like to dine out, and odds are they'll tell you Vögele, one of the area's oldest inns, where the menu features Tyrolean standards such as *canederli* (bread dumplings) with speck and venison. The classic wood-paneled dining room on the ground level is often packed, but don't despair—the restaurant has two additional floors. **Known for:** local dishes; friendly vibe; late dining. ⑤ *Average main: €18* ✉ *Goethestr 3, Bolzano* ☎ *0471/973938* ⊕ *www.voegele.it* ⊗ *Closed Sun.*

Hotels

★ Hotel Greif
$$$ | HOTEL | Individually designed guest rooms in a centuries-old Bolzano landmark feature modern furnishings with clean lines, as well as contemporary art paired with 19th-century paintings and sketches. **Pros:** central location; elegant decor; helpful staff. **Cons:** no on-site spa; rooms vary in size; some rooms have small windows. ⑤ *Rooms from: €207* ✉ *Piazza Walther 1, Bolzano* ☎ *0471/318000* ⊕ *www.greif.it* ⇌ *33 rooms* ⦿❘ *Free Breakfast.*

Parkhotel Laurin
$$$ | HOTEL | An exercise in art nouveau opulence, presiding over a large park in the middle of town, this elegant hotel features art-filled guest rooms, handsome public spaces, and an exceptional restaurant. **Pros:** convenient location; high standard of service; excellent restaurant. **Cons:** decor a bit old-fashioned; can be packed with business groups; rooms facing park can be noisy. ⑤ *Rooms from: €201* ✉ *Via Laurin 4, Bolzano* ☎ *0471/311000* ⊕ *www.laurin.it* ⇌ *100 rooms* ⦿❘ *Free Breakfast.*

Schloss Korb

$$$ | B&B/INN | This romantic 13th-century castle with crenellations and a massive tower is perched in a park amid vine-covered hills, viewed from some of the cozy guest rooms through Romanesque arched windows. **Pros:** romantic setting; very nice indoor and outdoor pools; charming traditional furnishings. **Cons:** A/C cannot be adjusted; need a car to get around; not all rooms are in the castle. ⑤ *Rooms from: €208* ✉ *Via Castel d'Appiano 5, Missiano* ☎ *0471/636000* ⊕ *www. schloss-hotel-korb.com* ⊘ *Closed Nov.– Mar.* ↩ *49 rooms* ⑩ *Free Breakfast.*

Nightlife

Grifoncino

COCKTAIL LOUNGES | The Hotel Greif's sleek, modern cocktail bar (where the actual bar is made out of empty bottles) serves the best libations in town. The drinks menu betrays a particular fondness for gin, but the staff also excel at making cocktails tailored to your preferences. ✉ *Via della Rena 28, Bolzano* ☎ *0471/318000* ⊕ *www.grifoncino.it.*

Parkhotel Laurin Bar

LIVE MUSIC | The Laurin Bar hosts jazz combos on Friday between October and May and a jazz pianist every Saturday evening. In summer, the bar moves outside to the pretty garden, where a DJ spins tunes on Thursday night. ✉ *Via Laurin 4, Bolzano* ☎ *0471/311000* ⊕ *www. laurin.it.*

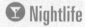 Activities

BIKING

Alp Bike

BIKING | If you're in decent shape, one great way to see some of the surrounding castles, lakes, and forested valleys of the Dolomites is by bike. Alp Bike leads various guided excursions at all levels and almost daily, but you must reserve a week or more ahead for more ambitious trips. It is suggested that you email

(*info@alpbike.it*), since they are often away from the office. They can help with bike rentals as well. ✉ *Via Castel Flavon 101, Bolzano* ☎ *338/1126584* ⊕ *www. alpbike.it.*

Shopping

CRAFTS

Artigiani Atesini

CRAFTS | This is the largest store for locally made handcrafted goods. ✉ *Via Portici 39, Bolzano* ☎ *0471/978590.*

MARKETS

Christkindlmarkt (*Christmas market*)

MARKET | FAMILY | From the end of November to the first week after New Year's there's a traditional Christkindlmarkt in Piazza Walther, with stalls selling all kinds of Christmas decorations and local handcrafted goods. ✉ *Piazza Walther, Bolzano.*

Piazza della Vittoria

MARKET | A weekly flea market takes place Saturday morning in Piazza della Vittoria. ✉ *Piazza della Vittoria, Bolzano.*

Bormio

97 km (60 miles) northwest of Madonna di Campiglio, 100 km (62 miles) southwest of Merano.

At the foot of Stelvio Pass, Bormio is the most famous ski resort on the western side of the Dolomites, with 38 km (24 miles) of long pistes and a 5,000-plus-foot vertical drop. In summer its cool temperatures and clean air entice Italians away from cities on the humid Lombard plain. This dual-season popularity supports the plentiful shops, restaurants, and hotels in town. Bormio has been known for the therapeutic qualities of its waters since the Roman era, and there are numerous spas.

GETTING HERE AND AROUND

Take the SS239 North toward Dimaro. Turn onto the SS42 and follow it for 41 km (25 miles). Turn right onto Via Roma, and, after 2 km (1 mile), turn right onto Via Valtellina for 24 km (15 miles), and then turn right at SP78. Merge onto the SS38, and follow it to Bormio. In the summertime, you can choose to turn off the SS42 at Ponte di Legno, onto the SS300, and follow it to the end in Bormio. This takes you through Stelvio National Park. The nearest railway is in Tirano, which is half an hour away by bus. Tirano is serviced by Trenitalia, as well as the UNESCO World Heritage–designated Rhaetian Railway.

VISITOR INFORMATION **Bormio Tourism Office.** ⊠ *Via Roma 131/B, Bormio* ☎ *0342/903300* ⊕ *www.bormio.eu.*

Sights

Bagni Vecchi (*Old Baths*)

HOT SPRING | Ancient Roman baths predate the thermal springs, caves, and waterfalls that are now known as the Bagni Vecchi. Leonardo da Vinci soaked here in 1493, and today you can book a package that includes a massage and lunch, or book massages and treatments separately. Each of the six spa centers offers a different treatment regimen, including such possibilities as thermal baths, sauna, and aromatherapy, depending on the desired outcome (purification, toning, or regeneration, for example). ⊠ *Via Bagni Nuovi 7, Molina* ☎ *0342/910131* ⊕ *www.bagnidibormio.it* ☞ *At the time of this writing, spa services only available to guests staying at the Bagni Vecchi Hotel.* ☏ *€48–€54.*

Bormio Terme

HOT SPRING | FAMILY | From outdoor swimming pools to private baths, there are plenty of ways to enjoy the healing qualities of the thermal waters. General admission gets you four hours in the pools, saunas, and Turkish baths, and more hours can be purchased as needed. Spa and beauty treatments are also available; book ahead to avoid disappointment. You do not need to pay for the pools if you are only enjoying spa treatments. ⊠ *Via Stelvio 14, Bormio* ☎ *0342/901325* ⊕ *www.bormioterme.it* ☏ *€26.*

Parco Nazionale dello Stelvio

NATIONAL PARK | FAMILY | The Alps' (and Italy's) biggest national park is spread over 1,350 square km (520 square miles) and four provinces. Opened in 1935 to preserve flora and protect fauna, today it has more than 1,200 types of plants, 600 different mushrooms, and more than 160 species of animals, including the chamois, ibex, and roe deer. There are many entrances to the park and a dozen visitor centers. ■TIP→ **Bormio makes a good base for exploring—the closest entrance to town is the year-round gateway at Torre Alberti.** ⊠ *Via Roma 131, Bormio* ☎ *0473/830430* ⊕ *www.stelviopark.bz.it* ☏ *Free.*

Restaurants

Ristorante Caffe Kuerc

$$ | NORTHERN ITALIAN | This building was for centuries where justice was publicly served to accused witches, among others. Today, it's a great place to enjoy bewitching specialties like bresaola with lemon and olive oil, or *pizzoccheri* (buckwheat pasta) with garlic and winter vegetables. **Known for:** interesting history; nice location; pizza. ⑤ *Average main: €17* ⊠ *Piazza Cavour 8, Bormio* ☎ *0342/910787* ⊗ *Closed Tues.*

Alto Adige and The Heart of the Dolomites

Zuckerhutl
3,507m

Hochfeiler ▲
3,510m

TO INNSBRUCK

Vipiteno

AUSTRIA

ALPS

Granatenkogel ▲
3,304m

Hochwilde ▲
3,842m

GIOGAIA DI TESSA

Naturno
(Naturns)

Tirolo

Merano (Meran)

Castel Juval

Castel
Trauttmansdorff

Museo
Agricolo di
Brunnenburg

Lana

Gargazzone

Caldaro
(Kaltern)

Cles

Madonna
di Campiglio

Pinzolo

Cma. Brenta
3,150m

Mezzolombardo

Cavalese

Ora

Bolzano

Cornedo

Abbazia di
Novacella

Bressanone
(Brixen)

Ortisei
(St. Ulrich)

Brunico
(Bruneck)

Croda d. Becco
2,810m

Tre Cime
di Lavaredo

TO AURONZO

Col
Vare

Misurina

Corvara

Passo di Sella

Col
Bodella

Canazei

SELLA MT. RANGE

Passo Pordoi

Arabba

Cortina
d'Ampezzo

DOLOMITES

VENETO

Vigo di
Fassa

Predazzo

San Martino

Laste delle Sute
2,616m

TRENTINO

Trento

0   10 mi
0   10 km

Hotels

La Genzianella

$$ | HOTEL | Unpretentious Alpine chic meets contemporary decor, with warm pine, ceramics, rich textiles, and wood-beamed ceilings—and all but one of the guest rooms have balconies. **Pros:** great for bikers; excellent on-site restaurant; handy to slopes and town. **Cons:** rooms can be compact; some beds are two twins pushed together; no pool. $ *Rooms from: €162* ✉ *Via Zandilla 6, Bormio* ☎ *0342/904485* ⊕ *www.genzianella.com* ☾ *Closed May and mid-Sept.– Dec.* ⤳ *39 rooms* ⦿ *Free Breakfast.*

Activities

SKIING

Funivia (cable car)

SKIING & SNOWBOARDING | FAMILY | You can buy a ski pass (€42–€44 per day) and pick up a trail map at the base of the funivia, in the center of town, before connecting to the Bormio 2000 station (6,600 feet) on Vallecetta, the main resort mountain. From there, you can ski down intermediate trails (the majority of Bormio's runs), use the extensive lift network to explore secondary ski areas, or get another funivia up to the Bormio 3000 station at Cima Bianca (9,800 feet) for more challenging terrain. The cable car also runs July to mid-September, when it is used by mountain bikers to reach long trails through breathtaking Alpine terrain; less ambitious visitors can wander around and then ride the cable car back down.

✉ *Via Battaglion Morbegno 25, Bormio* ☎ *0342/901451* ⊕ *www.bormioski.eu.*

Merano (Meran)

29 km (18 miles) north of Bolzano, 16 km (10 miles) east of Naturno.

The second-largest town in Alto Adige, Merano (Meran) was once the capital of the Austrian region of Tyrol. When the town and surrounding area were ceded to Italy as part of the 1919 Treaty of Versailles, Innsbruck became Tyrol's capital. Merano continued to be known as a spa town, attracting European nobility for its therapeutic waters and its "grape cure," which consists simply of eating the grapes grown on the surrounding hillsides. Sheltered by mountains, Merano has an unusually mild climate, with summer temperatures rarely exceeding 80°F (27°C) and winters that usually stay above freezing, despite the skiing within easy reach. Along the narrow streets of Merano's old town, houses have little towers and huge wooden doors, and the pointed arches of the Gothic cathedral sit next to neoclassical and art nouveau buildings. Merano serves as a good respite from mountain adventures, or from the bustle of nearby Trento and Bolzano.

GETTING HERE AND AROUND

By car from Bolzano, take the SP165 to the SP117 toward Merano (29 km [18 miles]). There is regular service by Trenitalia to the train station in Merano from all points in Italy.

VISITOR INFORMATION

CONTACT Merano Tourism Office. ✉ *Corso Libertà 45, Merano* ☎ *0473/272000* ⊕ *www.merano-suedtirol.it.*

◉ Sights

Castel Trauttmansdorff

GARDEN | FAMILY | This Gothic castle was restored in the 19th century and now serves as a museum that celebrates more than 200 years of tourism in South Tyrol. But the real draw is the expansive garden, where exotic flora is organized by country of origin. The castle is about 2 km (1 mile) southeast of town on the Sentiero di Sissi; you can also take Bus No. 4 or 1B from the station. ✉ *Via Valentino 51a, Merano* ☎ *0473/255600* ⊕ *www.trauttmansdorff.it* ☉ *Closed mid-Nov.–Mar.* 🎟 *€15.*

Duomo

CHURCH | The 14th-century Gothic cathedral, with a crenellated facade and an ornate campanile, sits in the heart of the old town. The Capella di Santa Barbara, just behind the Duomo, is an octagonal church containing a 15th-century pietà. ■**TIP**➔ **Mass is held in German only.** ✉ *Piazza del Duomo, Merano* ☎ *0473/230174* ⊕ *www.stadtpfarre-meran.it* 🎟 *Free.*

Museo Agricolo di Brunnenburg

HISTORY MUSEUM | FAMILY | Overlooking the town, atop Mt. Tappeinerweg, is Castel Fontana, which was the home of poet Ezra Pound from 1958 to 1964. Still in the Pound family, the castle now houses the Museo Agricolo di Brunnenburg, devoted to Tyrolean country life. Among its exhibits are a smithy and a room with Pound memorabilia. ✉ *Via Castello 17, Tirolo* ✛ *Take Bus No. 3, which departs every hr on the hr from Merano to Dorf Tirol (20 mins)* ☎ *339/1803086* ⊕ *www.brunnenburg.net* 🎟 *€6* ☉ *Closed Fri.–Sat.*

7

The Dolomites MERANO (MERAN)

★ Promenades

PROMENADE | A stroll along one of Merano's well-marked, impossibly pleasant promenades may yield even better relaxation than time in its famous spa. **Passeggiata Tappeiner** (Tappeiner's Promenade) is a 3-km (2-mile) path with panoramic views from the hills north of the Duomo and diverse botanical pleasures along the way. **Passeggiata d'Estate** (Summer Promenade) runs along the shaded south bank of the Passirio River, and the **Passeggiata d'Inverno** (Winter Promenade), on the exposed north bank, provides more warmth and the Wandelhalle—a sunny area decorated with idyllic paintings of surrounding villages. The popular Austrian empress Sissi (Elisabeth of Wittelsbach, 1837–98) put Merano on the map as a spa destination; a trail named in her honor, the **Sentiero di Sissi** (Sissi's Walk), follows a path from Castel Trauttmansdorff to the heart of Merano. ✉ *Merano.*

Terme di Merano

HOT SPRING | FAMILY | This sprawling spa complex has 25 pools (including a brine pool with underwater music) and five saunas (with an indoor "snow room" available for cooling down). Along with the family-friendly options for bathing, personalized services for grown-ups include traditional cures using local products, such as grape-based applications and whey baths. ✉ *Piazza Terme 9, Merano* ☎ *0473/252000* ⊕ *www.termemerano. it* ✉ *€16 for 3 hours in thermal baths; €23 for 3 hours in thermal baths and saunas; €28 for full day's use of baths and saunas.*

🍴 Restaurants

Bistro 7

$$ | ITALIAN | A hip young crowd frequent the ground-floor bar of this modern bistro in the town's central arcade. Upstairs in the stylish dining room, an older crowd enjoys both contemporary cooking—heavy on beef, venison, and other meat specialties, including calf's liver—and attentive service. **Known for:** central location; welcoming atmosphere; fine wines. ⑤ *Average main: €24* ✉ *Lauben 232, Merano* ☎ *0473/210636* ⊕ *www. bistrosieben.it* ⊘ *Closed Sun.*

Restaurant Sigmund

$$ | ITALIAN | Smack-dab on Merano's popular Corso della Libertà, this unassuming restaurant has an inviting terrace where you can people-watch and soak up some sun while enjoying local specialties with seasonal twists, such as a springtime menu with all things asparagus. The interior's wood-beamed ceilings and candlelit tables make it the perfect setting for a romantic dinner. ⑤ *Average main: €20* ✉ *Freiheitsstr. 2, Merano* ☎ *0473/237749* ⊕ *www.restaurantsigmund.com* ⊘ *Closed Wed.*

Saxifraga

$$ | ITALIAN | To reach this charming eatery, which occupies an enviable position overlooking Merano and the peaks enveloping the town, climb the stairs behind the Duomo or hike up along the Passeggiata Tappeiner. The kitchen serves well-prepared dumplings, pasta, and other local specialties—just don't leave without trying the homemade breads. **Known for:** beautiful views; charcuterie and cheeses; delicious desserts. ⑤ *Average main: €17* ✉ *Via Monte San Zeno 33, Passeggiata Tappeiner (Tappeiner's Promenade), Merano* ☎ *0473/239249* ⊕ *www. saxifraga.it* ⊘ *Closed Tues. and Nov.–Mar. No dinner Oct. and Apr.–May.*

Stumbling on Ötzi

It was at the Similaun rifugio in September 1991 that a German couple arrived talking of a dead body they'd discovered near a "curious pickax." The couple, underestimating the age of the corpse by about 5,300 years, thought it was a matter for the police. This was to be the world's introduction to Ötzi, the oldest mummy ever found. World-famous mountaineers Reinhold Messner and Hans Kammerlander happened to

be passing through the same rifugio during a climbing tour, and a few days later they were on the scene, freeing the iceman from the ice, and Ötzi's remarkable story was under way.

Today, you can see Ötzi on display, along with his longbow, ax, and clothes, at Bolzano's Museo Archeologico dell'Alto Adige, where he continues to be preserved at freezing temperatures.

★ Sissi

\$\$\$ | NORTHERN ITALIAN | The sterile surroundings of this restaurant, a short walk from Via dei Portici, belie its culinary delights—namely, rustic regional dishes re-energized and prepared with precision. Menus change according to the chef's whim and the season, but they always include a modernized *vitello tonnato* (veal with tuna sauce), delightful homemade pasta and dumplings, and decadent meat dishes, such as veal stewed in Lagrein, the area's renowned red wine. **Known for:** highly polished service; varied tasting menu; fantastic wine list. ⑤ *Average main: €32* ⊠ *Via Galilei 44, Merano* ☎ *0473/231062* ⊕ *www.sissi.andreafenoglio.com* ⊘ *Closed Mon. No lunch Tues.*

Coffee and Quick Bites

Vinothek Relax

\$\$ | NORTHERN ITALIAN | If you have difficulty choosing from the long list of tasty pizzas here, ask the friendly English-speaking staff for help with the menu. You're unlikely to find a better selection of wine, or a more pleasant environment for sampling. **Known for:** helpful service; large

choice of wines; top-notch pizzas and local cuisine. ⑤ *Average main: €15* ⊠ *Via Cavour 31, opposite Palace Hotel, Merano* ☎ *0473/236735* ⊕ *www.weine-relax.it* ⊘ *Closed Sun. and 2 wks in Feb. and Mar.*

🛏 Hotels

Hotel Terme Merano

\$\$\$\$ | HOTEL | If you're in Merano to pamper yourself, you can't do much better than the Hotel Terme: as its name suggests, it's connected to the expansive Terme di Merano (a stay here includes free, unlimited access via a "bathrobe tunnel"), and it also has the rooftop Sky Spa with indoor and outdoor pools and saunas. **Pros:** very central location; well-equipped gym; delicious breakfast offerings. **Cons:** staff can be unfriendly at times; accommodations above bar can be noisy; rooms on the plain side. ⑤ *Rooms from: €354* ⊠ *Piazza Terme 1, Merano* ☎ *0473/259000* ⊕ *www.hoteltermemerano.it* ⤴ *139 rooms* ⦿ *Free Breakfast.*

Did You Know?

There are three different hiking areas in Naturno: in the valley, wide easy paths traverse apple orchards and meadows; on the slopes of the Sonnenberg, trails run along ancient irrigation channels; the most popular hiking trail around Naturno is the Merano High Mountain Trail, a long-distance tour between mountain huts.

Meisters Hotel Irma

$$$ | RESORT | This goal of this hotel, opened in 1924, is to relax the body and the spirit—and it certainly makes a smashing effort by offering year-round outdoor pools, an indoor pool, a delightful spa, and beautiful park surroundings. **Pros:** great service; nearby hiking and bicycling trails; spectacular gardens and spa. **Cons:** outside of town; outlying suites may have poor Wi-Fi connection; expensive restaurant and bar. $ *Rooms from: €212* ✉ *Via Belvedere 17, Merano* ☎ *0473/212000* ⊕ *www.hotel-irma. com* ⊘ *Closed mid-Nov.–mid-Mar.* ⇨ *69 rooms* ⦿ *Free Breakfast.*

 ## Shopping

Via dei Portici (*Laubengasse*)

NEIGHBORHOODS | Merano's narrow, arcaded main shopping street runs west from the cathedral. Here you can find regional products—wood carvings, Tyrolean-style clothing, embroidery, cheeses, salami, and fruit schnapps—alongside standard clothing-boutique stock. ✉ *Via dei Portici, Merano.*

Naturno (Naturns)

44 km (27 miles) northwest of Bolzano, 61 km (38 miles) east of Passo dello Stelvio.

As the name suggests, Naturno is a great location for a nature-based vacation; you can access a number of hiking trails to explore the area by foot. City planners have redesigned the town, reducing traffic and making the town more pedestrian-friendly. The locals take great pride in their produce; the fresh fruit, wine, and cheeses of this area are alone worth the drive.

GETTING HERE AND AROUND

By car from Bolzano, take the SS42 to the SS38 toward Merano. Naturno is 15 km (9 miles) past Merano. The town is very pedestrian-friendly, so talk to your hotel about where to leave your car, or head straight to a parking garage. Naturno is easily accessible by train from Bolzano or Merano.

VISITOR INFORMATION

CONTACT Naturno Tourism Office. ✉ *Piazza Municipio 1, Naturno* ☎ *0473/666077* ⊕ *www.naturns.it.*

 ## Sights

FORST Brewery

BREWERY | The source of the full-flavor beer served throughout the region is the striking FORST Brewery, on the road connecting Naturno and Merano. Tours can be arranged if you call ahead, but you can turn up between late May and September to sample the product line. In high season, cross a flower-lined covered wooden bridge to reach the delightful beer garden. ✉ *Via Venosta 9, Lagundo* ☎ *0473/447727* ⊕ *www.forst.it* ⊘ *Closed late Sept.–late May.*

★ Messner Mountain Museum Juval (*Castel Juval*)

ART MUSEUM | Since 1983 this 13th-century castle in the hills above the hamlet of Stava has been the summer home of the South Tyrolese climber and polar adventurer Reinhold Messner—the first climber to conquer Everest solo. Part of the castle has been turned into one of six in Messner's chain of mountain museums, where guided tours are required to view his collection of Tibetan art and masks from around the world. (Note that the tours are in German or Italian only, though you can pick up an English information booklet to follow along.) It's a 10-minute shuttle ride from the parking lot below or a 60- to 90-minute hike on local trails; wear sturdy shoes, even if you take the shuttle, as the paths are uneven. ✉ *Juval 3, Castelbello* ☎ *348/4433871, 0471/631264* ⊕ *www.messner-mountain-museum.it/juval/museum* ⊘ *Closed Wed. and Nov.–Mar. and July* ⦿ *€10.*

San Procolo (*Prokolus*)

CHURCH | Frescoes here are some of the oldest in the German-speaking world, dating from the 8th century. A small, modern museum offers multimedia installations (in Italian or German only) presenting four epochs in the region's history: ancient, medieval, Gothic, and the era of the Great Plague of 1636 (which claimed a quarter of Naturno's population, some of whom are buried in the church's cemetery). There are leaflets and other information in English on request. ⊠ *Via San Procolo, Naturno* ☎ *348/673139* ⊕ *www.procolo.org* ⊙ *Closed Mon., Wed., Fri., Sat., and Nov.–Mar.* 🍽 *€6.*

🍴 Restaurants

⭐ Schlosswirt Juval

$$ | NORTHERN ITALIAN | Reinhold Messner's restored farmhouse, which is below Castel Juval, holds an old-style restaurant serving traditional local dishes. Not to be missed are the smoked hams and flavorful cheeses provided by the farm outside; they are well paired with the estate's Castel Juval wine. **Known for:** local wine; mountaintop dining; farm-to-table fare. ⑤ *Average main: €22* ⊠ *Juval 2, Castelbello* ☎ *0473/668056* ⊕ *www.schlosswirtjuval.it* ⊙ *Closed Wed. and Nov.–Mar.; dinner by reservation only.*

Caldaro (Kaltern)

15 km (9 miles) south of Bolzano.

This vineyard village, with clear views of castles high up in the surrounding mountains, represents the centuries of division that forged the unique character of the area. Caldaro architecture is famous for the way it blends Italian Renaissance elements of balance and harmony with the soaring windows and peaked arches of the Germanic Gothic tradition—the church of Santa Caterina, on the main square, is a good example.

The warmest bathing lake in the Alps is just 4 km (2½ miles) away.

GETTING HERE AND AROUND
By car from Bolzano, follow the SS42 south toward Caldaro. This road is famously known as the Strada del Vino (Wine Road), and you will pass several vineyards along the way. If you head straight to the Wine Museum in Caldaro, you can pick up maps and plan a route through the vineyards based on specific tastes.

VISITOR INFORMATION
Caldaro Tourism Office. ⊠ *Piazza Principale 8, Caldaro* ☎ *0471/963169* ⊕ *www.kaltern.com.*

👁 Sights

⭐ Elena Walch

WINERY | This sustainably farmed 60-hectare (148-acre) property produces some of the region's most renowned wines, in paricular Gewürztraminer and Pinot Nero. It's overseen by Elena herself along with her daughters Julia and Karoline. Stop by their gorgeous Castel Ringberg site for tastings in their wine shop, a tour that includes a short vineyard hike (May through October, by reservation), or lunch at their Ostaria al Castello, which has panoramic views over the vines and down to Lake Caldaro. A second vineyard site closer to Tramin, with a wine shop and a bistro, is open daily year-round. ⊠ *Castel Ringberg, San Giuseppe al Lago 1, Caldaro* ☎ *0471/960010* ⊕ *www.elenawalch.com* ⊙ *Castel Ringberg wine shop and osteria closed Mon.–Thurs. and Nov.–Mar.*

⭐ South Tyrolean Wine Museum

OTHER MUSEUM | Head here to learn how local wine has historically been made, stored, served, and worshipped, through a series of entertaining exhibits. ⊠ *Via dell'Oro 1, near main square, Caldaro* ☎ *0471/963168* ⊕ *www.museo-del-vino.it* 🍽 *€6* ⊙ *Closed Sun., Mon., and mid-Nov.–Mar.*

Bressanone (Brixen)

42 km (25 miles) northeast of Bolzano.

Bressanone is an important artistic center and was the seat of prince-bishops for centuries. Like their counterparts in Trento, these medieval administrators had the delicate task of serving two masters—the pope (the ultimate spiritual authority) and the Holy Roman Emperor (the civil and military power), who were virtually at war throughout the Middle Ages. Bressanone's prince-bishops became experts at tact and diplomacy.

The Brixen Card offers free transportation throughout Alto Adige (Südtirol/South Tyrol) and grants entry to more than 80 museums, plus free guided tours and discounts at partner venues; it's free to guests of local hotels.

GETTING HERE AND AROUND

Driving from Bolzano, follow the SS12 northeast 42 km (26 miles) to Bressanone. Trains run from Bolzano, as does SAD Bus No. 350.

VISITOR INFORMATION

CONTACT Bressanone Tourism Office.
✉ *Viale Ratisbona 9, Bressanone* ☎ *0472/275252* ⊕ *www.brixen.org.*

Sights

Abbazia di Novacella

CHURCH | This Augustinian abbey founded in 1142 has been producing wine for at least nine centuries and is most famous for the delicate stone-fruit character of its dry white Sylvaner. As you wander the delightful grounds, note the progression of Romanesque, Gothic, and Baroque building styles. Guided tours of the abbey, in various languages, depart daily, except Sunday. Guided tours of the vineyard are also available, in English, by reservation. ✉ *Via Abbazia 1, 3 km (2 miles) north of Bressanone, Varna* ☎ *0472/836189* ⊕ *www.abbazianovacella.it* ✉ *Abbey tour, €10; wine tastings with vineyard tour, €15* ⊙ *Closed Sun., and Mon. Jan.–Mar.*

Duomo

CHURCH | The imposing town cathedral was built in the 13th century but acquired a Baroque facade 500 years later; its 14th-century cloister is decorated with medieval frescoes. Guided tours are available from Easter to November 1 on Tuesday, Thursday, and Saturday at 10:30, as well as during the Christmas season on weekdays at 3, Saturday at 10:30 and 3, and Sunday at 2. ✉ *Piazza Duomo 1, Bressanone* ☎ *0472/834034* ✉ *Free.*

Museo Diocesano (*Diocesan Museum*)

ART MUSEUM | The Bishop's Palace houses an abundance of local medieval art, in particular Gothic wood carvings—statues and liturgical objects collected from the cathedral treasury. During the Christmas season, curators arrange the museum's large collection of antique Nativity scenes; look for the shepherds wearing Tyrolean hats. ✉ *Palazzo Vescovile 2, Bressanone* ☎ *0472/830505* ⊕ *www.hofburg.it* ✉ *€10 in summer, €8 in winter.*

Restaurants

Fink

$$ | NORTHERN ITALIAN | This warm, wood-paneled upstairs dining room is under the arcades of the pedestrians-only town center. In addition to hearty Tyrolean specialties, there's an affordable daily set menu, as well as homemade pastries. **Known for:** central location; local specialties; bustling atmosphere. ⑤ *Average main: €18* ✉ *Via Portici Minori 4, Bressanone* ☎ *0472/834883* ⊕ *www.restaurant-fink.it* ⊙ *Closed Wed.*

Hotels

★ Hotel Elephant

$$$ | HOTEL | At this cozy inn—over 450 years old and still one of the region's best—each room is unique, and many are filled with antiques and paintings. **Pros:** lovely ambience; lavish breakfast; good restaurants. **Cons:** rooms vary in size; Wi-Fi can be unreliable; some bathrooms are small. *$ Rooms from: €204 ⊠ Via Rio Bianco 4, Bressanone ☎ 0472/832750 ⊕ www.hotelelephant. com ➩ 44 rooms ⦿ Free Breakfast.*

Brunico (Bruneck)

33 km (20 miles) east of Bressanone, 65 km (40 miles) northwest of Cortina d'Ampezzo.

Located in the heart of the Val Pusteria, this quiet and quaint town is divided by the Rienza River. The modern part of Brunico is on one side of the river, and on the other is the medieval quarter, nestled below a 13th-century bishop's castle.

GETTING HERE AND AROUND

From Bressanone follow the E66 east for 30 km (19 miles) to Brunico. If driving from Cortina d'Ampezzo, take the SR48 over the Passo Falzarego and continue to the SP244 toward Brunico. There are bus (SAD) and train (Trenitalia) connections available at Bolzano.

VISITOR INFORMATION

CONTACT Brunico Tourism Office. ⊠ *Piazza Municipio 7, Brunico* ☎ *0474/555722* ⊕ *www.bruneck.com.*

Sights

★ Lumen Museum

ART MUSEUM | Take a cable car to the top of Kronplatz to reach this 19,375-square-foot museum dedicated to mountain photography (actually, you have your choice of eight different cable cars, two from the town of Brunico). Once inside, you'll find pictures from alpine photography's early days all the way to the present, taken by photographers from mountainous regions throughout the world and displayed across four floors. Lumen also houses AlpiNN, a casual restaurant from critically acclaimed chef Norbert Niederkofler of St. Hubertus fame. Note that the museum can be difficult to access in winter if you're not a skier; it's down a slight, rather terrifying incline from the top of the mountain. Be aware that the museum closes at 4 pm (last admission at 3:30), so that you won't miss the last cable car back down. ⊠ *Kronplatz–Plan de Corones Mountain Station, Brunico ⊕ Take a cable car up to Kronplatz* ☎ *0474/431090* ⊕ *www.lumenmuseum. it* ⊠ *€17* ⊗ *Closed mid-Apr.–May and mid-Oct.–Nov.*

Messner Mountain Museum Corones

OTHER MUSEUM | High atop the Mountain Station Kronplatz–Plan de Corones, almost 7,500 feet above Brunico, the newest museum from mountaineer Reinhold Messner displays climbing equipment and other alpine paraphernalia from the 1800s until now. It also examines all facets of mountaineering through painting, sculpture, and other media. Equally interesting is the museum's Zaha Hadid–designed concrete building: its sloped roof makes it seem like a miniature mountain, and its outdoor lookout point affords magnificent vistas. Note that the museum closes at 4 pm (last admission at 3:30), so that you won't miss the last cable car back down. ⊠ *Kronplatz–Plan de Corones Mountain Station, Brunico ⊕ Take a cable car up to Kronplatz* ☎ *0474/501350* ⊕ *www.messner-mountain-museum.it/en/corones/ museum* ⊠ *€10* ⊗ *Closed mid-Apr.–early June and mid-Oct.–late Nov.*

★ Messner Mountain Museum Ripa

OTHER MUSEUM | FAMILY | This fascinating, comprehensive museum within the 13th-century Bruneck Castle looks at the lives of mountain-dwelling people

om Europe, Asia, Africa, and South
America through artifacts, tools, statues,
paintings, living spaces, and more. Part
of the experience is reaching the castle
itself: it's a 15-minute hike up to it on a
path accessed just off Brunico's pedes-
rian area. ⊠ *Schlossweg 2, Brunico*
☏ 0474/410220 ⊕ www.messner-moun-
ain-museum.it/en/ripa/museum ⊠ €11
⊘ Closed Tues., late Apr.–mid-May, and
Nov.–early Dec.

outh Tyrolean Folklore Museum

MUSEUM VILLAGE | FAMILY | A re-crea-
on of a medieval rural village is built
round a 300-year-old mansion. The
wood-carving displays are especially
nteresting. ⊠ *Herzog-Diet-Str. 24, Bru-*
ico ☏ 0474/552087 ⊕ www.volkskun-
Nemuseum.it ⊠ €9 ⊘ Closed Mon. and
Nov.–mid-Apr.

Restaurants

Oberraut

$ | ITALIAN | Drive up into the hills about
2 minutes northeast of Brunico to reach
his charming chalet-style family-run
eatery, which has an expansive terrace with great views overlooking the
mountains. Hearty dishes use local
ngredients—including meat from their
arm, vegetables from their gardens and
greenhouses, and grain from their own
mill—and the delightful servers are happy
o recommend seasonal specialties.
Known for: zero-kilometer philosophy;
deer and beef dishes; alpine vistas. ⑤ *Av-*
erage main: €20 ⊠ *Via Ameto 1, Brunico*
☏ 0474/559977 ⊕ oberraut.it ⊘ Closed
Thurs.

Hotels

Das Majestic

$$$ | HOTEL | Right in front of the Plan de
Corones, this is a great base for a skiing
or hiking vacation, with bus service to the
ski slopes and a spa and pools on-site
to unwind after a big day out. **Pros:** nice
ndoor and outdoor pools; spacious

rooms; convenient for skiers and hikers.
Cons: far from town center; meal portions
are a little small; no covered parking.
⑤ *Rooms from: €282* ⊠ *Via Im Gelände*
20, Brunico ☏ 0474/410993 ⊕ www.
hotel-majestic.it ⇄ 60 rooms ⦿| *Free*
Breakfast ⊘ Closed Easter–May.

Misurina

115 km (71 miles) east of Bolzano.

Nestled on the shores of Lake Misurina, among the Dolomites, Misurina's
high altitude, low air humidity, and total
absence of dust mites and air pollution
has some saying that the "Pearl of the
Dolomites" has some of the purest air in
the world. The town itself is rather small,
but it's a perfect base to explore Lake
Misurina and the Tre Cime of Lavaredo. The surrounding mountains are rich in
history and artifacts from the First World
War and earlier conflicts. Along some
of the hikes and *vie ferrate* (mountain
paths with steel cables and fixed anchors
and ladders), you can explore caves and
trenches complete with informational
placards giving details about troop positions and fighting.

GETTING HERE AND AROUND

From Brunico, drive southeast on the
SS49/E66 to Dobbiaco. Turn right onto
SS51 and drive for 13 km (8 miles).
Turn left onto 48bis in the direction of
Auronzo. Arrive at Lago di Misurina in 6
km (4 miles).

VISITOR INFORMATION

CONTACT Misurina Tourism Office. ⊠ *Via*
Monte Piana 2, Misurina ☏ 0435/39016,
0435/99603 ⊕ www.auronzomisurina.it.

Sights

Tre Cime di Lavaredo

MOUNTAIN | FAMILY | Without a doubt, the
Three Peaks—Cima Piccola (9,373 feet),
Cima Grande (9,839 feet), and Cima
Ovest (9,753 feet)—are the symbol of

the Dolomite UNESCO World Heritage Site. From the town of Misurina, only two of the Tre Cime are visible. In order to get up close and personal, drive or take a bus along the dedicated toll road (open May through October; car parking €30). Once at the top, follow Footpath 101 from Rifugio Auronzo to Forcella Laveredo (easy) for about an hour. There are many other footpaths and vie ferrate which allow you to climb the cime and access the base. Rifugi offer hot meals without a reservation, as well as dorm-style lodging, which is best reserved in advance. ⊠ *Parco Naturale Tre Cime, Auronzo di Cadore* ☎ *0474/710310* ⊕ *www.tre-cime.info.*

 ## Restaurants

Malga Rin Bianco

$$$ | **NORTHERN ITALIAN** | **FAMILY** | For fresh, properly cooked regional food, this *malga* (Alpine hut) with great mountain views can't be beat—just make a reservation, especially in winter, when you must be transported over on a snowmobile by day and a shuttle at night (in summer, you can drive all the way). Salamis and cheeses are made on-site, and the bar serves both commercial and homemade grappas, many of which are brewed with local herbs. **Known for:** great views; mountain location; local food. ⑤ *Average main: €26* ⊠ *Via Monte Piana 35, Strada Tre Cime, Misurina* ☎ *0320/5699375, 0435/39048* ⊕ *www.rinbianco.com* ⊗ *Closed 1st 3 wks in Apr.*

Hotels

Chalet Lago Antorno

$$ | **B&B/INN** | **FAMILY** | Located in a quiet, panoramic spot, this chalet is ideal for exploring the mountains or simply relaxing amid the beauty of the Alps. **Pros:** typical decor and regional flavor; idyllic mountain setting; family-run. **Cons:** some rooms are small; away from town center; minimum night stays in peak season. ⑤ *Rooms from: €140*

⊠ *Località Lago Misurina, Misurina* ☎ *0320/9625700* ⊕ *www.lagoantorno. it* ⊗ *Closed Apr.–May and mid-Oct.–Nov* ➦ *10 rooms* ⑩ *Free Breakfast.*

The Grand Hotel Misurina

$$ | **HOTEL** | **FAMILY** | On the shores of beautiful Lake Misurina and just a few kilometers from renowned winter resort Cortina d'Ampezzo, this grand hotel has simply furnished rooms that range from standard fare to full apartments. **Pros:** located in town center; shuttle to ski areas; perfect for large groups. **Cons:** rooms have simple furnishings; dated decor; no Wi-Fi in rooms. ⑤ *Rooms from: €125* ⊠ *Via Monte Piana 21, Misurina* ☎ *0435/39191* ⊕ *www.grandhotelmisurina.com* ⊗ *Closed Nov. and Apr.* ➦ *125 rooms* ⑩ *Free Breakfast.*

 ## Activities

BIKING

Cycling enthusiasts flock to the Dolomites for the challenging mountain terrain, and much of the region is used by Olympic athletes to train. In addition, several important cycling races (such as the Giro di Italia) take place in this area. Some of the descents along gravelly roads set off a rush of adrenaline, while others follow paved roads and bike paths. The Auronzo-Misurina Cycle Track provides about 32 km (20 miles) of bicycle path between the two towns.

SKIING

Two major ski lifts service the area: the Col de Varda lift in Misurina, and the Monte Agudo lift in Auronzo di Cadore (about a 30-minute drive from Misurina), which takes you from Taiarezze (2,952 feet) to Rifugio Monte Agudo (5,160 feet). The views from Auronzo differ from Misurina in that all Tre Cime are visible. Restaurants and maps are available at the top.

The craggy peaks around Canazei are particularly stunning at sunset.

Col de Varda

SKIING & SNOWBOARDING | FAMILY | The major ski lift servicing the area from Misurina climbs to Col de Varda, with a summit of 6,909 feet. Rifugio Col de Varda, at the top, has a bar and restaurant, as well as rooms to rent. In the summer, the area is an excellent starting point for great hiking and biking excursions. At any time of the year, the views of Lake Misurina, Mt. Cristallo, the Sesto Dolomites, and the Cadini, Sorapiss, and Tofane massifs are breathtaking. ✉ *Misurina* ☎ *0435/39041* ⊕ *www.rifugiocoldevarda. it* ✉ *€11.50 round-trip.*

Monte Cristallo

SKIING & SNOWBOARDING | Some of the most impressive views (and steepest slopes) are on Monte Cristallo. ✉ *Misurina.*

Canazei

45 km (28 miles) southwest of Misurina.

Of the year-round resort towns in the Val di Fassa, Canazei is the most popular. The mountains around this small town are threaded with hiking trails and ski slopes, set amid large clutches of conifers.

GETTING HERE AND AROUND

Bus service from Bolzano and Bressanone (the nearest train stations) is infrequent, and schedules are often interrupted or canceled. By car from the A22 autostrada, take the Bolzano Nord exit onto the SS241. Cross the Passo Costalunga into the Val di Fassa. From the town of Vigo, follow signs for Canazei.

VISITOR INFORMATION

CONTACT Canazei Tourism Office. ✉ *Piazza Marconi 5, Canazei* ☎ *0462/609600* ⊕ *www.fassa.com.*

Ortisei (St. Ulrich)

28 km (17 miles) northwest of Canazei.

Ortisei (St. Ulrich), the jewel in the crown of Val Gardena's resorts, is a hub of activity in both summer and winter; there are hundreds of miles of hiking trails and accessible ski slopes. Ortisei has been a family-friendly mountain vacation destination since the 1930s. The most famous cable car in the area, the Alpe di Siusi, operates in summer and winter. As the largest village in the Val Gardena, Ortisei makes a picturesque and practical base for exploring much of the heart of the Dolomites.

For centuries Ortisei has also been famous for the expertise of its wood carvers, and there are still numerous workshops. Apart from making religious sculptures—particularly the wayside calvaries you come upon everywhere in the Dolomites—Ortisei's carvers were long known for producing wooden dolls, horses, and other toys. As itinerant peddlers, they traveled every spring on foot with their loaded packs as far as Paris, London, and St. Petersburg. Shops in town still sell woodcrafts.

GETTING HERE AND AROUND

By car from Bolzano, take the SS12 to the SS242 in the direction of Ortisei. From Canazei, follow the SS242 north to Ortisei. Bus service is available on the Val Gardena network from Bolzano and Bressanone.

VISITOR INFORMATION

CONTACT Ortisei Tourist Office. ⊠ *Via Rezia 1, Ortisei* ☎ *0471/777600, 0471/777777 Val Gardena* ⊕ *www.valgardena.it.*

Sights

Alpe di Siusi Cable Car

TRANSPORTATION | FAMILY | First opened in 1935, the cable car from Ortisei to Alpe di Siusi climbs more than 6,100 feet to the widest plateau in Europe. There are more than 57 square km (22 square miles) of Alpine pastures lined with summertime hiking trails. In the winter, 20 ski lifts and cross-country ski paths keep active visitors happy. There is a restaurant at the top of the Mt. Seuc ski lift, or you can pick up a map at the tourist office in Ortisei listing the mountain huts and restaurants that can be reached on foot. Opening days and times depend on the season and daily weather conditions; check the website or call ahead to avoid disappointment. ⊠ *Setil Str. 9, Ortisei* ☎ *0471/797897* ⊕ *www.alpedisiusi-seiseralm.com* ▭ *€20.90 round-trip.*

Museo della Val Gardena

ART MUSEUM | FAMILY | Fine historic and contemporary examples of local woodworking are on display here, as well as a retrospective on the life of local film director Luis Trenker. ⊠ *Via Rezia 83, Ortisei* ☎ *0471/797554* ⊕ *www.museumgherdeina.it* ☉ *Closed mid-Apr.–mid-May and mid-Oct.–mid-Dec.; closed Sat. and Sun. mid-May–mid-Oct.* ▭ *€8.*

Hotels

Cavallino Bianco Family Spa Grand Hotel

$$$$ | RESORT | FAMILY | With delicate wooden balconies and an eye-catching wooden gable, the pink Cavallino Bianco (Little White Horse) looks like a gigantic dollhouse, and it is, in fact, marketed toward families. **Pros:** excellent family facilities; laundry facilities; cheerful rooms. **Cons:** fixed arrival/departure dates in winter; some lower-level rooms face garage; in the busy town center. ⑤ *Rooms from: €584* ⊠ *Via Rezia 22,*

Ortisei ☎ 0471/783333 ⊕ www.cavalli-
no-bianco.com ⊗ Closed mid-Apr.–mid-
May ⇨ 104 rooms ⊖ All-Inclusive.

Hotel Garni Planaces

$ | B&B/INN | This clean and spacious
B&B is just a short walk from ski lifts
and the bus stop, and all guests have
access to the spa and pool areas. **Pros:**
well maintained; good value for the area;
very clean. **Cons:** simple furnishings;
fewer amenities than at higher-priced
hotels; rooms can feel small with ski
gear. ⑤ Rooms from: €140 ⊠ Via Rezia
212, Ortisei ☎ 0471/796159 ⊕ www.
garniplanaces.it ⊗ Closed Apr.–late Jun.
and mid-Oct.–early Dec. ⇨ 9 rooms, 4
apartments ⊖ Free Breakfast.

Hotel Grones

$$$$ | HOTEL | FAMILY | The attention to
detail at this family-run hotel, located just
a few minutes' walk from the ski slopes
or downtown, makes it a great base for a
mountain vacation. **Pros:** shuttle service
to ski stations; spa with nice indoor pool;
friendly staff. **Cons:** bed linens/bath towels could be higher quality; it's an uphill
walk from town; mandatory half board.
⑤ Rooms from: €318 ⊠ 110 Stufan St.,
Ortisei ☎ 0471/797040 ⊕ www.grones.
info/en ⇨ 25 rooms ⊖ Free Breakfast
⊗ Closed Apr.–May and early-Oct.–early
Dec.

 Activities

SKIING

With almost 600 km (370 miles) of
accessible downhill slopes and more
than 90 km (56 miles) of cross-country
skiing trails, Ortisei is one of the most
popular ski resorts in the Dolomites. Prices are good, and facilities are among the
most modern in the region. In warmer
weather, the slopes surrounding Ortisei
are a popular hiking destination, as well
as a playground for vehicular mountain
adventures like biking, rafting, and
paragliding.

Sella Ronda

SKIING & SNOWBOARDING | FAMILY | An
immensely popular ski route, the Sella
Ronda relies on well-placed chairlifts to
connect 26 km (16 miles) of downhill
skiing around the colossal Sella massif,
passing through several towns along the
way. You can ski the loop, which requires
intermediate ability and a full day's effort,
either clockwise or counterclockwise.
Going with a guide is recommended.
⊠ Ortisei ⊕ www.sella-ronda.info.

Corvara

*29 km (18 miles) east of Ortesei (St.
Ulrich).*

Corvara is the main town of the Alta
Badia, known for its prime skiing and
hiking location in the middle of the
Sella Ronda. The first chairlift in Italy
opened here in 1946, and today, there
are two cable cars—the Col Alto and the
Boè—along with 12 chairlifts, making
Corvara a convenient base for an active
holiday in winter or summer. Corvara is
also the start of the First World War Ski
Tour, a 49-mile route around Col di Lana
that takes you past wartime relics like
trenches and forts. The town itself is
pleasant and walkable, with a smattering
of restaurants, bars, and ski rental and
sporting goods stores.

GETTING HERE AND AROUND

To get to Corvara from Bolzano, take the
A22 north to Bressanone/Pusteral. Turn
right on the SS244, and take it all the
way to Corvara. From Ortisei, take the
SS242 to the SS243 into Corvara. Buses
arrive many times daily from Bolzano and
Bressanone.

VISITOR INFORMATION

CONTACTS Corvara Tourist Office. ⊠ Str.
Col Alt 36, Corvara ☎ 0471/836176
⊕ www.altabadia.org.

Sights

Boè Cable Car

TRANSPORTATION | FAMILY | This cable car takes hikers and skiers from Corvara up Piz Boè, the highest mountain of the Sella group, at 10,341 feet. Once at the first station, you can hike the Sella Ronda, ski back down, or ride a chairlift farther up to the Vallon Peak for more challenging skiing or hiking in the warmer months. Paragliding is also popular from the Vallon area. ⊠ *Strada Burjé* ☎ *0471/836266* ⊕ *www.moviment.it/en/boe-ski-lift-corvara.php* ⊠ *€17.70 round-trip.*

Col Alto Cable Car

TRANSPORTATION | FAMILY | The site of Italy's first chairlift in 1946 now has modern yellow eight-seater cable cars that ascend to a height of 6,562 feet. From there you have access to ski lifts that take you all over the Alta Badia region and, in summer, to trails that include a 6-mile route to the Rifugio Pralongià. You can rent skis and snowboards at the Ski Service Colalto, located at the bottom of the lift. ⊠ *Str. Col Alt 36, Corvara* ☎ *0471/830264* ⊕ *www.moviment.it/en/col-alt-ski-lift-corvara.php* ⊠ *€12.70 round-trip.*

🍴 Restaurants

La Stüa de Michil

$$$$ | ITALIAN | You'll feel like you're dining in a traditional Alto Adige hut at the Perla hotel's critically acclaimed restaurant, which features wood-beamed ceilings. Menu items are complex, modern takes on regional cuisine: even a simple veal dish might be served with almond foam and black truffle. **Known for:** daring ingredient combinations; romantic atmosphere; interesting wine pairings (not all Italian). ⑤ *Average main: €80* ⊠ *Strada Col Alt 105, San Cassiano* ☎ *0471/831000* ⊕ *www.laperlacorvara. it* ⊗ *Closed Sun., Apr.–late June, and late Sept.–early Dec.*

★ Ristorante Refugio Col Alt

$$ | ECLECTIC | From town, take the Col Alt cable car—or a snowcat (by reservation only) for dinner on Wednesday and Friday—to this surprisingly modern restaurant with amazing panoramas from 6,562 feet. The wide-ranging menu features everything from salads to hearty fried potatoes, eggs, and bacon (perfect after a morning of skiing), and the interesting wine list is heavy on natural producers, since the affable owner is a fan and often has local winemakers in for tastings. **Known for:** memorable wines at affordable prices; unbeatable vistas; an enormous terrace. ⑤ *Average main: €22* ⊠ *Monte Cabinovia, Strada Col Alt 1, Corvara* ⊹ *Take the Col Alt cable car* ☎ *0471/836324* ⊕ *rifugiocolalt. it* ⊗ *Closed mid-Apr.–late June and late Sept.–early Dec.*

★ St. Hubertus

$$$$ | MODERN ITALIAN | In a laid-back, welcoming setting at the Rosa Alpina hotel, chef Norbert Niederkofler oversees one of the Alto Adige's most highly regarded restaurants, where seasonal products sourced exclusively from the region are transformed into delicacies on an 11-course tasting menu. Servers thoroughly explain the provenance of the seemingly simple yet multilayered dishes, which can be paired with wines from all over the world, though there's a slant toward small local producers. **Known for:** zero-waste philosophy, all parts of ingredients are used; hyperlocal cuisine; bold use of fermentation. ⑤ *Average main: €280* ⊠ *Hotel & Spa Rosa Alpina, Strada Micurá de Rü 20, 7.5 km (4.5 miles) east of Corvara, San Cassiano* ☎ *0471/849500* ⊕ *www.st-hubertus.it* ⊗ *Closed Mon., Tues., early Oct.–early Dec., and Apr.– early June. No dinner Sun. late June.– early Sept. in the Piz Sorega mountain hut.*

🛏 Hotels

iasa Salares

$ | HOTEL | FAMILY | This refined, ameni-
es-filled hotel has a distinctly Germanic
ibe and lots of mountain atmosphere—
rom its outdoor hot tub and sauna to
s simple guest rooms, with light-wood
aneling, white accents, and balconies,
o its underground fondue room–wine
ellar (24,000 bottles with a focus on
iodynamic producers). **Pros:** a number of
op-notch dining choices; more afforda-
le than comparable hotels; lovely spa.
Cons: some rooms feel a bit cramped;
ervice can be standoffish; not ski-in,
ki-out. **$** *Rooms from: €194* ✉ *Strada
Prè de Vì 31, Località Armentarola, 10 km
(6 miles) east of Corvara, San Cassiano*
☎ *0471/849445* ⊕ *www.ciasasalares.
it* ⊗ *Closed Apr.–mid-June* ➡ *50 rooms*
⊙∣ *Free Breakfast.*

★ Hotel & Spa Rosa Alpina

$$$ | HOTEL | FAMILY | The Rosa Alpina
offers everything you need for a relaxed
mountain stay: chic yet homey Alpine
decor, guest rooms with working fireplaces and balconies, a spa, both family and
adults-only pools, and the St. Hubertus
restaurant, one of the region's most
renowned. **Pros:** private cinema; bountiful
breakfast selection; perfect blend of
refinement and mountain flavor. **Cons:**
can hear noise in rooms from outside and
within hotel; overnight guests not guaranteed St. Hubertus reservations; no A/C.
$ *Rooms from: €595* ✉ *Strada Micurà de
Rü 20, San Cassiano* ✛ *7.5 km (4.5 miles)
east of Corvara* ☎ *0471/849500* ⊕ *www.
rosalpina.it* ⊗ *Closed early Oct.–early
Dec. and Apr.–early June* ➡ *52 rooms*
⊙∣ *Free Breakfast.*

★ La Perla

$$$$ | HOTEL | Best described as "Alpine
country chic," this luxe yet rustic fami-
y-run hotel has spacious wood-latticed
rooms with mountain-view balconies,
a spa, lots of cozy sitting areas, and a
much-lauded restaurant. **Pros:** extremely

friendly service; ski-in, ski-out; convenient location next to both the mountains
and town. **Cons:** expensive drinks; no
mini-bar in rooms; Wi-Fi can be iffy at
times. **$** *Rooms from: €420* ✉ *Strada Col
Alt 105, Corvara* ☎ *0471/831000* ⊕ *www.
laperlacorvara.it* ⊗ *Closed Apr.–mid-June
and late Sept.–early Dec.* ➡ *50 rooms*
⊙∣ *All-Inclusive.*

🏃 Activities

HIKING

Corvara offers hikes for all levels, including the popular Col Alt Pralongià hike—an
easy, level hike that passes through pasture lands—as well as a number of walks
in the Puez-Odle nature reserve. Hikers
looking for more challenging, steeper
routes should start at the top of the Boè
cable car.

SKIING

Alta Badia

SKIING & SNOWBOARDING | The Alta Badia
ski area, which includes 53 ski lifts and
130 km (80 miles) of slopes, is cheaper
and more Austrian in character than the
more famous ski destinations in this
region. Groomed trails for cross-country
skiing (usually loops marked off by the
kilometer) accommodate differing degrees
of ability. Inquire at the local tourist office.
✉ *Corvara* ☎ *0471/836176 Corvara tourism office* ⊕ *www.altabadia.org.*

Cortina d'Ampezzo

38 km (24 miles) east of Corvara.

The archetypal Dolomite resort, Cortina
d'Ampezzo entices those seeking both
relaxation and adventure. The town is the
western gateway to the Strade Grande
delle Dolomiti and actually crowns the
northern Veneto region and an area
known as Cadore in the northernmost
part of the province of Belluno. Like Alto
Adige to the west, Cadore (birthplace of
the Venetian Renaissance painter Titian)

was on the Alpine front during World War
I, and was the scene of many battles that
have been commemorated in refuges
and museums. Although its appeal to
younger Italians has been eclipsed by the
steeper, sleeker Madonna di Campiglio,
Cortina remains, for many, Italy's most
idyllic incarnation of an Alpine ski town.

GETTING HERE AND AROUND

To drive to Cortina d'Ampezzo from Trento
or Bolzano, take the A22 autostrada north
to Bressanone/Pustertal. Turn right on
the SS49/E66, then right on to the SS51
and follow it into Cortina. The Dolomiti
Bus provides service to and from Cortina,
but it's not very convenient or reliable.
The town itself is pedestrian friendly and
has local bus service to area ski slopes.
Beware of taxis, as the rates are very
high—and the fare may begin from the
taxi's point of origin, not necessarily
where you get in the vehicle.

CONTACT Cortina d'Ampezzo Tourism Office.
✉ *Corso Italia 81, Cortina d'Ampezzo*
📞 *0436/869086* ⊕ *www.dolomiti.org/en/
cortina.*

👁 Sights

Surrounded by mountains and dense
forests, the "Queen of the Dolomites" is
in a lush meadow 4,000 feet above sea
level. The town hugs the slopes beside
a fast-moving stream, and a public park
extends along one bank. Higher in the
valley, luxury hotels and the villas of the
rich are identifiable by their attempts to
hide behind stands of firs and spruces.
The bustling center of Cortina d'Ampezzo has little nostalgia, despite its alpine
appearance, with its tone set by shops
and cafés as chic as their well-dressed
patrons. Unlike neighboring resorts that
have a strong Germanic flavor, Cortina
d'Ampezzo is unapologetically Italian and
distinctly fashionable.

🍴 Restaurants

La Tavernetta

$$ | **NORTHERN ITALIAN** | These Tirole-
an-style wood-paneled dining rooms near
the Olympic ice-skating rink are a Cortina
institution. Join the local clientele in
sampling terrific pizza along with house
specialties such as pasta with pork,
radicchio, and ricotta, and ravioli with
beetroot. **Known for:** house-made des-
serts; typical dishes; nice wine selection.
Ⓢ *Average main: €15* ✉ *Via Castello 53,
Cortina d'Ampezzo* 📞 *0436/868102.*

Ristorante Lago Pianozes

$$$ | **NORTHERN ITALIAN** | The owner of this
small, endearing establishment—just
outside Cortina and beside picturesque
Lago Pianozes—is friendly and knowledgeable, not only about the food and
wine but also about the region. The
menu varies according to the seasons,
always incorporating local recipes. **Known
for:** friendly staff; delightful location; local
dishes. Ⓢ *Average main: €28* ✉ *Campo
di Sotto Pianozes 1, Cortina d'Ampezzo*
📞 *0436/5601* ⊗ *Closed Tues.*

🛏 Hotels

Corona

$$$ | **HOTEL** | Modern art adorns the small
but comfortable pine-paneled rooms at
this inviting lodge, once owned by noted
ski instructor Luciano Rimoldi; ski slopes
and the town center are a 10-minute walk
away. **Pros:** friendly staff; ski shuttle stops
out front; quiet location. **Cons:** outside the
town center; dated decor; small rooms.
Ⓢ *Rooms from: €233* ✉ *Via Val di Sotto
12, Cortina d'Ampezzo* 📞 *0436/3251*
🍴 *Free Breakfast* ⊗ *Closed Apr.–May
and mid-Sept.–Nov.* ⊐ *44 rooms.*

★ Cristallo, a Luxury Collection Resort & Spa

$$$$ | RESORT | This luxury grande dame, now run by Marriott, is lauded for its service, spa, and more—the architecture was immortalized in 1963's *The Pink Panther*. **Pros:** stellar food and service; wonderful atmosphere; great spa. **Cons:** not in town; not accessible for all budgets; high parking fee. *⑤ Rooms from: €718 ⊠ Via R. Menardi 42, Cortina d'Ampezzo ☎ 0436/881111 ⊕ www.cristallo.it ⬎ 74 rooms ⑩ Free Breakfast ☉ Closed Nov. and Apr.–June.*

De la Poste

$$ | HOTEL | Loyal skiers return year after year to this old-school mountain retreat, where each unique room has antiques in characteristic Dolomite style (almost all have wooden balconies) and the main terrace bar is one of Cortina's social centers. **Pros:** professional service; lively atmosphere; charging stations for electric cars. **Cons:** street noise can be an issue; dated furnishings; a bit stuffy. *⑤ Rooms from: €130 ⊠ Piazza Roma 14, Cortina d'Ampezzo ☎ 0436/4271 ⊕ www.delaposte.it ☉ Closed Apr.–May and mid-Oct.–early Dec. ⬎ 72 rooms ⑩ Free Breakfast.*

Miramonti Majestic

$$$ | RESORT | A touch of luxurious formality rather than rustic charm comes through in the imperial Austrian design of this century-old landmark tucked into a magnificent mountain valley. **Pros:** magnificent location; great pool and spa; loads of old-world charm in lounges and guest rooms alike. **Cons:** shows a few signs of wear; Wi-Fi can be iffy; about 1 km (½ mile) outside town center. *⑤ Rooms from: €286 ⊠ Località Peziè 103, Cortina d'Ampezzo ☎ 0436/4201 ⊕ www.miramontimajestic.it ☉ Closed Apr.–June and Sept.–mid-Dec. ⬎ 122 rooms ⑩ Free Breakfast.*

⚐ Activities

HIKING AND CLIMBING

Cortina has more than 400 km (249 mi) of hiking routes, ranging from forests to alpine lakes, including the popular Lake Sorapis, famous for its amazing blue colors. Hiking information is available from the excellent local tourism office.

Gruppo Guide Alpine Cortina Scuola di Alpinismo (*Mountaineering School*)

HIKING & WALKING | This group organizes climbing trips and trekking adventures. *⊠ Corso Italia 69/a, Cortina d'Ampezzo ☎ 0436/868505 ⊕ www.guidecortina. com.*

SKIING

Cortina's long and picturesque ski runs will delight intermediates, but advanced skiers may pine for steeper terrain, which can be found only off-piste. Efficient ski-bus service connects the town with the high-speed chairlifts and gondolas that ascend in all directions from the valley.

Dolomiti Superski Pass

SKIING & SNOWBOARDING | FAMILY | The Dolomiti Superski Pass provides access to the surrounding Dolomites, with 450 lifts and gondolas serving 1,200 km (750 miles) of trails. There's also a Dolomiti Supersummer Pass, good from mid-May to early November. Buy the passes at the ticket office next to the bus station and at other outlets in the Dolomites. *⊠ Via Marconi 15, Cortina d'Ampezzo ☎ 0471/795397 ⊕ www.dolomitisuperski. com ⬛ Superski: €56–€62 for one day, lower rates for longer durations. Supersummer: €47 for one day.*

Faloria Gondola

SKIING & SNOWBOARDING | FAMILY | The Faloria gondola runs from the center of town. From its top you can get up to most of the central mountains. *⊠ Via Ria de Zeta 10, Cortina d'Ampezzo ☎ 0436/5889 ⊕ www.cortinacube.it ⬛ €22.50–€23.50 round-trip.*

Passo Falzarego

SKIING & SNOWBOARDING | The topography of the Passo Falzarego ski area, 16 km (10 miles) east of town, is dramatic. From here, a cable car takes you to one of the highest points in the Dolomites (Rifugio Lagazuoi)—where, on a clear day, you'll experience some of the best views. It's also easy to see why this was such a deadly area for soldiers in the Great War. Hiking is uneven in places, and there are vie ferrate that require the use of helmets and flashlights; other paths lead to tunnels that don't require helmets. ✉ *Cortina d'Ampezzo* ☎ *0436/867301* ⊕ *www.lagazuoi.it* 🎫 *€18.50–€19.50 round-trip.*

Chapter 8

MILAN, LOMBARDY, AND THE LAKES

Updated by
Elizabeth Shemaria

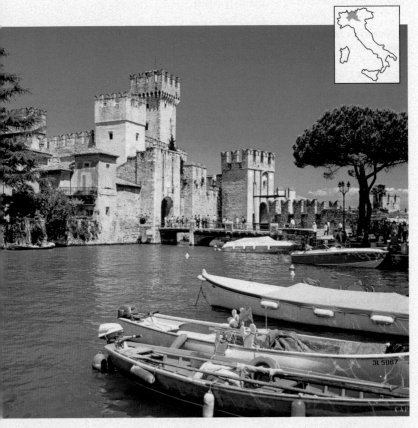

👁 Sights	🍴 Restaurants	🛏 Hotels	🛍 Shopping	🍸 Nightlife
★★★★☆	★★★★☆	★★★★☆	★★★★★	★★★☆☆

WELCOME TO MILAN, LOMBARDY, AND THE LAKES

TOP REASONS TO GO

★ **Lake Como, one of the most beautiful lakes in the world:** Ferries crisscross the waters, taking you from picture-book villages to stately villas to Edenic gardens—all against the backdrop of the snowcapped Alps.

★ **Leonardo's *The Last Supper*:** Behold one of the world's most famous works of art for yourself.

★ **The sky's no limit:** A funicular ride in Bergamo whisks you up to the magnificent medieval city.

★ **Milan alla moda:** As you window-shop the afternoon away in Milan's Quadrilatero shopping district, catch a glimpse of fashion's latest trends.

★ **A night at La Scala:** What the Louvre is to art, Milan's La Scala is to the world of opera.

★ **Lake Garda and Lake Maggiore:** The former is great for outdoors enthusiasts; the latter has plentiful islands to explore.

★ **Cremona's violins:** If you are in the market for a violin, you'll find the world's best here in more than 150 shops.

1 Milan. The international fashion capital.

2 Bergamo. A charming medieval quarter.

3 Pavia. See the 15th-century monastery.

4 Cremona. The birthplace of the violin.

5 Mantua. The Palazzo Ducale is a must.

6 Lake Iseo and Franciacorta. Lovely views and quaint restaurants.

7 Sirmione. A bustling spa town.

8 Malcesine. A favorite of sailors and hikers.

9 Riva del Garda. Stroll, sunbathe, or windsurf.

10 Gargnano. Don't miss the pleasant beach.

11 Gardone Riviera. A lovely town set against the Alps.

12 Bellagio. The belle of Lake Como.

13 Tremezzo. Explore two 18th-century villas.

14 Cernobbio. Villa d'Este hotel commands pride of place.

15 Como. A former silk town, with an urban vibe.

16 Stresa and the Isole Borromee. Grand hotels abound here.

17 Verbania. Gorgeous gardens and villas.

8

SWITZERLAND

Chiavenna

36

A L P S

Sondrio

Edolo

38

Morbegno

Lake
Como

340

Bellagio

12

TRENTINO-
ALTO ADIGE

42

Darfo-Boario

Riva del
Garda

36

LOMBARDY

9

bbio

Lecco

Malcesine

39

42

8

342

Bergamo

Lago
d'Iseo

Gargnano

10

2

6

za

A4

A4

510

Gardone Riviera

11

11

Brescia

Lago
Garda

235

Milan

11

7

Sirmione

415

Crema

VENETO

Melegnano

A21

236

A1

Lodi

River

9

River

Mantua

5

via

4

10

Po

Cremona

21

Po

EMILIA-
ROMAGNA

0   20 mi

0   20 km

EATING WELL IN MILAN, LOMBARDY, AND THE LAKES

Lombardy may well offer Italy's most varied, rich, and refined cuisine. Local cooking is influenced by the neighboring regions of the north; foreign conquerors have left their mark; and today, business visitors, industrious immigrants, and well-traveled Milanese are likely to find more authentic ethnic cuisine in Milan than in any other Italian city.

Milan runs counter to many established Italian dining customs. A "real" traditional Milanese meal is a rarity; instead, Milan offers a variety of tastes, prices, and opportunities, from expense-account elegance in fancy restaurants to abundant *aperitivo*-hour nibbles. The city's cosmopolitan nature means trends arrive here first, and things move fast. Meals are not the drawn-out pastime they tend to be elsewhere in Italy. But the food is still consistently good: competition among restaurants is fierce and the local clientele is demanding, which means you can be reasonably certain that if a place looks promising, it won't disappoint.

THE COTOLETTA QUESTION

Everyone has an opinion on *cotoletta*, the breaded veal cutlet known across Italy as *una Milanese*. It's clearly related to Austria's Wiener schnitzel, but did the Austrians introduce it when they seized Milan, or did they take it home when they left? Some think it's best with fresh tomato and arugula on top; others find this sacrilege. Two things unite all camps: the meat must be well beaten until it's thin, and it must never leave a grease spot after it's fried.

REGIONAL SPECIALTIES

Ask an Italian what Lombards eat, and you're likely to hear *cotoletta*, *càsoeûla*, and *risotto giallo*—all dishes that reinforce Lombardy's status as the crossroads of Italy. *Cotoletta alla Milanese* may very well have Austrian roots. *Càsoeûla* is a cabbage-and-pork stew that resembles French cassoulet, though some say it has Spanish origins. *Risotto giallo* (also known as *risotto Milanese*) is colorful and perfumed with exotic saffron.

BUTTER AND CHEESE

Geography and a strong agricultural tradition mean that animal products are more common here than in southern Italy; butter and cream, for example, take the place of olive oil. One rare point of agreement about *cotoletta* is that it's cooked in butter, and the first and last steps of risotto making—toasting the rice, then letting it "repose" before serving—use ample amounts of butter. And the second-most-famous name in Italian cheese (after Parmesan) is likely Gorgonzola, named for a town near Milan; the best now comes from Novara.

RISOTTO

Rice is Lombardy's answer to pasta, and the region is the center of Italian (and European) rice production. From

Milan's risotto giallo with its saffron tint, to Mantua's risotto with pumpkin or sausage, there's no end to the variety. Canonical risotto should be *all'onda,* flowing off the spoon like a wave. In keeping with the Italian tradition of wasting nothing, yesterday's risotto is flattened in a pan and fried in butter to produce *riso al salto,* which at its best has a crispy crust and a tender middle.

PANETTONE

Panettone, a tall, fluffy yeast bread, is flavored with sweet candied fruit. Invented in Milan, it graces nearly every table during the Christmas holiday. Consumption begins on December 7, Milan's patron saint's day, and goes until supplies run out at January's end.

WINE

The Franciacorta region around Brescia makes highly regarded sparkling wines, often called the "Champagne of Italy" since they're produced using the same labor-intensive method. The Valtellina area to the northeast of Milan produces two notable reds from the *nebbiolo* grape: Valtellina Superiore and the intense dessert wine Sforzato di Valtellina. Lake breezes yield crisp, smooth whites from the shores of Lake Garda.

Lombardy is one of Italy's most dynamic regions, offering everything from world-class ski slopes to summer lake resorts, and Milan is the pulse of the nation—commercial, fashionable, and forward-looking. The Renaissance cities of the Po Plain—Pavia, Cremona, and Mantua—offer the romantic Italy visitors dream about, embracing their past by preserving national treasures while keeping an eye on the present.

Topping any list of the region's attractions are the glacial lakes at the very feet of the Alps, praised as the closest thing to paradise by writers throughout the ages, from Virgil to Hemingway.

Millions of travelers have concurred: for sheer beauty, the lakes of northern Italy—Como, Maggiore, Garda, Iseo, and Orta—have few equals. Along their shores are 18th- and 19th-century villas, exotic formal gardens, sleepy villages, and dozens of Belle Époque–era resorts that were once Europe's most fashionable and that still retain a powerful allure.

Milan can be disappointingly modern and congested—a little too much like the place you've come to Italy to escape—but its historic buildings and art collections in many ways rival those of Florence and Rome. And if you love to shop, Milan is one of the world's great fashion centers, offering experiences and goods for every taste, from Corso Buenos Aires, which has a higher ratio of stores per square foot than anywhere else in Europe, to the edgy street-style of Corso di Porta Ticinese and upscale Via Montenapoleone, where there's no limit on what you can spend. Milan is home to global fashion giants such as Armani, Prada, Versace, Salvatore Ferragamo, and Ermenegildo Zegna; behind them stand a host of less famous designers who help fill all those fabulous shops.

MAJOR REGIONS

Milan. Long the country's capital of commerce, finance, fashion, and media, Milan is also Italy's transport hub, with the biggest international airport, the most rail connections, and the best subway system.

The Po Plain, Lake Garda, and Lake Iseo. Italy's wealthiest, most populous region is home not only to Milan, but also to nearby medieval towns that once rivaled Milan in power. Bergamo, set against the Bergamese Alps, is a modern town connected by funicular to its lovely ancient counterpart. Pavia is celebrated for its extraordinarily detailed Carthusian

monastery, and Cremona for its incomparable violin-making tradition. Picturesque
Mantua was the home of the fantastically
wealthy Gonzaga dynasty for almost 300
years.

An hour's drive from Milan, sleepy Lake
Iseo merits a stop for waterfront eateries
amid picture-postcard settings. It's also
on the northern edge of the Franciacorta
region, home to production of Italy's
up-and-coming sparkling wine.

Lake Garda is the region's biggest and,
by most accounts, cleanest lake. The
terrain is flat at its southern base—home
to the enchanting former Roman resort
town of Sirmione—and mountainous
at its northern tip, where dramatic Riva
del Garda sits. Places of note include
summer resort Malcesine, port town
Gargnano (known for its association
with Mussolini), and quaint 19th-century
Gardone Riviera.

Lakes Como and Maggiore. Palatial villas,
rose-laden belvederes, and majestic
Alpine vistas are among the treasures
of Lake Como—Europe's deepest lake.
Many travelers head directly to boats
for Bellagio and the *centro di lago,* the
beautiful center region of the lake's
three branches. Seasonal car ferries and
vaporetti also make it easy to reach the
towns of Cernobbio and Tremezzo. Don't
bypass the walled city of Como, which
has a medieval town center and pretty
lakefront. Magnificently scenic Lake
Maggiore has a unique geographical
position: its mountainous western shore
is in Piedmont, its lower eastern shore
is in Lombardy, and its northern tip is
in Switzerland. The better-known resort
towns, Stresa and Verbania, are on its
western shore, with access to the lake's
Borromean Islands.

Planning

Making the Most of Your Time

Italy's commercial hub isn't usually at
the top of the list for visiting tourists, but
Milan is the nation's most modern city,
with its own sophisticated appeal: its
fashionable shops rival those of New York
and Paris, its soccer teams are Italy's
answer to the Yankees and the Mets, its
opera performances set the standard for
the world, and its art treasures are well
worth the visit.

The biggest draw in the region, though,
is the Lake District. Throughout history, the magnificently beautiful lakes of
Como, Garda, Maggiore, Iseo, and Orta
have attracted their fair share of well-
known faces—from Winston Churchill
and Russian royalty to George Clooney
and Madonna. Each lake town has its
own history and distinct character. If
you have limited time, visit the lake you
think best suits your style, but if you have
time to spare, make the rounds to two or
three to get a sense of their contrasts.

Getting Here and Around

AIR
The region's main international gateway
airport is Aeroporto Malpensa (www.
milanomalpensa-airport.com), 48 km (30
miles) northwest of Milan. Some international and domestic flights also fly into
more central Aeroporto Linate (www.
milanolinate-airport.com), 7 km (4 miles)
east of Milan, while European low-cost
carriers like Ryanair use Aeroporto Milano
Bergamo Orio al Serio (www.milanberga-
moairport.it), 55 km (34 miles) northeast
of Milan and 5 km (3 miles) south of
Bergamo.

BOAT

Frequent daily ferry and hydrofoil services link the lakeside towns and villages. Residents take them to get to work and school, while visitors use them for exploring the area. There are also special round-trip excursions, some with (optional) dining service on board.

BOAT CONTACT Navigazione Laghi.
☎ *800/551801 within Italy* ⊕ *www.navigazionelaghi.it.*

BUS

Bus service isn't the best way to travel between cities here because trains are faster, cheaper, and more convenient. There's regular bus service for reaching and traveling between the small towns on the lakes. It's less convenient than going by boat or by car, and it's used primarily by locals (particularly school-children), but sightseers can use it as well. The bus service around Lake Garda serves mostly towns on the western shore.

BUS CONTACTS Arriva Italia.
☎ *035/289000 Bergamo, 02/070166 Cremona, 031/8412 1000 Como* ⊕ *www.arriva.it.* **Autostradale.** ☎ *02/30089000* ⊕ *www.autostradale.it.*

CAR

Getting almost anywhere by car is a snap, as several major highways intersect at Milan, all connected by the *tangenziale,* the city's ring road. The A4 autostrada runs west to Turin and east to Venice; the A1 leads south to Bologna, Florence, and Rome; the A7 angles southwest down to Genoa. The A8 goes northwest toward Lake Maggiore, and the A9 runs north past Lake Como and into Switzerland's southernmost tip.

To get around the lakes themselves by car, you have to follow secondary roads. The SP572 follows the southern and western shores of Lake Garda, the SS45bis edges the northernmost section of the western shore, and the SR249 runs along the eastern shore. Around Lake Como, follow the SS340 along the western shore, the SS36 on the eastern shore, and the SP583 on the lower arms. The SS33 and SS34 trace the western shore of Lake Maggiore. The SP469 runs on the western side of Lake Iseo, while the SP510 borders the east. Although the roads around the lakes can be beautiful, they're full of harrowing twists and turns, making for a slow, challenging drive—often with an Italian speed racer on your tail.

CAR CONTACT ACI (Automobile Club d'Italia). ☎ *803/116* ⊕ *www.aci.it.*

TRAIN

Milan's majestic Central Station (Milano Centrale), 3 km (2 miles) northwest of the Duomo, has frequent service within the region to Como, Bergamo, Brescia, Sirmione, Pavia, Cremona, and Mantua. There are plenty of signs to help you get around, but its sheer size requires considerable amounts of walking and patience, so allow for some extra time here.

Tickets bought without a reservation need to be validated by stamping them in yellow machines on the train platforms. Tickets with reservations don't require validation. When in doubt, validate—it can't hurt. For general information on trains and schedules, as well as online ticket purchases, visit the website of the Italian national railway, **Ferrovie dello Stato (FS)**.

Restaurants

You'll find lots of traditional northern Italian restaurants in this region, and can pretty much count on menus divided into pasta, fish, and meat options. As in the rest of Italy, it's common for dishes to feature seasonal and local ingredients. Meal prices in Milan tend to be higher than in the rest of the region (and quite high for European cities in general), though this is also where you'll see examples of the latest food trends and more adventurous choices on the menus.

Restaurant reviews have been shortened. For full information, visit Fodors.com.

Hotels

Given that this is the wealthiest part of Italy, most hotels here cater to a clientele willing to pay for extra comfort. Outside Milan, many are converted villas with well-landscaped grounds. Most of the famous lake resorts are expensive; many smaller lakeside hotels are more reasonably priced. Local tourism offices throughout the region are an excellent source of information about affordable lodging.

Please note that the time for "high season" can vary here—in the lakes it's the height of summer, not surprisingly, but in Milan it depends on what fairs and exhibitions are being staged. Prices in almost all hotels can go up dramatically during Salone, the furniture and design fair in early April. Fashion, travel, and tech fairs also draw big crowds throughout the year, raising prices. In contrast to other cities in Italy, however, you can often find discounts on weekends. The lakes, including Maggiore and Garda have little to offer except quiet from November to March, when most gardens, hotels, and restaurants are closed.

Hotel reviews have been shortened. For full information, visit Fodors.com.

WHAT IT COSTS in Euros

$	$$	$$$	$$$$
RESTAURANTS			
under €15	€15–€24	€25–€35	over €35
HOTELS			
under €125	€125–€200	€201–€300	over €300

Milan

Rome may be bigger and wield political power, but Milan and the affluent north are what really make the country go. Leonardo da Vinci's *The Last Supper* and other great works of art are here, as well as a spectacular Gothic Duomo, the finest of its kind. Milan even reigns supreme where it really counts (in the minds of many Italians), routinely trouncing the rest of the nation with its two premier soccer teams.

And yet, Milan hasn't won the battle for hearts and minds when it comes to tourism. Most visitors prefer Tuscany's hills and Venice's canals to Milan's hectic efficiency and wealthy indifference, and it's no surprise that in a country of medieval hilltop villages and skilled artisans, a city of grand boulevards and global corporations leaves visitors asking the real Italy to please stand up. They're right, of course: Milan is more European than Italian, a new buckle on an old boot, and although its old city can stand cobblestone to cobblestone against the best of them, seekers of Roman ruins and fairy-tale towns may pass. But Milan's secrets reveal themselves slowly to those who look. A side street conceals a garden complete with flamingos (Giardini Invernizzi, on Via dei Cappuccini, just off Corso Venezia; closed to the public, but you can still catch a glimpse), and a renowned 20th-century-art collection hides modestly behind an unspectacular facade a block from Corso Buenos Aires (the Casa-Museo Boschi di Stefano). Visitors tempted by world-class shopping will appreciate Milan's European sophistication while discovering unexpected facets of a country they may have only thought they knew.

Virtually every invader in European history—Gaul, Roman, Goth, Lombard, and Frank—as well as a long series of rulers from France, Spain, and Austria, took a turn at ruling the city. After being completely sacked by the Goths in AD 539 and by the Holy Roman Empire under Frederick Barbarossa in 1157, Milan became one of the first independent city-states of the Renaissance. Its heyday of self-rule proved comparatively brief. From 1277 until 1500 it was ruled first by the Visconti and then the Sforza dynasties. These families were known, justly or not, for a peculiarly aristocratic mixture of refinement, classical learning, and cruelty; much of the surviving grandeur of Gothic and Renaissance art and architecture is their doing. Be on the lookout in your wanderings for the Visconti family emblem—a viper, its jaws straining wide, devouring a child.

GETTING HERE AND AROUND
BICYCLE

The city center is compact and walkable; trolleys and trams make it even more accessible, and the efficient Metropolitana (subway) and buses provide access to locations farther afield. Driving in Milan is difficult and parking a real pain, so a car is a liability. In addition, drivers within the second ring of streets (the *bastioni*) must pay a daily congestion charge on weekdays between 7:30 am and 7:30 pm (until 6 pm on Thursday). You can pay the charge at news vendors, tobacconists, Banca Intesa Sanpaolo ATMs, or online at areac.atm-mi.it/Areac/iweb/Acquisto. aspx; parking meters and parking garages in the area also include it in the cost. There is also a public bike sharing system called BikeMi.

CONTACT BikeMi. ☎ *02/48607607* ⊕ *www.bikemi.com.*

PUBLIC TRANSPORTATION

A standard public transit ticket within the central zones of Milan costs €2 and is valid for a 90-minute trip on a subway, bus, or tram. An all-inclusive subway, bus, and tram pass costs €7 for 24 hours or €12 for 48 hours. Another option is a Carnet (€18), good for 10 tram, bus, or subway rides. Individual tickets and passes can be purchased from news vendors, tobacconists, at ticket machines at all subway stops, at ticket offices at the Duomo and other subway stops, and on your phone via the ATM Milano app. You can also pay for the subway using a contactless card at the turnstile.

Once you have your ticket, either stamp it or insert it into the slots in station turnstiles or on poles inside trolleys and buses. (Electronic tickets won't function if they become bent or demagnetized. If you have a problem, contact a station manager, who can usually issue a new ticket.) Trains run from 6 am to 12:30 am.

CONTACTS ATM. (*Azienda Trasporti Milanesi*) ☎ *02/48607607* ⊕ *www.atm. it/en.* **Radiobus.** ☎ *02/48034803* ⊕ *www. atm.it/en.*

TAXI

Taxi fares in Milan are higher than in American cities; a short ride can run about €15 during rush hour or fashion week. You can get a taxi at a stand with an orange "Taxi" sign, or by calling one of the taxi companies. Most also have apps you can download to order taxis from your phone; some let you text or use WhatsApp to hail a cab. Dispatchers may speak some English; they'll ask for the phone number you're calling from, and they'll tell you the number of your taxi and how long it'll take to arrive. If you're in a restaurant or bar, ask the staff to call a cab for you.

CONTACTS 026969. ☎ *02/6969* ⊕ *www.026969.it.* **Autoradiotaxi.** ☎ *02/8585* ⊕ *www.028585.it.* **Radio Taxi Freccia.** ☎ *02/4000* ⊕ *www.024000.it.* **Taxiblu.** ☎ *02/4040* ⊕ *www.taxiblu.it.*

TOURS

CONTACT City Sightseeing Milano. ☎ *02/867131* ⊕ *www.city-sightseeing.it/ en/milan.*

CONTACT Milan Tourism Office. ✉ *Piazza del Duomo 14, next to Palazzo Reale, Duomo* ☎ *02/88455555* ⊕ *www.yesmilano.it.*

Duomo

Milan's main streets radiate out from the massive Duomo, a late-Gothic cathedral begun in 1386. Heading north is the handsome Galleria Vittorio Emanuele II, an enclosed shopping arcade that opens at one end to the world-famous opera house known as La Scala. Via Manzoni leads northeast from La Scala to the Quadrilatero della Moda, or fashion district. Heading northeast from the Duomo is the pedestrian-only street Corso Vittorio Emanuele II. Northwest of the Duomo is Via Dante, at the top of which is the imposing outline of the Castello Sforzesco.

◉ Sights

Battistero Paleocristiano/Baptistry of San Giovanni alle Fonti

CHURCH | More specifically known as the Baptistry of San Giovanni alle Fonti, this 4th-century baptistry is one of two that lie beneath the Duomo. Although opinion remains divided, it is widely believed to be where Ambrose, Milan's first bishop and patron saint, baptized Augustine. Tickets also include a visit to the Duomo and its museum. ✉ *Piazza del Duomo, enter through Duomo* ☎ *02/72022656* ⊕ *www.duomomilano.it* 🎫 *€10, including admission to Duomo and museum; €20, including Duomo, museum, and roof* Ⓜ *Duomo.*

★ Duomo

CHURCH | There is no denying that for sheer size and complexity, the Duomo is unrivaled in Italy. It is the second-largest church in the country—the largest being St. Peter's in Rome—and the fourth largest in the world. This intricate Gothic structure has been fascinating and exasperating visitors and conquerors alike since it was begun by Gian Galeazzo Visconti III (1351–1402), first duke of Milan, in 1386. Consecrated in the 15th or 16th century, it was not completed until just before the coronation of Napoléon as king of Italy in 1809. The building is adorned with 135 marble spires and 2,245 marble statues. The oldest part is the apse. Its three colossal bays of curved and counter-curved tracery—especially the bay adorning the exterior of the stained-glass windows—should not be missed. At the end of the southern transept down the right aisle lies the tomb of Gian Giacomo Medici. The tomb owes some of its design to Michelangelo but was executed by Leone Leoni (1509–90) and is generally considered his masterpiece; it dates from the 1560s. Directly ahead is the Duomo's most famous sculpture, the gruesome but anatomically instructive figure of San Bartolomeo (St. Bartholomew), who was flayed alive. As you enter the apse to admire those splendid windows, glance at the sacristy doors to the right and left of the altar. The lunette on the right dates from 1393 and was decorated by Hans von Fernach. The one on the left also dates from the 14th century and is ascribed jointly to Giacomo da Campione and Giovannino de' Grassi. The roof is worth a look: walk out the left (north) transept to the stairs and elevator. As you stand among the forest of marble pinnacles, remember that virtually every inch of this gargantuan edifice, including the roof itself, is decorated with precious white marble dragged from quarries near Lake Maggiore by Duke Visconti's team along road laid fresh for the purpose and through the newly dredged canals. Exhibits at the Museo del Duomo shed light on the cathedral's history and include some of the treasures removed from the exterior for preservation purposes, while the early Christian Baptistry of St. John can be seen in the archaeological

Sights ▼

1 Battistero Paleocristiano/
Baptistry of San Giovanni
alle Fonti **H5**

2 Duomo **H5**

3 Galleria Vittorio
Emanuele II....................... **G3**

4 Milano Osservatorio-
Fondazione Prada **G4**

5 Museo del Novecento **G6**

6 Palazzo Reale **H7**

7 Pinacoteca Ambrosiana **D6**

8 Santa Maria Presso
San Satiro **E7**

Restaurants ▼

1 Giacomo Arengario............... **G6**

2 La Vecchia Latteria................ **E7**

3 Piz **D7**

Quick Bites ▼

1 Camparino in Galleria **G5**

2 Piccolo Peck **E6**

3 Rinascente Food &
Restaurants **H5**

Hotels ▼

1 Hotel Gran Duca di York............ **C6**

2 Hotel Spadari al Duomo............ **E6**

3 Hotel Star............................ **D3**

4 Maison Milano |
UNA Esperienze **F6**

5 Park Hyatt Milan.................... **F4**

6 Room Mate Giulia.................. **F5**

area underneath the cathedral. ⊠ *Piazza del Duomo, Duomo* ☎ *02/361691* ⊕ *www.duomomilano.it* ✆ *Cathedral €5; museum €5; cathedral, museum, and archaeological area €10; stairs to roof €15; elevator €20* Ⓜ *Duomo.*

★ Galleria Vittorio Emanuele II

STORE/MALL | This spectacular late-19th-century Belle Époque tunnel is essentially one of the planet's earliest and most select shopping malls, with upscale tenants that include Gucci, Prada, and Versace. This is the city's heart, midway between the Duomo and La Scala. It teems with life, which makes for great people-watching from the tables that spill out from bars and restaurants, where you can enjoy an overpriced coffee. Books, clothing, food, hats, and jewelry are all for sale. Known as Milan's "parlor," the Galleria is often viewed as a barometer of the city's well-being. The historic, if somewhat overpriced and inconsistent, Savini Restaurant hosts the beautiful and powerful of the city, just across from McDonald's. Even in poor weather the great glass dome above the octagonal center is a splendid sight. The paintings at the base of the dome represent Europe, Asia, Africa, and the Americas. Those at the entrance arch are devoted to science, industry, art, and agriculture. And the floor mosaics are a vastly underrated source of pleasure, even if they are not to be taken too seriously. Be sure to follow tradition and spin your heels once or twice on the more "delicate" parts of the bull beneath your feet in the northern apse; the Milanese believe it brings good luck. ⊠ *Piazza del Duomo* Ⓜ *Duomo.*

Milano Osservatorio—Fondazione Prada

OTHER MUSEUM | This contemporary photography exhibition space, developed in partnership with Fondazione Prada, is spread over two floors in the Galleria Vittorio Emanuele II. Exhibitions, which rotate several times a year, explore the cultural and social implications of photography. The space itself, bombed after World War II and then fully restored, is worth visiting just for the unique view of the Galleria dome through the large windows. You can reach the gallery via the elevator next to the Prada store. A ticket for the Osservatorio includes entry to the main Fondazione Prada museum (good for seven days). ⊠ *Galleria Vittorio Emanuele II, Piazza del Duomo, Duomo* ☎ *02/56662611* ⊕ *www.fondazioneprada. org/visit/milano-osservatorio* ✆ *€10; €15, including Fondazione Prada* ⊗ *Closed Tues.* Ⓜ *Duomo.*

Museo del Novecento

ART MUSEUM | Ascend a Guggenheim-esque spiral walkway to reach the modern works at this petite yet dense collection of Italian contemporary art, adjacent to the Duomo. The museum highlights 20th-century Italian artists, including a strong showing of Futurists, like Boccioni and Severini, and sculptures from Marini, along with a smattering of works by other European artists, including Picasso, Braque, and Matisse. ⊠ *Via Marconi 1, Duomo* ☎ *02/88444061* ⊕ *www.museodelnovecento.org* ✆ *€10 (free every 1st and 3rd Tues. of month after 2 and 1st Sun. of month)* ⊗ *Closed Mon. morning* Ⓜ *Duomo.*

★ Palazzo Reale

ART MUSEUM | Elaborately decorated with painted ceilings and grand staircases, this former royal palace close to the Duomo is almost worth a visit in itself; however, it also functions as one of Milan's major art galleries, with a focus on modern artists. Recent exhibitions have highlighted works by Picasso, Chagall, Warhol, Pollock, and Kandinsky. Check the website before you visit to see what's on; purchase tickets online in advance to save time in the queues, which are often long and chaotic. ⊠ *Piazza del Duomo 12, Duomo* ☎ *02/884 45 181* ⊕ *www.palazzorealemilano.it* ✆ *Varies by exhibition* ⊗ *Closed Mon. morning* Ⓜ *Duomo.*

Pinacoteca Ambrosiana

ART MUSEUM | Cardinal Federico Borromeo, one of Milan's native saints, founded this picture gallery in 1618 with the addition of his personal art collection to a bequest of books to Italy's first public library. The core works of the collection include such treasures as Caravaggio's *Basket of Fruit,* Raphael's monumental preparatory drawing (known as a "cartoon") for *The School of Athens,* which hangs in the Vatican, and Leonardo da Vinci's *Portrait of a Musician.* The highlight for many is Leonardo's *Codex Atlanticus,* which features thousands of his sketches and drawings. In addition to works by Lombard artists are paintings by Botticelli, Luini, Titian, and Jan Brueghel. A wealth of charmingly idiosyncratic items on display include 18th-century scientific instruments and gloves worn by Napoléon at Waterloo. Access to the library, the Biblioteca Ambrosiana, is limited to researchers who apply for entrance tickets. ⊠ *Piazza Pio XI 2, Duomo* 🕿 *02/806921* 🌐 *www. ambrosiana.it/en* 🎫 *€15* 🕓 *Closed Mon.* Ⓜ *Duomo.*

Santa Maria Presso San Satiro

CHURCH | Just a few steps from the Duomo, this architectural gem was first built in 876 and later perfected by Bramante (1444–1514), demonstrating his command of proportion and perspective—hallmarks of Renaissance architecture. Bramante tricks the eye with a famous optical illusion that makes a small interior seem extraordinarily spacious and airy, while accommodating a beloved 13th-century fresco. ⊠ *Via Torino 17–19, Duomo* 🕿 *02/874683* Ⓜ *Duomo; Tram No. 2, 3, 4, 12, 14, 19, 20, 24, or 27.*

Restaurants

Giacomo Arengario

$$$ | ITALIAN | Join businesspeople, ladies who lunch, and in-the-know travelers at this elegant restaurant atop the Museo del Novecento and with a glorious Duomo view (be sure to request a window table, though, or risk being relegated to a viewless back room). To complement the vistas, choose from a selection of well-prepared seafood, pasta, and meat courses for lunch and dinner; the servers are happy to recommend pairings from the extensive wine list. **Known for:** wine pairings; amazing Duomo views from tables by the windows; contemporary Milanese dishes. ⑤ *Average main: €30* ⊠ *Via Marconi 1, Duomo* 🕿 *02/72093814* 🌐 *giacomoarengario.com* Ⓜ *Duomo.*

La Vecchia Latteria

$$ | VEGETARIAN | In its two small dining rooms, this family-owned lunch spot serves an impressive amount of vegetarian cuisine. Nestled on a small street just steps away from the Duomo, it offers an array of freshly prepared seasonal selections from a daily-changing menu; try the *misto forno* (mixed plate), which offers a taste of several different small dishes. **Known for:** retro '50s atmosphere; Italian-focused vegetarian cuisine; daily-changing tasting menu. ⑤ *Average main: €15* ⊠ *6 Via dell'Unione, Duomo* 🕿 *02/874401* 🕓 *Closed Sun. No dinner* Ⓜ *Duomo or Missori.*

Piz

$ | PIZZA | FAMILY | Fun, lively, and full of locals, this casual and inexpensive pizzeria on a side street near the Duomo has just three kinds of thin-crust pizza on the menu—luckily, all are excellent. Choose from margherita, bianca (white, with no tomato), and marinara (with no mozzarella); although you'll inevitably need to wait, you'll likely get a free glass of prosecco and a slice of pizza with cheese while you do. **Known for:** bustling vibe; seasonal changing bianca pizza; free before- and after-dinner drinks. ⑤ *Average main: €9*

✉ *Via Torino 34, Duomo* ☎ *02/86453482*
Ⓜ *Duomo; Tram No. 2, 3, or 14.*

Coffee and Quick Bites

Camparino in Galleria

$$$ | CAFÉ | One thing has remained
constant in the Galleria: the Camparino,
whose inlaid counter, mosaics, and
wrought-iron fixtures have been welcom-
ing tired shoppers since 1867. It's been
given a fresh twist by star chef Davide
Oldani with a menu of Pan'cot—roasted
bread topped with veggies, fish, or meat,
to be enjoyed with a Campari aperitif—
served in pretty Bar di Passo downstairs,
while a more extensive range of Campari
cocktails paired with food for aperitivo
or dinner is available in elegant Sala
Spiritello upstairs. **Known for:** contempo-
rary versions of Campari cocktails; prime
people-watching; high-end aperitivo.
⑤ *Average main: €30* ✉ *Galleria Vittorio
Emanuele, Piazza del Duomo 21, Duomo*
☎ *02/86464435* ⊕ *www.camparino.it*
Ⓜ *Duomo.*

Piccolo Peck

$$ | SANDWICHES | The café at this foodie
paradise near the Duomo features
Italian specialty foods such as excellent
cheeses, charcuterie, vegetables in olive
oil, seafood, and sandwiches. It also rein-
terprets classic dishes like Russian salad
and paté, which can be washed down
with a fine selection of wines by the
glass or a bottle from its cellar of global
labels. **Known for:** casual atmosphere;
wide bakery selection, including classic
brioche; delicious Italian treats from the
famed Peck deli. ⑤ *Average main: €20*
✉ *Via Spadari 9, Duomo* ☎ *02/8023161*
⊕ *www.peck.it/en/restaurants/picco-
lo-peck* Ⓜ *Tram No. 2, 12, 14, 16, or 19.*

Rinascente Food & Restaurants

$ | ECLECTIC | The seventh floor of this
famous Italian department store is a
gourmet food market surrounded by several small restaurants that can be a good
option for lunch, an aperitivo overlooking

the Duomo, or dinner after a long day
of shopping. There are several places
to eat, including the popular mozzarella
bar Obica, God Save the Food for juices
and healthy bowls, De Santis for "slow
food" sandwiches, and the sophisticated
Maio restaurant. **Known for:** inexpensive
meals and snacks; terrace overlooking
the Duomo; culinary gifts to take home.
⑤ *Average main: €10* ✉ *Piazza Duomo,
Duomo* ☎ *02/8852454* ⊕ *www.rinas-
cente.it* Ⓜ *Duomo.*

Hotels

Hotel Gran Duca di York

$$ | HOTEL | The spare but classically ele-
gant and efficient rooms at this hotel are
arranged around a courtyard—four have
private terraces—and offer good value for
pricey Milan. **Pros:** good breakfast; central
location; friendly staff. **Cons:** many rooms
on the small side; limited amenities (no
restaurant or gym); showers can be tiny.
⑤ *Rooms from: €191* ✉ *Via Moneta 1,
Duomo* ☎ *02/874863* ⊕ *www.ducadiyork.
com* ⌁ *33 rooms* ¶⦶ *Free Breakfast*
Ⓜ *Cordusio or Duomo; Tram No. 2, 12,
14, 16, or 27.*

Hotel Spadari al Duomo

$$$ | HOTEL | That this chic city-center inn
is owned by an architect's family comes
through in details like the custom-de-
signed furniture and paintings by young
Milanese artists in the stylish guest
rooms. **Pros:** good breakfast; attentive
staff; central location. **Cons:** no restaurant; street noise can be a problem;
some rooms on the small side. ⑤ *Rooms
from: €260* ✉ *Via Spadari 11, Duomo*
☎ *02/72002371* ⊕ *www.spadarihotel.com*
¶⦶ *Free Breakfast* ⌁ *40 rooms* Ⓜ *Duomo;
Tram No. 2, 3, 12, 14, 16, 24, or 27.*

Hotel Star

$ | HOTEL | The price is extremely reason-
able, the staff are helpful, and the rooms
are well equipped and comfortable, some
with touches like whirlpool tubs and
balconies. **Pros:** breakfast is included;

centrally located near key attractions; reasonably priced. **Cons:** street noise can be an issue; quirky animal prints in some rooms not for everyone; some bathrooms are extremely small. $ *Rooms from: €115 ⊠ Via dei Bossi 5, Duomo ☎ 02/801501 ⊕ www.hotelstar.it ➨ 30 rooms* ⏐Ⓞ⏐ *Free Breakfast.*

Maison Milano | UNA Esperienze

$$$ | **HOTEL** | Inside this faithfully restored palazzo dating from the early 1900s, spaciousness is accentuated with soft white interiors, muted fabrics and marble, and contemporary lines. **Pros:** the warmth of a residence and the luxury of a design hotel; friendly staff; lovely bathrooms. **Cons:** no restaurant or bar; not much of a lobby; breakfast not included. $ *Rooms from: €239 ⊠ Via Mazzini 4, Duomo ☎ 02/726891 ⊕ www.gruppouna.it/esperienze/maison-milano* ⏐Ⓞ⏐ *No Meals ➨ 27 rooms* Ⓜ *Duomo; Tram No. 2, 3, 12, 14, 16, 24, or 27.*

★ Park Hyatt Milan

$$$$ | **HOTEL** | Extensive use of warm travertine stone and modern art creates a sophisticated yet inviting backdrop at the Park Hyatt, where spacious, opulent guest rooms have walk-in closets and bathrooms with double sinks, glass-enclosed rain showers, and separate soaking tubs. **Pros:** excellent restaurant; central location; contemporary decor and amenities. **Cons:** very expensive; not particularly intimate; some rooms showing a little wear. $ *Rooms from: €1,400 ⊠ Via Tommaso Grossi 1, Duomo ☎ 02/88211234 ⊕ milan.park.hyatt.com ➨ 106 rooms* ⏐Ⓞ⏐ *No Meals* Ⓜ *Duomo; Tram No. 1.*

★ Room Mate Giulia

$$$ | **HOTEL** | For hip, affordable, design-focused lodging with a friendly feel and prime location right next to the Galleria and around the corner from the Duomo, you can't do much better than the city's first outpost from Spanish hotel chain Room Mate. **Pros:** relatively affordable rates for Milan; fresh, appealing design;

amazing location. **Cons:** gym on the small side; breakfast room a bit cramped; busy location means some noise in rooms. $ *Rooms from: €249 ⊠ Via Silvio Pellico 4, Duomo ☎ 02/80888900 ⊕ www.room-matehotels.com/en ➨ 85 rooms* ⏐Ⓞ⏐ *No Meals* Ⓜ *Duomo; Tram No. 1.*

ⓨ Nightlife

Bar STRAF

BARS | This architecturally stimulating but dimly lit place has such artistic features as recycled fiberglass panels and vintage 1970s furnishings. The music is an eclectic mix of chill-out tunes during the daytime, with more upbeat and vibrant tracks pepping it up at night. Located on a quiet side street near the Duomo, STRAF draws a young and lively, if tourist-heavy, crowd. ⊠ *Via San Raffaele 3, Duomo ☎ 02/805081 ⊕ www.straf.it/bar* Ⓜ *Duomo.*

🎭 Performing Arts

Conservatorio

MUSIC | The two halls belonging to the Conservatorio host some of the leading names in classical music. Series are organized by several organizations, including the venerable chamber music society the **Società del Quartetto**. ⊠ *Via del Conservatorio 12, Duomo ☎ 02/762110, 02/795393 Società del Quartetto ⊕ www.consmilano.it* Ⓜ *San Babila; Tram No. 9, 12, 23, or 27; Bus No. 60 or 73.*

★ Teatro alla Scala

OPERA | You need know nothing of opera to sense that La Scala is closer to a cathedral than a concert hall. Hearing opera sung in this magical setting is an unparalleled experience: it is, after all, where Verdi established his reputation and where Maria Callas sang her way into opera lore. It stands as a symbol—both for the performer who dreams of singing here and for the opera buff—and its notoriously demanding audiences are apt to jeer performers who do not measure up. If you are lucky enough to be here during opera season, do whatever is necessary to attend. Tickets go on sale two months before the first performance and are usually sold out the same day. The opening gala is December 7, the feast day of Milan patron St. Ambrose, and performances run all year, except for the end of July and August, and major holidays. For tickets, visit the Box Office at Largo Ghiringhelli 1, Piazza della Scala, every day from 12 to 6 pm and two hours before the beginning of each performance, for same-day shows. Tickets are also available online. Tickets purchased online can be presented at the entrance with your smartphone or tablet. Although you might not get seats for the more popular operas with big-name stars, it is worth trying; ballets are easier. There are also 140 reduced-visibility balcony tickets available for each performance on a first-come, first-served basis; for evening operas and ballets, registration for the list begins at 1 pm, and ticket recipients (with a maximum of two tickets per person) are announced at 5:30 pm. At the Museo Teatrale alla Scala you can admire an extensive collection of librettos, paintings of the famous names of Italian opera, posters, costumes, antique instruments, and design sketches for the theater. It is also possible to take a look at the theater itself. Special exhibitions reflect current productions. ⊠ *Piazza della Scala, Largo Ghiringhelli 1, Duomo* ☎ *02/72003744 theater, 02/88797473 museum* ⊕ *www.teatroallascala.org* ➥ *Museum €9.75* Ⓜ *Duomo or Cordusio; Tram No. 1.*

🛍 Shopping

Borsalino

HATS & GLOVES | The kingpin of milliners, Borsalino has managed to stay trendy since it opened in 1857. ⊠ *Galleria Vittorio Emanuele II 92, Duomo* ☎ *02/89015436* ⊕ *www.borsalino.com* Ⓜ *Duomo; Tram No. 1.*

Gucci

MIXED CLOTHING | This Florence-born brand attracts lots of fashion-forward tourists in hot pursuit of its monogrammed bags, shoes, and accessories. ⊠ *Galleria Vittorio Emanuele II, Duomo* ☎ *02/8597991* ⊕ *www.gucci.com* Ⓜ *Duomo; Tram No. 1.*

La Rinascente

DEPARTMENT STORE | The flagship location of this always bustling and very central department store—adjacent to both the Duomo and the Galleria Vittorio Emanuele II—carries a wide range of Italian and international brands (both high-end and casual) for men, women, and children. There's also a fine selection of beauty and home products. ⊠ *Piazza Duomo, Duomo* ☎ *02/9138 7388* ⊕ *www.rinascente.it* Ⓜ *Duomo; Tram No. 1, 2, 12, 14, 16, or 27.*

Trussardi

JEWELRY & WATCHES | This family-run label offers sleek, fashion-forward accessories, leather goods, and clothes at its flagship store. ⊠ *Piazza della Scala 5, Duomo* ☎ *02/80688242* ⊕ *www.trussardi.com* Ⓜ *Duomo; Tram No. 1.*

Castello

This 15th-century castle is home to crypts, battlements, tunnels, and an interesting array of museums.

👁 Sights

Castello Sforzesco

HISTORIC SIGHT | Wandering the grounds of this tranquil castle and park near the center of Milan is a great respite from the often-hectic city, and the interesting museums inside are an added bonus. The castle's crypts and battlements, including a tunnel that emerges well into the Parco Sempione behind, can be visited with privately reserved guides from Ad Artem or Opera d'Arte. For the serious student of Renaissance military engineering, the Castello must be something of a travesty, so often has it been remodeled or rebuilt since it was begun in 1450 by the condottiere, or mercenary, who founded the city's second dynastic family: Francesco Sforza, fourth duke of Milan. Although today "mercenary" has a pejorative ring, during the Renaissance, all Italy's great soldier-heroes were professionals hired by the cities and principalities they served. Of them—and there were thousands—Francesco Sforza (1401–66) is considered one of the greatest, most honest, and most organized. It is said he could remember the names not only of all his men but of their horses as well. His rule signaled the enlightened age of the Renaissance but preceded the next foreign rule by a scant 50 years. Since the turn of the 20th century, the Castello has been the depository of several city-owned collections of Egyptian and other antiquities, musical instruments, arms and armor, decorative arts and textiles, prints and photographs, paintings, and sculpture. Highlights include the Sala delle Asse, a frescoed room attributed to Leonardo da Vinci (1452–1519), and Michelangelo's unfinished *Rondanini Pietà*, believed to be his last work—an astounding achievement for a man nearly 90, and a moving coda to his life—which is housed in the Museo Pietà Rondanini. The *pinacoteca* (picture gallery) features 230 paintings from medieval times to the 18th century, including works by Antonello da Messina, Canaletto, Andrea Mantegna, and Bernardo Bellotto. The Museo dei Mobili e delle Sculture Lignee (Furniture Museum), which illustrates the development of Italian furniture design from the Middle Ages to the present, includes a delightful collection of Renaissance treasure chests of exotic woods with tiny drawers and miniature architectural details. A single ticket purchased in the office in an inner courtyard admits visitors to these separate installations, which are dispersed around the castle's two immense courtyards. ⊠ *Piazza Castello, Castello* ☏ *02/88463700* ⊕ *www.*

milanocastello.it ⊠ *Castle free, museums €10 (free every 1st and 3rd Tues. of month after 2, and €5 1st Sun. of month)* ☉ *Museums closed Mon.* Ⓜ *Cadorna, Lanza, or Cairoli; Tram No. 1, 2, 4, 12, 14, or 19; Bus No. 18, 37, 50, 58, 61, or 94.*

Performing Arts

Teatro Dal Verme

CONCERTS | Frequent classical, rock, and jazz concerts by international artists are staged here from October to May. ⊠ *Via San Giovanni sul Muro 2, Castello* ☏ *02/87905* ⊕ *www.dalverme.org* Ⓜ *Cairoli; Tram No. 1 or 4.*

Sempione

Just beyond the Sforzesco Castle grounds is a large park that holds an aquarium, the Triennale museum, and the Torre Branca.

◉ Sights

Acquario Civico di Milano

(*Civic Aquarium of Milan*)
AQUARIUM | **FAMILY** | The third oldest aquarium in Europe, opened in 1906, is known as much for its art nouveau architecture as for its small but interesting collection of marine life. You'll find 36 pools that house more than 100 species of fish, including an emphasis on Italian freshwater fish and their habitat, and one tank of species from the Red Sea. ⊠ *Viale Gerolamo Gadio 2, Sempione* ☏ *02/88465750* ⊕ *www.acquariocivicomilano.eu* ⊠ *€5; free every 1st and 3rd Tues. of month after 2 and 1st Sun. of month* ☉ *Closed Mon.* Ⓜ *Lanza; Tram No. 2, 4, 12, or 14; Bus No. 57.*

Parco Sempione

CITY PARK | **FAMILY** | Originally the gardens and parade grounds of the Castello Sforzesco, this open space was reorganized during the Napoleonic era, when the arena on its northeast side was constructed, and then turned into a park during the building boom at the end of the 19th century. It is still the lungs of the city's fashionable western neighborhoods, and the **Aquarium** still attracts Milan's schoolchildren. The park became a bit of a design showcase in 1933 with the construction of the Triennale. ✉ *Sempione* 🎫 *Free* Ⓜ *Cairoli, Lanza or Cadorna; Tram No. 1, 2, 4, 12, 14, 19, or 27; Bus No. 43, 57, 61, 70, or 94*

Torre Branca

VIEWPOINT | It is worth visiting Parco Sempione just to see the Torre Branca. Designed by the architect Gio Ponti (1891–1979), who was behind so many of the projects that made Milan the design capital that it is, this steel tower rises 330 feet over the Triennale. Take the elevator to get a nice view of the city, then have a drink at the glitzy Just Cavalli Restaurant and Club at its base. ✉ *Parco Sempione, Sempione* ☎ *02/3314120* ⊕ *museobranca.it/torre-branca-2/* 🎫 *€6* 🕐 *Closed Sun. and Mon.; closed Mon., Tues., Thurs., and Fri. mid-Sept.–mid-May* Ⓜ *Cadorna; Tram No. 1; Bus No. 61.*

Triennale Design Museum

ART MUSEUM | In addition to honoring Italy's design talent, the Triennale also offers a regular series of exhibitions on design from around the world. A spectacular bridge entrance leads to a permanent collection, an exhibition space, and a stylish café and rooftop restaurant with expansive views. The Triennale also manages the fascinating museum-studio of designer Achille Castiglioni, in nearby Piazza Castello (hour-long guided tours Tuesday–Friday at 10, 11, and noon; €15. Call or email in advance to book: *02/8053606, info@achillecastiglioni.it*). ✉ *Via Alemagna 6, Sempione* ☎ *02/72434244* ⊕ *www.triennale.org* 🎫 *€12* 🕐 *Closed Mon.* Ⓜ *Cadorna; Bus No. 61.*

Brera

To the north of the Duomo lie the winding streets of this elegant neighborhood, once the city's bohemian quarter.

Sights

⭐ **Pinacoteca di Brera** (*Brera Gallery*)
ART MUSEUM | The collection here is star-studded even by Italian standards. The museum has nearly 40 rooms, arranged in chronological order—so pace yourself. One highlight is the somber, moving *Cristo Morto* (*Dead Christ*) by Mantegna, which dominates Room VI with its sparse palette of umber and its foreshortened perspective. Mantegna's shocking, almost surgical precision tells of an all-too-human agony. It's one of Renaissance painting's most quietly wondrous achievements, finding an unsuspected middle ground between the excesses of conventional gore and beauty in representing the Passion's saddest moment. Room XXIV offers two additional highlights of the gallery: Raphael's (1483–1520) *Sposalizio della Vergine* (*Marriage of the Virgin*), with its mathematical composition and precise, alternating colors, portrays the betrothal of Mary and Joseph. *La Vergine con il Bambino e Santi* (*Madonna with Child and Saints*), by Piero della Francesca (1420–92), is an altarpiece commissioned by Federico da Montefeltro (shown kneeling, in full armor, before the Virgin); it was intended for a church to house the duke's tomb. Room XXXVIII houses one of the most romantic paintings in Italian history: *Il Bacio*, by Francesco Hayez (1791–1882), depicts a couple from the Middle Ages engaged in a passionate kiss. The painting was meant to portray the patriotic spirit of Italy's Unification and freedom from the Austro-Hungarian Empire. ✉ *Via Brera 28, Brera* ☎ *02/722631* ⊕ *www.pinacotecabrera.*

org 🖼 *€15* ⏱ *Closed Mon.* Ⓜ *Montenapo-leone or Lanza; Tram No. 1, 4, 12, 14, or 27; Bus No. 61.*

🍴 Restaurants

⭐ Cittamani

$$ | **MODERN INDIAN** | Celebrity chef Ritu Dalmia runs well-regarded Italian restaurants in India, so it's no surprise that her first restaurant in Italy offers a mash-up of modern Indian food with Italian and international ingredients; even the decor, with shelves of pottery and terrazzo floors, is a cultural combo. Look for unexpected flavors and a mix of small plates, more substantial mains, and utterly delicious fusion desserts. **Known for:** sleek contemporary setting; Indian food quite different from the norm; nontraditional naans. 💲 *Average main: €21* ✉ *Piazza Mirabello 5, Brera* ☎ *02/38240935* ⊕ *www.cittamani.com* ⏱ *Closed Mon.* Ⓜ *Moscova or Turati; Bus No. 43 or 94.*

Fioraio Bianchi Caffè

$$$ | **MODERN ITALIAN** | A French-style bis-tro in the heart of Milan, Fioraio Bianchi Caffè was opened more than 40 years ago by Raimondo Bianchi, a great lover of flowers; in fact, eating at this restaurant is a bit like dining in a Parisian boutique with floral decor. Despite the French atmosphere, the dishes have Italian flair and ensure a classy, inventive meal. **Known for:** great spot for morning coffee and pastries; charming, flower-filled, shabby-chic setting; creative Italian-style bistro food. 💲 *Average main: €28* ✉ *Via Montebello 7, Brera* ☎ *02/29014390* ⊕ *www.fioraiobianchicaffe.it* ⏱ *Closed 3 wks in Aug.* Ⓜ *Turati.*

Coffee and Quick Bites

N'Ombra de Vin

$ | **WINE BAR** | This enoteca serves wine by the glass and, in addition to the plates of *salumi* (Italian cold cuts) and cheese nibbles, has light food and not-so-light desserts. It's a great place for peo-ple-watching on Via San Marco, while indoors offers a more dimly lit, romantic setting; check out the impressive vaulted basement, where bottled wines and spir-its are sold. **Known for:** Italian and French wines; solid tapas dishes; atmospheric setting in an old Augustinian refectory. 💲 *Average main: €14* ✉ *Via S. Marco 2, Brera* ☎ *02/6599650* ⊕ *www.nom-bradevin.it* Ⓜ *Lanza, Turati, or Montenapo-leone; Tram No. 1, 2, 4, 12, or 14.*

🛏 Hotels

Bulgari Hotel Milano

$$$$ | **HOTEL** | Housed in an 18th-century palazzo on a quiet street a short stroll from the shops of Brera and Monte-napoleone, the Bulgari offers up chic yet restrained rooms, an enormous garden, and a celebrity-chef-helmed restaurant. **Pros:** excellent spa, with heated pool, sauna, and Jacuzzi; convenient location for sightseeing; trendy and fashionable guests. **Cons:** extremely expensive; service not quite up to par; rooms are a bit bland. 💲 *Rooms from: €750* ✉ *Via Privata Fratelli Gabba 7b, Brera* ☎ *02/8058051* ⊕ *www.bulgarihotels. com/en_US/milan* ⮐ *61 rooms* 🍴◯ *No Meals* Ⓜ *Montenapoleone.*

Nightlife

Il Bar at Bulgari Hotel Milano

BARS | Having drinks or a light lunch at the Bulgari Hotel bar lets you step off the asphalt and into one of the city's most impressive private urban gardens—even indoors you seem to be outside, separated from the elements by a spectacular wall of glass. The Bar is a great place to run into international hotel guests and jet-setting Milanese, and the staff mix up a wide range of traditional and novel drinks—including the Bulgari Cocktail with gin, Aperol, and orange, pineapple, and lime juices. ⊠ *Via Privata Fratelli Gabba 7/b, Brera* ☎ *02/8058051* ⊕ *www.bulgarihotels.com/en_US/milan/bar-and-restaurant/il-bar* Ⓜ *Montenapoleone; Tram No. 1.*

Shopping

With its narrow streets and outdoor cafés, Brera is one of Milan's most charming neighborhoods. Wander through it to find smaller shops with some appealing offerings from lesser-known names that cater to the well-heeled taste of this upscale area. The densest concentration is along Via Brera, Via Solferino, and Corso Garibaldi.

Mercato di Via S. Marco

MARKET | The Monday- and Thursday-morning markets here cater to the wealthy residents of the central Brera neighborhood. In addition to food stands where you can get cheese, roast chicken, and dried beans and fruits, there are several clothing and shoe stalls that are important stops for some of Milan's most elegant women. ⊠ *Via San Marco, near Via Castelfidardo, Brera* Ⓜ *Lanza; Tram No. 2, 4, 12, or 14.*

Sant'Ambrogio

If the part of the city to the north of the Duomo is dominated by shopping, Sant'Ambrogio and other parts to the south are known for art. The most famous piece is *Il Cenacolo*—known in English as *The Last Supper*. If you have time for nothing else, make sure you see this masterpiece, which is housed in the refectory of Santa Maria delle Grazie. Reservations are required to see it, and you should make yours at least three weeks before you depart for Italy, so you can plan the rest of your time in Milan.

Sights

Basilica di Sant'Ambrogio

(*Basilica of St. Ambrose*)
CHURCH | Milan's bishop, St. Ambrose (one of the original Doctors of the Catholic Church), consecrated this church in AD 387. St. Ambroeus, as he is known in Milanese dialect, is the city's patron saint, and his remains—dressed in elegant religious robes, a miter, and gloves—can be viewed inside a glass case in the crypt below the altar. Until the construction of the more imposing Duomo, this was Milan's most important church. Much restored and reworked over the centuries (the gold-and-gem-encrusted altar dates from the 9th century), Sant'Ambrogio still preserves its Romanesque characteristics, including 5th-century mosaics. The church is often closed for weddings on Saturday. ⊠ *Piazza Sant'Ambrogio 15, Sant'Ambrogio* ☎ *02/86450895* ⊕ *www.basilicasantambrogio.it* Ⓜ *Sant'Ambrogio; Bus No. 50, 58, or 94.*

Chiesa di San Maurizio al Monastero Maggiore

CHURCH | Next to the Museo Civico Archeologico, you'll find this little gem of a church, constructed starting in 1503 and decorated almost completely with magnificent 16th-century frescoes.

The modest exterior belies the treasures inside, including a concealed back room once used by nuns that includes a fascinating fresco of Noah loading the ark with animals, including two unicorns. ⊠ *Corso Magenta 15, Sant'Ambrogio* ☎ *02/88445208* Ⓜ *Cadorna or Cairoli; Tram No. 16 or 27; Bus No. 50, 58, or 94.*

★ The Last Supper/Il Cenacolo/Santa Maria delle Grazie

CHURCH | Leonardo da Vinci's *The Last Supper,* housed in this church and former Dominican monastery, has had an almost unbelievable history of bad luck and neglect. Its near destruction in an American bombing raid in August 1943 was only the latest chapter in a series of misadventures, including—if one 19th-century source is to be believed—being whitewashed over by monks. Well-meant but disastrous attempts at restoration have done little to rectify the problem of the work's placement: it was executed on a wall unusually vulnerable to climatic dampness. Yet Leonardo chose to work slowly and patiently in oil pigments, which demand dry plaster, instead of proceeding hastily on wet plaster according to the conventional fresco technique. After years of restorers patiently shifting from one square centimeter to another, Leonardo's masterpiece is finally free of centuries of retouching, grime, and dust. Astonishing clarity and luminosity have been regained. Despite Leonardo's carefully preserved preparatory sketches, in which the apostles are clearly labeled by name, there still remains some small debate about a few identities in the final arrangement. There can be no mistaking Judas, however—small and dark, his hand calmly reaching forward to the bread, isolated from the terrible confusion that has taken the hearts of the others. Art historian Frederick Hartt offers an elegantly terse explanation for why the composition works: it combines "dramatic confusion" with "mathematical order." Certainly, the amazingly skillful and unobtrusive repetition of threes—in

the windows, in the grouping of the figures, and in their placement—adds a mystical aspect to what at first seems simply the perfect observation of spontaneous human gesture. Reservations are required to view the work. Viewings are in 15-minute timed-entry slots, and visitors must arrive 20 minutes before their assigned time in order not to lose their place. Reservations can be made online. Reserve at least three weeks ahead if you want a Saturday slot, two weeks for a weekday slot. Some city bus tours include a visit in their regular circuit, which may be a good option. The painting was executed in what was the order's refectory, which is now referred to as the Cenacolo Vinciano. Take a moment to visit Santa Maria delle Grazie itself. It's a handsome, completely restored church with a fine dome and a cloister, both of which Bramante added around the time Leonardo was commissioned to paint *The Last Supper.* ⊠ *Piazza Santa Maria delle Grazie 2, off Corso Magenta, Sant'Ambrogio* ☎ *02/92800360 reservations, 02/4676111 church* ⊕ *www. cenacolovinciano.net* ⊙ *Closed Mon.* ⊠ *Last Supper €15 (free 1st Sun. of month)* Ⓜ *Cadorna or Conciliazione; Tram No. 18.*

Museo Civico Archeologico

(*Municipal Archaeological Museum*)
HISTORY MUSEUM | Appropriately situated in the heart of Roman Milan, this museum housed in a former monastery displays everyday utensils, jewelry, silver plate, and several fine examples of mosaic pavement from Mediolanum, the ancient Roman name for Milan. The museum opens into a garden that is flanked by the square tower of the Roman circus and the polygonal Ansperto tower, adorned with frescoes dating to the end of the 13th and 14th centuries that portray St. Francis and other saints receiving the stigmata. ⊠ *Corso Magenta 15, Sant'Ambrogio* ☎ *02/88445208* ⊕ *www.museoarcheologicomilano.it* ⊠ *€5 (free every 1st and 3rd Tues. of*

Castello, Sempione, Brera, Sant'Ambrogio, Fiera and San Siro

KEY

- **1** Sights
- **1** Restaurants
- **1** Quick Bites
- **1** Hotels

Sights ▼

1. Acquario Civico di Milano **C2**
2. Basilica di Sant'Ambrogio **C5**
3. Castello Sforzesco **C3**
4. Chiesa di San Maurizio al Monastero Maggiore ... **C4**
5. The Last Supper/ Il Cenacolo/Santa Maria delle Grazie **B3**
6. Museo Civico Archeologico **C4**
7. Museo Nazionale della Scienza e Tecnologia Leonardo da Vinci **B5**
8. Parco Sempione **C2**
9. Pinacoteca di Brera **D2**
10. Torre Branca **B2**
11. Triennale Design Museum **B2**

Restaurants ▼

1. Al Rifugio Pugliese **A4**
2. Cittamani **E1**
3. Fioraio Bianchi Caffe ... **E1**
4. Taverna Moriggi **C4**

Quick Bites ▼

1. N'Ombra de Vin **E2**

Hotels ▼

1. Antica Locanda Leonardo **B4**
2. Bulgari Hotel Milano **E3**

month after 2) ⊘ *Closed Mon.* Ⓜ *Cadorna or Cairoli; Tram No. 16 or 27; Bus No. 50, 58, or 94.*

Museo Nazionale della Scienza e Tecnologia Leonardo da Vinci (*National Museum of Science and Technology*)

SCIENCE MUSEUM | **FAMILY** | This converted cloister is best known for the collection of models based on Leonardo da Vinci's sketches. One of the most visited rooms features interactive, moving models of the famous *vita aerea* (aerial screw) and *ala battente* (beating wing), thought to be forerunners of the modern helicopter and airplane, respectively. The museum also houses a varied collection of industrial artifacts, including trains, and several reconstructed workshops, including a watchmaker's, a lute maker's, and an antique pharmacy. Reserve tickets for the celebrated Italian-built submarine, the S-506 *Enrico Toti,* online or by phone to avoid disappointment. Displays also illustrate papermaking and metal founding, which were fundamental to Milan's—and the world's—economic growth. There's a bookshop and a bar. ■ **TIP→ Avoid this museum on weekends. It's a popular spot for families, and there are long lines on those days.** ⊠ *Via San Vittore 21, Sant'Ambrogio* ☎ *02/02485551* ⊕ *www. museoscienza.org* 🎫 *€10, €18 including tour of submarine (€20 when reserved in advance)* ⊘ *Closed Mon.* Ⓜ *Sant'Ambrogio; Bus No. 50, 58, or 94.*

 Restaurants

Taverna Moriggi

$$ | **MILANESE** | This wood-paneled traditional Milanese taverna near the stock exchange, within a house from the 14th century, is the perfect spot to enjoy a mix of both traditional and more innovative fare. Pasta, risotto, and more robust secondi like tenderloin with a Barolo wine reduction are available at both lunch and dinner; a reservation is a good idea. **Known for:** historical setting; well-prepared risotto and cotoletta alla Milanese; fantastic wine selection. Ⓢ *Average main: €21* ⊠ *Via Morigi 8, Sant'Ambrogio* ☎ *02/36755232* ⊕ *www.tavernamoriggi. com* ⊘ *Closed Mon. No lunch Tues.* Ⓜ *Cairoli or Cordusio; Tram 1, 2, 4, 12, 14, 16, or 27.*

 Hotels

Antica Locanda Leonardo

$ | **HOTEL** | A feeling of relaxation prevails in this 19th-century building, and the neighborhood—the church that houses *The Last Supper* is a block away—is one of Milan's most desired and historic. **Pros:** friendly, helpful staff; very quiet and homey; breakfast is ample. **Cons:** old-fashioned decor; more like a bed-and-breakfast than a hotel; breakfast is an extra fee. Ⓢ *Rooms from: €118* ⊠ *Corso Magenta 78, Sant'Ambrogio* ☎ *02/48014197* ⊕ *www.anticalocandaleonardo.com* ⊘ *Closed 1st wk in Jan. and 3 wks in Aug.* 🛏 *16 rooms* ⦿| *No Meals* Ⓜ *Conciliazione, Sant'Ambrogio, or Cadorna; Tram No. 1, 16, 19, or 27.*

Fiera and San Siro

Fiera is a quiet suburb northwest of the city center. Neighboring San Siro is home to Stadio Meazza (commonly known as San Siro Stadium), where AC and Inter Milan play their home matches.

Restaurants

Al Rifugio Pugliese

$$ | **SOUTHERN ITALIAN** | Outside the center of town, this is a fun place to sample specialties from the Puglia region of southern Italy. These include homemade orecchiette and other pastas served with a variety of sauces; dishes are piled high, so share or come with a big appetite. **Known for:** lively atmosphere; more than 10 different salads; burrata dishes. Ⓢ *Average main: €20* ⊠ *Via Costanza 2, Fiera* ☎ *02/48000917* Ⓜ *Wagner; Tram No. 14, 16, or 19.*

Activities

San Siro Stadium (Stadio Meazza)

SOCCER | AC Milan and Inter Milan, two of the oldest and most successful teams in Europe, vie for the heart of soccer-mad Lombardy. For residents, the city is *Milano* but the teams are *Milan,* a vestige of their common founding as the Milan Cricket and Football Club in 1899. When an Italian-led faction broke off in 1908, the new club was dubbed F. C. Internazionale (or "Inter") to distinguish it from the bastion of English exclusivity that would become AC Milan (or simply "Milan"). Since then, the picture has become more clouded: although Milan used to pride itself as the true team of the city and of its working class, and Inter more persuasively claimed pan-Italian support, the divide among the fan base is not so clear-cut. AC Milan and Inter Milan share the use of San Siro Stadium (Stadio Meazza) during their August–May season. With more than 60,000 of the 80,000 seats appropriated by season-ticket holders and another couple of thousand allocated to visiting fans, tickets to Sunday games can be difficult to come by. You can purchase advance AC Milan tickets online at the club's website (www.acmilan.com), at the Casa Milan ticket office at Via Aldo Rossi 8, at Banca Popolare di Milano branches, or at VivaTicket sales points. They're also sold at the stadium booth on match days. For true fans, the AC Milan headquarters, called Casa Milan, includes a museum with interactive exhibits, a store selling team merchandise, and a restaurant. Inter tickets are available on the club's website (www.inter.it). If you're a soccer fan but can't get in to see a game, consider taking one of the stadium tours (www.sansirostadium.com/en/museum-tour/tour). ⊠ *Piazzale Angelo Moratti, San Siro* ☎ *02/48798201* ⊕ *www.sansirostadium.com* Ⓜ *San Siro Stadio; Tram No. 16; Bus No. 49.*

Quadrilatero

Via Manzoni, which lies northeast of La Scala, leads to Milan's Quadrilatero della Moda, or fashion district.

◉ Sights

Museo Bagatti Valsecchi

HISTORIC HOME | Glimpse the lives of 19th-century Milanese aristocrats in a visit to this lovely historic house museum, once the home of two brothers, Barons Fausto and Giuseppe Bagatti. Family members inhabited the house until 1974; it opened to the public as a museum in 1984. The house is decorated with the brothers' fascinating collection of 15th- and 16th-century Renaissance art, furnishings, and objects, including armor, musical instruments, and textiles. The detailed audio guide included with admission provides a thorough insight into the history of the artworks and intriguing stories of the family itself. ⊠ *Via Gesu 5, Quadrilatero* ☎ *02/76006132* ⊕ *museobagattivalsecchi.org* ◷ *Closed Mon.* ⊠ *€10* Ⓜ *Montenapoleone; Tram No. 1.*

Museo Poldi-Pezzoli

ART MUSEUM | This exceptional museum, opened in 1881, was once a private residence and collection, and contains not only pedigreed paintings but also porcelain, textiles, and a cabinet with scenes from Dante's life. The gem is undoubtedly *Portrait of a Lady,* by Piero del Pollaiolo (1431–98), one of the city's most prized treasures and the source of the museum's logo. The collection also includes masterpieces by Botticelli (1445–1510), Andrea Mantegna (1431–1506), Giovanni Bellini (1430–1516), and Fra Filippo Lippi (1406–69). ⊠ *Via Manzoni 12, Quadrilatero* ☎ *02/794889* ⊕ *www.museopoldipezzoli.it* ⊠ *€10* ◷ *Closed Tues.* Ⓜ *Montenapoleone or Duomo; Tram No. 1.*

Restaurants

Don Carlos

$$$$ | **ITALIAN** | One of the few restaurants open after La Scala lets out, Don Carlos, in the Grand Hotel et de Milan, is nothing like its indecisive operatic namesake (whose betrothed was stolen by his father). Flavors are bold, presentation is precise and full of flair, service is attentive, and the walls are blanketed with sketches of the theater. **Known for:** veal Milanese; late-night hours; homemade pasta. $ *Average main: €39* ⊠ *Via Manzoni 29, Quadrilatero* ☎ *02/72314640* ⊗ *No lunch* Ⓜ *Montenapoleone; Tram No. 1 or 2.*

★ Seta

$$$$ | **MODERN ITALIAN** | Modern Italian cuisine made using interesting ingredients is the draw at this restaurant with sophisticated brown-and-green decor in Milan's Mandarin Oriental Hotel. The best way to experience the intricate dishes is through the seven-course tasting menu; for a less expensive option, opt for the three-course "carte blanche" lunch menu. **Known for:** top-notch service; wonderful Italo-centric wine list; ultra-creative dishes. $ *Average main: €120* ⊠ *Via Andegari 9, Quadrilatero* ☎ *02/87318897* ⊕ *www.mandarinoriental.com/milan/ la-scala/fine-dining/restaurants/italian-cuisine/seta* ⊗ *Closed Sun.,1st wk of Jan., and three wks in Aug.* Ⓜ *Montenapoleone; Tram No. 1.*

☕ Coffee and Quick Bites

Chic & Go Milano

$ | **MODERN ITALIAN** | Step into these stylish and trendy surroundings for a quick sandwich as exquisite as the fashions in the nearby shops. Though the lobster panini will run you a pretty penny, other top-notch items—like crab, salmon, prosciutto, Angus tartare, and mozzarella di bufala—are not a bad deal. **Known for:** convenient location near shopping; gourmet sandwiches; regional meats. $ *Average main: €8* ⊠ *Via Montenapoleone 25, Quadrilatero* ☎ *02/782648* ⊕ *www.chic-and-go.com* Ⓜ *Montenapoleone; Tram No. 1.*

🛏 Hotels

★ Armani Hotel Milano

$$$$ | **HOTEL** | Located in Milan's fashion district, this minimalist boutique hotel looks like it has been plucked from the pages of a sleek shelter magazine, and it should: it was designed by fashion icon Giorgio Armani to evoke the same sculptural, streamlined aesthetic—and tailored comfort—as his signature clothing. **Pros:** great location near major shopping streets; complimentary (except for alcohol) minibar; lovely spa area and 24-hour gym. **Cons:** some noise issues from neighboring rooms; breakfast (only included in some rates) not up to par; a few signs of wear and tear. $ *Rooms from: €760* ⊠ *Via Manzoni 31, Quadrilatero* ☎ *02/88838888* ⊕ *www.armanihotelmilano.com* ⇨ *95 rooms* ⦿ *No Meals* Ⓜ *Montenapoleone.*

Four Seasons Hotel Milano

$$$$ | **HOTEL** | Built in the 15th century as a convent, with a colonnaded cloister, this sophisticated retreat in the heart of Milan's upscale shopping district certainly exudes a feeling that is anything but urban. **Pros:** quiet, elegant setting that feels removed from noisy central Milan; friendly and helpful staff; large rooms. **Cons:** decor is a bit old-fashioned; breakfast isn't included in the rate; expensive. $ *Rooms from: €810* ⊠ *Via Gesù 6–8, Quadrilatero* ☎ *02/77088* ⊕ *www.fourseasons.com/milan* ⇨ *118 rooms* ⦿ *No Meals* Ⓜ *Montenapoleone; Tram No. 1.*

Grand Hotel et de Milan

$$$$ | **HOTEL** | Only blocks from La Scala, you'll find everything you would expect from a traditionally elegant European hotel, where tapestries and persimmon velvet enliven a 19th-century look without sacrificing dignity and luxury.

Quadrilatero

KEY

- ① Sights
- ① Restaurants
- ① Quick Bites
- ① Hotels

Sights	
1	Museo Bagatti Valsecchi **C3**
2	Museo Poldi-Pezzoli.... **B4**

Restaurants	
1	Don Carlos............... **B3**
2	Seta **B3**

Quick Bites	
1	Chic & Go Milano........ **C3**

Hotels	
1	Armani Hotel Milano **C2**
2	Four Seasons **D3**
3	Grand Hotel et de Milan **C3**
4	Hotel Senato **D2**
5	Mandarin Oriental, Milan **B3**

Pros: traditional and elegant; staff go above and beyond to meet guest needs; great location off Milan's main shopping streets. **Cons:** gilt decor may not suit those who like more modern design; no spa; some small rooms. $ *Rooms from: €466* ⊠ *Via Manzoni 29, Quadrilatero* ☎ *02/723141* ⊕ *www.grandhoteletdemilan.it* ➟ *72 rooms and 23 suites* ❘❙❘ *Free Breakfast* Ⓜ *Montenapoleone.*

Hotel Senato

$$$ | HOTEL | The central courtyard of this boutique hotel near Milan's fashion district is covered in a layer of water, a cheeky nod to the Naviglio Grande canal that once ran in front of the 19th-century palace, which now has a sleek, minimalist design and artsy touches like brass ginkgo biloba–leaf lamps, serpentine mosaic floor patterns, and flowers and music selected by "curators." Relatively simple white-on-white guest rooms have black and gray accents, high ceilings, oak parquet floors, and white Carrara marble bathrooms; try for a room with a private terrace overlooking the peaceful courtyard. **Pros:** convenient location; lovely breakfast buffet with local products; cool designer touches. **Cons:** some rooms on the small side; basic gym facilities; noise can be an issue. $ *Rooms from: €286* ⊠ *Via Senato 22, Quadrilatero* ☎ *02/781236* ⊕ *www.senatohotelmilano.it* ➟ *43 rooms* ❘❙❘ *Free Breakfast* Ⓜ *Turati or Palestro; Tram No. 1; Bus No. 61 or 94.*

★ Mandarin Oriental, Milan

$$$$ | HOTEL | FAMILY | A sense of refined luxury pervades the guest rooms and public spaces of this sophisticated hotel, located just off the main Via Montenapoleone shopping street; from the elegant bedrooms with super-comfortable beds and oversize bathrooms with underfloor heating to the highly rated restaurant and one of the largest spas in Milan (9,700 square feet), you'll be taken care

of here. **Pros:** tranquil spa and 24-hour fitness center; wonderful and attentive service; top restaurant on-site. **Cons:** can be difficult to find; very expensive; only some rooms have views. $ *Rooms from: €700* ⊠ *Via Andegari 9, Quadrilatero* ☎ *02/87318888* ⊕ *www.mandarinoriental.com* ➟ *104 rooms* ❘❙❘ *No Meals* Ⓜ *Montenapoleone; Tram No. 1.*

🍸 Nightlife

Armani/Bamboo Bar

BARS | The Bamboo Bar at the Armani Hotel Milano has kept Milan abuzz since its opening in 2011. With high ceilings, louvered windows, and expansive views of the city's rooftops, this modern architectural marvel is a great spot to enjoy a relaxing cup of tea or a pre-dinner aperitivo. ⊠ *Via Manzoni 31, Quadrilatero* ☎ *02/88838888* ⊕ *www.armanihotelmilano.com* Ⓜ *Montenapoleone; Tram No. 1.*

🛍 Shopping

The heart of Milan's shopping reputation is the Quadrilatero della Moda district, north of the Duomo. Here the world's leading designers compete for shoppers' attention, showing off their ultrastylish clothes in stores that are works of high style themselves. It's difficult to find any bargains, but regardless of whether you're making a purchase, the area is a great place for window-shopping and people-watching.

Armani Megastore

OTHER SPECIALTY STORE | Armani Junior, Emporio Armani, Armani Fiori (flowers), Armani Dolci (chocolate), and Armani Libri (books) are all under this monumental store's roof. ⊠ *Via Manzoni 31, Quadrilatero* ☎ *02/62312600* ⊕ *www.armani.com* Ⓜ *Montenapoleone; Tram No. 1.*

★ DMAG Outlet

JEWELRY & WATCHES | This store has some of the best prices in the area for luxury items, such as Prada, Gucci, Lanvin, and Cavalli. DMAG has two other locations, at Via Forcella 13 and Via Bigli 4. ✉ *Via Manzoni 44, Quadrilatero* ☎ *02/36514365* ⊕ *www.dmag.eu* Ⓜ *Montenapoleone; Tram No. 1.*

★ Dolce & Gabbana

JEWELRY & WATCHES | This fabulous duo has created an empire based on sultry designs for men and women. The gorgeous three-story flagship store features clothing for both, plus accessories. ✉ *Via della Spiga 2, Quadrilatero* ☎ *02/795747* ⊕ *www.dolcegabbana.it* Ⓜ *San Babila; Tram No. 61 or 94.*

Dondup

MIXED CLOTHING | Started in 1999, Dondup is a Milanese brand that has captured the essence of casual chic. But it's no longer just a brand for denim lovers: its flagship store houses menswear, women's wear, accessories, and shoe collections. ✉ *Via della Spiga 50, Quadrilatero* ☎ *02/20242232* ⊕ *www.dondup.com* Ⓜ *Montenapoleone; Tram No. 1.*

Giorgio Armani

MIXED CLOTHING | Find Armani's apparel and accessories for both men and women in the brand's newest boutique. ✉ *Via Sant'Andrea 9, Quadrilatero* ☎ *02/76003234* ⊕ *www.armani.com* Ⓜ *San Babilo.*

Missoni

MIXED CLOTHING | Famous for their kaleidoscope-pattern knits, this family-run brand sells whimsical designs for men and women. ✉ *Via Sant'Andrea 2, Quadrilatero* ☎ *02/76003555* ⊕ *www.missoni.com* Ⓜ *Montenapoleone or San Babila; Tram No. 1.*

Miu Miu

MIXED CLOTHING | Prada's more upbeat, youthful brand has a wide offering of boldly printed women's fashions and accessories. ✉ *Via Sant'Andrea 21, Quadrilatero* ☎ *02/76001799* ⊕ *www.miumiu.com* Ⓜ *Montenapoleone, San Babila, or Palestro; Tram No. 1.*

Moschino

MIXED CLOTHING | Known for its bold prints, colors, and appliqués, Moschino is a brand for daring fashionistas. ✉ *Via Sant'Andrea 25, Quadrilatero* ☎ *02/76022639* ⊕ *www.moschino.com* Ⓜ *Montenapoleone, San Babila, or Palestro; Tram No. 1.*

Prada

MIXED CLOTHING | Founded in Milan, Prada has several locations throughout the city. Its stores on Via Montenapoleone showcase its women's (Via Montenapoleone 8) and men's fashions (Via Montenapoleone 6). ✉ *Via Montenapoleone 8, Quadrilatero* ☎ *02/7771771* ⊕ *www.prada.com* Ⓜ *Montenapoleone, San Babila, or Palestro; Tram No. 1.*

Roberto Cavalli

MIXED CLOTHING | Famous for his wild-animal prints, Roberto Cavalli creates sexy designs for men and women. ✉ *Via Montenapoleone 6/A, Quadrilatero* ☎ *02/7630771* ⊕ *www.robertocavalli.com* Ⓜ *San Babila.*

Salvatore Ferragamo Donna

WOMEN'S CLOTHING | This Florence-based brand is a leader in leather goods and accessories, and carries designs for women in this store. ✉ *Via Montenapoleone 3, Quadrilatero* ☎ *02/76000054* ⊕ *www.ferragamo.com* Ⓜ *San Babila.*

Salvatore Ferragamo Uomo

MEN'S CLOTHING | Ferragamo's men's accessories, leather goods, and ties are a staple for Milan's male fashion set. ✉ *Via Montenapoleone 20/4, Quadrilatero* ☎ *02/76006660* ⊕ *www.ferragamo.com* Ⓜ *Montenapoleone; Tram No. 1.*

Tod's

MIXED CLOTHING | This leather-goods leader sells luxury handbags as well as a variety of shoes for men and women. It also offers complete lines of men's and women's clothing. ⊠ *Via Montenapo-leone 13, Quadrilatero* ☎ *02/76002423* ⊕ *www.tods.com* Ⓜ *Montenapoleone, San Babila, or Palestro; Tram No. 1.*

Valentino

MIXED CLOTHING | Even after the departure of its founding father, Valentino Gara-vani, this fashion brand still flourishes. ⊠ *Via Montenapoleone 20, Quadrilatero* ☎ *02/76006182* ⊕ *www.valentino.com* Ⓜ *Montenapoleone; Tram No. 1.*

Versace

MIXED CLOTHING | Run by flamboyant Donatella Versace and known for its rock-and-roll styling, the first store of this fashion house opened on Via della Spiga in 1978, not far from its current location in the Quadrilatero della Moda shopping district. ⊠ *Via Monte Napole-one, 11, Quadrilatero* ☎ *02/7600 8528* ⊕ *www.versace.com* Ⓜ *San Babila or Montenapoleone.*

Porta Garibaldi

This stylish, upscale, and buzzing district is home to the emblematic 10 Corso Como concept store and the colorful and lively Piazza Gae Aulenti, which is a study in Milan's modern architecture, includ-ing the 757-foot UniCredit Tower. New construction, stylish restaurants, and urban parks provide a modern break from historical sight-seeing.

◉ Sights

ADI Design Museum Compasso d'Oro

OTHER MUSEUM | More than 350 of the most renowned Italian industrial design objects from the last 65 years are showcased in this former Enel electricity plant (with two original transformers still visible in one gallery), which opened as a museum in 2021. The items in the per-manent collection were selected during biennial judging for Compasso d'Oro (golden compass) awards from 1954 until today. Some of the exhibits are grouped by category, like cars (1960 Abarth-Fiat Monza Zagato, 1959 Fiat 500, and 2014 Ferrari F12berlinetta) and coffee makers (Alessi's 9090 from 1979 and Napoletana from 1981). There's even a 1960 Flying Dutchman boat from Alpa. There are also playful groupings by color, such as 1970's orange winners (Soriana sofa from Cas-sina and Elvi's 390 automatic processing unit). One of the galleries is dedicated to "grandfathers of design," such as Giulio Castelli, founder of Milan-based furniture maker Kartell, and Camillo Olivetti and his eponymous information technology company, which started out making typewriters (its Lettera 22, which won in 1954, is also on display). Peruse a design library in the bookstore and sip coffee or wine in the cafe, taking a seat in more than a dozen chairs from various Italian designers. ⊠ *Piazza Compasso d'Oro, 1, Garibaldi* ☎ *02/36693790* ⊕ *www. adidesignmuseum.org* 🎫 *€12* ⊙ *Closed Mon.* ☞ *Tickets may be purchased online, or at the museum with a credit card or mobile wallet (no cash accepted).* Ⓜ *Garibaldi.*

Piazza Gae Aulenti

PLAZA/SQUARE | Welcome to the modern era. The piazza named for the famed Italian female architect is a stroll into the future of architectural design. Here you'll find Italy's tallest skyscraper (the 757-foot mirrored and spired Unicredit Tower), IBM Studios (a curved and wood-slatted innovation lab), a Tesla dealership, and an LED tree surrounded by reflective pools. Nearby are Bosco Verticale—two apartment buildings covered in more than 900 hanging trees—part of Stefano Boeri's "Vertical Forest" project, which launched in 2014 to improve air quality in cities (the studio has since created similar structures in more than 20 loca-tions across the globe). Stroll through a botanical garden, Biblioteca degli Alberi (library of trees), and join locals picnicking when the weather cooperates. ⊠ *Piazza Gae Aulenti, Garibaldi* Ⓜ *Garibaldi.*

Porta Garibaldi and Repubblica

KEY
- ❶ Sights
- ❶ Restaurants
- ❶ Quick Bites
- ❶ Hotels

Sights ▼	Restaurants ▼	Quick Bites ▼	Hotels ▼
1 ADI Design Museum Compasso d'Oro **B3**	1 Ceresio 7 Pools & Restaurant **B2**	1 Pavè **E4**	1 Hotel Principe di Savoia Milano **D3**
2 Piazza Gae Aulenti....... **C2**	2 Ratanà **D2**	2 Zàini **C3**	2 Hotel Viu Milan........... **A3**
			3 ME Milan Il Duca **D4**
			4 Westin Palace **E4**

🍴 Restaurants

★ Ceresio 7 Pools & Restaurant

$$$$ | CONTEMPORARY | Book well in advance for one of Milan's most fashionable eateries, where the tables are lacquered red and modern artwork crowds the walls—exactly what you'd expect from the twin brothers, Dean and Dan Caten, behind the fashion label Dsquared2. The food cred matches the scene—with fresh, creative, sophisticated pastas and other dishes. **Known for:** swimming pools and terrace views; place for seeing and being seen; luxe ingredients like lobster, king crab, and truffles. $ *Average main: €36* ⊠ *Via Ceresio 7, Garibaldi* ☎ *02/31039221* ⊕ *www.ceresio7.com* Ⓜ *Garibaldi; Tram No. 2, 4, 12, or 14; Bus No. 37 or 190.*

Ratanà

$$ | NORTHERN ITALIAN | Chef Cesare Battisti infuses the Milanese dishes of his childhood with a contemporary twist at this lively restaurant. Its two patios face a park with skyline views, and its dining room is decorated with vintage items (like an Olivetti typewriter and Scandalli accordion). **Known for:** more than 500 wines; meat- and fish-focused menu with contemporary and traditional dishes; setting in a former historical house. $ *Average main: €24* ⊠ *Via Gaetano de Castillia, 28, Garibaldi* ☎ *02/87128855* ⊕ *www.ratana.it* ⊗ *2 wks in Aug. and 2 wks in Dec.* Ⓜ *Gioia.*

☕ Coffee and Quick Bites

Zàini

$ | BAKERY | The Zàini family opened its chocolate factory here in 1913, on a side street off Corso Como. Today, its black-and-white marble-tile–floored and chandelier-lit cafe, is found just past flagship stores for Dsquared2 and Moschino. **Known for:** elegant breakfast or aperitivo spot; decadent hot chocolate; artfully wrapped chocolate gifts. $ *Average main: €10* ⊠ *Via Carlo de Cristoforis, 5, Garibaldi* ☎ *02/694914449* ⊕ *www.zainispa.com* Ⓜ *Garibaldi.*

🛏 Hotels

Hotel Viu Milan

$$$ | HOTEL | A short walk from trendy Corso Como and the historic Cimitero Monumentale, this sleek business-focused hotel features vertical gardens outside and contemporary Italian-designed furnishings within—but its true pièce de résistance is an inviting rooftop pool with panoramic views. **Pros:** stylish modern decor; spacious bathrooms; high-quality food. **Cons:** hotel has a signature scent, which may bother perfume-averse guests; rooftop terrace sometimes not useable due to events; out-of-the-way location for central Milan. $ *Rooms from: €240* ⊠ *Via Aristotile Fioravanti 6, Garibaldi* ☎ *02/80010910* ⊕ *www.hotelviumilan.com* ⇆ *124 rooms* ⎮⊙⎮ *No Meals* Ⓜ *Monumentale; Tram No. 10, 12, or 14.*

🍸 Nightlife

Blue Note

LIVE MUSIC | The first European branch of the famous New York nightclub features regular performances by some of the most famous names in jazz, as well as blues and rock concerts. Dinner is also available. ⊠ *Via Borsieri 37, Garibaldi* ☎ *02/69016888* ⊕ *www.bluenotemilano.com* Ⓜ *Isola; Tram No. 7, 31, or 33.*

Dry Milano

BARS | A hot spot for both classic and creative cocktails, this trendy industrial space packed with hip locals has a pizza joint in the back if you get hungry. There's a second location at Viale Vittorio Veneto 28. ⊠ *Via Solferino 33, Garibaldi* ☎ *02/63793414* ⊕ *www.drymilano.it* Ⓜ *Moscova, Turati, or Repubblica; Tram No. 1, 9, or 33; Bus No. 37.*

Shopping

★ 10 Corso Como

OTHER SPECIALTY STORE | A shrine to Milan's creative fashion sense, the concept store 10 Corso Como was founded by the former fashion editor and publisher Carla Sozzani. The clothing and design establishment also includes a restaurant-café, gallery, bookstore, and small hotel. There's also a second store at Via Tazzoli 3. ✉ *Corso Como 10, Corso Como* ☎ *02/290113581* ⊕ *www.10corsocomo. com* Ⓜ *Porta Garibaldi.*

Repubblica

Some of the city's best restaurants and hotels can be found around the Piazza della Repubblica.

Coffee and Quick Bites

★ Pavè

$ | **BAKERY** | Your main problem at Pavè will be deciding what to order among rows of cakes, tarts, classic Italian brioches (with sweet fillings like cream and jam), and other pastries. When everything is this drool-worthy, your best strategy is to come with friends and share your favorites. **Known for:** sandwiches and crostini on housemade bread; vegan pastries; chocolate and fruit-filled tarts. ⑤ *Average main: €10* ✉ *Via Felice Casati, 27, Repubblica* ☎ *02/37905491* ⊕ *www.pavemilano.com* ⊗ *No dinner* Ⓜ *Repubblica.*

Hotels

Hotel Principe di Savoia Milano

$$$$ | **HOTEL** | Milan's grande dame has all the exquisite trappings of a traditional luxury hotel: lavish mirrors, drapes, and carpets; limousine services; and some of the city's largest guest rooms, outfitted with eclectic fin-de-siècle furnishings.

Pros: substantial health club–spa; shuttle to Duomo and shopping district; close to Central Station. **Cons:** located in a not-very-central or attractive neighborhood; breakfast and other meals overly expensive; showing a bit of wear and tear. ⑤ *Rooms from: €400* ✉ *Piazza della Repubblica 17, Repubblica* ☎ *02/62301* ⊕ *www.dorchestercollection.com/en/ milan/hotel-principe-di-savoia* ↪ *301 rooms* ❖❖ *No Meals* Ⓜ *Repubblica; Tram No. 1, 9, or 33.*

ME Milan Il Duca

$$$$ | **HOTEL** | The first Italian outpost of the Spanish hotel brand ME by Meliá has a lively party atmosphere, with rousing music playing in the lobby, a design-conscious vibe, and a happening rooftop bar with panoramic city views. **Pros:** great rooftop bar; young, vibrant atmosphere; spacious rooms. **Cons:** no spa; may feel overdesigned to some; can be noisy. ⑤ *Rooms from: €328* ✉ *Piazza della Repubblica 13, Repubblica* ☎ *02/35403218* ⊕ *www.melia.com/en/ hotels/italy/milan/me-milan-il-duca/index. htm* ↪ *132 rooms* ❖❖ *No Meals* Ⓜ *Repubblica; Tram No. 1, 5, 9, 10, or 33.*

Westin Palace

$$$$ | **HOTEL** | Don't be fooled by the functional 1950s-era exterior of one of Milan's premier business addresses: inside, rooms have a contemporary look with soothing gray walls and brown marble bathrooms. **Pros:** full-service hotel with extensive amenities; good-size gym open 24/7; renovated rooms in both modern and more traditional styles. **Cons:** Wi-Fi can be spotty in some rooms; not in the most central or attractive location; lacking in local character. ⑤ *Rooms from: €313* ✉ *Piazza della Repubblica 20, Repubblica* ☎ *02/63361* ⊕ *www.marriott.com/hotels/ travel/milwi-the-westin-palace-milan* ↪ *231 rooms* ❖❖ *Free Breakfast* Ⓜ *Repubblica; Tram No. 1, 5, 9, or 33.*

Nightlife

Radio Rooftop Bar

COCKTAIL LOUNGES | Some of Milan's most beautiful people congregate for an Aperol spritz and a selection of international tapas on this terrace with panoramic views of the city. Located at the top of the ME Milan Il Duca, the bar has heat lamps to keep visitors here even in cooler weather. You can also enjoy lunch Monday through Friday. ⊠ *Piazza della Repubblica 13, Repubblica* ☎ *02/84220109* ⊕ *www.radiorooftop.com/milan* Ⓜ *Repubblica; Tram No. 1, 5, 9, 10, or 33.*

Shopping

Antonioli

MIXED CLOTHING | Antonioli raises the bar for Milan's top trendsetters. Uniting the most cutting-edge looks of each season, it is among the fashion-forward concept stores in the city. Aside from Italian brands like Valentino, it also stocks a competitive international array of designers, like Ann Demeulemeester, Rick Owens, Givenchy, Jil Sander, Maison Margiela, and Vetements. ⊠ *Via Pasquale Paoli 1, Centro Direzionale* ☎ *02/36561860* ⊕ *www.antonioli.eu* Ⓜ *Porta Genova; Tram No. 2; Bus No. 47 or 74.*

Cinque Giornate

Located just east of the city center, Cinque Giornate marks the location of the Five Days revolt against Austrian rule in Milan.

Restaurants

Da Giacomo

$$$ | **ITALIAN** | The fashion and publishing crowds, as well as international bankers and businesspeople, favor this Tuscan-Ligurian restaurant. The emphasis is on fish, and with its tile floor and bank of fresh seafood, the place has a refined neighborhood-bistro style. **Known for:** extensive wines, cocktails, and after-dinner drinks; sophisticated dining; specialty gnocchetti alla Giacomo (with seafood and tomato). $ *Average main: €32* ⊠ *Via P. Sottocorno 6, entrance in Via Cellini, Cinque Giornate* ☎ *02/76023313* ⊕ *www. giacomoristorante.com* Ⓜ *Tram No. 9, 12, 23, or 27; Bus No. 60 or 73.*

Palestro

Nestled just below the Giardini Pubblici Indro Montanelli park, Palestro is filled with galleries, museums, and historical landmarks.

Sights

GAM: Galleria d'Arte Moderna/Villa Reale

HISTORIC HOME | One of the city's most beautiful buildings is an outstanding example of neoclassical architecture, built between 1790 and 1796 as a residence for a member of the Belgiojoso family. After it was donated to Napoléon, who lived here briefly with Empress Josephine, it became known as the Villa Reale. Its residential origins are evident in its elegant proportions and private back garden. The museum provides a unique glimpse of the splendors hiding behind Milan's discreet and often stern facades. The collection consists of works donated by prominent Milanese art collectors. It emphasizes 18th- and 19th-century Italian works, but also has a smattering of 20th-century Italian pieces as well as some international works by Van Gogh and Picasso, among others. The museum also presents regularly scheduled rotating exhibitions. ⊠ *Via Palestro 16, Palestro* ☎ *02/88445947* ⊕ *www.gam-milano.com* 🎫 *€5 (Free every 1st and 3rd Tues. of month after 2)* ⊘ *Closed Mon.* Ⓜ *Palestro or Turati; Tram No. 1 or 2; Bus No. 94 or 61.*

Cinque Giornate, Palestro,
Porta Venezia, Buenos Aires,
Loreto, and Bicocca

Sights ▼

1 Casa-Museo
  Boschi di Stefano....... **D2**

2 GAM: Galleria d'Arte
  Moderna./Villa Reale .. **B3**

3 Giardini Pubblici
  Indro Montanelli **C3**

4 Pirelli
  HangarBicocca.........**C1**

5 Villa Necchi
  Campiglio **C4**

Restaurants ▼

1 Da Abele................. **D1**

2 Da Giacomo **D5**

3 Joia........................**C2**

4 LùBar.....................**C3**

Quick Bites ▼

1 Marghe **D2**

Villa Necchi Campiglio

NOTABLE BUILDING | In 1932, architect Piero Portaluppi designed this sprawling estate in an art deco style, with inspiration coming from the decadent cruise ships of the 1920s. Once owned by the Necchi Campiglio industrial family, the tasteful and elegant home—which sits on Via Mozart, one of Milan's most exclusive streets—is a reminder of the refined, modern culture of the nouveaux riches who accrued financial power in Milan during that era. There is also a cafe on the grounds that is open 10 am–6 pm. ■ TIP→ **Tours of the estate last about one hour; English-speaking tours are offered Wed.–Sat. between 10:30 am and 2:15 pm.** ⊠ *Via Mozart 14, Palestro* ☎ *02/76340121* ⊕ *www.fondoambiente.it/villa-necchi-campiglio-eng* ☑ *€14 or €20 for guided visits; garden-only €4.* ☉ *Closed Mon. and Tues.* Ⓜ *Palestro, San Babila, or Montenapoleone; Bus No. 54, 61, or 94.*

Porta Venezia

This district is home to parks and gardens, museums, galleries, and one end of the famed Corso Buenos Aires shopping street.

◉ Sights

Giardini Pubblici Indro Montanelli

(*Public Gardens Indro Montanelli*)

GARDEN | FAMILY | Giuseppe Piermarini, architect of La Scala, laid out these gardens across Via Palestro from the Villa Reale in 1770. Designed as public pleasure gardens, today they are still popular with families who live in the city center. Generations of Milanese have taken pony rides and gone on the miniature train and merry-go-round. The park also contains a small planetarium and the **Museo Civico di Storia Naturale** (Municipal Natural History Museum). ⊠ *Corso Venezia 55,* *Porta Venezia* ☎ *02/88463337* ⊕ *www.assodidatticamuseale.it* ☑ *Gardens free, museum €5 (free every 1st and 3rd Tues. of month after 2 and 1st Sun. of month)* ☉ *Museum closed Mon.* Ⓜ *Palestro; Tram No. 9, 29, or 30.*

🍴 Restaurants

Joia

$$$$ | VEGETARIAN | At this hushed, haute-cuisine vegetarian haven near Piazza della Repubblica, delicious dishes—all without eggs and many without flour—are served in a minimalist beige room that puts the focus solely on the artistry of the food. Vegetarians, who often get short shrift in Italy, will marvel at the variety of culinary offerings made from many organic and biodynamic ingredients. **Known for:** well-thought-out wine selection; imaginative presentations; ever-changing menu. ⑤ *Average main: €40* ⊠ *Via Panfilo Castaldi 18, Porta Venezia* ☎ *02/29522124* ⊕ *joia.it* ☉ *Closed 2 wks in Aug. and Dec. 24–Jan.6* Ⓜ *Repubblica or Porta Venezia; Tram No. 1, 5, 9, or 33.*

LùBar

$$ | SICILIAN | Dining at LùBar, which was started by three children of Milan fashion designer Luisa Beccaria and which is tucked into the side of the Galleria d'Arte Moderna, feels like eating inside a greenhouse—only with fashionable people among the trees and plants. The cozy, chic environs lend themselves perfectly to nibbling on small plates of modern Sicilian food—for lunch, an afternoon snack, or a light dinner—all served on Caltagirone ceramics straight from Sicily. ⑤ *Average main: €16* ⊠ *Via Palestro 16, Porta Venezia* ☎ *02/83527769* ⊕ *www.lubar.it* Ⓜ *Palestro or Turati; Tram No. 1 or 2; Bus No. 94 or 61.*

🛍 Shopping

Milan has several shopping streets that serve nearby residential concentrations. **Corso Buenos Aires** begins in the Porta Venezia area, and runs northeast from the Giardini Pubblici. The wide and busy street is lined with affordable shops. It has the highest concentration of clothing stores in Europe, so be prepared to give up halfway. Avoid weekends after 3, when it seems the entire city is here looking for bargains.

Buenos Aires

This street in northeastern Milan is one of the busiest in the city and has over 350 stores and outlets to choose from.

👁 Sights

Casa-Museo Boschi di Stefano (*Boschi di Stefano House and Museum*)
HISTORIC HOME | To most people, Italian art means Renaissance art, but the 20th century in Italy was also a time of artistic achievement. An apartment on the second floor of a stunning art deco building designed by Milan architect Portaluppi houses this collection, which was donated to the city of Milan in 2003 and is a tribute to the enlightened private collectors who replaced popes and nobles as Italian patrons. The walls are lined with the works of postwar greats, such as Fontana, de Chirico, and Morandi. Along with the art, the museum holds distinctive postwar furniture and stunning Murano glass chandeliers. ✉ *Via Jan 15, Buenos Aires* ☎ *02/88463614* ⊕ *www. fondazioneboschidistefano.it* ✉ *Free* ⊘ *Closed Mon.* Ⓜ *Lima; Tram No. 33; Bus No. 60.*

☕ Coffee and Quick Bites

★ **Marghe**
$ | **NEOPOLITAN** | At Marghe, crafting Neopolitan-style pizza is art—as the line of people outside the restaurant each night suggests. Put your name down (they don't accept reservations), or better, arrive right before they open at 7:30 pm to grab a table in the rustic and lively dining room with exposed concrete walls, floral tiled floors, and pendant lights, where pizzas are delivered quickly and piping hot. **Known for:** pizza made from type 1 flour and dough that rises for 48 hours; ingredients from Naples and the Amalfi Coast; local atmosphere. ⑤ *Average main: €10* ✉ *Via Plinio 6, Buenos Aires* ☎ *02/54118711* ⊕ *www. marghepizza.com* Ⓜ *Lima.*

Loreto

Located in the northeastern part of the city, Piazzale Loreto has a rather grim recent history: In August 1944, the Gestapo in Milan publicly executed 15 Italian resistance fighters here. Less than a year later, Benito Mussolini and a number of other high-ranking fascists, were captured and shot, with their bodies displayed here. There are no placards or signs to mark this history, and the square itself has since been widened to accomodate more traffic.

🍴 Restaurants

Da Abele
$ | **ITALIAN** | The superb risotto dishes at this neighborhood trattoria change with the season; you'll find at least three on the menu—meat, fish, and vegetarian—and it's tempting to try them all. The setting is relaxed and the service is informal. **Known for:** reasonable prices; meat-focused main courses like tripe;

cozy neighborhood favorite. $ *Average main: €13* ✉ *Via Temperanza 5, Loreto* ☎ *02/2613855* ⊕ *www.trattoriadaabele.it* ⊘ *Closed Mon. No dinner weekdays and Sun.* Ⓜ *Pasteur.*

Bicocca

This university and business district plays host to musicals and concerts as well as art installations.

👁 Sights

Pirelli HangarBicocca

ARTS CENTER | Anselm Kiefer's *The Seven Heavenly Palaces*—seven cement towers extending 43–52 feet high, along with five of Kiefer's large-scale paintings—is the must-see permanent installation at this impressive gallery in a former train factory. There are also temporary exhibitions of contemporary art through-out the year; check the website for the latest showings. ✉ *Via Chiese 2, Bicocca* ☎ *02/66111573* ⊕ *www.hangarbicocca. org* 🎟 *Free* ⊘ *Closed Sat.–Tues.* Ⓜ *Via Chiese; Bus No. 87 or 51.*

Porta Romana

Home to some of Milan's wealthiest residents, Porta Romana is a hip and vibrant neighborhood.

👁 Sights

⭐ **Fondazione Prada**

ART MUSEUM | New structures of metal and glass and revamped buildings once part of a distillery from the 1910s now contain this museum's roughly 205,000 square feet. The modern art showcased here is not for the faint of heart. Permanent pieces, such as *Haunted House*, featuring works by Louise Bourgeois and Robert Gober, are avant-garde and challenging, and temporary exhibitions highlight cutting-edge Italian and international

Formula 1 Racing

Italian Grand Prix. Italy's Formula 1 fans are passionate and huge numbers converge in early September for the Italian Grand Prix, held 15 km (9 miles) northeast of Milan in Monza. The racetrack was built in 1922 within the **Parco di Monza**. Check the website for dates, as well as for special category races, like classic cars and motorcycles. Visitors are allowed to zoom around the track on certain days—guided by a professional driver, of course. ✉ *Monza Eni Circuit, Via Vedano 5, Parco di Monza, Monza* ⊕ *www. monzanet.it.*

artists. Don't hesitate to ask one of the helpful, knowledgeable staffers for guidance navigating the expansive grounds, which can be confusing. And don't miss the Wes Anderson–designed café, Luce Bar, for a drink or snack, or the Restaurant Torre for an aperitivo or a full meal with panoramic views from on high. The Fondazione is a hike from the city center; expect a 10-minute walk from the metro station to the galleries. ✉ *Largo Isarco 2, Porta Romana* ☎ *02/56662611* ⊕ *www. fondazioneprada.org* 🎟 *€15 for full visit admission, which includes a ticket to Milano Osservatorio; €8-10 for temporary exhibitions or permanent projects only.* ⊘ *Closed Tues.* Ⓜ *Lodi TIBB; Tram No. 24; Bus No. 65.*

🍽 Restaurants

U Barba

$ | **NORTHERN ITALIAN** | Simple, fresh, authentic Ligurian (in that region's dialect the name means "the uncle") specialties will take you back to lazy summer days on the Italian Riviera—even during

Porta Romana, Ticinese, Navigli, and Tortona

Milan's gray winters. Such coastal classics as *trofie al pesto* (an egg-free pasta served with pesto) and *bagnun di acciughe* (anchovy soup), coupled with a basket of warm focaccia, or a side of *farinata* (a chickpea pancake) reign supreme in this Milan favorite. **Known for:** focaccia and farinata; fresh pasta, also available to take home; charming setting with vintage furniture. $ *Average main: €14 ⊠ Via Pier Candido Decembrio 33, Porta Romana ☎ 02/45487032 ⊕ www. ubarba.it ⊗ Closed Mon. No lunch Tues.– Fri. Ⓜ Lodi TIBB; Tram No. 16; Bus No. 90.*

Ticinese

This boho district is also home to the Basilica di San Lorenzo Maggiore and the Basilica di Sant'Eustorgio.

Sights

MUDEC (Museo delle Culture)

ART MUSEUM | Home to a permanent collection of ethnographic displays as well as temporary exhibitions of big-name artists such as Basquiat and Miró, MUDEC is in the vibrant and developing Zona Tortona area of the city. British architect David Chipperfield designed the soaring space in a former factory. The permanent collection includes art, objects, and documents from Africa, Asia, and the Americas. Book in advance for the most popular temporary exhibits. There's also a highly rated restaurant, Enrico Bartolini Mudec, as well as a more casual bistro. ⊠ *Via Tortona 56, Ticinese ☎ 02/54917 ⊕ www.mudec.it ☜ Permanent collection free, special exhibitions €10–€17 ⊗ Closed Mon. until 2:30 pm Ⓜ Sant'Agostino or Porta Genova; Tram No. 2 or 14; Bus No. 68 or 90/91.*

San Lorenzo Maggiore alle Colonne

CHURCH | Sixteen ancient Roman columns line the front of this sanctuary; 4th-century Paleo-Christian mosaics survive in the Cappella di Sant'Aquilino (Chapel of

"Let's Go to the Columns"

Andiamo al Le Colonne, in Milanese youthspeak, is the cue to meet up at the sober Roman columns in front of the Basilica San Lorenzo Maggiore. Attracted to the Corso di Porta Ticinese by its bars and shops, hipsters spill out on the street to chat and drink. Neighbors may complain about the noise and confusion, but students and nighthawks find it indispensable for socializing at all hours. It's a street—no closing time.

St. Aquilinus). ⊠ *Corso di Porta Ticinese 35, Ticinese ☎ 02/89404129 ⊕ www. sanlorenzomaggiore.com ☜ Mosaics €2 Ⓜ Missori.*

🍴 Restaurants

★ [bu:r] di Eugenio Boer

$$$$ | **MODERN ITALIAN** | Named after the phonetic spelling of the Dutch-Italian chef's last name, this innovative, high-concept restaurant, whose quiet dining rooms are done up in gray and gold, offers a choice of interesting tasting menus and à la carte options. Boer's contemporary Italian food is beautifully presented and full of complex flavors, and the well-matched wines lean toward the natural. **Known for:** helpful and well-informed service; personalized cuisine; traditional dishes with an ultramodern spin. $ *Average main: €65 ⊠ Via Mercalli ang. Via SF D'Assisi, Ticinese ☎ 02/62065383 ⊕ www.restaurantboer.com ⊗ Closed Sun. No lunch. Ⓜ Crocetta; Tram No. 15; Bus No. 94.*

Hotels

★ The Yard

$$$ | HOTEL | The decor in this eclectic, extremely hip hotel at the foot of the lively Corso di Porta Ticinese and by the Navigli canals features sports memorabilia from golf, horseback riding, boxing, and others. **Pros:** very friendly staff; contemporary flair; interesting location near many restaurants and bars. **Cons:** about a half-hour hike from the Duomo and central attractions; lacking some of the amenities of large hotels; bar noise can be heard in some rooms. $ *Rooms from: €229* ⊠ *Piazza XXIV Maggio 8, Porta Ticinese* ☎ *02/89415901* ⊕ *www.theyardmilano.com* ⤵ *32 rooms* ⦿ *Free Breakfast* Ⓜ *Tram No. 3 or 9.*

Navigli

One of the oldest neighborhoods in the city, Navigli is a quiet, artistic hub by day and a lively hot spot by night.

⊙ Sights

★ Navigli District

HISTORIC DISTRICT | In medieval times, a network of *navigli,* or canals, crisscrossed the city. Almost all have been covered over, but two—Naviglio Grande and Naviglio Pavese—are still navigable. The area's chock-full of boutiques, art galleries, cafés, bars, and restaurants, and at night the Navigli serves up a scene about as close as you will get to southern Italian–style street life in Milan. On weekend nights, it is difficult to walk among the youthful crowds thronging the narrow streets along the canals. Check out the antiques fair on the last Sunday of the month from 9 to 6. ■**TIP→ During the summer months, be sure to put on some mosquito repellent.** ⊠ *South of Corso Porta Ticinese, Navigli* Ⓜ *Porta Genova; Tram No. 2, 3, 9, 14, 15, 29, or 30.*

Nightlife

Rita

BARS | Though it's a bit difficult to find, on a side street in the popular aperitivo haunt of Navigli, the expertly mixed cocktails, well-prepared snacks, and excellent playlist make this classic worth the hunt. It also serves burgers, sandwiches, and more substantial plates for dinner. ⊠ *Via Angelo Fumagalli 1, Navigli* ☎ *02/837 2865* Ⓜ *Porta Genova; Tram No. 2.*

★ Ugo Bar

BARS | Flanked by a long bar and tables lit by candles, and featuring floral wallpaper and eclectic framed paintings of animals, this bar has a moody living-room vibe. It's a charming place for a drink, if you can squeeze past the crowds. There is also a handful of outdoor tables for prime people-watching. ⊠ *Via Corsico 12, Navigli* ☎ *02/39811557* ⊕ *www.ugobar.it* Ⓜ *Porta Genova; Tram No. 9 or 10.*

Performing Arts

Auditorium di Milano Fondazione Cariplo

CONCERTS | This modern hall, known for its excellent acoustics, is home to the **Orchestra Sinfonica di Milano Giuseppe Verdi** (Symphonic Orchestra) and **Coro Sinfonico di Milano Giuseppe Verdi** (Symphonic Choir). The season, which runs from September to June, includes many top international performers and rotating guest conductors. ⊠ *Largo Gustav Mahler, at Corso San Gottardo, Navigli* ☎ *02/83389401* ⊕ *www.laverdi.org* Ⓜ *Tram No. 3 or 15; Bus No. 59 or 91.*

Tortona

Tortona's former factories, warehouses, and workshops are now a creative hub packed with shops, studios, and the MUDEC, a museum with modern and contemporary art and special exhibitions.

Sights

★ Armani/Silos

OTHER MUSEUM | About 600 pieces, from about 1980 to the present, by famed Milanese fashion designer Giorgio Armani are displayed on four floors of this airy 48,000-square-foot museum, housed in a 1950s building that was formerly a Nestlé cereal storage facility. The collection is divided by theme: Ethnicities; Androgynous, including many of Armani's famous suits; and Stars, with clothes worn to the Oscars and other celebrity-studded events. A digital archive lets you explore Armani's full body of work, and a café lets you stop for a restorative espresso. Temporary exhibitions explore photography, architecture, and other themes related to design. ⊠ *Via Bergognone 40, Ticinese* ☎ *02/91630010* ⊕ *www.armanisilos.com* ⊠ *€12* ⊘ *Closed Mon. and Tues.* Ⓜ *Sant'Agostino or Porta Genova; Tram No. 2 or 14; Bus No. 68 or 90/91.*

Hotels

Hotel Magna Pars Suites Milano

$$$$ | **HOTEL** | Next to the trendy Navigli canals area, this ultrastylish all-suites boutique hotel in a former perfume factory has Italian-designed furnishings; paintings by local Brera Academy artists; and sleek, white accommodations—each with its own signature scent (such as fruity, woodsy, or floral) and all overlooking one of two tranquil courtyards. **Pros:** wonderful food at the attached restaurant; modern, design-y feel; attentive service. **Cons:** a bit of a trek to central attractions; spa on the small side; perfumed rooms not for everyone. ⑤ *Rooms from: €327* ⊠ *Via Forcella 6, Tortona* ☎ *02/8338371* ⊕ *www.magnapars-suitesmilano.it* ⋈ *60 suites* ⏹ *No Meals* Ⓜ *Porta Genova; Tram No. 2, 9, or 19.*

Bergamo

52 km (32 miles) northeast of Milan.

If you're driving from Milan to Lake Garda, the perfect deviation from your autostrada journey is the lovely medieval town of Bergamo, which is also a wonderful side trip by train from Milan. With direct service from Milan, you'll be whisked from the restless pace of city life to the medieval grandeur of Bergamo Alta in less than an hour.

From behind a set of battered Venetian walls high on an Alpine hilltop, Bergamo majestically surveys the countryside. Behind are the snowcapped Bergamese Alps, and two funiculars connect the modern **Bergamo Bassa** (Lower Bergamo) to the ancient **Bergamo Alta** (Upper Bergamo). Bergamo Bassa's long arteries and ornate piazzas speak to centuries of prosperity, but it's nonetheless overshadowed by Bergamo Alta, whose magnificent architecture has a fairy-tale allure.

GETTING HERE AND AROUND

Bergamo is along the A4 autostrada. By car from Milan, take the A51 out of the city to pick up the A4; the drive is 52 km (32 miles) and takes about 45 minutes. By train, Bergamo is about one hour from Milan and 1½ hours from Sirmione.

VISITOR INFORMATION

CONTACTS Bergamo Tourism Office. ⊠ *Torre del Gombito, Via Gombito 13, Bergamo Alta, Bergamo* ☎ *035/242226* ⊕ *www.visitbergamo.net.*

Sights

Accademia Carrara

ART MUSEUM | Bergamo is home to an art collection that's surprisingly rewarding given its size and remote location. Many of the Venetian masters are represented—Mantegna, Bellini, Carpaccio (circa 1460–1525/26), Tiepolo (1727–1804), Francesco Guardi (1712–93), and Canaletto (1697–1768), as well as Botticelli

The medieval town of Bergamo at sunrise

(1445–1510). ✉ *Piazza Carrara 82, Bergamo Bassa, Bergamo* ☎ *035/234396 Mon.–Fri., 035/4122097 Sat.–Sun.* ⊕ *www.lacarrara.it* ✉ *€10* ☽ *Closed Tues.*

Campanone

VIEWPOINT | The massive 13th-century Torre Civica (Civic Tower), known as the Campanone, offers a great view of the two cities. Climb the stairs or take an elevator to the top of the tower, where the bells ring every half hour and then 100 times each night at 10 to commemorate the closure of the city gates during Venetian rule. ✉ *Piazza Vecchia, Bergamo Alta, Bergamo* ☎ *035/247116* ✉ *€5* ☽ *Closed Mon.*

Cappella Colleoni

CHURCH | Bergamo's **Duomo** and **Battistero** are the most substantial buildings in Piazza Duomo. But the most impressive structure is the Cappella Colleoni, which boasts a kaleidoscope of marble decoration and golden accents. ✉ *Piazza Duomo, Bergamo* ☎ *035/210061* ☽ *Closed Mon.*

🍴 Restaurants

★ Al Donizetti

$$ | NORTHERN ITALIAN | Find a table in the back of this central, cheerful restaurant before choosing local cured meats and cheeses to accompany your wine. A few versions of polenta, daily pastas, and other heartier dishes are also available; just save room for the desserts, which go well with the sweet wines. **Known for:** chocolate desserts; beef tartare; 900-bottle wine selection with many by-the-glass. ⑤ *Average main: €20* ✉ *Via Gombito 17/a, Bergamo Alta, Bergamo* ☎ *035/242661* ⊕ *www.donizetti.it* ☽ *Closed Tues.*

Da Ornella

$$ | NORTHERN ITALIAN | The vaulted ceilings of this popular trattoria on the upper town's main street are marked with ancient graffiti, created by (patiently) holding candles to the stone overhead. The house specialties are simple but tasty: polenta *taragna* (with buckwheat flour) cooked with butter and cheese and served with rabbit, chicken, or sliced mushrooms with oil, garlic, and parsley. **Known for:** casoncelli (meat-filled pasta from Lombardy) dell'Ornella; local salame; historical setting. $ *Average main: €15* ✉ *Via Gombito 15, Bergamo Alta, Bergamo* ☎ *035/232736* ◷ *Closed Thurs.*

Vineria Cozzi

$$ | WINE BAR | The wine list at this romantic but informal *vineria* (wine bar) is exceptional—both by the glass and by the bottle—and there's also an array of flavorful foods, from snacks to sumptuous full-course meals typical of the region. The atmosphere is warm and charming, harking back more than 150 years to when the spot was first established in Bergamo as a lively meeting place. **Known for:** polenta dishes as starters and mains; quirky historical decorations; cellar with more than 300 wines. $ *Average main: €18* ✉ *Via B. Colleoni 22, Bergamo Alta, Bergamo* ☎ *035/238836* ⊕ *www.vineriacozzi.it.*

 Hotels

Excelsior San Marco

$$ | HOTEL | Some of the comfortable (if generic) rooms at this Bergamo Bassa hotel a short walk from the funicular have balconies with amazing upper town views. **Pros:** modern surroundings; panoramic views from rooftop restaurant; convenient location with parking. **Cons:** many bathrooms on the small side; rooms a little dated; hotel decor is nothing special. $ *Rooms from: €175* ✉ *Piazza della Repubblica 6, Bergamo Bassa, Bergamo* ☎ *035/366111* ⊕ *www.hotelsanmarco. com* ➥ *154 rooms* ⦿| *Free Breakfast.*

Mercure Bergamo Centro Palazzo Dolci

$ | HOTEL | Set in a restored 19th-century palazzo, this Bergamo Basso hotel has modern comforts and a friendly, efficient staff, making it a good choice for both business and leisure travelers. **Pros:** convenient to train station, airport, and some shopping; bountiful breakfast buffet; good value. **Cons:** basic rooms; no parking on-site; no restaurant. $ *Rooms from: €104* ✉ *Viale Papa Giovanni XXIII 100, Bergamo Bassa, Bergamo* ☎ *035/227411* ⊕ *www.hotelpalazzodolci.it/en/* ➥ *92 rooms* ⦿| *Free Breakfast.*

Pavia

40 km (25 miles) south of Milan.

Pavia was once Milan's chief regional rival. The city dates from at least the Roman era and was the capital of the Lombard kings for two centuries (572–774). It was at one time known as "the city of a hundred towers," but only a few have survived the passing of time. Its prestigious university was founded in 1361 on the site of a 10th-century law school, but it has roots that can be traced to antiquity.

GETTING HERE AND AROUND

By car from Milan, start out on the A7 autostrada and exit onto the A53 as you near Pavia; the drive is 40 km (25 miles) and takes about 45 minutes. Pavia is 30–40 minutes by train from Milan and 1½ hours (by slower regional service) from Cremona. The Certosa is 30 minutes by train from Milan Rogoredo station.

VISITOR INFORMATION

CONTACT Pavia Tourism Office. ✉ *Palazzo del Broletto, Via Paratici 21, Pavia* ☎ *0382/399343* ⊕ *www.visitpavia.com.*

 Sights

Castello Visconteo

CASTLE/PALACE | The town's 14th-century fortress-castle now houses the local Museo Civico (Municipal Museum), with a Romanesque and Renaissance sculpture gallery, an archaeological collection, and a large picture gallery displaying works by Correggio, Bellini, Tiepolo, Hayez, Pellizza da Volpedo, and la Foppa, among others. ✉ *Viale XI Febbraio 35, near Piazza Castello, Pavia* ☎ *0382/399770* ⊕ *www.museicivici. pavia.it* ⊗ *Closed Tues.* ▣ *€10.*

Certosa di Pavia (*Carthusian monastery*) **HISTORIC SIGHT** | The main draw in Pavia is its *certosa* (Carthusian monastery), 9 km (5½ miles) north of the city center. Its elaborate facade shows the same relish for ornamentation as Milan's Duomo. The Certosa di Pavia's extravagant grandeur was due in part to the plan to have it house the tombs of the family of the first duke of Milan, Gian Galeazzo Visconti (who died during a plague, at age 49, in 1402). The best marble was used, taken undoubtedly by barge from the quarries of Carrara, roughly 240 km (150 miles) away. Although the floor plan is Gothic—a cross shape divided into a series of squares—the gorgeous fabric that rises above it is triumphantly Renaissance. On the facade, in the lower frieze, are medallions of Roman emperors and Eastern monarchs; above them are low reliefs of scenes from the life of Christ and from the career of Gian Galeazzo Visconti. The first duke was the only Visconti to be interred here, and not until some 75 years after his death, in a tomb designed by Gian Cristoforo Romano. Look for it in the right transept. In the left transept is a more appealing tomb—that of a rather stern middle-aged man and a beautiful young woman. The man is Ludovico il Moro Sforza, seventh duke of Milan, who commissioned Leonardo to paint *The Last Supper.* The woman is Ludovico's wife, Beatrice d'Este (1475–97), one of the most celebrated women of her day, the embodiment of brains, culture, birth, and beauty. Married when he was 40 and she was 16, they had enjoyed six years together when she died while delivering a stillborn child. Ludovico commissioned the sculptor Cristoforo Solari to design a joint tomb for the high altar of Santa Maria delle Grazie in Milan. Originally much larger, the tomb for some years occupied the honored place as planned.

Then, for reasons that are still mysterious, the Dominican monks sold the tomb to their Carthusian brothers in Pavia and part of it and its remains were lost. ✉ *Certosa, Località Monumento 4, 9 km (5½ miles) north of Pavia, Pavia* ☎ *0382/925613* ⊕ *www.certosatourism.it* ⊗ *Closed Mon.* ▣ *Free.*

San Pietro in Ciel d'Oro
CHURCH | This basilica, a Romanesque masterpiece, houses the tomb of Christianity's most celebrated convert, St. Augustine (354–430), who rests in an intricately carved white-marble Gothic ark on the high altar. ✉ *San Pietro in Ciel d'Oro 2, Pavia* ☎ *0382/303036* ⊕ *santagostinopavia.wordpress.com* ⊗ *Closed daily noon–3.*

🍴 Restaurants

Locanda Vecchia Pavia al Mulino
$$$ | NORTHERN ITALIAN | Amid sophisticated art nouveau surroundings, you can order creative versions of traditional Lombard cuisine. All fish dishes are done with verve, as are the *lasagnette di pasta fresca alla robiola spinaci* (lasagna with soft cheese and spinach), *nocette d'agnello* (noisette of lamb), and veal-shank stew. **Known for:** veranda (summer only) with a view of Certosa di Pavia; Pavese wines; tasting menu with Lombard dishes and homemade pasta. ⑤ *Average main: €31* ✉ *Via al Monumento 5, Certosa di Pavia* ☎ *0382/925894* ⊗ *Closed Mon., Aug., and Jan. No dinner Sun.*

Cremona

85 km (53 miles) east of Pavia, 100 km (62 miles) southeast of Milan.

Cremona is a classical-music lover's dream. With violin shops on every block along its crooked old streets, it is where the world's best violins are crafted. Andrea Amati (1510–80) invented the modern instrument here in the 16th

The Po Plain, Lake Garda, and Lake Iseo

TRENTINO ALTO ADIGE

Riva del Garda
Limone
Malcesine
Tignale
Monte Baldo
A22
Gargnano
Gardone Riviera
Salò
Punta di San Vigilio
Bardolino
TO VERONA
TO VENICE
Sirmione
Desenzano
Mantua

Lake Garda

Darfo-Boario
Sale Marasino
Sarezzo
Brescia
Monte Isola
Lake Iseo
Borgonato
Franciacorta
Cortefranco
Erbusco
Ca' del Bosco
Cortefranco

LOMBARDY

Oglio

Cremona

Bergamo
Sarnico
Casalpusterlengo
TO PARMA

Adda
Crema
Treviglio
Lodi
Melegnano

Lecco
Giussano
Monza
Milan
Rozzano
Certosa di Pavia
Pavia

Como
Buccinasco
Legnano
Lainate
Rho

Aeroporto Malpensa

Mortara

Ticino

10 mi
10 km

century. Though cognoscenti continue to revere the Amati name, it was an apprentice of Amati's nephew for whom the fates had reserved wide and lasting fame. In a career that spanned an incredible 68 years, Antonio Stradivari (1644–1737) made more than 1,200 instruments—including violas, cellos, harps, guitars, and mandolins, in addition to his fabled violins. They remain the most coveted, most expensive stringed instruments in the world.

Strolling about this quiet medium-size city, you can't help noting that violin making continues to flourish. There are, in fact, more than 150 *liutai* (violin makers), many of them graduates of the Scuola Internazionale di Liuteria (International School of Violin Making). You're usually welcome in these ateliers, where traditional craftsmanship reigns supreme, especially if you're contemplating the acquisition of your own instrument; the tourist office can provide addresses.

Cremona's other claim to fame is *torrone* (nougat), which is said to have been created here in honor of the marriage of Bianca Maria Visconti and Francesco Sforza, which took place in October 1441. The new confection, originally prepared by heating almonds, egg whites, and honey over low heat, and shaped and named after the city's tower, was created in symbolic celebration. The annual Festa del Torrone is held in the main piazza over the third or fourth week of November.

GETTING HERE AND AROUND
By car from Milan, start out on the A1 autostrada and switch to the A21 at Piacenza; the drive is about 100 km (62 miles) and takes about 1½ hours. From Pavia, take the SP617 to the A21; the trip is 85 km (53 miles) and takes about an hour. By train, Cremona is about an hour from Milan and 1½ hours from Desenzano, near Sirmione on Lake Garda.

CONTACT Cremona Tourism Office. ⊠ *Piazza del Comune 5, Cremona* ☎ *0372/407081* ⊕ *www.turismocremona.it.*

 ## Sights

Duomo
CHURCH | Cremona's Romanesque Duomo was consecrated in 1190. It's an impressive structure in a breathtaking piazza, and certainly one of the most beautiful churches in Italy. Here you can find the *Story of the Virgin Mary and the Passion of Christ,* the central fresco of an extraordinary cycle commissioned in 1514 and featuring the work of local artists, including Boccaccio Boccaccino, Giovanni Francesco Bembo, and Altobello Melone. ⊠ *Piazza del Comune, Cremona* ☎ *0373/495011* ⊕ *www.diocesidicrema. it.*

★ Museo del Violino
OTHER MUSEUM | At this lovely and informative museum dedicated to all things violin, even those not already enamored by the instrument will find something to appreciate. Historic violins made in Cremona by masters, including Stradivari, are presented as works of art; be sure to get the audio guide included with admission to listen to recordings as you stroll. An audio chamber lets you hear a musical performance in "3D audio"—and if you're lucky, there will be a live concert going on at the innovative on-site auditorium, where the seats wrap around the stage and musicians for an immersive experience. ⊠ *Palazzo dell'Arte, Piazza Marconi 5, Cremona* ☎ *0372/801801, 0372/080809 tickets* ⊕ *www.museodelviolino.org* ⊒ *€12* ⊙ *Closed Mon.*

No. 1 Piazza Roma
PLAZA/SQUARE | Legendary violin maker Antonio Stradivari lived, worked, and died near the verdant square at Piazza Roma 1 (not open to the public). According to local lore, Stradivari kept each instrument in his bedroom for a month before

varnishing it, imparting part of his soul before sealing and sending it out into the world. In the center of the park is Stradivari's grave, marked by a simple tombstone. ⊠ *Piazza Roma 1, Cremona.*

Piazza del Comune

PLAZA/SQUARE | The Duomo, tower, baptistery, and Palazzo Communale (city hall) surround this distinctive and harmonious square: the combination of old brick, rose- and cream-color marble, terra-cotta, and old copper roofs brings Romanesque, Gothic, and Renaissance together with unusual success. ⊠ *Piazza del Comune 8, Cremona.*

Torrazzo (*Big Tower*)

NOTABLE BUILDING | Dominating Piazza del Comune is perhaps the tallest campanile in Italy, visible for a considerable distance across the Po Plain. The tower's astronomical clock is the 1583 original. Climb the 500-plus steps to the top for amazing views; along the way, you can stop at the Museo Verticale for informative displays on astronomy and ancient methods of measuring time. ⊠ *Piazza del Comune, Cremona* ☎ *0372/495011* ⊕ *www.dioce-sidicremona.it/museoverticale* ⌨ *€5 (€6 with baptistery)* ⊗ *Closed daily 1–2:30 and Mon. in Jan.–Feb.*

Restaurants

La Sosta

$$ | NORTHERN ITALIAN | This osteria looks to the 16th century for culinary inspiration, with excellent homemade salami and two popular primi—*gnocchi vecchia Cremona* (stuffed with sausage and baked with poppy seeds, sesame, and Parmigiano-*Reggiano*) and *marubini Cremonesi ai tre brodi* (stuffed meat ravioli in broth)—made according to time-tested recipes. Order the tiramisu and an accompanying dessert wine for a perfect finish. **Known for:** extensive wine cellar with dessert wines; cheese tasting menu; Cremonese sausage and veal ossobuco. ⑤ *Average main: €22* ⊠ *Via*

Sicardo 9, Cremona ☎ *0372/456656* ⊕ *www.osterialasosta.it* ⊗ *Closed Mon. and 3 wks in Aug. No dinner Sun.*

Coffee and Quick Bites

★ **Pasticceria Duomo**

$ | CAFÉ | This portal to the past opened in 1883 and still serves up such handmade local delights as *pan torrone* (a loaf cake made with chunks of nougat) and *torta cremona* (a cake made with almond flour and filled with Amarena cherries). A relaxing stop between visiting museums, it's the perfect place to have a cappuccino and sit by the fireplace. **Known for:** seasonal decorated cakes and pastries; Old World charm; *torrone* (nougat) in many shapes and sizes. ⑤ *Average main: €10* ⊠ *Via Boccaccino 6, Cremona* ☎ *0372/22273* ⊕ *www.pasticceriaduomo. it* ⊗ *Closed Tues.*

Hotels

Delle Arti Design Hotel

$$ | HOTEL | With modern interiors and eclectic but comfortable designer furniture, this aptly named hotel makes a nice counterpoint to the historical surroundings of Cremona. **Pros:** convenient central location; good breakfast options; friendly staff. **Cons:** small bathrooms; hallways can be a little dark; starting to show its age. ⑤ *Rooms from: €135* ⊠ *Via Bonomelli 8, Cremona* ☎ *0372/23131* ⊕ *www.dellearti.com* ⑩ *Free Breakfast* ⇥ *33 rooms.*

Hotel Impero

$ | HOTEL | Just a few minutes' walk from the Duomo and the Museo del Violino, this comfortable hotel with functional yet pleasant rooms (the best of which overlook the piazza) is well equipped to satisfy both leisure and business travelers. **Pros:** highly professional staff; spacious rooms; central location. **Cons:** breakfast is basic; outside noise can be a problem, especially on weekends; rooms are a little bland and outdated. ⑤ *Rooms* *from: €97* ⊠ *Piazza della Pace 21, Cremona* ☎ *0372/413013* ⊕ *www.hotelimpero.cr.it* ⤳ *53 rooms* ◎I *Free Breakfast.*

 ## Shopping

Sperlari

FOOD | Sperlari and parent company Fieschi have grown into a confectionery empire, but it all started at this handsome shop, which has been selling Cremona's famous nougat and its best *mostarda* (a preserved-fruit condiment served alongside meat and cheese) since 1836. While shopping for these items—as well as teas, marmalades, and other Italian delights—be sure to check out the historical product display at the back of the store. ⊠ *Via Solferino 25, Cremona* ☎ *0372/22346* ⊕ *www.sperlari1836.com.*

Mantua

192 km (119 miles) southeast of Milan.

Mantua (Mantova in Italian) stands tallest among the ancient walled cities of the Po Plain; it may not be flashy or dramatic, but its beauty is subtle and deep, hiding a rich trove of artistic, architectural, and cultural gems beneath its slightly somber facade. Its fortifications are circled on three sides by the passing Mincio River, which long provided Mantua with protection, fish, and a steady stream of river tolls on its meandering way from Lake Garda to the Po.

Mantua first came to prominence in Roman times as the home of Virgil, but its grand monuments date from the glory years of the Gonzaga dynasty. From 1328 until 1708, when the Austrian Hapsburgs sacked the city, Gonzaga dukes and marquesses reigned over a wealthy independent commune, and the arts thrived in the relative peace. Raphael's star pupil, Andrea Mantegna, who served as court painter for 50 years, was the best known of a succession of the artists

and architects who served Mantua through the years; some of his finest work, including his only surviving fresco cycle, can be seen here. Giulio Romano (circa 1499–1546), Mantegna's apprentice, built his masterpiece, Palazzo Te, on an island in the river. Leon Battista Alberti (1404–72), who designed two impressive churches in Mantua, was widely emulated later in the Renaissance.

GETTING HERE AND AROUND

Mantua is 5 km (3 miles) west of the A22 autostrada. The drive from Milan, following the A4 to the A22, takes a little more than two hours. The drive from Cremona, along the SP10, is 1¼ hours. Most trains arrive in just under 2 hours from Milan, depending on the type of service, and in about 1½ hours from Desenzano, near Sirmione on Lake Garda, via Verona.

VISITOR INFORMATION

CONTACT Mantua Tourism Office. ⊠ *Piazza A. Mantegna 6, Mantua* ☎ *0376/432432* ⊕ *www.turismo.mantova.it.*

 ## Sights

Be sure to pick up a Mantova Sabbioneta Card (www.mantovacard.it) at the tourism office, the Palazzo Ducale, or the Palazzo Te. It entitles you to visit 11 museums for one price and also includes access to city buses.

Casa del Mantegna

HISTORIC HOME | Serious Mantegna aficionados will want to visit the house the artist designed and built around an intriguing circular courtyard, which is usually open to view. The exterior is interesting for its unusual design, and the interior, with its hidden frescoes, can be seen by appointment or during occasional art exhibitions. Hours and prices vary depending on the exhibition. ⊠ *Via Acerbi 47, Mantua* ☎ *0376/360506* ⊕ *www.casadelmantegna.it* 🎟 *Varies by exhibition* ☉ *Closed Mon.*

★ Palazzo Ducale

CASTLE/PALACE | The 500-room palace that dominates the Mantua skyline was built for the Gonzaga family, though much of the art within the castle was sold or stolen as the dynasty waned in power and prestige. A glimpse of past grandeur can still be spotted in the Camera degli Sposi (literally, the "Wedded Couple's Room") where Duke Ludovico and his wife held court. Mantegna painted the hall over a nine-year period at the height of his power, finishing at age 44. He made a startling advance in painting by organizing the picture plane in a way that systematically mimics the experience of human vision. The circular trompe l'oeil around the vaulted ceiling is famous for the many details that attest to Mantegna's greatness: the three-dimensional quality of the seven Caesars (the Gonzagas saw themselves as successors to the Roman emperors and paid homage to classical culture throughout the palazzo); the self-portrait of Mantegna (in purple, on the right side of the western fresco); and the dwarf peering out from behind the dress of Ludovico's wife (on the northern fresco). Only 25 people at a time are allowed in the Camera degli Sposi, and for only five minutes at a time (though sometimes longer in low season); reservations are recommended, either by phone or online (www.ducalemantova.org). ⊠ *Piazza Sordello 40, Mantua* ☎ *041/2411897* ⊕ *www.mantovaducale. beniculturali.it* ⤢ *€13. Free 1st Sun. of month* ◷ *Closed Mon.*

★ Palazzo Te

CASTLE/PALACE | One of the greatest of all Renaissance palaces, built between 1525 and 1535 by Federico II Gonzaga, is the Mannerist masterpiece of artist-architect Giulio Romano, who created a pavilion where the strict rules of courtly behavior could be relaxed for libertine pastimes. Romano's purposeful breaks with classical tradition are lighthearted and unprecedented; note, for example, the "slipping" triglyphs along the upper edge of the inside courtyard. Two highlights are the Camera di Amore e Psiche (Room of Cupid and Psyche), which depicts a wedding set among lounging nymphs, frolicking satyrs, and even a camel and an elephant; and the gasp-inducing Camera dei Giganti (Room of the Giants) that shows Jupiter expelling the Titans from Mount Olympus. The scale of the latter is overwhelming; the floor-to-ceiling work completely envelops the viewer. The room's rounded corners, and the river rock covering the original floor, were meant to make it seem cavelike. It is a "whisper chamber" in which words softly uttered in one corner can be heard in the opposite one. Note the graffiti from as far back as the 17th century. ⊠ *Viale Te 13, Mantua* ☎ *0376/323266* ⊕ *www. palazzote.it* ⤢ *€12.*

Sant'Andrea

CHURCH | Mantegna's tomb is in the first chapel to the left in this basilica, most of which was built in 1472. The current structure, a masterwork by the architect Alberti, is the third built on this spot to house the relic of the Precious Blood: the crypt holds two reliquaries containing earth believed to be soaked in the blood of Christ, brought to Mantua by Longinus, the soldier who pierced his side. They are displayed only on Good Friday. ⊠ *Piazza di Mantegna 1, Mantua* ☎ *0376/320220* ⊕ *www.parrocchiasantanselmomantova.it.*

🍴 Restaurants

Ambasciata

$$$$ | NORTHERN ITALIAN | Heralded as one of Italy's classic gourmet restaurants, Ambasciata (Italian for "embassy") emphasizes elegance in tiny Quistello, 20 km (12 miles) southeast of Mantua. Those who are willing to make the trek (and pay the bill) can opt for the tasting menu with an ever-changing array of traditionally inspired creations, such as the famed *tortelli di zucca* (pumpkin tortelli with pumpkin cream and

Parmigiano-Reggiano), or mains like guinea fowl with *mostarda* (a sweet and sour mustard from Mantua) and roast pigeon with 25-year reserve balsamic vinegar. **Known for:** attentive service; intricate cuisine coupled with classics; whimsical setting. $ *Average main: €55* ✉ *Piazzetta Ambasciatori del Gusto, 1, Quistello* ☎ *376/619169* ⊕ *www.ristorantelambasciata.eu* ⊙ *Closed Tues. No dinner Mon.*

 Hotels

Casa Poli

$$ | HOTEL | FAMILY | A refreshing minimalist influence, attention to detail, and creative touches (like the room number projected onto the hall floor) create a welcoming ambience with contemporary flair. **Pros:** tasteful and modern; families welcome; attentive staff. **Cons:** no on-site restaurant; some traffic noise in front-facing rooms; although convenient, not in the absolute center of the city. $ *Rooms from: €125* ✉ *Corso Garibaldi 32, Mantua* ☎ *0376/288170* ⊕ *www.hotelcasapoli.it* ⇌ *27 rooms* ⊚ *Free Breakfast.*

Lake Iseo and Franciacorta

GETTING HERE AND AROUND
Frequent trains make the hour-long trip from Milano Centrale to Brescia. From there, hourly trains run to the town of Iseo (about half an hour) and then up Lake Iseo's eastern shore. You'll need a car to reach the western side or the Franciacorta wine region just south of the lake.

To drive from Milan or Bergamo, take the A4/E64; exit at Rovato on SP51 in the direction of Iseo. The trip takes about 1 hour and 20 minutes from Milan and 30 minutes from Bergamo. Ferries run from Sulzano, Sale Marasino, Iseo, and Tavernola Bergamasca to Monte Isola.

CONTACTS Lake Iseo and Franciacorta Tourism Office. ✉ *Lungolago Marconi 2/c* ☎ *030/3748733* ⊕ *www.visitlakeiseo.info.*

 Sights

Ca' del Bosco

WINERY | Modern sculptures adorn the grounds of this respected Franciacorta winery (one of the largest in the region). Enjoyable hour-long cellar tours conclude with a tasting; information about tour availability can be requested online. ✉ *Via Albano Zanella 13, Erbusco* ☎ *030/7766111* ⊕ *www.cadelbosco. com* ⊠ *From €20* ⊙ *Closed weekdays 12:30–2.*

★ Monte Isola

ISLAND | The largest island within any European lake, Monte Isola allows no cars (except authorized vehicles), making it the perfect place for leisurely walks and bike rides. The main towns are Siviano, with medieval mansions; Peschiera Maraglio, an old fishing village with 16th-century homes and the Church of St. Michele; and Carzano, with the 18th-century San Giovanni Battista church. Walk around the water and stop at the many restaurants and gelaterie, or, for more exercise, trek uphill to admire the views back to the shore. Frequent ferries from Sulzano stop at Peschiera Maraglio, and ferries from Sale Marasino arrive at Carzano; there are less frequent ferries from Iseo and Tavernola Bergamasca. ✉ *Monte Isola* ⊕ *www. navigazionelagoiseo.it.*

 Restaurants

★ Due Colombe Ristorante Al Borgo Antico

$$$ | NORTHERN ITALIAN | Visitors to Lake Iseo would do well to follow the locals' lead by sampling the delightful cooking at this cozy restaurant just south of the lake. The elegant dining area, with wood-beam ceilings and stone walls, is juxtaposed with the thoroughly modern menu, which offers a selection of "classic" and "creative" dishes. **Known for:** more than 900 wines to select from; countryside setting; Franciacorta sauces. ⑤ *Average main: €25* ⊠ *Via Foresti 13, Borgonato* ☎ *030/9828227* ⊕ *www. duecolombe.com* ⊗ *Closed Mon.–Wed. No dinner Sun.*

Hotels

★ L'Albereta

$$$$ | HOTEL | Set in an early-20th-century villa amid Franciacorta's hilly vineyards, this Relais & Chateaux property is a true sanctuary, with an enormous spa, a botanical garden, and vast, sculpture-filled grounds to explore. **Pros:** beautiful surroundings; cozy, calm, and luxurious atmosphere; excellent on-site restaurants. **Cons:** not all rooms have Lake Iseo views; rooms quite varied in terms of size and level of renovation; breakfast not included. ⑤ *Rooms from: €414* ⊠ *Via Vittorio Emanuele 23, Erbusco* ☎ *030/7760550* ⊕ *www.albereta.it* ⤴ *57 rooms* ⦿ *No Meals.*

Sirmione

138 km (86 miles) east of Milan.

Dramatically rising out of Lake Garda is the enchanting town of Sirmione. "*Paene insularum, Sirmio, insularumque ocelle,*" wrote Catullus in a homecoming poem: "It is the jewel of both peninsulas and islands." The forbidding Castello Scaligero stands guard behind the small bridge connecting Sirmione to the mainland; beyond, cobbled streets wind their way through medieval arches past lush gardens, stunning lake views, and gawking crowds. Originally a Roman resort town, Sirmione served under the dukes of Verona and later Venice as Garda's main point of defense. It has now reclaimed its original function, bustling with visitors in summer. Cars aren't allowed into town; parking is available by the tourist office at the entrance.

GETTING HERE AND AROUND

The town of Sirmione, at the south end of the lake, is 10 km (6 miles) from Desenzano, which has regular train service; it's about 1 hour and 20 minutes by train from Milan and 25 minutes from Verona. The A4 autostrada passes to the south of the lake, and the A22 runs north–south about 10 km (6 miles) from the eastern shore.

VISITOR INFORMATION

CONTACT Sirmione Tourism Office. ⊠ *Viale Marconi 8, Sirmione* ☎ *030/3748721, 030/3748722* ⊕ *www.sirmionebs.it.*

Sights

Bardolino

TOWN | This small town—one of the most popular summer resorts on the lake—is 32 km (20 miles) north of Sirmione along Lake Garda's eastern shore, at the wider end. It's most famous for its red wine, which is light, dry, and often slightly sparkling; the Festa dell'Uva e del Vino (Grape and Wine Festival), held here in early October, is a great excuse to indulge in the local product. Bardolino has two handsome Romanesque churches, both near the center: San Severo, from the 11th century, and San Zeno, from the 9th. ⊠ *Bardolino* ⊕ *www.bardolinoweb.com.*

Castello Scaligero di Sirmione

CASTLE/PALACE | As hereditary rulers of Verona for more than a century before they lost control of the city in 1402, the Della Scala counted Garda among their possessions. It was they who built this lakeside redoubt, along with almost all the other castles on the lake. You can go inside to take in a lake view from the tower, or you can swim at the nearby beach. ⊠ *Piazza Castello, Sirmione* ☎ *030/916468* ⓔ *€6* ⊗ *Closed Mon.*

Grotte di Catullo (*Grottoes of Catullus*)
RUINS | Locals will almost certainly tell you that these romantic lakeside ruins were once the site of the villa of Catullus (87–54 BC), one of the greatest pleasure-seeking poets of all time. Modern-day archaeology, however, does not concur, and there is some consensus that this was the site of two villas of slightly different periods, dating from about the 1st century AD. But never mind—the view through the cypresses and olive trees is lovely, and even if Catullus didn't have a villa here, he is closely associated with the area and undoubtedly did have a villa nearby. The ruins are at the top of the isthmus and are poorly signposted: walk through the historic center and past the various villas to the top of the spit; the entrance is on the right. Alternately, take a bus from town for a small fee. A small museum offers a brief overview of the ruins (on the far wall). ⊠ *Piazzale Orti Manara, Sirmione* ☎ *030/916157* ⊕ *www. grottedicatullo.beniculturali.it* 🎫 *€8 (free 1st Sun. of month)* 🕙 *Closed Tues.*

🍴 Restaurants

La Rucola 2.0
$$$$ | **MODERN ITALIAN** | Next to the castle and tucked into three charming rooms, this elegant, intimate restaurant is considered by many to be Sirmione's finest. Its creative menu has an appealing mix of fish (from the lake or the sea), meat, and vegetarian dishes, all accompanied by a good choice of wines; opt for one of the three-, five-, or seven-course tasting menus to fully experience the chef's sophisticated creations. **Known for:** meat, fish, and carte blanche tasting menus; fantastic wine list; open kitchen. ⑤ *Average main: €40* ⊠ *Vicolo Strentelle 3, Sirmione* ☎ *030/916326* ⊕ *www.ristorantelarucola.it* 🕙 *Closed Thurs.*

Ristorante Al Pescatore
$$ | **SEAFOOD** | Freshwater fish is the specialty at this simple, popular restaurant in Sirmione's historic center. Try the grilled trout with a bottle of local white, and then settle your meal with a walk in the nearby park. **Known for:** inexpensive meals; grilled fresh fish from the lake; extensive variety of pasta and seafood. ⑤ *Average main: €15* ⊠ *Via Giovanni Piana 20/22, Sirmione* ☎ *030/916216* ⊕ *www.ristorantealpescatore.com* 🕙 *Closed Thurs.*

🛏 Hotels

Hotel Sirmione e Promessi Sposi
$$$ | **HOTEL** | A homey feel with comfortable beds and upholstered furnishings with matching drapery, along with a luxurious thermal spa, keeps many guests returning year after year. **Pros:** nice spa area; next to the lake and near Castello; beautiful grounds. **Cons:** hotel could use a refresh; not all rooms have lake views; service can be indifferent. ⑤ *Rooms from: €203* ⊠ *Piazza Castello 19, Sirmione* ☎ *030/916331, 030/9904922 booking* ⊕ *www.termedisirmione.com* 🛌 *100 rooms* ⑪ *Free Breakfast.*

★ **Palace Hotel Villa Cortine**
$$$$ | **HOTEL** | This former private villa in a secluded park would be ostentatious if it weren't for the bucolic lakeside setting, the charming decor of the older rooms, and the accommodating staff. **Pros:** lovely pool area; an opulent experience; beautiful grounds. **Cons:** no gym; no spa at hotel but thermal baths a short walk away; very expensive. ⑤ *Rooms from: €530* ⊠ *Viale C. Gennari 2, Sirmione* ☎ *030/9905890* ⊕ *www. palacehotelvillacortine.com* 🕙 *Closed mid-Oct.–Apr.* 🛌 *54 rooms* ⑪ *Free Breakfast.*

Malcesine

63 km (39 miles) northeast of Sirmione, 180 km (112 miles) northeast of Milan.

Malcesine is one of the loveliest areas along the upper eastern shore of Lake Garda. It's principally known as a summer resort, with sailing and windsurfing schools. It tends to be crowded, but there are nice walks from the town toward the mountains. In winter, several lifts and more than 11 km (7 miles) of runs of varying degrees of difficulty serve skiers.

VISITOR INFORMATION

CONTACT Malcesine Tourism Office.
✉ *Via Gardesana 238, Malcesine* ☎ *045/7400044* ⊕ *www.visitmalcesine. com.*

 ## Sights

Castello di Malcesine

CASTLE/PALACE | Dominating the town is a 12th-century castle built by Verona's dynastic Della Scala family. It now contains a small museum of natural history. ✉ *Via Castello 39, Malcesine* ☎ *045/6570333* 🎫 *€6* ⊙ *Closed early Nov.–mid-Mar.*

Monte Baldo

MOUNTAIN | The futuristic *funivia* (cable car), which zips visitors to the top of Monte Baldo (7,276 feet), is unique because it rotates. After a 10-minute ride, you're high in Veneto where you can take a stroll and enjoy spectacular views of the lake. Ride the cable car down or bring along a mountain bike (or even a hang glider) for the descent. In the winter, there's skiing, snowboarding, and snowshoeing. ✉ *Via Navene Vecchia 12, Malcesine* ☎ *045/7400206* ⊕ *www. funiviedelbaldo.it* 🎫 *€22 round-trip (Malcesine–Monte Baldo)* ⊙ *Closed early Nov.–mid-Dec. and mid-Mar.–late Mar.*

Riva del Garda

18 km (11 miles) north of Malcesine, 180 km (112 miles) northeast of Milan.

Riva del Garda is set on the northern tip of Lake Garda, against a dramatic backdrop of jagged cliffs and miles of beaches. The old city, surrounding a pretty harbor, was built up during the 15th century, when it was a strategic outpost of the Venetian Republic.

VISITOR INFORMATION

CONTACT Riva del Garda Tourism Office.
✉ *Largo Medaglie d'Oro al Valor Militare 5, Riva del Garda* ☎ *0464/554444* ⊕ *www.gardatrentino.it.*

 ## Sights

Piazza III Novembre

PLAZA/SQUARE | This lakeside piazza, the heart of Riva del Garda, is surrounded by medieval palazzi. Standing there and looking out over the lake, you can understand why Riva del Garda has become a windsurfing destination: air currents ensure good breezes on even the most sultry midsummer days. ✉ *Piazza III Novembre, Riva del Garda.*

Torre Apponale

VIEWPOINT | Predating the Venetian period by three centuries, this sturdy tower looms above the medieval residences of the main square; its crenellations recall its defensive purpose. You can climb the 165 steps to see the view from the top. ✉ *Piazza III Novembre, Riva del Garda* ☎ *0464/573869* ⊕ *www.gardatrentino. it* 🎫 *€2* ⊙ *Closed mid-Nov.–mid-Mar. and Mon. mid-Mar.–May and early Nov.*

 ## Restaurants

Ristorante Castel Toblino

$$$ | **NORTHERN ITALIAN** | A lovely stop for a drink or a romantic dinner, this 16th-century castle is right on a lake in Sarche, about 20 km (12 miles) north of Riva oward Trento. Dishes highlight seasonal ocal ingredients, including mountain cheeses, salmon, trout, duck, and deer. **Known for:** fish tasting menu; wine ist featuring Trentino varieties; castle setting. $ *Average main: €25 ⊠ Localita' Castel Toblino, 1, Sarche ☏ 0461/864036 ⊕ www.casteltoblino.com ⊗ Closed Tues. and mid-Oct.–late Mar.*

Hotels

Du Lac et du Parc Grand Resort
$$$ | **RESORT** | **FAMILY** | Highly personal-zed service and well-appointed guest rooms (including bungalows perfect for families) are among the hallmarks of Riva's largest resort; another is the beautifully manicured 17-acre garden with more than 200 species of plants. **Pros:** lovely spa area; pampering and indulgent staff; lush, expansive grounds with two swimming pools, plus kids' pool. **Cons:** can hear noise in some rooms; no beach of its own; not that cozy. $ *Rooms from: €253 ⊠ Viale Rovereto 44, Riva del Garda ☏ 0464/566600 ⊕ www.dulacetduparc. com ⊷ 163 rooms ⦿ Free Breakfast ⊗ Closed mid-Nov.–late Mar.*

Hotel Sole
$$ | **HOTEL** | A 15th-century palazzo in the center of town is the setting for this classic, comfortable, and relatively affordable hotel, where front rooms have terraces with breathtaking lake views and the rooftop terrace is a perfect retreat from summer's crowded beaches. **Pros:** comfortable beds; prime location on the lake; modern hotel con-veniences. **Cons:** not for those looking for ultracontemporary design; some-times taken over by tour groups; food gets mixed reviews. $ *Rooms from: €133 ⊠ Piazza III Novembre 35, Riva del Garda ☏ 0464/552686, 0464/557809 booking office ⊕ www.hotelsoleriva.it ⊗ Closed Nov.–Dec. 21 and early Jan.– Mar. ⊷ 80 rooms ⦿ Free Breakfast.*

★ Lido Palace
$$$$ | **HOTEL** | In a 19th-century lakeside palace, Riva's most chic hotel has a high-end spa; sleek public spaces with turquoise mod couches and classic floor-to-ceiling windows; and contemporary guest rooms, where slate floors and brown-and-gray color schemes are offset by crisp white linens. **Pros:** top-notch food; friendly service; gorgeous spa and pools. **Cons:** on the pricey side; not all rooms have lake views or balconies; coffee- or tea-making facilities in room only on request. $ *Rooms from: €381 ⊠ Viale Carducci 10, Riva del Garda ☏ 0464/021899 ⊕ www.lido-palace.it ⦿ Free Breakfast ⊗ Closed mid-Jan.–late Mar. ⊷ 44 rooms.*

★ Luise
$$ | **HOTEL** | **FAMILY** | Outdoor perks here include a big garden, a large swimming pool, and free bikes to explore paths around the lake; interior draws include unique design touches—such as the lobby's collection of vintage luggage labels—and spacious rooms, all with comfy beds and a playful vibe and some with a whirlpool tub and a balcony. **Pros:** great for kids; pleasant service; reasona-bly priced. **Cons:** 10-minute walk to center of Riva; some rooms can be noisy; no gym. $ *Rooms from: €164 ⊠ Viale Rov-ereto 9, Riva del Garda ☏ 0464/550858 ⊕ www.hotelluise.com ⊗ Closed mid-Nov.–late Mar. ⊷ 68 rooms ⦿ Free Breakfast.*

Gargnano

30 km (19 miles) southwest of Riva del Garda, 144 km (89 miles) northeast of Milan.

This small port town was an important Franciscan center in the 13th century. Today, it comes alive in the summer, when German tourists, many of whom have villas here, crowd the small pebble beach. An Austrian flotilla bombarded the town in 1866, and some of the houses still bear marks of cannon fire. Mussolini owned two houses in Gargnano: one has been restored and reopened as the luxury hotel Villa Feltrinelli.

VISITOR INFORMATION

CONTACT Gargnano Tourism Office. ⊠ *Piazza Boldini 2, Gargnano* ☎ *0365/791243* ⊕ *www.gargnanosulgarda.it.*

Restaurants

La Tortuga

$$$$ | NORTHERN ITALIAN | This rustic trattoria is more sophisticated than it first appears: not only does it serve local dishes with novel twists, but it also has an extensive wine cellar. *Capesante scottate con salse ai diversi sapori* (seared scallops with different sauces) and *palette di piccoli campioni di lago e di mare* (mixed lake and sea fish) are worthy introductions to regional delights. **Known for:** delightful service; fish and meat tasting menu; extensive cheese selection. $ *Average main: €35* ⊠ *Via XXIV Maggio 5, Gargnano* ☎ *0365/71251* ⊕ *www.ristorantelatortuga.it* ⊗ *Closed Tues. and Dec.–Mar. No lunch Mon.–Sat.*

Hotels

Garni Bartabel

$ | HOTEL | The small rooms at this cozy main-street inn—where breakfast is served on an elegant lake-view terrace—have attractive Venetian-style furnishings and pastel color schemes. **Pros:** very attractive lake views; delicious breakfast; a bargain for this area. **Cons:** few luxuries; not all rooms have lake views or terraces; can hear road noise. $ *Rooms from: €82* ⊠ *Via Roma 39, Gargnano* ☎ *0365/71300* ⊕ *www.hotelbartabel.it* ⊗ *Closed Nov.–Mar.* ⇌ *11 rooms* ⦿ *Free Breakfast.*

Lefay Resort & Spa Lago di Garda

$$$$ | RESORT | The first thing you'll notice about this elegant resort in the hills above Gargnano are the stupendous lake and mountain views; the second thing will be its enormous spa, which is so filled with amenities (heated indoor-outdoor pool, saunas, well-equipped lake-view gym open 24 hours, extensive treatment menu) that you might just want to stay all day—and some guests do. **Pros:** fabulously relaxing spa; delicious breakfast buffet; lovely location. **Cons:** prices for food and drink excessively high; restaurant not up to standards of rest of hotel; village of Gargnano is down a steep and twisty road. $ *Rooms from: €630* ⊠ *Via Angelo Feltrinelli 136, Gargnano* ☎ *0365/241800* ⊕ *lagodigarda. lefayresorts.com* ⊗ *Closed early Jan.– early Feb.* ⇌ *93 rooms* ⦿ *Free Breakfast.*

Villa Feltrinelli

$$$$ | HOTEL | This 1892 art nouveau villa hotel, named for the Italian publishing family who once vacationed here, has attracted the likes of Winston Churchill, D. H. Lawrence, and Benito Mussolini to its private lake-view gardens; extensive library; sumptuous and palatial rooms (as befits the final bill); and overall opulent interior of frescoed ceilings, wood paneling, and antique ceramics. **Pros:** amazing service; first-class luxury hotel; like stepping into a bygone era. **Cons:** no gym; one of the most expensive hotels on the lake (or elsewhere); some find the attitude a bit arrogant. $ *Rooms from: €1650* ⊠ *Via Rimembranza 38/40, Gargnano* ☎ *0365/798000* ⊕ *www.villafeltrinelli. com* ⊗ *Closed mid-Oct.–mid-Apr.* ⇌ *20 suites* ⦿ *Free Breakfast.*

Gardone Riviera

12 km (7 miles) southwest of Gargnano, 139 km (86 miles) northeast of Milan.

Now pleasantly faded, this once fashionable 19th-century resort is best known these days for the hilltop estate of the poet Gabriele D'Annunzio, made as an elaborate memorial to himself. The middle-European appearance of ts towers and palaces helps set this lakeside town apart from the rest of Italy. With the Italian Alps in the background and crystalline lake views in the summer, it's a gorgeous, albeit underappreciated, destination.

Sights

Heller Garden

GARDEN | More than 2,000 alpine, subtropical, and Mediterranean species thrive at the Giardino Botanico Heller. ✉ Via Roma 2, Gardone Riviera ☎ 0366/410877 ⊕ www.hellergarden. com ⏱ Closed Nov.–Feb. 🎟 €12.

Il Vittoriale

HISTORIC HOME | The estate of the larger-than-life Gabriele D'Annunzio (1863–1938)—one of Italy's major modern poets, and later war hero and supporter of Mussolini—is filled with the trappings of his conquests in art, love, and war. His eccentric house crammed with quirky memorabilia can only be seen during a 35-minute guided tour (available in English), and the extensive gardens are definitely worth a stroll, particularly to see the curious full-size warship's prow. There's also an imposing mausoleum, made of white marble, along with three museums showcasing personal items from D'Annunzio's exploits, including the newest one devoted to his cars. ✉ Via Vittoriale 12, Gardone Riviera ☎ 0365/296511 ⊕ www.vittoriale.it ⏱ House closed Mon. Nov.–Feb. 🎟 €16 for park, museums, and guided tour of house; €12 for park only.

Salò Market (Mercato Di Salò)

MARKET | Four km (2½ miles) south of Gardone Riviera is the enchanting lakeside town of Salò, which history buffs may recognize as the capital of the ill-fated Social Republic, set up in 1943 by the Germans after they liberated Mussolini from the Gran Sasso. Every Saturday morning an enormous market is held in the Piazza Mario Pedrazzi, with bargains on household goods, clothing, food, and other items. In August or September a vendor often sells locally foraged tartufi neri (black truffles) at affordable prices. ✉ Piazza Mario Pedrazzi, Salò.

🍴 Restaurants

★ Ristorante Lido 84

$$$$ | MODERN ITALIAN | Dining in this bright, airy space feels like enjoying a meal in a fabulous friend's modern lake cottage—if the friend had floor-to-ceiling windows overlooking Lake Garda and a top-notch chef on hand. For an adventure in flavors from across the country, choose from two tasting menus (either "the classics" or one with "surprise" dishes chosen by the chef) and complement your meal with Italian or international wines in four- or five-glass pairings. **Known for:** exquisite lake setting; unusual ingredients from all across Italy; rose cake with zabaglione. $ Average main: €36 ✉ Corso Zanardelli 196, Gardone Riviera ☎ 0365/20019 ⊕ www.ristorantelido84.com ⏱ Closed Tues., Wed., and early Jan.–mid-Feb.

🛏 Hotels

★ Grand Hotel Fasano

$$$ | HOTEL | Used as a hunting lodge in the 19th century, the Fasano has matured into a seasonal hotel with high standards, opulent rooms, and many amenities—including an Aveda Destination Spa and a well-regarded restaurant, Il Fagiano, in addition to more casual eateries (one a short walk away). **Pros:** relaxing surroundings; gorgeous spa; exquisitely stylish rooms. **Cons:** food gets mixed reviews; not all rooms have lake views; staff can seem indifferent. $ Rooms from: €270 ✉ Corso Zanardelli 190, Gardone Riviera ☎ 0365/290220 ⊕ www.ghf.it ⇄ 79 rooms 🍴 Free Breakfast ⏱ Closed Nov.–Mar.

Lakes Como and Maggiore

Grand Hotel Gardone

$$$ | HOTEL | Attractive gardens surround this majestic 1800s palace, where the service is top-notch, many of the rooms have balconies overlooking the water, and a large pool and terrace sit near the gorgeous lake. **Pros:** lakeside pool; well-appointed; expansive, well-manicured grounds. **Cons:** some rooms could use an update; not much to do in the immediate area; service can be hit-or-miss. $ *Rooms from: €263* ✉ *Via Zanardelli 84, Gardone Riviera* ☎ *0365/20261* ⊕ *www.grandhotelgardone.it* ⊘ *Closed mid-Oct.–Apr.* ⇱ *164 rooms* ⊙¶ *Free Breakfast.*

Villa del Sogno

$$$$ | HOTEL | A narrow winding road takes you from town to this imposing villa, now a luxurious hotel retreat thanks to its valley and lake views and its peaceful grounds, which have an outdoor pool and a tennis court. **Pros:** endless amenities; expansive terrace overlooking the lake; individually decorated rooms. **Cons:** staff can be indifferent; remote location; food gets mixed reviews. $ *Rooms from: €355* ✉ *Via Zanardelli 107, Gardone Riviera* ☎ *0365/290181* ⊕ *www.villadelsogno. it* ⊘ *Closed Nov.–mid-Apr.* ⇱ *38 rooms* ⊙¶ *Free Breakfast.*

Villa Fiordaliso

$$$ | HOTEL | A fine restaurant and five tastefully furnished guest rooms are housed in the pink-and-white lakeside villa given to Benito Mussolini's mistress, Claretta Petacci, by Il Duce himself—indeed, the expensive Claretta Suite is probably where they conducted their affair. **Pros:** elaborate breakfast spread; combines cinematic charm with the intimacy of a B&B; amazing setting on

the lake. **Cons:** can sometimes be noisy; short on amenities (no spa or pool); may be too small for some people. ⑤ *Rooms from: €250 ⊠ Corso Zanardelli 150, Gardone Riviera ☎ 0365/20158 ⊕ www.villafiordaliso.it ⊗ Closed mid.-Oct.–mid-Mar. ⇨ 5 rooms ⊙⊢ Free Breakfast.*

Bellagio

30 km (19 miles) northeast of Como, 56 km (35 miles) northwest of Bergamo.

Sometimes called the prettiest town in Europe, Bellagio always seems perfectly adorned, with geraniums ablaze in every window and bougainvillea veiling its staircases, or *montées*. At dusk Bellagio's nightspots—including the wharf, where an orchestra may be serenading dancers under the stars—beckon you to come and make merry. It's an impossibly enchanting location, one that inspired the French composer Gabriel Fauré to call Bellagio "a diamond contrasting brilliantly with the sapphires of the three lakes in which it is set."

GETTING HERE AND AROUND

Boats can take you from here to Tremezzo, where Napoléon's worst Italian enemy, Count Sommariva, resided at Villa Carlotta; and a bit farther south of Tremezzo, to Villa del Balbianello. Check with the tourist office for the hours of the launch to Tremezzo.

VISITOR INFORMATION

CONTACT Bellagio Tourism Office. ⊠ *Piazza della Chiesa 14, Bellagio ☎ 031/951555 ⊕ www.bellagiolakecomo.com.*

 Sights

Villa Melzi

GARDEN | The famous gardens of the Villa Melzi were once a favorite picnic spot for Franz Liszt, who advised author Louis de Ronchaud in 1837, "When you write the story of two happy lovers, place them on the shores of Lake Como. I do not know

of any land so conspicuously blessed by heaven." The gardens are open to the public, and though you can't get into the 19th-century villa, don't miss the lavish Empire-style family chapel. The Melzi were Napoléon's greatest allies in Italy (the family has passed down the name "Josephine" to the present day). Guided tours are available with advance booking. ⊠ *Lungo Lario Manzoni, Bellagio ☎ 0333/031 950318 guided tour bookings ⊕ www.giardinidivillamelzi.it ⊗ Closed Nov.–late Mar. ☞ €8.*

Villa Monastero

GARDEN | By ferry from Bellagio it's a quick trip across the lake to Varenna. The principal sight here is the spellbinding garden of the Villa Monastero, which, as its name suggests, was originally a monastery. There's also a house museum where you can admire 18th-century furnishings, as well as an international science and convention center. ⊠ *Viale Giovanni Polvani 4, Varenna ☎ 0341/295450 ⊕ www.villamonastero.eu ☞ Garden €8, garden and house €10 ⊗ Garden and house closed Mon.–Sat. early Nov.–Feb. (except Dec 26–Jan. 6). House also closed Mon.–Thurs. in Mar.–Apr., Mon.–Wed. in May, and Mon. in June, Sept., and Oct.*

Villa Serbelloni Garden

GARDEN | This property of the Rockefeller Foundation has celebrated gardens on the site of Pliny the Elder's villa, overlooking Bellagio. There are only two 1½-hour-long guided visits per day, at 11 am (Tue.–Sun.) and 3:30 pm (Fri.–Sun.), with a maximum of 30 people each, and in May they tend to be booked by whole groups. It's wise to arrive early to sign up at the starting point, at the Bellagio tourist office in the medieval tower in St. Giacomo Square. The garden also closes due to bad weather, so call in advance. ⊠ *Piazza della Chiesa 14, Bellagio ☎ 031/951555 ⊕ www.bellagiolakecomo.com/en/bellagio-lake-como-italy/POI-points-of-interest/villa-serbelloni-garden ☞ €9 ⊗ Closed Mon. and early Nov.–mid-Mar.*

Restaurants

★ Ristorante La Punta

$$ | ITALIAN | When tourist-heavy Bellagio starts to wear you down, seek respite at this charming restaurant located on the town's very northernmost point, a scenic 10-minute walk from the center, with amazing lake views of Varenna to the north and Tremezzo to the west. As you might expect, the menu is heavy on lake fish; although the dishes aren't innovative, they're fresh and well prepared, and the view makes the experience even better. **Known for:** friendly service; super-fresh fish; superlative Lake Como views. $ *Average main: €23* ✉ *Via Eugenio Vitali 19, Bellagio* ☎ *031/951888* ⊕ *www.ristorantelapunta.it* ⊗ *Closed Nov.–Feb.*

🏨 Hotels

Du Lac

$$ | HOTEL | Most of the modern, inviting guest rooms at this comfortable, good-value old hotel—owned by an Anglo-Italian family and right in the center of Bellagio's action—have lake and mountain views, and the rooftop terrace garden is a perfect spot for drinks or dozing. **Pros:** friendly service; pleasant on-site restaurant; fabulous buffet breakfast. **Cons:** some of the decor could use a refresh; beds too hard for some; the boat dock right in front of the hotel can be noisy. $ *Rooms from: €195* ✉ *Piazza Mazzini 32, Bellagio* ☎ *031/950320* ⊕ *www.bellagiohoteldulac.com* ⊗ *Closed Nov.—Mar.* ⇌ *41 rooms* ⦿ *Free Breakfast.*

★ Grand Hotel Villa Serbelloni

$$$$ | HOTEL | The 19th-century luxury at this grand lake hotel—originally designed to cradle nobility and still a refined haven for the discreetly wealthy—has not so much faded as mellowed: guest rooms remain immaculate and plush; public areas are still awash with gilt ornamentation and marble; and breakfast is served in a ballroom. **Pros:** old-world grandeur; great

pools; lovely gardens. **Cons:** expensive food and drink; staff helpfulness varies widely; could use some sprucing up. $ *Rooms from: €618* ✉ *Via Roma 1, Bellagio* ☎ *031/950216* ⊕ *www.villaserbelloni.com* ⊗ *Closed Nov.–early Apr.* ⇌ *94 rooms* ⦿ *Free Breakfast.*

Hotel Belvedere

$$$$ | HOTEL | FAMILY | In Italian, *belvedere* means "beautiful view," and it's an apt name for this enchanting spot, where the modern rooms have classic touches such as antique furniture, decorative tiles, and marble bathrooms. **Pros:** great views; has a spa and a lovely pool; attention to detail. **Cons:** fewer on-site amenities than other similarly priced hotels; must request a lake-view balcony room in advance; a climb from the waterfront. $ *Rooms from: €448* ✉ *Via Valassina 31, Bellagio* ☎ *031/950410* ⊕ *www.belvederebellagio.com* ⊗ *Closed Nov.–Mar.* ⇌ *63 rooms* ⦿ *Free Breakfast.*

Hotel Florence

$$ | HOTEL | Most of the large and comfortable rooms in this 1880s villa across from the ferry stop are furnished with interesting antiques and have splendid views of the lake. **Pros:** lovely bar with outdoor lake-facing seating; central location; appealing public spaces. **Cons:** some baths only have hand-held showers; location may feel too central if you're looking to get away from it all; hotel could use an update. $ *Rooms from: €160* ✉ *Piazza Mazzini 46, Bellagio* ☎ *031/950342* ⊕ *www.hotelflorencebellagio.it* ⊗ *Closed mid-Oct.–Apr.* ⇌ *30 rooms* ⦿ *Free Breakfast.*

Tremezzo

34 km (21 miles) north of Cernobbio, 78 km (48 miles) north of Milan.

The dreamy lakeside town of Tremezzo is close to two outstanding and magical villas, as well as sprawling gardens and one of the lake's grandest hotels.

Sights

Villa Carlotta

GARDEN | If you're lucky enough to visit Tremezzo in late spring or early summer, you will find the magnificent Villa Carlotta a riot of color, with more than 14 acres of azaleas and dozens of varieties of rhododendrons in full bloom. The height of the blossoms is late April to early May. The villa was built between 1690 and 1743 for the luxury-loving marquis Giorgio Clerici. The garden's collection is remarkable, particularly considering the difficulties of transporting delicate plants before the age of aircraft. Palms, banana trees, cacti, eucalyptus, a sequoia, orchids, and camellias are among the more than 500 species. The villa's interior is worth a visit, particularly if you have a taste for the romantic sculptures of Antonio Canova (1757–1822). The best known is his *Cupid and Psyche,* which depicts the lovers locked in an odd but graceful embrace, with the young god above and behind, his wings extended, while Psyche awaits a kiss that will never come. The villa can be reached by boat from Bellagio and Como. ⊠ *Via Regina 2, Tremezzo* ☎ *0344/40405* ⊕ *www.villacarlotta.it* 🎫 *€12* ⊙ *Closed early Nov.–Mar. (except Dec. 5–8 or by appointment).*

★ Villa del Balbianello

HISTORIC HOME | The relentlessly picturesque Balbianello may be the most magical house in all of Italy; you probably know it from cameos in the movies *Casino Royale* and *Star Wars Episode II: Attack of the Clones.* It sits on its own little promontory, Il Dosso d'Avedo, around the bend from the tiny fishing village of Ossuccio. The villa is composed of loggias, terraces, and *palazzini* (tiny palaces), all spilling down verdant slopes to the shore, where you'll find an old Franciscan church, a magnificent stone staircase, and a statue of San Carlo Borromeo blessing the waters. The villa is usually reached from Como and Bellagio by boat, which leaves you at the village of Lenno. From there, marked signs lead you to the villa—it's either accessible by foot via a 20-minute walk or a more challenging 45-minute hike, or there is boat service from Bellagio (€9.20 roundtrip) or Como (€16.60 roundtrip), with a one-day ticket to travel around the islands running €23.30. ⊠ *Il Dosso d'Avedo, ferry stop Lenno, Lenno* ⊕ *5 km (3 miles) southwest of Tremezzo* ☎ *0344/56110* ⊕ *www.fondoambiente.it/luoghi/villa-del-balbianello* ⊙ *Closed Mon., Wed., and early Jan.–mid-Mar.* 🎫 *€22 villa and gardens, includes 1-hr guided tour; €11 gardens only.*

Restaurants

★ La Locanda dell'Isola Comacina

$$$$ | **ITALIAN** | For an unforgettable dining experience, head to Sala Comacina (a 10-minute drive south of Tremezzo) and take a five-minute speedboat ride to Lake Como's only island, Isola Comacina. Here you'll be treated to the same set menu that's been served at La Locanda since 1947: veggie antipasti; thinly sliced prosciutto and bresaola; grilled trout; fried chicken with salad; Parmesan cheese sliced from an enormous wheel; and oranges or peaches with ice cream, while charismatic owner Benvenuto Puricelli regales you with tales of the island's history. **Known for:** brandied coffee set afire with a dramatic flourish; wonderful scenery, history, and lore; rustic, tasty set menus. ⑤ *Average main: €80* ⊠ *Isola Comacina* ☎ *0344/55083, 0344/56755* ⊕ *comacina.it* ⊙ *Closed Tues. (except in summer) and Nov.–Feb.*

Hotels

★ Grand Hotel Tremezzo

$$$$ | **RESORT** | Creature comforts in this turn-of-the-20th-century building—one of the top grand hotels on the lake—include a lush park, three heated swimming pools (one of them floats on pontoons on the lake), a small private beach, and sumptuous guest rooms where old-world style meets modern amenities. **Pros:** lakeside location with beautiful views; attractive spa; gracious service. **Cons:** very expensive; somewhat busy road between hotel and lake; not well situated if you're looking for shopping or nightlife. ⓢ *Rooms from: €890 ⊠ Via Regina 8, Tremezzo ☎ 0344/42491 ⊕ www.grandhotel-tremezzo.com ⊗ Closed mid-Nov.–early Apr. ⇥ 90 rooms ⓞ Free Breakfast.*

Hotel Rusall

$$ | **B&B/INN** | Amid a large garden on the hillside above Tremezzo, this hotel offers small, private, comfortably simple rooms; a pool with a nice view; and a popular restaurant that serves tasty Italian classics. **Pros:** good on-site restaurant; lovely walks into town and in the countryside; more intimate than grander lake hotels. **Cons:** rooms are fairly basic; takes some effort to reach and walk to town; air-conditioning can be an issue in rooms and common areas. ⓢ *Rooms from: €135 ⊠ Via San Martino 2, Tremezzo ☎ 0344/40408 ⊕ www.rusallhotel.com ⊗ Closed Jan.–Feb. ⇥ 23 rooms ⓞ Free Breakfast.*

Cernobbio

5 km (3 miles) north of Como, 53 km (34 miles) north of Milan.

The legendary resort of Villa d'Este is reason enough to visit this jewel on the lake, but the town itself is worth a stroll. The place still has a neighborhood feel to it, especially on summer evenings and weekends, when the piazza is full of families and couples strolling.

VISITOR INFORMATION

CONTACT Cernobbio Tourism Office.
⊠ *Largo Alfredo Campanini, 1, Cernobbio ☎ 347/8818532 ⊕ www.comune.cernobbio.co.it.*

🍴 Restaurants

Il Gatto Nero

$$$ | **NORTHERN ITALIAN** | Reservations are a good idea for this longtime favorite in the hills above Cernobbio. The lake view is splendid, and specialties include homemade pastas and fish dishes with a dash of international flair. **Known for:** lovely terrace; classic (veal) and non-classic (tuna) Cotoletta alla Milanese; high-end wine selection. ⓢ *Average main: €28 ⊠ Via Monte Santo 69, Cernobbio ☎ 031/512042 ⊕ www.ristorantegattonero.it ⊗ Closed Jan.–mid-Mar. No lunch weekdays mid-to-late Mar.*

Lido di Cernobbio

$$ | **ITALIAN** | Right next to the Cernobbio ferry stop, this pretty restaurant offers a nice selection of local wines and, whenever possible, uses local ingredients in its pizza, pasta, fish, and meat dishes. Though the modern gray interior is pleasant, try for a table on the terrace, and note that, in season, you can rent a sunbed and use the pools (one for adults and one for kids) before or after your meal. **Known for:** family-friendly atmosphere; lovely lake scenery; solid Italian dishes. ⓢ *Average main: €20 ⊠ Piazza Risorgimento 5, Cernobbio ☎ 031/4446437 ⊕ www.lidodicernobbio.com ⊗ Closed Wed., Thurs., and Nov.–Mar. No lunch Tue. and Fri.*

★ Materia

$$$ | **MODERN ITALIAN** | This aesthetically simple bistro-style restaurant, spruced up with modern art, draws a mainly local crowd for some of the most inventive food creations and presentation in the Como region. The imaginative Asian-inspired cuisine (think steamed partridge with smoked eel butter), makes good use of local ingredients like lake fish, and the frequently changing surprise five-, seven-, or twelve-course tasting menus are a particular delight, especially when paired with the mostly natural wines on offer. **Known for:** seasonally changing dishes; Italian and international wines from small producers; use of organic herbs and vegetables from their greenhouse. $ Average main: €30 ☒ Via Cinque Giornate 32, Cernobbio ☎ 031/2075548 ⊕ www.ristorantemateria.it ⊙ Closed Mon. No lunch Tues.

☕ Coffee and Quick Bites

◀ Giardino
$$ | **NORTHERN ITALIAN** | "The Garden" has an expansive patio that's a shady respite from the summer sun. Though mainly known for its pizza, the restaurant also has an extensive menu of fish and meat dishes. **Known for:** fun vibe; extensive outdoor seating; tasty pizza. $ Average main: €16 ☒ Via Regina 73, Cernobbio ☎ 031/511154 ⊕ www.giardinocernobbio.com ⊙ Closed Wed. Nov.–Feb.

🛏 Hotels

★ Villa d'Este
$$$$ | **HOTEL** | Europe's rich and famous have long favored this hotel, one of Italy's grandest, where rooms are done in Empire style; a broad veranda sweeps out to the lakefront; a swimming pool extends above the water; a restaurant offers top-notch views and cuisine; there are four private villas; and pavilions, miniature forts, and other follies ensure whimsical garden walks. **Pros:** amazing grounds; excellent restaurant; fine service. **Cons:** all this grandness comes with a hefty price tag; not all rooms have lake views; may feel too formal for some. $ Rooms from: €920 ☒ Via Regina 40, Cernobbio ☎ 031/3481 ⊕ www.villadeste.it ⊙ Closed mid-Nov.–mid-Mar. ⇄ 152 rooms and 4 private villas ⏅ Free Breakfast.

Como

5 km (3 miles) south of Cernobbio, 30 km (19 miles) southwest of Bellagio, 49 km (30 miles) north of Milan.

Como commands the south shore of the lake. In its center, elegant cobblestone pedestrian streets wind their way past parks and bustling cafés. However, it's only partly a resort: the city also has an industrial heritage, deeply rooted in the production of textiles, particularly silk and the silk trade. If traveling by car, leave it at the edge of the town center in the well-lit underground parking facility right on the lake.

VISITOR INFORMATION
CONTACT Como Tourism Office. ☒ Via Albertolli 7, Como ☎ 031/304137, 031/4493068, 031/269712 ⊕ www.visitcomo.eu/en.

Sights

Duomo
CHURCH | The splendid 15th-century Renaissance-Gothic Duomo was begun in 1396. The facade was added in 1455, and the transepts were completed in the mid-18th century. The dome was designed by Filippo Juvarra (1678–1736), chief architect of many of the sumptuous palaces of the royal house of Savoy. The facade has statues of two of Como's most famous sons, Pliny the Elder and Pliny the Younger, whose writings are among the most important documents from antiquity. Inside, the works of art include Luini's *Holy Conversation,* a fresco cycle by Morazzone, and the *Marriage of the Virgin Mary* by Ferrari. ☒ Piazza del Duomo, Como ☎ 031/3312275 ⊕ www.cattedraledicomo.it.

Museo Didattico della Seta (*Silk Museum*)
OTHER MUSEUM | From silkworm litters to textile finishing machinery to temporary exhibitions, this small but complete collection preserves the history of a manufacturing region that continues to supply a large proportion of Europe's silk. The friendly staffers will give you an overview of the museum; they are also happy to provide brochures and information about local retail shops. The location isn't well marked: follow the textile school's driveway around to the low-rise concrete building on the left, and take the shallow ramp down to the entrance. ⊠ *Via Castelnuovo 9, Como* ☎ *031/303180* ⊕ *www.museosetacomo.com* ⏱ *Closed Mon.* 🎫 *€10.*

San Fedele

CHURCH | At the heart of Como's medieval quarter, the city's first cathedral is well worth a peek. The apse walls and ceiling are completely frescoed, as are the ceilings above the altar. ⊠ *Piazza San Fedele, Como* ☎ *031/267295* ⊕ *www.parrocchiasanfedelecomo.it.*

Sant'Abbondio

CHURCH | If you head into Como's industrial quarter, you will come upon this church, a gem of Romanesque architecture begun by Benedictine monks in 1013 and consecrated by Pope Urban II in 1095. Inside, the five aisles converge on a presbytery with a semicircular apse decorated with a cycle of 14th-century frescoes by Lombard artists heavily influenced by the Sienese school. To see them, turn right as you enter. In the nave, the cubical capitals are the earliest example of this style in Italy. ⊠ *Via Regina Teodolinda 35, Como* ☎ *031/304518* ⊕ *www.santabbondio.eu* 🎫 *Free.*

 Restaurants

⭐ Feel Como

$$$ | MODERN ITALIAN | Your palate will travel from the lakes (eel with leek) to the countryside (hay risotto) to the mountains (tripe), all from the comfort of your table, at this cozy stone-arched eatery tucked into Como's commercial district. Expect creative takes on Italian cuisine, like deconstructed ravioli, using both local and more exotic ingredients, best sampled with a tasting menu focused on either fish, meat, or a mix. **Known for:** extensive wine list; witty variations on local cuisine; gorgeous platings. $ *Average main: €28* ⊠ *Via Generale Armando Diaz 54, Como* ☎ *0334/7264545* ⊕ *www.feelcomo.com* ⏱ *Closed Sun. No lunch Tues.–Thurs.*

Rivenoteca

$$$ | NORTHERN ITALIAN | A former 17th-century convent is now a lively enoteca run by Alberto and Catia Rivetti, with more than 600 wines, as well as spirits and beers—all from Northern Italy. Old and new merge in this warm and friendly spot with sage and rose walls, an original decorative ceiling, and a hallway with an automatic dispenser with more than 30 wines available on-demand—get up from your seat to taste as many wines as you'd like using a pre-paid card. **Known for:** entirely Lombard-focused cuisine; local wines and spirits, including from the owners' Rivetti winery; dispenser for wines "on demand" in three sizes, or by the bottle. $ *Average main: €25* ⊠ *Via A. Diaz 56, Como* ☎ *33/56688743* ⊕ *www. rivenoteca.it* ⏱ *Closed Tues.*

 Hotels

Albergo Terminus

$$$$ | HOTEL | In addition to Lake Como panoramas, this early-20th-century art nouveau landmark has marbled public spaces and guest rooms with floral fabrics, walnut wardrobes, and silk-covered sofas. **Pros:** bountiful breakfast buffet; old-world charm; right on the lake. **Cons:** decor in some rooms seems dated; limited number of lake-view rooms; noise from the restaurant and outside can be an issue. $ *Rooms from: €402* ⊠ *Lungo Lario Trieste 14, Como* ☎ *031/329111* ⊕ *www.albergoterminus.it* 🛏 *50 rooms* 🍽 *Free Breakfast.*

I Sereno Lago di Como

$$$$ | **HOTEL** | Throughout this, the first European outpost of the luxe Il Sereno Hotel in St. Barths, you'll find floor-to-ceiling lake-view windows and an understated retro-mod aesthetic, with a muted palette of browns and grays complementing a panoply of wood, stone, leather, and copper accents. **Pros:** hushed elegance throughout; fabulous views; cool modern design. **Cons:** can be difficult to find; not for lovers of historical villas; extremely expensive. ⑤ *Rooms from: €850* ✉ *Via Torrazza 10, Como* ☎ *031/5477800* ⊕ *www.ilsereno.com* ⊙ *Closed Nov.–mid-Mar.* ⇆ *30 rooms* ⑽ *Free Breakfast.*

Mandarin Oriental, Lago di Como

$$$$ | **HOTEL** | The nine 19th-century villas that comprise this Lake Como outpost of the extravagant Mandarin chain have been thoroughly updated for the 21st century, offering a quiet setting (just north of the busy town of Como) and luxurious amenities that include a 14,000-square-foot spa and a swimming pool that "floats" above the lake. **Pros:** complimentary minibar; amazingly peaceful setting; fabulous wellness facilities. **Cons:** food not up to par; location a bit isolated from other towns; service can be haphazard. ⑤ *Rooms from: €850* ✉ *Via E. Caronti 69, Blevio* ☎ *031/32513035* ⊕ *www.mandarinoriental.com/lake-como/blevio/luxury-hotel* ⊙ *Closed mid-Nov.–mid-Mar.* ⇆ *75 rooms* ⑽ *Free Breakfast.*

Posta Design Hotel

$$ | **HOTEL** | Just a block from the lake, on downtown Como's pedestrian-only Piazza Volta, this boutique hotel has a minimalist modern interior that's in perfect keeping with its exterior—the 1931 building that houses it was designed by Rationalist architect Giuseppe Terragni. **Pros:** comfortable rooms; central location; friendly service. **Cons:** Internet must be logged into each time; rooms on lower floors can be noisy; sparse amenities (no minibars in rooms, no breakfast, no gym). ⑤ *Rooms from: €151* ✉ *Via Garibaldi 2, Como* ☎ *031/2769011* ⊕ *www.postadesignhotel.com* ⇆ *14 rooms* ⑽ *No Meals.*

★ Vista Palazzo Lago di Como

$$$$ | **HOTEL** | A 19th-century lakefront palazzo steps from pedestrian-only Piazza Cavour has been transformed into an elegant in-town hotel, where a sweeping staircase leads to spacious, sophisticated white-and-gray guest rooms that have pops of color, parquet floors, walk-in closets, and sumptuous marble bathrooms with deep soaking tubs. **Pros:** lovely views from most rooms; friendly and helpful service; great central location. **Cons:** not everyone wants to stay in Como town; breakfast can be a bit sparse; lakefront rooms can be noisy. ⑤ *Rooms from: €800* ✉ *Piazza Cavour 24, Como* ☎ *031/5375241* ⊕ *vistalagodicomo.com* ⇆ *18 rooms* ⑽ *Free Breakfast.*

🏃 Activities

Lake Como has lots of ways to stay active and outdoors, from windsurfing at the lake's northern end, to boating, sailing, and Jet Skiing at Como and Cernobbio. The lake is also quite swimmable in summer. For hikers there are lovely paths all around the lake. For an easy trek, take the funicular up to Brunate, and walk along the mountain to the lighthouse for a stunning view of the lake.

Stresa and the Isole Borromee

80 km (50 miles) northwest of Milan.

One of the better known resorts on the western shore, Stresa is a tourist town, which provided Hemingway with one of the settings in *A Farewell to Arms*. It has capitalized on its central lakeside position, though the luxurious elegance that distinguished its heyday has faded; grand hotels are still grand, but traffic now encroaches on their parks and gardens.

The best way to escape to yesteryear is to head for the Isole Borromee (Borromean Islands) in Lake Maggiore. Boats to the three islands depart every 15–30 minutes from the dock at Stresa's Piazza Marconi, as well as from Piazzale Lido at the northern end of the promenade. There's also a boat from Verbania; check locally for the seasonal schedule. Although you can hire a private boat, it's cheaper and just as convenient to use the regular service. Make sure you buy a ticket allowing you to visit all the islands—Bella, dei Pescatori, and Madre. The islands take their name from the Borromeo family, which has owned them since the 12th century.

GETTING HERE AND AROUND

Trains run regularly from Milan to the town of Stresa on Lake Maggiore; the trip takes 1–1½ hours, depending on the type of train. By car from Milan to Stresa, take the A8 autostrada to the A8dir, and from the A8dir take the A26; the drive is about 1¼ hours.

VISITOR INFORMATION

CONTACTS Isole Borromee Information. ☎ 0323/933478 ⊕ www.isoleborromee. it. **Stresa Tourism Office.** ✉ Piazza Marconi 16, Stresa ☎ 0323/31308, 0323/30150 ⊕ www.stresaturismo.it.

 # Sights

Funivia

VIEWPOINT | For amazing views, take the *funivia*, a cable car that takes you to heights from which you can see seven lakes: Maggiore, Orta, Mergozzo, Varese, Camabbio, Monate, and Biandronno. Situated between Lakes Maggiore and Orta, it offers tourists 360-degree views of the Po Plain right across to the distant Alpine peaks. At the top, nature- and adventure-lovers can rent mountain bikes and ride on properly marked paths, while others can just relax at a local restaurant.

✉ Piazzale Lido 8, Stresa ☎ 0323/30295 ⊕ www.stresa-mottarone.it ☞ €20 round-trip.

Isola Bella (*Beautiful Island*)

ISLAND | The most famous of the three Isole Borromee (Borromean Islands), and the first that you'll visit, is named after Isabella, whose husband, Carlo III Borromeo (1538–84), built the palace and terraced gardens here for her as a wedding present. Before Count Carlo began his project, the island was rocky and almost devoid of vegetation; the soil for the garden had to be transported from the mainland. For a splendid view of the lake, wander up the 10 terraces of the gardens, where peacocks roam among the scented shrubs, statues, and fountains. Visit the palazzo to see the rooms where famous guests—including Napoléon and Mussolini—stayed in 18th-century splendor. Those three interlocked rings on walls and even streets represent the powerful Borromeo, Visconti, and Sforza families. ✉ Isola Bella ☎ 0323/933478 ⊕ www.isoleborromee.it ☞ Garden and palazzo €18 ⊗ Closed late Oct.–late Mar.

★ Isola dei Pescatori (*Island of the Fishermen, also known as Isola Superiore*)

ISLAND | Stop for a while at the smallest Borromean island, less than 100 yards wide and only about ½ km (¼ mile) long. It's the perfect place for a seafood lunch before, after, or in between your visit to the other two islands. Of the 10 or so restaurants on this tiny island, the two worth visiting are Ristorante Verbano (0323/30408) and Ristorante Belvedere (0323/32292). The island's little lanes strung with fishing nets and dotted with shrines to the Madonna are the definition of picturesque; little wonder that in high season the village is crowded with postcard stands. ✉ Isola dei Pescatori.

★ Isola Madre (*Mother Island*)

GARDEN | All of this Borromean island is a botanical garden, with a season that stretches from late March to late October due to the climatic protection of the mighty Alps and the tepid waters of Lago Maggiore. The cacti and palm trees here, so far north and so near the border with Switzerland, are a beautiful surprise. Take time to see the profusion of exotic trees and shrubs running down to the shore in every direction. Two special times to visit are April, for the camellias, and May, for azaleas and rhododendrons. Also on the island is a 16th-century palazzo, where the Borromeo family still lives for part of the year. The palazzo has an antique puppet theater on display, complete with string puppets, prompt books, and elaborate scenery designed by Alessandro Sanquirico, who was a scenographer at La Scala in Milan. ✉ *Isola Madre* ☎ *0323/933479* ⊕ *www.isoleborromee.it* ✉ *€15* ⊙ *Closed late Oct.–late Mar.*

Parco Villa Pallavicino

GARDEN | As you wander around the palms and semitropical shrubs, don't be surprised if you're followed by a peacock or even an ostrich: they're part of the zoological garden and are allowed to roam almost at will. From the top of the hill on which the villa stands you can see the gentle hills of the Lombardy shore of Lake Maggiore and, nearer and to the left, the jewel-like Isole Borromee. In addition to a bar and restaurant, the grounds also have picnic spots. ✉ *Via Sempione 8, Stresa* ☎ *0323/933479* ⊕ *www.isoleborromee.it* ✉ *€12* ⊙ *Closed early Nov.–mid-Mar.*

 Restaurants

⭐ **Ristorante LaStresa**

$$ | **NORTHERN ITALIAN** | The nondescript exterior of this buzzy eatery on one of Stresa's main streets belies its chic, stylish interior. Dishes made with seasonal ingredients dominate the menu, but, no matter the season, you'll find local lake fish, both marinated and panfried, as well as a solid list of wines from throughout the region and across Italy. **Known for:** Piedmont dessert sampler; locals' favorite; friendly, knowledgeable

waitstaff. **$** *Average main: €20* ✉ *Via Principessa Margherita 22, Stresa* ☎ *0323/33240* ⊕ *www.ristorantelastresa. it* ⊙ *Closed Tues. Sept.–June.*

 Hotels

⭐ **Grand Hotel des Iles Borromees**

$$$$ | **HOTEL** | This palatial, Liberty-style hotel has catered to a demanding European clientele since 1863, and although its spacious salons and guest rooms still have lavish turn-of-the-last-century furnishings, there are signs of modernity, including a redesigned bar (Hemingway Bar), low-calorie and gluten-free options at the restaurant, and extensive wellness treatments. **Pros:** bygone-era grace and style plus modern amenities; nice pool and spa selection; sumptuous rooms, particularly the fabulous Hemingway Suite. **Cons:** Internet can be on the slow side; decor may be over the top for some; bathrooms could use a refresh. **$** *Rooms from: €314* ✉ *Corso Umberto I 67, Stresa* ☎ *0323/938938* ⊕ *www. borromees.com* ➳ *179 rooms* ⭐⊙ *Free Breakfast* ⊙ *Closed Dec.–Jan.*

Verbania

16 km (10 miles) north of Stresa, 95 km (59 miles) northwest of Milan.

The quaint town of Verbania is across the Gulf of Pallanza from its more touristy neighbor, Stresa. It is known for the Villa Taranto, which has magnificent botanical gardens. With its majestic gardens and greenery, Verbania is often called the Garden of Lake Maggiore.

👁 **Sights**

Santa Caterina del Sasso Ballaro

CHURCH | Near the town of Laveno, this beautiful lakeside hermitage was constructed in the 12th century by a local merchant to express his gratitude for having been saved from the wrath of a storm. Seemingly carved out of its supporting cliff, it's particularly striking as you approach it by boat or ferry, although, after docking, you'll need to climb 80 steps to reach the hermitage. Alternatively, park in the lot above and walk down a 268-step staircase; there's also an elevator, though it's not as scenic an option. ⊠ *Via Santa Caterina 13, Laveno* ☎ *0332/647172* ⊕ *www.santacaterinadel-sasso.com* ☉ *Closed weekdays Nov.– Feb.* 🎟 *Free.*

Villa Taranto

GARDEN | FAMILY | The Villa Taranto was acquired in 1931 by Scottish captain Neil McEachern, who helped make the magnificent gardens here what they are today, adding terraces, waterfalls, more than 3,000 plant species from all over the world—including 300 varieties of dahlias—and broad meadows sloping gently to the lake. While the gardens can be visited, the villa itself is not open to the public. ⊠ *Via Vittorio Veneto 111, Verbania* ☎ *0323/556667* ⊕ *www.villataranto.it* 🎟 *€11* ☉ *Closed early Nov.–early Apr.*

Hotels

Il Chiostro

$ | HOTEL | Using space formed from a 17th-century monastery merged with an adjoining 19th-century textile factory, this hotel offers plain, functional rooms, some overlooking a lovely garden. **Pros:** affordable for the area; friendly, efficient staff; lovely breakfast. **Cons:** limited amenities; rooms are fairly plain; small bathrooms. ⑤ *Rooms from: €90* ⊠ *Via Fratelli Cervi 14, Verbania* ☎ *0323/404077* ⊕ *www. chiostrovb.it* ⇪ *104 rooms* ⑩ *Free Breakfast.*

Il Sole di Ranco

$$ | HOTEL | For more than 170 years the same family has run this elegant inn—about an hour's drive from Verbania on the banks of the lake opposite Stresa—where guest rooms are in two late-19th-century villas surrounded by a garden and the chef does the family proud in the exceptional restaurant. **Pros:** lovely pool area; classic lake setting; tranquil grounds. **Cons:** decor on the old-fashioned side; far from the tourist center (hotel offers tours with private drivers); restaurant a bit pricey. ⑤ *Rooms from: €190* ⊠ *Piazza Venezia 5, Ranco* ☎ *0331/976507* ⊕ *www.ilsolediranco.it* ⇪ *14 rooms* ⑩ *Free Breakfast* ☉ *Closed Jan.–early Feb.*

PIEDMONT AND THE VALLE D'AOSTA

Updated by
Patricia Rucidlo

 Sights
★★★☆☆

 Restaurants
★★★★★

 Hotels
★★★★☆

 Shopping
★★☆☆☆

 Nightlife
★☆☆☆☆

WELCOME TO
PIEDMONT AND THE VALLE D'AOSTA

TOP REASONS TO GO

★ **Sacra di San Michele:** Explore one of the country's most spectacularly situated religious monuments.

★ **Castello di Fénis:** This castle transports you back in time to the Middle Ages.

★ **Monte Bianco:** A cable-car ride over a snowcapped mountain will take your breath away.

★ **Turin's Museo Egizio:** A surprising treasure—one of the world's richest collections of Ancient Egyptian art outside Cairo, Egypt.

★ **Regal wines:** Some of Italy's most revered reds—led by Barolo, the "king of wines"—come from the hills of southern Piedmont.

★ **Turin's Galleria Sabauda:** Witness to the regal splendor of the reigning House of Savoy, this museum is famed for its spectacular collection of old masters.

1 Turin. Neoclassical piazzas and Baroque palazzi have been restored in grand style.

2 Asti. Home of its namesake *spumante*, a sweet sparkling wine.

3 Alba. A city that's renowned for its truffles and mushrooms.

4 The Barolo Region. This is where nebbiolo grapes become celebrated wines.

5 Bard. A strategic medieval town with an impressive fortress.

6 Breuil-Cervinia/The Matterhorn. This skier's paradise straddles the Swiss border.

7 Castello di Fénis. Castello di Fénis is embellished with many towers.

8 Aosta. This is one of Italy's most livable cities.

9 Courmayeur/Monte Bianco. A cozy mountain town, popular with skiers and hikers.

10 Venaria Reale. An expansive 16th-century Savoy palace.

11 Rivoli. The storybook town of Rivoli is a highlight.

12 Sacra di San Michele. This 11th-century abbey once controlled 176 churches in Italy, France, and Spain.

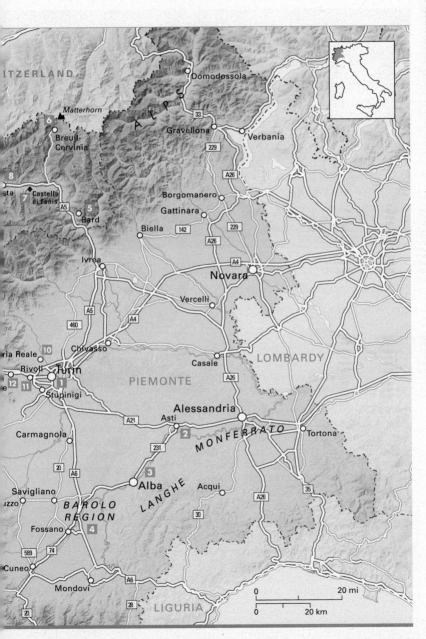

SWITZERLAND

Matterhorn

Domodossola

A L P S

33

Gravellona

6 Breuil-Cervinia

Verbania

229

A26

8

sta

7 Castello di Fenis

A5

Borgomanero

5 Bard

Gattinara

Biella   142

229

A26

Ivrea

A4

Novara

A5

Vercelli

A4

460

ria Reale **10**

Chivasso

LOMBARDY

Rivoli

Turin

Casale

A26

e **12**

11 **1**

PIEMONTE

Stupinigi

Alessandria

A21

Asti

2

Carmagnola

231

MONFERRATO

Tortona

3

20

A6

Alba

Acqui

Savigliano

LANGHE

A26

uzzo

BAROLO REGION

30

35

Fossano **4**

589 74

Cuneo

A6

Mondovì

28

LIGURIA

20

0   20 mi

0   20 km

EATING AND DRINKING WELL IN PIEDMONT AND THE VALLE D'AOSTA

In Piedmont and the Valle d'Aosta you can find rustic specialties from farmhouse hearths, fine cuisine with a French accent, and everything in between. The Piedmontese take their food and wine very seriously.

There's a significant concentration of upscale restaurants in Piedmont, with refined cuisine designed to showcase the region's fine wines. Wine-oriented menus are prevalent both in cities and in the country, where even simply named trattorias may offer a *menu di degustazione* (a multicourse tasting menu that highlights the chef's specialties) accompanied by wine pairings.

In Turin the ritual of the *aperitivo* (aperitif) has been finely tuned, and most cafés from the early evening onward provide lavish buffets that are included in the price of a cocktail—a respectable substitute for dinner if you're traveling on a limited budget. As a result, restaurants in Turin tend to fill only after 9 pm.

GREAT GRISSINI

Throughout the region—and especially in Turin—you'll find that most meals are accompanied by *grissini* (bread sticks). When they are freshly made and hand-rolled, these renditions are a far cry from the thin and dry, plastic-wrapped versions available elsewhere. Grissini were invented in Turin in the 17th century to ease the digestive problems of little Prince Vittorio Amedeo II (1675–1730). Napoléon called them *petits batons* and was supposedly addicted to them.

TRUFFLES

The *tartufo* (truffle) is a peculiar delicacy—a gnarly clump of fungus that grows wild in forests a few inches underground. It's hunted down using truffle-sniffing dogs. The payoff is a powerful, perfume flavor that makes gourmets swoon and for which they are willing to pay a small fortune. Although truffles are more abundant farther south in Umbria, the most coveted ones are the *tartufi bianchi* (white truffles) from Alba in Piedmont. A thin shaving of truffle often tops pasta dishes; they're also used to flavor soups and other dishes.

POLENTA AND PASTA

The area's best-known dish is probably polenta, creamy cornmeal served with *carbonada* (a meat stew), melted cheese, or wild mushrooms. *Agnolotti*—crescent-shape pasta stuffed with meat filling—is another specialty, often served with the pan juices of roast veal. Agnolotti *del plin* is a smaller version topped with melted butter and shaved truffles.

CHEESE

In keeping with their northern character, Piedmont and the Valle d'Aosta are both known for *fonduta,* a version of fondue made with melted cheese, eggs, and sometimes grated truffles.

Fontina and ham also often deck out the ubiquitous French-style crepes *alla valdostana,* served casserole-style.

MEAT

The locally raised beef of Piedmont is some of Italy's most highly prized; it's often braised or stewed with the region's hearty red wine. In winter, *bollito misto* (various meats, boiled and served with a rich sauce) shows up on many menus, and *fritto misto,* a combination of fried meats and vegetables, is another specialty.

DESSERTS AND SWEETS

Although desserts here are less sweet than in some other Italian regions, treats like *panna cotta* (a puddinglike cooked cream), *torta di nocciole* (hazelnut torte), and *bonet* (a pudding made with hazelnuts, cocoa, milk, and macaroons) are delights. Turin is renowned for its delicate pastries and fine chocolates—especially for *gianduiotti,* made with hazelnuts.

WINE

Piedmont is one of Italy's most important wine regions, producing full-bodied reds, such as Barolo, Barbaresco, freisa, barbera, and the lighter dolcetto. Asti Spumante, a sweet sparkling wine, comes from the region, while the Valle d'Aosta is famous for brandies made from fruits or herbs.

Northwest Italy's Piedmont and Valle d'Aosta regions come with a large dose of mountain splendor, bourgeois refinement, culinary achievement, and scenic beauty. Two of Europe's most famous peaks, Monte Bianco (Mont Blanc) and Monte Cervino (the Matterhorn), straddle the Valle d'Aosta's borders with France and Switzerland, and the region draws skiers and hikers from all over. You can ascend the mountains by cable car, or, if you're an experienced climber, make a go of it with professional guides. For the less actively inclined, a visit to the mountain museum in Bard might well do the trick.

To the south, the mist-shrouded lowlands skirting the Po River are home to Turin, a city that may not have the artistic treasures of Rome or the cutting-edge style of Milan, but has developed a sense of urban sophistication that makes it a pleasure to visit. The first capital of unified Italy and the fourth-largest city in the country, it was once overlooked on tourist itineraries as a mere industrial center (Fiat is based here), but the 2006 Winter Olympic Games put Turin on many tourists' map. Still, despite its higher profile and its many excellent museums, cafés, and restaurants, Turin never feels overrun.

Farther south, vineyards carpet the rolling hills of the Langhe and Monferrato regions, where Barolo, Barbaresco, and Asti Spumante wines—some of Italy's finest—are produced. It's here, as well, that the prized white truffle of Alba is found and celebrated during an autumn fair.

Piedmont has the longest border with France of any region, and the fact of its having been ruled by the French Savoy for centuries is revealed in a Gallic influence in all walks of life—especially in food and architecture. Turin's mansard roofs and porticoed avenues can make a walk through its streets feel like a stroll down a Parisian boulevard. Food is richer, creamier, and perhaps more refined than in many other parts of Italy, and the standard of service, even in simple restaurants, is often very high.

MAJOR REGIONS

Southeast of Turin—in the hilly, wooded Monferrato area, and farther south in the Langhe near Alba—the landscape is a patchwork of vineyards and dark woods, dotted with hill towns, castles like medieval Castello di Fénis, and fortresses like the one in Bard. This area produces some of Italy's most famous red wines, as well as sparkling whites like Asti Spumante. And in those dark woods are secret places where hunters and their dogs unearth the precious aromatic truffles that are worth their weight in gold at Alba's truffle fair.

In the Valle d'Aosta, a semiautonomous bilingual region near the French–Swiss border, the unspoiled beauty of the Alps' highest peaks, the Matterhorn and Mont Blanc, competes with the magnificent scenery of Italy's oldest national park, Gran Paradiso. Luckily, the region is so small that you don't have to choose—you can fit skiing, après-ski in the villages of Breuil-Cervinia or Courmayeur, and viewing wild ibex into one memorable trip. Aosta is also known as one of Italy's most livable cities.

The main Aosta Valley, largely on an east–west axis, is hemmed in by high mountains where glaciers have gouged out 14 tributary valleys, six to the north and eight to the south. A car is helpful, but although distances are relatively short as the crow flies, steep slopes and winding roads add to your mileage and travel time. Coming up from Turin, beyond Ivrea, the road takes you through steep ravines guarded by brooding, romantic castles. Pont St. Martin, about 18 km (11 miles) north of Ivrea, is the beginning of bilingual (Italian and French) territory.

As you head west from Turin into the Colline ("little hills"), castles and medieval fortifications begin to pepper the former dominion of the House of Savoy, and the Alps come into better and better view. In this region lie the storybook medieval town of Rivoli; 12th-century abbeys like Sacra di San Michele; a 16th-century Savoy hunting lodge, Venaria Reale; and, farther west in the mountains, the ski resort of Sestriere, one of the venues used during the 2006 Winter Games.

Planning

Making the Most of Your Time

Turin needs at least two or three days to visit properly. If you have extra time, visit one of the magnificent palaces built by the Savoy family. They surround Turin in the so-called *corona di delizie* (crown of delights) and make for an easy day trip.

Plan on several days to visit the Langhe and Monferrato areas. The towns of Alba and Asti should not be missed, but neither should the smaller wine towns that dot the rolling hills of both regions. You'll need your own car here, but the rewards are great views, great food, and great wine. If coming in September and October, when there are festivals in both Alba and Asti, make sure to book your trip well in advance.

Unless you are planning on a skiing or hiking holiday, the Valle d'Aosta requires less time to visit. The emphasis here is on the natural beauty of the mountains, but if you are driving between France and Italy, the region certainly merits a one- or two-night stopover, in either Courmayeur or Aosta; be sure not to miss Castello di Fénis and the Forte di Bard on your way.

Getting Here and Around

BUS

Turin's main bus station is on the corner of Corso Inghilterra and Corso Vittorio Emanuele. There's also a major bus station at Aosta, across the street from the train station.

BUS CONTACTS GTT. ⊠ *Turin* ☎ *800/019152 toll-free in Italy* ⊕ *www. gtt.to.it/cms.* **SADEM.** ⊠ ☎ *800/801600 toll-free in Italy* ⊕ *www.sadem.it.* **SAVDA.** ⊠ *Aosta* ☎ *0165/367011* ⊕ *www.savda.it.*

CAR

Like any mountainous region, the Italian Alps can be tricky to navigate by car. Roads that look like highways on the map can be narrow and twisting, with steep slopes and cliffside drops. Generally, roads are well maintained, but the distance covered by all of those curves tends to take longer than you might expect, so it's best to figure in extra time for getting around. This is especially true in winter, when weather conditions can slow traffic and close roads. Check with local tourist offices or, in a pinch, with the police to make sure roads are passable and safe.

For travel across the French, Swiss, and Italian borders in Piedmont and the Valle d'Aosta, only a few routes are usable year-round: the 12-km (7-mile) Mont Blanc tunnel connecting Chamonix with Courmayeur; the Colle del Gran San Bernardo/Col du Grand-Saint-Bernard (connecting Martigny to Aosta on Swiss highway E27 and Italian highway SS27, with 6 km [4 miles] of tunnel); and the Traforo del Fréjus (between Modane and Susa, with 13 km [8 miles] of tunnel). Other passes become increasingly unreliable between November and April.

TRAIN

Turin is on the main Paris–Rome TGV express line and is also connected with Milan, 90 minutes away on the fast train. The fastest (Frecciarossa) trains cover the 667-km (414-mile) trip to Rome in just over four hours; other trains take between five and seven hours.

Services to the larger cities east of Turin are part of the extensive and reliable train network of the Lombard Plain. In the mountains to the west of the region's capital, however, train service begins to peter out in favor of bus connections; information about train-bus mountain services can be obtained from train stations and tourist information offices, or by contacting FS–Trenitalia, the Italian national train service.

TRAIN CONTACTS Italo. ☎ *89020* ⊕ *www. italotreno.it/en.* **Trenitalia.** ☎ *199892021 toll-free in Italy* ⊕ *www.trenitalia.com.*

Restaurants

In this region's restaurants you'll taste a difference between the mountain and the city, but the hearty peasant fare served in tiny stone villages and the French-accented delicacies of the plain are both eminently satisfying.

Restaurant reviews have been shortened. For full information, visit Fodors.com.

Hotels

High standards and opulence are characteristic of Turin's better hotels, and the same is true at top mountain resorts. Hotels in Turin and other major towns are generally geared to business travelers; make sure to ask whether lower weekend rates or special deals for two- or three-night stays are available.

Summer vacationers and winter skiers keep occupancy rates and prices high at resorts during peak seasons. Many mountain hotels require guests to pay for either half or full board and insist on a stay of several nights; some have off-season rates that can reduce the cost by a full price category. If you're planning to ski, ask about packages that give you a discount on lift tickets.

Hotel reviews have been shortened. For full information, visit Fodors.com.

WHAT IT COSTS in Euros			
$	$$	$$$	$$$$
RESTAURANTS			
under €15	€15–€24	€25–€35	over €35
HOTELS			
under €125	€125–€200	€201–€300	over €300

Turin

Turin (Torino, in Italian) is roughly in the center of Piedmont–Valle d'Aosta and 128 km (80 miles) west of Milan; it's on the Po River, on the edge of the Po Plain, which stretches east all the way to the Adriatic. Turin's flatness and wide, angular tree-lined boulevards are a far cry from Italian *metropoli* to the south; the region's decidedly northern European bent is quite evident in its nerve center. Aside from its role as northwest Italy's major industrial, cultural, intellectual, and administrative hub, Turin also has a reputation as Italy's capital of black magic and the supernatural. This distinction is enhanced by the presence of Turin's most famous and controversial relic, the Sacra Sindone (Shroud of Turin), still believed by many Catholics to be Christ's burial shroud. (For its part, the Vatican has not taken an official position on its authenticity.)

GETTING HERE AND AROUND

Turin is well served by the Italian autostrada system and can be reached easily by car from all directions: from Milan on the A4 (2 hours); from Bologna (4 hours) and Florence (5 hours) on the A1 and A21; from Genoa on the A6 (2 hours). Bus service to and from other major

Italian cities is also plentiful, and Turin can be reached by fast train service from Paris in less than six hours. Fast train service also connects the city with Milan, Genoa, Bologna, Florence, and Rome.

VISITOR INFORMATION

The city's tourist office organizes group and personal guided tours. It also provides maps and details about a wide range of thematic self-guided walks through town. The Torino+Piemonte Card, which provides discounts on transportation and museum entrances for one-, two-, three-, or five-day visits, can be purchased here.

CONTACT Turin Tourist Information Center. ✉ *Piazza Castello, at Via Garibaldi, Turin* ☎ *011/535181* ⊕ *www.turismotorino.org.*

◉ Sights

DOWNTOWN TURIN

Many of Turin's major sights are clustered around Piazza Castello, and others are on or just off the portico-lined Via Roma, one of the city's main thoroughfares, which leads 1 km (½ mile) from Piazza Castello south to Piazza Carlo Felice, a landscaped park in front of the train station. First opened in 1615, Via Roma was largely rebuilt in the 1930s, during the Mussolini era.

Duomo di San Giovanni

CHURCH | The most impressive part of Turin's 15th-century cathedral is the shadowy black-marble-walled **Cappella della Sacra Sindone** (Chapel of the Holy Shroud), where the famous relic is housed in a sealed casket. The chapel was designed by the priest and architect Guarino Guarini (1604–83), a genius of the Baroque style who was official engineer and mathematician to the court of Duke Carlo Emanuele II of Savoy. The Sacra Sindone is a 12-foot-long sheet of linen, thought by millions to be the burial shroud of Christ, bearing the light imprint of his crucified body. The shroud first made an appearance around the middle

426

Sights ▼

1 Borgo
  Medievale .. **B8**
2 Duomo di San
  Giovanni **B2**
3 Galleria Civica
  d'Arte Moderna
  e Comtempora-
  nea (GAM).. **A5**
4 Galleria
  Sabauda **B2**
5 Gran Madre
  di Dio **D5**
6 Mole
  Antonelliana **C3**
7 Museo d'Arte
  Orientale.... **A2**
8 Museo dell'
  Automobile... **A9**
9 Museo di
  Antichità **B2**
10 Museo
  Egizio **B3**
11 Palazzo
  Carignano... **B3**
12 Palazzo
  Madama **B3**
13 Palazzo
  Reale **B2**
14 Parco del
  Valentino.... **B7**
15 Piazza San
  Carlo......... **B4**
16 Pinacoteca
  Agnelli....... **A9**
17 San
  Lorenzo **B2**
18 Sassi-Superga
  Cog Train.... **D2**

Restaurants ▼

1 Al
  Garamond... **B4**
2 Casa Vicina... **A9**
3 Consorzio ... **A3**
4 Da Mauro ... **B4**
5 Del Cambio... **B3**
6 L'Agrifoglio... **B5**
7 Pastificio
  Defilippis.... **A4**
8 Trattoria
  Anna........ **A2**
9 Vintage
  1997.......... **A3**

Quick Bites ▼

1 Al Bicerin..... **A1**

Hotels ▼

1 Genio......... **A5**
2 Grand Hotel
  Sitea......... **B4**
3 Victoria **B4**

of the 15th century, when it was presented to Ludovico of Savoy in Chambéry. In 1578 it was brought to Turin by another member of the Savoy royal family, Duke Emanuele Filiberto. It was only in the 1990s that the Catholic Church began allowing rigorous scientific study of the shroud. Not surprisingly, the results have been hazy, bolstering both sides of the argument. On one hand, three separate university teams—in Switzerland, Britain, and the United States—have concluded, as a result of carbon-14 analysis, that the cloth dates from between 1260 and 1390. On the other hand, they are unable to explain how medieval forgers could have created the shroud's image, which resembles a photographic negative, and how they could have had the knowledge or means to incorporate traces of Roman coins covering the eyelids and endemic Middle Eastern pollen woven into the cloth. Either way, the shroud continues to be revered as a holy relic, exhibited to the public on very rare occasions. ⊠ *Piazza San Giovanni, Centro* ☎ *011/4361540* ⊕ *www.duomoditorino.it.*

Galleria Civica d'Arte Moderna e Contemporanea (GAM)

ART MUSEUM | In 1863 Turin was the first Italian city to begin a public collection devoted to contemporary art. Housed in a modern building on the edge of downtown, a permanent display of more than 600 paintings, sculptures, and installation pieces provides an exceptional glimpse of how Italian contemporary art has evolved since the late 1800s. The futurist, pop, neo-Dada, and Arte Povera movements are particularly well represented, and the gallery has a fine video and art film collection. ⊠ *Via Magenta 31, Centro* ☎ *011/5211788* ⊕ *www.gamtorino.it* 🖃 *€10* 🕙 *Closed Mon.–Tues.*

Galleria Sabauda

ART MUSEUM | Housed in the restored Manica Nuova (new wing) of the Palazzo Reale, the gallery displays some of the most important paintings from the vast collections of the house of Savoy. The collection is particularly rich in Dutch and Flemish paintings: note the *Stigmate di San Francesco* (*St. Francis Receiving the Stigmata*) by Jan van Eyck (1395–1441), in which the saint receives the marks of Christ's wounds while a companion cringes beside him. Other Dutch masterpieces include paintings by Anthony van Dyck (1599–1641) and Rembrandt (1606–69). *L'arcangelo Raffaele e Tobiolo* (*Tobias and the Angel*) by Piero del Pollaiuolo (circa 1443–96) is showcased, and other featured Italian artists include Fra Angelico (circa 1400–55), Andrea Mantegna (1431–1506), and Paolo Veronese (1528–88). ⊠ *Piazetta Reale 1, Centro* ☎ *011/19560449* ⊕ *www.museireali. beniculturali.it* 🖃 *€15, includes Palazzo Reale, Armeria Reale, and the Cappella della Sindone* 🕙 *Closed Mon.*

Mole Antonelliana

NOTABLE BUILDING | You can't miss the unusual square dome and thin, elaborate spire of this Turin landmark above the city's rooftops. This odd structure, built between 1863 and 1889, was intended to be a synagogue, but costs escalated and eventually it was bought by the city. In its time it was the tallest brick structure in the world, and it is still the tallest building in Italy. You can take the crystal elevator to reach the terrace at the top of the dome for an excellent view of the city, the plain, and the Alps beyond. Also worth a visit is the Mole Antonelliana's **Museo Nazionale del Cinema** (National Cinema Museum), which covers more than 34,000 square feet and houses many items of film memorabilia as well as a film library with some 7,000 titles. ⊠ *Via Montebello 20, Centro* ☎ *011/8138563* ⊕ *www.museocinema.it* 🖃 *Museum €11, elevator €8; combination ticket €15* 🕙 *Closed Tues.*

Museo d'Arte Orientale

ART MUSEUM | Housed in the magnificently renovated 17th-century Palazzo Mazzonis, this is a beautifully displayed collection of Southeast Asian, Chinese, Japanese, Himalayan, and Islamic art, including sculptures, paintings, and ceramics. Highlights include a towering 13th-century wooden statue of the Japanese temple guardian Kongo Rikishi and a sumptuous assortment of Islamic manuscripts. ⊠ *Via San Domenico 11, Centro* 🕾 *011/4436932* ⊕ *www.maotorino.it* 🎫 *€10* ⊗ *Closed Tues.*

Museo di Antichità

ART GALLERY | A small but fascinating collection of artifacts found at archaeological sites in and around Turin is displayed here. A spiral ramp winds down through the subterranean museum; and, as in a real archaeological site, the deeper you go, the older the objects on display. A life-size silver bust of the Roman emperor Lucius Verus (AD 161–169) is one of the masterpieces of the collection. ⊠ *Via XX Settembre 88, Centro* 🕾 *011/19560449* ⊕ *www.museireali.beniculturali.it/museo-antichita* ⊗ *Closed Mon.* 🎫 *€15, includes Galleria Sabauda, Armeria Reale, and Palazzo Reale.*

★ Museo Egizio

ART MUSEUM | The Egyptian Museum's superb collection includes statues of pharaohs and mummies and entire frescoes taken from royal tombs—it's one of the world's finest and largest museums of its kind. The striking sculpture gallery, designed by the Oscar-winning production designer Dante Ferretti, is a veritable who's who of ancient Egypt. Look for the magnificent 13th-century BC statue of Ramses II and the fascinating Tomb of Kha. The latter was found intact with furniture, supplies of food and clothing, writing instruments, and a complete set of personal cosmetics and toiletries. The museum is housed in the **Palazzo dell'Accademia delle Scienze,** a Baroque tour de force designed by the priest and architect Guarino Guarini. ⊠ *Via Accademia delle Scienze 6, Centro* 🕾 *011/4406903* ⊕ *www.museoegizio.it* 🎫 *€12.*

Palazzo Carignano

CASTLE/PALACE | Half of this building is the Baroque triumph of Guarino Guarini, the priest and architect who designed many of Turin's most noteworthy buildings. Built between 1679 and 1685, his red-brick palace later played an important role in the creation of the modern-day nation. Vittorio Emanuele II of Savoy (1820–78), the first king of a united Italy, was born here, and, after a 19th-century neoclassical extension, Italy's first parliament met here between 1860 and 1865. The palace now houses the Museo del Risorgimento, a museum honoring the 19th-century movement for Italian unity. ⊠ *Via Accademia delle Scienze 5, Centro* ⊹ *Entrance at Piazza Carlo Alberto, 8* 🕾 *011/5621147* ⊕ *www.museorisorgimentotorino.it* ⊗ *Closed Mon.* 🎫 *€10.*

Palazzo Madama

CASTLE/PALACE | In the center of Piazza Castello, this castle was named for the Savoy queen Maria Cristina, who made it her home in the 17th century. The building incorporates the remains of a Roman gate with late-medieval and Renaissance additions, and the monumental Baroque facade and grand entrance staircase were added by Filippo Juvarra (1678–1736). The palace now houses the Museo Civico d'Arte Antica, whose collections comprise more than 30,000 items dating from the Middle Ages to the Baroque era. The paintings, sculptures, illuminated manuscripts, and various decorative objects on display illustrate almost 10 centuries of Italian and European artistic production. Works by Jan van Eyck and Orazio Gentileschi (1563–1639) highlight the collection. ⊠ *Piazza Castello 10, Centro* 🕾 *011/4433501* ⊕ *www.palazzomadamatorino.it* 🎫 *Staircase and courtyard free, museum €10* ⊗ *Closed Tues.*

Palazzo Reale

CASTLE/PALACE | This 17th-century palace, a former Savoy royal residence, is an imposing work of brick, stone, and marble that stands on the site of one of Turin's ancient Roman city gates. In contrast to its sober exterior, the two main floors of the palace's interior are swathed in luxurious rococo trappings, including tapestries, gilt ceilings, and sumptuous 17th- to 19th-century furniture. The second floor has several royal apartments, and you can head down to the basement and the old kitchens to see where food for the last kings of Italy was once dished up. The surrounding gardens were laid out in the late 17th century by André Le Nôtre, landscape designer at Versailles. The **Armeria Reale** (Royal Armory) wing holds one of Europe's most extensive collections of arms and armor. Note that certain parts of the palace are closed on varying days. ⊠ *Piazzetta Reale 1, Centro* ☎ *011/19560449* ⊕ *www.ilpalazzorealeditorino.it* ✉ *€15, includes Armeria Reale, Galleria Sabauda, and Museo Archeologico* ⊗ *Closed Mon.*

Piazza San Carlo

PLAZA/SQUARE | Surrounded by shops, arcades, fashionable cafés, and elegant Baroque palaces, this is one of the most beautiful squares in Turin. In the center stands a statue of Duke Emanuele Filiberto of Savoy, the victor at the battle of San Quintino, in 1557. The melee heralded the peaceful resurgence of Turin under the Savoy after years of bloody dynastic fighting. The fine bronze statue erected in the 19th century is one of Turin's symbols. At the southern end of the square, framing the continuation of Via Roma, are the twin Baroque churches of San Carlo and Santa Cristina. ⊠ *Piazza San Carlo, Centro.*

San Lorenzo

CHURCH | Architect, priest, and mathematician Guarino Guarini was in his mid-sixties when he began this church in 1668. The masterful use of geometric forms and the theatrical control of light and shadow show him working at his mature and confident best. ■TIP→ **Stand in the center of the church and look up into the cupola to appreciate the full effect.** ⊠ *Via Palazzo di Città 4, Centro* ☎ *011/4361527* ⊕ *www.sanlorenzo.torino.it.*

ALONG THE PO

The Po River is narrow and unprepossessing here in Turin, only a hint of the broad waterway that it becomes as it flows eastward toward the Adriatic. It's flanked, however, by formidable edifices, a park, and a lovely pedestrian path.

Borgo Medievale

TOWN | FAMILY | Along the banks of the Po, this complex, built for a General Exhibition in 1884, is a faithful reproduction of a typical Piedmont village in the Middle Ages. Craft shops, houses, a church, and stores are clustered in the narrow lanes, and in the center of the village is the **Rocca Medievale,** a medieval castle that's its main attraction. ⊠ *Viale Virgilio 107, San Salvario* ☎ *011/01167101* ⊕ *www.borgomedievaletorino.it* ✉ *Village free, Rocca Medievale and garden €5.*

Gran Madre di Dio

CHURCH | On the east bank of the Po, this neoclassical church is modeled after the Pantheon in Rome. It was built between 1827 and 1831 to commemorate the return of the house of Savoy to Turin after the fall of Napoleon's empire. ⊠ *Piazza Gran Madre di Dio 4, Borgo Po* ☎ *011/8193572.*

★ Museo dell'Automobile

ART MUSEUM | FAMILY | No visit to this motor city would be complete without a pilgrimage to see the perfectly preserved Bugattis, Ferraris, and Isotta Fraschinis at this museum. Here you can get an idea of the importance of Fiat—and cars in general—to Turin's economy. There's a collection of antique cars from as early as 1896, and displays show how the city has changed over the years as a result of the auto industry. ⊠ *Corso Unità d'Italia*

40, Millefonti ☎ 011/677666 ⊕ www.
museoauto.it ☑ €12.

Parco del Valentino

CITY PARK | This pleasant riverside park
is a great place to stroll, bike, or jog.
Originally the grounds of a relatively
simple hunting lodge, the park owes its
present arrangement to Madama Maria
Cristina of France, who received the land
and lodge as a wedding present after her
marriage to Vittorio Amedeo I of Savoy.
With memories of 16th-century French
châteaux in mind, she began work in
1620 and converted the lodge into a magnificent palace, the **Castello del Valentino.**
The building, now home to the University
of Turin's Faculty of Architecture, is not
open to the public. Next to the palace are
the university's **botanical gardens,** established in 1729, where local and exotic
flora can be seen in a hothouse, herbar-
ium, and arboretum. ⊠ *Viale Mattioli 25,
San Salvario* ☎ 011/6705970 *botanical
gardens* ⊕ *www.comune.torino.it* ⊙ *Botanical gardens closed Nov.–mid-Apr.*
☑ *Botanical gardens €5.*

★ Pinacoteca Agnelli

ART MUSEUM | This gallery was opened
by Gianni Agnelli (1921–2003), the head
of Fiat and patriarch of one of Italy's
most powerful families, just four months
before his death. The emphasis here is
on quality rather than quantity: 25 works
of art from the Agnelli private collection
are on permanent display, along with
temporary exhibitions. There are four
magnificent scenes of Venice by Canaletto (1697–1768); two splendid views
of Dresden by Canaletto's nephew, Bernardo Bellotto (1720–80); several works
by Manet (1832–83), Renoir (1841–1919),
Matisse (1869–1954), and Picasso (1881–
1973); and fine examples of the work of
Italian futurist painters Balla (1871–1958)
and Severini (1883–1966). The gallery
is on the top floor of the **Lingotto,** a
former Fiat factory that was completely

transformed between 1982 and 2002
by architect Renzo Piano. The multilevel
complex now holds a shopping mall,
several movie theaters, restaurants, two
hotels, and an auditorium. ■TIP→ **Don't
miss the beautifully preserved spiral ramps
that once took cars up and down the original building.** ⊠ *Via Nizza 230, Lingotto*
☎ 011/0062713 ⊕ *www.pinacoteca-agnel-
li.it* ⊙ *Closed Mon.* ☑ *€12.*

Sassi-Superga Cog Train

OTHER ATTRACTION | FAMILY | The 18-minute
ride from Sassi up the Superga hill is a
real treat on a clear day. The view of the
Alps is magnificent at the hilltop **Parco
Naturale Collina Torinese,** a tranquil retreat
from the bustle of the city. If you feel like
a little exercise, you can walk back down
to Sassi (about two hours) on one of the
well-marked wooded trails that start from
the upper station. Other circular trails
lead through the park and back to Superga. Note that a bus replaces the train on
Wednesday, although the ride up the hill
is still just as lovely. ⊠ *Piazza G. Modena,
Sassi* ☎ 011/0672000 ⊕ *www.gtt.to.it/
cms/turismo/sassisup* ☑ *€4 one-way on
weekdays, €6 one-way on weekends*
⊙ *Closed Wed.*

🍴 Restaurants

★ Al Garamond

$$ | PIEDMONTESE | The well-spaced tables
and the ancient brick vaulting in this
small, bright space set the stage for
game, meat, fish, and seafood dishes
served with creative flair. The level of
service is very high, even by demand-
ing Turin standards. **Known for:** mix of
traditional and inventive dishes; merg-
ing Sicilian and Piedmontese cuisine;
chef's table experience. ⑤ *Average
main: €24* ⊠ *Via G. Pomba 14, Centro*
☎ 011/8122781 ⊕ *www.algaramond.it*
⊙ *Closed Sun., Aug., and Jan. 7–14. No
lunch Sat.*

★ Casa Vicina

$$$$ | PIEDMONTESE | Hidden away in the basement of the Eataly Lingotto food emporium, this is one of Turin's top destinations for fine dining, and while the starkly modern and windowless decor might seem claustrophobic to some, the food makes up for everything. Traditional Piedmontese dishes are served up with creative style and the wine list is an encyclopedia, with many small but notable wineries included. **Known for:** layered bagna càuda served in a martini glass; fresh agnolotti pasta; fixed-price tasting and gastronomic menus. $ *Average main: €45* ✉ *Via Nizza 224, Lingotto* ☎ *011/19506840* ⊕ *www.casavicina.com* ☾ *Closed Mon. No dinner Sun.*

Consorzio

$$ | PIEDMONTESE | Extremely popular for lunch during the week, this lively and informal osteria is in Turin's business district. The service is relaxed, the decor is low-key, the menu highlights organic meats and vegetables from Piedmont, and there's a good selection of local wines. **Known for:** creative presentation; wide selection of cheeses from across Europe; Piedmont dishes like *torino di verdura* (vegetable flan). $ *Average main: €21* ✉ *Via Monte di Pietà 23, Centro* ☎ *011/2767661* ⊕ *www.ristoranteconsorzio.it* ☾ *Closed Sun. No lunch Sat.*

Da Mauro

$$ | TUSCAN | After a flux of Tuscan migrants moved to Turin in the '60s, Da Mauro was one of the first restaurants to cater to their tastes, mixing Tuscan dishes into the largely Piedmontese menu. Service is brisk and efficient for a local crowd at lunch and dinner—it's not the place to come for a slow-paced meal. **Known for:** Tuscan specialties; fresh pasta dishes like agnolotti al ragù; affordable menu. $ *Average main: €15* ✉ *Via Maria Vittoria 21, Centro* ☎ *011/8170604* ⊕ *www.ristorante-da-mauro.business.site* ☾ *Closed Mon.*

Del Cambio

$$$$ | PIEDMONTESE | Set in a palace dating from 1757, this is one of Europe's most beautiful and historic restaurants, with decorative moldings, mirrors, and hanging lamps that look as they did when Italian national hero Cavour dined here more than a century ago. The cuisine draws heavily on Piedmontese tradition and is paired with fine regional wines. **Known for:** inventive meat dishes; traditional pastas; elegant presentation and thematic tasting menus. $ *Average main: €43* ✉ *Piazza Carignano 2, Centro* ☎ *011/546690* ⊕ *www.delcambio.it* ☾ *Closed Mon. No lunch Tues.–Wed. No dinner Sun.*

L'Agrifoglio

$$ | PIEDMONTESE | This local favorite has a bright contemporary setting, with green and cream walls and just 10 tables, and it stays open late for post-movie and -theater crowds. Specialties change with the seasons and include risotto, fresh pasta, and a fine cheese selection. **Known for:** house-made pastas; roasted meats carved on the spot; traditional Piedmontese antipasti. $ *Average main: €20* ✉ *Via Andrea Provana 7, Centro* ☎ *011/8136837* ⊕ *www.lagrifoglioristorante.com* ☾ *Closed Mon. and 2 wks in Aug. No dinner Sun.*

Pastificio Defilippis

$$ | PIEDMONTESE | Famous for freshly made seasonal pasta dishes since 1872, this shop serves a packed lunch crowd all week long, with outdoor seating in the summer. Secondi and dolci are also available, but pasta is the main event. **Known for:** wide variety of pasta from Piedmont and across Italy; traditional agnolotti; vegetarian, meat, and seafood sauces. $ *Average main: €16* ✉ *Via Lagrange 39, Centro* ☎ *011/542137* ⊕ *www.pastificiodefilippis.it.*

Trattoria Anna

$ | **SEAFOOD** | If you are hankering for something different from the usual meat-based Piedmontese cuisine, give this simple, extremely popular family-run spot a try. They serve only seafood, and they do it well. **Known for:** mixed grilled fish; Ligurian-style dishes; linguine Trattoria Anna, with prawns, pesto, and cherry tomatoes. $ *Average main: €14* ✉ *Via Gian Francesco Bellezia 20, Centro* ☎ *011/4362134* ⊕ *www.trattorianna.com* ⊘ *Closed Mon. and 2 wks in Aug. No lunch.*

Vintage 1997

$$$ | **NORTHERN ITALIAN** | The first floor of an elegant town house in the center of Turin makes a fitting location for this sophisticated restaurant. There's an excellent wine list with regional, national, and international vintages well represented, and tasting menus, including a nine-course feast that covers the full range of the restaurant's cuisine and desserts. **Known for:** tasting menus from three to nine courses; Piedmontese roasted veal; selection of rare cheeses. $ *Average main: €30* ✉ *Piazza Solferino 16/h, Centro* ☎ *011/535948* ⊕ *www.vintage1997.com* ⊘ *Closed Sun. No lunch Sat.*

☕ Coffee and Quick Bites

Al Bicerin

$ | **CAFÉ** | A chocolate lover's pilgrimage to Turin inevitably leads to this café where Nietzsche, Puccini, Dumas, and the political reformer Cavour have all sipped. If you order the house specialty, bicerin (a hot drink with layers of chocolate, coffee, and cream), or a flavored *zabaioni* (warm eggnog), and browse the collection of chocolate goodies including chocolate-flavored pasta, you'll understand why. **Known for:** wide assortment of creative sweet drinks; elegant presentation; traditional Gianduiotto chocolates. $ *Average main: €6* ✉ *Piazza della Consolata 5, Centro* ☎ *011/4369325* ⊕ *www.bicerin.it* ⊘ *Closed Wed. and Aug.*

Hotels

The Turin Tourist Information Center provides a booking service for accommodations in the city and throughout the region. Book hotels through them at least 48 hours in advance, B&Bs at least seven days in advance.

Genio

$ | **HOTEL** | Although they're just steps away from the main train station, these spacious and tastefully decorated rooms are a quiet haven from the bustle of the city. **Pros:** abundant breakfast; spacious rooms and bathrooms; convenient location. **Cons:** entrance and lobby area could be updated; neighborhood is a bit seedy; street noise in some rooms. $ *Rooms from: €83* ✉ *Corso Vittorio Emanuele II 47, Centro* ☎ *011/6505771* ⊕ *www.hotel-genio.it* ⇆ *115 rooms* ⦿ *Free Breakfast.*

Grand Hotel Sitea

$ | **HOTEL** | One of the city's finest hotels, the Sitea is in the historic center and decorated in a warm classical style; the common areas and guest rooms are elegant, spacious, and comfortable. **Pros:** well-appointed rooms; large bathrooms; central location. **Cons:** spotty Wi-Fi connection; carpets are a little worn; air-conditioning and street noise can be loud in some rooms. $ *Rooms from: €103* ✉ *Via Carlo Alberto 35, Centro* ☎ *011/5170171* ⊕ *www.grandhotelsitea.it* ⇆ *120 rooms* ⦿ *Free Breakfast.*

★ Victoria

$$ | **HOTEL** | Style, attention to detail, and comfort are hallmarks of this retreat that's furnished like a refined English home. **Pros:** tranquil location in the center of town; wonderful breakfast; excellent spa facilities. **Cons:** standard rooms are small; parking nearby can be difficult; not all rooms have views. $ *Rooms from: €135* ✉ *Via Nino Costa 4, Centro* ☎ *011/5611909* ⊕ *www.hotelvictoria-torino.com* ⇆ *106 rooms* ⦿ *Free Breakfast.*

Piedmont

Nightlife

Two areas of Turin are enormously popular nightlife destinations: the Quadrilatero, to the north of the city center, and the Murazzi embankment, near the Ponte Vittorio Emanuele I. The center of town is also popular, especially earlier in the evening.

Caffè Elena

WINE BARS | This wine bar is a trendy place for an aperitif or for a drink before going out to a show or dancing. It's in the large piazza at the end of Via Po. ⊠ *Piazza Vittorio Veneto 5, Centro* ☏ *3295767414* ⊕ *www.caffeelena.it.*

Pastis

GATHERING PLACES | The Quadrilatero Romano, which roughly corresponds to the grid pattern of Roman Turin near Piazza della Repubblica, is a hopping area filled with nightclubs and ethnic restaurants. Places open and close with startling frequency here, but Pastis has shown considerable staying power. ⊠ *Piazza Emanuele Filiberto 9b, Centro* ☏ *011/5211085* ⊕ *www.pastistorino.com.*

🎭 Performing Arts

MUSIC

Lingotto Musica

MUSIC | Classical music concerts are held at this theater designed by Renzo Piano in the renovated Lingotto building; internationally famous conductors and orchestras are frequent guests. ⊠ *Via Nizza 280, Lingotto* ☏ *011/6313721* ⊕ *www. lingottomusica.it.*

MITO Settembre Musica Festival

MUSIC | Running for three weeks in September, this popular festival of classical music is held in a variety of venues around town. The program of performances and tickets becomes available in June each year. ✉ *Urban Lab, Piazza Palazzo di Città 8/F, ticket office, Turin* ☎ *011/24787* ⊕ *www.mitosettembremusica.it.*

OPERA

Teatro Regio

OPERA | Premieres at the Teatro Regio, one of Italy's leading opera houses, sell out well in advance. You can buy tickets for most performances at the box office or on the website, where discounts are often offered on the day of the performance. The season runs from October through July. ✉ *Piazza Castello 125, Centro* ☎ *011/8815241* ⊕ *www.teatroregio.torino.it.*

 # Shopping

Many people know that Turin produces more than 75% of Italy's cars, but they're often unaware that it's also a hub for clothing manufacturing. Top-quality boutiques stocking local, national, and international lines are clustered along Via Roma and Via Garibaldi. Piazza San Carlo, Via Po, and Via Maria Vittoria are lined with antiques shops, some of which specialize in 18th-century furniture and domestic items.

CHOCOLATE

The Italian tradition of making chocolate began in Turin during the early 17th century. Chocolate at that time was an aristocratic drink, but in the 19th century a Piedmontese invention made it possible to further refine cocoa to create solid bars and candies.

Peyrano

CHOCOLATE | The most famous of all Turin chocolates is the wedge-shape gianduiotto, flavored with hazelnuts and first concocted in 1867. The tradition has been continued at this family-run shop, where 60 types of chocolates are made. ✉ *Corso Moncalieri 47, Centro* ☎ *011/6602202* ⊕ *www.peyrano.com.*

Stratta

CHOCOLATE | In business since 1836, this famed shop sells confectionery of all kinds—not just the chocolates in the lavish window displays but also fancy cookies, rum-laced fudges, and magnificent cakes. ✉ *Piazza San Carlo 191, Centro* ☎ *011/547920* ⊕ *www.stratta1836.it.*

MARKETS

Balon Flea Market

MARKET | Go to this famous market for bargains on secondhand books, antiques, and clothing. There is good browsing to be had among the stands, which spill out of Borgo Dora onto the surrounding side streets. During the second weekend of every month, the market extends its hours into Sunday, becoming the so-called Gran Balon. (Be aware, however, that the market is also famous for its pickpockets.) ✉ *Borgo Dora, Centro* ⊕ *www.balon.it.*

★ Mercato di Porta Palazzo

MARKET | For food lovers, people-watchers, or anyone interested in the lively local scene, the immensely popular market in this huge square to the north of town is not to be missed. Outdoors, the keepers of hundreds of vegetable stands vie with one another to create the most appetizing displays. Indoors, the meat vendors provide an equally tantalizing array of local products, while the fishmongers proudly display the fresh catch of the day. ✉ *Piazza della Repubblica, Centro* ⊕ *www.scopriportapalazzo.com.*

Skiing in Piedmont and the Valle d'Aosta

Skiing is the major sport in both Piedmont and the Valle d'Aosta. Excellent facilities abound at resort towns such as Courmayeur and Breuil-Cervinia. The so-called Via Lattea (Milky Way)—five skiing areas near Sestriere with 400 km (almost 250 miles) of linked runs and more than 100 ski lifts—provides practically unlimited skiing. Lift tickets, running around €40 for a day's pass, are a good deal compared to those at major U.S. resorts.

To Italian skiers, a weeklong holiday on the slopes is known as a *settimana* *bianca* (white week). Ski resort hotels in Piedmont and the Valle d'Aosta encourage these getaways by offering six- and seven-day packages, and though they're designed with the domestic market in mind, you can get a bargain by taking advantage of them. The packages usually (though not always) include half or full board.

You should have your passport with you if you plan a day trip into Switzerland—although the odds are that you won't be asked to show it.

SPECIALTY FOOD AND DELIS

Borgiattino

FOOD | Specialty food stores and delicatessens abound in central Turin, but for a truly spectacular array of cheeses and other delicacies, this should be your first stop. ⊠ *Corso Vinzaglio 29, Centro* ☎ *011/5629075* ⊕ *www.borgiattino.com.*

Eataly

FOOD | Now with branches in Milan, Florence, Bologna, New York, and Tokyo, this is probably Turin's most famous food emporium. In addition to the market, there are kitchenware and cookbook stores, plus a wine bar and several different counters and restaurants serving hamburgers, haute cuisine, and lots more in between. ⊠ *Via Nizza 230, Lingotto* ☎ *011/19506801* ⊕ *www.eataly.net.*

Activities

BICYCLING

Ufficio Iniziative Ambientali (*Office for Environmental Initiatives*)

BIKING | Turin has about 160 km (100 miles) of bike paths running through the city and its parks. Bicycles are available for daily rental at stands throughout the city year-round. ⊠ *Piazza San Giovanni 5, Madonna di Campagna* ☎ *011/4420177.*

Asti

60 km (37 miles) southeast of Turin.

Asti is best known outside Italy for its wines—excellent reds as well as the famous sparkling white *spumante.* The town itself has some impressive reminders of the days when its strategic position on trade routes between Turin, Milan, and Genoa gave it broad economic power. In the 12th century Asti began to develop as a republic, at a time when other Italian cities were also flexing their economic and military muscles. It flourished in the following century, when the inhabitants began erecting lofty towers (west end of Corso Vittorio Alfieri) for its defense. As in Pavia, near Milan, this gave rise to the medieval nickname "City of a Hundred Towers." In the center of Asti some of these remain, among them the 13th-century **Torre Comentina** and the well-preserved **Torre Troyana,** a tall, slender tower attached to the **Palazzo Troya.** The 18th-century church of **Santa Caterina** has incorporated one of Asti's medieval towers, the **Torre Romana** (itself built on an ancient Roman base), as its bell tower. Corso Vittorio Alfieri is Asti's main thoroughfare, running west–east across the city. This road, known in medieval times as Contrada Maestra, was built by the Romans.

GETTING HERE AND AROUND

Asti is less than an hour away from Turin by car on the A21 autostrada. GTT bus service connects the two towns, but isn't direct. Train service to Asti, on the other hand, is frequent and fast.

VISITOR INFORMATION

CONTACT Asti Tourism Office. ⊠ *Piazza Alfieri 34, Asti* ☎ *0141/530357* ⊕ *www. astiturismo.it.*

Sights

Duomo

CHURCH | Dedicated to the Assumption of the Virgin, the Duomo is an object lesson in Italian Gothic architecture. Completed in the early 14th century, it is decorated so as to emphasize geometry and verticality: pointed arches and narrow vaults are completely covered with frescoes that direct your gaze upward. The porch on the south side of the cathedral facing the square was built in 1470; it represents the Gothic style at its most florid and excessive. ⊠ *Piazza Cattedrale, Asti* ☎ *0141/592924.*

San Secondo

CHURCH | This Gothic church is dedicated to Asti's patron saint, believed by some to have been decapitated by the Emperor Hadrian on this very spot. San Secondo is also the patron of the city's favorite folklore and sporting event, the annual Palio di Asti, a colorful medieval-style horse race that's similar to Siena's. It's held each year on a Sunday in early September in the vast Campo del Palio to the south of the church. ⊠ *Piazza San Secondo, Asti* ☎ *0141/530066.*

Restaurants

L'Angolo del Beato

$$ | PIEDMONTESE | At this Asti institution, in a building that dates to the 12th century (as you'll see from the exposed brick walls and original wood-beamed ceiling), you'll find that regional specialties are the main attractions. There's also an extensive list of several hundred Piedmont wines. **Known for:** tajarin pasta; roasted meats; vegetables with *bagna càuda* (anchovies, garlic, butter, and olive oil) antipasto. ⑤ *Average main: €16* ⊠ *Vicolo Cavalleri 2, Asti* ☎ *0141/531668* ⊕ *www. angolodelbeato.it* ⊘ *Closed Sun., 1st wk of Jan., and 10 days in Aug.*

Hotels

Reale

$ | B&B/INN | Spacious rooms in an 18th-century building on Asti's main square are eclectically decorated, with a mix of contemporary and period furniture. **Pros:** rooms with balconies; central location; historical details add character. **Cons:** lobby area is a little worn; limited parking; rooms facing the main square can be noisy. ⑤ *Rooms from: €95* ⊠ *Piazza Alfieri 5, Asti* ☎ *0141/532279* ⊕ *www. hotelristorantereale.it* ⊷ *26 rooms* ⑩ *Free Breakfast.*

Relais Sant'Uffizio

$$ | HOTEL | You may be surprised to learn that this now delightfully peaceful and elegant retreat—with a luxurious spa and swimming pool, surrounded by vineyards and rolling hills—was once home to the Inquisition in the 16th century. **Pros:** tranquil and beautiful location; good value for the amenities; excellent spa and exercise facilities. **Cons:** soundproofing could be better in some rooms; some rooms are a walk from the main building; a bit isolated, 20 km (12 miles) north of Asti. ⑤ *Rooms from: €136* ⊠ *Strada Sant Uffizio 1, Cioccaro di Penango, Asti* ☎ *0141/916292* ⊕ *www.relaissantuffizio. com* ⊷ *41 rooms* ⑩ *Free Breakfast.*

Alba

30 km (18 miles) southwest of Asti.

This small town has a gracious atmosphere and a compact core, studded with medieval towers and Gothic buildings. In addition to being a wine center for the region, Alba is known as the "City of the White Truffle" for dirty little tubers that cost as much as €2,200 a pound. For picking out your truffle and having a few wisps shaved on top of your food, expect to shell out an extra €16 or so—which may be worth it, at least once.

GETTING HERE AND AROUND
By car from Turin follow the A6 autostrada south to Marene and then head east on the A33, which connects Asti and Alba. GTT offers frequent bus service between Alba and Turin—the journey takes approximately 1½ hours. Direct trains run to Alba from Turin's Lingotto station; the trip takes about an hour.

VISITOR INFORMATION
CONTACT Alba Tourism Office. ✉ *Piazza Risorgimento 2, Alba* ☎ *0173/35833* ⊕ *www.langheroero.it.*

🍴 Restaurants

L'inedito: Vigin Mudest
$$ | **PIEDMONTESE** | Delicious regional specialties with tartufo-focused and fixed-price tasting menus are served at this bustling family-run restaurant in the center of Alba. Outdoor seating is available in summer. **Known for:** risotto al Barolo; carne cruda all'albese (Alba-style beef carpaccio); fresh tajarin. ⑤ *Average main: €18* ✉ *Via Vernazza 11, Alba* ☎ *0173/441701* ⊕ *www.lineditoviginmudest.it* ⊗ *Closed Wed.*

La Libera
$$ | **PIEDMONTESE** | Modern and subdued, this small spot on a quiet backstreet is conducive to a leisurely meal while trying a huge selection of Barolo wines. On the menu you'll find Piedmontese starters and pastas and a variety of tasty meat dishes, and there's also a superb selection of local cheeses. **Known for:** locally sourced meat and produce; tajarin al ragù; Piedmontese wines and cheeses. ⑤ *Average main: €18* ✉ *Via Elvio Pertinace 24a, Alba* ☎ *0173/293155* ⊕ *www.lalibera.com* ⊗ *Closed Sun., 3 wks in Aug., and late Dec.–mid-Jan.*

★ Massimo Camia
$$ | **PIEDMONTESE** | Chef Massimo Camia's restaurant is in an elegant and modern space, with views of the Barolo vineyards that surround the Damilano winery; the service is impeccable and the food is divine. The restaurant is outside the town of La Morra, a 20-minute drive to the southwest of Alba. **Known for:** amuse-bouche and wine pairings; inventive meat, seafood, and game dishes; extensive cheese menu. ⑤ *Average main: €16* ✉ *SP122 (Alba–Barolo), La Morra* ☎ *0173/56355* ⊕ *www.massimocamia.it* ⊗ *Closed Tues.*

Osteria dell'Arco
$$ | **PIEDMONTESE** | Delicious, hearty dishes using local ingredients are served here in a lovely setting with wine bottles lining the walls. In addition to lots of game meats, you'll find a nice selection of seafood dishes with a hint of Liguria. **Known for:** meat and fish crudos; house-made pastas; Slow Food movement cooking. ⑤ *Average main: €15* ✉ *Piazza Savona 5, Alba* ☎ *0173/363974* ⊕ *www.osteriadellarco.it* ⊗ *Closed Sun. Dec.–Sept.*

Vincafè
$$ | **WINE BAR** | This excellent *enoteca,* with a contemporary casual atmosphere, has a whole range of Piedmont specialties to pair with local wines. You'll find more than 60 labels, as well as grappas and liqueurs, on the menu. **Known for:** late-night dining; Piedmontese crudos; Langhe wine pairings. ⑤ *Average main: €16* ✉ *Via Emanuele 12, Alba* ☎ *0173/364603* ⊕ *www.vincafe.com.*

Hotels

Locanda del Pilone

$$$ | B&B/INN | It would be hard to imagine a more commanding position for these simply but tastefully decorated accommodations and the Michelin-starred restaurant above Alba. **Pros:** abundant breakfast; spectacular location with a 360-degree view; excellent restaurant. **Cons:** parking can be challenging; while not far from Alba, you do need a car to get around; rooms near common areas can be noisy. $ *Rooms from: €205 ⊠ Località Madonna di Como 34, Alba* ☎ *0173/366616* ⊕ *www.locandadelpilone.it* ⊗ *Closed Jan.–Mar.* ⌁ *8 rooms* ⦿ *Free Breakfast.*

Villa Beccaris

$$$ | HOTEL | This beautiful property consists of an old villa and two newer buildings in the heart of one of the Langhe's most charming villages. **Pros:** lovely gardens and pool area; nice views; located in a village with good restaurants. **Cons:** spotty Wi-Fi; some rooms are noisy; the classic rooms are on the small side. $ *Rooms from: €230 ⊠ Via Bava Beccaris 1, Monforte d'Alba* ☎ *0173/78158* ⊕ *www.villabeccaris.com* ⊗ *Closed Jan. 8–Feb. 8* ⌁ *23 rooms* ⦿ *Free Breakfast.*

The Barolo Region

17 km (11 miles) southwest of Alba, 72 km (45 miles) southeast of Turin.

The Langhe district may not get as much attention as other wine-producing regions in Italy, but the payoff for a visit can be just as satisfying. Try to schedule a day trip to one or several of the wine estates here.

GETTING HERE AND AROUND

The easiest way to reach Barolo and its wineries is to drive from Alba.

 Sights

Famiglia Anselma

WINERY | Probably best for wine lovers who have at least reached an intermediate level of fandom, this winery is known for its steadfast commitment to producing only Barolo—nothing else—and for its policy of holding wines for several years before release. The winemaker here, Maurizio Anselma, is something of a prodigy in the Barolo world, and he's quite open to visitors. ⊠ *Località Castello della Volta, Barolo* ☎ *0173/560511* ⊕ *www.anselma.it* ⌁ *Reservations essential.*

Marchesi di Barolo

WINERY | Right in the town of Barolo, this wine estate makes an easy, if touristy, option for getting to know the local wines. In the estate's user-friendly enoteca you can taste wine, buy some of the thousands of bottles from vintages going way back, and look at display bottles, including an 1859 Barolo. Marchesi di Barolo's *cantine* (wine cellars), at Via Roma 1, are open daily. ⊠ *Via Roma 1, Barolo* ☎ *0173/564491* ⊕ *www.marchesibarolo.com.*

Rocche dei Manzoni

WINERY | A good, accessible example of the new school of local wine making is this estate, about 6 km (4 miles) south of Barolo. The facade of the *cantina* (wine cellar) is like a Roman temple of brick, complete with imposing columns. Rocche dei Manzoni's reds include five Barolos, one dolcetto, two Langhe Rossos, two Langhe DOCs, and two barberas. ⊠ *Località Manzoni Soprani 3, Monforte d'Alba* ☎ *0173/78421* ⊕ *www.barolobig.com.*

Valle d'Aosta

Bard

65 km (40 miles) north of Turin.

This small medieval town clings to a rocky crag that almost completely blocks the entrance to the Valle d'Aosta from Piedmont. Recognized for its strategic importance since prehistoric times, the location was first fully fortified by the Romans, and then by the Ostrogoths in the 6th century. As befits its military heritage, the village is rather gray and somber, but the magnificent fortress that sits atop it makes a visit well worthwhile.

GETTING HERE AND AROUND

Bard is just off the A5 autostrada, which runs north from Turin into the Valle d'Aosta—by car the trip takes about an hour. There are trains about every two hours from Turin and more regular service to and from Aosta. Traveling to Bard by bus is not a viable option.

◉ Sights

★ Forte di Bard

MILITARY SIGHT | FAMILY | A few minutes beyond the French-speaking village of Pont St. Martin, you pass through the narrow Gorge de Bard to reach the fortress that has stood guarding the valley entrance for more than eight centuries. In 1800, Napoléon entered Italy through this valley, using the cover of darkness to get his artillery units past the castle unnoticed. Ten years later he remembered this inconvenience and had the fortress destroyed. It was rebuilt in the 19th century and now houses the lavishly multimedia **Museo delle Alpi**, dedicated to the history and culture of the Alps and the Valle d'Aosta region. There's also a fun section for young children that's dedicated to the geology and history of the region. ✉ *Bard* ☎ *0125/833811* ⊕ *www.fortedibard.it* 🎟 *€9, childrens' museum €5.*

Breuil-Cervinia/ The Matterhorn

50 km (30 miles) north of Bard, 116 km (72 miles) north of Turin.

Sitting in a huge natural basin at the foot of the Matterhorn, this town, once a high Alpine pasture, grew to become one of Europe's most famous ski areas when a road connecting it to the Valle d'Aosta was completed in 1934. It bustles in the winter and has become a popular spot for hikers in the summer, but it's sleepy for much of the rest of the year.

GETTING HERE AND AROUND
From Aosta take the A5 autostrada and then the SR46 (1 hour); from Turin take the A5 and then the SR46 (90 minutes). SADEM has regular bus service from Turin; SAVDA buses travel here from Milan. Breuil-Cervinia isn't on a train line.

Sights

Matterhorn (*Monte Cervino in Italian; Mont Cervin in French*)
MOUNTAIN | The famous peak straddles the border between Italy and Switzerland, and all sightseeing and skiing facilities are operated jointly. Splendid views of the peak can be seen from Plateau Rosa and the Cresta del Furggen, both of which can be reached by cable car from the center of Breuil-Cervinia. Although many locals complain that the tourist facilities and condominiums have changed the face of their beloved village, the cable car does give access to climbing and off-trail skiing on ridges that were once inaccessible. ✉ *Breuil-Cervinia* ⊕ *www.lovevda.it.*

Road to Gaul

Between Bard and the town of Donnas, 5 km (3 miles) south along the SS26, you can walk a short but fascinating stretch of a 1st-century Roman consular road that passed this way en route to France. Still showing the deeply worn tracks left by the passage of cart and chariot wheels, this section includes an archway carved through solid rock (used during the Middle Ages as the Donnas city gate) and a milestone ("XXXVI," counting 36 Roman miles from Aosta).

Hotels

Cime Bianche
$$$ | B&B/INN | This calm, quiet mountain lodge offers commanding views of the Matterhorn and surrounding peaks from the balconies of its simply furnished wood-paneled guest rooms (price includes two meals). **Pros:** lovely views; next to the ski slopes; great restaurant. **Cons:** busy during the ski season; lobby is showing wear; location is far from everything but the slopes. ⑤ *Rooms from: €240* ✉ *Frazione La Vieille 44, Breuil-Cervinia* ⊕ *near ski lift* ☎ *0166/949046* ⊕ *www.hotelcimebianche.com* ⦁⦁ *Free Breakfast* ⊙ *Closed May–June* ⤴ *13 rooms.*

Hermitage
$$$$ | RESORT | The entryway's marble relief of St. Theodolus reminds you that this was once a hermitage, but asceticism has given way to comfort and elegance—a fire is always glowing in the enormous hearth, the dining room is candlelit, the bright bedrooms have balconies, and the suites have antique fireplaces and 18th-century furnishings. **Pros:** frequent shuttle service into town and to ski lifts; refined atmosphere; superlative

The mighty Matterhorn straddles Switzerland and Italy and has one of the highest summits in Europe.

staff. **Cons:** located 2 km (1 mile) from the town center; expensive for the area; books up quickly. $ *Rooms from: €419* ✉ *Via Piolet 1, Località Chapellette, Breuil-Cervinia* ☎ *0166/948998* ⊕ *www. hotelhermitage.com* ⊘ *Closed May, June, and Sept.–Nov.* 🛏 *47 rooms* ❤️ *Free Breakfast.*

Les Neiges d'Antan

$$$$ | **B&B/INN** | In an evergreen forest at Perrères, just outside Cervinia, this family-run inn is quiet and cozy, with three big fireplaces and a nice view of the Matterhorn. **Pros:** excellent restaurant; well-designed spa facilities; secluded and beautiful setting. **Cons:** no elevator; 5 km (3 miles) outside Breuil-Cervinia (a car is essential); entrance and lobby areas are showing some wear. $ *Rooms from: €480* ✉ *Frazione Cret de Perrères 10, Breuil-Cervinia* ☎ *0166/948775* ⊕ *www. lesneigesdantan.com* ❤️ *Free Breakfast* ⊘ *Closed May–June* 🛏 *24 rooms.*

 Activities

CLIMBING

Serious climbers can make the ascent of the Matterhorn from Breuil-Cervinia after registering with the local mountaineering officials at the tourist office. This ascent is for experienced climbers only. Less demanding hikes follow the lower slopes of the Marmore river valley, south of town.

Società delle Guide Alpine

SNOW SPORTS | The Society's guides are available to accompany you on treks and also lead skiing, canyoning, and ice-climbing excursions. ✉ *Strada Villair 2, Courmayeur* ☎ *0165/842064* ⊕ *www. lovevda.it.*

SKIING

About 60 lifts and a few hundred miles of ski runs, ranging from beginner to expert, make Breuil-Cervinia one of the best and most popular resort areas in Italy. Because the slopes border a glacier, there's skiing year-round.

Castello di Fénis

34 km (21 miles) northwest of Bard, 104 km (65 miles) north of Turin.

The tiny town of Fénis owes its origins to the presence of the medieval castle that once provided shelter for the local peasants who lived nearby. Today, the population of the town is less than 2,000, most either farmers or part of the tourist industry.

GETTING HERE AND AROUND

To reach the castle by car, take the Nus exit from the A5 autostrada. SAVDA buses provide infrequent service between Aosta and Fénis. It's about a 10-minute train ride from Aosta to the train station in Nus, a 2-km (1-mile) walk from the castle.

 Sights

★ **Castello di Fénis**

CASTLE/PALACE | **FAMILY** | The best-preserved medieval fortress in the Valle d'Aosta, this many-turreted castle was built in the mid-14th century by Aimone di Challant, a member of a prolific family related to the Savoys. The castle, which used a double ring of walls for its defense, would make a perfect setting for a fairy tale, given its pointed towers, portcullises, and spiral staircases. The 15th-century courtyard surrounded by wooden balconies is elegantly decorated with well-preserved frescoes. Inside you can see the kitchen, with an enormous fireplace that provided central heat in winter; the armory; and the spacious, well-lighted rooms used by the lord and lady of the manor. If you have time to visit only one castle in the Valle d'Aosta, this should be it. ⊠ *Località Chez-Sapin 1, Fénis* ☎ *0165/764263* ⊕ *www.lovevda.it* ☜ *€7* ⊘ *Closed Mon. Oct.–Mar.*

Aosta

12 km (7 miles) west of Castello di Fénis, 113 km (70 miles) north of Turin.

Aosta stands at the junction of two of the important trade routes that connect France and Italy, the valleys of the Rhône and the Isère. Its significance as a trading post was recognized by the Romans, who built a garrison here in the 1st century BC, and the present-day layout of the streets is the clearest example you'll find of Roman urban planning in Italy. Well-preserved Roman walls form a perfect rectangle around the center, and the regular pattern of streets reflects its role as a military stronghold. Although its gray-stone buildings and slate roofing give the town a rather cold feeling, Aosta has recently begun to appear on several lists as one of the most livable towns in Italy.

GETTING HERE AND AROUND

Aosta is off the A5 autostrada and can easily be reached by car or bus from Milan and Turin. SAVDA buses regularly travel to and from Milan, Turin, and Chamonix in France. Train service is also available from Turin (2 hours) and from Milan (3 hours), but you'll have to transfer.

VISITOR INFORMATION

CONTACT Aosta Tourism Office. ⊠ *Piazza Porta Praetoria 3, Aosta* ☎ *0165/236627* ⊕ *www.regione.vda.it.*

 Sights

Arco di Augusto

NOTABLE BUILDING | At the eastern entrance to town, and commanding a fine view over Aosta and the mountains, stands the Arco di Augusto (Arch of Augustus), built in 25 BC to mark Rome's victory over the Celtic Salassi tribe. (The sloping roof was added in 1716 in an attempt to keep rain from seeping between the stones.) ⊠ *Piazza Arco d'Augusto, Aosta.*

Collegiata di Sant'Orso

CHURCH | This church has layers of history literally visible in its architecture. Originally there was a 6th-century chapel on this site, founded by the Archdeacon Orso, a local saint. Most of the structure was destroyed or hidden when an 11th-century church was erected over it. That church, in turn, was encrusted with Gothic and, later, Baroque features, resulting in a jigsaw puzzle of styles that surprisingly manage to work together. The 11th-century features are almost untouched in the crypt, and if you go up the stairs on the left from the main church you can see the 11th-century frescoes (ask the sacristan, who'll let you in). These restored frescoes depict the life of Christ and the apostles; although only the tops are visible, you can see the expressions on the faces of the disciples. Take the outside doorway to the right of the main entrance to see the church's crowning glory, its 12th-century cloister, enclosed by some 40 stone columns with masterfully carved capitals depicting scenes from the Old and New Testaments and the life of St. Orso. The turrets and spires of Aosta peek out above. ⊠ *Via Sant'Orso 14, Aosta* ☎ *0165/238515* ⊕ *www.diocesiaosta.it.*

Duomo

CHURCH | Aosta's cathedral dates from the 10th century, but all that remains from that period are the bell towers. The decoration inside is primarily Gothic, but the main attraction of the cathedral predates that era by 1,000 years: among the many ornate objects housed in the treasury is a carved ivory diptych from AD 406 portraying the Roman emperor Honorius. ⊠ *Piazza Papa Giovanni XXIII, Aosta* ☎ *0165/40251* ⊕ *www.cattedralea-osta.it* ☎ *Duomo free, treasury €5.*

Roman Porta Pretoria

NOTABLE BUILDING | This huge gateway, regally guarding the city, is a remarkable relic from the Roman era. The area between the massive inner and outer walls was used as a small parade ground for the changing of the guard. ⊠ *West end of Via Sant'Anselmo, Aosta* ⊕ *www. lovevda.it.*

Teatro Romano

RUINS | The 72-foot-high ruin of the facade of the Teatro Romano guards the remains of the 1st-century-BC amphitheater, which once held 20,000 spectators. Only a bit of the outside wall and seven of the amphitheater's original 60 arches remain. The latter, once incorporated into medieval buildings, are being brought to light by ongoing archaeological excavations. ⊠ *Via Porta Praetoria at Via Baillage, Aosta* ⊕ *www.lovevda.it* ☎ *€7, includes church of San Lorenzo, archaeological museum, and crypt* ⊗ *Closed Mon. Oct.–Mar.*

🍴 Restaurants

Praetoria

$$ | NORTHERN ITALIAN | Just outside the Porta Pretoria, this simple and unpretentious restaurant serves hearty local dishes, including homemade pastas and desserts. **Known for:** savory crepes; polenta with a variety of sauces and accompaniments; apple tart with vanilla sauce. ⑤ *Average main: €24* ⊠ *Via Sant'Anselmo 9, Aosta* ☎ *0165/35473* ⊕ *www.trattoriapraetoria.it* ⊗ *Closed Wed.*

Vecchio Ristoro

$ | NORTHERN ITALIAN | The elegant, intimate spaces of this converted mill are furnished with antiques, and a traditional ceramic stove provides additional warmth in cool weather. The chef-proprietor takes pride in creative versions of regional recipes and decadent desserts. **Known for:** game and polenta dishes; regional tasting menus; chocolate desserts. ⑤ *Average main: €10* ⊠ *Via Tourneuve 4, Aosta* ☎ *0165/33238* ⊕ *www.ristorante-vecchioristoro.it* ⊗ *Closed Wed. and Nov. No dinner Sun.*

Hotels

Le Miramonti

$$ | B&B/INN | On the banks of a branch of the Dora Baltea River, this establishment offers the alpine interiors, traditional furnishings, and homey comforts needed for a relaxing evening after a day of strenuous activity. **Pros:** spa and swimming pool; friendly, efficient service; excellent location for outdoor sports. **Cons:** rooms near the river may seem noisy to some; isolated location in a small village; some rooms and bathrooms are small. $ *Rooms from: €190* ✉ *Via Piccolo San Bernardo 3, La Thuile* ☎ *0165/883084* ⊕ *www.lemiramonti.it* ♻ *Closed mid-Apr.–early July and mid-Sept.–early Dec.* 🛏 *40 rooms* ❍| *Free Breakfast.*

★ Milleluci

$$ | B&B/INN | At this small and inviting family-run hotel overlooking Aosta, guest rooms are bright and charmingly decorated; some have balconies and all have splendid views of the city and mountains. **Pros:** cozy and traditionally decorated rooms; panoramic views; great spa amenities. **Cons:** no A/C; 1 km (½ mile) north of town, so a car is needed to get around; small bathrooms. $ *Rooms from: €200* ✉ *Località Porossan Roppoz 15, Aosta* ☎ *0165/235278* ⊕ *www.hotelmilleluci.com* 🛏 *28 rooms* ❍| *Free Breakfast* ♻ *Closed.*

Courmayeur/ Monte Bianco

35 km (22 miles) northwest of Aosta, 150 km (93 miles) northwest of Turin.

The main attraction of Courmayeur is a knock-'em-dead view of Europe's highest peak, Monte Bianco. The celebrities and the wealthy who come here these days are following a tradition that dates back to the late 17th century, when Courmayeur's natural springs first began to attract visitors. The spectacle of the Alps gradually surpassed the springs as the biggest draw: the Alpine letters of the English poet Percy Bysshe Shelley were almost advertisements for the region. Since 1965, when the Mont Blanc Tunnel opened, ever-increasing numbers of travelers have passed through the area, and it's now hugely popular with both skiers in winter and hikers during the summer. Planners have managed to keep some restrictions on wholesale development within the town, and its angled rooftops and immaculate cobblestone streets maintain a cozy feeling.

GETTING HERE AND AROUND

Courmayeur is on the A5 autostrada and can easily be reached by car from both Turin and Milan by way of Aosta. SAVDA buses run regularly from both Turin and Milan. Train service isn't available.

VISITOR INFORMATION

CONTACT Courmayeur Tourism Office. ✉ *Piazzale Monte Bianco 10, Courmayeur* ☎ *0165/842060* ⊕ *www.courmayeur-montblanc.it.*

Sights

Monte Bianco (*Mont Blanc*)

MOUNTAIN | Monte Bianco's attraction is not so much its shape, which is much less distinctive than that of the Matterhorn, as it is its expanse and the awesome vistas from the top. You can reach the summit via a cable car that ascends from Entrèves, just below the Mont Blanc Tunnel. In summer, if so inclined, you can then switch cable cars and descend into Chamonix, in France. In winter you can ski parts of the route off-piste. The Funivia Entrèves whisks you up first to the Pavillon du Mont Fréty in just four minutes—a starting point for many beautiful hikes—and then in six minutes to the spectacular viewing platform at Punta Helbronner (more than 11,000 feet), which is also the border post with France. The next stage up (in summer only) is on the Télépherique de l'Aiguille du Midi, as you pass into French territory. The trip is particularly impressive; you dangle over a huge glacial snowfield (more than 2,000 feet below) and make your way slowly to the viewing station above Chamonix. It's one of the most dramatic rides in Europe. From this point you're looking down into France, and if you change cable cars at the Aiguille du Midi station, you can make your way down into Chamonix itself. ⊠ *SS26, Courmayeur* ☎ *0165/89196 in Courmayeur, 0450/532275 in Chamonix* ⊕ *www.montebianco.com* 🎫 *€55 round-trip to Punta Helbronner* ⊗ *Closed Nov. and depending on weather conditions and demand.*

Parco Nazionale del Gran Paradiso

NATIONAL PARK | Cogne, 52 km (32 miles) southeast of Courmayeur, is the gateway to this huge park, which was once the domain of King Vittorio Emanuele II (1820–78). Bequeathed to the nation after World War I, it is one of Europe's most rugged and unspoiled wilderness areas, with wildlife and many plant species protected by law. The park is one of the few places in Europe where you can see the ibex (a mountain goat with horns up to 3 feet long) and the chamois (a small antelope). The park, which is 703 square km (271 square miles), is open free of charge throughout the year; there's an information office in Cogne. ■**TIP→ Try to visit in May, when spring flowers are in bloom and most of the meadows are clear of snow.** ⊠ *Villaggio Cogne 81, Cogne* ☎ *0165/753011* ⊕ *www.pngp.it.*

 Hotels

Auberge de la Maison

$$ | HOTEL | Most guest rooms here have balconies with spectacular views of Monte Bianco, and the plush fabrics, wood-burning stoves, and Alpine prints on the walls give the feeling of a cozy country inn. **Pros:** charming decor; secluded location in the center of Entrèves; hotel spa. **Cons:** not all standard

rooms have views of Monte Bianco; minimum stay in high seasons (summer and winter); spa and pool can be crowded and loud in high season. ⑤ *Rooms from: €166* ⊠ *Via Passerin d'Entrèves 16, Courmayeur* ☎ *0165/869811* ⊕ *www.aubergemaison.it* ⊗ *Closed 15 days in May and 20 days in Nov.* ⇥ *33 rooms* ¶○¶ *Free Breakfast.*

Croux

$$ | HOTEL | Half the guest rooms at this bright and comfortable hotel have balconies, the other half have great views of the mountains, and all have contemporary furnishings. **Pros:** great views; shuttle to ski lifts; central location. **Cons:** some rooms are noisy; on a busy road; rooms are simple and could use a revamp. ⑤ *Rooms from: €180* ⊠ *Via Croux 8, Courmayeur* ☎ *0165/846735* ⊕ *www.hotelcroux.it* ⊗ *Closed mid-Apr.–mid-June and Oct.–Nov.* ⇥ *28 rooms* ¶○¶ *Free Breakfast.*

Royal e Golf

$$$ | HOTEL | With wide terraces and wood paneling, this longtime landmark in the center of Courmayeur is one of the most elegant spots in town, and the cheery guest rooms have plenty of amenities. **Pros:** abundant breakfast buffet; central location on main traffic-free street; panoramic views. **Cons:** fee for spa and swimming pool; standard rooms can be small and outdated; no A/C. ⑤ *Rooms from: €239* ⊠ *Via Roma 87, Courmayeur* ☎ *0165/831611* ⊕ *www.hotelroyalegolf.com* ⊗ *Closed Easter–mid-June and mid-Sept.–Nov.* ⇥ *86 rooms* ¶○¶ *Free Breakfast.*

★ Villa Novecento

$ | B&B/INN | Run with friendly charm and efficiency, the Novecento is a peaceful haven with the style of a comfortable mountain lodge, complete with a log fire in winter, traditional fabrics, wooden furnishings, and early-19th-century prints. **Pros:** away from the main tourist area; frequent shuttle to the slopes and town; good restaurant and excellent breakfast. **Cons:** no A/C; parking is limited; spotty Wi-Fi. Ⓢ *Rooms from: €117* ✉ *Viale Monte Bianco 64, Courmayeur* ☎ *0165/843000* ⊕ *www.villanovecento. it* ⊗ *Closed Nov. and mid-Apr.–mid-May* ↪ *22 rooms* ⁇ *Free Breakfast.*

 Activities

SKIING
Funivie Courmayeur/Mont Blanc
SNOW SPORTS | Courmayeur pales in comparison to its French neighbor, Chamonix, in both the quality and the number of its ski runs. But with good natural snow cover, the trails and vistas are spectacular. A huge gondola leads from the center of Courmayeur to Plan Chécrouit, where other gondolas and lifts lead to the slopes. The skiing around Monte Bianco is particularly good, and the off-piste options are among the best in Europe. The routes from Cresta d'Arp (the local peak) to Dolonne, and from La Palud into France, should be done with a guide. Contact the Courmayeur tourist office for complete information about lift tickets, ski runs, and weather conditions. ✉ *Strada Dolonne La Villette 1, Courmayeur* ☎ *0165/846658 tourist office* ⊕ *www.lovevda.it.*

Società delle Guide Alpine (*Alpine Guide Society*)
SKIING & SNOWBOARDING | The society provides Alpine guide services year-round. ✉ *Strada Villair 2, Courmayeur* ☎ *0165/842064* ⊕ *www.guidecourmayeur.com.*

Venaria Reale

10 km (6 miles) northwest of Turin.

This immense palace was built in the 16th century as a hunting lodge.

GETTING HERE AND AROUND
Starting in Turin, from the north side of Piazza della Repubblica, take Bus No. 11 to reach Venaria; the trip takes approximately 40 minutes. By car, follow Corso Regina Margherita to the A55 autostrada. Head north and leave the highway at the Venaria exit, following signs for the Venaria Reale.

 Sights

★ Reggia di Venaria Reale
ART MUSEUM | Extensive Italianate gardens surround this 16th-century hunting lodge built for Carlo Emanuele II of Savoy. Inside, its Great Gallery is worthy of Versailles. The basements now house a historical exhibition that relates the story of the House of Savoy. The upper floors are reserved for changing exhibitions. ✉ *Piazza della Repubblica 4, Venaria Reale* ☎ *011/4992333* ⊕ *www.lavenaria.it* ⛉ *€20* ⊗ *Closed Mon.*

Rivoli

16 km (10 miles) southwest of Venaria, 13 km (8 miles) west of Turin.

The Savoy court was based in Rivoli in the Middle Ages, and the town retains several remnants from that richly dramatic period.

GETTING HERE AND AROUND

GTT buses and trams regularly link central Turin with Rivoli; the journey takes just over one hour. By car, follow Corso Francia from central Turin all the way to Rivoli; unless there's a lot of traffic, the trip should take a half hour.

Sights

★ **Museo d'Arte Contemporanea** (*Museum of Contemporary Art*)

ART MUSEUM | The Baroque castle of Rivoli now houses a fascinating museum of contemporary art. The building was begun in the 17th century and then redesigned, but never finished, by Juvarra in the 18th century; it was finally converted into a museum in the late 20th century by the minimalist Turin architect Andrea Bruno. ⊠ *Piazzale Mafalda di Savoia, Rivoli* ☎ *011/9565222* ⊕ *www.castellodirivoli.org* ⌑ *€8.50 (varies for temporary exhibitions)* ⊗ *Closed Mon.–Wed.*

Sacra di San Michele

26 km (17 miles) west of Rivoli, 43 km (27 miles) west of Turin.

Perhaps best known as inspiration for the setting of Umberto Eco's novel *The Name of the Rose*, this abbey was built on Monte Pirchiriano in the 11th century so it would stand out: it occupies the most prominent location for miles around, hanging over a 3,280-foot bluff.

GETTING HERE AND AROUND

Unless you want to do a 14-km (9-mile) uphill hike from the town of Avigliana, a car is essential for an excursion here—take the Avigliana Est exit from the A32 autostrada (Torino–Bardonecchia).

Sights

Sacra di San Michele

CHURCH | To reach the church, you must climb 150 steps, from the Porta dello Zodiaco, a splendid Romanesque doorway decorated with the signs of the zodiac. On the left side of the interior are 16th-century frescoes representing New Testament themes; on the right are depictions of the founding of the church. ⊠ *Via Sacra di San Michele 14, Sant'Ambrogio di Torino* ☎ *011/939130* ⊕ *www. sacradisanmichele.com* ⊗ *Closed Mon. in Jan. and Feb.* ⌑ *€8.*

Chapter 10

THE ITALIAN RIVIERA

Updated by
Patricia Rucidlo

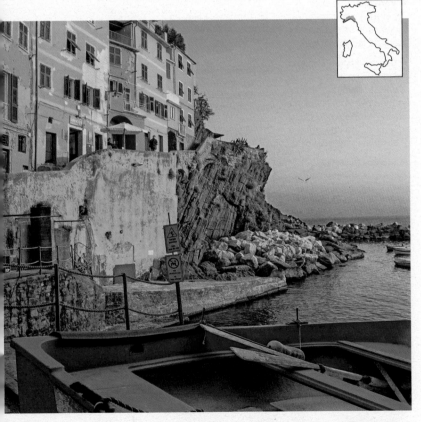

⊙ Sights	🍴 Restaurants	🛏 Hotels	🛍 Shopping	▼ Nightlife
★★★☆☆	★★★★☆	★★★★☆	★☆☆☆☆	★☆☆☆☆

WELCOME TO
THE ITALIAN RIVIERA

TOP REASONS TO GO

★ **The Cinque Terre:** Hike the famous Cinque Terre trails past gravity-defying vineyards, colorful, rock-perched villages, and the deep blue Mediterranean Sea.

★ **Portofino:** See the world through rose-tinted sunglasses at this glamorous little harbor village.

★ **Genoa's historical center and port:** From the palaces of Via Garibaldi to the labyrinthine backstreets of the old city to the world-class aquarium, the city is full of surprising delights.

★ **Giardini Botanici Hanbury:** A spectacular natural setting harbors one of Italy's largest, most exotic botanical gardens, near Bordighera.

★ **Pesto:** The basil-rich sauce was invented in Liguria, and it's never been equaled elsewhere.

1 Riomaggiore. The first of the Cinque Terre villages has a small harbor and coastal views.

2 Manarola. Terraced vineyards, olive trees, and pastel houses fill the town.

3 Corniglia. Climb (365 steps) to the most remote Cinque Terre town.

4 Vernazza. Enjoy its lively piazza and a postcard-worthy port view.

5 Monterosso al Mare. Come here for festivals, beaches, clear water, and plentiful accomodations.

6 Lerici. White-sand beaches, hiking trails, and seaside cafés are memorable.

7 La Spezia. This busy port city has outdoor markets and palm-lined streets.

8 Portovenere. Quaint passageways and a castle distinguish the port town.

9 Levanto. This makes an ideal base for diving, surfing, hiking, and day trips around Liguria.

10 Sestri Levante. The small seaside village is framed by two bays.

11 Chiavari. Ancient, twisting streets give character to this fishing town.

12 Santa Margherita Ligure. Palm trees, attractive hotels, and a yacht-filled marina add appeal.

13 Portofino. This vacation spot for the rich and famous has a castle, cliffside gardens, and fancy boutiques.

14 Camogli. Multicolor houses and a picturesque historical fishing port are draws here.

15 Genoa. Palaces, superb pesto, and a rich maritime history mark the birthplace of Christopher Columbus.

16 Nervi. A promenade and parks enhance this resort near busy Genoa.

17 Finale Ligure. Explore the Riviera di Ponente in the villages of Finalmarina, Finalpia, and Finalborgo.

18 Albenga. Narrow Roman-era streets, a Romanesque cathedral, and quaint shops and cafés fill this medieval town.

19 Imperia. This center of olive oil production has 17th- and 18th-century palaces.

20 San Remo. The largest resort in the Riviera di Ponente is known for its casino, glamorous hotels, and seaside promenades.

21 Bordighera. Its many English residents give this town a distinct personality, and it's near a famous botanical garden.

EATING AND DRINKING WELL IN THE ITALIAN RIVIERA

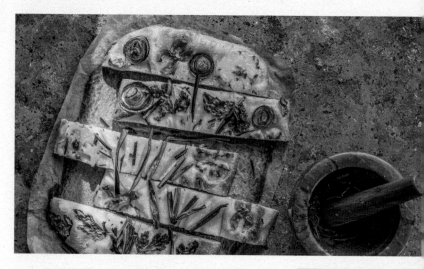

Ligurian cuisine might surprise you. As you'd expect, given the long coastline, it employs all sorts of seafood, but its real claim to fame is the exemplary use of vegetables and herbs.

Basil is practically revered in Genoa—the word is derived from the Greek *basileus,* meaning "king"—and the city is considered the birthplace of pesto, the basil-rich pasta sauce. This and other herbs (laurel, fennel, and marjoram) are cultivated, but also grow wild on the sun-kissed hillsides. Naturally, seafood plays a prominent role on the menu, appearing in soups, salads, and pasta dishes. Vegetables—particularly artichokes, eggplant, and zucchini—are abundant, and usually prepared with liberal amounts of olive oil and garlic.

Like much of Italy, Liguria has a wide range of eating establishments from cafeteria-like *tavole calde* to family-run trattorias to sophisticated *ristoranti.* Lunch is served between 12:30 and 2:30 and dinner between 7:30 and 11. Also popular, especially in Genoa, are *enoteche* (wine bars), which serve simply prepared light meals late into the night.

FABULOUS FOCACCIA

When you're hankering for a snack, turn to bakeries and small eateries serving focaccia. The flatbread is more dense and flavorful here than what's sold as focaccia in American restaurants—it's the region's answer to pizza, usually eaten on the go. It comes simply salted and drizzled with olive oil; flavored with rosemary and olives; covered with cheese or anchovies; and even *ripiena* (stuffed), usually with cheese or vegetables and herbs.

ANTIPASTI

Seafood antipasti are served in abundance at most Ligurian restaurants. Typical dishes include marinated anchovies from Monterosso, *cozze ripiene* (mussel shells stuffed with minced mussel meat, prosciutto, Parmesan, herbs, and bread crumbs), and *soppressata di polpo* (flattened octopus in olive oil and lemon sauce).

PASTA

Liguria's classic sauce is pesto, made from basil, garlic, olive oil, pine nuts, and hard cheese. It's usually served with *trenette* (similar to spaghetti) or the slightly sweet *testaroli* (a flat pasta made from chestnut flour). You can also find *pansotti* (triangular pockets filled with a cheese mixture), and *trofie* (short twists) with *salsa di noci,* a rich sauce of garlic, walnuts, and cream that, as with pesto, is ideally pounded with mortar and pestle. Spaghetti *allo scoglio* has an olive oil, tomato, and white-wine-based sauce containing an assortment of local *frutti di mare* (seafood) like shrimp, clams, mussels, and cuttlefish.

FISH AND MEAT

Fish is the best bet for a second course: the classic preparation is a whole grilled or baked whitefish—branzino and *orata* (dorado) are good

choices—served *alle Ligure,* with olives, potatoes, tomatoes, Ligurian spices, and a drizzle of olive oil. A popular meat dish is *cima alla Genovese,* a veal roll stuffed with a mixture of eggs and vegetables, served as a cold cut.

PANIGACCI

One of the real treats of the region is *panigacci.* Small, terra-cotta dishes known as *testine* are placed in a wood-burning oven or fire to heat at the highest of temperatures. Then balls of dough are laid in the dishes, which are stacked one on top of the other in order to flatten and cook the dough. Panigacci are usually served with *stracchino* cheese, pesto or nut sauce, and cold cuts.

WINE

Local vineyards produce mostly light and refreshing whites, such as *pigato* from the Ponente and *vermentino* from the Levante, although both light reds and appealing *rosato* (Italian rosé) are on the rise. Rossese di Dolceacqua, from near the French border, is considered the best red wine the region has to offer, but for a more robust accompaniment to meats, opt for the full-bodied reds of the neighboring Piedmont region. For a postdinner or dessert wine, try the *sciacchetrà,* made exclusively in the Cinque Terre.

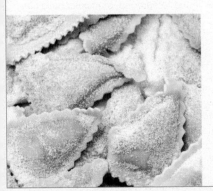

Nestled between the south of France and the Tuscan border lies the region of Liguria, with verdant and lush mountains to the north and east, and the sapphire-blue Mediterranean to the south and west. In between is a land of lush vegetation, medieval hilltop hamlets, panoramic vistas, colorful seaside villages, pristine beaches, and one of Italy's most underrated cities, Genoa.

There is plenty to do—from hiking and biking, to water sports and fishing, to eating (very) well—and plenty to see, including some of Italy's most aesthetically pleasing architecture. It's also easy to just enjoy la dolce vita along this coast, better known as the Italian Riviera.

The Italian Riviera oozes charm and irresistible allure, with many seaside resort towns and colorful villages that stake intermittent claim to the rocky shores of the Ligurian Sea and seem like the long-lost cousins of newer seaside paradises found elsewhere. It has been a haven for artists, writers, celebrities, and royalty since the 1800s, and continues to fascinate visitors throughout the year due to its mild climate. Here the grandest palazzi share space with frescoed, angular *terratetti* (tall, skinny houses). The rustic and elegant, the provincial and chic, the small-town and cosmopolitan all collide here in a sun-drenched blend that defines the Italian side of the Riviera. There are chic resort towns such as San Remo and Portofino, the unique beauty and outdoor adventures of the Cinque Terre, numerous quaint seaside and

hilltop villages to explore, plus the history and architectural charm of Genoa. Mellowed by balmy breezes blowing in from the sea, travelers bask in the sun, explore the picturesque fishing villages, and pamper themselves at the resorts that dot this ruggedly beautiful landscape.

MAJOR REGIONS

The beautiful **Cinque Terre** is the heart of the Italian Riviera. In their rugged simplicity, the five old fishing towns of **Monterosso al Mare, Vernazza, Corniglia, Manarola,** and **Riomaggiore** seem to mock the glitzy neighboring resorts. With a blue sea in the foreground, multicolor buildings emerge almost seamlessly from cliffs, and rocky mountains rise precipitously to vineyards and olive groves. The terrain is so steep that for centuries, footpaths were the only way to get around. Since its 1997 UNESCO World Heritage designation, the Cinque Terre have become one of Italy's most popular destinations. Eastward from Genoa to Lerici (encompassing the Cinque Terre and a naval port, **La Spezia**) stretches the **Riviera di Levante** (Riviera of the Rising Sun). It has a raw, unpolished feel, and its rugged coastline is dotted with colorful fishing villages like **Camogli, Portovenere, Chiavari,** and **Sestri Levante.** It also has one of Europe's well-known playgrounds for the rich and famous, the inlet of **Portofino,** and nearby **Santa Margherita Ligure** is popular with well-to-do Italians. From this area's twisting roads, the hills plummet sharply to the sea. Beaches tend to be rocky, yet there are some lovely sandy stretches in **Lerici,** Monterosso al Mare, **Levanto,** and Paraggi (near Portofino).

The seaside city of **Genoa** (Genova in Italian), birthplace of Christopher Columbus, has a long history as a major trading station, and in the Middle Ages and the Renaissance Genoa became a wealthy, prestigious commercial center. Its bankers, merchants, and princes adorned their city with palaces, churches, and impressive art collections. Today Genoa is a cultural center worth a look. Nearby **Nervi** is a stately resort town.

West of Genoa, the **Riviera di Ponente** (Riviera of the Setting Sun) covers the narrow strip of northwest Liguria from Genoa to the French border. The sapphire Mediterranean Sea to one side and the verdant foothills of the Alps on the other allow for temperate weather, which is why it's also called the Riviera dei Fiori (Riviera of the Flowers). There is also olive-growing in **Imperia.** Once filled with seaside villages and elegant homes, this area struggles to balance natural beauty with resort development, as in glitzy **San Remo.** Highly populated resorts and some overly industrialized areas are jammed into the thin stretch of white-sand and pebble beaches. There are still several worthwhile villages, like **Finale Ligure, Albegna,** and **Bordighera,** along the sea and hinterland. Bordighera is near Giardini Botanici Hanbury, one of Italy's most beautiful grouping of gardens. The Riviera di Levante may retain more of its natural beauty, but the Ponente remains popular with visitors looking for sunshine, nightlife, and relaxation.

Planning

When to Go

The Italian Riviera is extremely seasonal, apart from Genoa, a city with year-round cultural attractions. The region has a typical Mediterranean climate with warm summers and rainy winters, making high season (Easter and June–August in particular) the best time to visit, though it can be really crowded as well as lively. From April to October, the area bustles with shops, cafés, clubs, and restaurants that stay open late. The rest of the year, the majority of resorts close down, and you'll be hard-pressed to find accommodations or restaurants open.

Planning Your Time

Your first decision, particularly given limited time, is between the two Rivieras. The Riviera di Levante (east of Genoa) is more rustic and has a more distinct personality, with the unique Cinque Terre, ritzy Portofino, and the panoramic Gulf of Poets. The Riviera di Ponente (west of Genoa) is a classic European resort experience with many white-sand beaches and more nightlife and accommodation choices—similar to, but not as glamorous as, the French Riviera across the border.

In either case, your second decision is whether to visit Genoa. Despite its rough exterior and (diminishing) reputation as a seamy port town, Genoa's artistic and cultural treasures are significant—you won't find anything remotely comparable elsewhere in the region. Unless your goal is to avoid urban life entirely, consider a night or two in the city.

Getting Here and Around

BUS

Generally speaking, buses are a difficult way to come and go in Liguria. Although there are local buses that run between villages along the Riviera Ponente, it's not an extensive network and can be a challenge to navigate.

BUS CONTACTS ATP. ☎ *0185/3731* ⊕ *www.atpesercizio.it.* **Volpibus.** ☎ *010/561661* ⊕ *www.gruppostat.com/ autolinee-locali.*

CAR

With the freedom of a car, you could drive from one end of the Riviera to the other on the autostrada in about three hours. Two good roads run parallel to each other along the coast of Liguria. Closer to shore and passing through all the towns and villages is the SS1, or Via Aurelia, which was laid out by the ancient Romans and has excellent views at almost every turn. It gets very crowded in July and August. More direct and higher up than SS1 are autostradas A10, west of Genoa, and A12, to the south—engineering wonders with literally hundreds of long tunnels and towering viaducts. These routes save time on weekends, in summer, and on days when festivals slow traffic in some resorts to a standstill.

TRAIN

Train travel on the national railway, Ferrovie dello Stato is by far the most convenient mode of transportation throughout the region. It takes 3½ hours for an express train to cover the entire Ligurian coast. Local trains take upward of five hours or more to get from one end of the coast to the other, stopping in or near all the towns along the way. For schedules, check www.trenitalia.com/en.

Hiking

Walking Liguria's extensive network of trails while taking in the gorgeous views is a major outdoor activity and regional attraction. The mild climate and laid-back state of mind can lull you into underestimating just how strenuous such walks can be. Wear good shoes, use sunscreen, and carry plenty of water—you'll be glad you did. Trail maps are available from tourist information offices, or upon entry to the Cinque Terre National Park.

On the Portofino promontory, the relatively easy walk to the Abbazia di San Fruttuoso is popular, and there's a more challenging hike from Ruta to the top of Monte Portofino and back down to Camogli. From Genoa, you can take the Zecca–Righi funicular up to Righi and walk along the ring of fortresses that used to defend the city.

Walking tours can introduce you to lesser-known aspects of the region. For the Cinque Terre and the rest of the Province of La Spezia, the **Cooperativa Arte e Natura** (*Viale Amendola 172, La Spezia; 0187/739410;* www.cinqueterrexperience.com) is a good source for English-speaking and other foreign-language guides. A full day costs €255, and a three-hour tour is €170; these prices are for a group of up to 35 people.

Restaurants

While fine dining can be found in Liguria, you are more likely to enjoy a casual atmosphere, often with an amazing sea view. Expect both the decor and dishes to be simple but flavorful; fish and seafood are highlights here.

Restaurant reviews have been shortened. For full information, visit Fodors. com.

Hotels

Liguria's lodging may be a step behind more developed areas like Positano and Taormina, so be sure to reserve its better accommodations (and the relatively limited options in the Cinque Terre) far in advance. Lodging tends to be pricey in high season, particularly June to August.

Hotel reviews have been shortened. For full information, visit Fodors.com.

WHAT IT COSTS in Euros			
$	$$	$$$	$$$$
RESTAURANTS			
under €15	€15–€24	€25–€35	over €35
HOTELS			
under €125	€125–€200	€201–€300	over €300

Riomaggiore

17 km (11 miles) southwest of La Spezia, 101 km (60 miles) southeast of Genoa.

At the eastern end of the Cinque Terre, Riomaggiore is built into a river gorge (hence the name, which means "major river") and is easily accessible from La Spezia by train or car. The landscape is terraced and steep—be prepared for many stairs!—and leads to a small harbor, protected by large slabs of alabaster and marble that serve as tanning beds for sunbathers. The harbor is also the site of several outdoor cafés with fine views. According to legend, the settlement of Riomaggiore dates as far back as the 8th century, when Greek religious refugees came here to escape persecution by the Byzantine emperor.

. The village is divided into two parts. If you arrive by train, you will have to pass through a tunnel that flanks the train tracks to reach the historic side of town. To avoid the crowds and get a great view of the Cinque Terre coast, walk straight uphill as soon as you exit the station. This winding road takes you over the hill to the 14th-century **church of St. John the Baptist,** toward the medieval town center and the Genovese-style tower houses that dot the village. Follow Via Roma (the Old Town's main street) downhill, pass under the train tracks, and you'll arrive in the charming fishermen's port. Lined with traditional fishing boats and small trattorias, this is a lovely spot for a romantic lunch or dinner. Unfortunately, Riomaggiore doesn't have as much old-world charm as its sister villages; its easy accessibility has brought traffic and more construction here than elsewhere in the Cinque Terre.

GETTING HERE AND AROUND
The enormous parking problems presented by these cliff-dwelling villages have been mitigated somewhat by a large, covered parking structure at La Spezia Centrale station, which costs €2.30 per hour in summer. It's clean and secure (you cannot enter without a ticket code to open the door), and it's open 24/7. This is a good backup solution for those with cars, although others may choose to take a day trip from Pisa or Lucca and rely on bus and train services. Arrive early, as it can fill up by mid-morning, especially in high season.

Sights

Riomaggiore

TOWN | This village at the eastern end of the Cinque Terre is built into a river gorge (hence the name, which means "river major"). It has a tiny harbor protected by large slabs of alabaster and marble, which serve as tanning beds for sunbathers, as well as being the site of several outdoor cafés with fine views. According to legend, the settlement of Riomaggiore dates as far back as the 8th century, when Greek religious refugees came here to escape persecution by the Byzantine emperor. ✉ *Stazione Ferroviaria, Riomaggiore* ☎ *0187/762187* ⊕ *www.turismoinliguria.it.*

Accessing Cinque Terre Trails

When to Go

The ideal times to visit the Cinque Terre are September and May, when the weather is mild and the summer tourist season isn't in full swing (June through August can be unbearably hot and crowded).

Getting Here and Around

There is now a local train between La Spezia and Levanto that stops at each of the Cinque Terre villages, and runs approximately every 30 minutes throughout the day. Tickets for each leg of the journey (€1.90–€2.20) are available at all five train stations. In Corniglia, the only one of the Cinque Terre that isn't at sea level, a shuttle service (€1.50) is provided for those who don't wish to climb (or descend) the 300-plus steps that link the train station with the clifftop town.

Along the Cinque Terre coast two ferry lines operate. From June to September, Golfo Paradiso runs from Genoa and Camogli to Monterosso al Mare and Vernazza (a one-day ticket costs €38). The smaller but more frequent Golfo dei Poeti stops at each village from Lerici (east of Riomaggiore) to Monterosso, with the exception of Corniglia, four times a day (a one-day ticket costs €35).

Admission

Entrance tickets for using the trails are available at ticket booths located at the start of each section of Trail No. 2, and at information offices in the Levanto, Monterosso, Vernazza, Corniglia, Manarola, Riomaggiore, and La Spezia train stations. A one-day pass costs €7.50, which includes a trail map and an information leaflet; a two-day pass is €14.50.

The Cinque Terre Card combines park entrance fees with unlimited daily use of the regional train between La Spezia, the five villages, and Levanto just north of Monterosso, and costs €16 for a one-day pass and €29 for a two-day pass.

For More Information

www.cinqueterre.com; www.lecinqueterre.org; www.parconazionale-5terre.it; www.rebuildmonterosso.com; www.savevernazza.com; www.littleparadiso.com (blog).

🍴 Restaurants

Dau Cila

$$ | **LIGURIAN** | There's wonderful seaside dining on Riomaggiore harbor, with a menu of local Ligurian dishes and an extensive wine list. ■**TIP→ On bad-weather days, take advantage of the lovely dining room with vaulted ceilings, built into the rock. Known for:** local flavors; sea views; extensive wine list. $ *Average main: €22* ⊠ *Via San Giacomo 65, Riomaggiore* ☎ *0187/760032* ⊘ *Closed Tues.*

Manarola

16 km (10 miles) southwest of La Spezia, 117 km (73 miles) southeast of Genoa.

The enchanting pastel houses of Manarola spill down a steep hill overlooking a spectacular turquoise swimming cove and a bustling harbor. The whole town is built on black rock. Above the town, ancient terraces still protect abundant vineyards and olive trees. This village is the center of wine and

Continued on page 462

HIKING THE CINQUE TERRE

FIVE REMOTE VILLAGES MAKE ONE MUST-SEE DESTINATION

"Charming" and "breathtaking" are adjectives that get a workout when you're traveling in Italy, but it's rare that both apply to a single location. The Cinque Terre is such a place, and this combination of characteristics goes a long way toward explaining its tremendous appeal.

The area is made up of five tiny villages (Cinque Terre literally means "Five Lands") clinging to the cliffs along a gorgeous stretch of the Ligurian coast. The terrain is so steep that for centuries footpaths were the only way to get from place to place. It just so happens that these paths provide beautiful views of the rocky coast tumbling into the sea, as well as access to secluded beaches and grottoes.

Backpackers "discovered" the Cinque Terre in the 1970s, and its popularity has been growing ever since. Despite summer crowds, much of the original appeal is intact. Each town has maintained its own distinct charm, and views from the trails in between are as breathtaking as ever.

Monterosso

Corniglia

Terracing around Cornigl

HIKING THE CINQUE TERRE

Monterosso—Vernazza Trail

The most demanding portion of the trail. Often narrow, with significant climbs and descents, particularly near Vernazza. Your labors are rewarded with the Trail No. 2's best views.

Vernazza—Corniglia Trail

Ups and downs interspersed with olive groves and terraced vineyards.

Mount Malpertuso

Mount Castello

Mount Gaginara

Le Stalle

Trail No 8a

(Red Trail)

Drignana

38

370

Madonna di Soviore

1hr 30min

Trail No 1

Trail No 89

51

Trail No 8

Santuario del Reggio

1hr

Santuario Bernardino

1hr

S. Bernardo

Trail No 8

Trail No 7

3 km/2 mi–1 hr 30 min

Trail No 2 (Blue Trail)

3 km/2 mi–2 hrs

Guvano Beach

Vernazza

Palma Pt

del Frate Island

Molinara Pt

Monterosso al Mare

0 — 1 mi

0 — 1 km

FERRY TO LEVANTO

Monterosso

The most resort-like of the villages, with the largest beach.

Vernazza

Pretty and visitor-friendly. The best spot for lingering in a café and watching waves crash against the shore.

THE CLASSIC HIKE

Hiking is the most popular way to experience the Cinque Terre, and Trail No. 2, the Sentiero Azzurro (Blue Trail), is the most traveled path. To cover the entire trail is a full day: it's approximately 13 km (8 miles) in length, takes you to all five villages, and requires about five hours, not including stops, to complete. The best approach is to start at the eastern-most town of Riomaggiore and warm up your legs on the easiest segment of the trail. As you work your way west, the hike gets progressively more demanding. Between Corniglia and Manarola take the ferry (which provides its own beautiful views) or the inland train running between the towns instead.

Manarola

Along Lovers' Lane

Via dell'Amore

Corniglia—Manarola Trail
This section of the trail is currently closed.

Manarola—Riomaggiore Trail
Known as the Via dell'Amore (Lovers' Lane). A wide, paved, flat path with fine views.

KEY

··········	Major footpaths
- - - - -	Sanctuary footpaths
– – – – –	Connecting footpaths
45min	Hiking times
☩	Sanctuaries

Mount Capri

Mount Cuna

Mount Galera

Mount Grosso

Trail No 6

1 (Red Trail)

Trail No 7a

Trail No 6d

Trail No 02

1hr 30min

Madonna della Salute ☩
1hr

Volastra

3 km/2 mi–1 hr

Trail No. 2 (Blue Trail) (this section closed)

Spiaggione di Corniglia

51

370

Trail No 3

Madonna di Montenero
☩ 45min

370

TO LA SPEZIA →

Corniglia

Luogo Pt

Manarola ○
Trail No 2 (Blue Trail)
30min

Buonfiglio Pt

Via dell' Amore

Riomaggiore

Ligurian Sea

Torre Guardiola

C di M Nero

Corniglia
Perched on a cliff 500 ft. above the sea, reached by a switchback path (or by shuttle bus).

Manarola
The most photogenic of the villages, best seen from the cemetery a few minutes up the path toward Corniglia.

Riomaggiore
Cliff-clinging buildings are almost as striking as those in Manarola. Stairs to the left of the train station entrance cross over the tracks and lead to the trailhead.

BEYOND TRAIL NO.2

Trail No. 2 is just one of a network of trails crisscrossing the hills. If you're a dedicated hiker, spend a few nights and try some of the other routes. Trail No. 1, the Sentiero Rosso (Red Trail), climbs from Portovenere (east of Riomaggiore) and returns to the sea at Levanto (west of Monterosso al Mare). To hike its length takes from 9 to 12 hours; the ridge-top trail provides spectacular views from high above the villages, each of which can be reached via a steep path. Other shorter trails go from the villages up into the hills, some leading to religious sanctuaries. Trail No. 9, for example, starts from the old section of Monterosso and ends at the Madonna di Soviore Sanctuary.

Hiking the Cinque Terre

Though often described as relaxing and easy, the Cinque Terre also have several hiking options if you wish to exert yourself a little. Many people do not realize just how demanding parts of these trails can be—it's best to come prepared. We recommend bringing a Cinque Terre Card and cash (smaller shops, eateries, and the park entrances do not accept credit cards).

When all trails are completely open, a hike through the entire region takes about four to five hours; add time for exploring each village and taking a lunch break—it's an all-day, if not two-day, trek. We recommend an early start, especially in summer when midday temperatures can rise to 90ºF. Note that only Sentiero Azzurro (Trail No. 2) requires the Cinque Terre Card. The other 20-plus trails in the area are free. All trails are well marked with a red-and-white sign. Trails from village to village get progressively steeper from south (Riomaggiore) to north (Monterosso). If you're a day-tripper with a car, use the underground lot at La Spezia Centrale train station (€2.30 per hour in summer) and take the train to Riomaggiore (6–8 minutes).

Our Favorites

Other trails to consider include **Monterosso to Santuario Madonna di Soviore,** a fairly strenuous but rewarding 1½ hours up to a lovely 8th-century sanctuary. There is also a restaurant and a priceless view. **Riomaggiore to Montenero and Portovenere** is one hour up to the sanctuary and another three

hours to Portovenere, passing through some gorgeous, less-traveled terrain. **Manarola to Volastra to Corniglia** runs high above the main trail and through vineyards and lesser-known villages. **Monterosso to Levanto** is a good 2½-hour hike, passing over Punta Mesco with glorious views of the Cinque Terre to the south, Corsica to the west, and the Alps to the north.

Each town has something that passes for a beach (usually with lots of pebbles or slabs of terraced rock), but there is only one option for both sand and decent swimming—in Monterosso, just across from the train station. It's equipped with chairs, umbrellas, and snack bars.

Precautions

If you're hitting the trails, carry water with you, wear sturdy shoes (hiking boots are best), and have a hat and sunscreen handy. Note that the lesser-used trails aren't as well maintained as Trail No. 2. If you're undertaking the full Trail No. 1 hike, bring something to snack on as well as your water bottle. Note that currently the Via dell'Amore and the portion of Trail No. 2 between Manarola and Corniglia are closed indefinitely due to landslides.

■ TIP➔ **Check weather reports, especially in late fall and winter; thunderstorms can make shelterless trails slippery and dangerous. Rain in October and November can cause landslides and close trails altogether.**

olive oil production in the region, and its streets are lined with shops selling local products.

Surrounded by steep terraced vineyards, Manarola's one road tumbles from the **Chiesa di San Lorenzo** (14th century) high above the village, down to the rocky port. Since the Cinque Terre wine cooperative is located in **Groppo,** a hamlet overlooking the village (reachable by foot or by the green Park bus; ask at Park offices for schedules), the vineyards are accessible. If you'd like to snap a shot of the most famous view of the town, you can walk from the port area to the cemetery above. Along the way you'll pass the town's playground, uncrowded bathrooms, and a tap with clean drinking water.

 Sights

Manarola

TOWN | Enchanting pastel houses spill down a steep hill overlooking a spectacular turquoise swimming cove and a bustling harbor. The whole town is built on black rock. Above the town, ancient terraces still protect abundant vineyards and olive trees. This village is the center of the wine and olive oil production of the region, and its streets are lined with shops selling local products. ⊠ Manarola ⊕ *www.turismoinliguria.it, www.parconazionale5terre.it.*

 Hotels

★ La Torretta

$$$ | **HOTEL** | One of the Cinque Terre's few "boutique" hotels is in a 17th-century tower that sits high on the hill above the rainbow-hue village of Manarola, with truly lovely views of the terraced vineyards, colorful village homes, and the Mediterranean sea; inside, decor is chic, sleek, and antiques-bedecked. **Pros:** no-smoking policy; stellar staff; free luggage transfer. **Cons:** steep walk up to the hotel; books up quickly; strict no-refund policy.

⑤ *Rooms from: €250* ⊠ *Vico Volto 20, Cinque Terre, Manarola* ☎ *0187/920327* ⊕ *www.torrettas.com* ☉ *Closed Dec.– Feb.* ⇩ *15 rooms* ⑩ *Free Breakfast.*

Corniglia

27 km (17 miles) northwest of La Spezia, 100 km (60 miles) southeast of Genoa.

The buildings, narrow lanes, and stairways of Corniglia are strung together amid vineyards high on the cliffs. On a clear day, views of the entire coastal strip are excellent, from Elba in the south to the Italian Alps in the north. The high perch and lack of harbor make this farming community the most remote and therefore least crowded of the Cinque Terre. In fact, the 365 steps that lead up from the train station to the town center dissuade many tourists from making the hike to the village. You can also take the green Park bus, but they run infrequently and are usually packed with tired hikers.

Corniglia is built along one road edged with small shops, bars, gelaterias, and restaurants. Midway along Via Fieschi is the **Largo Taragio,** the main square and heart of the village. Shaded by leafy trees and umbrellas, this is a lovely spot for a mid-hike gelato break. Here you'll find the 14th-century **Chiesa di San Pietro.** The church's rose window of marble imported from Carrara is impressive, particularly considering the work required to get it here!

 Sights

Corniglia

TOWN | Stone buildings, narrow lanes, and stairways are strung together amid vineyards high on the cliffs; on a clear day views of the entire coastal strip are excellent. The high perch and lack of harbor make this farming community the most remote of the Cinque Terre. ⊠ *Corniglia* ☎ *0187/762600* ⊕ *www.parconazionale-5terre.it.*

San Pietro

CHURCH | On a pretty pastel square sits the 14th-century church of San Pietro. The rose window of marble imported from Carrara is impressive, particularly considering the work required to get it here. ⊠ *Main Sq., Corniglia.*

Vernazza

27 km (17 miles) west of La Spezia, 96 km (59 miles) southeast of Genoa.

With its narrow streets and small squares, Vernazza is arguably the most charming of the Cinque Terre towns, and usually the most crowded. Historically, it was the most important of them and—since Vernazza was the only one fortunate enough to have a natural port—the wealthiest, as evinced by the elaborate arcades, loggias, and marble work lining Via Roma and Piazza Marconi.

The village's pink slate-roof houses and colorful squares contrast with the remains of the medieval fort and castle, including two towers, in the Old Town. The Romans first inhabited this rocky spit of land in the 1st century. Today, Vernazza has a fairly lively social scene. **Piazza Marconi** looks out across Vernazza's small sandy beach to the sea, toward Monterosso. The numerous restaurants and bars crowd their tables and umbrellas on the outskirts of the piazza, creating a patchwork of sights and sounds that form one of the most unique and beautiful places in the world.

◉ Sights

If mass is not going on (a cord blocks the entrance if it is), take a peek into the **church of St. Margaret of Antioch,** where little has changed since its enlargement in the 1600s. This 14th-century edifice has simple interiors but truly breathtaking views toward the sea: a stark contrast to the other, elaborate churches of the Cinque Terre.

On the other side of the piazza, stairs lead to a lookout **fortress and cylindrical watchtower,** built in the 11th century as protection against pirate attacks. For a small fee you can climb to the top of the tower for a spectacular view of the coastline.

Vernazza

TOWN | With narrow streets and small squares, the village that many consider to be the most charming of the five towns has the best access to the sea—a geographic reality that made the village wealthier than its neighbors, as evidenced by the elaborate arcades, loggias, and marble work. The village's pink, slate-roof houses and colorful squares contrast with the remains of the medieval fort and castle, including two towers, in the old town. The Romans first inhabited this rocky spit of land in the 1st century. Today Vernazza has a fairly lively social scene. It's a great place to refuel with a hearty seafood lunch or linger in a café between links of the seaside hike. ⊠ *Vernazza ⊕ www.turismoinliguria. it, www.parconazionale5terre.it.*

🍴 Restaurants

Gambero Rosso

$$ | **LIGURIAN** | Relax on Vernazza's main square at this fine trattoria looking out onto the church of Santa Maria d'Antiochi. Enjoy such delectable dishes as shrimp salad, vegetable torte, and squid-ink risotto. **Known for:** pesto dishes; piazza view; fresh seafood. ⑤ *Average main: €22* ⊠ *Piazza Marconi 7, Vernazza* ☎ *0187/812265* ⊕ *www.ristorantegamberorosso.net* ⊗ *Closed Thurs. and Nov.–Mar.*

★ Ristorante Belforte

$$ | **LIGURIAN** | High above the sea in one of Vernazza's remaining medieval stone towers is this unique spot serving delicious Cinque Terre cuisine such s branzino *sotto sale* (cooked under alt), stuffed mussels, and *insalata di olpo* (octopus salad). The setting is nagnificent, so try for an outdoor table. **nown for:** lively atmosphere; incredi-le views; octopus salad. $ *Average nain: €20* ⊠ *Via Guidoni 42, Vernazza* ☎ *0187/812222* ⊕ *www.ristorantebel-orte.it* ☾ *Closed Tues. and Nov.–Easter.*

Hotels

a Malà

$$ | **B&B/INN** | A cut above other lodging ptions in the Cinque Terre, these small uest rooms are equipped with flat-creen TVs, air-conditioning, marble howers, and comfortable bedding nd have views of the sea or the port, vhich can also be enjoyed at their most ewitching from a shared terrace literally uspended over the Mediterranean. **Pros:** elpful, attentive staff; views; clean, resh-feeling rooms. **Cons:** child-friendly either a pro or a con); books up quickly; ome stairs are involved. $ *Rooms rom: €250* ⊠ *Giovanni Battista 29, Vernazza* ☎ *334/2875718* ⊕ *www.lamala. t* ☾ *Closed Jan. 8–Mar. 1* ⇥ *4 rooms* ⦿| *Free Breakfast.*

Monterosso al Mare

32 km (20 miles) northwest of La Spezia, 39 km (55 miles) southeast of Genoa.

t's the combined draw of beautiful peaches, rugged cliffs, crystal-clear tur-quoise waters, and plentiful small hotels nd restaurants that has made Monteros-so al Mare the largest of the Cinque Terre villages (population 1,800) and also the usiest in midsummer.

And Monterosso has festivals enough to match its size. They start with the Lemon Feast on the Saturday before Ascension Sunday. Then, on the second Sunday after Pentecost, comes the Flower Festival of Corpus Christi: during the afternoon, the streets and alleyways of the historic center are decorated with thousands of colorful flower petals, set in beautiful designs, over which an evening procession passes. Finally, the Salted Anchovy and Olive Oil Festival takes place each year during the second weekend of September.

◉ Sights

Heading west from the train station, you pass through a tunnel and exit into the *centro storico* (historic center) of the village. Nestled into the wide valley that leads to the sea, Monterosso is built above numerous streams, which have been covered to make up the major streets of the village. Via Buranco, the oldest street in Monterosso, leads to the most characteristic piazza of the village, Piazza Matteotti. Locals pass through here daily to shop at the supermarket and butcher. This piazza also contains the oldest and most typical wineshop in the village, Enoteca da Eliseo—stop here between 6 pm and midnight to share tables with fellow tourists and locals over a bottle of Cinque Terre wine. There's also the **Chiesa di San Francesco**, built in the 12th century and an excellent example of the Ligurian Gothic style. Its distinctive black stripes and marble rose window make it one of the most photographed sites in the Cinque Terre.

Fegina, the newer side of the village (and site of the train station), has relatively modern homes ranging from the Liberty style (art nouveau) to the early 1970s. At the far eastern end of town, you'll run into a private sailing club sheltered by a vast rock carved with an impressive statue of Neptune. From here, you can reach the challenging trail to Levanto (a great 2½-hour hike). This trail has the added bonus of a five-minute detour to the **ruins of a 14th-century monastery**. The expansive view from this vantage point allowed the monks who were housed here to easily scan the waters for enemy ships that might invade the villages and alert residents to coming danger. Have your camera ready for this Cinerama-like vista.

Although it has the most nightlife in the Cinque Terre (thanks to its numerous wine bars and pubs), Monterosso is also the most family-friendly. With its expanse of free and equipped beaches, extensive pedestrian areas, large children's play park, and summer activities, Monterosso is a top spot for kids.

The **local outdoor market** is held on Thursday and attracts crowds of tourists and villagers from along the coast to shop for everything from pots, pans, and underwear to fruits, vegetables, and fish. Often a few stands sell local art and crafts, as well as olive oil and wine.

🍴 Restaurants

Enoteca Internazionale

$ | **WINE BAR** | Located on the main street, this bar offers a large selection of wines, both local and from farther afield, plus delicious light fare; its umbrella-covered patio is a welcoming spot to recuperate after a day of hiking. Susanna, the owner, is a certified sommelier who's always forthcoming with helpful suggestions on pairing local wines with their tasty bruschettas. **Known for:** helpful staff; extensive wine list; patio dining. $ *Average main: €13* ✉ *Via Roma 62, Monterosso al Mare* ☎ *0187/817278* ⊕ *www.enotecaint-ernazionale.com* ⊗ *Closed Jan.–Feb.*

★ Miky

$$$ | **SEAFOOD** | This is arguably the best restaurant in Monterosso, specializing in tasty, fresh seafood dishes like grilled calamari and monkfish ravioli. The *catalana* (poached lobster and shrimp with sliced raw fennel and carrot) is a winner. **Known for:** fine dining; sunny seaside setting; fresh seafood. $ *Average main: €33* ✉ *Via Fegina 104, Monterosso al Mare* ☎ *0187/817608* ⊕ *www.ristorantemiky.it* ⊗ *Closed mid-Nov.–mid-Mar.*

 ## 🛏 Hotels

Bellambra B&B

$ | **B&B/INN** | Modern rooms with charm and comfort in the heart of the old town make this a terrific base for exploring the Cinque Terre. **Pros:** an apartment can sleep up to 6 people; location; spacious rooms and bathrooms. **Cons:** books up quickly; no elevator with steep, narrow stairs; can be a bit noisy. $ *Rooms from: €120* ✉ *Via Roma 64, Monterosso al Mare* ☎ *39/3920121912* ⊕ *www.bellambra5terre.com* �763 *4 rooms* ⦿ *No Meals.*

Il Giardino Incantato

$$ | **B&B/INN** | With wood-beam ceilings and stone walls, the stylishly restored and updated rooms in this 16th-century house in the historic center of Monterosso ooze comfort and old-world charm. **Pros:** gorgeous garden; excellent hosts; spacious rooms. **Cons:** some rooms are small; books up quickly; no views. $ *Rooms from: €180* ✉ *Via Mazzini 18, Monterosso al Mare* ☎ *0187/818315* ⊕ *www.ilgiardinoincantato.net* ⦿ *Free Breakfast* ⊗ *Closed Nov.–Easter* �763 *4 rooms.*

Porto Roca

$$$$ | **HOTEL** | Far from the madding crowds, one of Cinque Terre's only high-end hotels is perched on the famous terraced cliffs right over the main beach, with large balconies to savor panoramic views of the magnificent sea. **Pros:** unobstructed sea views; pool; tranquil location. **Cons:** somewhat removed from town; back-facing rooms can be a bit dark; some of the rooms could use a revamp. $ *Rooms from: €380* ✉ *Via Corone 1, Monterosso al Mare* ☎ *0187/817502* ⊕ *www.portoroca.it* �763 *43 rooms* ⦿ *Free Breakfast* ⊗ *Closed Nov.–Easter.*

erici

06 km (66 miles) southeast of Genoa, 5 km (40 miles) west of Lucca.

erici, part of the Riviera di Levante, is n the spectacular Bay of La Spezia, therwise known as the Gulf of Poets, nd is famous for its natural beauty. ear Liguria's border with Tuscany, nis picturesque village dates back to edieval times when, under the rule f Pisa, it fought cross-bay battles with ne Genovese town of Portovenere, as ell as with local pirates. The town is et on a magnificent coastline of gray iffs jutting down into a crystal clear ea and surrounded by a national park nat is like an unframed painting of pine rests, olive trees, and tiny colorful amlets. The waterfront piazza is filled /ith trompe-l'oeil frescoed buildings, and easide cafés line a charming little harbor nat holds sailboats and *gozzi*, the typical mall fishing boats of the area.

everal white-sand beaches and bathing stablishments dot the 2-km (1-mile) /alk along the bay from the village enter to nearby San Terenzo. From the illage, you can also reach some beautiful iking trails that head southeast to both easide and hilltop villages like Fiascheri- o, Tellaro, and Montemarcello.

ETTING HERE AND AROUND

y car, Lerici is less than a 10-minute rive west from the A12, with plenty of lue signs indicating the way. There's a arge parking (fee) lot about a 10-minute valk along the seaside promenade from ne center. By train, the closest station s either Sarzana (10-minute drive) or La pezia Centrale (20-minute drive) on the nain north–south line between Genoa nd Pisa.

ISITOR INFORMATION

CONTACT Lerici Tourism Office. *⊠ Piazza Bacigalupi 9, Lerici ☎ 0187/9601 ⊕ www. comune.lerici.sp.it.*

Sights

Castello di Lerici

CASTLE/PALACE | The promontory is dominated by this 13th-century Pisan castle, which now houses a museum of art and paleontology, a superb location for weddings—it overlooks the entire Gulf of Poets. *⊠ Piazza S. Giorgio 1, Lerici ☎ €5.*

Restaurants

Bonta Nascoste

$$ | ITALIAN | In the local dialect, *bonta nascoste* means "hidden goodness," a reference to its back-alleyway location and consistently delicious dishes, which include fresh pasta, local fish, and a handful of meat choices. There are only eight tables (and a couple more outside in summer), so reserve ahead. **Known for:** crudo; inventive seafood dishes, at a price; cozy atmosphere. $ *Average main: €20 ⊠ Via Cavour 52, Lerici ☎ 0187/965500 ⊕ www.bontanascoste.it.*

Il Frantoio

$$ | LIGURIAN | Located in a former olive-oil mill (the enormous wood grinder still sits in the middle of the dining room), this is a no-frills but fine-food restaurant serving excellent antipasti *al mare* and homemade pasta dishes. You can eat very well for a bit less than most of the touristy spots in town. **Known for:** variety of fresh seafood; generous portions of fish soup; elegant yet rustic setting. $ *Average main: €20 ⊠ Via Cavour 21, Lerici ☎ 0187/964174.*

★ La Caletta

$$ | LIGURIAN | This family-run trattoria is so popular that it's one of the few restaurants in Tellaro to stay open year-round, serving delectable dishes in a warm and friendly atmosphere. Do not miss the seafood antipasto with its assortment of marine treats, the homemade pasta dishes, and the always-recommended catch of the day. **Known for:** tartare dishes; lovely terrace in the warmer months;

fresh fish tasting menu. $ *Average main:*
€16 ✉ *Via Fiascherino 100, Tellaro* ✛ *3 km
(2 miles) south of Lerici* ☎ *0187/964000*
⊕ *www.osterialacaletta.com* ⊗ *Closed
Tues. except in summer.*

★ Locanda Miranda

$$$ | LIGURIAN | Perched amid the clus-
tered old houses in seaside Tellaro, 4 km
(2½ miles) southeast of Lerici, this small,
unpretentious family-run restaurant with
wooden tables and plenty of windows
has become a foodie destination. The
imaginative seafood-focused menu
changes often, and the pretty building
also houses a small inn with seven
charming and comfortable rooms. **Known
for:** pasta and risotto paired with seafood;
cozy dining room; locally sourced fish.
$ *Average main: €30* ✉ *Via Fiascherino
92, Lerici* ☎ *0187/964012* ⊕ *www.locan-
damiranda.com* ⊗ *Closed Nov.*

🛏 Hotels

★ Doria Park

$$$ | HOTEL | FAMILY | Its location—set
amid hills of olive trees yet steps from
the village center—makes this hotel
with bright rooms and contemporary
furnishings one of the best places to
stay in Lerici. **Pros:** sea views; free
parking and convenient location near
town and the beach; comfortable beds.
Cons: some furnishings in common areas need updating; expensive restaurant
stairs, narrow paths, and elevator are
not equipped for people with mobility
issues. $ *Rooms from: €209* ✉ *Via Car-
panini 9, Lerici* ☎ *0187/967124* ⊕ *www.
doriaparkhotel.it* ⇌ *46 rooms* ⦿⦿ *Free
Breakfast.*

lorida

$ | HOTEL | FAMILY | Prepare to relax at his family-run seaside establishment, where one pleasure is lounging on one of the deck chairs on the hotel's rooftop solarium and enjoying its sea views. **Pros:** abundant breakfast; beachfront location; bay views from some rooms. **Cons:** spotty Wi-Fi connection; rooms on the side have no view and can be noisy; small beds in some rooms. $ *Rooms from:* *€190* ✉ *Lungomare Biaggini 35, Lerici* 📞 *0187/967332* ⊕ *www.hotelflorida.it* ⊘ *Closed approximately Dec.15–Jan. 15* 🛏 *44 rooms* ✸ *Free Breakfast.*

La Spezia

11 km (7 miles) northwest of Lerici, 103 km (64 miles) southeast of Genoa.

La Spezia is sometimes thought of as nothing but a large, industrialized naval port en route to the Cinque Terre and Portovenere; it does possess some charm, however, and it also gives you a look at a less tourist-focused part of the Riviera. Its palm-lined promenade, fertile citrus parks, renovated Liberty-style palazzi, and colorful balcony-lined streets make parts of La Spezia surprisingly beautiful. Monday through Saturday mornings, you can stroll through the fresh fish, produce, and local cheese stalls at the outdoor market on Piazza Cavour, and on Friday take part in the busy flea market on Via Garibaldi. There's also Porto Mirabello, a newly built tourist port with a pool club, shops, and several restaurants that overlook the fleet of superyachts.

GETTING HERE AND AROUND

By car, take the exit for La Spezia off the A12. La Spezia Centrale train station is on the main north–south railway line between Genoa and Pisa.

VISITOR INFORMATION

CONTACT La Spezia Tourism Office. ✉ *Via del Prione 222, La Spezia* 📞 *0187/026152* ⊕ *www.myspezia.it.*

Sights

Castello di San Giorgio

CASTLE/PALACE | FAMILY | The remains of this massive 13th-century castle, atop a small hill above the modern town, now house a small museum dedicated to local archaeology. ✉ *Via XXVII Marzo, La Spezia* 📞 *0187/751142* ⊕ *museodelcastello.spezianet.it* 🎫 *€5.50* ⊘ *Closed Mon. afternoon and Tues.*

Restaurants

La Pia Centenaria

$ | PIZZA | Considered an institution, this white-walled, simply decorated *farinateria* and pizzeria dates back to 1887. During the lunch hour, you will probably find a line out the door, while inside—and on the patio in summer—locals munch on *farinata* (a chickpea pancake and a Ligurian delicacy) and thick-crust pizza served hot out of the wood-burning oven. **Known for:** variety of pizza toppings; affordable lunch menu; traditional Ligurian recipes. $ *Average main: €8* ✉ *Via Magenta 12, La Spezia* 📞 *0187/739999* ⊕ *www.lapia.it.*

Portovenere

12 km (7 miles) south of La Spezia, 114 km (70 miles) southeast of Genoa.

The colorful facades and pedestrian-only *calata* (promenade) make Portovenere the quintessential Ligurian seaside village; it's often called the "sixth town" of the Cinque Terre—but with half the crowds. As a UNESCO World Heritage Site, Portovenere is lined with tall, thin *terratetto* houses (townhouses), which date from as far back as the 11th century and which were connected in a wall-like formation to protect against attacks by Pisans and local pirates. Its tiny *carruggi* (alleylike passageways) lead to an array of charming shops, homes, and gardens, and eventually to the village's impressive **Castle Doria**, high on the olive-tree-covered hill. To the west, standing guard over the Mediterranean, is the picturesque medieval **Chiesa di San Pietro**, once the site of a temple to Venus (Venere in Italian), from which Portovenere gets its name. Nearby, in a rocky area leading to the sea, is Byron's Cave, one of the poet's favorite spots for swimming out into the sea.

GETTING HERE AND AROUND

By car from the port city of La Spezia, follow the blue signs for Portovenere. It's about a 20-minute winding drive along the sea through small fishing villages. From La Spezia train station you can hire a taxi for about €30. By bus from Via Garibaldi in La Spezia (a 10-minute walk from the train station) it takes about 30 minutes.

VISITOR INFORMATION

CONTACT Portovenere Tourist Office. ✉ *Piazza Bastreri 7, Portovenere* ☎ *0187/790691.*

 Sights

Grotto Arpaia

CAVE | Near the entrance to the huge, strange Grotto Arpaia, at the base of the sea-swept cliff, is a plaque recounting the strength and courage of Lord Byron (1788–1824) as he swam across the gulf to the village of San Terenzo, near Lerici, to visit his friend Shelley (1792–1822). The poet is said to have written his lengthy narrative poem *Childe Harold's Pilgrimage* in Portovenere. ✉ *Portovenere.*

San Pietro

CHURCH | With its black-and-white-striped exterior, this 13th-century Gothic church is a spectacular landmark recognizable from far out at sea and upon entering the village. It is built on the site of an ancient pagan shrine, on a formidable solid mass of rock above the Grotto Arpaia. There's a fantastic view of the Cinque Terre coastline from the front porch of the church. ✉ *Waterfront promenade, Portovenere* ☎ *0187/790691.*

 Restaurants

Bacicio

$ | WINE BAR | Tucked away on Portovenere's main caruggio, this enoteca and antipasto bar is popular with locals and tourists looking for quality regional dishes, fresh fish, and a lengthy wine list. The owner designed the entire place right down to the tables and chairs made from anchors and old boats. **Known for:** generous portions at reasonable prices; anchovies cooked many ways; fresh fish crostini. $ *Average main: €13* ✉ *Via Cappellini 17, Portovenere* ☎ *0187/79303* 🕙 *Closed Thurs.*

★ Il Timone

$ | LIGURIAN | FAMILY | Find some of the best food in Portovenere at this airy, affordable, and casual portside restaurant. The menu is typical "Ligure," ranging from meat to pasta with seafood and also offers farinata, focaccia, and pizza. **Known for:** Ligurian farinata and pizza; comfortable patio in summer; all-inclusive tasting menus. $ *Average main: €11* ✉ *Via Olivo 29, Portovenere* ☎ *347/3472601008* ⊕ *www.pizzeriailtimone.it* 🕙 *Closed Tues., Nov., and mid-Jan.–Feb.*

Locanda Lorena

$$ | LIGURIAN | Across the small bay of Portovenere lies the rugged island of Palmaria, where there are only a few restaurants (making for high prices), including this place with lovely seafront views and headliners like fresh pasta and local fish. To get here, take the restaurant's free Riva boat from the Portovenere jetty. **Known for:** incredible Portovenere views; quaint seaside setting; catch of the day specials. $ *Average main: €17* ✉ *Palmaria Island, Portovenere* ☎ *0187/792370* ⊕ *www.locandalorena.com* 🕙 *Closed Nov.*

🖺 Hotels

rand Hotel Portovenere

\$\$ | HOTEL | This 13th-century Franciscan onvent turned elegant hotel incorporates modern enhancements while etaining the structure's impressive rose cade, arches, and frescoes. **Pros:** shute service to a private beach; excellent cation and views; comfortable beds and pacious rooms. **Cons:** some room amenies are limited, no in-room tea or coffee aker; updated rooms bring hefty rates; xpensive restaurant and bar. ⑤ *Rooms om: €327 ⊠ Via Giuseppe Garibaldi 5, ortovenere ☎ 0187/777751 ⊕ www. ortoveneregrand.com* ✠ *Free Breakfast* ⊙ *Closed Nov.–mid-Mar.* 🖙 *52 rooms.*

otel Belvedere

\$ | HOTEL | True to its name (which means "nice view"), the best rooms in his sunny Liberty-style building face the ay of Portovenere, with lovely vistas of almaria Island and the Gulf of Poets. **ros:** sea views from the terrace and ome rooms; good value for the location espite plain decor; ideal location to each town and ferry terminal. **Cons:** poms facing the street are noisy; limited arking; parts of the hotel could use a hakeover. ⑤ *Rooms from: €180 ⊠ Via Giuseppe Garibaldi 26, Portovenere ☎ 0187/790608 ⊕ www.belvedereporto- enere.it* ⊙ *Closed Nov.–mid-Mar.* 🖙 *17 poms* ✠ *Free Breakfast.*

evanto

7 km (29 miles) northwest of Porto- venere, 60 km (36 miles) southeast of Genoa.

lestled at the end of a valley of pine orests, olive groves, vineyards, and medieval villages lies this sunny seaside own, an alternative and usually less xpensive base for exploring the Cinque erre and the Riviera di Levante.

GETTING HERE AND AROUND

By car, take the Carodanno/Levanto exit off the A12 for 25 minutes to the town center. By train, Levanto is on the main north–south railway, one stop north of Monterosso.

VISITOR INFORMATION

CONTACT Levanto Tourism Office. ⊠ *Piazza Cavour 1, Levanto* ☎ *0187/808125* ⊕ *www.visitlevanto.it.*

Sights

With its long sandy beach, colorful old quarter, and breathtakingly beautiful hiking paths, Levanto has become a haven not only for sun worshippers but also for divers, surfers, and hikers. The path between Levanto and Monterosso al Mare, about a 2½-mile hike, is freely accessible. This is also an ideal starting point for day trips by train or boat to many interesting places along the Riviera, such as Portovenere, Lerici, Tellaro, and Fiascherino, in the direction of La Spezia; and Portofino, Santa Margherita, Camogli, and Sestri Levante, in the direction of Genoa.

Sestri Levante

37 km (22 miles) northwest of Levanto and 28 km (17 miles) southeast of Santa Margherita Ligure.

Halfway between the Cinque Terre and Portofino lies this lovely seaside resort. The old village is on a peninsula with the beautiful Baia del Silenzio on one side and the Baia delle Favole and promenade on the other. The Baia delle Favole (*favole* means "fairy tales") was named in honor of the Danish author Hans Christian Andersen, who visited Sestri for a short time.

GETTING HERE AND AROUND

By car, it is a five-minute drive off the A12. The Sestri Levante train station is on the main north–south train line between Genoa and Pisa; it's just a five-minute walk to the beach and old village.

VISITOR INFORMATION

CONTACT Sestri Levante Tourist Office.
✉ *Corso Colombo 50, Sestri Levante*
☎ *0185/478530* ⊕ *www.sestri-levante.
net.*

Beaches

Baia del Silenzio

BEACH | The Bay of Silence is a sandy
cove east of the pedestrian-only street
in the old town, with pastel-color bars
and restaurants edging the sand and
bobbing boats dotting the horizon. It's
a picture-postcard public beach and an
idyllic setting for a dip in the Mediterranean, frequented mostly by locals and
some visiting crowds in summer. You can
also take a short walk up to the Convento
dei Cappuccini, a church dedicated to the
Virgin Mary. The monastery was built at
the end of the 17th century and offers
a spectacular panoramic view. ✉ *Sestri
Levante.*

Restaurants

Cantina del' Polpo

$$ | **LIGURIAN** | The Ballarini family runs
three restaurants in Sestri Levante, and
this cozy former cantina with wood
paneling, a fireplace, local maritime
memorabilia, and red-checkered tablecloths serves some of the best dishes
in town. Using the bounty of the two
bays that frame the village, they create
inventive tasting menus and standout
mains, which, in addition to expertly seasoned fish, include homemade pastas,
like the gnocchi. **Known for:** hard-to-find
regional wines; creative seafood-focused
tasting menus at affordable prices;
friendly staff. ⑤ *Average main: €20* ✉ *Via
Camillo Benso Cavour 2, Sestri Levante*
☎ *0185/485296* ⊕ *www.cantinadelpolpo.
it* ⊙ *Closed Tues. and Nov.*

Hotels

Grand Hotel dei Castelli

$$$ | **B&B/INN** | You can see the Baia delle
Favole from this castle-turned-hotel on
a promontory, and you just might feel
you've been transported to a fairy tale
here. **Pros:** private inlet; grand setting
with spectacular views of the two bays;
beautiful grounds. **Cons:** steep walk (or
slow elevator) down to the beach; some
rooms and public areas have a dated feel
a bit far from the train station, so a car is
best. ⑤ *Rooms from: €300* ✉ *Via Peniso
la di Levante 26, Liguria* ☎ *0185/487020*
⊕ *www.hoteldeicastelli.it/en* ⊙ *Closed
Nov.–mid-Mar.* ⇆ *50 rooms* � ❍ *Free
Breakfast.*

Chiavari

*8 km (5 miles) northwest of Sestri Levante
38 km (23 miles) southeast of Genoa.*

Chiavari is a fishing town (rather than
village) of considerable character, with
narrow, twisting streets and a good
harbor. Chiavari's citizens were intrepid
explorers, and many emigrated to South
America in the 19th century. The town
boomed, thanks to the wealth of the
returning voyagers, but Chiavari retains
many medieval traces in its buildings.

GETTING HERE AND AROUND

By car, take the Chiavari exit off the A12.
The Chiavari train station is located on
the main north–south train line between
Genoa and Pisa.

VISITOR INFORMATION

Chiavari Tourism Office. Chiavari Tourism Office (Corso Assaroti 1, Chiavari
☎ *0185/325216* ⊕ *www.comune.chiavari.*

je.it.) ✉ *via della Cittadella, Chiavari* ☎ *0185/365400* ⊕ *www.chiavariturismo.it.*

Sights

Museo Archeologico

ART MUSEUM | A worthy collection in the town center displays objects from an 8th-century BC necropolis, or ancient cemetery, excavated nearby. ✉ *Via Costaguta 4, Chiavari* ☎ *0185/320829* ⊕ *www. musei.liguria.beniculturali.it/musei* ⊘ *Closed Mon.* 🎫 *€3.*

Santa Margherita Ligure

21 km (13 miles) west of Chiavari, 31 km (19 miles) southeast of Genoa.

A beautiful old resort town favored by well-to-do Italians, Santa Margherita Ligure has everything a Riviera playground should have—plenty of palm trees and attractive hotels, cafés, and a marina packed with yachts. Some of the older buildings have trompe-l'oeil frescoed exteriors that are typical of this part of the Riviera. For many people, this pleasant, convenient base represents the perfect balance on the Italian Riviera: more spacious than the Cinque Terre; less glitzy than San Remo; more relaxing than Genoa and environs; and ideally situated for day trips, such as an excursion to Portofino.

GETTING HERE AND AROUND

By car, take the Rapallo exit off the A12 and follow the blue signs, about a 10-minute drive. The Santa Margherita Ligure train station is on the main north–south line between Genoa and Pisa.

VISITOR INFORMATION

CONTACT Santa Margherita Ligure Tourism Office. ✉ *Piazza Vittorio Veneto, Santa Margherita Ligure* ☎ *0185/287485* ⊕ *www.smlturismo.it.*

🍴 Restaurants

Oca Bianca

$$ | EUROPEAN | In a departure from the local norm, the menu at Oca Bianca has no seafood to offer; instead, meat dishes are the specialty, along with a few pastas. Choices may include mouthwatering preparations of beef, lamb, duck, and pork, and there is an extensive wine list from its next-door cantina. **Known for:** classic sauces for meat dishes; lively outdoor seating in summer; multiple steak preparations. ⑤ *Average main: €20* ✉ *Via XXV Aprile 21, Santa Margherita Ligure* ☎ *0185/288411* ⊕ *www.ristoranteocabianca.it* ⊘ *Closed Tues.*

★ U Giancu

$$ | LIGURIAN | Although the walls of Fausto Oneto's restaurant are covered in original cartoons, and a playground is the main feature of the outdoor seating area, this chef-owner is completely serious about his cooking, which follows the seasons. His own garden provides the freshest possible vegetables, the wine list (ask to visit the cantina) is excellent, and there are lively morning Ligurian cooking lessons. **Known for:** vegetables fresh from the restaurant's garden; lamb dishes; creative and playful setting. ⑤ *Average main: €20* ✉ *Via San Massimo 78, Località San Massimo* ☎ *0185/261212* ⊕ *www.ugiancu.it* ⊘ *Closed Wed. and Nov. No lunch Mon.–Fri.*

Hotels

Grand Hotel Miramare

$$$$ | RESORT | Classic Riviera elegance prevails at this palatial hotel overlooking the bay, where antique furniture and crystal chandeliers fill the high-ceiling rooms. **Pros:** top-notch service close to the beach; well-maintained rooms and marble bathrooms; spa and wellness center. **Cons:** beach is run by different management than the hotel; sea access is down the grand entrance staircase and across a busy street; traffic in summer from the road in front of the hotel. ⑤ *Rooms from: €361* ✉ *Via Milite Ignoto 30, Santa Margherita Ligure* ☎ *0185/287013* ⊕ *www.grandhotelmiramare.it* ☽ *Closed Jan. 7–Mar.* ⇌ *78 rooms* ⑩ *Free Breakfast.*

Hotel Continental

$$$$ | **HOTEL** | A stately seaside mansion surrounded by a lush garden shaded by tall palms and pine trees offers stylish accommodations done in a blend of classic furnishings, mostly inspired by the 19th century. **Pros:** private beach; lovely location; panoramic views from some rooms and the dining area. **Cons:** located off a road that gets busy in high season; rooms in the annex need to be refurbished; beach access included in room rates, but lounge chairs and cabanas are extra. ⑤ *Rooms from: €320* ✉ *Via Pagana 8, Santa Margherita Ligure* ☎ *0185/286512* ⊕ *www.hotel-continental.it* ☽ *Closed Jan.–Feb.* ⇌ *68 rooms* ⑩ *Free Breakfast.*

Hotel Jolanda

$$ | **HOTEL** | They may not have sea views, but the stylish, comfortable, and spacious rooms here are decorated in a contemporary style, and some have large balconies. **Pros:** spa and massage options; reasonable rates in a high-price area; outdoor areas for dining and relaxing. **Cons:** indoor common areas feel cramped; no sea view; parking is limited and expensive. ⑤ *Rooms from: €200* ✉ *Via Luisito Costa 6, Santa Margherita Ligure* ☎ *0185/287512* ⊕ *www.hoteljolanda.it* ⇌ *45 rooms* ⑩ *Free Breakfast.*

Santa Margherita Palace

$$$$ | **HOTEL** | Just a short walk from the old town, this well-kept and well-equipped hotel offers modern rooms with contemporary furnishings, an abundant breakfast, and two spas. **Pros:** modern bathrooms (some rooms have Jacuzzis); nice-size rooms with plenty of storage; helpful staff. **Cons:** no beach access; the neighborhood is less charming than the old town and seaside; outdoor spaces in common areas are a bit closed in due to the location. ⑤ *Rooms from: €400* ✉ *Via Roma 9, Santa Margherita Ligure* ☎ *0185/287139* ⊕ *www.santamargheritapalace.com* ⇌ *57 rooms* ⑩ *Free Breakfast.*

Portofino

5 km (3 miles) southeast of Santa Margherita Ligure, 36 km (22 miles) east of Genoa.

One of the most-photographed villages along the coast, with a decidedly romantic and affluent aura, Portofino has long been a popular destination for the rich and famous. Once an ancient Roman colony and taken by the Republic of Genoa in 1229, it has also been ruled by the French, English, Spanish, and Austrians, as well as by marauding bands of 16th-century pirates. Elite British tourists first flocked to the lush harbor in the mid-1800s. Some of Europe's wealthiest drop anchor in Portofino in summer, but they stay out of sight by day, appearing in the evening after buses and boats have carried off the day-trippers.

There's not actually much to *do* in Portofino other than stroll around the wee harbor, see the castle, walk to Punta del Capo, browse at the pricey boutiques, and sip a coffee while people-watching. However, weaving through picture-perfect cliffside gardens and gazing at yachts framed by the sapphire Ligurian Sea and the cliffs of Santa Margherita can make for quite a relaxing afternoon. There are also several tame, photo-friendly hikes into the hills to nearby villages.

Unless you're traveling on a deluxe budget, you may want to stay in Camogli or Santa Margherita Ligure rather than at one of Portofino's few very expensive hotels. Restaurants and cafés are good but also pricey: don't expect to have a beer here for much under €10.

By car, exit at Rapallo off the A12 and follow the blue signs (about a 20-minute drive mostly along the coast). Trying to reach Portofino by bus or car on the single narrow road can be a nightmare in summer and on holiday weekends.

The nearest train station is Santa Margherita Ligure. No trains go directly to Portofino: you must stop at Santa Margherita, then take public Bus No. 82 from there (€3). Alternatively, you can take a boat from Santa Margherita.

Portofino can be reached from Santa Margherita on foot: it's about a 60-minute walk along the sea, but be aware that many parts of the narrow road have no sidewalk.

VISITOR INFORMATION

CONTACT Portofino Tourism Office. ✉ *Via Roma 35, Portofino* ☎ *0185/269024* ⊕ *www.turismoinliguria.it.*

Sights

Abbazia di San Fruttuoso (*Abbey of San Fruttuoso*)

CHURCH | A medieval stronghold built by the Benedictines of Monte Cassino protects a minuscule fishing village that can be reached only on foot or by water—a 20-minute boat ride from Portofino and also reachable from Camogli, Santa Margherita Ligure, and Rapallo. The restored abbey is now the property of a national conservation fund (FAI) and occasionally hosts temporary exhibitions; it also contains the tombs of some illustrious members of the Doria family. Plan on spending a few hours enjoying the abbey and grounds, and perhaps lunching at one of the modest beachfront trattorias nearby (open only in summer). Boatloads of visitors can make this place very crowded very fast; you might appreciate it most off-season. ✉ *Portofino* ⊕ *15-min boat ride or 2-hr walk northwest of Portofino* ☎ *0185/772703* 💶 *€7.50* ⊗ *Closed Mon. Nov.–Feb.*

Castello Brown

CASTLE/PALACE | From the harbor, follow the signs for the climb to Castello Brown—the most worthwhile sight in Portofino—with its medieval relics, impeccable gardens, and sweeping views, as well as a video room that recounts the village's history. The castle was founded in the Middle Ages but restored in the 16th through 18th centuries. In true Portofino form, it was owned by Genoa's English consul from 1870 until it opened to the public in 1961. ✉ *Above harbor, Via alla Penisola 1, Portofino* ☎ *335/3662120565* ⊕ *www.castellobrown.com* ⊗ *Closed Mon.–Fri. Nov.–mid Mar.* 💶 *€5.*

San Giorgio

CHURCH | This small church, sitting on a ridge above Portofino, is said to contain the relics of its namesake, brought back from the Holy Land by the Crusaders. Portofino enthusiastically celebrates St. George's Day every April 23. ✉ *Above harbor, Salita San Giorgio, Portofino.*

Beaches

Paraggi

BEACH | The only sand beach near Portofino is at Paraggi, a cove on the road between Santa Margherita Ligure and Portofino. The bus will stop here on request. **Amenities:** umbrella and chair rentals, bars and restaurants on the beach. **Best for:** relaxing; snorkeling. ✉ *Via Strada Provinciale, Portofino.*

Punta Portofino

VIEWPOINT | Pristine views can be had from the deteriorating *faro* (lighthouse) at Punta Portofino, a 15-minute walk along the point that begins at the southern end of the port. Along the seaside path you can see numerous impressive, sprawling private residences behind high iron gates. **Amenities:** beautiful view. **Best for:** relaxing. ✉ *Viale Rainusso 1, Portofino.*

🍴 Restaurants

Canale

$ | BAKERY | If the staggering prices at virtually all of Portofino's cafés and restaurants are enough to ruin your appetite, join the long line outside this family-run bakery where you will find affordable and delicious eats worth waiting for. At this takeaway spot, the focaccia is baked on-site and served fresh, along with all kinds of sandwiches and other refreshments. **Known for:** delicious pastries; cash-only takeout; friendly staff. $ *Average main: €10* ✉ *Via Roma 30, Portofino* ☎ *0185/269248* ⊕ *www.panificiocanale.it* ☾ *Closed Wed. and Nov.*

Ristorante Puny

$$$ | LIGURIAN | If you want to be in the middle of everything and dine well, and don't mind spending a small fortune, then you'll want (and need) a reservation at this waterfront restaurant in Portofino. Quite simply, it's *the* place to be seen while dining on baked fish and homemade pasta dishes. **Known for:** dining right on the port; *pappardelle al portofino* (with tomato and pesto sauce); baked mini octopus. $ *Average main: €30* ✉ *Piazza Martiri dell'Olivetta 4–5, on harbor, Portofino* ☎ *0185/269037* ☾ *Closed Thurs.*

🛏 Hotels

Belmond Hotel Splendido

$$$$ | HOTEL | FAMILY | This 1920s luxury hotel oozes charm, taste, and lovely scenery, with a particular attention to color—from the coordinated floral linens in corals and gold in the guest rooms to the fresh flowers in the reception rooms and on the large terrace. **Pros:** rooms have garden or sea views; attentive staff; lovely manicured grounds. **Cons:** location makes it a hike to get to the center of Portofino; pool and other common areas can be noisy because of the kid-friendly atmosphere; be prepared to spend upward of €100 for a simple lunch for two. $ *Rooms from: €1000* ✉ *Salita*

Baratta 16, Portofino ☎ *0185/267801* ⊕ *www.belmond.com/hotel-splendido-portofino* ☾ *Closed Nov.–Mar.* 🛏 *108 rooms* ⦿| *Free Breakfast.*

Eight Hotel Portofino

$$$$ | HOTEL | At this intimate hotel, comfortable and soothingly designed guest rooms—some with canopy beds, pastel walls, and ultramodern bathrooms—are spread across two small 19th-century townhouses on a quiet backstreet. **Pros:** comfortable beds and a choice of pillows; walking distance to the harbor and village; rooftop garden. **Cons:** no sea views; some lower-level rooms don't receive much light; some rooms are small. $ *Rooms from: €830* ✉ *Via Del Fondaco 11, Portofino* ☎ *0185/26991* ⊕ *www. eighthotels.it* ☾ *Closed Nov.–Easter* 🛏 *18 rooms* ⦿| *Free Breakfast.*

🏃 Activities

HIKING

If you have the stamina, you can hike to the Abbazia di San Fruttuoso from Portofino. It's a steep climb at first, and the walk takes about 2½ hours one-way. If you're extremely ambitious and want to make a day of it, you can hike another 2½ hours all the way to Camogli. Much more modest hikes from Portofino include a one-hour uphill walk to Cappella delle Gave, a bit inland in the hills, from where you can continue downhill to Santa Margherita Ligure (another 1½ hours); there is also a gently undulating paved trail leading to the beach at Paraggi (½ hour). Finally, there's a 2½-hour hike from Portofino that heads farther inland to Ruta, through Olmi and Pietre Strette. The trails are well marked, and maps are available at the tourist information offices in Rapallo, Santa Margherita Ligure, Portofino, and Camogli.

Camogli

15 km (9 miles) northwest of Portofino, 20 km (12 miles) southeast of Genoa.

Camogli, at the edge of the large promontory and nature reserve known as the Portofino Peninsula, has always been a town of sailors. By the 19th century it was leasing its ships throughout the continent. Today, multicolor houses, staircases with incredible sea views, and a massive 17th-century seawall mark this appealing harbor community, which is perhaps as beautiful as Portofino but without the glamour. When exploring on foot, don't miss the antiquated second harbor, reached through a narrow archway at the northern end of the first one.

GETTING HERE AND AROUND
By car, exit the A12 at Recco and follow the blue signs. There are several parking lots (fee) near the village center. Camogli is on the main north–south railway line between Genoa and La Spezia.

VISITOR INFORMATION
CONTACT Camogli Tourism Office. ⊠ *Via XX Settembre 33/R, Camogli* ☎ *0185/7771066* ⊕ *www.camogliturismo.it.*

Sights

Ruta
TRAIL | The footpaths that leave from Ruta, 4 km (2½ miles) east of Camogli, thread through rugged terrain and contain a multitude of plant species. Weary hikers are sustained by stunning views of the Riviera di Levante from various vantage points along the way. ⊠ *Camogli.*

San Rocco, San Nicolò, and Punta Chiappa
TOWN | From Camogli, you can reach these hamlets along the western coast of the peninsula either on foot or by boat. They're more natural and less fashionable than those facing south on the eastern coast. In the small Romanesque church at San Nicolò, sailors who survived dangerous voyages came to offer thanks. ⊠ *Camogli.*

Restaurants

Revello
$ | LIGURIAN | You'll know this focacceria and pasticceria by the line out the door, as you walk along the beach before entering the archway to the old port. This tiny spot—where you can see focaccia being baked through a window into its kitchen—specializes in Liguria's favorite bread, farinata (baked late afternoons from October to March) and several flavors of *camogliesi* (rum-filled is the original), a sweet that the shop's owner, Giacomo, invented in 1970. **Known for:** no seating, so take your treats away; Camogliesi sweets; wide variety of focaccia flavors. ⑤ *Average main: €5* ⊠ *Via Giuseppe Garibaldi 183, Camogli* ☎ *0185/770777* ⊕ *www.revello-camogli.com* ⊙ *Closed 10 days in Jan.*

Vento Ariel
$$ | SEAFOOD | This small, friendly restaurant serves some of the best seafood in town on the covered terrace or the indoor patio with wicker chairs, where you can watch the bustling activity in the old port. Only the freshest catches are presented; try the mixed grilled fish or any of the pastas. **Known for:** relaxed atmosphere; outdoor seating with views; spaghetti *alle vongole* (clams). ⑤ *Average main: €20* ⊠ *Calata Porticciolo 1, Camogli* ☎ *0185/771080* ⊕ *www.ventoariel.it* ⊙ *Closed weekdays Nov.–Jan.*

Hotels

Cenobio dei Dogi
$$$ | HOTEL | Perched majestically above Camogli's beaches, the former summer palace of Genoa's doges features many guest rooms with expansive balconies and commanding vistas of the city's port. **Pros:** location and setting are wonderful; private beach; pool and gardens. **Cons:** neighborhood is less charming than the old town; old-fashioned decor; seems overbooked in high season. ⑤ *Rooms from: €270* ⊠ *Via Nicolò Cuneo 34, Camogli* ☎ *0185/7241* ⊷ *100 rooms* ⑩ *Free Breakfast.*

★ Locanda I Tre Merli

$$$ | B&B/INN | In a typical Ligurian terratetto on the old port, this charming *locanda,* or inn, is reminiscent of old-world voyages but with the amenities to make it a comfortable and relaxing stop for today's traveler. **Pros:** friendly staff; small spa with whirlpool tub and Turkish bath; quaint port location and views. **Cons:** can be a bit noisy in the summer months; located right on the port, so you have to park a distance away; narrow corridors. $ *Rooms from: €260* ✉ *Via Scalo 5, Camogli* ☎ *0185/776752* ⊕ *www.locandaitremerli.com* 🛏 *5 rooms* ⅓○⅓ *Free Breakfast.*

Villa Rosmarino

$$$ | B&B/INN | A beautiful Ligurian villa in the Camogli hills offers chic, contemporary, and comfortable accommodations, along with well-manicured gardens and outdoor sitting areas, arbors, and a welcoming pool. **Pros:** friendly staff; modern furnishings; pleasant outdoor pool and garden. **Cons:** the hike uphill is not ideal in summer months; some rooms are small and have minimal storage; parking can be challenging. $ *Rooms from: €270* ✉ *Via Figari 38, Camogli* ☎ *0185/771580* ⊕ *www.villarosmarino.com* ⊗ *Closed Nov.–Feb.* 🛏 *6 rooms* ⅓○⅓ *Free Breakfast.*

Genoa

20 km (12 miles) northwest of Camogli, 144 km (89 miles) south of Milan.

Genoa (Genova in Italian) was the birthplace of Christopher Columbus, but the city's proud history predates the famous explorer by hundreds of years. Genoa was already an important trading station by the 3rd century BC, when the Romans conquered Liguria. The Middle Ages and the Renaissance saw it rise to become a jumping-off place for the Crusaders, a commercial center of tremendous wealth and prestige, and a strategic bone of international contention. A network of fortresses defending the city connected by a wall second only in length to the Great Wall of China was constructed in the hills above, and Genoa's bankers, merchants, and princes adorned the city with palaces, churches, and impressive art collections.

Crammed into a thin crescent of land between sea and mountains, Genoa expanded up rather than out, taking on the form of a multilayer wedding cake, with churches, streets, and entire residential neighborhoods built on others' rooftops. Public elevators and funiculars are as common as buses and trains.

With its impressive palaces and museums, the largest medieval city center in Europe, and an elaborate network of ancient hilltop fortresses, Genoa may be just the dose of culture you're looking for. Europe's biggest boat show, the annual Salone Nautico Internazionale, is held here. Fine restaurants are abundant, and classical dance and music are richly represented. The Teatro Carlo Felice is the local opera venue, and it's where the internationally renowned annual Niccolò Paganini Violin Contest takes place.

GETTING HERE AND AROUND

By car, take the Genoa Ovest exit off the A12 and take the upper bridge (*sopraelevata*) to the second exit, Genova Centro–Piazza Corvetto. Be forewarned: driving in Genoa is harrowing and best avoided whenever possible. If you want to see the city on a day trip, go by train; regular service operates from Genoa's two stations. If you're staying in the city, park in a garage or by valet and travel by foot and taxi throughout your stay.

The best way by far to get around Genoa is on foot, with the occasional assistance of public transportation. Many of the more interesting districts are either entirely closed to traffic, have roads so narrow that no car could fit, or are, even at the best of times, blocked by gridlock. Although it might seem a daunting task, exploring the city is made simple by its geography. The historical center of Genoa occupies a relatively narrow strip of land running between the mountains and the sea. You can easily visit the most important monuments in one or two days. The main bus station in Genoa is at Piazza Principe. Local buses operated by the municipal transport company, AMT, serve the steep valleys that run to one of the towns along the western coast. Tickets may be bought at local bus stations or at newsstands. (You must have a ticket before you board.) This company also operates the funicular railways and the elevators that service the steeper sections of the city.

TRANSPORTATION CONTACTS AMT.
☒ *Palazzo Ducale, Molo* ☎ *010/5582414* ⊕ *www.amt.genova.it.* **Stazione Principe.** ☒ *Piazza del Principe, San Teodoro* ☎ ⊕ *www.trenitalia.com.*

VISITOR INFORMATION
CONTACTS Genoa Tourism Offices. ☒ *Via Garibaldi 12r, Maddalena* ☎ *010/5572903* ⊕ *www.visitgenoa.it.*

 ## Sights

THE MEDIEVAL CORE AND POINTS ABOVE
Castelletto
VIEWPOINT | To reach this charming neighborhood high above the city center, you take one of Genoa's historical municipal elevators that whisk you skyward from Piazza del Portello, at the end of Galleria Garibaldi, for a spectacular view of the old city. ☒ *Piazza del Portello, Castelletto* ☒ *€1.50 for municipal elevator.*

Cimitero Monumentale di Staglieno
CEMETERY | One of the most famous of Genovese landmarks is this bizarrely beautiful cemetery; its fanciful marble and bronze sculptures sprawl haphazardly across a hillside on the outskirts of town. A pantheon holds indoor tombs and some remarkable works like an 1878 *Eve* by Villa. Don't miss Rovelli's

1896 **Tomba Raggio,** which shoots Gothic spires out of the hillside forest. The cemetery began operation in 1851 and has been lauded by such visitors as Mark Twain and Evelyn Waugh. It covers a good deal of ground (allow at least half a day to explore). Take Bus Nos. 13 or 14 from the Stazione Genova Brignole, Bus No. 34 from Stazione Principe, or a taxi. ☒ *Piazzale Resasco 2, Piazza Manin* ☎ *010/5576400* ⊕ *www.staglieno. comune.genova.it* ☒ *Free.*

Ferrovia Genova–Casella
TRAIN/TRAIN STATION | **FAMILY** | The Genova–Casella Railroad is a good way to get a sense of the rugged landscape around Genoa; the train departs about every hour. In operation since 1929, it runs from Piazza Manin in Genoa (follow Via Montaldo from the center of town, or take Bus No. 34 or 36 to the piazza) through the beautiful countryside above the city, arriving in the rural hill town Casella. The tiny train traverses precarious switchbacks that afford sweeping views of the Ligurian hills. In **Casella Paese** (the last stop) you can hike, eat lunch, or check out the view and ride back. **Canova** (two stops from the end of the line) is the start of two possible hikes: a two-hour (one-way) trek to a small sanctuary, **Santuario della Vittoria,** and a grueling four-hour hike to the hill town of **Creto.** Another worthwhile stop is **Sant'Olcese Tullo,** where you can take a half-hour (one-way) walk through the **Sentiero Botanico di Ciaé,** a botanical garden and forest refuge with a tiny medieval castle. ☒ *Piazza Manin* ☎ *010/5582414* ⊕ *www.ferroviagenova-casella.it* ☒ *€4 one way.*

Galleria Nazionale di Palazzo Spinola
ART MUSEUM | Housed in the richly adorned Palazzo Spinola north of Piazza Soziglia, this beautiful museum contains masterpieces by Luca Giordano and Guido Reni. The *Ecce Homo,* by Antonello da Messina (1430–79), is a hauntingly beautiful painting, of historical interest

0   300 Meters

0   300 yards

Sights ▼

1 Acquario di Genova E5
2 Castelletto H4
3 Childhood Home of Christopher
   Columbus I7
4 Cimitero Monumentale di
   Staglieno J5
5 Consorzio Liguria Viamare B3
6 Ferrovia Genova-Casella J5
7 Galata Museo del Mare C3
8 Galleria Nazionale di Palazzo
   Spinola F5
9 Granarolo Funicular A1
10 The Harbor E6
11 Il Bigo E6
12 Loggia dei Mercanti F5
13 Mercato Orientale J7
14 Museo d'Arte Orientale
   Chiossone I4
15 Museo dell'Accademia Ligustica
   di Belle Arti H6
16 Palazzo Bianco G4
17 Palazzo dell'Università E2
18 Palazzo Ducale H6
19 Palazzo Reale D2
20 Palazzo Tursi G4
21 Porta Soprana H7
22 San Donato G7
23 San Lorenzo G6
24 San Matteo H6
25 San Siro G4
26 Sant'Agostino G8
27 Santa Maria di Castello F7
28 Santissima Annunziata
   del Vastato F3
29 Zecca-Righi funicular G3

Restaurants ▼

1 Da Gaia F3
2 I Cuochi H6
3 Il Genovese J7
4 Trattoria Ugo G7

Quick Bites ▼

1 I Canovacci H5
2 Spin Ristorante-Enoteca J9

Hotels ▼

1 Best Western Hotel Metropoli I5
2 Best Western Plus City Hotel I5
3 Grand Hotel Savoia C1
4 Hotel Bristol Palace I7
5 Hotel Palazzo Grillo G5
6 Melià Genova J9

because it was the Sicilian Antonello who first brought Flemish oil paints and techniques to Italy from his sojourns in the Low Countries. ⊠ *Piazza Pellicceria 1, Maddalena* ☎ *010/2705300* ⊕ *www.palazzospinola.beniculturali.it* 🔳 *€4* ⊗ *Closed Sun.–Tue.*

Granarolo Funicular

OTHER ATTRACTION | FAMILY | Take a cog railway up the steeply rising terrain to another part of the city's fortified walls. It takes 15 minutes to hoist you from Stazione Principe to **Porta Granarolo,** 1,000 feet above, where the sweeping view gives you a sense of Genoa's size. The funicular departs about every 40 minutes. ⊠ *Piazza del Principe, San Teodoro* ☎ *010/5582414* ⊕ *www.amt.genova.it* 🔳 *€.90.*

Loggia dei Mercanti

MARKET | This merchants' row dating from the 16th century is lined with shops selling local foods and gifts, as well as flowers and vintage books and records. ⊠ *Piazza Banchi, Maddalena.*

Museo d'Arte Orientale Chiossone

ART MUSEUM | One of Europe's most noteworthy collections of Japanese, Chinese, and Thai objects is housed in galleries in the Villetta di Negro park on the hillside above Piazza Portello. There's also a fine view of the city from the museum's terrace. ⊠ *Piazzale Mazzini 4, Maddalena* ☎ *010/542285* ⊕ *www.museidigenova.it/it/content/museo-darte-orientale* 🔳 *€5* ⊗ *Closed Mon.*

Palazzo Bianco

CASTLE/PALACE | It's difficult to miss the splendid white facade of this town palace and museum as you walk down Via Garibaldi (also known as Strada Nuova), one of Genoa's most important streets. The building houses a fine collection of 16th- and 17th-century art, with the Spanish and Flemish schools well represented. There's also a textiles collection. ⊠ *Via Garibaldi 11, Maddalena* ☎ *010/5572193* ⊕ *www.museidigenova.it* 🔳 *€9, includes*

Palazzo Rosso and Palazzo Doria Tursi ⊗ *Closed Mon.–Wed.*

Palazzo dell'Università

COLLEGE | Built in the 1630s as a Jesuit college, this has been Genoa's university since 1803. The exterior is unassuming, but climb the stairway flanked by lions to visit the handsome courtyard, with its portico of double Doric columns. ⊠ *Via Balbi 5, Pré* ☎ *010/20991* ⊕ *www.unige.it.*

Palazzo Tursi

GOVERNMENT BUILDING | In the 16th century, wealthy resident Nicolò Grimaldi had a palace built of pink stone quarried in the region, and today it has been reincarnated as Genoa's Palazzo Municipale (Municipal Building). Most of the goings-on inside are the stuff of local politics and quickie weddings, but you can visit the richly decorated **Sala Paganini,** where the famous Guarnerius violin that belonged to Niccolò Paganini (1782–1840) is typically displayed, and the gardens that connect the palace with the neighboring Palazzo Bianco. There is also a collection of five centuries worth of coins, as well as ceramics that were used in homes and pharmacies. ⊠ *Via Garibaldi 9, Maddalena* ☎ *010/2759185* ⊕ *www.museidigenova.it* 🔳 *€9, includes Palazzo Bianco and Palazzo Rosso* ⊗ *Closed Mon.–Wed.*

★ Palazzo Reale

CASTLE/PALACE | Lavish rococo rooms provide sumptuous display space for paintings, sculptures, tapestries, and Asian ceramics. The 17th-century palace—also known as Palazzo Balbi Durazzo—was built by the Balbi family, enormously wealthy Genovese merchants. Its regal pretensions were not lost on the Savoy, who bought the palace and turned it into a royal residence in the early 19th century. The gallery of mirrors and the ballroom on the upper floor are particularly decadent. ■TIP➔ **The formal gardens provide a welcome respite from the bustle of the city, as well as great views of the harbor.** ⊠ *Via Balbi 10, Pré* ☎ *010/2710236*

⊕ *www.palazzorealegenova.beniculturali.
it* 🎫 €4 ⊘ *Closed Sun.–Tues.*

San Siro

CHURCH | Genoa's oldest church was a Benedictine monastery and the city's cathedral from the 4th to the 9th century. It was rebuilt in the 16th and 17th centuries, and you can see excellent examples of Caravaggism—works reflecting the style of Caravaggio (1571–1610)—in the frescoes that decorate its chapels. ✉ *Via San Siro 3, Maddalena* ☎ *010/2461674.*

Santissima Annunziata del Vastato

CHURCH | Exuberantly frescoed vaults decorate the 16th- to 17th-century church, which is an excellent example of Genovese Baroque architecture. ✉ *Piazza della Nunziata, Pré* ☎ *010/2465525.*

Zecca-Righi Funicular

OTHER ATTRACTION | A seven-stop commuter funicular begins at Piazza della Nunziata and ends at a high lookout on the fortified gates in the 17th-century city walls. Ringed around the circumference of the city are a number of huge fortresses; this gate was part of the city's system of defenses. From Righi you can undertake scenic all-day hikes from one fortress to the next. ✉ *Piazza della Nunziata, Pré* ☎ *010/5582414* ⊕ *www.amt.genova.it* 🎫 *€.90.*

SOUTHERN DISTRICTS AND THE AQUARIUM

Inhabited since the 6th century BC, the oldest section of Genoa lies on a hill to the southwest of the Caruggi District. Today, apart from a section of 9th-century wall near Porta Soprana, there's little to show that an imposing castle once stood here. Though the neighborhood is quite run-down, some of Genoa's oldest churches make it a worthwhile excursion. Heading down the hill, you can stroll along the harbor. Once squalid and unsafe, the port was given a complete overhaul during Genoa's preparations for the Columbus quincentennial celebrations of 1992, and additional restorations in 2003 and 2004 have done much to revitalize the waterfront. You can easily reach the port on foot by following Via San Lorenzo downhill from Genoa's cathedral, Via delle Fontane from Piazza della Nunziata, or any of the narrow vicoli that lead down from Via Balbi and Via Pré.

Acquario di Genova

OTHER ATTRACTION | **FAMILY** | Europe's biggest aquarium is the third-most-visited museum in Italy and a must for children. Fifty tanks of marine species, including sea turtles, dolphins, seals, eels, penguins, jellyfish, and sharks, share space with educational displays, touch pools, and re-creations of marine ecosystems, among them a tank of coral from the Indian Ocean, and a wall that replicates a forest in Madagascar. The Aquarium Village complex (additional cost) includes two biospheres with tropical plants and birds, as well as a virtual reality room. If arriving by car, take the Genova Ovest exit from the autostrada. ✉ *Ponte Spinola, Porto Vecchio* ☎ *010/2345678* ⊕ *www.acquariodigenova.it* 🎫 *€18–€29.*

Childhood Home of Christopher Columbus

HISTORIC HOME | The ivy-covered remains of this fabled medieval house—just a very small portion of it—stand in the gardens below the Porta Soprana. A small collection of objects and reproductions relating to the life and travels of Columbus are on display inside. ✉ *Piazza Dante, Molo* ☎ *010/4490128* ⊕ *www.coopculture.it* 🎫 *€5* ⊘ *Closed Sat.–Wed.*

Consorzio Liguria Viamare

OTHER ATTRACTION | Boat tours of the harbor, operated by the Consorzio Liguria Viamare, launch from the aquarium pier and last about an hour. The tours include a visit to the breakwater outside the harbor, the Bacino delle Grazie, and the Molo Vecchio (Old Port). There are also daily excursions down the coast as far as the Cinque Terre and Portovenere. ✉ *via Marina d'Italia, Porto Vecchio* ☎ *010/256775* ⊕ *www.liguriaviamare.it* 🎫 *€8.*

Galata Museo del Mare

OTHER MUSEUM | FAMILY | Devoted to the city's seafaring history, this museum is probably the best way, at least on dry land, to get an idea of the changing shape of Genoa's busy port. Highlighting the displays is a full-size replica of a 17th-century Genovese galleon. ⊠ *Calata de Mari 1, Ponte dei Mille* ☎ *010/2345655* ⊕ *www.galatamuseodelmare.it* ⊘ *Closed Mon.–Wed.* ⊠ *€13.*

The Harbor

OTHER ATTRACTION | A boat tour (with Consorzio Liguria Viamare, for example) gives you a good perspective on the layout of the harbor, which dates to Roman times. The Genoa inlet, the largest along the Italian Riviera, was also used by the Phoenicians and Greeks as a harbor and a staging area from which they could penetrate inland to form settlements and to trade. The port is guarded by the Diga Foranea, a striking 5-km-long (3-mile-long) wall built into the ocean. The **Lanterna,** a lighthouse more than 360 feet tall, was built in 1544; it's one of Italy's oldest lighthouses and a traditional emblem of Genoa. ⊠ *Porto Vecchio.*

Il Bigo

VIEWPOINT | FAMILY | Designed by world-renowned architect Renzo Piano, this spiderlike white structure was erected in 1992 to celebrate the Columbus quincentenary. You can take its **Ascensore Panoramico Bigo** (Bigo Panoramic Elevator) up 650 feet for a 360-degree view of the harbor, city, and sea. In winter there's an ice-skating rink next to the elevator, in an area covered by sail-like awnings. Check the website for seasonal opening hours. ⊠ *Ponte Spinola, Porto Vecchio* ☎ *010/23451* ⊕ *www.acquariodigenova.it/ bigo-panoramic* ⊠ *Elevator €4.40* ⊘ *See website for seasonal hrs.*

Mercato Orientale

MARKET | A bustling place, this produce, fish, and meat market in a former church cloister has added a second-floor bar, restaurant, and cooking school. Experience the sensory overload of colorful everyday Genovese life while watching the merchants and buyers banter over prices on the ground floor, and then head upstairs for a drink, a cooking lesson, or to try authentic Ligurian cuisine. ⊠ *Via XX Settembre, Portoria* ⊕ *www.moggenova. it* ⊘ *Closed Sun.*

Museo dell'Accademia Ligustica di Belle Arti

ART MUSEUM | Founded in 1751, the city's art school has a museum with a collection of paintings from the 16th to the 19th century. Genovese artists of the Baroque period are particularly well represented. ⊠ *Largo Pertini 4, Portoria* ☎ *010/506131* ⊕ *www.museo.accademialigustica.it* ⊠ *€5* ⊘ *Closed Sun. and Mon.*

Palazzo Ducale

ART GALLERY | This palace was built in the 16th century over a medieval hall, and its facade was rebuilt in the late 18th century and later restored. It now houses temporary exhibitions and a restaurant-bar serving fusion cuisine. Reservations are recommended to visit the dungeons and tower. Guided tours of the palace, its prison tower, and its exhibitions are available. ⊠ *Piazza Matteotti 9, Portoria* ☎ *010/8171600* ⊕ *www.palazzoducale. genova.it* ⊠ *€8 – €12* ⊘ *Closed Mon.*

Porta Soprana

NOTABLE BUILDING | A striking 12th-century twin-tower structure, this medieval gateway stands on the spot where a road from ancient Rome entered the city. It is just steps uphill from Columbus's boyhood home. ⊠ *Piazza Dante, Molo.*

San Donato

CHURCH | Although somewhat marred by 19th- and 20th-century restorations, the 12th-century San Donato, with its original portal and octagonal campanile, is a fine example of Genovese Romanesque architecture. Inside, an altarpiece by the Flemish artist Joos van Cleve (circa 1485–1540) depicts the Adoration of the Magi. ✉ *Piazza San Donato, Portoria* ☎ *010/2468869* ⊕ *www.sandonato.org.*

San Lorenzo

ART MUSEUM | Contrasting black slate and white marble, so common in Liguria, embellishes the cathedral at the heart of medieval Genoa, inside and out. Consecrated in 1118, the church honors St. Lawrence, who passed through the city on his way to Rome in the 3rd century. For hundreds of years the building was used for state purposes, such as civic elections, as well as religious. Note the 13th-century Gothic portal, the fascinating twisted barbershop columns, and the 15th- to 17th-century frescoes inside. The last campanile dates from the early 16th century. The Museo del Tesoro di San Lorenzo (San Lorenzo Treasury Museum) inside has some stunning pieces from medieval goldsmiths and silversmiths, work for which medieval Genoa was renowned. ✉ *Piazza San Lorenzo, Molo* ☎ *010/2091863* ⊕ *www.museidigenova.it* 🎟 *Cathedral free, museum €6.*

San Matteo

CHURCH | This typically Genovese black-and-white-striped church dates from the 12th century; its crypt contains the tomb of Andrea Doria (1466–1560), the Genovese admiral who maintained the independence of his native city. The well-preserved Piazza San Matteo was, for 500 years, the seat of the Doria family, which ruled Genoa and much of Liguria from the 16th to the 18th century. The square is bounded by 13th- to 15th-century houses decorated with portals and loggias. ✉ *Piazza San Matteo, Maddalena* ☎ *010/2474361.*

Sant'Agostino

ART MUSEUM | This 13th-century Gothic church was damaged during World War II, but it still has a fine campanile with a Moorish inlaid marble design, and two well-preserved cloisters (one of which is the only triangular cloister in Europe) that house a museum displaying pieces of medieval architecture, sculptures, and frescoes. Highlights of the collection are the enigmatic fragments of a tomb sculpture by Giovanni Pisano (circa 1250–1315). ✉ *Piazza Sarzano 35/R, Molo* ☎ *010/2511263* ⊕ *www.museidigenova. it/it/content/museo-di-santagostino* 🎟 *€5* ☉ *Closed Mon.*

Santa Maria di Castello

ART MUSEUM | One of Genoa's most significant religious buildings, an early-Christian church, was rebuilt in the 12th century and finally completed in 1513. You can visit the adjacent cloisters and see the fine artwork in the museum. Hours vary during religious services. ✉ *Salita di Santa Maria di Castello 15, Molo* ☎ *347/9956740* ⊕ *www.santamariadicastello.it* 🎟 *Free.*

🍽 Restaurants

Da Gaia

$ | LIGURIAN | For a truly Genovese experience, this unassuming restaurant, located in the basement of an old palazzo in the heart of the centro storico between Strada Nuova and the port, is just the place. You'll find some of the best, most authentic food in the city, with a focus on fish, meat dishes, and, of course, pesto. **Known for:** Genovese dishes; cozy, old-world atmosphere; stuffed anchovies. 💲 *Average main: €14* ✉ *Vico dell'Argento, Maddalena* ☎ *010/2461629* ☉ *Closed 2d week of Jan. and last week in Aug. No dinner Sun.*

I Cuochi

$$ | LIGURIAN | This cozy bistro-style restaurant is popular with locals and visitors alike for its refined, almost elegant menu of primarily seafood dishes, with a few pastas and meats. The decor is art nouveau with exposed brick walls, round tables with candles, and white tablecloths. **Known for:** contemporary Ligurian dishes; artistically presented seafood and desserts; romantic setting. 💲 *Average main: €18* ✉ *Vico del Fieno 18r, Maddalena* ☎ *010/2476170* ☉ *Closed Sun.*

The Art of the Pesto Pestle

You may have known Genoa primarily for its salami or its brash explorer, but the city's most direct effect on your life away from Italy may be through its cultivation of one of the world's best pasta sauces. The sublime blend of basil, extra-virgin olive oil, garlic, pine nuts, and grated pecorino and Parmigiano-Reggiano cheeses that forms *pesto alla Genovese* is one of Italy's crowning culinary achievements, a concoction that the late Italian food guru Marcella Hazan called "the most seductive of all sauces for pasta." Ligurian pesto is served only over spaghetti, gnocchi, lasagna, or—most authentically—*trenette* (a flat, spaghetti-like pasta) or *trofie*

(short, doughy pasta twists), typically mixed with boiled potatoes and green beans. Pesto is also occasionally used to flavor minestrone.

The small-leaf basil grown in the region's sunny seaside hills is considered by many to be the best in the world, and pesto sauce was invented primarily as a showcase for that singular flavor. The simplicity and rawness of pesto is one of its virtues, as cooking (or even heating) basil ruins its delicate flavor. In fact, pesto aficionados refuse even to subject the basil leaves to an electric blender; Genovese (and other) foodies insist that true pesto can be made only with mortar and pestle.

Il Genovese

$ | **LIGURIAN** | At this bright and friendly trattoria with a maritime theme, you can dine on some of the city's best pesto and Ligurian dishes in a casual, comfortable setting. The staff are knowledgeable about the region's specialties and the wines on the always interesting menu, and even if you don't order a pesto dish, they'll bring you some to sample before your meal. **Known for:** good value for the price; award-winning pesto; local atmosphere near Brignole station. ⑤ *Average main: €12* ✉ *Via Galata 35r, Brignole* ☎ *010/3478009701* ⊕ *www.ilgenovese. com* ⊙ *Closed Sun.*

Trattoria Ugo

$ | **LIGURIAN** | Wood paneling, lanterns hanging from the ceiling, and communal tables, as well as delicious dishes, add to the old-world Genovese charm of this unassuming trattoria. It's particularly popular at lunchtime for the small menu that changes daily and includes homemade pastas, a variety of fresh seafood offerings, and perfectly baked

desserts. **Known for:** excellent octopus dishes and pesto; affordable prices; local, friendly atmosphere. ⑤ *Average main: €12* ✉ *Via dei Gustiniani 86/r, Maddalena* ☎ *010/2469302* ⊙ *Closed Sun. and Mon.*

☕ Coffee and Quick Bites

I Canovacci

$ | **ITALIAN** | There's a steady crowd of regulars at this modern and homey lunch spot and dry goods store on a typical vicolo. The reasonably priced, good-value daily menu follows the seasons, with generous portions of fish and pasta, sandwiches, vegetables, and homemade desserts. **Known for:** vegetarian options; seasonal ingredients, some of which are also sold in its grocery store; efficient and friendly staff. ⑤ *Average main: €10* ✉ *Via dei Macelli di Soziglia 60, Maddalena* ☎ *010/0985417* ⊙ *Closed Sun. No dinner.*

Spin Ristorante-Enoteca

$$ | **LIGURIAN** | Dishes are created specifically to complement wines at this casually elegant enoteca with dark wood

tables and bottle-lined walls in the heart of the modern town. The Ligurian menu varies daily, but the real draw is the vast wine list, including biodynamic selections. **Known for:** Ligurian seafood dishes; wines take precedence; elegant setting in an otherwise brash part of town. ⑤ *Average main: €15* ✉ *Via C. Barabino 120/R, Foce* ☎ *010/594513* ⊕ *www.spinristorante-enoteca.com.*

 ## Hotels

Best Western Hotel Metropoli

$ | HOTEL | FAMILY | A classic Genovese building tucked away on a side street, with the original staircase from the 1900s, is home to a welcoming inn on the border of the historic district and Via Garibaldi. **Pros:** generous breakfast and snacks and coffee served in the afternoon; most rooms and bathrooms are large; great room layouts for families. **Cons:** breakfast can often cost extra; rooms facing the piazza can be noisy; parking is off-site. ⑤ *Rooms from: €73* ✉ *Piazza Fontane Marose, Portoria* ☎ *010/2468888* ⊕ *www.hotelmetropoli.it* ➯ *48 rooms* ⑪ *Free Breakfast.*

Best Western Plus City Hotel

$ | HOTEL | At this good-value chain offering in the heart of the city, an ordinary apartment-building exterior gives way to a polished lobby and modern rooms, some with spectacular views. **Pros:** great views from the top floor suites; gym and spa; convenient location near shopping. **Cons:** dark decor in some rooms; regular rooms are small; lower-level windows open directly onto neighboring buildings. ⑤ *Rooms from: €110* ✉ *Via San Sebastiano 6, Portoria* ☎ *010/584707* ⊕ *www.bwcityhotel-ge.it* ➯ *65 rooms* ⑪ *No Meals.*

★ Grand Hotel Savoia

$ | HOTEL | As you enter this 1890s-vintage hotel above Piazza Acquaverde, you'll be transported from the modern city to a more glamorous era, thanks to

details such as the original marble floors and lush gilt and richly colored velvet furniture in common areas. **Pros:** convenient location near Stazione Principe; comfortable rooms with luxury amenities; rooftop restaurant and bar. **Cons:** breakfast not included in all rates; rooms on lower floors face next-door buildings; Principe station area not the best in the city. ⑤ *Rooms from: €119* ✉ *Via Arsenale di Terra 5, Genoa* ☎ *010/27721* ⊕ *www.grandhotelsavoiagenova.it* ➯ *117 rooms* ⑪ *No Meals.*

Hotel Bristol Palace

$$ | HOTEL | One of Europe's gracious 19th-century grand hotels, the Bristol Palace guards its reputation for courtesy, service, and elegance, offering mostly spacious, handsomely furnished, high-ceilinged guest rooms and lovely public spaces. **Pros:** beautiful period details in some rooms; outdoor terrace is lovely in summer months; in the heart of the shopping district. **Cons:** parking is a bit expensive; on a busy street that can be noisy; some standard rooms are small. ⑤ *Rooms from: €144* ✉ *Via XX Settembre 35, Portoria* ☎ *010/592541* ⊕ *www.hotelbristolpalace.com* ➯ *133 rooms* ⑪ *Free Breakfast.*

Hotel Palazzo Grillo

$ | HOTEL | Formerly the Grillo family palace, this sumptuously comfortable boutique hotel integrates architectural details from the 1500s to the 1700s—like an original marble entryway and staircase, frescoed ceilings, and frieze details in some rooms—with clean-lined modern luxury. **Pros:** terrace with cathedral views; comfortable rooms with large bathrooms and high-end mattresses; modern furnishings and attention to aesthetic details. **Cons:** breakfast costs a lot extra; location on piazza and next to a church can be a bit noisy; parking can be difficult in the old town. ⑤ *Rooms from: €123* ✉ *Piazza delle Vigne 4, Maddalena* ☎ *010/2477356* ⊕ *www.hotelpalazzogrillo.it* ➯ *25 rooms* ⑪ *No Meals.*

Melià Genova

$$ | **HOTEL** | Modern, bright, and sleekly decorated guest rooms and the on-site gourmet restaurant add allure to this five-star chain hotel in the modern part of the city. **Pros:** top-of-the-line contemporary style and amenities at a good price for the area; 24-hr gym; spa with a heated pool. **Cons:** bit of a walk to the port and centro; hotel parking is expensive; street noise can be heard from some rooms. ⑤ *Rooms from: €196* ⊠ *Via Corsica 4, Carignano* ☎ *010/5315111* ⊕ *www.melia-hotels.com* ⮢ *99 rooms* ⏐◉⏐ *Free Breakfast.*

 Performing Arts

Teatro Carlo Felice

OPERA | The World War II–ravaged opera house in Genoa's modern center, Piazza de Ferrari, was rebuilt and reopened in 1991 to host the fine Genovese opera company; its massive tower has been the subject of much criticism. Lavish productions of old favorites and occasional world premieres are staged from October to May. ⊠ *Piazza de Ferrari, Passo Eugenio Montale 4, Portoria* ☎ *010/5381* ⊕ *www.carlofelicegenova.it.*

 Shopping

Liguria is famous for fine lace, silver-and-gold filigree work, and ceramics. Also look for bargains in velvet, macramé, olivewood, and marble. Genoa is the best spot to find all these specialties. In the heart of the medieval quarter, Via Soziglia is lined with shops selling handicrafts and tempting foods. Via XX Settembre and Via Roma are famous for their exclusive shops. High-end shops line Via Luccoli. The best shopping area for trendy-but-inexpensive Italian clothing is near San Siro, on Via San Luca.

CLOTHING AND LEATHER GOODS

Pescetto

MIXED CLOTHING | Look for designer clothes, perfumes, and fancy gifts like high-end soaps and silk scarves at Pescetto. ⊠ *Via Scurreria 8, Molo* ☎ *010/2473433* ⊕ *www.pescetto.it.*

JEWELRY

Codevilla

JEWELRY & WATCHES | Established in 1830, Codevilla is known as one of the best jewelers in the city. They sell top-of-the-line watches and custom jewelry. ⊠ *Via Roma 83/85r, Maddalena* ☎ *010/8938278* ⊕ *www.luigicodevilla.it/codevilla.*

WINES

Vinoteca Sola

WINE/SPIRITS | The owner of this shop specializes in discovering the best wines from across Italy. During the fall you can taste the latest wines, and all year you can purchase your favorites and have them shipped home. You can even buy futures for vintages to come. ⊠ *Piazza Colombo 13–15/R, near Stazione Brignole, Brignole* ☎ *010/561329* ⊕ *www.vinotecasola.it.*

Nervi: Side Trip from Genoa

11 km (7 miles) east of Genoa.

The identity of this stately late-19th-century resort, famous for its 1½-km-long (1-mile-long) seaside **Passeggiata Anita Garibaldi,** its palm-lined roads, and its 300 acres of parks rich in orange trees, is given away only by the sign on the sleepy train station. Although Nervi is technically part of Genoa, its peace and quiet are as different from the city's hustle and bustle as its clear blue water is from the crowded port. From the centrally located train station, walk east along the seaside promenade to reach the beaches, a cliff-side restaurant, and the 2,000 varieties of rose in the public **Parco Villa Grimaldi,** all the while enjoying one of the most

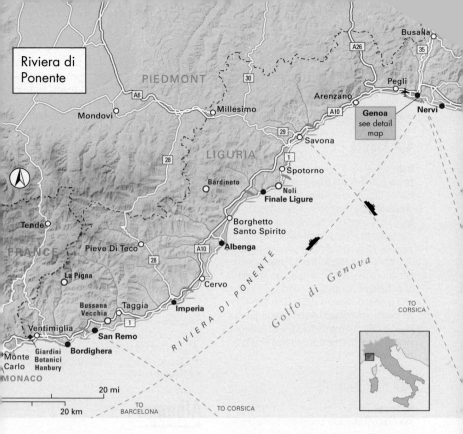

Riviera di Ponente

PIEDMONT

LIGURIA

Riviera di Ponente

Golfo di Genova

breathtaking views on the Riviera. Nervi and the road between it and Genoa are known for their nightlife in summer.

GETTING HERE

By car, exit the A12 at Genova Nervi and follow the "Centro" signs. The Nervi train station is on the main north–south line, and you can also take the commuter trains from Genova Principe and Brignole. Nervi can also be reached on Bus No. 15 from Genoa's Piazza Cavour.

Finale Ligure

72 km (44 miles) southwest of Genoa.

Lovely Finale Ligure is actually made up of three small villages—Finalmarina, Finalpia, and Finalborgo—and makes a wonderful base for exploring the Riviera di Ponente. The former two have fine

sandy beaches and a mix of traditional and modern resort amenities. Finalborgo, less than 1 km (½ mile) inland, is an attractive medieval walled village with nice shops and restaurants. Just above is a hauntingly well-preserved medieval settlement, planned to a rigid blueprint, with 15th-century walls. The surrounding countryside is pierced by deep, narrow valleys and caves; the limestone outcroppings provide the warm pinkish stone found in many buildings in Genoa. Rare reptiles lurk among the exotic flora.

GETTING HERE AND AROUND

By car, take the Finale Ligure exit off the A10 and follow the "Centro" signs. Finale Ligure is on the main train line between Genoa and France.

CONTACT Finale Ligure Tourism Office.
✉ *Via San Pietro 14, Finale Ligure*
☎ *019/681019* ⊕ *turismo.comunefinaleligure.it.*

Sights

Noli

TOWN | Just 9 km (5½ miles) northeast of Finale Ligure, the ruins of a castle loom benevolently over Noli, a tiny medieval gem. It's hard to imagine that this charming seaside village was—like Genoa, Venice, Pisa, and Amalfi—a prosperous maritime republic in the Middle Ages. Let yourself get lost among its labyrinth of cobblestone streets filled with shops and cafés or enjoy a day in the sun on its lovely stretch of beach. If you don't have a car, get a bus for Noli at Spotorno, where local trains stop. ✉ *Noli* ⊕ *www.tpllinea.it.*

Restaurants

Ai Torchi

$$$ | **LIGURIAN** | You could easily become a homemade-pesto snob at this restored 5th-century olive oil mill–turned–chic restaurant in the historical center of Finalborgo. The high prices are justified by excellent seafood and meat dishes as well as the lovely setting. **Known for:** traditional Ligurian cuisine with a contemporary twist; airy and modern dining area; delicious fresh fish and vegetables. ⑤ *Average main: €25* ✉ *Via dell'Annunziata 12, Finale Ligure* ☎ *019/690531* ⊕ *www.ristoranteaitorchi.com* ⊗ *Closed Tues. and Jan. 10–Feb. 10.*

🛏 Hotels

Ca de' Tobia

$ | **B&B/INN** | This lovely little guesthouse on the seafront promenade of Noli is stylishly done with wood floors, splashes of bright colors, and modern decor. **Pros:** great breakfast and aperitivo; easy beach access; modern furniture and bathrooms. **Cons:** street noise; a bit more expensive than comparable hotels in town; parking can be a challenge. ⑤ *Rooms from: €100* ✉ *Via Aurelia 35, Noli* ☎ *019/7485845* ⊕ *www.cadetobia.it* ➯ *6 rooms* ⑩ *Free Breakfast.*

Punta Est

$$ | **HOTEL** | **FAMILY** | The grand former home of a musician and composer, this 18th-century villa perched on a fragrant hillside above white-sand beaches has since had a wing added, creating a wonderful retreat from the crowds at the water's edge. **Pros:** relaxing pool and gardens; dining on the terrace with views; close to the beach. **Cons:** parking can be a challenge; some rooms are a bit outdated; some noisy rooms because of their proximity to the terrace. ⑤ *Rooms from: €200* ✉ *Via Aurelia 1, Finale Ligure* ☎ *39/019600611* ⊕ *www.puntaest.com* ⊗ *Closed mid-Oct.–mid-Apr.* ➯ *36 rooms* ⑩ *Free Breakfast.*

Albenga

20 km (12 miles) southwest of Finale Ligure, 90 km (55 miles) southwest of Genoa.

Albenga has a medieval core, with narrow streets laid out by the ancient Romans. A network of alleys is punctuated by centuries-old towers surrounding the 12th-century Romanesque cathedral, along with a late-14th-century campanile and a baptistery dating to the 5th century. It's a nice place to take an afternoon stroll and explore the many quaint shops and cafés.

GETTING HERE AND AROUND

By car, take the Albenga exit off the A10 and follow the "Centro" signs. Albenga is on the main train line between Genoa and France.

VISITOR INFORMATION
CONTACT Albenga Tourism Office. ✉ *Piazza San Michele 17, Albenga* ☎ *0182/5621* ⊕ *www.comune.albenga.sv.it.*

Sights

Bardineto

TOWN | For a look at some of the Riviera's mountain scenery, make an excursion by car to this attractive village in the middle of an area rich in mushrooms, chestnuts, a wide variety of potatoes, and blueberries, as well as local cheeses. A ruined castle stands above the village. From Borghetto Santo Spirito (between Albenga and Finale Ligure), drive inland 25 km (15 miles). ✉ *Piazza della Chiesa 6, Bardineto* ⊕ *www.comune.bardineto.sv.it.*

Imperia

34 km (21 miles) southwest of Albenga, 116 km (71 miles) southwest of Genoa.

Imperia actually consists of two towns: Porto Maurizio, a medieval town built on a promontory, and Oneglia, now an industrial center for oil refining and pharmaceuticals. Porto Maurizio has a virtually intact medieval center, an intricate spiral of narrow streets and stone portals, and some imposing 17th- and 18th-century palaces. There's little of interest in modern Oneglia, except the olive oil museum.

GETTING HERE AND AROUND

By car, take the Imperia Est exit off the A10 and follow the signs for "Centro" or "Porto Maurizio." Both Imperia and Porto Maurizio are on the main rail line between Genoa and France.

VISITOR INFORMATION
Imperia Tourism Office. ✉ *Largo San Francesco, Imperia* ☎ *0183/701609* ⊕ *iatimperia.business.site.*

Sights

Museo dell'Olivo

OTHER MUSEUM | Imperia is king when it comes to olive oil, and the story of the olive is the theme of this small museum. Displays of the history of the olive tree, farm implements, presses, and utensils show how olive oil has been made in many countries throughout history. A multilingual audio guide is also available. ✉ *Via Garessio 13, Imperia* ☎ *0183/295762* ⊕ *www.museodellolivo.com* ⊙ *Closed Sun.* 🎟 *€5.*

Hotels

Relais San Damian

$$ | **B&B/INN** | At this charming all-suites inn, set among olive trees high above Porto Maurizio and the Mediterranean Sea, the proprietors are more than happy to assist you in planning your days in the area. **Pros:** free parking; large suites and plenty of outdoor space, including infinity pool; garden or sea views from all suites. **Cons:** difficult to reach without a car; limited amenities (no TVs or phones); decor in some suites could be updated. 💲 *Rooms from: €190* ✉ *Strada Vasia 47, Imperia* ☎ *0183/280309* ⊕ *www.san-damian.com* 🛏 *10 suites* ¹⊙¹ *Free Breakfast* ⊙ *Closed Nov.–Easter.*

San Remo

*36 km (22 miles) southwest of Imperia,
146 km (90 miles) southwest of Genoa.*

Once the crown jewel of the Riviera di
Ponente, San Remo is still the area's
largest resort, lined with polished hotels,
exotic gardens, and seaside promenades.
Renowned for its VIP crowd, glittering casino, annual music festival, and
romantic setting, San Remo maintains
remnants of its glamorous past from the
late 19th century to World War II, but it
also suffers from the same epidemic of
overbuilding that has changed so much
of the Ponente for the worse. Still, it
continues to be a lively town, even in the
off-season.

The Mercato dei Fiori, Italy's most
important wholesale flower market, is
held here in a market hall between Piazza
Colombo and Corso Garibaldi, though it's
open to dealers only. More than 20,000
tons of carnations, roses, mimosa flowers, and innumerable other kinds of cut
flowers are dispatched from here each
year. As the center of northern Italy's
flower-growing industry, the town is surrounded by hills where verdant terraces
are now blanketed with plastic to form
immense greenhouses.

GETTING HERE AND AROUND
By car, take the San Remo exit off the
A10 and follow the "Centro" signs. San
Remo is on the main train line between
Genoa and France.

VISITOR INFORMATION
CONTACT San Remo Tourism Office. ⊠ *Corso Garibaldi 1, San Remo* ☎ *0184/580500*
⊕ *www.turismoinliguria.it.*

Sights

Bussana Vecchia
TOWN | In the hills where flowers are
cultivated for export, this self-conscious-
ly picturesque former ghost town is a
flourishing artists' colony. The town was
largely destroyed by an earthquake in
1877, when the inhabitants packed up
and left en masse. For almost a century
the houses, church, and crumbling bell
tower were empty shells, overgrown by
weeds and wildflowers. Since the 1960s,
painters, sculptors, artisans, and bric-a-
brac dealers have restored the dwellings
as houses and studios. You need a car to
visit the town. ⊠ Bussana Vecchia ✛ *8
km (5 miles) east of San Remo* ⊕ *www.
bussanavecchia.it.*

Chiesa Russa Ortodossa
CHURCH | This onion-dome Russian
Orthodox church testifies to a long
Russian presence on the Italian Riviera.
Russian empress Maria Alexandrovna,
wife of Czar Alexander I, built a sum-
merhouse here, and in winter San Remo
was a popular destination for other royal
Romanovs. The church was consecrated
in 1913. ⊠ *Via Nuvoloni 2, San Remo*
☎ *0184/531807* ⊕ *www.chiesarussasan-
remo.it* ✒ *€1 donation.*

La Pigna *(The Pinecone)*
TOWN | San Remo's old town climbs
upward to Piazza Castello, which offers a
splendid view of the town and sea below.
Some lovely old palazzi and squares have
been restored, and the neighborhood
gives you a sense of what it was like to
live in San Remo centuries ago. ⊠ *San
Remo* ⊕ *www.turismoinliguria.it.*

Did You Know?

The gorgeous Hanbury
Botanic Gardens were
completely devastated
in World War II. In 1960,
Lady Hanbury sold the
property to the State
of Italy and in 1987, the
University of Genoa
began restoration. Today
it's considered one of the
most beautiful gardens
in Italy.

San Remo Casinò

CASINO | In addition to gaming, this lovely 1905 art nouveau landmark offers two restaurants, bars, and a theater that hosts concerts. Admission is free, but if you want to try your luck at the gaming tables, bets begin at around €10, depending on the time of day or night. ■ **TIP→ Dress is elegant, with jacket and tie requested at the French gaming tables.** ✉ *Corso Inglesi 18, San Remo* ☎ *0184/5951* ⊕ *www.casinosanremo.it.*

Restaurants

Nuovo Piccolo Mondo

$ | **LIGURIAN** | Vintage wooden furniture evokes the homey charm of this small family-run trattoria. A faithful clientele keeps the kitchen busy, so get here early to grab a table and order Ligurian specialties—fresh pasta, pesto, and vegetable and seafood dishes. **Known for:** local atmosphere; *sciancui* (flat pasta with beans, tomatoes, zucchini, and pesto); *polpo e patate* (stewed octopus with potatoes). $ *Average main: €13* ✉ *Via Piave 7, San Remo* ☎ *0184/509012* ⊘ *Closed Sun.*

Taverna al 29

$$$ | **LIGURIAN** | At the entrance of the old town is this intimate and comfortable restaurant that focuses on traditional seafood recipes, such as a soup featuring anchovies. The tavern's cuisine is typical of the Riviera di Ponente, and they also serve a good variety of gluten-free dishes. **Known for:** traditional yet varied menu; cozy old-world atmosphere; desserts paired with a digestif. $ *Average*

main: €32 ✉ *Piazza Cassini 5, San Remo* ☎ *0184/570034* ⊘ *Closed Sun., Wed., and Oct.–May. No lunch.*

 ## Hotels

Hotel Paradiso

$$$ | **HOTEL** | There's an air of seclusion and a respite from hectic San Remo in these bright, well-equipped rooms—some with balconies and sea views—that face a quiet, palm-fringed garden and pool. **Pros:** secluded yet near town; nice pool and private beach; on-site restaurant and bar. **Cons:** paid parking; steep walk up some stairs and a hill from town; some bathrooms are dated. $ *Rooms from: €240* ✉ *Via Roccasterone 12, San Remo* ☎ *0184/571211* ⊕ *www.paradisohotel.it* ⌾ *Free Breakfast* ⊘ *Closed mid-Oct.–Dec. 15* ⇆ *41 rooms.*

Royal Hotel San Remo

$$$ | **HOTEL** | With its heated seawater swimming pool in a tropical garden and guest rooms (some with sea views) with an attention to traditional design and modern amenities, this is considered one of Liguria's most luxurious resorts. **Pros:** the glamour of yesteryear with high-end amenities; relaxing pool open April through October; reasonable prices given the surroundings and closeness to casino. **Cons:** pool area can be crowded in high season; some bathrooms could be updated; expensive on-site meals and beverages. $ *Rooms from: €270* ✉ *Corso Imperatrice 80, San Remo* ☎ *0184/5391* ⊕ *www.royalhotelsanremo.com* ⊘ *Closed mid-Nov.–Feb. 1* ⇆ *127 rooms* ⌾ *Free Breakfast.*

Bordighera

12 km (7 miles) southwest of San Remo, 155 km (96 miles) southwest of Genoa.

Bordighera is an attractive seaside resort with panoramas (on a clear day) from Genoa to Monte Carlo. A large English colony settled here in the second half of the 19th century and is still very much in evidence today; you regularly find people taking afternoon tea in the cafés, and streets are named after Queen Victoria and Shakespeare.

GETTING HERE AND AROUND

By car, take the Bordighera exit off the A10 and follow the signs for "Centro," about a 10-minute drive. Bordighera is on the main railway line between Genoa and France.

VISITOR INFORMATION

CONTACT Bordighera Tourism Office.
✉ *Via Vittorio Emanuele 172, Bordighera* ☎ *0184/262882* ⊕ *www.bordighera.it.*

Sights

★ Giardini Botanici Hanbury

GARDEN | Mortola Inferiore is the site of the world-famous Hanbury Botanical Gardens, one of the largest and most beautiful in Italy. Planned and planted in 1867 by a wealthy English merchant, Sir Thomas Hanbury, and his botanist brother, Daniel, the terraced gardens contain species from five continents, including many palms and succulents. ✉ *Corso Montecarlo 43, Località Mortola Inferiore, Ventimiglia* ☎ *0184/229507* ⊕ *www.giardinihanbury.com* ☞ *€9.*

Lungomare Argentina

PROMENADE | Running parallel to the ocean, Lungomare Argentina is a pleasant 1½-km (1-mile) promenade, which begins at the western end of the town and provides good views westward to the French Côte d'Azur. ✉ *Bordighera.*

Restaurants

★ Magiargè

$$ | LIGURIAN | A mix of great charm and great food make this small, bustling osteria in the historic center an absolute dining delight. Dishes are Ligurian with a focus on local fish, and the list of local wines, including organic selections, is excellent. **Known for:** multicourse set menus of Ligurian specialties; cozy dining room with curved archways; salt cod with chickpea polenta. ⑤ *Average main: €18* ✉ *Via Dritta 2, Bordighera* ☎ *0184/262946* ⊕ *www.magiarge.it* ☉ *Closed Mon. No lunch Aug.*

Chapter 11

EMILIA–ROMAGNA

11

Updated by
Elizabeth Shemaria

◉ Sights	🍴 Restaurants	🛏 Hotels	🛍 Shopping	🍸 Nightlife
★★★★☆	★★★★★	★★★★☆	★★★☆☆	★☆☆☆☆

WELCOME TO EMILIA-ROMAGNA

TOP REASONS TO GO

★ **The signature food of Emilia:** This region's food—prosciutto crudo, Parmesan cheese, balsamic vinegar, and above all, pasta—makes the trip to Italy worthwhile.

★ **Mosaics that take your breath away:** The intricate tiles in Ravenna's Mausoleo di Galla Placidia, in brilliantly well-preserved colors, depict vivid portraits and pastoral scenes.

★ **Arguably Europe's oldest wine bar:** Nicolaus Copernicus tippled here while studying at Ferrara's university in the early 1500s—Enoteca al Brindisi, in the historic center, has been pouring wine since 1435.

★ **The nightlife of Bologna:** This red-roof city has had a lively student culture since the university—Europe's oldest—was founded in the late 11th century.

★ **The medieval castles of San Marino:** Its three castles dramatically perch on a rock more than 3,000 feet above the flat landscape of Romagna.

1 Piacenza. With its majestic piazzas, fine cathedral, and palatial museum, this town at Emilia's northwestern end makes a fitting introduction to the region.

2 Busseto. Opera aficionados visit to pay homage to one of Italy's greatest composers, Giuseppe Verdi.

3 Parma. Internationally known for its foodstuffs, Parma also boasts a battery of sights.

4 Modena. Endowed with a compact, beautifully preserved city center and a magnificent cathedral, this town repays a leisurely wander.

5 Bologna. Emilia's principal cultural and intellectual center is famed for its arcaded sidewalks, medieval towers, and sublime restaurants.

6 Ferrara. This prosperous, tidy town north of Bologna has a rich medieval past and distinctive cuisine.

7 Imola. There is plenty more to this place than its famous Formula One racetrack, including an attractive city center.

8 Faenza. This handsome setttlement has bequeathed its name to the majolica ceramics, or *faience*, for which it is best known.

9 Rimini. A beach resort on the Adriatic coast, Rimini has noteworthy Roman and Renaissance monuments.

10 San Marino. Officially an independent republic, this quirky enclave is a tourist hot spot.

11 Ravenna. The main attractions of this well-preserved Romagna city are its mosaics—glittering treasures left from Byzantine rule.

EATING AND DRINKING WELL IN EMILIA-ROMAGNA

Italians rarely agree about anything, but many concede that some of the country's finest foods originated in Emilia-Romagna. Tortellini, fettuccine, Parmesan cheese, prosciutto crudo, and balsamic vinegar are just a few of the Italian delicacies born here.

One of the beauties of Emilia-Romagna is that its exceptional food can be had without breaking the bank. Many trattorias serve up classic dishes, mastered over the centuries, at reasonable prices. Cutting-edge restaurants and wine bars are often more expensive; their inventive menus are full of *fantasia*—reinterpretations of the classics. For the budget-conscious, Bologna, a university town, has great places for cheap eats.

Between meals, you can sustain yourself with the region's famous sandwich, the *piadina*. It's made with pitalike thin bread, usually filled with prosciutto or mortadella, cheese, and vegetables, then put under the grill and served hot, with the cheese oozing at the sides. These addictive sandwiches can be savored at sit-down places or ordered to go.

THE REAL RAGÙ

Emilia-Romagna's signature dish is *tagliatelle al ragù* (flat noodles with meat sauce), known as "spaghetti Bolognese" most everywhere else. This *primo* (first course) is on every menu, and no two versions are the same. The sauce starts in a sauté pan with finely diced carrots, onions, and celery. Purists add nothing but minced beef, but some use *guanciale* (pork cheek), sausage, veal, or chicken. Regular ministrations of broth are added, and sometimes wine, milk, or cream.

PORK PRODUCTS

It's not just mortadella and cured pork products like prosciutto crudo and *culatello* that Emilia-Romagnans go crazy for—they're wild about the whole hog. You'll frequently find cotechino and zampone, both *secondi* (second courses), on menus. *Cotechino* is a savory, thick, fresh sausage served with lentils on New Year's Eve (the combination is said to augur well for the new year) and with mashed potatoes year-round. *Zampone*, a stuffed pig's foot, is redolent of garlic and deliciously fatty.

BOLLITO MISTO

The name means "mixed boil," and they do it exceptionally well in this part of Italy. According to Emilia-Romagnans, *bollito misto* was invented here, although other Italians—especially those from Milan and Piedmont—might dispute this claim. Chicken, beef, tongue, and zampone are tossed into a stockpot and boiled; they're then removed from the broth and served with a fragrant *salsa verde* (green sauce), made with parsley and spiced with anchovies, garlic, and capers. This simple yet rich dish is usually served with mashed potatoes on the side, and savvy diners will mix some of the piquant salsa verde into the potatoes as well.

STUFFED PASTA

Among the many Emilian variations on stuffed pasta, *tortellini* are the smallest. *Tortelli* and *cappellacci* are larger pasta "pillows," about the size of a brussels sprout, but with the same basic form as tortellini. They're often filled with pumpkin or spinach and cheese. *Tortelloni* are, in theory, even bigger, although their size varies. Stuffed pastas are generally served simply, with melted butter, sage, and Parmigiano-Reggiano cheese or, in the case of tortellini, *in brodo* (in beef, chicken, or capon broth or some combination thereof), which brings out the subtle richness of the filling.

WINES

Emilia-Romagna's wines accompany the region's fine food rather than vying with it for accolades. The best-known is *Lambrusco,* a sparkling red produced on the Po Plain that has some admirers and many detractors. It's praised for its tartness and condemned for the same; it does, however, pair brilliantly with the local fare. The region's best wines include Sangiovese di Romagna (somewhat similar to Chianti), from the Romagnan hills, and barbera from the Colli Piacentini and Apennine foothills. Castelluccio, Bonzara, Zerbina, Leone Conti, and Tre Monti are among the region's top producers.

Gourmets the world over claim that Emilia-Romagna's greatest contribution to humankind has been gastronomic. Birthplace of fettuccine, tortellini, lasagna, prosciutto, and Parmigiano-Reggiano cheese, the region has a spectacular culinary tradition. But there are many reasons to come here aside from the desire to be well fed: Parma's Correggio paintings, Giuseppe Verdi's villa at Sant'Agata, the medieval splendor of Bologna's palaces, Ferrara's medieval alleys, the rolling hills of the Romagna countryside, and, perhaps foremost, the Byzantine beauty of mosaic-rich Ravenna—glittering as brightly today as it did 1,500 years ago.

As you travel through Emilia, the western half of the region, you'll encounter the sprawling plants of Italy's industrial food giants, like Barilla and Fini, standing side by side with the fading villas and farmhouses that have long punctuated the flat, fertile land of the Po Plain. Bologna, the principal city of Emilia, is a busy cultural and, increasingly, business center, less visited but in many ways just as engaging as the country's more famous tourist destinations—particularly given its acknowledged position as the leading city of Italian cuisine. The rest of the region follows suit: eating is an essential part of any Emilian experience.

The area's history is laden with culinary legends, such as how the original tortellino was modeled on the shape of Venus's navel and the original *tagliolini* (long, thin egg pasta) was served at the wedding banquet of Annibale Bentivoglio and Lucrezia d'Este—a marriage uniting two of the most powerful noble families in the region. You'll need to stay focused just to make sure you try all the basics: Parma's famed prosciutto and Parmigiano-Reggiano cheese, Modena's balsamic vinegar, the ragù whose poor imitations are known worldwide as "Bolognese"—and, of course, the best pasta in the world.

The historic border between Emilia to the west and Romagna to the east lies near the fortified town of Dozza. Emilia is flat, but just east of the Romagnan border the landscape gets hillier and more sparsely settled, in places covered with evergreen forests and steaming natural springs. Finally, it flattens again into the low-lying marshland of the Po Delta, which meets the Adriatic Sea. Each autumn, in both Romagna and Emilia, the trademark fog rolls in off the Adriatic to hang over the flatlands in winter, coloring the region with a spooky, gray glow.

MAJOR REGIONS

The westernmost part of the region, **Emilia,** is richly redolent of the history and culture of northern Italy. The Via Emilia, an ancient Roman road, runs through Emilia's heart in a straight shot from medieval Piacenza, southeast of Milan, through Bologna, home to one of the world's first universities and still one of Italy's great cities, and ultimately to Romagna and the Adriatic Coast. On the way you encounter many of Italy's cultural riches—notably the culinary and artistic treasures of Parma and Modena. Take time to veer into the countryside, with its ramshackle farmhouses and 800-year-old abbeys, and to detour north to the birthplace and home of Giuseppe Verdi at Busseto. Northeast of Bologna, explore the mist-shrouded tangle of streets in Ferrara's charismatic old town.

The mostly rural **Romagna** has rolling hills dotted with handsome farmhouses, giving way at its eastern end to the lively resorts and sandy beaches of the Adriatic coast. Imola, most famed for its Formula One racetrack, is traditionally regarded as the western gateway to Romagna. From here it's a short hop to Faenza, home to dozens of shops selling its well-known ceramics. Most visitors to Romagna make a beeline for Ravenna, the site of shimmering Byzantine mosaics, though you'll also find absorbing historical remnants at Rimini, a beach resort. The mini-state of San Marino, to the south, is a curiosity worth a brief detour for its castles.

Planning

When to Go

Extending along the valley of the River Po, Emilia-Romagna's predominantly flat and featureless landscape is subject to hot summers and cold, foggy winters. It's humid year-round, so rain is always a possibility and fairly common during the winter months. Tourism is mainly cultural in the region and thus isn't particularly subject to seasonal variations, though you can expect to see some resorts along the Romagna coast close in winter, particularly around Rimini.

Planning Your Time

Plan on spending at least two days in Bologna, the region's cultural and historical capital. You shouldn't miss Parma, with its stunning food and graceful public spaces. Also plan on visiting Ferrara, a misty, mysterious medieval city. If you have time, go to Ravenna for its memorable Byzantine mosaics and Modena for its harmonious architecture and famous balsamic vinegar.

If you have only a few days in the region, it's virtually impossible to do all five of those cities justice. If you're a dedicated gourmand (or *buona forchetta*, as Italians say), move from Bologna west along the Via Emilia (SS9) to Modena and Parma. If you're more interested in architecture, art, and history, choose the eastern route, heading north on the A13 to Ferrara and then southeast on the SS16 to Ravenna.

If you have more time, you won't have to make such tough choices. You can start in Milan, go east, and finish on the Adriatic—or vice versa.

Getting Here and Around

CAR

Driving is the best way to get around Emilia-Romagna. Roads are wide, flat, and well marked; distances are short; and beautiful farmhouses and small villages offer undemanding detours.

A car is particularly useful for visiting the spa towns of Romagna, which aren't well connected by train. Historic centers are off-limits to cars, but they're also quite walkable, so you may just want to park your car and get around on foot once you arrive.

Entering Emilia-Romagna by car is as easy as it gets. Coming in from the northwest on the Autostrada del Sole (A1), you'll first hit Piacenza, a mere 45-minute drive southeast of Milan. On the other side of the region, Venice is about an hour from Ferrara by car on the A13.

Bologna is on the autostrada, so driving between cities is a breeze, though take special care if you're coming from Florence, as the road is winding and the drivers speed. The Via Emilia (SS9), one of the oldest roads in the world, runs through the heart of the region. Although less scenic, the A1 autostrada, which runs parallel to the Via Emilia from Bologna, can get you where you're going about twice as fast. From Bologna, the A13 runs north to Ferrara, and the A14 takes you east to Ravenna. Much of the historic center of Bologna is closed off to cars daily from 7 am to 8 pm.

TRAIN

When it comes to public transportation in the region, trains are better than buses—they're fairly efficient and quite frequent, and most stations aren't too far from the center of town. The railroad track follows the Via Emilia (SS9). In Emilia it generally takes 30–60 minutes to get from one major city to the next. To reach Ferrara or Ravenna, you typically have to change to a local train at Bologna. Ferrara is a half hour north of Bologna on the train, and Ravenna is just over an hour east.

Bologna is an important rail hub for northern Italy and has frequent, fast service to Milan, Florence, Rome, and Venice. The routes from Bologna to the south usually go through Florence, about 40 minutes away on a high-speed train. The high-speed Frecciarossa train service cuts the time from Milan to Bologna to only one hour. On the northeastern edge of the region, Venice is 1½ hours east of Ferrara by train. Check the website of the state railway, the **Trenitalia** (aka Ferrovie dello Stato or FS; *www.trenitalia.com/en.html*) for information, or stop in a travel agency as many sell train tickets (without a markup) and agents often speak English **Italo** (*www.italotreno.it/en*), a privately owned high-speed train line, competes with the state-sponsored service. Italo's Milan–Rome line makes stops in Reggio Emilia, Bologna, and Florence; the Venice–Naples line stops in Padua, Bologna, Florence, and Rome. Some of these also stop at secondary stations.

Restaurants

Dining options range from mom-and-pop-style informal trattorias to three-star Michelin restaurants. Food in Emilia-Romagna is not for the faint of heart (or those on diets): it is rich, creamy, and cheesy. Local wines pair remarkably well with this sumptuous fare. You may want to rethink Lambrusco, as it marries well with just about everything on the menu.

Restaurant reviews have been shortened. For full information, visit Fodors.com.

Hotels

Emilia-Romagna has a reputation for demonstrating a level of efficiency uncommon in most of Italy. Even the smallest hotels are usually well run, with high standards of quality and service. Bologna is very much a businessperson's city, and many hotels here cater to the business traveler, but there are smaller, more intimate hotels as well. It's smart to book in advance—the region hosts many fairs and conventions that can fill up hotels even during low season.

Hotel reviews have been shortened. For full information, visit Fodors.com.

WHAT IT COSTS in Euros

	$	$$	$$$	$$$$
RESTAURANTS				
	under €15	€15–€24	€25–€35	over €35
HOTELS				
	under €125	€125–€200	€201–€300	over €300

Piacenza

67 km (42 miles) southeast of Milan, 150 km (93 miles) northwest of Bologna.

Piacenza has always been associated with industry and commerce. Its position on the Po River has made it an important inland port since the earliest times; the Etruscans, and then the Romans, had thriving settlements here. As you approach the city today, you could be forgiven for thinking that it holds little of interest. Piacenza is surrounded by ugly industrial suburbs (with particularly unlovely concrete factories and a power station), but if you forge ahead you'll discover a well-preserved medieval center and an unusually clean city. Its prosperity is evident in the great shopping along Corso Vittorio Emanuele II.

GETTING HERE AND AROUND

Regional trains run often from Milan to Piacenza and take a little less than an hour, and Frecciarossa trains make it from Milan to Bologna in an hour. Services from Bologna to Piacenza take about 1½ hours and closer to 2 hours on some regional trains. Both have frequent service. Piacenza is easily accessible by car via the A1, either from Milan or from Bologna. If you're coming from Milan, take the Piacenza Nord exit; from Bologna, the Piacenza Est exit.

VISITOR INFORMATION

CONTACT Piacenza Tourism Office. ⊠ *Piazza Cavalli 10, Piacenza* ☎ *0523/492001* ⊕ *www.comune.piacenza.it.*

Sights

Duomo

CHURCH | Attached like a sinister balcony to the bell tower of Piacenza's 12th-century Duomo is a *gabbia* (iron cage), where miscreants were incarcerated naked and subjected to the scorn of the crowd in the marketplace below. Inside the cathedral, less evocative but equally impressive medieval stonework decorates the pillars and the crypt, and there are extravagant frescoes in the dome of the cupola begun by Morazzone (1573–1626). Guercino (1591–1666) completed them upon Morazzone's death. If you're feeling strong, you can climb 136 steps to the cupola for a closer view. The Duomo can be reached by following Via XX Settembre from Piazza dei Cavalli. ⊠ *Piazza Duomo, Piacenza* ☎ *331/4606435* ⊕ *www.cattedralepiacenza.it* ⊠ *Free; cupola €10.*

Musei di Palazzo Farnese

ART MUSEUM | The eclectic city-owned museum of Piacenzan art and antiquities is housed in the vast Palazzo Farnese, a monumental palace commissioned by the ruling family that, although construction began in 1558, was never completed as planned. The highlight

Emilia-Romagna Through the Ages

Ancient History. Emilia-Romagna owes its beginnings to a road. In 187 BC the Romans built the Via Aemilia—a long road running northwest from the Adriatic port of Rimini to the central garrison town of Piacenza—and it was along this central spine that the primary towns of the region developed.

Despite the unifying factor of what came to be known as the Via Emilia, this section of Italy has had a fragmented history. Its eastern part, roughly the area from Faenza to the coast (known as Romagna), looked first to the Byzantine east and then to Rome for art, political power, and, some say, national character. The western part, from Bologna to Piacenza (Emilia), looked more to the north with its practice of self-government and dissent.

Bologna was founded by the Etruscans and eventually came under the influence of the Roman Empire. The Romans established a garrison here, renaming the old Etruscan settlement Bononia. It was after the fall of Rome that the region began its fragmentation. Romagna, centered in Ravenna, was ruled from Constantinople. Ravenna eventually became the capital of the empire in the west in the 5th century, passing to papal control in the 8th century. Even today, the city is filled with reminders of two centuries of Byzantine rule.

Family Ties. The other cities of the region, from the Middle Ages on, became the fiefdoms of important noble families—the Este in Ferrara and Modena, the Pallavicini in Piacenza, and the Bentivoglio in Bologna. Today all these cities bear the marks of their noble patrons. When in the 16th century the papacy managed to exert its power over the entire area, some of these cities were divided among the papal families—hence the stamp of the Farnese family on Parma and Piacenza.

A Leftward Tilt. Emilia-Romagna (and Bologna, in particular) has an established and hearty tradition of rebellion and dissent. The Italian socialist movement was born in this region, as was Benito Mussolini. In keeping with the political climate of his home state, he was a firebrand socialist during the early part of his career. Despite having Mussolini as a native son, Emilia-Romagna didn't take to fascism: it was here that the anti-fascist resistance was born, and during World War II the region suffered terribly at the hands of the fascists and the Nazis.

of the museum's collection is the tiny 2nd-century-BC Etruscan Fegato di Piacenza, a bronze tablet shaped like a *fegato* (liver), marked with the symbols of the gods of good and ill fortune. By comparing this master "liver" with one taken from the body of a freshly slaughtered sacrifice, priests predicted the future. The collection also contains Botticelli's beautiful *Madonna and Child with St.* *John the Baptist.* Because it's under glass, you have the rare opportunity of getting very close to the piece to admire the artist's brushwork. Reserve ahead for free 1½-hour guided tours (May–Oct. Sat. and Sun. 10 am–4:30 pm). ⊠ *Piazza Cittadella 29, Piacenza* ☎ *0523/492658* ⊕ *www.palazzofarnese.piacenza.it* 🎟 *€6* ⊗ *Closed Mon.*

Piazza dei Cavalli (*Square of the Horses*)
PLAZA/SQUARE | The hub of the city is the Piazza dei Cavalli, with the flamboyant equestrian statues from which the piazza takes its name. These are depictions of Ranuccio Farnese (1569–1622) and, on the left, his father, Alessandro (1545–92). The latter was a beloved ruler, enlightened and fair; Ranuccio, his successor, less so. Both statues are the work of Francesco Mochi, a master Baroque sculptor. Dominating the square is the massive 13th-century **Palazzo Pubblico,** also known as Il Gotico. This two-tone, marble-and-brick, turreted and crenellated building was the seat of town government before Piacenza fell under the iron fists of the ruling Pallavicini and Farnese families. ⊠ *Piazza dei Cavalli, Piacenza.*

Busseto

30 km (19 miles) southeast of Piacenza, 25 km (16 miles) south of Cremona in Lombardy.

Sleepy Busseto's greatest claim to fame is local son Giuseppe Verdi (1813–1901), who was not exactly born here—he was born in Le Roncole, a stone's throw away. However, he always considered this town his home. It's in the middle of cultivated countryside, and was known since Carolingian times as Buxetum. In 1533 it attracted the attention of Hapsburg emperor Charles V, who became lord of the city. Now it attracts opera lovers who wish to walk in the grand maestro's footsteps—either by hearing one of his works at the local theater or by touring either of his country estates.

GETTING HERE AND AROUND

If you're coming by car from Parma, drive along the A1/E35 and follow signs for the A15 in the direction of Milan/La Spezia. Choose the exit in the direction of Fidenza/Salsomaggiore Terme, following signs to the SP12, which connects to the SS9W. At Fidenza, take the SS588 heading north, which will take you into Busseto. If you're without a car, you'll have to take a bus from Piacenza or Parma, as there's no train service.

VISITOR INFORMATION

CONTACT Busseto Tourism Office. ⊠ *Piazza G. Verdi 10, Busseto* ☎ *0524/92487* ⊕ *www.bussetolive.com.*

 Sights

Teatro Verdi

HISTORIC SIGHT | In the center of Busseto is the lovely Teatro Verdi, dedicated, as you might expect, to the works of the hamlet's famous son. Guided tours (in both English and Italian) of the well-preserved, ornate, 19th-century-style theater are offered every half hour. Check with the Busseto tourist office for the performance schedule. ⊠ *Piazza G. Verdi 10, Busseto* ☎ *0524/92487* ⊕ *www.bussetolive.com* ⊠ *Tours €4* ☉ *Closed Mon.*

Villa Pallavicino

HISTORIC HOME | Busseto's main claim to fame is its native son, master composer Giuseppe Verdi (1813–1901). The 15th-century Villa Pallavicino is where Verdi worked and lived with his mistress (and later wife) Giuseppina Strepponi. Today it displays the maestro's piano, scores, composition books, and walking sticks. ⊠ *Via Ziliani 1, Busseto* ☎ *0524/931002* ⊕ *www.museogiuseppeverdi.it* ⊠ *€9* ☉ *Closed Mon.*

Villa Verdi

HISTORIC HOME | For Verdi lovers, Villa Verdi (also known as Villa Sant'Agata) is a veritable shrine. It's the grand country home Verdi built for himself in 1849—and the place where some of his greatest works

were composed. Visits are by tour only. ⊠ *Via Verdi 31, 4 km (2½ miles) north of Busseto on SS588, toward Cremona, Sant'Agata* ☎ *0523/830000* ⊕ *www.villaverdi.org* ⊠ *Tours €9* ☉ *Closed weekdays Nov.–Feb. and Mon. Mar.–Oct.*

Parma

40 km (25 miles) southeast of Busseto, 97 km (60 miles) northwest of Bologna.

Parma stands on the banks of a tributary of the Po River. Despite damage during World War II, much of the stately historic center seems untouched by modern times. This is a prosperous city, and it shows in its well-dressed residents, clean streets, and immaculate piazzas.

Bursting with gustatory delights, Parma draws crowds for its sublime cured pork product, *prosciutto crudo di Parma* (known locally simply as "prosciutto crudo"). The pale-yellow Parmigiano-Reggiano cheese produced here and in nearby Reggio Emilia is the original—and best—of a class known around the world as Parmesan.

Almost every major European power has had a hand in ruling Parma at one time or another. The Romans founded the city—then little more than a garrison on the Via Emilia—after which a succession of feudal lords held sway. In the 16th century came the ever-conniving Farnese family, which died out in 1731 on the death of Antonio Farnese. It then went to the Spanish before falling into French hands in 1796. In 1805 Marie-Louise (better known to the Parmigiani as Maria Luigia), the wife of Napoléon, took command of the city. She was a much-beloved figure in her adopted town until her death in 1847.

GETTING HERE AND AROUND

Train service, via Frecciabianca, Intercity, and Regionale trains, runs frequently from Milan and Bologna. It takes around

1¼ hours from Milan and slightly less than an hour on fast trains from Bologna. By car, Parma is just off the A1 autostrada, halfway between Bologna and Piacenza.

VISITOR INFORMATION

CONTACT Parma Tourism Office. ⊠ *Piazza Garibaldi 1, Parma* ☎ *0521/218889* ⊕ *www.parmawelcome.it.*

◉ Sights

Battistero (*Baptistery*)

CHURCH | Baptisms still happen (one Saturday and one Sunday a month) in this baptistery, which has a simple pink-stone Romanesque exterior and an uplifting Gothic interior. The doors are richly decorated with figures, animals, and flowers, and inside, the building is adorned with stucco figures (probably carved by Antelami) showing the months and seasons. Early-14th-century frescoes depicting scenes from the life of Christ grace the walls. ⊠ *Piazza del Duomo, Parma* ☎ *0521/208699* ⊕ *www.piazzaduomoparma.com* ⊠ *€12.*

★ **Camera di San Paolo**

HISTORIC SIGHT | This was the reception room for the erudite abbess Giovanna da Piacenza, who hired Correggio in 1519 to provide its decoration: mythological scenes are depicted in glorious frescoes of the *Triumphs of the Goddess Diana,* the *Three Graces,* and the *Three Fates.* ⊠ *Via Melloni 3, off Strada Garibaldi, near Piazza Pilotta, Parma* ☎ *0521/287195* ⊠ *€6* ☉ *Closed Sun.*

Duomo

CHURCH | The magnificent 12th-century cathedral has two vigilant stone lions standing guard beside the main door; inside is some notable art in styles from medieval to Mannerist. The arch of the entrance is decorated with a delicate frieze of figures representing the months of the year, a motif repeated inside the baptistery. Some of the church's original artwork still survives, notably the simple yet evocative *Descent from the Cross,* a carving in the right transept by Benedetto Antelami (active 1178–1230), whose masterwork is this cathedral's baptistery. It's an odd juxtaposition to turn from his austere work to the exuberant fresco in the dome, the *Assumption of the Virgin* by Antonio Allegri, better known to us as Correggio (1494–1534). The fresco was not well received when it was unveiled in 1530. "A mess of frogs' legs," the bishop of Parma is said to have called it. Today Correggio is acclaimed as one of the leading masters of Mannerist painting. ■ TIP→ **The fresco is best viewed when the sun is strong, as this building is not particularly well lit.** ⊠ *Piazza del Duomo, Parma* ☎ *0521/208699* ⊕ *www.piazzaduomoparma.com.*

Museo del Parmigiano Reggiano

OTHER MUSEUM | **FAMILY** | The trademark crumbly cheese is the focus of this museum, which is part of the collective known as Musei del Cibo whose goal is to showcase the region's most famous foods. There's a video that demonstrates the process of making Parmigiano-Reggiano and some 120 exhibits that explore the history of the cheese. Tastings are also offered, and cheese is available to purchase. Audio guides are available and can also be downloaded for free on the museum's website. Reservations are advisable for a guided tour in English, which should be booked at least 48 hours in advance by contacting prenotazioni.parmigianoreggiano@museidelcibo.it. ⊠ *Corte Castellazzi, Via Volta 5, Soragna* ✛ *28 km (17 miles) NW of Parma* ☎ *340/1939057* ⊕ *www.museidelcibo.it* ⊠ *€5* ☉ *Closed weekdays, and Dec. 9–Feb. 28.*

Museo del Pomodoro

OTHER MUSEUM | **FAMILY** | It's hard to imagine what Italian cuisine would be like without the New World tomato. This museum in Collecchio, part of the collective known as Musei del Cibo, explains all the mysteries. There are about a hundred exhibits explaining the history of the tomato, its farming, and its processing. If you want to book a guided tour, it's necessary to call or email prenotazioni. pomodoro@museidelcibo.it at least 15 days in advance. ⊠ *Corte di Giarola, Strada Giarola 11, Collecchio* ✛ *12 km (7 miles) from Parma* ☎ *0521/678174* ⊕ *www.museidelcibo.it* 🎟 *€5* ⊙ *Closed weekdays, and Dec. 9—Feb. 28.*

Museo del Prosciutto di Parma

OTHER MUSEUM | FAMILY | Part of the collective known as Musei del Cibo, which works to showcase the region's most famous foods, this museum offers an in-depth look at Italy's most famous cured pork product. It offers tastings, a bit of history on prosciutto, and a tour through the process of making it. A gift shop ensures that you can take some of this marvelous product home. ■TIP→ **Call or email prenotazioni.prosciutto@museidelcibo.it at least 48 hours ahead for a guided tour in English.** ⊠ *c/o Ex Foro Boario, Via Bocchialini 7, Parma* ✛ *Langhirano, 22 km (13 miles) from Parma* ☎ *0521/931800* ⊕ *www.museidelcibo.it* 🎟 *€5* ⊙ *Closed Dec. 9–Feb. 28.*

Museo del Salame di Felino

OTHER MUSEUM | FAMILY | This museum, part of the Musei del Cibo collective that works to showcase the region's most famous food, is all about cured meats. There are tastings, a bit of history, and a tour through the process of making these specialties. Guided tours in English are available upon request. ■TIP→ **Tours must be booked at least 48 hours in advance by emailing prenotazioni.salame@museidelcibo.it.** ⊠ *Strada al Castello 1, Parma* ✛ *near Castello di Felino, 17 km (10 miles) southwest of Parma* ☎ *340/1939057* ⊕ *www.museidelcibo.it* 🎟 *€5* ⊙ *Closed weekdays and Dec. 9–Feb 28.*

★ Pilotta Museums

ART GALLERY | With one ticket, you can visit the Pilotta museums: the National Gallery, Archeological museum, Palatina Library, Bodoniano museum, and Farnese Theatre. The Galleria Nazionale may be the biggest draw as it contains masterpieces by Correggio, Parmigianino, Leonardo da Vinci, El Greco, and Bronzino. It's on the piano nobile of the massive and somewhat forbidding Palazzo della Pilotta, constructed on the riverbank in 1618. The palazzo takes its name from the game *pilotta,* a sort of handball played within the palace precincts in the 17th century. Continuing your visit, you'll find the Baroque Teatro Farnese, built in 1617–18. Made entirely of wood, it was largely destroyed in a 1944 Allied bombing raid, but it's been flawlessly restored. In the Archeological Museum see Etruscan, Roman, and Egyptian artifacts; the Palatina Library houses more than 500 religious manuscripts; and the Bodoniano museum covers printmaking. ⊠ *Piazza della Pilotta 15, Parma* ☎ *0521/220400* ⊕ *www.pilotta.beniculturali.it* 🎟 *€12* ⊙ *Closed Mon.*

Piazza del Duomo

PLAZA/SQUARE | This spacious cobblestone piazza contains the cathedral and the Battistero, plus the Palazzo del Vescovado (Bishop's Palace). Behind the Duomo is the Baroque church of San Giovanni Evangelista. ⊠ *Parma.*

Piazza Garibaldi

PLAZA/SQUARE | This piazza is the heart of Parma, where people gather to pass the time of day, start their *passeggiata* (constitutional), or simply hang out; the square and nearby Piazza del Duomo make up one of the loveliest historic centers in Italy. Strada Cavour, leading off the piazza, is Parma's prime shopping street. It's also crammed with wine bars teeming with locals, so it's a perfect place to stop for a snack or light lunch or a drink. ⊠ *Parma.*

San Giovanni Evangelista

CHURCH | Beyond the elaborate Baroque facade of San Giovanni Evangelista, the Renaissance interior reveals several works by Correggio: *St. John the Evangelist* (in the lunette above the door in the left transept) is considered among his finest. More work by Correggio can be seen in the cupola and in the fifth chapel on the right. Also in this church, under the arches in the first, second, and fourth chapels on the left, are works by Parmigianino (1503–40), a contemporary of Correggio's. While you are here, enter the building on your left for a moment of contemplation, visiting the attached Benedictine monastery and St. John's Cloister (free entry, closed Thursday through Sunday). ⊠ Piazzale San Giovanni 1, Piazza del Duomo, Parma ☎ 0521/235311 ⊕ www.monasterosangiovanni.com.

Santa Maria della Steccata

CHURCH | Dating from the 16th century, this delightful church has one of Parma's most recognizable domes. In the dome's large arch there's a wonderful decorative fresco by Francesco Mazzola, better known as Parmigianino. He took so long to complete it that his patrons briefly imprisoned him for breach of contract. ⊠ Piazza Steccata 9, off Via Dante near Piazza Garibaldi, Parma ☎ 0521/380500 ⊕ www.diocesi.parma.it.

🍴 Restaurants

La Filoma

$$ | EMILIAN | FAMILY | The dining room here evokes the turn of the 19th century with its high ceilings, chandeliers, and damask drapes. The food shines, from the classic anolini in brodo di manzo e cappone (a local variation on tortellini in brodo) to the exquisite roast veal stuffed with prosciutto and Parmigiano-Reggiano. **Known for:** excellent wine list; regional specialties that don't break the bank; Parmigiana di melanzane and other options for vegetarians. ⑤ Average main: €16 ⊠ Borgo XX Marzo 15, Parma ☎ 0521/206181 ⊕ www.ristorantelafiloma.it ⊗ Closed Wed. and 10 days in July.

La Forchetta

$$ | ITALIAN | Sicily-born Parma transplant Angelo Cammarata makes magic in his small eatery on the ground floor of a 16th-century palazzo, where the menu teems with Parma classics as well as modern takes on Sicilian dishes. Creatures from the sea play a starring role—try the terrific starter of blanched shrimp. **Known for:** lip-smacking cannoli; cozy interior; great fish dishes. ⑤ Average main: €18 ⊠ Borgo San Biagio 6/D, Parma ☎ 0521/208812 ⊕ www.laforchettaparma.it ⊗ Closed Tues.

La Greppia

$$ | EMILIAN | Little-known by tourists but popular with locals in the know, this small and select restaurant just down the street from Palazzo della Pilotta in the historic center offers up traditional Parmesan cooking with stylistic flourishes. The chef has a nice touch with classics like anolini ripieni di stracotto in brodo di cappone (dumplings stuffed with stewed meat in a capon stock) but also prepares innovative dishes. **Known for:** superb antipasti and desserts; impeccable service; good gluten-free choices. ⑤ Average main: €17 ⊠ Strada Garibaldi 39, Parma ☎ 0521/233686 ⊕ facebook.com/lagreppiaparma ⊗ Closed Thurs.

★ Ristorante Parizzi

$$$ | EMILIAN | Chef-owner Marco Parizzi is the third-generation cook in this elegant restaurant, originally his grandfather's salumeria (delicatessen), where he now serves a mix of Parmense classics and contemporary creations. The anolini alla parmigiana in brodo di manzo e gallina (pasta with Parmigiano-Reggiano in broth) is a more typical dish, while the faraona in crosta di frutta secca (guinea fowl cooked with dried fruits and mushroom sauce) is a flight of fancy. **Known for:** inventive terra (earth) and mare (sea) tasting menus; affordable, well-curated wine list; special menu with white truffles from Alba in autumn. $ *Average main: €26* ✉ *Strada della Repubblica 71, Parma* ☎ *0521/285952* ⊕ *www.ristoranteparizzi.it* ⊙ *Closed Mon., Aug., and Jan. 8–15.*

☕ Coffee and Quick Bites

Enoteca Antica Osteria Fontana

$ | **WINE BAR** | This old-school *enoteca* (wine bar) is one of Parma's liveliest, drawing in a mix of intellectuals and gregarious twentysomethings, who often spill out onto the street, wine glasses in hand. Grab a table inside and feast on inexpensive tartines or grilled panini, whose seemingly endless options include coppa, pancetta, and Gorgonzola. **Known for:** teeming with happy locals; culatello cured ham; wide selection of wine bottles to go. $ *Average main: €9* ✉ *Strada Farini 24/a, near Piazza Garibaldi, Parma* ☎ *0521/286037* ⊙ *Closed Sun. and Mon.*

★ Tabarro

$ | **EMILIAN** | Convivial, lively, and full of locals, this favorite little wine bar on one of Parma's main drags has a couple of keg tables outside, a few stools on the ground floor, and several more small tables upstairs. The menu is based largely on cheese and pork products (equine as well: people in this part of the world like to eat horse) and is designed to pair with, and accentuate, the fine wines on offer. **Known for:** the ebullient host; international wine list; delicious crostini. $ *Average main: €12* ✉ *Strada Farini 5/b, Parma* ☎ *0521/200223* ⊕ *www.tabarro. net* ⊙ *Closed Tues. No lunch Sun., Mon., and Wed.–Fri.*

★ TCafè

$ | **EMILIAN** | The beauty of TCafè is that it does just about everything: the festivities begin with breakfast and end with an evening aperitivo all with a view of Parma's cathedral from its outdoor patio—weather permitting. Locals flock to this place, which once housed the aristocratic Dalla Rosa Prati's art collection, to catch up on gossip, and have lunch, which offers local specialties (among them plates of mortadella and culatello), a soup of the day, sandwiches, and tasty salads like the one with smoked duck breast. **Known for:** views of Parma's cathedral; late-night and early-morning dining; artisanal beers. $ *Average main: €9* ✉ *Strada al Duomo 7, Parma* ☎ *0521/386429* ⊕ *www.palazzodallarosaprati.it.*

Hotels

★ Palazzo dalla Rosa Prati

$ | **HOTEL** | Marchese Vittorio dalla Rosa Prati has converted part of his family's 15th-century palace on Piazza del Duomo into luxurious, self-catering accommodations, and those with connecting rooms are ideal for families. **Pros:** room service of continental breakfast included in the price; spacious, well-appointed rooms with small kitchenettes; historical setting. **Cons:** parking can sometimes be a problem; staff leave at 8 pm; Wi-Fi slow in some rooms. $ *Rooms from: €109* ✉ *Strada al Duomo 7, Parma* ☎ *0521/386429* ⊕ *www.palazzodallarosaprati.it* ⤴ *19 rooms* ⑩ *No Meals.*

Parizzi Suites and Studio

$ | **B&B/INN** | A 17th-century palace has been refurbished with 21st-century amenities to provide a lovely place to rest one's head: the suites are under the same management as the Parizzi restaurant (it's a shared entrance), so you can just glide downstairs for a marvelous meal. **Pros:** breakfast served in rooms; central location; great staff. **Cons:** might be too chic for some; no parking; inadequate, overpriced breakfasts. $ *Rooms from: €75* ✉ *Strada della Repubblica 71, Parma* ☎ *0521/207032* ⊕ *www.parizzisuite.com* ⤴ *13 suites* ⑩ *No Meals.*

Continued on page 518

EMILIA
ONE TASTE AT A TIME

4 towns, dozens of foods, and a mouthful of flavors you'll never forget

Imagine biting into the silkiest prosciutto in the world or the most delectable homemade tortellini you've ever tasted. In Emilia, Italy's most famous food region, you'll discover simple tastes that exceed all expectations. Beginning in Parma and moving eastward to Bologna, you'll find the epicenters of such world-renowned culinary treats as *prosciutto crudo*, Parmigiano-Reggiano, *aceto balsamico*, and tortellini. The secret to this region is not the discovery of new and exotic delicacies, but rather the rediscovery of foods you thought you already knew—in much better versions than you've ever tasted before.

TASTE 1 | PROSCIUTTO CRUDO

From Piacenza to the Adriatic, ham is the king of meats in Emilia-Romagna, but nowhere is this truer than in **Parma.**

Parma is the world's capital of *prosciutto crudo*, raw cured ham (*crudo* for short). Ask for *crudo di Parma* to signal its local provenance; many other regions also make their own crudo.

CRUDO LANGUAGE

It's easy to get confused with the terminology. Crudo is the product that Americans simply call "prosciutto" or the Brits might call "Parma ham." *Prosciutto* in Italian, however, is a more general term that means any kind of ham, including *prosciutto cotto*, or simply *cotto*, which means "cooked ham." Cotto is an excellent product and frequent pizza topping that's closer to (but much better than) what Americans would put in a deli sandwich.

Crudo is traditionally eaten in one of three ways: in a dry sandwich (*panino*); by itself as an appetizer, often with shaved butter on top; or as part of an appetizer or snack platter of assorted *salumi* (cured meats).

WHAT TO LOOK FOR

For the best crudo di Parma, look for slices, always cut to order, that are razor thin and have a light, rosy red color (not dark red). Don't be shy about going into a simple *salumeria* (a purveyor of cured meats) and ordering crudo by the pound. You can enjoy it straight out of the package on a park bench—and why not?

BEST SPOT FOR A SAMPLE

You can't go wrong with any of Parma's famed salumerie, but **Salumeria Garibaldi** is one of the town's oldest and most reliable. You'll find not only spectacular prosciutto crudo, but also delectable cheeses, wines, porcini mushrooms, and more.

LEARN MORE

For more information on crudo di Parma, contact the **Consorzio del Prosciutto di Parma** through the tourist office, or stop by the famous store, La Prosciutteria.

Quality testing

Greasing the ham

Fire branding

Quality trademark

A cut above

TASTE 2 | PARMIGIANO-REGGIANO

From Parma, it's only a half-hour trip east to **Reggio Emilia**, the birthplace of the crumbly and renowned Parmigiano-Reggiano cheese. Reggio (not to be confused with Reggio di Calabria in the south) is a charming little Emilian town that has been the center of production for this legendary cheese for more than 70 years.

Warming milk in copper cauldrons

SAY CHEESE

Grana is the generic Italian term for hard, aged, full-flavored cheese that can be grated. Certain varieties of Pecorino Romano, for example, or Grana Padano, also fall under this term, but Parmigiano-Reggiano, aged for as long as four years, is the foremost example.

Breaking up the curds

NOT JUST FOR GRATING

In Italy, Parmigiano-Reggiano is not only grated onto pasta, but also often served by itself in chunks, either as an appetizer—perhaps accompanied by local salumi (cured meats)—or even for dessert, when it might be drizzled with honey or Modena's balsamic vinegar.

Placing cheese in molds

MEET THE MAKERS

If you're a cheese enthusiast, you shouldn't miss the chance to take a free two-hour guided tour of a Parmigiano-Reggiano–producing farm. You'll witness the entire process and get to meet the cheesemakers. Tours can be arranged by contacting the **Consorzio del Formaggio Parmigiano-Reggiano** in Reggio Emilia at least 20 days in advance. (Ask specifically for an English-language tour if that's what you want.)

Aging cheese wheels

BEST SPOT FOR A SAMPLE

The production of Parmigiano-Reggiano is heavily controlled by the Consorzio del Formaggio, so you can buy the cheese at any store or supermarket in the region and be virtually guaranteed equal quality and price. For a more distinctive shopping experience, however, try buying Parmigiano-Reggiano at the street market on Reggio's central square. The market takes place on Tuesday and Friday from 8 am to 1 pm year-round. You can pick up a small piece to eat while you're in Italy, or have larger pieces shrink-wrapped to take home.

Parmigiano-Reggiano

TASTE 3 | ACETO BALSAMICO DI MODENA

Tasting *tradizionale* vinegar

Modena is home to *Aceto Balsamico Tradizionale di Modena*, a kind of balsamic vinegar unparalleled anywhere else on Earth. The balsamic vinegar you've probably tried—even the pricier versions sold at specialty stores—may be good on salads, but it bears only a fleeting resemblance to the real thing.

HOW IS IT MADE?

The *tradizionale* vinegar that passes strict government standards is made with Trebbiano grape must, which is cooked over an open fire, reduced, and fermented from 12 to 25 or more years in a series of specially made wooden casks. As the vinegar becomes more concentrated, so much liquid evaporates that it takes more than 6 gallons of must to produce one quart of vinegar 12 years later. The result is an intense and syrupy concoction best enjoyed sparingly on grilled meats, strawberries, or Parmigiano-Reggiano cheese. The vinegar has such a complexity of flavor that some even drink it as an after-dinner liqueur.

Wooden casks for fermenting

BEST SPOT FOR A SAMPLE

The **Consorzio Produttori Aceto Balsamico Tradizionale di Modena** offers tours and tastings by reservation only. The main objective of the consortium is to monitor the quality of the authentic balsamic vinegar, made by only a few licensed restaurants and small producers.

The consortium also limits production, keeping prices sky high. Expect to pay €60 for a 100-ml (3.4 oz) bottle of tradizionale, which is generally aged 12 to 15 years, or €90 and up for the older tradizionale extra vecchio variety, which is aged 25 years.

But perhaps the best place to sample this vinegar, in its various stages and permutations, is in situ—that is, in any one of Modena's remarkable restaurants. You can have a simple trattoria meal at Ermes, whose recipes rely heavily on that liquid gold. Or you can splurge at Osteria Francescana, where three-starred Michelin chef Massimo Bottura works miracles with local ingredients.

OTHER TASTES OF EMILIA

■ **Cotechino:** a sausage made from pork and lard, a specialty of Modena

■ **Culatello de Zibello:** raw cured ham produced along the banks of the Po River, and cured and aged for more than 11 months

■ **Mortadella:** soft, smoked sausage made with beef, pork, cubes of pork fat, and seasonings, a specialty of Bologna

■ **Ragù:** a sauce made from minced pork and beef, simmered in milk, onions, carrots, and tomatoes

■ **Salama da sugo:** salty, oily sausage aged and then cooked, a specialty of Ferrara

■ **Tortelli and cappellacci:** pasta pillows with the same basic form as tortellini, but stuffed with cheese and vegetables

TASTE 4 | TORTELLINI

The venerable city of **Bologna** is called "the Fat" for a reason: this is the birthplace of tortellini, not to mention other specialties such as mortadella and ragù. Despite the city's new reputation for chic nightclubs and flashy boutiques, much of the food remains as it ever was.

Simple beginnings

You'll find the many Emilian variations on stuffed pasta all over the region, but they're perhaps at their best in Bologna, especially the native tortellini.

INSPIRED BY THE GODS

According to one legend, tortellini was inspired by the navel of Venus, goddess of love. As the story goes, Venus and some other gods stopped at a local inn for the night. A nosy chef went to their room to catch a glimpse of Venus. Peering through the keyhole, he saw her lying only partially covered on the bed. He was so inspired after seeing her perfect navel that he created a stuffed pasta, tortellini, in its image.

Stretching the dough

ON THE MENU

Tortellini is usually filled with beef (sometimes cheese), and is served two ways: *asciutta* is "dry," meaning it is served with a sauce such as ragù, or perhaps just with butter and Parmigiano. *Tortellini in brodo* is immersed in a lovely, savory beef broth.

Adding the filling

Tortellini alla panna contains a meat filling and is sauced with cream. Aficionados, however, argue frequently about what to stuff into these little bundles, and probably no two cooks do it the same. Some purists insist that only beef will do; others mix it up with sausages, mortadella, spices, and cheese (usually Parmigiano).

Shaping each piece

BEST SPOT TO BUY

Don't miss **Tamburini**, Bologna's best specialty food shop, where aromas of Emilia-Romagna's famous specialties waft out through the room and into the streets.

Tortellini di Bologna

Modena

56 km (35 miles) southeast of Parma, 38 km (24 miles) northwest of Bologna.

Modena is famous for local products: Maserati, Ferrari, and opera star Luciano Pavarotti, born near here and buried in his family plot in Montale Rangone in 2007. However, it's Modena's heavenly scented balsamic vinegar, aged up to 40 years, that's probably its greatest achievement. The town has become another Emilian food mecca, with terrific restaurants and *salumerie* (delicatessens) at every turn. Although surrounded by modern industrial sprawl, the city's small historic center is filled with narrow medieval streets, pleasant piazzas, and typical Emilian architecture.

GETTING HERE AND AROUND

Modena, on the Bologna–Milan line, is easily accessible by train, and it's an easy walk from the station to the centro storico. The Intercity connection from Florence takes about 90 minutes. By car, Modena is just off the A1 autostrada.

TOURS

Consorzio Produttori Aceto Balsamico Tradizionale di Modena

FOOD AND DRINK | TOURS | Connoisseurs of balsamic vinegar can arrange visits to local producers through the Consorzio. It's best to contact the organization via its website to obtain a list of producers offering tours. ⊠ *Strada Vaciglio Sud 1085/1, Modena* ☎ *059/395633* ⊕ *www.balsamico.it* ✉ *Free.*

VISITOR INFORMATION

CONTACT Modena Tourism Office. ⊠ *Piazza Grande 14, Modena* ☎ *059/2032660* ⊕ *www.visitmodena.it.*

 Sights

Duomo

CHURCH | Begun by the architect Lanfredo in 1099 and consecrated in 1184, the 12th-century Romanesque cathedral has medieval sculptures depicting scenes from Genesis on the facade, but walk around to the Piazza Grande side as well to see the building's marvelous arcading. It's a rare example of a cathedral having more than one principal view. The interior, completely clad in brick, imparts a sober and beautiful feel. An elaborate gallery has scenes of the Passion of Christ carved by Anselmo da Campione and his assistants circa 1160–80. The tomb of San Geminiano is in the crypt. The white-marble bell tower is known as **La Torre Ghirlandina** (the Little Garland Tower) because of its distinctive weather vane. ⊠ *Piazza Grande, Modena* ☎ *059/216078* ⊕ *www.duomodimodena.it.*

Museo Enzo Ferrari

OTHER MUSEUM | FAMILY | The home of the much revered founder of the Ferrari automobile marque, Enzo Ferrari, has been imaginatively enlarged and converted into a museum dedicated to his life and work. Besides the various trophies and engines on display, visitors can view an absorbing video that tells the Ferrari story and see the restored workshop belonging to Enzo's father, Alfredo, and, in a futuristic pavilion built alongside, a grand array of contemporary and vintage cars. ■**TIP→ A joint ticket is available with the Museo Ferrari in Maranello.** ⊠ *Via Paolo Ferrari 85, Modena* ☎ *059/4397979* ⊕ *www.museiferrari.com* ✉ *€17, combination ticket with Museo Ferrari in Maranello €24.*

Museo Ferrari

OTHER MUSEUM | FAMILY | This museum has become a pilgrimage site for auto enthusiasts. It takes you through the illustrious history of Ferrari, from early 1951 models to the present—the legendary F50 and cars driven by Michael Schumacher in Formula One victories being highlights. You can also take a look at the glamorous life of founder Enzo Ferrari (a re-creation of his office is on-site) and get a glance at the production process. ⊠ *Via Dino Ferrari 43, Maranello* ✣ *In Maranello, 17 km (11 miles) south of Modena* ☎ *0536/949713* ⊕ *www.museiferrari.com* ✉ *€17, combination ticket with Museo Enzo Ferrari in Modena €24.*

Palazzo dei Musei

ART MUSEUM | Modena's principal museum, housed in the Palazzo dei Musei and located just a short walk from the Duomo, has a collection assembled in the mid-17th century by Francesco d'Este (1610–58), Duke of Modena. The **Galleria Estense** is named in his honor. The gallery also houses the **Biblioteca Estense,** a huge collection of illuminated manuscripts, of which the best known is the beautifully illustrated *Bible of Borso d'Este* (1455–61). A map dated 1501 was one of the first in the world to show that Columbus had discovered America. To get here, follow the Via Emilia, which runs through the heart of the town, to Via di Sant'Agostino. ⊠ *Largo Porta Sant'Agostino 337, Modena* ☎ *059/2033125* ⊕ *www.palazzodeimuseimodena.it* ✉ *€6.*

🍴 Restaurants

Aldina

$$ | EMILIAN | On the second floor of a building across from the covered market, steps from the Piazza Grande, this simple, typical trattoria is in the very nerve center of the city. Here you'll find exemplary preparations of the region's crown jewels: tortellini in brodo, tagliatelle al ragù, and roasted meats. **Known for:** tortellini in brodo; authentically old-fashioned character; inexpensive regional food loved by locals. ⑤ *Average main: €20* ⊠ *Via Albinelli 40, Modena* ☎ *059/236106* ⊕ *www.trattoriaaldina.it* ▭ *No credit cards* ⊗ *Closed Sun. Aug. No dinner Mon.–Thurs.*

★ Hosteria Giusti

$$$ | EMILIAN | In the back room of the Salumeria Giusti, established in 1605 and reportedly the world's oldest deli, you'll find just four tables in a room tastefully done with antique furnishings. You'll also find some of the best food in Emilia-Romagna—perfectly executed takes on traditional dishes such as *gnocco fritto* (fried dough) stuffed with pancetta or prosciutto, and *anolini in brodo di Cappone* (pasta in possibly the most fragrant broth in the world). **Known for:** popular and busy; gnocco fritto with prosciutto; cozy setting. ⑤ *Average main: €26* ⊠ *Via Farini 75 and Vicolo Squallore 46, Modena* ☎ *059/222533* ⊕ *www.hosteriagiusti.it* ⊗ *Closed Sun. and Mon., Aug., and Dec. No dinner.*

★ Mon Café

$ | ECLECTIC | Locals love this lively café because it does just about everything and does it well, beginning at 7 in the morning with excellent coffee and tasty breakfast pastries and ending long after dark with *aperitivi*, cocktails, and dinner. The fairly limited menu includes Italian tapas and starters and mains with vegetarian and fish options. **Known for:** atmospheric interior; fresh fruit cocktails; excellent service. ⑤ *Average main: €14* ⊠ *Corso Canalchiaro 128, Modena* ☎ *059/223257* ⊗ *Closed Mon. No dinner Sun.*

★ Osteria Francescana

$$$$ | EMILIAN | Chef-proprietor Massimo Bottura has done stints with Adrià and Ducasse, takes inspiration from music and literature, and pours all these influences into creating some of the most memorable food in all of Italy while remaining true to his Modenese roots. The restaurant contains only 12 tables and although it's possible to order à la carte, most everyone opts for the twelve-course tasting menu with the accompanying wine pairing. **Known for:** reservations required months in advance; five stages of Parmesan signature dish; a chef who makes food art. ⑤ *Average* *main: €110* ⊠ *Via Stella 22, Modena* ☎ *059/223912* ⊕ *www.osteriafrances-cana.it* ⊘ *Closed Sun., Mon., and 2 wks in Aug.*

Trattoria Ermes

$$ | **EMILIAN** | Mercurial host Ermes Rinaldi greets you as you walk in and seats you wherever he happens to have room: it doesn't matter that you might be put with people you don't know, since the host feels this quasi-communal style of lunching encourages conviviality. In the kitchen, Bruna, Ermes's wife, turns out splendid versions of *cucina casalinga modenesi* (home cooking, Modena-style). **Known for:** slapdash service; popular with everyone from businesspeople in suits to construction workers; primi and secondi change daily. Ⓢ *Average main: €18* ⊠ *Via Ganaceto 89–91, Modena* ☎ *059/238065* ⊘ *Closed Sun. No dinner.*

☕ Coffee and Quick Bites

Archer

$$ | **ITALIAN** | Bibliophile proprietor (she named her establishment after a Henry James heroine) Marina Bersani presides over this sleek wine bar. High ceilings provide plenty of places to store her vast collection of unique wines, and the short-but-sweet menu offers lots of traditional classics like *affettati misti* (sliced, cured pork products), as well as cheese plates. **Known for:** outdoor seating; unique wines; crostini for snacking. Ⓢ *Average main: €15* ⊠ *Via Cesare Battisti 54, Modena* ☎ *059/237656* ⊘ *Closed Mon. and 3 wks in Aug.*

Hotels

La Maison du Charme

$$ | **B&B/INN** | Gracious host Maria Luisa Valentini has turned part of her family's early-20th-century villa into a charming bed-and-breakfast complete with peri-od-appropriate furniture and bright aqua walls. **Pros:** intimate experience; historic ambience; quiet location, yet close to the center. **Cons:** steps to climb and no eleva-tor; antique furniture not always practical or usable; books up quickly. Ⓢ *Rooms from: €125* ⊠ *Via Usiglio 12, Modena* ☎ *349/1984584* ⊕ *www.bblamaison-ducharmemodena.it* ⌁ *2 suites* ⦿ *Free Breakfast.*

Phi Hotel Canalgrande

$$ | **HOTEL** | In a calm location within easy walking distance of Modena's main tour-ist attractions, this hotel housed in an old palazzo has plenty of old-world character in the form of antique paintings, fancy plasterwork, and trompe l'oeil in the pub-lic rooms. **Pros:** secure garage parking; great central position; spacious gardens. **Cons:** service is sometimes poor; dated in parts; inadequate soundproofing in some rooms. Ⓢ *Rooms from: €132* ⊠ *Corso Canalgrande 6, Modena* ☎ *059/217160* ⊕ *www.hotelcanalgrandemodena.com* ⌁ *67 rooms* ⦿ *Free Breakfast.*

★ Quartopiano

$$ | **B&B/INN** | Proprietor Antonio di Resta shows his impeccable sense of style and love of all things French in a lovely little bed-and-breakfast just a few steps from the Duomo. **Pros:** intimate setup in the heart of town; owner provides helpful local advice; lovely bath products and fluffy towels. **Cons:** breakfast in a sepa-rate establishment; space a bit cramped; with only two rooms, it books up quickly. Ⓢ *Rooms from: €140* ⊠ *Via Bonacorsa 27, Modena* ☎ *348/0189112* ⊕ *www.bbquar-topiano.it* ⌁ *2 rooms* ⦿ *Free Breakfast.*

Bologna

Bologna, a city rich with cultural jewels, has long been one of the best-kept secrets in northern Italy. Tourists in the know bask in the shadow of its leaning medieval towers and devour the city's wonderful food.

The charm of the centro storico, with its red-arcaded passageways and side-walks, can be attributed to wise city counselors who, at the beginning of the 13th century, decreed that roads couldn't be built without *portici* (porticoes). Were these counselors to return to town eight centuries later, they'd marvel at how little has changed.

Bologna, with a population of about 388,000, has a university-town vibe—and it feels young and lively in a way that many other Italian cities don't. It also feels full of Italians in a way that many other towns, thronged with tourists, don't. Bolognesi come out at aperitivo time, and you might be struck by the fact that it's not just youngsters who are out for the passeggiata or a glass of wine with affettati misti.

From as early as the Middle Ages the town was known as "Bologna the Fat" for the agricultural prosperity that resulted in a well-fed population. In the 21st century Bolognese food remains, arguably, the best in Italy. With its sublime cuisine, lively spirit, and largely undiscovered art, Bologna is a memorable destination.

GETTING HERE AND AROUND

Frequent train service from Florence to Bologna makes getting here easy. The Italo and Frecciarossa and Frecciargento (high-speed trains) run several times an hour and take just under 40 minutes. Otherwise, you're left with the *regionale* (regional) trains, which putter along and get you to Bologna in around 1¾ hours. The historic center is an interesting and relatively effortless walk from the station—though it takes about 20 minutes.

If you're driving from Florence, take the A1, exiting onto the A14, and then get on the RA1 to Exit 7–Bologna Centrale. The trip takes about an hour. From Milan, take the A1, exiting to the A14 as you near the city; from there, take the A13 and exit at Bologna; then follow the RA1 to Exit 7–Bologna Centrale. The trip takes just under three hours.

VISITOR INFORMATION
CONTACTS Bologna Tourism Offices.
✉ *Aeroporto di Bologna, Bologna* ☎ *051/6472201* ⊕ *www.bolognawelcome.com.*

Sights

Piazza Maggiore and the adjacent Piazza del Nettuno are the historic centers of the city. Arranged around these two squares are the imposing Basilica di San Petronio, the massive Palazzo Comunale, the Palazzo del Podestà, the Palazzo Re Enzo, and the Fontana del Nettuno—one of the most visually harmonious groupings of public buildings in the country. From here, sights that aren't on one of the piazzas are but a short walk away, along delightful narrow cobblestone streets or under the ubiquitous arcades that double as municipal umbrellas. Take at least a full day to explore Bologna; it's compact and lends itself to easy exploration, but there's plenty to see.
■TIP→ **The first Sunday of the month is free at many museums.**

Basilica di San Petronio

CHURCH | Construction on this vast cathedral began in 1390; and the work, as you can see, still isn't finished more than 600 years later. The wings of the transept are missing and the facade is only partially decorated, lacking most of the marble that was intended to adorn it. The main doorway was carved in 1425 by the great Sienese master Jacopo della Quercia. Above the center of the door is a Madonna and Child flanked by saints Ambrose and Petronius, the city's patrons. Michelangelo, Giulio Romano, and Andrea Palladio (among others), submitted designs for the facade, which were all eventually rejected. The Bolognesi had planned an even bigger church—you can see the columns erected to support the larger version outside the east end—but had to tone down construction when the university seat was established next door in 1561. The **Museo di San Petronio** contains

Bologna

Sights ▼

1 Basilica di
San Petronio **B3**

2 Fontana del Nettuno... **C3**

3 Le Due Torri............. **C3**

4 MAMbo.................. **B1**

5 Museo Internazionale
e Biblioteca della
Musica di Bologna **D4**

6 Palazzo Comunale **B3**

7 Palazzo del Podestà..... **C3**

8 Palazzo Re Enzo.......... **C3**

9 Pinacoteca Nazionale.. **E2**

10 San Domenico **C4**

11 Santo Stefano........... **D4**

12 Torre dell'Orologio
(Clock Tower)........... **B3**

13 Università di Bologna ... **E2**

Restaurants ▼

1 Da Cesari **B4**

2 Da Gianni a la Vecia
Bulagna.................... **C3**

3 Drogheria della Rosa... **D4**

4 Ristorante I Portici....... **C1**

5 RIstorante Marconi..... **A4**

6 Trattoria del Rosso....... **C2**

7 Trattoria di Via Serra **C1**

Quick Bites ▼

1 Sfoglia Rina.............. **C3**

2 Tamburini **C3**

Hotels ▼

1 Art Hotel Novecento ... **B3**

2 Art Hotel Orologio **B3**

3 Hotel Corona D'Oro...... **C3**

models showing how it was originally supposed to look. The most important art in the church is in the fourth chapel on the left: these frescoes by Giovanni di Modena date to 1410–15. ✉ *Piazza Maggiore* ☎ *051/231415* ⊕ *www.basilicadisanpetronio.org* ✆ *Free* ◔ *Museo di San Petronio closed Mon.*

Fontana del Nettuno

FOUNTAIN | Sculptor Giambologna's elaborate 1563–66 Baroque fountain and monument to Neptune occupying Piazza Nettuno has been aptly nicknamed "Il Gigante" (The Giant). Its exuberantly sensual mermaids and undraped god of the sea drew fire when it was constructed—but not enough, apparently, to dissuade the populace from using the fountain as a public washing stall for centuries. ✉ *Piazza del Nettuno, Piazza Maggiore.*

Le Due Torri

NOTABLE BUILDING | Two landmark medieval towers, mentioned by Dante in *The Inferno*, stand side by side in the compact Piazza di Porta Ravegnana. Once, every family of importance had a tower as a symbol of prestige and power (and as a potential fortress). Now only 24 remain out of nearly 100 that once presided over the city. Torre Garisenda (late 11th century), which tilts 10 feet off perpendicular, was shortened to 157 feet in the 1300s and is now closed to visitors. Torre degli Asinelli (1119) is 318 feet tall and leans 7½ feet. If you're up to a serious physical challenge—and not claustrophobic—you may want to climb its 498 narrow, wooden steps to get the view over Bologna. ✉ *Piazza di Porta Ravegnana, East of Piazza Maggiore* ⊕ *www.duetorribologna.com* ✆ *€5.*

MAMbo

ART MUSEUM | The museum—the name stands for Museo d'Arte Moderna di Bologna, or Bologna's Museum of Modern Art—houses a permanent collection of modern art (defined as post–World War II until five minutes ago) and stages a revolving series of temporary exhibitions by cutting-edge artists. All of this is set within a remarkable space: you might have a hard time telling that the sleek minimalist structure was built in 1915 as the Forno del Pane, a large bakery that made bread for city residents. A bookshop and a restaurant complete the complex, the latter offering Sunday brunch and delicious aperitivi. ✉ *Via Don Minzoni 14, Bologna* ☎ *051/6496611* ⊕ *www.mambo-bologna.org* ✆ *€6* ◔ *Closed Mon.*

Museo Internazionale e Biblioteca della Musica di Bologna

OTHER MUSEUM | The music museum in the spectacular Palazzo Aldini-Sanguinetti, with its 17th- and 18th-century frescoes, offers among its exhibits a 1606 harpsichord and a collection of beautiful music manuscripts dating from the 1500s. ✉ *Strada Maggiore 34, University area* ☎ *051/2757711* ⊕ *www.museibologna.it* ◔ *Closed Mon.* ✆ *€5.*

Palazzo Comunale

GOVERNMENT BUILDING | When Bologna was an independent city-state, this huge palace dating from the 13th to 15th century was the seat of government—a function it still serves today in a building that is a mélange of styles. Over the door is a statue of Bologna-born Pope Gregory XIII (reigned 1572–85), most famous for reorganizing the calendar. There are good views from the upper stories. The first-floor Sala Rossa (Red Room) and the Sala del Consiglio Comunale (City Council Hall) are open with advance request and during some exhibitions. Within the palazzo are two museums. The Collezioni Comunali d'Arte exhibits medieval paintings as well as some Renaissance works by Luca Signorelli (circa 1445–1523) and Tintoretto (1518–94). Underground caves and the foundations of the old cathedral can be visited by appointment; contact the tourist office. The old stock exchange, part of the Palazzo Comunale, which you enter from Piazza Nettuno, has been turned into a library. Dubbed the Sala

Borsa, it has an impressive interior court-yard. ✉ *Piazza Maggiore 6, Piazza Maggiore* ☎ *051/2193998 Collezioni Comunali d'Arte, 051/2194400 Sala Borsa* ⊕ *www.museibologna.it* ✉ *Collezioni Comunali d'Arte €6; Sala Borsa free* ⊙ *Collezioni Comunali d'Arte closed Mon.; Sala Borsa closed Sun.*

Palazzo del Podestà

NOTABLE BUILDING | This classic Renaissance palace facing the Basilica di San Petronio was erected from 1484–94, and attached to it is the soaring Torre dell'Arengo. The bells in the tower have rung whenever the city has celebrated, mourned, or called its citizens to arms. It's not open to the public. ✉ *Piazza Maggiore 1, Piazza Maggiore.*

Palazzo Re Enzo

CASTLE/PALACE | Built in 1244, this palace became home to King Enzo of Sardinia, who was imprisoned here in 1249 after he was captured during the fierce battle of Fossalta. He died here 23 years later. The palace has other macabre associations as well: common criminals received last rites in the tiny courtyard chapel before being executed in Piazza Maggiore. The courtyard is worth a peek, but the palace merely houses government offices as well as special events. ✉ *Piazza del Nettuno 1/c, Piazza Maggiore* ☎ *051/6583121.*

Pinacoteca Nazionale

ART GALLERY | Bologna's principal art gallery contains many works by the immortals of Italian painting; its prize possession is the *Ecstasy of St. Cecilia* by Raphael (1483–1520). There's also a beautiful polyptych by Giotto (1267–1337), as well as *Madonna with Child and Saints Margaret, Jerome, and Petronius* (altarpiece of St. Margaret) by Parmigianino (1503–40); note the rapt eye contact between St. Margaret and the Christ child. ✉ *Via delle Belle Arti 56, University area* ☎ *051/4209411* ⊕ *www.pinacotecabologna.beniculturali.it* ⊙ *Closed Mon.* ✉ *€6.*

San Domenico

CHURCH | The tomb of St. Dominic, who died here in 1221, is called the **Arca di San Domenico,** and is found in this church in the sixth chapel on the right. Many artists participated in its decoration, notably Niccolò di Bari, who was so proud of his 15th-century contribution that he changed his name to Niccolò dell'Arca to recall this famous work. The young Michelangelo (1475–1564) carved the angel on the right and the image of San Petronio. In the right transept of the church is a tablet marking the last resting place of hapless King Enzo, the Sardinian ruler imprisoned in the Palazzo Re Enzo. The attached museum contains religious relics. ✉ *Piazza San Domenico 13, off Via Garibaldi, South of Piazza Maggiore* ☎ *051/6400411* ⊕ *www.sandomenicobologna.it.*

★ Santo Stefano

CHURCH | This splendid and unusual basilica contains between four and seven connected churches (authorities differ). A 4th-century temple dedicated to Isis originally occupied this site, but much of what you see was erected between the 10th and 12th centuries. The oldest existing building is **Santi Vitale e Agricola,** parts of which date from the 5th century. The exquisite beehive-shape San Sepolcro contains a Nativity scene much loved by Bologna's children, who come at Christmastime to pay their respects to the Christ child. Just outside the church, which probably dates from the 5th century (with later alterations), is the **Cortile di Pilato** (Pilate's Courtyard), named for the basin in the center. Despite the fact that the basin was probably crafted around the 8th century, legend has it that Pontius Pilate washed his hands in it after condemning Christ. Also in the building are a museum displaying various medieval religious works and its shop, which sells honey, shampoos, and jams made by the monks. ✉ *Piazza Santo Stefano, Via Santo Stefano 24, University area* ☎ *320/9065699* ⊕ *www.santostefanobologna.it* ⊙ *Closed during services.*

Torre dell'Orologio (Clock Tower)

CLOCK | For a spectacular view of Piazza Maggiore and the Bolognesi hills from two terraces as well as a look at how Bologna's oldest clock keeps the city punctual, climb the Torre dell'Orologio, or d'Arccursio tower. Opened to the public in 2021, it was built in 1249 as University of Bologna law professor Accursio da Bagnolo's monumental timepiece for his home in the piazza. The clock mechanism you'll see dates from 1773, as found on the horologist's inscription "Rinaldo Gandofli Accademic Clementi Fece 1773," among the clock's movement, gears, and swinging pendulum. An audio guide for your mobile phone, accessible via a QR code, shares the story of the tower and the clock's history. ⊠ *Piazza Maggiore, 6, Bologna* ☎ *051/658 3111* ⊕ *www.bolognawelcome.com* ✆ *€8* ☉ *Closed Mon.* ⌨ *Reservations required.*

Università di Bologna

COLLEGE | Take a stroll through the streets of the university area: a jumble of buildings, some dating as far back as the 15th century and most to the 17th and 18th. The neighborhood, as befits a college town, is full of bookshops, coffee bars, and inexpensive restaurants. Though not particularly distinguished, they're characteristic of student life in the city. Try eating at the *mensa universitaria* (cafeteria) if you want to strike up a conversation with local students (most speak English). Political slogans and sentiments are scrawled on walls all around the university and tend to be ferociously leftist, sometimes juvenile, and often entertaining. Among the university museums, the most interesting is the **Museo di Palazzo Poggi,** which displays scientific instruments plus paleontological, botanical, and university-related artifacts. ⊠ *Via Zamboni 33, University area* ☎ *051/2099610 museum* ⊕ *www. museopalazzopoggi.unibo.it* ☉ *Closed Mon.* ✆ *€5 museum.*

🍴 Restaurants

★ Da Cesari

$$ | EMILIAN | Host Paolino Cesari has been presiding over his eatery since 1962, and he and his staff go out of their way to make you feel at home. The food's terrific, and if you love pork products, try anything on the menu with *mora romagnola:* Paolino has direct contact with the people who raise this breed that nearly became extinct (he calls it "my pig"). **Known for:** traditional setting; pork dishes like flavorful salame; wine list with lots of local bottles. ⑤ *Average main: €18* ⊠ *Via de' Carbonesi 8, South of Piazza Maggiore* ☎ *051/237710* ⊕ *www.da-cesari.it* ☉ *Closed Sun., Aug., and 1 wk in Jan.*

★ Da Gianni a la Vecia Bulagna

$$ | EMILIAN | At the bottom of an alley off Piazza Maggiore, this unassuming place—known to locals as simply "Da Gianni"—is all about food. The usual starters are on hand—including a tasty *tortellini in brodo*—in addition to daily specials; *bollito misto* (mixed boiled meat) is a fine option here, and the *cotechino con puré di patate* (pork sausage with mashed potatoes) is elevated to sublimity by the accompanying salsa verde. **Known for:** busy local spot; tortellini in brodo; efficient and friendly service. ⑤ *Average main: €16* ⊠ *Via Clavature 18, Piazza Maggiore* ☎ *051/229434* ⊕ *www. trattoria-gianni.it* ☉ *Closed Mon. and 1 wk early Jan. No dinner Sun.*

Drogheria della Rosa

$$ | EMILIAN | Chef Emanuele Addone, who presides over his intimate little restaurant set in an ex-pharmacy, hits the food markets every day and buys what looks good, ensuring seasonality. He sauces his tortelli stuffed with *squacquerone* and *stracchino* (two creamy, fresh cow's-milk cheeses) with artichokes, zucchini flowers, or mushrooms, depending on the time of year. **Known for:** no written menu; idiosyncratic surroundings; seasonal filled tortelli. ⑤ *Average* main: €18 ✉ Via Cartoleria 10, University area ☎ 051/222529 ⊕ www.drogheriadel-larosa.it ⊘ Closed Sun.

Ristorante I Portici

$$$$ | EMILIAN | The frescoed ceiling, parquet flooring, and live classical music are clues that this sophisticated restaurant (part of the hotel of the same name) occupies a former theater and *café-chantant,* or musical venue, from the late 19th century. It's the perfect setting for an evening of fine dining featuring mainly Emilian dishes with modern touches—and even the odd southern influence picked up by the award-winning chef Emanuele Petrosino from his years working in Naples. **Known for:** sophisticated culinary offerings; refined and attentive service; sumptuous surroundings in a former theater. $ Average main: €43 ✉ Via dell'Indipendenza 69, North of Piazza Maggiore ☎ 051/42185 ⊕ www.iporticihotel.com ⊘ Closed Sun. and Mon. No lunch.

Ristorante Marconi

$$$ | EMILIAN | Siblings Aurora and Massimo Mazzucchelli have succeeded in enticing a steady stream of Bolognesi to their celebrated eatery 15 km (9 miles) south of the city to sample their startlingly modern gourmet creations. Ingredients are fresh, rich, and well balanced in dishes featuring pigeon breast and eel, while flavorsome desserts include a sorbet of the day. **Known for:** discreet but attentive service; sober style; intriguing and unusual dishes in tasting menus. $ Average main: €30 ✉ Via Porrettana 291, Sasso Marconi ☎ 051/846216 ⊕ www.ristoran-temarconi.it ⊘ Closed Mon. and 10 days in Aug. No dinner Sun.

Trattoria del Rosso

$ | EMILIAN | Here, in the mirrored interior, a mostly young crowd chows down on classic regional fare at affordable prices. Nimble staff bearing multiple plates sashay neatly between the closely spaced tables delivering such standards as *tortellini in brodo* and *Cotoletta alla Bolognese* (veal with Parmigiano-Reggiano and

prosciutto). **Known for:** fun atmosphere; student haunt with great-value regional food; affordable wine list. $ Average main: €10 ✉ Via Augusto Righi 30/A, University area ☎ 051/236730 ⊘ Closed Mon. No dinner Sun.

Trattoria di Via Serra

$$ | EMILIAN | At this simple trattoria off the main tourist circuit, much care has been taken with the decor: the rooms, overseen by host Flavio, are small and intimate, and the wooden walls painted a creamy whitish gray. Chef Tommaso gives equal care to the menu and deftly turns out Bolognese classics, as well as dishes with a modern twist—among the antipasti, his *tosone fresco avvolto nella pancetta* incorporates Parmigiano-Reggiano, unsmoked bacon, and greens. **Known for:** convivial atmosphere; all locally sourced ingredients; modern riffs on classic dishes. $ Average main: €18 ✉ Via Serra 9B, Bologna ☎ 051/6312330 ⊕ www.trattoriadiviaserra.it ⊘ Closed Mon.

☕ Coffee and Quick Bites

Sfoglia Rina

$ | ITALIAN | FAMILY | The *pastaio* (pasta-maker) tradition in this bright honeycomb tiled pasta shop and restaurant—which often has a line around the block—started nearly 60 years ago in a town about six miles southwest of Bologna. There, Rina De Franceschi rolled *sfoglia* (dough) following family recipes. **Known for:** affordable and wide-ranging menu; fresh pasta in many varieties; weekly vegetarian-friendly specials. $ Average main: €10 ✉ Via Castiglione, 5/b, Bologna ☎ 051/9911710 ⊕ www.sfogliarina.it.

Tamburini

$$ | WINE BAR | Two small rooms inside plus kegs and bar stools outside make up this lively, packed little spot. The overwhelming plate of *affettati misti* is crammed with top-quality local cured

meats and succulent cheeses, and the adjacent salumeria offers many wonderful items to take away. **Known for:** lively atmosphere with a vast wine selection; cheese and cured meat plates; abundant portions. $ *Average main: €15* ⊠ *Via Caprarie 1, Piazza Maggiore* ☎ *051/234726* ⊕ *www.tamburini.com.*

Hotels

★ Art Hotel Novecento

$$ | **HOTEL** | This swank place, with decor inspired by European design of the 1930s, is in a little piazza just minutes from Piazza Maggiore. **Pros:** spacious single rooms ideal for solo travelers; sumptuous buffet breakfast; friendly, capable concierge service. **Cons:** cheapest doubles are small; the piazza outside can get noisy; expensive parking. $ *Rooms from: €139* ⊠ *Piazza Galileo 4/3, Piazza Maggiore* ☎ *051/7457311* ⊕ *www.art-hotel-novecento.com* ❍I *Free Breakfast* ⌐ *24 rooms.*

★ Art Hotel Orologio

$$ | **HOTEL** | **FAMILY** | The location of this stylish and welcoming family-run hotel can't be beat: it's right around the corner from Piazza Maggiore on a quiet piazza. **Pros:** central location; welcomes all animals; family-friendly rooms. **Cons:** needs some updating; pet-friendly environment may not appeal to allergy sufferers; limited facilities. $ *Rooms from: €185* ⊠ *Via IV Novembre 10, Piazza Maggiore* ☎ *051/7457411* ⊕ *www.art-hotel-orologio. com* ⌐ *32 rooms* ❍I *Free Breakfast.*

Hotel Corona D'Oro

$$$ | **HOTEL** | Elegance and historic charm are the keynotes of this central lodging, converted from a medieval palazzo and just a short stroll from Piazza Maggiore and all the main attractions. **Pros:** spacious and silent rooms; historic character; helpful, friendly staff. **Cons:** some rooms are small; no restaurant; steps on some floors are not ideal for anyone with mobility issues. $ *Rooms from: €208* ⊠ *Via*

Oberdan 12, Bologna ☎ *051/7457611* ⊕ *www.hco.it* ⌐ *40 rooms* ❍I *Free Breakfast.*

Nightlife

As a university town, Bologna has long been known for its busy nightlife. By as early as 1300, it was said to have 150 taverns, and most of the city's current 200-plus pubs and bars are frequented by students and young adults—with the university area forming the hub. The pedestrian zone on Via del Pratello, lined with plenty of bars, also has a hopping nightlife scene, as does Via delle Moline, with its cutting-edge cafés and bars. A more upscale, low-key evening experience can be had at one of Bologna's many wine bars, where the *apericena* (snack accompaniments) are often substantial enough to constitute dinner.

BARS

Bar Calice

BARS | A year-round indoor-outdoor operation (with heat lamps), this bar is extremely popular with thirtysomethings, sometimes pushing baby carriages. Its large menu includes raw oysters. There's also a dining room upstairs. ⊠ *Via Clavature 13, at Via Marchesana, Piazza Maggiore* ☎ *051/236523.*

Le Stanze

BARS | At Le Stanze you can sip an aperitivo or a late-night drink amid a young and noisy clientele. The decor includes 17th-century frescoes in what was once the private chapel of the Palazzo Bentivoglio. The adjoining restaurant offers a small selection of Bologna favorites. ⊠ *Via del Borgo di San Pietro 1, University area* ☎ *051/228767* ⊕ *www.lestanzecafe.it.*

★ Nu Lounge Bar

BARS | This high-energy tiki bar draws a cocktail-loving crowd that enjoys fun drinks such as "Hellvis," made with lime, agave syrup, rum, grenadine, ginger, and Angostura. ⊠ *Via de' Musei 6, off*

Buca San Petronio, Piazza Maggiore
☎ 051/222532 ⊕ www.nuloungebar.com.

Osteria del Sole

WINE BARS | Although "osteria" in an establishment's name suggests that food will be served, such is not the case here. This place is all about drinking wine; the entrance door has warnings such as "He who doesn't drink will please stay outside" and "Dogs who don't drink are forbidden to come in." It's been around since 1465, and locals pack in, bearing food from outside to accompany the wine. ⊠ Vicolo Ranocchi 1/d, Piazza Maggiore ☎ 347/9680171 ⊕ www.osteriadelsole.it.

CAFÉS

★ Zanarini

CAFÉS | Chic Bolognesi congregate at this bar that serves coffee in the morning and swank aperitivi in the evening. Tasty sandwiches and pastries are also available. ⊠ Piazza Galvani 1, Piazza Maggiore ☎ 051/2750041.

MUSIC VENUES

Cantina Bentivoglio

LIVE MUSIC | With live music including jazz staged nearly every evening, Cantina Bentivoglio is one of Bologna's most renowned nightspots. You can enjoy light and more substantial meals here as well. ⊠ Via Mascarella 4/B, University area ☎ 051/265416 ⊕ www.cantinabentivoglio.it.

Osteria Buca delle Campane

LIVE MUSIC | In a 13th-century building, this underground tavern has good, inexpensive food, and the after-dinner scene is popular with locals, including students, who come to listen to the live music on weekends and some other nights. The kitchen stays open until long past midnight. Reservations are strongly advised. ⊠ Via Benedetto XIV 4, University area ☎ 051/220918 ⊕ www.bucadellecampane.it.

Performing Arts

MUSIC AND OPERA

Teatro Comunale

MUSIC | This 18th-century theater presents concerts by Italian and international orchestras throughout the year, but the highly acclaimed opera performances from January to July and October to December are the main attraction. Reserve seats for those performances well in advance. ⊠ Largo Respighi 1, University area ☎ 051/529019 ⊕ www.tcbo.it.

🛍 Shopping

CLOTHING

Castel Guelfo The Style Outlets

OUTLET | If you don't feel like paying Galleria Cavour prices, this mall is about 20 minutes outside Bologna. It includes more than 50 stores, among them such top brands as Swarovski. ⊠ Via del Commercio 4/2, Loc. Poggio Piccolo, Castel Guelfo ⊹ Take the A14 toward Imola, Castel San Pietro Terme exit; 299 m (980 feet) after tollbooth, turn right onto Via San Carlo ☎ 0542/670765 ⊕ www.thestyleoutlets.it.

Galleria Cavour

MALL | One of the most upscale malls in Italy, the Galleria houses many of the fashion giants, including Armani, Gucci, Saint Laurent, and Tod's. ⊠ Via Luigi Carlo Farini, South of Piazza Maggiore ⊕ www.galleriacavour.it.

WINE AND FOOD

Bologna is a good place to buy wine. Several shops have a bewilderingly large selection—to go straight to the top, ask the managers which wines have won the prestigious Tre Bicchieri (Three Glasses) award from Gambero Rosso's wine bible, Vini d'Italia.

Eataly

FOOD | At this lively shop—the original location in the now international Italian cuisine empire—with an attached bookstore, you can grab a bite to eat or have a glass f wine while stocking up on high-qual-y olive oil, vinegar, cured meats, and rtisanal pasta. On the top floor, you can ave a full-fledged trattoria meal. There's a econd entrance on Via Pescherie Vecchie. ⊠ Via degli Orefici 19, Piazza Maggiore ☎ 051/0952820 ⊕ www.eataly.net.

noteca Italiana

VINE/SPIRITS | Consistently recognized s one of the best wine stores in the ountry, Enoteca Italiana lives up to its eputation—as it says, "every good bottle as a good story"—with shelves lined vith excellent selections from all over taly at reasonable prices. In addition, the lelicious plates of cured meats served vith wines by the glass, make a great ght lunch. ⊠ Via Marsala 2/b, North of Piazza Maggiore ☎ 051/235989 ⊕ www. enotecaitaliana.it.

a Baita Vecchia Malga

FOOD | Fresh tagliolini, tortellini, and other Bolognese pasta delicacies are sold here, along with sublime food to eat at small ables here or take away. The cheese counter is laden with superlative local specimens. ⊠ Via Pescherie Vecchie 3/a, Piazza Maggiore ☎ 051/223940 ⊕ www. vecchiamalganegozi.com.

Majani

CANDY | Classy Majani has been produc-ing chocolate since 1796. Its staying power may be attributed to high-quality confections that are as pretty to look at as they are to eat. ⊠ Via de' Carbonesi 5, Piazza Maggiore ☎ 051/234302 ⊕ www. majani.it.

Mercato delle Erbe

FOOD | This food market and food hall that opened in 1910 bustles year-round. ⊠ Via Ugo Bassi 23, Piazza Maggiore ☎ 335/4112427 ⊕ www.mercatodelleerbe.it.

Mercato di Mezzo

FOOD | This former fruit and vegetable market has morphed into a food hall. Various stalls offer a wide range of Italian and Romagnolo cuisine from pasta to fish to pizza and cured meats and cheeses. Order from whatever place strikes your fancy, and sit anywhere there's room. There's a second entrance on Via Pescherie Vecchie. ⊠ Via Clavature 12, Piazza Maggiore ☎ 051/228782.

Paolo Atti & Figli

FOOD | This place has been producing some of Bologna's finest pastas, cakes, and other delicacies since 1868. There's a second branch at Via Drapperie 6. ⊠ Via Caprarie 7, Piazza Maggiore ☎ 051/220425 ⊕ www.paoloatti.com.

★ Roccati

CANDY | Sculptural works of chocolate, as well as basic bonbons and simpler sweets, have been crafted here since 1909. ⊠ Via Clavature 17/a, Piazza Maggiore ☎ 051/261964 ⊕ www.roccaticioccolato.com.

Ferrara

47 km (29 miles) northeast of Bologna, 74 km (46 miles) northwest of Ravenna.

When the legendary Ferrarese filmmaker Michelangelo Antonioni called his beloved hometown "a city that you can see only partly, while the rest disappears to be imagined," perhaps he was referring to the low-lying mist that rolls in off the Adriatic each winter and shrouds Ferrara's winding knot of medieval alleyways, turreted palaces, and ancient wine bars—once frequented by the likes of Copernicus—in a ghostly fog. But perhaps Antonioni was also suggesting that Ferrara's striking beauty often conceals a dark and tortured past.

Today you're likely to be charmed by Ferrara's prosperous air and meticulous cleanliness, its excellent restaurants and chic bars (for coffee and any other liquid refreshment), and its lively wine-bar scene. You'll find aficionados gathering outside any of the wine bars near the Duomo even on the foggiest of weeknights. Although Ferrara is a UNE-SCO World Heritage Site, the city draws amazingly few tourists—which only adds to its appeal.

GETTING HERE AND AROUND

Train service is frequent from Bologna (usually three trains per hour) and takes either a half hour or 50 minutes, depending on which train type you take. It's around 35 minutes from Florence to Bologna, and then about a half hour from Bologna to Ferrara. The walk from the station is easy (about 20 minutes) and not particularly interesting. You can also take Bus No. 1, No. 6, No. 9, or No. 11 from the station to the center; buy your ticket at the newsagent inside and remember to stamp your ticket upon boarding the bus.

If you're driving from Bologna, take the RA1 out of town, then the A13 in the direction of Padua, exiting at Ferrara Nord. Follow the SP19 directly into the center of town. The trip should take about 45 minutes.

VISITOR INFORMATION

CONTACT Ferrara Tourism Office. ⊠ *Castello Estense, Piazza Castello, Ferrara* ☎ *0532/209370* ⊕ *www.ferrarainfo.com.*

 Sights

Casa Romei

CASTLE/PALACE | Built by the wealthy banker Giovanni Romei (1402–83), this vast structure with a graceful courtyard ranks among Ferrara's loveliest Renaissance palaces. Mid-15th-century frescoes adorn rooms on the ground floor; the piano nobile contains detached frescoes from local churches as well as lesser-known Renaissance sculptures. The Sala delle Sibille has a very large 15th-century fireplace and beautiful coffered wood ceilings. ⊠ *Via Savonarola 30, Ferrara* ☎ *0532/234130* ⊕ *www.ferraraterraeacqua.it* ☑ *€3 (free 1st Sun. of the month Oct.–Mar.).*

★ Castello Estense

CASTLE/PALACE | The former seat of Este power, this massive castle dominates the center of town, a suitable symbol for the ruling family: cold and menacing on the outside, lavishly decorated within. The public rooms are grand, but deep in the bowels of the castle are dungeons where enemies of the state were held in wretched conditions. The prisons of Don Giulio, Ugo, and Parisina have some fascinating features, like 15th-century graffiti. Lovers Ugo and Parisina (stepmother and stepson) were beheaded in 1425 because Ugo's father, Niccolò III, didn't like the fact that his son was cavorting with his stepmother. The castle was established as a fortress in 1385, but work on its luxurious ducal quarters continued into the 16th century. Representative of Este grandeur are the Sala dei Giochi, painted with athletic scenes, and the Sala dell'Aurora, decorated to show the times of the day. The terraces of the castle and the hanging garden have fine views of the town and countryside. You can traverse the castle's drawbridge and wander through many of its arcaded passages whenever the castle gates are open. ⊠ *Piazza Castello, Ferrara* ☎ *0532/419180* ⊕ *www.castelloestense.it* ☑ *€12.*

Duomo

CHURCH | The magnificent Gothic cathedral, a few steps from the Castello Estense, has a three-tier facade of slender arches and beautiful sculptures over the central door. Work began in 1135 and took more than 100 years to complete. The interior was completely remodeled in the 17th century. At this writing, the facade is scaffolded and the interior closed as part of a major restoration. ⊠ *Piazza della Cattedrale, Modena* ☎ *0532/207449* ⊕ *www.cattedralediferrara.it.*

Museo della Cattedrale

ART MUSEUM | Some of the original decorations of the town's main church, the former church, and the cloister of San Romano reside in the Museo della Cattedrale, across the piazza from the Duomo. Inside you'll find 22 codices commissioned between 1477 and 1535; early-13th-century sculptures by the Maestro dei Mesi; a mammoth oil on canvas by Cosmè Tura from 1469; and an exquisite Jacopo della Quercia, the *Madonna della Melagrana*. Although this last work dates from 1403 to 1408, the playful expression on the Christ child seems very 21st century. ⊠ *Via San Romano 1, Ferrara* 🕾 *0532/761299* ⊕ *www.artecultura.fe.it* 🎫 *€6* ⊘ *Closed Mon.*

Museo Nazionale dell'Ebraismo Italiano e della Shoah (*Museum of Italian Judaism and the Shoah*)

OTHER MUSEUM | The collection of ornate religious objects and multimedia installations at this museum (commonly known as MEIS) bears witness to the long history of the city's Jewish community. This history had its high points—1492, for example, when Ercole I invited the Jews to come over from Spain—and its lows, notably 1627, when Jews were enclosed within the ghetto, where they were forced to live until the advent of a united Italy in 1860. The triangular warren of narrow cobbled streets that made up the ghetto originally extended as far as Corso Giovecca (originally Corso Giudecca, or Ghetto Street). When it was enclosed, the neighborhood was restricted to the area between Via Scienze, Via Contrari, and Via di San Romano. The museum is located about a 15-minute walk from the former Jewish ghetto. Guided tours may be booked in advance by emailing or calling the museum. ⊠ *Via Piangipane, 81, 44121 Ferrara FE, Ferrara* 🕾 *0532/769137* ⊕ *www.meisweb.it* 🎫 *€10* ⊘ *Closed Mon.*

Palazzina di Marfisa d'Este

CASTLE/PALACE | On the busy Corso Giovecca, this grandiose 16th-century palace belonged to a great patron of the arts. It has painted ceilings, fine 16th-century furniture, and a garden containing a grotto and an outdoor theater. ⊠ *Corso Giovecca 170, Ferrara* 🕾 *0532/244949* ⊕ *www.artecultura.fe.it* ⊘ *Closed Mon.* 🎫 *€4.*

Palazzo dei Diamanti (*Palace of Diamonds*)

ART MUSEUM | Named for the 8,500 small pink-and-white marble pyramids (or "diamonds") that stud its facade, this building was designed to be viewed in perspective—both faces at once—from diagonally across the street. Work began in the 1490s and finished around 1504. Inside the palazzo is the Pinacoteca Nazionale and Modern and Contemporary Art Gallery, which host temporary exhibits. ⊠ *Corso Ercole I d'Este 21, Ferrara* 🕾 *0532/244949* ⊕ *www.palazzodiamanti. it* 🎫 *€6* ⊘ *Closed Mon.*

★ Palazzo Schifanoia

HISTORIC SIGHT | The oldest, most characteristic area of Ferrara is south of the Duomo, stretching between the Corso Giovecca and the city's ramparts. Here various members of the Este family built pleasure palaces, the best known of which is the Palazzo Schifanoia (*schifanoia* means "carefree" or, literally, "fleeing boredom"). Begun in the late 14th century, the palace was remodeled between 1464 and 1469. Inside is Museo Schifanoia, with its lavish interior—particularly the Salone dei Mesi, which contains an extravagant series of frescoes showing the months of the year and their mythological attributes. ⊠ *Via Scandiana 23, Ferrara* 🕾 *0532/244949* ⊕ *www.artecultura.fe.it* 🎫 *€10* ⊘ *Closed Mon.*

Via delle Volte

STREET | One of the best-preserved medieval streets in Europe, the Via delle Volte clearly evokes Ferrara's past. The series of ancient *volte* (arches) along the narrow cobblestone alley once joined the merchants' houses on the south side of the street to their warehouses on the north side. The street ran parallel to the banks of the Po River, which was home to Ferrara's busy port. ⊠ *Ferrara*.

🍽 Restaurants

★ Enoteca al Brindisi

$ | **WINE BAR** | Ferrara is a city of wine bars, beginning with this one (allegedly Europe's oldest), which opened in 1435—Copernicus drank here while a student in the late 1400s, and the place still has an undergraduate aura. The twentysomething staff pours well-chosen wines by the glass, and they serve *cappellacci di zucca* (pasta stuffed with squash or pumpkin) with two different sauces (ragù or butter and sage). **Known for:** full of locals, students, and visitors; set menus at great prices; marvelous salads. ⑤ *Average main: €12* ⊠ *Via Adelardi 11, Ferrara* ☎ *0532/473744* ⊕ *www. albrindisi.net* ⊗ *Closed Mon. and 1 wk late Jan.*

Il Mandolino

$$ | **EMILIAN** | At this idiosyncratic trattoria on the historic Via delle Volte try tearing your attention away from the countless paintings, photographs, and musical instruments that cover the walls, and instead focusing on the excellent fare on offer. Typical dishes include the classic *cappellacci di zucca*, and the lasagna may be one of the best you'll ever have. **Known for:** friendly staff; fascinating decor; local home cooking like excellent lasagna. ⑤ *Average main: €15* ⊠ *Via delle Volte 52, Ferrara* ☎ *0532/760080* ⊕ *www. ristoranteilmandolino.it* ⊗ *Closed Tues. No dinner Sun. and Mon.*

Il Sorpasso

$$ | **EMILIAN** | Named after a 1962 cult movie, *Il Sorpasso* (*The Easy Life*) serves terrific, honestly priced food in an unassuming space: white walls lined with movie posters, and white floors. No matter—the fine cooking and the sourcing of local ingredients whenever possible help this trattoria surpass many others. **Known for:** vegan and vegetarian options; excellent pastas and desserts; using local ingredients whenever possible. ⑤ *Average main: €15* ⊠ *Via Saraceno 118, Ferrara* ☎ *0532/790289* ⊕ *www.trattoriailsorpasso.it* ⊗ *Closed Tues. No dinner Mon.*

L'Oca Giuliva

$$ | **EMILIAN** | Food, service, and ambience harmonize blissfully at this casual but elegant restaurant inside a 12th-century building. The chef shows a deft hand with area specialties and shines with the fish dishes. **Known for:** tasting menus; creative antipasti and seafood dishes; *cappellacci di zucca* (pumpkin-stuffed pasta). ⑤ *Average main: €20* ⊠ *Via Boccacanale di Santo Stefano 38/40, Ferrara* ☎ *0532/207628* ⊕ *www. ristorantelocagiuliva.it* ⊗ *Closed Tues.*

Molto Più Che Centrale

$ | **EMILIAN** | A winning combination of traditional and innovative dishes is the big draw at this stylish restaurant spread over two floors. With red and white walls adorned with splashy modern art, and elegant wooden tables and chairs, the ambience is colorful and contemporary without being garish. **Known for:** attentive waitstaff; local dishes with modern flourishes; upbeat, contemporary setting. ⑤ *Average main: €14* ⊠ *Via Boccaleone 8, Ferrara* ☎ *0532/1880070* ⊗ *Closed Thurs.*

★ Quel Fantastico Giovedì

$$ | **EMILIAN** | Locals and other cognoscenti frequent this sleek eatery just minutes away from Piazza del Duomo, where chef Gabriele Romagnoli uses prime local ingredients to create gustatory sensations on a menu that changes daily. Fish and seafood figure prominently among his dishes, such as with a *gratinato* (similar to a French au gratin) with seafood. **Known for:** excellent service; seasonal menu; notable fish and seafood dishes. ⑤ *Average main: €15* ⊠ *Via Castelnuovo 9, Ferrara* ☎ *0532/760570* ⊕ *www.quelfantasticogiovedi.it* ⊗ *Closed Wed. No lunch Thurs.*

Hotels

Hotel Annunziata

$ | **HOTEL** | Brightly colored fittings enliven the white-walled, hardwood-floor guest rooms—think minimalism with a splash—at this hotel on a quiet little piazza near the forbiddingly majestic Castello Estense. **Pros:** perfect location (you can't get much more central); terrific buffet breakfast; stellar staff. **Cons:** annex 500 feet from main building; some rooms have uninspiring views; few facilities and limited public spaces. ⑤ *Rooms from: €74* ⊠ *Piazza Repubblica 5, Ferrara* ☎ *0532/201111* ⊕ *www.annunziata.it* ⊷ *27 rooms* ⦿❘ *Free Breakfast.*

⭐ **Locanda Borgonuovo**

$ | **B&B/INN** | In the early 18th century this lodging began life as a convent (later suppressed by Napoléon), but now it's a delightful city-center bed-and-breakfast, popular with performers at the city's Teatro Comunale. **Pros:** knowledgeable local advice; bicycles can be borrowed for free; phenomenal breakfast featuring local foods and terrific cakes made in-house. **Cons:** must reserve far in advance as this place books quickly; steep stairs to reception area and rooms; decor may be a bit over-fussy for some. ⑤ *Rooms from: €100* ⊠ *Via Cairoli 29, Ferrara* ☎ *0532/211100* ⊕ *www.borgonuovo.com* ⊷ *5 rooms* ⦿❘ *Free Breakfast.*

Maxxim Hotel

$ | **HOTEL** | **FAMILY** | Though given a stylish modern makeover, the courtyards, vaulted brick lobby, and breakfast room of this 15th-century palazzo retain much of their lordly Renaissance flair. **Pros:** tasteful modern makeover; beyond-helpful staff; good choice for families. **Cons:** occasional noise from neighboring rooms; split-level loft rooms impractical for some; some bathrooms are on the small side. ⑤ *Rooms from: €64* ⊠ *Via Ripagrande 21, Ferrara* ☎ *0532/1770700* ⊕ *www.maxxim.it* ⊷ *40 rooms* ⦿❘ *Free Breakfast.*

Imola

82 km (51 miles) south of Ferrara, 42 km (26 miles) southeast of Bologna.

Affluent Imola, with its wide and stately avenues, lies on the border between Emilia and Romagna. It was populated as early as the Bronze Age, came under Roman rule, and was eventually annexed to the Papal States in 1504. Imola is best known for its Formula One auto-racing tradition: the San Marino Grand Prix was held here every spring from 1981 until 2006. Auto-racing as a serious sport in Imola dates to 1953, when, with the support of Enzo Ferrari, the racetrack just outside the city center was inaugurated. The venue sometimes returns to the Formula One calendar, but you'll more likely find yourself in Imola shopping for its well-known ceramics or sampling the cuisine at the town's world-famous restaurant, San Domenico.

GETTING HERE AND AROUND

Local trains from Bologna run often and take 20–30 minutes. If you're driving from Bologna, take the RA1 to the A14 (following signs for Ancona). Take the exit for Imola. If you're coming from Milan, you can catch the Frecciarossa to Bologna (a little over an hour), and then transfer to the local train.

VISITOR INFORMATION

CONTACT Imola Tourism Office. ⊠ *Galleria del Centro Cittadino, Via Emilia 135, Imola* ☎ *0542/602207* ⊕ *www.visitareimola.it.*

🍴 Restaurants

⭐ **San Domenico**

$$$$ | **MODERN ITALIAN** | Year after year this restaurant defends its position as one of Italy's most refined dining destinations, and heads of state, celebrities, and lovers of fine food venture here to savor chef Valentino Marcattilii's wondrous creations. Typical of these is his memorable *uovo in raviolo San Domenico,* in which a large

raviolo is stuffed with a raw egg yolk—it cooks only a little, then spills out and mixes with Parmigiano-Reggiano, butter, and black truffles (depending on the season). **Known for:** impeccable service; creative destination dining worth the price; ravioli filled with egg yolk. $ *Average main: €50* ✉ *Via G. Sacchi 1, Imola* ☏ *0542/29000* ⊕ *www.sandomenico.it* ⊘ *Closed Mon. No dinner Sun. Closed Sun. and Mon. Jun.–Aug. No lunch Sat. Jun.–Aug.*

Faenza

16 km (10 miles) southeast of Imola, 49 km (30 miles) southeast of Bologna.

In the Middle Ages, Faenza was the crossroads between Emilia-Romagna and Tuscany, and the 15th century saw many Florentine artists working in town.

In 1509, when the Papal States took control, Faenza became something of a backwater. It did, however, continue its 12th-century tradition of making top-quality glazed earthenware. In the 16th century local artists created a color called *bianchi di Faenza* (Faenza white), which was widely imitated and wildly desired all over Europe. The Frenchified *faience*, referring to the color and technique, soon entered the lexicon, where it remains to this day. In the central **Piazza del Popolo**, dozens of shops sell local ceramics.

GETTING HERE AND AROUND

Trains run frequently from Bologna to Faenza, making the trip in 25–45 minutes. There's also sporadic service from Florence, a beautiful ride of under two hours. The walk to the centro storico, though easy, isn't especially interesting.

By car it takes about an hour from Bologna. Follow the SP253 to the RA1, at which point pick up on the A14/E45 heading in the direction of Ancona. Exit and take the SP8 into Faenza.

VISITOR INFORMATION

CONTACT Faenza Tourism Office. ✉ *Voltone della Molinella 2, Faenza* ☎ *0546/25231* ⊕ *www.prolocofaenza.it.*

 Sights

Museo Internazionale delle Ceramiche

ART MUSEUM | One of the largest ceramics museums in the world has a well-labeled, well-lit collection, with objects from the Renaissance among its highlights. Although the emphasis is clearly on local work, the rest of Italy and the globe are also represented. Don't miss the 20th- and 21st-century galleries, which prove that decorative arts often surpass their practical limitations and become genuinely sculptural. ✉ *Viale Baccarini 19, Faenza* ☎ *0546/697311* ⊕ *www.micfaenza.org* 💶 *€10* 🕙 *Closed Mon.*

🍴 Restaurants

Marianaza

$ | ITALIAN | A large open-hearth fireplace dominates this simple trattoria, and wonderful aromas of grilled meats and garlic greet you as you walk in. Marianaza successfully showcases the best of *la cucina romagnola* (the cuisine of Romagna): the extraordinary primi are mostly made with fresh pasta—tagliatelle or garganelli (egg-based and tubular)—while secondi rely heavily on the grill. **Known for:** Romagna specialties; good-value grilled meats; fresh pasta. $ *Average main: €14* ✉ *Via Torricelli 21, Faenza* ☎ *0546/681461* ⊕ *www.marianaza.com* 🕙 *Closed Tues. and Wed.*

Rimini

70 km (43½ miles) southeast of Faenza, 52 km (32 miles) southeast of Ravenna, 121 km (75 miles) southeast of Bologna.

Rimini is one of the most popular summer resorts on the Adriatic Coast and one of the most popular in Italy. July and August are the most crowded, packed with people who don't mind crammed beaches and not-terribly-blue water. In the off-season (October through March), Rimini is a cold, windy fishing port with few places open. Any time of year, one of Rimini's least touristy areas is the port; rambling down the **Via Sinistra del Porto** or **Via Destra del Porto** past all the fishing boats, you're far from the crush of sunbathers.

The town stands at the junction of two great Roman consular roads, the Via Emilia and the Via Flaminia. In Roman times it was an important port, making it a strategic and commercial center. From the 13th century onward, Rimini was controlled by the Malatesta family, an unpredictable clan equally capable of grand gestures and savage deeds.

GETTING HERE AND AROUND

Trains run hourly from Ravenna to Rimini and take about an hour. By car from Ravenna, take the SS16/E55, then follow the SS3bis/E45/E55 in the direction of Roma/Ancona. Follow directions for Ancona Nord, then follow signs for Ancona. Take the A14/E55 to the Rimini Nord exit, then the SP136 to the SS16, and follow signs for the center of town. Alternatively, take the coastal road, SS16, which hugs the shoreline much of the way, passing through Cervia. Though only 52 km (32 miles), this scenic route is naturally slower (beware of fog in winter). The coast north of Rimini is lined with dozens of small resort towns, but only one really has any charm—the seaport of Cesenatico—the others are mini-Riminis, and in summer the narrow road is hopelessly clogged with traffic.

There's frequent train service (usually three or four trains per hour) from Bologna to Rimini. It takes 1–2 hours, depending upon which train you choose. By car from Bologna, take the SP253 out of town, pick up the RA1, and then enter the A14 heading toward Ancona. Get off at the Rimini Nord exit, follow the SP136 to the SS16 to the center of town.

VISITOR INFORMATION

CONTACT Rimini Tourism Office. ⊠ *Piazzale Federico Fellini 3, Rimini* ☎ *0541/53399* ⊕ *www.riminiturismo.it.*

Sights

Arco d'Augusto

HISTORIC SIGHT | Rimini's oldest monument is the Arco d'Augusto, now stranded in the middle of a square just inside the city ramparts. It was erected in 27 BC, making it among the oldest surviving ancient Roman arches. ⊠ *Largo Giulio Cesare at Corso d'Augusto, Rimini.*

Tempio Malatestiano

CHURCH | The Malatesta family constructed the Tempio Malatestiano, also called the Basilica Cattedrale, with a masterful facade by Leon Battista Alberti (1404–72). Inside, the chapel to the right of the high altar contains a wonderful (if faded) fresco by Piero della Francesca (1420–92) depicting Sigismondo Malatesta kneeling before a saint. The two greyhounds in the right corner are significantly less faded than the rest. ⊠ *Via IV Novembre 35, Rimini* ☎ *0541/1835101* ⊕ *www.diocesi.rimini.it* ▱ *Free.*

Restaurants

La Marianna

$ | **ITALIAN** | It's all about fish at this welcoming spot, and aside from vegetable side dishes and dessert there's little on the menu that wasn't recently swimming (or lurking) in the sea. Locals flock here, and with good reason— the food is excellent, and the prices are reasonable. ⑤ *Average main: €14* ⊠ *Viale Tiberio 19, Rimini* ☎ *0541/22530* ⊕ *www.trattorialamarianna.it.*

Hotels

Grand Hotel Rimini

$$$$ | **HOTEL** | **FAMILY** | This 1908 extravaganza, made famous by Federico Fellini in his film *Amarcord*, is grander than ever with ongoing restorations that keep the place completely current while maintaining its hyperluxe old-world charm. **Pros:** sumptuous buffet breakfast that starts early (7 am) and ends late (11 am); amenities including everything from a spa and a private beach to programs for children in summer; the American Bar. **Cons:** not always worthy of five-star status annex rooms outdated; 1 kilometer from Rimini's historic center. ⑤ *Rooms from: €333* ⊠ *Parco Federico Fellini, Rimini* ☎ *0541/56000* ⊕ *www.grandhotelrimini. com* ❍ *Free Breakfast* ▱ *172 rooms.*

San Marino

20 km (12½ miles) southwest of Rimini, 139 km (86 miles) southeast of Bologna.

The world's smallest and oldest republic, as San Marino dubs itself, is surrounded entirely by Italy. It consists of three ancient castles perched on sheer cliffs rising implausibly out of the flatlands of Romagna, and a tangled knot of cobblestone streets below that are lined with tourist boutiques, cheesy hotels and restaurants, and gun shops. A visit here is justified, however, by the sweeping views from the castle of the countryside. The 3,300-foot-plus precipices will make jaws drop and acrophobes quiver.

Visiting San Marino in winter (off-season) increases the appeal of the experience, as tourist establishments shut down and you more or less have the castles to yourself. In August every inch of walkway on the rock is mobbed with sightseers. Don't worry about changing money, nowing passports, and the like (although the tourist office in Piazza Garibaldi will stamp your passport for €5). San Marino is, for all practical purposes, Italy—except, that is, for its majestic perch, its lax gun laws, and its high national voter turnout rate.

GETTING HERE AND AROUND

To get to San Marino by car, take highway SS72 west from Rimini. From Borgo Maggiore, at the base of the rock, a cable car will whisk you up to the town. Alternatively, you can drive up the winding road; public parking is available. There is a regular bus service to and from Rimini, with service sometime every hour throughout the year (less frequent service on Sunday); a one-way ticket from Rimini to San Marino costs €5. The trip takes about 45 minutes.

VISITOR INFORMATION

CONTACT San Marino Tourism Office. ✉ Piazza Garibaldi, San Marino ☎ 054/9885431 ⊕ www.visitsanmarino.com.

 ## Sights

Piazza della Libertà
PLAZA/SQUARE | One must-see is the Piazza della Libertà, where the Palazzo Pubblico is guarded by soldiers in green uniforms. As you'll notice by peering into the shops along the old town's winding streets, the republic is famous for crossbows and other items (think fireworks or firearms) that are illegal almost everywhere else. ✉ San Marino.

★ Tre Castelli
CASTLE/PALACE | San Marino's headline attractions are its Tre Castelli—medieval architectural wonders that appear on every coat of arms in the city—and some spectacular views. Starting in the center of town, walk a few hundred yards past the trinket shops, along a paved clifftop ridge, from the 10th-century **Rocca della Guaita** to the 13th-century **Rocca della Cesta** (containing a museum of ancient weapons; worthwhile mostly for the views from its terraces and turrets) and finally to the 14th-century **Rocca Montale** (closed to the public), the most remote of the castles. Every step of the way affords spectacular views of Romagna and the Adriatic—it's said that on a clear day you can see Croatia. The walk makes for a good day's exercise, but is by no means arduous. Even if you arrive after visiting hours, it's supremely rewarding. ✉ San Marino ☎ 0549/991369 ⊕ www.cultura.sm ✉ La Torre Guaita and La Torre Cesta €4.50 each, €6.50 for both.

Ravenna

80 km (50 miles) northwest of San Marino, 93 km (58 miles) southeast of Ferrara.

A small, quiet, and well-heeled city, Ravenna has brick palaces, cobblestone streets, magnificent monuments, and spectacular Byzantine mosaics. The high point in its civic history occurred in the 5th century, when Pope Honorious moved his court here from Rome. Gothic kings Odoacer and Theodoric ruled the city until it was conquered by the Byzantines in AD 540. Ravenna later fell under the sway of Venice, and then, inevitably, the Papal States.

Because Ravenna spent much of its past looking east, its greatest art treasures show that Byzantine influence. Churches and tombs with the most unassuming exteriors contain within them walls covered with sumptuous mosaics. These beautifully preserved Byzantine mosaics put great emphasis on nature, which you can see in the delicate rendering of sky, earth, and animals. Outside Ravenna, the town of Classe hides even more mosaic gems.

GETTING HERE AND AROUND

By car from Bologna, take the SP253 to the RA1, and then follow signs for the A14/E45 in the direction of Ancona. From here, follow signs for Ravenna, taking the A14dir Ancona–Milano–Ravenna exit. Follow signs for the SS16/E55 to the center of Ravenna. From Ferrara the drive is more convoluted, but also more interesting. Take the SS16 to the RA8 in the direction of Porto Garibaldi, taking the Roma/Ravenna exit. Follow the SS309/E55 to the SS309dir/E55, taking the SS253 Bologna/Ancona exit. Follow the SS16/E55 into the center of Ravenna.

By train, there are one or two services hourly from Bologna, taking 70 minutes.

VISITOR INFORMATION

CONTACT Ravenna Tourism Office. ⊠ *Piazza San Francesco 7, Ravenna* ☎ *0544/35755* ⊕ *www.turismo.ra.it.*

 Sights

★ Basilica di San Vitale

CHURCH | The octagonal church of San Vitale was built in AD 547, after the Byzantines conquered the city, and its interior shows a strong Byzantine influence. The area behind the altar contains the most famous works, depicting Emperor Justinian and his retinue on one wall, and his wife, Empress Theodora, with her retinue, on the opposite one. Notice how the mosaics seamlessly wrap around the columns and curved arches on the upper sides of the altar area. ■TIP→ **School groups can sometimes swamp the site from March through mid-June.** ⊠ *Via San Vitale, off Via Salara, Ravenna* ☎ *0544/541688 for info, 800/303999 for info (toll-free)* ⊕ *www.ravennamosaici.it* ⊠ *€10.50 combination ticket, includes 4–5 diocesan monuments.*

★ Battistero Neoniano

CHURCH | Next door to Ravenna's 18th-century cathedral, the baptistery has one of the town's most important mosaics. It dates from the beginning of the 5th century AD, with work continuing through the century. In keeping with the building's role, the great mosaic in the dome shows the baptism of Christ, and beneath are the Apostles. The lowest register of mosaics contains Christian symbols, the Throne of God, and the Cross. Note the naked figure kneeling next to Christ—he is the personification of the River Jordan. ⊠ *Piazza Duomo, Ravenna* ☎ *0544/541688 for info, 800/303999 for info (toll-free)* ⊕ *www.ravennamosaici.it* ⊠ *€10.50 combination ticket, includes 4–5 diocesan monuments.*

Classis Ravenna–Museo della Città e del Territorio

OTHER MUSEUM | FAMILY | In Classe, a short distance outside Ravenna, this museum dazzlingly illustrates the history of Ravenna and its environs from the pre-Roman era to the Lombard conquest in AD 751. The museum occupies a refurbished sugar refinery, and with the help of multimedia presentations and panels in Italian and English, it chronicles the Roman, Ostrogoth, and Byzantine periods. Displays include bronze statuettes, stone sculptures, glassware, and mosaic fragments. A separate room summarizes the building's more recent history. It's an easy walk from Sant'Apollinare in Classe. ■TIP→ **To get here from Ravenna, take Bus No. 4 from the station or the local train to Classe, or use the cycle path from the city center.** ⊠ *Via Classense 29, off SS71, Classe* ☎ *0544/473717* ⊕ *www.classisravenna.it* ⊠ *€5 (€12 including Sant'Apollinare in Classe)* ⊗ *Closed Mon Nov.–late Dec. and 10 days Jan.*

Domus dei Tappeti di Pietra
(House of the Stone Carpets)

RUINS | This archaeological site with lovely mosaics was uncovered in 1993 during digging for an underground parking garage near the 18th-century church of Santa Eufemia. Ten feet below ground level lie the remains of a Byzantine palace dating from the 5th and 6th centuries AD. Its beautiful and well-preserved network of floor mosaics displays elaborately designed patterns, creating the effect of luxurious carpets. ☒ *Via Barbiani 16, enter through Sant'Eufemia church, Ravenna* ☎ *0544/32512* ⊕ *www.domusdeitappetidipietra.it* ☒ *€4.*

★ Mausoleo di Galla Placidia

CHURCH | The little tomb and the great church stand side by side, but the tomb predates the Basilica di San Vitale by at least 100 years: these two adjacent sights are decorated with the best-known, most elaborate mosaics in Ravenna. Galla Placidia was the sister of the Roman emperor Honorius, who moved the imperial capital to Ravenna in AD 402. This mid-5th century mausoleum is her memorial. The simple redbrick exterior only serves to enhance by contrast the richness of the interior mosaics, in deep midnight blue and glittering gold. The tiny central dome is decorated with symbols of Christ, the evangelists, and striking gold stars. Eight of the Apostles are represented in groups of two on the four inner walls of the dome; the other four appear singly on the walls of the two transepts. There are three sarcophagi in the tomb, none of which are believed to actually contain the remains of Galla Placidia. ■TIP→ **Visit early or late in the day to avoid the school groups that can sometimes swamp the Mausoleo from March through mid-June.** ☒ *Via San Vitale, 17, off Via Salara, Ravenna* ☎ *0544/541688 for info, 800/303999 for info (toll-free)* ⊕ *www.ravennamosaici.it* ☒ *€10.50 combination ticket, includes 4–5 diocesan monuments (€2 supplement for mausoleum).*

Museo Nazionale di Ravenna *(National Museum of Ravenna)*

OTHER MUSEUM | Next to the Church of San Vitale and housed in a former Benedictine monastery, the museum contains artifacts from ancient Rome, Byzantine fabrics and carvings, and pieces of early Christian art. The collection is well displayed and artfully lighted. In the first cloister are marvelous Roman tomb slabs from excavations nearby; upstairs, you can see a reconstructed 18th-century pharmacy. ☒ *Via San Vitale 17, Ravenna* ☎ *0544/213902* ⊕ *www.ravennantica.it/en/ravenna-national-museum-museo-nazionale-di-ravenna/* ☒ *€6* ⊘ *Closed Mon.*

Sant'Apollinare in Classe

CHURCH | This church about 5 km (3 miles) southeast of Ravenna is landlocked now, but when it was built, it stood in the center of the busy shipping port known to the ancient Romans as Classis. The arch above and the area around the high altar are rich with mosaics. Those on the arch, older than the ones behind it, are considered superior. They show Christ in Judgment and the 12 lambs of Christianity leaving the cities of Jerusalem and Bethlehem. In the apse is the figure of Sant'Apollinare himself, a bishop of Ravenna, and above him is a magnificent Transfiguration against blazing green grass, animals in odd perspective, and flowers. ☒ *Via Romea Sud 224, off SS71, Classe* ☎ *0544/527308* ☒ *€5 or €9 including Classis Ravenna museum* ⊘ *Closed Mon.*

★ Sant'Apollinare Nuovo

CHURCH | The mosaics displayed in this church date from the early 6th century, making them slightly older than those in San Vitale. Since the left side of the church was reserved for women, it's only fitting that the mosaics on that wall depict 22 virgins offering crowns to the Virgin Mary. On the right wall, 26 men carry the crowns of martyrdom; they approach Christ, surrounded by angels. ☒ *Via Roma 53, at Via Guaccimanni,*

Ravenna

KEY

1 Exploring Sights

1 Restaurants

1 Hotels

TO TRAIN & BUS STATIONS

KEY

i Tourist information

0   150 yards

0   150 meters

Sights ▼

1 Basilica di San Vitale... **B2**
2 Battistero Neoniano.... **B4**
3 Classis Ravenna – Museo della Città e del Territorio **E5**
4 Domus dei Tappeti di Pietra **A2**
5 Mausoleo di Galla Placidia **B1**
6 Museo Nazionale di Ravenna.............. **B2**
7 Sant'Apollinare in Classe................... **E5**
8 Sant'Apollinare Nuovo **E4**
9 Tomba di Dante **D4**

Restaurants ▼

1 Bella Venezia............ **C3**
2 Ca' de Vèn **C4**
3 Osteria del Tempo Perso.................... **B2**

Hotels ▼

1 Albergo Cappello **C3**
2 Hotel Sant'Andrea...... **A3**

Ravenna 🕾 *800/303999 for info (toll-free),*
0544/541688 for info ⊕ www.ravenna-
mosaici.it 🎫 €10.50 combination ticket,
includes 4–5 diocesan monuments.

omba di Dante

OMB | Exiled from his native Florence,
the author of *The Divine Comedy* died
here in 1321, and Dante's tomb is
in a small neoclassical building next
door to the large church of St. Francis.
The Florentines have been trying to
reclaim their famous son for hundreds
of years, but the Ravennans refuse to
give him up, arguing that since Florence
did not welcome Dante in life, it does
not deserve him in death. Perhaps as
penance, every September the Florentine
government sends olive oil that's used
to fuel the light hanging in the chapel's
center. ⊠ *Via Dante Alighieri 9, Ravenna*
🕾 *0544/215676* 🎫 *Free.*

🍴 Restaurants

Bella Venezia

$$ | **ITALIAN** | Pastel walls, crisp white
tablecloths, and warm light provide
the backdrop for some seriously good
Romagnolo dishes. The menu offers local
specialties, but also gives a major nod
to Venice—Ravenna's conqueror of long
ago. **Known for:** family-owned and operated; truffle dishes, depending on the
season; outdoor dining. 💲 *Average main:*
€15 ⊠ Via IV Novembre 16, Ravenna
🕾 *0544/212746 ⊕ www.ristorantebel-*
lavenezia.it ⊗ Closed Sun. No lunch Sat.

Ca' de Vèn

$$ | **ITALIAN** | These buildings, joined by
a glass-ceilinged courtyard, date from
the 15th century, so the setting itself is
reason enough to come; that the food
is so good makes a visit here all the
more satisfying. At lunchtime Ca' de Vèn

teems with locals tucking in to *piadine* (a
typical Romagnolo flatbread) stuffed or
topped with various ingredients, and the
grilled dishes—including *tagliata di pollo*
(sliced chicken breast tossed with arugula and set atop exquisitely roasted potatoes)—are among the highlights. **Known
for:** majestic, high-ceilinged lively setting;
grilled meats; weekly menu of Romagnolo specialties. 💲 *Average main: €16 ⊠ Via
Corrado Ricci 24, Ravenna* 🕾 *0544/30163
⊕ www.cadeven.it ⊗ Closed Mon.*

Osteria del Tempo Perso

$$ | **ITALIAN** | A couple of jazz-, rock-, and
food-loving friends joined forces to open
this smart little restaurant in the center.
The interior's warm terra-cotta-sponged
walls give off an orange glow, and wine
bottles line the walls, interspersed with
photographs of musical greats—but the
food is what counts. **Known for:** fine wine
list; housemade pastas; terrific seafood
dishes. 💲 *Average main: €20 ⊠ Via Gam-
ba 12, Ravenna* 🕾 *0544/215393 ⊕ www.
osteriadeltempoperso.it ⊗ No lunch
weekdays.*

Hotels

Albergo Cappello

$$ | **HOTEL** | Originally opened in the late
19th century and restored a century
later, this small, charming place exhibits
a Venetian influence, with Murano chandeliers hanging from the high coffered
wood ceilings in common rooms. **Pros:**
wine bar and good restaurant; good
location in historic area and near sights;
accommodating staff. **Cons:** occasional
street noise in some rooms; only seven
rooms; parking sometimes hard to find.
💲 *Rooms from: €134 ⊠ Via IV Novembre
41, Ravenna* 🕾 *0544/219813 ⊕ www.
albergocappello.it ⊅ 7 rooms* 🍴 *Free
Breakfast.*

Hotel Sant'Andrea

$ | **B&B/INN** | **FAMILY** | For a quiet and welcoming lodging on a residential street a stone's throw from the Basilica di San Vitale, look no further—it even has a delightful garden. **Pros:** cheery and helpful staff; quiet neighborhood; good-size guest rooms and family suites, some with terraces. **Cons:** reception closes at 9 pm; can get a little noisy; few facilities. ⑤ *Rooms from: €93* ✉ *Via Carlo Cattaneo 33, Ravenna* ☎ *0544/215564* ⊕ *www. santandreahotel.com* 🛏 *12 rooms* ❑ *Free Breakfast.*

Performing Arts

Teatro di Tradizione Dante Alighieri

ARTS CENTERS | Operas and dance productions are staged here from November to April. If your Italian is up to it, you could also attend any of the theatrical productions. ✉ *Via Mariani 2, Ravenna* ☎ *0544/249244* ⊕ *www.teatroalighieri. org.*

Chapter 12

FLORENCE

Updated by
Patricia Rucidlo

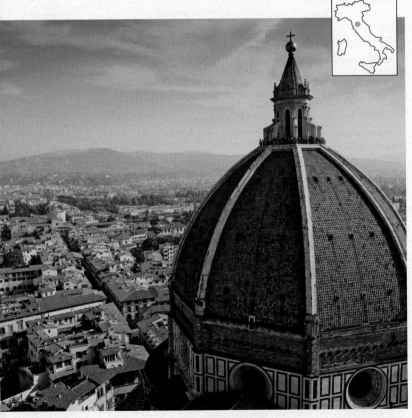

⊙ Sights	🍴 Restaurants	🛏 Hotels	🛍 Shopping	🍸 Nightlife
★★★★★	★★★★★	★★★★★	★★★★★	★★★★☆

WELCOME TO FLORENCE

TOP REASONS TO GO

★ **Galleria degli Uffizi:** Italian Renaissance art doesn't get much better than this vast collection bequeathed in 1737 by the last Medici, Anna Maria Luisa.

★ **Brunelleschi's Dome:** His work of engineering genius is the city's undisputed centerpiece.

★ **Michelangelo's *David*:** One look, up close, and you'll know why this is one of the world's most famous sculptures.

★ **The view from Piazzale Michelangelo:** From this perch the city is laid out before you. The colors at sunset heighten the experience.

★ **Piazza Santa Croce:** After you've had your fill of Renaissance masterpieces, idle here and watch the world go by.

1 Around the Duomo. You're in the heart of Florence here. Among the numerous highlights are the city's greatest museum (the Uffizi) and arguably its most impressive square (Piazza della Signoria).

2 San Lorenzo. The complex of the basilica of San Lorenzo, the Palazzo Medici-Riccardi, and the Galleria dell'Accademia bears the imprints of the Medici and of Michelangelo, culminating in the latter's masterful statue of *David*. Just to the north, the former convent of San Marco is an oasis of artistic treasures decorated with ethereal frescoes.

3 Santa Maria Novella. This part of town includes the train station, 16th-century palaces, and the city's swankest shopping street, Via Tornabuoni.

4 Santa Croce. The district centers on its namesake basilica, which is filled with the tombs of Renaissance (and other) luminaries. The area is also known for its leather shops.

5 The Oltrarno. Across the Arno you encounter the massive Palazzo Pitti and the narrow streets of the Santo Spirito neighborhood.

EATING AND DRINKING WELL IN FLORENCE

In Florence, simply prepared meats, grilled or roasted, are the culinary stars, usually paired with seasonal vegetables like artichokes or porcini. *Bistecca* is popular here, but there's plenty more that tastes great on the grill, too.

Traditionalists go for their gustatory pleasures in *trattorie* and *osterie*, places where decor is unimportant and place mats are mere paper. Culinary innovation comes slowly in this town, though some cutting-edge restaurants have been appearing.

By American standards, Florentines eat late: 1:30 or 2 pm is typical for lunch and 9 pm for dinner is considered early. Consuming a *primo*, *secondo*, and *dolce* is largely a thing of the past. For lunch, many Florentines simply grab a panino and a glass of wine at a bar. Those opting for a simple trattoria lunch often order a plate of pasta and dessert.

STALE AND STELLAR

Stale bread is the basis for three classic Florentine primi: *pappa al pomodoro, ribollita,* and *panzanella.* Pappa is made with either fresh or canned tomatoes and that stale bread. Ribollita is a vegetable soup with *cavolo nero* (Tuscan kale) and cannellini beans, thickened with bread. Panzanella is reconstituted Tuscan bread combined with tomatoes, cucumber, and basil. They all are enhanced with a generous application of fragrant Tuscan olive oil.

A CLASSIC ANTIPASTO: CROSTINI DI FEGATINI

This beloved dish consists of a chicken-liver spread, served warm or at room temperature, on toasted, garlic-rubbed bread. It can be served smooth, like a pâté, or in a chunkier, more rustic version. It's made by sautéing chicken livers with finely diced carrot and onion, enlivened with the addition of wine, broth, or Marsala reductions, and mashed anchovies and capers.

A CLASSIC SECONDO: BISTECCA FIORENTINA

The town's culinary pride and joy is a thick slab of beef, resembling a T-bone steak, from large white oxen called Chianina. The meat's slapped on the grill and served rare, sometimes with a pinch of salt.

It's always seared on both sides, and just barely cooked inside.

A CLASSIC CONTORNO: CANNELLINI BEANS

Simply boiled, they provide the perfect accompaniment to bistecca. The small white beans are best when they go straight from the garden into the pot. They should be anointed with a generous dose of Tuscan olive oil; the combination is oddly felicitous, and it goes a long way toward explaining why Tuscans are referred to as *mangiafagioli* (bean eaters) by other Italians.

A CLASSIC DOLCE: BISCOTTI DI PRATO

These are sometimes the only dessert on offer. *Biscotti* means twice-cooked (or, in this case, twice-baked). They are hard almond cookies that soften considerably when dipped languidly into *vin santo* ("holy wine"), a sweet dessert wine, or into a simple *caffè*.

A CLASSIC WINE: CHIANTI CLASSICO

This blend from the region just south of Florence relies mainly on the local, hardy *sangiovese* grape; it's aged for at least one year before hitting the market. (*Riserve*—reserve—is aged at least an additional six months.)

Chianti is usually the libation of choice for Florentines. Traditionalists opt for the younger, fruitier (and usually less expensive) versions often served in straw flasks. You can sample Chianti Classico all over town, and buy it in local supermarkets.

Its magical combination of beauty and history has drawn people to Florence for centuries, and then it draws them back again. It offers myriad moments of personal illumination before its palazzi, its churches, and its art museums, as well as in interaction with the people you meet there.

Florence has captivated visitors for ages now, probably ever since the powerful Medici family first staged jousts and later lavish pageants to celebrate their weddings. Its mostly sober beauty continued to attract people from all over Europe intent on taking in the achievements of the past on their Grand Tour of Europe. Sometimes this heady combination of art and beauty has proven overwhelming, as it did for French author and diplomat Stendhal in 1817, whose visit to the church of Santa Croce occasioned palpitations and a fainting spell. Today, however, visitors are more often overwhelmed by the press of their own numbers intent on taking it all in before moving on to the next stop on their tightly scheduled tours. Florence has always been visitor-friendly—the historical center of the city can be crossed on foot in less than half an hour, and the picturesque surrounding hills are a short bus ride away. But the flood of tourists has made the natives more reticent. A visitor is more likely to bump into or to exchange views with other visitors than with native Florentines, all busy catering to tourists' needs. Few Florentines, these days, can afford to live in the center where they work. Even the university has pulled out to a suburb. By day, the city is overrun with bus-loads of processing day-trippers; come evening by droves of U.S. study-abroad students intent on immersion in the native *aperitivo* culture. Where have all the Italians gone, you wonder? Fear not, they still come out on Sundays to walk in family groups along the major shopping streets, school groups still pack museums, and they still hold parades in Renaissance costume to mark various historical or religious occasions. *Caffè* culture still thrives. All this will be revealed to the attentive visitor who sees past the crowds and takes the time to look around the corner onto a quieter street, piazza, or neighborhood.

When the sun sets over the Arno and, as Mark Twain described it, "overwhelms Florence with tides of color that make all the sharp lines dim and faint and turn the solid city to a city of dreams," it's hard not to fall under the city's spell.

Planning

Making the Most of Your Time

With some planning, you can see Florence's most famous sights in a couple of days. Start off at the city's most awe-inspiring architectural wonder, the **Duomo,** climbing to the top of the dome if you have the stamina (and are not claustrophobic: it gets a little tight going up and coming back down). On the same piazza, check out Ghiberti's bronze doors at the **Battistero.** (They're actually high-quality copies; the Museo dell'Opera del Duomo has the originals.) Set aside the afternoon for the **Galleria degli Uffizi,** making sure to reserve tickets in advance.

On Day 2, visit Michelangelo's *David* in the **Galleria dell'Accademia**—reserve tickets here, too. Linger in **Piazza della Signoria,** Florence's central square, where a copy of *David* stands in the spot the original occupied for centuries, then head east a couple of blocks to **Santa Croce,** the city's most artistically rich church. Double back and walk across Florence's landmark bridge, the **Ponte Vecchio.**

Do all that, and you'll have seen some great art, but you've just scratched the surface. If you have more time, put the **Bargello,** the **Museo di San Marco,** and the **Cappelle Medicee** at the top of your list. When you're ready for an art break, stroll through the **Boboli Gardens** or explore Florence's lively shopping scene, from the food stalls of the **Mercato Centrale** to the chic boutiques of the **Via Tornabuoni.**

HOURS
Florence's sights keep tricky hours. Some are closed Wednesday, some Monday, some every other Monday. Quite a few shut their doors each day (or on most days) by 2 in the afternoon. Things get even more confusing on weekends. Make it a general rule to check the hours closely for any place you're planning to visit; if it's someplace you have your heart set on seeing, it's worthwhile to call to confirm.

Here's a selection of major sights that might not be open when you'd expect (consult the Sight listings within this chapter for the full details). And be aware that, as always, hours can and do change. Also note that on the first Sunday of the month, all state museums are free. That means that the Accademia and the Uffizi, among others, do not accept reservations. Unless you are a glutton for punishment (i.e., large crowds), these museums are best avoided on that day.

The **Accademia** and the **Uffizi** are both closed Monday.

The **Battistero** is open Monday through Saturday 8:15–10:15 and 11:15–8; Sunday 8:30–2.

The **Bargello** closes at 1:50 pm, and is closed entirely on alternating Sundays and Mondays. However, it's often open much later during high season and when there's a special exhibition on.

The **Cappelle Medicee** are closed alternating Sundays and Mondays (those Sundays and Mondays when the Bargello is open).

The **Duomo** closes at 4:30 on Thursday, as opposed to 5 other weekdays, 4:45 Saturday, and Sunday it's open only 1:30–4:45. The dome of the Duomo is closed Sunday.

Museo di San Marco closes at 1:50 weekdays but stays open until 4:45 weekends—except for alternating Sundays and Mondays, when it's closed entirely.

Palazzo Medici-Riccardi is closed Wednesday.

RESERVATIONS

At most times of day you'll see a line of people snaking around the Uffizi. They're waiting to buy tickets, and you don't want to be one of them. Instead, call ahead for a reservation (055/294883; reservationists speak English). You'll be given a reservation number and a time of admission—the sooner you call, the more time-slots you'll have to choose from. Go to the museum's reservation door 10 minutes before the appointed hour, give the clerk your number, pick up your ticket, and go inside. (Know that often in high season, there's at least a half-hour wait to pick up the tickets and often an even longer wait to get into the museum.) You'll pay €4 for this privilege, but it's money well spent. You can also book tickets online through the website (www. uffizi.it/en/the-uffizi); the booking process takes some patience, but it works.

Use the same reservation service to book tickets for the Galleria dell'Accademia, where lines rival those of the Uffizi. (Reservations can also be made for the Palazzo Pitti, the Bargello, and several other sights, but they usually aren't needed—although, lately, in summer, lines can be long at Palazzo Pitti.) An alternative strategy is to check with your hotel—many will handle reservations.

Getting Here and Around

AIR

To get into the city center from the airport by car, take the autostrada A11. A SITA bus will take you directly from the airport to the center of town. Buy the tickets within the train station.

AIR CONTACTS Aeroporto A. Vespucci. ⊠ *10 km (6 miles) northwest of Florence, Florence* ☎ *055/30615* ⊕ *www.aeroporto. firenze.it.* **Aeroporto Galileo Galilei.** ⊠ *12 km (7 miles) south of Pisa and 80 km (50 miles) west of Florence, Florence* ☎ *050/849300* ⊕ *www.pisa-airport.com.*

BIKE AND MOPED

Brave souls (cycling in Florence is difficult at best) may rent bicycles at easy-to-spot locations at Fortezza da Basso, the Stazione Centrale di Santa Maria Novella, and Piazza Pitti. Otherwise, try **Alinari** (Via San Zanobi 40/r, San Marco; 055/280500). You'll be up against hordes of tourists and those pesky *motorini* (mopeds). (For a safer ride, try Le Cascine, a former Medici hunting ground turned into a large public park with paved pathways.) The historic center can be circumnavigated via bike paths lining the *viali*, the ring road surrounding the area. If you want to go native and rent a noisy Vespa (Italian for "wasp") or other make of motorcycle or *motorino*, you can do so at **Massimo** (Via Campo d'Arrigo 102/B, 055/573689).

BUS

Florence's flat, compact city center is made for walking, but when your feet get weary you can use the efficient bus system, which includes small electric buses making the rounds in the center. Buses also climb to Piazzale Michelangelo and San Miniato south of the Arno.

Maps and timetables for local bus service are available for a small fee at the ATAF (Azienda Trasporti Area Fiorentina), or for free at visitor information offices. Tickets must be bought in advance from tobacco shops, newsstands, automatic ticket machines near main stops, or ATAF booths. The ticket must be canceled in the small validation machine immediately upon boarding.

You have several ticket options, all valid for one or more rides on all lines. A €1.50 ticket is good for ninety minutes from the time it is first canceled. Another option is to buy a booklet of 10 tickets, each good for 70 minutes, for €14.

Long-distance buses provide inexpensive service between Florence and other cities in Italy and Europe. **Bus Italia** (Via

Santa Caterina da Siena 17/r, 055/47821) is the major line.

CAR

Florence is connected to the north and south of Italy by the Autostrada del Sole (A1). It takes about 1½ hours of driving on scenic roads to get to Bologna (although heavy truck traffic over the Apennines often makes for slower going), about 3 hours to Rome, and 3–3½ hours to Milan. The Tyrrhenian Coast is an hour west on the A11.

An automobile in Florence is a major liability. If your itinerary includes parts of Italy where you'll want a car (such as Tuscany), pick the vehicle up on your way out of town.

TAXI

Taxis usually wait at stands throughout the city (in front of the train station and in Piazza della Repubblica, for example), or you can call for one (055/4390 or 055/4242). The meter starts at €3.30 from any taxi stand; if you call Radio Dispatch (that means that a taxi comes to pick you up wherever it is you are), it starts at €5.50. Extra charges apply at night, on Sunday, for radio dispatch, and for luggage. Single women traveling after 9 pm seeking taxis are entitled to a 10% discount on the fare; you must, however, request it.

TRAIN

Florence is on the principal Italian train route between most European capitals and Rome, and within Italy it is served frequently from Milan, Venice, and Rome by Intercity (IC) and nonstop Eurostar trains. Avoid trains that stop only at the Campo di Marte or Rifredi station, which are not convenient to the city center.

TRAIN CONTACTS Italo. ⊠ *Florence* ☎ *892020* ⊕ *www.italotreno.it.* **Stazione Centrale di Santa Maria Novella.** ⊠ *Florence* ☎ *892021* ⊕ *www.trenitalia.com.*

Restaurants

Florence's popularity with tourists means that, unfortunately, there's a higher percentage of mediocre restaurants here than you'll find in most Italian towns (Venice, perhaps, might win that prize). Some restaurant owners cut corners and let standards slip, knowing that a customer today is unlikely to return tomorrow, regardless of the quality of the meal. So, if you're looking to eat well, it pays to do some research, starting with the recommendations here. Dining hours start at around 1 for lunch and 8 for dinner. Many of Florence's restaurants are small, so reservations are a must. You can sample such specialties as creamy *fegatini* (a chicken-liver spread) and *ribollita* (minestrone thickened with bread and beans and swirled with extra-virgin olive oil) in a bustling, convivial trattoria, where you share long wooden tables set with paper place mats, or in an upscale *ristorante* with linen tablecloths and napkins.

Restaurants reviews have been shortened. For full information, visit Fodors.com.

WHAT IT COSTS in Euros			
$	$$	$$$	$$$$
AT DINNER			
under €15	€15–€24	€25–€35	over €35

Hotels

Florence is equipped with hotels for all budgets; for instance, you can find both budget and luxury hotels in the *centro storico* (historic center) and along the Arno. Florence has so many famous landmarks that it's not hard to find lodging with a panoramic view. The equivalent of the genteel *pensioni* of yesteryear can still be found, though they are now officially classified as "hotels." Generally small and intimate, they often have a quaint appeal that usually doesn't preclude modern plumbing. Florence's importance not only as a tourist city but also as a convention center and the site of the Pitti fashion collections guarantees a variety of accommodations.

The high demand also means that, except in winter, reservations are a must. If you find yourself in Florence with no reservations, go to **Consorzio ITA** (Stazione Centrale, Santa Maria Novella, 055/282893). You must go there in person to make a booking.

Hotel reviews have been shortened. For full information, visit Fodors.com.

WHAT IT COSTS in Euros

$	$$	$$$	$$$$
FOR TWO PEOPLE			
under €125	€125–€200	€201–€300	over €300

Shopping

Window-shopping in Florence is like visiting an enormous contemporary-art gallery. Many of today's greatest Italian artists are fashion designers, and most keep shops in Florence. Discerning shoppers may find bargains in the street markets.

■TIP➜ **Do not buy any knockoff goods from any of the hawkers plying their fake Prada (or any other high-end designer) on the streets. It's illegal, and fines are astronomical if the police happen to catch you. (You pay the fine, not the vendor.)**

Shops are generally open 9–1 and 3:30–7:30, and are closed Sunday and Monday mornings most of the year. Summer (June to September) hours are usually 9–1 and 4–8, and some shops close Saturday afternoon instead of Monday morning. When looking for addresses, you'll see two color-coded numbering systems on each street. The red numbers are commercial addresses and are indicated, for example, as "31/r." The blue or black numbers are residential addresses. Most shops take major credit cards and ship purchases, but because of possible delays it's wise to take your purchases with you.

Visitor Information

The Florence tourist office, known as the APT (Azienda di Promozione Turistica; 055/290832), has branches next to the Palazzo Medici-Riccardi, across the street from Stazione di Santa Maria Novella (the main train station), and at the Bigallo, in Piazza del Duomo. The offices are generally open from 9 in the morning until 7 in the evening. The multilingual staff will give you directions and the latest on happenings in the city. It's particularly worth a stop if you're interested in finding out about performing-arts events. The APT website (feelflorence.it) provides information in both Italian and English.

Around the Duomo

The heart of Florence, stretching from the Piazza del Duomo south to the Arno, is as dense with artistic treasures as any place in the world. Its churches, medieval towers, Renaissance palaces, and world-class museums and galleries contain some of the most outstanding achievements of Western art.

Much of the centro storico is closed to automobile traffic, but you still must dodge mopeds, cyclists, and masses of fellow tourists as you walk the narrow streets, especially in the area bounded by the Duomo, Piazza della Signoria, Galleria degli Uffizi, and the Ponte Vecchio. Via dei Calzaiuoli, between Piazza del Duomo and Piazza della Signoria, is the city's favorite *passeggiata* (constitutional).

Sights

Bargello

ART MUSEUM | This building started out as the headquarters for the Capitano del Popolo (Captain of the People) during the Middle Ages, and was later a prison. Today it houses the Museo Nazionale, home to what is probably the finest collection of Renaissance sculpture in Italy. Masterpieces by Michelangelo (1475–1564), Donatello (circa 1386–1466), and Benvenuto Cellini (1500–71) are remarkable; the works are distributed among an eclectic collection of arms, ceramics, and miniature bronzes, among other things. In 1401 Filippo Brunelleschi (1377–1446) and Lorenzo Ghiberti (circa 1378–1455) competed to earn the most prestigious commission of the day: the decoration of the north doors of the Baptistery in Piazza del Duomo. For the contest, each designed a bronze bas-relief panel depicting the sacrifice of Isaac; the panels are displayed together in the room devoted to the sculpture of Donatello, on the upper floor. According to Ghiberti, the judges chose him, though Brunelleschi maintained that they were both hired for the commission. See whom you believe after visiting. ⊠ *Via del Proconsolo 4, Bargello* ☎ *055/294883* ⊕ *www.museodelbargello.it* ⊘ *Closed 1st, 3rd, 5th Mon. of month; closed 2nd and 4th Sun. of month* ⊡ *€8.*

Battistero (*Baptistery*)

RELIGIOUS BUILDING | The octagonal Baptistery is one of the supreme monuments of the Italian Romanesque style and one of Florence's oldest structures. Local legend has it that it was once a Roman temple dedicated to Mars (it wasn't), and modern excavations suggest that its foundations date from the 1st century AD. The round Romanesque arches on the exterior date from the 11th century, and the interior dome mosaics from the beginning of the mid-13th century are justly renowned, but—glittering beauties though they are—they could never outshine the building's famed bronze Renaissance doors decorated with panels crafted by Lorenzo Ghiberti. These doors—or at least copies of them—on which Ghiberti worked most of his adult life (1403–52), are on the north and east sides of the Baptistery. The Gothic panels on the south door were designed by Andrea Pisano (circa 1290–1348) in 1330. Ghiberti's original doors were removed to protect them from the effects of pollution and acid rain and have been beautifully restored. Ghiberti's north doors depict scenes from the life of Christ; his later east doors (dating 1425–52), facing the Duomo facade, render scenes from the Old Testament. Both merit close examination, for they are very different in style and illustrate the artistic changes that marked the beginning of the Renaissance. Look at the far right panel of the middle row on the earlier (1403–24) north doors (*Jesus Calming the Waters*). Ghiberti here captured the chaos of a storm at sea with great skill and economy, but the artistic conventions he used are basically pre-Renaissance: Jesus is the most important figure, so he is the largest; the disciples are next in size, being next in importance; the ship on which they founder looks like a mere toy. The exquisitely rendered panels on the east doors are larger, more expansive, more sweeping—and more convincing. The middle panel on the left-hand door tells the story of Jacob and Esau, and the various episodes of the story—the selling of the birthright, Isaac ordering Esau to go hunting, the blessing of Jacob, and so forth—have been merged into a single beautifully realized street scene. Ghiberti's use of perspective suggests depth: the background architecture looks far more credible than on the north-door panels, the figures in the foreground are grouped realistically, and the naturalism and grace of the poses (look at Esau's left leg and the dog next to him) have nothing to do with the sacred message being conveyed. Although the religious

Around the Duomo

content remains, the figures and their place in the natural world are given new prominence, and are portrayed with a realism not seen in art since the fall of the Roman Empire nearly a thousand years before. As a footnote to Ghiberti's panels, one small detail of the east doors is worth a special look. To the lower left of the Jacob and Esau panel, Ghiberti placed a tiny self-portrait bust. From either side, the portrait is extremely appealing—Ghiberti looks like everyone's favorite uncle—but the bust is carefully placed so that you can make direct eye contact with the tiny head from a single spot. When that contact is made, the impression of intelligent life—of *modern* intelligent life—is astonishing. It's no wonder that these doors received one of the most famous compliments in the history of art from an artist known to be notoriously stingy with praise: Michelangelo declared them so beautiful that they could serve as the Gates of Paradise. ✉ *Piazza del Duomo, Duomo* ☎ *055/2302885* ⊕ *www.operaduomo. firenze.it* 🎫 *€10.*

Campanile

NOTABLE BUILDING | The Gothic bell tower designed by Giotto (circa 1266–1337) is a soaring structure of multicolor marble originally decorated with sculptures by Donatello and reliefs by Giotto, Andrea Pisano, and others (which are now in the Museo dell'Opera del Duomo). A climb of 414 steps rewards you with a close-up of Brunelleschi's cupola on the Duomo next door and a sweeping view of the city. ✉ *Piazza del Duomo, Duomo* ☎ *055/2302885* ⊕ *www.operaduomo. firenze.it* 🎫 *€15.*

★ Duomo (*Cattedrale di Santa Maria del Fiore*)

CHURCH | In 1296 Arnolfo di Cambio (circa 1245–circa 1310) was commissioned to build "the loftiest, most sumptuous edifice human invention could devise" in the Romanesque style on the site of the old church of Santa Reparata. The immense Duomo was consecrated in 1436, but work continued over the centuries. The imposing facade dates only from the 19th century; its neo-Gothic style somewhat complements Giotto's genuine Gothic 14th-century campanile. The real glory of the Duomo, however, is Filippo Brunelleschi's dome, presiding over the cathedral with a dignity and grace that few domes to this day can match. Brunelleschi's **cupola** was an ingenious engineering feat. The space to be enclosed by the dome was so large and so high above the ground that traditional methods of dome construction—wooden centering and scaffolding—were of no use whatsoever. So Brunelleschi developed entirely new building methods, which he implemented with equipment of his own design (including a novel scaffolding method). Beginning work in 1420, he built not one dome but two, one inside the other, and connected them with ribbing that stretched across the intervening empty space, thereby considerably lessening the crushing weight of the structure. He also employed a new method of bricklaying, based on an ancient herringbone pattern, interlocking each course of bricks with the course below in a way that made the growing structure self-supporting. The result was one of the great engineering breakthroughs of all time: most of Europe's later domes, including that of St. Peter's in Rome, were built employing Brunelleschi's methods, and today the Duomo has come to symbolize Florence in the same way that the Eiffel Tower symbolizes Paris. The Florentines are justly proud of it, and to this day the Florentine phrase for "homesick" is *nostalgia del cupolone* (homesick for the dome). The interior is a fine example of Florentine Gothic. Much of the cathedral's best-known art has been moved to the nearby Museo dell'Opera del Duomo. Notable among the works that remain, however, are two massive equestrian frescoes honoring

Florence Through the Ages

Guelph vs. Ghibelline. Although Florence can lay claim to a modest importance in the ancient world, it didn't come into its own until the Middle Ages. In the early 1200s the city, like most of the rest of Italy, was rent by civic unrest. Two factions, the Guelphs and the Ghibellines, competed for power. The Guelphs supported the papacy, and the Ghibellines supported the Holy Roman Empire. Bloody battles—most notably one at Montaperti in 1260—tore Florence and other Italian cities apart. By the end of the 13th century the Guelphs ruled securely, and the Ghibellines had been vanquished. This didn't end civic strife, however: the Guelphs split into the Whites and the Blacks for reasons still debated by historians. Dante, author of *The Divine Comedy*, was banished from Florence in 1301 because he was a White.

The Guilded Age. Local merchants had organized themselves into guilds by some time beginning in the 12th century. In 1250, they proclaimed themselves the *primo popolo* (literally, "first people"), making a landmark attempt at elective, republican rule. Though the episode lasted only 10 years, it constituted a breakthrough in Western history. Such a daring stance by the merchant class was a by-product of Florence's emergence as an economic powerhouse. Florentines were papal bankers; they instituted the system of international letters of credit; the gold florin became the international standard of currency. With this economic strength came a building boom. Sculptors such as Ghiberti and Donatello decorated the new churches; painters such as Giotto and Masaccio frescoed their walls.

Mighty Medici. Though ostensibly a republic, Florence was blessed (or cursed) with one very powerful family, the Medici, who came to prominence in 1434 and were initially the de facto rulers and then the absolute rulers of Florence for several hundred years. It was under patriarch Cosimo il Vecchio (1389–1464) that the Medici's position in Florence was securely established. Florence's golden age occurred during the reign of his grandson Lorenzo de' Medici (1449–92). Lorenzo was not only an astute politician but also a highly educated man and a great patron of the arts. Called "Il Magnifico" (the Magnificent), he gathered around him poets, artists, philosophers, architects, and musicians.

Lorenzo's son Piero (1471–1503) proved inept at handling the city's affairs. He was run out of town in 1494, and Florence briefly enjoyed its status as a republic while dominated by the Dominican friar Girolamo Savonarola (1452–98). After a decade of internal unrest, the republic fell and the Medici returned to power, but Florence never regained its former prestige. By the 1530s most of the major artistic talent had left the city—Michelangelo, for one, had settled in Rome. The now-ineffectual Medici, eventually attaining the title of grand dukes, remained nominally in power until the line died out in 1737, after which time Florence passed from the Austrians to the French and back again until the unification of Italy (1865–70), when it briefly became the capital under King Vittorio Emanuele II.

famous soldiers: Niccolò da Tolentino, painted in 1456 by Andrea del Castagno (circa 1419–57), and Sir John Hawkwood, painted 20 years earlier by Paolo Uccello (1397–1475); both are on the left nave. A 1995 restoration repaired the dome and cleaned the vastly crowded fresco of the Last Judgment, executed by Giorgio Vasari (1511–74) and Zuccaro, on its interior. Originally Brunelleschi wanted mosaics to cover the interior of the great ribbed cupola, but by the time the Florentines got around to commissioning the decoration, 150 years later, tastes had changed. Too bad: it's a fairly dreadful Last Judgment and hardly worth the effort of craning your neck to see it. You can explore the upper and lower reaches of the cathedral. The remains of a Roman wall and an 11th-century cemetery have been excavated beneath the nave; the way down is near the first pier on the right. The **climb to the top of the dome** (463 steps) is not for the faint of heart, but the view is superb. ✉ *Piazza del Duomo, Florence* ☎ *055/2302885* ⊕ *www.operaduomo.firenze.it* ✷ *Closed Sun. morning.*

★ Galleria degli Uffizi

ART MUSEUM | The venerable Uffizi Gallery occupies two floors of the U-shape Palazzo degli Uffizi, designed by Giorgio Vasari (1511–74) in 1560 to hold the *uffici* (administrative offices) of the Medici Grand Duke Cosimo I (1519–74). Among the highlights are Paolo Uccello's *Battle of San Romano*, its brutal chaos of lances one of the finest visual metaphors for warfare ever captured in paint (it returned from a glorious restoration in 2012); the *Madonna and Child with Two Angels,* by Fra Filippo Lippi (1406–69), in which the impudent eye contact established by the angel would have been unthinkable prior to the Renaissance; *The Birth of Venus* and *Primavera*, by Sandro Botticelli (1445–1510), the goddess of the former seeming to float on air and the fairy-tale charm of the latter exhibiting the painter's idiosyncratic genius at its zenith; the portraits of the Renaissance

duke Federico da Montefeltro and his wife Battista Sforza, by Piero della Francesca (circa 1420–92); *Madonna of the Goldfinch*, by Raphael (1483–1520), distinguished by the brilliant blues that decorate the sky, as well as the eye contact between mother and child, both clearly anticipating the painful future; Michelangelo's *Doni Tondo*; the *Venus of Urbino*, by Titian (circa 1488/90–1576); and the splendid *Bacchus*, by Caravaggio (circa 1571/72–1610). In the last two works, the approaches to myth and sexuality are diametrically opposed (to put it mildly). Late in the afternoon is the least crowded time to visit. For a €4 fee, advance tickets can be reserved by phone, online, or, once in Florence, at the Uffizi reservation booth (Consorzio ITA, Piazza Pitti, 055/294883), at least one day in advance of your visit. Keep the confirmation number and take it with you to the door at the museum marked "Reservations." In the past, you were ushered in almost immediately. But overbooking (especially in high season) has led to long lines and long waits even with a reservation. Taking photographs in the Uffizi has been legal since 2014, and has contributed to making what ought to be a sublime museum-going experience more of a day at the zoo. ✉ *Piazzale degli Uffizi 6, Piazza della Signoria* ☎ *055/294883* ⊕ *www.uffizi.firenze.it; www.polomuseale.firenze.it for reservations* ✇ *From €20* ✷ *Closed Mon.*

Mercato Nuovo (*New Market*)

MARKET | **FAMILY** | The open-air loggia, built in 1551, teems with souvenir stands, but the real attraction is a copy of Pietro Tacca's bronze *Porcellino* (which translates as "little pig" despite the fact the animal is, in fact, a wild boar). The *Porcellino* is Florence's equivalent of the Trevi Fountain: put a coin in his mouth, and if it falls through the grate below (according to one interpretation), it means you'll return to Florence someday. What you're seeing is a copy of a copy: Tacca's original version, in the Museo Bardini, is actually a copy of an ancient Greek work. ✉ *Via Por Santa Maria at Via Porta Rossa, Piazza della Repubblica* 🕙 *Closed Sun.*

★ Museo dell'Opera del Duomo (*Cathedral Museum*)

ART MUSEUM | A seven-year restoration of this museum and its glorious reopening in October 2015 have given Florence one of its most modern, up-to-date museums. Exhibition space has doubled in size, and the old facade of the cathedral, torn down in the 1580s, has been re-created with a 1:1 relationship to the real thing. Both sets of Ghiberti's doors adorn the same room. Michelangelo's *Pietà* finally has the space it deserves, as does Donatello's *Mary Magdalene*. ✉ *Piazza del Duomo 9, Duomo* 🕾 *055/2302885* ⊕ *www.operaduomo.firenze.it* 🎟 *€5* 🕙 *Closed Tues.–Fri.*

Orsanmichele

PUBLIC ART | This multipurpose structure began as an 8th-century oratory and then in 1290 was turned into an open-air loggia for selling grain. Destroyed by fire in 1304, it was rebuilt as a loggia-market. Between 1367 and 1380 the arcades were closed and two stories were added above; finally, at century's end it was turned into a church. Inside is a beautifully detailed 14th-century Gothic tabernacle by Andrea Orcagna (1308–68). The exterior niches contain sculptures (all copies) dating from the early 1400s to the early 1600s by Donatello and Verrocchio (1435–88), among others, which were paid for by the guilds. Although it is a copy, Verrocchio's *Doubting Thomas* (circa 1470) is particularly deserving of attention. Here you see Christ, like the building's other figures, entirely framed within the niche, and St. Thomas standing on its bottom ledge, with his right foot outside the niche frame. This one detail, the positioning of a single foot, brings the whole composition to life. It's possible to see the original sculptures at the **Museo di Orsanmichele,** which is open

Monday only. ✉ *Via dei Calzaiuoli, Piazza della Repubblica* 🕾 *055/284944* ⊕ *www. polomuseale.firenze.it* 🕙 *Closed Tues.– Sun.* 🎟 *Free.*

Palazzo Davanzati

CASTLE/PALACE | The prestigious Davizzi family owned this 14th-century palace in one of Florence's swankiest medieval neighborhoods (it was sold to the Davanzati in the 15th century). The place is a delight, as you can wander through the surprisingly light-filled courtyard, and climb the steep stairs to the piano nobile (there's also an elevator), where the family did most of its living. The beautiful *Sala dei Pappagalli* (Parrot Room) is adorned with trompe-l'oeil tapestries and gaily painted birds. ✉ *Piazza Davanzati 13, Piazza della Repubblica* 🕾 *055/0649460* ⊕ *www.polomuseale.firenze.it* 🎟 *€6* 🕙 *Closed Tues. and 1st, 3rd, 5th Sun. of month.*

Palazzo Vecchio (*Old Palace*)

CASTLE/PALACE | FAMILY | Florence's forbidding, fortress-like city hall was begun in 1299, presumably designed by Arnolfo di Cambio, and its massive bulk and towering campanile dominate Piazza della Signoria. It was built as a meeting place for the guildsmen governing the city at the time; today it is still City Hall. The interior courtyard is a good deal less severe, having been remodeled by Michelozzo (1396–1472) in 1453; a copy of Verrocchio's bronze *puttino* (cherub), topping the central fountain, softens the space. (The original is upstairs.) The main attraction is on the second floor: two adjoining rooms that supply one of the most startling contrasts in Florence. The first is the opulently vast **Sala dei Cinquecento** (Room of the Five Hundred), named for the 500-member Great Council, the people's assembly established after the death of Lorenzo the Magnificent, that met here. Giorgio Vasari and others decorated the room, around 1563–65, with gargantuan frescoes

12

Florence AROUND THE DUOMO

Continued on page 565

THE DUOMO
FLORENCE'S BIGGEST MASTERPIECE

For all its monumental art and architecture, Florence has one undisputed centerpiece: the Cathedral of Santa Maria del Fiore, better known as the Duomo. Its cupola dominates the skyline, presiding over the city's rooftops like a red hen over her brood. Little wonder that when Florentines feel homesick, they say they have "nostalgia del cupolone."

The Duomo's construction began in 1296, following the design of Arnolfo da Cambio, Florence's greatest architect of the time. By modern standards, construction was slow and haphazard—it continued through the 14th and into the 15th century, with some dozen architects having a hand in the project.

In 1366 Neri di Fioravante created a model for the hugely ambitious cupola: it was to be the largest dome in the world, surpassing Rome's Pantheon. But when the time finally came to build the dome in 1418, no one was sure how—or even if—it could be done. Florence was faced with a 143-ft hole in the roof of its cathedral, and one of the greatest challenges in the history of architecture.

Fortunately, local genius Filippo Brunelleschi was just the man for the job. Brunelleschi won the 1418 competition to design the dome, and for the next 18 years he oversaw its construc-

tion. The enormity of his achievement can hardly be overstated. Working on such a large scale (the dome weighs 37,000 tons and uses 4 million bricks) required him to invent hoists and cranes that were engineering marvels. A "dome within a dome" design and a novel herringbone bricklaying pattern were just two of the innovations used to establish structural integrity. Perhaps most remarkably, he executed the construction without a supporting wooden framework, which had previously been thought indispensable.

Brunelleschi designed the lantern atop the dome, but he died soon after its first stone was laid in 1446; it wouldn't be completed until 1461. Another 400 years passed before the Duomo received its façade, a 19th-century neo-Gothic creation.

DUOMO TIMELINE

1296 Work begins, following design by Arnolfo di Cambio.

1302 Arnolfo dies; work continues, with sporadic interruptions.

1331 Management of construction taken over by the Wool Merchants guild.

1334 Giotto appointed project overseer, designs campanile.

1337 Giotto dies; Andrea Pisano takes leadership role.

1348 The Black Plague; all work ceases.

1366 Vaulting on nave completed; Neri di Fioravante makes model for dome.

1417 Drum for dome completed.

1418 Competition is held to design the dome.

1420 Brunelleschi begins work on the dome.

1436 Dome completed.

1446 Construction of lantern begins; Brunelleschi dies.

1461 Antonio Manetti, a student of Brunelleschi, completes lantern.

1469 Gilt copper ball and cross added by Verrocchio.

1587 Original façade is torn down by Medici court.

1871 Emilio de Fabris wins competition to design new facade.

1887 Facade completed.

WHAT TO LOOK FOR INSIDE THE DUOMO

The interior of the Duomo is a fine example of Florentine Gothic with a beautiful marble floor, but the space feels strangely barren—a result of its great size and the fact that some of the best art has been moved to the nearby Museo dell'Opera del Duomo.

Notable among the works that remain are two towering equestrian frescoes of famous mercenaries: Niccolò da Tolentino (1456), by Andrea del Castagno, and Sir John Hawkwood (1436), by Paolo Uccello. There's also fine terra-cotta work by Luca della Robbia. Ghiberti, Brunelleschi's great rival, is responsible for much of the stained glass, as well as a reliquary urn with gorgeous reliefs. A vast fresco of the Last Judgment, painted by Vasari and Zuccari, covers the dome's interior. Brunelleschi had wanted mosaics to go there; it's a pity he didn't get his wish.

In the crypt beneath the cathedral, you can explore excavations of a Roman wall and mosaic fragments from the late sixth century; entry is near the first pier on the right. On the way down you pass Brunelleschi's modest tomb.

1. Entrance; stained glass by Ghiberti

2. Fresco of Niccolò da Tolentino by Andrea del Castagno

3. Fresco of John Hawkwood by Paolo Uccello

4. Dante and the Divine Comedy by Domenico di Michelino

5. Lunette: Ascension by Luca della Robbia

6. Above altar: two angels by Luca della Robbia. Below the altar: reliquary of St. Zenobius by Ghiberti.

7. Lunette: Resurrection by Luca della Robbia

8. Entrance to dome

9. Bust of Brunelleschi by Buggiano

10. Stairs to crypt

11. Campanile

500 Feet

300 Feet

MAKING THE CLIMB

Climbing the 463 steps to the top of the dome is not for the faint of heart—or for the claustrophobic—but those who do it will be awarded a smashing view of Florence ❶. Keep in mind that the way up is also the way down, which means that while you're huffing and puffing in the ascent, people very close to you in a narrow staircase are making their way down ❷.

300 Feet

75 Feet

DUOMO BASICS

• Even first thing in the morning during high season (May through September), a line is likely to have formed to climb the dome. Expect an hour wait.

• For an alternative to the dome, consider climbing the less trafficked campanile, which gives you a view from on high of the dome itself.

• Dress code essentials: covered shoulders, no short shorts, and hats off upon entering.

THE CRYPT

The crypt is worth a visit: computer modeling allows visitors to see its ancient Roman fabric and subsequent rebuilding. A transparent plastic model shows exactly what the earlier church looked like.

BRUNELLESCHI vs. GHIBERTI
The Rivalry of Two Renaissance Geniuses

In Renaissance Florence, painters, sculptors, and architects competed for major commissions, with the winner earning the right to undertake a project that might occupy him (and keep him paid) for a decade or more. Stakes were high, and the resulting rivalries fierce—none more so than that between Filippo Brunelleschi and Lorenzo Ghiberti.

The two first clashed in 1401, for the commission to create the bronze doors of the Baptistery. When Ghiberti won, Brunelleschi took it hard, fleeing to Rome, where he would remain for 15 years. Their rematch came in 1418, over the design of the Duomo's cupola, with Brunelleschi triumphant. For the remainder of their lives, the two would miss no opportunity to belittle each other's work.

FILIPPO BRUNELLESCHI (1377–1446)

MASTERPIECE: The dome of Santa Maria del Fiore.

BEST FRIENDS: Donatello, whom he stayed with in Rome after losing the Baptistery doors competition; the Medici family, who rescued him from bankruptcy.

SIGNATURE TRAITS: Paranoid, secretive, bad tempered, practical joker, inept businessman.

SAVVIEST POLITICAL MOVE: Feigned sickness and left for Rome after his dome plans were publicly criticized by Ghiberti, who was second-in-command. The project proved too much for Ghiberti to manage on his own, and Brunelleschi returned triumphant.

MOST EMBARRASSING MOMENT: In 1434 he was imprisoned for two weeks for failure to pay a small guild fee. The humiliation might have been orchestrated by Ghiberti.

OTHER CAREER: Shipbuilder. He built a huge vessel, *Il Badalone*, to transport marble for the dome up the Arno. It sank on its first voyage.

INSPIRED: The dome of St. Peter's in Rome.

LORENZO GHIBERTI (1378–1455)

MASTERPIECE: The Gates of Paradise, the ten-paneled east doors of the Baptistery.

BEST FRIEND: Giovanni da Prato, an underling who wrote diatribes attacking the dome's design and Brunelleschi's character.

SIGNATURE TRAITS: Instigator, egoist, know-it-all, shrewd businessman.

SAVVIEST POLITICAL MOVE: During the Baptistery doors competition, he had an open studio and welcomed opinions on his work, while Brunelleschi labored behind closed doors.

OTHER CAREER: Collector of classical artifacts, historian.

INSPIRED: *The Gates of Hell* by Auguste Rodin.

The Gates of Paradise detail

elebrating Florentine history; depictions of battles with nearby cities predominate. Continuing the martial theme, the room lso contains Michelangelo's *Victory*, ntended for the never-completed tomb f Pope Julius II (1443–1513), plus other culptures of decidedly lesser quality. In omparison, the little **Studiolo**, just off the Sala dei Cinquecento's entrance, was private room meant for the duke and hose whom he invited in. Here's where he melancholy Francesco I (1541–87), son of Cosimo I, stored his priceless reasures and conducted scientific experiments. Designed by Vasari, it was decorated by him, Giambologna, and many others. Spectacular 360-degree views may be had from the battlements (only 77 steps) and from the tower (223 more). ⊠ *Piazza della Signoria, Piazza della Signoria* ☎ *055/2768325* ⊕ *museicivicifiorentini.comune.fi.it* 🖂 *From €12.50.*

Piazza della Repubblica

PLAZA/SQUARE | The square marks the site of the ancient forum that was the core of the original Roman settlement. While the street plan around the piazza still reflects the carefully plotted Roman military encampment, the Mercato Vecchio (Old Market), which had been here since the Middle Ages, was demolished and the current piazza was constructed between 1885 and 1895 as a neoclassical showpiece. The piazza is lined with outdoor cafés, affording an excellent opportunity for people-watching. ⊠ *Florence.*

Piazza della Signoria

PLAZA/SQUARE | Here, in 1497 and in 1498, the famous "bonfire of the vanities" took place, when the fanatical Dominican friar Savonarola induced his followers to hurl their worldly goods into the flames; it was also here, a year later, that he was hanged as a heretic and, ironically, burned. A plaque in the piazza pavement marks the spot of his execution. Cellini's famous bronze *Perseus* holding the severed head of Medusa is among the most important sculptures in the Loggia dei

Lanzi. Other works include *The Rape of the Sabine Women* and *Hercules and the Centaur*, both late-16th-century works by Giambologna (1529–1608). In the square, the Neptune Fountain, created between 1550 and 1575 by Bartolomeo Ammannati, dominates. The Florentines call it il Biancone, which may be translated as "the big white man" or "the big white lump." Giambologna's equestrian statue, to the left of the fountain, portrays Grand Duke Cosimo I. Occupying the steps of the Palazzo Vecchio is a copy of Michelangelo's *David,* as well as Baccio Bandinelli's *Hercules.* ⊠ *Florence.*

Ponte Vecchio (*Old Bridge*)

BRIDGE | This charmingly simple bridge was built in 1345 to replace an earlier bridge swept away by a flood. Its shops first housed butchers, then grocers, blacksmiths, and other merchants. But in 1593, the Medici grand duke Ferdinand I (1549–1609), whose private corridor linking the Medici palace (Palazzo Pitti) with the Medici offices (the Uffizi) crossed the bridge atop the shops, decided that all this plebeian commerce under his feet was unseemly. So he threw out the butchers and blacksmiths and installed 41 goldsmiths and eight jewelers. The bridge has been devoted solely to these two trades ever since. The Corridoio Vasariano (Piazzale degli Uffizi 6, Piazza della Signoria, 055/294883), the private Medici elevated passageway, was built by Vasari in 1565. Though the ostensible reason for its construction was one of security, it was more likely designed so that the Medici family wouldn't have to walk amid the commoners. Take a moment to study the Ponte Santa Trinita, the next bridge downriver, from either the bridge or the corridor. It was designed by Bartolomeo Ammannati in 1567 (probably from sketches by Michelangelo), blown up by the retreating Germans during World War II, and painstakingly reconstructed after the war. The view from the Ponte Santa Trinita is beautiful, which might explain why so many young lovers seem to hang out there. ⊠ *Florence.*

Restaurants

Coquinarius

$$ | ITALIAN | This rustically elegant space, which has served many purposes over the past 600 years, offers some of the tastiest food in town at great prices. It's the perfect place to come if you aren't sure what you're hungry for, as they offer a little bit of everything: salad lovers will have a hard time choosing from among the lengthy list (the Scozzese, with poached chicken, avocado, and bacon, is a winner); those with a yen for pasta will face agonizing choices (the ravioli with pecorino and pears is particularly good). **Known for:** service can be inconsistent; marvelous salads; reasonably priced wine list. ⑤ *Average main: €18* ⊠ *Via delle Oche 15/r, Duomo* ☎ *055/2302153* ⊕ *www. coquinarius.it* ⊘ *No lunch Mon.–Fri.*

★ Gucci Osteria

$$$ | FUSION | Chef/artist/visionary Massimo Bottura has joined forces with creative folk at Gucci to make a marvelous menu that is both classic and innovative. Though he's trained with Ducasse and Adrià, he says his major influence was his grandmother's cooking. **Known for:** outdoor seating in one of Florence's most beautiful squares; tortellini in crema di Parmigiano Reggiano; an ever-changing creative menu. ⑤ *Average main: €35* ⊠ *Piazza della Signoria 10, Piazza della Signoria* ☎ *055/75927038* ⊕ *www.gucci.com.*

★ Rivoire

$$ | ITALIAN | One of the best spots in Florence for people-watching offers stellar service, light snacks, and terrific aperitivi. It's been around since the 1860s, and has been famous for its hot and cold chocolate (with or without cream) for more than a century. **Known for:** the view on the piazza; hot chocolate; friendly bartenders. ⑤ *Average main: €15* ⊠ *Via Vaccphereccia 4/r, Piazza della Signoria* ☎ *055/214412* ⊕ *www.rivoire.it* ⊘ *Closed Mon.*

Coffee and Quick Bites

★ 'ino

$ | ITALIAN | Serving arguably the best panini in town, proprietor Alessandro Frassica sources only the very best ingredients. Located right behind the Uffizi, 'ino is a perfect place to grab a tasty sandwich and glass of wine before forging on to the next museum. **Known for:** sourcing the best ingredients; bread; interesting ingredient combinations. ⑤ *Average main: €8* ⊠ *Via dei Georgofili 3/r–7/r, Piazza della Signoria* ☎ *055/214154* ⊕ *www.inofirenze.com* ⊘ *Closed Mon.*

Hotels

Hotel degli Orafi

$$$$ | HOTEL | A key scene in *A Room with a View* was shot in this pensione, which is today a luxury hotel adorned with chintz and marble. **Pros:** stellar Arno views; quiet location during the evenings; rooftop bar. **Cons:** some street noise in river-facing rooms; on the path of many tour groups during the day; somewhat pricey. ⑤ *Rooms from: €389* ⊠ *Lungarno Archibusieri 4, Piazza della Signoria* ☎ *055/26622* ⊕ *www.hoteldegliorafi.it* ⇒ *50 rooms* ⑩ *Free Breakfast.*

Hotel Helvetia and Bristol

$$$$ | HOTEL | From the cozy yet sophisticated lobby with its stone columns to the guest rooms decorated with prints, you might feel as if you're a guest in a sophisticated manor house. **Pros:** central location; old-world charm; excellent restaurant. **Cons:** books up quickly; breakfast is not always included in the price of a room; rooms facing the street get some noise. ⑤ *Rooms from: €684* ⊠ *Via dei Pescioni 2, Piazza della Repubblica* ☎ *055/26651* ⊕ *www.starhotelscollezione.com* ⇒ *82 rooms* ⑩ *No Meals.*

otel Renaissance

| **HOTEL** | Nestled in an old building st a stone's throw from the main civic quare (Piazza Signoria), this charming tle boutique hotel offers peace in quiet egance. **Pros:** the location; the staff; e sumptuous breakfast. **Cons:** some reet noise in some rooms; steps up to e elevator; books up quickly. $ *Rooms om:* €180 ✉ *Via della Condotta 4, Piazza lla Signoria* ☎ *055/213996* ⊕ *www. otelrenaissancefirenze.com* 🛏 *9 rooms* | *Free Breakfast.*

In Piazza della Signoria

$ | **B&B/INN** | In this home that is part f a 15th-century palazzo, a cozy feeling ermeates the charming rooms, all of hich are uniquely decorated and loving- furnished; some have damask curtains, thers fanciful frescoes in the bathroom. **ros:** some rooms easily accommodate ree; marvelous staff; tasty breakfast ith a view of Piazza della Signoria. **Cons:** ome of the rooms have steps up into howers and bathtubs; short flight of airs to reach elevator; books up quickly uring high season. $ *Rooms from:* 300 ✉ *Via dei Magazzini 2, Piazza della ignoria* ☎ *055/2399546* ⊕ *www.inpiazza- ellasignoria.com* 🛏 *13 rooms* ⦿ *Free reakfast.*

Nightlife

ard Rock Cafe

VE MUSIC | Hard Rock packs in young lorentines and travelers eager to sample he music hall chain's take on classic merican grub. ✉ *Via De' Brunelleschi Piazza della Repubblica, Piazza della epubblica* ☎ *055/277841* ⊕ *www. ardrock.com.*

ab

ANCE CLUBS | Yab never seems to go out f style, though it increasingly becomes he haunt of Florentine high school and niversity students intent on dancing and oing vodka shots. ✉ *Via Sassetti 5/r,*

Piazza della Repubblica ☎ *055/215160* ⊕ *www.yab.it.*

Performing Arts

Orchestra da Camera Fiorentina

MUSIC | This orchestra performs various concerts of classical music throughout the year at Orsanmichele, the grain mar- ket–turned–church. ✉ *Via Monferrato 2, Piazza della Signoria* ☎ *783374* ⊕ *www. orchestrafiorentina.it.*

🛍 Shopping

★ Bernardo

MEN'S CLOTHING | Come here for men's trousers, cashmere sweaters, and shirts with details like mother-of-pearl buttons. ✉ *Via Porta Rossa 87/r, Piazza della Repubblica* ☎ *055/283333* ⊕ *www. bernardofirenze.it.*

Cabó

MIXED CLOTHING | Missoni knitwear is the main draw at Cabó. ✉ *Via Porta Rossa 77–79/r, Piazza della Repubblica* ☎ *055/215774.*

Carlo Piccini

JEWELRY & WATCHES | Still in operation after four generations, this Florentine institution sells antique jewelry and makes pieces to order; you can also get old jewelry reset here. ✉ *Ponte Vecchio 31/r, Piazza della Signoria* ☎ *055/292030.*

Diesel

MIXED CLOTHING | Trendy Diesel started in Vicenza; its gear is on the "must have" list of many Italian teens. ✉ *Via degli Speziali 16/r, Piazza della Signoria* ☎ *055/2399963* ⊕ *www.diesel.com.*

Mandragora Art Store

SOUVENIRS | This is one of the first attempts in Florence to cash in on the museum-store craze. In store are reproductions of valued works of art and jewelry. ✉ *Piazza del Duomo 50/r, Duomo* ☎ *055/2654384* ⊕ *www.mandragora.it.*

Mercato dei Fiori (*flower market*)

MARKET | Every Thursday morning from September through June the covered loggia in Piazza della Repubblica hosts a Mercato dei Fiori; it's awash in a lively riot of plants, flowers, and difficult-to-find herbs. ⊠ *Piazza della Repubblica.*

Mercato del Porcellino

MARKET | **FAMILY** | If you're looking for cheery, inexpensive trinkets to take home, roam through the stalls under the loggia of the Mercato del Porcellino. ⊠ *Via Por Santa Maria at Via Porta Rossa, Piazza della Repubblica.*

Oro Due

JEWELRY & WATCHES | Gold jewelry and other beauteous objects are priced according to the level of craftsmanship and the price of gold bullion that day. ⊠ *Via Lambertesca 12/r, Piazza della Signoria* ☎ *055/292143* ⊘ *Closed Sun.*

Patrizia Pepe

WOMEN'S CLOTHING | The Florentine designer has clothes for mostly really thin young people, especially for women with a tiny streak of rebelliousness. Sizes run extremely small. ⊠ *Via Strozzi 13/r, Duomo* ☎ *055/2302518* ⊕ *www.patrizia-pepe.com.*

★ Pegna

FOOD | Looking for some cheddar cheese to pile in your panino? Pegna has been selling both Italian and non-Italian food since 1860. ⊠ *Via dello Studio 8, Duomo* ☎ *055/282701* ⊕ *www.pegna.it.*

★ Penko

JEWELRY & WATCHES | Renaissance gold-smiths provide the inspiration for this dazzling jewelry with a contemporary feel. ⊠ *Via dell'Oca 20–22/r, Duomo* ☎ *055/2052577* ⊕ *www.paolopenko.com.*

Spazio A

WOMEN'S CLOTHING | For cutting-edge fashion, these fun and funky window displays merit a stop. The shop carries such well-known designers as Alberta Ferretti and Moschino, as well as lesser-known Italian, English, and French designers. ⊠ *Via Porta Rossa 109–115/r, Piazza della Repubblica* ☎ *055/6582109.*

San Lorenzo

A sculptor, painter, architect, and poet, Florentine native son Michelangelo was a consummate genius, and some of his finest creations remain in his hometown. The Biblioteca Medicea Laurenziana is perhaps his most fanciful work of architecture. A key to understanding Michelangelo's genius can be found in the magnificent Cappelle Medicee, where both his sculptural and architectural prowess can be clearly seen. Planned frescoes were never completed, sadly, for they would have shown in one space the artistic triple threat that he certainly was. The towering yet graceful *David*, perhaps his most famous work, resides in the Galleria dell'Accademia.

After visiting San Lorenzo, resist the temptation to explore the market that surrounds the church: the market is open until 7 pm, while the churches and museums you may want to visit are not. Come back to the market later, after other sites have closed. Note that the Museo di San Marco closes at 1:50 on weekdays.

◉ Sights

Biblioteca Medicea Laurenziana
(*Laurentian Library*)

LIBRARY | Michelangelo the architect was every bit as original as Michelangelo the sculptor. Unlike Brunelleschi (the architect of the Spedale degli Innocenti), however, he wasn't obsessed with proportion and perfect geometry. He was interested in experimentation and invention and in the expression of a personal vision that was at times highly idiosyncratic. It was never more idiosyncratic than in the Laurentian Library, begun in 1524 and finished in 1568 by Bartolomeo Ammannati

Its famous **vestibolo,** a strangely shaped anteroom, has had scholars scratching their heads for centuries. In a space more than two stories high, why did Michelangelo limit his use of columns and pilasters to the upper two-thirds of the wall? Why didn't he rest them on strong pedestals instead of on huge, decorative curlicue scrolls, which rob them of all visual support? Why did he recess them into the wall, which makes them look weaker still? The architectural elements here do not stand firm and strong and tall as inside San Lorenzo next door; instead, they seem to be pressed into the wall as if into putty, giving the room a soft, rubbery look that is one of the strangest effects ever achieved by 16th-century architecture. It's almost as if Michelangelo intentionally flouted the conventions of the High Renaissance to see what kind of bizarre, mannered effect might result. His innovations were tremendously influential, and produced a period of architectural experimentation. As his contemporary Giorgio Vasari put it, "Artisans have been infinitely and perpetually indebted to him because he broke the bonds and chains of a way of working that had become habitual by common usage." The anteroom's staircase (best viewed straight on), which emerges from the library with the visual force of an unstoppable lava flow, has been exempted from the criticism, however. In its highly sculptural conception and execution, it is quite simply one of the most original and fluid staircases in the world. ⊠ *Piazza San Lorenzo 9, entrance to left of San Lorenzo, San Lorenzo* ⊕ *www. bmlonline.it* ⊠ *Special exhibitions €3* ⊗ *Closed weekends.*

Cappelle Medicee (*Medici Chapels*)
CHURCH | This magnificent complex includes the **Cappella dei Principi,** the Medici chapel and mausoleum that was begun in 1605 and kept marble workers busy for several hundred years, and the **Sagrestia Nuova** (New Sacristy), designed by Michelangelo and so called

to distinguish it from Brunelleschi's Sagrestia Vecchia (Old Sacristy) in San Lorenzo. Michelangelo received the commission for the New Sacristy in 1520 from Cardinal Giulio de' Medici (1478–1534), who later became Pope Clement VII. The cardinal wanted a new burial chapel for his cousins Giuliano, Duke of Nemours (1478–1534), and Lorenzo, Duke of Urbino (1492–1519), and he also wanted to honor his father, also named Giuliano, and his uncle, Lorenzo il Magnifico. The result was a tour de force of architecture and sculpture. Architecturally, Michelangelo was as original and inventive here as ever, but it is, quite properly, the powerfully sculpted tombs that dominate the room. The scheme is allegorical: on the tomb on the right are figures representing Day and Night, and on the tomb to the left are figures representing Dawn and Dusk; above them are idealized sculptures of the two men, usually interpreted to represent the active life and the contemplative life. But the allegorical meanings are secondary; what is most important is the intense presence of the sculptural figures and the force with which they hit the viewer. ⊠ *Piazza di Madonna degli Aldobrandini, San Lorenzo* ☎ *055/294883 reservations* ⊕ *www.cappellemedicee.it* ⊠ *€9* ⊗ *Closed 1st, 3rd, and 5th Mon., and 2nd and 4th Sun. of month.*

Galleria dell'Accademia (*Accademia Gallery*)
ART MUSEUM | FAMILY | The collection of Florentine paintings, dating from the 13th to 18th century, is largely unremarkable, but the sculptures by Michelangelo are worth the price of admission. The unfinished *Slaves,* fighting their way out of their marble prisons, were meant for the tomb of Michelangelo's overly demanding patron Pope Julius II (1443–1513). But the focal point is the original *David,* moved here from Piazza della Signoria in 1873. *David* was commissioned in 1501 by the Opera del Duomo (Cathedral Works Committee), which gave the

26-year-old sculptor a leftover block of marble that had been ruined 40 years earlier by two other sculptors. Michelangelo's success with the block was so dramatic that the city showered him with honors, and the Opera del Duomo voted to build him a house and a studio in which to live and work. Today *David* is beset not by Goliath but by tourists, and seeing the statue at all—much less really studying it—can be a trial. Save yourself a long wait in line by reserving tickets in advance. A plexiglass barrier surrounds the sculpture, following a 1991 attack on it by a self-proclaimed hammer-wielding art anarchist who, luckily, inflicted only a few minor nicks on the toes. The statue is not quite what it seems. It is so poised and graceful and alert—so miraculously alive—that it is often considered the definitive sculptural embodiment of High Renaissance perfection. But its true place in the history of art is a bit more complicated. As Michelangelo well knew, the Renaissance painting and sculpture that preceded his work were deeply concerned with ideal form. Perfection of proportion was the ever-sought Holy Grail; during the Renaissance, ideal proportion was equated with ideal beauty, and ideal beauty was equated with spiritual perfection. But *David,* despite its supremely calm and dignified pose, departs from these ideals. Michelangelo didn't give the statue perfect proportions. The head is slightly too large for the body, the arms are too large for the torso, and the hands are dramatically large for the arms. The work was originally commissioned to adorn the exterior of the Duomo and was intended to be seen from a distance and on high. Michelangelo knew exactly what he was doing, calculating that the perspective of the viewer would be such that, in order for the statue to appear proportioned, the upper body, head, and arms would have to be bigger, as they are farther away from the viewer. But he also did it to express and embody, as powerfully as possible in a single figure, an entire biblical story. David's hands *are* big, but so was Goliath, and these are the hands that slew him. Music lovers might want to check out the Museo degli Instrumenti Musicali contained within the Accademia; its Stradivarius is the main attraction. ⊠ *Via Ricasoli 60, San Marco* ☎ *055/294883 reservations, 055/2388609 gallery* ⊕ *www.polomuseale.firenze.it* ⊠ *€12; reservation fee €4* ☉ *Closed Mon.*

★ Mercato Centrale

MARKET | FAMILY | Some of the food at this huge, two-story market hall is remarkably exotic. The ground floor contains meat and cheese stalls, as well as some very good bars that have panini. In 2014, a second-floor food hall opened, eerily reminiscent of food halls everywhere. The quality of the food served, however, more than makes up for this. The downstairs market is closed on Sundays: the upstairs food hall is always open. ⊠ *Piazza del Mercato Centrale, San Lorenzo* ☎ *2399798,* ⊕ *www.mercatocentrale.it.*

Museo di Casa Martelli

HISTORIC HOME | The wealthy Martelli family, long associated with the all-powerful Medici, lived, from the 16th century, in this palace on a quiet street near the basilica of San Lorenzo. The last Martelli died in 1986, and in October 2009 the *casa-museo* (house-museum) opened to the public. It's the only nonreconstructed example of such a house in all of Florence, and for that reason alone it's worth a visit. The family collected art, and while most of the stuff is B-list, a few gems by Beccafumi, Salvatore Rosa, and Piero di Cosimo adorn the walls. Reservations are essential, and you will be shown the glories of this place by well-informed, English-speaking guides. ⊠ *Via Zanetti 8, San Lorenzo* ☎ *055/294883* ⊕ *www.polomuseale.firenze.it* ☉ *Closed Mon.–Wed., Fri., and 1st, 3rd, and 5th Sun. of month.*

Museo di San Marco

ART MUSEUM | A Dominican convent adjacent to the church of San Marco now

Florence's Trial by Fire

One of the most striking figures of Renaissance Florence was Girolamo Savonarola, a Dominican friar who, for a moment, captured the spiritual conscience of the city. In 1491 he became prior of the convent of San Marco, where he adopted a life of austerity and delivered sermons condemning Florence's excesses and the immorality of his fellow clergy. Following the death of Lorenzo de' Medici in 1492, Savonarola was instrumental in the re-formation of the republic of Florence, ruled by a representative council with Christ enthroned as monarch. In one of his most memorable acts he urged Florentines to toss worldly possessions—from sumptuous dresses to Botticelli paintings—onto a "bonfire of the vanities" in Piazza della Signoria. Savonarola's antagonism toward church hierarchy led to his undoing: he was excommunicated in 1497, and the following year was hanged and burned on charges of heresy. Today, at the Museo di San Marco, you can visit Savonarola's cell.

houses this museum, which contains many stunning works by Fra Angelico (circa 1400–55), the Dominican friar famous for his piety as well as for his painting. When the friars' cells were restructured between 1439 and 1444, he decorated many of them with frescoes meant to spur religious contemplation. His unostentatious and direct paintings exalt the simple beauties of the contemplative life. Fra Angelico's works are everywhere, from the friars' cells to the superb panel paintings on view in the museum. Don't miss the famous *Annunciation*, on the upper floor, and the works in the gallery off the cloister as you enter. Here you can see his beautiful *Last Judgment*; as usual, the tortures of the damned are far more inventive and interesting than the pleasures of the redeemed. ⊠ *Piazza San Marco 1, San Lorenzo* ☎ *055/294883* ⊕ *www.polomuseale.firenze.it* ✉ *€8* ⊗ *Closed 1st, 3rd, and 5th Sun., and 2nd and 4th Mon. of month.*

Palazzo Medici-Riccardi

CASTLE/PALACE | The main attraction of this palace, begun in 1444 by Michelozzo for Cosimo de' Medici, is the interior chapel, the so-called **Cappella dei Magi** on the piano nobile. Painted on its walls is Benozzo Gozzoli's famous *Procession of the Magi*, finished in 1460 and celebrating both the birth of Christ and the greatness of the Medici family. Gozzoli wasn't a revolutionary painter, and today is considered by some not quite first-rate because of his technique, which was old-fashioned even for his day. Gozzoli's gift, however, was for entrancing the eye, not challenging the mind, and on those terms his success here is beyond question. Entering the chapel is like walking into the middle of a magnificently illustrated children's storybook, and this beauty makes it one of the most enjoyable rooms in the city. ⊠ *Via Cavour 1, San Lorenzo* ☎ *055/2768224* ⊕ *www. palazzomediciriccardi.it* ⊗ *Closed Wed.* ✉ *€7.*

San Lorenzo

CHURCH | Filippo Brunelleschi designed this basilica, as well as that of Santo Spirito in the Oltrarno, in the 15th century. He never lived to see either finished. The two interiors are similar in design and effect. San Lorenzo, however, has a grid of dark, inlaid marble lines on the floor, which considerably heightens the dramatic effect. The grid makes the rigorous geometry of the interior immediately

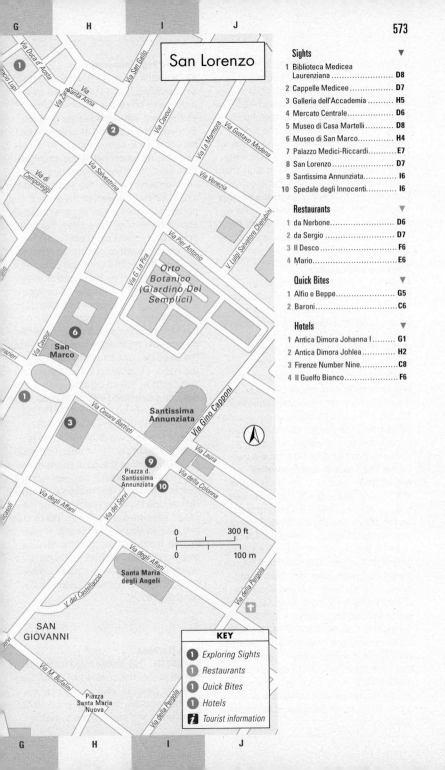

San Lorenzo

Sights ▼

Restaurants ▼

Quick Bites ▼

Hotels ▼

KEY

- 1 *Exploring Sights*
- 1 *Restaurants*
- 1 *Quick Bites*
- 1 *Hotels*
- 🛈 *Tourist information*

visible, and is an illuminating lesson on the laws of perspective. If you stand in the middle of the nave at the church entrance, on the line that stretches to the high altar, every element in the church—the grid, the nave columns, the side aisles, the coffered nave ceiling—seems to march inexorably toward a hypothetical vanishing point beyond the high altar, exactly as in a single-point-perspective painting. Brunelleschi's **Sagrestia Vecchia** (Old Sacristy) has stucco decorations by Donatello; it's at the end of the left transept. ⊠ *Piazza San Lorenzo, San Lorenzo* 🚇 *€7* ⊘ *Closed Sun.*

Santissima Annunziata

CHURCH | Dating from the mid-13th century, this church was restructured in 1447 by Michelozzo, who gave it an uncommon (and lovely) entrance cloister with frescoes by Andrea del Sarto (1486–1530), Pontormo (1494–1556), and Rosso Fiorentino (1494–1540). The interior is a rarity for Florence: an overwhelming example of Baroque. But it's not really a fair example, because it's merely 17th-century Baroque decoration applied willy-nilly to an earlier structure—exactly the sort of violent remodeling exercise that has given Baroque a bad name. The **Cappella dell'Annunziata,** immediately inside the entrance to the left, illustrates the point. The lower half, with its stately Corinthian columns and carved frieze bearing the Medici arms, was commissioned by Piero de' Medici in 1447; the upper half, with its erupting curves and impish sculpted cherubs, was added 200 years later. Fifteenth-century-fresco enthusiasts should also note the very fine *Holy Trinity with St. Jerome* in the second chapel on the left. Done by Andrea del Castagno (circa 1421–57), it shows a wiry and emaciated St. Jerome with Paula and Eustochium, two of his closest followers. This church, unlike many others in Florence, is highly active: please do not enter if Mass is in progress. ⊠ *Piazza di Santissima Annunziata, San Lorenzo.*

Spedale degli Innocenti

ART MUSEUM | **FAMILY** | The building built by Brunelleschi in 1419 to serve as an orphanage takes the historical prize as the very first Renaissance building. Brunelleschi designed its portico with his usual rigor, constructing it from the two shapes he considered mathematically (and therefore philosophically and aesthetically) perfect: the square and the circle. Below the level of the arches, the portico encloses a row of perfect cubes; above the level of the arches, the portico encloses a row of intersecting hemispheres. The entire geometric scheme is articulated with Corinthian columns, capitals, and arches borrowed directly from antiquity. At the time he designed the portico, Brunelleschi was also designing the interior of San Lorenzo, using the same basic ideas. But because the portico was finished before San Lorenzo, the Spedale degli Innocenti can claim the honor of ushering in Renaissance architecture. The 10 ceramic medallions depicting swaddled infants that decorate the portico are by Andrea della Robbia (1435–1525/28), done in about 1487. Within the Spedale degli Innocenti is a small museum, or Pinacoteca (€7; Mon.–Fri. 9–1). Most of the objects are minor works by major artists, but well worth a look is Domenico Ghirlandaio's (1449–94) *Adorazione dei Magi* (*Adoration of the Magi*), executed in 1488. His use of color, and his eye for flora and fauna, shows that art from north of the Alps made a great impression on him. ⊠ *Piazza di Santissima Annunziata 12, San Lorenzo* 🕾 *055/20371* ⊕ *www.istitutodeglinnocenti.it* 🚇 *€10.*

🍽 Restaurants

★ da Nerbone

$ | **TUSCAN** | This *tavola calda* (cafeteria) in the middle of the covered Mercato Centrale has been serving up food to Florentines who like their tripe since 1872. Tasty primi and secondi are available every day, but cognoscenti come for the *panino con il lampredotto* (tripe sandwich). **Known for:** favorite dishes sell out; tripe sandwich; frequented by locals (and everyone else). $ *Average main: €10 ⊠ Mercato San Lorenzo, Florence ⊗ Closed Sun. No dinner.*

★ da Sergio

$ | TUSCAN | Run by the Gozzi family for just over a hundred years, the food here is delicious, affordable, and just across the way from the basilica of San Lorenzo. The menu is short, and changes daily. **Known for:** lunch only; ever-changing menu; local favorite. $ *Average main: €10 ⊠ Piazza San Lorenzo 8/r, San Lorenzo ☎ 281941 ⊗ Closed Sun. No dinner Mon.–Thurs.*

Il Desco

$ | TUSCAN | The Bargiacchi family, also proprietors of the lovely hotel Guelfo Bianco just next door, source much of what is on the frequently changing menu from their organic farm in the Tuscan countryside. The menu plays to all tastes—Tuscan classics such as *peposo* (a hearty, black pepper–filled beef stew) can be found, as well as vegetarian dishes. **Known for:** clever wine list; just a few tables; fine vegetarian and vegan dishes. $ *Average main: €14 ⊠ Via Cavour 55/r, San Lorenzo ☎ 055/288330 ⊕ www. ildescofirenze.it.*

★ Mario

$ | TUSCAN | Florentines flock to this narrow family-run trattoria near San Lorenzo to feast on Tuscan favorites served at simple tables under a wooden ceiling dating from 1536. A distinct cafeteria feel and genuine Florentine hospitality prevail: you'll be seated wherever there's room, which often means with strangers. **Known for:** festive atmosphere; grilled meats; roasted potatoes. $ *Average main: €13 ⊠ Via Rosina 2/r, corner of Piazza del Mercato Centrale, San Lorenzo ☎ 055/218550 ⊕ www.trattoriamario.com ⊗ Closed Sun. and Aug. No dinner.*

☕ Coffee and Quick Bites

Alfio e Beppe

$ | ITALIAN | Watch chickens roast over high flames as you decide which of the other delightful things you're going to eat with it. The beauty of this place is that it's open on Sunday when most things are not. **Known for:** roasted dishes; grilled vegetables; open Sunday. $ *Average main: €9 ⊠ Via Cavour 118–120/r, San Marco ☎ 055/214108 ⊗ Closed Sat.*

★ Baroni

$ | INTERNATIONAL | The cheese collection at Baroni may be the most comprehensive in Florence. They also have high-quality truffle products, vinegars, and other delicacies. **Known for:** products packed for shipping; expansive cheese selection; top-notch foodstuffs. $ *Average main: €10 ⊠ Mercato Central, enter at Via Signa, San Lorenzo ☎ 055/289576 ⊕ www.baronialimentari.it.*

🛏 Hotels

Antica Dimora Johanna I

$ | B&B/INN | Savvy travelers and those on a budget should look no further, as this *residenza* is a tremendous value for quality and location, and though it's very much in the centro storico, the place is rather homey. **Pros:** many great, inexpensive restaurants nearby; morning tea and coffee served in your room; in a quiet neighborhood. **Cons:** no credit cards; staff go home at 7 pm; might be too removed for some. $ *Rooms from: €110 ⊠ Via Bonifacio Lupi 14, San Marco ☎ 055/481896 ⊕ www.antichedimorefiorentine.it ⤺ 10 rooms ⦿| Free Breakfast.*

★ Antica Dimora Johlea

$ | B&B/INN | Lively color runs rampant on the top floor of this 19th-century palazzo, with a charming flower-filled rooftop terrace where you can sip a glass of wine while taking in a view of Brunelleschi's cupola. **Pros:** honor bar; great staff; cheerful rooms. **Cons:** narrow staircase to get to roof terrace; staff goes home at 7:30; steps to breakfast room. $ *Rooms from: €119* ✉ *Via San Gallo 80, San Marco* ☎ *055/4633292* ⊕ *www. antichedimorefiorentine.it* ⤴ *6 rooms* ⦿I *Free Breakfast.*

Firenze Number Nine

$$$ | **HOTEL** | Those wanting an elegant hotel with a walk-in gym in the historic center have found their match: swank reception rooms, vividly decorated, have comfortable couches to sink into, and works by contemporary artists adorn the walls. **Pros:** sumptuous breakfast; location; walk-in gym and spa. **Cons:** might be too trendy for some; some street noise; books up quickly. $ *Rooms from: €300* ✉ *del Conti 9, San Lorenzo* ☎ *055/293777* ⊕ *www.firenzenumber-nine.com* ⤴ *45 rooms* ⦿I *Free Breakfast.*

Il Guelfo Bianco

$$ | **HOTEL** | The 15th-century building has all modern conveniences, but Renaissance charm still shines in the high-ceiling rooms. **Pros:** sumptuous breakfast; great staff; restaurant Il Desco is on-site. **Cons:** might be too removed for some; rooms facing the street can be noisy; not all rooms are well lit. $ *Rooms from: €140* ✉ *Via Cavour 29, San Marco* ☎ *055/288330* ⊕ *www.ilguelfobianco.it* ⦿I *Free Breakfast* ⤴ *40 rooms.*

 ## Nightlife

Kitsch

BARS | Choose from indoor or outdoor seating and take advantage of the great list of wines by the glass. At aperitivo time €12 will buy you a truly tasty cocktail and give you access to the tremendous buffet; it's so good, you won't need dinner afterward—in fact, they called it "Apericena." That means, roughly, drink and dinner. ✉ *Via San Gallo 22/r, San Marco* ☎ *055/3841358* ⊕ *www.kitschfirenze. com.*

 ## Shopping

Mercato Centrale

MARKET | FAMILY | This huge indoor food market offers a staggering selection of all things edible. Downstairs is full of vendors hawking their wares—meat, fish, fruit, vegetables; upstairs (daily 8 am–midnight) is full of food stalls serving up the best of what Italy has to offer. ✉ *Piazza del Mercato Centrale, San Lorenzo* ☎ *2399798* ⊕ *www.mercato-centrale.it* ⊗ *Downstairs closed Sun. and after 2 pm Mon.–Sat.*

Mercato di San Lorenzo

MARKET | FAMILY | The clothing and leather-goods stalls of the Mercato di San Lorenzo in the streets next to the church of San Lorenzo have bargains for shoppers on a budget. ✉ *Florence.*

Santa Maria Novella

Piazza Santa Maria Novella is a gorgeous, pedestrian-only square, with grass (laced with roses) and plenty of places to sit and rest your feet. The streets in and around the piazza have their share of architectural treasures, including some of Florence's most tasteful palaces. Between Santa Maria Novella and the Arno is Via Tornabuoni, Florence's swankiest shopping street.

 ## Sights

Museo Novecento

ART MUSEUM | It began life as a 13th-century Franciscan hostel offering shelter to tired pilgrims. It later became a convalescent home, and in the late 18th century it was a school for poor girls. Now the former Ospedale di San Paolo houses a museum devoted to Italian art of the 20th century. Admittedly, most of these artists are not exactly household names, but the museum is so beautifully well done that it's worth a visit. The second floor contains works by artists from the second half of the century; start on the third floor, and go directly to the collection of Alberto della Ragione, a naval engineer who was determined to be on the cutting edge of art collecting. ⊠ *Piazza Santa Maria Novella 10, Santa Maria Novella* ☏ *055/286132* ⊕ *www.museonovecento.it* ⊠ *€9.50* ⊗ *Closed Thurs.*

Museo Salvatore Ferragamo

ART MUSEUM | Almost like a shrine to footwear, the shoes in this dramatically displayed collection were designed by Salvatore Ferragamo (1898–1960) beginning in the early 20th century. Born in southern Italy, Ferragamo jump-started his career in Hollywood by creating shoes for the likes of Mary Pickford and Rudolph Valentino. He then returned to Florence and set up shop in the 13th-century Palazzo Spini Ferroni. The collection includes about 16,000 shoes, and those on exhibition are frequently rotated. Special exhibitions are also mounted here and are well worth visiting—past shows have been devoted to Audrey Hepburn, Greta Garbo, and Marilyn Monroe. ⊠ *Via dei Tornabuoni 2, Santa Maria Novella* ☏ *055/3562846* ⊕ *www.ferragamo.com* ⊠ *€8.*

Museo Stibbert

ART MUSEUM | Frederick Stibbert (1838–1906), born in Florence to an Italian mother and an English father, liked to collect things. Over a lifetime of doing so, he amassed some 50,000 objects. This museum, which was also his home, displays many of them. He had a fascination with medieval armor and also collected costumes, particularly Uzbek costumes, which are exhibited in a room called the Moresque Hall. These are mingled with an extensive collection of swords, guns, and other devices whose sole function was to kill people. The paintings, most of which date from the 15th century, are largely second-rate. The house itself is an interesting amalgam of neo-Gothic, Renaissance, and English eccentric. To get here, take Bus No. 4 (across the street from the station at Santa Maria Novella) and get off at the stop marked "Fabbroni 4," then follow signs to the museum. ⊠ *Via Federico Stibbert 26, Florence* ☏ *055/486049* ⊕ *www.museostibbert.it* ⊠ *€6* ⊗ *Closed Thurs.*

Palazzo Strozzi

HISTORIC HOME | The Strozzi family built this imposing palazzo in an attempt to outshine the nearby Palazzo Medici. Based on a model by Giuliano da Sangallo (circa 1452–1516) dating from around 1489 and executed between 1489 and 1504 under il Cronaca (1457–1508) and Benedetto da Maiaino (1442–97), it was inspired by Michelozzo's earlier Palazzo Medici-Riccardi. The palazzo's exterior is simple, severe, and massive: it's a testament to the wealth of a patrician, 15th-century Florentine family. The interior courtyard, entered from the rear of the palazzo, is another matter altogether. It is here that the classical vocabulary—columns, capitals, pilasters, arches, and cornices—is given uninhibited and powerful expression. The palazzo frequently hosts blockbuster art shows. ⊠ *Via Tornabuoni, Piazza della Repubblica* ☏ *055/2645155* ⊕ *www.palazzostrozzi.org* ⊠ *Free.*

Santa Maria Novella

CHURCH | The facade of this church looks distinctly clumsy by later Renaissance standards, and with good reason: it is an architectural hybrid. The lower half was completed mostly in the 14th century; its pointed-arch niches and decorative marble patterns reflect the Gothic style of the day. About 100 years later (around 1456), architect Leon Battista Alberti was called in to complete the job. The marble decoration of his upper story clearly defers to the already existing work below, but the architectural motifs he added evince an entirely different style. The central doorway, the four ground-floor half-columns with Corinthian capitals, the triangular pediment atop the second story, the inscribed frieze

Santa Maria Novella

immediately below the pediment—these are borrowings from antiquity, and they reflect the new Renaissance style in architecture, born some 35 years earlier at the Spedale degli Innocenti. Alberti's most important addition—the S-curve scrolls (called volutes) surmounting the decorative circles on either side of the upper story—had no precedent whatsoever in antiquity. The problem was to soften the abrupt transition between wide ground floor and narrow upper story. Alberti's solution turned out to be definitive. Once you start to look for them, you will find scrolls such as these (or sculptural variations of them) on churches all over Italy, and every one of them derives from Alberti's example here. The architecture of the interior is, like that of the Duomo, a dignified but somber example of Florentine Gothic. Exploration is essential, however, because the church's store of art treasures is remarkable. Highlights include the 14th-century stained-glass rose window depicting the *Coronation of the Virgin* (above the central entrance); the Cappella Filippo Strozzi (to the right of the altar), containing late-15th-century frescoes and stained glass by Filippino Lippi; the *cappella maggiore* (the area around the high altar), displaying frescoes by Ghirlandaio; and the Cappella Gondi (to the left of the altar), containing Filippo Brunelleschi's famous wood crucifix, carved around 1410 and said to have so stunned the great Donatello when he first saw it that he dropped a basket of eggs. Of special interest for its great historical importance and beauty is Masaccio's *Trinity,* on the left-hand wall, almost halfway down the nave. Painted around 1426–27 (at the same time he was working on his frescoes in Santa Maria del Carmine), it unequivocally announced the arrival of the

Renaissance. The realism of the figure of Christ was revolutionary in itself, but what was probably even more startling to contemporary Florentines was the barrel vault in the background. The mathematical rules for employing single-point perspective in painting had just been discovered (probably by Brunelleschi), and this was one of the first works of art to employ them with utterly convincing success. In the first cloister is a faded and damaged fresco cycle by Paolo Uccello depicting tales from Genesis, with a dramatic vision of the Deluge (at this writing, in restoration). Earlier and better-preserved frescoes painted in 1348–55 by Andrea da Firenze are in the chapter house, or the **Cappellone degli Spagnoli** (Spanish Chapel), off the cloister ✉ *Piazza Santa Maria Novella 19, Florence* ☎ *055/219257 museo* ⊕ *www.smn. it/en* 🎫 *€7.50* ⊘ *Closed Tues.–Wed. and Sat.–Sun. Closed Thurs.–Fri. Apr.–Sept.*

Santa Trinita

CHURCH | Started in the 11th century by Vallombrosian monks and originally Romanesque in style, the church underwent a Gothic remodeling during the 14th century. (Remains of the Romanesque construction are visible on the interior front wall.) The major works are the fresco cycle and altarpiece in the Cappella Sassetti, the second to the high altar's right, painted by Ghirlandaio between 1480 and 1485. His work here possesses such graceful decorative appeal as well as a proud depiction of his native city (most of the cityscapes show 15th-century Florence in all her glory). The wall frescoes illustrate scenes from the life of St. Francis, and the altarpiece, depicting the *Adoration of the Shepherds,* veritably glows. ✉ *Piazza Santa Trinita, Santa Maria Novella* ⊘ *Closed Sun. 10:45–4.*

Meet the Medici

The Medici were the dominant family of Renaissance Florence, wielding political power and financing some of the world's greatest art. You'll see their names at every turn around the city. These are some of the more notable family members:

Cosimo il Vecchio (1389–1464), incredibly wealthy banker to the popes, was the first in the family line to act as de facto ruler of Florence. He was a great patron of the arts and architecture; he was the moving force behind the family palace and the Dominican complex of San Marco.

Lorenzo il Magnifico (1449–92), grandson of Cosimo il Vecchio, presided over a Florence largely at peace with her neighbors. A collector of cameos, a writer of sonnets, and a lover of ancient texts, he was the preeminent Renaissance man and, like his grandfather, the de facto ruler of Florence.

Leo X (1475–1521), also known as Giovanni de' Medici, became the first Medici pope, helping extend the family power base to include Rome and the Papal States. His reign was characterized by a host of problems, the biggest one being a former friar named Martin Luther.

Catherine de' Medici (1519–89) was married by her great uncle Pope Clement VII to Henry of Valois, who later became Henry II of France. Wife of one king and mother of three, she was the first Medici to marry into European royalty. Lorenzo il Magnifico, her great-grandfather, would have been thrilled.

Cosimo I (1537–74), the first grand duke of Tuscany, should not be confused with his ancestor Cosimo il Vecchio.

12

Florence SANTA MARIA NOVELLA

Restaurants

Cantinetta Antinori

$$$ | TUSCAN | After a morning of shopping on Via Tornabuoni, stop for lunch in this 15th-century palazzo in the company of Florentine ladies and men who come to see and be seen over lunch. The panache of the food matches its clientele: expect treats such as *tramezzino con pane di campagna al tartufo* (country pâté with truffles served on bread) and the *insalata di gamberoni e gamberetti con carciofi freschi* (crayfish and prawn salad with shaved raw artichokes). **Known for:** high prices to match the excellent food and wine; chic clientele; most ingredients come from the family farm. $ *Average main: €28* ✉ *Piazza Antinori 3, Santa Maria Novella* ☎ *055/292234* ⊕ *www.cantinetta-antinori.com* ⊗ *Closed Sun., 20 days in Aug., and Dec. 25–Jan. 6.*

La Spada

$ | ITALIAN | FAMILY | Near Santa Maria Novella is La Spada. Walk in and inhale the fragrant aromas of meats cooking in the wood-burning oven. **Known for:** aromatic pastas; adherence to Tuscan cuisine; grilled meats. $ *Average main: €11* ✉ *Via della Spada 62/r, Santa Maria Novella* ☎ *055/218757.*

★ Mangiafoco

$$ | TUSCAN | Created by Francesco and Elisa in 2001, this small, brightly painted spot in the heart of the centro storico on a romantic medieval side street serves Tuscan classics *con fantasia* (with fantasy).

The menu changes daily, reflecting both what's in season and the whims of the chef. **Known for:** creative, seasonal menu changes daily; phenomenal wines by the glass and by the bottle; great service. $ *Average main: €20* ⊠ *Borgo Santi Apostoli 26/r, Santa Maria Novella* 🕾 *055/2658170* ⊕ *www.mangiafoco.com.*

Obicà

$$ | ITALIAN | Mozzarella takes center stage at this sleek eatery on Florence's swankiest street. The cheese, along with its culinary cousin *burrata* (a fresh cheese filled with cream), arrives daily from southern Italy to become the centerpiece for various salads and pastas. **Known for:** outdoor seating in nice weather; mozzarella-laden menu; outstanding pizza and desserts. $ *Average main: €20* ⊠ *Via Tornabuoni 16, Santa Maria Novella* 🕾 *055/2773526* ⊕ *www.obica.com.*

Osteria delle Belle Donne

$ | TUSCAN | Down the street from the church of Santa Maria Novella, this gaily decorated spot, always festooned with some sort of creative decoration (ropes of garlic and other vegetables have figured in the past) has an ever-changing menu and stellar service led by the irrepressible Giacinto. The menu offers Tuscan standards, but shakes things up with alternatives such as *sedani con bacon, verza, e uova* (thick noodles sauced with bacon, cabbage, and egg); when avocados are ripe, they're on the menu, too (either with cold boiled shrimp or expertly grilled chicken breast). **Known for:** dessert; many dishes not typical of Tuscany; seasonal ingredients. $ *Average main: €13* ⊠ *Via delle Belle Donne 16/r, Santa Maria Novella* 🕾 *055/2382609* ⊕ *www.casatrattoria.com.*

★ Procacci

$$ | ITALIAN | At this classy Florentine institution dating to 1885, try one of the truffle panini and swish it down with a glass of prosecco. **Known for:** serene (but tiny) space; pane tartufato; excellent wines by the glass. $ *Average main: €15* ⊠ *Via Tornabuoni 64/r, Santa Maria Novella* 🕾 *055/211656* ⊕ *www.procacci1885.it* ⊘ *Closed Sun.*

Vincanto

$$$ | ITALIAN | It opens at 11 am and closes at midnight: this is a rarity in Florentine dining. They do a little bit of everything here, including fine pastas, salads, pizzas, and even an American-style breakfast. **Known for:** outside terrace with views of a beautiful square; a wide-ranging menu; kitchen stays open. $ *Average main: €28* ⊠ *Piazza Santa Maria Novella 23/r, Santa Maria Novella* 🕾 *055/2679300* ⊕ *www.ristorantevincanto.com.*

Hotels

Alessandra

$$ | B&B/INN | FAMILY | An aura of grandeur pervades these clean, ample rooms a block from the Ponte Vecchio. **Pros:** tiny terrace allows for solitude while sipping a glass of wine; several rooms have views of the Arno; the spacious suite is a bargain. **Cons:** two rooms do not have en suite baths; stairs to elevator; some street noise. $ *Rooms from: €145* ⊠ *Borgo Santi Apostoli 17, Santa Maria Novella* 🕾 *055/283438* ⊕ *www.hotelalessandra.com* ⊘ *Closed Dec. 10–28* 🛏 *30 rooms* ⊰⊘⊱ *Free Breakfast.*

Antica Torre di Via Tornabuoni

$$$$ | B&B/INN | If you're looking for a room with a view you'll find it here, where just about every room looks out onto the awe-inspiring Duomo or the Arno (some even have small terraces). **Pros:** views of the Arno and Duomo; rooftop terrace with restaurant; tasteful decor. **Cons:** some street noise; books up very quickly; no staff after 7 pm. $ *Rooms from: €395* ⊠ *Via Tornabuoni 1, Santa Maria Novella* 🕾 *055/2658161* ⊕ *www.tornabuoni1.com* 🛏 *24 rooms* ⊰⊘⊱ *Free Breakfast.*

Gallery Hotel Art

$$$$ | HOTEL | High design resides at this art showcase near the Ponte Vecchio, where sleek, uncluttered rooms are dressed mostly in neutrals and luxe touches, such as leather headboards and kimono robes, abound. **Pros:** artistic touches; the in-house Fusion Bar serves delightful cocktails; trendy atmosphere. **Cons:** might be too trendy for some; books up quickly; some street noise. $ *Rooms from: €350* ⊠ *Vicolo dell'Oro 5, Santa Maria Novella* ☎ *055/27263* ⊕ *www.lungarnocollection.com* ⤴ *74 rooms* ⦿ *No Meals.*

Nuova Italia

$ | HOTEL | FAMILY | The genial Viti family oversees these clean and simple rooms near the train station and well within walking distance of the sights. **Pros:** great for those on a budget; reasonable rates; close to everything. **Cons:** the neighborhood is highly trafficked; no elevator; some street noise. $ *Rooms from: €54* ⊠ *Via Faenza 26, Santa Maria Novella* ☎ *055/268430* ⊕ *www.hotel-nuovaitalia. com* ⦿ *Free Breakfast* ⊙ *Closed Dec. 20–Dec. 27* ⤴ *20 rooms.*

★ The Place Firenze

$$$$ | HOTEL | Hard to spot from the street, this sumptuous place provides all the comforts of a luxe home away from home—expect soothing earth tones in the guest rooms, free minibars, crisp linens, and room service offering organic dishes. **Pros:** private, intimate feel; small dogs allowed; stellar staff. **Cons:** breakfast at a shared table; books up quickly; might be too trendy for some. $ *Rooms from: €442* ⊠ *Piazza Santa Maria Novella 7, Florence* ☎ *055/2645181* ⊕ *www. theplacefirenze.com* ⤴ *20 rooms* ⦿ *Free Breakfast.*

Torre Guelfa

$$ | B&B/INN | If you want a taste of medieval Florence, try one of these character-filled guest rooms—some with canopied beds, some with balconies—housed within a 13th-century tower. **Pros:**

some family-friendly triple and quadruple rooms; rooftop terrace with tremendous views; wonderful staff. **Cons:** some street noise; 72 steps to get to the terrace; books up quickly. $ *Rooms from: €199* ⊠ *Borgo Santi Apostoli 8, Santa Maria Novella* ☎ *055/2396338* ⊕ *www.hotel-torreguelfa.com* ⤴ *39 rooms* ⦿ *Free Breakfast.*

🎭 Performing Arts

Maggio Musicale Fiorentino

MUSIC | After some delay due to funding issues, a new music hall opened in 2014; the area is called the Parco della Musica (Music Park), and was designed by Paolo Desideri and associates. Maggio Musicale has taken up residence there, and continues to hold forth at the Teatro Comunale (Corso Italia 16, Lungarno North, 055/287222). Within Italy you can purchase tickets from late April through July directly at the box office or by phone (055/2779309). You can also buy them online. ⊠ *Via Alamanni 39, Florence* ☎ *055/2001278* ⊕ *www.operadifirenze.it.*

Tuscany Hall

FESTIVALS | This large exhibition space, formerly Teatro Saschall, hosts many events throughout the year, including a big and boisterous Christmas bazaar run by the Red Cross, visiting rock stars, and trendy bands from all over Europe. ⊠ *Lungarno Aldo Moro 3, Santa Maria Novella* ☎ *055/6504112* ⊕ *www.tuscanyhall.it.*

🛍 Shopping

Alberto Cozzi

STATIONERY | You'll find an extensive line of Florentine papers and paper products here. The artisans in the shop rebind and restore books and works on paper. Their hours are tricky, so it's best to call first before stopping by. ⊠ *Via del Parione 35/r, Santa Maria Novella* ☎ *055/294968.*

★ Angela Caputi

JEWELRY & WATCHES | Angela Caputi wows Florentine cognoscenti with her highly creative, often outsize plastic jewelry. A small, but equally creative, collection of women's clothing made of fine fabrics is also on offer. ✉ *Borgo Santi Apostoli 44/46, Florence* ☎ *055/292 993* ⊕ *www.angelacaputi.com.*

Antica Officina del Farmacista Dr. Vranjes

PERFUME | Dr. Vranjes elevates aromatherapy to an art form with scents for the body and home. ✉ *Via della Vigna Nuova 30/r, Florence* ☎ *055/0945851* ⊕ *www.drvranjes.it.*

Cellerini

LEATHER GOODS | In a city where it seems just about everybody wears an expensive leather jacket, Cellerini is an institution. ✉ *Via del Sole 9/r, Santa Maria Novella* ☎ *055/282533* ⊕ *www.cellerini.it.*

Emilio Pucci

WOMEN'S CLOTHING | The aristocratic Marchese di Barsento, Emilio Pucci, became an international name in the late 1950s when the stretch ski clothes he designed for himself caught on with the *dolce vita* crowd—his pseudopsychedelic prints and "palazzo pajamas" became all the rage. ✉ *Via Tornabuoni 20–22/r, Santa Maria Novella* ☎ *055/2658082* ⊕ *www.emiliopucci.com.*

Ferragamo

LEATHER GOODS | This classy institution, in a 13th-century palazzo, displays designer clothing and accessories, though elegant footwear still underlies the Ferragamo success. ✉ *Via Tornabuoni 14/r, Santa Maria Novella* ☎ *055/292123* ⊕ *www.ferragamo.com.*

Gatto Bianco

JEWELRY & WATCHES | This contemporary jeweler has breathtakingly beautiful pieces worked in semiprecious and precious stones. ✉ *Borgo Santi Apostoli 12/r, Santa Maria Novella* ☎ *055/282989* ⊕ *www.gattobiancogioielli.com.*

Giotti

LEATHER GOODS | You'll find a full line of leather goods, including clothing. ✉ *Piazza Ognissanti 3–4/r, Lungarno North* ☎ *055/294265* ⊕ *www.bottegagiotti.com/collection.*

★ Loretta Caponi

MIXED CLOTHING | Synonymous with Florentine embroidery, the luxury lace, linens, and lingerie have earned the eponymous signora worldwide renown. There's also beautiful (and expensive) clothing for children. ✉ *Via delle Belle Donne 28/r, Santa Maria Novella* ☎ *055/213668* ⊕ *www.lorettacaponi.com.*

★ Officina Profumo Farmaceutica di Santa Maria Novella

PERFUME | The essence of a Florentine holiday is captured in the sachets of this art nouveau emporium of herbal cosmetics and soaps that are made following centuries-old recipes created by friars. It celebrated its 400th birthday in 2012. ✉ *Via della Scala 16, Santa Maria Novella* ☎ *055/216276* ⊕ *www.smnovella.it.*

★ Pineider

STATIONERY | Although it has shops throughout the world, Pineider started out in Florence in 1774 and still does all its printing here. Stationery and business cards are the mainstay, but the stores also sell fine-leather desk accessories as well as a less stuffy, more lighthearted line of products. ✉ *Piazza Rucellai 4/7/r, Santa Maria Novella* ☎ *055/284656* ⊕ *www.pineider.com.*

Principe

DEPARTMENT STORE | This Florentine institution sells casual clothes for men, women, and children at far-from-casual prices. It also has a great housewares department. ✉ *Via del Sole 2, Santa Maria Novella* ☎ *055/292843* ⊕ *www.principedifirenze.com.*

Tiffany

JEWELRY & WATCHES | One of Florence's oldest jewelers has supplied Italian (and other) royalty with finely crafted gems for centuries. Its selection of antique-looking classics has been updated with contemporary silver. ⊠ *Via Tornabuoni 37/r, Santa Maria Novella* ☎ *800/215506* ⊕ *www.tiffany.it.*

Santa Croce

The Santa Croce quarter, on the southeast fringe of the historic center, was built up in the Middle Ages outside the second set of medieval city walls. The centerpiece of the neighborhood was (and is) the basilica of Santa Croce, which could hold great numbers of worshippers; the vast piazza could accommodate any overflow and also served as a fairground and, allegedly since the middle of the 16th century, as a playing field for no-holds-barred soccer games. A center of leatherworking since the Middle Ages, the neighborhood is still packed with leatherworkers and leather shops.

 Sights

Casa Buonarroti
ART MUSEUM | If you really enjoy walking in the footsteps of the great genius, you may want to complete the picture by visiting the Buonarroti family home. Michelangelo lived here from 1516 to 1525, and later gave it to his nephew, whose son, called Michelangelo il Giovane (Michelangelo the Younger) turned it into a gallery dedicated to his great-uncle. The artist's descendants filled it with art treasures, some by Michelangelo himself. Two early marble works—the *Madonna of the Stairs* and *Battle of the Centaurs*—demonstrate his genius. ⊠ *Via Ghibellina 70, Santa Croce* ☎ *055/241752* ⊕ *www.casabuonarroti.it* ☎ *€8* ⊗ *Closed Tues.*

Piazza Santa Croce
PLAZA/SQUARE | Originally outside the city's 12th-century walls, this piazza grew with the Franciscans, who used the large square for public preaching. During the Renaissance it was used for

giostre (jousts), including one sponsored by Lorenzo de' Medici. Lined with many palazzi dating from the 15th and 16th centuries, the square remains one of Florence's loveliest piazze and is a great place to people-watch. ⊠ *Florence.*

★ **Santa Croce**
CHURCH | Like the Duomo, this church is Gothic, but, like the Duomo, its facade dates from the 19th century. As a burial place, the church probably contains more skeletons of Renaissance celebrities than any other in Italy. The tomb of Michelangelo is on the right at the front of the basilica; he is said to have chosen this spot so that the first thing he would see on Judgment Day, when the graves of the dead fly open, would be Brunelleschi's dome through Santa Croce's open doors. The tomb of Galileo Galilei (1564–1642) is on the left wall; he was not granted a Christian burial until 100 years after his death because of his controversial contention that Earth was not the center of the universe. The tomb of Niccolò Machiavelli (1469–1527), the political theoretician whose brutally pragmatic philosophy so influenced the Medici, is halfway down the nave on the right. The grave of Lorenzo Ghiberti, creator of the Baptistery doors, is halfway down the nave on the left. Composer Gioachino Rossini (1792–1868) is buried at the end of the nave on the right. The monument to Dante Alighieri (1265–1321), the greatest Italian poet, is a memorial rather than a tomb (he is buried in Ravenna); it's on the right wall near the tomb of Michelangelo. The collection of art within the complex is by far the most important of any church in Florence. The most famous works are probably the Giotto frescoes in the two chapels immediately to the right of the high altar. They illustrate scenes from the lives of St. John the Evangelist and St. John the Baptist (in the right-hand chapel), as well as those from the life of St. Francis (in the left-hand chapel). Time has not been kind to these frescoes; through the centuries, wall tombs were

KEY
- Sights
- Restaurants
- Quick Bites
- Hotels

placed in the middle of them, they were whitewashed and plastered over, and in the 19th century they suffered a clumsy restoration. But the reality that Giotto introduced into painting can still be seen. He did not paint beautifully stylized religious icons, as the Byzantine style that preceded him prescribed; he instead painted drama—St. Francis surrounded by grieving friars at the very moment of his death. This was a radical shift in emphasis: before Giotto, painting's role was to symbolize the attributes of God; after him, it was to imitate life. His work is indeed primitive compared with later painting, but in the early 14th century it caused a sensation that was not equaled for another 100 years. He was, for his time, the equal of both Masaccio and Michelangelo. Among the church's other highlights are Donatello's *Annunciation,* a moving expression of surprise (on the right wall two-thirds of the way down the nave); 14th-century frescoes by Taddeo Gaddi (circa 1300–66) illustrating scenes from the life of the Virgin Mary, clearly showing the influence of Giotto (in the chapel at the end of the right transept); and Donatello's *Crucifix,* criticized by Brunelleschi for making Christ look like a peasant (in the chapel at the end of the left transept). Outside the church proper, in the Museo dell'Opera di Santa Croce off the cloister, is the 13th-century *Triumphal Cross* by Cimabue (circa 1240–1302), badly damaged by the flood of 1966. A model of architectural geometry, the Cappella Pazzi, at the end of the cloister, is the work of Brunelleschi. ✉ *Piazza Santa Croce 16, Santa Croce* ☎ *055/2466105* ⊕ *www.santacroceopera. it* 🎫 *Church and museum €8* ⊗ *Closed Sun. morning and Tues.*

Sinagoga

SYNAGOGUE | Jews were well settled in Florence by the end of the 14th century, but by 1574 they were required to live within the large "ghetto" at the north side of today's Piazza della Repubblica, by decree of Cosimo I. Construction of the modern Moorish-style synagogue began in 1874 as a bequest of David Levi, who wished to endow a synagogue "worthy of the city." Falcini, Micheli, and Treves designed the building on a domed Greek cross plan with galleries in the transept and a roofline bearing three distinctive copper cupolas visible from all over Florence. The exterior has alternating bands of tan travertine and pink granite, reflecting an Islamic style repeated in Giovanni Panti's ornate interior. Of particular interest are the cast-iron gates by Pasquale Franci, the eternal light by Francesco Morini, and the Murano glass mosaics by Giacomo dal Medico. The gilded doors of the Moorish ark, which fronts the pulpit and is flanked by extravagant candelabra, are decorated with symbols of the ancient Temple of Jerusalem and bear bayonet marks from vandals. The synagogue was used as a garage by the Nazis, who failed to inflict much damage in spite of an attempt to blow up the place with dynamite. Only the columns on the left side were destroyed, and even then, the Women's Balcony above did not collapse. Note the Star of David in black and yellow marble inlay on the floor. The original capitals can be seen in the garden. ✉ *Via Farini 4, Santa Croce* ☎ *055/245253* ⊕ *www.jewishflorence. it* 🎫 *Synagogue and museum €6.50* ⊗ *Closed Sat. and Jewish holidays.*

🍴 Restaurants

Antico Noe

$$ | TUSCAN | The short menu at the one-room eatery relies heavily on seasonal ingredients picked up daily at the market. Although the secondi are good, the antipasti and primi really shine. **Known for:** artichoke dishes; porcini dishes; attention to seasonal vegetables. ⑤ *Average main: €20* ✉ *Volta di San Piero 6/r, Santa Croce* ☎ *055/2340838* ⊗ *No dinner Sun. Closed 2 wks in Aug.*

Continued on page 595

WHO'S WHO IN RENAISSANCE ART

Michelangelo. Leonardo da Vinci. Raphael. This heady triumvirate of the Italian Renaissance is synonymous with artistic genius. Yet they are only three of the remarkable cast of characters whose work defines the Renaissance, that extraordinary flourishing of art and culture in Italy, especially in Florence, as the Middle Ages drew to a close. The artists were visionaries, who redefined painting, sculpture, architecture, and even what it means to be an artist.

THE PIONEER. In the mid-14th century, a few artists began to move away the flat, two-dimensional painting of the Middle Ages. Giotto, who painted seemingly three-dimensional figures who show emotion, had a major impact on the artists of the next century.

THE GROUNDBREAKERS. The generations of Brunelleschi and Botticelli took center stage in the 15th century. Ghiberti, Masaccio, Donatello, Uccello, Fra Angelico, and Filippo Lippi were other major players. Part of the Renaissance (or "re-birth") was a renewed interest in classical sources—the texts, monuments, and sculpture of Ancient Greece and Rome. Perspective and the illusion of three-dimensional space in painting was another discovery of this era, known as the Early Renaissance. Suddenly the art appearing on the walls looked real, or more realistic than it used to.

Roman ruins were not the only thing to inspire these artists. There was an incredible exchange of ideas going on. In Santa Maria del Carmine, Filippo Lippi was inspired by the work of Masaccio, who in turn was a friend of Brunelleschi. Young artists also learned from the masters via the apprentice system. Ghiberti's workshop (bottega in Italian) included, at one time or another, Donatello, Masaccio, and Uccello. Botticelli was apprenticed to Filippo Lippi.

THE BIG THREE. The mathematical rationality and precision of 15th-century art gave way to what is known as the High Renaissance. Leonardo, Michelangelo, and Raphael were much more concerned with portraying the body in all its glory and with achieving harmony and grandeur in their work. Oil paint, used infrequently up until this time, became more widely employed: as a result, Leonardo's colors are deeper, more sensual, more alive. For one brief period, all three were in Florence at the same time. Michelangelo and Leonardo surely knew one another, as they were simultaneously working on frescoes (never completed) inside Palazzo Vecchio.

When Michelangelo left Florence for Rome in 1508, he began the slow drain of artistic exodus from Florence, which never really recovered her previous glory.

A RENAISSANCE TIMELINE

IN THE WORLD

Black Death in Europe kills one third of the population, 1347-50.

Joan of Arc burned at the stake, 1431.

IN FLORENCE

Founding of the Medici bank, 1397.

Medici family made official papal bankers.

1434, Cosimo il Vecchio becomes de facto ruler of Florence. The Medici family will dominate the city until 1494.

Dante, a native of Florence, writes *The Divine Comedy*, 1302-21.

1300

1400

IN ART

EARLY RENAISSANCE

GIOTTO (ca. 1267-1337)

Masaccio and Masolino fresco Santa Maria del Carmine, 1424-28.

Giotto fresoes in Santa Croce, 1320-25.

BRUNELLESCHI (1377-1446)

LORENZO GHIBERTI (ca. 1381-1455)

DONATELLO (ca. 1386-1466)

PAOLO UCCELLO (1397-1475)

1334, 67-year-old Giotto is appointed chief architect of Santa Maria del Fiore, Florence's Duomo (below). He begins to work on the Campanile, which will be completed in 1359, after his death.

FRA ANGELICO (ca. 1400-1455)

MASACCIO (1401-1428)

FILIPPO LIPPI (ca. 1406-1469)

Donatello sculpts hi⌐ bronze *David*, ca. 144⌐

Fra Angelico frescoes friars' cells in San Marco, c 1438-45.

Ghiberti wins the competition for the Baptistery doors (above) in Florence, 1401.

Uccello's Sir John Hawkwood, ca. 1436.

Brunelleschi wins the competition for the Duomo's cupola (right), 1418.

Gutenberg Bible is printed, 1455.

Columbus discovers America, 1492.

Martin Luther posts his 95 theses on the door at Wittenberg, kicking off the Protestant Reformation, 1517.

Constantinople falls to the Turks, 1453.

Machiavelli's *Prince* appears, 1513.

Copernicus proves that the earth is not the center of the universe, 1530-43.

Lorenzo "il Magnifico" (right), the Medici patron of the arts, rules in Florence, 1449-92.

Two Medici popes Leo X (1513-21) and Clement VII (1523-34) in Rome.

Catherine de'Medici becomes Queen of France, 1547.

1450   **1500**   **1550**

HIGH RENAISSANCE   MANNERISM

Fra Filippo Lippi's *Madonna and Child*, ca. 1452.

1508, Raphael begins work on the chambers in the Vatican, Rome.

Giorgio Vasari publishes his first edition of *Lives of the Artists*, 1550.

1504, Michelangelo's *David* is put on display in Piazza della Signoria, where it remains until 1873.

Botticelli paints the *Birth of Venus*, ca. 1482.

Michelangelo begins to fresco the Sistine Chapel ceiling, 1508.

BOTTICELLI (ca. 1444-1510)

LEONARDO DA VINCI (1452-1519)

RAPHAEL (1483-1520)

MICHELANGELO (1475-1564)

Leonardo paints *The Last Supper* in Milan, 1495-98.

Giotto's *Nativity*   Donatello's *St. John the Baptist*   Ghiberti's Gates of Paradise

GIOTTO (CA. 1267-1337)

Painter/architect from a small town north of Florence.

He unequivocally set Italian painting on the course that led to the triumphs of the Renaissance masters. Unlike the rather flat, two-dimensional forms found in then prevailing Byzantine art, Giotto's figures have a fresh, life-like quality. The people in his paintings have bulk, and they show emotion, which you can see on their faces and in their gestures. This was something new in the late Middle Ages. Without Giotto, there wouldn't have been a Raphael.

In Florence: **Santa Croce; Uffizi; Campanile; Santa Maria Novella**
Elsewhere in Italy: **Scrovegni Chapel, Padua; Vatican Museums, Rome**

FILIPPO BRUNELLESCHI (1377-1446)

Architect/engineer from Florence.

If Brunelleschi had beaten Ghiberti in the Baptistery doors competition in Florence, the city's Duomo most likely would not have the striking appearance and authority that it has today. After his loss, he sulked off to Rome, where he studied the ancient Roman structures first-hand. Brunelleschi figured out how to vault the Duomo's dome, a structure unprecedented in its colossal size and great height. His Ospedale degli Innocenti employs classical elements in the creation of a stunning, new architectural statement; it is the first truly Renaissance structure.

In Florence: **Duomo; Ospedale degli Innocenti; San Lorenzo; Santo Spirito; Baptistery Doors Competition Entry, Bargello; Santa Croce**

LORENZO GHIBERTI (CA. 1381-1455)

Sculptor from Florence.

Ghiberti won a competition—besting his chief rival, Brunelleschi—to cast the gilded bronze North Doors of the Baptistery in Florence. These doors, and the East Doors that he subsequently executed, took up the next 50 years of his life. He created intricately worked figures that are more true-to-life than any since antiquity, and he was one of the first Renaissance sculptors to work in bronze. Ghiberti taught the next generation of artists; Donatello, Uccello, and Masaccio all passed through his studio.

In Florence: **Door Copies, Baptistery; Original Doors, Museo dell'Opera del Duomo; Baptistry Door Competition Entry, Bargello; Orsanmichele**

DONATELLO (CA. 1386-1466)

Sculptor from Florence.

Donatello was an innovator who, like his good friend Brunelleschi, spent most of his long life in Florence. Consumed with the science of optics, he used light and shadow to create the effects of nearness and distance. He made an essentially flat slab look like a three-dimensional scene. His bronze is probably the first free-standing male nude since antiquity. Not only technically brilliant, his work is also emotionally resonant; few sculptors are as expressive.

In Florence: ***David*, Bargello; St. Mark, Orsanmichele; Palazzo Vecchio; Museo dell'Opera del Duomo; San Lorenzo; Santa Croce**
Elsewhere in Italy: **Padua; Prato; Venice**

Fra Angelico's *The Deposition*   Masaccio's *Trinity*   Filippo Lippi's *Madonna and Child*

PAOLO UCCELLO (1397-1475)
Painter from Florence.
Renaissance chronicler Vasari once observed that had Uccello not been so obsessed with the mathematical problems posed by perspective, he would have been a very good painter. The struggle to master single-point perspective and to render motion in two dimensions is nowhere more apparent than in his battle scenes. His first major commission in Florence was the gargantuan fresco of the English mercenary Sir John Hawkwood (the Italians called him Giovanni Acuto) in Florence's Duomo.

In Florence: **Sir John Hawkwood, Duomo; Battle of San Romano, Uffizi; Santa Maria Novella**

Elsewhere in Italy: **Urbino, Prato**

FRA ANGELICO (CA. 1400-1455)
Painter from a small town north of Florence.
A Dominican friar, who eventually made his way to the convent of San Marco, Fra Angelico and his assistants painted frescoes for aid in prayer and meditation. He was known for his piety; Vasari wrote that Fra Angelico could never paint a crucifix without a tear running down his face. Perhaps no other painter so successfully translated the mysteries of faith and the sacred into painting. And yet his figures emote, his command of perspective is superb, and his use of color startles even today.

In Florence: **Museo di San Marco; Uffizi**

Elsewhere in Italy: **Vatican Museums, Rome; Fiesole; Cortona; Perugia; Orvieto**

MASACCIO (1401-1428)
Painter from San Giovanni Valdarno, southeast of Florence.
Masaccio and Masolino, a frequent collaborator, worked most famously together at Santa Maria del Carmine. Their frescoes of the life of St. Peter use light to mold figures in the painting by imitating the way light falls on figures in real life. Masaccio also pioneered the use of single-point perspective, masterfully rendered in his His friend Brunelleschi probably introduced him to the technique, yet another step forward in rendering things the way the eye sees them. Masaccio died young and under mysterious circumstances.

In Florence: **Santa Maria del Carmine; Trinity, Santa Maria Novella**

FILIPPO LIPPI (CA. 1406-1469)
Painter from Prato.
At a young age, Filippo Lippi entered the friary of Santa Maria del Carmine, where he was highly influenced by Masaccio and Masolino's frescoes. His religious vows appear to have made less of an impact; his affair with a young nun produced a son, Filippino (Little Philip, who later apprenticed with Botticelli), and a daughter. His religious paintings often have a playful, humorous note; some of his angels are downright impish and look directly out at the viewer. Lippi links the earlier painters of the 15th century with those who follow; Botticelli apprenticed with him.

In Florence: **Uffizi; Palazzo Medici Riccardi; San Lorenzo; Palazzo Pitti**

Elsewhere in Italy: **Prato**

Botticelli's *Primavera*

Leonardo's *Portrait of a Young Woman*

Raphael's *Madonna on the Meadow*

BOTTICELLI (CA. 1444-1510)

Painter from Florence.

Botticelli's work is characterized by stunning, elongated blondes, cherubic angels (something he undoubtedly learned from his time with Filippo Lippi), and tender Christs. Though he did many religious paintings, he also painted monumental, nonreligious panels—his *Birth of Venus* and *Primavera* being the two most famous of these. A brief sojourn took him to Rome, where he and a number of other artists frescoed the Sistine Chapel walls.

In Florence: **Birth of Venus, Primavera, Uffizi; Palazzo Pitti**

Elsewhere in Italy: **Vatican Museums, Rome**

LEONARDO DA VINCI (1452-1519)

Painter/sculptor/engineer from Anchiano, a small town outside Vinci.

Leonardo never lingered long in any place; his restless nature and his international reputation led to commissions throughout Italy, and took him to Milan, Vigevano, Pavia, Rome, and, ultimately, France. Though he is most famous for his mysterious *Mona Lisa* (at the Louvre in Paris), he painted other penetrating, psychological portraits in addition to his scientific experiments: his design for a flying machine (never built) predates Kitty Hawk by nearly 500 years. The greatest collection of Leonardo's work in Italy can be seen on one wall in the Uffizi.

In Florence: **Adoration of the Magi, Uffizi**

Elsewhere in Italy: **Last Supper, Santa Maria delle Grazie, Milan**

RAPHAEL (1483-1520)

Painter/architect from Urbino.

Raphael spent only four highly productive years of his short life in Florence, where he turned out made-to-order panel paintings of the *Madonna and Child* for a hungry public; he also executed a number of portraits of Florentine aristocrats. Perhaps no other artist had such a fine command of line and color, and could render it, seemingly effortlessly, in paint. His painting acquired new authority after he came up against Michelangelo toiling away on the Sistine ceiling. Raphael worked nearly next door in the Vatican, where his figures take on an epic, Michelangelesque scale.

In Florence: **Uffizi; Palazzo Pitti**

Elsewhere in Italy: **Vatican Museums, Rome**

MICHELANGELO (1475-1564)

Painter/sculptor/architect from Caprese.

Although Florentine and proud of it (he famously signed his St. Peter's *Pietà* to avoid confusion about where he was from), he spent most of his 89 years outside his native city. He painted and sculpted the male body on an epic scale and glorified it while doing so. Though he complained throughout the proceedings that he was really a sculptor, Michelangelo's Sistine Chapel ceiling is arguably the greatest fresco cycle ever painted (and the massive figures owe no small debt to Giotto).

In Florence: **David, Galleria dell'Accademia; Uffizi; Casa Buonarroti; Bargello**

Elsewhere in Italy: **St. Peter's Basilica, Vatican Museums, and Piazza del Campidoglio in Rome**

⚓ Cibrèo

$$$ | TUSCAN | This upscale trattoria serves sumptuous options like the creamy crostini *di fegatini* (with a savory chicken-liver spread) and melt-in-your-mouth desserts. Many Florentines hail this as the city's best restaurant, and justifiably so: chef-owner Fabio Picchi knows Tuscan food better than anyone, and though there's not a pasta dish to be seen on the menu (he argues that Florence doesn't really have any native pasta dishes), his deep understanding of Tuscan food shines through. **Known for:** multilingual staff; authentic Tuscan food; no written menu. $ *Average main: €40* ✉ *Via A. del Verrocchio 8/r, Santa Croce* ☎ *055/2341100.*

Cibrèo Trattoria

$$ | TUSCAN | This intimate little trattoria, known to locals as Cibreino, shares its kitchen with the famed Florentine culinary institution from which it gets its name. It's the same kitchen, shorter menu, and is not nearly as expensive. **Known for:** go early to avoid a wait; excellent meal at a moderate price; clever riffs on classic dishes. $ *Average main: €15* ✉ *Via dei Macci 118, Santa Croce* ☎ *055/2341100* ⏱ *Closed Sun., Mon., and July 25–Sept. 5.*

da Rocco

$ | TUSCAN | At one of Florence's biggest markets you can grab lunch to go, or you can cram yourself into one of the booths and pour from the straw-cloaked flask (wine here is *da consumo,* which means they charge you for how much you drink). Food is abundant, Tuscan, and fast; locals pack in. **Known for:** takeout; tasty food at rock-bottom prices; ever-changing menu. $ *Average main: €7* ✉ *Mercato Sant'Ambrogio, Piazza Ghiberti, Santa Croce* ☎ ⏱ *Closed Sun. No dinner.*

Ditta Artigianale

$ | ITALIAN | This place is always crowded with mostly young folk lingering over non-Italian cups of coffee. Light lunch and brunch are also on offer, and in between there's a steady supply of cakes, cookies, and croissants. **Known for:** long opening hours; non-Italian coffee; tasty food. $ *Average main: €12* ✉ *Via de'Neri 32, Santa Croce* ☎ *055/2741541* ⊕ *www.dittaartigianale.it.*

Enoteca Pinchiorri

$$$$ | ITALIAN | A sumptuous Renaissance palace with high frescoed ceilings and bouquets in silver vases provides the backdrop for this restaurant, one of the most expensive in Italy. Some consider it one of the best, and others consider it inauthentic as the cuisine extends far beyond Italian. **Known for:** exorbitantly high prices; wine cellar; creative food. $ *Average main: €103* ✉ *Via Ghibellina 87, Santa Croce* ☎ *055/242777* ⊕ *www.enotecapinchiorri.it* ⏱ *Closed Sun., Mon., and Aug. No lunch* 👔 *Jacket required.*

Kome

$$ | JAPANESE | If you're looking for a break from the ubiquitous ribollita, stop in at this eatery, which may be the only Japanese restaurant in the world to be housed in a 15th-century Renaissance palazzo. High, vaulted arches frame the kaiten sushi conveyor belt. **Known for:** ramen noodles; creative sushi; Japanese barbecue prepared table-side. $ *Average main: €16* ✉ *Via de' Benci 41/r, Santa Croce* ☎ *055/2008009* ⊕ *www.kome-firenze.it* ⏱ *No lunch Sun.*

★ La Giostra

$$$ | ITALIAN | This clubby spot, whose name means "carousel" in Italian, was created by the late Prince Dimitri Kunz d'Asburgo Lorena and is now expertly run by Soldano and Dimitri, his friendly twin sons. The ever-changing menu almost always has vegetarian and vegan options. **Known for:** vegetarian and vegan options; sublime tiramisù and a wonderfully gooey Sacher torte; carefully curated wine list. $ *Average main: €34* ✉ *Borgo Pinti 12/r, Santa Croce* ☎ *055/241341* ⊕ *www.ristorantelagiostra.com.*

Coffee and Quick Bites

★ Perché No!

$ | CAFÉ | FAMILY | They've been making ice cream at this much-loved-by-Florentines place since 1939. Such continuity is the reason why this might be the best gelateria in the historic center. **Known for:** unusual flavors and vegan options; gelati made daily; one of the oldest gelaterias in the city. $ *Average main: €3* ✉ *Via dei Tavolini 19r, Santa Croce* ☎ *055/2398969* ⊕ *www.percheno.firenze.it.*

Hotels

The Four Seasons

$$$$ | HOTEL | This 15th-century palazzo in Florence's center is perhaps the most luxurious show in town; many guest rooms have original 17th-century frescoes, while some face the garden and others face quiet interior courtyards. **Pros:** a Michelin-starred restaurant; pool and state-of-the-art spa; 11-acre garden. **Cons:** breakfast not included; small rooms; splashing children in the pool can be a nuisance for some. $ *Rooms from: €850* ✉ *Borgo Pinti 99e, Santa Croce* ☎ *055/26261* ⊕ *www.fourseasons.com/florence* ⇄ *117 rooms* ⊚ *No Meals.*

Hotel Regency

$$$$ | HOTEL | Rooms dressed in richly colored fabrics and antique-style furniture remain faithful to the premises' 19th-century origins as a private mansion; meanwhile, the noise and crowds of Florence seem far from this stylish retreat in a residential district near the Sinagoga, though you're not more than 10 minutes from the Accademia and Michelangelo's *David.* Across the street is Piazza d'Azeglio, a small public park that somehow evokes 19th-century middle Europe. **Pros:** the lovely restaurant Il Relais le Jardin on-site; faces one of the few green parks in the center of Florence; quiet neighborhood. **Cons:** rooms facing the park can be noisy; somewhat removed from the city center; books up quickly. $ *Rooms from:*

€350 ✉ *Piazza d'Azeglio 3, Santa Croce* ☎ *055/245247* ⊕ *www.regency-hotel.com* ⇄ *31 rooms* ⊚ *Free Breakfast.*

La Casa per Ferie Borgo Pinte delle Oblate dell'Assunzione

$ | B&B/INN | Nuns run this convent holiday house, minutes from the Duomo, with spotlessly clean, simple rooms; some have views of the cupola, and others look out onto a carefully tended garden where you are welcome to relax. **Pros:** a soothing, somewhat untended garden; great location and (mostly) quiet rooms; Mass held daily. **Cons:** rooms facing the street can be noisy; some have observed that there's hall noise; rooms are frugal. $ *Rooms from: €90* ✉ *Borgo Pinti 15, Santa Croce* ☎ *055/2480582* ⊕ *www.oblate.it* ⇄ *40 rooms* ⊚ *Free Breakfast.*

★ Monna Lisa

$$ | HOTEL | Although some rooms are small, they are tastefully decorated, and best of all, housed in a 15th-century palazzo that retains some of its wood-coffered ceilings from the 1500s, as well as its original staircase. **Pros:** garden; lavish buffet breakfast; cheerful multilingual staff. **Cons:** street noise in some rooms; rooms in annex are less charming than those in palazzo; thin walls have been noted. $ *Rooms from: €150* ✉ *Borgo Pinti 27, Santa Croce* ☎ *055/2479751* ⊕ *www.monnalisa.it* ⇄ *45 rooms* ⊚ *Free Breakfast.*

★ Morandi alla Crocetta

$$ | B&B/INN | You're made to feel like friends of the family at this charming and distinguished residence, furnished comfortably in the classic style of a gracious Florentine home and former convent. **Pros:** affable staff; historic touches like 17th-century fresco fragments; interesting, offbeat location near the sights. **Cons:** some say breakfast could be better; far from the "true" historical center; books up quickly. $ *Rooms from: €170* ✉ *Via Laura 50, Santissima Annunziata*

☎ 055/2344747 ⊕ www.hotelmorandi.it
⤴ 10 rooms |◎| Free Breakfast.

 Nightlife

Jazz Club
DANCE CLUBS | Enjoy live music in this small basement club. ✉ Via Nuova de' Caccini 3, at Borgo Pinti, Santa Croce.

Rex
BARS | A trendy, artsy clientele frequents this bar at aperitivo time; around 10 pm, the place is packed with mostly young folks sipping artfully made cocktails. ✉ Via Fiesolana 23–25/r, Santa Croce ☎ 055/2480331 ⊕ www.rexfirenze.com.

Sant'Ambrogio Caffè
BARS | Come here when it's summer for outdoor seating with a view of an 11th-century church (Sant'Ambrogio) directly across the street. Come here when it's not for perfectly mixed drinks and a lively atmosphere filled with (mostly) locals. ✉ Piazza Sant'Ambrogio 7–8/r, Santa Croce ☎ 055/2477277.

Performing Arts

Amici della Musica
MUSIC | This organization sponsors classical and contemporary concerts at the Teatro della Pergola (Box office, Via delle Carceri 1, 055/210804). ✉ Via Pier Capponi 41, Florence ⊕ www.amicimusica.fi.it.

Orchestra della Toscana
MUSIC | The concert season of the Orchestra della Toscana runs from November to June. ✉ Via Ghibellina, Santa Croce ☎ 055/234 0710 ⊕ www.orchestradellatoscana.it.

Shopping

Mercato di Sant'Ambrogio
MARKET | FAMILY | It's possible to strike gold at this lively market, where clothing stalls abut the fruits and vegetables. ✉ Piazza Ghiberti, off Via dei Macci, Santa Croce.

Paolo Carandini
OTHER ACCESSORIES | Stop in here for exquisite leather objects such as picture frames, jewelry boxes, and desk accessories. ✉ Borgo Allegri 7/r, Santa Croce ☎ 055/3347355954 ⊕ www.paolocarandini.net.

★ **Scuola del Cuoio**
LEATHER GOODS | A consortium of leatherworkers ply their trade at Scuola del Cuoio (Leather School), in the former dormitory of the convent of Santa Croce; high-quality, fairly priced jackets, belts, and purses are sold here. ✉ Piazza Santa Croce 16, Florence ☎ 055/244533 ⊕ www.scuoladelcuoio.com.

The Oltrarno

A walk through the Oltrarno (literally "the other side of the Arno") takes in two very different aspects of Florence: the splendor of the Medici, manifest in the riches of the mammoth Palazzo Pitti and the gracious Giardino di Boboli; and the charm of the Oltrarno, a slightly gentrified but still fiercely proud working-class neighborhood with artisans' and antiques shops.

Farther east across the Arno, a series of ramps and stairs climb to Piazzale Michelangelo, where the city lies before you in all its glory (skip this trip if it's a hazy day). More stairs (behind La Loggia restaurant) lead to the church of San Miniato al Monte. You can avoid the long walk by taking Bus No. 12 or 13 at the west end of Ponte alle Grazie and getting off at Piazzale Michelangelo; you still have to climb the monumental stairs to and from San Miniato, but you can then take the bus from Piazzale Michelangelo back to the center of town. If you decide to take a bus, remember to buy your ticket before you board.

The Oltrarno

F   **G**   **H**   **I**   **J**

Piazza della Signoria
Piazza San Firenze
V. del Gondi
V. dei Leoni
Via dell'Anguillara
Via della Torta

Por Santa V. Vaccherccia
Ch d. Baroncelli

Via d. Ninna
Borgo del Greci
Piazza Santa Croce

Galleria degli Uffizi
Via d'Vinegla
Via dei Neri
V.le Rustici
Via del Benci
Via San Giuseppe
V. dei Macci

Via Lambertesca
Piazza degli Uffizi
Via del Neri
V. de' Brache
Via del Benci
Borgo Santa Croce

Lungarno Archibusieri
Via del Saponai
V. d. N' Neri
Santa Croce
SANTA CROCE
Via delle Casine

Piazza d. Giudici
V. del Vagellal
Via Antonio Magliabechi

Piazza Mentana
V. di Malenchini
Corso del Tintori
Piazza Cavalleggeri
Via Tripoli

Lungarno Generale Armando Diaz
Lungarno della Grazie
Lungarno della Zecca Vecchia

Fiume Arno
Ponte alle Grazie

Coasta de Magnoli
Lungarno Torrigiani
Via de' Bardi

Coasta di San Giorgio
Via dei Renai
Piazza N. Demidoff
Lungarno Serristori
Via d. Giardino Serriston
Piazza Giuseppe Poggi

Costa di San Giorgio
Via di San Niccolo
Via di San Niccolo

olo della Cava
Via di San Niccolo
SAN NICCOLO
Via S. Miniato
Via del Bastioni
V. Giuseppe Poggi

Via Forte di San Giorgio
Via di Belvedere
Piazzale Michelangelo

Forte i Belvedere (San Giorgio)
Via di Belvedere

Via di San Leonardo
V. dell'Erta Canina
V. d. S. Salvatore al Monte
V. Monte alle Croci

Via dell'Erta Canina
Viale Galileo Galilei
Via delle Porte

KEY

- ① Exploring Sights
- ① Restaurants
- ① Quick Bites
- ① Hotels

1   **2**   **3**   **4**   **5**   **6**   **7**

600

 Sights

Giardino Bardini

GARDEN | Garden lovers, those who crave a view, and those who enjoy a nice hike should visit this lovely villa and garden, whose history spans centuries. The villa had a walled garden as early as the 14th century; the "Grand Stairs"—a zigzag ascent well worth scaling—have been around since the 16th. The garden is filled with irises, roses, and heirloom flowers, and includes a Japanese garden and statuary. A very pretty walk (all for the same admission ticket) takes you through the Giardino di Boboli and past the Forte Belvedere to the upper entrance to the giardino. ⊠ Via de'Bardini, San Niccolò ☎ 055/2638599 ⊕ www.villabardini. it ⊠ €10 ☉ Closed 1st and last Mon. of month.

Giardino di Boboli (Boboli Gardens)

GARDEN | The main entrance to these landscaped gardens is from the right side of the courtyard of Palazzo Pitti. The gardens began to take shape in 1549, when the Pitti family sold the palazzo to Eleanor of Toledo, wife of the Medici grand duke Cosimo I. Niccolò Tribolo (1500–50) laid out the first landscaping plans, and after his death, Ammannati, Giambologna, Bernardo Buontalenti (circa 1536–1608), Giulio (1571–1635), and Alfonso Parigi (1606–56), among others, continued his work. Italian landscaping is less formal than French, but still full of sweeping drama. A copy of the famous *Morgante,* Cosimo I's favorite dwarf astride a particularly unhappy tortoise, is near the exit. Sculpted by Valerio Cioli (circa 1529–99), the work seems to illustrate the perils of culinary overindulgence. A visit here can be disappointing because the gardens are somewhat sparse, but the pleasant walk offers excellent views. ⊠ Enter through Palazzo Pitti, Florence ☎ 055/294883 ⊕ www. polomuseale.firenze.it ⊠ €10 combined ticket, Giardino Bardini ☉ Closed 1st and last Mon. of month.

Museo Bardini

ART MUSEUM | The 19th-century collector and antiquarian Stefano Bardini turned his palace into his own private museum. Upon his death, the collection was turned over to the state and includes an interesting assortment of Etruscan pieces, sculpture, paintings, and furniture that dates mostly from the Renaissance and the Baroque. ⊠ Piazza de' Mozzi 1, Florence ☎ 055/2342427 ⊕ museicivicifiorentini.comune.fi.it ⊠ €7 ☉ Closed Tues.–Thurs.

Palazzo Pitti

ART MUSEUM | This enormous palace is one of Florence's largest architectural set pieces. The original palazzo, built for the Pitti family around 1460, comprised only the main entrance and the three windows on either side. In 1549, the property was sold to the Medici, and Bartolomeo Ammannati was called in to make substantial additions. Although he apparently operated on the principle that more is better, he succeeded only in producing proof that more is just that: more. Today, the palace houses several museums: The **Museo degli Argenti** displays a vast collection of Medici treasures, including exquisite antique vases belonging to Lorenzo the Magnificent. The **Galleria del Costume** showcases fashions from the past 300 years. The **Galleria d'Arte Moderna** holds a collection of 19th- and 20th-century paintings, mostly Tuscan. Most famous of the Pitti galleries is the **Galleria Palatina,** which contains a broad collection of paintings from the 15th to 17th century. The rooms of the Galleria Palatina remain much as the Lorena, the rulers who took over after the last Medici died in 1737, left them. Their floor-to-ceiling paintings are considered by some to be Italy's most egregious exercise in conspicuous consumption, aesthetic overkill, and trumpery. Still, the collection possesses high points, including a number of portraits by Titian and an unparalleled collection of paintings by Raphael. The price of admission to the Galleria

Palatina also allows you to explore the former **Appartamenti Reali,** containing furnishings from a remodeling done in the 19th century. ⊠ *Piazza Pitti, Florence* ☎ *055/294883* ⊕ *www.polomuseale. firenze.it* ✉ *From €16* ⊗ *Closed Mon.*

Piazzale Michelangelo

PLAZA/SQUARE | FAMILY | From this lookout you have a marvelous view of Florence and the hills around it, rivaling the vista from the Forte di Belvedere. A copy of Michelangelo's *David* overlooks outdoor cafés packed with tourists during the day and with Florentines in the evening. In May the **Giardino dell'Iris** (Iris Garden) off the piazza is abloom with more than 2,500 varieties of the flower. The **Giardino delle Rose** (Rose Garden) on the terraces below the piazza is also in full bloom in May and June. ⊠ *Florence.*

San Miniato al Monte

CHURCH | This church, like the Baptistery a fine example of Romanesque architecture, is one of the oldest churches in Florence, dating from the 11th century. A 12th-century mosaic topped by a gilt bronze eagle, emblem of San Miniato's sponsors, the Calimala (cloth merchants' guild), crowns the lovely green-and-white marble facade. Inside are a 13th-century inlaid-marble floor and apse mosaic. Artist Spinello Aretino (1350–1410) covered the walls of the Sagrestia with frescoes depicting scenes from the life of St. Benedict. The Cappella del Cardinale del Portogallo (Chapel of the Portuguese Cardinal) is one of the richest 15th-century Renaissance works in Florence. It contains the tomb of a young Portuguese cardinal, Prince James of Lusitania, who died in Florence in 1459. Its glorious ceiling is by Luca della Robbia, and the sculpted tomb by Antonio Rossellino (1427–79). Every day at 5:30 pm, the monks fill the church with the sounds of Gregorian chanting, and say Mass in Latin. ⊠ *Viale Galileo Galilei, Piazzale Michelangelo, Oltrarno* ☎ *055/2342731* ⊕ *www.sanminiatoalmonte.it.*

Santa Felicita

CHURCH | This late Baroque church (its facade was remodeled between 1736 and 1739) contains the mannerist Jacopo Pontormo's *Deposition,* the centerpiece of the Cappella Capponi (executed 1525–28) and a masterpiece of 16th-century Florentine art. The remote figures, which transcend the realm of Renaissance classical form, are portrayed in tangled shapes and intense pastel colors (well preserved because of the low lights in the church), in a space and depth that defy reality. Note, too, the exquisitely frescoed *Annunciation,* also by Pontormo, at a right angle to the *Deposition.* The granite column in the piazza was erected in 1381 and marks a Christian cemetery. ⊠ *Piazza Santa Felicita, Via Guicciardini, Palazzo Pitti* ⊗ *Closed Sun.*

Santa Maria del Carmine

CHURCH | The Cappella Brancacci, at the end of the right transept of this church, houses a masterpiece of Renaissance painting: a fresco cycle that changed the course of Western art. Fire destroyed most of the church in the 18th century; miraculously, the Brancacci Chapel survived almost intact. The cycle is the work of three artists: Masaccio and Masolino (1383–circa 1447), who began it around 1424, and Filippino Lippi, who finished it some 50 years later, after a long interruption during which the sponsoring Brancacci family was exiled. It was Masaccio's work that opened a new frontier for painting, as he was among the first artists to employ single-point perspective; tragically, he died in 1428 at the age of 27, so he didn't live to experience the revolution his innovations caused. Masaccio collaborated with Masolino on several of the frescoes, but his style predominates in the *Tribute Money,* on the upper-left wall; *St. Peter Baptizing,* on the upper altar wall; the *Distribution of Goods,* on the lower altar wall; and the *Expulsion of Adam and Eve,* on the chapel's upper-left entrance pier. If you look closely at the last painting and compare it with some of the chapel's other works, you should see a pronounced difference. The figures of Adam and Eve possess a startling presence primarily thanks to the dramatic way in which their bodies seem to reflect light. Masaccio here shaded his figures consistently, so as to suggest a single, strong source of light within the world of the painting but outside its frame. In so doing, he succeeded in imitating with paint the real-world effect of light on mass, and he thereby imparted to his figures a sculptural reality unprecedented in his day. These matters have to do with technique, but with the *Expulsion of Adam and Eve* his skill went beyond mere technical innovation. In the faces of Adam and Eve, you see more than finely modeled figures; you see terrible shame and suffering depicted with a humanity rarely achieved in art. Reservations to see the chapel are mandatory, but can be booked on the same day. ✉ *Piazza del Carmine, Santo Spirito* ☎ *055/2768224 reservations* ⊕ *www.museicivicifiorentini.comune.fi.it* 🖃 *€4.50* ⏱ *Closed Tues.*

Santo Spirito

CHURCH | The plain, unfinished facade gives nothing away, but the interior, although it appears chilly compared with later churches, is one of the most important examples of Renaissance architecture in Italy. The interior is one of a pair designed in Florence by Filippo Brunelleschi in the early decades of the 15th century (the other is San Lorenzo). It was here that Brunelleschi supplied definitive solutions to the two major problems of interior Renaissance church design: how to build a cross-shape interior using classical architectural elements borrowed from antiquity and how to reflect in that interior the order and regularity that Renaissance scientists (among them Brunelleschi himself) were at the time discovering in the natural world around them. Brunelleschi's solution to the first problem was brilliantly simple: turn a Greek temple inside out. While ancient Greek temples were walled buildings surrounded by classical colonnades, Brunelleschi's churches were classical arcades surrounded by walled buildings. This brilliant architectural idea overthrew the previous era's religious taboo against pagan architecture once and for all, triumphantly claiming that architecture for Christian use. Brunelleschi's solution to the second problem—making the entire interior orderly and regular—was mathematically precise: he designed the ground plan of the church so that all its parts were proportionally related. The transepts and nave have exactly the same width; the side aisles are precisely half as wide as the nave; the little chapels off the side aisles are exactly half as deep as the side aisles; the chancel and transepts are exactly one-eighth the depth of the nave; and so on, with dizzying exactitude. For Brunelleschi, such a design technique was a matter of passionate conviction. Like most theoreticians of his day, he believed that mathematical regularity and aesthetic beauty were flip sides of the same coin, that one was not possible without the other. In the refectory, adjacent to the church, you can see Andrea Orcagna's highly damaged fresco of the Crucifixion. ✉ *Piazza Santo Spirito, Oltrarno* ☎ *055/210030* ⊕ *www.basilicasantospirito.it* ⏱ *Church closed Wed.*

🍴 Restaurants

Alla Vecchia Bettola

$$ | TUSCAN | The name doesn't exactly mean "old dive," but it comes pretty close. The recipes here come from "wise grandmothers" and celebrate Tuscan food in its glorious simplicity—prosciutto is sliced with a knife, portions of grilled meat are tender and ample, service is friendly, and the wine list is well priced and good. **Known for:** just outside the centro storico but worth the taxi ride; grilled meats; firmly Tuscan menu. ⑤ *Average main: €15* ✉ *Viale Vasco Pratolini, Oltrarno* ☎ *055/224158* ⏱ *Closed Sun. and Mon.*

★ Il Santo Bevitore

$$ | TUSCAN | Florentines and other lovers of good food flock to "The Holy Drinker" for tasty, well-priced dishes. Unpretentious white walls, dark wood furniture, and paper place mats provide the simple decor; start with the exceptional *verdure sott'olio* (vegetables in oil) or the *terrina di fegatini* (a creamy chicken-liver spread) before sampling any of the divine pastas. **Known for:** friendly waitstaff; pasta; verdure sott'olio. $ *Average main: €18* ⊠ *Via Santo Spirito 64/66r, Santo Spirito* ☎ *055/211264* ⊕ *www.ilsantobevitore. com* ☉ *No lunch Sun.*

La Bottega del Buon Caffè

$$$$ | MODERN ITALIAN | This restaurant is a symphony in gustatory pleasures in a room with exposed sandy brick walls and high, luminous windows. Executive chef Antonello Sardi is young and gifted, as is his ace brigade. **Known for:** stupendous wine list; farm to table; cutting-edge fare. $ *Average main: €44* ⊠ *Lungarno, Cellini, 69/r, Oltrarno* ☎ *055/5535677* ⊕ *www. borgointhecity.com.*

★ La Casalinga

$ | TUSCAN | *Casalinga* means "housewife," and this place, which has been around since 1963, has the nostalgic charm of a mid-century kitchen with Tuscan comfort food to match. If you eat ribollita anywhere in Florence, eat it here—it couldn't be more authentic. **Known for:** often packed; ribollita; liver, Venetian style. $ *Average main: €13* ⊠ *Via Michelozzi 9/r, Santo Spirito* ☎ *055/218624* ⊕ *www. trattorialacasalinga.it* ☉ *Closed Sun., 1 wk at Christmas, and 3 wks in Aug.*

Osteria Antica Mescita San Niccolò

$ | TUSCAN | Always crowded, always good, and always inexpensive, the osteria is next to the church of San Niccolò, and, if you sit in the lower part, you'll find yourself in what was once a chapel dating from the 11th century. The subtle but dramatic background is a nice complement to the food, which is simple Tuscan at its best. **Known for:** delicious soup; outdoor seating in a small, lovely square; great, simple salads. $ *Average main: €11* ⊠ *Via San Niccolò 60/r, San Niccolò* ☎ *055/2342836* ⊕ *www.osteri-asanniccolo.it.*

Zeb

$ | TUSCAN | Incredibly tasty and gently priced, Zeb stands for *zuppa e bollito* (soup and boiled things) and nothing at this small *alimentari* (delicatessen) disappoints. It's home-style Tuscan cuisine at its very best, served in unpretentious, intimate surroundings: there's room for only about 15 guests. **Known for:** lovely wine list; fantastic soup; terrific pasta. $ *Average main: €13* ⊠ *Via San Miniato 2, Oltrarno* ☎ *055/2342864* ⊕ *www. zebgastronomia.com* ☉ *Closed Wed.*

☕ Coffee and Quick Bites

Gelateria la Carraia

$ | ITALIAN | FAMILY | Although it's a bit of a haul to get here (it's at the foot of Ponte Carraia, two bridges down from the Ponte Vecchio), you'll be well rewarded for doing so. They do standard flavors, and then creative ones such as *limone con biscotti* (lemon sorbet with cookies), and they do both of these very well. **Known for:** every flavor is delicious; super-creamy gelato; generous €1 tasting cones. $ *Average main: €3* ⊠ *Piazza Nazario Sauro 2, Santo Spirito* ☎ *055/280695* ⊕ *www. lacarraiagroup.eu.*

🛏 Hotels

Hotel Silla

$ | HOTEL | Rooms in this 15th-century palazzo, entered through a courtyard lined with potted plants and sculpture-filled niches, are simply furnished; some have views of the Arno, others have stuccoed ceilings. **Pros:** cordial, friendly staff; great breakfast; in the middle of everything except the crowds. **Cons:** could use an update; small rooms; street noise. $ *Rooms from: €92* ⊠ *Via de' Renai 5, San Niccolò* ☎ *055/2342888*

⊕ *www.hotelsilla.it* ⤷ *39 rooms* ¶ ◎¶ *Free Breakfast.*

Lungarno

$$$$ | **HOTEL** | Many rooms and suites here have private terraces that jut out right over the Arno, granting stunning views of the Palazzo Vecchio and the Lungarno; a studio suite in a 13th-century tower preserves details like exposed stone walls and old archways, and looks over a little square with a medieval tower covered in jasmine. **Pros:** upscale without being stuffy; lovely views of the Arno; Borgo San Jacopo, its one-starred Michelin restaurant. **Cons:** street noise happens; walls can be thin; rooms without Arno views feel less special. ⑤ *Rooms from: €472* ⊠ *Borgo San Jacopo 14, Oltrarno* ☎ *055/27261* ⊕ *www.lungarnocollection. com* ⤷ *63 rooms* ¶ ◎¶ *Free Breakfast.*

Nightlife

Montecarla

GATHERING PLACES | People sip cocktails against a backdrop of exotic flowers, leopard-print chairs and chintz, surrounded by red walls on the two crowded floors at Montecarla. ⊠ *Via de' Bardi 2, San Niccolò* ☎ *055/2480918.*

Zoe

GATHERING PLACES | Though it's called a *caffetteria,* and coffee is served (as well as terrific salads and burgers at lunchtime), Zoe's fine cocktails are the real draw for elegant Florentines who come here to see and be seen. ⊠ *Via de' Renai 13/r, San Niccolò* ☎ *055/243111* ⊕ *www. zoebar.it.*

Shopping

★ Giulio Giannini e Figlio

STATIONERY | One of Florence's oldest paper-goods stores is *the* place to buy the marbleized stock, which comes in many shapes and sizes, from flat sheets to boxes and even pencils. ⊠ *Piazza Pitti*

37/r, Oltrarno ☎ *055/212621* ⊕ *www. giuliogiannini.it.*

★ Il Torchio

STATIONERY | Photograph albums, frames, diaries, and other objects dressed in handmade paper are high quality, and the prices lower than usual. ⊠ *Via dei Bardi 17, San Niccolò* ☎ *055/2342862* ⊕ *www. legatoriailtorchio.com.*

Maçel

WOMEN'S CLOTHING | Browse collections by lesser-known Italian designers, many of whom use the same factories as the A-list, at this women's clothing shop. ⊠ *Via Guicciardini 128/r, Palazzo Pitti* ☎ *055/287355.*

★ Madova

HATS & GLOVES | Complete your winter wardrobe with a pair of high-quality leather gloves, available in a rainbow of colors and a choice of linings (silk, cashmere, and unlined), from Madova. They've been in business for 100 years. ⊠ *Via Guicciardini 1/r, Palazzo Pitti* ☎ *055/2396526* ⊕ *www.madova.com.*

Santo Spirito flea market

MARKET | **FAMILY** | The second Sunday of every month brings the Santo Spirito flea market. On the third Sunday of the month, vendors at the Fierucola organic fest sell such delectables as honeys, jams, spice mixes, and fresh vegetables. ⊠ *Santo Spirito, Florence.*

A Side Trip from Florence

Fiesole

A half-day excursion to Fiesole, in the hills 8 km (5 miles) above Florence, gives you a pleasant respite from museums and a wonderful view of the city. From here the view of the Duomo gives you a new appreciation for what the Renaissance accomplished. Fiesole began life as an ancient Etruscan and later Roman village that held some power until it succumbed to barbarian invasions. Eventually it gave up its independence in exchange for Florence's protection. The medieval cathedral, ancient Roman amphitheater, and lovely old villas behind garden walls are clustered on a series of hilltops. A walk around Fiesole can take from one to two or three hours, depending on how far you stroll from the main piazza.

GETTING HERE AND AROUND

The trip from Florence by car takes 20–30 minutes. Drive to Piazza Liberta and cross the Ponte Rosso heading in the direction of the SS65/SR65. Turn right on to Via Salviati and continue on to Via Roccettini. Make a left turn to Via Vecchia Fiesolana, which will take you directly to the center of town. There are several possible routes for the two-hour walk from central Florence to Fiesole. One route begins in a residential area of Florence called Salviatino (Via Barbacane, near Piazza Edison, on the No. 7 bus route), and after a short time, offers peeks over garden walls of beautiful villas, as well as the view over your shoulder at the panorama of Florence in the valley.

VISITOR INFORMATION

CONTACT Fiesole Tourism Office. ✉ *Via Portigiani 3, Fiesole* ☎ *055/5961311* ⊕ *www.fiesoleforyou.it.*

Sights

Anfiteatro Romano (*Roman Amphitheater*) **RUINS** | The beautifully preserved 2,000-seat Anfiteatro Romano, near the Duomo, dates from the 1st century BC and is still used for summer concerts. To the right of the amphitheater are the remains of the Terme Romani (Roman Baths), where you can see the gymnasium, hot and cold baths, and rectangular chamber where the water was heated. A beautifully designed Museo Archeologico,

its facade evoking an ancient Roman temple, is built amid the ruins and contains objects dating from as early as 2000 BC. The nearby Museo Bandini is filled with the private collection of Canon Angelo Maria Bandini (1726–1803); he fancied 13th- to 15th-century Florentine paintings, terra-cotta pieces, and wood sculpture, which he later bequeathed to the Diocese of Fiesole. ✉ *Via Portigiani 1, Fiesole* ☎ *055/5961293* ⊕ *www.museidifiesole.it* ⊘ *Museo Bandini closed Mon.–Thurs.* 🎟 *€12, includes access to archaeological park and museums.*

Badia Fiesolana

CHURCH | From the church of San Domenico it's a five-minute walk northwest to the Badia Fiesolana, which was Fiesole's original cathedral. Dating to the 11th century, it was first the home of the Camaldolese monks. Thanks to Cosimo il Vecchio, the complex was substantially restructured. The facade, never completed owing to Cosimo's death, contains elements of its original Romanesque decoration. ✉ *Via della Badia dei Roccettini 11, Fiesole* ☎ *055/46851* ⊕ *www.eui.eu* ⊘ *Closed Sat. afternoon and Sun.*

Duomo

CHURCH | A stark medieval interior yields many masterpieces. In the raised presbytery, the **Cappella Salutati** was frescoed by 15th-century artist Cosimo Rosselli, but it was his contemporary, sculptor Mino da Fiesole (1430–84), who put the town on the artistic map. The Madonna on the altarpiece and the tomb of Bishop Salutati are fine examples of the artist's work. ✉ *Piazza Mino da Fiesole, Fiesole.*

San Domenico

CHURCH | If you really want to stretch your legs, walk 4 km (2½ miles) toward the center of Florence along Via Vecchia Fiesolana, a narrow lane in use since Etruscan times, to the church of San Domenico. Sheltered in the church is the *Madonna and Child with Saints* by

Fra Angelico, who was a Dominican friar here before he moved to Florence. ✉ *Piazza San Domenico, off Via Giuseppe Mantellini, Fiesole* ⊗ *Closed Sun.*

San Francesco

CHURCH | This lovely hilltop church has a good view of Florence and the plain below from its terrace and benches. Off the little cloister is a small, eclectic museum containing, among other things, two Egyptian mummies. Halfway up the hill you'll see sloping steps to the right; they lead to a fragrant wooded park with trails that loop out and back to the church. ✉ *Fiesole.*

 Restaurants

La Reggia degli Etruschi

$$ | **ITALIAN** | Located on a steep hill on the way up to the church of San Francesco, this lovely little eatery is certainly worth the trek. Indulge in inventive reworkings of Tuscan classics, like the *mezzaluna di pera a pecorino* (little half-moon pasta stuffed with pear and pecorino) sauced with Roquefort and poppy seeds. **Known for:** small terrace with outdoor seating; out-of-the-way location; good wine list and friendly service. ⑤ *Average main: €21* ✉ *Via San Francesco, Fiesole* ☎ *055/59385* ⊕ *www. lareggiadeglietruschi.com.*

 Hotels

Villa San Michele

$$$$ | **HOTEL** | The cypress-lined driveway provides an elegant preamble to this incredibly gorgeous (and very expensive) hotel nestled in the hills of Fiesole. **Pros:** stunning views; exceptional convent conversion; shuttle bus makes frequent forays to and from Florence. **Cons:** you must either depend upon the shuttle bus or have a car; money must be no object; some rooms are small. ⑤ *Rooms from: €769* ✉ *Via Doccia 4, Fiesole* ☎ *055/5678200* ⊕ *www.belmond.com* ⇦ *45 rooms* ⑩ *Free Breakfast* ⊗ *Closed Nov.–Easter.*

Chapter 13

TUSCANY

Updated by
Patricia Rucidlo

⊙ Sights	🍴 Restaurants	🛏 Hotels	🛍 Shopping	🍸 Nightlife
★★★★★	★★★★★	★★★★☆	★★★☆☆	★★★☆☆

WELCOME TO TUSCANY

TOP REASONS TO GO

★ **Piazza del Campo, Siena:**
Sip a cappuccino or enjoy some gelato as you take in the spectacle in and of this shell-shape piazza.

★ **Piero della Francesca's True Cross frescoes, Arezzo:**
If your Holy Grail is great Renaissance art, seek out these 12 enigmatic scenes in Arezzo's Basilica di San Francesco.

★ **San Gimignano:** Grab a spot at sunset on the steps of the Collegiata as flocks of swallows swoop in and out of the famous medieval towers.

★ **Wine tasting in Chianti:**
Sample the fruits of the region's gorgeous vineyards, either at the wineries themselves or in the wine bars found in the towns.

★ **Leaning Tower of Pisa:**
It may be touristy, but it's still a whole lot of fun to climb to the top and admire the view.

1 **Lucca.** See 16th-century ramparts.

2 **Pisa.** Its bell tower is known the world over.

3 **Chianti.** A picturesque wine region.

4 **Volterra.** Breathtaking hilltop views.

5 **San Gimignano.** Lovely hill town.

6 **Colle di Val d'Elsa.** Laid-back hill town.

7 **Siena.** An enchanting medieval city.

8 **Arezzo.** Visit for the sublime frescoes.

9 **Cortona.** Sits above the flat Valdichiana.

10 **Montepulciano.** Its higher altitude means cooler summers.

11 **Pienza.** An ideal city planned by Pope Pius II.

12 **Montalcino.** Famed for its robust red wine.

13 **Abbazia di Sant'Antimo.** A Roman-esque abbey.

EATING AND DRINKING WELL IN TUSCANY

The influence of the ancient Etruscans—who favored the use of fresh herbs—is still felt in Tuscan cuisine three millennia later. Simple and earthy, Tuscan food celebrates the seasons with fresh vegetable dishes, wonderful bread-based soups, and meats perfumed with sage, rosemary, and thyme.

Throughout Tuscany there are excellent upscale restaurants that serve elaborate dishes, but to get a real taste of the flavors of the region, head for the family-run trattorias found in every town. The service and setting are often basic, but the food can be memorable.

Few places serve lighter fare at midday, so expect substantial meals at lunch and dinner, especially in out-of-the-way towns. Dining hours are fairly standard: lunch between 12:30 and 2, dinner between 7:30 and 10.

HOLD THE SALT

Tuscan bread is famous for what it's missing: salt. That's because it's intended to pick up seasoning from the food it accompanies, not be eaten alone. That doesn't mean Tuscans don't like to start a meal with bread, but usually it's prepared in some way. It can be grilled and drizzled with olive oil (*fettunta*), covered with chicken liver spread (*crostino con fegatini*), or toasted, rubbed with garlic, and topped with tomatoes (*bruschetta*).

AFFETTATI MISTI

The name, roughly translated, means "mixed cold cuts," and it's something Tuscans do exceptionally well. A platter of cured meats, served as an antipasto, is sure to include *prosciutto crudo* (cured pork, cut paper-thin) and *salame* (dry sausage, prepared in dozens of ways—some spicy, some sweet). The most distinctly Tuscan affettati are made from *cinta senese* (a once nearly extinct pig found only in the heart of the region) and *cinghiale* (wild boar, which roam all over Italy). You can eat these delicious slices unadorned or layered on a piece of bread.

PASTA

Restaurants throughout Tuscany serve dishes similar to those in Florence, but they also have their own local specialties. Many recipes are from the *nonna* (grandmother) of the restaurant's owner, handed down over time but never written down.

Look in particular for pasta creations made with *pici* (a long, thick, hand-rolled spaghetti). *Pappardelle* (a long, ribbonlike pasta noodle) is frequently paired with sauces made with game, such as *lepre* (hare) or cinghiale. In the northwest, a specialty of Lucca is *tordelli di carne al ragù* (meat-stuffed pasta with a meat sauce).

MEAT

Bistecca fiorentina (a thick T-bone steak, grilled rare) is the classic meat dish of Tuscany, but there are other specialties as well. Many menus will include *tagliata di manzo* (thinly sliced, roasted beef, drizzled with olive oil), *arista di maiale* (roast pork with sage and rosemary), and *salsiccia e fagioli* (pork sausage and beans). In the southern part of the region, don't be surprised to find *piccione* (pigeon), which can be roasted, stuffed, or baked.

WINE

Grape cultivation here also dates from Etruscan times, and vineyards are abundant, particularly in Chianti. The resulting medium-body red wine is a staple on most tables; however, you can select from a multitude of other varieties, including such reds as Brunello di Montalcino and Vino Nobile di Montepulciano and such whites as vermentino and vernaccia.

Super Tuscans (a fanciful name given to a group of wines by American journalists) now command attention as some of the best produced in Italy; they have great depth and complexity. The dessert wine *vin santo* is made throughout the region, and is often sipped with *biscotti* (twice-baked almond cookies), perfect for dunking.

Midway down the Italian peninsula, Tuscany (Toscana in Italian) is distinguished by rolling hills, snowcapped mountains, dramatic cypress trees, and miles of coastline on the Tyrrhenian Sea—which all adds up to gorgeous views at practically every turn. The beauty of the landscape proves a perfect foil for the region's abundance of superlative art and architecture. It also produces some of Italy's finest wines and olive oils. The combination of unforgettable art, sumptuous landscapes, and eminently drinkable wines that pair beautifully with its simple food makes a trip to Tuscany something beyond special.

Many of Tuscany's cities and towns have retained the same fundamental character over the past 500 years. Civic rivalries that led to bloody battles centuries ago have given way to soccer rivalries. Renaissance pomp lives on in the celebration of local feast days and centuries-old traditions such as the Palio in Siena and the Giostra del Saracino (Joust of the Saracen) in Arezzo. Often, present-day Tuscans look as though they might have served as models for paintings produced hundreds of years ago. In many ways, the Renaissance lives on in Tuscany.

MAJOR REGIONS

Hill Towns Southwest of Florence. The search for the best tiny hill town always leads to San Gimignano, known as the "medieval Manhattan" for its 13th-century stone towers.

Southern Tuscany. Among the highlights of Tuscany's southern reaches are the wine-producing centers of Montalcino and Montepulciano.

Planning

Making the Most of Your Time

Tuscany isn't the place for a jam-packed itinerary. One of the greatest pleasures here is indulging in rustic hedonism, marked by long lunches and showstopping sunsets. Whether by car, by bike, or on foot, you'll want to get out into the glorious landscape, but it's smart to keep your plans modest. Set a church or a hill town or an out-of-the-way restaurant as your destination, knowing that half the pleasure is in getting there—admiring as you go the stately palaces, the tidy geometry of row upon row of grapevines, and the fields vibrant with red poppies, sunflowers, and yellow broom.

You'll need to devise a strategy for seeing the sights. Take Siena: this beautiful, art-filled town simply can't be missed; it's compact enough that you can see the major sights on a day trip, and that's exactly what most people do. Spend the night, though, and you'll get to see the town breathe a sigh and relax on the day-trippers' departure. In Pisa, the famous tower and the rest of the Camposanto are not only worth seeing but a must-see, a highlight of any trip to Italy. But nearby Lucca must not be overlooked either. In fact, this walled town has greater charms than Pisa does, making it a better choice for an overnight, so you should come up with a plan that takes in both places.

Getting Here and Around

BUS

Buses are a reliable but time-consuming means of getting around the region because they tend to stop in every town. Trains are a better option in virtually every respect when you're headed to Pisa, Lucca, Arezzo, and other cities with good rail service. But for most smaller towns, buses are the only option. Be aware that making arrangements for bus travel, particularly for a non–Italian speaker, can be a test of patience.

BUS CONTACTS CPT. ✉ *Pisa* ☎ *050/884111* ⊕ *www.cttnord.it.* **Bus Italia.** ✉ *Via Santa Caterina da Siena 17/r, Florence* ⊕ *www.fsbusitalia.it.* **Tra-In.** ☎ *0577/204111* ⊕ *www.trainspa.it.*

CAR

Driving is the only way (other than hiking or biking) to reach many of Tuscany's small towns and vineyards. The cities west of Florence are easily accessed by the A11, which leads to Lucca and then to the sea. The A1 takes you south from Florence to Arezzo and Chiusi (where you turn off for Montepulciano). Florence and Siena are connected by a *superstrada* and also the scenic Via Cassia (SR2) and even more panoramic Strada Chiantigiana (SR222), both of which thread through Chianti, skirting rolling hills and vineyards. The hill towns north and west of Siena lie along superstradas and winding local roads—all are well marked, but you should still arm yourself with a good map.

TRAIN

Trains on Italy's main north–south rail line stop in Florence as well as Prato, Arezzo, and Chiusi. Another major line connects Florence with Pisa, and the coastal line between Rome and Genoa passes through Pisa as well. There's regular, frequent hourly service from Florence to Lucca, and several trips a day between Florence and Siena. Siena's train station is 2 km (1 mile) north of the *centro storico* (historic center), but cabs and city buses are readily available, as is a very handy funicular.

For other parts of Tuscany—Chianti, Montalcino, and Montepulciano, for example—you're better off traveling by bus or by car. Train stations, when they exist, are far from the historic centers (usually in the valleys below hill towns), and service is infrequent.

TRAIN CONTACT Trenitalia. ☎ *892021 toll-free in Italy* ⊕ *www.trenitalia.com.*

Restaurants

A meal in Tuscany traditionally consists of five courses, and every menu you encounter will be organized along this plan of antipasto, primo, secondo, contorno, and dolce. The crucial rule of restaurant dining is that you should order at least two courses. Otherwise, you'll likely end up with a lonely piece of meat and no sides.

Restaurant reviews have been shortened. For full information, visit Fodors.com.

Hotels

A visit to the Tuscan countryside is a trip into absolute beauty. There are plenty of good hotels in the larger towns, but the classic experience is to stay in one of the rural accommodations—often converted private homes, sometimes working farms or vineyards (known as *agriturismi*)

Although it's tempting to think you can stumble upon a little out-of-the-way hotel at the end of the day, you're better off not testing your luck. Make reservations before you go. If you don't have a reservation, you may be able to get help finding a room from the local tourist office.

Hotel reviews have been shortened. For full information, visit Fodors.com.

WHAT IT COSTS in Euros			
$	$$	$$$	$$$$
RESTAURANTS			
under €15	€15–€24	€25–€35	over €35
HOTELS			
under €125	€125–€200	€201–€300	over €300

Visitor Information

Many towns in Tuscany have tourist information offices, which can be useful resources for trip-planning advice (and sometimes maps). Such offices are typically open from 8:30 to 1 and 3:30 to 6 or 7; those in smaller towns are usually closed Saturday afternoon and Sunday, and often shut down entirely from early November through Easter.

The tourist information office in Greve is an excellent source for general information about the Chianti wine region and its hilltop towns. In Siena, the centrally located tourist office in Piazza del Campo has information about Siena and its province. Both offices book hotel rooms for a nominal fee. Offices in smaller towns can also be a good place to check if you need last-minute accommodations.

Lucca

Ramparts built in the 16th and 17th centuries enclose a charming fortress town filled with churches (99 of them), terra-cotta–roofed buildings, and narrow cobblestone streets, along which locals maneuver bikes to do their daily shopping. Here Caesar, Pompey, and Crassus agreed to rule Rome as a triumvirate in 56 BC; Lucca was later the first Tuscan town to accept Christianity. The town still has a mind of its own, and when most of Tuscany was voting communist as a matter of course, Lucca's citizens rarely followed suit. The famous composer Giacomo Puccini (1858–1924) was born here; he is celebrated during the summer Opera Theater and Music Festival of Lucca. The ramparts circling the centro storico are the perfect place to stroll, bicycle, or just admire the view.

GETTING HERE AND AROUND

You can reach Lucca easily by train from Florence; the centro storico is a short walk from the station. If you're driving, take the A11/E76.

VISITOR INFORMATION

CONTACT Lucca Tourism Office. ⊠ Piazzale Verdi ☎ 0583/583150 ⊕ www.luccaturismo.it.

◉ Sights

Traffic (including motorbikes) is restricted in the walled historic center of Lucca. Walking is the best, most enjoyable way to get around. Or you can rent a bicycle; getting around on bike is easy, as the center is quite flat.

Duomo

CHURCH | The blind arches on the cathedral's facade are a fine example of the rigorously ordered Pisan Romanesque style, in this case happily enlivened by an extremely varied collection of small, carved columns. Take a closer look at the decoration of the facade and that of the portico below; they make this one of the most entertaining church exteriors in Tuscany. The Gothic interior contains a moving Byzantine crucifix—called the Volto Santo, or Holy Face—brought here, according to legend, in the 8th century (though it probably dates from between the 11th and early 13th century). The masterpiece of the Sienese sculptor Jacopo della Quercia (circa 1371–1438) is the marble Tomb of Ilaria del Carretto (1407–08). ⊠ Piazza San Martino, Lucca ☎ 0583/919175 ⊕ www.museocattedrale-lucca.it ⊠ €9.

Museo Nazionale di Villa Guinigi

ART MUSEUM | On the eastern end of the historic center, this sadly overlooked museum has an extensive collection of local Etruscan, Roman, Romanesque, and Renaissance art. The museum represents an overview of Lucca's artistic traditions from Etruscan times until the 17th century, housed in the 15th-century former villa of the Guinigi family. ⊠ Via della Quarquonia 4, Lucca ☎ 0583/496033 ⊕ www.polomusealetoscana.beniculturali.it ⊠ €4 ☉ Closed Mon., Wed., and Fri. morning. Closed Sat.–Sun.

★ Passeggiata delle Mura

CITY PARK | FAMILY | Any time of day when the weather is nice, you can find the citizens of Lucca cycling, jogging, strolling, or kicking a soccer ball in this green, beautiful, and very large circular park—neither inside nor outside the city but rather right atop and around the ring of ramparts that defines Lucca. Sunlight streams through two rows of tall plane trees to dapple the passeggiata delle mura (walk on the walls), which is 4.2 km (2½ miles) in length. Ten bulwarks are topped with lawns, many with picnic tables and some with play equipment for children. Be aware at all times of where the edge is—there are no railings, and the drop to the ground outside the city is a precipitous 40 feet. ⊠ Lucca.

Lucca

KEY

- ① Sights
- ① Restaurants
- ① Quick Bites
- ① Hotels

Sights ▶

1 Duomo............................**D1**
2 Museo Nazionale
di Villa Guinigi..............**G1**
3 Passeggiata delle
Mura.............................**G3**
4 Piazza dell'Anfiteatro
Romano.........................**E1**
5 San Frediano.................**D1**
6 San Michele in Foro......**D2**
7 Torre Guinigi.................**E2**

Restaurants ▶

1 Buca di
Sant'Antonio..................**C2**
2 Il Giglio..........................**D3**

Quick Bites ▶

1 Blend.............................**D2**
2 Gelateria Veneta...........**C3**

Hotels ▶

1 Albergo San
Martino..........................**D3**
2 Alla Corte degli
Angeli.............................**D1**
3 La Luna..........................**D1**
4 Palazzo Alexander.........**B1**
5 Piccolo Hotel
Puccini...........................**C2**

Piazza dell'Anfiteatro Romano

PLAZA/SQUARE | **FAMILY** | Here's where the ancient Roman amphitheater once stood; some of the medieval buildings built over the amphitheater retain its original oval shape and brick arches. ⊠ *Piazza Anfiteatro, Lucca.*

San Frediano

CHURCH | A 14th-century mosaic decorates the facade of this church just steps from the Anfiteatro. Inside are works by Jacopo della Quercia (circa 1371–1438) and Matteo Civitali (1436–1501), as well as the lace-clad mummy of St. Zita (circa 1218–78), the patron saint of household servants. ⊠ *Piazza San Frediano, Lucca* ☎ *3498440290* ⊕ *www.sanfredianolucca.com* 🔁 *€3.*

San Michele in Foro

CHURCH | The facade here is even more fanciful than that of the Duomo. Its upper levels have nothing but air behind them (after the front of the church was built, there were no funds to raise the nave), and the winged Archangel Michael, who stands at the very top, seems precariously poised for flight. The facade, heavily restored in the 19th century, displays busts of such 19th-century Italian patriots as Garibaldi and Cavour. Check out the superb Filippino Lippi (1457/58–1504) panel painting of Saints Jerome, Sebastian, Rocco, and Helen in the right transept. ⊠ *Piazza San Michele, Lucca.*

Torre Guinigi

NOTABLE BUILDING | **FAMILY** | The tower of the medieval Palazzo Guinigi contains one of the city's most curious sights: a grove of ilex trees has grown at the top of the tower, and their roots have pushed their way into the room below. From the top you have a magnificent view of the city and the surrounding countryside. (Only the tower is open to the public, not the palazzo.) ⊠ *Via Sant'Andrea, Lucca* ☎ *0583/48090* 🔁 *€5.*

🍴 Restaurants

★ Buca di Sant'Antonio

$$ | **TUSCAN** | The staying power of Buca di Sant'Antonio—it's been around since 1782—is the result of superlative Tuscan food brought to the table by waitstaff who don't miss a beat. The menu includes the simple but blissful *tortelli lucchesi al sugo* (meat-stuffed pasta with a tomato-and-meat sauce), as well as more daring dishes such as roast *capretto* (kid goat) with herbs. **Known for:** classy, family-run ambience; superlative pastas; excellent sommelier. ⑤ *Average main: €20* ⊠ *Via della Cervia 3, Lucca* ☎ *0583/55881* ⊕ *www.bucadisantantonio.com* 🕙 *Closed Mon., 1 wk in Jan., and 1 wk in July. No dinner Sun.*

★ Il Giglio

$$$ | **TUSCAN** | Cutting-edge divine food (along with Tuscan classics) are served in this one-room space; the roaring fireplace dominates. In the summer, there's seating outdoors on a pretty little piazza. **Known for:** fine service; creative menu and ingredients; the wine list, especially its selection of local wines. ⑤ *Average main: €28* ⊠ *Piazza del Giglio 2, Lucca* ☎ *0583/494508* ⊕ *www.ristorantegiglio. com* 🕙 *Closed Wed. and 15 days in Nov. No dinner Tues.*

☕ Coffee and Quick Bites

Blend

$ | **ITALIAN** | If you're looking for a lovely spot to recharge, stop by this place (just around the corner from the Duomo), and have a fantastic sandwich, or a glass of wine, or a tasty salad, a coffee, or dessert. It's open from late morning to late in the evening. **Known for:** open late; near the Duomo; good salads. ⑤ *Average main: €7* ⊠ *Piazza S. Giusto 8, Duomo.*

Gelateria Veneta

$ | ITALIAN | FAMILY | This place makes outstanding gelato, sorbet, and ices (some sugar-free). They prepare their confections three times a day, using the same recipes with which the brothers Arnoldo opened the place in 1927. **Known for:** delicious ices on a stick; longtime institution and a favorite with locals; sorbet-stuffed frozen fruits. ⑤ *Average main: €3* ✉ *Via V. Veneto 74, Lucca* ☎ *0583/467037* ⊕ *www.gelateriaveneta.net* ◷ *Closed Nov.–Mar.*

Hotels

★ Albergo San Martino

$ | B&B/INN | FAMILY | The brocade bedspreads of this inn in the heart of the centro storico are fresh and crisp, the proprietor friendly, the breakfast, served in a cheerful apricot room, more than ample. **Pros:** friendly staff; comfortable beds; great breakfast, including homemade cakes and pastries. **Cons:** surroundings are pleasant and stylish though not luxurious; parking is difficult; slightly noisy during Lucca Music Festival. ⑤ *Rooms from: €89* ✉ *Via della Dogana 9, Lucca* ☎ *0583/469181* ⊕ *www.albergosanmarti-no.it* ⇝ *18 rooms* †⊙† *Free Breakfast.*

Alla Corte degli Angeli

$$ | B&B/INN | This charming hotel with a friendly staff is right off the main shopping drag, Via Fillungo. **Pros:** many rooms are connecting, making them good for families; fantastic on-site restaurant; great location. **Cons:** books up quickly; some rooms have tubs but no showers; not all rooms are created equal. ⑤ *Rooms from: €180* ✉ *Via degli Angeli 23, Lucca* ☎ *0583/469204, 0583/991989* ⊕ *www.allacortedegliangeli.it* ⇝ *21 rooms* †⊙† *Free Breakfast.*

La Luna

$$ | B&B/INN | On a quiet, airy courtyard close to the Piazza del Mercato, this hotel, run by the Barbieri family for more than four decades, occupies two renovated wings of an old building. **Pros:** central location; professional staff; the annex has wheelchair-accessible rooms. **Cons:** street noise can be a bit of a problem; some rooms feel dated; may be too central for some. ⑤ *Rooms from: €160* ✉ *Corte Compagni 12, at Via Fillungo, Lucca* ☎ *0583/493634, 0583/490021* ⊕ *www. hotellaluna.it* †⊙† *Free Breakfast* ◷ *Closed Jan. 7–31* ⇝ *29 rooms.*

Palazzo Alexander

$$ | HOTEL | The building, dating from the 12th century, has been restructured to create the ease common to Lucchesi nobility: timbered ceilings, warm yellow walls, and brocaded chairs adorn the public rooms, and guest rooms have high ceilings and that same glorious damask. **Pros:** a short walk from San Michele in Foro; intimate feel; gracious staff. **Cons:** books up quickly; some complain of too-thin walls; might be too quiet for some. ⑤ *Rooms from: €160* ✉ *Via S. Giustina 48, Lucca* ☎ *0583/583571* ⊕ *www.hotel-palazzoalexander.it* ⇝ *13 rooms* †⊙† *Free Breakfast.*

Piccolo Hotel Puccini

$ | HOTEL | Steps away from the busy square and church of San Michele al Foro, this little hotel is quiet, calm, and affordable and a great deal: wallpaper, hardwood floors, and throw rugs are among the handsome decorations. **Pros:** quiet, central location; cheery, English-speaking staff; good value. **Cons:** some rooms are on the dark side; books up quickly; many wish the breakfast was more copious. ⑤ *Rooms from: €90* ✉ *Via di Poggio 9, Lucca* ☎ *0583/55421* ⊕ *www.hotelpuccini.com* ⇝ *14 rooms* †⊙† *Free Breakfast.*

Shopping

Lucca's justly famed olive oils are available throughout the city (and exported around the world).

★ Antica Bottega di Prospero

FOOD | Stop by this shop for top-quality local food products, including farro, dried porcini mushrooms, olive oil, and wine. ⊠ *Via San Lucia 13, Lucca* ☎ *0583/494 875.*

★ Caniparoli

CHOCOLATE | Chocolate lovers will be pleased with the selection of artisanal chocolates, marzipan delights, and gorgeous cakes. Creations become even more fanciful during two big Christian holidays: Christmas and Easter. ⊠ *Via San Paolino 44, Lucca* ☎ *0583/53456* ⊕ *www. caniparoliocioccolateria.it.*

★ Enoteca Vanni

WINE/SPIRITS | A huge selection of wines, as well as an ancient cellar, make this place worth a stop. For the cost of the wine only, tastings can be organized through the shopkeepers and are held in the cellar or outside in a lovely little piazza. All of this can be paired with *affettati misti* (sliced cured meats) and cheeses of the highest caliber. ⊠ *Piazza San Salvatore 7, Lucca* ☎ *0583/491902* ⊕ *www.enotecavanni.com.*

★ Pasticceria Taddeucci

FOOD | A particularly delicious version of *buccellato*—the sweet, anise-flavored bread with raisins that is a Luccan specialty—is baked at Pasticceria Taddeucci. ⊠ *Piazza San Michele 34, Lucca* ☎ *0583/494933* ⊕ *www.buccellatotaddeucci.com.*

🏃 Activities

A good way to spend the afternoon is to go biking around the large path atop the city's ramparts. There are two good spots right next to each other where you can rent bikes. The prices are about the same (about €16 per day and €4 per hour for city bikes) and they are centrally located, just beside the town wall.

Poli Antonio Biciclette

BIKING | This is the best option for bicycle rental on the east side of town. ⊠ *Piazza Santa Maria 42, Lucca East* ☎ *0583/493787* ⊕ *www.biciclettepoli. com.*

Pisa

If you can get beyond the kitsch of the stalls hawking cheap souvenirs around the Leaning Tower, you'll find that Pisa has much to offer. Its treasures aren't as abundant as those of Florence, to which it is inevitably compared, but the cathedral-baptistery-tower complex of Piazza del Duomo, known collectively as the Campo dei Miracoli (Field of Miracles), is among the most dramatic settings in Italy.

Pisa may have been inhabited as early as the Bronze Age. It was certainly populated by the Etruscans and, in turn, became part of the Roman Empire. In the early Middle Ages this city on the Arno River flourished as an economic powerhouse—along with Amalfi, Genoa, and Venice, it was one of the four maritime republics. The city's economic and political power ebbed in the early 15th century as it fell under Florence's domination, though it enjoyed a brief resurgence under Cosimo I de' Medici in the mid-16th century. Pisa sustained heavy damage during World War II, but the Duomo and the Leaning Tower were spared, along with some other grand Romanesque structures.

GETTING HERE AND AROUND

Pisa is an easy hour's train ride from Florence. By car it's a straight shot on the Firenze–Pisa–Livorno ("Fi-Pi-Li") autostrada. The Pisa–Lucca train runs frequently and takes about 30 minutes.

Campo Santo translates literally to "holy field" because it's supposedly built around a shipload of sacred soil from Golgotha, the site where Jesus was crucified.

VISITOR INFORMATION

CONTACT Pisa Tourism Office. ✉ *Piazza del Duomo 7, Pisa* ☎ *050/550100* ⊕ *www.turismo.pisa.it.*

 Sights

Pisa, like many Italian cities, is best explored on foot, and most of what you'll want to see is within walking distance. The views along the Arno River are particularly grand and shouldn't be missed—there's a feeling of spaciousness that isn't found along the Arno in Florence.

As you set out, note that there are various combination-ticket options for sights on the Piazza del Duomo.

Battistero

NOTABLE BUILDING | This lovely Gothic baptistery, which stands across from the Duomo's facade, is best known for the pulpit carved by Nicola Pisano (circa 1220–84; father of Giovanni Pisano) in 1260. Every half hour, an employee will dramatically close the doors, then intone, thereby demonstrating how remarkable the acoustics are in the place. ✉ *Piazza del Duomo, Pisa* ☎ *050/835011* ⊕ *www.opapisa.it* 🎫 *€5, discounts available if bought in combination with tickets for other monuments.*

Camposanto

CEMETERY | According to legend, the cemetery—a walled structure on the western side of the Piazza dei Miracoli—is filled with earth that returning Crusaders brought back from the Holy Land. Contained within are numerous frescoes, notably *The Drunkenness of Noah,* by Renaissance artist Benozzo Gozzoli (1422–97), and the disturbing *Triumph of Death* (14th century; artist uncertain), whose subject matter shows what was on people's minds in a century that saw the ravages of the Black Death. ✉ *Piazza del Duomo, Pisa* ☎ *050/835011* ⊕ *www.opapisa.it* 🎫 *€5.*

Duomo

CHURCH | Pisa's cathedral brilliantly utilizes the horizontal marble-stripe motif (borrowed from Moorish architecture) that became common on Tuscan cathedrals. It is famous for the Romanesque panels on the transept door facing the tower that depict scenes from the life of Christ. The beautifully carved 14th-century pulpit is by Giovanni Pisano. ⊠ *Piazza del Duomo, Pisa* ☎ *050/835011* ⊕ *www.opapisa.it.*

★ Leaning Tower (Torre Pendente)

NOTABLE BUILDING | Legend holds that Galileo conducted an experiment on the nature of gravity by dropping metal balls from the top of the 187-foot-high Leaning Tower of Pisa. Historians, however, say this legend has no basis in fact—which isn't quite to say that it's false. Work on this tower, built as a *campanile* (bell tower) for the Duomo, started in 1173: the lopsided settling began when construction reached the third story. The tower's architects attempted to compensate through such methods as making the remaining floors slightly taller on the leaning side, but the extra weight only made the problem worse. The settling continued, and by the late 20th century it had accelerated to such a point that many feared the tower would simply topple over, despite all efforts to prop it up. The structure has since been firmly anchored to the earth. The final phase to restore the tower to its original tilt of 300 years ago was launched in early 2000 and finished two years later. The last phase removed some 100 tons of earth from beneath the foundation. Reservations, which are essential, can be made online or by calling the Museo dell'Opera del Duomo; it's also possible to arrive at the ticket office and book for the same day. Note that children under eight years of age are not allowed to climb. ⊠ *Piazza del Duomo, Pisa* ☎ *050/835011* ⊕ *www.opapisa.it* ◻ *€18.*

Museo Nazionale di San Matteo

ART MUSEUM | On the north bank of the Arno, this museum contains some beautiful examples of local Romanesque and Gothic art. Here you'll find very few visitors, and stunning works by Donatello and Benozzo Gozzoli (among others). ⊠ *Piazza Matteo in Soarta 1, Pisa* ☎ *050/541865* ⊕ *www.polomusealetoscana.beniculturali.it* ◻ *€5* ◷ *Closed Sun.*

Piazza dei Cavalieri

PLAZA/SQUARE | The piazza, with its fine Renaissance Palazzo dei Cavalieri, Palazzo dell'Orologio, and Chiesa di Santo Stefano dei Cavalieri, was laid out by Giorgio Vasari in about 1560. The square was the seat of the Ordine dei Cavalieri di San Stefano (Order of the Knights of St. Stephen), a military and religious institution meant to defend the coast from possible invasion by the Turks. Also in this square is the prestigious Scuola Normale Superiore, founded by Napoléon in 1810 on the French model. Here graduate students pursue doctorates in literature, philosophy, mathematics, and science. In front of the school is a large statue of Ferdinando I de' Medici dating from 1596. On the extreme left is the tower where the hapless Ugolino della Gherardesca (died 1289) was imprisoned with his two sons and two grandsons—legend holds that he ate them. Dante immortalized him in Canto XXXIII of his *Inferno*. Duck into the Church of Santo Stefano (if you're lucky enough to find it open) and check out Bronzino's splendid *Nativity of Christ* (1564–65). ⊠ *Piazza dei Cavalieri, Pisa.*

🍴 Restaurants

★ Beny

$$$ | TUSCAN | Apricot walls hung with etchings of Pisa make this small, single-room restaurant warmly romantic. Husband and wife Damiano and Sandra Lazzerini have been running the place for two decades, and it shows in their

Pisa

Marches
◆ Pisa
Tuscany
Umbria

Via Ugo Rindi
Via Piave
Via Contessa Matilde
Piazza Manin
Via Bonanno Pisano
V. Santa Maria
Via Roma
V. della Faggiola
Via Cardinale Pietro Maffi
Via Luigi Bianchi
Via Francesco Rismondo
Via Lucchese
Via del Brennero
Via San Zeno
Via Ghioste Carducci
Via Filippo Buonarroti
Via San Lorenzo
Via Savi
Via Derna
Via Santa Maria
Via Risorgimento
Via Roma
Via Renato Fucini
Via Santa Cecilia
Vicolo dei Rustici
Via San Francesco
V. Ettore Sighieri
V. Mario Lalli
Via Enrico Fermi
Via Trieste
Via Voltorno
Via Nicola Pisano
Piazza Dante
Via San Frediano
Borgo Stretto
V. Giuseppe Verdi
Via Palestro
Lungarno Antonio Pacinotti
Lungarno Gambacorti
Ponte Solferino
Via La Maddalena
V. Giuseppe Mazzini
V. la Nunziatina
Ponte di Mezzo
Lungarno Mediceo
Fiume Arno
Lungarno Galileo Galilei
Via San Martino
Ponte delle Fortezza
Lungarno Sidney Sonnino
Via Francesco Crispi
Via San Paolo
Via Sant'Antonio
Via del Carmine
Via Giovanni Bovio
Ponte della Cittadella
Via Francesco Niosi
Via Enzo Zerboglio
Via Nino Bixio
Corso Italia
Via Filippo Turati
Via Giordano Bruno
Piazza Vittorio
Via Cesare Battisti
Via Benedetto Croce
Viale Francesco Bonaini

0   1,000 ft
0   200 m

KEY

1 *Exploring Sights*

1 *Restaurants*

1 *Hotels*

obvious enthusiasm while talking about the menu (fish is a focus) and daily specials, which often astound. **Known for:** terrific wine list; superb fish dishes; gracious service. ⑤ *Average main: €27* ✉ *Piazza Gambacorti 22, Pisa* ☎ *050/25067* ☾ *Closed Sun. and 2 wks in mid-Aug. No lunch Sat.*

La Pergoletta

$$ | **TUSCAN** | **FAMILY** | On an old town street named for its beautiful towers, this small, simple restaurant is in one such tower itself. It's a place where Pisans come to celebrate. **Known for:** gracious waitstaff; creative, inventive menu; festive atmosphere. ⑤ *Average main: €16* ✉ *Via delle Belle Torri 36, Pisa* ☎ *050/542458* ⊕ *www.ristorantelapergoletta.com* ☾ *Closed Mon. and 1 wk in Aug. No lunch Sat.*

Osteria dei Cavalieri

$ | **ITALIAN** | This charming white-wall restaurant, a few steps from Piazza dei Cavalieri, is reason enough to come to Pisa. They can do it all here—serve up exquisitely grilled fish dishes, please vegetarians, and prepare tagliata for meat lovers. **Known for:** vegetable tasting menu; land tasting menu; sea tasting menu. ⑤ *Average main: €14* ✉ *Via San Frediano 16, Pisa* ☎ *050/580858* ⊕ *www.osteriacavalieri.pisa.it* ☾ *Closed Sun., 2 wks in Aug., and Dec. 29–Jan. 7. No lunch Sat.*

 Hotels

Royal Victoria

$ | **HOTEL** | In a pleasant palazzo facing the Arno, a 10-minute walk from the Campo dei Miracoli, the hotel has room styles that range from the 1800s, complete with frescoes, to the 1920s; the most charming are in the old tower. **Pros:** old-world charm; friendly staff; lovely views of the Arno from many rooms. **Cons:** rooms a little worn; rooms vary significantly in size; not all rooms have views of the Arno. ⑤ *Rooms from: €60* ✉ *Lungarno Pacinotti*

12, Pisa ☎ *050/940111* ⊕ *www.royalvictoria.it* ⤴ *38 rooms* ⦿| *Free Breakfast.*

 Performing Arts

Fondazione Teatro di Pisa

THEATER | Pisa has a lively performing-arts scene, most of which happens at the 19th-century Teatro Verdi. Music and dance performances are presented from September through May. Contact Fondazione Teatro di Pisa for schedules and information. ✉ *Via Palestro 40, Lungarni* ☎ *050/941111* ⊕ *www.teatrodipisa.pi.it.*

Chianti

This is the heartland: both sides of the Strada Chiantigiana (SR222) are embraced by glorious panoramic views of vineyards, olive groves, and castle towers. Traveling south from Florence, you first reach the aptly named one-street town of Strada in Chianti. Farther south, the number of vineyards on either side of the road dramatically increases—as do the signs inviting you in for a free tasting. Beyond Strada lies Greve in Chianti, completely surrounded by wineries and filled with wineshops. There's art to be had as well: Passignano, west of Greve, has an abbey that shelters a 15th-century *Last Supper* by Domenico and Davide Ghirlandaio. Farther still, along the Strada Chiantigiana, are Panzano and Castellina in Chianti, both hill towns. It's from near Panzano and Castellina that branch roads head to the other main towns of eastern Chianti: Radda in Chianti, Gaiole in Chianti, and Castelnuovo Berardenga.

The Strada Chiantigiana gets crowded during the high season, but no one is in a hurry. The slow pace gives you time to soak up the beautiful scenery.

Greve in Chianti

40 km (25 miles) north of Siena, 28 km (17½ miles) south of Florence.

If there is a capital of Chianti, it is Greve, a friendly market town with no shortage of cafés, enoteche, and crafts shops lining its streets.

GETTING HERE AND AROUND

Driving from Florence or Siena, Greve is easily reached via the Strada Chiantigiana (SR222). SITA buses travel frequently between Florence and Greve. Tra-In and SITA buses connect Siena and Greve, but a direct trip is virtually impossible. There is no train service to Greve.

VISITOR INFORMATION

CONTACT Greve in Chianti Tourism Office.
✉ *Piazza Matteotti 11, Greve in Chianti* ☎ *055/8546299* ⊕ *www.greve-in-chianti. info.*

 Sights

Montefioralle

TOWN | A tiny hilltop hamlet, about 2 km (1 mile) west of Greve in Chianti, Montefioralle is the ancestral home of Amerigo Vespucci (1454–1512), the mapmaker, navigator, and explorer who named America. (His cousin-in-law Simonetta may have been the inspiration for Sandro Botticelli's *The Birth of Venus,* painted sometime in the 1480s.)

Piazza Matteotti

PLAZA/SQUARE | Greve's gently sloping and asymmetrical central piazza is surrounded by an attractive arcade with shops of all kinds. In the center stands a statue of the discoverer of New York harbor, Giovanni da Verrazzano (circa 1480–1527). Check out the lively market held here on Saturday morning. ✉ *Greve in Chianti.*

🍴 Restaurants

Da Padellina

$ | TUSCAN | Locals don't flock to this restaurant on the outskirts of Strada in Chianti for the art on the walls, some of it questionable, most of it kitsch, but instead for the bistecca fiorentina. As big as a breadboard and served rare, one of these justly renowned steaks is enough to feed a family of four, with doggie bags willingly provided if required. **Known for:** great grilled meats; large, diverse wine list; unpretentious local choice. $ *Average main: €10* ✉ *Via Corso del Popolo 54, 10 km (6 miles) north of Greve, Greve in Chianti* ☎ *055/858388* ⊙ *Closed Thurs.*

Enoteca Fuoripiazza

$ | TUSCAN | Detour off Greve's flower-strewn main square for food that relies heavily on local ingredients (like cheese and salami produced nearby). The lengthy wine list provides a bewildering array of choices to pair with *affettati misti* (cured meats) or one of their primi—the *pici* (a thick, short noodle) are deftly prepared here. **Known for:** attentively prepared food; local cheese and salami; alfresco dining. $ *Average main: €14* ✉ *Via I Maggio 2, Greve in Chianti* ☎ *055/8546313* ⊕ *www.enotecafuoripiazza.it* ⊙ *Closed Mon.*

★ Ristoro di Lamole

$$ | TUSCAN | Up a winding road lined with olive trees and vineyards, this place is worth the effort it takes to find. The view from the outdoor terrace is divine, as is the simple, exquisitely prepared Tuscan cuisine: start with the bruschetta drizzled with olive oil or the sublime *verdure sott'olio* (marinated vegetables) before moving on to any of the fine secondi. **Known for:** sweeping view from the terrace; your hosts Paolo and Filippo; *coniglio* (rabbit) is a specialty. $ *Average main: €20* ✉ *Via di Lamole 6, Località Lamole, Greve in Chianti* ☎ *055/8547050* ⊕ *www.ristorodilamole.it* ⊙ *Closed Wed. and Nov.–Apr.*

Hotels

Albergo del Chianti

$$ | B&B/INN | FAMILY | Simple but pleasant-
ly decorated bedrooms with plain modern
cabinets and wardrobes and wrought-iron
beds have views of the town square
or out over the tile rooftops toward the
surrounding hills. **Pros:** swimming pool;
central location; best value in Greve. **Cons:**
small bathrooms; rooms facing the piazza
can be noisy; remote: a car is a necessity.
⑤ *Rooms from: €145* ✉ *Piazza Matteotti 86, Greve in Chianti* ☎ *055/853763*
⊕ *www.albergodelchianti.it* ⊘ *Closed
Jan.–beginning Mar.* ⛵ *22 rooms* ⎮⦿⎮ *Free
Breakfast.*

★ Villa Bordoni

$$$ | B&B/INN | Scottish expats David
and Catherine Gardner transformed
a ramshackle 16th-century villa into a
stunning retreat where no two rooms
are alike—all have stenciled walls; some
have four-poster beds, others small mez-
zanines. **Pros:** wonderful hosts; splendidly isolated in the hills above Greve;
beautiful decor. **Cons:** need a car to get
around; on a long and bumpy dirt road;
books up quickly. ⑤ *Rooms from: €235*
✉ *Via San Cresci 31/32, Greve in Chianti*
☎ *055/8546230* ⊕ *www.villabordoni.com*
⊘ *Closed Dec.–Feb.* ⛵ *11 rooms* ⎮⦿⎮ *Free
Breakfast.*

★ Villa Il Poggiale

$$ | B&B/INN | FAMILY | Renaissance gar-
dens, beautiful rooms with high ceilings
and elegant furnishings, a panoramic
pool, and expert staff are just a few of the
things that make a stay at this 16th-cen-
tury villa memorable. **Pros:** exceptionally
professional staff; beautiful gardens and
panoramic setting; elegant historical
building. **Cons:** some rooms face a country
road and may be noisy during the day;
private transportation necessary; it may
be too isolated for some. ⑤ *Rooms from:
€142* ✉ *Via Empolese 69, 20 km (12
miles) northwest of Greve, San Casciano
Val di Pesa, San Casciano Val di Pesa*
☎ *055/828311* ⊕ *www.villailpoggiale.
it* ⊘ *Closed Jan. and Feb.* ⛵ *26 rooms*
⎮⦿⎮ *Free Breakfast.*

Panzano

*7 km (4½ miles) south of Greve, 36 km
(22 miles) south of Florence.*

The magnificent views of the valleys of
the Pesa and Greve Rivers easily make
Panzano one of the prettiest stops in
Chianti. The triangular Piazza Bucciarelli is
the heart of the new town. A short stroll
along Via Giovanni da Verrazzano brings
you up to the old town, Panzano Alto,
which is still partly surrounded by medieval walls. The town's 13th-century castle
is now almost completely absorbed by
later buildings (its central tower is now a
private home).

GETTING HERE AND AROUND
From Florence or Siena, Panzano is
easily reached by car along the Strada Chiantigiana (SR222). SITA buses
travel frequently between Florence and
Panzano. From Siena, the journey by bus
is extremely difficult because SITA and
Tra-In do not coordinate their schedules.
There is no train service to Panzano.

 Sights

San Leolino

CHURCH | Ancient even by Chianti
standards, this hilltop church probably
dates from the 10th century, but was
completely rebuilt in the Romanesque
style sometime in the 13th century. It
has a 14th-century cloister worth seeing.
The 16th-century terra-cotta tabernacles
are attributed to Giovanni della Robbia,
and there's also a remarkable triptych
(attributed to the Master of Panzano) that
was executed sometime in the mid-14th
century. Open days and hours are unpredictable; check with the tourist office in
Greve in Chianti for the latest. ✉ *Località
San Leolino, Panzano.*

Restaurants

★ **Officina della Bistecca**

$$ | **ITALIAN** | **FAMILY** | Local butcher and restaurateur Dario Cecchini has extended his empire of meat to include this space located directly above his butcher's shop. Here, you'll find only four items on the menu: the Dario DOC, a half-pound burger, without bun, served with roasted potatoes and onions; the Super Dario, the former with salad and beans added; the Welcome, with four different dishes of beef and pork served with fresh garden vegetables; and a vegetarian dish. **Known for:** enormously popular, especially in summer; the best burger in Italy; performing waitstaff. $ *Average main: €15* ✉ *Via XX Luglio 11, Panzano* ☎ *055/852020* ⊕ *www.dariocecchini.com* ⊗ *Closed Sun.*

Hotels

★ **Villa Le Barone**

$$$ | **B&B/INN** | Once the home of the Viviani della Robbia family, this 16th-century villa in a grove of ancient cypress trees retains many aspects of a private country dwelling, complete with homey guest quarters. **Pros:** wonderful restaurant; great base for exploring the region; beautiful location. **Cons:** a car is a must; some rooms are a bit small; 15-minute walk to nearest town. $ *Rooms from: €289* ✉ *Via San Leolino 19, Panzano* ☎ *055/852621* ⊕ *www.villalebarone.com* ❑ *Free Breakfast* ⊗ *Closed Oct.–Easter* ➔ *28 rooms.*

Radda in Chianti

26 km (15 miles) southeast of Panzano, 55 km (34 miles) south of Florence.

Radda in Chianti sits on a ridge stretching between the Val di Pesa and Val d'Arbia. It is easily reached by following the SR429 from Castellina. It's another one of those tiny villages with steep streets for strolling; follow the signs that point you toward the *camminamento medioevale,* a covered 14th-century walkway that circles part of the city inside the walls.

GETTING HERE AND AROUND

Radda can be reached by car from either Siena or Florence along the SR222 (Strada Chiantigiana), and from the A1 autostrada. Three Tra-In buses make their way from Siena to Radda. One morning SITA bus travels from Florence to Radda. There is no train service convenient to Radda.

VISITOR INFORMATION

CONTACT Radda in Chianti Tourism Office.
✉ *Piazza Castello 6, Radda in Chianti* ☎ *0577/738494* ⊕ *www.chianti.com.*

 Sights

Badia a Coltibuono (*Abbey of the Good Harvest*)

GARDEN | This Romanesque abbey has been owned by internationally acclaimed cookbook author Lorenza de' Medici's family for more than a century and a half (the family isn't related to the Florentine Medici). Wine has been produced here since the abbey was founded by Vallombrosan monks in the 11th century. Today the family continues the tradition, making wines, cold-pressed olive oil, and various flavored vinegars. Don't miss the jasmine-draped courtyard and the inner cloister with its antique well. ✉ *Località Badia a Coltibuono, 4 km (2½ miles) north of Gaiole, Gaiole in Chianti* ☎ *0577/74481 tours* ⊕ *www. coltibuono.com* ✉ *Abbey €7* ⊗ *Closed Jan. 7–mid-Mar.*

★ **Castello di Brolio**

CASTLE/PALACE | If you have time for only one castle in Tuscany, this is it. At the end of the 12th century, when Florence conquered southern Chianti, Brolio became Florence's southernmost outpost, and it was often said, "When Brolio growls, all Siena trembles." It was built about AD 1000 and owned by the monks of the Badia Fiorentina. The "new" owners, the Ricasoli family, have been in possession since 1141. Bettino Ricasoli (1809–80), the so-called Iron Baron, was one of the founders of modern Italy and is said to have invented the original formula for Chianti wine. Brolio, one of Chianti's best-known labels, is still justifiably famous. The grounds are worth visiting, even though the 19th-century manor house is not open to the public. The entrance fee includes a wine tasting in the enoteca. A small museum, where the Ricasoli Collection is housed in a 12th-century tower, displays objects that relate the long history of the family and the origins of Chianti wine. There are two apartments here available for rent by the week. ⊠ *Località Madonna a Brolio, 2 km (1 mile) southeast of Gaiole, Gaiole in Chianti* ☎ *0577/7301* ⊕ *www.ricasoli.com* 🎫 *€7.50 gardens* ⊘ *Closed Dec. Museum closed Mon.*

Palazzo del Podestà

GOVERNMENT BUILDING | Radda's town hall (aka Palazzo Comunale), in the middle of town, was built in the second half of the 14th century and has served the same function ever since. Fifty-one coats of arms (the largest is the Medici's) are imbedded in the facade, representing the past governors of the town, but unless you have official business, the building is closed to the public. ⊠ *Piazza Ferrucci 1, Radda in Chianti.*

🍴 Restaurants

Osteria Le Panzanelle

$ | TUSCAN | Silvia Bonechi's experience in the kitchen—with the help of a few precious recipes handed down from her grandmother—is one of the reasons for the success of this small restaurant in the tiny hamlet of Lucarelli; the other is the front-room hospitality of Nada Michelassi. These two *panzanelle* (women from Panzano) serve a short menu of tasty and authentic dishes at what the locals refer to as *il prezzo giusto* (the right price). **Known for:** unpretentious atmosphere; fine home cooking; good wine list. ⑤ *Average main: €13* ⊠ *Località Lucarelli 29, 8 km (5 miles) northwest of Radda on the road to Panzano, Radda in Chianti* ☎ *0577/733511* ⊕ *www.lepanzanelle.it* ⊘ *Closed Mon. and Jan. and Feb.*

 ## Hotels

La Bottega di Giovannino

$ | B&B/INN | This is a fantastic place for the budget-conscious traveler, as rooms are immaculate and most have a stunning view of the surrounding hills. **Pros:** super value; great location in the center of town; close to restaurants and shops. **Cons:** basic decor; books up quickly; some rooms are small. ⑤ *Rooms from: €60* ⊠ *Via Roma 6–8, Radda in Chianti* ☎ *0577/735601* ⊕ *www.labottegadigiovannino.it* 🛏 *12 rooms* ⊙❙ *Free Breakfast.*

★ La Locanda

$$$ | B&B/INN | At an altitude of more than 1,800 feet, this converted farmhouse is probably the loftiest luxury inn in Chianti. **Pros:** wonderful host; idyllic setting; panoramic views. **Cons:** isolated location; on a very rough gravel access road; need a car to get around. ⑤ *Rooms from: €220* ⊠ *Località Montanino di Volpaia, off Via della Volpaia, 13 km (8 miles) northwest of Radda, Radda in Chianti* ☎ *0577/738833* ⊕ *www.lalocanda.it* 🛏 *7 rooms* ❙⊙❙ *Free Breakfast* ⊙ *Closed mid-Oct.–mid-Apr.*

Palazzo San Niccolò

$ | HOTEL | The wood-beam ceilings, terra-cotta floors, and some of the original frescoes of a 19th-century town palace remain, but the marble bathrooms have all been updated, some with Jacuzzi tubs. **Pros:** pool (though a car is necessary to get there); central location; friendly staff. **Cons:** room sizes vary; some rooms face a main street; some street noise in some rooms. ⑤ *Rooms from: €91* ⊠ *Via Roma 16, Radda in Chianti*

☎ 0577/735666 ⊕ www.hotelsanniccolo.
com ⊙ Closed Nov.–Mar. 🛏 18 rooms
🍽 Free Breakfast.

⭐ **Relais Fattoria Vignale**

$$$ | B&B/INN | A refined and comfortable
country house offers numerous sitting
rooms with terra-cotta floors and attractive stonework, as well as wood-beamed
guest rooms filled with simple wooden
furnishings and handwoven rugs. **Pros:**
intimate public spaces; nice grounds and
pool; excellent restaurant. **Cons:** a car is
necessary; annex across a busy road;
single rooms are small. **⑤** *Rooms from:*
€214 ✉ Via Pianigiani 9, Radda in Chianti
☎ 0577/738300 hotel, 0577/738094
restaurant ⊕ www.vignale.it ⊙ Closed
Nov.–Mar. 🛏 41 rooms 🍽 No Meals.

Castellina in Chianti

*13 km (8 miles) south of Panzano, 59 km
(35 miles) south of Florence, 22 km (14
miles) north of Siena.*

Castellina in Chianti—or simply Castellina—is on a ridge above three valleys: the
Val di Pesa, Val d'Arbia, and Val d'Elsa. No
matter what direction you turn, the panorama is bucolic. The strong 15th-century
medieval walls and fortified town gate give
a hint of the history of this village, which
was an outpost during the continuing wars
between Florence and Siena. In the main
square, the Piazza del Comune, there's a
15th-century palace and a 15th-century fort
constructed around a 13th-century tower. It
now serves as the town hall.

GETTING HERE AND AROUND
As with all the towns along the Strada
Chiantigiana (SR222), Castellina is an easy
drive from either Siena or Florence. From
Siena, Castellina is well served by the
local Tra-In bus company. However, only
one bus a day travels here from Florence.
The closest train station is at Castellina
Scalo, some 15 km (9 miles) away.

VISITOR INFORMATION
**CONTACT Castellina in Chianti Tourism
Office.** ✉ Via Ferruccio 40, Castellina in
Chianti ☎ 0577/741392.

🍴 Restaurants

Albergaccio
$$$ | TUSCAN | The fact that the dining
room can seat only 35 guests makes a
meal here an intimate experience, and
the ever-changing menu mixes traditional
and creative dishes. In late September
and October *zuppa di funghi e castagne*
(mushroom and chestnut soup) is a
treat; grilled meats and seafood are on
the list throughout the year. **Known for:**
marvelous waitstaff; creative menu;
superb wine list. **⑤** *Average main: €25*
✉ Via Fiorentina 63, Castellina in Chianti
☎ 0577/741042 ⊕ www.albergacciocast.
com ⊙ Closed Sun.

Ristorante Le Tre Porte
$$ | TUSCAN | Grilled meat dishes are the
specialty at this popular restaurant, with
a bistecca fiorentina (served very rare, as
always) taking pride of place; paired with
grilled fresh porcini mushrooms when
in season (spring and fall), it's a heady
dish. The panoramic terrace is a good
choice for dining in summer. **Known for:**
fine wine list with lots of local bottles;
views from the terrace; their way with
mushrooms. **⑤** *Average main: €17* ✉ Via
Trento e Trieste 4, Castellina in Chianti
☎ 0577/741163 ⊕ www.treporte.com.

Sotto Le Volte
$$ | TUSCAN | As the name suggests,
you'll find this small restaurant under the
arches of Castellina's medieval walkway,
and the eatery's vaulted ceilings make
for a particularly romantic setting. The
menu is short and eminently Tuscan, with
typical soups and pasta dishes. **Known
for:** unique setting; attentive waitstaff;
flair for Tuscan classics. **⑤** *Average main:
€17* ✉ Via delle Volte 14–16, Castellina in Chianti ☎ 0577/741299 ⊕ www.

Sights ▼

1 Duomo **B3**
2 Museo Etrusco Guarnacci .. **C4**
3 Pinacoteca . **B2**
4 Porta all'Arco Etrusco...... **B3**
5 Teatro Romano **B2**

Restaurants ▼

1 Da Badò **D5**
2 Il Sacco Fiorentino .. **B3**

Hotels ▼

1 Etruria **B3**

Volterra

ristorantesottolevolte.it ☒ *Closed Wed. and Jan.–Mar.*

 Hotels

★ **Palazzo Squarcialupi**

$$ | **B&B/INN** | In this lovely 15th-century palace, spacious rooms have high ceilings, tile floors, and 18th-century furnishings, and many have views of the valley below. **Pros:** nice spa, pool, and grounds; great location in town center; elegant public spaces. **Cons:** across from a busy restaurant; on a street with no car access; rooms facing the street can experience some noise. ⑤ *Rooms from: €140* ☒ *Via Ferruccio 22, Castellina in Chianti* ☎ *0577/741186* ⊕ *www.squarcialupirelaxinchianti.com* ☒ *Closed Nov.–Mar.* ↪ *17 rooms* ⏍ *Free Breakfast.*

Volterra

30 km (18 miles) southwest of San Gimignano.

As you approach the town through bleak, rugged terrain, you can see that not all Tuscan hill towns rise above rolling green fields. Volterra stands mightily over Le Balze, a stunning series of gullied hills and valleys formed by erosion that has slowly eaten away at the foundation of the town—now considerably smaller than it was during its Etruscan glory days some 2000 years ago. The town began as the northernmost of the 12 cities that made up the Etruscan League, and excavations in the 18th century revealed a bounty of relics, which are on exhibit at the impressively overstocked Museo Etrusco Guarnacci. The Romans and later the Florentines laid siege to the town to ecure its supply of minerals and stones, particularly alabaster, which is still worked into handicrafts on sale in many of the shops around town.

GETTING HERE AND AROUND

By car, the best route from San Gimignano follows the SP1 south to Castel San Gimignano and then the SS68 west to Volterra. Coming from the west, take the SS1, a coastal road to Cecina, then follow the SS68 east to Volterra. Either way, there's a long, winding climb at the end of your trip. Traveling to Volterra by bus or train is complicated; avoid it if possible, especially if you have lots of luggage. From Florence or Siena the journey by public transit is best made by bus and involves a change in Colle di Val d'Elsa. From Rome or Pisa, it is best to take the train to Cecina and then take a bus to Volterra or a train to the Volterra-Saline station. The latter is 10 km (6 miles) from town.

VISITOR INFORMATION

CONTACT Volterra Tourism Office. ✉ *Piazza dei Priori 10, Volterra* ☎ *0588/86150* ⊕ *www.provolterra.it.*

 # Sights

Duomo

CHURCH | Behind the textbook 13th-century Pisan–Romanesque facade is proof that Volterra counted for something during the Renaissance, when many important Tuscan artists came to decorate the church. Three-dimensional stucco portraits of local saints are on the gold, red, and blue ceiling (1580) designed by Francesco Capriani, including St. Linus, the successor to St. Peter as pope and claimed by the Volterrans to have been born here. The highlight of the Duomo is the brightly painted, 13th-century, wooden, life-size *Deposition* in the chapel of the same name. The unusual Cappella dell'Addolorata (Chapel of the Grieved) has two terra-cotta Nativity scenes; the depiction of the arrival of the Magi has a background fresco by Benozzo Gozzoli. ✉ *Piazza San Giovanni, Volterra.*

★ Museo Etrusco Guarnacci

ART MUSEUM | An extraordinary collection of Etruscan relics is made all the more interesting by clear explanations in English. The bulk of the collection is comprised of roughly 700 carved funerary urns. The oldest, dating from the 7th century BC, were made from tufa (volcanic rock), a handful are made of terra-cotta, and the vast majority—from the 3rd to 1st century BC—are from alabaster. The urns are grouped by subject and taken together form a fascinating testimony about Etruscan life and death. Some illustrate domestic scenes, others the funeral procession of the deceased. Greek gods and mythology, adopted by the Etruscans, also figure prominently. The sculpted figures on many of the covers may have been made in the image of the deceased, reclining and often holding the cup of life overturned. Particularly well known is *Gli Sposi* (Husband and Wife), a haunting, elderly duo in terra-cotta. The *Ombra della Sera* (Evening Shadow)—an enigmatic bronze statue of an elongated, pencil-thin male nude—highlights the collection. Also on display are Attic vases, bucchero ceramics, jewelry, and household items. ✉ *Via Don Minzoni 15, Volterra* ☎ *0588/86347* ⊕ *www.comune. volterra.pi.it* ✉ *From €8.*

Pinacoteca

ART MUSEUM | One of Volterra's best-looking Renaissance buildings contains an impressive collection of Tuscan paintings arranged chronologically on two floors. Head straight for Room 12, with Luca Signorelli's (circa 1445–1523) *Madonna and Child with Saints* and Rosso Fiorentino's later *Deposition.* Though painted just 30 years apart, they serve to illustrate the shift in style from the early 16th-century Renaissance ideals to full-blown mannerism: the balance of Signorelli's composition becomes purposefully skewed in Fiorentino's painting, where the colors go from vivid but realistic to emotively bright. Other important paintings in the small museum include Ghirlandaio's

Apotheosis of Christ with Saints and a polyptych of the *Madonna and Saints* by Taddeo di Bartolo, which once hung in the Palazzo dei Priori. ⊠ *Via dei Sarti 1, Volterra* ☎ *0588/87580* ⊕ *www.comune. volterra.pi.it* 🎫 *From €8.*

Porta all'Arco Etrusco

RUINS | Even if a good portion of the arch was rebuilt by the Romans, three dark and weather-beaten 4th-century-BC heads (thought to represent Etruscan gods) still face outward to greet those who enter here. A plaque on the outer wall recalls the efforts of the locals who saved the arch from destruction by filling it with stones during the German withdrawal at the end of World War II. ⊠ *Via Porta all'Arco, Volterra.*

Teatro Romano

RUINS | Just outside the walls past Porta Fiorentina are the ruins of the 1st-century-BC Roman theater, one of the best preserved in Italy, with adjacent remains of the Roman *terme* (baths). You can enjoy an excellent bird's-eye view of the theater from Via Lungo le Mura. ⊠ *Viale Francesco Ferrucci, Volterra* 🎫 ⊘ *Closed weekdays Nov.–Mar.* 🎫 *From €5.*

 ## Restaurants

Da Badò

$ | TUSCAN | This is the best place in town to eat traditional food elbow-to-elbow with the locals. Da Badò is family-run, with Lucia in the kitchen and her sons Giacomo and Michele waiting tables. **Known for:** local favorite; excellent traditional dishes; small menu. ⑤ *Average main: €14* ⊠ *Borgo San Lazzaro 9, Volterra* ☎ *0588/80402* ⊕ *www.trattoriadabado. com* ⊘ *Closed Wed.*

Il Sacco Fiorentino

$$ | TUSCAN | This lovely trattoria has been around for a long time, and with good reason. Here they turn out Tuscan classics, relying heavily on the local cheese (pecorino) and local meats (especially wild boar, among others). **Known for:**

excellent wine list; inventive food; tranquil setting. ⑤ *Average main: €15* ⊠ *Via Giusto Turazza 13, Volterra* ☎ *0588/88537* ⊘ *Closed Wed.*

 ## Hotels

Etruria

$ | B&B/INN | The rooms are modest and there's no elevator, but the central location, the ample buffet breakfast, and the modest rates make this a good choice for those on a budget. **Pros:** great central location; tranquil garden with rooftop views; friendly staff. **Cons:** no elevator; books up quickly as it's good value; some rooms can be noisy during the day. ⑤ *Rooms from: €83* ⊠ *Via Matteotti 32, Volterra* ☎ *0588/87377* ⊕ *www.albergoetruria.it* ⦿ *Free Breakfast* ⊘ *Closed Jan. and Feb.* ⇌ *18 rooms.*

San Gimignano

14 km (9 miles) northwest of Colle di Val d'Elsa, 38 km (24 miles) northwest of Siena, 54 km (34 miles) southwest of Florence.

When you're on a hilltop surrounded by soaring medieval towers silhouetted against the sky, it's difficult not to fall under the spell of San Gimignano. Its tall walls and narrow streets are typical of Tuscan hill towns, but it's the medieval "skyscrapers" that set the town apart from its neighbors. Today 14 towers remain, but at the height of the Guelph–Ghibelline conflict there was a forest of more than 70, and it was possible to cross the town by rooftop rather than by road. The towers were built partly for defensive purposes—they were a safe refuge and useful for pouring boiling oil on attacking enemies—and partly for bolstering the egos of their owners, who competed with deadly seriousness to build the highest tower in town.

San Gimignano

KEY

1 Exploring Sights
1 Restaurants
1 Hotels

0   1/8 mile
0   1/8 kilometer

Today San Gimignano isn't much more than a gentrified walled city, touristy but still very much worth exploring because, despite the profusion of cheesy souvenir shops lining the main drag, there's some serious Renaissance art to be seen here. Tour groups arrive early and clog the wine-tasting rooms—San Gimignano is famous for its light, white *vernaccia*—and art galleries for much of the day, but most sights stay open through late afternoon, when all the tour groups have long since departed.

San Gimignano is particularly beautiful in the early morning. Take time to walk up to the *rocca* (castle), at the highest point of town. Here you can enjoy 360-degree views of the surrounding countryside. Apart from when it's used for summer outdoor film festivals, it's always open.

GETTING HERE AND AROUND

You can reach San Gimignano by car from the Florence–Siena superstrada. Exit at Poggibonsi Nord and follow signs for San Gimignano. Although it involves changing buses in Poggibonsi, getting to San Gimignano by bus from Florence is a relatively straightforward affair. SITA operates the service between Siena or Florence and Poggibonsi. From Siena, Tra-In offers direct service to San Gimignano several times daily. You cannot reach San Gimignano by train.

VISITOR INFORMATION

CONTACT San Gimignano Tourism Office.
✉ *Piazza Duomo 1, San Gimignano*
☎ *0577/940008* ⊕ *www.sangimignano. com.*

Sights

★ Collegiata

CHURCH | The town's main church is not officially a duomo (cathedral), because San Gimignano has no bishop. But behind the simple facade of the Romanesque Collegiata lies a treasure trove of fine frescoes, covering nearly every part of the interior. Bartolo di Fredi's 14th-century fresco cycle of Old Testament scenes extends along one wall. Their distinctly medieval feel, with misshapen bodies, buckets of spurting blood, and lack of perspective, contrasts with the much more reserved scenes from the Life of Christ (attributed to 14th-century artist Lippo Memmi) painted on the opposite wall just 14 years later. Taddeo di Bartolo's otherworldly *Last Judgment* (late 14th century), with its distorted and suffering nudes, reveals the great influence of Dante's horrifying imagery in Inferno. Proof that the town had more than one protector, Benozzo Gozzoli's arrow-riddled St. Sebastian was commissioned in gratitude after the locals prayed to the saint for relief from plague. The Cappella di Santa Fina is decorated with a fresco cycle by Domenico Ghirlandaio illustrating the life of St. Fina. ⊠ *Piazza Pecori 1–2, entrance on left side of church, San Gimignano* ☎ *0577/286300* ⊕ *www.duomosangimignano.it* ⊠ *€3* ⊘ *Closed Thurs. and Jan. 1 and Dec. 25.*

Museo Civico

CASTLE/PALACE | The impressive civic museum occupies what was the "new" Palazzo del Popolo; the Torre Grossa is adjacent. Dante visited San Gimignano for only one day as a Guelph ambassador from Florence to ask the locals to join the Florentines in supporting the pope—just long enough to get the main council chamber, which now holds a 14th-century *Maestà* by Lippo Memmi, named after him. Off the stairway is a small room containing the racy frescoes by Memmo di Filippuccio (active 1288–1324), depicting the courtship, shared bath, and wedding of a young, androgynous-looking couple. That the space could have been a private room for the commune's chief magistrate may have something to do with the work's highly charged eroticism. Upstairs, paintings by famous Renaissance artists Pinturicchio (*Madonna Enthroned*) and Benozzo Gozzoli (*Madonna and Child*), and two large *tondi* (circular paintings) by Filippino Lippi (circa 1457–1504) attest to the importance and wealth of San Gimignano. Admission includes the steep climb to the top of the **Torre Grossa,** which on a clear day has spectacular views. ⊠ *Piazza Duomo 2, San Gimignano* ☎ *0577/990312* ⊕ *www. sangimignanomusei.it* ⊠ *€9 cumulative ticket.*

Sant'Agostino

CHURCH | Make a beeline for Benozzo Gozzoli's superlative 15th-century fresco cycle depicting scenes from the life of St. Augustine. The saint's work was essential to the early development of church doctrine. As thoroughly discussed in his autobiographical *Confessions* (an acute dialogue with God), Augustine, like many saints, sinned considerably in his youth before finding God. But unlike the lives of other saints, where the story continues through a litany of deprivations, penitence, and often martyrdom, Augustine's life and work focused on philosophy and the reconciliation of faith and thought. Benozzo's 17 scenes on the choir wall depict Augustine as a man who traveled and taught extensively in the 4th and 5th centuries. The 15th-century altarpiece by Piero del Pollaiolo (1443–96) depicts *The Coronation of the Virgin* and the various protectors of the city. On your way out of Sant'Agostino, stop in at the **Cappella di San Bartolo,** with a sumptuously elaborate tomb by Benedetto da Maiano (1442–97). ⊠ *Piazza Sant'Agostino 10, San Gimignano* ⊕ *www.sangimignano.com* ⊠ *Free.*

Restaurants

★ Cum Quibus

$$$ | ITALIAN | Without a doubt, this is among the most creative food happening in Tuscany. Lorenzo (in the front) has put together a menu that's Tuscan but not: it's rare to see bok choy incorporated into any dish, but here it's done with élan. **Known for:** two marvelous tasting menus; amazing wine list with prices to suit all budgets; incorporation of non-Tuscan ingredients into Tuscan food. ⑤ *Average main: €25* ✉ *Via San Martino 17, San Gimignano* ☎ *0577/943199* ⊕ *www.cumquibus.it* ⊗ *Closed Tues. and Jan.–Feb.*

Osteria del Carcere

$$ | ITALIAN | Although it calls itself an *osteria* (tavern), this place much more resembles a wine bar, with a bill of fare that includes several different types of pâtés and a short list of seasonal soups and salads. The sampler of goat cheeses, which can be paired with local wines, should not be missed. **Known for:** housed in a former jail; excellent chef-proprietor; inventive dishes. ⑤ *Average main: €16* ✉ *Via del Castello 13, San Gimignano* ☎ *0577/941905* ⊗ *Closed Wed. and early Jan.–Mar. No lunch Thurs.*

🛏 Hotels

La Collegiata

$$$ | HOTEL | After serving as a Franciscan convent and then the residence of the noble Strozzi family, the Collegiata has been converted into a fine hotel, with no expense spared in the process. **Pros:** wonderful staff; gorgeous views from terrace; elegant rooms in main building. **Cons:** service can be impersonal; long walk into town; some rooms are dimly lit. ⑤ *Rooms from: €220* ✉ *Località Strada 27, 1 km (½ mile) north of San Gimignano town center, San Gimignano* ☎ *0577/943201* ⊕ *www.lacollegiata.it* ⊗ *Closed Nov.–Mar.* ⇆ *20 rooms* ❑ *Free Breakfast.*

Pescille

$ | B&B/INN | A rambling farmhouse has been transformed into a handsome hotel with understated contemporary furniture in the bedrooms and country-classic motifs such as farm implements hanging on the walls in the bar. **Pros:** 10-minute walk to town; splendid views; quiet atmosphere. **Cons:** there's an elevator for luggage but not for guests; furnishings a bit austere; a vehicle is a must. ⑤ *Rooms from: €89* ✉ *Località Pescille, 4 km (2½ miles) south of San Gimignano, San Gimignano* ☎ *0577/940186* ⊕ *www.pescille.it* ⊗ *Closed mid-Oct.–Easter* ⇆ *38 rooms* ❑ *Free Breakfast.*

Torraccia di Chiusi

$$ | B&B/INN | FAMILY | A perfect retreat for families, this tranquil hilltop *agriturismo* (farm stay) offers simple, comfortably decorated accommodations on extensive grounds 5 km (3 miles) from the hubbub of San Gimignano. **Pros:** delightful countryside view; great walking possibilities; family-run hospitality. **Cons:** 30 minutes from the nearest town on a winding gravel road; might be too remote for some; need a car to get here. ⑤ *Rooms from: €160* ✉ *Località Montauto, San Gimignano* ☎ *0577/941972* ⊕ *www.torracciadichiusi.it* ⇆ *11 rooms* ❑ *Free Breakfast.*

Colle di Val d'Elsa

12 km (7 miles) west of Monteriggioni, 25 km (16 miles) northwest of Siena, 51 km (32 miles) south of Florence.

Most people pass through on their way to and from popular tourist destinations Volterra and San Gimignano—a shame, since Colle di Val d'Elsa has a lot to offer. It's another town on the Via Francigena that benefited from trade along the pilgrimage route to Rome. Colle got an extra boost in the late 16th century when it was given a bishopric, probably related to an increase in trade when nearby San Gimignano was cut off from the well-traveled road. The town is arranged on two levels, and from the 12th century onward the flat lower portion was given over to a flourishing papermaking industry; today the area is mostly modern, and efforts have shifted toward the production of fine glass and crystal.

GETTING HERE AND AROUND

You can reach Colle di Val d'Elsa by car on either the SR2 from Siena or the Florence–Siena superstrada. Bus service to and from Siena and Florence is frequent.

VISITOR INFORMATION

CONTACT Colle di Val d'Elsa Tourism Office. ⊠ *Piazza Arnolfo di Cambio 10, Colle di Val d'Elsa* ☎ *0577/292222* ⊕ *www. terresiena.it.*

👁 Sights

Make your way from the newer lower town (Colle Bassa) to the prettier, upper part of town (Colle Alta). The best views of the valley are to be had from Viale della Rimembranza, the road that loops around the western end of town, past the church of San Francesco. The early-16th-century Porta Nuova was inserted into the preexisting medieval walls, just as several handsome Renaissance palazzi were placed into the medieval neighborhood to create what is now called the Borgo. The Via Campana, the main road, passes through the facade of the surreal Palazzo Campana, an otherwise unfinished building that serves as a door connecting the two parts of the upper town. Via delle Volte, named for the vaulted arches that cover it, leads straight to Piazza del Duomo. There is a convenient parking lot off the SS68, with stairs leading up the hill. Buses arrive at Piazza Arnolfo, named after the town's favorite son, Arnolfo di Cambio (circa 1245–1302), the early-Renaissance architect who designed Florence's Duomo and Palazzo Vecchio (but sadly nothing here).

Chiesa di Santa Caterina

CHURCH | Visit this 15th-century church to view the excellent stained-glass window in the apse, executed by Sebastiano Mainardi (circa 1460–1513), as well as a haunting *Pietà* created by local artist Zacchia Zacchi (1473–1544). ⊠ *Via Campana 35, Colle di Val d'Elsa.*

Duomo

CHURCH | Several reconstructions have left little to admire of the once-Romanesque Duomo. Inside is the **Cappella del Santo Chiodo** (Chapel of the Holy Nail), built in the 15th century to hold a nail allegedly from the cross upon which Christ was crucified. (Perhaps it inspired the locals to go into the nail-making business, which became another of the town's flourishing industries.) ⊠ *Piazza del Duomo, Colle di Val d'Elsa.*

Museo San Pietro

ART MUSEUM | The museum of sacred art displays religious relics as well as triptychs from the Sienese and Florentine schools dating from the 14th and 15th centuries. It also contains the town's tribute to Arnolfo di Cambio, with photos of the buildings he designed for other towns. Down Via del Castello, at No. 63, is the house-tower where Arnolfo was born in 1245. (It's not open to the public.) ⊠ *Via Gracco del Secco 102, Colle di Val d'Elsa* ☎ *0577/286300* ⊕ *www.museisenesi.org* ⊠ *€6, includes the Museo Archeologico.*

Hotels

Palazzo San Lorenzo

$ | B&B/INN | A 17th-century palace in the historic center of Colle boasts rooms that exude warmth and comfort, with light-color wooden floors, soothingly tinted fabrics, and large windows. **Pros:** extremely well maintained; central location; indoor pool. **Cons:** some of the public spaces feel rather sterile; caters to business groups; a car is a necessity. ⑤ *Rooms from: €113* ⊠ *Via Gracco del Secco 113, Colle di Val d'Elsa* ☎ *0577/923675* ⊕ *www.palazzosanlorenzo.it* ⊅ *48 rooms* ¶◎¶ *Free Breakfast.*

Siena

With its narrow streets and steep alleys, a Gothic Duomo, a bounty of early Renaissance art, and the glorious Palazzo Pubblico overlooking its magnificent Campo, Siena is often described as Italy's best-preserved medieval city. It is also remarkably modern: many shops sell clothes by up-and-coming designers. Make a point of catching the *passeggiata* (evening stroll), when locals throng the Via di Città, Banchi di Sopra, and Banchi di Sotto, the city's three main streets.

Victory over Florence in 1260 at Montaperti marked the beginning of Siena's golden age. Even though Florentines avenged the loss twenty-nine years later, Siena continued to prosper. During the following decades Siena erected its greatest buildings (including the Duomo); established a model city government presided over by the Council of Nine; and became a great art, textile, and trade center. All of these achievements came together in the decoration of the Sala della Pace in Palazzo Pubblico. It makes you wonder what greatness the city might have gone on to achieve had its fortunes been different, but in 1348 a plague decimated the population, brought an end to the Council of Nine, and left Siena economically vulnerable. Siena succumbed to Florentine rule in the mid-16th century, when a year-long siege virtually eliminated the native population. Ironically, it was precisely this decline that, along with Sienese pride, prevented further development, to which we owe the city's marvelous medieval condition today.

But although much looks as it did in the early 14th century, Siena is no museum. Walk through the streets and you can see that the medieval *contrade*—17 neighborhoods into which the city has been historically divided—are a vibrant part of modern life. You may see symbols of the *contrada* emblazoned on banners and engraved on building walls: Tartuca (turtle), Oca (goose), Istrice (porcupine), Torre (tower)—among others. The Sienese still strongly identify themselves with the contrada where they were born and raised; loyalty and rivalry run deep. At no time is this more visible than during the centuries-old Palio, a twice-yearly horse race held in the Piazza del Campo, but you need not visit then to come to know the rich culture of Siena, evident at every step.

GETTING HERE AND AROUND

From Florence, the quickest way to Siena is via the Florence–Siena superstrada. Otherwise, take the Via Cassia (SR2) for a scenic route. Coming from Rome, leave the A1 at Valdichiana, and follow the Siena–Bettole superstrada. SITA provides excellent bus service between Florence and Siena. Because buses are direct and speedy, they are preferable to the train, which sometimes involves a change in Empoli.

If you come by car, you're better off leaving it in one of the parking lots around the perimeter of town. Driving is difficult or impossible in most parts of the city center. Practically unchanged since medieval times, Siena is laid out in a "Y" over the slopes of several hills, dividing the city into *terzi* (thirds).

BUS CONTACT Tra-In. ☎ *0577/204111* ⊕ *www.trainspa.it.*

TIMING

It's a joy to walk in Siena—hills notwithstanding—as it's a rare opportunity to stroll through a medieval city rather than just a town. (There is quite a lot to explore, in contrast to tiny hill towns that can be crossed in minutes.) The walk can be done in as little as a day, with minimal stops at the sights. But stay longer and take time to tour the churches and museums, and to enjoy the streetscapes themselves. Many of the sites have reduced hours Sunday afternoon and Monday.

VISITOR INFORMATION

CONTACT Siena Tourism Office. ⊠ *Piazza del Duomo 2, Siena* ☎ *0577/280551* ⊕ *www.terresiena.it.*

 Sights

Battistero

RELIGIOUS BUILDING | The Duomo's 14th-century Gothic Baptistery was built to prop up the apse of the cathedral. There are frescoes throughout, but the highlight is a large bronze 15th-century baptismal font designed by Jacopo della Quercia (1374–1438). It's adorned with bas-reliefs by various artists, including two by Renaissance masters: the *Baptism of Christ* by Lorenzo Ghiberti (1378–1455) and the *Feast of Herod* by Donatello. ⊠ *Piazza San Giovanni, Città* ☎ *0577/286300* ⊕ *www.operaduomo.siena.it* 🎟 *€20 combined ticket includes the Duomo, Cripta, and Museo dell'Opera.*

★ Cripta

CEMETERY | After it had lain unseen for possibly 700 years, a crypt was rediscovered under the grand *pavimento* (floor) of the Duomo during routine excavation work and was opened to the public in 2003. An unknown master executed the breathtaking frescoes here sometime between 1270 and 1280. They retain their original colors and pack an emotional punch even with sporadic damage. The *Deposition/Lamentation* gives strong evidence that the Sienese school could paint emotion just as well as the Florentine school—and did it some 20 years before Giotto. ⊠ *Scale* *di San Giovanni, Città ⊕ Down steps to right side of cathedral ☎ 0577/286300 ⊕ www.operaduomo.siena.it ✉ €20 combined ticket includes the Duomo, Battistero, and Museo dell'Opera.*

★ Duomo

CHURCH | Siena's cathedral is beyond question one of the finest Gothic churches in Italy. The multicolor marbles and painted decoration are typical of the Italian approach to Gothic architecture—lighter and much less austere than the French. The amazingly detailed facade has few rivals. It was completed in two brief phases at the end of the 13th and 14th centuries. The statues and decorative work were designed by Nicola Pisano and his son Giovanni, although most of what we see today are copies, the originals having been removed to the nearby Museo dell'Opera. The gold mosaics are 18th-century restorations. The Campanile (no entry) is among central Italy's finest, the number of windows increasing with each level, a beautiful and ingenious way of reducing the weight of the structure as it climbs to the heavens. The Duomo's interior, with its dark green–and–white striping throughout and illusionistically coffered and gilded dome, is simply striking. Step in and look back up at a copy of Duccio's (circa 1255–1319) panels of stained glass that once filled the circular entrance window—the originals are now in the Museo dell'Opera Metropolitana. Finished in 1288, the window is the oldest example of stained glass in Italy. The Duomo is most famous for its unique and magnificent inlaid-marble floors, which took almost 200 years to complete. More than 40 artists contributed to the work, made up of 56 separate compositions depicting biblical scenes, allegories, religious symbols, and civic emblems. The floors are covered for most of the year for conservation purposes, but are unveiled during September and October. The Duomo's carousel pulpit, also much appreciated, was carved by Nicola Pisano (circa 1220–84) around 1265; the Life of Christ is depicted on the rostrum frieze. In striking contrast to all the Gothic decoration in the nave are the magnificent Renaissance frescoes in the Biblioteca Piccolomini, off the left aisle. Painted by Pinturicchio (circa 1454–1513) and completed in 1509, they depict events from the life of Aeneas Sylvius Piccolomini (1405–64), who became Pope Pius II in 1458. The frescoes are in excellent condition, and have a freshness rarely seen in work so old. The Duomo is grand, but the medieval Sienese people had even bigger plans. They wanted to enlarge the building by using the existing church as a transept for a new church, with a new nave running toward the southeast, to make what would be the largest church in the world. But only the side wall and part of the new facade were completed when the Black Death struck in 1348, decimating Siena's population. The city fell into decline, funds dried up, and the plans were never carried out. (The dream of building the biggest church was actually doomed to failure from the start—subsequent attempts to get the project going revealed that the foundation was insufficient to bear the weight of the proposed structure.) The beginnings of the new nave, extending from the right side of the Duomo, were left unfinished, perhaps as a testament to unfulfilled dreams, and ultimately enclosed to house the adjacent Museo dell'Opera. The Cripta was discovered during routine preservation work on the church and has been opened to the public. The last entrance to the Duomo is 30 minutes before closing. ✉ *Piazza del Duomo, Città* ☎ *0577/286300* ⊕ *www.operaduomo. siena.it* ✉ *€20 combined ticket includes Cripta, Battistero, and Museo dell'Opera.*

★ Museo dell'Opera

ART MUSEUM | Part of the unfinished nave of what was to have been a new cathedral, the museum contains the Duomo's treasury and some of the original decoration from its facade and interior. The

Siena

KEY
- **1** Exploring Sights
- **1** Restaurants
- **1** Hotels

Sights ▼		Restaurants ▼	Hotels ▼
1 Battistero **C4**	7 Pinacoteca Nazionale **C5**	1 Liberamente Osteria **C4**	1 Grand Hotel Continental **C3**
2 Cripta **B4**	8 San Domenico **B3**	2 Osteria Il Grattacielo **C3**	2 Palazzo Ravizza **B5**
3 Duomo **B4**	9 Santa Maria della Scala **B4**	3 Trattoria Papei **C4**	
4 Museo dell'Opera **C4**			
5 Palazzo Pubblico **C4**			
6 Piazza del Campo **C4**			

first room on the ground floor displays weather-beaten 13th-century sculptures by Giovanni Pisano (circa 1245–1318) that were brought inside for protection and replaced by copies, as was a tondo of the *Madonna and Child* (now attributed to Donatello) that once hung on the door to the south transept. The masterpiece is unquestionably Duccio's *Maestà,* one side with 26 panels depicting episodes from the Passion, the other side with a *Madonna and Child Enthroned.* Painted between 1308 and 1311 as the altarpiece for the Duomo (where it remained until 1505), its realistic elements, such as the lively depiction of the Christ child and the treatment of interior space, proved an enormous influence on later painters. The work originally decorated the Duomo's high altar, before being displaced by Duccio's *Maestà.* There is a fine view from the tower inside the museum. ⊠ *Piazza del Duomo 8, Città* ☎ *0577/286300* ⊕ *www.operaduomo.siena.it* ✉ *€20 combined ticket includes the Duomo, Cripta, and Battistero.*

Palazzo Pubblico

GOVERNMENT BUILDING | The Gothic Palazzo Pubblico, the focal point of the Piazza del Campo, has served as Siena's town hall since the 1300s. It now also contains the Museo Civico, with walls covered in early Renaissance frescoes. The nine governors of Siena once met in the Sala della Pace, famous for Ambrogio Lorenzetti's frescoes called *Allegories of Good and Bad Government*, painted in the late 1330s to demonstrate the dangers of tyranny. The good government side depicts utopia, showing first the virtuous ruling council surrounded by angels and then scenes of a perfectly running city and countryside. Conversely, the bad government fresco tells a tale straight out of Dante. The evil ruler and his advisers have horns and fondle strange animals, and the town scene depicts the seven mortal sins in action. The **Torre del Mangia,** the palazzo's famous bell tower, is named after one of its first bell ringers,

Giovanni di Duccio (called Mangiaguadagni, or earnings eater). The climb up to the top is long and steep, but the view makes it worth every step. ⊠ *Piazza del Campo 1, Città* ☎ *0577/292232* ⊕ *www. comune.siena.it* ✉ *Museum €10, ticket sales end 30 mins before closing; tower €10, ticket sales end 45 mins before closing.*

★ Piazza del Campo

PLAZA/SQUARE | The fan-shape Piazza del Campo, known simply as il Campo (The Field), is one of the finest squares in Italy. Constructed toward the end of the 12th century on a market area unclaimed by any contrada, it's still the heart of town. The bricks of the Campo are patterned in nine different sections—representing each member of the medieval Government of Nine. At the top of the Campo is a copy of the early 15th-century **Fonte Gaia** by Siena's greatest sculptor, Jacopo della Quercia. The 13 sculpted reliefs of biblical events and virtues that line the fountain are 19th-century copies; the originals are in the museum complex of Santa Maria della Scala. On Palio horserace days (July 2 and August 16), the Campo and all its surrounding buildings are packed with cheering, frenzied locals and tourists craning their necks to take it all in. ⊠ *Piazza del Campo, Città.*

Pinacoteca Nazionale

ART MUSEUM | The superb collection of five centuries of local painting in Siena's national picture gallery can easily convince you that the Renaissance was by no means just a Florentine thing. Accordingly, the most interesting section of the collection, chronologically arranged, has several important firsts. Room 1 contains a painting of the *Stories of the True Cross* (1215) by the so-called Master of Tressa, the earliest identified work by a painter of the Sienese school, and is followed in Room 2 by late-13th-century artist Guido da Siena's *Stories from the Life of Christ,* one of the first paintings ever made on canvas (earlier painters used wood panels). Rooms 3 and 4 are dedicated to Duccio, a student of Cimabue (circa 1240–1302) and considered to be the last of the proto-Renaissance painters. Ambrogio Lorenzetti's landscapes in Room 8 are among the first truly secular paintings in Western art. Among later works in the rooms on the floor above, keep an eye out for the preparatory sketches used by Domenico Beccafumi (1486–1551) for the 35 etched marble panels he made for the floor of the Duomo. ⊠ *Via San Pietro 29, Città* ☎ *0577/286143* ⊕ *www.pinacote-canazionale.siena.it* ⊠ *€8* ⊗ *Closed Mon.*

San Domenico

CHURCH | Although the Duomo is celebrated as a triumph of 13th-century Gothic architecture, this church, built at about the same time, turned out to be an oversize, hulking brick box that never merited a finishing coat in marble, let alone a graceful facade. Named for the founder of the Dominican order, the church is now more closely associated with St. Catherine of Siena. Just to the right of the entrance is the chapel in which she received the stigmata. On the wall is the only known contemporary portrait of the saint, made in the late 14th century by Andrea Vanni (circa 1332–1414). Farther down is the famous **Cappella delle Santa Testa,** the church's official shrine. Catherine, or bits and pieces of her, was literally spread all over the country—a foot is in Venice, most of her body is in Rome, and only her head (kept in a reliquary on the chapel's altar) and her right thumb are here. She was revered throughout the country long before she was officially named a patron saint of Italy in 1939. On either side of the chapel are well-known frescoes by Sodoma (aka Giovanni Antonio Bazzi, 1477–1549) of *St. Catherine in Ecstasy.* Don't miss the view of the Duomo and town center from the apse-side terrace. ⊠ *Piazza San Domenico, Camollia* ☎ *0577/286848* ⊕ *www.basilicacateriniana.com.*

★ Santa Maria della Scala

HISTORIC SIGHT | For more than 1,000 years, this complex across from the Duomo was home to Siena's hospital, but now it serves as a museum to display some terrific frescoes and other Sienese Renaissance treasures. Restored 15th-century frescoes in the Sala del Pellegrinaio (once the emergency room) tell the history of the hospital, which was created to give refuge to passing pilgrims and to those in need, and to distribute charity to the poor. Incorporated into the complex is the church of the Santissima Annunziata, with a celebrated *Risen Christ* by Vecchietta (also known as Lorenzo di Pietro, circa 1412–80). Down in the dark, Cappella di Santa Caterina della Notte is where St. Catherine went to pray at night. The displays—including the *bucchero* (dark, reddish clay) ceramics, Roman coins, and tomb furnishings—are clearly marked and can serve as a good introduction to the history of regional excavations. Don't miss della Quercia's original sculpted reliefs in the subterranean archaeological museum, from the Fonte Gaia. Although the fountain has been faithfully copied for the Campo, there's something incomparably beautiful about the real thing. ⊠ *Piazza del Duomo 2, Città* ☎ *0577/534511* ⊕ *www.santamariadellascala.com* ⊠ *€9.* ⊗ *Closed Tues.*

🍽 Restaurants

Liberamente Osteria

$ | ITALIAN | Though the food here is rather good, the real reasons to come are the exquisitely crafted cocktails and the view, which just happens to be of Il Campo, arguably the prettiest square in all of Italy. Tasty little nibbles accompany the generously proportioned aperitivi. **Known for:** facility with rum-based drinks; opens early (9 am) and closes late (2 am); variations on the spritz. $ *Average main: €7* ⊠ *Il Campo 27, Siena* ☎ *0577/274733* ⊕ *www.liberamenteosteria.it.*

Osteria Il Grattacielo

$ | TUSCAN | If you're wiped out from too much sightseeing, consider a meal at this hole-in-the-wall restaurant where locals congregate for a simple lunch over a glass of wine. There's a collection of *verdure sott'olio*, a wide selection of *affettati misti*, and various types of frittatas, and all of this can be washed down with the cheap, yet eminently drinkable, house red. **Known for:** usually filled with local men arguing about the Palio; simple, good-value food; earthy ambience. ⑤ *Average main: €10 ⊠ Via Pontani 8, Camollia ☎ 331/7422835.*

Trattoria Papei

$ | TUSCAN | The menu hasn't changed for years, and why should it? This place has been in the Papei family for three generations, and they know how to turn out Sienese specialties: their reasonable prices and fine, basic fare is what draws locals to the place. ⑤ *Average main: €11 ⊠ Piazza del Mercato 6, Città ☎ 0577/280894* ⊕ *www.anticatrattoriapapei.com.*

 # Hotels

Grand Hotel Continental

$$$ | HOTEL | Pope Alexander VII of the famed Sienese Chigi family gave this palace to his niece as a wedding present in 1600; through the centuries it has been a private family home as well as a grand hotel exuding elegance from the stately pillared entrance to the crisp-linen sheets. **Pros:** luxurious accommodations; first-rate concierge; great location on the main drag. **Cons:** breakfast costs extra; lots of noise if your room is street-side; sometimes stuffy atmosphere. ⑤ *Rooms from: €297 ⊠ Banchi di Sopra 85, Camollia ☎ 0577/56011 ⊕ www.starhotelscollezione.com ⇦ 51 rooms ¶○¶ No Meals.*

★ Palazzo Ravizza

$$ | HOTEL | This charming palazzo exudes a sense of an age gone by; its guest rooms have high ceilings, antique furnishings, and bathrooms decorated with hand-painted tiles. **Pros:** pleasant garden with a view beyond the city walls; professional staff; 10-minute walk to the center of town. **Cons:** somewhat removed from the center of things; some rooms are a little cramped; not all rooms have views. ⑤ *Rooms from: €139 ⊠ Pian dei Mantellini 34, Città ☎ 0577/280462* ⊕ *www.palazzoravizza.it ⇦ 41 rooms* ¶○¶ *Free Breakfast.*

Arezzo

63 km (39 miles) northeast of Siena, 81 km (50 miles) southeast of Florence.

Arezzo is best known for the magnificent Piero della Francesca frescoes in the church of San Francesco. It's also the birthplace of the poet Petrarch (1304–74), the Renaissance artist and art historian Giorgio Vasari, and Guido d'Arezzo (aka Guido Monaco), the inventor of contemporary musical notation. Arezzo dates from pre-Etruscan times, when around 1000 BC the first settlers erected a cluster of huts. Arezzo thrived as an Etruscan capital from the 7th to the 4th century BC, and was one of the most important cities in the Etruscans' anti-Roman 12-city federation, resisting Rome's rule to the last.

The city eventually fell and in turn flourished under the Romans. In 1248 Guglielmino degli Ubertini, a member of the powerful Ghibelline family, was elected bishop of Arezzo. This sent the city headlong into the enduring conflict between the Ghibellines (pro-emperor) and the Guelphs (pro-pope). In 1289 Florentine Guelphs defeated Arezzo in a famous battle at Campaldino. Among the Florentine soldiers was Dante Alighieri (1265–1321), who often referred to Arezzo in his *Divine Comedy*. Guelph–Ghibelline wars continued to plague Arezzo until the end of the 14th century, when Arezzo lost its independence to Florence.

GETTING HERE AND AROUND

Arezzo is easily reached by car from the A1, the main highway running between Florence and Rome. Direct trains connect Arezzo with Rome (2½ hours) and Florence (1 hour). Direct bus service is available from Florence, but not from Rome.

VISITOR INFORMATION

CONTACT Arezzo Tourism Office. ✉ Piazza Libertà 1, Arezzo ☎ 0575/377 678 ⊕ *www.arezzointuscany.it.*

◉ Sights

★ Basilica di San Francesco

CHURCH | The famous Piero della Francesca frescoes depicting *The Legend of the True Cross* (1452–66) were executed on the three walls of the Capella Bacci, the apse of this 14th-century church. What Sir Kenneth Clark called "the most perfect morning light in all Renaissance painting" may be seen in the lowest section of the right wall, where the troops of Emperor Maxentius flee before the sign of the cross. Reservations are recommended

June through September. ✉ *Piazza San Francesco 2, Arezzo* ☎ *0575/352727* ⊕ *www.pierodellafrancesca-ticketoffice. it* ⌨ *€8.*

Duomo

CHURCH | Arezzo's medieval cathedral at the top of the hill contains a fresco of a tender *Maria Maddalena* by Piero della Francesca (1420–92); look for it in the north aisle next to the large marble tomb near the organ. Construction of the Duomo began in 1278 but twice came to a halt, and the church wasn't completed until 1510. The ceiling decorations and the stained-glass windows date from the 16th century. The facade, designed by Arezzo's Dante Viviani, was added later (1901–14). ✉ *Piazza del Duomo 1, Arezzo.*

Museo Archeologico

ART MUSEUM | The Archaeological Museum in the **Convento di San Bernardo,** just outside the **Anfiteatro Romano,** exhibits a fine collection of Etruscan bronzes. ✉ *Via Margaritone 10, Arezzo* ☎ *0575/20882* ⊕ *www.polomusealetoscana.beniculturali.it* ⌨ *€6* ⊙ *Closed Wed. and Fri.–Sun.*

Piazza Grande

PLAZA/SQUARE | With its irregular shape and sloping brick pavement, framed by buildings of assorted centuries, Arezzo's central piazza echoes Siena's Piazza del Campo. Though not quite so magnificent, it's lively enough during the outdoor antiques fair the first weekend of the month and when the **Giostra del Saracino** (Saracen Joust), featuring medieval costumes and competition, is held here on the third Saturday of June and on the first Sunday of September. ✉ *Piazza Grande, Arezzo.*

Santa Maria della Pieve (*Church of Saint Mary of the Parish*)

CHURCH | The curving, tiered apse on Piazza Grande belongs to a fine Romanesque church that was originally an Early Christian structure, which had been constructed over the remains of a Roman temple. The church was rebuilt in Romanesque style in the 12th century. The splendid facade dates from the early 13th century but includes granite Roman columns. A magnificent polyptych, depicting the Madonna and Child with four saints, by Pietro Lorenzetti (circa 1290–1348), embellishes the high altar. ✉ *Corso Italia 7, Arezzo.*

🍴 Restaurants

Caffè dei Costanti

$ | ITALIAN | Outdoor seating on Arezzo's main pedestrian square and a tasty range of chef's salads (named after the servers) make this a very pleasant spot for a light lunch during a tour of town. If you're here in the early evening, the dei Costanti serves up an ample buffet of snacks to accompany predinner aperitifs. **Known for:** tasty snacks; very fine cappuccini; perfect location across from Basilica di San Francesco. ⑤ *Average main: €6* ✉ *Piazza San Francesco 19, Arezzo* ☎ *0575/1824075* ⊕ *www.caffedeicostanti.it* ⊙ *Closed Wed.*

★ I Tre Bicchieri

$$ | SEAFOOD | Chef Luigi Casotti hails from Amalfi and this shows through in his fine adaptations of dishes, notably seafood, more commonly served near the Bay of Naples. Two well-priced tasting menus are available. **Known for:** notable chef; creative menu including two tasting menus; superlative wine list. ⑤ *Average main: €19* ✉ *Piazzetta Sopra i Ponti 3–5, Arezzo* ☎ *0575/26557* ⊕ *www. ristoranteitrebicchieri.com* ⊙ *Closed Sun. (except 1st weekend of month).*

La Torre di Gnicche

$ | ITALIAN | Wine lovers shouldn't miss this wine bar/eatery, just off Piazza Grande, with more than 700 labels on the list. Seasonal dishes of traditional fare, such as *acquacotta del casentino* (porcini mushroom soup) and *baccalà in umido* (salt-cod stew), are served in the simply decorated, vaulted dining room. **Known for:** outdoor seating in warm weather; the extensive wine list,

Cortona

KEY

1 Exploring Sights

1 Restaurants

1 Hotels

with many choices by the glass; an ever-changing menu. $ *Average main: €9* ✉ *Piaggia San Martino 8, Arezzo* ☎ *0575/352035* ⊕ *www.latorredignicche. it* ⊗ *Closed Wed. and Jan.*

 Hotels

★ **Calcione**

$ | B&B/INN | FAMILY | This six-century-old family estate (circa 1483) now houses sophisticated rustic lodgings; many of the apartments have open fireplaces, and the stone houses have a private pool (the rest share the estate pool). **Pros:** quiet, beautiful, remote setting; houses sleep up to 17; private lakes for fishing and windsurfing. **Cons:** no A/C; private transportation is a must—nearest village is 8 km (5 miles) away; minimum one-week stay in season. $ *Rooms from: €100*

✉ *Località Il Calcione 102, 26 km (15 miles) southwest of Arezzo, Lucignano* ☎ *0575/837153* ⊕ *www.calcione.com* ⊗ *Closed Dec.–Feb.* ⇥ *30 rooms* ⦿ *No Meals.*

★ **Il Borro**

$$$$ | HOTEL | The location has been described as "heaven on earth," and a stay at this elegant Ferragamo estate, with a 10-bedroom villa (rented out as a single unit) that was once a luxurious hunting lodge, and nearby a medieval village is sure to bring similar descriptions to mind. **Pros:** unique setting and atmosphere; exceptional service; great location for exploring eastern Tuscany. **Cons:** not all suites have country views; off the beaten track, making private transport a must; very expensive. $ *Rooms from: €690* ✉ *Località Il Borro 1, outside village of San Giustino Valdarno, 20 km (12 miles)* *northwest of Arezzo* ☎ *055/977053* ⊕ *www.ilborro.it* ⊘ *Closed Dec.–Mar.* ⇥ *61 rooms* ⵔⵗ *Free Breakfast.*

Shopping

Ever since Etruscan goldsmiths set up their shops here more than 2,000 years ago, Arezzo has been famous for its jewelry. Today the town lays claim to being one of the world's capitals of jewelry design and manufacture, and you can find an impressive display of big-time baubles in the town center's shops.

Arezzo is also famous, at least in Italy, for its antiques dealers. The first weekend of every month, between 8:30 and 5:30, a popular and colorful flea market selling antiques and not-so-antique items takes place in the town's main square, **Piazza Grande,** and in the streets and parks nearby.

Cortona

29 km (18 miles) south of Arezzo, 79 km (44 miles) east of Siena, 117 km (73 miles) southeast of Florence.

Brought into the limelight by Frances Mayes's book *Under the Tuscan Sun* and a subsequent movie, Cortona is no longer the destination of just a few specialist art historians and those seeking reprieve from busier tourist venues. The main street, Via Nazionale, is now lined with souvenir shops and fills with crowds during summer. Although the main sights of Cortona make braving the bustling center worthwhile, much of the town's charm lies in its maze of quiet back-streets. It's here that you will see laundry hanging from windows, find children playing, and catch the smell of simmering pasta sauce. Wander off the beaten track and you won't be disappointed.

GETTING HERE AND AROUND

Cortona is easily reached by car from the A1 autostrada: take the Valdichiana exit toward Perugia, then follow signs for Cortona. Regular bus service, provided by Etruria Mobilità, is available between Arezzo and Cortona (one hour). Train service to Cortona is made inconvenient by the location of the train station, in the valley 3 km (2 miles) steeply below the town itself. From there, you have to rely on bus or taxi service to get up to Cortona.

VISITOR INFORMATION

CONTACT Cortona Tourism Office. ⊠ *Piazza Signorelli 9, Cortona* ☎ *0575/637223* ⊕ *www.comunedicortona.it.*

Sights

Museo Diocesano

ART MUSEUM | Housed in part of the original cathedral structure, this nine-room museum houses an impressive number of large, splendid paintings by native son Luca Signorelli (1445–1523), as well as a beautiful *Annunciation* by Fra Angelico (1387/1400–55), which is a delightful surprise in this small town. The church was built between 1498 and 1505 and restructured by Giorgio Vasari in 1543. Frescoes depicting sacrifices from the Old Testament by Doceno (1508–56), based on designs by Vasari, line the walls. ⊠ *Piazza Duomo 1, Cortona* ☎ *0575/62830* ⊕ *www.cortonatuseibellezza.it* ⵔ *€6* ⊘ *Closed Mon.–Thurs. Nov.–Mar.*

Santa Maria al Calcinaio

CHURCH | Legend has it that the image of the Madonna appeared on a wall of a medieval *calcinaio* (lime pit used for curing leather), the site on which the church was then built between 1485 and 1513. The linear gray-and-white interior recalls Florence's Duomo. Sienese architect Francesco di Giorgio (1439–1502) most likely designed the sanctuary: the church is a terrific example of Renaissance

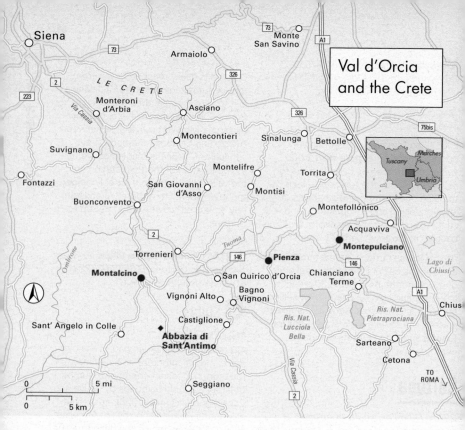

Val d'Orcia and the Crete

architectural principles. ⊠ *Località Il Calcinaio 227, 3 km (2 miles) southeast of Cortona's center, Cortona.*

🍴 Restaurants

Osteria del Teatro

$$ | TUSCAN | Photographs from theatrical productions spanning many years line the walls of this tavern off Cortona's large Piazza del Teatro. The food is simply delicious—try the *filetto al lardo di colonnata e prugne* (beef cooked with bacon and prunes); service is warm and friendly.
Known for: pretty dining room; food that's in season; lively atmosphere. ⑤ *Average main: €18* ⊠ *Via Maffei 2, Cortona* ☎ *0575/630556* ⊕ *www.osteria-del-teatro.it* ☉ *Closed Wed. and 2 wks in Nov.*

🛏 Hotels

★ Il Falconiere

$$$$ | B&B/INN | Accommodation options at this sumptuous property include rooms in an 18th-century villa, suites in the *chiesetta* (chapel, or little church), or for more seclusion, Le Vigne del Falco suites at the far end of the property. **Pros:** elegant, but relaxed; attractive setting in the valley beneath Cortona; excellent service. **Cons:** might be too isolated for some; a car is a must; some find rooms in main villa a little noisy. ⑤ *Rooms from: €330* ⊠ *Località San Martino 370, 3 km (2 miles) north of Cortona, Cortona* ☎ *0575/612679* ⊕ *www.ilfalconiere.it* ☉ *Closed Nov. 3–Mar. 27* ⇨ *34 rooms* ❂ *Free Breakfast.*

Montepulciano

610 km (6 miles) northeast of Chianciano Terme, 65 km (40 miles) southeast of Siena, 114 km (70 miles) southeast of Florence.

Perched on a hilltop, Montepulciano is made up of a pyramid of redbrick buildings set within a circle of cypress trees. At an altitude of almost 2,000 feet, it is cool in summer and chilled in winter by biting winds sweeping down its spiraling streets. The town has an unusually harmonious look, the result of the work of three architects: Antonio da Sangallo "il Vecchio" (circa 1455–1534), Vignola (1507–73), and Michelozzo (1396–1472). The group endowed it with fine palaces and churches in an attempt to impose Renaissance architectural ideals on an ancient Tuscan hill town.

GETTING HERE AND AROUND
From Rome or Florence, take the Chiusi–Chianciano exit from the A1 (Autostrada del Sole). From Siena, take the SR2 south to San Quirico and then the SP146 to Montepulciano. Tra-In offers bus service from Siena to Montepulciano several times a day. Montepulciano's train station is in Montepulciano Stazione, 10 km (6 miles) away.

VISITOR INFORMATION
CONTACT Montepulciano Tourism Office. ✉ *Piazza Don Minzoni 1, Montepulciano* ☎ *0578/757341* ⊕ *www.prolocomontepulciano.it.*

Sights

Duomo
CHURCH | On the Piazza Grande the unfinished facade of Montepulciano's cathedral doesn't measure up to the beauty of its neighboring palaces. On the inside, however, its Renaissance roots shine through. The high altar has a splendid triptych painted in 1401 by Taddeo di Bartolo (circa 1362–1422), and you can see fragments of the tomb of Bartolomeo Aragazzi, secretary to Pope Martin V, which was sculpted by Michelozzo between 1427 and 1436. ✉ *Piazza Grande, Montepulciano.*

Piazza Grande
PLAZA/SQUARE | Filled with handsome buildings, this large square on the heights of the old historic town is Montepulciano's pièce de résistance. ✉ *Piazza Grande, Montepulciano.*

★ San Biagio
CHURCH | Designed by Antonio da Sangallo il Vecchio, and considered his masterpiece, this church sits on the hillside below the town walls and is a model of High Renaissance architectural perfection. Inside the church is a painting of the Madonna that, according to legend, was the only thing remaining in an abandoned church that two young girls entered on April 23, 1518. The girls saw the eyes of the Madonna moving, and that same afternoon so did a farmer and a cow, who knelt down in front of the painting. In 1963 the image was proclaimed the Madonna del Buon Viaggio (Madonna of the Good Journey), the protector of tourists in Italy. ✉ *Via di San Biagio, Montepulciano* ☎ *0578/286300* ⊕ *www.tempiosanbiagio.it* 🎫 *€3.50.*

Restaurants

★ La Grotta
$$ | **TUSCAN** | You might be tempted to pass right by the innocuous entrance across the street from San Biagio, but you'd miss some fantastic food. This tasty menu relies heavily on local classics turned out to perfection. **Known for:** stellar service; creative menu; local wine list. $ *Average main: €22* ✉ *Via di San Biagio 15, Montepulciano* ☎ *0578/757479* ⊕ *www.lagrottamontepulciano.it* ⊘ *Closed Wed. and Jan. 15–Mar. 15.*

★ Osteria del Conte

$ | ITALIAN | As high in Montepulciano as you can get, just behind the Duomo, this small and intimate restaurant is expertly run by the mother-and-son team of Lorena and Paolo Brachi. Passionate about the food they prepare, both have a flair for the region's traditional dishes—the pici *all'aglione* (with garlic sauce) and the *filetto ai funghi porcini* (steak with porcini mushrooms) are mouthwateringly good. **Known for:** attentive service; fine home cooking; good local wines. $ *Average main: €13 ⊠ Via di San Donato 19, Montepulciano ☎ 0578/756062 ⊕ www.osteriadelconte.it ⊗ Closed Mon. No dinner Sun.*

Hotels

La Terrazza

$ | B&B/INN | FAMILY | On a quiet street in the upper part of town, these unpretentious lodgings are given sparkle by the welcoming and friendly service of the owners, Roberto and Vittoria Giardinelli. **Pros:** great value for money; friendly family atmosphere; quiet central location. **Cons:** no night porter; no A/C; books up quickly. $ *Rooms from: €95 ⊠ Via del Piè al Sasso 16, Montepulciano ☎ 0578/757440 ⊕ www.laterrazzadi-montepulciano.it ⊶ 14 rooms ⊠ Free Breakfast.*

★ Podere Dionora

$$$ | B&B/INN | At this secluded and serene country inn, earth-tone fabrics complement antiques in the individually decorated rooms, all of which have functioning fireplaces. **Pros:** attentive service; secluded setting; great views. **Cons:** need a car to get around; long walk to the nearest town; books up quickly. $ *Rooms from: €270 ⊠ Via Vicinale di Poggiano 9, 3 km (2 miles) east of Montepulciano town center, Montepulciano ☎ 0578/717496 ⊕ www.dionora.it ⊗ Closed mid-Dec.–mid-Mar. ⊶ 6 rooms ⊠ Free Breakfast.*

Pienza

12 km (7 miles) west of Montepulciano, 52 km (31 miles) southeast of Siena, 120 km (72 miles) southeast of Florence.

Pienza owes its appearance to Pope Pius II (1405–64), who had grand plans to transform his hometown of Corsignano—its former name—into a compact model Renaissance town. The man entrusted with the transformation was Bernardo Rossellino (1409–64), a protégé of the great Renaissance architectural theorist Leon Battista Alberti (1404–72). His mandate was to create a cathedral, a papal palace, and a town hall that adhered to the vainglorious pope's principles. Gothic and Renaissance styles were fused, and the buildings were decorated with Sienese paintings. The net result was a project that expressed Renaissance ideals of art, architecture, and civilized good living in a single scheme: it stands as an exquisite example of the architectural canons that Alberti formulated in the early Renaissance and that were utilized by later architects, including Michelangelo, in designing many of Italy's finest buildings and piazzas. Today the cool nobility of Pienza's center seems almost surreal in this otherwise unpretentious village, renowned for its smooth sheep's-milk pecorino cheese.

GETTING HERE AND AROUND

From Siena, drive south along the SR2 to San Quirico d'Orcia and then take the SP146. The trip should take just over an hour. Tra-In shuttles passengers between Siena and Pienza. There is no train service to Pienza.

VISITOR INFORMATION

CONTACT Pienza Tourism Office. ⊠ *Piazza Dante 18, Pienza ☎ 0578/748359 ⊕ www.pienza.info.*

Sights

Duomo

CHURCH | This 15th-century cathedral was built by the architect Bernardo Rossellino (1409–64) under the influence of Leon Battista Alberti. The travertine facade is divided in three parts, with Renaissance arches under the pope's coat of arms encircled by a wreath of fruit. Inside, the cathedral is simple but richly decorated with Sienese paintings. The building's perfection didn't last long—the first cracks appeared immediately after the building was completed, and its foundations have shifted slightly ever since as rain erodes the hillside behind. You can see this effect if you look closely at the base of the first pier as you enter the church and compare it with the last. ⊠ *Piazza Pio II* ☎ *0578/749071* ⊕ *www. pienza.org.*

Museo Diocesano

ART MUSEUM | This museum sits to the left of Pienza's Duomo. It's small but has a few interesting papal treasures and rich Flemish tapestries. The most precious piece is a rare mantle woven in gold with pearls and embroidered religious scenes that belonged to Pope Pius II. ⊠ *Corso Il Rossellino 30, Pienza* ☎ *0578/749905* ⊕ *www.palazzoborgia.it* 🎫 *€10* ⊗ *Closed Tues.*

Palazzo Piccolomini

CASTLE/PALACE | In 1459 Pius II commissioned Bernardo Rossellino to design the perfect palazzo for his papal court. The architect took Florence's Palazzo Rucellai by Alberti as a model and designed this 100-room palace. Three sides of the building fit perfectly into the urban plan around it, while the fourth, looking over the valley, has a lovely loggia uniting it with the gardens in back. Guided tours departing every 30 minutes take you to visit the papal apartments, including a beautiful library, the Sala delle Armi (with an impressive weapons collection), and the music room, with its extravagant wooden ceiling forming four letter Ps, for Pope, Pius, Piccolomini, and Pienza. The last tour departs 30 minutes before closing. ⊠ *Piazza Pio II, Pienza* ☎ *0577/286300* ⊕ *www.palazzopiccolominipienza.it* 🎫 *€7* ⊗ *Closed early Jan.– mid-Feb., mid-Nov.–late Nov., and Tues.*

Restaurants

La Chiocciola

$ | **TUSCAN** | Take the few minutes to walk from the old town for typical Pienza fare, including homemade pici with hare or wild-boar sauce. The restaurant's version of *formaggio in forno* (baked cheese) with assorted accompaniments such as fresh porcini mushrooms is reason enough to venture here. **Known for:** good wine list; beloved by locals; simple, well-prepared food. ⓢ *Average main: €14* ⊠ *Via Mencatelli 2, Pienza* ☎ *0578/748683* ⊕ *www.trattorialachiocciola.it* ⊗ *Closed Fri.*

Osteria Sette di Vino

$ | **TUSCAN** | Tasty dishes based on the region's cheeses are the specialty at this simple and inexpensive osteria on a quiet, pleasant square in the center of Pienza. Try versions of pici or the starter of radicchio baked quickly to brown the edges. **Known for:** lively proprietor; bean soup; pecorino tasting menu. ⓢ *Average main: €7* ⊠ *Piazza di Spagna 1, Pienza* ☎ *0578/749092* ⊗ *Closed Wed., July 1–15, and Nov.*

Climb to the top of La Fortezza for the views and then slake your thirst in the on-site enoteca.

Montalcino

19 km (12 miles) northeast of Bagno Vignoni, 41 km (25½ miles) south of Siena, 109 km (68 miles) south of Florence.

Tiny Montalcino, with its commanding view from high on a hill, can claim an Etruscan past. It saw a fair number of travelers, as it was directly on the road from Siena to Rome. During the early Middle Ages it enjoyed a brief period of autonomy before falling under the orbit of Siena in 1201. Now Montalcino's greatest claim to fame is that it produces Brunello di Montalcino, one of Italy's most esteemed reds. Driving to the town, you pass through the brunello vineyards. You can sample the excellent but expensive red in wine cellars in town or visit a nearby winery, such as Fattoria dei Barbi, for a guided tour and tasting; you must call ahead for reservations.

GETTING HERE AND AROUND

By car, follow the SR2 south from Siena, then follow the SP45 to Montalcino. Several Tra-In buses travel between Siena and Montalcino daily, making a tightly scheduled day trip possible. There is no train service available.

VISITOR INFORMATION

CONTACT Montalcino Tourism Office.
✉ *Costa del Municipio 1, Montalcino* ☎ *0577/849331* ⊕ *www.prolocomontalcino.com.*

Sights

La Fortezza

CASTLE/PALACE | FAMILY | Providing refuge for the last remnants of the Sienese army during the Florentine conquest of 1555, the battlements of this 14th-century fortress are still in excellent condition. Climb up the narrow, spiral steps for the 360-degree view of most of southern

Tuscany. An enoteca for tasting wines is on-site. ✉ *Piazzale Fortezza, Montalcino* ☎ *0577/849221* 🎫 *Fortress free, walls €4* 🕐 *Closed Mon. Nov.–Mar.*

Museo Civico e Diocesano d'Arte Sacra
ART MUSEUM | This fine museum is housed in a building that once belonged to 13th-century Augustinian friars. The ticket booth is in the glorious refurbished cloister, and the sacred art collection, gathered from churches throughout the region, is displayed on two floors in former monastic quarters. Although the art here might be called B-list, a fine altarpiece by Bartolo di Fredi (circa 1330–1410), the *Coronation of the Virgin*, makes dazzling use of gold. In addition, there's a striking 12th-century crucifix that originally adorned the high altar of the church of Sant'Antimo. Also on hand are many wood sculptures, a typical medium in these parts during the Renaissance. ✉ *Via Ricasoli 31, Montalcino* ☎ *0577/846014* ⊕ *www.museisenesi.org* 🎫 *€4.50* 🕐 *Closed Mon.*

🍴 Restaurants

Il Grappolo Blu
$ | **ITALIAN** | Any one of this restaurant's *piatti tipici* (typical plates) is worth trying: the local specialty, pici *all'aglione* (thick, long noodles served with sautéed cherry tomatoes and many cloves of garlic), is done particularly well. The chef also has a deft touch with vegetables; if there's fennel on the menu, make sure to try it. **Known for:** convivial atmosphere; great quality and price;

kind, caring staff. **⑤** *Average main: €14* ✉ *Scale di Via Moglio 1, Montalcino* ☎ *0577/847150* ⊕ *www.grappoloblu.it.*

Taverna dei Barbi
$$ | **TUSCAN** | Set among the vineyards that produce excellent Brunello—as well as its younger cousin, Rosso di Montalcino—is this rustic taverna with a large stone fireplace. The estate farm produces many of the ingredients used in such traditional specialties as *stracotto nel brunello* (braised beef cooked with beans in Brunello wine). **Known for:** the superb staff; heavenly aromas coming from grilled meat on a spit; fantastic wines. **⑤** *Average main: €18* ✉ *Podere Podernuovo 170, Montalcino* ☎ *0577/847143* ⊕ *www.fattoriadeibarbi. it* 🕐 *Closed Wed. No dinner Tues.*

🛏 Hotels

La Crociona
$ | **B&B/INN** | **FAMILY** | A quiet and serene family-owned farm in the middle of a small vineyard with glorious views houses guests in lovely apartments that can sleep up to five people. **Pros:** friendly atmosphere; peaceful location; great for families or small groups. **Cons:** need a car to get around; no A/C; family-friendly might not be to everyone's taste. **⑤** *Rooms from: €95* ✉ *Località La Croce 15, Montalcino* ☎ *0577/848007* ⊕ *www.lacrociona.com* 🛏 *7 apartments.*

Abbazia di Sant'Antimo

10 km (6 miles) south of Montalcino, 51 km (32 miles) south of Siena, 19 km (74 miles) south of Florence.

GETTING HERE AND AROUND

The Abbazia di Sant'Antimo, nestled below the town of Castelnuovo dell'Abate, is a 15-minute drive from Montalcino. Tra-In bus service is extremely limited, and the abbey cannot be reached by train.

Sights

★ Abbazia di Sant'Antimo

CHURCH | It's well worth your while to go out of your way to visit this 12th-century Romanesque abbey, as it's a gem of pale stone in the silvery green of an olive grove. The exterior and interior sculpture is outstanding, particularly the nave capitals, a combination of French, Lombard, and even Spanish influences. The sacristy (seldom open) forms part of the primitive Carolingian church (founded in AD 781), its entrance flanked by 9th-century pilasters. The small vaulted crypt dates from the same period. ✉ *Castelnuovo dell'Abate* ☎ *0577/286300* ⊕ *www. antimo.it.*

Chapter 14

UMBRIA AND THE MARCHES

Updated by
Liz Humphreys

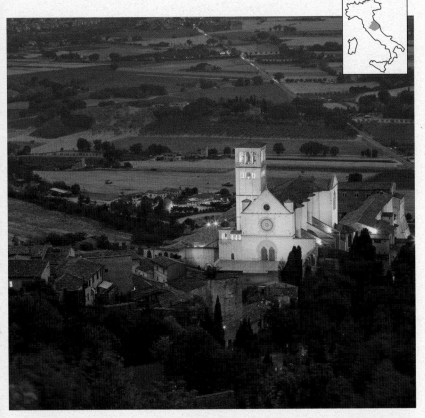

👁 Sights	🍴 Restaurants	🛏 Hotels	🛍 Shopping	🍸 Nightlife
★★★★★	★★★★★	★★★★★	★★★☆☆	★★☆☆☆

WELCOME TO
UMBRIA AND THE MARCHES

TOP REASONS TO GO

★ **Palazzo Ducale, Urbino:** A visit here reveals more about the ideals of the Renaissance than a shelf of history books could.

★ **Assisi, shrine to St. Francis:** Recharge your soul in this rose-color hill town with a visit to the gentle saint's majestic basilica, adorned with great frescoes.

★ **Spoleto, Umbria's musical Mecca:** Crowds descend and prices ascend here during summer's Festival dei Due Mondi, but Spoleto's hushed charm enchants year round.

★ **Tantalizing truffles:** Are Umbria's celebrated "black diamonds" coveted for their pungent flavor, their rarity, or their power in the realm of romance?

★ **Orvieto's Duomo:** Arresting visions of heaven and hell on the facade and brilliant frescoes within make this Gothic cathedral a dazzler.

1 Perugia. Umbria's largest town.

2 Assisi. The city of St. Francis.

3 Gubbio. A medieval mountainous town in North Umbria.

4 Deruta. A 14th-century town famous for its ceramics.

5 Spello. A hilltop town known for its cuisine.

6 Montefalco. Its nickname is the "balcony over Umbria."

7 Spoleto. Come to see the Piazza del Duomo.

8 Todi. Considered Umbria's prettiest hill town.

9 Orvieto. Carved out of volcanic rock and known today for wine and shoe shopping.

10 The Valnerina. Valley of the River Nera.

11 Urbino. See the Palazzo Ducale here.

12 Loreto. Home to the House of the Virgin Mary.

13 Ascoli Piceno. A major producer of fruit and olives in the region.

EATING AND DRINKING WELL IN UMBRIA AND THE MARCHES

Central Italy is mountainous, and its food is hearty and straightforward, with a stick-to-the-ribs quality that sees hardworking farmers and artisans through a long day's work and helps them make the steep climb home at night.

In restaurants here, as in much of Italy, you're rewarded for seeking out the local cuisines, and you'll often find better and cheaper food if you're willing to stray a few hundred yards from the main sights. Spoleto is noted for its good food and service, probably a result of high expectations from the international arts crowd. For gourmet food, however, it's hard to beat Spello, which has both excellent restaurants and first-rate wine merchants.

A rule of thumb for eating well throughout Umbria is to order what's in season; stroll through local markets to see what's for sale. A number of restaurants in the region offer *degustazione* (tasting) menus, which give you a chance to try different local specialties without breaking the bank.

TASTY TRUFFLES

More truffles are found in Umbria than anywhere else in Italy. Spoleto and Norcia are prime territory for the *tartufo nero* (reddish-black interior and fine white veins), prized for its extravagant flavor and intense aroma.

The mild summer truffle, *scorzone estivo* (black outside and beige inside), is in season from May through December. The *scorzone autunnale* (burnt brown color and visible veins inside) is found from October through December.

OLIVE OIL

Nearly everywhere you look in Umbria, olive trees grace the hillsides. The soil of the Apennines allows the olives to ripen slowly, guaranteeing low acidity, a cardinal virtue of fine oil. Look for restaurants that proudly display their own oil, often a sign that they care about their food.

Umbria's finest oil is found in Trevi, where the local product is intensely green and fruity. You can sample it in the town's wine bars, which often offer olive-oil tastings.

PORK PRODUCTS

Much of traditional Umbrian cuisine revolves around pork. It can be cooked in wood-fired stoves, sometimes basted with a rich sauce made from innards and red wine. The roasted pork known as *porchetta* is grilled on a spit and flavored with fennel and herbs, leaving a crisp outer sheen.

The art of pork processing has been handed down through generations in Norcia, so much so that charcuterie producers throughout Italy are often known as *norcini*. Don't miss *prosciutto di Norcia*, which is aged for two years.

LENTILS AND SOUPS

The town of Castelluccio di Norcia is particularly known for its lentils and

its farro (an ancient grain used by the Romans, similar to wheat), and for a variety of beans used in soups. Throughout Umbria, look for *imbrecciata*, a soup of beans and grains, delicately flavored with local herbs. Other ingredients that find their way into thick Umbrian soups are wild beet, sorrel, mushrooms, spelt, chickpeas, and the elusive, fragrant saffron, grown in nearby Cascia.

WINE

Sagrantino grapes are the star in Umbria's most notable red wines. For centuries they've been used in Sagrantino *passito,* a semisweet wine made by leaving the grapes to dry for a period after picking in order to intensify their sugar content. In recent decades, Montefalco Sagrantino *secco* (dry) has occupied the front stage. Both passito and secco have a deep red-ruby color, with a full body and rich flavor.

The abundance of *enotecas* (wineshops and wine bars) has made it easier to arrange wine tastings. Many also let you sample different olive oils on toasted bread, known as bruschetta. Some wine information centers, such as La Strada del Sagrantino in the town of Montefalco, will help set up appointments for tastings.

Birthplace of saints and home to some of the country's greatest artistic treasures, central Italy is a collection of misty green valleys and picture-perfect hill towns laden with centuries of history.

Umbria and the Marches are the Italian countryside as you've imagined it: verdant farmland, steep hillsides topped with medieval fortresses, and winding country roads. No single town here has the extravagant wealth of art and architecture of Florence, Rome, or Venice, but this works in your favor; small jewels of towns feel knowable, not overwhelming. And the cultural cupboard is far from bare. Orvieto's cathedral and Assisi's basilica are two of the most important sights in Italy, while Perugia, Todi, Gubbio, and Spoleto are rich in art and architecture.

East of Umbria, the Marches (Le Marche to Italians) stretch between the Apennines and the Adriatic Sea. It's a region of great turreted castles on high peaks defending passes and roads—a testament to the centuries of battle that have taken place here. Rising majestically in Urbino is a splendid palace, built by Federico da Montefeltro, where the humanistic ideals of the Renaissance came to their fullest flower, while the town of Ascoli Piceno can lay claim to one of the most beautiful squares in Italy. Virtually every small town in the region has a castle, church, or museum worth a visit—but even without them, you'd still be compelled to stop for the interesting streets, panoramic views, and natural beauty.

MAJOR REGIONS

Umbria's largest town, **Perugia,** is home to some of Perugino's great frescoes. **Assisi,** the city of St. Francis, is a major pilgrimage site but still maintains its medieval hill-town character. The quiet towns lying around Perugia include **Deruta,** which produces exceptional ceramics **Spoleto** includes the Piazza del Duomo, the Filippo Lippi frescoes in the cathedral, and the massive castle towering over the town. Of central Italy's many hill towns, none has a more impressive setting than **Orvieto,** perched on a plateau 1,000 feet above the surrounding valley. East of Umbria, the steep, twisting roads of this region lead to well-preserved medieval towns before settling down to the sandy beaches of the Adriatic.

Planning

Making the Most of Your Time

Umbria is a nicely compact collection of character-rich hill towns; you can settle in one, then explore the others, as well as the countryside and forest in between, on day trips.

Perugia, Umbria's largest and liveliest city, is a logical choice for your base, particularly if you're arriving from the north. If you want something a little quieter, virtually any other town in the region will uit your purposes; even Assisi, which overflows with bus tours during the day, is delightfully quiet in the evening and early morning. Spoleto and Orvieto are the most developed towns to the south, but they're still of modest proportions.

If you have the time to venture farther afield, consider trips to Gubbio, northeast of Perugia, and Urbino, in the Marches. Both are worth the time it takes to reach them, and both make for pleasant overnight stays. In southern Umbria, Valnerina and the Piano Grande are out-of-the-way spots with the region's best hiking.

Getting Here and Around

BUS

Perugia's bus station is in Piazza Partigiani, which you can reach by taking the escalators from the town center.

Local bus services between all the major and minor towns of Umbria are good. Some of the routes in rural areas are designed to serve as many places as possible and are, therefore, quite roundabout and slow. Schedules change often, so consult with local tourist offices before setting out.

BUS CONTACTS Flixbus. ⊕ *www.flixbus. com.* **Sulga Line.** ☎ *075/5009641* ⊕ *www. sulga.eu.*

CAR

On the western edge of the region is the Umbrian section of the Autostrada del Sole (A1), Italy's principal north–south highway. It links Florence and Rome with Orvieto and passes near Todi and Terni. The S3 intersects with the A1 and leads on to Assisi and Urbino. The Adriatica superhighway (A14) runs north–south along the coast, linking the Marches to Bologna and Venice.

The steep hills and deep valleys that make Umbria and the Marches so idyllic also make for challenging driving. Fortunately, the area has an excellent, modern road network, but be prepared for tortuous mountain roads if your explorations take you off the beaten track. Central Umbria is served by a major highway, the S75bis, which passes along the shore of Lake Trasimeno and ends in Perugia. Assisi is served by the modern highway S75; the S75 connects to the S3 and S3bis, which cover the heart of the region. Major inland routes connect coastal A14 to large towns in the Marches, but inland secondary roads in mountain areas can be winding and narrow.

TRAIN

Several direct daily trains run by the Italian state railway, **Trenitalia** (892021, www.trenitalia.com), link Florence and Rome with Perugia and Assisi, and local service to the same area is available from Terontola (on the Rome–Florence line) and from Foligno (on the Rome–Ancona line). Intercity trains between Rome and Florence make stops in Orvieto, and the main Rome–Ancona line passes through Narni, Terni, Spoleto, and Foligno.

Restaurants

As befits a landlocked territory, the cuisine of Umbria is firmly based on its fresh agricultural produce. Consequently, most restaurants in the region offer menus that are strictly seasonal, though locals have ensured that the food most associated with Umbria—*tartufi,* or truffles—is available year round thanks to their mastery of freezing, drying, and preserving techniques. Truffles may be added to a variety of dishes, not least the local pastas *stringozzi* (also written *strengozzi* or *strangozzi*) and *ombrichelli*. Lamb, pork, and boar are the most common meats consumed in Umbria, while lentils grown around Castelluccio are also highly prized. Seafood from the Adriatic predominates in the coastal Marches region, often made into *brodetto,* a savory fish soup. Inland, Ascoli Piceno is renowned for its stuffed green olives.

Restaurant reviews have been shortened. For full information, visit Fodors.com.

Hotels

Virtually every older town, no matter how small, has some kind of hotel. A trend, particularly around Gubbio, Orvieto, and Todi, is to convert old villas, farms, and monasteries into first-class hotels. The natural splendor of the countryside more than compensates for the distance from town—provided you have a car. Hotels in town tend to be simpler than their country cousins, with a few notable exceptions in Spoleto, Gubbio, and Perugia.

Hotel reviews have been shortened. For full information, visit Fodors.com.

WHAT IT COSTS in Euros			
$	$$	$$$	$$$$
RESTAURANTS			
under €15	€15–€24	€25–€35	over €35
HOTELS			
under €125	€125–€200	€201–€300	over €300

Visitor Information

Umbria Regional Tourism Office. ⊠ *Piazza Matteotti 18, Perugia* ☎ *075/5736458* ⊕ *www.umbriatourism.it.*

Perugia

Perugia is a majestic, handsome, wealthy city, and with its trendy boutiques, refined cafés, and grandiose architecture, it doesn't try to hide its affluence. A student population of around 30,000 means that the city, with a permanent population of about 165,000, is abuzz with activity throughout the year. Umbria Jazz, one of the region's most important music festivals, attracts music lovers from around the world every July, and Eurochocolate, the international chocolate festival, is an irresistible draw each October for anyone with a sweet tooth.

GETTING HERE AND AROUND

The best approach to the city is by train. The area around the station doesn't attest to the rest of Perugia's elegance, but buses running from the station to Piazza d'Italia, the heart of the old town, are frequent. If you're in a hurry, take the *minimetro,* a one-line subway, to Stazione della Cupa. If you're driving to Perugia and your hotel doesn't have parking facilities, leave your car in one of the lots close to the center. Electronic displays indicate the location of lots and the number of spaces free. If you park in the Piazza Partigiani, take the escalators that pass through the fascinating subterranean excavations of the Roman foundations of the city and lead to the town center.

👁 Sights

Collegio del Cambio (*Bankers' Guild Hall*)
HISTORIC SIGHT | These elaborate rooms, on the ground floor of the **Palazzo dei Priori,** served as the meeting hall and chapel of the guild of bankers and money changers. Most of the frescoes were completed by the most important Perugian painter of the Renaissance, Pietro Vannucci, better known as Perugino. He included a remarkably honest self-portrait on one of the pilasters. The iconography includes common religious themes, such as the Nativity and the Transfiguration seen on the end walls. On the left wall are female figures representing the virtues, and beneath them are the heroes and sages of antiquity. On the right wall are figures presumed to have been painted in part by Perugino's most famous pupil, Raphael. (His hand, experts say, is most apparent in the figure of Fortitude.) The *cappella* (chapel) of San Giovanni Battista has frescoes painted by Giannicola di Paolo, another student of

Perugino's. ⊠ *Corso Vannucci 25, Perugia* ☎ *075/5728599* ⊕ *www.collegiodelcambio.it* ⊗ *Closed Sun. afternoon, also Mon. afternoon Nov.–Mar.* 🎫 *€4.50.*

Corso Vannucci

STREET | A string of elegantly connected palazzi expresses the artistic nature of this city center, the heart of which is concentrated along Corso Vannucci. Stately and broad, this pedestrian-only street runs from Piazza Italia to Piazza IV Novembre. Along the way, the entrances to many of Perugia's side streets might tempt you to wander off and explore. But don't stray too far as evening falls, when Corso Vannucci fills with Perugians out for their evening *passeggiata*, a pleasant predinner stroll that may include a pause for an aperitif at one of the many bars that line the street. ⊠ *Perugia.*

Duomo

CHURCH | Severe yet mystical, the Cathedral of San Lorenzo is most famous for being the home of the wedding ring of the Virgin Mary, stolen by the Perugians in 1488 from the nearby town of Chiusi. The ring, kept high up in a red-curtained vault in the chapel immediately to the left of the entrance, is stored under lock and key—15 locks, to be precise—most of the year. It's shown to the public on July 30 (the day it was brought to Perugia) and the second-to-last Sunday in January (Mary's wedding anniversary). The cathedral itself dates from the Middle Ages, and has many additions from the 15th and 16th centuries. The most visually interesting element is the altar to the Madonna of Grace; an elegant fresco on a column at the right of the entrance of the altar depicts La Madonna delle Grazie. Sections of the church may be closed to visitors during religious services. The **Museo Capitolare** displays a large array of precious objects associated with the cathedral, including vestments, vessels, and manuscripts. Outside the Duomo is the elaborate **Fontana Maggiore,** which dates from 1278. It's adorned with zodiac figures and symbols of the seven arts. ⊠ *Piazza IV Novembre, Perugia* ☎ *075/5723832* ⊕ *www.cattedrale.perugia.it* 🏛 *Museum €6* ⊗ *Museum closed Mon. Nov.–Mar.*

★ Galleria Nazionale dell'Umbria

ART MUSEUM | The region's most comprehensive art gallery is housed on the fourth floor of the **Palazzo dei Priori.** Enhanced by skillfully lit displays and computers that allow you to focus on the works' details and background information, the collection includes work by native artists—most notably Pintoricchio (1454–1513) and Perugino (circa 1450–1523)—and others of the Umbrian and Tuscan schools, among them Gentile da Fabriano (1370–1427), Duccio (circa 1255–1318), Fra Angelico (1387–1455), Fiorenzo di Lorenzo (1445–1525), and Piero della Francesca (1420–92). In addition to paintings, the gallery has frescoes, sculptures, and some superb examples of crucifixes from the 13th and 14th centuries. Some rooms are dedicated to Perugia itself, showing how the medieval city evolved. ⊠ *Corso Vannucci 19, Perugia* ☎ *075/58668415* ⊕ *www.gallerianazionaledellumbria.it* 🏛 *€8* ⊗ *Closed Mon.*

Museo Archeologico Nazionale

HISTORY MUSEUM | An excellent collection of Etruscan artifacts from throughout the region sheds light on Perugia as a flourishing Etruscan city long before it fell under Roman domination in 310 BC. Little else remains of Perugia's mysterious ancestors, although the Arco di Augusto, in Piazza Fortebraccio, the northern entrance to the city, is of Etruscan origin. ⊠ *Piazza G. Bruno 10, Perugia* ☎ *075/5727141* ⊕ *www.polomusealeumbria.beniculturali.it* 🏛 *€5* ⊗ *Closed Mon.*

Palazzo dei Priori (*Palace of the Priors*)

GOVERNMENT BUILDING | A series of elegant connected buildings, the palazzo serves as Perugia's city hall and houses three of the city's museums. The buildings string along Corso Vannucci and wrap around the Piazza IV Novembre, where the original entrance is located. The steps here lead to the **Sala dei Notari** (Notaries' Hall). Other entrances lead to the **Galleria Nazionale dell'Umbria,** the **Collegio del Cambio,** and the **Collegio della Mercanzia.** The Sala dei Notari, which dates back to the 13th century and was the original meeting place of the town merchants, had become the seat of the notaries by the second half of the 15th century. Wood beams and an interesting array of frescoes attributed to Maestro di Farneto embellish the room. Coats of arms and crests line the back and right lateral walls; you can spot some famous figures from Aesop's *Fables* on the left wall. The palazzo facade is adorned with symbols of Perugia's pride and past power: the griffin is the city symbol, and the lion denotes Perugia's allegiance to the Guelph (or papal) cause. ⊠ *Piazza IV Novembre 25, Perugia* 🏛 *Free.*

Rocca Paolina

CASTLE/PALACE | A labyrinth of little streets, alleys, and arches, this underground city was originally part of a fortress built at the behest of Pope Paul III between 1540 and 1543 to confirm papal dominion over the city. Parts of it were destroyed after the end of papal rule, but much still remains. Begin your visit by taking the escalators that descend through the subterranean ruins from Piazza Italia down to Via Masi. In the summer this is the coolest place in the city. ⊠ *Piazza Italia, Perugia* 🏛 *Free.*

🍽 Restaurants

Antica Trattoria San Lorenzo

$$ | UMBRIAN | Both the food and the service are outstanding at this popular small, brick-vaulted eatery next to the

Umbria Through the Ages

The earliest inhabitants of Umbria, the Umbri, were thought by the Romans to be the most ancient inhabitants of Italy. Little is known about them; with the coming of Etruscan culture the tribe fled into the mountains in the eastern portion of the region. The Etruscans, who founded some of the great cities of Umbria, were in turn supplanted by the Romans. Unlike Tuscany and other regions of central Italy, Umbria had few powerful medieval families to exert control over the cities in the Middle Ages—its proximity to Rome ensured that it would always be more or less under papal domination.

In the center of the country, Umbria has for much of its history been a battlefield where armies from north and south clashed. Hannibal destroyed a Roman army on the shores of Lake Trasimeno, and the bloody course of the interminable Guelph–Ghibelline conflict of the Middle Ages was played out here. Dante considered Umbria the most violent place in Italy. Trophies of war still decorate the Palazzo dei Priori in Perugia, and the little town of Gubbio continues a warlike rivalry begun in the Middle Ages—every year it challenges the Tuscan town of Sansepolcro to a cross-bow tournament. Today the bowmen shoot at targets, but neither side has forgotten that 500 years ago they were shooting at each other.

In spite of—or perhaps because of—this bloodshed, Umbria has produced more than its share of Christian saints. The most famous is St. Francis, the decidedly pacifist saint whose life shaped the Church of his time. His great shrine at Assisi is visited by hundreds of thousands of pilgrims each year. St. Clare, his devoted follower, was Umbria-born, as were St. Benedict, St. Rita of Cascia, and the patron saint of lovers, St. Valentine.

Duomo. Particular attention is paid to adapting traditional Umbrian cuisine to the modern palate, and there's also a nice variety of seafood dishes on the menu—the *pacchero di Gragnano* (pasta with smoked eggplant, cod, clams, scampi, and prawns) is a real treat. ⑤ *Average main: €22* ✉ *Piazza Danti 19/a, Perugia* ☎ *075/5721956* ⊕ *www.anticatrattori-asanlorenzo.com.*

Dal Mi' Cocco

$$ | UMBRIAN | A great favorite with Perugia's university students, it is fun, crowded, and inexpensive; you may find yourself seated at a long table with other diners, but some language help from your neighbors could come in handy—the menu is in pure Perugian dialect. Fixed-price meals change with the season, and each day of the week brings some new creation *dal cocco* (from the "coconut," or head) of the chef. ⑤ *Average main: €15* ✉ *Corso Garibaldi 12, Perugia* ☎ *075/5732511* ⊙ *Closed Mon. and late July–mid-Aug.*

Ristorante La Rosetta

$$ | ITALIAN | The dining room of the hotel of the same name is a peaceful, elegant spot for travelers seeking to get away from the bustle of central Perugia; in winter you dine inside under medieval vaults, and in summer, in the cool courtyard. The food is simple but reliable, and flawlessly served. ⑤ *Average main: €18* ✉ *Piazza d'Italia 19, Perugia* ☎ *075/3747858* ⊕ *www.ristorantelarosettaperugia.com.*

Ristorante La Taverna

$$ | UMBRIAN | Medieval steps lead to a rustic two-story space where wine bottles and artful clutter decorate the walls. The regional menu features lots of delicious house-made pastas and grilled meats prepared by chef Claudio, served up in substantial portions, plus generous shavings of truffle in season. $ *Average main: €22* ⊠ *Via delle Streghe 8, off Corso Vannucci, Perugia* ☎ *075/5724128* ⊕ *www.ristorantelataverna.com.*

★ Osteria a Priori

$ | MODERN ITALIAN | This charming wine-and-olive-oil shop with a restaurant (with vaulted ceilings and exposed brick) tucked into the back offers up small plates using ingredients with a "zero-kilometer" philosophy: everything comes from local and artisanal Umbrian producers. Regional cheeses, homemade pastas, and slow-cooked meats steal the show and, as might be expected, the selection of wine is top-notch. $ *Average main: €12* ⊠ *Via dei Priori 39, Perugia* ☎ *075/5727098* ⊕ *www.osteriaapriori.it* ⊗ *Closed Sun.*

Hotels

Alla Posta dei Donini

$ | HOTEL | Beguilingly comfortable guest rooms are set on lovely grounds, where gardeners go quietly about their business. **Pros:** great restaurant; plush atmosphere; a quiet and private getaway. **Cons:** uninteresting village; outside Perugia; spa sometimes overcrowded. $ *Rooms from: €119* ⊠ *Via Deruta 43, 15 km (9 miles) south of Perugia, San Martino in Campo* ☎ *075/609132* ⊕ *www.postadonini.it* ⌁ *48 rooms* ❖ *No Meals.*

Locanda della Posta

$$ | HOTEL | Renovations have left the lobby and other public areas rather bland, but the rooms in this converted 18th-century palazzo are soothingly decorated in muted colors. **Pros:** exudes good taste and refinement; some fine views; central location. **Cons:** some small rooms; some street noise; no public areas. $ *Rooms from: €134* ⊠ *Corso Vannucci 97, Perugia* ☎ *075/5728925* ⊕ *www.locandadellapostahotel.it* ⌁ *17 rooms* ❖ *Free Breakfast.*

Sina Brufani

$$ | HOTEL | Though a tad old-fashioned, this elegant centrally located hotel dating from 1884 is the most upscale accommodation in town. **Pros:** excellent views from many rooms; wonderful location; unique spa area. **Cons:** in-house restaurant not up to par; could use a refresh; service can be hit-or-miss. $ *Rooms from: €185* ⊠ *Piazza Italia 12, Perugia* ☎ *075/5732541* ⊕ *www.sinahotels.com/ en/h/sina-brufani-perugia* ⌁ *94 rooms* ❖ *No Meals.*

Tre Vaselle

$$ | HOTEL | Rooms spread throughout four stone buildings are spacious and graced with floors of typical red-clay Tuscan tiles. **Pros:** nice pool; perfect for visiting the Torgiano wine area and Deruta; friendly staff. **Cons:** in center of uninspiring village; somewhat far from Perugia; service occasionally falters. $ *Rooms from: €145* ⊠ *Via Garibaldi 48, Torgiano* ☎ *075/9880447* ⊕ *www.3vaselle.it* ⌁ *51 rooms* ❖ *No Meals.*

🍸 Nightlife

With its large student population, the city has plenty to offer in the way of bars and clubs. The best ones are around the city center, off Corso Vannucci.

🛍 Shopping

Take a stroll down any of Perugia's main streets, including Corso Vannucci, Via dei Priori, Via Oberdan, and Via Sant'Ercolano, and you'll see many well-known designer boutiques and specialty shops.

The most typical thing to buy in Perugia is some Perugina chocolate, which you can find almost anywhere. The best-known chocolates made by Perugina

now owned by Nestlé) are the choco-
late-and-hazelnut-filled nibbles called Baci
(literally, "kisses"). They're wrapped in
silver foil that includes a sliver of paper,
like the fortune in a fortune cookie, with
multilingual romantic sentiments or
sayings.

Assisi

The small town of Assisi is one of the
Christian world's most important pilgrimage sites and home of the Basilica di
San Francesco—built to honor St. Francis
(1182–1226) and erected in swift order
after his death. The peace and serenity
of the town are a welcome respite after
the hustle and bustle of some of Italy's
major cities.

Like most other towns in the region,
Assisi began as an Umbri settlement in
the 7th century BC and was conquered
by the Romans 400 years later. The town
was Christianized by St. Rufino, its patron
saint, in the 3rd century, but it's the spirit
of St. Francis, a patron saint of Italy and
founder of the Franciscan monastic order,
that's felt throughout its narrow medieval
streets. The famous 13th-century basilica
was decorated by the greatest artists of
the period.

GETTING HERE AND AROUND

Assisi lies on the Terontola–Foligno rail
line, with almost hourly connections
to Perugia and direct trains to Rome
and Florence several times a day. The
Stazione Centrale is 4 km (2½ miles)
from town, with a bus service about
every half hour. Assisi is easily reached
from the A1 autostrada (Rome–Florence)
and the S75b highway. The walled town
is closed to traffic, so cars must be left in
the parking lots at Porta San Pietro, near
Porta Nuova, or beneath Piazza Matteotti.
Pay your parking fee at the *cassa* (ticket
booth) before you return to your car to
get a ticket to insert in the machine that

will allow you to exit. It's a short but
sometimes steep walk into the center
of town; frequent minibuses (buy tickets
from a newsstand or tobacco shop
near where you park your car) make the
rounds of weary pilgrims.

◉ Sights

Assisi is pristinely medieval in architecture and appearance, owing in large part
to relative neglect from the 16th century
until 1926, when the celebration of the
700th anniversary of St. Francis's death
brought more than 2 million visitors.
Since then, pilgrims have flocked here in
droves, and today several million arrive
each year to pay homage. But not even
the constant flood of visitors to this town
of 30,000 residents can spoil the singular
beauty of this significant religious center,
the home of some of the Western tradition's most important works of art. The
hill on which Assisi sits rises dramatically from the flat plain, and the town is
dominated by a medieval castle at the
very top.

Even though Assisi is sometimes
besieged by busloads of sightseers who
clamor to visit the famous basilica, it's
difficult not to be charmed by the tranquility of the town and its medieval architecture. Once you've seen the basilica,
stroll through the town's narrow winding
streets to see beautiful vistas of the
nearby hills and valleys peeking through
openings between the buildings.

★ Basilica di San Francesco

CHURCH | The basilica isn't one church but
two: the Gothic church on the upper level, and the Romanesque church on the
lower level. Work on this two-tiered mon-
olith was begun in 1228. Both churches
are magnificently decorated artistic treas-
ure-houses, covered floor to ceiling with
some of Europe's finest frescoes: the
Lower Basilica is dim and full of candle-
light shadows, while the Upper Basilica

Continued on page 672

Assisi

Basilica di San Francesco
see feature in this chapter

Rocca Maggiore

Anfiteatro Romano

KEY

- **1** Exploring Sights
- **1** Restaurants
- **1** Hotels
- Steps

TO SANTA MARIA
DEGLI ANGELI
AND TRAIN STATION

TO
SAN DAMIANO

Sights ▶

1 Basilica
di San Francesco......**A1**
2 Basilica di Santa
Chiara......**F2**
3 Cattedrale di San
Rufino......**F2**
4 Eremo delle Carceri......**H2**

5 Santa Maria Sopra
Minerva......**E2**

Restaurants ▶

1 Buca di
San Francesco......**D2**
2 La Pallotta......**E2**
3 Osteria Piazzetta
dell'Erba......**E2**
4 Ristorante
San Francesco......**A3**

Hotels ▶

1 Castello di Petrata......**G1**
2 Hotel Umbra......**E2**
3 Nun Assisi Relais
& Spa Museum......**G1**

200 yards

200 meters

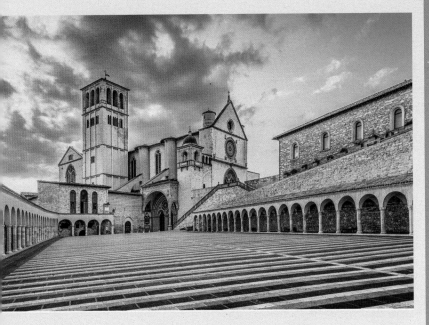

ASSISI'S BASILICA DI SAN FRANCESCO

The legacy of St. Francis, founder of the Franciscan monastic order, pervades Assisi. Each year the town hosts several million pilgrims, but the steady flow of visitors does nothing to diminish the singular beauty of one of Italy's most important religious centers. The pilgrims' ultimate destination is the massive Basilica di San Francesco, which sits halfway up Assisi's hill, supported by graceful arches.

The basilica is not one church but two. The Romanesque Lower Church came first; construction began in 1228, just two years after St. Francis's death, and was completed within a few years. The low ceilings and candlelit interior make an appropriately solemn setting for St. Francis's tomb, found in the crypt below the main altar. The Gothic Upper Church, built only half a century later, sits on top of the lower one, and is strikingly different, with soaring arches and tall stained-glass windows (the first in Italy). Inside, both churches are covered floor to ceiling with some of Europe's finest frescoes: the Lower Church is dim and full of candlelit shadows, and the Upper Church is bright and airy.

VISITING THE BASILICA

THE LOWER CHURCH

The most evocative way to experience the basilica is to begin with the dark Lower Church. As you enter, give your eyes a moment to adjust. Keep in mind that the artists at work here were conscious of the shadowy environment—they knew this was how their frescoes would be seen.

In the first chapel to the left, a superb fresco cycle by Simone Martini depicts scenes from the life of St. Martin. As you approach the main altar, the vaulting above you is decorated with the Three Virtues of St. Francis (poverty, chastity, and obedience) and St. Francis's Triumph, frescoes attributed to Giotto's followers. In the transept to your left, Pietro Lorenzetti's Madonna and Child with St. Francis and St. John sparkles when the sun hits it. Notice Mary's thumb; legend has it Jesus is asking which saint to bless, and Mary is pointing to Francis. Across the way in the right transept, Cimabue's Madonna Enthroned Among Angels and St. Francis is a famous portrait of the saint. Surrounding the portrait are painted scenes from the childhood of Christ, done by the assistants of Giotto. Nearby is a painting of the crucifixion attributed to Giotto himself.

You reach the crypt via stairs midway along the nave—on the crypt's altar, a stone coffin holds the saint's body. Steps up from the transepts lead to the cloister, where there's a gift shop, and the treasury, which contains holy objects.

THE UPPER CHURCH

The St. Francis fresco cycle is the highlight of the Upper Church. (*See facing page.*) Also worth special note is the 16th-century choir, with its remarkably delicate inlaid wood. When a 1997 earthquake rocked the basilica, the St. Francis cycle sustained little damage, but portions of the ceiling above the entrance and altar collapsed, reducing their frescoes (attributed to Cimabue and Giotto) to rubble. The painstaking restoration is ongoing. ⚠ **The dress code is strictly enforced—no bare shoulders or bare knees.**

FRANCIS, ITALY'S PATRON SAINT

PREGANDO ASPETTERO CHE TORNI

St. Francis was born in Assisi in 1181, the son of a noblewoman and a well-to-do merchant. His troubled youth included a year in prison. He planned a military career, but after a long illness Francis heard the voice of God, renounced his father's wealth, and began a life of austerity. His mystical embrace of poverty, asceticism, and the beauty of man and nature struck a responsive chord in the medieval mind; he quickly attracted a vast number of followers. Francis was the first saint to receive the stigmata (wounds in his hands, feet, and side corresponding to those of Christ on the cross). He died on October 4, 1226, in the Porziuncola, the secluded chapel in the woods where he had first preached the virtue of poverty to his disciples. St. Francis was declared patron saint of Italy in 1939, and today the Franciscans make up the largest of the Catholic orders.

THE UPPER CHURCH'S ST. FRANCIS FRESCO CYCLE

The 28 frescoes in the Upper Church depicting the life of St. Francis are the most admired works in the entire basilica. They're also the subject of one of art history's biggest controversies. For centuries they thought to be by Giotto (1267-1337), the great early Renaissance innovator, but inconsistencies in style, both within this series and in comparison to later Giotto works, have thrown their origin into question. Some scholars now say Giotto was the brains behind the cycle, but that assistants helped with the execution; others claim he couldn't have been involved at all.

Two things are certain. First, the style is revolutionary—which argues for

Giotto's involvement. The tangible weight of the figures, the emotion they show, and the use of perspective all look familiar to modern eyes, but in the art of the time there was nothing like it. Second, these images have played a major part in shaping how the world sees St. Francis. In that respect, who painted them hardly matters.

Starting in the transept, the frescoes circle the church, showing events in the saint's life (and afterlife). Some of the best are grouped near the church's entrance—look for the nativity at Greccio, the miracle of the spring, the death of the knight at Celano, and, most famously, the sermon to the birds.

The St. Francis fresco cycle
1. Homage of a simple man
2. Giving cloak to a poor man
3. Dream of the palace
4. Hearing the voice of God
5. Rejection of worldly goods
6. Dream of Innocent III
7. Confirmation of the rules
8. Vision of flaming chariot
9. Vision of celestial thrones
10. Chasing devils from Arezzo
11. Before the sultan
12. Ecstasy of St. Francis
13. Nativity at Greccio
14. Miracle of the spring
15. Sermon to the birds
16. Death of knight at Celano
17. Preaching to Honorius III
18. Apparition at Arles
19. Receiving the stigmata
20. Death of St. Francis
21. Apparition before Bishop Guido and Fra Agostino
22. Verification of the stigmata
23. Mourning of St. Clare
24. Canonization
25. Apparition before Gregory IX
26. Healing of a devotee
27. Confession of a woman
28. Repentant heretic freed

is bright and airy. In the **Upper Church,** the magnificent frescoes from 13th-century Italian painter Giotto, painted when he was only in his twenties, show that he was a pivotal artist in the development of Western painting. He broke away from the stiff, unnatural styles of earlier generations to move toward realism and three-dimensionality. The **Lower Church** features frescoes by celebrated Sienese painters Simone Martini and Pietro Lorenzetti, as well as by Giotto (or his assistants). The basilica's dress code is strictly enforced—no bare shoulders or bare knees are permitted. ⊠ *Piazza di San Francesco, Assisi* ☎ *075/8190084* ⊕ *www.sanfrancescoassisi.org* ⊠ *Free.*

Basilica di Santa Chiara

CHURCH | The lovely, wide piazza in front of this church is reason enough to visit. The red-and-white-striped facade frames the piazza's panoramic view over the Umbrian plains. Santa Chiara is dedicated to St. Clare, one of the earliest and most fervent of St. Francis's followers and the founder of the order of the Poor Ladies— or Poor Clares—which was based on the Franciscan monastic order. The church contains Clare's body, and in the **Cappella del Crocifisso** (on the right) is the cross that spoke to St. Francis. A heavily veiled nun of the Poor Clares order is usually stationed before the cross in adoration of the image. ⊠ *Piazza Santa Chiara, Assisi* ☎ *075/812216* ⊕ *www.assisisantachiara. it* ⊠ *Free.*

Cattedrale di San Rufino

CHURCH | St. Francis and St. Clare were among those baptized in Assisi's Cattedrale, which was the principal church in town until the 12th century. The baptismal font has since been redecorated, but it's possible to see the crypt of St. Rufino, the bishop who brought Christianity to Assisi and was martyred on August 11, 238 (or 236 by some accounts), as well as climb to the bell tower. Admission to the crypt includes the small Museo della Cattedrale, with its detached frescoes

and artifacts. ⊠ *Piazza San Rufino, Assisi* ☎ *075/812712* ⊕ *www.assisimuseodiocesano.it* ⊠ *Church free, Crypt and Museum €3.50, Bell Tower and Museum €4, Bell Tower €1.50* ⊘ *Bell tower closed Wed.*

Eremo delle Carceri

RELIGIOUS BUILDING | About 4 km (2½ miles) east of Assisi is a monastery set in a dense wood against Monte Subasio: the Hermitage of Prisons. This was the place where St. Francis and his followers went to "imprison" themselves in prayer. The only site in Assisi that remains essentially unchanged since St. Francis's time, the church and monastery are the kinds of tranquil places that St. Francis would have appreciated. The walk out from town is very pleasant, and many trails lead from here across the wooded hillside of Monte Subasio (now a protected forest), with beautiful vistas across the Umbrian countryside. True to their Franciscan heritage, the friars here are entirely dependent on alms from visitors. ⊠ *Via Santuario delle Carceri, 4 km (2½ miles) east of Assisi, Assisi* ☎ *075/812301* ⊠ *Donations accepted.*

Santa Maria Sopra Minerva

CHURCH | Dating from the time of the Emperor Augustus (27 BC–AD 14), this structure was originally dedicated to the Roman goddess of wisdom, and in later times it was used as a monastery and prison before being converted into a church in the 16th century. The expectations raised by the perfect classical facade are not met by the interior, which was subjected to a thorough Baroque transformation in the 17th century. ⊠ *Piazza del Comune, Assisi* ☎ *075/812361* ⊠ *Free.*

 Restaurants

Buca di San Francesco

$ | **UMBRIAN** | In summer, dine in a cool green garden; in winter, under the low brick arches of the cozy cellars.

The unique settings and the first-rate fare make this central restaurant one of Assisi's busiest; try the namesake homemade spaghetti *alla buca,* served with a roasted mushroom sauce. **Known for:** warm and welcoming service; cozy atmosphere; historical surroundings. $ *Average main: €14* ✉ *Via Eugenio Brizi 1, Assisi* ☎ *075/812204* ⊕ *bu-ca-di-san-francesco.business.site* ⊙ *Closed Mon. and 10 days in late July.*

La Pallotta

$$ | **UMBRIAN** | At this homey, family-run trattoria with a crackling fireplace and stone walls, the women do the cooking and the men serve the food; try the *strangozzi alla pallotta* (thick spaghetti with a pesto of olives and mushrooms). Connected to the restaurant is an inn whose eight rooms have firm beds and some views across the rooftops of town. $ *Average main: €15* ✉ *Vicolo della Volta Pinta 3, Assisi* ☎ *075/8155273* ⊕ *www.trattoriapallotta.it* ⊙ *Closed Tues.*

Osteria Piazzetta dell'Erba

$$ | **UMBRIAN** | Hip service and sophisticated presentations attract locals, who enjoy Italian cuisine with unusual twists (think porcini mushroom risotto with blue cheese and blueberries), a nice selection of salads—unusual for an Umbrian restaurant—and intriguing desserts. The enthusiastic young team keep things running smoothly and the energy high. **Known for:** intimate ambience; friendly staff; inventive dishes. $ *Average main: €18* ✉ *Via San Gabriele dell'Addolorata 15/b, Assisi* ☎ *075/815352* ⊕ *www.osteriapiazzettadellerba.it/en* ⊙ *Closed Mon. and a few wks in Jan. or Feb.*

Ristorante San Francesco

$$ | **UMBRIAN** | An excellent view of the Basilica di San Francesco from the covered terrace is just one reason to enjoy this traditional restaurant, where Umbrian dishes are made with aromatic locally grown herbs. Menus change seasonally and include a fine selection of pastas and mains; appetizers and desserts are also especially good. **Known for:** pleasant staff; excellent location; pleasing desserts. $ *Average main: €20* ✉ *Via di San Francesco 52, Assisi* ☎ *075/813302* ⊕ *www.ristorantesanfrancesco.com* ⊙ *Closed Wed. Nov.–Easter and 1–2 wks early July.*

Hotels

Advance reservations are essential at Assisi's hotels between Easter and October and over Christmas. Latecomers are often forced to stay in the modern town of Santa Maria degli Angeli, 8 km (5 miles) away. As a last-minute option, you can always inquire at restaurants to see if they're renting out rooms.

Until the early 1980s, pilgrim hostels outnumbered ordinary hotels in Assisi, and they present an intriguing and economical alternative to conventional lodgings. They're usually called *conventi* or *ostelli* ("convents" or "hostels") because they're run by convents, churches, or other Catholic organizations. Rooms are spartan but peaceful. Check with the tourist office for a list.

★ Castello di Petrata

$$ | **HOTEL** | Wood beams and sections of exposed medieval stonework add a lot of character to this fortress built in the 14th century, while comfortable couches turn each individually decorated room into a delightful retreat. **Pros:** peaceful pool; great views of town and countryside; medieval character. **Cons:** far from Assisi town center; slightly isolated; limited choices in restaurant. $ *Rooms from: €171* ✉ *Via Petrata 25, Località Petrata, Assisi* ☎ *075/815451* ⊕ *www.castellopetrata.it* ⊙ *Closed Sun.–Wed. Jan.–mid-Mar.* ⇌ *20 rooms* ⦿ *Free Breakfast.*

Hotel Umbra

$ | **HOTEL** | Rooms on the upper floors of this charming 16th-century town house near Piazza del Comune look out over the Assisi rooftops to the valley below, as does the sunny, vine-covered terrace. **Pros:** excellent valley views from some rooms; very central; pleasant small garden. **Cons:** some small rooms; difficult parking; uninspiring breakfasts. $ *Rooms from: €100* ✉ *Via degli Archi 6, Assisi* ☎ *075/812240* ⊕ *www.hotelumbra.it* ⊘ *Closed Nov.–late Mar.* ⇱ *24 rooms* ⦿ *Free Breakfast.*

★ Nun Assisi Relais & Spa Museum

$$$$ | HOTEL | A monastery built in 1275 has been converted into a thoroughly contemporary, high-end place to stay with a fabulous spa carved out of 2,000-year-old Roman baths and within walking distance of Assisi's restaurants and shops. **Pros:** wonderful place to relax; fantastic blend of the historic and modern; excellent restaurant. **Cons:** on-site parking costs extra; on the expensive side; split-level rooms with stairs difficult for those with mobility issues. $ *Rooms from: €328* ✉ *Via Eremo delle Carceri 1A,* *Assisi* ☎ *075/8155150* ⊕ *www.nunassisi.* *com* ⇱ *18 rooms* ⦿ *Free Breakfast.*

Gubbio

35 km (22 miles) southeast of Città di Castello, 39 km (24 miles) northeast of Perugia, 92 km (57 miles) east of Arezzo.

There's something otherworldly about this jewel of a medieval town tucked away in a mountainous corner of Umbria. Even at the height of summer, the cool serenity and quiet of Gubbio's streets remain intact. The town is perched on the slopes of Monte Ingino, meaning the streets are dramatically steep. Gubbio's relatively isolated position has kept it free of hordes of high-season visitors, and most of the year the city lives up to its Italian nickname, "La Città del Silenzio"

(City of Silence). Parking in the central Piazza dei Quaranta Martiri—named for 40 hostages murdered by the Nazis in 1944—is easy and secure, and it's wise to leave your car in the piazza and explore the narrow streets on foot.

At Christmas, kitsch is king. From December 7 to January 10, colored lights are strung down the mountainside in a shape resembling an evergreen, the world's largest Christmas tree.

GETTING HERE AND AROUND

The closest train station is Fossato di Vico, about 20 km (12 miles) from Gubbio. Twelve daily buses (five on Sunday) connect the train station with the city, a 30-minute trip. If you're driving from Perugia, take the SS298, which rises steeply up toward the Gubbio hills. The trip will take you one hour. There are also 11 buses a day (4 on Sunday) that leave from Perugia's Piazza Partigiani, the main Perugia bus terminal.

VISITOR INFORMATION

CONTACT Gubbio Tourism Office. ✉ Via della Repubblica 15, Gubbio ☎ 075/9220693 ⊕ www.comune.gubbio.pg.it.

Sights

Basilica di Sant'Ubaldo

CHURCH | Gubbio's famous *ceri*—three 16-foot-tall pillars crowned with statues of Saints Ubaldo, George, and Anthony—are housed in this basilica atop Monte Ingino. The pillars are transported to the Palazzo dei Consoli on the first Sunday of May, in preparation for the Festa dei Ceri, one of central Italy's most spectacular festivals. ✉ Monte Ingino, Gubbio ☎ 075/9273872 🎟 Free.

Duomo

CHURCH | On a narrow street on the highest tier of the town, the Duomo dates from the 13th century, with some Baroque additions—in particular, a lavishly decorated bishop's chapel. ✉ Via Ducale, Gubbio 🎟 Free.

Funicular

TRANSPORTATION | **FAMILY** | For a bracing ride to the top of Monte Ingino, hop on the funicular that climbs the hillside just outside the city walls at the eastern end of town. It's definitely not for those who suffer from vertigo. Operating hours vary considerably from month to month; check the funicular's website. ✉ Via San Girolamo, Gubbio ☎ 075/9277507 ⊕ www.funiviagubbio.it 🎟 From €4.

Palazzo dei Consoli

HISTORY MUSEUM | Gubbio's striking Piazza Grande is dominated by this medieval palazzo, attributed to a local architect known as Gattapone, who is still much admired by today's residents (though some scholars have suggested that the palazzo was in fact the work of another architect, Angelo da Orvieto). In the Middle Ages the Parliament of Gubbio assembled in the palace, which has become a symbol of the town and now houses a museum with a collection famous chiefly for the Tavole Eugubine. These seven bronze tablets are written in the ancient Umbrian language, employing Etruscan and Latin characters, and provide the best key to understanding this obscure tongue. Also in the museum is a fascinating miscellany of rare coins and earthenware pots. A lofty loggia provides exhilarating views over Gubbio's roofscape and beyond. For a few days at the beginning of May, the palace also displays the famous *ceri,* the ceremonial wooden pillars at the center of Gubbio's annual festivities. ✉ Piazza Grande, Gubbio ☎ 075/9274298 ⊕ www.palazzodeiconsoli.it 🎟 €7.

Palazzo Ducale

CASTLE/PALACE | This scaled-down copy of the Palazzo Ducale in Urbino (Gubbio was once the possession of that city's ruling family, the Montefeltro) contains a small museum and a courtyard. Some of the public rooms offer magnificent views. ✉ Via Federico da Montefeltro, Gubbio ☎ 075/9275872 ⊕ www.comune.gubbio.pg.it 🎟 €5 ⊘ Closed Mon. morning Nov.–Mar.

Restaurants

Grotta dell'Angelo

$$ | UMBRIAN | The rustic trattoria sits in the lower part of the old town near the main square; the few outdoor tables are in high demand in the summer. The menu features simple local specialties, including *capocollo* (a type of salami), stringozzi, and lasagna *tartufata* (with truffles). **Known for:** good antipasti and grilled meats; homey atmosphere; reasonable prices. ⑤ *Average main: €15 ⊠ Via Gioia 47, Gubbio* ☎ *075/9271747* ⊕ *www.grottadellangelo.it* ⊘ *Closed Tues. and Jan. 7–Feb. 7.*

★ Taverna del Lupo

$$ | UMBRIAN | One of the city's most famous taverns, this traditional spot has a menu that includes such indulgences as lasagna made in the Gubbian fashion, with ham and truffles. The *suprema di faraono* (guinea fowl in a delicately spiced sauce) is a specialty. ⑤ *Average main: €19 ⊠ Via Ansidei 21, Gubbio* ☎ *075/9274368* ⊕ *www.tavernadellupo.it.*

🛏 Hotels

★ Castello di Petroia

$ | HOTEL | This atmospheric 12th-century castle 15 km (9 miles) from Gubbio offers spacious antiques-filled rooms, some with decorated or beamed ceilings and stained glass, and excellent in-house dining for both dinner and breakfast. **Pros:** charming atmosphere; outdoor swimming pool, in season; lovely breakfast buffet with handmade cakes and jams. **Cons:** temperature can be difficult to regulate in guest rooms; beds could be comfier; decor is on the simple side. ⑤ *Rooms from: €120 ⊠ Località Petroia, Gubbio* ☎ *075/920287* ⊕ *www.petroia. it* ⊘ *Closed early Jan.–early Mar.* 🛏 *13 rooms* ⑩ *Free Breakfast.*

Hotel Bosone Palace

$ | HOTEL | A former palace is now home to an elegant, if faded, hotel, where elaborate frescoes grace the ceilings of the two enormous suites and delightful breakfast room. **Pros:** low rates; friendly welcome; excellent location. **Cons:** dated bathrooms; some noise in tourist season; cheapest rooms are cramped and lack A/C. ⑤ *Rooms from: €74 ⊠ Via XX Settembre 22, Gubbio* ☎ *075/9220688* ⊕ *www.hotelbosone.com* ⑩ *Free Breakfast* ⊘ *Closed early Jan.–mid-Feb.* 🛏 *30 rooms.*

Deruta

7 km (4½ miles) south of Torgiano, 19 km (11 miles) southeast of Perugia.

This 14th-century medieval hill town is most famous for its ceramics. A drive through the countryside to visit the ceramics workshops is a good way to spend a morning, but be sure to stop in the town itself.

GETTING HERE AND AROUND

From Perugia follow the directions for Rome and the E45 highway; Deruta has its own exits. There are also trains from the smaller St. Anna train station in Perugia. Take the train in the direction of Terni, and get off at Deruta.

VISITOR INFORMATION

CONTACT Deruta Tourism Office. ⊠ *Piazza dei Consoli 4, Deruta* ☎ *075/9711559.*

Sights

Museo Regionale della Ceramica (*Regional Ceramics Museum*)

HISTORY MUSEUM | It's only fitting that Deruta is home to an impressive ceramics museum, which is housed in the 14th-century former convent of San Francesco. The museum tells the history of ceramics, with panels (in Italian and English) explaining artistic techniques and production processes, and also holds the country's largest collection of Italian ceramics—nearly 8,000 pieces are on display. The most notable are the

Renaissance vessels using the *lustro* technique, which originated in Arab and Middle Eastern cultures some 500 years before coming into use in Italy in the late 1400s. Lustro, as the name sounds, gives the ceramics a rich finish, which is accomplished with the use of crushed precious materials such as gold and silver. ⊠ *Largo San Francesco, Deruta* ☎ *075/9711000* ⊕ *www.museocerami-cadideruta.it* 🎟 *€7, includes Pinacoteca Comunale* ⊘ *Closed Mon. and Tues. Oct.–May; Mon.–Fri. June; Mon.–Wed. July; Mon. Aug.–Sept.*

Pinacoteca Comunale

ART MUSEUM | The 14th-century Palazzo dei Consoli houses Deruda's Municipal Picture Gallery, open Sunday from March through October. A rich collection of works displayed over two floors includes frescoes and paintings by the Renaissance artists Perugino and L'Alunno, among other works from local churches. Upstairs, the Pascoli Collection features 17th- and 18th-century canvases, donated by a descendant of the prominent art collector and writer Lione Pascoli. Artists represented include Giovanni Battista Gaulli, Sebastiano Conca, and Francesco Trevisani. ⊠ *Piazza dei Consoli 15, Deruta* ☎ *075/9711000* ⊕ *www.museoceramica-dideruta.it* 🎟 *€7, includes Museo Regionale Della Ceramica* ⊘ *Closed Mon.–Sat. and Nov.–Feb.*

🛍 Shopping

Deruta is home to more than 70 ceramics shops. They offer a range of ceramics, including extra pieces from commissions for well-known British and North American tableware manufacturers. If you ask, most owners will take you to see where they actually throw, bake, and paint their wares. A drive along **Via Tiberina Nord** takes you past one shop after another.

Spello

12 km (7 miles) southeast of Assisi, 33 km (21 miles) north of Spoleto.

Only a few minutes from Assisi by car or train, this hilltop town at the edge of Monte Subasio makes an excellent strategic base for exploring nearby towns, with well-appointed hotels. Spello's art scene includes first-rate frescoes by Pinturicchio and Perugino, and contemporary artists can be observed at work in studios around town. If antiquity is your passion, the town also has some intriguing Roman ruins. And the warm, rosy-beige tones of the local *pietra rossa* stone on the buildings brighten even cloudy days.

GETTING HERE AND AROUND

Spello is an easy half-hour drive from Perugia. From the E45 highway, take the exit toward Assisi and Foligno. Merge onto the SS75 and take the Spello exit. There are also regular trains on the Perugia–Assisi line. Spello is 1 km (½ mile) from the train station, and buses run every 30 minutes for Porta Consolare. From Porta Consolare, continue up the steep main street that begins as Via Consolare and changes names several times as it crosses the little town, following the original Roman road. As it curves around, notice the winding medieval alleyways to the right and the more uniform Roman-era blocks to the left.

VISITOR INFORMATION

CONTACT Spello Tourism Office. ⊠ *Piazza Matteotti 3, Spello* ☎ *0742/301009* ⊕ *www.prospello.it.*

👁 Sights

Santa Maria Maggiore

CHURCH | The two great Umbrian artists hold sway in this 16th-century basilica. Pinturicchio's vivid frescoes in the Cappella Baglioni (1501) are striking for their rich colors, finely dressed figures, and complex symbolism. Among Pinturicchio's finest works are the *Nativity, Christ Among the Doctors* (on the far left side is a portrait of Troilo Baglioni, the prior who commissioned the work), and the *Annunciation* (look for Pinturicchio's self-portrait in the Virgin's room). The artist painted them after he had already won great acclaim for his work in the Palazzi Vaticani in Rome for Borgia Pope Alexander VI. Two pillars on either side of the apse are decorated with frescoes by Perugino (circa 1450–1523). ✉ *Piazza Matteotti 18, Spello* ☎ *0742/301792* ⊕ *www.smariamaggiore.com.*

Hotels

Hotel Palazzo Bocci

$ | **HOTEL** | Lovely sitting areas, a reading room, bucolic ceiling and wall frescoes, and a garden terrace all add quiet and elegant charm to this 14th-century building, where several rooms have valley views. **Pros:** abundant breakfasts; central location; splendid views of the valley from public areas and some rooms. **Cons:** not all rooms have views; noisy in summer months; needs a brush-up. ⑤ *Rooms from: €105* ✉ *Via Cavour 17, Spello* ☎ *0742/301021* ⊕ *www.palazzobocci.com* ⑪ *Free Breakfast* ⤳ *23 rooms.*

La Bastiglia

$ | **HOTEL** | Polished wood planks and handwoven rugs have replaced the rustic flooring of a former grain mill, and comfortable sitting rooms and cozy bedrooms are filled with a mix of antique and modern pieces. **Pros:** fine views from top-floor rooms, some with terraces; lovely terrace restaurant; leisure and wellness facilities. **Cons:** no elevator and plenty of steps, so pack light; some shared balconies; mix of modern and antique decor not congenial to all. ⑤ *Rooms from: €95* ✉ *Piazza Vallegloria, Spello* ☎ *0742/651277* ⊕ *www.labastiglia. com* ☾ *Closed 3 wks in Jan.* ⤳ *33 rooms* ⑪ *Free Breakfast.*

Montefalco

6 km (4 miles) southeast of Bevagna, 34 km (21 miles) south of Assisi.

Nicknamed the "balcony over Umbria" for its high vantage point over the valley that runs from Perugia to Spoleto, Montefalco began as an important Roman settlement situated on the Via Flaminia. The town owes its current name ("Falcon's Mount") to Emperor Frederick II (1194–1250). Obviously a greater fan of falconry than Roman architecture, he destroyed the ancient town, which was then called Coccorone, in 1249, and built in its place what would later become Montefalco. Aside from a few fragments incorporated in a private house just off Borgo Garibaldi, no traces remain of the old Roman center. However, Montefalco has more than its fair share of interesting art and architecture and is well worth the drive up the hill. Montefalco is also a good place to stop for a meal, as is close-by Bevagna: here you need go no farther than the main squares to find a restaurant or bar with a hot meal, and most establishments—both simple and sophisticated—offer a splendid combination of history and small-town hospitality.

GETTING HERE AND AROUND

If you're driving from Perugia, take the E45 toward Rome. Take the Foligno exit, then merge onto the SP445 and follow it into Montefalco. The drive takes around 50 minutes. The nearest train station is in Foligno, about 7 km (4½ miles) away. From there you can take a taxi or a bus into Montefalco.

VISITOR INFORMATION

CONTACT La Strada del Sagrantino.
✉ *Piazza del Comune 17, Montefalco* ☎ *0742/378490* ⊕ *www.stradadelsagrantino.it.*

The Sagrantino Story

Sagrantino grapes have been used for the production of red wine for centuries. The wine began centuries ago as Sagrantino *passito*, a semisweet version in which the grapes are left to dry for a period after picking to intensify the sugar content. One theory traces the origin of Sagrantino back to ancient Rome in the works of Pliny the Elder, the author of the *Natural History*, who referred to the Itriola grape that some researchers think may be Sagrantino. Others believe that in medieval times Franciscan friars returned from Asia Minor with the grape. ("Sagrantino" perhaps derives from *sacramenti*, the religious ceremony in which the wine was used.)

The passito is still produced today, and is preferred by some. But the big change in Sagrantino wine production came in the past decades, when Montefalco Sagrantino *secco* (dry) came onto the market. Both passito and secco have a deep ruby-red color that tends toward garnet highlights, with a full body and rich flavor.

For the dry wines, producers not to be missed are Terre di Capitani, Antonelli, Perticaia, and Caprai. Try those labels for the passito as well, in addition to Ruggeri and Scacciadiavoli. Terre di Capitani is complex and has vegetable and mineral tones that join tastes of wild berries, cherries, and chocolate—this winemaker pampers his grapes and it shows. Antonelli is elegant, refined, and rich. Perticaia has a full, rounded taste. Caprai is bold and rich in taste, and has the largest market share, including a high percentage exported to the United States. The Ruggeri passito is one of the best, so don't be put off by its homespun label.

At La Strada del Sagrantino in Montefalco's main square, you can pick up a map of the wine route, set up appointments, and book accommodations. Some wineries are small and not equipped to receive visitors. Visit the local enoteche, and ask the sommeliers to guide you to some smaller producers you'll have difficulty finding elsewhere.

🍴 Restaurants

★ Enoteca L'Alchimista
$ | UMBRIAN | "The Alchemist" is an apt name, as the chef's transformations are magical, and everything can be paired with wines from their extensive selection. Though pasta, veggie, and meat dishes change seasonally, the homemade gnocchi in Sagrantino sauce, always on offer, wins raves from guests, plus all the delicious desserts are made on the premises. **Known for:** refined but relaxed dining; extensive wine list; congenial setting and atmosphere. ⑤ *Average main: €14* ⊠ *Piazza del Comune 14, Montefalco* ☎ *0742/378558*

⊕ *www.ristorantealchimista.it* ⊗ *Closed Tues. and Feb.*

★ Redibis
$$ | MODERN ITALIAN | Housed in a Roman theater built in the 1st century AD, but brought up-to-date with mid-century modern furniture and sleek chandeliers, the atmosphere is as unique as the food. The seasonally changing menu, featuring mainly zero kilometer products, aims to adapt ancient ingredients like Roveja wild peas of Colfiorito to sophisticated modern tastes, while offering a fine selection of Umbrian wines. ⑤ *Average main: €22* ⊠ *8 km (5 miles) northwest of Montefalco, Via dell' Anfiteatro 3, Montefalco*

☎ 0742/362120 ⊕ www.ristoranteredibis.
it ⊗ Closed Tues.

 Hotels

★ Palazzo Bontadosi Hotel & Spa

$$$ | HOTEL | This charming boutique
hotel set inside an 18th-century palace
overlooking the main square includes
spacious rooms with original frescoes
and beamed ceilings contrasted with
modern furnishings. **Pros:** friendly
service; sophisticated design-focused
vibe; spa in medieval cellars has a private
Turkish bath and whirlpool. **Cons:** limited
spa facilities; rooms facing the square
can be noisy; small breakfast selection. ⑤ *Rooms from: €209* ⊠ *Piazza del
Comune 19, Montefalco* ☎ *0742/379357*
⊕ *www.hotelbontadosi.it* ⬏ *12 rooms*
†⊙† *Free Breakfast.*

Villa Pambuffetti

$$ | HOTEL | If you want to be pampered in
the refined atmosphere of a private villa,
this is the spot, with the warmth of a
fireplace in the winter, a pool to cool you
down in summer, and cozy reading nooks
and guest rooms year-round. **Pros:** peaceful gardens; cooking courses offered;
excellent dining room. **Cons:** outside the
town center; can get crowded on weekends; slightly dated feel. ⑤ *Rooms from:
€130* ⊠ *Viale della Vittoria 20, Montefalco*
☎ *0742/379417* ⊕ *www.villapambuffetti.it*
⬏ *15 rooms* †⊙† *Free Breakfast.*

Spoleto

For most of the year, Spoleto is one more
in a pleasant succession of sleepy hill
towns, resting regally atop a mountain.
But for three weeks every summer the
town shifts into high gear for a turn in the
international spotlight during the Festival
dei Due Mondi (Festival of Two Worlds),
an extravaganza of theater, opera, music,
painting, and sculpture. As the world's
top artists vie for honors, throngs of
art aficionados vie for hotel rooms. If

you plan to spend the night in Spoleto
during the festival, make sure you have
confirmed reservations, or you may find
yourself scrambling at sunset.

Spoleto has plenty to lure you during the
rest of the year as well: the final frescoes
of Filippo Lippi, beautiful piazzas and
streets with Roman and medieval attractions, and superb natural surroundings
with rolling hills and a dramatic gorge.
Spoleto makes a good base for exploring
all of southern Umbria, as Assisi, Orvieto,
and the towns in between are all within
easy reach.

GETTING HERE AND AROUND

Spoleto is an hour's drive from Perugia.
From the E45 highway, take the exit
toward Assisi and Foligno, then merge
onto the SS75 until you reach the Foligno
Est exit. Merge onto the SS3, which
leads to Spoleto. There are regular trains
on the Perugia–Foligno line. From the
train station it's a 15-minute uphill walk
to the center, so you'll probably want to
take a local bus or a taxi.

VISITOR INFORMATION

CONTACT Spoleto Tourism Office. ⊠ *Largo
Ferrer 6, off Corso Mazzini, Spoleto*
☎ *0743/218620* ⊕ *www.comune.spoleto.
pg.it/turismoecultura.*

 Sights

The walled city is set on a slanting hillside, with the most interesting sections
clustered toward the upper portion.
Parking options inside the walls include
Piazza Campello (just below the Rocca)
on the southeast end, Via del Trivio to the
north, and Piazza San Domenico on the
west end. You can also park at Piazza della Vittoria farther north, just outside the
walls. There are also several well-marked
lots near the train station. If you arrive by
train, you can walk 1 km (½ mile) from
the station to the entrance to the lower
town. Regular bus connections are every
15–30 minutes.

KEY

1 *Exploring Sights*

1 *Restaurants*

1 *Hotels*

Spoleto

0 100 yards

0 100 meters

Like most other towns with narrow, winding streets, Spoleto is best explored on foot. Bear in mind that much of the city is on a steep slope, so there are lots of stairs and steep inclines. The well-worn stones can be slippery even when dry; wear rubber-sole shoes for good traction. Several pedestrian walkways cut across Corso Mazzini, which zigzags up the hill, and three escalators connect the main car parks with the upper town. A €9.50 combination ticket purchased at any of the town's museums allows you entry to all the main museums and galleries over seven days.

Casa Romana

RUINS | Spoleto became a Roman colony in the 3rd century BC, but the best excavated remains date from the 1st century AD. Best preserved among them is the Casa Romana. According to an inscription, it belonged to Vespasia Polla, the mother of Emperor Vespasian (one of the builders of the Colosseum and perhaps better known by the Romans for taxing them to install public toilets, later called "Vespasians"). The rooms, arranged around a large central atrium built over an *impluvium* (rain cistern), are decorated with black-and-white geometric mosaics. ✉ *Palazzo del Municipio, Via Visiale 9, Spoleto* ☎ *0743/40255* ⊕ *www.spoleto-card.it* 🎫 *€3* ⏱ *Closed Mon.–Thu.*

★ Duomo

CHURCH | The 12th-century Romanesque facade received a Renaissance face-lift with the addition of a loggia in a rosy pink stone, creating a stunning contrast in styles. One of the finest cathedrals in the region is lit by eight rose windows that are especially dazzling in the late afternoon sun. The original floor tiles remain from an earlier church destroyed by Frederick I (circa 1123–90). Above the church's entrance is Bernini's bust of Pope Urban VIII (1568–1644), who had the church redecorated in 17th-century Baroque; fortunately he didn't touch the 15th-century frescoes painted in the apse by Fra Filippo Lippi (circa 1406–69) between 1466 and 1469. These immaculately restored masterpieces—the Annunciation, Nativity, and Dormition—tell the story of the life of the Virgin. The Coronation of the Virgin, adorning the half dome, is the literal and figurative high point. Portraits of Lippi and his assistants are on the right side of the central panel. The Florentine artist-priest, "whose colors expressed God's voice" (the words inscribed on his tomb), died shortly after completing the work. His tomb, which you can see in the right transept (note the artist's brushes and tools), was designed by his son, Filippino Lippi (circa 1457–1504). ⊠ *Piazza del Duomo, Spoleto* ☏ *0577/286300* ⊕ *www. duomospoleto.it* ⊠ *Free.*

La Rocca Albornoz

CASTLE/PALACE | Built in the mid-14th century for Cardinal Egidio Albornoz, this massive fortress served as a seat for the local pontifical governors, a tangible sign of the restoration of the Church's power in the area when the pope was ruling from Avignon. Several popes spent time here, and one of them, Alexander VI, in 1499 sent his capable teenage daughter Lucrezia Borgia (1480–1519) to serve as governor for three months. The Gubbio-born architect Gattapone (14th century) used the ruins of a Roman acropolis as a foundation and took materials from many Roman-era sites, including the Teatro Romano. La Rocca's plan is long and rectangular, with six towers and two grand courtyards, an upper loggia, and inside some grand reception rooms. In the largest tower, Torre Maestà, you can visit an apartment with some interesting frescoes. The fortress also contains the Museo Nazionale del Ducato, 15 rooms

dedicated to the art of the duchy of Spoleto during the Middle Ages. If you phone in advance, you may be able to secure an English-speaking guide. ⊠ *Piazza Campello, Spoleto* ☏ *0743/224952* ⊕ *www.asso-roccaspoleto.it* ⊗ *Closed Tue. and Wed.* ⊠ *€7.50, including the Museo Nazionale del Ducato.*

★ **Ponte delle Torri** (*Bridge of the Towers*)
BRIDGE | Standing massive and graceful through the deep gorge that separates Spoleto from Monteluco, this 14th-century bridge is one of Umbria's most photographed monuments, and justifiably so. Built over the foundations of a Roman-era aqueduct, it soars 262 feet above the forested gorge—higher than the dome of St. Peter's in Rome. Sweeping views over the valley and a pleasant sense of vertigo make a walk across the bridge a must, particularly on a starry night. ⊠ *Via del Ponte, Spoleto* ⊠ *Free.*

Teatro Romano

RUINS | The Romans who colonized the city in 241 BC constructed this small theater in the 1st century AD; for centuries afterward it was used as a quarry for building materials. The most intact portion is the hallway that passes under the *cavea* (stands). The rest was heavily restored in the early 1950s and serves as a venue for Spoleto's Festival dei Due Mondi. The theater was the site of a gruesome episode in Spoleto's history: during the medieval struggle between Guelph (papal) and Ghibelline (imperial) forces, Spoleto took the side of the Holy Roman Emperor. Afterward, 400 Guelph supporters were massacred in the theater, their bodies burned in an enormous pyre. In the end, the Guelphs were triumphant, and Spoleto was incorporated into the states of the Church in 1354. Through a door in the west portico of the adjoining building is the **Museo Archeologico,** with assorted artifacts found in excavations primarily around Spoleto and Norcia. The collection contains Bronze Age and Iron Age artifacts from Umbrian and pre-Roman eras. The highlight is the stone tablet inscribed on both sides with the Lex Spoletina (Spoleto Law). Dating from 315 BC, this legal document prohibited the desecration of the woods on the slopes of nearby Monteluco. ⊠ *Piazza della Libertà, Spoleto* ☎ *0743/223277* ⊕ *www.spoletocard.it* ⊡ *€4* ⊙ *Closed Mon. and Tue.*

🍴 Restaurants

★ Apollinare
$$ | UMBRIAN | Low wooden ceilings and flickering candlelight make this monastery from the 10th and 11th centuries Spoleto's most romantic spot; in warm weather you can dine under a canopy on the piazza across from the archaeological museum. The kitchen serves sophisticated, innovative variations on local dishes, including long, slender *strengozzi* pasta with such toppings as cherry tomatoes, mint, and a touch of red pepper, or (in season) porcini mushrooms or truffles. ⑤ *Average main: €16* ⊠ *Via Sant'Agata 14, Spoleto* ☎ *0743/223256* ⊕ *www.ristoranteapollinare.it* ⊙ *Closed Tues.*

⬤ Tartufo
$$ | UMBRIAN | As the name indicates, dishes prepared with truffles are the specialty here—don't miss the risotto al tartufo. Incorporating the ruins of a Roman villa, the surroundings are rustic on the ground floor and more modern upstairs; in summer, tables appear outdoors and the traditional fare is spiced up to appeal to the cosmopolitan crowd attending (or performing in) the Festival dei Due Mondi. **Known for:** abundant portions, well presented; recipes incorporating truffles; charming staff. ⑤ *Average main: €18* ⊠ *Piazza Garibaldi 24, Spoleto* ☎ *0743/40236* ⊕ *www.ristoranteiltartufo. it* ⊙ *Closed Mon. and early Jan.–early Feb. No dinner Sun.*

⬤ Tempio del Gusto
$ | UMBRIAN | In charming shabby-chic environs, this welcoming eatery near the Arco di Druso (ancient Roman arch) serves up Italian with a subtle twist. Along with an extensive selection of thoughtfully chosen Umbrian wines, you'll find lots of veggie options, mounds of truffles in season, and, to finish things off, a superlative version of Spoleto sponge cake. ⑤ *Average main: €14* ⊠ *Via Arco di Druso 11, Spoleto* ☎ *0743/47121* ⊕ *www.iltempiodelgusto.com* ⊙ *Closed Thurs.*

Ristorante Il Panciolle
$ | UMBRIAN | A small garden filled with lemon trees in the heart of Spoleto's medieval quarter provides one of the most appealing settings you could wish for. Dishes change throughout the year, and may include pastas served with asparagus or mushrooms, as well as grilled meats; more expensive dishes prepared with fresh truffles are also available in season. ⑤ *Average main: €14* ⊠ *Via Duomo 3/5, Spoleto* ☎ *0743/45677* ⊕ *www.ilpanciolle.it* ⊙ *Closed Wed. Sept.–Mar.*

🛏 Hotels

★ Hotel San Luca
$ | HOTEL | Hand-painted friezes decorate the walls of the spacious guest rooms, and elegant comfort is the grace note throughout—you can sip afternoon tea in oversize armchairs by the fireplace, or take a walk in the sweet-smelling rose garden. **Pros:** very helpful staff; spacious rooms; close to escalators for exploring city. **Cons:** no restaurant; can feel soulless in winter; outside the town center. ⑤ *Rooms from: €91* ⊠ *Via Interna delle Mura 21, Spoleto* ☎ *0743/223399* ⊕ *www.hotelsanluca.com* ⇆ *35 rooms* ⦿ *Free Breakfast.*

★ Palazzo Leti Residenza d'Epoca
$ | HOTEL | Fabulously landscaped gardens, complete with fountains and sculptures, along with panoramic views provide a grand entrance to this late 13th-century residence turned charming

hotel high up in Spoleto's old town. **Pros:** friendly owners happy to help; feels like a private hideaway; unbeatable views. **Cons:** often booked far in advance; reaching on-site parking can be tricky; few amenities (no restaurant, gym, or spa). ⑤ *Rooms from: €109* ✉ *Via degli Eremiti 10, Spoleto* ☎ *0743/224930* ⊕ *www.palazzoleti.com* ⤳ *12 rooms* ⑪ *Free Breakfast.*

Todi

34 km (22 miles) south of Perugia, 34 km (22 miles) northeast of Orvieto.

As you stand on Piazza del Popolo, looking out onto the Tiber Valley below, it's easy to see why Todi is often described as Umbria's prettiest hill town. Legend has it that the town was founded by the Umbri, who followed an eagle who had stolen a tablecloth. They liked this lofty perch so much that they settled here for good. The eagle is now perched on the insignia of the medieval palaces in the main piazza.

GETTING HERE AND AROUND
Todi is best reached by car, as the town's two train stations are way down the hill and connected to the center by infrequent bus service. From Perugia, follow the E45 toward Rome. Take the Todi/Orvieto exit, then follow the SS79bis into Todi. The drive takes around 40 minutes.

VISITOR INFORMATION
CONTACT Todi Tourism Office. ✉ *Piazza del Popolo 29–30, Todi* ☎ *0758/8956227* ⊕ *www.visitodi.eu.*

Sights

Duomo

CHURCH | One end of the Piazza del Popolo is dominated by this 12th-century Romanesque-Gothic masterpiece, built over the site of a Roman temple. The simple facade is enlivened by a finely carved rose window. Look up at that window as you step inside and you'll notice its peculiarity: each "petal" of the rose has a cherub's face in the stained glass. Also take a close look at the capitals of the double columns with pilasters: perched between the acanthus leaves are charming medieval sculptures of saints—Peter with his keys, George and the dragon, and so on. You can see the rich brown tones of the wooden choir near the altar, but unless you have binoculars or request special permission in advance, you can't get close enough to see all the exquisite detail in this Renaissance masterpiece of woodworking (1521–30). The severe, solid mass of the Duomo is mirrored by the Palazzo dei Priori (1595–97) across the way. ⊠ *Piazza del Popolo, Todi* ☎ *075/8943041* ⊕ *www.chiesaditodi.it* 🎟 *Free.*

Piazza del Popolo

PLAZA/SQUARE | Built above the Roman Forum, Piazza del Popolo is Todi's high point, a model of spatial harmony with stunning views onto the surrounding countryside. In the best medieval tradition, the square was conceived to house both the temporal and the spiritual centers of power. ⊠ *Todi* 🎟 *Free.*

🍴 Restaurants

Ristorante Umbria

$$ | **UMBRIAN** | Todi's most popular restaurant for more than four decades is reliable for its sturdy country food and the wonderful view from the terrace; because it has only 16 tables outside, make sure you reserve ahead. In winter, try lentil soup, risotto with saffron and porcini mushrooms, or wild boar with polenta; steaks, accompanied by a rich dark-brown wine sauce, are good any time of year. **Known for:** friendly atmosphere; traditional Umbrian dishes; terrific vista from terrace. $ *Average main:* €15 ⊠ *Via San Bonaventura 13, Todi* ☎ *075/8942737* ⊕ *www.ristoranteumbria.it* 🕙 *Closed Tues. and 3–4 wks in Jan. and Feb.*

🛏 Hotels

★ Relais Todini

$$ | **HOTEL** | Inside a 14th-century manor house 9 km (6 miles) southeast of Todi, this elegant hotel sits adjacent to working vineyards (don't forget to sample the Todini wines) and features such welcome amenities as a spa, outdoor pool, and gym. **Pros:** walking paths around the grounds; quiet location; lots of public spaces to relax in. **Cons:** price on the high side; decor feels a bit worn; reception not staffed 24/7. $ *Rooms from: €146* ⊠ *Frazione Collevalenza, Todi* ☎ *075/887521* ⊕ *www.relaistodini.it* 🛏 *12 rooms* ⧓ *Free Breakfast.*

Residenza San Lorenzo Tre

$ | **HOTEL** | Filled with antique furniture, paintings, and period knickknacks, 19th-century charm pairs with magnificent views over valleys and hills at this property. **Pros:** spectacular views; excellent central location; old-world atmosphere. **Cons:** long flight of steps to enter; few modern amenities; small, basic bathrooms. $ *Rooms from: €95* ⊠ *Via San Lorenzo 3, Todi* ☎ *075/8944555* ⊕ *www.sanlorenzo3.it* 🛏 *6 rooms* ⧓ *Free Breakfast.*

Orvieto

30 km (19 miles) southwest of Todi, 81 km (51 miles) west of Spoleto.

Carved out of an enormous plateau of volcanic rock high above a green valley, Orvieto has natural defenses that made the high walls seen in many Umbrian towns unnecessary. The Etruscans were the first to settle here, digging a honeycombed network of more than 1,200 wells and storage caves out of the soft stone. The Romans attacked, sacked, and destroyed the city in 283 BC; since then, it has grown up out of the rock into an enchanting maze of alleys and squares. Orvieto was solidly Guelph in the Middle Ages, and for several hundred years popes sought refuge in the city, at times needing protection from their enemies, at times seeking respite from the summer heat of Rome.

When painting his frescoes inside the Duomo, Luca Signorelli asked that part of his contract be paid in Orvietan wine, and he was neither the first nor the last to appreciate the region's popular white. In past times the caves carved underneath the town were used to ferment the Trebbiano grapes used in making Orvieto Classico; now local wine production has moved out to more traditional vineyards, but you can still while away the afternoon with tastings at any number of shops in town.

GETTING HERE AND AROUND
Orvieto is well connected by train to Rome, Florence, and Perugia. It's also adjacent to the A1 autostrada that runs between Florence and Rome. Parking areas in the upper town tend to be crowded. A better idea is to follow the signs for the Porta Orvetiana parking lot, then take the funicular that carries people up the hill.

VISITOR INFORMATION
The Carta Orvieto Unica (single ticket) is expensive but a great deal if you want to visit everything. For €20 you get admission to 11 museums and monuments, including the three major sights in town—Cappella di San Brizio (at the Duomo), Museo Etrusco Claudio Faina, and Orvieto Underground—along with entry to the Torre del Moro, with views of Orvieto, plus a bus and funicular pass.

CONTACT Orvieto Tourism Office. ✉ *Piazza del Duomo 24, Orvieto* ☎ *0763/341772* ⊕ *www.liveorvieto.com.*

 ## Sights

★ Duomo
CHURCH | Orvieto's stunning cathedral was built to commemorate the Miracle at Bolsena. In 1263 a young priest who questioned the miracle of transubstantiation (in which the Communion bread and wine become the flesh and blood of Christ) was saying Mass at nearby Lago di Bolsena. A wafer he had just blessed suddenly started to drip blood, staining the linen covering the altar. Thirty years later, construction began on a duomo in Orvieto to celebrate the miracle and house the stained altar cloth. Inside, the cathedral is rather vast and empty; the major works are in the transepts. To the left is the **Cappella del Corporale**, where the square linen cloth (*corporale*) is kept in a golden reliquary that's modeled on the cathedral and inlaid with enamel scenes of the miracle. In the right transept is the **Cappella di San Brizio**, which holds one of Italy's greatest fresco cycles, notable for its influence on Michelangelo's *Last Judgment*, as well as for the extraordinary beauty of the figuration. In these works, a few by Fra Angelico and the majority by Luca Signorelli, the damned fall to hell, demons breathe fire and blood, and Christians are martyred. ✉ *Piazza del Duomo, Orvieto* ☎ *0763/342477* ⊕ *www.opsm.it* 🎟 *€5, including Cappella di San Brizio.*

Museo Etrusco Claudio Faina
HISTORY MUSEUM | This superb private collection, beautifully arranged and presented, goes far beyond the usual museum offerings of a scattering of local remains. The collection is particularly rich in Greek- and Etruscan-era pottery, from large Attic amphorae (6th–4th century BC) to Attic black- and red-figure pieces to Etruscan *bucchero* (dark-reddish clay) vases. Other interesting pieces in the

collection include a 6th-century sarcophagus and a substantial display of Roman-era coins. ✉ *Piazza del Duomo 29, Orvieto* ☎ *0763/341216* ⊕ *www.museofaina.it* 🎫 *€5* ⊗ *Closed Mon.–Thurs.*

Orvieto Underground

RUINS | More than just about any other town, Orvieto has grown from its own foundations. The Etruscans, the Romans, and those who followed dug into the tufa (the same soft volcanic rock from which catacombs were made) to create more than 1,000 separate cisterns, caves, secret passages, storage areas, and production areas for wine and olive oil. Much of the tufa removed was used as building blocks for the city that exists today, and some was partly ground into *pozzolana*, which was made into mortar. You can see the labyrinth of dugout chambers beneath the city on the Orvieto Underground tour, which runs daily at 11, 12:15, 4, and 5:15 (more frequently in busy periods) from Piazza del Duomo 23. ✉ *Orvieto* ☎ *0763/344891* ⊕ *www.orvietounderground.it* 🎫 *Tours €7.*

Pozzo della Cava

RUINS | If you're short on time but want a quick look at the cisterns and caves beneath the city, head for the Pozzo della Cava, an Etruscan well for spring water. ✉ *Via della Cava 28, Orvieto* ☎ *0763/342373* ⊕ *www.pozzodellacava.it* 🎫 *€4.*

🍴 Restaurants

Le Grotte del Funaro

$ | **UMBRIAN** | Dine inside tufa caves under central Orvieto, where the two windows afford splendid views of the hilly countryside. The traditional Umbrian food is reliably good, with simple grilled meats and vegetables and pizzas—oddly, though, the food is outclassed by an extensive wine list, with top local and Italian labels and quite a few rare vintages. **Known for:** good choice of wines; unusual setting; crusty pizzas. ⑤ *Average main: €14* ✉ *Via*

Ripa Serancia 41, Orvieto ☎ *0763/343276* ⊕ *www.grottedelfunaro.com* ⊗ *Closed Mon. and 10 days in July.*

Ristorante Maurizio

$$ | **UMBRIAN** | Off a busy pedestrian street near the Duomo, this welcoming family-owned restaurant has an uber-contemporary look, but is actually housed in a 14th-century medieval building with arched ceilings. The Martinelli family's own products, including balsamic vinegar, olive oil, and pasta, are used in their robustly flavored dishes, and you can also sample their own well-regarded Montefalco wines. ⑤ *Average main: €16* ✉ *Via del Duomo 78, Orvieto* ☎ *0763/341114, 0763/343212* ⊕ *www.ristorante-maurizio.com.*

Trattoria La Grotta

$$ | **UMBRIAN** | The vaulted, plant-filled dining area with white walls adorned with paintings, antique vases, and other knick-knacks makes a congenial setting for this small, rustic-style trattoria that is lauded for its homemade pasta, perhaps with an artichoke, duck, or wild-boar sauce. Roast lamb, veal, and pork are all good, and the desserts are supplied by Orvieto's most eminent pasticceria. ⑤ *Average main: €16* ✉ *Via Luca Signorelli 5, Orvieto* ☎ *0763/341348* ⊕ *www.trattorialagrottaorvieto.com* ⊗ *Closed Tues.*

Hotels

Hotel Palazzo Piccolomini

$ | **HOTEL** | This 16th-century family palazzo has been beautifully restored, with inviting public spaces and handsome guest quarters where contemporary surroundings are accented with old beams, vaulted ceilings, and other distinctive touches. **Pros:** good location; private parking; efficient staff. **Cons:** four-star category not completely justified; underwhelming breakfasts; some rooms and bathrooms are small. ⑤ *Rooms from: €120* ✉ *Piazza Ranieri 36, Orvieto* ☎ *0763/341743*

Hiking the Umbrian Hills

Magnificent scenery makes the heart of Italy excellent walking, hiking, and mountaineering country. In Umbria, the area around Spoleto is particularly good; several pleasant, easy, and well-signed trails begin at the far end of the Ponte alle Torri bridge over Monteluco. From Cannara, an easy half-hour walk leads to the fields of Pian d'Arca, the site of St. Francis's sermon to the birds. For slightly more arduous walks, you can follow the saint's path, uphill from Assisi to the Eremo delle Carceri, and then continue along the trails that crisscross Monte Subasio. At 4,250 feet, the treeless summit affords views of Assisi, Perugia, far-off Gubbio, and the distant mountain ranges of Abruzzo.

For even more challenging hiking, the northern reaches of the Valnerina are exceptional; the mountains around Norcia should not be missed. Throughout Umbria and the Marches, you'll find that most recognized walking and hiking trails are marked with the distinctive red-and-white blazes of the Club Alpino Italiano. Tourist offices are a good source for walking and climbing itineraries to suit all ages and levels of ability, while bookstores, *tabacchi* (tobacconists), and *edicole* (newsstands) often have maps and hiking guides that detail the best routes in their area. Depending on the length and location of your walk, it can be important that you have comfortable walking shoes or boots, appropriate attire, and plenty of water to drink.

⊕ *www.palazzopiccolomini.it* ⤳ *33 rooms* ⏍*Free Breakfast.*

★**Locanda Palazzone**
$$$ | HOTEL | Spending the night in this 13th-century building just 5 km (3 miles) northwest of Orvieto is like staying in a sophisticated country home, with vineyard views, a private chef, and two-level rooms with modern furnishings. **Pros:** tasty meals served nightly; tranquil surroundings; extremely friendly owners and staff. **Cons:** limited public spaces to lounge in; no à la carte menus; split-level rooms can be difficult for those with mobility issues or young children.
Ⓢ *Rooms from: €234* ⊠ *Località Rocca Ripesena 68, Orvieto* ☏ *0763/393614* ⊕ *www.locandapalazzone.it* ⤳ *7 rooms* ⏍*Free Breakfast.*

The Valnerina

The Valnerina is 27 km (17 miles) southeast of Spoleto.

The Valnerina (the valley of the River Nera, to the southeast of Spoleto) is the most beautiful of central Italy's many well-kept secrets. The twisting roads that serve the rugged landscape are poor, but the drive is well worth the effort for its forgotten medieval villages and dramatic mountain scenery.

GETTING HERE AND AROUND
You can head into the area from Terni on the S209, or on the SP395bis north of Spoleto, which links the Via Flaminia (S3) with the middle reaches of the Nera Valley through a tunnel.

Sights

Cascata delle Marmore

WATERFALL | FAMILY | The road east of Terni (SS Valnerina) leads 10 km (6 miles) to the Cascata delle Marmore (Waterfalls of Marmore), which, at 541 feet, are the highest in Europe. A canal was dug by the Romans in the 3rd century BC to prevent flooding in the nearby agricultural plains. Nowadays the waters are often diverted to provide hydroelectric power for Terni, reducing the roaring falls to an unimpressive trickle, so check with the information office at the falls (there's a timetable on their website) or with Terni's tourist office before heading here. On summer evenings, when the falls are in full spate, the cascading water is floodlit to striking effect. The falls are usually at their most energetic at midday and at around 4 pm. This is a good place for hiking, except in December and January, when most trails may be closed. ⊠ *SP79, 10 km (6 miles) east of Terni* ☎ *0744/67561* ⊕ *www.cascatadellemarmore.info* ⊘ *Closed weekdays in Jan.* ⊠ *€10.*

Norcia

TOWN | The birthplace of St. Benedict, Norcia is best known for its Umbrian pork and truffles. Norcia exports truffles to France and hosts a truffle festival, the Sagra del Tartufo, every February. The surrounding mountains provide spectacular hiking. ⊹ *42 km (25 miles) east of Spoleto, 67 km (42 miles) northeast of Terni.*

★ Piano Grande

VIEWPOINT | A spectacular mountain plain 25 km (15 miles) to the northeast of the valley, Piano Grande is a hang glider's paradise and a wonderful place for a picnic or to fly a kite. It's also nationally famous for the quality of the lentils grown here, which are a traditional part of every Italian New Year's feast. ⊠ *Terni.*

Urbino

75 km (47 miles) north of Gubbio, 116 km (72 miles) northeast of Perugia, 230 km (143 miles) east of Florence.

Majestic Urbino, atop a steep hill with a skyline of towers and domes, is something of a surprise to come upon. Though quite remote, it was once a center of learning and culture almost without rival in western Europe. The town looks much as it did in the glory days of the 15th century: a cluster of warm brick and pale stone buildings, all topped with russet-color tile roofs. The focal point is the immense and beautiful Palazzo Ducale.

The city is home to the small but prestigious Università di Urbino—one of the oldest in the world—and the streets are usually filled with students. Urbino is very much a college town, with the usual array of bookshops, bars, and coffeehouses. In summer the Italian student population is replaced by foreigners who come to study Italian language and arts at several prestigious private fine-arts academies.

Urbino's fame rests on the reputation of three of its native sons: Duke Federico da Montefeltro (1422–82), the enlightened warrior-patron who built the Palazzo Ducale; Raffaello Sanzio (1483–1520), or Raphael, one of the most influential painters in history and an embodiment of the spirit of the Renaissance; and the architect Donato Bramante (1444–1514), who translated the philosophy of the Renaissance into buildings of grace and beauty. Unfortunately there's little work by either Bramante or Raphael in the city, but the duke's influence can still be felt strongly.

GETTING HERE AND AROUND

Take the SS3bis from Perugia, and follow the directions for Gubbio and Cesena. Exit at Umbertide and take the SS219, then the SS452, and at Calmazzo, the SS73bis to Urbino.

The Marches

VISITOR INFORMATION

CONTACT Urbino Tourism Office. ✉ *Via Puccinotti 35, Urbino* ☎ *0722/2613* ⊕ *www.turismo.marche.it.*

Sights

Casa Natale di Raffaello (*House of Raphael*)

HISTORIC HOME | This is the house in which the painter was born and where he took his first steps in painting, under the direction of his artist father. There's some debate about the fresco of the Madonna here; some say it's by Raphael, whereas others attribute it to the father—with Raphael's mother and the young painter himself standing in as models for the Madonna and Child. ✉ *Via Raffaello 57, Urbino* ☎ *0722/320105* ⊕ *www.casaraffaello.com* ✉ *€3.50.*

★ **Palazzo Ducale** (*Ducal Palace*)

ART MUSEUM | The Palazzo Ducale holds a place of honor in the city. If the Renaissance was, ideally, a celebration of the nobility of man and his works, of the light and purity of the soul, then there's no place in Italy, the birthplace of the Renaissance, where these tenets are better illustrated. From the moment you enter the peaceful courtyard, you know you're in a place of grace and beauty, the harmony of the building reflecting the high ideals of the time. Today the palace houses the **Galleria Nazionale delle Marche** (National Museum of the Marches), with a superb collection of paintings, sculpture, and other objets d'art. Some works were originally the possessions of the Montefeltro family; others were brought here from churches and palaces throughout the region. Masterworks in the collection include Paolo Uccello's

Profanation of the Host, Titian's *Resur-ection* and *Last Supper,* and Piero della Francesca's *Madonna of Senigallia.* But the gallery's highlight is Piero's enigmatic work long known as *The Flagellation of Christ.* Much has been written about this painting, and few experts agree on its meaning. Academic debates notwith-standing, the experts agree that the work is one of the painter's masterpiec-es. ⊠ *Piazza Rinascimento 13, Urbino* ☎ *0722/2760* ⊕ *www.gallerianazionale-marche.it* 🎟 *€8* ⊗ *Closed Mon.*

Restaurants

La Fornarina

$$ | ITALIAN | Locals often crowd this small, two-room trattoria near the Piazza della Repubblica. The specialty is meaty country fare, such as *coniglio* (rabbit) and *vitello alle noci* (veal cooked with walnuts) or *ai porcini* (with mushrooms); there's also a good selection of pasta dishes. $ *Average main: €18* ⊠ *Via Mazz-ini 14, Urbino* ☎ *0722/320007.*

Osteria Angolo Divino

$$ | ITALIAN | Starred chef Tiziano Rossetti has taken over this long-standing res-taurant in the center of Urbino, where tradition still reigns supreme. Elegant versions of regional dishes feature lots of local ingredients, including truffles, forest mushrooms, game, and pork, along with a wine list focused on small producers from the Marche. $ *Average main: €23* ⊠ *Via S. Andrea 14, Urbino* ☎ *0722/327559* ⊕ *www.tizianorossetti. com/osterialangolodivino* ⊗ *Closed Wed. No lunch Thurs.*

🛏 Hotels

Hotel Bonconte

$ | HOTEL | Pleasant rooms just inside the city walls and close to the Palazzo Ducale are decorated with a smattering of antiques, and those in front have views of the valley below Urbino. **Pros:** good breakfast; pleasant views; central

but away from the bustle. **Cons:** some rooms are cramped; an uphill walk to town center; traffic noise in some rooms. $ *Rooms from: €110* ⊠ *Via delle Mura 28, Urbino* ☎ *0722/2463* ⊕ *www.viphotels.it* ⇆ *25 rooms* ⦿ *Free Breakfast.*

Loreto

31 km (19 miles) south of Ancona, 118 km (73 miles) southeast of Urbino.

There's a strong Renaissance feel about this hilltop town, which is home to one of the most important religious sites in Europe, the Santuario della Santa Casa (House of the Virgin Mary). Bramante and Sansovino gave the church its Renais-sance look, although many other artists helped create its special atmosphere. Today the town revolves around the religious calendar; if you can be here on December 10, you will witness the Feast of the Translation of the Holy House, when huge bonfires are lighted to cele-brate the miraculous arrival of the house in 1295.

GETTING HERE AND AROUND

If you're driving from Perugia, take the SS318 and then the SS76 highway to Fabriano and then on to Chiaravalle, where it merges with the A14 autostra-da. The drive takes around 2½ hours. Trains also go to Loreto, but the station is about a mile outside the town center. Regular buses leave from the station to the center.

VISITOR INFORMATION

CONTACT Loreto Tourism Office. ⊠ *Via Solari 3, Loreto* ☎ *071/970276* ⊕ *www. turismo.marche.it.*

⊙ Sights

Basilica della Santa Casa

CHURCH | Loreto is famous for one of the best-loved shrines in the world, that of the **Santuario della Santa Casa** (House of the Virgin Mary), within the Basilica della

Santa Casa. Legend has it that angels moved the house from Nazareth, where the Virgin Mary was living at the time of the Annunciation, to this hilltop in 1295. The reason for this sudden and divinely inspired move was that Nazareth had fallen into the hands of Muslim invaders, whom the angelic hosts viewed as unsuitable keepers of this important shrine. The house itself consists of three rough stone walls contained within an elaborate marble tabernacle. Built around this centerpiece is the giant basilica of the Holy House, which dominates the town. Millions of visitors come to the site every year (particularly at Easter and on the December 10 Feast of the Holy House), and the little town of Loreto can become uncomfortably crowded with pilgrims. Many great Italian architects—including Bramante, Antonio da Sangallo the Younger (1483–1546), Giuliano da Sangallo (circa 1445–1516), and Sansovino (1467–1529)—contributed to the design of the basilica. It was begun in the Gothic style in 1468 and continued in Renaissance style through the late Renaissance. ⊠ *Piazza della Madonna, Loreto* ☎ *071/9747155* ⊕ *www.santuariooloreto.it* ✉ *Free.*

Ascoli Piceno

88 km (55 miles) south of Loreto, 105 km (65 miles) south of Ancona.

Ascoli Piceno sits in a valley ringed by steep hills and cut by the Tronto River. In Roman times it was one of central Italy's best-known market towns, and today, with almost 52,000 residents, it's a major fruit and olive producer, making it one of the most important towns in the region. Despite growth during the Middle Ages and at other times, the streets in the town center continue to reflect the grid pattern of the ancient Roman city. You'll even find the word *rua,* from the Latin *ruga,* used for "street" instead of the

Italian *via.* Now largely closed to traffic, the city center is great to explore on foot

GETTING HERE AND AROUND
From Perugia take the SS75 to Foligno, then merge onto the SS3 to Norcia. From here take the SS4 to Ascoli Piceno. There are also trains, but the journey would be quite long, taking you from Perugia to Ancona before changing for Ascoli Piceno.

VISITOR INFORMATION
CONTACT Ascoli Piceno Tourism Office.
⊠ *Piazza Aringo 7, Ascoli Piceno*
☎ *0736/298916* ⊕ *www.visitascoli.it.*

 Sights

Piazza del Popolo
PLAZA/SQUARE | The heart of the town is the majestic Piazza del Popolo, dominated by the Gothic church of **San Francesco** and the **Palazzo del Popolo,** a 13th-century town hall that contains a graceful Renaissance courtyard. The square functions as the living room of the entire city and at dusk each evening is packed with people strolling and exchanging news and gossip—the sweetly antiquated ritual called the *passeggiata,* performed all over the country. ⊠ *Ascoli Piceno* ✉ *Free.*

 Hotels

Hotel Pennile
$ | **HOTEL** | This modern, affordable, family-run hotel in a quiet residential area outside the old city center is pleasantly set amid a grove of olive trees. **Pros:** easy parking; peaceful environment; a good budget option. **Cons:** no restaurant; distance from town center; basic buffet breakfast. ⑤ *Rooms from: €75* ⊠ *Via G. Spalvieri, Ascoli Piceno* ☎ *0736/41645* ⊕ *www.hotelpennile.it* ↪ *33 rooms* ⑩ *Free Breakfast.*

Chapter 15

NAPLES AND CAMPANIA

15

Updated by
Nick Bruno

⊙ Sights	🍴 Restaurants	🏨 Hotels	🛍 Shopping	🍸 Nightlife
★★★★★	★★★★★	★★★★☆	★★★★☆	★★★★☆

WELCOME TO NAPLES AND CAMPANIA

TOP REASONS TO GO

★ **Naples, Italy's most operatic city:** Walk through the energy, chaos, and beauty that is Spaccanapoli, the city's historic artery, and you'll create an unforgettable memory.

★ **Pompeii:** The excavated ruins of Pompeii offer a unique, occasionally spooky glimpse into everyday life—and sudden death—in Roman times.

★ **"The Living Room of the World":** Pose oh-so-casually with the beautiful people on La Piazzetta, the central crossroads of the island of Capri—a stage-set square that always seems ready for a gala performance.

★ **Ravello:** High above the famously blue Bay of Salerno, this Amalfi Coast charmer is a contender for the title of "most beautiful village in the world."

★ **Positano, a world made of stairs:** Built like a vertical amphitheater, Positano's only job is to look enchanting on the Amalfi Coast—and it does that very well.

1 Naples. Italy's third-largest city is lush, chaotic, friendly, amusing, confounding, and very beautiful.

2 Herculaneum. The famous archaeological site was once a wealthy seaside resort.

3 Pompeii. The most famous dig of all—the one that arguably kickstarted archaeological studies—is Pompeii.

4 Vesuvius. Dominating the skyline southeast of Naples is the destructive Vesuvius caldera.

5 Oplontis. Fascinating lesser-known ruins.

6 Ischia. More than twice the size of Capri, lesser-known Ischia has volcanic-sand beaches, thermal hot-spring spas, and fewer day-trippers.

7 Procida. Sun, cliffs, and sea combine to create the distinctive atmosphere so memorably immortalized in the film *Il Postino.*

8 Capri. The rocky island mixes natural beauty and *dolce vita* glamour.

9 Sorrento. Perched over the Bay of Naples with an incomparable view of Mt. Vesuvius, this Belle Époque resort town is sheer delight.

10 Positano. The ultimate pastel-brushed, tumbling-to-the-seaside village moves between sophisticated-luxe, beachcomber casual, and selfie-reverential posing.

11 Conca Dei Marini. Put on the map by 1960s jet-setters, this tiny but exceedingly picturesque harbor hideaway rubs shoulders with the luminous Emerald Grotto.

12 Amalfi. This buzzy resort is threaded with beguiling, rambling passages, testimony to its Norman and Arab-Sicilian past. The glory of the city's days as a medieval maritime republic is most evident in its fantastic cathedral.

13 Ravello. Just beyond the Valley of the Dragon lies Ravello, perched "closer to the sky than the sea" atop Monte Cereto and set over the breathtaking Bay of Salerno. Ravello is one of Italy's most beautiful towns.

14 Paestum. With its Greek temples and Roman ruins in flowery meadows, this vision of a lost city makes a rousing finale to any Grand Tour.

MOLISE

PUGLIA

A1

87

ZIO

372 Telese

Teano

7

Benevento

Grottaminarda

A1

Caserta

7

A16

Nola

Avellino

Naples

4 Mt. Vesuvius

Pozzuoli

A30

1

2

5 3 Pompeii

Herculaneum

Oplontis

A3

PROCIDA

7

Castellammare

SORRENTINE PENINSULA

Salerno

6

Golfo di Nápoli

13

Eboli

ISCHIA

12 Ravello

Sorrento Positano

10

Amalfi

Battipaglia

9

11

8

Concha dei Marini

Golfo di Salerno

18

CAPRI

Paestum

14

Agropoli

Castellabate

0   20 mi

0   20 km

EATING AND DRINKING WELL IN NAPLES AND CAMPANIA

Think of Neapolitan food and you conjure up images of pasta, pizza, and tomatoes. The stereotype barely scratches the surface of what's available in Naples—to say nothing of the rest of Campania, where the cuisine reflects an enormously diverse landscape.

The region is known for its enclaves of gastronomy, notable among them the tip of the Sorrentine Peninsula. You may well come across *cucina povera*, a cuisine inspired by Campania's *contadino* (peasant) roots, with all the ingredients sourced from a nearby garden. Expect to see roadside stalls selling stellar local produce, including *annurca* apples (near Benevento), giant lemons (Amalfi Coast), roasted chestnuts (especially near Avellino), and watermelons (the plains around Salerno). Try to get to one of the local *sagre*, village feasts celebrating a *prodotto tipico* (local specialty), which could be anything from snails to wild boar to cherries to (commonly) wine.

PIZZA

Naples is the undisputed homeland of pizza, and you'll usually encounter it here in two classic forms: *margherita* and *marinara*. Given the larger-than-your-plate portions of standard pizzas, some choose to ask for a *mignon* (kid's portion), or even to share, divided between two plates. Take-away outlets in most town centers sell pizza by the slice, along with the usual range of fried *arancini* (rice balls) and *crocchè di patate* (potato fritters).

COFFEE

Given the same basic ingredients—coffee grounds, water, a machine—what makes *caffè* taste so much better in Naples than elsewhere remains a mystery. If you find the end product too strong, ask to have it with a dash of milk (caffè *macchiato*) or a little diluted (caffè *lungo*). Many bars serve with sugar already added, so if you want it without, request *senza zucchero* or *amaro*.

BUFFALO

Long feted for the melt-in-your-mouth mozzarella cheese made from its milk (pictured below), the river buffalo is also the source of other culinary delights. Throughout the region, look for buffalo ricotta and mascarpone, as well as buffalo *provola* and *scamorza*, which may be lightly smoked (resulting in a golden crust). Caserta has more mature *nero di bufala* (aged like sheep's cheese), while around Salerno you'll find smoked *caciocavallo* cheese as well as *carne di bufala* (buffalo meat).

THE ORAL TRADITION

Locals in Campania like to bypass the restaurant menu and ask what the staff recommend. Take this approach and you'll often wind up with a daily special or the house specialty. Although you're unlikely to get multilingual staff outside the larger hotels and main tourist areas, the person you talk to will spare no effort to get the message across.

WINE

Wine in Campania has an ancient pedigree. Some say fancifully that Campania's undisputed king of reds, the *aglianico*, got its name from the word "Hellenic"; and *fiano*, the primary white grape, closely resembles the Roman variety *apianus*. Horace, the Latin poet, extolled the virtues of drinking wine from Campania. A century later, Pliny the Elder was harsher in his judgment.

In recent decades, though, Campania has gained respect for its boutique reds. Due to the rugged landscape, small farms, and limited mechanization, prices can be relatively high, but the quality is high as well.

A region of evocative names—Capri, Sorrento, Pompeii, Positano, Amalfi— Campania conjures up visions of cliff-shaded, sapphire-hue coves, sun-dappled waters, and mighty ruins. More travelers visit this corner than any other in southern Italy, and it's no wonder.

Home to Vesuvius, the area's unique geology is responsible for Campania's photogenic landscape. A spectacular coastline stretches out along a deep blue sea, punctuated by rocky islands.

Through the ages, the area's temperate climate, warm sea, fertile soil, and natural beauty have attracted Greek colonists, then Roman emperors—who called the region "Campania Felix," or "the happy land"—and later Saracen raiders and Spanish invaders. The result has been a rich and varied history, reflected in everything from architecture to mythology. The highlights span millennia: the near-intact Roman towns of Pompeii and Herculaneum, the Greek temples in Paestum, the Norman and Baroque churches in Naples, the white-dome fisherman's houses of Positano, the *dolce vita* resorts of Capri. Campania piles them all onto one mammoth must-see sandwich.

The region's complex identity is most intensely felt in its major metropolis, Naples. Few who visit remain ambivalent. You needn't participate in the mad whirl of the city, however. The best pastime in Campania is simply finding a spot with a stunning view and indulging in *il dolce far niente* ("the sweetness of doing nothing").

MAJOR REGIONS

Volcanic ash and mud preserved the Roman towns of **Herculaneum** and **Pompeii** almost exactly as they were on the day **Mt. Vesuvius** erupted in AD 79, leaving them not just archaeological ruins but museums of daily life in the ancient world. The two cities and the volcano that buried them can be visited from either Naples or Sorrento, thanks to the Circumvesuviana, the suburban railroad that provides fast, frequent, and economical service.

Capri may get star billing among the islands that line the Bay of Naples, but **Ischia** and **Procida** also have their own lower-key appeal. Once entirely dependent on its thermal springs, Ischia is now the archaeological front-runner in the bay, thanks to the noted museum in Lacco Ameno. Procida has opened up to tourism, sparking rejuvenation through culture as *Capitale Italiana della Cultura 2022*, while opening access to its chief natural asset, the unspoiled isle of Vivara.

As the hub for a whole banquet of must-see sites—Pompeii and Naples to the north, Capri to the west, and the Amalfi Coast to the south—the beautiful, Belle Époque resort town of **Sorrento** is unequaled. The rest of the Sorrentine Peninsula, with plains and limestone outcroppings, watchtowers and Roman ins, groves and beaches, monasteries and villages, winding paths leading to isolated coves, and panoramic views of the bays of both Naples and Salerno, remains relatively undiscovered.

One of the most gorgeous places on earth is the corner of the Campania region called the Amalfi Coast. The justly famed jewels along the water are **Positano**, **Amalfi**, and **Ravello**. Considering the natural splendor of this region, it's no surprise that it has some of the most beautiful beaches in the world. White, sunbaked villages rise above cliffs hollowed out with grottoes and crystal lagoons lapped by emerald green water. Larger beaches, like those in Positano and Amalfi, are easily accessible, but the magic often lies in finding hidden coves and scenic spots, such as the picture-perfect Marina di Praia.

Planning

Making the Most of Your Time

In Campania there are three primary travel experiences: Naples, with its restless exuberance; the resorts (Capri, Sorrento, the Amalfi Coast), dedicated to leisure and indulgence; and the archaeological sites (Pompeii, Herculaneum, Paestum), where the ancient world is frozen in time. Each is wonderful in its own way. If you have a week, you can get a good taste of all three. With less time, you're better off choosing between them rather than stretching yourself thin.

Pompeii, being a day trip, is the simplest to plan for. To get a feel for Naples, you should give it a couple of days at a minimum. The train station makes a harsh first impression (an overhaul has softened the blow), but the city grows on you as you take in the sights and interact with the locals.

That said, many people bypass Naples and head right for the resorts. These places are all about relaxing—you'll miss the point if you're in a rush. Although Sorrento isn't as spectacular as Positano or Capri, it makes a good base because of its central location.

DISCOUNTS AND DEALS

Government-run sites are free on the first Sunday of each month—good for those on a budget, but less so for avoiding crowds. The **Campania ArteCard** with app entitles users to free or discounted admission to about four dozen museums and monuments in Naples and beyond. These are the main passes: Naples, three days (€21), has two sights included and up to 50% off the rest, plus transportation; Campania region, three days (€32), including Pompeii and other Bay of Naples sights and Ravello and Paestum with two sights included and others up to 50% off, plus transportation; Campania region, seven days (€34), with five sights included and many others up to 50% off, but no transportation. For longer stays the new 365 Gold Pass allows two entries to principle attractions and up to 50% off entry to others over an entire year (€43). Other benefits (which vary depending on the pass) include discounts on audio guides, theater and ferry tickets, city tours, and other activities. Visitors aged 18–25 receive generous discounts (10 free admissions) with the 3-day Napoli Young card (€12) and 365 Gold Pass Young (€33) for twice entry to the Artecard circuit sights over a year.

Confusingly, in 2019 the e-commerce driven **Naples Pass** (app only) was introduced in conjunction with Arte-Card. It includes some free sights, tours and transport (except the Lite), adding discounts. A warning: the poorly written, biased guide nudges the user to use certain affiliated businesses. It's pricey too: the cheapest three-day option Naples Pass Lite is €49 while the seven-day Whole Campania is €88. For more information, visit the www.campaniartecard.it and www.naplespass.eu, or the tourist office in the Piazza Garibaldi station, which distributes a helpful booklet about the various passes.

Getting Here and Around

BOAT

Several companies offer a variety of fast craft and passenger and car ferries connecting the islands of Capri, Ischia, and Procida with Naples and Pozzuoli year-round. Hydrofoils and other fast craft leave from Naples's Molo Beverello, adjacent to Piazza Municipio, with some departures in high season also from Mergellina, about 1½ km (1 mile) west of Piazza Municipio. Slower car ferries leave from the berths at Calata Porta di Massa, a 10-minute walk, or 3-minute shuttle bus ride, east of Molo Beverello.

Information on departures is published every day in the local paper, *Il Mattino*. Alternatively, ask at the tourist office or at the port, check websites, or contact these companies directly. Always double-check schedules in stormy weather.

BOAT CONTACTS Alilauro.
☎ *081/4972252* ⊕ *www.alilauro.it.* **Caremar.** ☎ *081/18966690* ⊕ *www.caremar.it.* **Gescab.** (*NLG*) ☎ *081/8071812 Sorrento office, 081/4285555 Naples Port office* ⊕ *www.gescab.it.* **SNAV.** ☎ *081/4285555* ⊕ *www.snav.it.*

BUS

Within Campania there's an extensive network of local buses, although finding information about it can be trying.

BUS CONTACT SITA Buses.
☎ *342/6256442* ⊕ *www.sitasudtrasporti.it.*

CAR

You can get along fine without a car in Campania, and there are plenty of reasons not to have one. Much of Naples is pedestrianized, meaning motorized arteries are often bottlenecked; you can't bring a car to Capri (except in winter, when everything's closed); and parking in the towns of the Amalfi Coast is hard to come by and expensive.

Italy's main north–south route, the A1 (aka the Autostrada del Sole), connects Rome with Naples and Campania. In good traffic the drive to Naples from Rome takes a little more than two hours. The A3 autostrada, a somewhat perilous continuation of the A1, runs south from Naples through Campania and into Calabria. Herculaneum (Ercolano) and Pompeii (Pompei) both have marked exits off the A3. For Vesuvius, take the Portici Ercolano exit. For the Sorrento Peninsula and the Amalfi Coast, exit at Castellammare di Stabia. To get to Paestum, take the A3 to the Battipaglia exit, and follow the road to Capaccio Scalo–Paestum. Roads on the Sorrento Peninsula and Amalfi Coast are narrow and twisting, but they have outstanding views.

If you come to Naples by car, find a garage, agree on the rate, and leave it there for the duration of your stay. (If you park on the street, you run the risk of theft.)

NAPLES GARAGE CONTACTS Garage Cava. ✉ *Via Mergellina 6, Mergellina* ☎ *081/660023* ⊕ *www.garagecava.it* Ⓜ *Mergellina.* **Petraglia.** ✉ *Via Ferraris 42, Piazza Garibaldi* ☎ *081/3602840* ⊕ *www.garagepetraglia.it* Ⓜ *Garibaldi.* **Turistico.** ✉ *Via de Gasperi 14, near port, Toledo* ☎ *081/5525442* ⊕ *www.garageturistico.it* Ⓜ *Municipio/Università.*

TAXI

You may be able to hail a taxi if you see one driving, but your best bet is to call Radio Taxi or ask someone at your hotel to book one. Taxi ranks can be found outside the central Piazza Garibaldi train station and the port (Molo Beverello), as well as throughout the city. Watch out for overcharging at three locations: the airport, the railway station, and the ydrofoil marina. The fixed rate (be sure o ask for *tariffa predeterminata*!) from ne airport to the central station is €18, vhich covers three people, two large eces of luggage, and two small pieces. ity Airport Taxis offers a private service.

sk for *il tariffario*, the tariff information neet of the Comune di Napoli with ommon fixed-rate journeys when taking taxi, as drivers may invent an exorbitant rice, even hiding the tariff sheet—trips round the city should cost €8–€10. You an of course request that the meter is witched on; this often results in your aying less. Taxis charge approximately 3.50 initially (more on Sunday, holidays, nd after 10 pm), then €0.05 per 48 neters (or 8 seconds of idling). A copy f the latest tariff sheet can be down-oaded at www.comune.napoli.it/taxi. Other options besides Radio Taxi include Consorttaxi (081/2222), La Partenope 081/0101), and La 570 (081/5707070). In summer, many cabs in Naples have no ir-conditioning, so you can bake if caught n a traffic jam.

AXI CONTACTS City Airport Taxis.
✉ *Naples* ⊕ *www.city-airport-taxis.com.* **Radio Taxi Napoli.** ✉ *Naples* ☎ *081/8888* ⊕ *www.taxinapoli.it.*

TRAIN

There are up to five trains every hour between Rome and Naples. Both the Alta Velocità Frecciarossa and Italo trains (the fastest types of train service) make the trip in a little more than an hour, with the ntercity taking two. All trains to Naples stop at the refurbished but forever scuzzy Stazione Centrale.

The efficient (though run-down) suburban Circumvesuviana runs from Naples's Porta Nolana and stops at Stazione Centrale before continuing to Herculaneum, Pompeii, and Sorrento. Travel time between Naples and Sorrento on the Circumvesuviana line is about 75 minutes.

For ticketing purposes, the region is divided into travel zones by distance from Naples. If you're traveling from Naples to anywhere else in Campania, be sure to ask for a *biglietto integrato*. It's slightly more expensive than the direct ticket (about €1 more), but there will be no need to buy a separate ticket for your subway, tram, or bus ride to the train station as the biglietto integrato covers the whole journey. An *integrato* ticket to Herculaneum costs €2.70, to Pompeii €3.50, and to Sorrento €4.90. Choose a cheaper *corso semplice* direct ticket if no changes required

TRAIN CONTACTS Circumvesuviana.
☎ *800/211388* ⊕ *www.eavsrl.it.* **Trenitalia and Italo.** ✉ *Piazza Garibaldi, Naples* ☎ *892021 Trenitalia (in Italy: fee), 06/68475475 Trenitalia: from abroad, 892020 Italo (in Italy: fee), 06/8937 1892 Italo (from abroad)* ⊕ *www.trenitalia.com, www.italotreno.it.*

Restaurants

As the birthplace of pizza, Naples prides itself on its vast selection of pizzerias, the most famous of which—Da Michele (where Julia Roberts filmed her pizza scene in *Eat Pray Love*) or Sorbillo—deserve the designation of "incomparable." Many Neapolitans make lunch their big meal of the day, and then have a pizza for supper.

Dining on the Amalfi Coast, Capri, Ischia and Procida revolves largely around seafood. Dishes are prepared using the short, rolled handmade *scialatielli* or large *paccheri* pasta and adorned with local *vongole* (clams) or *cozze* (mussels) and other shellfish. Octopus, squid, and the fresh fish of the season are always on the menu for the second course. Cetara has been famous for its *alici* (anchovies) since Roman times, and even produces alici bread. Eateries range from beach-side trattorias to beacons of fine dining with stupendous views.

Restaurant reviews have been shortened. For full information, visit Fodors.com.

Hotels

Most parts of Campania have accommodations in all price categories, but they tend to fill up in high season, so reserve well in advance. In summer, on the coast and the islands, hotels that serve meals often require you to take half board.

Hotel reviews have been shortened. For full information, visit Fodors.com.

WHAT IT COSTS in Euros			
$	$$	$$$	$$$$
RESTAURANTS			
under €15	€15–€24	€25–€35	over €35
HOTELS			
under €125	€125–€200	€201–€300	over €300

Tours

City Sightseeing

BUS TOURS | Close to the port, beside the main entrance to Castel Nuovo, is the terminal for double-decker buses belonging to City Sightseeing. For €23 you can take two different excursions, giving you reasonable coverage of the downtown sights and outlying attractions like the Museo di Capodimonte. ⊠ *Piazza Municipio, Naples* ☏ *055961237, 39/3248114807 WhatsApp/Cellphone* ⊕ *www.napoli.city-sightseeing.it.*

Lino Tour

GUIDED TOURS | Lino Tour offers tailor-made tours of the attractions in and around Naples. ⊠ *Naples* ☏ *081/8772244* ⊕ *www.linotourcarservice.com.*

Naples

Located under the shadow of Vesuvius, Naples is the most vibrant city in Italy—a steaming, bubbling, reverberating minestrone in which each block is a small village and everything seems to be a backdrop for an opera not yet composed

It's said that northern Italians vacation here to remind themselves of the time when Italy was *molto italiana—really* Italian. In this respect, Naples (Napoli in Italian) doesn't disappoint: Neapolitan rainbows of laundry wave in the wind over alleyways, mothers caress children, men break out into impromptu arias at sidewalk cafés, and street scenes offer an intricate theatre of human exchanges.

Everywhere contrasting elements of faded gilt and romance, grandeur and squalor form a pageant of pure *Napoletanità*, a distillation of *Italianità*—Italy at its most Italian.

As the historic capital of the region known as Campania, Naples has been perpetually and tumultuously in a state of flux. Neapolitans are instinctively the most hospitable of people, and they've often paid a price for being so, having unwittingly extended a warm welcome to wave after wave of invaders. Lombards, Goths, Normans, Swabians, Spanish viceroys and kings, and Napoleonic generals arrived in turn; most of them proved to be greedy and self-serving. Still, if these foreign rulers bled the populace dry with taxes, they left the impoverished city with a rich architectural inheritance.

Much of that inheritance is on display in the Centro Storico neighborhood, where the Piazza del Gesù Nuovo and the surrounding blocks are a showplace for the city's most beloved churches. Compared to most great metropolises of the world, Naples has little tourist infrastructure, forcing you to become a native very quickly, which you will if you spend enough time wandering through the grid-like narrow streets of the old center.

GETTING HERE AND AROUND

Public transportation in Naples is decent, and includes two subway lines, three funiculars, and a multitude of buses. Tickets cost €1.10 per journey (€1.30 on Metro Linea 2), but a Ticket Integrato Campania costs €1.60 and is valid for 90 minutes on all transport for as far as Pozzuoli to the west and Portici to the east; €4.50 buys a *biglietto giornaliero* (all-day ticket).

Now with a couple of art-decorated stations (Toledo and Università) voted among Europe's most attractive, Naples's Metropolitana provides fairly frequent service and can be the fastest way to get across the traffic-clogged city. Linea 1, Metropolitana Collinare, links the hill area of the Vomero and beyond with the National Archaeological Museum and Piazza Municipio near the port, as well as Stazione Centrale. The older Linea 2 stretches from the train station to Pozzuoli. Trains on both lines run 5:45 am–11 pm. To check journey costs and download the app visit www.unicocampania.it.

Bus service is viable, especially with the introduction of larger buses on the regular R1, R2, R3, and R4 routes. Electronic signs display wait times at many stops. Three tram routes now thread through the streets with new tram rolling stock introduced in 2020, but the service is unreliable and regularly suspended.

VISITOR INFORMATION

The numerous tourist offices in Naples aren't always open when they claim to be, but most are generally open Monday–Saturday 8:30–8 (Sunday 8:30–2) except where noted. The AACST specializes in information on old Naples but generally just supplies brochures. A second office, which is closed on Sunday, is handily located inside the Palazzo Reale. There's an EPT (Ente Provinciale per il Turismo; open daily 9–6) office in Stazione Centrale staffed by a welcoming team of helpers. Pick up a free map and the latest "Art in Campania" brochure listing key venues and possible savings through the Campania ArteCard.

CONTACTS Azienda Autonoma di Soggiorno Cura e Turismo di Napoli. ⊠ *Via San Carlo 9, Piazza Plebiscito* ☎ *081/402394* ⊕ *www.inaples.it.* **EPT.** ⊠ *Stazione Centrale, Piazza Garibaldi* ☎ *081/268779* ⊕ *www.eptnapoli.info* Ⓜ *Garibaldi.* **I Naples.** ⊠ *Piazza del Gesù 7, Centro Storico* ☎ *081/5512701* ⊕ *www.inaples.it.*

Centro Storico

To experience the true essence of Naples, you need to explore the Centro Storico, an unforgettable neighborhood that is the heart of old Naples. This is the Naples of peeling building facades and hanging laundry, with small alleyways fragrant with fresh flowers laid at the many shrines to the Blessed Virgin. Here the cheapest pizzerias in town feed the locals like kings, and the raucous street carnival of Neapolitan daily life is punctuated with oases of spiritual calm. All the contradictions of Naples—splendor and squalor, palace and slum, triumph and tragedy—meet here and sing a full-throated chorale. But the Centro Storico is not simply picturesque. It also contains some of Naples's most important sights, including a striking conglomeration of churches—Lombard, Gothic, Renaissance, Baroque, Rococo, and neoclassical. There are the majolica-adorned cloister of Santa Chiara; the sumptuous church of the Gesù Nuovo; two opera-set piazzas; the Duomo, where the Festa di San Gennaro is celebrated every September; the Museo Cappella Sansevero; the greatest painting in Naples—Caravaggio's *Seven Acts of Mercy* altarpiece—on view at the museum complex of Pio Monte; and Via Gregorio Armeno, where shops devoted to *Presepe crèche* (Nativity scene statues) make every day a rehearsal for

Campania Through the Ages

Ancient history. Lying on Mediterranean trade routes plied by several pre-Hellenic civilizations, Campania was settled by the ancient Greeks from approximately 800 BC onward. Here myth and legend blend with historical fact. The town of Herculaneum is said—rather improbably—to have been established by Hercules himself; and Naples in ancient times was called Parthenope, the name attributed to one of the sirens who preyed on hapless sailors in antiquity.

Thanks to archaeological research, some of the layers of myth have been stripped away to reveal a pattern of occupation and settlement well before Rome became established. Greek civilization flourished for hundreds of years all along this coastline, but there was nothing in the way of centralized government until centuries later when the Roman Republic, uniting all Italy for the first time, absorbed the Greek colonies with little opposition. Generally, the peace of Campania was undisturbed during these centuries of Roman rule.

Foreign influences. Naples and Campania, like Italy in general, decayed along with the Roman Empire and was thereafter squabbled over by Europe's foreign dynasties. Naples regained some importance under the rule of the Angevins in the latter part of the 13th century and continued its progress in the 1440s under Aragonese rule. The nobles who served under the Spanish viceroys in the 16th and 17th centuries enjoyed their pleasures, even as Spain milked the area for taxes.

After a short Austrian occupation, Naples became the capital of the Kingdom of the Two Sicilies, which the Bourbon kings established in 1738. Their rule was generally benevolent as far as Campania was concerned, and their support of papal authority in Rome was important in the development of the country as a whole. Their rule was important artistically, too, contributing to the architecture of the region, and attracting great musicians, artists, and writers who were drawn by the easy life at court. Finally, Giuseppe Garibaldi launched his famous expedition, and in 1860 Naples was united with the rest of Italy.

Modern times. Things were relatively tranquil through the years that followed—with visitors thronging to Capri, Sorrento, Amalfi, and, of course, Naples—until World War II. Allied bombings did considerable damage in and around Naples. At the fall of the Fascist government, the sorely tried Neapolitans rose up against Nazi occupation troops and in four days of street fighting drove them out of the city. A monument was raised to the *scugnizzo* (the typical Neapolitan street urchin), celebrating the youngsters who participated in the battle. With the end of the war, artists, tourists, writers, and other lovers of beauty returned to the Campania region.

As time passed, some parts of Campania gained increased attention from visitors, while others lost their cachet. Years of misgovernment have left their mark, yet the region's cultural and natural heritage is finally being revalued as local authorities and inhabitants recognize the importance of the area's largest industry—tourism.

Christmas. And even though this was the medieval center of the city, the city's flagship museum of modern art, the Madre, is here, and night owls will find that many of Naples's most cutting-edge clubs and bars are hidden among its nooks and alleys. For soccer fanatics, there is even a shrine to Diego Maradona, and intriguing, edgy graffitti mixing modern and ancient motifs abound.

 ## Sights

Duomo

CHURCH | Hemmed in on three sides, this cathedral is a trip through the city's history. Although the cathedral was established in the 1200s, the building you see was erected a century later and has since undergone radical changes—especially during the Baroque period. Inside, ancient columns salvaged from pagan buildings rise to the 350-year-old richly decorated false wooden ceiling (the original Gothic ceiling is 6 meters higher). Off the left aisle, step down into the 4th-century church of **Santa Restituta,** which was incorporated into the cathedral. Though Santa Restituta was redecorated in the late 1600s in the prevalent Baroque style, the **Battistero** (Baptistery) is the oldest in the Western world, with what some claim to be the most beautiful mosaics in Italy. On the right aisle of the cathedral, in the **Cappella del Tesoro di San Gennaro,** multicolor marbles and frescoes honor Saint Januarius, the miracle-working patron saint of Naples, whose altar and relics are encased in silver. Three times a year—on September 19 (his feast day); on the Saturday preceding the first Sunday in May, which commemorates the transfer of his relics to Naples; and on December 16—his dried blood, contained in two sealed vials, is believed to liquefy during rites in his honor; the rare occasions on which it does not liquefy portend ill, as in 1980, the year of the Irpinia earthquake. The most spectacular painting on display is Ribera's *San Gennaro in the Furnace* (1647), depicting the saint emerging unscathed from the furnace while his persecutors scatter in disarray. These days large numbers of devout Neapolitans offer up prayers in his memory. The **Museo del Tesoro di San Gennaro** houses a rich collection of treasures associated with the saint. Paintings by Solimena and Luca Giordano hang alongside statues, busts, candelabras, and tabernacles in gold, silver, and marble by Cosimo Fanzago and other 18th-century Baroque masters. ⊠ *Via Duomo 149, Centro Storico* ☎ *081/449097 Duomo, 081/294980* ⊕ *www.museosangennaro.it* ☑ *Museum €5; 'Full Experience' guided tour and museums €8.*

Gesù Nuovo

CHURCH | A stunning architectural contrast to the plain Romanesque frontage of other nearby churches, the oddly faceted stone facade of this elaborate Baroque church dates to the late 16th century. Originally a palace, the building was seized by Pedro of Toledo in 1547 and donated to the Jesuits on the condition the facade remain intact. Recent research has revealed that the symbols on the stones out front are Aramaic musical notes that produce a 45-minute concerto. Behind the entrance is Francesco Solimena's action-packed *Heliodorus' Eviction from the Temple.* The bulk of the interior decoration took more than 40 years and was completed only in the 18th century. You can find the work of familiar Baroque sculptors (Naccherino, Finelli) and painters inside. The gracious *Visitation* above the altar in the second chapel on the right is by Massimo Stanzione, who also contributed the fine frescoes in the main nave: they're in the presbytery (behind and around the main altar). Don't miss the votive chapel dedicated to the surgeon and university teacher Saint Giuseppe Moscato, along with a re-creation of his studio. Here hundreds of tiny silver images have been hung on the walls to give thanks to the saint, who was canonized in 1987, for his

Centro Storico

KEY

Ⓜ Line 1 Metropolitana Collinare

Ⓜ Line 2 Metropolitana FS

① Sights

① Restaurants

① Quick Bites

① Hotels

assistance in medical matters. On the opposite far left corner a smaller chapel similarly gives thanks to San Ciro (Saint Cyrus), also a doctor. Farther down are impressive statues of David and Jeremiah by Fanzago. Left of the altar the wooden heads of various saints are aligned like gods in an antique theater. ⊠ *Piazza Gesù Nuovo, Centro Storico* ☎ *081/5578111* ⊕ *www.gesunuovo.it.*

Madre (*Museum of Contemporary Art Donnaregina*)

ART GALLERY | With 8,000 square meters (86,111 square feet) of exhibition space, a host of young and helpful attendants, and occasional late-night events, the Madre is one of the most visited museums in Naples. Most of the artworks on the first floor were installed in situ by their creators, but the second-floor gallery exhibits works by international and Italian contemporary artists. The museum also hosts temporary shows by major international artists. ⊠ *Via Settembrini 79, San Lorenzo, Centro Storico* ☎ *081/19978017* ⊕ *www. madrenapoli.it/en* ⊠ *€8* ☉ *Closed Tues.*

★ **Museo Cappella Sansevero**
(*Sansevero Chapel Museum*)

NOTABLE BUILDING | The dazzling funerary chapel of the Sangro di Sansevero princes combines noble swagger, overwhelming color, and a touch of the macabre—which expresses Naples perfectly. The chapel was begun in 1590 by Prince Giovan Francesco di Sangro to fulfill a vow to the Virgin if he were cured of a dire illness. The seventh Sangro di Sansevero prince, Raimondo, had the building modified in the mid-18th century and is generally credited for its current Baroque styling, the noteworthy elements of which include the splendid marble-inlay floor. A larger-than-life figure, Prince Raimondo was believed to have signed a pact with the devil allowing him to plumb nature's secrets. He commissioned the young sculptor Giuseppe Sanmartino to create numerous works, including the chapel's centerpiece, the remarkable *Veiled Christ,*

which has a seemingly transparent marble veil. If you have the stomach for it, take a look in the crypt, where some of the anatomical experiments conducted by the prince are gruesomely displayed. ⊠ *Via Francesco de Sanctis 19, off Vicolo Domenico Maggiore, Centro Storico* ☎ *081/5518470* ⊕ *www.museosansevero. it* ⊠ *€8* ☉ *Closed Tues.*

★ **Napoli Sotterranea**
(*Underground Naples*)

HISTORIC SIGHT | FAMILY | Fascinating 90-minute tours of a portion of Naples' fabled underground city provide an initiation into the complex history of the city center. Efforts to dramatize the experience—amphoras lowered on ropes to draw water from cisterns, candles given to navigate narrow passages, objects shifted to reveal secret passages—combine with enthusiastic English-speaking guides to make this particularly exciting for older children. A short descent delivers you to a section of a 400-km (249-mile) system of quarries and aqueducts used from Greek times until the 1845 cholera epidemic, including a highly claustrophobic 1-km (½-mile) walk with only a candle to light your way. At the end of the aqueduct, you come first to a Greek and then a much larger Roman cistern. Near the entrance is the War Museum, which displays uniforms, armed transportation vehicles, and weapons from World War II. Returning aboveground your guide leads you to a small apartment where you step down to a section of an amphitheater where Nero famously performed three times. During one of his performances an earthquake struck and—so Suetonius relates—the emperor forbade the 6,000 spectators to leave. The rumbling, he insisted, was only the gods applauding his performance. A room at the end of the tour contains examples of that most Neapolitan of art forms, *il presepe* (the crib). Be prepared on the underground tour to go up and down many steps and crouch in very narrow corridors. Temperatures in summer will be much lower below than at street level, so bring a sweater. ⊠ *Piazza San Gaetano 68, along Via dei Tribunali, Centro Storico* ☎ *081/296944* ⊕ *www. napolisotterranea.org* 🎫 *€10.*

Monumento Nazionale dei Girolamini

RELIGIOUS BUILDING | *I Girolamini* is another name for the Oratorians, followers of St. Philip Neri, to whom the splendid church I Girolamini is dedicated. The church is part of a larger complex managed as the Monumento Nazionale dei Girolamini. The Florentine architect Giovanni Antonio Dosio designed I Girolamini, which was erected between 1592 and 1619; the dome and facade were rebuilt (circa 1780) in the most elegant neoclassical style after a design by Ferdinando Fuga. Inside the entrance wall is Luca Giordano's grandiose fresco (1684) of Christ chasing the money-changers from the temple. The intricate carved-wood ceiling, damaged by Allied bombs in 1943, has now been restored to its original magnificence. The Oratorians also built the Casa dei Padri dell'Oratorio (House of the Oratorio Fathers). Step through its gate to see the two cloisters, from the 16th and the 17th centuries, the latter designed by Dosio and other Florentine architects. The gallery in this section contains 16th- and 17th-century paintings by Ribera, Reni, and other Baroque masters. One of Europe's most gloriously decorated 18th-century libraries, the Biblioteca dei Girolamini (Girolamini Library: closed for restoration) helped make this an intellectual nexus during the Renaissance and Baroque periods. The ticket office is on Via Duomo, behind the church. Ongoing restoration works mean that visits are only via pre-booked tours so contact ahead for upcoming dates and times. ⊠ *Via Duomo 142, Centro Storico* ☎ *081/294444* ⊕ *www.bibliotecadeigirolamini.beniculturali.it* 🎫 *€8.*

★ Pio Monte della Misericordia

NOTABLE BUILDING | One of the Centro Storico's defining sites, this octagonal church was built around the corner from the Duomo for a charitable institution seven noblemen founded in 1601. The institution's aim was to carry out acts of Christian charity like feeding the hungry, clothing the poor, nursing the sick, sheltering pilgrims, visiting prisoners, and burying the indigent dead—acts immortalized in the history of art by Caravaggio's famous altarpiece depicting the *Sette Opere della Misericordia* (*Seven Acts of Mercy*). In this haunting work, the artist has brought the Virgin, borne atop the shoulders of two angels, down into the streets of Spaccanapoli, populated by figures in whose spontaneous and passionate movements the people could see themselves. The original church was considered too small and was destroyed in 1658 to make way for a new church that was designed by Antonio Picchiatti and built between 1658 and 1672. Pride of place is given to the great Caravaggio above the altar, but there are other important Baroque paintings on view here. Some hang in the church—among them seven other works of mercy depicted individually by Caravaggio acolytes— while other works, including a wonderful self-portrait by Luca Giordano, are in the adjoining *pinacoteca* (picture gallery). ∎TIP➔ **Step into the choral chamber for a bird's-eye view of the Sette Opere della Misericordia.** ⊠ *Via Tribunali 253, Centro Storico* ☎ *081/446973* ⊕ *www.piomontedellamisericordia.it* 🎫 *€8.*

★ San Lorenzo Maggiore

NOTABLE BUILDING | One of the city's unmissable sights has a travel-through-time descent to Roman and Greek times, as well as the grandest medieval church of the Decumano Maggiore. The Archaeological Area explores the original streets below the bustling Centro Storico, first with the Roman law courts and then down a level to the streets, markets, and workshops on the *cardo* (north–south road) crossing the *decumani* (east–west road) of the 1st century BC Neapolis. The church of San Lorenzo features a very unmedieval facade of 18th-century splendor. Due to the effects and threats of earthquakes, the church was reinforced and reshaped along Baroque lines in the 17th and 18th centuries. Begun by Robert d'Anjou in 1270 on the site of a previous 6th-century church, the church has a single, barnlike nave that reflects the Franciscans' desire for simple spaces with enough room to preach to large crowds. A grandiose triumphal arch announces the transept, and the main altar (1530) is the sculptor Giovanni da Nola's masterpiece; this is a copy of the original, now disappeared, pedestal. Also found here is the church's most important monument: the tomb of Catherine of Austria (circa 1323), by Tino da Camaino, among the first sculptors to introduce the Gothic style into Italy. The apse, designed by an unknown French architect of great caliber, is pure French Angevin in style, complete with an ambulatory of nine chapels covered by a magnificent web of cross arches. The left transept contains the 14th-century funerary monument of Carlo di Durazzo and yet another Cosimo Fanzago masterpiece, the Cappellone di Sant'Antonio. Tickets to the scavi also give access to the Museo dell'Opera di San Lorenzo, installed in the 16th-century palazzo around the *torre campanaria* (bell tower). In Room 1 ancient remains from the Greek agora beneath combine with modern maps to provide a fascinating impression of import and export trends in the 4th century BC. The museum also contains ceramics dug up from the Swabian period, many pieces from the early Middle Ages, large tracts of mosaics from the 6th-century basilica, and helpful models of how the ancient Roman forum and nearby buildings must have looked. An app is available to do further justice to a place that exists in several historical dimensions. ⊠ *Via dei Tribunali 316, Centro Storico* ☎ *081/2110860* ⊕ *www.laneapolis-sotterrata.it* 🎟 *Excavations and museum €9* Ⓜ *Cavour, Dante.*

★ **Santa Chiara**

NOTABLE BUILDING | Offering a stark and telling contrast to the opulence of the nearby Gesù Nuovo, Santa Chiara is the leading Angevin Gothic monument in Naples. The fashionable house of worship for the 14th-century nobility and a favorite Angevin church from the start, the church of St. Clare was intended to be a great dynastic monument by Robert d'Anjou. His second wife, Sancia di Majorca, added the adjoining convent for the Poor Clares to a monastery of the Franciscan Minors so she could vicariously satisfy a lifelong desire for the cloistered seclusion of a convent. This was the first time the two sexes were combined in a single complex. Built in a Provençal Gothic style between 1310 and 1328 (probably by Gagliardo Primario) and dedicated in 1340, the church had its aspect radically altered, as did so many others, in the Baroque period. A six-day fire started by Allied bombs on August 4, 1943, put an end to all that, as well as to what might have been left of the important cycle of frescoes by Giotto and his Neapolitan workshop. The church's most important tomb towers behind the altar. Sculpted by Giovanni and Pacio Bertini of Florence (1343–45), it is, fittingly, the tomb of the founding king: the great Robert d'Anjou, known as the Wise. Nearby are the tombs of Carlo, duke of Calabria, and his wife, Marie de Valois, both by Tino da Camaino. Around the left side of the church is the Chiostro delle Clarisse, the most famous cloister in Naples. Complemented by citrus trees, the benches and octagonal columns comprise a light-handed masterpiece of painted majolica designed by Domenico Antonio Vaccaro, with a delightful profusion of landscapes and light yellow, azure, and green floral motifs realized by Donato and Giuseppe Massa and their studio (1742). ⊠ *Piazza Gesù Nuovo, Centro Storico* ☎ *081/5516673* ⊕ *www.monasterodisantachiara.it* 🎟 *Museum and cloister €6* Ⓜ *Dante, Università.*

🍴 Restaurants

★ Di Matteo

$ | PIZZA | Every pizzeria along Via dei Tribunali is worth the long wait—and trust us, all the good ones will be jam-packed—but just one can claim to have served a U.S. President: Bill Clinton enjoyed a margherita here when the G8 was held in Naples in 1994. **Known for:** top value, including filling pizza fritta (fried); functional decor and pizzaioli working at front; funny pics of Clinton and the "Pizzaiolo del Presidente" Ernesto Cacialli in 1994. ⑤ *Average main: €6* ⊠ *Via Tribunali 94, Centro Storico* ☎ *081/455262* ⊕ *www.pizzeriadimatteo. com.*

Gino Sorbillo

$ | PIZZA | FAMILY | There are a few restaurants called Sorbillo along Via dei Tribunali; this is the one with the crowds waiting outside and is world-renowned. Order the same thing the locals come for: a basic Neapolitan pizza (try the unique pizza al pesto or the stunningly simple marinara—just tomatoes and oregano). **Known for:** head honcho Gino is a celebrity and pizza ambassador; the crowd waiting outside; leave your name at the door and listen to be called. ⑤ *Average main: €10* ⊠ *Via dei Tribunali 32, Centro Storico* ☎ *081/446643* ⊕ *www.sorbillo.it* ⊗ *Closed Sun.*

Palazzo Petrucci Pizzeria

$ | PIZZA | In a 17th-century mansion facing the grand Piazza San Domenico Maggiore, Palazzo Petrucci doesn't lack for dramatic settings for dining—under the vaulted ceiling of the former stables, near the pizzaiolo and oven action, outside in the piazza, or on the roof terrace at *giuglia* (obelisk) di San Domenico level. Expect classic *pizze, pizze fritte,* and some unusual topping combinations, alongside heaped salads and antipasti. **Known for:** grandest palazzo venue for a pizza feast; craft beer, pizze fritte, and vegan options; atmospheric views and sounds over the piazza. ⑤ *Average main: €9* ⊠ *Piazza San Domenico Maggiore 5–7, Centro Storico* ☎ *081/5512460* ⊕ *www. palazzopetruccipizzeria.it* ⊗ *Closed 2 wks in Aug.*

☕ Coffee and Quick Bites

★ Scaturchio

$ | CAFE | Established in 1905, this Neapolitan institution on Spaccanapoli is a buzzy place to sample some of the finest pastries in town—plus it also makes classic savory dishes, ice cream, and mighty decent caffè. **Known for:** zucchine a scapece, arancini, and other savory bites; sumptuous babà, sfogliatelle, and pastiera; Ministeriale liquor-filled chocolates. ⑤ *Average main: €6* ⊠ *Piazza San Domenico Maggiore 19, Centro Storico* ☎ *081/551 6944* ⊕ *www.scaturchio.it.*

🛏 Hotels

Costantinopoli 104

$$ | HOTEL | An oasis of what Italians call *stile liberty* (art nouveau style), with impressive stained-glass fittings and striking artwork, this serene, elegant hotel is well placed for touring the Museo Archeologico Nazionale and the Centro Storico. **Pros:** pleasant service; convenient Centro Storico location; pool (a rarity in Neapolitan hotels) and garden. **Cons:** some rooms suffer from nightlife disturbance from Piazza Bellini; hotel can be difficult to find (look for the sign that reads Villa Spinelli, the place's former name); rooms getting dated. ⑤ *Rooms from: €184* ⊠ *Via Costantinopoli 104, Centro Storico* ☎ *081/5571035* ⊕ *costantinopoli104.it* ⑩ *Free Breakfast* ⤵ *19 rooms.*

★ Hotel Palazzo Decumani

$$ | HOTEL | This contemporary upscale hotel near the Centro Storico's major sights occupies an early-20th-century palazzo, but you won't find heavy, ornate furnishings—the emphasis is on light and space, both in short supply in old Naples.

Pros: service on par with fancier hotels; guests-only lounge-bar; large rooms and bathrooms. **Cons:** some may find decor a tad sparse; can be hard to find—follow signs from Corso Umberto; sound-proofing not the best. $ *Rooms from:* €190 ⊠ *Piazzetta Giustino Fortunato 8, Centro Storico* ☎ *081/4201379* ⊕ *www. palazzodecumani.com* ⊙| *Free Breakfast* ⇨ *28 rooms.*

⛒ Shopping

Ferrigno

OTHER SPECIALTY STORE | Shops selling Nativity scenes cluster along the Via San Gregorio Armeno off Spaccanapoli, and they're all worth a glance. The most famous is Ferrigno. Although Maestro Giuseppe Ferrigno died in 2008, the family business continues, still faithfully using 18th-century techniques. ⊠ *Via San Gregorio Armeno 8, Centro Storico* ☎ *081/5523148* ⊕ *www.arteferrigno.it.*

Ospedale delle Bambole

TOYS | **FAMILY** | In the courtyard of the 16th-century Palazzo Marigliano is this world-famous hospital for dolls. In business since 1850, it's a wonderful place to take kids (and their injured toys). It's closed Sunday. ⊠ *Via San Biagio dei Librai 39, Centro Storico* ☎ *081/18639797* ⊕ *ospedaledellebambole.com.*

Museo Archeologico Nazionale

It's only fitting that the Museo Archeologico Nazionale—the single most important and remarkable museum of Greco-Roman antiquities in the world (in spite of itself, some observers say)—sits in the upper *decumanus,* or neighborhood, of ancient Neapolis, the district colonized by the ancient Greeks and Romans. Happily, it's almost always open (its core collection, that is). But if two hours is your limit for gazing at ancient

art, nearby you can discover some of the lesser-known delights of medieval and Renaissance Naples, along with the city's lush botanical gardens. Along the way are churches that are repositories for magnificent 15th- and 16th-century art and sculpture.

⊙ Sights

★ **Museo Archeologico Nazionale** (*National Museum of Archaeology*)
HISTORY MUSEUM | Also known as MANN, this legendary museum has experienced something of a rebirth in recent years. Its unrivaled collections include world-renowned archaeological finds that put most other museums to shame, from some of the best mosaics and paintings from Pompeii and Herculaneum to the legendary Farnese collection of ancient sculpture. The core masterpiece collection is almost always open to visitors, while seasonal exhibitions feature intriguing cultural events, collaborations, and contemporary artists. Some of the newer rooms, covering archaeological discoveries in the Greco-Roman settlements and necropolises in and around Naples, have helpful informational panels in English. ⊠ *Piazza Museo 19, Centro Storico* ☎ *081/4422111149 from overseas and cell phones* ⊕ *mannapoli.it* ⊠ *€10* ⊙ *Closed Tues.* Ⓜ *Museo.*

Toledo

Naples's setting on what is possibly the most captivating bay in the world has long been a boon for its inhabitants—the expansive harbor has always brought great mercantile wealth to the city—and, intermittently, a curse. Throughout history, a who's who of Greek, Roman, Norman, Spanish, and French despots has quarreled over this gateway to Campania. Each set of conquerors recognized that the area around the city harbor—today occupied by the Molo Beverello hydrofoil terminal and the 1928

Stazione Marittima—functioned as a veritable welcome mat to the metropolis and consequently should be a fitting showcase of regal authority. This had become imperative because of explosive population growth, which, by the mid-16th century, had made Naples the second-largest city in Europe, after Paris. With the mass migration of the rural population to the city, Naples had grown into a capricious, unplanned, disorderly, and untrammeled capital. Thus, the central aim of the ruling dynasties became the creation of a *Napoli nobilissima*—a "most noble" Naples.

Sights

★ Castel Nuovo

CASTLE/PALACE | Known to locals as Maschio Angioino, in reference to its Angevin builders, this imposing castle is now used more for marital than military purposes—a portion of it serves as a government registry office. A white four-tiered triumphal entrance arch, ordered by Alfonso of Aragon after he entered the city in 1443 to seize power from the increasingly beleaguered Angevin Giovanna II, upstages the building's looming Angevin stonework. At the arch's top, as if justifying Alfonso's claim to the throne, the Archangel Michael raises his right arm to slay a demon. Across the courtyard within the castle, up a staircase, is the Sala Grande, also known as the Sala dei Baroni, which has a stunning vaulted ceiling 92 feet high. In 1486, local barons hatched a plot against Alfonso's son, King Ferrante, who reacted by inviting them to this hall for a wedding banquet, which promptly turned into a mass arrest. (Ferrante is also said to have kept a crocodile in the castle as his pet executioner.) You can also visit the Sala dell'Armeria, where a glass floor reveals recent excavations of Roman baths from the Augustan period, with resin plaster casts of the skeletons also found here (the originals are in the Museo Archeologico Nazionale). In the next room on the left, the Cappella Palatina, Niccolò di Tommaso's frescoes adorn the walls along with a few tiny remaining fragments of the famous Giotto pictures described by Petrarch. Before climbing to the castle's first-floor gallery, with its beautiful Renaissance-era masterpieces, check out the magnificent 16th-century Cappella delle Anime del Purgatorio and its richly decorated gold-plated altar. At the back of the courtyard are giant photographs of three Roman ships, wood amazingly intact, unearthed during recent digging of the nearby metro station and now hidden away for restoration. A few tour itineraries are offered, including one of the Beverello Tower, with its unrivaled views of Piazza Muncipio's Roman excavations and a vertigo-inducing look at the Sala dei Baroni and its ceiling. ☒ *Piazza Municipio, Toledo* ☏ *081/7957722* ⊕ *www.timelinenapoli.it* ✉ *From €6* ☾ *Closed Sun.*

Gallerie d'Italia Palazzo Zevallos Stigliano

ART GALLERY | Tucked inside this beautifully restored 17th-century palazzo, once a bank, is a small museum that's worth seeking out for its outstanding collection of 17th- and 18th-century paintings. Enter through Cosimo Fanzago's gargoyled doorway, and take the handsome elevator to the upper floor where a room on the right holds the star attraction, Caravaggio's last work, *The Martyrdom of Saint Ursula*. The saint here is, for dramatic effect, deprived of her usual retinue of a thousand followers. On the left, a face of pure spite, is the king of the Huns, who has just shot Ursula with an arrow after his proposal of marriage has been rejected. Free lunchtime concerts are sometimes held in the atrium of the palazzo. ☒ *Via Toledo 185, Toledo* ☏ *800/454229* ⊕ *www.palazzozevallos. com* ✉ *€5* ☾ *Closed Mon.* Ⓜ *Toledo.*

Galleria Umberto I

NOTABLE BUILDING | The galleria was erected during the "cleanup" of Naples following the devastating cholera epidemic of 1884, part of a massive urban-renewal plan that entailed the destruction of slum areas between the Centro Storico and the Palazzo Reale. With facades on Via Toledo—the most animated street in Naples at the time—the structure, built between 1887 and 1890 according to a design by Emanuele Rocco, had a prestigious and important location. As with its larger predecessor, the Galleria Vittorio Emanuele II in Milan, the Galleria Umberto Primo exalts the taste of the postunification commercial elite in a virtuoso display of late-19th-century technology clothed in traditional style. Here are the iron-ribbed glass barrel vault and 188-feet-high dome by Paolo Boubée, which represented the latest advance in modern form yet was layered over with the reassuring architectural ornament of the 14th century (another era when the bourgeoisie triumphed in Italy). ⊠ *Entrances on Via San Carlo, Via Toledo, Via Santa Brigida, and Via Verdi, Toledo* Ⓜ *Toledo.*

★ Palazzo Reale

CASTLE/PALACE | A leading Naples showpiece created as an expression of Bourbon power and values, the Palazzo Reale dates from 1600. Renovated and redecorated by successive rulers and once lorded over by a dim-witted king who liked to shoot his hunting guns at the birds in his tapestries, it is filled with salons designed in the most lavish 18th-century Neapolitan style. The Spanish viceroys originally commissioned the palace, ordering the Swiss architect Domenico Fontana to build a suitable new residence for King Philip III, should he ever visit Naples. He died in 1621 before ever doing so. The palace saw its greatest moment of splendor in the 18th century, when Charles III of Bourbon became the first permanent resident. The flamboyant Naples-born architect

Luigi Vanvitelli redesigned the facade, and Ferdinando Fuga, under Ferdinand IV, created the Royal Apartments, sumptuously furnished and full of precious paintings, tapestries, porcelains, and other objets d'art. To access these 30 rooms, climb the monumental Scalone d'Onore (Staircase). On the right is the Court Theater, built by Fuga for Charles III and his private opera company. Damaged during World War II, it was restored in the 1950s; note the resplendent royal box. Pass through three regal antechambers to Room VI, the Throne Room, the ponderous titular object dating to sometime after 1850. In the Ambassadors' Room, choice Gobelin tapestries grace the beige fabric walls and the ceiling honors Spanish military victories, painted by local artist Belisario Corenzio (1610–20). Room IX was bedroom to Charles's queen, Maria Cristina. The brilliantly gold private oratory has beautiful paintings by Francesco Liani (1760). The Great Captain's Room has ceiling frescoes by Battistello Caracciolo (1610–16); all velvet, fire, and smoke, they reveal the influence of Caravaggio's visit to the city. A wall-mounted, jolly series by Federico Zuccari depicts 12 proverbs. Room XIII was Joachim Murat's writing room when he was king of Naples; brought with him from France, some of the furniture is courtesy of Adam Weisweiler, cabinetmaker to Marie Antoinette. The huge Room XXII, painted in green and gold with kitschy faux tapestries, is known as the Hercules Hall, because it once housed the *Farnese Hercules,* an epic sculpture of the mythological Greek hero. Pride of place now goes to the Sèvres porcelain. The Palatine Chapel, also known as the Royal Chapel, redone by Gaetano Genovese in the 1830s, is gussied up with an excess of gold, although it has a stunning multicolored marble intarsia altar transported from a now-destroyed chapel in Capodimonte (Dionisio Lazzari, 1678). Also here is a Nativity scene with pieces sculpted by Giuseppe Sammartino

Sights ▼

1 Castel Nuovo **C5**
2 Galleria Umberto I ... **B5**
3 Galleria d'Italia Palazzo Zevallos Stigliano **B4**
4 Palazzo Reale **B6**
5 Piazza Plebiscito ... **B6**
6 Sant'Anna dei Lombardi (Chiesa di Monteoliveto **B1**
7 Teatro San Carlo and MeMus Museum **B5**
8 Via Toledo... **B6**

Restaurants ▼

1 A' Cucina Ra Casa Mia.... **A5**
2 Trattoria San Ferdinando . **A6**

Hotels ▼

1 Palazzo Turchini **C3**
2 Renaissance Naples Hotel Mediterraneo..... **B3**

KEY

⎓M⎓ Line 1 Metropolitana Collinare

⎓M⎓ Line 2 Metropolitana FS

1 Sights

1 Restaurants

1 Hotels

Toledo and the Port

Golfo di Napoli

and others. Another wing holds the Biblioteca Nazionale Vittorio Emanuele III. Starting out from Farnese bits and pieces, it was enriched with the papyri from Herculaneum found in 1752 and opened to the public in 1804. The sumptuous rooms can still be viewed, and there's a tasteful terrace that looks onto Castel Nuovo. ⊠ *Piazza Plebiscito, Toledo* ☎ *081/5808255, 848/082408 schools and guided tours* ⊕ *www.coopculture.it* 🖾 *€6* ☉ *Closed Wed.*

Piazza Plebiscito (*People's Square*)
PLAZA/SQUARE | After spending time as a parking lot, this square was restored in 1994 to one of Napoli Nobilissima's most majestic spaces, with a Doric semicircle of columns resembling Saint Peter's Square in Rome. The piazza was erected in the early 1800s under the Napoleonic regime, but after the regime fell, Ferdinand, the new King of the Two Sicilies, ordered the addition of the Church of San Francesco di Paola. On the left as you approach the church is a statue of Ferdinand and on the right one of his father, Charles III, both of them clad in Roman togas. Around dusk, floodlights come on, creating a magical effect. A delightful sea breeze airs the square, and most days one corner becomes an improvised soccer stadium where local youths emulate their heroes. ⊠ *Piazza Plebiscito, Toledo* Ⓜ *Toledo, Piazza Municipio.*

★ **Sant'Anna dei Lombardi**
(Chiesa di Monteoliveto)
CHURCH | Long favored by the Aragonese kings, this church, simple and rather anonymous from the outside, houses some of the most important ensembles of Renaissance sculpture in southern Italy. Begun with the adjacent convent of the Olivetani and its four cloisters in 1411, it was given a Baroque makeover in the mid-17th century by Gennaro Sacco. This, however, is no longer so visible because the bombs of 1943 led to a restoration favoring the original *quattrocento* (15th-century) lines. The wonderful

coffered wooden ceiling adds a bit of pomp. Inside the porch is the tomb of Domenico Fontana, one of the major architects of the late 16th century, who died in Naples after beginning the Palazzo Reale. On either side of the original entrance door are two fine Renaissance tombs. The one on the left as you face the door belongs to the Ligorio family (whose descendant Pirro designed the Villa d'Este in Tivoli) and is a work by Giovanni da Nola (1524). The tomb on the right is a masterpiece by Giuseppe Santacroce (1532) done for the del Pozzo family. To the left of the Ligorio Altar (the corner chapel on the immediate right as you face the altar) is the Mastrogiudice Chapel, whose altar contains precious reliefs of the Annunciation and *Scenes from the Life of Jesus* (1489) by Benedetto da Maiano, a great name in Tuscan sculpture. On the other side of the entrance is the Piccolomini Chapel, with a *Crucifixion* by Giulio Mazzoni (circa 1550), a refined marble altar (circa 1475), a funerary monument to Maria d'Aragona by another prominent Florentine sculptor, Antonello Rossellino (circa 1475), and on the right, a rather sweet fresco of the Annunciation by an anonymous follower of Piero della Francesca. The true surprises of the church are to the right of the altar, in the presbytery and adjoining rooms. The chapel just to the right of the main altar, belonging to the Orefice family, is richly decorated in pre-Baroque (1596–98) polychrome marbles and frescoes by Luis Rodriguez; from here you continue on through the Oratory of the Holy Sepulchre, with the tomb of Antonio D'Alessandro and his wife, to reach the church's showpiece: a potently realistic life-size group of eight terra-cotta figures by Guido Mazzoni (1492), which make up a Pietà; the faces are said to be modeled from people at the Aragonese court. Toward the rear of the church is Cappella dell'Assunta, with a fun painting in its corner of a monk by Michelangelo's student Giorgio Vasari, and the lovely Sacrestia Vecchia (Old Sacristy), adorned with one of the most successful decorative ensembles Vasari ever painted (1544) and breathtaking wood-inlay stalls by Fra' Giovanni da Verona and assistants (1506–10) with views of famous buildings. ⊠ *Piazza Monteoliveto 15, Toledo* ☎ *081/4420039* ⊕ *www.santannadeilombardi.com* ✉ *Side chapels, oratory, and sacristy €5* ⊗ *Side chapels, oratory, and sacristy closed Sun.*

Teatro San Carlo and MeMus Museum
NOTABLE BUILDING | Out of all the Italian opera houses, La Scala in Milan is the most famous, but San Carlo is more beautiful, and Naples is, after all, the most operatic of cities. The neoclassical structure, designed by Antonio Niccolini, was built in a mere nine months after an 1816 fire destroyed the original. Many operas were composed for the house, including Donizetti's *Lucia di Lammermoor* and Rossini's *La Donna del Lago*. In the theater, nearly 200 boxes are arranged on six levels, and the 1,115-square-meter (12,000-square-foot) stage permits productions with horses, camels, and elephants, and even has a backdrop that can lift to reveal the Palazzo Reale Gardens. Above the rich red-and-gold auditorium is a ceiling fresco by Giuseppe Cammarano representing Apollo presenting poets to Athena. Performance standards are among Europe's highest—even the great Enrico Caruso was hissed here. If you're not attending an opera, you can still see the splendid theater on a 30-minute guided tour and visit MeMus (Museo Memoria e Musica): San Carlo's theatrically lit museum and archive has props, costumes, stage sets, and multimedia and documents galore. English-language tours, which take place daily except on holidays, can be booked in advance on the theater's website. ⊠ *Via San Carlo 101–103, Toledo* ☎ *081/7972331 ticket office, 081/7972412 tours, 081/7972449 MeMus* ⊕ *www.teatrosancarlo.it* ✉ *From €6* ⊗ *MeMus closed Wed. and Aug.*

Via Toledo
HISTORIC DISTRICT | Sooner or later you'll wind up at one of the busiest commercial arteries, also known as Via Roma, which is thankfully closed to through traffic—at least along the stretch leading from the Palazzo Reale. Don't avoid dipping into this parade of shops and coffee bars where plump pastries are temptingly arranged. ⊠ *Via Toledo, Toledo* Ⓜ *Toledo.*

Restaurants

A' Cucina Ra Casa Mia
$ | SOUTHERN ITALIAN |Just off bustling Via Toledo on the basalti flagstones of a narrow Quartieri Spagnoli street, this small trattoria does superb-value, classic Neapolitan dishes. Take a seat at one of the small tables with checkered tablecloths and ask the amiable staff about the day's freshest seafood, meat, and vegetable dishes, while taking in the atmospheric surroundings. **Known for:** veggie and gluten-free options; fresh seafood pasta dishes; homey place popular with locals. Ⓢ *Average main: €13* ⊠ *Via Carlo De Cesare 14, Toledo* ☎ *081/4976297* ⊕ *www.acucinaracasamia.it* ⊗ *Closed Tues.*

Trattoria San Ferdinando
$$$ | SOUTHERN ITALIAN |This cheerful trattoria seems to be run for the sheer pleasure of it, and chatting locals give it a buzzy Neapolitan atmosphere. Try the excellent fish or the traditional (but cooked with a lighter modern touch) pasta dishes, especially those with *verdure* (fresh leafy vegetables) or with *patate con la provola* (potatoes and smoked mozzarella). **Known for:** near Teatro San Carlo; excellent, fresh seafood specialties; popular with locals in the evening, so reserve ahead. Ⓢ *Average main: €25* ⊠ *Via Nardones 117, Toledo* ☎ *081/421964* ⊕ *www.trattoriasanferdinando.com* ⊗ *Closed Sun. and last 3 wks of Aug. No dinner Sat. and Mon.*

Hotels

Palazzo Turchini

$ | **HOTEL** | Just a few minutes' walk from the Castel Nuovo, Palazzo Turchini is one of the city center's more attractive smaller hotels. **Pros:** more intimate than neighboring business hotels; rooftop terrace; good location for the port. **Cons:** rooms on the small and stuffy side; rooms a tad business-like; close to a busy traffic hub. $ *Rooms from: €118* ✉ *Via Medina 21, Toledo* ☎ *081/5510606* ⊕ *www.palazzoturchini.it* ¶◎¶ *Free Breakfast* ⬑ *27 rooms.*

Renaissance Naples Hotel Mediterraneo

$$$ | **HOTEL** | A modern, efficient business hotel, the Mediterraneo is within walking distance of both the Teatro San Carlo and the Centro Storico. **Pros:** convenient to the port; good for those who want a modern hotel; attractive rooftop breakfast terrace. **Cons:** not for those who want historic atmosphere; some of the rooms are poorly maintained; in a busy part of town. $ *Rooms from: €290* ✉ *Via Nuova Ponte di Tappia 25, Toledo* ☎ *081/7970001* ⊕ *www.mediterraneonapoli.com* ⬑ *189 rooms* ¶◎¶ *Free Breakfast.*

Shopping

Ascione

JEWELRY & WATCHES | A family firm established in 1855 and known for its traditionally made coral jewelry and artwork, Ascione has a showroom/gallery on the second floor of a shabby wing of the Galleria Umberto. A hidden secret, aficionados should not miss the guided tour (€5, book ahead) describing the company's rich history, with displays including Egypt's King Farouk's elaborate wedding gift to his bride Farida and what many consider the most beautiful cameo in existence. ✉ *Piazzetta Matilde Serao 19, Piazza Municipio* ☎ *081/4211111* ⊕ *www.ascione.it.*

Chiaia, Santa Lucia, and Nearby

The Lungomare is the city's grandest stretch of waterfront. In the 19th century, Naples's waterfront harbored the picturesque quarter that was called Santa Lucia, a district dear to artists and musicians and known for its fishermen's cottages. The fishermen were swept away when an enormous landfill project extended the land out to what is now Via Nazario Sauro and Via Partenope, the address for some of Naples's finest hotels. Huge stretches of the waterfront are blessedly traffic-free, only enhancing their distinctly Neapolitan charm. The area also boasts the chic Chiaia neighborhood surrounding Piazza dei Martiri and the gilded 19th-century Villa Pignatelli.

◉ Sights

Castel dell'Ovo (*Castle of the Egg*)

CASTLE/PALACE | The oldest castle in Naples, the 12th-century Castel dell'Ovo dangles over the Porto Santa Lucia on a thin promontory. Built atop the ruins of an ancient Roman villa, the castle these days shares its views with some of the city's top hotels. Its gigantic rooms, rock tunnels, and belvederes over the bay are among the most striking sights that Naples has to offer. Some rooms are given over to free temporary art and photography shows. You enter the castle through its main entrance, past its forbidding trio of cannons. On the right is a large picture of the castle in Renaissance times. Turn left and look through the battlements to the intimate Borgo Marinaro below. An elevator on the right ascends to the castle top, or you can also continue along the walkway overlooking the ramparts. The roof's Sala della Terrazze offers a postcard-come-true view of Capri. This is a peaceful spot for strolling and enjoying the views. As for the castle's name, the poet Virgil

Chiaia, Santa Lucia,
and Nearby

is supposed to have hidden inside the villa an egg that had protective powers as long as it remained intact. The belief was taken so seriously that to quell the people's panic after Naples suffered an earthquake, an invasion, and a plague in quick succession, its monarch felt compelled to produce an intact egg, solemnly declaring it to be the Virgilian original. ⊠ *Santa Lucia waterfront, Via Eldorado 3, off Via Partenope, Santa Lucia* ☎ *081/7956180* ⬛ *Free.*

★ **Lungomare** (*Seafront*)
PROMENADE | The first thing mayor Luigi de Magistris did after his 2011 election was to banish traffic from the city's seafront. Strolling, skating, or biking along Via Caracciolo and Via Partenope with Capri, Mt. Vesuvius, and the Castel dell'Ovo in your sights is a favorite Neapolitan pastime. ⊠ *Via Caracciolo, Chiaia.*

🍴 Restaurants

Amici Miei
$$$ | **SOUTHERN ITALIAN** | Favored by meat eaters who can't abide another bite of bream, this dimly lit cozy dining den is known for dishes such as tender carpaccio with fresh artichoke hearts. There are also excellent homemade pasta selections, including orecchiette with chickpeas or *alla barese* (with chewy green turnips), but the highlights are the extravagant grilled meat plates. **Known for:** superb, friendly service befitting the name; a choice of quality meat dishes; art nouveau decorative flourishes. ⑤ *Average main: €25* ⊠ *Via Monte di Dio 78, Chiaia* ☎ *081/7646063* ⊕ *www.ristoranteamicimiei.com* ☾ *Closed Mon. and late July–early Sept. No dinner Sun.*

Dora
$$$ | **SEAFOOD** | Despite its location up an unpromising-looking *vicolo* (alley) off the Riviera di Chiaia, this small restaurant has achieved cult status for its seafood platters. It's remarkable what owner-chef Giovanni can produce in his tiny kitchen:

start with linguine *alla Dora,* laden with local seafood and fresh tomatoes, and perhaps follow up with grilled *pezzogna* (blue-spotted bream). **Known for:** great service; freshest seafood, both raw and cooked; simple, attractive nautical-themed decor. ⑤ *Average main: €26* ⊠ *Via Fernando Palasciano 30, Chiaia* ☎ *081/680519* ⊕ *www.ristorantedora.it* ☾ *No dinner Sun., no lunch Mon.*

'O Tabaccaro
$ | **SEAFOOD** | If you're trying to keep to a budget but want to enjoy a seafood feast alongside the yachts of the Borgo Marinaro harbor, head to this former tobacco store. While your eyes feast on all the pretty boats, the Lungomare hotels, the Castel dell'Ovo, and Vesuvius, you can savor classic Neapolitan seafood spaghetti or an *impepata di cozze* (mussels with pepper and garlic). **Known for:** family service; relatively inexpensive fare; portside dining. ⑤ *Average main: €13* ⊠ *Via Luculliana 28, Santa Lucia* ☎ *081/7646352.*

★ **Pescheria Mattiucci**
$$ | **SOUTHERN ITALIAN** | In the evening, this fourth-generation fish shop becomes a trendy spot to enjoy an aperitif and a light meal. If you want to experience superb Neapolitan sushi and cold wine while sitting on a buoy stool, get here early: service is 7:30–10:30. **Known for:** fish lunches; pescheria counter displaying today's catch; intimate and small place, so get here early or call ahead for dinner. ⑤ *Average main: €15* ⊠ *Vico Belledonne a Chiaia 27, Chiaia* ☎ *081/2512215* ⊕ *www.pescheriamattiucci.com* ☾ *Closed Mon. No dinner Sun.*

★ **Umberto**
$$ | **SOUTHERN ITALIAN** | Run by the Di Porzio family since 1916, Umberto is one of the city's classic restaurants, combining the classiness of its neighborhood, Chiaia, and the friendliness one finds in other parts of Naples. Try the *paccheri 'do tre dita* ("three-finger" pasta with octopus, tomato, olives, and capers); it bears

the nickname of the original Umberto, who happened to be short a few digits. **Known for:** classic Neapolitan meat sauce alla Genovese; charming host Massimo organizes cultural events here; authentic Pizza DOC (smaller, with chunky cornicione rim). ⑤ *Average main: €17* ✉ *Via Alabardieri 30–31, Chiaia* ☎ *081/418555* ⊕ *www.umberto.it* ☽ *No lunch Mon.*

Coffee and Quick Bites

Gran Caffè Cimmino

$ | CAFÉ | Connoisseurs often say the most refined pastries in town can be found at Gran Caffè Cimmino. Many of the city's lawyers congregate here, to celebrate or commiserate with crisp, light cannoli; airy lemon eclairs; *choux* paste in the form of a mushroom laced with chocolate whipped cream; and delightful wild-strawberry tartlets. **Known for:** terrace for watching Chiaia's finest; Neapolitan breakfast favorite; babà to die for. ⑤ *Average main: €3* ✉ *Via G. Filangieri 12/13, Chiaia* ☎ *081/418303.*

🛏 Hotels

Chiaja Hotel de Charme

$ | HOTEL | This 18th-century palazzo has a great location and its apartments, all on the first floor, have plenty of atmosphere. **Pros:** some antiques in guest rooms; good location near Piazza del Plebiscito and the Palazzo Reale; on a bustling pedestrian-only street. **Cons:** even with A/C, some rooms get hot in summer; no views in a town with some great ones; entrance up a flight of stairs. ⑤ *Rooms from: €89* ✉ *Via Chiaia 216, Chiaia* ☎ *081/415555* ⊕ *www.hotelchiaia. it* ⦿ *Free Breakfast* ➱ *33 rooms.*

Grand Hotel Parker's

$$$ | HOTEL | A little up the hill from Chiaia, with fine views of the bay and distant Capri, this landmark hotel, first opened in 1870, continues to serve up a supremely elegant dose of old-style atmosphere to visiting VIPs. **Pros:** historic hotel; excellent

restaurant; fabulous views. **Cons:** not quite as grand as it once was; a very long walk or taxi ride from city center and seafront; terrace sometimes closed when hosting weddings. ⑤ *Rooms from: €250* ✉ *Corso Vittorio Emanuele 135, Chiaia* ☎ *081/7612474* ⊕ *www.grandhotelparkers.it* ➱ *79 rooms* ⦿ *Free Breakfast.*

★ Grand Hotel Vesuvio

$$$$ | HOTEL | You'd never guess from the modern exterior that this is the oldest of the city's great seafront hotels—the place where Enrico Caruso died, where Oscar Wilde dallied with lover Lord Alfred Douglas, and where Bill Clinton charmed the waitresses—fortunately, the spacious, soothing interior compensates for what's lacking on the outside. **Pros:** directly opposite Borgo Marinaro; luxurious atmosphere; historic setting and traditionally furnished rooms. **Cons:** reception staff can be snooty; spa and pool cost extra; not all rooms have great views. ⑤ *Rooms from: €340* ✉ *Via Partenope 45, Santa Lucia* ☎ *081/7640044* ⊕ *www.vesuvio.it* ➱ *181 rooms* ⦿ *Free Breakfast.*

★ Hotel Palazzo Alabardieri

$$ | HOTEL | Just off the chic Piazza dei Martiri, this is a solid choice among the city's smaller smart hotels—with comfortable guest rooms and a fab location for sights, shopping, and eating. **Pros:** polite, pleasant staff; impressive public salons; central yet quiet location. **Cons:** cell reception and A/C are patchy; no sea view; small rooms. ⑤ *Rooms from: €178* ✉ *Via Alabardieri 38, Chiaia* ☎ *081/415278* ⊕ *www.palazzoalabardieri. it* ⦿ *Free Breakfast* ➱ *44 rooms.*

Hotel Santa Lucia

$$$ | HOTEL | Neapolitan *lungomare* enchantment can be yours if you stay at this luxurious, quietly understated hotel that overlooks the port immortalized in the song "Santa Lucia." Hundreds of boats bob in the water, seafood restaurants line the harbor, and the medieval Castel dell'Ovo presides over it all. **Pros:**

ab pastries and baked goods; great views from most rooms; proximity to the port is convenient for trips to the islands. **Cons:** extra charges at breakfast; rooms can be small; not near a metro stop. $ *Rooms from: €210* ✉ *Via Partenope 46, Santa Lucia* ☎ *081/7640666* ⊕ *www.santalucia.it* ⤳ *90 rooms* ❢❍❢ *Free Breakfast.*

★ Il Transatlantico Napoli
$$ | **B&B/INN** | Enjoying perhaps the most enchanting setting in all of Naples, this modestly priced hotel tops many travelers' dream list of places to stay. **Pros:** fabulous location and views; boat hire available; reasonable prices for maritime-style rooms. **Cons:** sometimes loud music in the Borgo; no elevator; dated furniture and fabrics. $ *Rooms from: €140* ✉ *Via Luculliana 15, Santa Lucia* ☎ *081/7648842* ⊕ *www.transatlanticonapoli.com* ⤳ *8 rooms* ❢❍❢ *No Meals.*

Pinto-Storey Hotel
$ | **HOTEL** | The name combines a 19th-century Englishman who fell in love with Naples with a certain Signora Pinto; together they went on to establish this hotel that overflows with warmth, charm, and late-19th-century (but fully renovated) decor. **Pros:** traditional Anglophile atmosphere; safe neighborhood; near public transit. **Cons:** no views; not close to major sights; two-night minimum in high season. $ *Rooms from: €100* ✉ *Via G. Martucci 72, Chiaia* ☎ *081/681260* ⊕ *www.pintostorey.it* ⤳ *16 rooms* ❢❍❢ *No Meals.*

★ Weekend a Napoli
$ | **B&B/INN** | Patrizia and Paolo run this homey upscale B&B in a handsome stile-liberty (Italian art nouveau) palazzo on the well-to-do Vomero hill. **Pros:** home baking and cozy lounge; residential Vomero atmosphere; passionate, knowledgeable hosts. **Cons:** away from the downtown sights; basic rooms lack light and are noisy; some rooms have steps to mezzanine beds. $ *Rooms from: €120* ✉ *Via Enrico Alvino 157, Vomero* ☎ *081/5781010* ⊕ *weekendanapoli.com* ۞ *Closed Jan.* ⤳ *6 rooms* ❢❍❢ *Free Breakfast.*

◉ Nightlife

★ Enoteca Belledonne
WINE BARS | Between 8 and 9 in the evening, it seems as though the whole upscale Chiaia neighborhood has descended into this tiny space for an aperitivo. The small tables and low stools are notably uncomfortable, but the cozy atmosphere and the pleasure of being surrounded by glass-front cabinets full of wine bottles with beautiful labels more than makes up for it. Excellent local wines are available by the glass at great prices. ✉ *Vico Belledonne a Chiaia 18, Chiaia* ☎ *081/403162* ⊕ *www.enotecabelledonne.it.*

◉ Shopping

Marinella
MEN'S CLOTHING | Count the British royal family among the customers of this shop that has been selling old-fashioned made-to-measure ties for more than 100 years. ✉ *Via Riviera di Chiaia 287, Chiaia* ☎ *081/7642365* ⊕ *www.emarinella.com.*

Tramontano
LEATHER GOODS | Since 1865, this place has been crafting fine leather luggage, bags, belts, and wallets. ✉ *Via Chiaia 143, Chiaia* ☎ *081/414837* ⊕ *www. tramontano.it.*

Piazza Garibaldi

The first place many see in Naples thanks to the city's main train station, there is not a lot to hold your attention here. Recently completely rebuilt, it now features a swanky new underground shopping mall based around the train station, but is still a gathering point for street sellers and hawkers and is best avoided at night. The surrounding area has some notable churches as well as the famed Porta Capuana, one of the historic gates to the city walls.

Restaurants

Da Michele

$ | **PIZZA** | You may recognize Da Michele from the movie *Eat Pray Love,* but for more than 140 years before Julia Roberts arrived, this place was a culinary reference point. Despite offering only two types of pizza—marinara (with tomato, garlic, and oregano) and Margherita (with tomato, mozzarella, and basil)—plus a small selection of drinks, it still manages to draw long lines. **Known for:** long lines outside the humble, historic HQ; pizza purists' favorite; marinara and Margherita only. ⑤ *Average main: €6* ✉ *Via Sersale 1/3, off Corso Umberto, between Piazza Garibaldi and Piazza Nicola Amore, Piazza Garibaldi* ☏ *081/5539204* ⊕ *www.damichele.net* ⊘ *Closed Sun. and 2 wks in Aug.* Ⓜ *Garibaldi/Duomo.*

Mimì alla Ferrovia

$$ | | Patrons of this Neapolitan institution have included the filmmaker Federico Fellini and that truly Neapolitan comic genius and self-styled aristocrat, Totò. It's in a fairly seedy area so take a taxi, especially at night, but it's worth it to sample Mimì's classics such as pasta e fagioli and the sea bass *al presidente,* baked in a pastry crust and enjoyed by visiting Italian presidents. **Known for:** fresh fish on display from the market; crammed with washed-out photos of Italian VIPs; classic Neapolitan dishes. ⑤ *Average main: €18* ✉ *Via A. D'Aragona 19/21, Piazza Garibaldi* ☏ *081/5538525* ⊕ *www.mimiallaferrovia.it* ⊘ *Closed Sun. and last wk in Aug.*

Capodimonte and Vomero

The Parco di Capodimonte is the crowning point of the vast mountainous plain that slopes down through the city to the waterfront area. Nearly 5 km (3 miles) removed from the crowds in the Centro Storico, it is enjoyed by locals and visitors alike as a favored escape from the overheated city center. With views over the entire city and bay, the park was first founded in the 18th century as a hunting preserve by Charles of Bourbon. Before long, partly to house the famous Farnese collection that he had inherited from his mother, he commissioned a spectacular Palazzo Reale for the park. Today this palace is the Museo di Capodimonte, which contains among its treasures the city's greatest collection of old master paintings.

To the west is the largely residential Vomero. From the balcony belvedere of the Museo di San Martino, a rich spread of southern Italian amplitude fills the eye: hillsides dripping with luxuriant greenery interspersed with villainously ugly apartment houses, streets short and narrow—leading to an unspeakable as well as unsolvable traffic problem—countless church spires and domes, and far below, the reason it all works, the intensely blue Bay of Naples. To tie together the lower parts with Vomero, everyone uses the *funicolare*—the funicular system that runs on four separate routes up and down the hill.

◉ Sights

Castel Sant'Elmo

CASTLE/PALACE | Perched on the Vomero, this massive castle is almost the size of a small town. Built by the Angevins in the 14th century to dominate the port and the old city, it was remodeled by the Spanish in 1537. The parapets, configured in the form of a six-pointed star, provide fabulous views. The whole bay lies on one side; on another, the city spreads out like a map, its every dome and turret clearly visible; to the east is slumbering Vesuvius. Once a major military outpost, the castle these days hosts occasional cultural events. Its prison, the Carcere alto di Castel Sant'Elmo, is the site of the **Museo del Novecento Napoli,** which traces Naples' 20th-century artistic output, from the Futurist period through the 1980s. ✉ *Largo San Martino, Vomero*

848/800288, 081/5587708 ⊕ *www. coopculture.it* ☎ *€5* ⊗ *Museo del Novecento closed Tues.*

⭐ **Certosa e Museo di San Martino**

HISTORY MUSEUM | Atop a rocky promontory with a fabulous view of the entire city and majestic salons that would please any monarch, the Certosa di San Martino is a monastery that seems more like a palace. The *certosa,* or charter house, had been started in 1325, but by the 18th century, it had grown so sumptuous that Ferdinand IV was threatening to halt the religious order's government subsidy. Although the Angevin heritage can be seen in the pointed arches and cross-vaulted ceiling of the Certosa Church, over the years dour Gothic was traded in for varicolored Neapolitan Baroque. The sacristy leads into the Cappella del Tesoro, with Luca Giordano's ceiling fresco of Judith holding aloft Holofernes's head and paintings by Jusepe de Ribera (the *Pietà* over the altar is one of his masterpieces). The polychrome marble work of the architect and sculptor Cosimo Fanzago (1591–1678) is at its finest here, and he displays a gamut of sculptural skills in the Chiostro Grande (Great Cloister). Fanzago's ceremonial portals at each corner of the cloister are among the most spectacular of all Baroque creations, aswirl with Michelangelo-esque ornament. The nearby Museo dell'Opera, not always open, contains sociology-theme rooms that add up to a chronological tour of the city. One room has 13 gouaches of Vesuvius, and another has paintings depicting the Plague. The Quarto del Priore (Prior's Quarters), the residence of the only monk allowed contact with the outside world, is an extravaganza of salons filled with frescoes, majolica-tile floors, and paintings, plus extensive gardens where scenic *pergolati* (roofed balconies) overlook the bay. Entering from the Quarto del Priore side, you come upon two splendid gilded coaches and then the "Vessels of the King" naval museum, with a 20-meter (65-foot) boat occupying a whole room. Beyond this lie two rooms with Early Renaissance masterpieces; subsequent rooms hold works by later artists, including the tireless Luca Giordano. Past the library, with its heavenly majolica-tile floor, comes the Sezione Presepiale, the world's greatest collection of Christmas cribs. Pride of place goes to the *Presepe* (Nativity scene) of Michele Cuciniello. Equally amazing in its own way is a crib inside an eggshell. ⊠ *Piazzale San Martino 8, Vomero* ☎ *081/2294503* ⊕ *www. coopculture.it* ☎ *€6* Ⓜ *Vanvitelli.*

⭐ **Museo di Capodimonte**

ART MUSEUM | The grandiose, 18th-century, neoclassical, Bourbon royal palace houses fine and decorative art in 124 rooms. Capodimonte's greatest treasure is the excellent collection of paintings displayed in the Galleria Nazionale, on the palace's first and second floors. Aside from the artwork, part of the royal apartments still has a collection of beautiful antique furniture (most of it on the splashy scale so dear to the Bourbons) and a staggering range of porcelain and majolica from the various royal residences. Note that due to ongoing renovation works, the royal apartments will be without air-conditioning until 2022. The main galleries on the first floor are devoted to the Farnese collection, as well as work from the 13th to the 18th century, including many pieces by Dutch masters, as well as an El Greco and 12 Titian paintings. On the second floor look for stunning paintings by Simone Martini (circa 1284–1344) and Caravaggio (1573–1610). For a contrast, don't miss the contemporary art collection, including Warhol's iconic version of Vesuvius. The palace is in the vast Bosco di Capodimonte (Capodimonte Park), which served as the royal hunting preserve and later as the site of the Capodimonte porcelain works. Covering 331 acres, it's the largest green area in Naples and was declared Italy's most beautiful garden in 2014. ⊠ *Via Miano 2, Capodimonte* ☎ *081/7499111,*

848/800288 ⊕ *www.museocapodimonte.
beniculturali.it, www.amicidicapodimon-
te.org* ✉ *€14* ⊘ *Closed Wed.*

 Nightlife

Fonoteca

COCKTAIL LOUNGES | By day the city's best
independent record store, by night this
is *the* place to hear eclectic tunes and
mingle in Vomero. They serve decent
bar snacks, pasta dishes, cakes, and
drinks. ✉ *Via Morghen 31, Vomero*
☎ *081/5560338* ⊕ *www.fonoteca.net.*

Herculaneum

10 km (6 miles) southeast of Naples.

A visit to the archaeological site of
Herculaneum neatly counterbalances the
hustle of its larger neighbor, Pompeii.
Although close to the heart of busy
Ercolano—indeed, in places right under
the town—the ancient site seems worlds
apart.

GETTING HERE AND AROUND
To get to Herculaneum by car, take the
A3 Naples–Salerno autostrada and exit
at Ercolano. Follow signs for the "Scavi"
(excavations). The Circumvesuviana
railway connects Herculaneum to Naples,
Portici, Torre del Greco, Torre Annunziata,
Pompeii, and Sorrento.

 Sights

⭐ **Herculaneum Ruins**

RUINS | Lying more than 50 feet below the
present-day town of Ercolano, the ruins
of Herculaneum are set among the acres
of greenhouses that make this area an
important European flower-growing center.
In AD 79, the gigantic eruption of Vesuvius,
which also destroyed Pompeii, buried the
town under a tide of volcanic mud. The
semiliquid mass seeped into the crevices
and niches of every building, covering
household objects, enveloping textiles and
wood, and sealing all in a compact, airtight
tomb. Excavation began in 1738 under King
Charles of Bourbon, using tunnels. Digging
was interrupted but recommenced in 1828,
continuing into the following century. Today
less than half of Herculaneum has been
excavated. With contemporary Ercolano
and the unlovely Resina Quarter sitting on
top of the site, progress is limited. From
the ramp leading down to Herculaneum's
well-preserved edifices, you get a good
overall view of the site, as well as an idea
of the amount of volcanic debris that had
to be removed to bring it to light. About
5,000 people lived in Herculaneum when
it was destroyed, many of them fishermen
and craftsmen. Although Herculaneum had
only one-third the population of Pompeii
and has been only partially excavated,
what has been found is generally better
preserved. In some cases you can even
see the original wooden beams, doors,
and staircases. Unfortunately, the Villa dei
Papiri (Villa of Papyri) is currently closed
to the public—this excavation outside
the main site was built by Julius Caesar's
father-in-law (with a replica built by Paul
Getty in Malibu almost 2,000 years later).
The building is named for almost 2,000 carbonized papyrus scrolls dug up here in the
18th century, leading scholars to believe
that this may have been a study center or
library. Also worth special attention are the
carbonized remains within the Casa del
Tramezzo di Legno (House of the Wooden
Partition). Be sure to stock up on refresh-
ments beforehand; there is no food at the
archaeological site. At the entrance, pick
up a free map showing the gridlike layout
of the dig, which is divided into numbered
blocks, or insulae. Splurge on an audio
guide if available (€8 for one, €13 for two),
or join a group with a local guide (around
€15 per person). Most of the houses are
open, and a representative cross-section of
domestic, commercial, and civic buildings
can be seen. ✉ *Corso Resina 6, Ercolano*
☎ *081/7777008* ⊕ *ercolano.beniculturali.it*
✉ *€13* ⊘ *Closed Wed.*

Museo Archeologico Virtuale (MAV)

HISTORY MUSEUM | FAMILY | With dazzling "virtual" versions of Herculaneum's streets and squares and a multidimensional simulation of Vesuvius erupting, Herculaneum's 1st-century-meets-the-21st-century museum is a must for kids and adults alike. After stopping at the ticket office you descend, as in an excavation, to a floor below. You'll experience Herculaneum's Villa dei Papiri before and (even more dramatically) during the eruption, courtesy of special effects: enter "the burning cloud" of AD 79; then emerge, virtually speaking, inside Pompeii's House of the Faun, which can be seen both as it is and as it was for two centuries BC. The next re-creation is again Villa dei Papiri. Then comes a stellar pre- and post-flooding view of Baia's Nymphaeum, the now-displaced statues arrayed as they were in the days of Emperor Claudius, who commissioned them. Visitors here are invited to take a front-row seat for "Day and Night in the Forum of Pompeii," with soldiers, litter-bearing slaves, and toga-clad figures moving spectrally to complete the spell; or to make a vicarious visit to the Lupanari brothels, their various pleasures illustrated in graphic virtual frescoes along the walls. A wooden model of Herculaneum's theater, its virtual re-creation, reminds us that it was here that a local farmer, while digging a well, first came across what proved to be not merely a single building, but a whole town. Equally fascinating are the virtual baths. There's also a 3D film of Vesuvius erupting, replete with a fatalistic narrative and cataclysmic special effects: the words of Pliny the Younger provide a timeless commentary while the floor vibrates under your feet. ⊠ *Via IV Novembre 44, Ercolano* ☎ *081/7776843* ⊕ *www.museomav.it* ⛁ *€10* ⊗ *Closed Mon. Oct.–Feb.*

Pompeii

22 km (14 miles) southeast of Naples, 17 km (10.5 miles) southeast of Herculaneum.

Mention Pompeii and most travelers think of ancient Roman villas, prancing bronze fauns, plaster casts of writhing Vesuvius victims, and the fabled days of the emperors.

GETTING HERE AND AROUND

To get to Pompeii by car, take the A3 Napoli–Salerno highway to the Pompei exit and follow signs for the nearby "Scavi." There are numerous guarded parking lots near the Porta Marina, Piazza Essedra, and Anfiteatro entrances, where you can leave your vehicle for a fee.

Pompeii has two central Circumvesuviana railway stations served by two separate train lines. The Naples–Sorrento train stops at "Pompei Scavi–Villa dei Misteri," 100 yards from the Porta Marina ticket office of the archaeological site, while the Naples–Poggiomarino train stops at Pompei Santuario, more convenient for the Santuario della Madonna del Rosario and the hotels and restaurants in the modern town center. A third Ferrovie della Statale (FS) train station south of the town center is only convenient if arriving from Salerno or Rome.

Sights

★ Pompeii

RUINS | The site of Pompeii, the petrified memorial to Vesuvius's eruption in AD 79, is the largest, most accessible, and probably most famous excavation anywhere. A busy commercial center with a population of 10,000–20,000, ancient Pompeii covered about 170 acres on the seaward end of the fertile Sarno Plain. Today it's choked with both the dust of 25 centuries and more than 2 million visitors every year; only by escaping the hordes and lingering along its silent

Planning for Your Day in Pompeii

Getting There

The archaeological site of Pompeii has its own stop (Pompei–Villa dei Misteri) on the Circumvesuviana line to Sorrento, close to the main entrance at the Porta Marina, which is the best place from which to start a tour. If, like many visitors every year, you get the wrong train from Naples (stopping at the other "Pompei" station), all is not lost. There's another entrance to the excavations at the far end of the site, just a seven-minute walk to the Amphitheater.

Admission

Single tickets cost €16 (€10 reduced *afternoon admission fee* from 3:30 pm) and are valid for one full day. The site is open April–October, daily 9–7 (last admission at 5:30; although check ahead as it's closed Monday from early autumn through early June); and November–March, daily 9–5 (last admission at 3:30). For more information call 081/8575347 or visit www.pompeiisites.org.

What to Bring

The only restaurant inside the site is both overpriced and busy, so bring along water and snacks. There are some shady, underused picnic tables outside the Porta di Nola, to the northeast of the site. Luggage is not allowed in the site.

Timing

Visiting Pompeii does have its frustrating aspects: many buildings are blocked off by locked gates, and enormous group tours tend to clog up more popular attractions. But the site is so big that it's easy to lose yourself. To really see the site, you'll need four or five hours, a bit less if you hire a guide.

To get the most out of Pompeii, rent an audio guide and opt for one of the three itineraries (two hours, four hours, or six hours). If hiring a guide, make sure the guide is registered for an English tour and standing inside the gate; agree beforehand on the length of the tour and the price, and prepare yourself for sound bites of English mixed with dollops of hearsay. For a higher-quality (and more expensive) full-day tour, try Context Travel (www.contexttravel.com).

streets can you truly fall under the site's spell. On a quiet backstreet, all you need is a little imagination to picture life in this ancient town. Come in the late afternoon, when the site is nearly deserted, and you will understand the true pleasure of visiting Pompeii. If entering via Porta Marina, the revamped (2021) Antiquarium traces the history of Pompeii from the Samnite era (4th century BC) until AD 79. Among the artifacts displayed are the House of the Golden Bracelet frescoes, the *triclinium* (dining room) of the House of Menander, and the recently created casts of the Civita Giuliana villa victims. Get your bearings at the Foro (Forum), which served as Pompeii's cultural, political, commercial, and religious hub. You can still see some of the two stories of colonnades that used to line two sides of the square. Like the ancient Greek *agora* in Athens, the Forum was a busy shopping area, complete with public officials to apply proper standards of weights and measures. Fronted by an elegant portico on the eastern side of the forum is the Macellum, a covered meat and fish market dating to the 2nd century

BC. The nearby Terme del Foro (Forum Baths) offered a relaxing respite. It had underground furnaces, the heat from which circulated beneath the floor, rose through flues in the walls, and escaped through chimneys: temperature could be set for cold, lukewarm, or hot. On the southwestern corner is the Basilica, the city's law court and the economic center. These oblong halls were the model for early Christian churches, which had a nave (central aisle) and two side aisles separated by rows of columns. Several homes were captured in various states by the eruption of Vesuvius, each representing a different slice of Pompeiian life. The Casa del Poeta Tragico (House of the Tragic Poet) is a typical middle-class residence. On the floor is a mosaic of a chained dog and the inscription *cave canem* ("Beware of the dog"). The Casa dei Vettii (House of the Vettii) is the best example of a wealthy merchant's home. There's no more magnificently memorable evidence of Pompeii's devotion to the pleasures of the flesh than the frescoes on view at the Villa dei Misteri (Villa of the Mysteries), a palatial abode built at the far northwestern fringe of Pompeii. Unearthed in 1909 this villa had many rooms, all adorned with frescoes—the finest of which are in the triclinium. Painted in the most glowing Pompeiian red, the panels relate the saga of a young bride and her initiation into the mysteries of the cult of Dionysus, who was a god imported to Italy from Greece and then given the Latin name of Bacchus. Pompeii's other major edifice is the Anfiteatro (Amphitheater), once the ultimate entertainment venue for locals. It provided a range of experiences, though these essentially involved gladiators rather than wild animals. Built in about 70 BC, the oval structure was divided into three seating areas. There were two main entrances—at the north and south ends—and a narrow passage on the west called the Porta Libitinensis, through which the dead were most probably dragged out. To get the most out of Pompeii, rent an audio guide (€8 for one, €13 for two; you'll need to leave an ID card) and opt for one of the three itineraries (2 hours, 4 hours, or 6 hours). If hiring a guide, make sure the guide is registered for an English tour and standing inside the gate; agree beforehand on the length of the tour and the price. You can find a knowledgeable and qualified guide at www.vesuviusvspompeii.com or www.contexttravel.com. A few words about closures: which excavations are open or closed when you arrive might seem a caprice of the gods adorning many of the buildings' walls, but the actual determining factors include availability of staff, geological uncertainty, and restoration. Many excavations are closed long-term for restoration. The Casa del Fauno and Casa del Menandro are usually always open, however, as is the central core of the city, a visit requiring two or more hours itself. In 2019, La Schola Armaturarum—the so-called Casa dei Gladiatori (House of the Gladiators)—was reopened after water damage had caused its roof to collapse in 2010, an event that made world headlines and highlighted the need to better protect Pompeii's treasures. It's now open on Thursday, an emblem of revitalized preservation efforts and improved management. If you're lodging in the town of Pompei, note that there's a convenient entrance to the ruins near the amphitheater off Piazza Santa Immacolata. ⊠ *Pompei* ☎ *081/8575347* ⊕ *www.pompeiisites.org* ✉ *From €16.*

Continued on page 736

ANCIENT POMPEII
TOMB OF A CIVILIZATION

The site of Pompeii, petrified memorial to Vesuvius's eruption in AD 79, is the largest, most accessible, and probably most famous of excavations anywhere.

A busy commercial center with a population of 10,000–20,000, ancient Pompeii covered about 170 acres on the seaward end of the fertile Sarno Plain. Today Pompeii is choked with both the dust of 25 centuries and more than 2 million visitors every year; only by escaping the hordes and lingering along its silent streets can you truly fall under the site's spell. On a quiet backstreet, all you need is a little imagination to picture life in this ancient town. Come in the late afternoon when the site is nearly deserted and you will understand the true pleasure of visiting Pompei.

A FUNNY THING HAPPENS ON THE WAY TO THE FORUM

as you walk through Pompeii. Covered with dust and decay as it is, the city seems to come alive. Perhaps it's the familiar signs of life observed along the ancient streets: bakeries with large ovens just like those for making pizzas, *thermopolia* (snack bars) tracks of cart wheels cut into the road surface, graffiti etched onto the plastered surfaces of street walls. But a glance up at Vesuvius, still brooding over the scene like an enormous headstone, reminds you that these folks—whether imagined in your head or actually wearing a mantle of

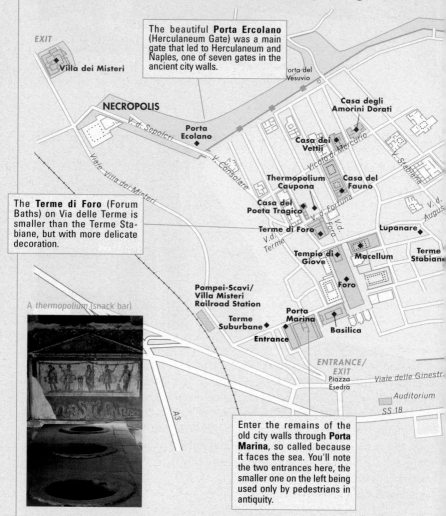

The beautiful **Porta Ercolano** (Herculaneum Gate) was a main gate that led to Herculaneum and Naples, one of seven gates in the ancient city walls.

The **Terme di Foro** (Forum Baths) on Via delle Terme is smaller than the Terme Stabiane, but with more delicate decoration.

Enter the remains of the old city walls through **Porta Marina**, so called because it faces the sea. You'll note the two entrances here, the smaller one on the left being used only by pedestrians in antiquity.

A *thermopolium* (snack bar)

EXIT

Villa dei Misteri

Porto del Vesuvio

NECROPOLIS

Casa degli Amorini Dorati

Porta Ecolano

Casa dei Vettii

Casa del Fauno

Thermopolium Caupona

Casa del Poeta Tragico

Terme di Foro

Lupanare

Tempio di Giove

Macellum

Terme Stabiane

Foro

Pompei-Scavi/ Villa Misteri Railroad Station

Terme Suburbane

Porta Marina

Basilica

Entrance

ENTRANCE/ EXIT

Piazza Esedra

Viale delle Ginestr

Auditorium

SS 18

V. d. Sepolcri

Viale Villa dei Misteri

V. Consolare

Vicolo di Mercurio

V. Stabiane

V. d. Fortuna

V. d. Fora

V. d. Terme

V. d. Augus

A3

lava dust—have not taken a breath for centuries. The town was laid out in a grid pattern, with two main intersecting streets. The wealthiest took a whole block for themselves; or built a house and rented out the front rooms, facing the street, as shops. There were good numbers of *tabernae* (taverns) and *thermopolia* on almost every corner, and frequent shows at the amphitheater.

Pompeii's cemetery, or Necropolis

The **Orto dei Fuggiaschi** (Garden of the Fugitives) contains poignant plaster casts of those overwhelmed by the eruption in AD 79 and left *in situ*. Many of the victims were claimed a day after the initial eruption not by the rain of lapilli and ash but by the first surge—a dense cloud of vapor, ash, and other solids that swept down the slopes of the volcano like a boiling avalanche at 40–50 miles per hour.

Togas, the required Roman attire, were washed and wool was dyed at . Urine was used to bleach and clean garments.

PUBLIC LIFE IN ANCIENT POMPEII

Forum

THE CITY CENTER

As you enter the ruins at Porta Marina, make your way uphill to the **Foro** (Forum), which served as Pompeii's commercial, cultural, political, and religious center. You can still see some of the two stories of colonnades that used to line the square. Like the ancient Greek *agora* in Athens, the Forum was a busy shopping area, complete with public officials to apply proper standards of weights and measures. Fronted by an elegant three-column portico on the eastern side of the forum is the **Macellum**, the covered meat and fish market dating to the 2nd century BC; here vendors sold goods from their reserved spots in the central market. It was also in the Forum that elections were held, politicians let rhetoric fly, speeches and official announcements were made, and worshippers crowded around the **Tempio di Giove** (Temple of Jupiter), at the northern end of the forum.

Basilica

On the southwestern corner is the **Basilica**, the city's law court and the economic center. These rectangular aisled halls were the model for early Christian churches, which had a nave (central aisle) and two side aisles separated by rows of columns. Standing in the Basilica, you can recognize the continuity between Roman and Christian architecture.

THE GAMES

The **Anfiteatro** (Amphitheater) was the ultimate in entertainment for Pompeiians and offered a gamut of experiences, but essentially this was for gladiators rather than wild animals. By Roman standards, Pompeii's amphitheater was quite small (seating 20,000). Built in about 70 BC,

Amphitheater

making it the oldest extant permanent amphitheater in the Roman world, it was oval and divided into three seating areas. There were two main entrances—at the north and south ends—and a narrow passage on the west called the Porta Libitinensis, through which the dead were probably dragged out. A wall painting found in a house near the theater (now in the Naples Museum) depicts the riot in the amphitheater in AD 59 when several citizens from the nearby town of Nocera were killed. After Nocerian appeals to Nero, shows were suspended for three years.

Fresco of Pyramus and Thisbe in the House of Loreius Tiburtinus

BATHS AND BROTHELS

In its day, Pompeii was celebrated as the Côte d'Azur, the Fire Island of the ancient Roman empire. Evidence of a Sybaritic bent is everywhere—in the town's grandest villas, in its baths and rich decorations, and murals reveal ing a worship of hedonism. Satyrs, bacchantes, hermaphrodites, and acrobatic couples are pictured.

The first buildings to the left past the ticket turnstiles are the **Terme Suburbane** (Suburban Baths), built—by all accounts without permission—right up against the city walls. The baths have eyebrow-raising frescoes in the *apodyterium* (changing room) that strongly suggest that more than just bathing and massaging went on here.

On the walls of **Lupanari** (brothels) are scenes of erotic games in which clients could engage. The **Terme Stabiane** (Stabian Baths) had underground furnaces, the heat from which circulated beneath the floor, rose through flues in the walls, and escaped through chimneys. The sequence of the rooms is standard: changing room (*apoditerium*), tepid (*tepidarium*), hot (*calidarium*), and cold (*frigidarium*). A vigorous massage with oil was followed by rest, and conversation.

Thanks to those deep layers of pyroclastic deposits from Vesuvius that protected the site from natural wear and tear over the centuries, graffiti found in Pompeii provide unique insights into the sort of things that the locals found important 2,000 years ago. A good many were personal and lend a human dimension to the disaster that not even the sights can equal.

At the baths: "What is the use of having a Venus if she's made of marble?"

At the entrance to the front lavatory at a private house: "May I always and everywhere be as potent with women as I was here."

On the Viale ai Teatri: "A copper pot went missing from my shop. Anyone who returns it to me will be given 65 bronze coins."

In the Basilica: "A small problem gets larger if you ignore it."

PRIVATE LIFE IN ANCIENT POMPEII

The facades of houses in Pompeii were relatively plain and seldom hinted at the care and attention lavished on the private rooms within. When visitors arrived they passed the shops and entered an atrium, from which the occupants received air, sunlight, and rainwater, the latter caught by the *impluvium*, a rectangular-shaped receptacle under the sloped roof. In the back was a receiving room, the *tablinum*,

House of Paquius Proculus

and behind was another open area, the peristyle. Life revolved around this uncovered inner courtyard, with rows of columns and perhaps a garden with a fountain. The atrium was surrounded by *cubicula* (bedrooms) and the *triclinium* (dining area). Interior floors and walls were covered with colorful marble tiles, mosaics, and frescoes.

Several homes were captured in various states by the eruption of Vesuvius, each representing a different slice of Pompeiian life. The **Casa del Fauno** (House of the Faun) displayed

wonderful mosaics, now at the Museo Archeologico Nazionale in Naples. The **Casa del Poeta Tragico** (House of the Tragic Poet) is a typical middle-class house. On the floor is a mosaic of a chained dog and the inscription *cave canem* ("Beware of the dog"). The **Casa degli Amorini Dorati** (House of the Gilded Cupids) is an elegant, well-preserved home with original decorations. Many paintings and mosaics were executed at **Casa del Menandro** (House of Menander), a patrician's villa named for a fresco of the Greek playwright. Two blocks beyond the Stabian Baths you'll notice on the left the current digs at the **Casa dei Casti Amanti** (House of the Chaste Lovers). A team of plasterers and painters were at work here when Vesuvius erupted, redecorating one of the rooms and patching up the cracks in the bread oven near the entrance—possibly caused by tremors a matter of days before.

Small Garden
Triclinium
Owner's Quarters
Kitchen
Servant's Quarters
Secondary Atrium
Entrance
Garden
Atrium
Peristyle
Impluvium

CASA DEI VETTII

The **House of the Vettii** (temporarily closed for restoration) is the best example of a house owned by wealthy *mercatores* (merchants). It contains vivid murals—a magnificent *pinacoteca* (picture gallery) within the very heart of Pompeii. The scenes here—except for those in the two wings

off the atrium—were all painted after the earthquake of AD 62. Once inside, look at the delicate frieze around the wall of the (on the right of the peristyle garden as you enter from the atrium), depicting cupids engaged in various activities, such as selling oils and perfumes,

working as goldsmiths and metalworkers, acting as wine merchants, or performing in chariot races. Another of the main attractions in the Casa dei Vettii is the small cubicle beyond the kitchen area (to the right of the atrium) with its faded erotic frescoes now protected by Perspex screens.

UNLOCKING THE VILLA DEI MISTERI

Villa dei Misteri

There is no more astounding, magnificently memorable evidence of Pompeii's devotion to the pleasures of the flesh than the frescoes on view at the **Villa dei Misteri** (Villa of the Mysteries), a palatial abode 400 yards outside the city gates, northwest of Porta Ercolano. Unearthed in 1909, this villa had many beautiful rooms painted with frescoes; the finest are in the *triclinium*. Painted in the most glowing Pompeiian reds and ochers, the panels may relate the saga of a young bride (Ariadne) and her initiation into the mysteries of the cult of Dionysus, who was a god imported to Italy from Greece and then given the Latin name of Bacchus. The god of wine and debauchery also represented the triumph of the irrational—of all those mysterious forces that no official state religion could fully suppress.

Pompeii's best frescoes, painted in glowing reds and oranges, retain an amazing vibrancy.

The frescoes in the Villa of Mysteries were painted circa 50 BC, most art historians believe, and represent the peak of the Second Style of Pompeiian wall painting. The triclinium frescoes are thought to have been painted by a local artist, although the theme may well have been copied from an earlier cycle of paintings from the Hellenistic period. In all there are 10 scenes, depicting children and matrons, musicians and satyrs, phalluses and gods. There are no inscriptions (such as are found on Greek vases), and after 2,000 years historians remain puzzled by many aspects of the triclinium cycle. Scholars endlessly debate the meaning of these frescoes, but anyone can tell they are among the most beautiful paintings left to us by antiquity. In several ways, the eruption of Vesuvius was a blessing in disguise, for without it, these masterworks of art would have perished long ago.

Vesuvius

8 km (5 miles) northeast of Herculaneum, 16 km (10 miles) east of Naples.

Vesuvius may have lost its plume of smoke for now, but it has lost none of its fascination—especially for those who live in the towns around the cone.

GETTING HERE AND AROUND

To arrive by car, take the A3 Napoli–Salerno autostrada to the Torre del Greco exit and follow Via E. De Nicola from the tollbooth and then signs for the Parco Nazionale del Vesuvio.

Vesuvio Express operates a shuttle-bus service (€10) departing every 40 minutes from Ercolano Circumvesuviana station. The vehicles thread their way rapidly up back roads, reaching the top in 20 minutes. Allow at least three hours for the journey, including a 30-minute walk to the crater on a soft cinder track.

BUS CONTACT Vesuvio Express. ✉ *Piazzale Stazione Circumvesuviano 7, Ercolano* ☎ *081/7393666.*

 Sights

Mt. Vesuvius

VOLCANO | Although Vesuvius's destructive powers are on hold, the threat of an eruption remains ever present. Seen from the other side of the Bay of Naples, Vesuvius appears to have two peaks: on the northern side is the steep face of Monte Somma, possibly part of the original crater wall in AD 79; to the south is the present-day cone of Vesuvius, which has actually formed within the ancient crater. The AD 79 cone would have been considerably higher, perhaps peaking at around 9,000 feet. The upper slopes bear the visible scars left by 19th- and 20th-century eruptions, the most striking being the lava flow from 1944 lying to the left (north side) of the approach road from Ercolano on the way up. As you tour the cities that felt the volcano's wrath,

you may be overwhelmed by the urge to explore Vesuvius itself, and it's well worth the trip. The view when the air is clear is magnificent, with the curve of the coast and the tiny white houses among the orange and lemon blossoms. When the summit becomes lost in mist, though, you'll be lucky to see your hand in front of your face. If you notice the summit clearing—it tends to be clearer in the afternoon—head for it. If possible, see Vesuvius after you've toured the ruins of buried Herculaneum to appreciate the magnitude of the volcano's power. Admission to the crater includes a compulsory guide, usually a young geologist who speaks a smattering of English. At the bottom you'll be offered a stout walking stick (a small tip is appreciated when you return it). The climb can be tiring if you're not used to steep hikes. Because of the volcanic stone you should wear athletic or sturdy shoes, not sandals. ☎ *081/2395653, 081/8653911* ⊕ *www.parconazionaledelvesuvio.it, www.guidevesuvio.it* 🎫 *€10.*

Oplontis (Torre Annunziata)

20 km (12 miles) southeast of Naples, 5 km (3 miles) west of Pompeii.

Surrounded by the fairly drab 1960s urban landscape of Torre Annunziata, Oplontis justifies its reputation as one of the more mysterious archaeological sites to be unearthed in the 20th century. The villa complex has been imaginatively ascribed—from a mere inscription on an amphora—to Nero's second wife, Poppaea Sabina. Her family was well known among the landed gentry of neighboring Pompeii, although, after a kick in the stomach from her emperor husband, she died some 15 years before the villa was overwhelmed by the eruption of 79.

GETTING HERE AND AROUND

By car, take the A3 Napoli–Salerno autostrada to the Torre Annunziata exit. Follow Via Veneto west, then turn left onto Via Sepolcri for the excavations. By train, take the Circumvesuviana railway to Torre Annunziata, the town's modern name (€2.80 from Naples).

 Sights

Oplontis

RUINS | For those overwhelmed by the throngs at Pompeii, a visit to the site of Oplontis offers a chance for contemplation and intellectual stimulation. What has been excavated so far of the Villa of the Empress Poppaea covers more than 7,000 square meters (75,000 square feet), and because the site is bound by a road to the west and a canal to the south, its full extent may never be known. Complete with porticoes, a large peristyle, a pool, baths, and extensive gardens, the villa is thought by some to have been a school for young philosophers and orators. Unlike Herculaneum and Pompeii, no skeletons were found here, leading scholars to conclude that the villa had been abandoned after the earthquake of AD 62 and was undergoing restructuring pending sale to another owner. You have to visit to appreciate the full range of Roman wall paintings; one highlight is found in Room 5, a sitting room that overlooked the sea. Here a painted window depicts the sanctuary of Apollo, while off to the left a peacock perches next to a theatrical mask. Owing to the second Pompeian style, the walls and their frescoed arches and columns seem to open out onto a scene beyond, as seen in the paintings in the triclinium (Room 6) and the cubiculum (Room 7). At the back, through a cooling garden planted with bay trees as in antiquity, is what would be an Olympic-size swimming pool. The adjacent guest rooms, or hospitalia, display murals of the fourth Pompeian style, dating them from AD 50

onward. With painted fruits and flowers, vegetation was guaranteed to flourish all year, and in the open *viridarium* (pleasure garden; Room 16) guests could compare painted flora and the odd bird with the real things. Room 21 is a Roman latrine, its ancient fittings clearly on view. ⊠ *Via Sepolcri 1, Torre Annunziata* ☎ *081/8575347* ⊕ *www.pompeiisites.org* 🎟 *From €5* ⏱ *Closed Tues.*

Ischia

45 mins by hydrofoil, 90 mins by car ferry from Naples, 60 mins by ferry from Pozzuoli.

Although Capri leaves you breathless with its charm and beauty, Ischia (pronounced "EES-kee-ah"), also called Isola Verde (Green Island)—not, as is often believed, because of its lush vegetation, but for its typical green tuff rock—takes time to cast its spell. In fact, an overnight stay is not long enough; you have to look harder here for the signs of antiquity, the traffic can be reminiscent of Naples, and the island displays all the hallmarks of rapid, uncontrolled urbanization. Ischia does have many jewels, though. There are the wine-growing villages beneath the lush volcanic slopes of Monte Epomeo, and unlike Capri, the island enjoys a life of its own that survives when the tourists head home.

Ischia is volcanic in origin, with thermal springs said to cure whatever ails you. Today the island's main industry, tourism, revolves around the more than 100 thermal baths, most of which are attached to hotels.

Much of the 37 km (23 miles) of coastline are punctuated with a continuum of *stabilimenti balneari* (private bathing establishments) in summer. However, there are also lots of public beaches set against the scenic backdrop of Monte Epomeo and its verdant slopes.

GETTING HERE AND AROUND

Ischia is well connected with the mainland in all seasons. The last boats leave for Naples and Pozzuoli at about 8 pm (though in the very high season there is a midnight sailing), and you should allow plenty of time for getting to the port and buying a ticket. Ischia has three ports—Ischia Porto, Casamicciola, and Forio (hydrofoils only)—so you should choose your ferry or hydrofoil according to your destination. Non-Italians can bring cars to the island relatively freely. Up-to-date schedules are published at www.traghetti-ischia.info.

Ischia's bus network reaches all the major sites and beaches on one of its 18 lines. The principal lines are CD and CS, circling the island in clockwise and counterclockwise directions—in the summer months runs continue until after midnight. The main bus terminus is in Ischia Porto at the start of Via Cosca, where buses run by the company EAV radiate out around the island. There are also convenient *fermate* (stops) at the two main beaches—Citara and Maronti—with timetables displayed at the terminus. Tickets cost €1.50 per ride, €1.80 for 100 minutes. A one-day pass is €4.50, a seven-day pass €14.50. Note that conditions can get hot and crowded at peak beach-visiting times.

VISITOR INFORMATION

CONTACT Azienda Autonoma di Cura, Soggiorno e Turismo. ⊠ *Via Iasolino 7, Ischia Porto* ☎ *081/5074211* ⊕ *www.infoischia-procida.it.*

Sights

Forio

TOWN | FAMILY | The far-western and southern coasts of Ischia are more rugged and attractive than other areas. Forio, at the extreme west, has a waterfront church, Chiesa del Soccorso, and is a good spot for lunch or dinner.

■**TIP→ Head to the whitewashed Soccorso**

church to watch a gorgeous sunset—perhaps the best spot on the island to do so. ⊠ *Forio.*

Giardini Poseidon Terme

OTHER ATTRACTION | FAMILY | The largest spa on the island has the added boon of a natural sauna hollowed out of the rocks. Here you can sit like a Roman senator on stone chairs recessed in the rock and let the hot water cascade over you. With countless thermally regulated pools, promenades, and steam pools, plus lots of kitschy toga-clad statues of the Caesars, Poseidon exerts a special pull on tourists, many of them grandparents shepherding grandchildren. On certain days, the place is overrun with people, so be prepared for crowds and wailing babies. ⊠ *Citara Beach, Forio* ☎ *081/9087111* ⊕ *www.giardiniposeidon-terme.com* 🎫 *From €33 all day* ⏰ *Closed Nov.–mid-Apr.*

Ischia Ponte

NEIGHBORHOOD | FAMILY | Most of the hotels are along the beach in the part of town called Ischia Ponte, which gets its name from the *ponte* (bridge) built by Alfonso of Aragon in 1438 to link the picturesque castle on a small islet offshore with the town and port. For a while the castle was the home of Vittoria Colonna, poetess, granddaughter of Renaissance Duke Federico da Montefeltro (1422–82), and platonic soul mate of Michelangelo, with whom she carried on a lengthy correspondence. You'll find a typical resort atmosphere in this area: countless cafés, shops, and restaurants, and a 1-km (½-mile) fine-sand beach.

Ischia Porto

TOWN | FAMILY | This is the island's largest town and the usual point of debarkation. It's no workaday port, however, but rather a lively resort with plenty of hotels, the island's best shopping area, and low, flat-roof houses on terraced hillsides overlooking the water. Its narrow streets and villas and gardens are framed by pines.

Monte Epomeo

VOLCANO | The inland town of Fontana is the base for excursions to the top of this long-dormant volcano that dominates the island landscape. You can reach its 2,589-foot peak in less than 1½ hours of relatively easy walking. ⊠ *Ischia.*

Sant'Angelo

TOWN | **FAMILY** | On the southern coast, this is a charming village with a narrow path leading to its promontory; the road doesn't reach all the way into town, so it's free of traffic. It's a five-minute boat ride from the beach of Maronti, at the foot of cliffs.

🍴 Restaurants

Da Cocò

$$ | **SOUTHERN ITALIAN** | This inviting restaurant with a terrace is on the causeway that links the Aragonese castle to the rest of Ischia. It's renowned for its fresh seafood, which is highly prized by the ischitani: shoreline classics dominate, including the antipasto *polipo con patate* (octopus with potatoes) and primo summer favorite *spaghetti allo scoglio.* **Known for:** good spot to just sit with an aperitivo and nibbles; magical setting near the castello; deliciously light lemon and almond cake. $ *Average main: €21* ⊠ *Via Aragonese 1, Ischia Ponte* ☎ *081/981823* ⊕ *www.ristorantecocoischia.it* ⊗ *Closed Jan. and Feb.*

O' Padrone Dò Mare

$$ | **SOUTHERN ITALIAN** | In a gorgeous seaside location just off the pedestrian stretch, this is the ideal place to enjoy fresh seafood—the name, "owner of the sea," says it all. For more than 70 years, O' Padrone Dò Mare has been an institution on the island, and locals and visitors crowd the terrace. **Known for:** spot-on fritto misto di mare seafood medley; local institution; cracking harbor views. $ *Average main: €15* ⊠ *Corso A. Rizzoli 6, Lacco Ameno* ☎ *081/900244* ⊗ *Closed Nov.–Mar.*

Umberto a Mare

$$$ | **SOUTHERN ITALIAN** | This iconic eatery has occupied the space below the Santuario del Soccorso since 1936, when the original Umberto began to grill the local catch on the seafront. The setting is divine, with a terrace overlooking the Bay of Citara and the green tuff *scogli innamorati* (lovers' rocks). **Known for:** decades-long reputation for exquisite seafood; breathtaking sunset sea views; changing displays of artworks. $ *Average main: €26* ⊠ *Via Soccorso 8, Forio* ☎ *081/997171* ⊕ *www.umbertoamare.it* ⊗ *Closed Nov.–Mar.*

☕ Coffee and Quick Bites

Angelina Bakery

$ | **BAKERY** | Two warm young people with a passion for traditional Neapolitan and internationally influenced, innovative baking, make this a fab pit-stop pasticceria, with a sunny terrace. Among the quirky treats are Guinness cake, apple maple cake, and cute tiramisu cakes that can be eaten in the cheery, pastel-shaded space or on the sunny terrace. **Known for:** sunny terrace; welcoming vibe; apple maple cake. $ *Average main: €3* ⊠ *Via S.Girardi 26, Casamicciola Terme* ☎ *348/399 2886* ⊗ *Closed Wed.*

🛏 Hotels

Albergo Il Monastero

$$ | **HOTEL** | The Castello Aragonese, on its own island, is the unrivaled location for this unique hotel with a peaceful ambience and simple but comfortable rooms overlooking the Mediterranean. **Pros:** situated inside the castle; great restaurant on terrace; stunning views and peaceful garden. **Cons:** some may not like the understated decor; perhaps too far from the town's action; a long way from the entrance to your room. $ *Rooms from: €150* ⊠ *Castello Aragonese 3, Ischia Ponte* ☎ *081/992435* ⊕ *www.*

albergoilmonastero.it |O| *Free Breakfast* 🌙 *Closed Nov.–late Apr.* 🛏 *21 rooms.*

★ Mezzatorre Resort & Spa

$$$$ | **HOTEL** | Far from the madding, sun-burned crowds—in a sleekly renovated former fortress on Punta Cornacchia above the Bay of San Montano—this luxurious getaway tempts its privileged guests to stay put and *relax*, with a glamorous heated pool overlooking a storybook cove, fine restaurants, spa treatments, and hundreds of pretty pine and pomegranate trees. **Pros:** shuttle provided from Lacco Ameno; tranquil retreat with wonderful views; good restaurants and spa. **Cons:** pricey; very isolated; far from the action. 🔒 *Rooms from: €612* ✉ *Via Mezzatorre 23, Forio* ☎ *081/986111* ⊕ *www.mezzatorre.it* 🌙 *Closed Nov.–Apr.* 🛏 *57 rooms* |O| *Free Breakfast.*

★ Terme Manzi

$$$ | **HOTEL** | Dating from the mid–19th century and set amid one of southern Italy's largest spas (the spot where Giuseppe Garibaldi bathed is conserved in a corner), this hotel is believed to have started the "thermal tourism" movement; as you'd expect, the decor is sybaritic, with hypercolorful mosaic columns, gilded Empire-style furniture, and lots of Las Vegas–ian glitz. **Pros:** wonderful indoor pool; range of soothing treatments; exceptional spa. **Cons:** set in a nondescript square; a bit far from beach; terrace restaurant noise might disturb guests in some rooms. 🔒 *Rooms from: €218* ✉ *Piazza Bagni 4, Casamicciola Terme* ☎ *081/994722* ⊕ *www.termemanzihotel.com* 🛏 *58 rooms* |O| *Free Breakfast.*

Procida

35 mins by hydrofoil, 1 hr by car ferry from Naples.

Lying barely 3 km (2 miles) from the mainland and 10 km (6 miles) from the nearest port (Pozzuoli), Procida is an island of enormous contrasts. It's the most densely populated island in Europe—just more than 10,000 people crammed into less than 3½ square km (2 square miles)—and yet there are oases like Marina Corricella and Vivara, which seem to have been bypassed by modern civilization. The inhabitants of the island—the Procidani—have an almost symbiotic relationship with the Mediterranean: many join the merchant navy, others either fish or ferry vacationers around local waters. And yet land traffic here can be more intense than on any other island in the Bay of Naples.

GETTING HERE AND AROUND

Procida's ferry timetable caters to the many daily commuters who live on the island and work in Naples or Pozzuoli. The most frequent—and cheapest—connections are from the Port of Pozzuoli. After stopping at Procida's main port, Marina Grande (also called Sancio Cattolico), many ferries and hydrofoils continue on to Ischia, for which Procida is considered a halfway house.

◉ Sights

★ Marina di Corricella

TOWN | **FAMILY** | Perched under the citadel of the Terra Murata, the Marina di Corricella is Procida's most memorable sight. Singled out for the waterfront scenes in *Il Postino* (*The Postman,* the 1995 Oscar winner for Best Foreign Film), this fishermen's cove is one of the most eye-popping villages in Campania—a rainbow-hued, horizontal version of Positano, comprising hundreds of traditional Mediterranean-style stone houses threaded by numerous *scalatinelle* staircase streets). ⊠ *Procida*.

🍴 Restaurants

La Conchiglia

$$ | **SOUTHERN ITALIAN** | A meal at this restaurant, on the beach about a half-mile east of Corricella, encapsulates Procida's seaside simplicity. Lapping waves and views of the marina and Capri form the backdrop for the fresh seafood and vegetable creations. **Known for:** boat trips and bathing nearby; beachside views and breezes through open windows; freshest ingredients. ⑤ *Average main: €20* ⊠ *Via Pizzaco 10, Procida* ☎ *081/8967602* ⊕ *www.laconchigliaristorante.com* ⊗ *Closed mid-Nov.–Mar.*

☕ Coffee and Quick Bites

Bar Dal Cavaliere

$ | **CAFÉ** | This busy café-bar has outside seating on the *basalti* flagstones with views of the port, so you can watch the boats coming in and out while munching on sfogliatella, panino, or a semi-freddo. **Known for:** stuzzichini snacks with beers and aperitivi; pastries sold by weight—great for groups; cheeky caffè near the ferry port. ⑤ *Average main: €5* ⊠ *Via Roma 42, Marina Grande, Procida* ☎ *081/8101074*.

Capri

Gorgeous grottoes, soaring conical peaks, caverns great and small, plus villas of the emperors and thousands of legends brush Capri with an air of whispered mystery. Emperor Augustus was the first to tout the island's pleasures by nicknaming it Apragopolis (City of Sweet Idleness), and Capri has drawn escapists of all kinds ever since. Ancient Greek and Roman goddesses were moved aside by the

likes of Jacqueline Onassis, Elizabeth Taylor, and Brigitte Bardot, who made the island into a paparazzo's playground in the 1960s. Today, new generations of glitterati continue to answer the island's call.

Life on Capri gravitates around the two centers of Capri Town (on the saddle between Monte Tiberio and Monte Solaro) and Anacapri, higher up (902 feet). The main road connecting Capri Town with the upper town of Anacapri is well plied by buses. On arriving at the main harbor, the Marina Grande, everyone heads for the famous funicular, which ascends (and descends) several times an hour. Once you're lofted up to Anacapri by bus, you can reach the island heights by taking the spectacular chairlift that ascends to the top of Monte Solaro (1,932 feet) from Anacapri's town center. Within Capri Town and Anacapri foot power is the preferred mode of transportation, as much for convenience as for the sheer delight of walking along these gorgeous streets and roads.

GETTING HERE AND AROUND

Capri is well connected with the mainland in all seasons, though there are more sailings April–October. Hydrofoils, Sea Cats, and similar vessels leave from Molo Beverello (below Piazza Municipio) in Naples, while far less frequent car ferries leave from Calata Porta di Massa, 1,000 yards to the east. There's also service to and from Sorrento's Marina Piccola. Much of Capri is pedestrianized, and a car is a great hindrance, not a help.

Several ferry and hydrofoil companies ply the waters of the Bay of Naples, making frequent trips to Capri. Schedules change from season to season; the tourist office's website (www.capritourism.com) gives updated departure times. However, you can't return to Naples after the last sailing (11 pm in high season, often 8 pm or even earlier in low season). There's little to be gained—sometimes nothing—from buying a round-trip ticket, which will just tie you down to the return schedule of

Capri

Grotta Azzurra

P. dell' Arcera

P. Trasete

P. Capocchia

Cala del Rio

P. Campetiello

Bagni di Tiberio

Villa San Michele

S. Constanzo

Phoenician Stairway

Villa di Damecuta

Casa Rossa

San Michele

Anacapri

Pagliaro

Piazza Vittoria

Segovia cable car

Monte Cappello

Monte S. Maria

Caprile

Materita

Santa Maria a Cetrella

Monte Solaro

Philosophical Park

P. del Tuono

P. del Pino

P. Carena

Lido del Faro

KEY

Ferry Lines

Villa Jovis

Monte Tiberio

Villa Lysis

P. del Capo

P. della Chiavica

Via Tiberio

Moneta

Arco Naturale

Via Mater Maria

Matermania

Grotta di Matermania

Villa Malaparte

P. Massullo

Monte Tuoro

Via Pizzolungo

Porto de Tragara

Monacone

Capri Town

La Piazzetta

Strada S Francesco Stairway

Santo Stefano

Via Tragara

Certosa di San Giacomo

Giardini di Augusto

Punta Tragara

La Fontelina

P. di Tragara

Faraglioni de Fuori

I Faraglioni

Marina Grande

Funicolare

Museo Caprense Ignazio Cerio

Via Krupp

Marina Piccola

P. Mulo

P. di Terita

P. Ventroso

NAPLES AND SORRENTO

TO

0   1000 yards

0   1000 meters

one line. However, book in advance in spring and summer for a Sunday return to the mainland.

VISITOR INFORMATION

CONTACTS Azienda Autonoma di Cura, Soggiorno e Turismo. ✉ *Banchina del Porto, Marina Grande* ☎ *081/8370686* ⊕ *www. capritourism.com.* **Azienda Autonoma di Cura, Soggiorno e Turismo.** ✉ *Piazza Umberto I, Capri* ☎ *081/8370686* ⊕ *www.capritourism.com.*

◉ Sights

★ Anacapri

TOWN | A tortuous road leads up to Anacapri, the island's "second city," about 3 km (2 miles) from Capri Town. To get here you can take a bus either from Via Roma in Capri Town or from Marina Grande (both €2), or a taxi (about €30 one-way; agree on the fare before starting out). Crowds are thick down Via Capodimonte leading to Villa San Michele and around Piazza Vittoria, the square where you catch the chairlift to the top of Monte Solaro. Via Finestrale leads to the noted **Le Boffe quarter,** centered on the Piazza Diaz. Le Boffe owes its name to the distinctive domestic architecture prevalent here, which uses vaults and sculpted groins instead of crossbeams. Elsewhere, Anacapri is quietly appealing. It's a good starting point for walks, such as the 80-minute round-trip journey to the **Migliara Belvedere,** on the island's southern coast.

Capri Town

TOWN | On arrival at the port, pick up the excellent map of the island at the tourist office. You may have to wait for the funicular railway (€2 one-way) to Capri Town, some 450 feet above the harbor. So this might be the time to splurge on an open-top taxi—it could save you an hour in line and a sweaty ride packed into a tiny, swaying bus. From the upper station, walk out into Piazza Umberto I, better known as the Piazzetta, the island's social hub.

Certosa di San Giacomo

HISTORIC SIGHT | An eerie atmosphere hangs around neglected corners of this once grand, palatial complex between the Castiglione and Tuoro hills, which was for centuries a Carthusian monastery dedicated to St. James. It was founded between 1371 and 1374, when Queen Giovanna I of Naples gave Count Giacomo Arcucci, her secretary, the land and the means to create it. The count himself then became devoutly religious and retired here until his death. After the monastery was sacked by the pirates Dragut and Barbarossa in the 16th century, it was heavily restored and rebuilt—thanks in part to heavy taxes exacted from the populace. The friars within were detested by many Capresi for refusing to open the gates to minister to the people when plague broke out. You enter the complex via a grandly imposing entryway, which leads to the Biblioteca Comunale Popolare Luigi Bladier (the public library) and the spacious church of San Giacomo (built in 1690, reopened after renovations in 2010). After admiring the church's Baroque frescoes, follow the signposts down toward the Parco, which leads down an avenue flanked by pittosporum and magnolia toward the tranquil monastery gardens and some welcome benches with stunning views. Take heed of the signs reminding you to watch your step, as the ground is uneven in places. Beyond a covered road lies the Chiostro Grande (Large Cloister)—originally the site of the monks' cells and now the home of a high school. Nearby is the 15th-century Chiostro Piccolo (Small Cloister). Both are often venues for summertime open-air concerts. The Quarto del Priore hosts occasional art exhibitions from international artists, but the showstopper here is the Museo Diefenbach, comprising a collection of restored large canvases by influential German painter K. W. Diefenbach, who visited Capri in 1900 and stayed until his death in 1913. For years, Diefenbach rivaled the Blue

Grotto for sheer picturesqueness—he was given to greeting visitors replete with flowing white beard, monk's cowl, and primitive sandals. ⊠ *Via Certosa, Capri* ☎ *081/8376218* ✉ *€4, with audio guide, combined ticket with Giardini di Augusto €5 (only available at the Giardini)* ☾ *Closed Mon.*

★ Giardini di Augusto
(*Gardens of Augustus*)

GARDEN | From the terraces of this beautiful public garden, you can see the village of Marina Piccola below—restaurants, cabanas, and swimming platforms huddle among the shoals—and admire the steep, winding Via Krupp, actually a staircase cut into the rock. Friedrich Krupp, the German arms manufacturer, loved Capri and became one of the island's most generous benefactors. Sadly, the path down to Marina Piccola is closed indefinitely due to the danger of rockfalls. ⊠ *Via Matteotti, beyond monastery of San Giacomo, Capri* ✉ *From €1.*

Grotta Azzurra

CAVE | Only when the Grotta Azzurra was "discovered" in 1826, by the Polish poet August Kopisch and Swiss artist Ernest Fries, did Capri become a tourist destination. The watery cave's blue beauty became a symbol of the return to nature and revolt from reason that marked the Romantic era, and it soon became a required stop on the Grand Tour. In reality, the grotto had long been a local landmark. During the Roman era—as testified by the extensive remains, primarily below sea level, and several large statues now at the Certosa di San Giacomo—it had been the elegant, mosaic-decorated nymphaeum of the adjoining villa of Gradola. Historians can't quite agree if it was simply a lovely little pavilion where rich patricians would cool themselves or truly a religious site where sacred mysteries were practiced. The water's extraordinary sapphire color is caused by a hidden opening in the rock that refracts the light. At highest illumination the very air inside seems tinted blue. The Blue Grotto can be reached from Marina Grande or from the small embarkation point below Anacapri on the northwest side of the island, accessible by bus from Anacapri. If you're pressed for time, however, skip this sometimes frustrating and disappointing excursion. You board one boat to get to the grotto, then transfer to a smaller boat that takes you inside. If there's a backup of boats waiting to get in, you'll be given precious little time to enjoy the gorgeous color of the water and its silvery reflections. ⊠ *Capri* ✉ *€15–€20 from Marina Grande via various companies, then €10 by rowboat with Coop. Battellieri.* ☾ *Excursions don't run if the sea is even minimally rough.*

★ I Faraglioni

NATURE SIGHT | Few landscapes set more artists dreaming than that of the famous Faraglioni—three enigmatic, pale-ocher limestone colossi that loom out of the sea just off the Punta Tragara on the southern coast of Capri. Soaring almost 350 feet above the water, the Faraglioni have become for most Italians a beloved symbol of Capri and have been poetically compared to Gothic cathedrals or modern skyscrapers. The first rock is called Faraglione di Terra, since it's attached to the land; at its base is the famous restaurant and bathing lido Da Luigi, where a beach mattress may accompany the luncheon menu. The second is called Faraglione di Mezzo, or Stella, and little boats can often be seen going through its picturesque tunnel, which was caused by sea erosion. The rock farthest out to sea is Faraglione di Scopolo and is inhabited by a wall lizard species with a striking blue belly, considered a local variant by biologists although legend has it that they were originally brought as pets from Greece to delight ancient Roman courtiers. ⊠ *End of Via Tragara, Capri.*

★ Marina Piccola

BEACH | FAMILY | A 10-minute ride from the main bus terminus in Capri (Piazzetta d'Ungheria), Marina Piccola is a delightfully picturesque inlet that provides the Capresi and other sun worshippers with their best access to reasonable beaches and safe swimming. The entire cove is lined with *stabilimenti*—elegant bathing lidos where the striped cabanas are often air-conditioned and the bodies can be Modigliani-sleek. The most famous of these lidos (there's a fee to use the facilities), found closest to the Faraglioni, is La Canzone del Mare, once presided over by the noted British music-hall singer Gracie Fields and for decades favored by the smart set, including Noël Coward and Emilio Pucci (who set up his first boutique here). La Canzone del Mare's seaside restaurant offers a dreamy view of the Faraglioni and a luncheon here, although pricey, can serve as an indelible Capri moment. Jutting out into the bay at the center of the marina is the Scoglio delle Sirene, or Sirens' Rock—a small natural promontory—which the ancients believed to be the haunt of the Sirens, the mythical temptresses whose song seduced Odysseus in Homer's *Odyssey*. This rock separates the two small beaches: Pennaulo, to the east, and Marina di Mulo, site of the original Roman harbor, to the west. The small church, Chiesa di Sant'Andrea, was built in 1900 to give the local fishermen a place of worship. ✉ *Via Marina Piccola, Capri.*

★ Monte Solaro

VIEWPOINT | An impressive limestone formation and the highest point on Capri (1,932 feet), Monte Solaro affords gasp-inducing views toward the bays of both Naples and Salerno. A serene 13-minute chairlift ride will take you right to the top (refreshments available at the bar), where you can launch out on a number of scenic trails on the western side of the island. Picnickers should note that even in summer it can get windy at this height, and there are few trees to provide shade or refuge. ✉ *Piazza Vittoria, Anacapri* ☎ *081/8370420* ⊕ *www.capriseggiovia.it* ☉ *Chairlift closed in adverse weather* 🎫 *€9 one-way, €12 return.*

★ Villa Jovis

RUINS | Named in honor of the ancient Roman god Jupiter, or Jove, the villa of the emperor Tiberius is riveted to the towering Rocca di Capri like an eagle's nest overlooking the strait separating Capri from Punta Campanella, the tip of the Sorrentine Peninsula. Lying near the easternmost point of the island, Villa Jovis is a powerful reminder of the importance of the island in Roman times. What makes the site even more compelling are the accounts of the latter years of Tiberius's reign from Capri (AD 27–37), written by authors and near-contemporaries Suetonius and Tacitus. This villa was famous for its sybaritic living, thus sounding a leitmotif whose echo can be heard at the luxurious hotels of today. There are remarkably few discrepancies between the accounts of the two historiographers. Both point to Tiberius's mounting paranoia in Rome, while Tacitus outlines his reason for choosing Capri (Annals, Book IV): "Presumably what attracted him was the isolation of Capreae. Harborless, it has few roadsteads even for small vessels; sentries can control all landings. In winter the climate is mild, since hills on the mainland keep off gales. In summer the island is delightful, since it faces west and has open sea all round. The bay it overlooks was exceptionally lovely, until Vesuvius's eruption transformed the landscape." Capri in Roman times was the site of 12 spacious villas, but Villa Jovis is both the best preserved and must have been the largest, occupying nearly 23,000 square feet. The entrance to the site lies just beyond the *pharos* (lighthouse) built under Tiberius and used until the 17th century to warn ships away from the narrows between Capri and the mainland. Pick up a site map at the ticket office, which gives a useful breakdown of the various areas of the villa to be visited. Nearby, you can find Salto di Tiberio (Tiberius's Leap), the place where ancient gossips believed Tiberius had enemies—among them his discarded lovers and even unfortunate cooks—hurled over the precipice into the sea some 1,000 feet below. After taking stock of this now-harmless viewing platform and its information panels, take the upper path past the baths complex around the palace residential quarters to view the heavily restored Chapel of Santa Maria del Soccorso and its large bronze statue of the Madonna, a gift to the island from the Caprese painter Guido Odierna in 1979. The walk around the perimeter of the site gives an idea of the overall layout of the palatial residence, which in places rose to five stories in height. From here descend some steps and then a ramp to the *ambulatio* (walkway), which offers additional spectacular views and plenty of shade, as well as a *triclinium* (dining room) halfway along. The center of the site is a complex devoted to cisterns. Unlike in Pompeii, there was no aqueduct up here to provide fresh running water, so the cisterns next to the bath complex were of prime importance. From La Piazzetta allow 45 minutes each way for the walk alone. ⊠ *Via A. Maiuri, Capri* ☎ *081/8374549* 🖭 *€6, with audioguide* ⊘ *Closed Jan.–Feb. and Tues. Oct.–Mar.*

★ Villa San Michele

HISTORIC HOME | From Anacapri's Piazza Vittoria, picturesque Via Capodimonte leads to Villa San Michele, the charming former home of Swedish doctor and philanthropist Axel Munthe (1857–1949), and which Henry James called "the most fantastic beauty, poetry, and inutility that one had ever seen clustered together." At the ancient entranceway to Anacapri at the top of the Scala Fenicia, the villa is set around Roman-style courtyards, marble walkways, and atria. Rooms display the doctor's varied collections, which range from bric-a-brac to antiquities. Medieval choir stalls, Renaissance lecterns, and gilded statues of saints

are all part of the setting, with some rooms preserving the doctor's personal memorabilia. A spectacular pergola path overlooking the entire Bay of Naples leads from the villa to the famous Sphinx Parapet, where an ancient Egyptian sphinx looks out toward Sorrento: you cannot see its face—on purpose. It is said that if you touch the sphinx's hindquarters with your left hand while making a wish, it will come true. The parapet is connected to the little Chapel of San Michele, on the grounds of one of Tiberius's villas. Besides hosting summer concerts, the Axel Munthe Foundation carries out ornithological research in the surrounding area and has an ecomuseum that fittingly reflects Munthe's fondness for animals. Here you can learn about various bird species—accompanied by their songs—found on Capri. Munthe bought up the hillside and made it a sanctuary for birds, and today this little realm is still an Eden. The foundation also organizes weekly guided visits (Thursday afternoon April–October, call to reserve a place) of the ruined Barbarossa castle, almost clinging to the side of the cliff above Villa San Michele. Dating to the late 10th century, when Capri was ruled by the ancient maritime republic of Amalfi, and named after the admiral of the Turkish fleet, Khair-Eddin, or Barbarossa (Redbeard), who stormed and took the castle in 1535, much of the original layout has been changed over the centuries. ⊠ *Viale Axel Munthe 34, Anacapri* ☎ *081/8371401* ⊕ *www.villasanmichele. eu* 🖭 *€10.*

🍽 Restaurants

Al Grottino

$$ | SOUTHERN ITALIAN | In a 14th-century building close to the Piazzetta, this small, friendly, family-run restaurant has arched ceilings, autographed photos of famous patrons, and lots of atmosphere. Specialties include scialatielli *ai fiori di zucchine e gamberetti* (with zucchini flowers and shrimp) and *cocotte* (pasta with mussels and clams), but the owner delights in taking his guests through the menu of regional dishes. **Known for:** gluten-free options; good value for Capri; Caprese specialties with the freshest ingredients. ⑤ *Average main: €20* ✉ *Via Longano 27, Capri* ☎ *081/8370584* ⊕ *www.ristorantealgrottino.net* ⊙ *Closed Nov.–late Mar.*

Aurora

$$$ | SOUTHERN ITALIAN | Often frequented by celebrities, whose photographs adorn the walls inside and out, the island's oldest restaurant offers courtesy and *simpatia* (irrespective of your star status), a sleekly minimalist interior, and tables outside along a chic thoroughfare. The cognoscenti start by sharing a pizza *all'Acqua*—thin-crust, with mozzarella and a sprinkling of *peperoncino* (chili)—but the *gnocchetti al pesto con fagiolini croccanti e pinoli* (dumplings with pesto, beans, and pine nuts) and homemade sweets are good, too. **Known for:** incredible wine cellar and choice; historic jet-set hangout; Papà Gennaro's unusually light pizza all'Acqua. ⑤ *Average main: €28* ✉ *Via Fuorlovado 18/22, Capri* ☎ *081/8370181* ⊕ *www.auroracapri.com* ⊙ *Closed Nov.–Easter.*

★ Da Gelsomina

$$$ | SOUTHERN ITALIAN | Amid its own terraced vineyards with inspiring views to the island of Ischia and beyond, this is much more than just a well-reputed restaurant. The owner's mother was a friend of Axel Munthe, and he encouraged her to open a food kiosk, which evolved into Da Gelsomina; today the specialties include *pollo a mattone,* chicken grilled on bricks, and locally caught rabbit. **Known for:** fresh produce and wine from their verdant gardens; opened in the 1960s with family links to Axel Munthe; chicken grilled on bricks. ⑤ *Average main: €35* ✉ *Via Migliara 72, Anacapri* ☎ *081/8371499* ⊕ *www.dagelsomina. com* ⊙ *Closed Nov.–Mar.*

★ Il Solitario

$$ | NEOPOLITAN | Tucked away from Via G. Orlandi, there's always a warm, relaxed family welcome and deliciously simple Caprese food here. **Known for:** cheery dining room and leafy pergola; grilled fish and meat; sumptuous ravioli. ⑤ *Average main: €16* ✉ *Via Giuseppe Orlandi 96, Anacapri* ☎ *081/8371382* ⊕ *www.ilsolitarioanacapri.com* ⊙ *No dinner Sun.*

La Canzone del Mare

$$$ | SOUTHERN ITALIAN | Although it's not primarily a restaurant, a luncheon dominated by fresh seafood and vegetables in the covered pavilion of this legendary bathing lido of the Marina Piccola is Capri at its most picture-perfect. With two seawater pools, a rocky beach, and I Faraglioni in the distance, it was the erstwhile haunt of Gracie Fields, Emilio Pucci, Noël Coward, and any number of 1950s and '60s glitterati. **Known for:** famous dolce vita–era haunt, now very crowded; open terrace overlooking Marina Piccola; sunset wine and peaches served with *stuzzichini* (appetizers). ⑤ *Average main: €35* ✉ *Via Marina Piccola 93, Capri* ☎ *081/8370104* ⊕ *www. lacanzonedelmare.com* ⊙ *Closed Oct.–mid-Apr. No dinner.*

★ La Capannina

$$$ | SOUTHERN ITALIAN | Near the busy piazzetta and long one of Capri's most celebrity-haunted restaurants, La Capannina has a discreet flower-decked veranda that's ideal for dining by candlelight. Specialties change daily depending on the season, but the menu always includes ravioli capresi, linguine *con lo scorfano* (with scorpion fish), and an exquisite "Pezzogna" (sea bream cooked whole and topped with a layer of potatoes). **Known for:** seafood dishes; walls strewn with photos of celebrity clientele; wine bar next door. ⑤ *Average main: €26* ✉ *Via Le Botteghe 12b, Capri* ☎ *081/8370732* ⊕ *www.capanninacapri. com* ⊙ *Closed Nov.–mid-Mar.*

15

Naples and Campania CAPRI

La Fontelina

$$$ | SOUTHERN ITALIAN | Given its position right on the water's edge, seafood is almost de rigueur here, but also expect fabulous fresh vegetable creations like *polpette di melanzane* (eggplant fritters), and then dip into the vegetable buffet. La Fontelina also functions as a lido, with steps and ladders into fathoms-deep blue water, and this location—accessible on foot from Punta Tragara or by boat from Marina Piccola (10 minutes; €25 up to four passengers)—makes it a good place to spend a delightfully comatose day. **Known for:** chef Mario's daily seafood specials; lunch stop for beach-club bathers; shuttle boat from Marina Piccola. $ *Average main: €28* ⊠ *Via Faraglioni 2, Capri* ☎ *081/8370845* ⊕ *www.fontelina-capri.com* ⊗ *Closed mid-Oct.–Easter. No dinner.*

Le Grottelle

$$$ | SOUTHERN ITALIAN | This extremely informal trattoria enjoys a distinctive setting up against limestone rocks not far from the Arco Naturale, with the kitchen in a cave at the back. Whether you stumble over it (and are lucky enough to get a table) or intentionally head for it after an island hike, Le Grottelle will prove memorable, thanks to the ambience, the views of Li Galli islands, and a menu that includes ravioli and local rabbit but is best known for seafood dishes such as linguine *con gamberetti e rucola* (with shrimp and arugula). **Known for:** cool grotto interiors; breathtaking cliff-clinging location; seafood dishes. $ *Average main: €25* ⊠ *Via Arco Naturale 13, Capri* ☎ *081/8375719* ⊗ *Closed Nov.–mid-Mar.*

☕ Coffee and Quick Bites

★ Buonocore

$ | ITALIAN | FAMILY | Follow your nose to this legendary, sweet-smelling Caprese fave for breakfast, beach picnics, and on-the-hoof snacks. Buonocore lures you down its steps on a Capri Town lane with all manner of pizze, panini, gelati, and paste, including their speciality almond and lemon Caprilú biscotti. **Known for:** very popular so may have to *fare la coda*; tempting smells of freshly made cones and pastries; small pizze to take away. $ *Average main: €8* ⊠ *Via Vittorio Emanuele 35, Capri Town* ☎ *081/8377826.*

Hotels

★ Caesar Augustus

$$$$ | HOTEL | A favorite of the Hollywood set, this landmark villa hotel is a Caprese paradise thanks to its breathtaking perch atop a cliff; its grand gardens, terraces, and pool; and its charming, casual-chic rooms with their plump chairs and fragrant bouquets. **Pros:** serene terrace views; infinity pool; summer concerts on-site. **Cons:** pricey; no kids under 10 allowed; a bit far from the action for some. $ *Rooms from: €700* ⊠ *Via G. Orlandi 4, Anacapri* ☎ *081/8373395* ⊕ *www.caesar-augustus.com* ⊗ *Closed Nov.–mid-Apr.* ⊸ *55 rooms* ⦿| *Free Breakfast.*

★ Capri Palace Jumeirah

$$$$ | RESORT | This Anacapri icon with unique design, spa, exquisite food, and luxurious retreat atmosphere throughout has amassed a noted art collection and even launched a fashion and home line and hosted A-list cultural events. **Pros:** award-winning spa and dining; stunning (and sometimes surprising) design; noted art collection. **Cons:** some may find the quiet Anacapri location removed from the action (and water); all that glam comes at a price; service can be slow. $ *Rooms from: €725* ⊠ *Via Capodimonte 14, Anacapri* ☎ *081/9780111* ⊕ *www.capripalace.com* ⊸ *78 rooms* ⦿| *Free Breakfast* ⊗ *Closed mid-Oct.–mid-Apr.*

★ Capri Tiberio Palace

$$$$ | HOTEL | Offering guests comfort, style, luxury, and sigh-inducing views since the 19th century, this hotel is a short walk from the piazzetta—near the action, but not quite in the thick of it.

Pros: traditional and kosher restaurant; pure luxury; friendly staff. Cons: some rooms are not as large as expected in a five-star; no port-to-door guest shuttle; tiny gym. ⑤ *Rooms from: €599* ⊠ *Via Croce 11–15, Capri* ☎ *081/9787111* ⊕ *www.capritiberiopalace.com* ⊘ *Closed Nov.–mid-Apr.* ⇨ *45 rooms* ⦿*I Free Breakfast.*

★ J. K. Place

$$$$ | HOTEL | Occupying an 1876 villa above Marina Grande harbor, southern Italy's most glamorous hotel makes other Capri accommodations seem dull. Pros: free shuttle to town; exquisite pool; pleasant walk to the magical Tiberio beach. Cons: only for high rollers; expensive; pool visible from main road. ⑤ *Rooms from: €1182* ⊠ *Via Provinciale Marina Grande 225, Capri* ☎ *081/8384001* ⊕ *www.jkcapri.com* ⇨ *22 rooms* ⦿*I Free Breakfast* ⊘ *Closed mid-Oct.–mid-Apr.*

La Tosca

$$ | HOTEL | Up a tiny side street above the Certosa, this simple, quiet hotel offers unassuming vibes, terrace views, and reasonable rates. Pros: quiet spot near Capri Town; simple, unadorned charm; pleasant, helpful owner. Cons: books up early; not all rooms have good views; rooms might seem to lack panache. ⑤ *Rooms from: €165* ⊠ *Via Birago 5, Capri* ☎ *081/8370989* ⊕ *www. latoscahotel.com* ⇨ *11 rooms* ⦿*I Free Breakfast* ⊘ *Closed Nov.–Feb.*

★ Punta Tragara

$$$$ | HOTEL | Designed by Le Corbusier, this former private villa was the site of a secret wartime meeting between Churchill and Eisenhower; today, it's one of Capri's most beautiful hotels, with a breathtaking location on Punta Tragara; public areas adorned with baronial fireplaces, gilded antiques, and travertine marble; and guest rooms that are simultaneously sumptuous and cozy-casual. Pros: wonderful views of the famed Faraglioni rocks; two gorgeous pools;

decadent and luxurious. Cons: small gym; a 15-minute walk from the center; some find the style dated (others find it a plus). ⑤ *Rooms from: €950* ⊠ *Via Tragara 57, Capri* ☎ *081/8370844* ⊕ *www.hoteltragara.com* ⊘ *Closed mid-Oct.–mid-Apr.* ⇨ *44 rooms* ⦿*I Free Breakfast.*

Quisisana

$$$$ | HOTEL | Some say Capri has three villages: Capri Town, Anacapri, and this landmark hotel, which looms large in island mythology, attracts utterly devoted guests, and has an enormous lobby and theater-cum-convention center that are 1930s jewels designed by noted modernist Gio Ponti. Pros: top spa facilities; luxe atmosphere on a large scale; stumbling distance from La Piazzetta. Cons: convention-size and far from cozy; minimum 3- or 5-night stay some periods; quality of customer service can be patchy. ⑤ *Rooms from: €490* ⊠ *Via Camerelle 2, Capri* ☎ *081/8370788* ⊕ *www.quisisana. com* ⊘ *Closed Nov.–mid-Mar.* ⇨ *147 rooms* ⦿*I Free Breakfast.*

Villa Krupp

$$ | B&B/INN | Occupying a beautiful house overlooking the idyllic Gardens of Augustus, this hostelry (once the home of Maxim Gorky, whose guests included Lenin) has comfy beds in plain but spacious rooms, some of which have south-facing terraces and awesome views. Pros: much-needed porter service; a historical home; stunning views. Cons: a lot of steps to negotiate; breakfast doesn't match the views; simple rooms. ⑤ *Rooms from: €170* ⊠ *Viale Matteotti 12, Capri* ☎ *081/8370362* ⊕ *www.villakrupp.com* ⊘ *Closed mid-Oct.–mid-Apr.* ⇨ *12 rooms* ⦿*I Free Breakfast.*

Villa Sarah

$$$ | HOTEL | This yellow, two-story, Mediterranean-style hostelry—complete with Capri's signature round windows and a setting amid lovely gardens in a pleasant residential district—has lots of Caprese spirit and simple but homey and brightly accented rooms that will make

you feel like a guest in a private villa. **Pros:** unfussy decor; gorgeous pool; lush gardens. **Cons:** many rooms tiny; a long and steep climb from the Piazzetta; small pool. ⑤ *Rooms from: €250* ⊠ *Via Tiberio 3/a, Capri* ☎ *081/8377817* ⊕ *www.villa-sarah.it* ⊘ *Closed Nov.–Mar.* ⤳ *20 rooms* ⊠⃝ *Free Breakfast.*

Sorrento

50 km (31 miles) south of Naples.

Winding along a cliff above a small beach and two harbors, the town is split in two by a narrow ravine formed by a former mountain stream. To the east, dozens of hotels line busy Via Correale along the cliff—many have "grand" included in their names, and some indeed are. To the west, however, is the historic sector, which still enchants. It's a relatively flat area, with winding, stone-paved lanes bordered by balconied buildings, some joined by medieval stone arches. The bustling, coach- and car-traffic–fringed central piazza is named after the poet Torquato Tasso, born here in 1544. Away from the vehicles this part of town is a delightful place to walk through. Craftspeople are often at work in their stalls and shops and are happy to let you watch; in fact, that's the point. Music spots and bars cluster in the side streets near Piazza Tasso.

GETTING HERE AND AROUND

From downtown Naples, take a Circum-vesuviana train from Stazione Centrale (Piazza Garibaldi) or a hydrofoil from Molo Beverello. If you're coming directly from the airport in Naples, pick up a direct bus to Sorrento. By car, take the A3 Naples–Salerno autostrada, exiting at Castel-lammare, and then following signs for Penisola Sorrentina, then for Sorrento.

VISITOR INFORMATION

CONTACT Azienda Autonoma di Soggiorno Sorrento-Sant'Agnello. ⊠ *Via L. De Maio 35, Sorrento* ☎ *081/8074033.*

 # Sights

Convento di San Francesco

RELIGIOUS BUILDING | Near the Villa Comunale gardens and sharing its view over the Bay of Naples, the convent is celebrated for its 12th-century cloister. Filled with greenery and flowers, the Moorish-style cloister has interlaced pointed arches of tufa rock, alternating with octagonal columns topped by elegant capitals, supporting smaller arches. The combination makes a suitably evocative setting for summer concerts and theatrical presentations. The church portal is particularly impressive, with the 16th-century door (moved from a church across the road in 1947) featuring *intarsia* (inlaid) work. The interior's 17th-century decoration includes an altarpiece, by a student of Francesco Solimena, depicting St. Francis receiving the stigmata. The convent is now an art school, where students' works are often exhibited. ⊠ *Piazza S. Francesco, Sorrento* ☎ *081/8781269* ⊠ *Free.*

Marina Grande

MARINA/PIER | Close to the historic quarter (but not that close—many locals prefer to use the town bus to shuttle up and down the steep hill), the port, or *borgo,* of the Marina Grande is Sorrento's fishing harbor. In recent years it has become unashamedly touristy, with outdoor restaurants and cafés encroaching on what little remains of the original harbor. Most establishments down here are geared to the English-speaking market—expect a "good evening" rather than a "buona sera" as you enter. The marina still remains a magical location for an evening out on the waterfront, but if you're interested in a dip—given the dubious sea-water quality here and the cramped conditions—head out instead toward Massa Lubrense and Nerano. Don't confuse this harbor with Marina Piccola, at the base of the cliff, below Piazza Tasso and the Hotel Excelsior Vittoria; that's the area where ferries and hydrofoils dock. ⊠ *Via del Mare, Sorrento.*

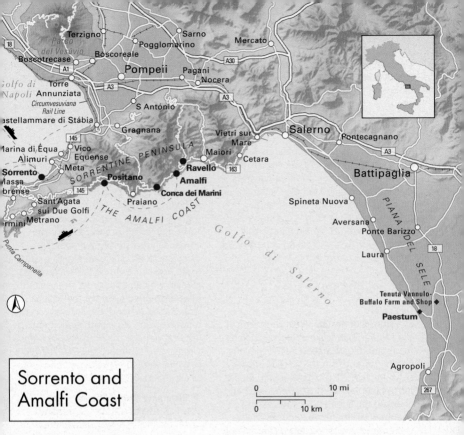

Sorrento and Amalfi Coast

Museo Correale di Terranova

ART MUSEUM | In an 18th-century villa with a lovely garden, on land given to the patrician Correale family by Queen Joan of Anjou in 1428, this museum is a highlight of Sorrento and a must for connoisseurs of the *seicento* (17th century). It has an eclectic private collection amassed by the count of Terranova and his brother—one of the finest devoted to Neapolitan paintings, decorative arts, and porcelains. Magnificent 18th- and 19th-century inlaid tables by Giuseppe Gargiulo, Capodimonte porcelains, and rococo portrait miniatures are reminders of the age when pleasure and delight were everything. Also on view are regional Greek and Roman archaeological finds, medieval marble work, glasswork, old master paintings, and 17th-century majolicas—even the poet Tasso's death mask. The building itself is fairly charmless,

with few period rooms, but the garden offers an allée of palm trees, citrus groves, floral nurseries, and an esplanade with a panoramic view of the Sorrento Coast. ✉ *Via Correale 50, Sorrento* ☎ *081/8781846* ⊕ *www.museocorreale.it* ⊙ *Closed Mon.* 🎫 *€8, €13 with guide.*

Sedile Dominova

NOTABLE BUILDING | Enchanting showpiece of the Largo Dominova—the little square that is the heart of Sorrento's historic quarter—the Sedile Dominova is a picturesque open loggia with expansive arches, balustrades, and a green-and-yellow-tile cupola, originally constructed in the 16th century. The open-air structure is frescoed with 18th-century trompe-l'oeil columns and the family coats of arms, which once belonged to the *sedile* (seat), the town council where nobles met to discuss civic problems as early as the

Angevin period. Today Sorrentines still like to congregate around the umbrella-topped tables near the tiny square. ✉ *Largo Dominova, at Via S. Cesareo and Via P.R. Giuliani, Sorrento* 🎫 *Free.*

Villa Comunale

VIEWPOINT | The largest public park in Sorrento sits on a cliff top overlooking the entire Bay of Naples. It offers benches, flowers, palms, and people-watching, plus a seamless vista that stretches from Capri to Vesuvius. From here steps lead down to Sorrento's main harbor, the Marina Piccola. ✉ *Adjoining church of San Francesco, Sorrento.*

Restaurants

Da Emilia

$$ | SOUTHERN ITALIAN | Near the steps of the Marina Grande, this reliable choice for seafood (established in 1947) might not be Sorrento's most visually prepossessing place, but its homespun, family feel—complete with wooden tables and checked tablecloths—is a refreshing change from the town's (occasionally pretentious) elegance. **Known for:** friendly and family-run; tasty and fresh seafood combos like mussels with Sorrentine lemons; harbor terrace above the rocks. ⑤ *Average main: €20* ✉ *Via Marina Grande 62, Sorrento* 🕾 *081/8072720* ⊕ *www.daemilia.it* ⊘ *Closed Nov.–Feb.*

★ Don Alfonso 1890

$$$$ | SOUTHERN ITALIAN | A gastronomic giant and pioneer in upscale farm-to-table cuisine (it even grows its own produce on a small farm nearby), Don Alfonso is considered one of Italy's best restaurants. It's a family affair, with mamma (Livia) handling the dining room, papà (former chef Alfonso Iaccarino) tending to the organic plot, one son working as the current chef (preparing classic dishes alongside edgier creations), and the other serving as maître d'. **Known for:** Punta Campanella local garden produce; stellar dining experience; slow food pioneer.

⑤ *Average main: €80* ✉ *Corso Sant'Agata 13, Sant'Agata sui Due Golfi* ✛ *SITA Bus to via Nastro Verde or taxi from Sorrento.* 🕾 *081/8780026* ⊕ *www.donalfonso.com* ⊘ *Closed Mon. and Tues. and Nov.–May. No lunch weekdays.*

★ Ristorante Bagni Delfino

$$ | SOUTHERN ITALIAN | At this informal, waterside restaurant and snack bar, you won't see many locals—they're unlikely to be impressed by the four-language menus—but the seafood platters are fresh and flavorful, and you can eat alfresco in the sunshine or inside a glass-enclosed dining area with a nautical motif. You can even go for a swim (just please, wait an hour or so after eating!). **Known for:** great views of the Marina Grande and beyond; bountiful portions; terrace beside a sunbathing/swimming jetty. ⑤ *Average main: €22* ✉ *Via Marina Grande 216, Sorrento* 🕾 *081/8782038* ⊕ *www.ristoranteildelfinosorrento.com* ⊘ *Closed Nov.–Mar.*

★ Ristorante Museo Caruso

$$$$ | SOUTHERN ITALIAN | Sorrentine favorites, including *acquerello* (fresh fish appetizer) and ravioli with crab and zucchini sauce, are tweaked creatively here. The staff is warm and helpful, the singer on the sound system is the long-departed "fourth tenor" himself, and the operatic memorabilia (including posters and old photos of Caruso) is displayed in a flattering blush-pink light. **Known for:** tasting menus; Caruso memorabilia aplenty; Torna a Surriento and the Neapolitan songbook. ⑤ *Average main: €45* ✉ *Via S. Antonino 12, Sorrento* 🕾 *081/8073156* ⊕ *www.ristorantemuseocaruso.com.*

Ristorante 'o Parrucchiano La Favorita

$$ | SOUTHERN ITALIAN | Opened in 1868 by an ex-priest (*'o parrucchiano* means "the priest" in the local dialect), this restaurant serves classic Sorrentine cuisine in an enchanting 19th-century setting: a sprawling, multilevel greenhouse, packed with tables and chairs amid fruit trees and enough tropical foliage to fill a Victorian conservatory. **Known for:** gorgeous setting but may disappoint food-wise; fecund greenhouse and terrace foliage and fruit; signature cannelloni created in 1870. ⑤ *Average main: €23* ✉ *Corso Italia 71, Sorrento* ☎ *081/8781321* ⊕ *www.parrucchiano. com* ⊗ *Closed Wed. mid-Nov.–mid-Mar.*

Coffee and Quick Bites

★ A'Marenna

$ | **ITALIAN | FAMILY |** Run with enthusiasm and love by two young Sorrentine women, this small rustic-styled bakery and bistro makes generously filled panini using fresh ingredients on ciabatta and *panuozzo* pizza-dough bread. It's also a fab spot to linger with some local wine and a cheese platter. **Known for:** vegan and veggie options; friendly service; local wines. ⑤ *Average main: €7* ✉ *Via Tasso 23, Sorrento* ☎ *081/18495183.*

Hotels

★ Bellevue Syrene

$$$$ | **HOTEL |** This luxurious retreat, magnificently set on a bluff high over the Bay of Naples, is one of Italy's most legendary hotels, complete with art deco touches throughout; lounges and salons decorated with avant-garde artwork and trompe-l'oeil frescoes; and guest rooms that range from sleekly modern to sumptuously fanciful. **Pros:** half board available; impeccable design elements; elegant common areas. **Cons:** parking is €25 a day; very expensive; small pool. ⑤ *Rooms from: €615* ✉ *Piazza della Vittoria 5, Sorrento* ☎ *081/8781024* ⊕ *www. bellevue.it* ⊗ *Closed Jan.–Mar.* ⇥ *49 rooms* ❤❤ *Free Breakfast.*

★ Excelsior Vittoria

$$$$ | **HOTEL |** Overlooking the Bay of Naples, this luxurious Belle Époque dream has been in the same family since 1834, which means that public spaces are virtual museums—with elegant Victorian love seats and stile

liberty (art nouveau) ornamentation—and guest rooms are spacious, with soigné furnishings and balconies and terraces that overlook gardens or the bay. **Pros:** grand spaces and handsome furnishings; beyond the protected gates, you're in the heart of town; gardens buffer city noise. **Cons:** not all rooms have sea views; front desk can be cold; some rooms are comparatively small. ⑤ *Rooms from: €480* ✉ *Piazza Tasso 34, Sorrento* ☎ *081/8777111* ⊕ *www.exvitt.it* ⊗ *Closed Jan.–Mar.* ⇥ *83 rooms* ❤❤ *Free Breakfast.*

La Favorita

$$$$ | **HOTEL |** The lobby might be a glamorous white-on-white extravaganza of Caprese columns, tufted sofas, shimmering crystal chandeliers, silver ecclesiastical objects, and gilded Baroque mirrors, but the charming staff ensure the vibe is elegantly casual, the guest rooms are well equipped and spacious, and the rooftop pool area has magnificent bay and Vesuvius vistas. **Pros:** idyllic garden; central location; beautiful terrace. **Cons:** lack of decent air-conditioning and room thermostat control; no views to speak of from guest rooms; rooms near the bar noisy after midnight. ⑤ *Rooms from: €400* ✉ *Via T. Tasso 61, Sorrento* ☎ *081/8782031* ⊕ *www.hotellafavorita. com* ⊗ *Closed Jan.–Mar.* ⇥ *85 rooms* ❤❤ *Free Breakfast.*

Settimo Cielo

$$$ | **HOTEL |** Even if your wallet won't allow a stay at one of Sorrento's grand hotels, Settimo Cielo—although dated and a hike away on Capo Sorrento—provides gorgeous views, pretty gardens, and a swimming pool. **Pros:** balcony options; plenty of parking; excellent views. **Cons:** very basic, dated rooms and breakfast; 15-minute walk along busy road into Sorrento; walls not soundproofed. ⑤ *Rooms from: €260* ✉ *Via Capo 27, Sorrento* ☎ *081/8781012* ⊕ *www.hotelsettimocielo.com* ⇥ *20 rooms* ❤❤ *Free Breakfast.*

Positano

14 km (9 miles) east of Sorrento, 57 km (34 miles) south of Naples.

When John Steinbeck visited Positano in 1953, he wrote that it was difficult to consider tourism an industry because "there are not enough [tourists]." Alas, there are more than enough now, and the town's vertical landscape with pastel-hue houses, drapes of bright pink bougainvillea, and sapphire-blue sea make it easy to understand why.

The most photographed fishing village in the world, this fabled locale is home to some 4,000 *Positanesi*, who are joined daily by hordes arriving from Capri, Sorrento, and Amalfi. The town clings to the Monti Lattari with arcaded, cubist buildings, set in tiers up the mountainside, in shades of rose, peach, purple, and ivory.

GETTING HERE AND AROUND

SITA buses leave from the Circumvesuviana train station in Sorrento. Buses also run from Naples and, in summer, Rome. There is a ferry from Sorrento in the summer months.

A word of advice: wear comfortable walking shoes and be sure your back and legs are strong enough to negotiate those picturesque but daunting and ladderlike scalinatelle. In the center of town, where no buses can go, you're on your own from Piazza dei Mulini. To begin your explorations, make a left turn onto the boutique-flanked Via dei Mulini and head down to the Palazzo Murat, Santa Maria Assunta, and the beach—one of the most charming walks of the coast.

VISITOR INFORMATION

CONTACT Azienda Autonoma Soggiorno e Turismo. ⊠ *Via Regina Giovanna 13, Positano* ☎ *089/875067* ⊕ *www.aziendaturismopositano.it.*

Sights

Palazzo Murat

NOTABLE BUILDING | Past a bevy of resort boutiques, head to Via dei Mulini to view the prettiest garden in Positano: the 18th-century courtyard of the Palazzo Murat, named for Joachim Murat, who sensibly chose the palazzo as his summer residence. This was where Murat, designated by his brother-in-law Napoléon as King of Naples in 1808, came to forget the demands of power and lead a simpler life. He built this grand abode (now a hotel) near the church of Santa Maria Assunta, just steps from the main beach. ⊠ *Via dei Mulini 23, Positano* ☎ *089/875177* ⊕ *www.palazzomurat.it.*

Santa Maria Assunta

CHURCH | The Chiesa Madre, or parish church of Santa Maria Assunta, lies just south of the Palazzo Murat, its green-and-yellow majolica dome topped by a perky cupola visible from just about anywhere in town. Built on the site of the former Benedictine abbey of Saint Vito, the 13th-century Romanesque structure was almost completely rebuilt in 1700. The last piece of the ancient mosaic floor can be seen under glass behind the altar. Note the carved wooden Christ, a masterpiece of devotional religious art, with its bathetic face and bloodied knees, on view before the altar. At the altar is a Byzantine 13th-century painting on wood of Madonna with Child, known popularly as the Black Virgin. A replica is carried to the beach every August 15 to celebrate the Feast of the Assumption. Legend claims that the painting was once stolen by Saracen pirates, who, fleeing in a raging storm, heard a voice from on high saying, "*Posa, posa*" (Put it down, put it down). When they placed the image on the beach near the church, the storm calmed, as did the Saracens. Embedded over the doorway of the church's bell tower, set across the tiny piazza, is a medieval bas-relief of fishes, a fox, and a pistrice (the mythical half-dragon,

Marina Grande Beach in Positano is a nice, long stretch of sand that attracts a cosmopolitan crowd.

half-dog sea monster). This is one of the few relics of the medieval abbey of Saint Vito. The Oratorio houses historic statues from the Sacristy; renovations to the Crypt have unearthed part of an extensive Roman Villa buried by the AD 79 eruption. ✉ *Piazza Flavio Gioia, Positano* ☎ *089/875480* 🌐 *www.chiesapositano.it.*

Spiaggia Grande

BEACH | FAMILY | The walkway from the Piazza Flavio Gioia leads down to Spiaggia Grande, Positano's main beach, bordered by an esplanade and some of the town's busiest restaurants. Surrounded by the spectacular amphitheater of houses and villas that leapfrog up the hillsides of Monte Comune and Monte Sant'Angelo, this remains one of the most picturesque beaches in the world. ✉ *Spiaggia Grande, Positano.*

★ Via Positanesi d'America

PROMENADE | FAMILY | Just before the ferry ticket booths to the right of Spiaggia Grande, a tiny road that is the loveliest seaside walkway on the entire coast rises up and borders the cliffs leading to Fornillo Beach. The road is named for the town's large number of 19th-century emigrants to the United States—Positano virtually survived during World War II thanks to the money and packages their descendants sent back home. Halfway up the path lies the Torre Trasita (Trasita Tower), the most distinctive of Positano's three coastline defense towers. Now a residence occasionally available for summer rental, the tower was used to spot pirate raids. As you continue along the Via Positanesi d'America, you'll pass a tiny inlet and an emerald cove before Fornillo Beach comes into view. ✉ *Via Positanesi d'America, Positano.*

🍽 Restaurants

Il Ritrovo

$$ | SOUTHERN ITALIAN | FAMILY | In the tiny town square of Montepertuso, 1,500 feet up the mountainside from Positano (call for the free shuttle service to and from), the Ritrovo has been noted for its cucina for more than 20 years. The menu showcases food from both the sea and the hills: try the *scialatielli ai frutti di mare* accompanied by well-grilled vegetables; the house specialty *zuppa saracena,* a paella-like affair brimming with assorted seafood; and the lemon tiramisu, perhaps paired with one of 80 different kinds of a homemade liqueur, including carob and chamomile options. **Known for:** amiable padrone Salvatò, who also runs a cooking school; airy, tranquil mountainside location; trademark *zuppa saracena* (seafood soup). ⑤ *Average main: €22* ✉ *Via Montepertuso 77, Montepertuso* ☎ *089/812005* ⊕ *www.ilritrovo. com* ⊙ *Closed mid-Jan.–mid-Feb.*

Lo Guarracino

$$ | SOUTHERN ITALIAN | This partly arbor-covered restaurant is a romantic place to enjoy *scialatielli di mare* (seafood pasta) above the waves, with a terrace vista that takes in the cliffs, the sea, the Li Galli islands, Spiaggia del Fornillo, and Torre Clavel. **Known for:** seafood and wood-fired pizza; romantic Robinson Crusoe–esque terrace; family-made liquori digestivi including a new wild-herb number (agrumi). ⑤ *Average main: €22* ✉ *Via Positanesi d'America 12, Positano* ☎ *089/875794* ⊕ *www.loguarracinopositano.it* ⊙ *Closed Jan.–Mar.*

Next2

$$$ | SOUTHERN ITALIAN | Wrought-iron gates open from scenic Via Pasitea into Next2's *bianco e nero*–chic courtyard, replete with a cocktail bar and a whiff of edgy, youthful swagger. You can watch the talented *squadra* at work in the open kitchen crafting elegant, subtly flavored creations such as the *pizza margherita*

starter, the seared tuna *secondo*, and—for those with bigger, bolder appetities—the *frittura di mare* (fried seafood medley). **Known for:** cocktails with novel, fresh infusions; delectable dessert pairings such as pear and walnut ice cream; exquisite-looking small-portioned dishes. ⑤ *Average main: €28* ✉ *Via Pasitea 242, Positano* ☎ *089/8123516* ⊙ *No lunch.*

☕ Coffee and Quick Bites

Paradise Lounge Bar

$ | SANDWICHES | FAMILY | With an outdoor terrace overlooking the Spiaggia Grande, this is an ideal stop for a coffee, a sandwich, or an ice cream. By night, MTV music pumps from the stereo and the clamor of sporting events blares from the four large-screen TVs, as movers, groovers, and soccer fans from around the globe sip cocktails after a hard day on the beach. **Known for:** pastries, pizza, and panini; fab gelato *artigianale*; warm counter service from Alessio and the team. ⑤ *Average main: €5* ✉ *Via del Saracino 32, Positano* ☎ *089/811915* ⊙ *Closed Mon.*

🏨 Hotels

Hotel Eden Roc

$$$ | HOTEL | The closest hotel to the Sponda bus stop, this luxury property (perfect for either couples or families) has spectacular views and service and spacious, pastel-hued guest rooms—all with terraces overlooking the town and some with whirlpool tubs. **Pros:** large rooms; good on-site amenities (gym, steam bath, wellness center, rooftop pool); magical views. **Cons:** on the main road (take care as you exit the hotel); some rooms are dated; a bit of a climb from the town center. ⑤ *Rooms from: €273* ✉ *Via G. Marconi 110, Positano* ☎ *089/875844* ⊕ *www.edenroc.it* ⊙ *Closed mid-Nov.–Feb.* ➷ *25 rooms* ⦿ *Free Breakfast.*

Hotel L'Ancora

$$$$ | **HOTEL** | Set back a little from the main road and a short walk up from the main beach, this hotel has commanding views and bright guest rooms decorated with local artwork and boldly patterned mosaic tile. **Pros:** not far from the Sponda bus stop; bright and sunny; all rooms have balconies or terraces and sea views. **Cons:** no on-site pool; a slight climb from the main drag; below-par breakfast. ⑤ *Rooms from: €430* ✉ *Via Cristoforo Colombo 36, Positano* ☎ *089/875318* ⊕ *www.hotelancorapositano.com* ⧖ *Free Breakfast* ⊘ *Closed Nov.–Mar.* ⬅ *18 rooms.*

La Fenice

$$ | **HOTEL** | This tiny, unpretentious hotel on the outskirts of Positano beckons with bougainvillea-laden views, castaway cottages, and a turquoise seawater pool—all perched over a private beach where a boat can whisk you away to Capri. **Pros:** secluded pool; small private beach with kayaks; 250 steps to private beach. **Cons:** roadside rooms are small and noisy; a 10-minute walk to town; lots of steps. ⑤ *Rooms from: €190* ✉ *Via G. Marconi 4, Positano* ☎ *089/875513* ⊕ *www.lafenicepositano.com* ⊘ *Sometimes closed Dec.–Feb.* ⬅ *14 rooms* ⧖ *Free Breakfast.*

★ Le Sirenuse

$$$$ | **HOTEL** | As legendary as its namesake sirens, this 18th-century palazzo has long set the standard for luxury in Italian hotels: it opened in 1951 with just 12 rooms (John Steinbeck stayed here while writing "Positano" for *Harper's Bazaar* in 1953) and now sprawls over eight floors, where extravagantly stylish guest rooms are accented with antiques and fine linens. **Pros:** gorgeous artworks around every corner; unrivaled views, including from poolside terrace; many rooms have whirlpool tubs. **Cons:** lower-priced rooms are small; a bit of a climb from the town center; can be noisy. ⑤ *Rooms from: €778* ✉ *Via Cristoforo Colombo 30, Positano* ☎ *089/875066* ⊕ *www.sirenuse.it* ⊘ *Closed Nov.–Mar.* ⬅ *58 rooms* ⧖ *Free Breakfast.*

Palazzo Murat

$$$$ | **HOTEL** | A central-yet-secreted location, an infinity pool below the cupola of Santa Maria Assunta, and a magical bougainvillea-draped patio garden are among the things that make the Murat an extraordinary place to stay. **Pros:** shops and passeggiata on the doorstep; once a regal residence; stunning garden and surroundings. **Cons:** constant stream of curious day-trippers; only five rooms have seaside views; not all balconies secluded. ⑤ *Rooms from: €560* ✉ *Via dei Mulini 23, Positano* ☎ *089/875177* ⊕ *www. palazzomurat.it* ⊘ *Closed Nov.–Mar.* ⬅ *31 rooms* ⧖ *Free Breakfast.*

🍸 Nightlife

L'Africana

DANCE CLUBS | Off a mile-long footpath from the Marina del Praia—or accessed via an elevator from Statale 163—L'Africana is a golden-oldie classic from the 1960s. With an open-to-the-sea atmosphere, a cave for a dance floor, and wildish shows with partial nudity, you can party the night away here, as Jackie Kennedy once did. The nightclub runs boats from Positano on Saturday—transfer can also be arranged from other points along the coast. Just ring them to get picked up. ✉ *Via Terramare 2, Praiano* ☎ *089/874858, 331/5330612 cell phone* ⊕ *www.africanafamousclub.com.*

Conca dei Marini

13 km (8 miles) east of Positano, 29 km (18 miles) east of Sorrento.

A longtime favorite of the off-duty rich and famous, Conca dei Marini (the name means "seafarers' basin") hides many of its charms, as any sublime hideaway should. On a curve in the road sits the village's most noteworthy attraction, the Emerald Grotto.

Sights

Grotta dello Smeraldo (*Emerald Grotto*)
NATURE SIGHT | **FAMILY** | The tacky road sign, squadron of tour buses, Dean Martino–style boatmen, and freeform serenading (Andrea is the king of the grotto crooners) scream tourist trap, but there is, nevertheless, a compelling, eerie *bellezza* in the rock formations and luminous waters here. The karstic cave was originally part of the shore, but the lowest end sank into the sea. Intense greenish light filters into the water from an arch below sea level and is reflected off the cavern walls. You visit the Grotta dello Smeraldo, which is filled with huge stalactites and stalagmites, on a large rowboat. Don't let the boatman's constant spiel detract from the experience— just tune out and enjoy the sparkles, shapes, and brilliant colors. The light at the grotto is best from noon to 3 pm. You can take an elevator from the coast road down to the grotto, or in the summer you can drive to Amalfi and arrive by boat (€10, excluding the grotto's €6 admission fee). Companies in Positano, Amalfi, and elsewhere along the coast provide passage to the grotto, but consider one of the longer boat trips that explore Punta Campanella, Li Galli, and the more secluded spots along the coast. ✉ *Via Smeraldo, west of Capo di Conca, Conca dei Marini* ☎ *089/831535* 💳 *€6* ☉ *Closed in adverse weather conditions.*

Hotels

★ **Monastero Santa Rosa Hotel & Spa**
$$$$ | **HOTEL** | One of Italy's most exclusive retreats—in a 17th-century monastery on dramatic coastal cliffs—this boutique hotel has just 20 rooms, all with vaulted ceilings, Italian antiques, modern amenities, sumptuous bathrooms, and dazzling views framed by Mediterranean gardens.
Pros: gorgeous gardens and infinity pool; excellent service; meticulously restored property with spa. **Cons:** some rooms could be more spacious; out of reach for many budgets; a bit remote. 💲 *Rooms from: €748* ✉ *Via Roma 2, Conca dei Marini* ☎ *089/8321199* 🌐 *www.monasterosantarosa.com* ☉ *Closed Nov.–mid-Apr.* 🛏 *20 rooms* ❧ *Free Breakfast.*

Amalfi

18 km (11 miles) east of Positano, 35 km (22 miles) east of Sorrento.

At first glance, it's hard to imagine that this resort destination was one of the world's great naval powers, and a sturdy rival of Genoa and Pisa for control of the Mediterranean in the 11th and 12th centuries. Once the seat of the Amalfi Maritime Republic, the town is set in a verdant valley of the Lattari Mountains, with cream-color and pastel-hue buildings tightly packing a gorge on the Bay of Salerno. The harbor, which once launched the greatest fleet in Italy, now bobs with ferries and blue-and-white fishing boats. The main street, lined with shops and *pasticcerie,* has replaced a raging mountain torrent, and terraced hills flaunt the green and gold of lemon groves. Bearing testimony to its great trade with Tunis, Tripoli, and Algiers, Amalfi remains honeycombed with Arab-Sicilian cloisters and covered passages. In a way Amalfi has become great again, showing off its medieval glory days with sea pageants, convents-turned-hotels, ancient paper mills, covered streets, and its glimmering cathedral.

GETTING HERE AND AROUND

From April to October the optimal way to get to Amalfi is by ferry from Salerno. SitaSud buses run from Naples and Sorrento throughout the year. By car, take the Statale 163 (Amalfitana) from outside Sorrento or Salerno, or take the Angri exit on the A3 autostrada and cross the mountainous Valico di Chiunsi.

VISITOR INFORMATION

CONTACT Amalfi Tourism Office. ✉ *Via delle Repubbliche Marinare 27,* ☎ *089/871107* ⊕ *www.amalfitouristoffice.it.*

 Sights

★ Duomo di Sant'Andrea

CHURCH | Complicated, grand, delicate, and dominating, the 9th-century Amalfi cathedral has been remodeled over the years with Romanesque, Byzantine, Gothic, and Baroque elements, but retains a predominantly Arab-Norman style. This intriguing blend of architectural styles easily confuses past and present, old and new, authentic and revival. The facade, with its glimmering mosaics, intricate patterns, and Arab design influences, is in fact no older than the 19th century. It was the master work of Neapolitan architect Errico Alvino, created during the height of Italy's fascination with Revivalism. The campanile, spliced with Saracen colors and intricate tile work, is the real deal and dates to the 13th century. The **Chiostro del Paradiso** (Paradise Cloister) is an Arab-Sicilian spectacular. Built around 1266 as a burial ground for Amalfi's elite, the cloister, the first stop on a tour of the cathedral, is one of southern Italy's architectural treasures. Its flower-and-palm-filled quadrangle has a series of exceptionally delicate intertwining arches on slender double columns. The chapel at the back of the cloister leads into the earlier (9th century) **basilica.** Romanesque in style, the structure has a nave, two aisles, and a high, deep apse. Note the 14th-century crucifixion scene by a student of Giotto. This section has now been transformed into a museum, housing sarcophagi, sculpture, Neapolitan goldsmiths' artwork, and other treasures from the cathedral complex. Steps from the basilica lead down into the **Cripta di Sant'Andrea** (Crypt of Saint Andrew). The cathedral above was built in the 13th century to house the saint's bones, which came from Constantinople and supposedly exuded a miraculous liquid believers call the "manna of Saint Andrew." Following the one-way traffic up to the cathedral itself, you finally get to admire the elaborate polychrome marbles and painted, coffered ceilings from its 18th-century restoration. Art historians shake their heads over this renovation, as the original decoration of the apse must have been one of the wonders of the Middle Ages. ✉ *Piazza Duomo, Amalfi* ☎ *089/871324* ⊕ *www.parrocchiaamalfi. com* ⏱ *Generally closed early Jan. and Feb. except for daily services* 🎫 *€4.*

★ Museo della Carta (*Paper Museum*)

HISTORY MUSEUM | **FAMILY** | Uphill from town, the Valle dei Mulini (Valley of the Mills) was for centuries Amalfi's center for papermaking, an ancient trade learned from the Arabs, who learned it from the Chinese. Beginning in the 12th century, former flour mills were converted to produce paper made from cotton and linen. The paper industry was a success, and by 1811 more than a dozen mills here, with more along the coast, were humming. Natural waterpower ensured that the handmade paper was cost-effective. Yet, by the late 1800s the industry had moved to Naples and other more geographically accessible areas. Flooding in 1954 closed most of the mills for good, and many have been converted into private housing. The Museo della Carta (Museum of Paper) opened in 1971 in a 15th-century mill. Paper samples, tools of the trade, old machinery, and the audiovisual presentation are all enlightening. You can also participate in a paper-making laboratory. ✉ *Via delle Cartiere 23, Amalfi* ☎ *089/8304561* ⊕ *www.*

museodellacarta.it ⊠ *€4.50, includes guided tour* ⊗ *Closed Feb. and Mon. Nov.–Jan.*

 Restaurants

La Caravella

$$$$ | SOUTHERN ITALIAN | Opened in 1959 and southern Italy's first restaurant to earn a Michelin star (in 1966), this atmospheric place—graced with frescoes, marble floors, vibrant ceramics, and fresh flowers—once had a gilded guest list that included Andy Warhol and Federico Fellini. The menu maintains dishes favored 50 years ago (picture slices of fish grilled in lemon leaves marinated with an almond and wild fennel sauce); there's also a tasting menu, but don't miss the antipasti. **Known for:** cheerful dining room; wine-dealer expertise; the Mezzogiorno's pioneering fine-dining eatery. $ *Average main: €60* ⊠ *Via Matteo Camera 12, near Arsenale, Amalfi* ☎ *089/871029* ⊕ *www. ristorantelacaravella.it* ⊗ *Closed Tues. and Nov. and Jan.*

 Coffee and Quick Bites

Andrea Pansa

$ | CAFÉ | Amalfi's historic pasticceria is famed for its candied fruits and assortment of tempting Neapolitan pastries. If you have no time to linger and indulge at their piazza tables, order at the bar for a cheaper stand-up caffè and *sfogliatella* pastry fix. **Known for:** excellent but pricey; *delizia di limone* cake; historic facade and interiors on Piazza Duomo. $ *Average main: €5* ⊠ *Piazza Duomo 40, Amalfi* ☎ *089/871065* ⊕ *www.pasticceriapansa.it.*

 Hotels

Albergo Sant'Andrea

$ | HOTEL | Just across from the magnificent steps leading to Amalfi's cathedral, this tiny, family-run *pensione* has a cute "Room with a View" lobby that's as big as a Victorian closet and guest rooms (most overlooking the Duomo) that range from cozy to vast. **Pros:** friendly, reliable budget option; great location on the main square; divine Duomo views. **Cons:** simple, dated decor; steep flight of steps to entrance; on the piazza, so expect noise. $ *Rooms from: €120* ⊠ *Via Duca Mansone I, Amalfi* ☎ *089/871145* ⊕ *www. albergosantandrea.it* ⊅ *8 rooms* ⦿| *Free Breakfast* ⊗ *Closed Feb. and Mar.*

★ Grand Hotel Convento di Amalfi

$$$$ | HOTEL | This fabled medieval monastery was lauded by such guests as Longfellow and Wagner, and though recently modernized, it still retains some of its historic charm, including Victorian lecterns, Savonarola chairs, and a celebrated Arab-Sicilian cloister; once stark monk cells are now comfy contemporary guest room cocoons, some with wicker settees and beds. **Pros:** sublime terrace and garden walkways; a slice of paradise; impeccable service. **Cons:** a 10-minute walk to town; traditionalists will miss some of its old-world charm; limited dining options. $ *Rooms from: €600* ⊠ *Via Annunziatella 46, Amalfi* ☎ *089/8736711* ⊕ *www.ghconventodiamalfi.com* ⊗ *Closed Jan.–mid-Mar.* ⊅ *53 rooms* ⦿| *Free Breakfast.*

Shopping

Leading off from Piazza Duomo is the main street of Amalfi, Via Lorenzo d'Amalfi, which is lined with some of the loveliest shops on the coast. While it can be crowded during the day, be sure to take a stroll along here in the evening.

Ravello's History

The town itself was founded in the 9th century, under Amalfi's rule. Residents prosperous from cotton tussled with the superpower republic and elected their own doge in the 11th century; *Amalfitani* dubbed them *rebelli* (rebels). In the 12th century, with the aid of the Norman King Roger, Ravello even succeeded in resisting Pisa's army for a couple of years, though the powerful Pisans returned to wreak destruction along the coast. Even so, Ravello's skilled seafaring trade with merchants and Moors from Sicily and points east led to a burgeoning wealth, which peaked in the 13th century, when there were 13 churches, four cloisters, and dozens of sumptuous villas. Neapolitan princes built palaces and life was privileged.

Ravello's bright light eventually diminished, first through Pisa's maritime rise in the 14th century, then through rivalry between its warring families in the 15th century. When the plague cast its shadow in the 17th century, the population plummeted from upward of 30,000 to perhaps a couple of thousand souls, where it remains today. When Ravello was incorporated into the diocese of Amalfi in 1804, a kind of stillness settled in. Despite the decline of its power and populace, Ravello's cultural heritage and special loveliness continued to blossom. Gardens flowered and music flowed in the ruined villas, and artists, sophisticates, and their lovers filled the crumbling palazzi. Grieg, Wagner, D. H. Lawrence, Chanel, Garbo and her companion, conductor Leopold Stokowski, and then, slowly, tourists, followed in their footsteps.

Ravello

5 km (3 miles) northeast of Amalfi, 40 km (25 miles) northeast of Sorrento.

Positano may focus on pleasure, and Amalfi on history, but cool, serene Ravello revels in refinement. Thrust over the S163 and the Bay of Salerno on a mountain buttress, below forests of chestnut and ash, above terraced lemon groves and vineyards, it early on beckoned the affluent with its island-in-the-sky views and secluded defensive positioning. Gardens out of the *Arabian Nights,* pastel palazzi, tucked-away piazzas with medieval fountains, architecture ranging from Romano-Byzantine to Norman-Saracen, and those sweeping blue-water, blue-sky vistas have inspired a panoply of large personalities. Today, many visitors flock here to discover this paradisiacal place, some to enjoy the town's celebrated two-month-long summer music festival (the Ravello Festival, www.ravellofestival. com), others just to stroll through the hillside streets to gape at the bluer-than-blue panoramas of sea and sky.

GETTING HERE AND AROUND
Buses from Amalfi make the 20-minute trip along white-knuckle roads. From Naples, take the A3 Naples–Salerno autostrada; then exit at Angri and follow signs for Ravello. The journey takes about 75 minutes. Save yourself the trouble of driving by hiring a car and driver.

VISITOR INFORMATION
CONTACT Azienda Autonoma Soggiorno e Turismo. ✉ *Piazza Fontana Moresca, 10, Ravello* ☎ *089/857096* ⊕ *www.ravello-time.it.*

Sights

Auditorium Oscar Niemeyer

ARTS CENTER | Crowning Via della Repubblica and the hillside, which overlooks the spectacular Bay of Salerno, Auditorium Oscar Niemeyer is a startling piece of modernist architecture. Designed with a dramatically curved, all-white roof by the Brazilian architect Oscar Niemeyer, it was conceived as an alternative indoor venue for concerts, including those of the famed Ravello Festival of music and arts, and is now also used as a cinema in the winter. The subject of much controversy since its first conception back in 2000, it raised the wrath of some locals who denounced such an ambitious modernist building in medieval Ravello. They need not have worried: the result, inaugurated in 2010, is a design masterpiece—a huge canopied roof suspended over a 400-seat concert area, with a giant eye-shape window allowing spectators to contemplate the extraordinary bay vista during performances. While only open during concerts and events, it is worth visiting to admire not only the architecture but also the impressive views from the large terrace, which is also a scenic setting for art exhibitions during the Ravello Festival. ⊠ *Via della Repubblica 12, Ravello.*

★ Duomo

CHURCH | Ravello's first bishop, Orso Papiciò, founded this cathedral in 1086. Rebuilt in the 12th and 17th centuries, it retains traces of medieval frescoes in the transept, a marble portal, and a three-story 13th-century bell tower playfully interwoven with mullioned windows and arches. The 12th-century bronze door has 54 embossed panels depicting Christ's life, and saints, prophets, plants, and animals, all narrating biblical lore. Ancient columns divide the nave's three aisles, and treasures include sarcophagi from Roman times and paintings by the southern Renaissance artist Andrea da Salerno. Most impressive are the two medieval pulpits: the earlier one (on your left as you face the altar) is inset with a mosaic scene of Jonah and the whale, symbolizing death and redemption. The more famous one opposite was commissioned by Nicola Rufolo in 1272 and created by Niccolò di Bartolomeo da Foggia, with exquisite mosaic work, bas-reliefs, and six twisting columns sitting on lion pedestals. An eagle grandly tops the inlaid marble lectern. A chapel to the left of the apse is dedicated to San Pantaleone, a physician beheaded in the 3rd century in Nicomedia. Every July 27 devout believers gather in hope of witnessing a miracle (similar to that of San Gennaro in Naples), in which the saint's blood, collected in a vial and set out on an inlaid marble altar, appears to liquefy and come to a boil. In the crypt is the **Museo del Duomo,** which displays religious treasures, including many from the 13th century during the reign of Frederick II of Sicily. ⊠ *Piazza del Duomo, Ravello* ☎ *089/858311* ⊕ *www.museoduomoravello.com* ✑ *€3.*

Giardini del Vescovo (*Monsignore*)

HISTORIC HOME | A one-time bishop's residence that dates from at least the 12th century, the Villa Episcopio (formerly Villa di Sangro) today hosts concerts and exhibitions and has an open-air theater in its splendid gardens—the same gardens where André Gide found inspiration for his novel *The Immoralist,* where Italy's King Vittorio Emanuele III abdicated in favor of his son in 1944, and where Jackie Kennedy enjoyed breaks from her obligations as First Lady during a much publicized 1962 visit. Wheelchair access is via a new ramp on via San Giovanni del Toro. ⊠ *Via Boccaccio, Ravello* ✑ *Free.*

Mamma Agata

SCHOOL | If you fancy learning how to make some of the things you've been eating, Mamma Agata, who has cooked for Elizabeth Taylor, Federico Fellini, Jackie Kennedy, and Marcello Mastroianni, will take you into her kitchen—with the almost obligatory stunning view—and walk you through the preparation of the area's pasta dishes and sweets. A morning session is followed by lunch—that you will have seen made. ⊠ *Piazza San Cosma 9, Ravello* ☎ *089/857845* ⊕ *www. mammaagata.com* ✉ *cooking class and lunch €250* ⊘ *Closed weekends, and Nov.–mid-Mar.*

★ **Museo del Corallo** (*Coral Museum*)
ART MUSEUM | To the left of the Duomo, the entrance to this private museum is through the tempting shop CAMO, and both are the creation of master-craftsman-in-residence Giorgio Filocamo. The museum celebrates the venerable tradition of Italian workmanship in coral, harvested in bygone centuries from the gulfs of Salerno and Naples and crafted into jewelry, cameos, and figurines. The fascinating collection, not confined solely to coral work, includes a painting of Sisto IV from the 14th century. Look also in particular for a carved Christ from the 17th century, for which the J. Paul Getty Museum offered $525,000 in 1987 (the offer was refused), and a tobacco box covered in cameos, one of only two in the world. There is also a statue of the Madonna dating to 1532. Giorgio has crafted coral for Pope John Paul II, the Clintons, and Princess Caroline, as well as numerous Hollywood stars. ⊠ *Piazza Duomo 9, Ravello* ☎ *089/857461* ⊕ *www. museodelcorallo.com* ✉ *Free.*

★ **Villa Cimbrone**
GARDEN | To the south of Ravello's main square, a somewhat hilly 15-minute walk along Via San Francesco brings you to Ravello's showstopper, the Villa Cimbrone, whose dazzling gardens perch 1,500 feet above the sea. This medieval-style fantasy was created in 1905 by England's Lord Grimthorpe and made world famous in the 1930s when Greta Garbo found sanctuary from the press here. The Gothic *castello-palazzo* sits amid idyllic gardens that are divided by the grand Avenue of Immensity pathway, leading in turn to the literal high point of

any trip to the Amalfi Coast—the **Belvedere of Infinity**. This grand stone parapet, adorned with stone busts, overlooks the entire Bay of Salerno and frames a panorama the late writer Gore Vidal, a longtime Ravello resident, described as the most beautiful in the world. The villa itself is now a five-star hotel. ⊠ *Via Santa Chiara 26, Ravello* ☎ *089/857459* ⊕ *www. villacimbrone.it* ✉ *€7.*

★ **Villa Rufolo**
GARDEN | Directly off Ravello's main piazza is the Villa Rufolo, home to enchanting gardens, many of which frame a stunning vista of the Bay of Salerno. If the master storyteller Boccaccio is to be believed, the villa was built in the 13th century by Landolfo Rufolo, whose immense fortune stemmed from trade with the Moors and the Saracens. Norman and Arab architecture mingle in a welter of color-filled gardens so lush the composer Richard Wagner used them as inspiration for Klingsor's Garden, the home of the Flower Maidens, in his opera *Parsifal*. Beyond the Arab-Sicilian cloister and the Norman tower lie the two terrace gardens. The lower one, the "Wagner Terrace," is often the site for Ravello Festival concerts, with the orchestra perched on a platform constructed over the precipice. Sir Francis Nevile Reid, a Scotsman, acquired the villa in 1851 and hired Michele Ruggiero, head of the excavations at Pompeii, to restore the villa to its full splendor and replant the gardens with rare cycads, cordylines, and palms. Highlights of the house are its Moorish cloister—an Arabic-Sicilian delight with interlacing lancet arcs and polychromatic palmette decoration—and the 14th-century Torre Maggiore, the so-called Klingsor's Tower, renamed in honor of Richard Wagner's landmark 1880 visit. ⊠ *Piazza del Duomo, Ravello* ☎ *089/857621* ⊕ *www.villarufolo. it* ✉ *€7, extra charge for concerts.*

Restaurants

Ristorante Pizzeria Vittoria

$$ | **PIZZA** | **FAMILY** | Just south of the Duomo, this airy, unfussy place with coved stone ceilings is a good bet for an informal bite. The *pizza al forno di legna* with fresh toppings is the star attraction: locals praise it, and even Gore Vidal allegedly approved. **Known for:** Campanian classics, including seafood frittura and eggplant parmigiana; extensive menu; very popular with locals and tourists. ⑤ *Average main: €18* ✉ *Via dei Rufolo 3, Ravello* ☎ *089/857947* ⊕ *www.ristorantepizzeriavittoria.it.*

🛏 Hotels

Hotel Parsifal

$$ | **HOTEL** | In 1288, this diminutive property overlooking the coastline housed an order of Augustinian friars; today the intact cloister hosts travelers intent on enjoying themselves under the coved ceilings of the former *eremitani scalzi* (shaved hermit) cells. **Pros:** open year-round; staying in a former Ravello convent; charming manager and his family dote on Americans. **Cons:** tiny rooms; very pricey in high season; minimum 3-night stay in some periods. ⑤ *Rooms from: €200* ✉ *Viale Gioacchino d'Anna 5, Ravello* ☎ *089/857144* ⊕ *www.hotelparsifal.com* ↝ *17 rooms* ⑩| *Free Breakfast.*

★ Hotel Villa Cimbrone

$$$$ | **HOTEL** | Suspended over the azure sea and set amid legendary rose-filled gardens, this Gothic-style castle was once home to Lord Grimthorpe and a hideaway for Greta Garbo; since the 1990s, it's been an exclusive if pricey visitors haven, with guest rooms ranging from palatial to cozy. **Pros:** surrounded by beautiful gardens; top-rated restaurant; gorgeous pool and views. **Cons:** special place comes at a price; daily arrival of respectful day-trippers; a longish hike from town center (porters can help with luggage). ⑤ *Rooms from: €540* ✉ *Via Santa Chiara 26, Ravello* ☎ *089/857459* ⊕ *www.villacimbrone.com* ☾ *Closed Nov.–mid-Apr.* ↝ *19 rooms* ⑩| *Free Breakfast.*

Villa Amore

$$ | **HOTEL** | A 10-minute walk from the Piazza Duomo, this secluded hotel with a garden is family-run and shares the same exhilarating view of the Bay of Salerno as Ravello's most expensive hotels. **Pros:** wonderful views; inexpensive alternative to its illustrious neighbors; great value restaurant. **Cons:** standard rooms are small; long flight of steps to reach entrance; away from the main drag. ⑤ *Rooms from: €180* ✉ *Via dei Fusco 5, Ravello* ☎ *089/857135* ⊕ *www.villaamore.it* ☾ *Closed Nov.–Mar.* ↝ *12 rooms* ⑩| *Free Breakfast.*

Paestum

99 km (62 miles) southeast of Naples.

For history buffs, a visit to Campania is not complete without seeing the ancient ruins of Paestum. A visit to the ruins to stroll past the incredibly well-preserved temples and see the top-notch collection at the Museo Nazionale is a great day trip from the Amalfi Coast or Naples.

GETTING HERE AND AROUND

By car, take the A3 autostrada south from Salerno, take the Battipaglia exit to SS18. Exit at Capaccio Scala. You can also take a CSTP or SCAT bus (departs hourly) or an FS train from Salerno. The archaeological site is a 10-minute walk from the station.

VISITOR INFORMATION

CONTACT Azienda Autonoma Soggiorno e Turismo di Paestum. (*Paestum Tourist Office*) ⊠ *Via Magna Grecia 887, Paestum* ☎ *0828/811016* ⊕ *www.infopaestum.it.*

 Sights

⭐ **Greek Temples**

RUINS | One of Italy's most majestic sights lies on the edge of a flat coastal plain: the remarkably preserved Greek temples of Paestum. This is the site of the ancient city of Poseidonia, founded by Greek colonists probably in the 6th century BC. When the Romans took it over in 273 BC, they Latinized the name to Paestum and changed the layout of the settlement, adding an amphitheater and a forum. Much of the archaeological material found on the site is displayed in the Museo Nazionale, and several rooms are devoted to the unique tomb paintings—rare examples of Greek and pre-Roman pictorial art—discovered in the area. At the northern end of the site opposite the ticket barrier is the Tempio di Cerere (Temple of Ceres). Built in about 500 BC, it is thought to have been originally dedicated to the goddess Athena. Follow the road south past the Foro Romano (Roman Forum) to the Tempio di Nettuno (Temple of Poseidon), a showstopping Doric edifice with 36 fluted columns and an entablature (the area above the capitals) that rivals those of the finest temples in Greece. Beyond is the so-called Basilica. It dates from the early 6th century BC. The name is an 18th-century misnomer, though, since it was, in fact, a temple to Hera, the wife of Zeus. Try to see the temples in the early morning or late afternoon. ⊠ *Via Magna Grecia, Paestum* ☎ *0828/811023 ticket office* ⊕ *www.museopaestum.beniculturali.it* 🎫 *Site and museum: Mar.-Nov. €12, Dec.-Feb. €6.*

⭐ **Tenuta Vannulo—Buffalo Farm and Shop**

FARM/RANCH | FAMILY | Foodies, families, and the curious flock to this novel farm attraction that celebrates humane animal husbandry, organic mozzarella di bufala, and other wonderful products. A tour of the ranch run by the Palmieri family—headed by the serene octogenerian Antonio—brings you nose to glistening snout with probably the most pampered buffalo in the world. Some 600 of them wallow in pools, get a mechanical massage, and flap their ears to classical music. The shop/restaurant is the place to taste and take away cheese, ice cream, yogurt, chocolate, and leather products. ⊠ *Contrada Vannulo, Via Galileo Galilei 101, Capaccio, Paestum* ☎ *0828/727894* ⊕ *www.vannulo.it* 🎫 *€5 guided tours; book in advance.*

 Hotels

Azienda Agrituristica Seliano

$ | B&B/INN | At this working farm about 3 km (2 miles) from Paestum's Greek temples, befriend the resident dogs so they will accompany you on country walks or bike rides, and opt for half-board to enjoy home-produced mozzarella and rich buffalo stew; you'll dine at a table with other guests before withdrawing to your charming wood-beamed guest room in one of the 19th-century baronial buildings. **Pros:** cooking classes; a great taste of a working farm; a banquet every evening. **Cons:** not for non–dog fans; confusing to find; dated decor. ⑤ *Rooms from: €90* ⊠ *Via Seliano, about 1 km (½ mile) down dirt track west off main road from Capaccio Scalo to Paestum, Paestum* ☎ *0828/723634* ⊕ *www.agriturismoseliano.it* ⊘ *Closed Nov.–Mar.* 🛏 *14 rooms* ⑩ *Free Breakfast.*

Chapter 16

PUGLIA, BASILICATA, AND CALABRIA

16

Updated by
Nick Bruno

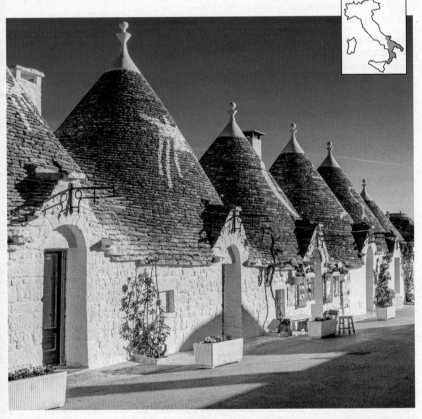

◉ **Sights**　　🍴 **Restaurants**　　🛏 **Hotels**　　🛍 **Shopping**　　🍸 **Nightlife**
★★★☆☆　　★★★★★　　★★★☆☆　　★★☆☆☆　　★☆☆☆☆

WELCOME TO
PUGLIA, BASILICATA, AND CALABRIA

TOP REASONS TO GO

★ **A wander through Sassi:** The Basilicata town of Matera is endowed with one of the most unusual landscapes in Europe—a complex network of ancient cave dwellings partially hewn from rock, some of which now house chic bars and restaurants.

★ **A trip to peasant-food heaven:** Dine on Puglia's famous puree of fava beans with chicory and olive oil in a humble country restaurant.

★ **Lecce and its Baroque splendors:** The beautiful, friendly city of Lecce might be known for its peculiar brand of fanciful Baroque architecture, but it's not yet famous enough to have lost its Pugliese charm.

★ **The trulli of the Valle d'Itria:** Strange conical houses—many of them still in use—dot the rolling countryside of Puglia, centering around Alberobello, a town still composed almost entirely of these *trulli*. They must be seen to be believed.

1 Bari. An atmospheric *centro storico* is a highlight of this busy Adriatic port.

2 Trani. Don't miss this harbor town's stunning cathedral.

3 Polignano a Mare. Steep cliffs draw thrill-seekers and those looking to relax overlooking gorgeous inlets.

4 Castel del Monte. This town's octagonal, epony-mous fortress is mysterious.

5 Mattinata. The Gulf of Manfredonia beaches here will dazzle you.

6 Vieste. The spectacular Gargano Promontory is the site of this resort town.

7 Alberobello. It's hard not to be enchanted by Alberobello's fairy-tale stone trulli.

8 Ostuni. The so-called Città Bianca (White City) is perched above azure waters.

9 Ceglie Messapica. The heart of this town is beguilingly medieval.

10 Martina Franca. Lose yourself in a maze of alleys and piazzas.

11 Taranto. An engaging archaeological museum is the main draw of this port town with a naval base.

12 Lecce. Here, it's all about Baroque beauty and lively locals.

13 Otranto. Look out over the sea from Otranto's medieval fortress.

14 Gallipoli. This fishing town is famed for its island *borgo antico*.

15 Matera. The so-called City of Sassi is filled with the intriguing cave dwellings.

16 Maratea. The mountains here seem to fall into the sea.

17 Diamante. This Calabrese resort is lively.

18 Castrovillari. For hiking, this gateway to mountainous Pollino National Park is a great hub.

19 Cosenza. Come to explore attractive medieval sights.

20 Camigliatello. The mountainous Sila National Park surrounds this town.

21 Crotone. The Treasure of Hera is among Crotone's draws.

22 Tropea. Gorgeous beaches will beckon you to Tropea.

23 Reggio Calabria. This busy port city plays footsie with Sicily.

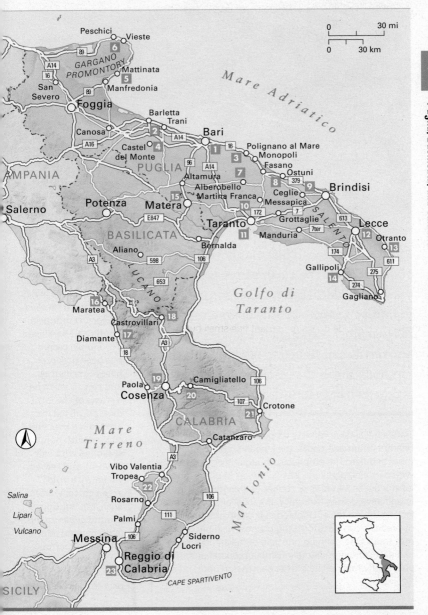

EATING AND DRINKING WELL IN PUGLIA, BASILICATA, AND CALABRIA

The Mediterranean diet was born in the South of Italy. The cuisine here is based on seasonal local produce, so don't expect to find, say, grapes in May or watermelon in November, although the mild climate and fertile soil, linked to modern farming methods, mean that most vegetable products have a long growing season.

Traditional cuisine reflects its peasant origins, with hearty homemade pasta, thick bean soups, and grilled meat and fish. The emphasis, though, is on vegetables, with zucchini, eggplant, beans, sweet peppers, and at least a dozen varieties of tomatoes transformed into imaginative dishes. Naturally, the local olive oil is never lacking on the table. Dribbled over soup or a thick chunk of bread, it can transform the plainest dish into a gourmet treat. One defining principle of Italian cooking is to use excellent ingredients in simple preparations. That philosophy reaches its purest expression here.

FABULOUS FAVA

Puré di fave e cicorielle, a puree of fava beans topped with sautéed chicory, is unique to Puglia and Basilicata. The simple recipe has been prepared here for centuries and continues to be a staple of the local diet. The dried favas are soaked overnight, cooked with potatoes, seasoned with salt and olive oil, and served warm with wild green chicory, often with a sprinkling of ground *peperoncino* (chili pepper). Mix it together before eating, and wash it down with a glass of *primitivo* or *aglianico*.

MEAT

In addition to its excellent beef, Basilicata is known for its *salsicce lucane* (sausages), seasoned with salt, cayenne pepper, and fennel seeds. Enormous grills are a feature of many of the region's restaurants, infusing the dining area with the aroma of freshly cooked meat. Adventurous eaters in Puglia should look for *turcinieddhri* (a blend of lamb's innards) and *pezzetti di cavallo* (braised horse meat).

PASTA

Puglia is the home of orecchiette with *cime di rapa* (broccoli rabe) and olive oil, a melodious dish that's wondrous in its simplicity. Try also cavatelli and *strascinati* (rectangles of pasta with one rough side and one smooth side).

PEPPERS

Calabria is known for its use of little hot peppers that can range from a mild sprinkling in tomato sauce to the tongue-scorching *'nduja* (spicy pork salami) paste. Local cured meats like *soppressata* (dried spicy salami) and *salsiccia piccante* (hot sausage), often sold by street vendors on a roll with peppers, onions, french fries, and mayonnaise, are all spiced with peperoncini.

SEAFOOD

Fish can be grilled (*alla griglia*), baked (*al forno*), roasted (*arrosto*), or steamed (*in umido*). Among the highlights are delicate *orata* (sea bream), branzino (sea bass), *gamberi rossi* (sweet red shrimp), and calamari. Puglia is the home of *cozze pelose* (hairy-shelled mussels), and Calabria's version of sushi is freshly caught *ricci di mare* (sea urchins), considered a delicacy—and an aphrodisiac!

WINES

Puglia produces around 17% of Italy's wine, more than the output of Australia. In the past, most of it was *vino sfuso* (jug wine), but over the past 15 years, producers have been concentrating on quality—with impressive results. The ancient *primitivo* grape (an ancestor of California's zinfandel) yields strong, heady wines like Primitivo di Manduria. The *negroamaro* grape is transformed into palatable *rosati* (rosés), as well as the robust Salice Salentino. Pair a dessert with the sweet red Aleatico di Puglia or Moscato di Trani.

In Basilicata, producers use the *aglianico* grape to outstanding effect in the prestigious Aglianico del Vulture. In Calabria, they've worked wonders with *gaglioppo*.

Venture off the traffic-filled highways and explore the countryside of Italy's boot, made up of three separate regions—Puglia, Basilicata, and Calabria—each one with its own character. This is Italy's deep south, where whitewashed buildings stand silently over three turquoise seas, castles guard medieval alleyways, and grandmothers dry their handmade orecchiette, the most Puglian of pastas, in the midafternoon heat.

At every turn, these three regions boast dramatic scenery. Geographical divides have preserved an astonishing cultural and linguistic diversity that's unequaled elsewhere on the Italian mainland. Southern Italians are extremely proud of their hometowns and will gladly direct you to some forgotten local chapel in an olive grove, an unmarked monument, or an obscure work of art. The Greek city-states of Magna Graecia (Greater Greece) once ruled here, and ancient names, such as Lucania, are still commonly used. It's here also that you'll find long-isolated hill communities where Albanian and Greek are still spoken by the descendants of 16th-century refugees from the Balkans.

One of southern Italy's most popular vacation destinations is the Gargano Promontory, where safe sandy shores and secluded coves are nestled between whitewashed coastal towns and craggy limestone cliffs. You'll also find many beautiful stretches of sandy beaches along the coast of the Salento Peninsula and the Mediterranean shoreline of Calabria and Basilicata. There are cultural gems everywhere, including Valle d'Itria's fairy-tale trulli, Matera's Sassi (a network of ancient dwellings carved out of rock), and the Baroque churches in the town of Lecce, the jewel of the south. Beyond the cities, seaside resorts, and the few major sights, there's a sparsely populated, sunbaked countryside where road signs are rare and expanses of silvery olive trees, vineyards of primitivo and aglianico, and giant prickly pear cacti fight their way through the rocky soil in defiance of the relentless summer heat.

MAJOR REGIONS

Bari and the Adriatic Coast. The busy port of Bari offers architectural nuggets in its labyrinthine old quarter. In nearby Trani a distinctive Apulian-Romanesque church stands by the sea, while Polignano a Mare has clifftop medieval charm above sparkling waters. For a unique excursion, head to Castel del Monte, home to an enigmatic 13th-century octagonal castle.

The Gargano Promontory. Amid the Foresta Umbra's landscape of craggy limestone, pine trees, and scrubby Mediterranean *macchia* (underbrush) are the beguiling coastal resorts of Vieste and Mattinata.

The Trulli District. The inland area southeast of Bari has a mostly flat, rock-strewn terrain that's been given over to olive cultivation. The area is also interspersed with idiosyncratic limestone habitations called *trulli*. The center of the Trulli District is Alberobello in the enchanting Valle d'Itria. Amid this fairy-tale-like landscape are the dazzling whitewashed hilltop market towns of Martina Franca, Ceglie Messapica, and Ostuni.

The Salento Peninsula. South of the Trulli District the monotony of endless olive trees is redeemed by an alluring coastline of dramatic sandstone cliffs and intimate fishing towns such as Otranto and Gallipoli. Taranto has a captivating archaeological museum amid its rusty, industrial surroundings, while Lecce is an oasis of grace and sophistication, with swirling Baroque architecture and a lively cultural scene.

Basilicata. Occupying the instep and part of the heel of Italy's boot, this and the neighboring Calabria region formed part of Magna Graecia, southern Italy's Greek colonies. Today, Basilicata attracts travelers in search of bucolic settings, great food, and archaeological treasures. The village of Aliano was made famous by writer Carlo Levi (1902–75). Matera, a recently rejuvenated city with Baroque splendor, is built on the side of a ravine honeycombed with Sassi that have been transformed into swanky homes, restaurants, and hotels. On a spectacularly mountainous section of the Tyrrhenian coast is the gorgeous resort Maratea.

Calabria. Italy's southernmost mainland region has fantastic beaches in lively resort communities such as Tropea and Diamante. Castrovillari, Cosenza, and Camigliatello are great rustic bases for exploring the Sila Mountains and Pollino National Park. Crotone was a major ancient cultural center, and, toward Sicily, the busy port of Reggio Calabria is home to two arresting ancient Greek statues, the *Bronzi di Riace*.

Planning

Making the Most of Your Time

If your priority is relaxing on the beach, plan on a few days at a seaside resort in one of the Gargano Promontory's fishing villages, such as Peschici, Rodi Garganico, and Vieste, and perhaps a further stay at one of the Calabrian coastal resorts, such as Diamante or Tropea, or Maratea in Basilicata.

Otherwise, choose a base like Polignano a Mare or Trani, especially if you land or dock in Bari. Take day trips out to the Valle d'Itria, or to the remarkable octagonal Castel del Monte. Then head east along the Adriatic route (SS16), stopping to see the idyllic hilltop Ostuni before continuing on to Lecce, where you'll want to spend at least two to three nights exploring the city's Baroque wonders and taking a day trip down to Otranto and Gallipoli.

Next, take regional roads and the Via Appia (SS7) to reach Matera, whose Sassi cave dwellings are a southern Italian highlight; allow at least two nights here. Then it's back out to the SS106 to Calabria, along the coast dotted with ancient Greek settlements, as far as Tropea. At this point, cut inland on the

SS107 across the Sila Massif, stopping at the hill resort of Camigliatello or carrying on to the more vibrant lowland Cosenza. Reggio Calabria is worthwhile just to see the celebrated Riace bronzes.

Getting Around

BUS

There is direct, if not always frequent, service between most destinations within Calabria, Puglia, and Basilicata. In many cases, bus service is the backup when problems with train service arise. Matera is linked with Bari by frequent Ferrovie Appulo Lucane trains and buses and with Taranto by SITA bus. In Calabria the Romano bus company runs a regular service between various towns. Ferrovie della Calabria operates many of the local routes.

BUS CONTACTS Bus Romano.
☎ *0962/21709* ⊕ *www.autolineer-omano.com.* **Ferrovie della Calabria.**
☎ *0961/896306, 328/2391123*
⊕ *www.ferroviedellacalabria.it.* **SITA.**
☎ *0835/385007 Matera Office,*
080/5790111 Puglia Regional Office, Bari,
0971/506811 Basilicata Regional Office,
Potenza ⊕ *www.sitasudtrasporti.it.*

CAR

Although roads are generally good in the south, and major cities are linked by fast autostradas, driving here is a major test of navigation skills. Driving into the center of many cities and towns can be particularly complicated, owing to mazes of one-way streets, pedestrianized zones, and limited parking facilities. The good news is that you can bypass many communities via ring roads. Also, if you're staying at an in-town hotel, check with the staff about parking: the more upscale properties often have garage facilities or valet services for guests.

If you're squeamish about getting lost, don't drive at night in the countryside—roads can be confusing without the visual aid of landmarks, and GPS is far from infallible. Also, Bari, Brindisi, and Reggio Calabria are notorious for car thefts and break-ins. In these cities, don't leave valuables in the car, and find a guarded parking space if possible.

The toll-free A3 autostrada (Napoli–Reggio Calabria) links Naples to the south, with major exits at Sicignano (for the interior of Basilicata and Matera), Cosenza (the Sila Massif and Crotone), and Pizzo (for Tropea). Parts of the A3 in northern Calabria cross uplands more than 3,000 feet high, and snow chains may be required during winter months. In the summer and during holiday weekends this is the main north–south route for Italy's sun seekers, so factor in plenty of time for delays and avoid peak travel times.

Take the SS18 for coastal destinations on the Tyrrhenian side and the E90 for the Ionian, alongside various state roads that crisscross toward the Adriatic. Given speed detectors and driver-tracking technology, it's best to stick to speed limits and be careful not to enter ZTL (*zona a traffico limitato*) restricted traffic areas (cameras are set up in towns such as Matera and Altamura): you'll be spared an unwelcome ticket when you get home.

TRAIN

Trenitalia runs to Calabria, either following the Ionian Coast as far as Reggio Calabria or swerving inland to Cosenza and the Tyrrhenian Coast.

TRAIN CONTACTS Ferrovie Appulo Lucane.
☎ *080/5725421, 800/050500 numero verde (toll-free)* ⊕ *www.ferrovieappulo-lucane.it.* **Ferrovie Sud-Est.** ☎ *800/079090 numero verde (toll-free)* ⊕ *www.fseon-line.it.* **Trenitalia.** ☎ *892021 (within Italy), 06/68475475 (from outside Italy)* ⊕ *www.trenitalia.com.*

Restaurants

Italy's southern region is home to numerous restaurants that feature home cooking or Slow Food–inspired menus, which boils down to everything is made with the freshest ingredients. Meals are meant to be enjoyed at leisure, however, and service is not swift. Whether you decide to dine in a well-known restaurant or at a humble country trattoria, plan to give some thought to your menu choices (it's expected) and ask questions (also expected).

Restaurant reviews have been shortened. For full information, visit Fodors.com.

Hotels

Hotels in the region range from grand upscale establishments to small and stylish bijou inns to family-run rural *agriturismi* (country hostelries, often part of farms) that compensate for a lack of amenities with their famous southern hospitality. *Fattorie* and *masserie* (small farms and grander farm estates) offering accommodations are listed at local tourist offices.

In beach areas such as the Gargano Promontory and Salento, campgrounds and bungalow lodgings are ubiquitous and popular with families and budget travelers. Note that many seaside hotels open up just for the summer season, when they often require several-day stays with full or half board. And do remember that in a region like this—blazingly hot in summer and chilly in winter—air-conditioning and central heating can be important.

Hotel reviews have been shortened. For full information, visit Fodors.com.

WHAT IT COSTS in Euros

	$	$$	$$$	$$$$
RESTAURANTS				
	under €15	€15–€24	€25–€35	over €35
HOTELS				
	under €125	€125–€200	€201–€300	over €300

Bari

260 km (162 miles) southeast of Naples, 450 km (281 miles) southeast of Rome.

The biggest city in the region, Bari is a major port and a transit point for travelers catching ferries across the Adriatic to Greece, Croatia, and Albania. It's also a cosmopolitan city with one of the most interesting historic centers in the region. In recent years, it has become a major center of pilgrimage for Russian Orthodox visitors, due to its connection with St. Nicholas, the patron saint of Russia, as well as of Bari. The old quarter of the city, around the basilica and the harbor castle, is a lively maze of whitewashed alleyways buzzing with bars, cafés, restaurants, and crafts shops. Most of the modern town is set out in a logical 19th-century grid, following the designs of Joachim Murat (1767–1815), Napoléon's brother-in-law and King of the Two Sicilies. The heart is **Piazza della Libertà,** where old and young gather in the evenings to stroll up and down and see and be seen.

GETTING HERE AND AROUND

By car, take the Bari-Nord exit from the A14 autostrada. Bari's train station is a hub for Puglia-bound trains. Alitalia and Ryanair fly to Bari Airport from Rome and Milan. Bari and Milan are also connected by easyJet.

VISITOR INFORMATION

CONTACT Bari Tourism Office. ⊠ *Piazza Moro 33/a, Bari* ☎ *080/5242361* ⊕ *www.viaggiareinpuglia.it.*

 Sights

★ Bari Vecchia and Via Sparano

HISTORIC DISTRICT | FAMILY | By day, you can lose yourself in the maze of white alleyways in Bari Vecchia, the old town stretching along the harbor, now humming with restaurants, cafés, and crafts shops. Residents tend to leave their doors wide open, so you catch a glimpse into the daily routine of southern Italy: matrons hand-rolling orecchiette, their grandchildren home from school for the midday meal, and workers busy patching up centuries-old arches and doorways. Back in the new town, join the evening passeggiata on pedestrian-only Via Sparano, then, when night falls, saunter out among the outdoor bars and restaurants in Piazza Mercantile, past Piazza Ferrarese at the end of Corso Vittorio Emanuele. ⊠ *Via Sparano, Bari.*

★ Basilica di San Nicola

CHURCH | The 11th-century Basilica di San Nicola, overlooking the sea in the *città vecchia* (old city), houses the bones of St. Nicholas, the inspiration for Santa Claus. His relics were stolen from Myra, in present-day Turkey, by a band of sailors from Bari and are now buried in the crypt. Because St. Nicholas is also the patron saint of Russia, the church draws both Roman Catholic and Russian Orthodox pilgrims; souvenir shops in the area display miniatures of the Western saint and his Eastern counterpart side by side. ⊠ *Largo Abate Elia 13, Piazza San Nicola, Bari* ☎ *080/5737111* ⊕ *www.basilicasannicola.it.*

Castello Svevo

CASTLE/PALACE | Looming over the cathedral is the symbol of Bari: huge Castello Svevo, which houses a number of archaeological and art collections within its evocative courtyards, towers, and rooms. The current building dates from the time of Holy Roman Emperor Frederick II (1194–1250), who rebuilt an existing Norman-Byzantine castle to his own exacting specifications. Designed more for power than beauty, it looks out beyond the cathedral to the small Porto Vecchio (Old Port). Inside are displays that include plaster-cast reproductions of the city's sculptural riches, Byzantine archaeological finds, photo collections from Bari's past, and historic ceramics and other precious objects. ⊠ *Piazza Federico II di Svevia, Bari* ☎ *080/8869304* ⊕ *www.musei.puglia.beniculturali.it* ⊠ *€6; €9 during exhibitions* ☉ *Closed Tues.*

Cattedrale di San Sabino

CHURCH | Bari's 12th-century cathedral is the seat of the local bishop and was the scene of many significant political marriages between important families in the Middle Ages. The cathedral is dedicated to San Sabino, a 6th-century bishop who apparently lived to be 105. The architecture reflects the Romanesque style favored by the Normans of that period. Visit the crypt with its ornate columns, polychrome marble altar, and silver-and-gold icon of Maria Santissima di Costantinopoli, also known as the Vergine Odegitria, patron of Bari along with San Nicola. ⊠ *Piazza dell'Odegitria, Bari* ☎ *080/5210605* ⊕ *www.arcidiocesibaribitonto.it.*

 Restaurants

Ristorante al Pescatore

$$$ | SEAFOOD | In the lively heart of the old town, opposite the castle, stands one of Bari's best seafood restaurants. Try the house specialty, *crudo di mare* (a platter of mixed local seafood), accompanied by a crisp salad and a carafe of uplifting Pugliese wine. **Known for:** *ricci di mare*—a taste of the Puglian sea; seafood antipasto (crudo misto); lively atmosphere with tables packed together. ⑤ *Average main: €27* ⊠ *Piazza Federico II di Svevia 6/8, Bari* ☎ *080/5237039* ⊕ *www.alpescatore-bari.com.*

Puglia

ISOLE TREMITI
I Cameroni
ISOLE S. DOMINO

TO TERMOLI

Rodi Garganico
Peschici
88
528
Foresta Umbra
Vieste
Mattinata
Monte Sant'Angelo
Manfredonia
L'Annunziata
Golfo di Manfredonia
Zapponeta
San Giovanni Rotondo
San Severo
Lucera
Foggia
Cerignola
Melfi
S. Angelo dei Lombardi
Barletta
Andria
Trani
Molfetta
Bari
Corato
Castel del Monte
Spinazzola
Gravina in Puglia
Santeramo in Colle
Gioia del Colle
Altamura
Matera
Potenza
Eboli
Battipaglia
Auletta
Salerno
Golfo di Salerno

CAMPANIA
BASILICATA
PUGLIA
GARGANO PROMONTORY
TRULLI DISTRICT
LUCANO

Polignano a Mare
Grotte di Castellana
Fasano
Ostuni
Alberobello
Locorotondo
Valle d'Itria
Martina Franca
Ceglie Messapica
Francavilla Fontana
Grottaglie
Masgafra
Taranto
Mare Grande
Mare Piccolo
Castellaneta Marina
Lido di Metaponto
Scanzano

Brindisi
Mesagne
Campi
Manduria
SALENTO
Lecce
Otranto
Santa Cesarea Terme
Castro
Leuca
Maglie
Nardo
Gallipoli

Golfo di Taranto

Adriatic Sea

KEY
Ferry lines

30 miles
50 km

611
16
101
275
274
123
7
174
7
100
16
16
16
16
27
141
90
160
17
655
168
97
170
96
271
A14
E55
106
106
653
598
92
407
96
7
7
91
407
164
A16
A3
18
166
91
90
A14
89
272
89
A16

Coffee and Quick Bites

★ Caffè Vergnano 1882 Amendola

$ | **SOUTHERN ITALIAN** | Grand stone rooms and a pretty terrazza sprouting olive trees make this a flexible and fab venue to breakfast, brunch, and lunch—and to socialize with evening drinks. As well as a constant stream of excellent caffè, they do a selection of pastries, great-value daily specials, and various snacks. **Known for:** evening buffet and DJ sets; historic stone building and courtyard seating; daily pasta, grilled meat, and veggie dishes. ⑤ *Average main: €8* ⊠ *Via Amendola 128/B, Bari* ☎ *080/5586586.*

🛏 Hotels

Palace Hotel

$$ | **HOTEL** | Common areas in this downtown landmark (est. 1956) have bright color schemes and baroque touches, and the spacious guest rooms have balconies and marble-lined bathrooms. The Murat rooftop restaurant has great views, especially from the outdoor terrace in summer, and serves regional cuisine. **Pros:** convenient location near both the medieval old town and the shops of the new city; comfortable, modern rooms; garage facilities. **Cons:** mainly geared to conferences and business clients; large, busy hotel (can feel impersonal); some bathrooms and rooms desperately need updating. ⑤ *Rooms from: €156* ⊠ *Via Lombardi 13, Bari* ☎ *080/5216551* ⊕ *www.palacehotelbari.com* ↗ *195 rooms* ⑪ *Free Breakfast.*

Trani

43 km (27 miles) northwest of Bari.

Trani has a harbor filled with fishing boats and a quaint old town with cobblestone streets, gleaming medieval churches, and palazzi built from local limestone. The town is also justly famous for its sweet dessert wine, Moscato di Trani. It's smaller than the other ports along this coast.

GETTING HERE AND AROUND

By car, take the Trani exit from the A14 autostrada. Frequent trains run from Bari

VISITOR INFORMATION

CONTACT Trani Tourism Office. ⊠ *Palazzo Palmieri, Piazza Trieste 10, Trani* ☎ *0883/588830.*

Sights

Castello

CASTLE/PALACE | One of Frederick II's most imposing fortresses, the quadrangular Trani Castle guarded the Adriatic sea route throughout the Middle Ages. It was the scene of several royal weddings of the Swabian and Anjou houses, as well as the place of imprisonment for life of Siffridina, Countess of Caserta, who had supported the losing Swabian dynasty against Charles I of Anjou. In the early 20th century it became a state prison and remained so until 1974. The ground floor contains a museum telling the story of the castle alongside archaeological finds, sculpture, and a wealth of ceramics. ⊠ *Piazza Re Manfredi 14, Trani* ☎ *0883/506603* ⊕ *www.castelloditrani. beniculturali.it* ⑤ *€5.*

★ Cattedrale

CHURCH | The stunning pinkish-white 11th-century cathedral, considered one of the finest in Puglia, is built on a spit of land jutting into the sea. Dedicated to St. Nicholas the Pilgrim, it was a favorite place of prayer for crusaders embarking for war in the Holy Land. Its lofty bell tower can be visited by request at the nearby Museo Diocesiano; the views are worth the climb. Group and other guided tours must be booked via the website. ⊠ *Piazza Duomo, Trani* ☎ *0883/500293* ⊕ *www.cattedraletrani.it* ⑤ *Free, bell tower €5.*

Museo Sinagoga Sant'Anna (*Synagogue Street and Sant'Anna Museum*)

SYNAGOGUE | In the 12th century one of the largest Jewish communities in southern Italy flourished here, and on Via Sinagoga two of the four synagogues still stand. The 13th-century Scolanova has been reconverted to a synagogue after a long period as a Christian church, while the former Sant'Anna now houses a museum of Trani's Jewish history.

TIP→ Contact the Trani Tourism Office to set up tours and visits. ⊠ *Via La Guidea 24, corner of Via San Martino, Trani* ☎ *0883/582470* ⊕ *www.fondazioneseca. it* ✉ *Donations accepted.*

Polo Museale Trani

OTHER MUSEUM | Four floors of the handsome 18th-century Palazzo Lodispoto, near the Duomo, contain two very different collections: the Museo Diocesano showcases Trani's wealth of religious artifacts, while the Museo della Macchina per Scrivere follows the evolution of the typewriter. Among the highlights in the former are fragments from the 6th-century basilica, medieval and Baroque architectural elements, and funereal treasures commissioned by Charles I of Anjou on the death of his son Philip. The latter collection has 400 examples of typewriters from around the world, including some iconic Olivetti models as well as those used to type Braille, Arabic, and Japanese. A reasonably priced café serves drinks and pastries. ⊠ *Palazzo Lodispoto, Piazza Duomo 8/9, Trani* ☎ *0883/582470* ⊕ *www.fondazioneseca. it* ✉ *Free* ⊗ *Closed Mon.*

 Hotels

Ibis Styles Trani

$ | HOTEL | Although this hotel caters mainly to business travelers, its location near the main sights in Trani's historic center makes it a decent option for tourists. **Pros:** parking in hotel garage; close to the train station and the old town; wheelchair accessible. **Cons:** often busy with conference delegates; functional but somewhat basic; breakfast disappointing. ⑤ *Rooms from: €61* ⊠ *Corso Imbriani 137, Trani* ☎ *0883/588010* ⊕ *www.accorhotels. com* ✒ *46 rooms* ⍾ *Free Breakfast.*

★ **Palazzo Filisio**

$$ | HOTEL | Superbly positioned in front of the Duomo on a quiet seaside piazza, this small, handsome, beautifully maintained hotel has guest rooms with contemporary wooden furniture, white and azure fabrics, and marbled bathrooms. **Pros:** most rooms have sea views; right next to the cathedral; superb breakfast and restaurant. **Cons:** often occupied by wedding parties; no parking outside hotel; books up in high season. ⑤ *Rooms from: €140* ⊠ *Piazza Mons. Addazzi 2, Trani* ☎ *0883/500931* ⊕ *www.palazzofilisio.it* ⍾ *Free Breakfast* ⊗ *Restaurant closed Mon.* ✒ *10 rooms.*

Polignano a Mare

35 km (22 miles) southeast of Bari, 14 km (9 miles) north of Castellana.

This well-preserved, whitewashed old town, perched on limestone cliffs overlooking the Adriatic, makes an atmospheric base for exploring the surrounding area. Film crews and adrenaline junkies come to experience the town's spectacular cliff-diving championships, which usually take place in early June. Other things have cemented Polignano's reputation for drama: it leapt to fame in 2013, when the cast of the popular soap *The Bold and the Beautiful* shot scenes on the Scalinata di Grottone. It's also the hometown of Domenico Modugno—author of the song "Nel blu, dipinto di blu" (aka "Volare")—who has a statue here in his honor.

GETTING HERE AND AROUND
From Bari, take the Polignano exit from the SS16. Frequent trains run from Bari.

VISITOR INFORMATION

CONTACT Polignano Tourism Office. ✉ *Via Martiri Di Dogali 2, Polignano a Mare* ☎ *080/4252336* ⊕ *www.polignanoamare. com.*

 Hotels

Borgobianco Resort & Spa

$$ | RESORT | FAMILY | Housed in a handsome masseria farmhouse building, this countryside resort provides a tranquil base for relaxing by the pool, eating al fresco in courtyards and terrace, and spa pampering. **Pros:** gorgeous pool, spa and outdoor spaces; cool whitewashed luxury in tranquil location; shuttle bus to town. **Cons:** service can be patchy; town not in easy walking distance; decor could be a tad soulless for some. ⑤ *Rooms from: €175* ✉ *Contrada Casello Cavuzzi, Polignano a Mare* ☎ *080/2049060* ⊕ *borgobianco.it* ❙⊘❙ *Free Breakfast* ⇥ *48 rooms.*

Hotel Covo dei Saraceni

$$ | HOTEL | It would be difficult to find a more romantic location than that occupied by this hotel, dramatically perched on the rocks above the narrow cove of Polignano. **Pros:** spa center in the hotel; magnificent sea views; decent buffet breakfast. **Cons:** some rooms have views of parking lot; popular for wedding receptions (can be busy); many rooms on the small side. ⑤ *Rooms from: €167* ✉ *Via Conversano 1, Polignano a Mare* ☎ *080/4241177* ⊕ *www.covodeisaraceni. com* ❙⊘❙ *Free Breakfast* ⇥ *32 rooms.*

Castel del Monte

56 km (35 miles) southwest of Bari.

The isolated Norman Castel del Monte dominates the surrounding countryside from the top of a 1,778-foot-high hill. The nearest town is Andria, 17 km (10½ miles) away, largely modern and congested—avoid traffic by taking the ring road around it.

GETTING HERE AND AROUND

Take the Andria-Barletta exit from the A14 autostrada, then follow the SS170di to Castel del Monte. From April through October there's minibus service from Piazza Bersaglieri d'Italia in Andria.

VISITOR INFORMATION

CONTACT Castel del Monte Tourism Office. ✉ *Via Vespucci 114, Andria* ☎ *0883/592283* ⊕ *www.proloco.andria. ba.it.*

 Sights

★ Castel del Monte

CASTLE/PALACE | Crowning an isolated hill 1,778 feet above sea level in the heart of the Alta Murgia National Park, this enigmatic octagonal fortress, built by Frederick II in the first half of the 13th century, has puzzled historians and researchers for centuries. Rooms are arranged in a seemingly illogical sequence through eight towers around a central courtyard. Recent interpretations suggest it was an elaborate cultural center conceived by Frederick to study various scientific disciplines of the Western and the Arabic worlds. Umberto Eco used it as his inspiration for riddles in *The Name of the Rose.* It's worth hiring the services of one of the authorized tour guides here to get a deeper insight into the mysteries of this unique monument. Note that if coming by car between April and September, you have to park in designated areas about a mile away and then take a shuttle bus. ✉ *On sign-posted minor road, 17 km (10½ miles) south of Andria, Andria* ☎ *0883/569997* ⊕ *www.casteldelmonte. beniculturali.it* ▣ *€7, €10 when there's an exhibition.*

Mattinata

138 km (86 miles) northwest of Bari.

The town of Mattinata is a good center for hikes in the Foresta Umbra and for

The imposing Castel del Monte is a 13th-century structure built by Emperor Frederick II on land he inherited from his mother, Constance of Sicily.

visiting the Santuario di San Michele. It also has attractive stretches of sandy beach.

GETTING HERE AND AROUND

From Foggia (the chief city in Puglia's northernmost province), take the winding SS89. Regular buses leave from Foggia's train station.

VISITOR INFORMATION

CONTACT Mattinata Tourism Office. ✉ Piazza Roma, Mattinata ☎ 0884/552430 Municipal Office ⊕ www.comune. mattinata.fg.it.

 Sights

Foresta Umbra

NATURE PRESERVE | In the middle of the Gargano Promontory is the majestic Foresta Umbra (Shady Forest), a dense growth of beech, maple, pine, and oak generally found in more northerly climates, thriving here because of the altitude, which reaches 3,200 feet above sea level. Between the trees in this national park are occasional dramatic

vistas opening out over the Golfo di Manfredonia. There are nature trails and picnic areas easily reached from Vieste, Peschici, and Mattinata. ✉ Visitor center, Laghetto Umbra, SP52bis, Monte Sant'Angelo ☎ 0884/708578 national park ⊗ Visitor center closed Oct.–Easter.

Santuario di San Michele

RELIGIOUS BUILDING | Pilgrims have flocked to the mountain community of Monte Sant'Angelo for nearly 1,500 years—among them St. Francis of Assisi and crusaders setting off for the Holy Land from the then-flourishing port of Manfredonia. Monte Sant'Angelo is centered on the Santuario di San Michele, built over the grotto where the archangel Michael is believed to have appeared before shepherds in the year 490. Walk down a long series of steps to get to the grotto itself; on its walls you can see the hand tracings left by pilgrims. The Sanctuary was declared a UNESCO World Heritage site in 2011. To learn more about the history and myth surrounding the site visit the adjoining Musei TECUM. ✉ Via

Reale Basilica 127, Monte Sant'Angelo ☎ *0884/561150* ⊕ *www.santuariosan-michele.it* ⊠ *Musei TECUM €5.*

Restaurants

Trattoria dalla Nonna

$$$ | SEAFOOD | FAMILY | Waves lap at the shore just inches from your table at this elegant but unpretentious trattoria, which often has a cozy fireplace ablaze in winter. You must follow a narrow twisting lane to get here, but it's worth the effort for specialties like the raw seafood antipasto, which features shellfish you might not find anywhere else. *Cozze pelose* (local mussels), hiding inside their spiked-hair shells, are briny and buttery, and big local oysters are all about rich texture. **Known for:** also run a B&B; unique cozze pelose mussels; fabulous sea views. $ *Average main: €26* ⊠ *Contrada Funni al Lido, Località Funni, off the main road (watch for signs), Mattinata* ☎ *0884/559205* ⊕ *www.dallanonna.it* ⊘ *No lunch Tues.*

Hotels

Baia delle Zagare

$$ | HOTEL | Overlooking one of the Gargano Peninsula's loveliest bays, this secluded cluster of whitewashed buildings houses simply furnished modern rooms, some of which have balconies. **Pros:** access to wonderful beach; incredible views and location; fab pool and gardens. **Cons:** rooms may be a tad sparse for some; impossible to get to without a car; lots of steps. $ *Rooms from: €155* ⊠ *Litoranea Mattinata–Vieste, 17 km (10 miles) northeast of Mattinata, Mattinata* ☎ *0884/550155* ⊕ *www.hotelbaia-dellezagare.it* ⊘ *Closed Oct.–mid May* ⤶ *143 rooms* ⏐Ol *Free Breakfast.*

Vieste

93 km (58 miles) northeast of Foggia, 179 km (111 miles) northwest of Bari.

This large whitewashed town jutting off the tip of the spur of Italy's boot is an attractive place to wander around. Although curvy mountain roads render it slightly less accessible from autostradas and main rail stations than, say, Mattinata, it is, nevertheless, a good base for exploring Gargano. The resort attracts legions of tourists in summer, some bound for the Isole Tremiti, a tiny archipelago connected to Vieste by regular ferries.

GETTING HERE AND AROUND

If you're driving from Foggia, take the winding SS89. Regular buses leave from Foggia's train station.

VISITOR INFORMATION

CONTACT Vieste Tourism Office. ⊠ *Piazza John Fitzgerald Kennedy, Vieste* ☎ *0884/708806* ⊕ *www.viaggiarein-puglia.it.*

Sights

Castello Svevo

CASTLE/PALACE | Originally built by Frederick II, this impressive structure was enlarged by the Spanish to defend against attacks from the Turks, and it has remained a military base ever since. It is only open to the public for guided visits and temporary exhibitions and events; call ahead for the latest information. ⊠ *Via Duomo, Vieste* ☎ *0884/708806* ⊕ *www.viaggiareinpuglia.it.*

Restaurants

★ Al Dragone

$$ | SOUTHERN ITALIAN | Dine on exquisite Gargano fare at this atmospheric eatery set

a natural grotto just next to the cathedral in the heart of the old center. The menu is dominated by locally caught fish, and though dishes draw on traditional recipes, you can expect the occasional innovation. ⓘ *Average main: €22* ✉ *Via Duomo 8, Vieste* ☎ *0884/701212* ⊕ *www.aldragone.it* ⊘ *Closed mid-Oct.–Mar. 1.*

🛏 Hotels

★ Navircri

| **B&B/INN** | **FAMILY** | Run by the friendly famiglia De Mauro, this modern B&B ticks all the boxes for those seeking great value in a tranquil, scenic setting near the beach. **Pros:** immaculate rooms; fab rooftop pool and Jacuzzi; great breakfast spread, including homemade jams. **Cons:** one triple doesn't have a balcony; having to walk to town and beach might not appeal to some; minimum night stays in high season. ⓢ *Rooms from: €75* ✉ *Via Saragat, Vieste* ☎ *0884/705022* ⊕ *www.bnbnavicri.it* ↪ *6* ⊗ *Free Breakfast.*

Alberobello

59 km (37 miles) southeast of Bari, 45 km (28 miles) north of Taranto.

With more than 1,000 trulli along its steep, narrow streets, Alberobello has been designated a UNESCO World Heritage site. It is one of the more popular and well-established destinations in Puglia, and has some excellent restaurants (and some less-than-excellent trinket shops).

GETTING HERE AND AROUND

By car, take the Monopoli exit from the SS16, follow the SP237 to Putignano, then SS172 to Alberobello. Trains run half-hourly from Bari to Putignano, where you then take a bus. The journey takes around two hours.

16

CONTACT Alberobello Tourism Office.
✉ *Via Monte Nero 1, Alberobello* ☎ *080/4322822* ⊕ *www.prolocoalberobello.it.*

👁 Sights

Alberobello–Martina Franca Road

SCENIC DRIVE | The trulli in Alberobello itself are impressive, but the most scenic concentration of these unique conical structures is along a 15-km (9-mile) stretch of the SS172 (Alberobello–Martina Franca) through the tranquil Valle d'Itria. Stop to visit some of the area's vineyards and oil mills—many of which have a welcoming open-door policy—surrounded by vast groves of ancient gnarled olive trees. ✉ *Alberobello.*

Trullo Sovrano

MUSEUM VILLAGE | **FAMILY** | Although this 18th-century house, Alberobello's largest trullo, originally belonged to a wealthy family, it has been furnished in a traditional style, providing insight into what everyday life was like in these unique beehive constructions. Guided tours are included with admission; there's an information center and shop, and gastronomic events are held in the garden. Check out the classic film *Casanova '70*, starring Marcello Mastroianni and Moira Orfei, which was partly filmed in and around the trullo. ✉ *Piazza Sacramento 10, Alberobello* ✛ *Follow Corso Vittorio Emanuele up past the obelisk and basilica* ☎ *080/4326030* ⊕ *www.trullosovrano.eu* ⓘ *€2.*

🍴 Restaurants

Il Poeta Contadino

$$$ | **SOUTHERN ITALIAN** | There are actually two eateries here, but far superior is the well-regarded Poeta Contadino, which specializes in regional cooking with a creative twist and offers a refined dining experience amid candlelight that casts shadows on ancient stone walls. If you're on a budget, though, the more affordable Osteria del Poeta also serves traditional dishes. **Known for:** stunning vaulted ceiling; exquisite seafood and meat dishes; extensive wine list. Ⓢ *Average main: €28* ✉ *Via Indipendenza 21–27, Alberobello* ☎ *080/4321917* ⊕ *www.ilpoetacontadino. it* ✆ *Closed Thurs.*

★ L'Aratro
$$ | SOUTHERN ITALIAN | Welcoming and rustic, this eatery is set inside adjoining trulli, complete with dark-wood beams, whitewashed walls, and a patio for summer dining. It's a certified Slow Food restaurant, so local ingredients figure prominently in the traditional, often seasonal dishes. **Known for:** gorgeous trulli venue; diligent use of local produce; classic regional fare. Ⓢ *Average main: €22* ✉ *Via Monte San Michele 25–29, Alberobello* ☎ *080/4322789* ⊕ *www. ristorantearatro.it.*

Coffee and Quick Bites

Principotto
$ | SOUTHERN ITALIAN | FAMILY | For a great-value on-the-hoof snack, pop into this tiny, popular place for filled *panzerotti* (deep-fried pockets), *friselle* (crunchy durum-wheat bread), and *schiacciatella Romana* (pizza-like flatbread). Check the board for daily specials, including meaty ragù sauces and seafood like *polpi* (octopus) to fill your freshly fried pockets. **Known for:** bar next door for a vino accompaniment; buzzy place with crowds spilling out; cime di rapa and other Pugliese produce. Ⓢ *Average main: €5* ✉ *Via Bissolati 16, Alberobello* ☎ *347/4529922.*

Hotels

★ Le Alcove
$$$ | HOTEL | This cluster of trulli has been transformed into luxury suites with original architectural features, modern comforts, and tasteful flourishes that make everything seem straight out of a lifestyle-magazine spread. **Pros:** heated floors; centrally located near the Trullo Sovrano; quaint, unusual accommodations. **Cons:** three rooms aren't in the main building; rooms are rather small; some rooms have a narrow, awkward metal staircase to upper areas. Ⓢ *Rooms from: €250* ✉ *Piazza Ferdinando IV 7, Alberobello* ☎ *080/4323754* ⊕ *www. lealcove.it* ⤳ *9 rooms* ⏺ *Free Breakfast.*

Ostuni

50 km (30 miles) west of Brindisi, 85 km (53 miles) southeast of Bari.

This sun-bleached medieval town lies on three hills not far from the coast. From a distance, Ostuni is a jumble of blazing white houses and churches spilling over a hilltop and overlooking the sea. Don't be surprised if you hear a lot of English and German spoken in the cobbled streets. The Città Bianca (White City), as it is called, has cast its spell on a large number of British and German nationals, who have bought second homes here. That doesn't mean that the town has lost its local flavor; fairs, religious festivals, and colorful traditional events are held as always with the same enthusiasm and fervor.

GETTING HERE AND AROUND
By car, take the Ostuni exit from the SS16. Trenitalia runs frequent trains from Bari. The station, however, is 5 km (3 miles) from the town—there is almost hourly local bus service.

VISITOR INFORMATION

CONTACT Ostuni Tourism Office. ✉ *Corso Mazzini 6, Ostuni* ☎ *0831/301268.*

 Sights

Ostuni Old Town

HISTORIC DISTRICT | Known as the Città Bianca for its dazzling white buildings and cobbled streets, Ostuni commands stupendous views out over the coast and the surrounding plain. Its unpolluted sea and clean beaches have earned it international Blue Flag recognition since 2008. The surrounding countryside contains a number of interesting 17th- and 18th-century masserie, many of which have been converted into agriturismi. ✉ *Ostuni* ⊕ *www.viaggiareinpuglia.it.*

Piazza Libertà

PLAZA/SQUARE | The city's main square divides the new town to the west and the old town to the east. The triangular piazza contains the town symbol: the towering Guglia di Sant'Oronzo (Spire of St. Oronzo), named after the patron of Ostuni, in whose honor an elaborate festival is held every year in late August. ✉ *Ostuni* ⊕ *www.viaggiareinpuglia.it.*

 Beaches

★ Torre Guaceto

BEACH | The transparent water and chalky sand of this marine reserve extend 12 miles along the coast and 4 miles inland, where the wetlands are a haven for wildlife. Those seeking a spectacular walk in an unspoiled expanse head to the Spiaggia delle Conchiglie, which consists of tiny white shells. Note: it's protected and off-limits to bathers. A shuttle bus operates from the main car park. **Amenities:** food and drink; lifeguards; parking (fee); toilets. **Best for:** snorkeling; sunrise; sunset; swimming; walking. ✉ *Riserva Naturale di Torre Gauceto, Ostuni* ⊕ *www.riservaditorreguaceto.it.*

 Restaurants

Osteria del Tempo Perso

$$ | SOUTHERN ITALIAN | On an old-town side street, this laid-back restaurant occupies two caves, where ancient rough-hewn stone walls contrast with elegant table settings. The service is friendly, and local, seasonal dishes include antipasti mainstays like eggplant Parmesan or salumi di Martina Franca, as well as both meat and fish *secondi.* **Known for:** local meat, including donkey; excellent changing menu; housemade pasta with classic Pugliese sauces. ⑤ *Average main: €20* ✉ *Via G. Tanzarella Vitale 47, Ostuni* ☎ *0831/304819* ⊕ *www.osteriadeltempoperso.com* ⊙ *Closed Mon. Sept.–June.*

🛏 Hotels

Hotel Relais Sant'Eligio

$ | HOTEL | Nestled in a valley just below Ostuni and surrounded by venerable olive trees, this stylish adaptation of a 16th-century posthouse—with characteristic stone archways and roughcasted walls—has whitewashed, simply furnished guest rooms whose beds have wrought-iron headboards. **Pros:** pleasant, modern environment with touches of old-world charm; fab views; free parking at hotel. **Cons:** showers lack decent water pressure; limited breakfast choice; outside the city walls and short walk uphill to the old center of Ostuni. ⑤ *Rooms from: €120* ✉ *Via Giosuè Pinto 50, Ostuni* ☎ *0831/1985171* ⊕ *www.santeligiorelais.it* ⇥ *22 rooms* ⑩ *Free Breakfast.*

La Terra Hotel

$$ | B&B/INN | It doesn't get more historic than this 14th-century noble residence, where spacious, tastefully decorated rooms and a cocktail-perfect, colonnaded rooftop loggia offer character and comfort aplenty. **Pros:** some rooms have superb views; inside the walls of the old city, near all sights; great seafood restaurant. **Cons:** street can be noisy in high season; parking outside town (with shuttle service); standard rooms look a bit tired. $ *Rooms from: €140* ✉ *Via Gaspare Petrarolo 16, Ostuni* ☎ *0831/336651* ⊕ *www.laterrahotel.it* 🛏 *17 rooms* ⦿ *Free Breakfast.*

Ceglie Messapica

11 km (7 miles) southwest of Ostuni, 18 km (11 miles) southeast of Martina Franca.

With its 14th-century Piazza Vecchia, tattered Baroque balconies, and lordly medieval castles, the little whitewashed town of Ceglie Messapica is the epitome of everyone's notion of the sleepy southern Italian town. Situated at the center of the triangle formed by Taranto, Brindisi, and Fasano, this town was once the military capital of the region, and often defended itself against invasions from the Taranto city-state, which wanted to clear a route to the Adriatic. Nowadays, Ceglie Messapica is a gourmet capital, with a surprising number of excellent restaurants.

GETTING HERE AND AROUND
By car, take the Ostuni exit from the SS16, and follow the SP22 to Ceglie Messapica. Ferrovie del Sud-Est runs frequent bus and train connections from Bari.

VISITOR INFORMATION
CONTACT Ceglie Messapica Tourism Office. ✉ *Via G. Elia 16, Ceglie Messapica* ☎ *0831/371003* ⊕ *www.ceglieturismo.it.*

 Restaurants

Al Fornello Da Ricci
$$$ | SOUTHERN ITALIAN | The cuisine served in the elegant dining room of this restaurant, complete with a verdant garden and run by a local couple—both creative chefs—marries exotic influences with tradition. It's a great place to splurge on a tasting menu; note, though, that hours can be erratic, especially during winter months, so call ahead. **Known for:** magical outside space; friendly service; imaginative dishes. $ *Average main: €28* ✉ *Via delle Grotte 11, Ceglie Messapica* ☎ *0831/377104* ⊕ *www.alfornellodaricci. com* ⊗ *Closed Mon.–Tues.*

★ **Cibus**
$ | SOUTHERN ITALIAN | Amid the stone vaults and vine-leafy, light-dappled courtyard of this highly acclaimed old-town osteria turned Slow Food destination, the freshest Pugliese meat and produce are transformed into exquisite tapas-like dishes. Be sure to ask the amiable owner to show you his wine cellar and equally impressive cheese larder, where he personally controls the maturing process. **Known for:** noteworthy wine and cheese; gorgeous setting; friendly service and Slow Food ethos. $ *Average main: €14* ✉ *Via Chianche di Scarano, Ceglie Messapica* ☎ *0831/388980* ⊕ *www. ristorantecibus.it* ⊗ *Closed Tues.*

Martina Franca

29 km (18 miles) southwest of Ostuni, 36 km (22 miles) north of Taranto.

Martina Franca is a beguiling town with a dazzling mixture of medieval and Baroque architecture in the light-color local stone. Developed as a military stronghold in the 14th century, all that remains of the defensive walls are the four gates that divide the old part from the modern suburbs. Lose yourself in the maze of twisting white alleyways, where erstwhile palaces jostle with ancient churches and narrow stairways leading up to humbler abodes. No longer a little-known backwater, the centro storico can be crowded with sightseers on the weekends. The positive side is that this has led to the emergence of top-quality restaurants, and you'll be spoiled for choice. Each July into early August, the town hosts the Valle d'Itria music festival, which showcases classical music and opera.

GETTING HERE AND AROUND

By car, take the Fasano exit from the SS16, then follow the SS172. The Ferrovie Sud-Est runs frequent trains and buses from Bari and Taranto.

VISITOR INFORMATION

CONTACT Martina Franca Tourism Office. ⊠ *Via Dott. Adolfo Ancona 5, Martina Franca* ☎ *366/1266045, 333/4378469 English-speaking contact* ⊕ *www.prolocomartinafranca.it.*

Sights

Basilica di San Martino

CHURCH | A splendid example of southern Italian Baroque architecture, the basilica contains rows of lavishly decorated altars in polychrome marbles, as well as treasures like the silver statues of the two patron saints, San Martino and Santa Comasia. To the right of the main altar note the illuminated niche with the sculpture of the Madonna Pastorella as a shepherd girl in a gown of cloth-of-gold, defending Christ's flock from demons. The elaborately sculpted facade is dominated by a dramatic image of St. Martin with his prancing horse in a shell-shape niche. Some interesting MuBA (Museo Basilica) exhibits in the adjacent Palazzo Stabile tell the story of Martina Franca through religious art and artifacts. ⊠ *Via Vittorio Emanuele 30, Martina Franca* ☎ *080/4302664* ⊕ *www.muba-sanmartino.it* 🎫 *€3 museum; €1.50 for guided tour* 🕐 *Museum closed Mon.*

🍴 Restaurants

⭐ Garibaldi Bistrot

$$ | MODERN ITALIAN | FAMILY | The location—right on the piazza by the Duomo, with tables outside and a cool white-washed dining room inside—is what initially draws people to this restaurant. But it's the tasty Pugliese produce used in simple salads, antipasti, pasta dishes, and classic seafood or meat mains that keeps people coming back. **Known for:** great service; heaping salads and bountiful bruschetta; stunning spot on the piazza. ⓢ *Average main: €17* ⊠ *Piazza Plebiscito 13, Martina Franca* ☎ *080/4837987.*

Taranto

100 km (62 miles) southeast of Bari, 40 km (25 miles) south of Martina Franca.

Taranto (stress the first syllable) was an important port even in Greek times, and it's still Italy's largest naval base. It lies toward the back of the instep of the boot on the broad Mare Grande bay, which is connected to a small internal Mare Piccolo basin by two narrow channels, one artificial and one natural. The old town is a collection of palazzi (in varying states of decay) along narrow cobblestone streets on an island between the two bodies of water, linked by causeways to the modern city, which stretches inward along the mainland. Circumnavigating the city can be quite tricky, with a confusing series of junctions and overpasses; take it as slowly as you can and follow the signs for the centro storico, where the main sights are situated.

GETTING HERE AND AROUND

By car, the A14 autostrada takes you almost directly to Taranto. Trenitalia runs frequent trains from Bari and Brindisi.

VISITOR INFORMATION

CONTACT Taranto Tourism Office. ⊠ *Castello Aragonese, Taranto* ☎ *389/9935679* ⊕ *www.prolocoditaranto.wordpress.com.*

Sights

Castel Sant'Angelo

CASTLE/PALACE | The monumental Castel Sant'Angelo, more commonly referred to as the Castello Aragonese, guards the drawbridge leading from the island center of Taranto to the newer city on the mainland. The castle is occupied by the Italian navy, but it's open to the public, and navy personnel conduct regular, free guided tours. The castle, built in its present form by King Ferdinand of Aragon, king of Naples, in the 15th century, contains ruins of older Greek, Byzantine, and Norman constructions as well as the Renaissance Chapel of San Leonardo. ⊠ *Piazza Castello 4, Taranto* ☎ *099/7753438* ⊕ *www.castelloaragone-setaranto.com* ⊠ *Free.*

★ MARTA—Museo Archeologico Nazionale Taranto

OTHER MUSEUM | Taranto's outstanding National Archaeological Museum (MAR-TA) occupies the historic premises of the ex-monastery of San Pasquale. The museum dates from 1887, and its collection of Greek and Roman antiquities is considered to be one of the most important in Italy. Many artifacts were discovered in the vicinity, testifying to the city's centuries-old importance as a port. Admire the rich cache of tomb goods, including magnificent gold jewelry, polychrome terra-cotta, objects in ivory and bone, and rare colored glass. A display of Jewish, Christian, and Muslim funeral epitaphs, dating from the 4th to 11th century, demonstrate the peaceful coexistence of the three religions in this multicultural Mediterranean hub from the Byzantine era to the Middle Ages. ⊠ *Via Cavour 10, Taranto* ☎ *099/4538639* ⊕ *www.museo-taranto.beniculturali.it* ⊠ *€8.*

San Domenico Maggiore

CHURCH | Taranto's most important monument is the ancient church and monastery of San Domenico in the heart of the centro storico. Situated on the narrow strip of land that divides Taranto's two bays, Mare Piccolo and Mare Grande, the present, rather neglected church rises over the ancient Greek acropolis of Taranto where the city is considered to have originated. The statue of Our Lady of Sorrows, much venerated by the local

people, stands in the last chapel on the left. Pop into the beautiful 13th-century cloister for a moment's respite from sightseeing. ⊠ *Via Duomo 33, Taranto* ☎ *099/4713511* ⊠ *Free* ⊘ *Erratic hours; cloister closed Sun.*

Restaurants

Al Gatto Rosso

$$$ | SOUTHERN ITALIAN | Set in a handsome stile liberty palazzo, with outdoor seating and a smart, minimalist dining room, the well-regarded "Red Cat" has been serving elegant seafood since 1952. The third-generation owner and head chef is renowned for his innovative dishes using the freshest fish and seasonal vegetables. **Known for:** near MARTA; delicious gelato and semifreddo desserts; raw seafood antipasti. ⑤ *Average main: €25* ⊠ *Via Cavour 2, Taranto* ☎ *340/5337800* ⊕ *www.ristorantegattorosso.com* ⊘ *Closed Mon.*

Hotels

Hotel Europa

$$ | HOTEL | The views are fantastic from this Belle Époque palazzo—situated on a point jutting out over Mar Piccolo, across from the old town—and most of the high-ceilinged guest rooms have little balconies where you can watch naval ships mingle with fishing boats in the port. **Pros:** some mini-apartments with kitchenettes; great location overlooking the bay; short walk to MARTA. **Cons:** steep stairs to mezzanine areas in some rooms; rooms a bit old-fashioned and on the small size; tricky parking in such a busy area. ⑤ *Rooms from: €140* ⊠ *Via Roma 1, Taranto* ☎ *099/4525994* ⊕ *www.hoteleuropataranto.it* ⑩ *Free Breakfast* ⊷ *43 rooms.*

Lecce

*40 km (25 miles) southeast of Brindisi,
87 km (54 miles) east of Taranto.*

Lecce is the crown jewel of the Mezzogiorno. The city is called "the Florence of the south," but that term doesn't do justice to Lecce's uniqueness in the Italian landscape. Although its pretty boutiques, lively bars, bustling streets, laid-back student cafés, and evening passeggiata draw comparisons to the cultural capitals of the north, Lecce's impossibly intricate Baroque architecture and its hyperanimated crowds are distinctively southern. The city is a cosmopolitan oasis two steps from the idyllic Otranto–Brindisi coastline and a hop from the olive groves of Puglia. Relatively undiscovered by foreign tourists, Lecce exudes an optimism and youthful joie de vivre unparalleled in any other Baroque showcase.

Summer is a great time to visit, when courtyards and piazzas throughout the city host dramatic productions or performances by rock and pop stars. Baroque music concerts are often held in Lecce's beautiful churches and cultural spaces.

GETTING HERE AND AROUND
By car from Bari, take the main toll-free coast road via Brindisi and continue along the SS613 to Lecce. Frequent trains run along the coast from Bari and beyond. The closest airport is in Brindisi.

VISITOR INFORMATION
CONTACT Lecce Tourism Office. ⊠ *Corso Vittorio Emanuele II 16, Lecce* ☎ *0832/682985* ⊕ *www.turismo.ilecce.it/infopoint.*

Sights

★ Duomo
CHURCH | Dominating a vast square concealed by a maze of alleyways, Lecce's magnificent cathedral of Santa Maria Assunta never fails to take visitors by surprise. The goal when building the 17th-century structure was to stun the faithful with a vision of opulence and power. Its sheer theatricality still leaves viewers open-mouthed, especially at night when the entire piazza is illuminated like a stage set. Constructed in rosy local stone, the church is flanked by the ornate Bishops' Palace, the seminary, and the 236-foot-high bell tower, which dominates the centro storico skyline. ⊠ *Piazza Duomo, off Corso Vittorio Emanuele II, Lecce* ☎ *0832/308557* ⊕ *www.cattedraledilecce.it.*

Piazza Sant'Oronzo
PLAZA/SQUARE | This is the buzzing hub of Lecce's social life in the heart of the maze of pedestrianized alleyways lined with cafés, little restaurants, and crafts shops. Named after Oronzo, the city's patron saint, who crowns a Roman column that once marked the end of the Via Appia Antica, the piazza is also occupied by another city symbol, the somewhat odd-looking 17th-century Sedile, formerly the town hall but now an art and exhibition center. The piazza revolves around the sunken hemicycle of the old Anfiteatro Romano, where the rows of seats are clearly visible. ⊠ *Piazza Sant'Oronzo, Lecce.*

Santa Croce
CHURCH | Although Lecce was founded before the time of the ancient Greeks, it's often associated with the term *Barocco leccese,* the result of a citywide impulse in the 17th century to redo the town in an exuberant fashion. But this was Baroque with a difference: generally, such architecture is heavy and monumental, but here it took on a lighter, more fanciful air, and the church of Santa Croce is a fine example, along with the adjoining Palazzo della Prefettura. The facade is a riot of sculptures of saints, angels, leaves, vines, and columns—all in glowing local honey-color stone, creating an overall lighthearted effect. ⊠ *Via Umberto I 3, Lecce* ☎ *0832/6931* ⊕ *basilicasantacrocelecce.it.*

🍴 Restaurants

Alle Due Corti

$$ | **SOUTHERN ITALIAN** | **FAMILY** | Renowned local culinary experts run this cove-ceilinged trattoria, where traditional Salentine cuisine is treated with both respect and originality. The white-walled interior is stark, but there's plenty of character in the simple, tasty fare and the gregarious chatter of local families. ⑤ *Average main: €16 ⊠ Corte dei Giugni 1, corner of Via Prato 42, Lecce ☎ 0832/242223 ⊕ www.alleduecorti.com ⊗ Closed Sun.*

Corte dei Pandolfi

$$ | **SOUTHERN ITALIAN** | Choose from a vast list of Salento's best wines, and feast on an unparalleled spread of artisanal *salumi* (cured meats) and local cheeses accompanied by delicious local honey and *mostarda* (preserved fruit). The seasonally changing menu of primi and secondi includes vegetarian specialties. ⑤ *Average main: €18 ⊠ Corte dei Pandolfi 3, Lecce ☎ 0832/332309 ⊕ www.cortedeipandolfi.com ⊗ Closed Mon.*

Le Zie

$$ | **SOUTHERN ITALIAN** | **FAMILY** | Local families favor this tiny old-fashioned trattoria, where no-frills charm is matched by wholesome, unfussy food. *Cucina casareccia* (home-cooked) specialties include *polpo in teglia* (stewed octopus), *baccalà al forno* (baked salt cod), and the ubiquitous rustic *purè di fave e cicoria* (bean puree with wild chicory). ⑤ *Average main: €16 ⊠ Via Costadura 19, Lecce ☎ 0832/245178 ⊗ Closed Mon. No dinner Sun.*

☕ Coffee and Quick Bites

★ Caffè Alvino

$ | **SOUTHERN ITALIAN** | This historic caffè-gelateria is in the heart of Lecce, with handsome interiors and seating out on Piazza Sant'Oronzo. From early morning to late at night this is a buzzy place where Leccesi come to meet and refuel on classic Salentino pastries like *pasticciotti* and *zeppole*. **Known for:** the late Anthony Bourdain was a fan; arguably the best pastries in town; ottimi coffee and gelato. ⑤ *Average main: €7 ⊠ Piazza Sant'Oronzo 30, Lecce ☎ 0832/246748.*

🛏 Hotels

★ 8piuhotel

$ | **HOTEL** | **FAMILY** | Its design is more "international style" than "rustic Pugliese," but this hotel offers superb value, combining contemporary creature comforts with fancy tech. **Pros:** abundant breakfast; on-site restaurant, Negroamaro; fitness center and guest cycles. **Cons:** lack of local character might not appeal to some; a bit out of town; tech overload. ⑤ *Rooms from: €94 ⊠ Viale del Risorgimento, Lecce ☎ 0832/306686 ⊕ www.8piuhotel.com ⇄ 83 rooms ⊗ Free Breakfast.*

Patria Palace

$$ | **HOTEL** | Lecce's grandest hotel—impeccable from top to bottom, with vaulted ceilings, frescoes, and antique furnishings—also happens to have a stellar location in front of the monumental Santa Croce Basilica, the crown jewel of Lecce Baroque. **Pros:** valet parking for guests; many sumptuous, high-ceilinged rooms; fabulous roof terrace. **Cons:** some rooms outdated and less grand; a few rooms overlook noisy backstreets; style of the lobby doesn't match that of the handsome facade. ⑤ *Rooms from: €160 ⊠ Piazzetta Riccardi 13, Lecce ☎ 0832/245111 ⊕ www.patriapalace.com ⇄ 67 rooms ⊗ Free Breakfast.*

Risorgimento Resort Lecce

$$ | **HOTEL** | Although this hotel has been a centro storico landmark since 1880, it feels unmistakably 21st century, with modern decor and vibrant color schemes. **Pros:** wellness spa; spacious

guest rooms; highly professional staff.
Cons: may be noisy in rooms at the front;
smart, international-style hotel without much local atmosphere; tiny gym.
$ *Rooms from: €139* ✉ *Via Augustus Imperatore 19, Lecce* ☎ *0832/246311* ⊕ *www.risorgimentoresort.it* ⇄ *47 rooms* ❍ *Free Breakfast.*

Otranto

36 km (22 miles) southeast of Lecce, 188 km (117 miles) southeast of Bari.

In one of the first great Gothic novels, Horace Walpole's *The Castle of Otranto*, published in 1764, the English writer immortalized this city and its mysterious medieval fortress, and indeed Otranto (stress the first syllable) has had more than its share of dark thrills. As the easternmost point in Italy—and therefore closest to the Balkan Peninsula—it's often borne the brunt of foreign invasions, including the massacre of 800 citizens by the Moors in 1480 because they refused to give up their faith. From here, you can see across the sea to Albania on a clear day. If you are a fan of the Neolithic, you will be interested in the Grotta dei Cervi, a few miles down the coast. The walls of the cave are covered with hundreds of prehistoric images, painted with red ocher and black bat guano.

GETTING HERE AND AROUND
By car from Lecce, take the southbound SS16 and exit at Maglie. To follow the coast, take the SS53 from Lecce, then follow the SS611 south. There's regular train service from Lecce on Ferrovie del Sud-Est.

VISITOR INFORMATION
CONTACT Otranto Tourism Office. ✉ *Piazza Castello, Otranto* ☎ *0836/801436* ⊕ *www.comune.otranto.le.it.*

 Sights

Castello Aragonese
CASTLE/PALACE | The massive Aragonese Castle is considered a masterpiece of 16th-century military architecture. Rebuilt by the Spanish viceroy Don Pedro di Toledo in 1535 after it was badly damaged in the siege of Otranto (1480), when invading Ottoman armies destroyed the city, its impressive walls and bastions dominate the port and seashore. Escape the heat with a walk around its cool interiors and snake around its recently landscaped moats. Various art and photographic exhibitions are held here in the summer. ✉ *Piazza Castello, Otranto* ☎ *0836/801436, 0836/210094* ⊕ *www.comune.otranto.le.it* 🎫 *€4.*

Cattedrale
CHURCH | By far the best sight in Otranto is the cathedral, Santa Maria Annunziata, consecrated in 1088. Its highlight is a 12th-century Pantaleone mosaic: covering the entire length of the nave, the sanctuary, and the apse, it depicts scenes from the Old Testament and traditional medieval chivalric tales and animals set alongside a Tree of Life. The walls behind the main altar are lined with glass cases containing the skulls and tibias of the 800 martyrs of Otranto, slain by the Ottomans after the seige of 1480 for not renouncing their faith. ✉ *Piazza Basilica, Otranto* ☎ *0836/801436* ⊕ *www.comune.otranto.le.it.*

 Hotels

Corte di Nettuno
$$ | HOTEL | Handily moored near the marina and the castello, this hotel has a nautical theme with wrought-iron gates in the shape of waves, a statue of the sea god Neptune at the entrance, the owner's maritime antiques throughout, and guest rooms accented by shades of blue.
Pros: decent food; good location near the marina and sights; quirky decor full of surprises. **Cons:** clinical feel in some

dated and gloomy rooms; some people may find the sea theme overly eccentric; lackadaisical service in low season. ⑤ *Rooms from: €150* ✉ *Via Madonna del Passo, Otranto* ☎ *0832/351321* ⊕ *www.cdshotels.it* ⊙ *Closed Nov.–Mar.* ⇱ *28 rooms* ❢❢❢ *Free Breakfast.*

Masseria Montelauro

$$$ | **B&B/INN** | **FAMILY** | Beautifully restored, with high-style interiors, this 19th-century former masseria is an oasis of comfort just a short drive from lovely Otranto. **Pros:** friendly, helpful service; interesting building; lovely grounds and pool. **Cons:** food is pricey; a car is absolutely necessary; some rooms rather stuffy. ⑤ *Rooms from: €204* ✉ *SP358, Località Montelauro, Otranto* ☎ *0836/806203* ⊕ *www.masseriamonte-lauro.it* ❢❢❢ *Free Breakfast* ⊙ *Closed Nov.–Apr.* ⇱ *29 rooms.*

Gallipoli

37 km (23 miles) south of Lecce, 190 km (118 miles) southeast of Bari.

The fishing port of Gallipoli, on the eastern tip of the Golfo di Taranto, is divided between a new town, on the mainland, and the beautiful fortified *borgo antico* (old town) across a 17th-century bridge, crowded onto its own small island in the gulf. The Greeks called it Kallipolis ("the fair city"), the Romans Anxa. Like the infamous Turkish town of the same name on the Dardanelles, the Italian Gallipoli occupies a strategic location and thus was repeatedly attacked through the centuries—by the Normans in 1071, the Venetians in 1484, and the British in 1809. Today life in Gallipoli revolves around fishing. Boats in primary colors breeze in and out of the bay during the day, and Gallipoli's fish market, below the bridge, throbs with activity all morning.

GETTING HERE AND AROUND

From Lecce, take the SS101. From Taranto, follow the coastal SS174. Frequent trains run from Lecce.

VISITOR INFORMATION

CONTACT Gallipoli Tourism Office. ✉ *Via Kennedy, Gallipoli* ☎ *0833/264283* ⊕ *www.prolocogallipoli.it.*

 # Sights

Castello Aragonese

CASTLE/PALACE | The massive bulk of Gallipoli's castle guards the entrance to the island of the *borgo antico*, which is linked to the new town by a bridge. Rising out of the sea, the present fortress, dating from the 17th to 18th century, is built on the foundations of an earlier Byzantine citadel. It has four towers, plus a separate fifth known as the Rivellino, where open-air shows are held in summer. A visit allows grandstand sea views, but there's little to see inside between exhibitions. ✉ *Rampa Castello, Gallipoli* ☎ *0833/262775* ⊕ *www.castellogallipoli.it* ⊙ *Closed Mon., and Tues.–Sun. 1–3* 🎫 *€7.*

Duomo

CHURCH | In the center of the *borgo antico*, Gallipoli's Duomo is a notable Baroque cathedral from the late 17th century, dedicated to Sant'Agata, patron saint of the city. Built in local limestone, the ornate facade is matched by an equally elaborate interior with columns and altars in fine polychrome marble and paintings by leading local Gallipoli and Neapolitan maestros of the time. Particularly interesting are the stone carvings that depict episodes from the city's history. ✉ *Via Duomo 1, Gallipoli* ☎ *0833/261987* ⊕ *www.cattedralegal-lipoli.it.*

a Purità

HURCH | A fine example of Gallipoli Baroque, the 17th-century Church of Santa Maria della Purità stands at the end of the borgo antico overlooking famed Purità Beach. It contains an eye-popping wealth of art and decoration, including the painting at the high altar by Luca Giordano, intricately carved wooden choir stalls, and a 19th-century majolica pavement. ⊠ *Riviera Nazario Sauro, Gallipoli* ☎ *0833/261699.*

Beaches

★ Beaches of Gallipoli

BEACH | FAMILY | Ample swimming and clean, fine-grained sand make Gallipoli's beaches a good choice for families. The 5-km (3-mile) strand reaches from Punta Pizzo to Lido San Giovanni and is divided among a series of bathing establishments, all of which provide sun beds, umbrellas, showers, changing facilities, and snack bars. Parco Gondar hosts a fun fair and music events. Water-sports equipment can be bought or rented at the waterfront shops in town. **Amenities:** food and drink; lifeguards; parking (fee); showers; toilets; water sports. **Best for:** partiers; snorkeling; sunset; swimming; walking; windsurfing. ⊕ *www.prolocogallipoli.it.*

Restaurants

Marechiaro

$$ | SEAFOOD | Built on wooden piles in the shadow of Aragonese Castle, this restaurant—in business for more than a century—seems to float like a ship in the bay by the bridge connecting new town with the island that contains the borgo antico. Its flower-filled terrace has outdoor tables in summer; in winter, eat inside and enjoy the view through panoramic windows. **Known for:** jetty terrace over the water; warm Gallipolino

welcome; freshest raw *ricci di mare* (sea urchins). ⑤ *Average main: €20* ⊠ *Lungomare Marconi, Gallipoli* ☎ *0833/266143* ⊕ *ristorantemarechiaro.net.*

Hotels

★ Relais Corte Palmieri

$ | HOTEL | Set in an aristocratic 18th-century house in the center of the borgo antico and near Purità Beach, the Relais Corte Palmieri has been tastefully renovated to meet modern standards while preserving its frescoes, mosaics, antique doors, and other historical features. **Pros:** on-site spa; individually decorated rooms; roof garden with spectacular views. **Cons:** parking is mighty tricky in narrow alleys; difficult to reach; noisy rooms streetside and near breakfast room. ⑤ *Rooms from: €110* ⊠ *Corte Palmieri 3, Gallipoli* ☎ *0833/265318* ⊕ *www.relaiscortepalmieri.it* ⊗ *Closed late Oct.–late Mar. or early Apr.* ⇆ *20 rooms* ⏹ *Free Breakfast.*

Matera

62 km (39 miles) south of Bari.

This town of unique Sassi (cave dwellings) is one of southern Italy's most intriguing places. The so-called New Town is full of elegant Baroque churches, palazzi, and broad piazzas, which are filled to bursting during the evening passeggiata. It's perched on the verge of a steep gully crowded with ancient rock churches, some of which you can tour, and other Sassi converted into modern-day homes as well as hotels and restaurants. This is a particularly good time to visit: Matera's designation as the European Capital of Culture for 2019 reenergized the community with investment, cultural initiatives, and plenty of buzz.

From Bari, take the SS96 to Altamura, then the SS99 to Matera. Roughly one train per hour (Ferrovie Appulo Lucane) leaves Bari Centrale for Matera.

CONTACT Proloco Matera Città dei Sassi Tourism Office). ⊠ *Via Lucana 184, Matera* 🕾 *328/9333548* ⊕ *www.prolocomat-era2019.it.*

 ## Sights

★ Duomo

CHURCH | Matera's splendidly restored cathedral, dedicated to the Madonna della Bruna and Sant'Eustachio, was built in the late 13th century and occupies a prominent position between the two Sassi. Lavishly decorated, it has a typical Puglian Romanesque flavor; inside, there's a recovered fresco, probably painted in the 14th century, showing scenes from the Last Judgment. On the Duomo's facade the figures of Sts. Peter and Paul stand on either side of a sculpture of Matera's patron, the Madonna della Bruna. ⊠ *Piazza Duomo, Matera* 🕾 *0835/332012* ⊕ *www.diocesimaterairsina.it.*

Museo Archeologico Nazionale Domenico Ridola

HISTORY MUSEUM | Named after local 19th-century medical doctor Domenico Ridola, who investigated archaeological sites in the surrounding area, the museum highlights his excavations of the remains of Paleolithic and Neolithic settlements, as well as a richly endowed 4th-century-BC tomb. Ridola's finds are on view in the museum, which is housed in the former monastery of Santa Chiara. The collection includes an extensive selection of prehistoric and classical artifacts, notably Bronze Age implements and beautifully decorated red-figure pottery from Magna Graecia. ⊠ *Via Ridola 24, Matera* 🕾 *0835/310058* ⊕ *www.basilicata.beniculturali.it* ⌨ *€2.50* 🕓 *Closed Mon. until 2.*

Museo Nazionale d'Arte Medievale e Moderna della Basilicata

ART MUSEUM | Housed within the handsome 17th-century Palazzo Lanfranchi, this museum is divided into three contrasting thematic sections: Sacred Art, Collectibles, and Contemporary Art. You may want to skim through the many restored artifacts from Basilicata's churches and the 300-plus works of the Neapolitan school: the main attraction are the paintings of Carlo Levi and his must-stop-to-absorb humanist masterpiece *Lucania '61.* ⊠ *Piazza G. Pascoli 1, Matera* 🕾 *0835/256211* ⊕ *www.musei-matera.it/palazzo-lanfanchi/* ⌨ *€3.*

MUSMA (Museo della Scultura Contemporanea)

ART GALLERY | Amid otherworldly cave interiors, medieval courtyards, frescoed corners, and the grand spaces of 17th-century Palazzo Pomarici, this museum charts the evolution of Italian sculpture from the early 1800s to the present. Innovative curation, atmospheric lighting, and eerie acoustics make for a one-of-a-kind gallery experience. ⊠ *Palazzo Pomarici, Via San Giacomo, Matera* 🕾 *366/9357768* ⊕ *www.musma.it* ⌨ *€7* 🕓 *Closed Mon.*

San Giovanni Battista

CHURCH | Considered a jewel of medieval architecture, the 13th-century Romanesque church of San Giovanni Battista was restored to its pre-Baroque simplicity in 1926. The elaborately carved portal is a riot of entwining stone vines, flowers, leaves, human figures, and allegorical creatures. Inside, the three naves are flanked by columns crowned with capitals, each one decorated with symbolic animal forms and other images—no two are alike. ⊠ *Via San Biagio, Matera* 🕾 *0835/334182.*

★ Sassi di Matera

HISTORIC DISTRICT | Matera's Sassi are piled chaotically atop one another down the sides of a steep ravine. Some date from Paleolithic times, when they were truly just caves. Over time, they were transformed into enclosed houses, which once presented the Dante-esque vision of squalor and poverty that was graphically described in Carlo Levi's 1945 memoir, *Christ Stopped at Eboli*. In the 1960s, most inhabitants moved into ugly apartment blocks. The 1993 designation as a UNESCO World Heritage site, however, resulted in a cleanup and gentrification, with hotels, bars, and restaurants taking over many structures. From the upper town, the Strada Panoramica walk offers stellar views of the two areas known as **Sasso Caveoso** and **Sasso Barisano**. Feel free to wander down amid the troglodytic abodes, which, in the words of travel writer H. V. Morton in his *A Traveller in Southern Italy*, "resemble the work of termites rather than of man." There are also more than 100 *chiese rupestri*, or rock-hewn churches, some of which have medieval frescoes and a few of which are open to the public. The most spectacular is **Santa Maria de Idris**, right on the edge of the Sasso Caveoso, near the ravine. Guided tours can be arranged through the tourist office. ✉ *Sasso Caveoso, Matera* ⊕ *www.prolocomatera2019.it.*

★ **Storica Casa Grotta di Vico Solitario**
MUSEUM VILLAGE | Head to this house-museum in the Sasso Caveoso district for moving insights into what peasant life was like in a limestone cave dwelling. The cramped quarters are filled with traditional utensils and furniture, the belongings of its last inhabitants, who left in 1956 as part of a forced relocation of some 15,000 Sassi residents to apartment blocks. With its rainwater cistern, hand loom, storage niches, and tiny kitchen area and other living spaces (for both the family and their animals), the cave also demonstrates the ingenuity that made living here possible. ✉ *Vicinato di vico Solitario 11, Matera* ☎ *0835/310118* ⊕ *www.casagrotta.it* ⫞ *€3.*

🍴 Restaurants

Il Terrazzino
$$ | SOUTHERN ITALIAN | The dining area is carved out of a cliff, and the terrace overlooks the famous Sassi ravine. From both you can enjoy such rustic specialties as *foglie d'ulivo* (stuffed olive leaves), *zuppa di grano e ceci* (cheese and chickpea soup), and *pignata* (lamb stew with seasonal vegetables). **Known for:** interesting interiors (including a spectacular three-level wine cellar); classic Basilicata meat dishes and fresh pasta; stupendous views. ⑤ *Average main: €17* ✉ *Vico S. Giuseppe 7, Matera* ☎ *0835/332503* ⊕ *www.ilterrazzino.org* ⊗ *No dinner Tues.*

★ Vitantonio Lombardo
$$$$ | MODERN ITALIAN | An open kitchen and contemporary table lamps heighten the culinary theater of Matera's fanciest restaurant, set in a cool, minimalist Rione Sassi grotto. The chef's innovative tasting menus feature vibrant seasonal creations served on artsy ceramics and in wooden bowls. **Known for:** glass-screened wine cellar; exquisite bread and olive oil; imaginative, changing tasting menu. ⑤ *Average main: €37* ✉ *Via Madonna delle Virtù 13/14, Matera* ☎ *0835/335475* ⊕ *www.vlristorante.it* ⊗ *Closed Tues. No lunch Wed.*

🛏 Hotels

★ Locanda di San Martino
$ | HOTEL | Situated at the bottom of the Sassi ravine on Via Fiorentini (limited car access), the Locanda is a more upscale cave-dwelling hotel, with all modern comforts, including an elevator to whisk you up the cliff to your room. **Pros:** on-site ancient Roman–style spa; convenient location if you come by car; comfortable rooms. **Cons:** limited parking nearby; rooms reached via outdoor walkway; spa may be a tad intimate for some. ⑤ *Rooms from: €116* ✉ *Via Fiorentini 71, Matera* ☎ *0835/256600* ⊕ *www.locandadisanmartino.it* ⇥ *40 rooms* ⧖ *Free Breakfast.*

★ Palazzo Margherita

$$$$ | HOTEL | On the main square in the town of Francis Ford Coppola's ancestors, a large palazzo has been transformed (by French designer Jacques Grange) into Basilicata's top lodging, complete with hidden gardens, spacious porticoes, frescoed ceilings, and Moroccan-tile floors. **Pros:** spacious rooms with lots of high-tech gadgetry; professional, courteous staff; a garden pool. **Cons:** private transport needed; film-star prices; not much to do in Bernalda. $ *Rooms from: €500* ⊠ *Corso Umberto 64, Bernalda* ✛ *A 40-min drive south of Matera: take the SS7 out of Matera heading for Potenza and then join the SS407 for Metaponto and Taranto. Look for the turnoff to Bernalda after 25 km (16 miles)* ☎ *0835/549060* ⊕ *www.thefamilycoppolahideaways.com/en/palazzo-margherita* ➳ *9 rooms* ⦿ *Free Breakfast.*

Palazzo Vicecconte

$$ | HOTEL | If cave-dwelling isn't your style, consider staying at this hotel in a former aristocratic residence—a lovingly restored property, where each unique guest room showcases oil paintings, antiques, and high vaulted frescoed ceilings. **Pros:** suites are especially spacious; an easy walk to most of the main sights; on a quiet square. **Cons:** exorbitant parking rates; rooms vary considerably in size; breakfast may disappoint. $ *Rooms from: €151* ⊠ *Via San Potito 7, Matera* ☎ *0835/330699* ⊕ *www.palazzovicecconte.it* ➳ *14 rooms* ⦿ *Free Breakfast.*

Sant'Angelo Resort

$$$ | HOTEL | Authentic rough-hewn walls and arches contrast with chic furnishings and modern amenities at this Sassi hotel, created by interior designer Stefano Tardito and situated across a piazza from the Church of San Pietro Caveoso. **Pros:** a more luxurious cave-dwelling experience; unrivaled views; atmospheric rooms with minimalist design. **Cons:** can feel stuffy and humid at times; no elevator and many steps to climb; lack of natural light. $ *Rooms from: €250* ⊠ *Piazza San Pietro Caveoso, Matera* ☎ *0835/314010* ⊕ *www.santangeloresort.it* ⦿ *Free Breakfast* ➳ *21 rooms.*

Sassi

$ | HOTEL | Opened in 1996, Sassi claims to be Matera's first "grotto hotel," with rooms inside a succession of caves that overlook the huddle of rooftops and stone stairs down to the valley floor of Sasso Barisano. **Pros:** good value; fabulous views (day or night); decent breakfast. **Cons:** rooms are spread out and not connected to each other; bathrooms are small and need a refresh; tricky access for less fit. $ *Rooms from: €98* ⊠ *Via San Giovanni Vecchio 89, Matera* ☎ *0835/331009* ⊕ *www.hotelsassi.it* ➳ *35 rooms* ⦿ *Free Breakfast.*

Maratea

217 km (135 miles) south of Naples.

The high, twisty road into the Maratea region affords breathtaking glimpses of the turquoise sea and a gigantic statue of Cristo Redentore (reminiscent of the one in Rio de Janeiro) atop a hill. Steep crags separate the area into villages that include Maratea Porto, Marina di Maratea, Fiumicello, and Cersuta. The main inland town of Maratea proper is a tumble of cobblestone streets, where the ruins of a much older settlement (Maratea Antica) can be seen. Between the rocky headlands, there's no shortage of secluded beaches, which can get crowded in August. A summer minibus service connects all the different points once or twice an hour.

GETTING HERE AND AROUND

By car, take the Lagonegro exit from the A3 autostrada and continue along the SS585. Intercity and regional trains from Reggio Calabria and Naples stop at Maratea. In the summer months there's a bus linking the train station to the upper town 4 km (2½ miles) away.

VISITOR INFORMATION

CONTACT APT Maratea (Azienda di Promozione Turistica). ✉ *Piazza Vitolo, Maratea* ☎ *0973/030366* ⊕ *www.aptbasilicata.it.*

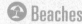 Beaches

Cala Jannita

BEACH | FAMILY | Maratea's dramatic rock topography is best experienced from this fab little bay and its Spiaggia Nera (Black Beach) with sparkling limpid waters and striking dark, volcanic pebbles. Bring sandals or shoes as it's a tricky approach. **Amenities:** food and drink; lifeguards; parking; showers; toilets. **Best for:** swimming. ✉ Maratea ☎ *393/8404975 Lido facilities.*

Restaurants

Da Cesare

$$ | SOUTHERN ITALIAN | With an open kitchen and a veranda—so you can keep an eye on both the chef and the azure waters of the Golfo di Policastro—there's always something to see at this family-run seafood restaurant. Even better: it serves some of the freshest catch in town, with specialties like linguine *con nero di seppia* (with cuttlefish ink sauce), grilled squid, and *grigliata mista* (mixed grilled fish and seafood). **Known for:** prominent position on coastal road; seafood dishes aplenty; open veranda with views. ⑤ *Average main: €21* ✉ *Via Nazionale Cersuta 52, on the SS18 (main coast road) in village of Cersuta, about 5 km (3 miles) north of Maratea, 3 km (2 miles) south of Acquafredda* ☎ *0973/871840* ⊗ *Closed Thurs. Nov.–Mar.*

Hotels

Villa Cheta Elite

$$ | HOTEL | FAMILY | This stile liberty villa in the seaside village of Acquafredda has original features and period pieces, a tranquil garden, a pool where you can idle the days away, and a flowery terrace for sunset dining. **Pros:** lovely art nouveau building; surrounded by Mediterranean greenery; beautiful coast and mountain views. **Cons:** nearest beach is far away; hotel is quite remote, so shops and the town require a car; steps up to entrance. ⑤ *Rooms from: €162* ✉ *Via Timpone 46, Località Acquafredda, Maratea* ☎ *0973/878134* ⊕ *www.villacheta.it* ⊗ *Closed Oct.–Apr.* ⑩ *Free Breakfast* ⇄ *22 rooms.*

Diamante

51 km (32 miles) south of Maratea, 225 km (140 miles) south of Naples.

A lively and attractive little resort on Calabria's north Tyrrhenian Coast, Diamante styles itself as "the town of murals and peperoncini." The old town center is accessed over a bridge across the Corvino River, which runs through town to the sea. The maze of alleyways and whitewashed houses is covered in murals by both local and international artists, many featuring fishing and religious themes, while strings of bright-red chili pods hang from doorways and balconies. The pedestrianized seafront promenade is the town hub, lined with small shops, ice cream parlors, and bars. Flanking the broad palm-lined promenade are sparkling beaches to the north and south and interesting archaeological remains in the nearby Cirella district. September's annual Peperoncino Festival is a major event, involving almost the entire town.

GETTING HERE AND AROUND

Driving from Maratea, take the SS18; from Cosenza, take the SS107 to Paola, then the SS18. Regional trains leave from Naples a few times a day, with regular service from Paola and Cosenza.

VISITOR INFORMATION

CONTACT Diamante Tourist Office. ⊠ *Via Gullo 1, Diamante* ☎ *0985/81130* ⊕ *www. prolocodiamante.it.*

 Restaurants

★ A' Cucchiarella

$$ | SEAFOOD | FAMILY | One of Diamante's most popular restaurants, in the old town center just off the seafront promenade, has atmospheric stone interiors. In the summer, sidewalk tables are the perfect relaxed place to watch the evening passeggiata while savoring exquisite fish dishes. **Known for:** handsome stone-walled dining rooms and a terrace; exceptional seafood; good vegetarian options. ⑤ *Average main: €18* ⊠ *Via Cavour 6, Diamante* ☎ *0985/877287* ◔ *Closed Mon.–Thurs. Oct.–Mar.*

La Guardiola

$ | ITALIAN | FAMILY | With its own private beach on the Diamante Riviera, La Guardiola is a great spot to go for a swim, enjoy a relaxing lunch, and indulge in a siesta under a beach umbrella. The menu has many pizza options, as well as dishes focusing on the catch of the day—perhaps spaghetti with sea urchins, fish-stuffed ravioli, or *stufata di alici alla diamantese* (fresh anchovy stew). **Known for:** beachside views and sunsets; spicy pizza *al peccati di gola* with *'nduja* (Calabrese pork salumi); evenings can be lively, with music and televised soccer matches. ⑤ *Average main: €14* ⊠ *Lungomare Riviera Bleu, Diamante* ☎ *0985/876759* ⊕ *www.laguardioladiamante.it.*

 Hotels

Grand Hotel San Michele

$ | HOTEL | Set in a Belle Époque–style villa surrounded by gardens, atop a cliff near the village of Cetraro, the San Michele offers Mediterranean charm and old-style elegance. **Pros:** pool and private beaches; beautiful setting; 9-hole golf course. **Cons:** breakfast lacks variety; some garden level accessed by steps; isolated, if you lack your own transport. ⑤ *Rooms from: €95* ⊠ *Località Bosco 8/9, 20 km (12 miles) south of Diamante on the SS18, Cetraro* ☎ *0982/91012* ⊕ *www.sanmichele.it* ◔ *Closed Nov.– Easter* ⇥ *65 rooms* ⦿ *Free Breakfast.*

Hotel Ferretti

$ | HOTEL | FAMILY | A visual stand-out on the coast just outside Diamante, this gleaming white 1970s wedding-cake structure is a good base for a relaxing stay away from the crowds and bustle. **Pros:** quirky architecture and decor; beach, pool, and tennis court; overlooks the sea. **Cons:** food is underwhelming; extra costs for leisure facilities; style might not appeal to everyone. ⑤ *Rooms from: €104* ⊠ *Via Poseidone 171, Diamante* ☎ *0985/81428* ⊕ *www.ferrettihotel.it* ⇥ *52 rooms* ⦿ *Free Breakfast.*

Castrovillari

68 km (43 miles) northeast of Diamante, 75 km (48 miles) northwest of Cosenza.

Stress the first *i* when you pronounce the name of this provincial Calabrian city, nestled in the deep valley beneath 7,375-foot Mt. Pollino. The town is notable as a venue for summer's Calabria-wide Peperoncino Jazz Festival (www.peperoncinojazzfestival.com). Its synagogue, which you can visit, dates from the early Middle Ages; its San Giuliano church from the 16th-century. The excellent restaurant La Locanda di Alia has also made

Castrovillari something of a gastronomic destination.

The city is also a great jumping-off point for exploring both the Albanian-speaking village of Cìvita and Pollino National Park, Italy's biggest national park and a walkers' paradise.

GETTING HERE AND AROUND
By car, take the A3 autostrada and exit at Frascineto-Castrovillari. Ferrovie della Calabria runs around four buses per day from Cosenza.

 ## Sights

Parco Nazionale del Pollino
NATIONAL PARK | FAMILY | Italy's largest national park straddles Calabria and Basilicata, rises to over 7,000 feet at Serra Dolcedorme, and offers many opportunities for outdoor enthusiasts. Its ancient wooded valleys are home to Europe's oldest tree, a 1,230-year-old Heldreich's pine. Hiking trails dot the landscape with excursions for most abilities—and there are popular picnicking viewpoints, often near *rifugi* (rustic hostels that tend to offer food). The Rifugio Biagio Longo near Castrolvillari is a good bet for those seeking to explore, and there's a Club Alpino contact number for those seeking a guide. For a more leisurely introduction, head to Rotonda in neighboring Basilicata, where the park headquarters and infopoint can put you in touch with outdoor centers and guides for rafting, hiking, climbing, and skiing. ⊠ *Via Cairoli 80, Castrovillari* ☏ *334/1005054 Club Alpino Italiano–Sezione di Castrovillari, 0973/669311 Ente Parco Nazionale del Pollino Infopoint* ⊕ *parcopollino.gov.it.*

 ## Restaurants

★ La Locanda di Alia
$$$ | MODERN ITALIAN | International food magazines have lauded this restaurant, where the wine cellar is well stocked and renowned chef-owner Gaetano Alia incorporates local produce and imaginative twists into the Calabrese dishes on the changing menu. La Locanda also has guest rooms in its adjoining Alia Jazz Hotel, which is surrounded by a lush garden and has a swimming pool. **Known for:** gorgeous setting with a leafy terrace; award-winning but unpretentious cuisine; candele pasta with spicy Calabrese 'nduja sauce. ⑤ *Average main: €26* ⊠ *Via Ietticelli 55, off the main street in Castrovillari (look for signs), Castrovillari* ☏ *0981/46370* ⊕ *www.locandadialia.it* ⊙ *No dinner Sun.*

🛏 Hotels

Alia Jazz Hotel
$ | B&B/INN | In addition to a theme that honors the international jazz festival held in the town every summer, the hospitable inn adjoining acclaimed Locanda di Alia restaurant has small but well-appointed and uniquely decorated guest rooms, each with a little sitting area and a modern bath equipped with a hydro-massage tub. **Pros:** local art in rooms; peaceful setting and informal atmosphere; fabulous homemade cakes, jams, and other culinary treats. **Cons:** rooms can be gloomy in winter; rooms in a row all at ground level; some rooms have a mezzanine-level bedroom. ⑤ *Rooms from: €100* ⊠ *Via Ietticelli 55, off the main street in Castrovillari (look for signs), Castrovillari* ☏ *0981/46370* ⊕ *aliahotel.business.site* ⌁ *14 rooms* ❤ *Free Breakfast.*

Cosenza

75 km (48 miles) southeast of Diamante, 185 km (115 miles) northeast of Reggio Calabria.

A construction boom in the 1950s and '60s encased Cosenza's medieval city—which winds up the hillsides between the Busento and Crati Rivers—in a sprawling, traffic-clogged modern town. Nevertheless, the steep, stair-filled centro storico truly hails from another age: wrought-iron balconies overlook narrow alleyways lined with old-fashioned storefronts and bars. The palazzi that line the route to the 12th-century Duomo, a UNESCO World Heritage monument, once housed nobility but today serve as studio spaces for many artists and artisans. The medieval castle, open to the public, crowns Pancrazio Hill, where the views of the town and the surrounding countryside are magnificent.

Cosenza is also the gateway to the cool and silent forests of the Sila mountains and villages like Rende (only 13 km [8 miles] away) and the Pollino National Park area (less than 80 km [50 miles]).

GETTING HERE AND AROUND

By car, take the Cosenza exit from the A3 autostrada. By train, change at Paola or Napoli on the main Rome–Reggio Calabria line. Regional trains run from Naples. Ferrovie della Calabria runs buses from Spezzano della Sila, Castrovillari, and Camigliatello.

VISITOR INFORMATION

CONTACT Cosenza Tourist Office. ✉ *Piazza XI Settembre, Cosenza* ☎ *328/1754422* ⊕ *www.cosenzaturismo.it.*

 Sights

Castello Svevo

CASTLE/PALACE | Castello Normanno Svevo crowns Pancrazio Hill above the old city, with views across to the Sila Mountains. Its origins are lost to memory: It may have been built by the Byzantines or the Saracens, and, before he was ousted by Normans, it was the residence of the Arab caliph Saati Cayti. What is known is that the castle takes its name from the great Swabian emperor Frederick II (1194–1250), who added two octagonal towers. Although extensively restored and open to the public, the castle still shows the considerable damage caused by successive earthquakes and a lightning strike that ignited gunpowder once stored within. ✉ *Via del Castello, Colle Pancrazio, Cosenza* ☎ *0984/1811234* ⊕ *www.castellocosenza.it* 🎟 *€4* ⊘ *Closed Mon.*

Duomo

CHURCH | Cosenza's original Duomo, probably built in the middle of the 11th century, was destroyed by an earthquake in 1184. A new cathedral was consecrated in the presence of Emperor Frederick II in 1222. After many Baroque additions, later alterations have restored some of the Provençal Gothic style. Inside, on the left of the main altar, you'll see the lovely monument to Isabella of Aragon, who died after falling from her horse en route to France in 1271. ✉ *Piazza del Duomo 1, Cosenza* ☎ *0984/77864* ⊘ *Closed daily noon–4:30 in summer, daily noon–3:30 in winter.*

Museo Diocesano di Cosenza

HISTORY MUSEUM | Situated between the archbishop's palace and the Duomo, the museum contains paintings, silverware, vestments, and other precious objects collected by the archbishops of Cosenza over centuries. Look for the filigreed silver cup known as "the Pope," two ivory statuettes attributed to the School of Michelangelo, the 15th-century "Torquemada" chalice, and paintings by Luca Giordano, Andrea Vaccaro, and Giuseppe Pascaletti. The heart of the museum contains the emblem of Cosenza and the city's greatest treasure: a unique reliquary cross dating back to the 13th century, which was donated by

Take a break from sightseeing and enjoy the great outdoors in La Fossiata nature preserve.

Frederick II of Swabia on the occasion of the consecration of the cathedral in 1222. ⊠ *Piazza Aulo Giano Parrasio 16, Cosenza* ☎ *0984/687750* ⊕ *www.museodiocesanocosenza.it* ☎ *Free* ⊘ *Closed Mon.–Sat. 12:30–3, and Sun. (except by appointment).*

🍴 Restaurants

Calabria Bella

$ | **SOUTHERN ITALIAN** | **FAMILY** | Don't let the small, unimposing entrance or the rusticity fool you: the clientele of this family-run restaurant nestled by the steps to the Duomo often includes celebrities. Cuisine is typical of the region, with ingredients like porcini mushrooms from the Sila forests and *strigoli* (bladder-campion seedpods) from nearby fields. **Known for:** generous house antipasto Calabria Bella; excellent, robust cucina calabrese; rustic interior and piazza seating. ⑤ *Average main: €14* ⊠ *Piazza Duomo 20, Cosenza* ☎ *0984/793531* ⊕ *www.ristorantecalabriabella.it.*

★ Hippocampus

$$$ | **SEAFOOD** | Renowned for its simply crafted dishes made with the freshest seasonal catch, Cosenza's best seafood restaurant has (appropriately enough) a minimalist, blue-and-white, nautical-theme interior. Guided by a waiter, you might start with a selection of antipasti to share, followed by a classic pasta allo scoglio and a main *fritto misto di mare* (medley of fried seafood). **Known for:** a chef happy to create vegetarian dishes; unfussy, welcoming vibe; exceptional, super-fresh seafood. ⑤ *Average main: €25* ⊠ *Via Piave 33, Cosenza* ☎ *0984/22103* ⊘ *Closed Mon. No dinner Sun.*

La Trattoria di Vincenzo

$ | **SOUTHERN ITALIAN** | **FAMILY** | This cheerful family-run hostelry a few miles outside Cosenza, in the hamlet of Castiglione Cosentino, offers an authentic Calabrian experience, with dishes highlighting *maialino nero* (local black pork), Podolica beef, truffles, pistachios, and wild mushrooms. In the homey dining room, locals feast enthusiastically—perhaps starting with a wooden board piled with *salumi* and *formaggi*—at tables adorned with brightly checked tablecloths. **Known for:** friendly and family-run; hunks of local black pork and Podolica beef sizzling at your table; Calabrian cured meats and cheeses. $ *Average main: €14* ⊠ *Via Ponte Crati 1, between SP229 and SP234, Castiglione Cosentino* ☎ *340 6211981 Cell* ⊙ *No dinner Sun.*

Hotels

Royal Hotel
$ | **HOTEL** | Like most hotels in Cosenza, the Royal caters mainly to a business clientele, yet it's nevertheless a good choice for a stopover: what it lacks in local flavor, it makes up for with functional whitewashed decor, spacious bathrooms, and reasonable room rates. **Pros:** good customer service; close to pedestrian-only shopping area; free parking. **Cons:** beige '70s time-capsule decor in parts; 20-min walk from centro storico; can be busy during events. $ *Rooms from: €78* ⊠ *Via delle Medaglie d'Oro 1, Cosenza* ☎ *0984/412165* ⊕ *www.hotelroyalcosenza.it* ⤵ *34 rooms* ⦿ *Free Breakfast.*

Camigliatello

30 km (19 miles) east of Cosenza.

Lined with chalets, Camigliatello is one of the Sila Massif's major resort towns. Most of the Sila isn't mountainous at all; rather, it's an extensive, sparsely populated plateau with areas of thick forest. There was, at one point, considerable deforestation, but in 1968 the area received a special designation as the Parco Nazionale della Sila, and strict rules have limited the felling of timber, which has allowed the forests to regenerate. There are well-marked trails through pine and beech woods and ample opportunities for horseback riding. Autumn sees droves of locals hunting mushrooms and gathering chestnuts; winter brings crowds to nearby ski slopes.

GETTING HERE AND AROUND
By car, take the Cosenza Nord exit from the A3 autostrada, then follow the SS107, or if you are following the SS106 along the Ionian Coast, branch off at Sibari and follow the signs.

VISITOR INFORMATION
CONTACT Camigliatello Tourism Office. ⊠ *Via Roma 5, Camigliatello* ☎ *0984/452850* ⊕ *www.prolococamigliatello.it.*

Sights

Il Treno della Sila
TRAIN/TRAIN STATION | **FAMILY** | In spring and summer, this narrow-gauge steam railway takes visitors through stunning countryside from Moccone to San Nicola (at 4,600 feet) via Camigliatello. The journey takes 40–50 minutes and costs €15 online or €17 on the train; check the website for schedules. ⊠ *Via Forgitelle 11, Camigliatello* ☎ *328/2391117* ⊕ *www.trenodellasila.it.*

★ **Parco Nazionale della Sila—La Fossiata**
NATIONAL PARK | Calabria's granite plateau of Sila National Park is a wonderful place for lovers of the wild outdoors. Rising to nearly 7,000 feet at its highest peak, Botte Donato, the park was inaugurated in 2002, with forests, valleys, and rivers home to 175 species of vertebrates, including the park's now protected symbol, *il lupo*, the wolf. A couple of miles east of Campigliatello is Lago Cecita, a good starting point for exploring La Fossiata, a lovely wooded conservation area within the park that has a rich variety of trees, some centuries old. The forestry commission office in nearby Cupone can provide tourist information, maps, and assistance, such as arranging guides. ⊠ *Via Nazionale, Lorica di San Giovanni in Fiore, Camigliatello* ☎ *0984/537109 Forestry Commission Office* ⊕ *www.parcosila.it* ⊙ *Office closed weekends.*

Hotels

Tasso

$ | **HOTEL** | **FAMILY** | On the edge of Camigliatello, less than 1 km (½ mile) from the ski slopes, this hotel is in a peaceful, picturesque location. **Pros:** conveniently located near the ski area; beautiful surroundings; lively evening and family entertainment. **Cons:** scant breakfast choice lacking Calabrese products; nondescript architecture and out-of-date decor; dated bathrooms. ⑤ *Rooms from: €90 ⊠ Via Torquato Tasso, Spezzano della Sila, Camigliatello* ☎ *0984/578113* ⊕ *www.hoteltasso.it* ⌁ *82 rooms* ⍩ *Free Breakfast.*

Crotone

105 km (65 miles) east of Cosenza, 150 km (94 miles) northeast of Locri.

One of the most important Magna Graecia colonies in Italy, Crotone was a major cultural center in the 5th century BC, when it was the home of thinkers like philosopher and mathematician Pythagoras. Sadly, modern development has eclipsed much of its former beauty, but it preserves something of an old-town feel, with its imposing 16th-century castle and an archaeological museum of some importance. Its coastal waters, stretching to Capo Rizzuto, make up Italy's largest protected marine area; and the island Castle Le Castella, 15 km (9 miles) from Crotone, is a vision out of a fairy tale.

GETTING HERE AND AROUND

By car, take the Cosenza Nord exit from the A3 autostrada, then follow the SS107. There are regular trains from Sibari.

VISITOR INFORMATION

CONTACT Crotone Tourism Office. ⊠ *Via Molo Sanità 2, Crotone* ☎ *329/8154963* ⊕ *www.prolocolecastella.it.*

Sights

Museo Archeologico Nazionale

HISTORY MUSEUM | Constructed to house the treasures found at the Sanctuary of Hera Lacinia, as well as many antiquities recovered from the surrounding seabed, the museum is situated in the heart of the old city of Crotone, close to the seafront castle. The most precious part of the collection is the so-called Treasure of Hera, with the goddess's finely wrought gold diadem and belt pendant. You can also see the rare 5th-century-BC bronze *askos* (container for oil) in the form of a mermaid, illegally exported to the United States and subsequently recovered by the Italian government from the Getty Museum in California. ⊠ *Via Risorgimento 121, Crotone* ☎ *0962/23082* ⊕ *musei. calabria.beniculturali.it* ⊗ *Closed Mon.* ⌨ *€4.*

★ Museo e Parco Archeologico Nazionale di Capo Colonna

RUINS | Il Santuario di Hera Lacinia (Sanctuary of Hera Lacinia) was once one of the most important shrines of Magna Graecia. Only one column remains standing, but the site (known as Capo Colonna because of that single pillar) occupies a stunning position on a promontory 11 km (7 miles) south of the town of Crotone. The ruins are part of a vast park, which also contains a well-appointed museum documenting finds from prehistory to the Roman era. The sanctuary itself, which dates from the 7th century BC, is fenced off for safety reasons, but a walkway allows viewing. ⊠ *Via Michele Di Donato, Capo Colonna, Crotone* ☎ *0962/934814* ⊕ *musei.calabria.beniculturali.it* ⌨ *Free* ⊗ *Closed Mon.*

Beaches

★ Capo Rizzuto—Spiagge Rosse

BEACH | FAMILY | If practicalities and time allow, make the short trip toward Capo Rizzuto just down the coast for some of the most fabulous bathing and snorkeling in the region. Among its bays and protected marine reserve waters is Spiagge Rosse, whose orange-red sand beach and crystalline waters make it the most alluring on this stretch of coast. **Amenities:** food and drink; lifeguards; parking (free); showers; toilets. **Best for:** snorkeling; swimming. ⊠ *Contrada Fratte, Capo Rizzuto, Crotone.*

 Hotels

Hotel Helios

$ | HOTEL | On the coastal road between Crotone and Capo Colonna, a little out of town and just 8 km (5 miles) from the Sanctuary of Hera Lacinia, the '70s-style Helios has crystal-clear shores nearby and a fab pool, terrace, restaurant, and snack bar—all on-site. **Pros:** on bus route into town and open year-round; efficient, courteous staff; elevated sea views. **Cons:** skimpy breakfasts; uninspiring architecture; rooms need a refresh. $ *Rooms from: €81* ⊠ *Viale Magna Grecia at Via Makalla 2, Crotone* ☎ *0962/901291* ⊕ *www.helioshotels.it* ⇲ *42 rooms* ⊙ *Free Breakfast.*

Tropea

120 km (75 miles) southwest of Cosenza, 107 km (66 miles) north of Reggio Calabria.

Ringed by cliffs and wonderful sandy beaches, the Tropea Promontory is still just beginning to be discovered by foreign tourists. The main town of Tropea, its old palazzi built in simple golden stone, easily wins the contest for prettiest town on Calabria's Tyrrhenian Coast. On a clear day the seaward views from the waterfront promenade take in Stromboli's cone and at least four of the other Aeolian Islands; you can visit them by motorboat, departing daily in summer. Accommodations are good, and beach addicts won't be disappointed by the choice of magnificent sandy bays within easy reach. The beach beside Santa Maria dell'Isola is said to be one of the Mediterranean's most beautiful, but there are other fine beaches south at Capo Vaticano and north at Briatico.

GETTING HERE AND AROUND

By car, exit the A3 autostrada at Pizzo and follow the southbound SP6/SS522. Eleven trains depart daily from Lamezia Terme.

VISITOR INFORMATION

CONTACT Tropea Tourism Office. ⊠ *Piazza Ercole 19–23, Tropea* ☎ *0963/61475* ⊕ *www.prolocotropea.eu.*

Sights

Cattedrale

CHURCH | In Tropea's beguiling warren of lanes, seek out the old Norman cathedral, whose main altar contains the locally revered icon of the Madonna di Romania, protectress of the city. Also of interest are the imposing 14th-century "Black Crucifix," in one of the side chapels, and the adjoining Museo Diocesano, which contains an archaeological section and a collection of sacred art, including a life-size statue of Santa Domenica in solid silver, dating from 1738. ■TIP→ **November through March, the cathedral is open for church services only, but if you're quiet and respectful, you can probably sneak a peek.** ⊠ *Largo Duomo, Tropea* ☎ *0963/61034* ⊙ *Closed Nov.–Mar., except for services* 🎫 *Cathedral free, Museo Diocesano €2.*

★ Santa Maria dell'Isola

VIEWPOINT | The sanctuary of Santa Maria dell'Isola is the symbol of Tropea, and it is easy to see why. Perched high on a rocky promontory and accessible only by a winding flight of stone steps cut into the cliffside, it dominates the sea view from Piazza Ercole, the main town square. Believed to date from the 4th century AD, it has been rebuilt many times and took its present form in the 18th century, after it was damaged by an earthquake. The inside of the church is unadorned, but visitors can climb up to the roof to admire the splendid view or wander through the pleasant garden set on the rocks behind the building. The beach below the rock has been classed among the 10 most beautiful beaches in Italy. ⊠ *Largo Marina dell'Isola, Tropea* ☎ *347/2541232* 🎫 *Church free, garden €2.*

Beaches

★ Marasusa

BEACH | **FAMILY** | The most famous of Calabria's beaches is backed by sheer cliffs topped by Tropea's stacked buildings—seemingly growing out of the rock. Beyond this popular vacation destination stretch sits the gleaming island promontory sanctuary of Santa Maria dell'Isola. For bathers, snorkelers, and frolickers the light-hued sand is quite-fine underfoot and the greenish-blue waters are wonderful. Adding to the drama is the smoking cone of island volcano Stromboli on the western horizon. **Amenities:** lifeguards; parking (free); showers; toilets. **Best for:** snorkeling; surfing; swimming; windsurfing. ⊠ *Via Lungomare, Tropea.*

🍽 Restaurants

Osteria Antico Androne

$$ | **SOUTHERN ITALIAN** | With intimate tables around the interior courtyard and mezzanine of the 18th-century Palazzo Teotino, this osteria is a truly atmospheric place to dine. The menu is a mix of traditional local dishes and classic southern Italian pasta combinations—with subtle Tropeana twists here and there. **Known for:** meat and vegetarian options; grilled and fried seafood; Calabrese fileja pasta with Tropea onions. ⑤ *Average main: €18* ⊠ *Via Boiano 6, Tropea* ☎ *349/2887969* ⊙ *Closed Mon.*

Pimm's

$$ | **SOUTHERN ITALIAN** | Since the 1960s, this basement restaurant in the historic center has offered Tropea's top seafood dining experience, with such specialties as pasta with monkfish and almond pesto, smoked swordfish and prawns on red Tropea onions, and gnocchi filled with tiny clams and creamed pistachio nuts. The splendid sea views from the rear windows (ask for the *tavolo in nicchia panoramica*) are a surprising—and substantial—reason to head here.

Known for: book a window table for the azure views; excellent fresh seafood; perched high above the beach. $ Average main: €20 ⊠ Largo Migliarese 2, at the foot of Corso Vittorio Emanuele, Tropea ☎ 0963/666105.

Hotels

★ Hotel Rocca della Sena

$$ | HOTEL | Overlooking Tropea's golden sands and azure waters, this intimate, self-styled boutique hotel—with modern, quirky, equatorial-themed rooms—is a reliable option. **Pros:** a terrace with a large whirlpool bath; tranquil location on Tropea's periphery; fab sea views. **Cons:** lack of bar menu options; standard rooms on the cramped and gloomy side; some may find the LED mood lighting and furnishings tacky. $ Rooms from: €199 ⊠ Via Paolo Orsi, Tropea ☎ 0963/62374 ⊕ www.hotelroccadellasena.it ۞ Closed Nov.–early Apr. ❍| Free Breakfast ⇥ 12 rooms.

Reggio Calabria

115 km (71 miles) south of Tropea, 499 km (311 miles) south of Naples.

This raw city is one of Italy's busiest ports, where you can find not only container ships and cranes but also a wonderful *lungomare* (promenade) made for lazy *passeggiatas*. Hydrofoils for Sicily depart from here; vehicle-carrying ferries depart from Villa San Giovanni, 13 km (8 miles) north.

Reggio Calabria is also a great base for visiting *borghi* (historic villages) like the beautiful town of Stilo, which is known for being the birthplace and home of the philosopher Tommaso Campanella (1568–1639), whose magnum opus was the socialistic *La Città del Sole* (*The City of the Sun*, 1602). Stilo is 138 km (86 miles) northeast of Reggio Calabria, along the Ionian coastal road, SS106. Regular trains run from Lamezia Terme.

GETTING HERE AND AROUND

The A3 autostrada runs directly to Reggio Calabria. A dozen direct trains depart from Naples and Rome daily. There are daily flights from Rome, Milan, Turin, Bergamo, and Bologna.

VISITOR INFORMATION

CONTACT I.A.T. Reggio Calabria Tourism Office. ⊠ Stazione Ferroviaria, Via Barlaam da Seminara 1, Reggio Calabria ☎ 0965/27120 ⊕ turismo.reggiocal.it.

Sights

★ Museo Nazionale della Magna Grecia

HISTORY MUSEUM | Reggio Calabria is home to one of southern Italy's most important archaeological museums. Its prize exhibit, of course, is the two ancient Greek statues known as the Bronzi di Riace, which were discovered by an amateur deep-sea diver off Calabria's Ionian Coast in 1972. After a lengthy but necessary conservation effort, these 5th-century-BC statues of two Greek warriors, thought to be the work of either Pheidias or Polykleitos, now take pride of place in their special temperature-controlled room, complete with earthquake-resistant bases. Visitors are allowed to view the bronzes in groups of 20, every 20 minutes. Make sure you have time to head upstairs to see the many other antiquities; there are descriptive panels in English and Italian. ⊠ Piazza de Nava 26, Reggio Calabria ☎ 0965/613988 ⊕ www.museoarcheologicoreggiocalabria.it ⊡ €8 ۞ Closed Mon.

Hotels

★ Hotel Medinblu

$ | HOTEL | The sleek, contemporary guest rooms at this hotel in an imaginatively renovated 1915 palazzo are warmed up a bit by fabrics with bold prints; fabulous public areas include a spacious roof terrace that serves cheeky aperitivi. **Pros:** central location; roof terrace breakfast and seasonal evening concerts; warm, professional customer service. **Cons:** some may find decor lacks character; traffic noise in some rooms; hotel's garage a short walk away. *$ Rooms from: €110 ⊠ Via Demetrio Tripepi 98, Reggio Calabria* ☎ *0965/312982 ⊕ www.hotelmedinblu. com ⇨ 33 rooms ⧉ Free Breakfast.*

SICILY

Updated by
Fergal Kavanagh

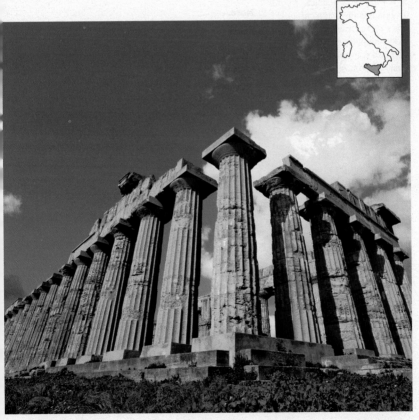

⦿ Sights	🍴 Restaurants	🛏 Hotels	🛍 Shopping	🍸 Nightlife
★★★★☆	★★★★★	★★★★☆	★★☆☆☆	★★☆☆☆

WELCOME TO SICILY

TOP REASONS TO GO

★ **Taormina, Sicily's most beautiful resort:** The view of the sea and Mt. Etna from its jagged cactus-covered cliffs is as close to perfection as a panorama can get.

★ **A walk on Siracusa's Ortygia Island:** Classical ruins rub elbows with faded seaside palaces and fish markets in Sicily's most striking port city, where the Duomo is literally built atop an ancient Greek temple.

★ **Palermo's palaces, churches, and crypts:** Virtually every great European empire ruled Sicily's strategically positioned capital at some point, and it shows most of all in the diverse architecture, from Roman to Byzantine to Arab-Norman.

★ **Valley of the Temples, Agrigento:** This stunning set of ruins is proudly perched above the sea in a grove full of almond trees; not even in Athens will you find Greek temples this finely preserved.

1 **Messina.**

2 **Taormina.**

3 **Castelmola.**

4 **Mt. Etna.**

5 **Acireale.**

6 **Catania.**

7 **Siracusa.**

8 **Ortygia.**

9 **Noto.**

10 **Scicli.**

11 **Modica.**

12 **Ragusa.**

13 **Caltagirone.**

14 **Piazza Armerina.**

15 **Enna.**

16 **Agrigento.**

17 **Selinunte.**

18 **Marsala.**

19 **Erice.**

20 **Segesta.**

21 **Monreale.**

22 **Palermo.**

23 **Cefalù.**

24 **Lipari.**

25 **Salina.**

26 **Panarea.**

27 **Stromboli.**

28 **Filicudi.**

Stromboli

Panarea

Salina

Filicudi

Alicudi

Lipari

AEOLIAN IS.

Vulcano

Villa San Giovanni

Mare Tirreno

Milazzo

Capo d'Orlando

Messina

Barcellona Pozzo di Gotto

Reggio di Calabria

Palermo

Bagheria

Cefalù

TYRRHENIAN COAST

116

Randazzo

Castelmola

Taormina

Termini Imerese

Mt. Etna 3,323m

Adrano

Paternò

Acireale

Mare Ionio

Enna

Catania

Caltanissetta

Piazza Armerina

Lentini

Canicattì

Augusta

grigento

Caltagirone

Siracusa

Ortygia

Licata

Gela

Vittoria

Ragusa

Modica

Noto

diterráneo

Scicli

Pachino

A20

A19

189

A20

23

A19

284

120

3

A18

2

4

5

6

15

640

14

417

194

13

626

123

16

115

115

124

12

11

10

9

8

7

Mare Mediterráneo

EATING AND DRINKING WELL IN SICILY

Sicilian cuisine is one of the oldest in existence, with records of cooking competitions dating to 600 BC. Food in Sicily today reflects the island's unique cultural mix, imaginatively combining fish, fruits, vegetables, and nuts with Italian pastas and Arab and North African elements—couscous is a staple in Palermo.

It's hard to eat badly here. From the lowliest of *trattorias* to the most highfalutin *ristorante*, you'll find classic dishes that have long been staples of the family dinner table—basically pasta and seafood. In more formal restaurants, you'll find greater attention to detail and a more sophisticated atmosphere, while less pretentious trattorias tend to be family-run affairs, often without so much as a menu to guide you. There's also a new wave of creative restaurants that have come up with interesting versions of old standbys, using local and often organic ingredients and changing their menus with the season. No matter where you choose to eat in the most gregarious of regions in the most convivial of countries, you can expect a lively dining experience.

SICILIAN MARKETS

Sicily's natural fecundity is evident wherever you look, from the prickly pears sprouting on roadsides, to the slopes of vineyards and citrus groves covering the interior, to the ranks of fishing boats moored in every harbor. You can come face-to-face with this bounty in the clamorous street markets of Palermo and Catania. Here, you'll encounter teetering piles of olives and oranges, enticing displays of cheeses and meats, plus pastries and sweets of every description.

WINES

The earthy *nero d'avola* grape bolsters many of Sicily's traditionally sunny, expansive reds, and it's often softened with fruity, bright *frappato* to make Sicily's only DOCG wine, Cerasuolo di Vittoria. Red wines from around Mt. Etna that use the grapes *nerello mascalese* and *nerello cappuccio* have also gained renown. Sicily produces crisp white varieties, too, such as *carricante, catarratto bianco, inzolia,* and *grillo.* When it comes to sweet accompaniments, the small island of Pantelleria produces the smooth *passito* dessert wine, made from *zibibbo* grapes, while the Aeolian Islands are known for Malvasia delle Lipari.

DELICIOUS FISH

Pasta *con le sarde*, with fresh sardines, olive oil, raisins, pine nuts, and wild fennel gets a different treatment at every restaurant. Grilled *tonno* (tuna) and *orata* (dorado) are coastal staples, while delicate *ricci* (sea urchins) are a specialty. King, however, is *pesce spada* (swordfish), best enjoyed *marinato* (marinated), *affumicato* (smoked), or as the traditional *involtini di pesce spada* (roulades).

LOCAL SPECIALTIES

In Catania, you'll be offered *caserecci alla Norma* (a short pasta with a sauce

of tomato, eggplant, salted ricotta, and basil). The *mandorla* (bitter almond), the pride of Agrigento, plays into everything from risotto *alle mandorle* (with almonds, butter, Grana cheese, and parsley) to incomparable almond granita—an absolute must in summer. Pistachios (pronounced *pistakkio*) produced around Bronte, on the lower slopes of Etna, go into pasta sauces as well as ice cream and granita, while capers from the Aeolian Islands add zest to salads and fish sauces.

SNACKS

Two favorite Sicilian snacks are *arancini* ("little oranges," or rice croquettes with a cheese or meat filling), and *panelle* (seasoned chickpea flour boiled to a paste, cooled, sliced, and fried). Other tidbits to look out for include special foods associated with festivals, such as the ominously named *ossa dei morti* ("bones of the dead," or rolled almond cookies). But the most eye-catching of all are the *frutta martorana*: sweet marzipan confections shaped to resemble fruits and temptingly arrayed in bars and *pasticcerie* (pastry shops). The Baroque town of Modica is famous for its chocolate, produced using an Aztec recipe.

The island of Sicily has an abundance of history. Some of the world's best-preserved Byzantine mosaics stand adjacent to magnificent Greek temples and Roman amphitheaters. Add the spectacular sight of Mt. Etna plus Sicily's unique cuisine—mingling Arab and Greek spices, Spanish and French techniques—and you understand why visitors continue to be drawn here.

Sicily has beckoned seafaring wanderers since the trials of Odysseus were first sung in Homer's *Odyssey*—an epic that is sometimes called the world's first travel guide. Strategically poised between Europe and Africa, this mystical land of three corners and a fiery volcano once hosted two of the most enlightened capitals of the West: Siracusa and Palermo. And it has been a melting pot of every great civilization on the Mediterranean—Greek and Roman, then Arab and Norman, and finally French, Spanish, and Italian. Invaders through the ages weren't just attracted by its strategic location, however; they recognized a paradise in Sicily's deep blue skies and temperate climate, in its lush vegetation and rich marine life—all of which prevail to this day.

In modern times, the traditional graciousness and nobility of the Sicilian people have survived alongside the destructive influences of the Mafia under Sicily's semiautonomous government. The island has more recently emerged as something of an international travel hot spot, drawing increasing numbers of visitors. Brits and Germans flock in ever-growing numbers to Agrigento and Siracusa, and in high season Chinese and American tour groups seem to outnumber the locals in Taormina and the Baroque hill towns. And yet, in Sicily's windswept heartland, vineyards, olive groves, and lovingly kept dirt roads leading to family farmhouses still tie Sicilians to the land and to tradition, forming a happy connectedness that can't be defined by economic measures.

MAJOR REGIONS

On Sicily's northeastern corner, lively and chaotic Messina commands an unparalleled position across from Calabria. Halfway down the coast, Catania has a gritty, vivacious charm and is a good base for exploring lofty Mt. Etna, unless you opt to stay at one of the cozy boutique hotels that have sprouted on the slopes of the volcano. The sparkling seaside of Taormina, unparalleled views from lofty Castelmola, and festive carnival floats of Acireale can all be explored nearby. To the south, the marvelous ruins of Siracusa await, combined with the seaside allure of the tiny island of Ortygia.

Sicily's pretty interior has grand architecture and unspoiled vistas—in particular, the UNESCO World Heritage–listed Baroque towns of Ragusa, Modica, Noto, Scicli, and Caltagirone. The Imperial Roman Villa outside Piazza Armerina is a showstopper, while the mountaintop city of Enna is shrouded in ancient mystery.

The crowning glory of western Sicily is the concentration of Greek temples at Agrigento, but the mark of ancient Greek culture also lingers in the cluster of ruined cliffside temples at Selinunte and at the splendidly isolated site of Segesta. The coastal town of Marsala offers tantalizing historical artifacts as well as its eponymous wine, while the cobblestone streets of hilltop Erice retain a strong medieval complexion. Palermo's crumbling splendor, tucked-away museums, and lively markets create an almost irresistible pull toward the Sicilian capital, and nearby Monreale's cathedral glitters with some of the finest mosaics in Italy.

Sicily's northern shore, the Tyrrhenian Coast, is mostly a succession of small holiday towns, but the biggest attraction is the old town of Cefalù, with one of the island's most remarkable cathedrals.

Off Sicily's northeast coast lies an archipelago of seven spectacular islands of volcanic origin. The Aeolian Islands (Isole Eolie), also known as the Lipari Islands (Isole Lipari), tempt with superb snorkeling in the clearest and cleanest of Italy's waters and challenging treks along rocky paths. Lipari is the largest of them and provides the widest range of lodging, so it's a good jumping-off point for day trips to the others. Most exclusive are Vulcano and Panarea: the former is noted for black-sand beaches and stupendous sunsets, as well as for the acrid smell of sulfur, whereas the latter is, according to some, the prettiest of the islands. Most remarkable is Stromboli, with its constant eruptions, while the greenest island—and the one with the best hiking—is Salina. The farthest are Filicudi and Alicudi, where electricity was introduced only in the 1980s.

Planning

Making the Most of Your Time

You should plan a visit to Sicily around Taormina, Siracusa, Agrigento, and Palermo—four don't-miss destinations. The best way to see them all is to travel in a circle. Start your circuit in the northeast in Taormina, worth at least a night or two. If you have time, stay also in Catania, a lively, fascinating city that's often overlooked. From there, connect to the Catania–Ragusa toll-free A18 autostrada and head toward the spectacular ancient Greek port of Siracusa, which merits at least two nights. If you have a couple more days, Siracusa makes a good base for visiting the Baroque towns of Noto, Ragusa, and Modica.

Next, backtrack north on the same highway, and take the A19 autostrada toward Palermo. Piazza Armerina's impressive mosaics and Enna, a sleepy mountaintop city, are worthwhile stops in the interior. Take the SS640 to the Greek temples of Agrigento. Stay here for a night before driving west along the coastal SS115, checking out Selinunte's ruins before reaching magical Erice, a good base for one night. You're now near some of Sicily's best beaches at San Vito Lo Capo.

Take the A29 to Palermo, the chaotic and wonderful capital city, to wrap up your Sicilian experience. Give yourself at least two days here—ideally, four or five. Or, if it's the warm season, consider heading east toward Milazzo and sailing to one of the lovely Aeolian Islands for a few days of leisure.

Getting Here and Around

BUS

Air-conditioned buses connect major and minor cities and are often faster and more convenient than local trains—still single track on many stretches—but also slightly more expensive. Various companies serve the different routes. SAIS runs frequently between Palermo and Catania, Messina, and other cities, in each case arriving at and departing from near the train stations.

BUS CONTACTS Cuffaro. ☎ *091/6161510* ⊕ *www.cuffaro.info.* **SAIS.** ☎ *800/211020 toll-free* ⊕ *www.saisautolinee.it.*

CAR

This is the ideal way to explore Sicily. Modern highways circle and bisect the island, making all main cities easily reachable. The E90 autostrada connects Messina and Palermo; Messina, Taormina, and Catania are linked by the A18; running through the interior, from Catania to west of Cefalù, is the A19; threading west from Palermo, the A29/E933 runs to Trapani, with a leg stretching down to Mazara del Vallo. In general, the south side of the island is less well served, though stretches of the SS115 west of Agrigento are relatively fast and traffic-free.

You'll likely hear stories about the dangers of driving in Sicily. In the big cities—especially Palermo, Catania, and Messina—streets can be a honking mess, with lane markings and stop signs taken as mere suggestions; you can avoid the chaos by driving through at off-peak times or on weekends. However, once outside the urban areas and resort towns, most of the highways and regional state roads are a driving enthusiast's dream—they're winding, sparsely populated, and reasonably well maintained, with striking new views around many bends. Obviously, don't leave valuables in your car, and make sure baggage is stowed out of sight, if possible.

TRAIN

There are direct express trains from Rome to Palermo, Catania, and Siracusa. The Rome–Palermo and Rome–Siracusa trips take at least 11 hours. After Naples, the run is mostly along the coast, so try to book a window seat on the right if you're not on an overnight train. At Villa San Giovanni, in Calabria, the train is separated and loaded onto a ferryboat to cross the strait to Messina—a favorite for kids.

There are no high-speed lines within Sicily, but main lines connect Messina, Taormina, Siracusa, Catania, and Palermo. The Messina–Palermo run, along the northern coast, is especially scenic. Secondary lines are generally very slow and unreliable. For schedules, check the website of the Italian state railway, Trenitalia.

TRAIN CONTACT Trenitalia. ☎ *892021 in Italy, 06/68475475 outside Italy* ⊕ *www. trenitalia.com.*

Restaurants

As befits a major city, Palermo has a huge selection of interesting and varied restaurants, while Catania is best known for its high-quality seafood. In the tourist-heavy coastal towns, dining can be hit or miss, while inland there has been a mini-explosion of new-wave gourmet restaurants in the Baroque towns of Ragusa, Modica, and especially Noto, as well as some intriguing options popping up on Mt. Etna. If you're staying in the countryside, country hotels and wineries are your best bets for a good meal.

Restaurant reviews have been shortened. For full information, visit Fodors.com.

Hotels

High-quality hotels tend to be confined to the major cities and resorts of Palermo, Catania, Taormina, Siracusa, Noto, and Agrigento, along with the odd beach resort. There are also numerous *agriturismo* lodgings (rural bed-and-breakfasts and country inns), some quite basic but others extremely luxe. These country houses usually also offer all-inclusive, full-board plans that can make for some of Sicily's most memorable meals.

Hotel reviews have been shortened. For full information, visit Fodors.com.

WHAT IT COSTS in Euros

	$	$$	$$$	$$$$
RESTAURANTS				
	under €15	€15–€24	€25–€35	over €35
HOTELS				
	under €125	€125–€200	€201–€300	over €300

Messina

8 km (5 miles) by ferry from Villa San Giovanni, 94 km (59 miles) northeast of Catania, 237 km (149 miles) east of Palermo.

Messina's ancient history recounts a series of disasters, but the city once vied with Palermo in a bid to become the capital, developing a fine university, a bustling commercial center, and a thriving cultural environment. At 5:20 am on December 28, 1908, Messina was reduced from a flourishing metropolis of 120,000 to a heap of rubble, shaken to pieces by an earthquake that turned into a tidal wave; 80,000 people died as a result, and the city was almost completely leveled. As you approach by ferry, you won't notice any outward indication of the disaster, except for the modern countenance of

a 3,000-year-old city. The somewhat flat look is a precaution of seismic planning: tall buildings are not permitted.

GETTING HERE AND AROUND

Frequent hydrofoils and ferries carry passengers and trains across the Strait of Messina from Villa San Giovanni, from just below the train station. There are also regular departures for foot passengers from Reggio Calabria. Cruise ships also stop in Messina's port.

VISITOR INFORMATION

CONTACT Messina Tourism Office. ✉ *Via dei Mille 270* ☎ *090/77611672* ⊕ *turismoecultura.cittametropolitana.me.it.*

 ## Sights

Duomo

CHURCH | The reconstruction of Messina's Norman and Romanesque cathedral, originally built by the Norman king Roger II and consecrated in 1197, has retained much of the original plan—including a handsome crown of Norman battlements, an enormous apse, and a splendid wood-beamed ceiling. The adjoining bell tower contains one of the largest and most complex mechanical clocks in the world: constructed in 1933, it has a host of gilded automatons (a roaring lion and crowing rooster among them) that spring into action every day at the stroke of noon. ✉ *Piazza del Duomo 29, Messina* ☎ *090/66841* ⊕ *www.diocesimessina.it* ⊘ *Closed daily 1–4.*

Museo Regionale di Messina

ART MUSEUM | One of Italy's most celebrated Renaissance painters, Caravaggio spent a good deal of time in Sicily toward the end of his life, while on the run after committing murder in Rome, and artworks he left behind him include two on display at this regional museum. The scandal-prone artist is best known for his religious works, which utilize dramatic shadows and heavenly lighting. The two here are the highlight of the collection, though there are also some interesting

Eastern Sicily,
the Tyrrhenian Coast,
and the Aeolian Islands

TO NAPLES

TO NAPLES

TO TROPEA

Stromboli

A E O L I A N   I S L A N D S

ALICUDI   **Filicudi**

Panarea

Salina

Lipari

Vulcano

T y r r h e n i a n

S e a

Golfo di Milazzo

Milazzo

Villa San Giovanni

CAPO D'ORLANDO

St Agata di Militello

113

A20

Patti

113

Messina

Cefalù

A20

Caldura

T Y R R H E N I A N   C O A S T

113

116

185

A18

114

106

Reggio di Calabria

Pizzo Carbonara

117

Randazzo

Castelmola

Taormina

120

120

Bronte

Linguaglossa

Giardini-Naxos

Nicosia

Mt. Etna

Milo

Riposto

A19

121

Adrano

Barone di Villagrande

Giarre

Zafferana Etnea

Trecastagni

Santa Maria La Scala

Enna

192

Biancavilla

Nicolosi

Acireale

Paternò

Aci Castello

Caltanisetta

A19

Aci Trezza

Villa Romana del Casale (Imperial Roman Villa)

191

288

Catania

Golfo di Catania

Casale

Piazza Armerina

117b

Agnone

626

Mazzarino

417

Palagonia

385

124

Caltagirone

194

Lentini

Augusta

Vizzini

Euryalus

Gela

Palazzolo Acreide

194

124

A18

115

Golfo di Gela

Vittoria

Ragusa

Siracusa with Ortigia Island see detail map

Comiso

Modica

Noto

Avola

115

Scicli

19

Golfo di Noto

E45

TO MALTA

Pachino

CAPO PASSERO

I o n i a n   S e a

0   20 mi

0   20 km

KEY

🚂 *Ferry lines*

⛷ *Ski Area*

archaeological pieces salvaged from shipwrecks and several works by Antonello da Messina. ⊠ *Viale della Libertà, 465, Messina* ☏ *090/361292* ⊕ *www.mume.in* ⊠ *€8* ⊘ *Closed Sun. morning and Mon.*

Taormina

43 km (27 miles) southwest of Messina.

The view of the sea and Mt. Etna from Taormina's jagged, cactus-covered cliffs is as close to perfection as a panorama can get—especially on clear days, when the snowcapped volcano's white puffs of smoke rise against the blue sky. Even when overrun with tourists, its natural beauty is hard to dispute. Writers have extolled Taormina's charms almost since it was founded in the 6th century BC by Greeks from nearby Naxos; Goethe and D. H. Lawrence were among its well-known enthusiasts. The town's boutique-lined main streets get old pretty quickly, but the many hiking paths that wind through the beautiful hills surrounding Taormina promise a timeless alternative. A trip up to stunning Castelmola (whether on foot or by car) should also be on your itinerary.

GETTING HERE AND AROUND

Buses from Messina or Catania arrive near the center of Taormina, while trains from these towns pull in at the station at the bottom of the hill. Local buses bring you the rest of the way. A cable car takes passengers up the hill from a parking lot about 2 km (1 mile) north of the train station.

VISITOR INFORMATION

CONTACT Taormina Tourism Office.
⊠ *Palazzo Corvaja, Piazza Santa Caterina* ☏ *0942/23243* ⊕ *www.comune.taormina. me.it.*

Sights

Castello Saraceno

MILITARY SIGHT | An unrelenting 20-minute walk up the Via Crucis footpath takes you to the church of the Madonna della Rocca, hollowed out of the limestone rock. Above it towers the 1,000-year-old stone walls of Castello Saraceno, which is built on the site of earlier Greek and Roman fortifications. Although the gate to the castle has been locked for decades, it's worth the climb just for the panoramic views. ⊠ *Monte Tauro, Taormina.*

Funivia

OTHER ATTRACTION | Taormina Mare is accessible by a *funivia,* or suspended cable car, that glides past incredible views on its way down to the beach at Mazzarò. It departs every 15 minutes, until 8 pm. In June, July, and August, the normal hours are extended until 1 am. ⊠ *Via L. Pirandello, downhill from town center toward bus station, Taormina* ☏ *0942/23906* ⊠ *€3 one-way, €10 day-ticket.*

Palazzo Corvaja

NOTABLE BUILDING | Many of Taormina's 14th- and 15th-century palaces have been carefully preserved. Especially beautiful is the Palazzo Corvaja, with characteristic black-lava and white-limestone inlays. Today it houses the tourist office and a museum dedicated to Sicilian art and traditions. ⊠ *Largo Santa Caterina, Taormina* ☏ *0942/620198.*

Teatro Greco

RUINS | The Greeks put a premium on finding impressive locations to stage their dramas, such as Taormina's hillside Teatro Greco. Beyond the columns, you can see the town's rooftops spilling down the hillside, the arc of the coastline, and Mt. Etna in the distance. The theater was built during the 3rd century BC and rebuilt by the Romans during the 2nd century AD. Its acoustics are exceptional: even today a stage whisper can be heard in the last rows. In summer, many music and dance performances are held in the Teatro Greco after sunset, when the marvelous vistas of the sparkling Ionian Sea are shrouded in darkness, but the glow of Sicily's most famous volcano can sometimes be seen in the distance. ✉ *Via Teatro Greco, Taormina* ☎ *0942/23220* ⊕ *www.parconaxostaormina.com* ✉ *€10.*

★ Villa Comunale

GARDEN | Stroll down Via Bagnoli Croce from the main Corso Umberto to the Villa Comunale to enjoy the stunning views from the seaside city's best terrace walkways. Also known as the Parco Duca di Cesarò, the lovely public gardens were designed by Florence Trevelyan Cacciola, a Scottish lady "invited" to leave England following a romantic liaison with the future Edward VII (1841–1910). Arriving in Taormina in 1889, she married a local professor and devoted herself to the gardens, filling them with native Mediterranean and exotic plants, ornamental pavilions, and fountains. ✉ *Via Bagnoli Croce, Taormina.*

 Beaches

Taormina Mare

BEACH | Below the main city of Taormina is Taormina Mare, where summertime beachgoers jostle for space on a pebble beach against the scenic backdrop of the aptly named Isolabella. The first section of beach is reserved for expensive resorts but the far end, next to Isolabella, has a large free area. The tiny "beautiful island" of Isolabella was once a private residence, but is now a nature preserve reached by walking along a narrow rocky path and visited for a small fee of €4. **Amenities:** none. **Best for:** walking. ✉ *Taormina* ⊕ *www.parconaxostaormina.com* ✉ *€4 for Isola Bella.*

🍴 Restaurants

Bella Blu

$ | SICILIAN | FAMILY | If you fancy a meal with a view but don't want to spend a lot, this casual and convivial seafood and pizza restaurant caters to an international crowd with multilingual staff and decent prices. Try the spaghetti with fresh clams and mussels or the pizza alla Norma (with ricotta, eggplant, and tomatoes) while you watch the funivia fly up and down from the beach, with the coastline in the distance. **Known for:** moderate prices; lovely views of the funivia and coast; tasty pizza. ⑤ *Average main: €14* ✉ *Via Pirandello 28, Taormina* ☎ *0942/24239* ⊕ *www.bellablutaormina.com* ☾ *Closed Jan.–Mar.*

L'Arco dei Cappuccini

$$ | SEAFOOD | Just off Via Costantino Patricio, by the far side of the Cappuccini arch, lies this diminutive restaurant. Outdoor seating and an upstairs kitchen help make room for a few extra tables—a necessity, as locals are well aware that neither the price nor the quality is equaled elsewhere in town. **Known for:** a great wine list; fine inexpensive dining; authentic local cooking. ⑤ *Average main: €16* ✉ *Via Cappuccini 7, off Via Costantino Patricio, Taormina* ☎ *392/2442484* ⊕ *www.ristorantearcodeicappuccini.com* ☾ *Closed Feb.*

Osteria RossoDiVino

$$ | SICILIAN | Run by two sisters, this intimate restaurant in a cobblestone courtyard just before the old city gate is one of the friendliest in town, with creative daily menus highlighting homemade pastas, seasonal produce from the market, and freshly caught fish; seating is primarily outdoors on the patio (bug spray is provided, if mosquitoes become an issue). As the name suggests, wine is a specialty, so let them recommend a glass or bottle. **Known for:** delicious modern Sicilian food; daily-changing menus; excellent wine choices. ⑤ *Average main: €18* ✉ *Vico de Spuches 8, Taormina* ☎ *0942/628653* ☾ *Closed Jan.–Feb and Tues.*

Coffee and Quick Bites

Pasticceria Etna

$ | BAKERY | Fans of marzipan will delight at the range of almond sweets on offer here in the shape of the ubiquitous *fico d'India* (prickly pear) and other fruit. A bock of almond paste makes a good souvenir—you can bring it home to make an almond latte or granita. **Known for:** homemade granita; almond sweets; fresh cannoli. ⑤ *Average main: €2* ⊠ *Corso Umberto I 112, Taormina* ☎ *0942/24735* ⊕ *www.pasticceriaetna.com.*

🛏 Hotels

★ Belmond Grand Hotel Timeo

$$$$ | HOTEL | On a princely perch overlooking the town, the Greek theater, and the bay, this truly grand hotel, Taormina's oldest, wears a graceful patina that suggests la dolce vita, with a splash of Baroque and a dash of Mediterranean design in the lobby, which has tile- and brickwork walls and vaulted ceilings. **Pros:** exemplary service; feeling of indulgence; amazing location with fantastic views. **Cons:** some parts of the hotel look a tad worn; very expensive; spa is on the small side. ⑤ *Rooms from: €736* ⊠ *Via Teatro Greco 59, Taormina* ☎ *0942/6270200* ⊕ *www.belmond.com/grand-hotel-timeo-taormina* ⊘ *Closed mid-Nov.–late Mar.* ⇥ *70 rooms* ⦿ *Free Breakfast.*

★ Belmond Villa Sant'Andrea

$$$$ | HOTEL | FAMILY | In a prime location on its own private beach at Taormina Mare, this elegant hotel in a late-1800s villa offers phenomenal views of the water, attentive service, and luxurious and comfortable guest rooms. **Pros:** Kids' Club from May to October; glorious private beach; flawless service. **Cons:** not so convenient for dining in Taormina town; limited on-site parking; pricey food and drinks. ⑤ *Rooms from: €802* ⊠ *Via Nazionale 137, Taormina* ☎ *0942/6271200* ⊕ *www.belmond.com/villa-sant-andrea-taormina-mare* ⊘ *Closed Nov.–mid-Apr.* ⇥ *71 rooms* ⦿ *Free Breakfast.*

Hotel Metropole Taormina

$$$$ | HOTEL | This trendy boutique hotel boasts a prime location, with the main shopping street of Corso Umberto on one side and sea views on the other. **Pros:** jazz shows a nice touch; amazing views from restaurant and pool; lovely spa and public areas. **Cons:** not all rooms have good views; expensive overall, with high prices particularly in the bar; bathrooms can be small and dark. ⑤ *Rooms from: €405* ⊠ *Corso Umberto 154, Taormina* ☎ *0942/24013* ⊕ *www.hotelmetropoletaormina.it* ⇥ *23 rooms* ⦿ *Free Breakfast* ⊘ *Closed Jan.–Mar.*

Hotel Villa Carlotta

$$$ | HOTEL | This small luxury hotel, in a former noble home a short walk from the center of town, has contemporary accommodations with calming neutral tones and a seamless mix of modern and period furniture, but the true allure of the property is in its incredible rooftop terrace and the attentive staff. **Pros:** relaxing pool and garden area; most rooms have sea views; fabulous breakfast on beautiful rooftop terrace. **Cons:** some rooms are a bit dark; not all rooms have balconies; no free parking. ⑤ *Rooms from: €290* ⊠ *Via Luigi Pirandello 81, Taormina* ☎ *0942/626058* ⊕ *www.hotelvillacarlottataormina.com* ⊘ *Closed mid-Nov.–mid-Mar.* ⇥ *29 rooms* ⦿ *No Meals.*

Hotel Villa Paradiso

$$$ | HOTEL | On the edge of the historic center, overlooking lovely public gardens and facing the sea, this under-the-radar family-run hotel was renovated in 2021 but maintains its antique furnishings, paintings, and Persian rugs, as well as its delightful service, good rooftop restaurant, and Etna views from many guest rooms. **Pros:** great rooftop views; good value; free 55 minutes of play time daily at tennis courts. **Cons:** only three free parking spaces (paid parking nearby);

not all rooms have views; the beach club fee is extra. $ *Rooms from: €259* ✉ *Via Roma 2, Taormina* ☎ *0942/23921* ⊕ *www.hotelvillaparadisotaormina.com* 🛏 *37 rooms* ❁ *Free Breakfast.*

Villa Ducale

$$$$ | **HOTEL** | The former summer residence of a local aristocrat has been converted into a luxurious hotel in which each individually styled guest room is furnished with antiques and has a balcony with a view, and the public spaces include an intimate wood-paneled library. **Pros:** away from the hubbub; personalized service; camera-ready views. **Cons:** some rooms are a bit dark; the restaurant menu can be limited; a 10- to 15-minute walk to the center of Taormina. $ *Rooms from: €320* ✉ *Via Leonardo da Vinci 60, Taormina* ☎ *0942/28153* ⊕ *www.villaducale.com* ☾ *Closed mid-Nov.–Mar.* 🛏 *17 rooms* ❁ *Free Breakfast.*

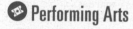 Performing Arts

Taormina Arte

ARTS FESTIVALS | The Teatro Greco and the Palazzo dei Congressi, near the entrance to the theater, are the main venues for the summer festival dubbed TaoArte, held each year between June and August. Performances encompass classical music, ballet, and theater. ✉ *Taormina* ☎ *391/7462146* ⊕ *www.taoarte.it.*

Castelmola

5 km (3 miles) west of Taormina.

Although many believe that Taormina has the most spectacular views, tiny Castelmola—floating 1,800 feet above sea level—takes the word "scenic" to a whole new level. Along the cobblestone streets within the ancient walls, 360-degree panoramas of mountain, sea, and sky are so ubiquitous that you almost get used to them (but not quite). Collect yourself with a sip of the sweet almond wine (best

En Route

The 50-km (30-mile) stretch of road between Taormina and Messina is flanked by lush vegetation and seascapes. Inlets are punctuated by gigantic, oddly shaped rocks.

served cold) made in local bars, or with lunch at one of the humble pizzerias or panino shops.

A 10-minute drive on a winding but well-paved road leads from Taormina to Castelmola; you must park in one of the public lots below the village and walk up to the center, only a few minutes away. On a nice day, hikers are in for a treat if they make the trip from Taormina on foot instead. It's a serious uphill climb, but the 1½-km (¾-mile) path offers breathtaking views, which compensate for the somewhat poor maintenance of the path itself. You'll begin at Porta Catania in Taormina, with a walk along Via Apollo Arcageta past the Chiesa di San Francesco di Paola on the left. The Strada Comunale della Chiusa then leads past Piazza Andromaco, revealing good views of the jagged promontory of Cocolonazzo di Mola to the north. Allow around an hour for the ascent, a half hour for the descent. There's another, slightly longer (2-km [1-mile]) path that heads up from Porta Messina past the Roman aqueduct, Convento dei Cappuccini, and the northeastern side of Monte Tauro. You could take one up and the other down. In any case, avoid the midday sun, wear comfortable shoes, and carry plenty of water with you.

GETTING HERE AND AROUND

Regular buses bound for Castelmola leave from Taormina's bus station on Via Pirandello.

Sights

★ Castello Normanno

RUINS | In all of Sicily there may be no spot more scenic than atop Castello Normanno, reached by a set of steep staircases rising out of the town center. From here you can gaze upon two coastlines, smoking Mt. Etna, and the town spilling down the mountainside. The area was fortified by the Byzantines in the 9th century and was later rebuilt by the Normans, but all that stands today are the remains of the 16th-century castle walls. Come during daylight hours to take full advantage of the vista. ⊠ *Castelmola.*

Restaurants

Il Vicolo

$ | **SICILIAN** | Located on a side street, this trattoria is one of the simpler dining choices in town, and also one of the better ones—what it lacks in views it makes up for with a pleasant rustic ambience plus a great selection of handmade pasta and, in the evening, *forno a legna* (from a wood-fired oven). (In winter, pizzas are served weekends only.) **Known for:** signature squid ragù; cozy environs; pasta and pizza. ⑤ *Average main: €12* ⊠ *Via Pio IX 26, Castelmola* ☎ *0942/28481, 331/9094077* ⊗ *Closed Tues. Sept.–June and 2 wks late Jan.–early Feb.*

Hotels

Villa Sonia

$$ | **HOTEL** | Many guest rooms at this well-situated hotel have private terraces with gorgeous grab-the-camera views of Etna without the crowds (or high prices) of nearby Taormina. **Pros:** friendly service; bus stop to Taormina outside door; on-site sauna and pool. **Cons:** not much to do in the evening; some rooms are quite small; iffy Wi-Fi. ⑤ *Rooms from: €139* ⊠ *Via Porta Mola 9, Castelmola* ☎ *0942/28082* ⊕ *www.hotelvillasonia. com* ⊗ *Closed Nov.–Dec. 20 and Jan. 8– mid-Mar* ➭ *44 rooms* ⦿ *Free Breakfast.*

Nightlife

Antico Caffè San Giorgio

BARS | This knickknack-filled bar has lorded over Castelmola's town square since 1907, and if you manage to resist the pull of the enchanting view on the terrace, you can explore the historic interior to learn more about the village's past. Try the *vino alle mandorle* (almond wine) from a recipe produced by the original owner more than a century ago, then follow luminaries such as Guglielmo Marconi, Winston Churchill, John D. Rockefeller, and John Steinbeck by signing the visitors' book. ⊠ *Piazza Sant'Antonino, Castelmola* ☎ *0942/28228* ⊕ *www.barsangiorgio.com.*

Bar Turrisi

BARS | Truly one of the most infamous places to have a drink in all of Italy, this humorous bar has cozy nooks and crannies on three levels—all decked out with phallus images of every size, shape, and color imaginable, from bathroom wall murals inspired by the brothels of ancient Greece to giant wooden carvings honoring Dionysus. If you can get past the design choices, the roof terrace has extraordinary views of Taormina and the coast, while a limited selection of hearty pasta dishes are served inside. ⊠ *Piazza del Duomo 19, Castelmola* ☎ *0942/28181* ⊕ *www.turrisibar.it.*

Mt. Etna

64 km (40 miles) southwest of Taormina, 30 km (19 miles) north of Catania.

The first time you see Mt. Etna, whether it's trailing clouds of smoke or emitting fiery streaks of lava, is certain to be unforgettable. The best-known symbol of Sicily and one of the world's major active volcanoes, Etna is the largest and highest volcano in Europe—the cone of the crater rises 10,902 feet above sea level. Although you'll get wonderful vantage points of Etna from Taormina, Castelmola, and Catania in particular, it also makes a rewarding day or overnight trip to see the mountain up close, with a hike or climb; you can find routes suitable for every fitness level. It's also become a popular destination for wine lovers thanks to the many boutique wineries on its slopes; most accept visitors with an appointment.

GETTING HERE AND AROUND

Reaching the lower slopes of Mt. Etna is easy, either by car or by bus from Catania. Getting to the more interesting, higher levels requires taking one of the stout four-wheel-drive minibuses that leave from Piano Provenzana on the north side and from Rifugio Sapienza on the south side. A cable car, called the Funivia dell'Etna, from Rifugio Sapienza takes you part of the way.

CABLE CAR Funivia dell'Etna.
☎ *095/914141, 095/914142* ⊕ *www.funiviaetna.com.*

TOURS

Club Alpino Italiano

ADVENTURE TOURS | A great resource for Mt. Etna climbing and hiking guides for those who have some experience and don't want a lot of hand-holding. ⊠ *Via Messina 593/a, Catania* ☎ *340/2326542* ⊕ *www.caicatania.it.*

Gruppo Guide Etna Nord

ADVENTURE TOURS | This group offers more personalized (and more expensive) services than others, including excursions well suited to novice climbers. Reserve ahead. ⊠ *Piazza Attilio Castrogiovanni 19, Linguaglossa* ☎ *095/7774502, 348/0125167* ⊕ *www.guidetnanord.com.*

VISITOR INFORMATION

CONTACT Nicolosi Tourism Office. (*Porta dell'Etna*) ⊠ *Piazza Vittorio Emanuele, Nicolosi* ☎ *095/914488* ⊕ *www.nicolosietna.it.*

Sights

★ Barone di Villagrande

WINERY | The oldest winery in Etna offers friendly and informative tours of its stunning property, followed by a tasting of five wines with food pairings or a more formal lunch; reservations are required. There are also four charming guest rooms overlooking the vineyards for overnight stays. ⊠ *Via del Bosco 25, Milo* ☎ *095/7082175* ⊕ *www.villagrande.it* 🏷 *€25 tour and tasting.*

Circumetnea

TRAIN/TRAIN STATION | Instead of climbing up Mt. Etna, you can circle it on this private railroad, which runs between Catania and Riposto, with a change at Randazzo. By following the base of the volcano, the Circumetnea stretches out a 31-km (19-mile) journey along the coastal road to 114 km (71 miles). The line was first constructed between 1889 and 1895 and remains small, slow, and single track, but it has some dramatic vistas of the volcano and goes through lava fields. The one-way trip takes about 3½ hours, with departures every 90 minutes or so. After you've made the trip, you can get back to where you started from on the much quicker, but less scenic, conventional rail service between Riposto and Catania. ⊠ *Via Caronda 352, Catania* ☎ *095/541111* ⊕ *www.circumetnea.it* 🏷 *€7.90 one-way* ⏱ *Closed Sun.*

★ Mt. Etna

VOLCANO | In 387 BC, Plato sailed in just to catch a glimpse of it; in the 9th century AD, the first granita of all was shaved off its snowy slopes; in 1669, it erupted continuously for four months and lava flows reached Catania; and in the 21st century, the volcano still grabs headlines on an annual basis. Etna has erupted a dozen times since 1971, most spectacularly in 1971, 1983, 2001, 2002, 2005, and 2015. There were also a pair of medium-size eruptions in 2008, one in 2009, and fairly constant eruptive activity during the summer of 2011, winter of 2013, summer of 2014, and winter of 2020. A BBC television crew was injured in a 2017 eruption and spewing ash caused airspace closure in 2018 and 2021. Travel in the proximity of the crater depends on Mt. Etna's temperament, but you can walk up and down the enormous lava dunes and wander over its moonlike surface of dead craters. The rings of vegetation change markedly as you rise, with vineyards and pine trees gradually giving way to growths of broom and lichen. ⊠ *Parco dell'Etna* ⊕ *www.parcoetna.it.*

Restaurants

★ Cave Ox

$ | PIZZA | This casual osteria is frequented by local winemakers who come for pizza dinners and rustic daily lunch specials, but most visitors are smitten with the small but amazing cellar focused on Etna natural wines. Everything's fresh, simple, and delicious—and made to pair with one of the delightful wines suggested by owner and wine enthusiast Sandro. **Known for:** local winemaker crowd; superlative selection of natural wines from Etna; filling lunches and pizza dinners. ⑤ *Average main: €9* ⊠ *Via Nazionale Solicchiata 159, Solicchiata* ☎ *0942/986171, 328/1349683* ⊕ *www.caveox.it* ⊘ *Closed Tues.*

Mt. Etna's Villages

The villages that surround Mt. Etna make good bases for visiting nearby cities like Catania, Acireale, and Taormina. **Zafferana Etnea** is famous for orange-blossom honey; **Nicolosi**, at nearly 3,000 feet, is known as La Porta dell'Etna (The Door to Etna); **Trecastagni** (The Three Chestnut Trees) has beautiful Renaissance churches; **Randazzo**, the largest of the surrounding towns, is the site of a popular wood, textile, and metalwork market; and **Bronte** is Italy's center of pistachio cultivation.

★ Shalai

$$ | **MODERN ITALIAN** | You might not expect to find a thoroughly contemporary restaurant on the slopes of Mt. Etna, but Shalai, in the boutique hotel of the same name, is truly a modern oasis, where young chef Giovanni Santoro prepares updated and beautifully presented versions of Sicilian classics. For the full Michelin-starred experience, choose from the six-course meat or fish tasting menus; to finish, the deconstructed cannoli are a true delight. ⑤ *Average main: €22* ⊠ *Via Marconi 25, Linguaglossa* ☎ *095/643128* ⊕ *www.shalai.it* ⊘ *No lunch weekdays.*

🛏 Hotels

★ Monaci delle Terre Nere

$$$$ | HOTEL | This cozy boutique hotel in the foothills of Mt. Etna features spacious rustic-chic rooms on a working organic farm with vineyards, along with an elegant Slow Food–inspired restaurant. **Pros:** black-lava-stone pool with countryside views; eco-conscious atmosphere; delicious food and wine on offer. **Cons:** not many restaurants in the area;

accommodations may be a little quirky for some; service can be hit or miss. $ *Rooms from: €370* ✉ *Via Monaci, Zafferana Etnea* ☎ *095/7083638* ⊕ *www. monacidelleterrenere.it* ⊗ *Closed Jan.– mid-Mar.* ⟿ *27 rooms* ⦶ *Free Breakfast.*

Acireale

40 km (25 miles) south of Taormina, 16 km (10 miles) north of Catania.

Acireale sits amid a clutter of rocky pinnacles and lush lemon groves. The craggy coast is known as the Riviera dei Ciclopi, after the legend narrated in *The Odyssey* in which the blinded Cyclops, Polyphemus, hurled boulders at the retreating Ulysses, thus creating spires of rock, or *faraglioni* (pillars of rock rising dramatically out of the sea). Tourism has barely taken off here, so it's a good destination if you feel like putting some distance between yourself and the busloads of tourists in Taormina, or if seeking an easy day trip from Catania. And though the beaches are rocky, there's good swimming here, too

GETTING HERE AND AROUND
Buses arrive frequently from Taormina and Catania. Acireale is on the main coastal train route, though the station is a long walk south of the center. Local buses pass every 20 minutes or so.

 Sights

Belvedere di Santa Caterina
VIEWPOINT | Lord Byron (1788–1824) visited the Belvedere di Santa Caterina to look out over the Ionian Sea during his Italian wanderings. Today, the viewing point is south of the old town, near the Terme di Acireale, off SS114, and is a tranquil spot for photos or quiet reflection on one of the several benches positioned toward the water. ✉ *Off SS114, Acireale.*

Duomo
RELIGIOUS BUILDING | With its cupola and twin turrets, Acireale's Duomo is an extravagant Baroque construction dating from the 17th century. In the chapel to the right of the altar, look for the 17th-century silver statue of Santa Venera (patron saint of Acireale) by Mario D'Angelo, and the early-18th-century frescoes by Antonio Filocamo. ✉ *Piazza del Duomo, Acireale* ☎ *095/601102* ⊕ *www. diocesiacireale.it.*

Santa Maria La Scala
MARINA/PIER | A half-hour's walk from Acireale's center, this picturesque harbor, with lava stone steps leading to the water, is filled with fishermen unloading brightly colored boats. Inexpensive lunches are served in the many restaurants along the harbor; your fresh fish dish is priced by weight. ✉ *Acireale.*

🍴 Restaurants

La Grotta
$$$ | **SEAFOOD** | Its dining room set in a cave above the harbor of Santa Maria La Scala, this rustic trattoria specializes in seafood. Try the *insalata di mare* (a selection of delicately boiled fish served with lemon and olive oil), pasta with clams or cuttlefish ink, or fish grilled over charcoal. **Known for:** unique cave setting; superfresh seafood; the catch of the day. $ *Average main: €26* ✉ *Via Scalo Grande 46, Acireale* ☎ *095/7648153* ⊕ *www. ristorantelagrotta.info* ⊗ *Closed Tues., and late Oct.*

☕ Coffee and Quick Bites

Bar Eldorado
$ | **SOUTHERN ITALIAN** | The delicious ice creams and granita *di mandora* (almond granita) at Eldorado invite a firsthand acquaintance. **Known for:** friendly staff; great ice creams; wonderful desserts. $ *Average main: €3* ✉ *Corso Umberto I 5, Acireale* ☎ *347/9717926.*

Performing Arts

Teatro dell'Opera dei Pupi

PUPPET SHOWS | FAMILY | Although it has died out in most other parts of the island, the puppet-theater tradition carries on in Acireale with a small but informative free exhibit at the Museo Opera dei Pupi, which recounts the history of the art and displays the puppets once used in widely beloved local perfomances. ✉ *Via Nazionale per Catania 195, Acireale* ☎ *095/7648035* ⊕ *www.operadeipupi. com* ✉ *€10 for guided tours, €15 for shows.*

Catania

16 km (10 miles) south of Acireale, 94 km (59 miles) south of Messina, 60 km (37 miles) north of Siracusa.

The chief wonder of Catania, Sicily's second city, is that it's there at all. Its successive populations were deported by one Greek tyrant, sold into slavery by another, and driven out by the Carthaginians. Every time the city got back on its feet it was struck by a new calamity: plague decimated the population in the Middle Ages, a mile-wide stream of lava from Mt. Etna swallowed part of it in 1669, and 25 years later a disastrous earthquake forced the Catanesi to begin again.

Today Catania is in the midst of yet another resurrection—this time from crime, filth, and urban decay. Although the city remains loud and full of traffic, signs of gentrification are everywhere. The elimination of vehicles from the Piazza del Duomo and the main artery of Via Etnea, and the cleaning of many of the historic buildings have added to its newfound charm. Home to what is arguably Sicily's best university, Catania is full of youthful exuberance, which comes through in the designer bistros, the chic osterias that serve wine, and the trendy ethnic boutiques that have

cropped up all over town. Even more impressive is the vibrant cultural life.

GETTING HERE AND AROUND

Catania is well connected by bus and train with Messina, Taormina, Siracusa, Enna, and Palermo. The airport of Fontanarossa serves as a transportation hub for the eastern side of the island. From here you can get buses to most major destinations without going into the city center.

VISITOR INFORMATION

CONTACT Catania Tourism Office. ✉ *Minoriti Palace, Via Etnea 63/65, Catania* ☎ *4014070* ⊕ *turismo.cittametropolitana. ct.it.*

⊙ Sights

Amenano River

NATURE SIGHT | This underground river flows beneath much of Catania. You can glimpse it at the Fontana dell'Amenano, but the best place to experience the river is at the bar-restaurant A Putia dell'Ostello. Here you can sit at an underground table as swirls of water rush by. If you're not planning to stay for a drink, someone from the bar will sell you a €1 ticket to walk into the cavelike seating area. Aside from the underground river, the bar area above ground is a lively, fun spot to hang out on a Monday evening when many other places are closed. ✉ *Piazza Currò 6, Catania* ☎ *095/7233010* ⊕ *aputiadellostello.business.site.*

Cattedrale di Sant'Agata (Duomo)

RELIGIOUS BUILDING | Giovanni Vaccarini designed the contrasting black lava and white limestone facade of the cathedral, which dominates the Piazza del Duomo and which houses the tomb of composer Vincenzo Bellini. Also of note are the three apses of lava that survive from the original Norman structure and a fresco from 1675 in the sacristy that portrays Catania's submission to Etna's attack. Guided tours of the cathedral, which is dedicated to Catania's protector, are available in English if reserved at least a week in advance. The cathedral's treasures are on view in the Museo Diocesano Catania (www.museodiocesanocatania.com), and underneath the cathedral are the ruins of Greco-Roman baths. ⊠ *Piazza del Duomo, bottom end of Via Etnea, Catania* ☎ *095/320044, 339/4859942 for tours* ⊕ *www.cattedralecatania.it* ⊠ *Museum €7, sacristy €2, baths €5; combined ticket €10.*

Centro Storico

HISTORIC DISTRICT | Black lava stone from Etna, combined with largely Baroque architecture, give Catania's historic center a very distinctive feel. After Catania's destruction by lava and earthquake at the end of the 17th century, the city was rebuilt and its informal mascot "U Liotru" (an elephant carved out of lava balancing an Egyptian obelisk) was placed outside the cathedral as a kind of talisman. This square also marks the entrance to Catania's famous *pescheria* (fish market) and is one of the few points in the city where you can see the Amenano River above ground. Another point of interest is Via Garibaldi, which runs from Piazza del Duomo up toward the impressively huge Porta Garibaldi, a black-and-white triumphal arch built in 1768 to commemorate the marriage of Ferdinando I. Also of note in the center are Castello Ursino, which is now a museum, the Greco-Roman theater off of Via Vittorio Emanuele II, and the Roman amphitheater in Piazza Stesicoro. ⊠ *Catania.*

Festa di Sant'Agata

OTHER ATTRACTION | Each February 3–5, the Festa di Sant'Agata honors Catania's patron saint with one of Italy's biggest religious festivals. The saint herself was first tortured, then killed, when she spurned a Roman suitor in favor of keeping her religious purity. Since then, the Catanesi have honored her memory by parading her relics through the streets of Catania on an enormous silver-encrusted carriage. The entire festival is highly affecting, even for nonbelievers, and is not to be missed by February visitors. ⊠ *Catania* ⊕ *www.festadisantagata.it.*

Via Etnea

STREET | With the ever-looming volcano perfectly framed at the end of the road, this main street is lined with cafés and stores selling high-street jewelry, clothing, and shoes. At sunset, it plays host to one of Sicily's most enthusiastic passeggiatas, in which Catanesi of all ages take part. It is closed to automobile traffic until 10 pm during the week and all day on weekends. ⊠ *Catania.*

 Restaurants

Il Sale Art Cafè

$ | SICILIAN | Arrive early to get your name on the list for a table and be prepared to wait, because Il Sale is always full to bursting, thanks to the elegant simplicity with which it lets the best Sicilian ingredients speak for themselves. Start with antipasti of delicious local cheeses and salami, and follow up with excellent primi and succulent meat dishes—or the more economical (and extremely popular) pizza—all paired with an excellent bottle from the digital wine list. **Known for:** buzzing crowd; creative presentation of local ingredients; unrivaled pizzas and focaccia. Ⓢ *Average main: €9* ⊠ *Via S. Filomena 10/12, Catania* ☎ *095/316888* ⊕ *ilsale.info.*

★ Osteria Antica Marina

$$ | SEAFOOD | Just steps from Catania's famous fish market, this bustling osteria makes a perfect stop for ultrafresh seafood, surrounded by an energetic mix of locals and in-the-know tourists. Antica Marina's famed for its linguine with sea urchin, but you also can't go wrong with any of the daily grilled fish specials which will be announced at your table (and priced based on the weight of the whole fish). **Known for:** straight-from-the-market fish; fresh seafood antipasti; scrumptious pastas. Ⓢ *Average main: €18* ⊠ *Via Pardo*

29, Catania ☎ *095/348197* ⊕ *www.antica-marina.it* ⏾ *Closed Wed.*

Trattoria La Canonica

$ | **ITALIAN** | **FAMILY** | More is more when it comes to decor at this cozy red-walled, knickknack-filled trattoria serving classic Sicilian dishes, just two minutes from the city's famous cathedral. The informal service and homey ambience make it feel like you are sitting down in a family kitchen for traditional plates like pasta alla Norma or seafood dishes, including *pepata di cozze* (peppery steamed mussels). **Known for:** eclectic interior design; central location; excellent versions of traditional dishes. $ *Average main: €14* ✉ *Via Raddusa 7, Catania* ☎ *334/8787190* ⊕ *ristorantelacanonica.eatbu.com* ⏾ *Closed Wed.*

Coffee and Quick Bites

Caffè del Duomo

$ | **CAFÉ** | Dive right into the hustle and bustle of Catania at Caffè del Duomo, which has handmade cookies and cakes and a great local atmosphere. The piazza-front location is the main draw, but the fantastic cannoli are another reason to stop for coffee and watch the world go by. **Known for:** typical Sicilian breakfast; handmade treats; great spot for people-watching. $ *Average main: €5* ✉ *Piazza Duomo 11–13, Catania* ☎ *095/7150556* ⊕ *www.caffedelduomocatania.com.*

Pasticceria Savia

$ | **CAFÉ** | The lively Pasticceria Savia makes superlative arancini with ragù. Or you could choose cannoli, granita, or other snacks to munch on while you people-watch from one of the streetside tables. **Known for:** lovely outdoor seating; arancini with ragù; typical Sicilian pastries like cannoli and *paste di mandorla* (almond paste). $ *Average main: €5* ✉ *Via Etnea 302–304 and Via Umberto 2, near Villa Bellini, Catania* ☎ *095/322335* ⊕ *www.savia.it* ⏾ *Closed Mon.*

Hotels

Romano House

$ | **HOTEL** | With a sleek minimalist design in a 17th-century palace and a convenient location in an increasingly trendy area not far from the train station, this boutique hotel caters to design aficionados on a budget. **Pros:** on-site restaurant and bar; use of private beach of its sister hotel, the Romano Palace; good-size rooms. **Cons:** neighborhood won't appeal to everyone; design sometimes wins over practicality in rooms; street noise can be a problem. $ *Rooms from: €119* ✉ *Via di Prima 20, Catania* ☎ *095/3520611* ⊕ *www.romanohouse.com* ⇌ *50 rooms* ❑ *No Meals.*

Una Hotel Palace

$$ | **HOTEL** | For great views of Etna, this centrally located hotel overlooking Catania's main shopping street has a rooftop terrace where you can enjoy breakfast or take in the scenery during happy hour over a cocktail and antipasti buffet. **Pros:** eager-to-please staff; extremely central location; amazing rooftop views. **Cons:** some noisy rooms; bit of a generic feel; fee for parking. $ *Rooms from: €148* ✉ *Via Etnea 218, Catania* ☎ *095/2505111* ⊕ *www.gruppouna.it/esperienze/palace-catania* ⇌ *94 rooms* ❑ *Free Breakfast.*

Nightlife

First Lounge Bar

BEER GARDENS | Breathing new life into the San Berillo district, First is an outdoor lounge-bar with a beer garden feel, original street art, and walls covered in potted plants. Stop in for a craft beer or a cocktail in the previously forgotten back alleys a few minutes from Teatro Massimo Bellini, and you will also likely be treated to art installations or live DJ sets, depending on the constantly updated cultural calendar of events. ✉ *Via Martinez 13, Catania* ☎ *320/7633921.*

Performing Arts

Teatro Massimo Bellini

OPERA | Opera season (October through June) attracts top singers and productions to the birthplace of the great composer Vincenzo Bellini. Guided tours of the theater's lavish interior, built in 1890, run Tuesday through Saturday from 9:30 to noon, as theater business permits; call first to ensure you can get a tour. Enter by the box office on Piazza Bellini. ⊠ *Via Perrotta 12, Catania* ☎ *095/7306111 for info, 095/7306135 box office, 344/2249701 for guided tours* ⊕ *www.teatromassimobellini.it* 🎟 *€6 guided tours.*

Shopping

I Dolci di Nonna Vincenza

CANDY | The selection of almond-based delights here may be small, but everything is fresh and phenomenally good. Ask for boxes of mixed cookies by weight, add in some marzipan treats dedicated to Catania's patron, Sant'Agata, and enjoy the grab-bag selection at your leisure later. International shipping is available. This is the original and most historic location, but other stores can be found on Via G. d'Annunzio 216/218, Via San Giuseppe la Rena 30, and at the Catania airport. ⊠ *Palazzo Biscari, Piazza San Placido 7, Catania* ☎ *095/7151844* ⊕ *www.dolcinonnavincenza.it.*

★ Outdoor Fish and Food Market

MARKET | Beginning behind the Fontana Amenano at the corner of Piazza Duomo and spreading westward between Via Garibaldi and Via Transito, this is one of Italy's most memorable markets. It's a feast for the senses, with ricotta, fresh produce, endless varieties of meats, thousands of just-caught fish (some still wriggling), plus a symphony of vendor shouts to fill the ears. The market is at its best in early morning and finishes up around 1 pm. ⊠ *Corner of Piazza Duomo, Catania* ☉ *Closed Sun.*

Siracusa

Siracusa, known to English speakers as Syracuse, is a wonder to behold. One of the great ancient capitals of Western civilization, the city was founded in 734 BC by Greek colonists from Corinth and soon grew to rival—and even surpass—Athens in splendor and power. It became the largest, wealthiest city-state in the West and a bulwark of Greek civilization. Although Siracusa lived under tyranny, rulers such as Dionysius filled their courts with Greeks of the highest cultural stature—among them the playwrights Aeschylus and Euripides and the philosopher Plato. The Athenians, who didn't welcome Siracusa's rise, set out to conquer Sicily, but the natives outsmarted them in what was one of the greatest military campaigns in ancient history (413 BC). The city continued to prosper until it was conquered two centuries later by the Romans.

Present-day Siracusa still has some of the finest examples of Baroque art and architecture; dramatic Greek and Roman ruins; and a Duomo that's the stuff of legend—a microcosm of the city's entire history in one building. The modern city also has a wonderful, lively Baroque old town worthy of extensive exploration, as well as pleasant piazzas, outdoor cafés and bars, and a wide assortment of excellent seafood. There are essentially two areas to explore in Siracusa: the Parco Archeologico (Archaeological Zone) on the mainland, and the island of Ortygia, the ancient city first inhabited by the Greeks, which juts out into the Ionian Sea and is connected to the mainland by two small bridges. Ortygia has become increasingly popular with tourists, and although it's filled with lots of modern boutiques (and tourist shops), it still retains its charm despite the crowds.

Although Ortygia, a compact area, is a pleasure to amble around without getting unduly tired, mainland Siracusa is a grid

Walk inside the Ear of Dionysius, the Greek god of wine, fertility, ritual madness, and religious ecstasy.

of wide modern avenues. At the northern end of Corso Gelone, above Viale Paolo Orsi, the orderly grid gives way to the ancient quarter of Neapolis, where the sprawling Parco Archeologico is accessible from Viale Teracati (an extension of Corso Gelone). East of Viale Teracati, about a 10-minute walk from the Parco Archeologico, the district of Tyche holds the archaeological museum and the church and catacombs of San Giovanni, both off Viale Teocrito (drive or take a taxi or city bus from Ortygia). Coming from the train station, it's a 15-minute trudge to Ortygia along Via Francesco Crispi and Corso Umberto. If you're not up for that, take one of the free electric buses leaving every 10 minutes from the station around the corner.

GETTING HERE AND AROUND

On the main train line from Messina and Catania, Siracusa is also linked to Catania and the nearby Val di Noto by frequent buses.

VISITOR INFORMATION

CONTACT Siracusa Tourism Office. ⊠ *Via Roma 31, Ortygia* ☎ *800931/055500 Toll free* ⊕ *www.siracusaturismo.net.*

Sights

ARCHAEOLOGICAL ZONE

Catacomba di San Giovanni
HISTORIC SIGHT | Not far from the Archaeological Park, off Viale Teocrito, the catacombs below the church of San Giovanni are one of the earliest known Christian sites in the city. Inside the crypt of San Marciano is an altar where St. Paul preached on his way through Sicily to Rome. The frescoes in this small chapel are mostly bright and fresh, though some dating from the 4th century AD show their age. To visit the catacombs, you must take a 45-minute guided tour (included with the admission price), which leaves about every half hour and is conducted in Italian and English. ⊠ *Piazza San Giovanni, Tyche* ☎ *0931/64694* ⊕ *www.kairos-web.com* ✉ *€8* ⊙ *Closed daily 12:30–2:30, and Mon. in winter.*

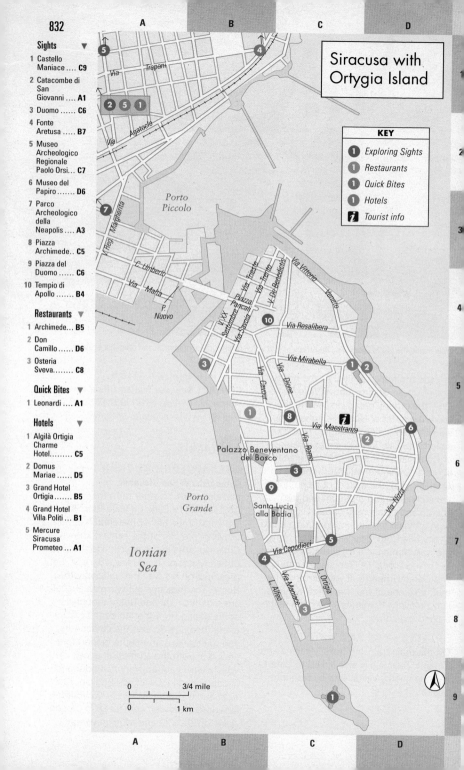

Sights ▼

1 Castello Maniace **C9**

2 Catacombe di San Giovanni **A1**

3 Duomo **C6**

4 Fonte Aretusa **B7**

5 Museo Archeologico Regionale Paolo Orsi... **C7**

6 Museo del Papiro **D6**

7 Parco Archeologico della Neapolis **A3**

8 Piazza Archimede.. **C5**

9 Piazza del Duomo **C6**

10 Tempio di Apollo **B4**

Restaurants ▼

1 Archimede.. **B5**

2 Don Camillo **D6**

3 Osteria Sveva........ **C8**

Quick Bites ▼

1 Leonardi **A1**

Hotels ▼

1 Algilà Ortigia Charme Hotel......... **C5**

2 Domus Mariae **D5**

3 Grand Hotel Ortigia....... **B5**

4 Grand Hotel Villa Politi ... **B1**

5 Mercure Siracusa Prometeo ... **A1**

Siracusa with Ortygia Island

KEY

1 Exploring Sights

1 Restaurants

1 Quick Bites

1 Hotels

i Tourist info

Via Trapani

Via Agatocle

Porto Piccolo

V. Reg. Magnenta

C. Umberto

Via Malta

P. Nuovo

Via Trieste

Via Trento

V. Di Benedictis

Via Vittorio

Veneto

Piazza Pancali

V. XX Settembre

Via Savoia

Via Resalibera

Via Mirabella

Via Cavour

Via Diana

Via Maestranza

Via Roma

Palazzo Beneventano del Bosco

Porto Grande

Santa Lucia alla Badia

Via Nizza

Via Capodieci

L. Ortigia

L. Alfeo

Via Mariniace

Ionian Sea

0   3/4 mile

0   1 km

Museo Archeologico Regionale Paolo Orsi

HISTORY MUSEUM | The impressive collection of Siracusa's splendid archaeological museum is organized by region and time period around a central atrium and ranges from Neolithic pottery to fine Greek statues and vases. Compare the Landolina Venus—a headless goddess of love who rises out of the sea in measured modesty (a 1st-century-AD Roman copy of the Greek original)—with the much earlier (300 BC) elegant Greek statue of Hercules in Section C. Of a completely different style is a marvelous fanged Gorgon, its tongue sticking out, that once adorned the cornice of the Temple of Athena to ward off evildoers. ✉ *Viale Teocrito 66, Tyche* ☎ *0931/489514* ⊕ *www.regione.sicilia.it/beniculturali/ museopaoloorsi* ✉ *€8, combined ticket with Parco Archeologico €13.50* ⊗ *Closed Sun. after 2 and Mon.*

★ Parco Archeologico della Neapolis

·**RUINS** | Siracusa is most famous for its dramatic set of Greek and Roman ruins, which are considered to be some of the best archeological sites in all of Italy and should be combined with a stop at the Museo Archeologico. If the park is closed, go up Viale G. Rizzo from Viale Teracati to the belvedere overlooking the ruins, which are floodlit at night. Before the park's ticket booth is the gigantic **Ara di Ierone** (Altar of Hieron), which was once used by the Greeks for spectacular sacrifices involving hundreds of animals. The first attraction in the park is the **Latomia del Paradiso** (Quarry of Paradise), a lush tropical garden full of palm and citrus trees. This series of quarries served as prisons for the defeated Athenians, who were enslaved; the quarries once rang with the sound of their chisels and hammers. At one end is the famous **Orecchio di Dionisio** (Ear of Dionysius), with an ear-shape entrance and unusual acoustics inside, as you'll hear if you clap your hands. The legend is that Dionysius used to listen in at the top of the quarry to hear what the slaves were plotting below. The **Teatro Greco** is the chief

monument in the Archaeological Park. Indeed it's one of Sicily's greatest classical sites and the most complete Greek theater surviving from antiquity. Climb to the top of the seating area (which could accommodate 15,000) for a fine view: all the seats converge upon a single point—the stage—which has the natural scenery and the sky as its backdrop. Hewn out of the hillside rock in the 5th century BC, the theater saw the premieres of the plays of Aeschylus, and Greek tragedies are still performed here every year in May and June. Above and behind the theater runs the Via dei Sepulcri, in which streams of running water flow through a series of Greek sepulchres. The well-preserved and striking **Anfiteatro Romano** (Roman Amphitheater) reveals much about the differences between the Greek and Roman personalities. Where drama in the Greek theater was a kind of religious ritual, the Roman amphitheater emphasized the spectacle of combative sports and the circus. This arena is one of the largest of its kind and was built around the 2nd century AD. The corridor where gladiators and beasts entered the ring is still intact, and the seats (some of which still bear the occupants' names) were hauled in and constructed on the site from huge slabs of limestone. ✉ *Viale Teocrito, Archaeological Zone, Siracusa* ☎ *0931/66206* ⊕ *www.regione.sicilia. it/beniculturali/museopaoloorsi* ✉ *€10, combined ticket with Museo Archeologico €13.50. Free 1st Sun. of month.*

ORTYGIA

Castello Maniace

CASTLE/PALACE | The southern tip of Ortygia island is occupied by this castle built by Frederick II (1194–1250), until recently an army barracks, from which there are fine sea views. There's also a small museum with information about the castle's history and artifacts found during excavations, though English translations are limited. ✉ *Via del Castello Maniace, Ortygia* ☎ *0931/4508211* ✉ *€4* ⊗ *Closed Mon., and Tues.–Sun. after 1 pm.*

★ Duomo

RELIGIOUS BUILDING | Siracusa's Duomo is an archive of more than 2,000 years of island history, and has creatively incorporated ruins through the many time periods it has survived, starting with the bottommost, where excavations have unearthed remnants of Sicily's distant past, when the Siculi inhabitants worshipped their deities here. During the 5th century BC (the same time as Agrigento's Temple of Concord was built), the Greeks erected a temple to Athena over it, and in the 7th century Siracusa's first Christian cathedral was built on top of the Greek structure. The massive columns of the original Greek temple were incorporated into the present structure and are clearly visible, embedded in the exterior wall along Via Minerva. The Greek columns were also used to dramatic advantage inside, where on one side they form chapels connected by elegant wrought-iron gates. The Baroque facade, added in the 18th century, displays a harmonious rhythm of concaves and convexes. In front, the sunkissed stone piazza is encircled by pink and white oleanders and elegant buildings ornamented with filigree grillwork, and is filled with frolicking children and street musicians. Check with the tourist office for guided tours of the underground tunnels, which are located to the right when you stand facing the cathedral. ⊠ *Piazza del Duomo, Ortygia* ☎ *0931/65328* 🖅 *€2.*

Fonte Aretusa

FOUNTAIN | A freshwater spring, the Fountain of Arethusa, sits next to the sea, studded with Egyptian papyrus that's reportedly natural. This anomaly is explained by a Greek legend that tells how the nymph Arethusa was changed into a fountain by the goddess Artemis (Diana) when she tried to escape the advances of the river god Alpheus. She fled from Greece, into the sea, with Alpheus in close pursuit, and emerged in Sicily at this spring. It's said if you throw a cup into the Alpheus River in Greece, it will emerge here at this fountain, which is home to a few tired ducks and some faded carp—but no cups. If you want to stand right by the fountain, you need to gain admission through the aquarium; otherwise look down on it from Largo Aretusa. ⊠ *Largo Aretusa, Ortygia* ⊕ *Off promenade along harbor* ☎ *0931/65861* ⊕ *www.fontearetusasiracusa.it* 🖅 *€5* ⊘ *Closed Tues.*

Museo del Papiro

OTHER MUSEUM | Housed in the 16th-century former convent of Sant'Agostino, the small but intriguing Papyrus Museum uses informative exhibits and videos to demonstrate how papyri are prepared from reeds and then painted—an ancient tradition in the city. Siracusa, it seems, has the only climate outside the Nile Valley in which the papyrus plant—from which the word "paper" comes—thrives. ⊠ *Via Nizza 14, Ortygia* ☎ *0931/22100* ⊕ *www.museodelpapiro.it* 🖅 *€5* ⊘ *Closed Mon.*

Piazza Archimede

PLAZA/SQUARE | The center of this piazza has a Baroque fountain, the Fontana di Diana, festooned with fainting sea nymphs and dancing jets of water. Look for the Chiaramonte-style **Palazzo Montalto,** an arched-window gem just off the piazza on Via Montalto. ⊠ *Piazza Archimede, Ortygia.*

Tempio di Apollo

RUINS | Scattered through the piazza just across the bridge to Ortygia are the ruins of a temple dedicated to Apollo, a model of which is in the Museo Archeologico. In fact, little of this noble Doric temple remains except for some crumbled walls and shattered columns; the window in the south wall belongs to a Norman church that was built much later on the same spot. ⊠ *Piazza Pancali, Ortygia.*

Restaurants

Archimede

$$ | PIZZA | Although the restaurant gets decidedly mixed reviews, the Archimede pizzeria offers well-made pizzas with classical names, such as the Teocrite, topped with fresh tomato, mozzarella, garlic, onion, and basil. For those who can't face the full-size offerings, mini pizzas are also available (albeit at the same price), and everyone should find enough space to sample one of the many bottled beers on the menu. **Known for:** good beer selection; satisfying pizzas; reasonable prices. ⑤ *Average main: €15* ✉ *Via Gemmellaro 8, Ortygia* ☎ *0931/69701.*

★ Don Camillo

$$ | SICILIAN | A gracious series of delicately arched rooms at this beloved local eatery are lined with wine bottles and sepia-tone images of the old town. Preparations bring together fresh seafood and inspired creativity: taste, for instance, the sublime spaghetti *delle Sirene* (with sea urchin and shrimp in butter) or *gamberoni* (prawns) prepared, unexpectedly (and wonderfully), in pork fat. **Known for:** excellent wine list; fish, meat, and vegetarian tasting menus; helpful service. ⑤ *Average main: €20* ✉ *Via Maestranza 96, Ortygia* ☎ *0931/67133* ⊕ *www.ristorantedoncamillosiracusa.it* ⊗ *Closed Sun., 2 wks in Jan., and 2 wks in July.*

Osteria Sveva

$ | SICILIAN | At this Slow Food tavern, conveniently located right behind the Castello Maniace, you can sit back and enjoy both surf and turf dishes in the studiously modern but minimalist surroundings. One major plus is that you can order half portions of several pasta dishes or opt for a secondo, like the unusual *pesce in crosta di patate* (grilled fish in a potato crust)—all served on hand-painted ceramic ware. **Known for:** charming setting on a square; authentic Sicilian dishes; good-value meals. ⑤ *Average*

main: €13 ✉ *Piazza Federico di Svevia 1, Ortygia* ☎ *0931/24663* ⊗ *Closed Nov. and Jan., and Wed. Sept. 15–June. No lunch June–Sept.*

Coffee and Quick Bites

Leonardi

$ | BAKERY | For some great Sicilian cakes and ice cream on your way to the Archaeological Park, visit this bar-cum-pasticceria. It's popular with locals, so you may have to line up for your cakes during holiday times. **Known for:** near the Archaeological Park; great coffee and cakes; a favorite of locals. ⑤ *Average main: €3* ✉ *Viale Teocrito 123, Siracusa* ☎ *0931/61411* ⊕ *www.pasticcerialeonardi.com.*

🛏 Hotels

★ Algilà Ortigia Charme Hotel

$$$$ | HOTEL | It's hard to say what's more charming about this boutique hotel: its location overlooking the sea on the edge of the old town, or its delightful interiors, including guest rooms done up in country-chic style, with a mix of modern amenities (Bvlgari toiletries, free minibar) and antique touches (wood-beamed ceilings, hand-painted tiles in the bathroom). **Pros:** eager-to-please service with valet parking (fee); wonderfully central location; prime water views. **Cons:** lots of stairs could be an issue for some; no spa, pool, or gym; not all rooms have sea views. ⑤ *Rooms from: €328* ✉ *Via Vittorio Veneto 93, Siracusa* ☎ *0931/465186* ⊕ *www.algila.it* ⇌ *54 rooms* ⦿❘ *Free Breakfast.*

Domus Mariae

$ | HOTEL | On Ortygia's eastern shore, this hotel, in an unusual twist, is owned by Ursuline nuns, who help to make the mood placid and peaceful—but the elegant accommodations are far from monastic. **Pros:** nice breakfast; enthusiastic staff; gorgeous sea views and rooftop terrace. **Cons:** small rooms; stairs to climb; not much street parking near the hotel. **⑤** *Rooms from: €119* ✉ *Via Vittorio Veneto 76, Ortygia* ☎ *0931/24854* ⊕ *www.domusmariaebenessere.com* ⇨ *12 rooms* ⑩ *Free Breakfast.*

Grand Hotel Ortigia

$$$ | **HOTEL** | An elegant though somewhat old-fashioned design of inlaid wood furniture and stained-glass windows prevails in the guest rooms at this venerable institution, which has enjoyed a prime position on the Porto Grande at the base of Ortygia since 1890. **Pros:** convenient location; wonderful seafront views from the restaurant; attentive service. **Cons:** small bathrooms; back rooms have no view; Wi-Fi weak in some rooms. **⑤** *Rooms from: €247* ✉ *Viale Mazzini 12, Ortygia* ☎ *0931/464600* ⊕ *www. grandhotelortigia.it* ⇨ *57 rooms* ⑩ *Free Breakfast.*

Grand Hotel Villa Politi

$$ | **HOTEL** | Winston Churchill, European royalty, and other VIPs have frequented the grand 18th-century Villa Politi. **Pros:** expansive outdoor pool and nearby private beach; excellent service; free parking in the hotel lot. **Cons:** not many restaurants in the neighborhood; a fair distance from the sights of Ortygia; not as sparkling and fresh as in the past. **⑤** *Rooms from: €180* ✉ *Via M. Politi 2, Archaeological Zone, Siracusa* ☎ *0931/412121* ⊕ *www.villapoliti.com* ⇨ *100 rooms* ⑩ *Free Breakfast.*

Mercure Siracusa Prometeo

$$ | **HOTEL** | The Mercure occupies a glass-fronted building along the busy Viale Teracati and, like most other hotels in the same chain, it's a slick operation with first-rate amenities. **Pros:** good parking; swimming pool on the roof; a two-minute walk from the archaeological site of Neapolis. **Cons:** a long way from the island of Ortygia; chain hotel with little character; €10 breakfast. **⑤** *Rooms from: €150* ✉ *Viale Teracati 20, Tyche* ☎ *0931/464646* ⊕ *www.hotelmercuresiracusa.com* ⇨ *93 rooms* ⑩ *No Meals.*

Performing Arts

Teatro Greco (*Greek Theater*)
CULTURAL FESTIVALS | From early May to mid-July, Siracusa's ancient Teatro Greco stages performances of classical tragedy and comedy. Tickets run €36–€73, with a small discount if you buy the ticket in person. ✉ *Teatro Greco, Archaeological Zone, Siracusa* ☎ *0931/487248 Ticket office* ⊕ *www.indafondazione.org.*

Noto

38 km (23 miles) southwest of Siracusa.

If Siracusa's Baroque beauties whet your appetite for that over-the-top style, head to Noto, a UNESCO World Heritage site. Lying about 40 minutes away on the A18, the compact and easy-to-navigate city is doable as a day trip—though staying overnight lets you see the lovely buildings glow in the setting sun after the tourist hordes have departed. Despite being decimated by an earthquake in 1693 and rebuilt in the prevailing fashion of the day, Noto has remarkable architectural integrity. A prime example of design from the island's Baroque heyday, it presents a pleasing ensemble of honey-color buildings, strikingly uniform in style but never dull. Simply walking Corso Vittorio Emanuele, the pedestrianized main street, qualifies as an aesthetic experience.

GETTING HERE AND AROUND

Trains leave from Siracusa at least 8 times daily (fewer trains on Sunday); there are also four trains a day from Ragusa, though the station is a bit outside of town. Buses depart numerous times a day from Siracusa, Catania, and Ragusa.

VISITOR INFORMATION

CONTACT Noto Tourism Office. ✉ *Corso Vittorio Emanuele 135, Noto* ☎ *339/4816218* ⊕ *www.notoinforma.it.*

Sights

Cattedrale di San Nicolò

RELIGIOUS BUILDING | Noto's domed cathedral (divine in more ways than one) is an undisputed highlight of the extraordinary Baroque architecture for which the town is world-famous. Climb the monumental staircase to get a glimpse of the interior—restored over a 10-year period after the dome collapsed in 1996—which is simple compared to the magnificent exterior, but still worth a look. ⊠ *Corso Vittorio Emanuele, Noto.*

Palazzo Nicolaci di Villadorata

CASTLE/PALACE | For a rare insight into the lifestyle of social climbers in the 18th century, this palace is a must-see. It contains about 90 rooms belonging to the noble Nicolaci family, and although only some are on view to the public, they include a splendid frescoed ballroom. Outside the palace, note the gorgeous balconies featuring mythical creatures. ⊠ *Via Corrado Nicolaci, Noto* ☏ *338/7427022* ⊕ *www.palazzonicolaci. it* 🎫 *€4.*

Restaurants

Anche gli Angeli

$$ | ITALIAN | Part concept store, part bar, and part fine gourmet dining experience, this unique eatery is built into a grotto underneath the Chiesa di San Carlo and specializes in deceptively simple grilled dishes and contemporary cocktails. **Known for:** high-end takes on local meat dishes; excellent drinks; beautiful design under historic arched ceiling. ⑤ *Average main: €17* ⊠ *Via Arnaldo da Brescia, 2, Noto* ☏ *0931/576023* ⊕ *www.anchegli-angeli.it.*

★ Ristorante Crocifisso

$$ | SICILIAN | Although getting to Crocifisso is a bit of a hike—it's away from Noto's tourist area and up a hill only accessible by many steps—intrepid diners will be rewarded with one of the Baroque town's finest restaurants, serving traditional dishes presented in a contemporary style in a beautiful modern dining room. With a wonderful wine list focused on Sicilian natural wines, a meal here is truly one to remember, even if the service tends to be a bit aloof. **Known for:** fantastic wine selection; superlative homemade pastas; new takes on classic Sicilian dishes. ⑤ *Average main: €18* ⊠ *Via Principe Umberto 48, Noto* ☏ *0931/968608, 338/8530241* ⊕ *www. ristorantecrocifisso.it* ☉ *Closed mid-Jan.– late Feb. and Wed. No lunch Thurs.*

★ Ristorante Manna

$$ | SICILIAN | The plain exterior here gives no hint of the sleek, cool design inside this welcoming restaurant just off of Noto's main street where all of the dishes—from fresh pastas to creative seafood and exceptional daily specials—shine a light on local ingredients. Although the small outdoor patio allows for great people-watching, it's inside that the restaurant really shines; the chic multilevel dining area highlights modern art, a stylish complement to the restaurant's thoroughly modern food. **Known for:** cool, contemporary setting; modern, creative Sicilian cuisine; delightful staff. ⑤ *Average main: €18* ⊠ *Via Rocco Pirri 19, Noto* ☏ *0931/836051* ⊕ *www.mannanoto.it* ☉ *Closed Nov., Jan., and Tues.*

Trattoria del Carmine

$ | SICILIAN | This family-run eatery in the center of town is known for low-key but reliable local dishes and a pleasant atmosphere. If you're not tempted by the fish of the day, you can choose between the various land-based dishes on offer, such as ravioli with pork ragù, roasted veal, and rabbit with olives and mint. **Known for:** affordable prices; traditional Sicilian dishes; generous portions. ⑤ *Average main: €8* ⊠ *Via Ducezio 1/a, Noto* ☎ *0931/838705* ⊕ *www.trattoriadelcarmine.it* ⊗ *Closed Mon. and mid-Jan.–mid-Mar.*

Coffee and Quick Bites

Caffè Sicilia

$ | **BAKERY** | When you need a break from the architectural eye candy, indulge in an edible sweet (and a restorative coffee or granita) at this wondrous cake shop. Their cannoli and gelato are particularly highly rated and considered some of the best in the country. **Known for:** homemade ice cream; almond granita; delicious cannoli. ⑤ *Average main: €5* ⊠ *Corso Vittorio Emanuele 125, Noto* ☎ *0931/835013* ⊕ *www.caffesicilia.it* ⊗ *Closed mid-Jan.–mid-Mar.*

🛏 Hotels

Gagliardi Boutique Hotel

$$$ | **HOTEL** | For an unbeatable location only a block from the main pedestrian street, visitors to Noto can't do better than this hotel with an industrial vibe and spacious minimalist rooms accented with chandeliers—all inside a former 18th-century palace. **Pros:** large rooms and good public spaces; extremely central location; friendly service. **Cons:** iffy Wi-Fi connection; only one room has a bathtub; short on amenities (no restaurant, spa, or pool). ⑤ *Rooms from: €228* ⊠ *Via Silvio Spaventa 41, Noto* ☎ *0931/839730* ⊕ *www.gagliardihotel.com* ⊶ *11 rooms* ⦿ *Free Breakfast.*

Masseria degli Ulivi

$$ | **B&B/INN** | **FAMILY** | Up on the Hyblean plateau, a good 15-minute drive north of Noto, this rural *masseria* (farm) is surrounded by tastefully designed two-story lodging and immersed in olive groves. **Pros:** courteous staff; excellent restaurant; airy breakfast room with patio. **Cons:** breakfast could be better; really need your own transport; rooms are sparsely decorated. ⑤ *Rooms from: €144* ⊠ *Contrada Porcari SS287, Villa Vela, Noto* ☎ *0931/813019* ⊕ *www.masseriadegliulivi.com* ⊗ *Closed Nov.–Mar.* ⊶ *34 rooms* ⦿ *Free Breakfast.*

Scicli

44 km (27 miles) west of Noto and 10 km (6 miles) south of Modica.

Overshadowed by its larger neighbors, Modica and Ragusa, Scicli is a Baroque beauty in its own right and one of the eight villages designated by UNESCO in the Val di Noto. In recent years, it has entered Italian popular culture as the filming location of the hugely popular Montalbano series, but its decorated stone palaces and unique Madonna delle Milizie (Virgin Mary of Militias) will delight visitors who may not yet know the Sicilian detective show.

GETTING HERE AND AROUND
Buses from Siracusa, Ragusa (by way of Modica) and Noto stop in Scicli on a regular basis.

Sights

Chiesa di San Bartolomeo

RELIGIOUS BUILDING | An enchanting fusion of the Baroque and rococo lies behind the lace grate doors of this church on the edge of the historic center. Inside the single-nave church is a wooden nativity scene that dates back to the 16th century. ⊠ *Via S. Bartolomeo, Scicli.*

Chiesa di San Matteo

VIEWPOINT | Scicli is a city of churches, honey-hued and all built after the devastating earthquake in the 17th century. The church of San Matteo is abandoned, but it's well worth climbing the shallow stairs up the steep hillside to take in the panoramic views of Scicli's old town from the terrace in front of the church. ⊠ *Via San Matteo, 9, Scicli.*

Chiesa di Sant'Ignazio

CHURCH | Founded in the 17th century as a Jesuit church, this was rebuilt following the 1693 earthquake. Housing the remains of Scicli's patron saint Guglielmo the hermit, a side chapel also hosts the life-size paper-mache statue of the Madonna *su cavallo* (on a horse), the Madonna delle Milizie. This is paraded through the streets on the last Saturday in May to celebrate her feast day. ⊠ *Piazza Italia, Scicli* ☎ *0932/931278.*

Modica

37 km (23 miles) west of Noto.

Modica and Ragusa are the two chief cities in Sicily's smallest province, and the centers of a region known as Iblea. The dry, rocky, and gentle countryside filled with canyons and grassy knolls is a unique landscape for Sicily. In Modica, the main artery—Corso Umberto I—is lined with shops and restaurants and is in the valley at the bottom of the town (called Modica Bassa), while the old town of Modica Alta is built atop a ridge. That's part of this UNESCO-listed area's charm; it's a joy to wander its steep 14th-century lanes traversed by endless staircases and lined with Baroque architecture. Modica is also famed for its chocolate—don't miss trying it at one of the many stores on Corso Umberto I.

GETTING HERE AND AROUND

Trains leave from Siracusa six times a day, while buses from Catania, Siracusa, Ragusa, and Noto also stop in Modica on a regular basis.

VISITOR INFORMATION

CONTACT Modica Tourism Office. ⊠ *Corso Umberto I 141, Modica* ☎ *346/6558227* ⊕ *comune.modica.gov.it/site/ufficio-turistico.*

 Sights

Cattedrale di San Pietro

RELIGIOUS BUILDING | Statues of the apostles line the staircase of Modica's cathedral, which was originally constructed in the 14th century, then rebuilt in an impressive Baroque style following its destruction in the 1693 earthquake. ⊠ *Corso Umberto I 120, Modica* ⊗ *Closed daily 12:30–3:30.*

★ Chiesa di San Giorgio

RELIGIOUS BUILDING | This lovely Baroque church in Modica Alta, dating from after the 1693 earthquake, is reached by climbing 250 steps that crisscross in a monumental staircase leading up to the main doors. It's worth the effort for the amazing views over the old town. ⊠ *Corso San Giorgio, Modica* ☎ *0932/941279* ⊗ *Closed daily 12:30–3:30.*

Museo del Cioccolato di Modica

OTHER MUSEUM | There is an abundance of choice when it comes to indulgent desserts in Sicily, but the chocolate of Modica—cooked at a low temperature and possessed of a distinctive granular texture—is prized above all others. It feels only natural, then, to find a museum in the center of the old town dedicated to the local sweet. The small exhibit (with English translation) follows the history of chocolate in general, before describing the way cacao beans first arrived in Modica, and how they were traditionally processed by being ground on a board made of volcanic stone. There is also an eccentric collection of sculptures and celebrity portraits made entirely of chocolate. ⊠ *Corso Umberto I 149, 1st fl., behind the Museo Civico, Modica* ☎ *347/4612771* ⊕ *museociocciolatomodica.business.site* 🎫 *€3* ⊙ *Closed Tues.– Sat. 2–4, Sun. afternoon, and Mon.*

Coffee and Quick Bites

Caffè dell'Arte

$ | ITALIAN | FAMILY | Across the street from the Museo del Cioccolato, this small coffee bar makes excellent granita. The shaved ice is often eaten for breakfast in the summer months with a soft brioche, and the toasted almond flavor here is particularly good. **Known for:** casual outdoor seating; hot chocolate; almond granita. Ⓢ *Average main: €5* ⊠ *Corso Umberto I 114, Modica* ☎ *0932/943257* ⊕ *caffedellarte.it* ⊙ *Closed Wed.–Mon. 1:30–3 and Tues.*

Pasticceria Di Lorenzo

$ | BAKERY | FAMILY | Wood-lined and unadorned, this family-run pastry shop is one of the best places to try Modica's signature crescent-shape cookies, the *'mpanatigghi*. These soft cookies are filled with a mixture of chocolate, almonds, and veal. The meat was added to the cookies as a way of making the snacks more nutritious on long voyages, and the blend works surprisingly well together. **Known for:** specialty cookies; chocolate squares; family-run. Ⓢ *Average main: €5* ⊠ *Corso Umberto I 225, Modica* ☎ *0932/945324* ⊕ *www.pasticceriadilorenzo.it* ⊙ *Closed Wed.*

🛍 Shopping

Modica is famous for its chocolate, which uses an ancient Aztec technique. Made at a low heat, it has a grainier consistency than most.

★ **Antica Dolceria Bonajuto**

CHOCOLATE | Bonajuto is the oldest chocolate producer in town, dating from 1880. This busy shop on Modica Bassa's main street lets you sample many varieties of their delightful product before you buy, and also makes renowned cannoli and candied orange peel. ⊠ *Corso Umberto I 159, Modica* ☎ *0932/941225* ⊕ *www.bonajuto.it.*

Ragusa

21 km (13 miles) northwest of Modica.

Ragusa, a modern city with a beautiful historic core, is known for some great local red wines and wonderful cheese—a creamy, doughy, flavorful version of *caciocavallo*, made by hand every step of the way. It also has some wonderful Baroque buildings with fabulous vantage points throughout its narrow, twisty, and steep old town.

GETTING HERE AND AROUND

Trains and buses leave from Siracusa four or five times daily.

VISITOR INFORMATION

CONTACT Ragusa Tourism Office. ⊠ *Piazza della Repubblica, Ragusa* ☎ *0932/684780.*

Sights

Basilica di San Giorgio

RELIGIOUS BUILDING | Designed by Rosario Gagliardi in 1738, the duomo is a fine example of the Sicilian Baroque. ⊠ *Salita Duomo 15, Ragusa* ☎ *0932/220085* ⊕ *www.diocesidiragusa.it* ⊙ *Closed daily noon–4.*

Giardino Ibleo

GARDEN | Set on the edge of the old town, Giardino Ibleo is a tranquil public garden lined with palm trees and dotted with fountains and churches along stone paths. The ambling walkways skirt the cliffside and offer dramatic views of the valley below. ⊠ *Via Giardino, Ragusa.*

Ibla

HISTORIC DISTRICT | The lovely historic center of Ragusa, known as Ibla, was completely rebuilt after the devastating earthquake of 1693. Its tumble of buildings are perched on a hilltop and suspended between a deep ravine and a sloping valley. The tiny squares and narrow lanes make for pleasant meandering, but expect plenty of stairs. ⊠ *Ragusa.*

🍴 Restaurants

Duomo

\$\$\$\$ | **SICILIAN** | In an understated palazzo on a cobblestone street near the Duomo, star chef Ciccio Sultano prepares imaginative and beautifully plated splurge-worthy dinners and a four-course set lunch menu (a terrific value) that include unforgettable variations on classic Sicilian cuisine. Although dishes can be ordered à la carte, tasting menus convey a fuller sense of the chef's signature style, which uses the finest ingredients from around the island in subtly extravagant combinations. **Known for:** imaginative wine pairings; intimate and elegant setting; spaghettone with yellowtail tuna and carrot sauce. ⑤ *Average main: €45* ⊠ *Via Capitano Bocchieri 31, Ragusa* ☎ *0932/651265* ⊕ *www.cicciosultano. it* ⊗ *Closed early Jan.–late Feb. and Sun. No lunch Mon., except in Aug. and Dec. 26–Jan. 6.*

Locanda Gulfi

\$\$ | **SICILIAN** | On the grounds of the expansive Gulfi winery, which produces well-regarded organic wines, you'll find a unique place for a sophisticated lunch or dinner, with sweeping views of the Chiaramonte hills and vineyards (about a half-hour drive north of Ragusa). The chef skillfully uses local ingredients to prepare Sicilian dishes with a twist in

the modern dining room which features handblown chandeliers and a design-focused black-and-red color scheme; in warmer months, enjoy your meal on the lovely terrace. **Known for:** vineyard views and an inn to stay the night; seasonal, local Sicilian dishes; renowned Gulfi wine. ⑤ *Average main: €18* ⊠ *C. da. Patria, Chiaramonte Gulfi, Chiaramonte Gulfi, Sicily* ☎ *0932/928081 reservations, 0932/921654 winery* ⊕ *www.locanda-gulfi.it.*

🛏 Hotels

★ Eremo della Giubiliana

\$\$ | **B&B/INN** | Set in the countryside, a 20-minute drive from Ragusa, this charming family-run monastery-turned-hotel features friendly service and a relaxed but luxurious vibe, with unique rooms in former monks' chambers that vary in size and layout but are all quiet and well appointed, with antiques, stone floors, wood-beamed ceilings, and tapestries; some also have fireplaces, whirlpools, and/or balconies. **Pros:** top-notch service; peaceful atmosphere; rooms filled with character. **Cons:** restaurant food could be better for the price; grounds, while lovely, could use better upkeep; no other nearby eateries due to remote location. ⑤ *Rooms from: €200* ⊠ *Contrada Giubiliana, Marina di Ragusa* ☎ *0932/669119* ⊕ *www.eremodellagiubiliana.it* ⤴ *24 rooms* ⑪ *Free Breakfast.*

La Moresca

\$\$ | **HOTEL** | If you plan on visiting Ragusa and Modica but want to stay by the water, you can't do better than this artsy boutique hotel on Sicily's southeastern coast—it's two blocks from the beach and a pleasant half-hour drive from either inland town. **Pros:** modern, large bedrooms; friendly and helpful staff; artsy vibe. **Cons:** town itself not so charming; parking can be an issue; no hotel restaurant other than breakfast. ⑤ *Rooms from:*

€200 ✉ *Via Dandolo 63, Marina di Ragusa* ☎ *0932/1915535* ⊕ *www.lamorescahotel. eu* ⍾⦿⍾ *Free Breakfast* ⤳ *15 rooms.*

★ Locanda Don Serafino
$$ | HOTEL | This small boutique hotel offers contemporary rooms and excellent service inside a historic manor house in the heart of Ragusa Ibla. **Pros:** valet parking service; modern design in a historic setting; incredibly attentive staff. **Cons:** some rooms are a few doors down from the main building; bathrooms can be small or quirky; steep stairs limit the accessibility of some rooms. ⑤ *Rooms from: €160* ✉ *Via XI Febbraio 15, Ragusa* ☎ *0932/220065 hotel, 0932/248778 restaurant* ⊕ *www.locandadonserafino.it* ⤳ *11* ⍾⦿⍾ *Free Breakfast.*

Caltagirone

66 km (41 miles) northwest of Ragusa.

Built over three hills, this charming Baroque town is a center of Sicily's ceramics industry. Here you can find majolica balustrades, tiled windowsills, and the monumental Scala Santa Maria del Monte.

GETTING HERE AND AROUND
Buses and trains from Catania stop in the lower town, which is a pleasant stroll from the center. Caltagirone is also well served by local buses and taxis. Connections by bus with Ragusa, Enna, and Piazza Armerina are less frequent.

VISITOR INFORMATION
CONTACT Caltagirone Tourism Office. ✉ *Via Volta Libertini 3, Caltagirone* ☎ *0933/53809* ⊕ *www.cittadicaltagirone.it.*

 Sights

Museo della Ceramica
OTHER MUSEUM | Caltagirone was declared a UNESCO World Heritage site for its ceramics as well as for its numerous Baroque churches. Although the museum offers little information in English about the beautiful items displayed in its many glass cases, you can still see one of Sicily's most extensive ceramics collections, ranging from Neolithic finds to red-figure pottery from 5th-century-BC Athens and 18th-century terra-cotta Nativity figures. ✉ *Via Roma, inside Giardini Pubblici, Caltagirone* ☎ *0933/58418, 0933/58423* ⊕ *www. poloregionalecatania.net/home/caltagirone_museo_it* ⊡ *€4.*

Scala Santa Maria del Monte
VIEWPOINT | While you can see examples of Caltagirone's long ceramic tradition throughout the city, the most impressive display can be found in the 142 individually decorated tiled steps of this monumental staircase leading up to the neglected Santa Maria del Monte church. On July 24 (the feast of San Giacomo, the city's patron saint) and again on August 15 (the feast of the Assumption), the stairs are illuminated with candles that form a tapestry design. Months of work go into preparing the 4,000 *coppi*, or cylinders of colored paper, that hold oil lamps—then, at 9:30 pm on the nights of July 24, July 25, August 14, and August 15, a squad of hundreds of youngsters (tourists are welcome to participate) spring into action to light the lamps, so that the staircase flares up all at once. ✉ *Begins at Piazza Municipio, Caltagirone.*

Shopping

Improntibarre Handcraft & Design Laboratory

CERAMICS | Of the numerous ceramic shops in Caltagirone's old center, this one 13 steps up Caltagirone's fabled ceramic staircase is one of the best, selling eye-catching work with a modern aesthetic that is inspired by the town's long artisan tradition. ✉ *Scala Santa Maria del Monte 5, Caltagirone* ☎ *0933/24427* ⊕ *www.improntabarre.it.*

Piazza Armerina

30 km (18 miles) northwest of Caltagirone.

A quick look around the fanciful town of Piazza Armerina is rewarding; it has a provincial warmth, and the crumbling yellow-stone architecture with Sicily's trademark bulbous balconies creates quite an effect. The greatest draw, however, lies just down the road: the ancient Roman mosaics at Villa Romana del Casale.

GETTING HERE AND AROUND

Piazza Armerina is linked to Catania, Enna, and Palermo by regular buses, with slightly less frequent buses also connecting to Caltagirone. There's no train station.

VISITOR INFORMATION

CONTACT **Piazza Armerina Tourism Office.** ✉ *Via Monsignore Sturzo 3, Piazza Armerina* ☎ *338/8524872.*

Sights

★ **Villa Romana del Casale (Imperial Roman Villa)**

HISTORIC HOME | The exceptionally well-preserved Imperial Roman Villa is thought to have been a hunting lodge of the emperor Maximian (3rd–4th century AD) and offers some of the best mosaics of the Roman world, artfully covering more than 12,000 square feet. The excavations were not begun until 1950, and most of the wall decorations and vaulting have been lost, but the shelter over the site hints at the layout of the original building. The mosaics were probably made by North African artisans; they're similar to those in the Tunis Bardo Museum, in Tunisia. The entrance was through a triumphal arch that led into an atrium surrounded by a portico of columns, which line the way to the *thermae,* or bathhouse. It's colorfully decorated with mosaic nymphs, a Neptune, and slaves massaging bathers. The peristyle leads to the main villa, where in the Salone del Circo you look down on mosaics illustrating scenes from the Circus Maximus in Rome. A theme running through many of the mosaics—especially the long hall flanking one entire side of the peristyle courtyard—is the capturing and shipping of wild animals, which may have been a major source of the owner's wealth. Yet the most famous mosaic is the floor depicting 10 girls wearing the ancient equivalent of bikinis, going through what looks like a fairly rigorous set of training exercises. ✉ *SP15, Contrada Casale, 4 km (2½ miles) southwest of Piazza Armerina, Piazza Armerina* ☎ *0935/680036 ticket office, 0935/687667 office* ⊕ *www.piazzaarmerina.org* ✉ *€10 (free 1st Sun. of month).*

Restaurants

★ **Al Fogher**

$$ | **MODERN ITALIAN** | This culinary beacon in Sicily's interior features ambitious—and successful—dishes with the creative flair of chef Angelo Treno, whose unforgettable pastas topped with truffles or caviar, for example, offer a decidedly different expression of traditional regional

ingredients. The unassuming and elegant dining room is inside an old railway house and is the perfect place to enjoy a bottle from the 500-label wine list; in cold weather, you can cozy up to a fireplace, but the terrace is the place to be in summer. **Known for:** well-thought-out wine list; sophisticated preparations; local ingredients. ⑤ *Average main: €18* ✉ *Contrada Bellia, near SS117bis, Aidone exit, about 1 km (½ mile) north of Piazza Cascino, Piazza Armerina* ☎ *0935/684123* ⊕ *alfogher.sicilia.restaurant* ⊘ *No dinner Sun.; no lunch Mon.*

Enna

33 km (21 miles) northwest of Piazza Armerina, 136 km (85 miles) southeast of Palermo.

Deep in Sicily's interior, the fortress city of Enna (altitude 2,844 feet) commands exceptional views of the surrounding rolling plains, and, in the distance, Mt. Etna. It's the highest provincial capital in Italy and, thanks to its central location, is nicknamed the "Navel of Sicily." Virtually unknown by tourists and relatively untouched by industrialization, this sleepy town charms and prospers in a distinctly old-fashioned Sicilian way. Enna makes a good stopover for the night or just for lunch, as it's right along the autostrada between Palermo and Catania.

GETTING HERE AND AROUND
Just off the A19 autostrada, Enna is easily accessible by car. With the train station 5 km (3 miles) below the upper town, the most practical public transportation is by bus from Palermo or Catania.

VISITOR INFORMATION
CONTACT Enna Tourism Office. ✉ *Via Roma 413, Enna* ☎ *0932/521243* ⊕ *www. provincia.enna.it.*

Sights

Castello di Lombardia
CASTLE/PALACE | Enna's narrow, winding streets are dominated at one end by the impressive cliff-hanging Castello di Lombardia, rebuilt by Frederick II to create an expansive summer residence on the foundations of an ancient Sicani fort raised more than 2,000 years ago. While there is little to see inside the castle, climb up the tower for great views from the dead center of the island—on a very clear day, you can see to all three coasts. Immediately to the south you see Lake Pergusa (dry, in late summer), now almost swallowed by Enna's sprawling suburbs and the racetrack around its perimeter. According to Greek mythology, this was where Persephone was abducted by Hades. While a prisoner in his underworld realm she ate six pomegranate seeds, and was therefore doomed to spend half of each year there. For the ancients, she emerged at springtime, triggering a display of wildflowers that can still be admired all over Sicily. ✉ *Piazza di Castello di Lombardia, Enna* ☞ *€3–€4 combined ticket with Torre di Federico II.*

Piazza Vittorio Emanuele
PLAZA/SQUARE | In town, head straight for Via Roma, which leads to Piazza Vittorio Emanuele—the center of Enna's shopping scene and evening passeggiata. The attached **Piazza Crispi,** dominated by what used to be the grand old Hotel Belvedere, affords breathtaking panoramas of the hillside and smoking Etna looming in the distance. The bronze fountain in the middle of the piazza is a reproduction of Gian Lorenzo Bernini's famous 17th-century sculpture *The Rape of Persephone,* a depiction of Hades abducting Persephone. ✉ *Piazza Vittorio Emanuele, Enna.*

Rocca di Cerere (*Rock of Demeter*)
VIEWPOINT | The Greek cult of Demeter, goddess of the harvest, was said to have centered on Enna, where its adherents

built a temple atop the Rocca di Cerere, protruding out on one end of town next to the Castello di Lombardia. The spot enjoys spectacular views of the expansive countryside and windswept Sicilian interior. ⊠ *Enna*

Torre di Federico II

VIEWPOINT | This mysterious octagonal tower stands above the lower part of town and has been celebrated for millennia as marking the exact geometric center of the island—thus the tower's (and the city's) nickname, Umbilicus Siciliae (Navel of Sicily). Climb the 97 steps of the spiral staircase for views over the city and beyond. ⊠ *Enna* ⊕ *www.torredienna. it* 🎟 *€2–€4 combined ticket with Castello di Lombardia.*

🍽 Restaurants

Centrale

$ | **SICILIAN** | Housed in an old palazzo, this casual place has served meals since 1889 and famously keeps a medieval specialty, *controfiletto all'Ennese* (a veal fillet with onions, artichokes, guanciale, and white wine), on the menu, in addition to a range of slightly more modern seasonal dishes. Choose from a decent selection of Sicilian wines to accompany your meal while you take in the large mirrored wall and local pottery. ⑤ *Average main: €13* ⊠ *Piazza VI Dicembre 9, Enna* 🕿 *0935/500963* ⊕ *www.ristorantecentrale.net* ⊗ *No lunch Sat. Sept.–Mar.*

Agrigento

95 km (59 miles) southwest of Enna.

Agrigento owes its fame almost exclusively to its ancient Greek temples—though it was also the birthplace of playwright Luigi Pirandello (1867–1936). Along the coast, around 12 km (7 miles) to the west of Agrigento near the town of Realmonte, you can view the Scala dei Turchi (Stairs of the Turks), which are

natural white cliffs eroded into unusual shapes. By visiting the beaches closest to the temples, near the town of San Leone, you can sunbathe beside the locals.

GETTING HERE AND AROUND

Driving from Enna, take the A19 autostrada 35 km (22 miles) southwest to Caltanissetta; then follow the SS640 to Agrigento. Motorists can also access the town easily via the coastal SS115 and, from Palermo, by the SS189. Buses and trains run from Enna, Palermo, and Catania; both bus and train stations are centrally located.

VISITOR INFORMATION

CONTACT Agrigento Tourism Office. ⊠ *Via Empedocle 73, Agrigento* 🕿 *0922/20391* ⊕ *www.visitsicily.info.*

Sights

Monastero di Santo Spirito

RELIGIOUS BUILDING | First built in 1299, these cloisters and courtyard, up the hill above the Valle dei Templi, near the modern city, are open to the public. However, most visitors stop by the adjacent abbey for a treat and tour of the church, so be sure to ring the doorbell and try the *kuskus*—a sweet dish made from pistachio nuts, almonds, and chocolate—that the Cistercian nuns prepare. ⊠ *Cortile Santo Spirito 9, off Via Porcello, Agrigento* 🕿 *0922/1552737, 349/4792401* ⊕ *www. monasterosspirito.wixsite.com/agrigento.*

★ Valle dei Templi

RUINS | The eight or so monuments within the Valley of the Temples, a UNESCO World Heritage site, are considered to be, along with the Acropolis in Athens, the finest Greek ruins in the world. Whether you first come upon the valley in the early morning light, bathed by golden floodlights after sunset, or at its very best in February, when the valley is awash in the fragrant blossoms of thousands of almond trees, it's easy to see why Akragas (Agrigento's Greek name) was celebrated by the poet Pindar as "the most beautiful city built by mortals." The temples were originally erected as a showpiece to flaunt the Greek victory over Carthage, and they have since withstood a later sack by the Carthaginians, mishandling by the Romans, and neglect by Christians and Muslims. Although getting to, from, and around the dusty ruins of the Valle dei Templi is pretty easy, this important archaeological zone still deserves several hours. The temples are a bit spread out, but the valley is all completely walkable and usually toured on foot. However, since there's only one hotel (Villa Athena) that's close enough to walk to the ruins, you'll most likely have to drive to reach the site. Parking is at the entrance to the temple area. The site, which opens at 8:30 am, is divided into western and eastern sections. For instant aesthetic gratification, walk through the eastern zone; for a more comprehensive tour, start way out at the western end and work your way back uphill. You'll want to spend time seeing the eight pillars of the Tempio di Ercole (Temple of Hercules) that make up Agrigento's oldest temple complex, dating from the 6th century BC, and the beautiful Tempio della Concordia (Temple of Concord), up the hill from the Temple of Hercules, perhaps the best-preserved Greek temple currently in existence. Other notable temples are the Tempio di Giunone (Temple of Juno), east on the Via Sacra from the Temple of Concord, which commands an exquisite view of the valley (especially at sunset), and the Tempio di Giove (Temple of Jupiter); though never completed, it was once considered the eighth wonder of the world. At the end of Via dei Templi, where it turns left and becomes Via Petrarca, stands the Museo Archeologico Regionale. An impressive collection of antiquities from the site includes vases, votives, everyday objects, weapons, statues, and models of the temples. Be sure to visit after you've seen the temples. ⊠ *Zona Archeologica, Via dei Templi,*

Agrigento ☎ *0922/1839996* ⊕ *www. parcovalledeitempli.it* ⊠ *€10, €13.50 with museum (free 1st Sun. of month).*

Restaurants

★ Il Re di Girgenti

$$ | SICILIAN | You wouldn't expect to find an ultramodern—even hip—place to dine within a few minutes' drive of Agrigento's ancient temples, yet Il Re di Girgenti offers up pleasing versions of Sicilian classics in a trendy, country-chic atmosphere (think funky black-and-white tile floors mixed with shelves lined with old-fashioned crockery) popular with young locals. The thoughtful wine list offers good prices on both local wines and those from throughout Sicily. **Known for:** delightful wine selections; Sicilian dishes with a twist; contemporary setting with lovely views. ⑤ *Average main: €22* ⊠ *Via Panoramica dei Templi 51, Agrigento* ☎ *0922/401388* ⊕ *www. ilredigirgenti.it* ⊗ *Closed Tues.*

Trattoria dei Templi

$$ | SICILIAN | Along a road on the way up to Agrigento proper from the temple area, this vaulted family-run restaurant serves up tasty traditional food, namely daily homemade pasta specials and plenty of fresh fish dishes, all prepared with Sicilian flair. Your best bet is to ask the advice of brothers Giuseppe and Simone, the owners and chief orchestrators in the restaurant, who can also help select a Sicilian wine to pair with your meal. **Known for:** good choice of local wines; exceptional antipasti, like carpaccio of *cernia* (grouper); fresh fish. ⑤ *Average main: €18* ⊠ *Via Panoramica dei Templi 15, Agrigento* ☎ *0922/403110* ⊗ *Closed Sun.*

🛏 Hotels

Foresteria Baglio della Luna

$$ | HOTEL | In the valley below the temples, fiery sunsets and moonlight cast a glow over the ancient 12th-century watchtower at the center of this farmhouse-hotel complex, which is composed of stone buildings surrounding a peaceful geranium- and ivy-filled courtyard and the garden beyond. **Pros:** top-notch restaurant; quiet setting; pretty gardens. **Cons:** no pool; hotel a little dark inside; location a bit remote. $ *Rooms from: €145* ✉ *Via Serafino Amabile Guastella 1, Contrada Maddalusa* ☎ *0922/511061* ⊕ *www.bagliodellaluna. com* ⊗ *Closed Dec.–Feb.* ⇆ *23 rooms* ❍❘ *Free Breakfast.*

★ **Villa Athena**

$$$$ | **HOTEL** | The 18th-century Villa Athena, updated into a sleek, luxurious place to stay, complete with gorgeous manicured gardens and swimming pool, holds a privileged position directly overlooking the Temple of Concordia, a 10-minute walk away—an amazing sight both during the day and when it's lit up at night. **Pros:** perfect location for the Valle dei Templi, with phenomenal temple views; good restaurant and spa; plenty of free parking. **Cons:** lobby on the small side; service a bit detached; lack of information on local attractions. $ *Rooms from: €420* ✉ *Via Passeggiata Archeologica 33, Agrigento* ☎ *0922/596288* ⊕ *www. hotelvillaathena.it* ⇆ *27 rooms* ❍❘ *Free Breakfast.*

Selinunte

100 km (62 miles) northwest of Agrigento, 114 km (71 miles) southwest of Palermo.

Numerous Greek temple ruins perch on a plateau overlooking an expanse of the Mediterranean at Selinunte (or Selinus). The town is named after a local variety of wild parsley (*Apium graveolens* or *petroselinum*) that in spring grows in profusion among the ruined columns and overturned capitals. Although there are a few places to stay right around Selinunte, many people see it as an easy—and richly rewarding—stopover along the road to or from Agrigento. It takes only an hour or two to see.

GETTING HERE AND AROUND

You can get here by bus or car via the town of Castelvetrano, 11 km (7 miles) north, which is itself accessible from Palermo by car on the A29 autostrada, as well as by bus and train.

VISITOR INFORMATION

CONTACT Selinunte Tourism Office. ✉ *Via Cantone 21, Marinella Selinunte* ☎ *0924/46117* ⊕ *en.visitselinunte.com.*

 Sights

★ Greek Temple Ruins

RUINS | Selinunte was one of the most superb colonies of ancient Greece. Founded in the 7th century BC, the city became the rich and prosperous rival of Segesta, which in 409 BC turned to the Carthaginians for help. The Carthaginians, in turn, sent an army to destroy the city. The temples were demolished, and the city was razed, and 16,000 of Selinunte's inhabitants were slaughtered. The remains of Selinunte are in many ways unchanged from the day of its sacking—burn marks still scar the Greek columns, and much of the site still lies in rubble at its exact position of collapse. The original complex held seven temples scattered over two sites separated by a harbor. Of the seven, only one—reconstructed in 1958—is whole. ■ **TIP→ This is a large archaeological site, so you might make use of the private navetta (shuttle) to save a bit of walking. Alternatively, if you have a car, you can visit the first temples close to the ticket office on foot and then drive westward to the farther site. Be prepared to show your ticket at various stages.** ✉ *SS115, 13 km (8 miles) southeast of Castelvetrano, Marinella Selinunte* ☎ *0924/46277* ⊠ *€6.*

Restaurants

Lido Zabbara

| SICILIAN | This eatery right on the beach at Selinunte is really no more than a glorified salad bar, although it does also serve a nice selection of grilled fish and seafood (often sardines). Serve yourself from the delicacies on the center spread; the lunch buffet is very affordable, while dinner doesn't cost much more, often served by the owner whose constant back-and-forth to look after customers has earned this place the nickname "Da Toyo." As a bonus, there are sun beds and umbrellas at reasonable prices if you want to unwind before the next archaeological bonanza. **Known for:** buffet of appetizers and salads; beachside dining; great value. $ *Average main:* €12 ⊠ *Via Pigafetta, Marinella Selinunte* ☎ *0924/46194* ⊗ *Closed Nov.–Mar.*

Marsala

38 km (55 miles) northwest of Selinunte.

Marsala is readily associated with its world-famous, richly colored eponymous fortified wine, and your main reason for stopping will likely be to visit some of the many wineries in the area. But this quiet seaside town, together with the nearby island of Mozia, was also once the main Carthaginian base in Sicily: it was from here that Carthage fought for supremacy over the island against Greece and Rome, leaving behind intriguing archaeological sites. In 1773, a British merchant named John Woodhouse happened upon the town and discovered that the wine here was as good as the port long imported by the British from Portugal. Two other wine merchants, Whitaker and Ingram, rushed in, and by 1800 Marsala was exporting wine all over the British Empire.

GETTING HERE AND AROUND

Buses and trains from Palermo, Trapani, and Castelvetrano stop in Marsala. Drivers can take the coastal SS115.

VISITOR INFORMATION

CONTACT Marsala Tourism Office. ⊠ *Via XI Maggio 100, Marsala* ☎ *0923/714097* ⊕ *www.turismocomunemarsala.com.*

Sights

Donnafugata Winery

WINERY | A respected Sicilian wine producer, the 160-year-old Donnafugata Winery is open for tastings and tours of its *cantina* (wine cellar); reservations are required and can be made online or by phone. It's an interesting look at the wine-making process in Sicily, and it ends with a sampling of several whites and reds, an optional food pairing, and a chance to buy. Don't miss the delicious, full-bodied red Mille e Una Notte, and the famous Ben Ryè Passito di Pantelleria, a sweet dessert wine made from dried grapes. ⊠ *Via Sebastiano Lipari 18, Marsala* ☎ *0923/724245, 0923/724263* ⊕ *www.donnafugata.it* 🎫 *Tastings €24–€48* ⊗ *Closed Sun.*

Museo Archeologico Baglio Anselmi

HISTORY MUSEUM | A sense of Marsala's past as a Carthaginian stronghold is captured by the well-preserved Punic warship displayed in the museum, along with some of the amphorae and other artifacts recovered from the wreck. The vessel, which was probably sunk during the great sea battle that ended the First Punic War in 241 BC, was dredged up from the mud near the Egadi Islands in the 1970s. There's also a good display of maritime and archaeological finds, as well as some Roman ruins with mosaics just beyond the museum's doors. ⊠ *Lungomare Boeo 30, Marsala* ☎ *0923/952535* ⊗ *Closed Sun. after 1:30 and Mon.* 🎫 *€4.*

Erice

45 km (28 miles) northeast of Marsala, 15 km (9 miles) northeast of Trapani.

Perched 2,450 feet above sea level, Erice is an enchanting medieval mountaintop aerie of palaces, fountains, and cobblestone streets. Shaped like an equilateral triangle, the town was the ancient landmark Eryx, dedicated to Aphrodite (Venus). When the Normans arrived, they built a castle on Monte San Giuliano, where today there's a lovely public park with benches and belvederes offering striking views of Trapani, the Egadi Islands offshore, and, on a very clear day, Cape Bon and the Tunisian coast. Because of Erice's elevation, clouds conceal much of the view for most of winter. Sturdy shoes (for the cobblestones) and something warm to wear are recommended.

GETTING HERE AND AROUND

Make your approach via Trapani, which is on the A29 autostrada and well connected by bus and train with Marsala and Palermo. Late March to early January a funivia runs from the outskirts of Trapani to Erice (Monday 1–9, Tuesday to Friday 8:30–8, weekends 9:30–8:30; extended hours from late June to mid-September; see www.funiviaerice.it for details). Going by car or bus from Trapani takes around 40 minutes.

 Sights

San Vito Lo Capo

TOWN | The cape that gives this town its name has a long sandy beach on a promontory overlooking a bay in the Gulf of Castellammare. San Vito Lo Capo is famous for its North African couscous, made with fish instead of meat. In late September it hosts the 10-day Cous Cous Fest (www.couscousfest.it), a serious international couscous competition and festival with live music and plenty of free tastings. San Vito is also one of the bases for exploring the Riserva dello Zingaro; this nature reserve—one of the few stretches of coastline in Sicily that is not built-up—is at its best in late spring, when both wildflowers and birds are plentiful. ⊠ *Capo San Vito, 40 km (25 miles) north of Erice, San Vito Lo Capo.*

 Restaurants

Monte San Giuliano

$ | SICILIAN | At this traditional restaurant near the main piazza, you can sit on a tree-lined patio overlooking the sea or in the white-walled dining room and munch on free *panelle* (chickpea fritters) while waiting for your main dish, which will be served tableside, spooned from the cooking pots to your plate by the friendly staff. The pastas are exemplary, but the specialty is the seafood couscous, served with a bowl of fish broth on the side.
Known for: extensive and interesting wine list; great pasta and couscous; charming setting. ⑤ *Average main: €12* ⊠ *Vicolo San Rocco 7, Erice* ☎ *0923/869595* ⊕ *www.montesangiuliano.it* ⊗ *Closed Mon., 2 wks in mid-Jan., and 1st 2 wks of Nov.*

☕ Coffee and Quick Bites

Pasticceria Grammatico

$ | BAKERY | Fans of Sicilian sweets make a beeline for this place, run by Maria Grammatico, who gained international fame with *Bitter Almonds,* her life story of growing up in a convent orphanage cowritten with Mary Taylor Simeti. Her almond-paste creations are works of art, molded into striking shapes, including dolls and animals. **Known for:** delicious sweets; uniquely shaped desserts; nice views. ⑤ *Average main: €5* ⊠ *Via Vittorio Emanuele 14, Erice* ☎ *0923/869390* ⊕ *www.mariagrammatico.it.*

Hotels

Hotel Elimo

| **HOTEL** | Like the town of Erice itself, the Hotel Elimo is old-fashioned and yet full of charm; eccentric knickknacks and artwork fill the lobby, and the 21 homey guest rooms are all different, many boasting terraces with views of either the cobblestone streets or the valleys below when they're not shrouded by clouds). **Pros:** lots of character; convenient location; helpful staff. **Cons:** noise in some rooms; rooms can feel a bit musty; small bathrooms. $ *Rooms from: €90* ⊠ *Via Vittorio Emanuele 75, Erice* ☎ *0923/869377* ⊕ *www.hotelelimo.it* ⊗ *Closed Jan.–Feb.* ⇄ *21 rooms* ⊚ *Free Breakfast.*

Moderno

$ | **HOTEL** | This delightful hotel has a creaky old feel to it, but that's part of the charm—the lobby area, scattered with books, magazines, and tchotchkes, calls to mind an elderly relative's living room; but the rooms themselves are simple, light, and comfortable. **Pros:** well-regarded restaurant; central location; great rooftop terrace. **Cons:** street-facing rooms can be noisy; very modest rooms; old-fashioned feel not for everyone. $ *Rooms from: €100* ⊠ *Via Vittorio Emanuele 67, Erice* ☎ *0923/869300* ⊕ *www.hotelmodernoerice.it* ⇄ *40 rooms* ⊚ *Free Breakfast.*

Shopping

Ceramica Ericina

CERAMICS | Among Italians, Erice is known for the quality and delicate floral designs of its majolica ceramics, which are unique to the city. This ceramics store is one of the best in the city. ⊠ *Via Gian Filippa Guarnotti 20, Erice* ☎ *0923/869126.*

Segesta

35 km (22 miles) southeast of Erice, 85 km (53 miles) southwest of Palermo.

Segesta is the site of one of Sicily's most impressive temples, constructed on the side of a barren windswept hill overlooking a valley of giant fennel. Virtually intact today, the temple is considered by some to be finer in its proportions and setting than any other Doric temple left standing.

GETTING HERE AND AROUND

Three or four daily buses travel from Trapani to Segesta. About as many trains from Palermo and Trapani stop at the Segesta–Tempio station, a 20-minute uphill walk from Segesta. The site is easily reached via the A29 autostrada.

Sights

★ **Tempio Dorico** (*Doric Temple*)

RUINS | Segesta's imposing temple was actually started in the 5th century BC by the Elymians, who may have been refugees from Troy—or at least non-Greeks, since it seems they often sided with Carthage. In any case, the style of the temple is in many ways Greek, but it was never finished; the walls and roof never materialized, and the columns were never fluted. Wear comfortable shoes, as you need to park your car in the lot at the bottom of the hill and walk about five minutes up to the temple. If you're up for a longer hike, a little more than 1 km (½ mile) away near the top of the hill are the remains of a fine theater with impressive views, especially at sunset, of the plains and the Bay of Castellammare. (There's also a shuttle bus for €1.50 that leaves every half hour.) Concerts and plays are staged here in summer. ⊠ *Calatafimi-Segesta* ☎ *0924/952356* ⊠ *€6.*

Monreale

*59 km (37 miles) northeast of Segesta,
10 km (6 miles) southwest of Palermo.*

Only a short drive from Palermo, the
sleepy town of Monreale is well worth
the effort just to see the spectacular gold
mosaics inside the Duomo. Try to arrive
early in the morning or later in the afternoon to avoid the tour-bus hordes.

GETTING HERE AND AROUND

You can reach Monreale on the frequent
buses that depart from Palermo's Piazza
Indipendenza. From Palermo, drivers can
follow Corso Calatafimi west, though the
going can be slow.

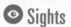 ## Sights

Cloister

VIEWPOINT | The lovely cloister of the
abbey adjacent to the Duomo was
built at the same time as the church
but enlarged in the 14th century. The
beautiful enclosure is surrounded by 216
intricately carved double columns, every
other one decorated in a unique glass
mosaic pattern. Afterward, don't forget
to walk behind the cloister to the belvedere, with stunning panoramic views
over the Conca d'Oro (Golden Conch) valley toward Palermo. ⊠ *Piazza del Duomo,
Monreale* ☎ *091/7489995* ⬚ *€6* ⊗ *Closed
Sun. after 1:30.*

★ Duomo

RELIGIOUS BUILDING | Monreale's splendid
cathedral is lavishly executed with mosaics depicting events from the Old and
New Testaments. It's a glorious fusion
of Eastern and Western influences,
widely regarded as the finest example of
Norman architecture in Sicily. After the
Norman conquest of Sicily the new princes showcased their ambitions through

monumental building projects. William II
(1154–89) built the church complex with
a cloister and palace between 1174 and
1185, employing Byzantine craftsmen.
The major attraction is the 68,220 square
feet of glittering gold mosaics decorating
the cathedral interior. Christ Pantocra-
tor dominates the apse area; the nave
contains narratives of the Creation; and
scenes from the life of Christ adorn the
walls of the aisles and the transept. The
painted wooden ceiling dates from 1816-
37. The roof commands a great view (a
reward for climbing 172 stairs). The wood
and metal organ, the only one in Europe
with six keyboards and 10,000 pipes,
was restored after lightning damage in
2015, and played by Mick Jagger on a
private visit in 2021. Bonnano Pisano's
bronze doors, completed in 1186, depict
42 biblical scenes and are considered
among the most important of medieval
artifacts. Barisano da Trani's 42 panels
on the north door, dating from 1179,
present saints and evangelists. ⊠ *Piazza
del Duomo, Monreale* ☎ *091/6404413,
327/3510886* ⊕ *www.monrealeduomo.it*
⬚ *€4* ⊗ *Closed Mon.–Sat. 12:30–2:30.*

Palermo

Once the intellectual capital of southern
Europe, Palermo has always been at
the crossroads of civilization. Favorably
located on a crescent bay at the foot of
Monte Pellegrino, it has attracted almost
every culture touching the Mediterranean
world. To Palermo's credit, it's absorbed
these diverse cultures into a unique personality that's at once Arab and Christian,
Byzantine and Roman, Norman and Italian. The city's heritage encompasses all
of Sicily's varied ages, but its distinctive
aspect is its Arab-Norman identity, an
improbable marriage that, mixed in with

Palermo

KEY
- Sights
- Restaurants
- Quick Bites
- Hotels

KEY
🛈 Tourist information

Sights

1 Catacombe dei Cappuccini A3
2 Cattedrale D2
3 Chiesa del Gesù E3
4 La Martorana E2
5 Museo Archeologico Regionale Salinas E1
6 Museo Internazionale delle Marionette Antonio Pasqualino G1
7 Palazzo Abatellis G2
8 Palazzo Reale C3
9 Piazza Pretoria E2
10 Quattro Canti E2
11 San Cataldo E2
12 San Giovanni degli Eremiti C3
13 Santa Caterina E2
14 Teatro Massimo D1

Restaurants

1 Casa del Brodo F2
2 Osteria dei Vespri F2
3 Piccolo Napoli E1
4 Pizzeria I Comparucci D1
5 Ristorante Cin Cin E1

Quick Bites

1 Antica Focacceria San Francesco F2
2 Cappadonia D2
3 Pani Ca Meusa F1

Hotels

1 Eurostars Centrale Palace E2
2 Grand Hotel Piazza Borsa F2
3 Hotel Principe di Villafranca D1
4 Le Terrazze D2
5 Massimo Plaza Hotel E1
6 Villa Igiea F1

0 _____ 300 yards
0 _____ 300 meters

Byzantine and Jewish elements, resulted in resplendent works of art. These are most notable in the churches, from small jewels such as San Giovanni degli Eremiti to larger-scale works such as the cathedral. No less noteworthy than the architecture is Palermo's chaotic vitality, on display at some of Italy's most vibrant outdoor markets, public squares, street bazaars, and food vendors, and, above all, in its grand, discordant symphony of motorists, motorcyclists, and pedestrians that triumphantly climaxes in the new town center each evening with Italy's most spectacular passeggiata.

GETTING HERE AND AROUND

Palermo is well connected by road and rail; its airport links it to other cities in Italy, as well as around Europe.

VISITOR INFORMATION

CONTACTS Palermo Tourism Office.
✉ Via Principe di Belmonte 92, Palermo ☎ 091/585172, 091/591698 Airport ⊕ www.cittametropolitana.pa.it/turismo.

Sights

Sicily's capital is a multilayered, vigorous metropolis with a strong historical profile; approach it with an open mind. You're likely to encounter some frustrating instances of inefficiency and, depending on the season, stifling heat. If you have a car, park it in a garage as soon as you can, and don't take it out until you're ready to depart.

Palermo is easily explored on foot, but you may choose to spend a morning taking a bus tour to help you get oriented. The Quattro Canti, or Four Corners, is the hub that separates the four sections of the old city: La Kalsa (the old Arab section) to the southeast, Albergheria to the southwest, Capo to the northwest, and Vucciria to the northeast. Each of these is a tumult of activity during the day, though at night the narrow alleys empty out and are best avoided in favor of the more animated avenues of the new city north

of Teatro Massimo. Sights to see by day are scattered along three major streets: Corso Vittorio Emanuele, Via Maqueda, and Via Roma. The tourist information office in Piazza Bellini will give you a map and a valuable handout that lists opening and closing times, which sometimes change with the seasons.

Catacombe dei Cappuccini

CEMETERY | The spookiest sight in all of Sicily, this 16th-century catacomb houses over 8,000 corpses of men, women, and young children—some in tombs but many mummified and preserved—hanging in rows on the walls, divided by social caste, age, or gender. Most wear signs indicating their names and the years they lived, and many are Capuchin friars, who were founders and proprietors of this bizarre establishment from 1599 to 1911. The site is still managed by the nearby Capuchin church, but was closed to new corpses when an adjacent cemetery was opened, making the catacombs redundant. Though memorable, this is not a spot for the faint of heart; children might be frightened or disturbed. ✉ Piazza Cappuccini 1, off Via Cappuccini, Near Palazzo Reale, Palermo ☎ 091/6527389 ⊕ www.catacombepalermo.it ☞ €3 ⊙ Closed daily 1–3 and Sun. after 1 pm late Oct.–late Mar.

Cattedrale

RELIGIOUS BUILDING | This church is a lesson in Palermitano eclecticism—originally Norman (1182), then Catalan Gothic (14th to 15th century), then fitted out with a Baroque and neoclassical interior (18th century). Its turrets, towers, dome, and arches come together in the kind of meeting of diverse elements that King Roger II (1095–1154), whose tomb is inside along with that of Frederick II, fostered during his reign. The exterior is more intriguing than the interior, but the back of the apse is gracefully decorated with interlacing Arab arches inlaid with limestone and black volcanic tufa. It's possible to visit the cathedral's roof (€5) for some fabulous city views. ✉ *Corso Vittorio Emanuele, Palermo* ☎ *091/334373* ⊕ *www.cattedrale. palermo.it* ⊘ *Closed Sun. after 1* ✉ *Free. €10 treasury, crypt, royal tombs, and roof visit; €5 treasury, crypt, and tombs; €5 roof visit only.*

Chiesa del Gesù

RELIGIOUS BUILDING | It is more than worth the short detour from the lively Ballarò Market to step into the serene Baroque perfection of Chiesa del Gesù (Church of Saint Mary of Gesù). The ornate church was built by the Jesuits not long after their arrival in Palermo in the late 16th century, and was constructed at the site of their religious seat in the city, so the chuch is also sometimes known as Casa Professa (mother house). The interior is almost completely covered with intricate marble bas-reliefs and elaborate black, tangerine, and cream stone work. The splendid church was severely damaged in World War II, but careful restoration has returned it to its shiny, swirling glory. ✉ *Piazza Casa Professa 21, Palermo* ☎ *338/4512011* ✉ *€2.*

★ La Martorana (*Santa Maria dell'Ammiraglio*)

RELIGIOUS BUILDING | One piazza over from the dancing nymphs of Fontana Pretoria, this church, with its elegant Norman campanile, was erected in 1143 but had its interior altered considerably during the Baroque period. High along the western wall, however, is some of the oldest and best-preserved mosaic artwork of the Norman period. Near the entrance is an interesting mosaic of King Roger II being crowned by Christ. In it Roger is dressed in a bejeweled Byzantine stole, reflecting the Norman court's penchant for all things Byzantine. Archangels along the ceiling wear the same stole wrapped around their shoulders and arms. The much plainer San Cataldo is next door. ✉ *Piazza Bellini 3, Quattro Canti* ☎ *345/8288231* ✉ *€2* ⊘ *Closed Sun. after 10:30 am and Mon.–Sat. 1:30–3:30.*

Museo Archeologico Regionale Salinas (*Salinas Regional Museum of Archaeology*)

HISTORY MUSEUM | This archaeology museum is the oldest public museum in Sicily, with a small but excellent collection, including a marvelously reconstructed Doric frieze from the Greek temple at Selinunte, which reveals the high level of artistic culture attained by the Greeks in Sicily some 2,500 years ago. There are also lion's head water spouts from 480 BC, as well as other excavated pieces from around Sicily, including Taormina and Agrigento, which make up part of an informative exhibition on the broader history of the island. After admiring the artifacts, wander through the two plant-filled courtyards, and be sure to check the website for special culture nights, when the museum is open late to host musical performances. ✉ *Piazza Olivella 24, Via Roma, Olivella* ☎ *091/6116807* ⊕ *www. regione.sicilia.it/beniculturali/salinas* ✉ *€6* ⊘ *Closed Sun. afternoon and Mon.*

Museo Internazionale delle Marionette Antonio Pasqualino

OTHER MUSEUM | FAMILY | This collection of more than 4,000 masterpieces showcasing the traditional Opera dei Pupi (puppet show), both Sicilian and otherwise, will delight visitors of all ages with their glittering armor and fierce expressions. The free audio guide to the colorful displays is only available in Italian, but the well-designed exhibits include video clips of the puppets in action, which requires no translation. There are also regular live performances in the museum's theater (stop by or call in advance to check times), which center on the chivalric legends of troubadours of bygone times. The museum can be hard to find: look for the small alley just off Piazzetta Antonio Pasqualino 5. ✉ *Piazzetta Antonio Pasqualino 5, near Via Butera, Kalsa* ☎ *091/328060* ⊕ *www. museodellemarionette.it/en* ✉ *€5* ⊘ *Sun. and Mon. after 2 pm.*

Palermo's Multicultural Pedigree

Palermo was first colonized by Phoenician traders in the 6th century BC, but it was their descendants, the Carthaginians, who built the important fortress here that caught the covetous eye of the Romans. After the First Punic War, the Romans took control of the city in the 3rd century BC. Following several invasions by the Vandals, Sicily was settled by Arabs, who made the country an emirate and established Palermo as a showpiece capital that rivaled both Córdoba and Cairo in the splendor of its architecture. Nestled in the fertile Conca d'Oro (Golden Conch) plain, full of orange, lemon, and carob groves and enclosed by limestone hills, Palermo became a magical world of palaces, mosques, minarets, and palm trees.

It was so attractive and sophisticated a city that the Norman ruler Roger de Hauteville (1031–1101) decided to conquer it and make it his capital (1072). The Norman occupation of Sicily resulted in Palermo's golden age (1072–1194), a remarkable period of enlightenment and learning in which the arts flourished. The city of Palermo, which in the 11th century counted more than 300,000 inhabitants, became the European center for the Norman court and one of the most important ports for trade between the East and West.

Eventually the Normans were replaced by the Swabian ruler Frederick II (1194–1250), the Holy Roman Emperor, and incorporated into the Kingdom of the Two Sicilies. You'll also see plenty of evidence in Palermo of the Baroque art and architecture of the long Spanish rule. The Aragonese viceroys also brought the Spanish Inquisition to Palermo, which some historians believe helped foster the protective secret societies that evolved into today's Mafia.

Palazzo Abatellis
CASTLE/PALACE | Housed in this late-15th-century Catalan Gothic palace with Renaissance elements is the **Galleria Regionale.** Among its treasures are the *Annunciation* (1474), a painting by Sicily's prominent Renaissance master Antonello da Messina (1430–79), and an arresting fresco by an unknown 15th-century painter, titled *The Triumph of Death,* a macabre depiction of the plague years. ✉ *Via Alloro 4, Kalsa* ☏ *091/6230011, 091/6230006 tickets* ⊕ *www.regione. sicilia.it/beniculturali/palazzoabatellis/english/home.htm* 🎫 *€8* ⊘ *Closed weekends after 1 pm and Mon.*

Palazzo Reale (*Royal Palace*)
CASTLE/PALACE | This historic palace, also called Palazzo dei Normanni (Norman Palace), was the seat of Sicily's semiautonomous rulers for centuries; the building is a fascinating mesh of 10th-century Norman and 17th-century Spanish structures. Because it now houses the Sicilian Parliament, parts of the palace are closed to the public from Tuesday to Thursday when the regional assembly is in session. The must-see **Cappella Palatina** (Palatine Chapel) remains open. Built by Roger II in 1132, it's a dazzling example of the harmony of artistic elements produced under the Normans and the interweaving of cultures in the court. Here the skill of French and Sicilian masons was brought to bear on the decorative purity of Arab ornamentation and the splendor of 11th-century Greek Byzantine mosaics. The interior is covered with glittering mosaics and capped by a splendid 10th-century Arab honeycomb stalactite wooden ceiling.

Biblical stories blend happily with scenes of Arab life—look for one showing a picnic in a harem—and Norman court pageantry. Upstairs are the royal apartments, including the **Sala di Re Ruggero** (King Roger's Hall), decorated with ornate medieval mosaics of hunting scenes—an earlier (1120) secular counterpoint to the religious themes seen elsewhere. During the time of its construction, French, Latin, and Arabic were spoken here, and Arab astronomers and poets exchanged ideas with Latin and Greek scholars in one of the most interesting marriages of culture in the Western world. The Sala is always included with entry to the palace or chapel and sometimes hosts special art exhibits. ✉ *Piazza Indipendenza, Albergheria* ☎ *091/7055611* ⊕ *www. federicosecondo.org* 🎫 *€18 Fri.–Mon., €13.50 Tues.–Thurs.* 🕓 *Closed Sun. after 1. Royal Apartments closed Tues.–Thurs.*

Piazza Pretoria

FOUNTAIN | The square's centerpiece, a lavishly decorated fountain with 500 separate pieces of sculpture and an abundance of nude figures, so shocked some Palermitans when it was unveiled in 1575 that it got the nickname "Fountain of Shame." It's even more of a sight when illuminated at night. ✉ *Piazza Pretoria, Quattro Canti.*

Quattro Canti

STREET | The Four Corners is the decorated intersection of two main thoroughfares: Corso Vittorio Emanuele and Via Maqueda. Four rather exhaust-blackened Baroque palaces from Spanish rule meet at concave corners, each with its own fountain and representations of a Spanish ruler, patron saint, and one of the four seasons. ✉ *Palermo.*

San Cataldo

RELIGIOUS BUILDING | Three striking Saracenic scarlet domes mark this church, built in 1154 during the Norman occupation of Palermo. The church now belongs to the Knights of the Holy Sepulchre and has a spare but intense stone interior. For a small discount, save and show your ticket after visiting La Martorana next door. ✉ *Piazza Bellini 3, Kalsa* ☎ *091/6077111* 🎫 *€3* 🕓 *Closed daily 12:30–3.*

San Giovanni degli Eremiti

RELIGIOUS BUILDING | Distinguished by its five reddish-orange domes and stripped-clean stone interior, this 12th-century church was built by the Normans on the site of an earlier mosque—one of 200 that once stood in Palermo. The emirs ruled Palermo for nearly two centuries and brought to it their passion for lush gardens and fountains. One is reminded of this while sitting in San Giovanni's delightful cloister of twin half columns, surrounded by palm trees, jasmine, oleander, and citrus trees. ✉ *Via dei Benedettini 14–20, Albergheria* ☎ *091/6515019* 🕓 *Closed Sun. afternoon* 🎫 *€6.*

Santa Caterina

RELIGIOUS BUILDING | The walls of this splendid Baroque church (1596) in Piazza Bellini are covered with extremely impressive decorative 17th-century inlays of precious marble. There is also a bakery selling delicacies made using the nuns' recipes. ✉ *Piazza Bellini, Quattro Canti* ☎ *091/2713837* ⊕ *www.monasterosanta-caterina.com* 🎫 *€3; €10 combined ticket, includes church, monastery, and rooftop.*

Teatro Massimo

PERFORMANCE VENUE | Construction of this formidable neoclassical theater, the largest in Italy, was started in 1875 by Giovanni Battista Basile and completed by his son Ernesto in 1897. A reconstruction project started in 1974 ran into severe delays, and the facility remained closed until just before its centenary, in 1997. Its interior is as glorious as ever, but the exterior remains more famous thanks to *The Godfather Part III*, which ended with a famous shooting scene on the theater's steps. Visits, by 30-minute guided tour only, are available in five languages, including English. ✉ *Piazza Verdi 9, Olivella* ☎ *091/8486000, 091/6053580 ticket office* ⊕ *www.teatromassimo.it* 🎫 *€8.*

🍴 Restaurants

Casa del Brodo

$$ | SICILIAN | On the edge of the Vucciria, this is one of Palermo's oldest restaurants, dating back to 1890, and still dear to the hearts of locals for its wintertime namesake dish, tortellini *in brodo* (in beef broth), the specialty of the house. There's an extensive antipasto buffet, and you can't go wrong with the *fritella di fave, piselli, carciofi e ricotta* (fried fava beans, peas, artichokes, and ricotta), but be sure to ask about the daily fixed-price meat and fish menus. **Known for:** good choice of meat and fish dishes; large selection of antipasti; tortellini in brodo. ⑤ *Average main: €15* ✉ *Corso Vittorio Emanuele 175, Vucciria* ☎ *091/321655* ⊕ *www. casadelbrodo.it* ⊗ *Closed Jan., Tues. Oct.–May, and Sun. June–Sept.*

Osteria dei Vespri

$$$$ | SICILIAN | This popular eatery occupies a cozy-but-elegant space on an unheralded piazza in the historic city center and splits its offerings between the winter menu (November–March) with traditional osteria fare, and a special larger tasting menu built around seasonal ingredients for the summer. Local seafood is a big draw here, and the homemade pastas won't disappoint, especially when paired with a selection from the extensive wine list. **Known for:** impressive wine cellar; tasting menus with local ingredients; local seafood. ⑤ *Average main: €70* ✉ *Piazza Croce dei Vespri 6, Kalsa* ☎ *091/6171631* ⊕ *www. osteriadeivespri.it* ⊗ *No lunch Sun. and Mon. Nov.–Apr.*

Piccolo Napoli

$$ | SEAFOOD | Founded in 1951, this is one of Old Palermo's most esteemed seafood eateries, and locals come at midday to feast on the freshest of fish, roasted or grilled, from a memorable buffet featuring baby octopus, raw *neonata*

(small fish like sardines but with a milder flavor), and chickpea fritters. There's also spaghetti with sea urchin or *casarecce* (partially rolled pasta) with swordfish and mint. **Known for:** local crowds; friendly staff; fresh fish and seafood. ⑤ *Average main: €16* ✉ *Piazzetta Mulino al Vento 4, Palermo* ☎ *333/3292576, 328/6044380* ⊗ *No dinner Sun.*

Pizzeria I Comparucci

$ | PIZZA | One of Palermo's best pizzerias serves delicious Neapolitan pies from a big oven in the open kitchen—the genius is in the crust, which is seared in a matter of seconds. The owners make their money on a quick turnover (so don't expect a long, leisurely meal), but the pizza is delicious and the place often serves until midnight—later than almost any other restaurant in the neighborhood. **Known for:** late-night dining; pizza, pizza, and more pizza; outdoor seating. ⑤ *Average main: €7* ✉ *Via Messina 36e, Libertà* ☎ *091/6090467* ⊕ *comparucci.it* ⊗ *No lunch.*

Ristorante Cin Cin

$$ | SICILIAN | The Sicilian-born owner of this charming restaurant near Palermo's main shopping street is known for creating lighter and more modern versions of traditional Sicilian dishes, including exemplary pasta with ultrafresh seasonal ingredients and creative takes on seafood-based main dishes. Don't miss the signature dessert, a heavenly semifreddo with flavors like pistachio and cinnamon, chocolate and hazelnut, and Marsala wine and raisin—and perhaps learn some of the secrets with a chef's private cooking class. **Known for:** top-notch cooking classes; modernized Sicilian flavors; delicious semifreddo. ⑤ *Average main: €16* ✉ *Via Manin 22, Libertà* ☎ *091/6124095* ⊕ *ristorantecincin.com* ⊗ *Closed Sun. No lunch.*

Desabout Desserts in Sicily

Sicily is famous for its desserts, none more so than the wonderful cannoli (singular *cannolo*), whose delicate pastry shells and just-sweet-enough ricotta filling, and local pistachio crumbles barely resemble their foreign impostors. They come in all sizes, from pinkie-size bites to holiday cannoli the size of a coffee table, but all should be freshly made to order (*espressi*).

Even your everyday bar will display a window piled high with dozens of varieties of ricotta-based desserts, including delicious fried balls of dough, like the cream-filled iris of Catania. The traditional cake of Sicily is the *cassata siciliana*, a rich, chilled sponge cake with sheep's-milk ricotta and candied fruit. Often bright green

thanks to a colored almond-based frosting, it's the most popular dessert at many Sicilian restaurants, and you shouldn't miss it. From behind bakery windows and glass cases beam tiny marzipan sweets fashioned into brightly colored apples, cherries, and even hamburgers and prosciutto.

If it's summer, do as the locals do and dip your morning brioche—the best in Italy—into a cup of brilliantly refreshing coffee- or almond-flavored granita (Italian shaved ice). Indeed, top-quality frozen treats remain prevalent throughout the island; the world's first granita is said to have been made by the Romans from the snow on the slopes of Mt. Etna mixed with fruit from the countryside.

☕ Coffee and Quick Bites

Antica Focacceria San Francesco

$ | SICILIAN | Turn-of-the-20th-century wooden cabinets, marble-top tables, and cast-iron ovens characterize this neighborhood bakery, celebrated for its Sicilian snacks and inexpensive meals. The big pot on the counter holds the delicious regional specialty *pani câ meusa* (boiled calf's spleen with caciocavallo cheese and salt), but the squeamish can opt for chickpea fritters or an enormous *arancino* (stuffed, fried rice ball). **Known for:** meat and pasta specialties; Sicilian street food; historic atmosphere. ⑤ *Average main: €6* ✉ *Via A. Paternostro 58, Kalsa* ☎ *091/320264* ⊕ *www.anticafocacceria.it* ⊘ *Closed 2 wks mid-Jan.*

Cappadonia

$ | ITALIAN | After experiencing the cozy but basic trattorias located down Palermo's twisting alleyways, take a sweet break at this modern gelateria along the

main drag, which serves exceptional gourmet ice cream. The flavors change with the seasons, but don't miss the tangerine sorbetto that bursts with sweet citrus tang or the classic zabaglione custard. **Known for:** delicious ice cream; seasonal flavors; central location. ⑤ *Average main: €3* ✉ *Via Vittorio Emanuele 401, Palermo* ☎ *392/5689784, 392/5759351* ⊕ *cappadonia.it.*

Pani Ca Meusa

$ | SICILIAN | A civic institution facing Palermo's old fishing port, this standing-room-only joint has been serving its titular calf's spleen sandwich for more than 70 years. The original owner's grandsons produce this local specialty sprinkled with a bit of salt and some lemon and served with or without cheese to a buzzing crowd of Palermo's well-weathered elders, and the sandwich here may very well beat Antica Focacceria San Francesco's for the title of best in town. **Known for:** no seating; calf's spleen sandwich; a bit of Sicilian history. ⑤ *Average main: €2* ✉ *Via Cala 62, Porta Carbone, Kalsa* ☎ *091/323433* ⏰ *Closed Sun.*

Hotels

★ Eurostars Centrale Palace

$ | **HOTEL** | A stone's throw from Palermo's main historic sites, this is the only hotel in the heart of the old town that was once a stately private palace; built in 1717, it weaves old-world charm with modern comfort. **Pros:** comfortable rooms; sparkling clean; in the center of it all. **Cons:** traffic noise; hotel showing its age; some rooms have no view. ⑤ *Rooms from: €112* ✉ *Corso Vittorio Emanuele 327, Vucciria* ☎ *091/8539* ⊕ *www.eurostarscentralepalace.com* ⟲ *104 rooms* ⦿ *Free Breakfast.*

Grand Hotel Piazza Borsa

$$ | **HOTEL** | Cleverly constructed within Palermo's historic stock exchange, this monastery-turned-hotel is ideally located in the old town, just around the corner from Antica Focacceria San Francesco. **Pros:** wellness center with fitness equipment, rare for Sicily hotels; very convenient location; interesting architecture. **Cons:** some noise issues in rooms; somewhat indifferent staff; building feels a bit sterile. ⑤ *Rooms from: €160* ✉ *Via dei Cartari 18, Kalsa* ☎ *091/320075* ⊕ *www.piazzaborsa.it* ⟲ *127 rooms* ⦿ *Free Breakfast.*

Hotel Principe di Villafranca

$$$ | **HOTEL** | Contemporary art mixed with antique furnishings, creamy marble floors, and vaulted ceilings evoke a luxurious private home in a residential area near Palermo's glitzy shopping district. **Pros:** quiet, center-adjacent location; appealing design; well-maintained building. **Cons:** the small car park cannot accommodate all; some rooms on the small side; some rooms can be noisy. ⑤ *Rooms from: €215* ✉ *Via G. Turrisi Colonna 4, Libertà* ☎ *091/6118523* ⊕ *www. principedivillafranca.it* ⟲ *32 rooms* ⦿ *Free Breakfast.*

★ Le Terrazze

$ | **B&B/INN** | Although just steps from the bustling Cattedrale area, complete calm envelops this small, beautifully restored B&B, named for its five lush roof terraces, all with sublime views. **Pros:** period-style rooms; convenient location; in summer, breakfast is served on the glorious rooftop. **Cons:** books up quickly; parking can be difficult; Wi-Fi is iffy. ⑤ *Rooms from: €110* ✉ *Via Pietro Novelli 14, Albergheria* ☎ *091/6520866, 320/4328567* ⊕ *www.leterrazzebb.it* ⟲ *3 rooms* ⦿ *Free Breakfast.*

Massimo Plaza Hotel

$$ | **HOTEL** | Small and select, this hotel enjoys one of Palermo's best locations—opposite the Teatro Massimo, on the border of the old and new towns—and has guest rooms that are spacious, comfortably furnished, and well insulated from the noise on pedestrianized Via Maqueda. **Pros:** tasty breakfast made to order; central location; low-season bargains. **Cons:** plain interiors; stairs (no elevator) up to the rooms; tiny breakfast room. ⑤ *Rooms from: €149* ✉ *Via Maqueda 437, Vucciria* ☎ *091/325657* ⊕ *www.massimoplazahotel.com* ⟲ *11 rooms* ⦿ *Free Breakfast.*

★ Villa Igiea

$$$$ | **HOTEL** | Completely renovated in 2020, this grande dame set in a private tropical garden at the edge of the bay—a local landmark for a century—still maintains a somewhat faded aura of luxury and comfort and retains its essential character. **Pros:** free shuttle to city center in the summer; historic building with lots of atmosphere; secluded setting.

Cons: a bit far from Palermo attractions; no amenities in the nearby area; price range out of reach for most. ⑤ *Rooms from: €620* ⊠ *Salita Belmonte 43, Palermo* ☎ *091/6312111* ⊕ *villa-igiea.com* ⊘ *Closed Jan.–mid-Mar.* ☞ *100 rooms* ⦿ *Free Breakfast.*

Nightlife

Each night between 6 and 9, Palermo's youth gather to shop, socialize, flirt, and plan the evening's affairs in an epic passeggiata along Via Ruggero Settimo (a northern extension of Via Maqueda) and filling Piazza Ruggero Settimo in front of Teatro Politeama. Some trendy bars also line Via Principe del Belmonte, intersecting with Via Roma and Via Ruggero Settimo.

BARS AND CAFÉS

★ Bocum

COCKTAIL LOUNGES | This multilevel cocktail bar between the Vucciria market and the marina is serious about mixology and has created a dedicated oasis in the city's trendiest area. Linger over complex cocktails while lounging on vintage chairs under sparkling chandeliers, all while rubbing elbows with Palermo's cool crowd as records spin on the retro turntable in the corner. ⊠ *Via dei Cassari 6, Vucciria* ☎ *091/332009.*

Santa Monica

PUBS | Immensely popular with the twenty- and thirtysomething crowd, who belly up to the bar for pizza, crepes, and excellent German-style draft beer, this pub is also a good place to watch televised soccer. ⊠ *Via E. Parisi 7, Libertà* ☎ *091/324735* ⊕ *www.santamonicaristorante.it.*

🎭 Performing Arts

CONCERTS AND OPERA

Teatro Massimo

CONCERTS | As the biggest theater in Italy, Teatro Massimo is truly larger than life. Concerts and operas are presented throughout the year, though in summer concerts are usually held outdoors. An opera at the Massimo is an unforgettable Sicilian experience. ⊠ *Piazza Verdi, at top of Via Maqueda, Palermo* ☎ *091/6053580 tickets, 091/8486000, 091/6053267 tours* ⊕ *www.teatromassimo.it* ☞ *Performances €22–€140, tours €8.*

Teatro Politeama Garibaldi

CONCERTS | The shamelessly grandiose, neoclassical Teatro Politeama Garibaldi, home of the Orchestra Sinfonica Siciliana, stages a season of opera and orchestral works from October through June. ⊠ *Piazza Ruggero Settimo, Libertà* ☎ *091/6072532* ⊕ *www.orchestrasinfonicasiciliana.it.*

PUPPET SHOWS

Figli d'Arte Cuticchio Association

PUPPET SHOWS | **FAMILY** | Palermo's tradition of puppet theater holds an appeal for children and adults alike, and street artists often perform outside the Teatro Massimo in summer. One of the most celebrated examples of the folk tradition is performed by the Figli d'Arte Cuticchio association, which hosts classic puppet shows from September to June. ⊠ *Via Bara all'Olivella 95, Kalsa* ☎ *091/323400* ⊕ *www.figlidartecuticchio.com* ☞ *€10.*

🛍 Shopping

North of Piazza Castelnuovo, Via della Libertà and the surrounding streets represent the luxury end of the shopping scale. A second nerve center for shoppers is the pair of parallel streets connecting modern Palermo with the train station, Via Roma and Via Maqueda, where boutiques and shoe shops become increasingly upscale as you move from the Quattro Canti past Teatro Massimo to Via Ruggero Settimo.

FOOD AND WINE

Enoteca Picone

WINE/SPIRITS | The best wineshop in town has been family run for four generations and stocks a fantastic selection of Sicilian and national wines. Although service can be curt, you can taste a selection of wines by the glass in the front of the store. There are tables in the back, where meats and cheeses are also served. ⊠ *Via Marconi 36, Libertà* ☎ *091/331300* ⊕ *www.enotecapicone.it.*

I Peccatucci di Mamma Andrea

OTHER FOOD & DRINK | The charming "Mamma Andrea's Small Sins" sells a plethora of mouthwatering original creations, including jams, preserves, and Sicilian treats like the superb marzipan *frutta martorana* (fruits and vegetables). ⊠ *Via Principe di Scordia 67, near Piazza Florio, Vucciria* ☎ *091/6111654* ⊕ *www.mammaandrea.com.*

Pasticceria Alba

OTHER SPECIALTY STORE | One of the most famous sweets shops in Italy, this is the place to find pastry favorites like cannoli and cassata siciliana, as well as excellent gelato in summer. There is also an on-site restaurant pizzeria. ⊠ *Piazza Don Bosco 7/C, off Via della Libertà near La Favorita Park, Libertà* ☎ *091/309016* ⊕ *www.pasticceriaalba.it.*

MARKETS

Ballarò Market

MARKET | Wind your way through the Albergheria district and this historic market, where the Saracens did their shopping in the 11th century—joined by the Normans in the 12th. The market's name is said to come from nearby Monreale, named Bahlara when Arab traders resided there, and it remains faithful to

their original commerce of fruit, vegetables, and grain. These days it sees more tourists than locals, but it's still fun to experience—just keep a close eye on your belongings in the crowd. And go early: the action dies out by 4 pm most days. ⊠ *Ballarò Market, Albergheria* ✛ *between La Martorana and Quattro Canti.*

Mercato del Capo

MARKET | Umbrella-covered stands crowd the narrow streets along Via Porta Carini and Via Beati Paoli, which are soon clogged with locals stopping to check out the daily fresh catch or haggle over household items at this traditional market. Less touristed than Palermo's other famous food markets, the atmosphere is lively without feeling showy, and there are excellent street food options tucked along the main artery—particularly the unmissable arancini at Da Arianna, a low-key eatery in the heart of the market. ⊠ *Via Porta Carini, Capo* ☽ *Closed Sun.*

Vucciria Market

MARKET | It's easy to see how this market got its name—*vucciria* translates to "voices" or "hubbub." Though now more for tourists than locals, Palermo's most established outdoor market, in the heart of the old town, is a maze of side streets around Piazza San Domenico, where hawkers deliver incessant chants from behind stands brimming with mounds of olives, blood oranges, fennel, and long-stem artichokes. Morning is the best time to see the market in full swing, but it takes on more of a street food atmosphere at night, when no-name bars open to sell cheap cocktails to the crowds gathering around the smoking grills that are wheeled outside after dark. ⊠ *Vucciria Market, Vucciria.*

Cefalù

70 km (43 miles) east of Palermo, 161 km (100 miles) west of Messina.

The coast between Palermo and Messina is dotted with charming villages. Tindari (which dates back to the early-Christian era) and Laghetti di Maranello are two that are worth a stop, but the jewel of the coast is Cefalù, a classically appealing old Sicilian town built on a spur jutting out into the sea.

GETTING HERE AND AROUND

Trains and buses run between Palermo and Messina, and stop at the station about a 10-minute walk from town. Drivers can take the A20 autostrada, though the traffic going in and out of Cefalù can be heavy in summer and the 50-minute train ride from Palermo may be the better option.

VISITOR INFORMATION

CONTACT Cefalù Tourism Office. ✉ *Corso Ruggeri 77, Cefalù* ☎ *0921/421050* ⊕ *cefalu.it.*

Sights

Duomo

RELIGIOUS BUILDING | Cefalù is dominated by a massive headland—*la rocca*—and a 12th-century Romanesque duomo, which is one of the finest Norman cathedrals in Italy. Roger II began the church in 1131 as an offering of thanks for having been saved here from a shipwreck. Its mosaics rival those of Monreale. (Whereas Monreale's Byzantine Christ figure is an austere and powerful image, emphasizing Christ's divinity, the Cefalù Christ is softer, more compassionate, and more human.) At the Duomo you must be respectfully attired—no shorts or beachwear permitted. ✉ *Piazza del Duomo, Cefalù* ☎ *0921/922021* ⊕ *www.cattedraledicefalu.com* ⏱ *Cloister closed weekends* 💶 *Cloister €3.*

Restaurants

Al Porticciolo

$$ | **SICILIAN** | Nicola Mendolia's seaside restaurant is comfortable, casual, and faithfully focused on food—primarily pizza, but with an extensive selection of seafood, pasta, and meat. Dark, heavy wooden tables create a comfortable environment filled with a mix of jovial locals and businesspeople, though you may opt to dine on the spacious terrace. **Known for:** local seafood; lovely terrace overlooking the water; high-quality pizza. 💲 *Average main: €17* ✉ *Via C. Ortolani di Bordonaro 66, Cefalù* ☎ *0921/921981* ⊕ *www.alporticcioloristorante.com.*

🛏 Hotels

Kalura

$$$ | **HOTEL** | This modern hotel is on a small promontory in Caldura, 2 km (1 mile) east of Cefalù, a few minutes away by taxi or a 30-minute walk, and offers bright and cheerful rooms, many with balconies overlooking the sea. **Pros:** family-friendly environment; good swimming; beautiful sea views. **Cons:** Wi-Fi only in lobby; outside town; minimum stay of two to seven nights in high season. 💲 *Rooms from: €209* ✉ *Via V. Cavallaro 13, Cefalù* ☎ *0921/421354* ⊕ *www.hotelkalura.com* ⏱ *Closed mid-Nov.–mid-Mar.* 🛏 *84 rooms* 🍴 *Free Breakfast.*

Lipari

2 hrs 10 mins from Milazzo by ferry, 1 hr by hydrofoil; 60–75 mins from Reggio di Calabria and Messina by ferry.

The largest and most developed of the Aeolians, Lipari welcomes you with distinctive pastel-color houses. Fields of spiky agaves dot the northernmost tip of the island, Acquacalda, indented with pumice and obsidian quarries. In the west is San Calogero, where you can explore hot springs and mud baths. From the red-lava base of the island rises a pla-teau crowned with a 16th-century castle and a 17th-century cathedral.

GETTING HERE AND AROUND

Ferries and hydrofoils from Milazzo, which is 41 km (25 miles) west of Messi-na, stop here. There's also ferry service from Reggio di Calabria and Messina.

Sights

★ Museo Archeologico Regionale Eoliano

HISTORY MUSEUM | This vast, multibuilding museum is terrific, with an intelligent-ly arranged collection of prehistoric finds—some dating as far back as 4000 BC—from various sites in the archipelago, as well as Greek and Roman artifacts, including an outstanding collection of Greek theatrical masks, and even interesting information on volcanoes. Basic descriptions about the exhibits are provided in English and Italian, though more comprehensive information is in Italian only. That said, there is so much to see, the museum is worth at least a few hours of your time. ⊠ *Via Castello 2, Lipari* ☎ *090/9880174* ⊙ *Closed Sun. after 1:30* 🎫 *€6.*

★ Vulcano

ISLAND | A popular day trip from Lipari is to visit the most notorious of the Aeolian Islands: Vulcano. True to its name—and the origin of the term—Vulcano has a profusion of fumaroles sending up jets of hot vapor, although the volcano itself has long been dormant. Visitors come to soak in the strong-smelling sulfur springs, or to sunbathe or walk on some of the archipelago's best beaches, though the volcanic black sand can be off-putting at first glance. Ascend to the crater (1,266 feet above sea level) on mule-back for eye-popping views or take a boat ride into the grottoes around the base. From

Capo Grillo you can see all the Aeolians. **Liberty Lines** has high-speed passenger vessels that make the crossing from Lipari in 10 minutes; frequent daily depar-tures are offered year-round. ⊠ *Vulcano, Lipari.*

Restaurants

★ Filippino

$$ | SICILIAN | Founded in 1910, Filippino is rightly rated as one of the archipelago's best dining venues—and you'll under-stand why, when you sample the catch of the day on the gorgeous terrace. *Zuppa di pesce* (fish soup) and the antipasto platter of smoked and marinated fish are absolute musts, but be sure to leave some room for the local version of cassata siciliana, accompanied by sweet Malvasia wine from Salina. **Known for:** scrumptious local desserts; pasta, soup, and risotto with fresh seafood; traditional Sicilian recipes. 💲 *Average main: €18* ⊠ *Piazza Mazzini Lipari, Lipari* ☎ *090/9811002* ⊕ *www.filippino.it* ⊙ *Closed Mon. Nov.–Jan.*

🛏 Hotels

Les Sables Noirs

$$ | HOTEL | Named for the black sands of the beach in front, this luxury hotel is superbly sited on the beautiful Porto di Ponente on the nearby island of Vulcano, and its cool modern furnishings and inviting pool and spa induce a sybaritic mood. **Pros:** five-minute walk to town; stunning beachfront location; delicious breakfasts. **Cons:** five-night minimum stay in August; no on-site restaurant; the spa is not included in the price. 💲 *Rooms from: €240* ⊠ *Porto di Ponente, Vulcano* ☎ *090/9850* ⊕ *www.lessablesnoirs. it* ⊙ *Closed mid-Oct.–Apr.* 🛏 *53 rooms* 🍴 *Free Breakfast.*

Salina

50 mins from Lipari by ferry, 20 mins by hydrofoil.

The second largest of the Aeolians, Salina is also the most fertile, which accounts for its excellent Malvasia dessert wine. Salina is the archipelago's lushest and highest island, too—Mt. Fossa delle Felci rises to more than 3,000 feet and offers a challenging two-hour hike to the summit—and the vineyards and fishing villages along its slopes add to the allure. Pollara, in the west of the island, has capitalized on its fame as one of the locations in the 1990s cult movie *Il Postino* (*The Postman*) and is an ideal location for an evening passeggiata on well-maintained paths along the volcanic terrain.

GETTING HERE AND AROUND

Ferries and hydrofoils arrive here from Lipari.

Hotels

Hotel Solemar

$ | **HOTEL** | In a valley between Salina's two mountains, this hotel has most of the hallmarks of Mediterranean charm—large terraces for contemplation, a location in a sleepy town, and pleasing local seafood served on summer evenings in the restaurant. **Pros:** terrific views; relaxed atmosphere; helpful staff. **Cons:** very simple decor; no pool; a 15-minute taxi ride from Salina's main port. ⑤ *Rooms from: €100* ✉ *Via Roma 8, Leni* ☎ *090/9809445* ⊕ *www.salinasolemar-hotel.it* ⊗ *Closed Nov.–Mar.* ➥ *14 rooms* � ○ *Free Breakfast.*

Panarea

2 hrs from Lipari by ferry, 25–50 mins by hydrofoil; 7–9 hrs from Naples by ferry.

Panarea is the second smallest of the islands but has some of the most dramatic scenery, including wild caves carved out of the rock and dazzling flora. The exceptionally clear water and the richness of life on the sea floor make Panarea especially suitable for underwater exploration, though there's little in the way of beaches. The outlying rocks and islets make a gorgeous sight, and you can enjoy the panorama on an easy excursion to the small Bronze Age village at Capo Milazzese.

GETTING HERE AND AROUND

Ferries and hydrofoils arrive here from Lipari and Naples.

Hotels

Hotel Raya

$$$$ | **HOTEL** | Although some visitors say it's resting on past laurels, Raya is perfectly in keeping with the elite style of Panarea—discreet and expensive, with a pool and terrace that enjoy views over the sea toward Stromboli. **Pros:** lovely pool area; great views of Stromboli; hippie-chic ambience. **Cons:** uphill trudge to rooms; snooty staff; in need of renovations. ⑤ *Rooms from: €500* ✉ *San Pietro, Panarea* ☎ *090/983013* ⊕ *www.hotelraya.it* ⊗ *Closed mid-Oct.–mid-Apr.* ➥ *34 rooms* ○ *Free Breakfast.*

Stromboli

3 hrs 45 mins from Lipari by ferry, 65–90 mins by hydrofoil; 9 hrs from Naples by ferry, 5 hrs by hydrofoil.

This northernmost of the Aeolians consists entirely of the cone of an active volcano. The view from the sea—especially at night, as an endless stream of glowing red-hot lava flows into the water—is unforgettable. Stromboli is in a constant state of mild dissatisfaction, and every now and then its anger flares up, so following a devastating eruption on July 3, 2019, which killed a hiker, authorities do not allow any ascents to the crater. The main town has a small selection of reasonably priced hotels and restaurants, and a choice of lively clubs and cafés. In addition to the island tour, excursions might include boat trips around the sea stack of Strombolicchio, which is all that remains of the original volcano that gave rise to Stromboli.

GETTING HERE AND AROUND

Ferries and hydrofoils arrive here from Lipari and Naples.

Sights

Pippo Navigazione

VOLCANO | The best way to see Stromboli's eruptions is with a boat tour such as those run by Pippo Navigazione. Boat trips include three-hour day cruises and night tours that explore the area where the lava reaches the sea. ⊠ *Porto Scari, Stromboli* ☎ *348/0559296 (Giovanni) 339/2229714 (Giovanni's mother).*

Filicudi

30–60 mins from Salina and Lipari by hydrofoil; 2 hrs from Cefalù and Palermo, 2 hrs from Milazzo, and 10 hrs from Naples by ferry.

Just a dot in the sea, Filicudi is famous for its unusual volcanic rock formations, the enchanting Grotta del Bue Marino (Grotto of the Sea Ox), and the crumbled remains of a prehistoric village at Capo Graziano. The island, which is spectacular for walking and hiking, is still a truly undiscovered, restful haven, and has a handful of hotels and *pensioni* as well as some more informal rooms with families who put up guests. Car ferries are available only in summer.

GETTING HERE AND AROUND

Ferries and hydrofoils arrive throughout the year from Salina and Lipari, and also in summer from Palermo, Cefalù, Milazzo, and Naples.

Hotels

La Canna

$$ | **HOTEL** | Set above the tiny port, commanding fabulous views of sea and sky from its flower-filled terrace, this hotel offers small but adequate guest rooms, kept clean and tidy by the family-friendly staff. **Pros:** great views; relaxing pool and lounge area; family-friendly atmosphere. **Cons:** half board required in peak season; an uphill climb from the port; no Wi-Fi in guest rooms. ⑤ *Rooms from: €160* ⊠ *Via Rosa 43, Filicudi Porto* ☎ *090/9889956* ⊕ *www.lacannahotel.it* ☉ *Closed mid-Oct.–mid-Apr.* ➦ *14 rooms* ⭘⏐ *No Meals.*

Chapter 18

SARDINIA

Updated by
Robert Andrews

 Sights
★★★☆☆

 Restaurants
★★★★☆

 Hotels
★★★★☆

 Shopping
★★☆☆☆

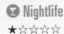 Nightlife
★☆☆☆☆

WELCOME TO SARDINIA

TOP REASONS TO GO

★ **Relax on idyllic beaches:** Covering more than 1,200 miles of coastline, Sardinia's beaches beckon with their turquoise waters, white sand, and rippled dunes.

★ **Discover natural beauty:** A network of trails explores Sardinia's resplendent mountains, deep gorges, lush forests, and cascading waterfalls.

★ **Explore charming towns and villages:** From coastal towns to rural villages, the island is dotted with a variety of settlements that take pride in their history and tradition. Each has its own culture, cuisine, and unique way of life.

★ **Dive or snorkel the outer reefs:** Crystalline waters, warm weather, and outer reefs make Sardinia a paradise for underwater adventurers. Sunken ships and marine reserves provide the ideal place to discover marine life.

★ **Savor Sardinian delicacies:** From pasta and prosciutto to lamb and cheese, the island's cuisine is sure to satisfy any appetite.

1 Cagliari. Sardinia's capital is a hive of cultural attractions, dining hot spots, and glamorous shops.

2 Pula. Just south of Cagliari, Pula is home to resorts, beaches, and a major archaeological site.

3 Sant'Antioco. A significant archaeological site and museum merit a visit on this west-coast island, once a major Carthaginian base.

4 San Pietro. This offshore isle makes a perfect bolt-hole, with its lively port and undeveloped beaches.

5 Costa Verde. A high, cliffy coastline and alluring beaches are the main attractions on Sardinia's "Green Coast."

6 Barumini. The island's ancient and enigmatic nuraghic culture are showcased at Su Nuraxi, just outside Barumini.

7 Oristano. Little visited by tourists, this provincial center makes an appealing base for the nearby Sinis Peninsula.

8 Tharros. Explore Carthaginian and Roman ruins at this site near the town of Oristano.

9 Nuoro. The largest inland town is a must-see for anyone interested in Sardinia's traditional culture.

10 Fonni. Near the island's highest peaks, Fonni makes an ideal hiking base.

11 Alghero. Alghero's historic center is a warren of traffic-free lanes lined with lively bars, shops, and restaurants.

12 Sassari. Sardinia's second city has an engaging old quarter.

13 Castelsardo. This former north coast stronghold is renowned for its basketware.

14 Santa Teresa Gallura. On the island's northern tip, this resort is surrounded by excellent beaches.

15 La Maddalena. Garibaldi's former home is a highlight of any tour of this archipelago.

16 Porto Cervo. Day-trippers are drawn to this jet-setter enclave on the famed Costa Smeralda.

17 Olbia. Sardinia's northern gateway is a short drive from some of Italy's most exclusive hotels and beaches.

EATING AND DRINKING WELL IN SARDINIA

Wining and dining in Sardinia is not just a richly delicious experience, it's also a way to have a close-up encounter with the history, geography, and cultural traditions of the island. Sardinian food has its own culinary identity, a complex and eclectic mix that makes for mouthwatering and often revelatory dishes.

Sardinia's proximity to North Africa and its long Spanish occupation mean that elements of both cultures can be found in the island's kitchens, including couscous and paella. There are also strong regional variations within Sardinia itself, as well as a traditional division between the land-based fare of the interior and the fresh seafood on the coasts. Wherever you go here, you'll find a strong emphasis on seasonal ingredients and ancient cooking techniques.

BREADS, CHEESES, AND SWEET SPECIALTIES

Sardinia has a strong tradition of bread-making and is famous for crispy paper-thin *pane carasau* flatbread (*carta di musica* in Italian).

Ever wondered about all those sheep roaming the rugged slopes of the interior? They're there to produce the raw materials for Italy's original and best pecorino. It's ubiquitous in Sardinia, and comes in various strengths and consistencies.

Sardinian desserts include *sospiri* (morsels of almond dough stuffed with citrus-infused almond paste), *torrone di mandorle* (almond nougat), and *seadas* (cheese-filled pastries topped with honey, also called *sebadas*). The *candelaus,* a fruit-and-almond dessert, and sweet ricotta-stuffed *pardula* cakes are popular in Cagliari. Unmissable is *amaro di corbezzolo,* made by bees that suck nectar from a plant known as *arbutus,* the tree strawberry.

MEAT

The most popular meat dishes are veal, roast *agnello* (lamb), and *porcheddu* (spit-roasted suckling pig). *Cavallo,* or *carne equino* (horse meat), is also commonly found on restaurant menus, particularly in Sassari, where it's generally served in the form of a *bistecca* (thin steak). Donkey (*asino*) and wild boar (*cinghiale*) are other Sardinian specialties. Sometimes cinghiale is roasted on a spit or prepared using the ancient Sardinian technique of *incarralzadu,* for which it's placed in a large hole lined with fragrant myrtle leaves. Another option is *suppa quata,* a hearty soup that's made from beef broth, bread, and aged pecorino cheese.

SEAFOOD

Whole fish are best eaten roasted or grilled, though you may also find them sautéed in pasta or incorporated into *copaxa de peix,* a fish soup from Alghero. The most famous Alghero dish is lobster, known as *langouste* or *aragosta.* Lobster doesn't appear on restaurant menus in winter—fortunately, the very time when *riccio di mare* (sea urchin), another local specialty, is best enjoyed. Winter is also the best season for *bottarga,* the dried, cured roe of gray mullet or tuna.

STARTERS

Opt for antipasti *di mare* or *di terra* to kick off your meal. Traditional pastas include *malloreddus* (small shells), *culurgiones* (ravioli), and *maccarones de busa* (thick pasta twists). Homemade pastas might be topped with a wild-boar sauce; *fregola,* a semolina pasta, is often served with *arselle* (clams).

WINE

Among the whites, the dry *torbato* of the Alghero Coast and the slightly sparkling *vermentino* from Gallura are standouts. The Oristano region produces the dry, sherrylike *vernaccia* (unrelated to the Tuscan variety), Bosa produces amber-tone *malvasia,* and Barbagia is one of the best sources of *cannonau,* a red wine with an ancient pedigree. The traditional liqueur *mirto,* which makes a fine after-dinner drink, is made from native wild myrtle berries.

The second-largest island in the Mediterranean, Sardinia remains unique and enigmatic with its rugged coastline and white-sand beaches, dramatic granite cliffs, and mountainous inland tracts. Glamorous resorts lie within a short distance of quiet, medieval villages, and ruined castles and ancient churches testify to an eventful history.

But although conquerors from all directions—Phoenicians, Carthaginians, Romans, Catalans, Pisans, Piemontese—have left their traces, no outside culture has had a dominant impact. Pockets of foreign influence persist along the coasts, but inland, a proud Sardinian culture flourishes.

As a travel destination, Sardinia's identity is split: the island has some of Europe's most expensive resorts, but it's also home to pristine terrain untouched by commercial development. Fine sand and clean waters draw summer sun worshippers to beaches that rank among the Mediterranean's best. Most famous are those along the Costa Smeralda (Emerald Coast), where the ultra-rich have anchored their yachts since the 1960s. Less exclusive beach holidays can be had elsewhere on the island at La Maddalena, Villasimius, and Pula, and there are wonderfully intact medieval towns—Cagliari, Oristano, Sassari—on or near the water.

Apart from the glamorous shores and upscale locales found in the east, most of Sardinia's coast is rugged and unreachable, a jagged series of wildly beautiful inlets accessible only by sea. Inland, Sardinia remains shepherd's country, silent and stark. Against this landscape are the striking and mysterious stone *nuraghi* (ancient defensive structures) that provide clues to the island's ancient culture. Found only on Sardinia, these sites have been included on the UNESCO World Heritage list, described as "the finest and most complete example of a remarkable form of prehistoric architecture."

MAJOR REGIONS

Cagliari and the Southern Coast. Sardinia's capital and largest city, Cagliari (pronounced *cahl*-yah-ree) contains the island's principal art and archaeology museums as well as an intact old citadel with lofty views of the sea, lagoons, and mountains. To the southwest is Pula, an inland resort within easy reach of good beaches and the excavations at Nora. West of Cagliari, the town of Sant'Antioco sits on an island of the same name that was once a major Carthaginian base and now preserves an absorbing archaeological site and museum.

Su Nuraxi to the Costa Smeralda. Inland and north of Cagliari, explore the apogee of the island's prehistoric nuraghic civilization at Su Nuraxi, just outside the village of Barumini. Northwest of here, Oristano makes an ideal stopover for exploring the Carthaginian and Roman archaeological ruins at Tharros. In the mountainous interior, Nuoro has a first-rate ethnographic museum highlighting Sardinia's traditional culture, while the village of Fonni is a convenient base for outdoor excursions. In the northwest, Sardinia's second city, Sassari, and the Spanish-influenced port and resort of Alghero both have excellent restaurants.

Castelsardo and Santa Teresa Gallura are popular north coast resorts—the first for its castle-museum, the second for its beaches. But the rugged granite landscape of Sardinia's northeast is probably best known for the Costa Smeralda, a short strip of elite hotels and beaches in an area with strict building codes that safeguard the environment. Porto Cervo is the hub of this, one of Europe's most prestigious summer destinations and long favored by the rich and famous. A major port and an airport are in nearby Olbia, which is worth a short visit to see the basilica of San Simplicio, a fine Romanesque church.

Planning

Getting Here and Around

AIR

Flying is by far the fastest and easiest way to get to the island. Sardinia's major airport, Aeroporto di Elmas, is in Cagliari, with smaller ones at Alghero (Aeroporto Fertilia) and Olbia (Aeroporto Costa Smeralda).

AIR CONTACTS Aeroporto di Alghero. ⊠ *Regione Nuraghe Biancu, 9½ km (6 miles) north of Alghero* ☎ *079/935011* ⊕ *www.aeroportodialghero.it.* **Aeroporto di Cagliari.** ⊠ *Via dei Trasvolatori, 8 km (5 miles) northwest of city center, Elmas*

☎ *070/211211* ⊕ *www.cagliariairport. it.* **Aeroporto di Olbia Costa Smeralda.** ⊠ *Strada Statale Orientale Sarda, 4 km (2½ miles) southeast of city center, Olbia* ☎ *0789/563444* ⊕ *www.geasar.it.*

BUS

Cagliari is linked with the other towns of Sardinia by a network of buses. All major cities and most local destinations are served by ARST. City buses in Cagliari, Olbia, Alghero, and Sassari operate on the same system as those on the mainland: buy your ticket first, at a tobacco shop or machine, and punch it in the machine on the bus.

BUS CONTACTS ARST. ☎ *351/8374226 in Italy, daily 7 am–8 pm* ⊕ *www.arst. sardegna.it.* **Cagliari Bus Station.** ⊠ *Piazza Matteotti, Cagliari* ☎ *070/6671824.*

CAR

Sardinia is about 270 km (167 miles) long from north to south, which takes 3–4 hours to drive on main roads; it's roughly 120 km (75 miles) across. Most of the ferries that connect the island with the mainland transport cars.

Roads are generally in good condition, with clear signposting. Superstrada double-lane routes are well developed. Expect winding inland mountain and coastal roads with hairpin turns. Most gas stations are closed in the afternoons, at night, and on Sunday, though at those times you can still use cash to automatically gas up. Try to avoid driving at night, when mountain roads are particularly hazardous and roadside facilities are infrequent, especially in the east. Fog may be an issue in winter.

TRAIN

Trenitalia, or Ferrovie dello Stato (FS), is the national railway of Italy. You can plan itineraries, purchase tickets, and look for special deals online. The Stazione Centrale in Cagliari is next to the bus station on Piazza Matteotti. There are fairly good connections between Olbia, Cagliari, Sassari, and Oristano. Service on

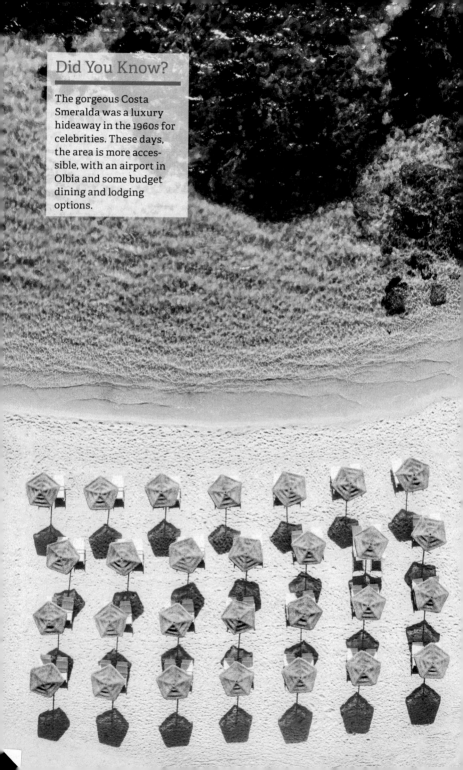

the few other local lines is infrequent and slow. The fastest train between Olbia and Cagliari takes 3½ hours. Local trains run by ARST connect Sassari with Alghero (around 40 minutes).

If you can stand a little agitation and are a fan of slow travel, consider taking a trip on the rickety old narrow-gauge railroad operated by Trenino Verde della Sardegna through the island's interior. The service, which started as a public transport utility in 1893, now only runs during the high season in the form of tourist excursions that take in some of Sardinia's most panoramic landscapes. The two Trenino Verde routes run between the mountain villages of Mandas (linked to Cagliari by local trains) and Sadali, and between Arbatax, a small port on the island's east coast, and the village of Gairo; each is a full-day excursion taking 11 and 10 hours respectively, and each includes guided tours of some of the places en route plus lunch stops. There are one to four departures weekly in summer.

TRAIN CONTACTS Trenitalia. ☎ *892021 in Italy, 06/68475475 from outside Italy* ⊕ *www.trenitalia.com.*

When to Go

The best time to visit Sardinia is Easter through September. European vacationers flock to the island for sunshine in July and August. Expect to pay the highest rates during these two peak summer months, when roads, tourist sites, and beaches are most crowded. From September to October, when accommodations start to shut down for the year, you'll find end-of-season deals and fewer tourists. Any other time of year, expect near ghost towns—with closed restaurants, hotels, and shops.

Restaurants

The full range of eateries can be found in every Sardinian town, from pizzerias to gourmet restaurants, and you'll be especially spoiled for choice in the island's capital, Cagliari, and the resort of Alghero, where good-value fixed-price menus are common. Seafood is ubiquitous, though the most authentic Sard cuisine is based on land products, such as lamb, boar, and suckling pig, not to mention mushrooms, artichokes, and other seasonal produce. Note that, as in other parts of Italy, fish dishes are often priced according to weight (usually by the *etto,* or 100 grams). Many places close in winter; in summer, book ahead to be sure of a table.

Restaurant reviews have been short-ened. For full information, visit Fodors. com.

Hotels

In Sardinia, there are numerous luxury resorts with stunning beachfront vistas, bed-and-breakfast inns in medieval villages, private villas tucked away on lush hills, modern hotels in the trendy capital, and farmhouses on tranquil mountainsides. During summer months, the most popular destination on the island is the Costa Smeralda in the east. High demand during July and August raises nightly rates to an astronomical range, above €1,500 for the most deluxe accommodations. Find more reasonable hotel rates in other parts of the island, which are equally breathtaking and less crowded. Plan dates well in advance, as many hotels close at the end of September until the following April or May.

Hotel reviews have been shortened. For full information, visit Fodors.com.

WHAT IT COSTS in Euros			
$	$$	$$$	$$$$
RESTAURANTS			
under €15	€15–€24	€25–€35	over €35
HOTELS			
under €125	€125–€200	€201–€300	over €300

Tours

Visos Viaggi
PRIVATE GUIDES | This travel agent and tour operator specializes in individual tours and villa and hotel accommodations. ✉ Via Puccini 41, Cagliari ☎ 070/658772 ⊕ www.visosviaggi.com.

Cagliari

268 km (166 miles) south of Olbia.

Known in the local dialect as Casteddu, the island's capital has a warren of pedestrianized streets at its heart and a range of impressive Italianate architecture, from modern to medieval. The city comprises nearly 160,000 people and has a busy commercial port and waterfront with broad avenues and arched arcades, while the old hilltop citadel (called, simply, Castello) makes a good starting point to a visit, not least for the Museo Archeologico located here. The imposing Bastione di Saint Remy and Mercato di San Benedetto (one of the best fish markets in Italy) are both must-sees.

GETTING HERE AND AROUND
The easiest way to arrive in Cagliari is by plane or boat. From the airport, it's easy to get into the city center by train. You can also rent a car at the airport; booking before arrival is highly recommended. If you arrive by boat, travel from Palermo (Sicily), Civitavecchia (Rome), or Naples. The port is quite near the city center.

Piazza Matteotti is the terminal for Cagliari's city buses, which are operated by Consorzio Trasporti e Mobilità (CTM). Buy tickets at the kiosk or machine here before boarding.

VISITOR INFORMATION
CONTACT Cagliari Tourism Office. ✉ *Palazzo Civico, Piazza Matteotti* ☎ *070/6777397* ⊕ *www.cagliariturismo.it/en.*

Sights

Anfiteatro Romano
RUINS | This substantial amphitheater arena dating from the 2nd century AD attests to the importance of this area to the Romans. You can tour the seating area but not (at least for the time being) the underground passages. ■ **TIP→ The site isn't suitable for people with mobility impairments. If you don't want to enter it, good views can be had from Viale Sant'Ignazio.** ✉ *Viale Sant'Ignazio da Laconi, Cagliari* ☎ *366/256–2826* ⊕ *www.beniculturalicagliari.it* 🎫 *€3.*

Castello
VIEWPOINT | Perched over the vast expanse of Cagliari and its port, this hillside quarter has narrow streets that hold ancient monuments and piazzas amid apartments with wash hung out to dry on elaborate wrought-iron balconies. The most impressive entrance is through the commanding late-19th-century archway of the Bastione di St. Remy on Piazza Costituzione. Entering this way means climbing numerous steps; if this is a problem, walk up Viale Regina Elena to find an elevator. At the top is an impressive panorama of the cityscape and the Gulf of Cagliari. From Piazza Palazzo, holding Cagliari's cathedral, you can walk to Piazza Indipendenza and the 14th-century limestone St. Pancras Tower, a twin of the nearby Elephant Tower. ✉ *Cagliari* ⊕ *www.comune.cagliari.it/portale.*

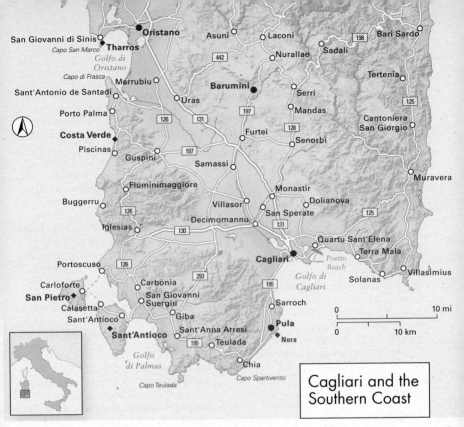

Cagliari and the Southern Coast

Duomo

CHURCH | The Cattedrale di Santa Maria, also known as the Duomo, was begun in the 12th century, but major renovation in the 17th century and reconstruction during the mid-1930s have left little of the original medieval church. The tiers of columns on the facade resemble those of medieval Romanesque Pisan churches, but only sections of the central portal, the bell tower, and the two side entrances are from the 13th century. Look for one of the most memorable features inside—the oversize marble pulpit sculpted in the 1300s and divided in half to fit into the church nave; it now lies on either side of the main entrance. ⊠ *Piazza Palazzo, Cagliari* ☎ *070/663837* ⊕ *www.duomodicagliari.it.*

Museo Archeologico

HISTORY MUSEUM | Built within the walls of the Pisan castle erected in the early 1300s, Cagliari's archaeological museum is the world's foremost authority on Sardinia's ancient nuraghic civilization, named after the curious stone towers, or *nuraghi*, that are unique to the island. Archaeologists date most of these enigmatic structures to about 1300–1200 BC, the same time the ancient Israelites were establishing themselves in Canaan. Among the highlights on display are bronze statuettes from nuraghic towers and tombs, and the much-celebrated Giganti di Mont'e Prama, giant nuraghic stone statues representing warriors and boxers, unearthed in the 1970s and only recently restored. Other items worth seeking out in the museum include a pearl-laden Phoenician faience necklace, finds from the Tuvixeddu necropolis, remnants from the archaeological site of Nora, and medieval gold coins. ⊠ *Cittadella dei Musei, Piazza Arsenale, Cagliari* ☎ *070/60518245* ⊕ *www.museoarcheocagliari.beniculturali.it* ⊠ *€7* ⊘ *Closed Mon.*

San Sperate

MUSEUM VILLAGE | Considered a *paese museo,* a "museum village," this small town 20 km (12 miles) northwest of Cagliari has houses whose walls have been brightened with murals by local artists and some well-known Italian painters. The first murals were painted in the 1960s, and colorful new trompe-l'oeil and other artistic renderings of daily life continue to transform the town into an open-air art gallery. Be on the lookout for the world-renowned artist Pinuccio Sciola's suggestive stone and bronze sculptures that also pay tribute to the region's ancient history. ⊠ *San Sperate* ✛ *SP4, off SS131* ⊕ *www.sansperate.net.*

 Beaches

★ Poetto Beach

BEACH | FAMILY | Only 5 km (3 miles) southeast of the city center, Poetto Beach is one of the most enticing spots to relax in summer for both locals and tourists. Its clean, shallow, turquoise waters stretch for some 8 km (5 miles), and the beach is lined with cafés, restaurants, snack bars, and parks. Beach chairs and umbrellas are available for rent for around €15. From the large, sandy shores, you can admire the pink flamingos that nest in the marshy reeds of the nearby Molentargius lagoon. ■**TIP→ Poetto is easy to reach on the frequent public transport services: take Bus PF or PQ from Piazza Matteotti. Amenities:** food and drink; lifeguards; showers; toilets; parking (fee in summer); water sports. **Best for:** swimming; walking; windsurfing. ⊠ *Cagliari* ✛ *By car, take Viale Diaz from Cagliari to Viale Poetto.*

Restaurants

★ Dal Corsaro

$$$$ | ITALIAN | This critically acclaimed and elegant but simply furnished restaurant near the port offers modern and creative Italian haute cuisine on three tasting menus. It shares an entrance and a kitchen with the more casual Fork bistro, where the à la carte and prix-fixe lunch menus include such traditional dishes as smoked swordfish carpaccio, seafood risotto, and veal shank with a beer sauce, and there's a separate oyster menu, too. **Known for:** good-value snack lunches at next-door Fork; eclectic tasting menus; adventurous and sophisticated cuisine. ⑤ *Average main: €100* ⊠ *Viale Regina Margherita 28, Cagliari* ☎ *070/664318* ⊕ *www.stefanodeidda.it* ⊘ *Closed Mon. and 2 wks in Jan.* ⋔ *Jacket required.*

Sa Ide e S'Ollia

$$$ | ITALIAN | Take a tour of contemporary Sardinian gastronomy in this trendsetting place that has become a huge hit with the *cagliaritani.* Small dishes on the tasting menus (€27 and €37, including drinks) consist of such bold pairings as *ravioli di cernia con fragole e gamberi* (fish ravioli with strawberries and prawns), *spezzatino di maiale con le cozze* (pork stew with mussels), and *cappuccino di seppie in crema di patate e bottarga* (cuttlefish with creamed potatoes and mullet roe). **Known for:** enthusiastic service; good-value set menus that include wine; innovative food pairings. ⑤ *Average main: €25* ⊠ *Corso Vittorio Emanuele II 370, Cagliari* ☎ *070/3510392* ⊘ *No dinner Sun.*

Su Cumbidu

$$ | ITALIAN | A meal at this restaurant in Cagliari's lively Marina quarter, near the port, makes for a quick and affordable introduction to Sardinia's rural cuisine. Dishes can be ordered as part of a fixed-price meal or separately, and portions are large, so go easy on antipasti to leave room for main courses of lamb, sausage, and the famous Sardinian *maialetto* (roast suckling pig, aka *porcheddu*). **Known for:** traditional meat-based dishes; range of set-price menus; casual, friendly atmosphere. $ *Average main: €15 ⊠ Via Napoli 13, Cagliari ☎ 070/670712 ⊕ www.sucumbidu.com.*

☕ Coffee and Quick Bites

Antico Caffè

$$ | **ITALIAN** | The gilded Antico Caffè once served as an intellectual haunt for famous writers like D. H. Lawrence and Grazia Deledda, who won the Nobel Prize in Literature in 1926. With its street-front terrace and polished-wood-and-brass interior, it has anchored the base of the Bastione di St. Remy since 1855, serving as a social center from breakfast time until well after midnight; the menu features local fish and meat specialties. You can also get pastas, salads, and such desserts as tiramisu and elaborate artisanal gelato *coupe* concoctions. **Known for:** swift lunches; traditional ambience; convenient location. $ *Average main: €18 ⊠ Piazza Costituzione 10/11, Cagliari ☎ 070/658206 ⊕ www.anticocaffe1855.it.*

Hotels

Hotel BJ Vittoria

$ | **B&B/INN** | The airy white rooms, period-style furnishings, and ceramic flooring make this third-floor pension directly opposite the port cozy and characterful. **Pros:** clean rooms; family atmosphere; central location near port. **Cons:** limited amenities; no parking; breakfast is not served in the hotel. $ *Rooms from: €110 ⊠ Via Roma 75, Cagliari ☎ 070/657970 ⊕ www.hotelbjvittoria.it ⇋ 14 rooms ꙰ Free Breakfast.*

Hotel Regina Margherita

$$ | **HOTEL** | Close to the port and the main downtown sights, this large, modern hotel attracts both vacationers and businesspeople with a quiet, friendly ambience and spacious, sober rooms. **Pros:** free parking; central location; higher rooms have harbor views. **Cons:**

few leisure facilities; lacks local character; breakfast sometimes disappoints. $ *Rooms from: €130 ⊠ Viale Regina Margherita 44, Cagliari ☎ 070/670342 ⊕ www.hotelreginamargherita.com ⇋ 100 rooms ꙰ Free Breakfast.*

Il Gallo Bianco

$ | **B&B/INN** | A broad sun terrace and white, plant-filled decor make this sleek boutique hotel a good choice, as do the spacious and surprisingly quiet—given the busy location—guest rooms, all of which have modern baths and some of which have private balconies. **Pros:** friendly staff; sun terrace; central location near the train and bus stations. **Cons:** no parking; breakfast is a bit basic; neighborhood is traffic-heavy and a bit run-down. $ *Rooms from: €100 ⊠ Via Roma 237, Cagliari ☎ 334/9533149 ⊕ www.gallobiancocagliari.it ⇋ 16 rooms ꙰ Free Breakfast.*

La Ghirlanda

$ | **B&B/INN** | At this quiet haven, spacious, high-ceilinged rooms decorated with taste and restraint make you feel as if you're a guest at a palazzo. **Pros:** elegant rooms; affable, helpful owners; convenient location near the port and bus and train stations. **Cons:** no parking; no views from the rooms; breakfast in a bar. $ *Rooms from: €85 ⊠ Via Lodovico Baylle 7, Cagliari ☎ 351/5364248 ⊕ www.bnblaghirlanda.com ⊙ Closed Nov.–Mar. ⇋ 3 rooms ꙰ No Meals.*

★ T Hotel

$$ | **HOTEL** | In the vicinity of Parco di Monte Claro, about a 15-minute taxi or bus ride from Cagliari's center, this trendy hotel offers contemporary styling and upscale guest rooms in a 15-floor circular tower with sweeping city views. **Pros:** great views from most rooms; outstanding service; free parking. **Cons:** constant bustle in public areas; spa facilities can get busy; 2 km (1¼ miles) from port. $ *Rooms from: €124 ⊠ Via Dei Giudicati 66, Cagliari ☎ 070/47400 ⊕ www.thotel.it ⇋ 207 rooms ꙰ Free Breakfast.*

Nightlife

Caffè de Candia

CAFÉS | Relax in the atmospheric interior or on the capacious terrace (open in summer only) of this café on the edge of Terrazza Umberto I. It's a great place to enjoy a cappuccino, snack lunch, cocktail, or glass of vermentino after exploring the Castello quarter. The bar is open daily from 7 am until 9 pm during the week (later in summer) and until 2 am on weekends; DJs occasionally take over in the evenings. It's closed on Monday in winter. ⊠ *Bastione di St. Remy, Via Mario de Candia 3, Cagliari* ☎ *070/6407572.*

Caffè dell'Elfo

CAFÉS | A central yet secluded location and a casual ambience attract local professionals and artists, who linger in the evening over good wine, snacks, and conversation. Open hours are reduced in winter. ⊠ *Salita Santa Chiara 4–6, off Piazza Yenne, Cagliari* ☎ *070/682399.*

Caffè Libarium Nostrum

CAFÉS | A dim bohemian haunt full of wooden beams and brick-lined nooks and crannies, Libarium Nostrum is one of Cagliari's coolest café-bars. It's an occasional venue for live music and DJs, but the real draw is the outdoor terrace high atop medieval ramparts, the perfect spot for enjoying cocktails and views. Panini and other snacks are available. ⊠ *Via Santa Croce 33/35, Cagliari* ☎ *346/5220212.*

Caffè Svizzero

BARS | Entering this antique, vaulted, and frescoed bar a stone's throw from the port is like stepping back into the 19th century. Order a steaming cappuccino, a glass of the local vermentino, or a freshly squeezed fruit juice, and nibble on a panino, a pizzetta, or a pastry. It's all served with politeness and heaps of old-fashioned charm. ⊠ *Largo Carlo Felice 6–8, Cagliari* ☎ *070/664578* ⊘ *Closed Sun.*

Performing Arts

The Teatro Lirico stages concerts with local and well-known European artists throughout the year. See www.teatroliricodicagliari.it or contact the tourist office for information.

Shopping

ISOLA

CRAFTS | The Istituto Sardo Organizzazione Lavoro Artigiano is a government-sponsored cooperative of artisans. Look for handmade ceramics, woven and wooden goods, baskets, metalwork, and beautiful gold filigree or precious stone jewelry. ⊠ *Via Bacaredda 176, Cagliari* ☎ *070/492756* ⊕ *www.isolacagliari.com.*

Sapori di Sardegna

OTHER SPECIALTY STORE | Drop into this shop for Sardinian food products, including local wines, artisanal biscuits, pecorino cheeses, carasau flatbread, honey, and olives. There's a great range of items, and the English-speaking staff are always willing to help you out. If you want to sample some of the foodstuffs first, try the branch nearby at Via Baylle 6, where snacks are served. ⊠ *Vico dei Mille 1, Cagliari* ☎ *070/6848747* ⊕ *www.saborescagliari.com.*

Activities

WINDSURFING

Windsurfing Club Cagliari

WINDSURFING | FAMILY | Sardinia has some of Europe's best windsurfing spots. This outfit located in Cagliari's beach resort of Poetto provides advice and courses for everyone from beginners to experts. ⊠ *Viale Marina Piccola, Cagliari* ☎ *070/372694* ⊕ *www.windsurfingclub.it.*

ula

*km (18 miles) southwest of Cagliari,
4 km (195 miles) southwest of Olbia.*

sort villages sprawl along the coast
uthwest of the capital, which has its
are of fine scenery and good beach-
. On the marshy shoreline between
gliari's Aeroporto di Elmas and Pula,
ge flocks of flamingos are a common
ht. Beaches and lodging catering to
mmer crowds are concentrated 4 km
½ miles) south of Pula, a little more
n 1½ km (1 mile) south of Nora, in
conglomeration that makes up Santa
argherita di Pula. South of here at
ia is one of Sardinia's most magnifi-
nt coastal stretches, with white-sand
aches, turquoise waters, placid coves,
d powdery dunes.

TTING HERE AND AROUND

om Cagliari, drive approximately 40
(25 miles) on the SS195. Follow
ections for Pula/Chia. From Olbia, take
131 toward Cagliari-Sassari; then,
low SS554 towards Pula/Chia. The jour-
y is approximately 300 km (190 miles).

Sights

Nora

SEUM VILLAGE | The narrow prom-
tory outside Pula was the site of a
oenician, Carthaginian, and then,
er, Roman settlement that was first
habited some 2,800 years ago. Nora
as a prime location as a stronghold and
important trading town; Phoenician
ttlers scouted for good harbors, cliffs
shelter their craft from the wind,
d an elevation from which they could
fend themselves. An old Roman paved
ad passes the temple ruins, which
clude baths, a Roman theater, and an
phitheater now reserved for summer
usic festivals. Extensive excavations
ve shed light on life in this ancient
y. The channels through which hot air
se to warm the Roman baths can still

be made out. Well-preserved multicolor
tiles illustrate the difference between
the style of the Carthaginians (simple
mosaics) and that of the Romans (more
elaborate designs). If the Mediterranean
is calm, you can peek under clear waters
along the shore for more ruins of the
ancient city which are now submerged
due to rising seas, earthquakes, and
erosion. Your ticket also allows entry to
the Torre di Coltellazzo, a 17th-century
Spanish watchtower that affords lofty
views of the whole site. ■ TIP→ **The site
opens at 9 am; guided tours, usually held on
the hour, begin at 10 am.** ⊠ *3 km (2 miles)
south of Pula* ☎ *070/9209138* 🎟 *€5, €6
with guided tour.*

Sant'Efisio

CHURCH | The simple 11th-century church
at the base of the Nora promontory is
key to one of the island's most colorful
annual events. A four-day procession during the Festa di Sant'Efisio accompanies
a statue of the martyred St. Efisius all the
way from Cagliari to here and back again.
The event culminates in a huge parade of
costumed Sardinians and decorated *trac-
cas* (ox-drawn carriages) along Cagliari's
main avenue. Try to catch this if you're in
southern Sardinia from May 1 to May 4.
⊠ *Nora Beach, 3 km (2 miles) south of
Pula* ☎ *347/1436054* ◷ *Closed weekdays
and Sat. morning.*

Beaches

★ Chia Beach

BEACH | FAMILY | Although there is a
perfectly serviceable sandy beach right
outside the archaeological site of Nora,
infintely more enticing is the series of
long expanses of sand 18 kilometers
farther south toward the cape of Capo
Spartivento, Sardinia's southernmost
tip. These can get very busy in July and
August, but there's plenty of space
for you to find your own patch on such
beaches as Su Giudeu, Sa Colonia, and
Cala Cipolla. With very little development
in these parts, the water is extremely

clean, and shallow enough to be ideal for families. Be aware, however, that you would do well to bring your own shade as there is little natural shade here and few opportunities to rent a parasol. **Amenities:** food and drink; lifeguards; toilets; parking (fee in summer). **Best for:** swimming; sunbathing, families. ⊠ *Santa Margherita di Pula* ✛ *By car, head south down the SS195 past Santa Margherita di Pula.*

 Restaurants

Su Furriadroxu

$$ | ITALIAN | Amid the lime and lemon trees in this courtyard restaurant in the center of Pula, you'll find down-home Sard cooking at its most authentic, with the accent firmly on meat dishes. The menu (in the local *campidanese* dialect alongside Italian) lists a selection of meaty fare, with pride of place going to the most famous of island dishes, *porceddu* (roast suckling pig), which you'll find displayed sizzling on a spit to satisfy the most purist of local gourmands.
Known for: carnivorous feast; authentic Campidanese cooking; traditional outdoor setting. Ⓢ *Average main: €16* ⊠ *Via XXIV Maggio 11, Pula* ☎ *070/9246148* ⊕ *www.sufurriadroxu.it* ⊗ *Closed Wed. in summer, Mon.–Thur. in winter. No lunch Mon.–Sat.*

🛏 Hotels

Costa dei Fiori

$$$ | HOTEL | FAMILY | Worry and stress seem to melt away upon arriving at this beach hideaway, where modern guest rooms with stone floors, big windows, and rural Sardinian touches are surrounded by peaceful gardens planted with pines and palms. **Pros:** good low-season rates; great leisure facilities; lovely grounds. **Cons:** you need a car; poor road access; the beach may disappoint. Ⓢ *Rooms from: €242* ⊠ *SS195 Km 33, Santa Margherita di Pula* ☎ *070/9245333* ⊕ *www.*

costadeifiori.it ⊗ *Closed mid-Oct.–late Apr.* ⊃ *82 rooms* ⦿ *Free Breakfast.*

★ Faro Capo-Spartivento

$$$$ | HOTEL | Atop a cliff at the end of a rocky track on Sardinia's southernmost tip, a working lighthouse dating from 1856 contains this unusual hotel—a self-described "door suspended between the sky and the sea"—where it's easy to switch off and tune out amid luxurious surroundings. **Pros:** unique character and setting; select and secluded; excellent restaurant. **Cons:** hard to find; remote and isolated location; extravagant rates. Ⓢ *Rooms from: €92* ⊠ *Viale Spartivento* ✛ *5 km (3 miles) southwest of Chia* ☎ *393/8276800* ⊕ *www.farocapospartivento.com* ⊃ *10 rooms.*

Is Molas Resort

$$ | HOTEL | FAMILY | If you love golf and stargazing, then the place to stay in southern Sardinia is this peaceful hotel, with 70 Mediterranean-style rooms and a 27-hole golf complex. **Pros:** tranquil setting with rural views; immediate access to golf course; freshwater pool. **Cons:** isolated location; lacks charm; poor soundproofing in some rooms. Ⓢ *Rooms from: €195* ⊠ *SS195, Località Is Molas, Pula* ☎ *070/9241006* ⊕ *www.ismolas.it* ⊗ *Closed Nov.–Mar.* ⊃ *70 rooms* ⦿ *Free Breakfast.*

Is Morus Relais

$$$ | RESORT | FAMILY | A luxurious, palm-filled garden enclave laced with undulating paths, the Is Morus sits on a sandy cove and has all the amenities of a fine beach resort. **Pros:** attentive staff; lovely grounds; large pool and poolside grill restaurant. **Cons:** needs modernizing; food overall could be improved; disappointing beach. Ⓢ *Rooms from: €294* ⊠ *SS195, Km 37.4, Santa Margherita di Pula* ☎ *070/921171, 070/921596* ⊕ *www.ismorus.it* ⊗ *Closed mid-Oct.–Mar.* ⊃ *6 rooms* ⦿ *Free Breakfast.*

Sant'Antioco

75 km (47 miles) west of Pula, 100 km (62 miles) west of Cagliari.

Off Sardinia's southwest coast is the sleepy island of Sant'Antioco—the most hectic activity seems to be the silent repairing of nets by local fishermen who have already pulled in their daily catch. It has become a popular holiday spot because of its good beaches. The island has been connected to the mainland since Roman times by a causeway that's still standing (the modern causeway that you cross runs parallel).

GETTING HERE AND AROUND

Sant'Antioco is about 90 minutes from Cagliari by bus or car. Drive on the SS130 as far as Iglesias, then the SS126 in the direction of Carbonia and Sant'Antioco.

 ## Sights

Calasetta

BEACH | On the island of Sant'Antioco, off the southwestern coast of Sardinia, the fishing village and port of Calasetta draws visitors year-round for its beautiful beaches and fresh-seafood dishes. The pristine beaches of Spiaggia Grande and Le Saline, alternating with rocky areas, dunes, and local vegetation, form a rugged paradise. Founded by Ligurian settlers who worked as coral and tuna fishermen, Calasetta is connected daily by ferry boats with the smaller island of San Pietro, which also keeps intact its Ligurian cultural history and dialect. ⊠ *10 km (6 miles) northwest of Sant'Antioco town, Sant'Antioco.*

Carbonia

MINE | If you like to seek out the esoteric, explore the rugged inland hills and town of Carbonia, less than 30 minutes' drive from Sant'Antioco and about an hour by car or train from Cagliari. Built in 1938 by Mussolini to serve as an administrative center of a once boom-ing coal-mining area, its time-frozen architecture—ordered rows of workers' houses around a core of monumental public buildings on the broad Piazza Roma—has been called an urban UFO set down in the Sardinian landscape. The Dopolavoro, on the piazza, was a fascist institution that organized coal workers' free time for them. Managers lived closest to the city center, while laborers lived in the shantytowns on the outskirts. Carbonia's coal industry was short-lived, and the enormous mines are long since abandoned; just outside town you can hear the wind whistle through their ghostly shells among rows of still-in-habited public housing projects. You can also tour the underground tunnels of the Grande Miniera di Serbariu. ⊠ *S126 at S78, Carbonia.*

Iglesias

BEACH | Perched at about 600 feet in the southwest hills of the island, this authen-tic Sardinian town 35 km (22 miles) north of Sant'Antioco has two notable medieval churches: the Cattedrale di Santa Chiara and Madonna delle Grazie. The town is famous for its theatrical, Spanish-in-flected Easter festivities. A short drive away, on the Costa Verde, you can enjoy unspoiled, uncrowded beaches, includ-ing the beautiful Masua cove at Porto Cauli beach. ⊠ *27 km (16 miles) north of Carbonia, Iglesias* ☎ *0781/274507 Tourist office* ⊕ *www.visitiglesias.comune. iglesias.ca.it.*

Monte Sirai

MILITARY SIGHT | Just outside Carbonia and strategically positioned atop a plateau that provides views inland and far out to sea, the remains of one of Sardinia's most important Carthaginian military strongholds were discovered by chance in 1962. The walls of Mt. Sirai were erect-ed around 375 BC, and they continued to function as impregnable fortress barriers until the Roman conquest in 238 BC. The ancient acropolis is spread across more than 400 acres, so bring your walking shoes. You can continue exploring at

Carbonia's Museo Archeologico Villa Sulcis to view a large collection of artifacts, some of them more than 4,000 years old. ✉ *Località Sirai, off SS126, Km 17, Località Sirai ✛ 1 km (½ mile) north of Carbonia, direction Sant'Antioco, Carbonia* ☎ *0781/665037 office, 345/7559751 site* ⊘ *Closed Mon. Sept.–June* ✉ *Site €6, museum €6, or €10 for both.*

Zona Archeologica

RUINS | The chief point of interest in Sant'Antioco island's eponymous main town is the Archaeological Zone at the top of the old section, which has terrific views of the Sardinian mainland. Here you can see a *tophet*—a Punic sanctuary, necropolis, and burial site—which is scattered with urns that contained the cremated remains of stillborn children. Below the site is Sant'Antioco's excellent archaeological museum that showcases artifacts from the tophet as well as from the Neolithic, Byzantine, and Roman eras. You can also visit a nearby ethnographic collection and a Piedmontese fort. Various combined tickets are available. ✉ *Via Sabatino Moscati, Sant'Antioco* ☎ *0781/82105, 389/7962114* ⊕ *www. mabsantantioco.it* ✉ *Archaeological zone €4, museum €6, combined tickets for both €7 or for ethnographic collection and Piedmontese fort €6.*

San Pietro

5 km (3 miles) northwest of Sant'Antioco.

A ferry at the small northern port of Calasetta connects Sant'Antioco with Carloforte, the main town on the smaller island of San Pietro. This classic little Italian port and its surrounding coastline are a favorite of wealthy Cagliarians, many of whom have built weekend cottages here. The best views are from Capo Sandalo, on San Pietro's rugged western coast, but head to the island's southern tip for the beaches. During daylight hours the

ferry departs approximately hourly in summer and every 90 minutes in winter—the trip takes 30 minutes.

GETTING HERE AND AROUND

Small car ferries connect San Pietro with Calasetta on Sant'Antioco, or Portoscuso near Iglesias on the Sardinian mainland. Round-trip tickets are about €9 per person, €20 for a car.

 Hotels

Hotel Hieracon

$ | HOTEL | This art nouveau–style hotel with modern whitewashed rooms sits on the harbor in Carloforte. **Pros:** helpful English-speaking staff; good location; pretty internal garden. **Cons:** cheaper rooms are cramped; few sea-facing rooms; limited Wi-Fi reception. ⑤ *Rooms from: €96* ✉ *Corso Cavour 62, Carloforte* ☎ *0781/854028* ⊕ *www.hotelhieracon. com* ⊘ *Closed early Oct.–late Apr.* ⇔ *23 rooms* ⑩ *Free Breakfast.*

Costa Verde

80 km (50 miles) northwest of Cagliari.

If you've come to Sardinia in search of untrammeled wilderness and sweeping sands as far as the eye can see, this semideserted coast is the place to find them. Hidden away in the forgotten southwest corner of the island, the Costa Verde, or Green Coast, is a succession of cliffs and beaches, many of them accessible only by bumpy, unpaved tracks. The effort is worth it. The dune-backed sands shelter rare grasses and birdlife, and the area offers magnificent swimming along stretches of beach that seem endless.

GETTING HERE AND AROUND

The best way to access the Green Coast is by car, though roads can be dangerously steep and winding. Take precautions and drive during daytime, also because roads and exits are poorly lit. Roads designated "SS" are developed freeways with fast-flowing traffic.

You can approach one of the most evocative stretches of the coast, Piscinas, either from the town of Guspini, on the straggling S126, or from a turnoff a couple of miles farther south, which leads through the abandoned mining town of Ingurtosu. It's a strange, ghostly cluster of chimneys and workers' dwellings, forlorn amid the encroaching scrubland. Drive down the dirt track another 10 km (6 miles) or so, through woods of juniper, to reach the sea.

 ## Hotels

Hotel Le Dune

$$$$ | **HOTEL** | A remote Green Coast oasis on lovely Piscinas Beach—between Capo Pecora and Capo Frasca—this luxury hotel occupies a former warehouse, built in the late 1800s to house minerals excavated from surrounding hills; although bamboo furnishings and neutral linens make the spacious guest rooms (some with sitting areas) feel contemporary, wagons, rails, and other mining remnants scattered about lend them historical allure. **Pros:** yoga sessions available; breathtaking setting; beachfront property. **Cons:** basic, overpriced rooms; remote location; no lounge. $ *Rooms from: €343* ✉ *Via Bau 1, Piscinas di Ingurtosu, Arbus* ☎ *070/977130, 340/2415287 mobile in Italy* ⊕ *www.ledunepiscinas.com* ⊗ *Closed Sept.–mid-May* ⇌ *27 rooms* ⦾| *Free Breakfast.*

Barumini

65 km (40 miles) north of Cagliari.

It's definitely worth a detour to the quiet village of Barumini to visit the extraordinary stone village-fortress of Su Nuraxi.

GETTING HERE AND AROUND

The best way to reach Su Nuraxi is by car. From the capital, follow SS131 to SS197. Direct buses to the site are few and far between.

 ## Sights

★ Su Nuraxi

RUINS | **FAMILY** | The most extensive of the island's 7,000 discovered nuraghi, Su Nuraxi is on the UNESCO World Heritage list. Concentric rings of thick stone walls conceal dark chambers and narrow passages in a central beehive-shape tower. In the ruins of the surrounding village there are benches, ovens, wells, and other Bronze Age remnants. The specific functions of individual nuraghi remain a mystery, as their construction predates written history. Though this particular type of construction is unique to Sardinia, similar buildings dating from the same era are found in Cyprus, the Balearic Islands off of Spain, and other parts of the Mediterranean. Visits are accompanied by a local guide and include explorations of the interior. Tours start every 30 minutes and last about 50 minutes. The same ticket includes entry to a museum and exhibition center in Barumini. ■**TIP**➔ **If you're driving from SS131, don't be misled to other, lesser nuraghi—follow the signs all the way to Barumini.** ✉ *Viale Su Nuraxi, Barumini*

✛ SP5 Barumini–Tuili, 1 km (½ mile) west of Barumini ☎ 070/9368128 ⊕ www.fondazionebarumini.it ✑ €14.

Oristano

25 km (16 miles) north of Giara di Gesturi, 93 km (58 miles) northwest of Cagliari.

The beautiful, small, colonial center exudes a distinct serenity. Oristano's evening passeggiata teems with vivacious children and has a relaxed friendliness about it. The city's star shone most brightly in the Middle Ages, when it was capital of an independent duchy led by Sardinia's own Joan of Arc–type heroine, Eleonora d'Arborea (circa 1340–1402), who is immortalized with her own piazza, the site of the city's town hall. Oristano is now the scene of a rousing series of horseback competitions, called Sa Sartiglia, marking the end of February's Carnival. The tradition—in which a rider must pierce a string-suspended star with his sword—began in 1350 as a wedding celebration of Judge Mariano II. It has since continued as an annual festival that is supposed to ensure a plentiful harvest.

GETTING HERE AND AROUND

Oristano is easily accessible and well connected to other major areas of Sardinia by car, train, or bus. Trains and buses travel between Cagliari, Sassari, Olbia, Nuoro, and other small towns several times per day. The central bus station is in the city center.

By car, follow the SS131 from major towns in the direction of Oristano.

Sights

Cabras

BEACH | FAMILY | Fishermen pole round-bottomed rush boats through shallow ponds teeming with eels, crayfish, and wildlife in the extensive marshlands outside this 11th-century town. Make a stop at the archaeological museum here for its awe-inspiring nuraghic statues, then drive north and west into the Sinis Peninsula to access the pristine beaches of Is Arutas, Maimoni, and Mari Ermi, characterized by fine white quartzified sand grains. ⊠ *SP3 off SP1, 10 km (6 miles) northwest of Oristano, Cabras.*

🍴 Restaurants

Cocco e Dessi

$$ | ITALIAN | The building dates from 1925 but the interior shows a diversity of styles, with the main dining area (one of five) inside a glass gazebo. Dishes featuring fresh catches of the day, vegetables, and herb-infused sauces are complemented by pizzas and pastas—just save room for the semifreddo with Cointreau or the chocolate ganache. **Known for:** great pizzas; quirky decor; convivial setting. Ⓢ *Average main: €18* ⊠ *Via Tirso 31, Oristano* ☎ *0783/252648* ⊕ *www.coccoedessi.it.*

Ristorante Craf da Banana

$$ | ITALIAN | The brick walls, dim lighting, and arched ceilings here make you feel as if you've stepped into a wine cellar. Aged photographs of Oristano's Sa Sartiglia jousting festival and specialty dishes from Oristano and Montiferru do a good job capturing local flavor. **Known for:** cozy, romantic atmosphere; traditional Sardinian dishes; historical setting. Ⓢ *Average main: €16* ⊠ *Via de Castro 34, Oristano* ☎ *0783/70669* ⊕ *www.ristorantedabananaoristano.it* ⏱ *No lunch Sun. June–Sept., no dinner Sun. Oct.–May.*

Trattoria Gino

$ | SEAFOOD | Light-color walls lined with bottles of wine and simple rows of tables deck out the single room of Trattoria Gino, beloved by locals, especially at lunch, and run by the same family for nearly a century. Although the lobster is a memorable splurge, consider trying the antipasto *di mare* (mixed seafood appetizer) or spaghetti *ai ricci* (with sea urchins). **Known for:** honest, local cooking;

cordial, attentive service; reasonable prices. $ *Average main: €14* ✉ *Via Tirso 13, Oristano* ☎ *0783/71428* ⊙ *Closed Sun. and mid-Aug.–mid-Sept.*

Coffee and Quick Bites

Bar Pasticceria Eleonora

$ | CAFÉ | Steps from the tourist office, you can take a refreshing afternoon break with a coffee and a pastry or panino. The friendly café has outdoor tables on the corner of Piazza Eleonora, which retains an old-world charm thanks to a neoclassical town hall, a marble monument to Giudichessa Eleonora carved by the Florentine sculptor Ulisse Cambi in 1881, and the 18th-century Mameli palace with its beautiful wrought-iron balconies. **Known for:** central people-watching spot; traditional local flavor; outdoor seating. $ *Average main: €10* ✉ *Piazza Eleonora d'Arborea 1, Oristano* ☎ *0783/71454* ⊙ *Closed Sun.*

Hotels

Mariano IV Palace Hotel

$ | HOTEL | This central downtown hotel has a reassuringly old-fashioned style, with its grand, columned exterior and elegant neoclassical lobby hung with chandeliers. **Pros:** convenient location; low online rates; good restaurant. **Cons:** no parking for cars; caters mostly to business travelers; dated feel. $ *Rooms from: €90* ✉ *Piazza Mariano 50, Oristano* ☎ *0783/360101* ⊕ *www.hotelmarianoiv. com* 🛏 *81 rooms* ❑ *Free Breakfast.*

Residenza d'Epoca Regina d'Arborea

$$ | HOTEL | One floor of a 19th-century palazzo, next to the town hall on Oristano's traffic-free main square, has been tastefully converted into a small but stylish guest house, with rich furnishings, chandeliers, antique murals, and domed ceilings. **Pros:** period character; helpful personnel; central location. **Cons:** not suitable for children; no car access possible; few facilities. $ *Rooms from:*

€150 ✉ *Piazza Eleonora d'Arborea 4, Oristano* ☎ *0783/302101* ⊕ *www.reginadarborea.com* ⊙ *Closed 10 days in Dec.* 🛏 *6 rooms* ❑ *Free Breakfast.*

Tharros

16 km (10 miles) west of Oristano, 52 km (32 miles) northwest of Barumini.

Spread across a thin tongue of land that dangles off the Sinis Peninsula, the archaeological site of Tharros ranks as one of Sardinia's most important Phoenician, Carthaginian, and Roman settlements. It's not hard to understand why this evocative site was selected by the ancients, given its sweeping views across the Gulf of Oristano, its defensibility, and the shelter it provides vessels. Founded around 800 BC, the city was finally abandoned in the 11th century AD, in favor of Oristano.

GETTING HERE AND AROUND
Whether you're heading to Tharros from the north or south, follow the SS131 to Oristano. Drive through Oristano toward Cabras, branching off on SP6 for San Giovanni di Sinis and Tharros. There's frequent bus service from Oristano.

Sights

Museo Civico di Cabras

HISTORY MUSEUM | This lagoon-side archaeological museum displays many of the better-preserved urns and other artifacts recovered from nearby excavation sites, including Tharros. It is also the main home of the Giganti di Mont'e Prama—unique nuragic stone statues recovered from the Sinis Peninsula in the 1970s but only recently viewable in their restored state. The visit takes about an hour. Buy a combination ticket to see the Museo Civico and the ruins at Tharros. ✉ *Via Tharros 121, off SP6, 10 km (6 miles) northwest of Oristano, Cabras* ☎ *0783/290636*

⊕ *www.museocabras.it* ☞ *€6.50; €10 combined ticket, includes Tharros.*

Tharros
RUINS | FAMILY | The spectacular site of the Carthaginian and Roman city of Tharros was, like Nora to the south, chosen because it commanded the best views of the gulf and could provide an easy escape route if inland tribes threatened. The Phoenician-Punic city planning here includes sophisticated water channeling and masonry foundations. Two reconstructed Corinthian columns stand as testament to the site's Roman history, and there are baths visible and mosaic fragments from the Roman city. Look for the Cardo Maximus, the main road of the city, built to last for centuries. As at Nora, many more ruins are submerged under water. A climb up the steep hill to a Spanish watchtower affords a scenic view over the Sinis Peninsula. There's a small souvenir shop and attached café for snacks and beverages. You can buy a combined ticket that also allows entry to the **Museo Civico di Cabras,** where some of the finds are displayed, though the best items are in Cagliari's archaeological museum. ⊠ *Off SP6, 16 km (10 miles) west of Oristano, 113 km (70 miles) northwest of Cagliari, San Giovanni di Sinis, Cabras* ☎ *0783/370019* ⊕ *www.tharros.sardegna.it* ☞ *€6.50; €10 combined ticket, includes Museo Civico di Cabras; tower €4.*

Nuoro

107 km (67 miles) northeast of Tharros, 181 km (113 miles) north of Cagliari.

The somewhat shabby provincial capital of Nuoro is on the edge of a gorge in the harsh mountainous area that culminates in Gennargentu, the island's highest massif (6,000 feet). Not much happens here; you can do some (relatively inexpensive) shopping amid strolling locals, or try the local Barbagia sausage,

which is great. Just 40 km (25 miles) east of Nuoro is the coastal town of Cala Gonone. Cradled on Orosei Bay, this popular holiday destination has white-sand beaches, mountain views, and regular boat trips to the mysterious water caves of Bue Marino.

GETTING HERE AND AROUND
From Cagliari, the drive to Nuoro takes about two hours. Take the SS131 toward Sassari/Oristano/Nuoro, then continue on SS131 DCN toward Nuoro/Olbia. After 55 km (34 miles), turn off, following signs for Nuoro Centro until you reach Nuoro.

VISITOR INFORMATION
CONTACT Nuoro Tourism Office. ⊠ *Piazza Italia 8, Nuoro* ☎ *0784/238878.*

 Sights

Monte Ortobene
MOUNTAIN | About 7 km (4 miles) northeast of Nuoro is Monte Ortobene, a granite peak at 2,900 feet offering lofty views over the gulch below. Here you can also see up close the imposing bronze statue of the Rendentore, or Christ the Redeemer, overlooking the city. Pilgrimages and masses take place in summer here. Picnic tables make this a favorite spot for an alfresco lunch throughout the year. The mountain is easily reachable from Nuoro by bus or car via SP45. ⊠ *Nuoro* ⊕ *www.comune.nuoro.it.*

★ **Museo Etnografico Sardo**
HISTORY MUSEUM | This ethnographic collection is a must for anyone interested in the cultural context of Sardinia's customs and traditions. Among the 8,000 items in the museum's collection, you can view domestic and agricultural implements, splendid jewelry, traditional musical instruments, and dozens of local costumes. Audioguides are available, and guided tours can be booked. The nearby park on Sant'Onofrio Hill affords magnificent views over Nuoro and the surrounding country. ■ **TIP➔ Entry to the museum is free on the first Sunday of the month.** ⊠ *Via*

A. Mereu 56 ☎ 0784/257035 ⊕ www.
isresardegna.it ☞ €5 ⊗ Closed Mon.

🍴 Restaurants

★ Il Portico

$$ | ITALIAN | Brotherly love (and owner-
ship) and quality seafood are among the
things that make this old-town restau-
rant so exceptional. Modern artwork,
stone pillars, and arched ceilings help to
provide a fitting setting for the predomi-
nantly traditional cuisine livened up with
modern elements. **Known for:** welcoming
atmosphere; innovative takes on tradi-
tional cuisine; locals' choice. ⑤ *Average
main: €15* ⊠ *Via Mons. Bua 13, Nuoro*
☎ *0784/232909* ⊕ *www.ilporticonuoro.it*
⊗ *Closed Mon., 2 wks July–Aug., and 2
wks Jan.–Feb. No dinner Sun.*

Il Rifugio

$$ | ITALIAN | FAMILY | At this family-run
local spot, the rustic dining area—with
terra-cotta floors, brick pillars, and a
wood-burning stove—is packed nearly
every night. The service, presentation,
and wine list are as exceptional as the
food: only the freshest local meats and
cheeses are served, and all the dishes
are made from scratch, including the pizza, the pasta, and the ice cream drizzled
with honey. **Known for:** amiable staff; boisterous and convivial air; unpretentious
but well-prepared local dishes. ⑤ *Average
main: €17* ⊠ *Via A. Mereu 28/36, Nuoro*
☎ *0784/232355* ⊕ *www.trattoriarifugio.
com* ⊗ *Closed Wed.*

🛏 Hotels

Casa Solotti

$ | B&B/INN | You don't have to venture far
out of Nuoro to appreciate its magnificent mountainous setting, and mountain
views don't get much grander than from
this excellent lodging immersed in the
oak forests of Monte Ortobene. **Pros:** terrific breakfasts; beautiful mountain views;
warm and friendly hospitality. **Cons:** not
ideal for anyone with impaired mobility;

En Route

On the way to the archaeological
ruins in Tharros you pass the ghost
town of **San Salvatore,** revived
briefly in the 1960s as a locale
for spaghetti Westerns and since
abandoned, except for a few days
every summer, when it is the focus
of a religious festival. The saloon
from the movie set still stands.

Among the dunes past San Salvatore
are large rush huts formerly used by
fishermen and now much in demand
as back-to-nature vacation homes.

The 5th-century church of **San
Giovanni di Sinis,** on the Sinis
Peninsula, is claimed to be the
oldest Christian church in Sardinia.

remote spot; few facilities. ⑤ *Rooms
from: €70* ⊠ *Località Monte Ortobene,
Nuoro* ☎ *0784/33954, 328/6028975*
⊕ *www.casasolotti.it* ⊗ *Closed mid-Nov.–
late Dec. and late Jan.–late Mar.* ⇆ *6
rooms* ⦿| *Free Breakfast.*

Euro Hotel

$ | HOTEL | Centrally located, this simple
block-style hotel—more or less standard
for provincial Nuoro—is ideal for a stopover; rooms are spacious and clean, with
parquet flooring and modern amenities.
Pros: near train station; amiable staff;
ample parking. **Cons:** outdated rooms; not
much character; no restaurant. ⑤ *Rooms
from: €80* ⊠ *Via Trieste 62, Nuoro*
☎ *0784/34071* ⊕ *www.eurohotelnuoro.it*
⇆ *54 rooms* ⦿| *Free Breakfast.*

★ Su Gologone Experience Hotel

$$$$ | HOTEL | Just southeast of Nuoro, in
the foothills of the Supramonte range,
Su Gologone combines luxury with
rural flavor in guest rooms that feel
like country retreats (exposed beams,
wooden chests, traditional Sardinian
fabrics) and a rustic restaurant that pairs

local *cannonau* reds with such Sardinian specialties as *maccarones de busa* (thick homemade pasta twists), *culurgiones* (ravioli), suckling pig, and, for dessert, *sebadas* (fried-dough pockets stuffed with cheese and lemon peel). **Pros:** museumlike decor; locally influenced restaurant; great location for hiking in the Supramonte Valley. **Cons:** many stairs to negotiate; used by groups and wedding parties; very remote. $ *Rooms from: €309* ⊠ *Località Su Gologone, Oliena* ☎ *0784/287512* ⊕ *www.sugologone.it* ⊗ *Closed early Nov.–Apr.* ⤳ *73 rooms* ⊚ *Free Breakfast.*

Fonni

30 km (19 miles) south of Nuoro, 137 km (85 miles) south of Olbia.

In the heart of the Barbagia region, Fonni is the highest town on the island. This mountainous district, including Monte Spada and the Bruncu Spina refuge on the Gennargentu massif, is Sardinia's most primitive. Life in some villages seems not to have changed much since the Middle Ages. Here a rigidly patriarchal society perpetuates age-old customs and obedience to rural traditions. Although as a tourist you may be looked at with curiosity, a smile can go a long way. High mountain roads wind and loop through the landscape; towns are small and undistinguished, their social fabric formed in complete isolation. On feast days elaborate local costumes are worn as an explicit statement of community identity.

GETTING HERE AND AROUND
To reach Fonni, the highest town in Sardinia, drive (or hire a car and driver) or take a bus from Nuoro. There is no train service.

From Nuoro, take SS389 from the junction of Mamoiada, or take SS128 to the town of Gavoi. From Cagliari, follow SS131, exiting toward the village of

Ottana. Continue on SS128, turning at Fonni. From Sassari, follow SS131 south, turning east onto SS129 at Macomer. Continue on SS128, following signs for Fonni.

Hotels

Hotel Sa Orte
$ | **HOTEL** | Close to the highest peaks of the Gennargentu range in the center of Sardinia, this hotel, a palazzo in the center of Fonni, provides a warm welcome at any time of the year. **Pros:** convenient for mountain excursions; generous breakfasts; affable staff. **Cons:** few facilities; some rooms are small and dark; no views. $ *Rooms from: €80* ⊠ *Via Roma 14, Fonni* ☎ *0784/58020* ⊕ *www.hotelsaorte.it* ⊚ *Free Breakfast* ⤳ *26 rooms.*

Shopping

Special candies made from honey and nougat are sold in hilltop **Tonara,** 15 km (9 miles) southwest of Fonni.

In the mountain village of **Aritzo,** about 45 km (28 miles) south of Fonni, high up in the Barbagia, look for handcrafted wooden utensils and furniture.

Alghero

137 km (85 miles) southwest of Olbia.

A tourist-friendly town of about 45,000 inhabitants, with a distinctly Spanish flavor, Alghero is also known as "Barcelonetta" (Little Barcelona) for its strong Catalan ties. Rich wrought-iron scrollwork decorates balconies and screened windows; Spanish motifs appear in stone portals and bell towers. The town was occupied in the 14th century by the Aragonese and Catalans, who constructed seaside ramparts and sturdy towers encompassing an inviting nucleus of narrow, winding streets with honey-color palazzi. The dialect spoken here is closer to Catalan than Italian, although you probably have to attend one of the masses conducted in Algherese (or listen in on stories swapped by older fishermen) to hear it.

Besides its historic architectural gems, such as the cathedral and Palazzo d'Albis, the fortified city is well worth a visit to simply stroll and discover local culture on narrow cobblestone streets. The city also has a reputation for serving great food at reasonable prices.

GETTING HERE AND AROUND

Alghero International Airport is 15 km (9 miles) from the city center, which you can reach by car, taxi, or public transport. Regional buses and local trains connect the town with Sassari, and there are buses to local villages. The closest passenger port to Alghero is Porto Torres, approximately 40 km (25 miles) away, with links to Genoa, Civitavecchia (Rome), Corsica and France.

VISITOR INFORMATION

CONTACT Alghero Tourism Office. ⊠ *Via Cagliari 2, Alghero* ☎ *079/979054* ⊕ *www.algheroturismo.eu.*

 Sights

Capo Caccia

NATURE SIGHT | Head 25 km (16 miles) west of Alghero for the spectacular heights of the imposing limestone headland of Capo Caccia. The rugged promontory, blanketed by thick maquis, forms part of the Porto Conte nature reserve and is home to deep caves such as the Grotta di Nettuno. Close by are the beaches of Porto Ferro, Cala Viola, and, on the beautiful Porto Conte inlet, Cala Dragunara. ⊠ *Alghero* ☎ *079/945005* ⊕ *www.algheroparks.it.*

★ **Grotta di Nettuno** (*Neptune's Cave*)
CAVE | FAMILY | At the base of a sheer cliff, the pounding sea has carved an entrance to a vast fantastic cavern filled with stunning water pools, stalactites,

and stalagmites. The dramatic cave and coves, discovered by fishermen in the 18th century, are popular tourist attractions for their sheer natural beauty. You must visit with a guide; tours start on the hour. It's possible to reach the caves by boat or by land. Between April and October, boat trips depart regularly from the port of Alghero for €16 round-trip (admission to the grotto is extra). To reach the grotto by land, you can descend the 654 dizzying steps of Escala del Cabirol ("Goat Steps"), which are cut into the steep cliff here. ■TIP→ **By public bus from Alghero's Via Catalogna, the trip to the top of the stairway takes about 50 minutes. Allow 15 minutes for the descent by foot.** ⊠ *Off SP55, 13 km (8 miles) west of Alghero, Alghero* ☎ *079/946540* ⊕ *www. grottadinettuno.it* ⊗ *Closed in rough seas and Wed. Nov.–Apr.* ⊠ *€14.*

Museo del Corallo

OTHER MUSEUM | The coast around Alghero is one of the Mediterranean's most abundant sources of red coral, the subject of this entertaining and informative museum housed in a Liberty-era villa near Piazza Sulis. Old photographs and films show the process of harvesting the substance, and there are impressive displays of coral jewelry and ornaments. ⊠ *Via Venti Settembre 8, Alghero* ☎ *079/9734045* ⊠ *€5* ⊗ *Closed Mon.*

Museo Diocesano d'Arte Sacra (*Diocesan Museum of Sacred Art*)

RELIGIOUS BUILDING | This cathedral museum is housed in a 13th-century church designed with Catalan Gothic architecture. The usual assortment of religious treasures—paintings, wooden sculptures, and bronze statues—is on display; look for the masterful 16th-century Catalan silverware, forged with intricate ancient motifs. ⊠ *Via Maiorca 1, Alghero* ☎ *079/9733041* ⊗ *Closed Sun. and Tues.* ⊠ *€4.*

Beaches

Le Bombarde and Lazzaretto Beaches

BEACH | FAMILY | A couple of kilometers north of Alghero's old town, backed by pine woods, Maria Pia beach offers a convenient though unspectacular spot for an afternoon of bathing and sunbathing, but if you don't mind going farther afield, head for the altogether superior beaches of Le Bombarde and Lazzaretto, on adjacent inlets 10 kms (6 miles) west of town. Sheltered from the wind and fully equipped with bars and facilities for renting pedalos and canoes, the beaches are similar in style—both curves of soft sand studded with a few rocks, and both packed in August. ■ TIP➜ **The beaches are easy to reach on the frequent tourist bus service, Il Trottolo. Amenities:** food and drink; lifeguards; sunloungers; showers; toilets; parking (fee in summer); water sports. **Best for:** swimming; snorkelling; windsurfing. ⊠ *Alghero* ✛ *By car, take Via Garibaldi and then SS127bis north and west along the coast toward Fertilia.*

🍴 Restaurants

Il Pavone

$$ | ITALIAN | Fresh flowers on white linen tablecloths add color to the bright glass-enclosed dining area of this delightful eatery on busy Piazza Sulis; gold-framed paintings and oversize wine bottles capped in wax add Italian charm—as does the seasonally changing menu of pasta and seafood dishes such as tagliatelle with shrimp or ravioli au gratin. The four-course prix-fixe menu (€50) includes an appetizer, two tastings of pasta, two of seafood or meat, and a traditional dessert. **Known for:** attentive and knowledgeable service; delicious mains and desserts; impressive wine list. ⑤ *Average main: €22* ⊠ *Piazza Sulis 3, Alghero* ☎ *079/979584* ⊗ *Closed 2 wks in Nov. No dinner Sun. late Nov.–Mar.*

La Lepanto

$$ | SEAFOOD | A covered veranda by the seafront marks out Alghero's top seafood restaurant, an expansive and sunny room complete with crustacean-filled aquarium. Summer sees crowds of both locals and tourists, many of whom come for the specialty *aragosta* (lobster) cooked different ways, including *alla catalana* (with tomato and onions) or with ricotta foam, parsley, basil, and tomato. **Known for:** central location; bright interior with covered veranda seating; superior seafood in all its forms. ⑤ *Average main: €18* ⊠ *Via Carlo Alberto 135, Alghero* ☎ *079/979116* ⊕ *www.lalepanto.com* ⊗ *Closed Jan.– mid-Mar. and Tues. in Oct.–Dec. and late Mar.*

Mabrouk

$$$$ | ITALIAN | There's always a lively crowd at this backstreet trattoria, where diners pack into three rooms to enjoy the same multi-course set menu. If this seems limiting, think again—you'll be presented with a range of fresh, delicious, seasonally appropriate dishes (perhaps prawns, squid, swordfish, or sea bass) in abundant portions. **Known for:** vivacious atmosphere; prix-fixe menus with unlimited drinks; fresh seafood. ⑤ *Average main: €45* ⊠ *Via Santa Barbara 4, Alghero* ☎ *079/970000* ⊗ *Closed Nov.– Feb. No lunch.*

☕ Coffee and Quick Bites

Bar Pasticceria Ciro

$ | ITALIAN | For a delicious cannolo, fruit tart or *bignè* (cream puff), local cognoscenti make a beeline for this traditional bar and pastry shop, where the sweet delights displayed are made with the lightest pastry and the freshest fillings. Good coffees, ice creams, and sandwiches are also available, and there are tables inside and out back. **Known for:** cordial service; light pastries; old-fashioned style. ⑤ *Average main: €5* ⊠ *Via Sassari*

35/b, Alghero ☎ *079/979960* ⊘ *Closed Mon.*

Cafè Latino

$ | **ITALIAN** | In prime position on Alghero's broad city walls, with views down to the yachting marina and across to Capo Caccia, this makes a wonderful place to pause by day or night with a spritz or fruit juice. The menu has a number of food items, too. **Known for:** friendly service; superb views over the port; good selection of snacks and cocktails. $ *Average main: €10* ✉ *Bastioni Magellano 10, Alghero* ☎ *079/6766044* ⊕ *www.cafelatino.it* ⊘ *Closed Jan.–mid-Feb. and Tues. mid-Feb.–May and Oct.–Dec.*

Gelateria K2

$ | **ITALIAN** | Traditional and more unusual flavors jostle for space at this highly rated ice cream parlor, an obligatory stop on any passeggiata in the old town. Among the favorites are fig, *nocciola* (hazelnut), and pistachio. **Known for:** ample choice; superb flavors; lactose- and gluten-free options. $ *Average main: €4* ✉ *Via Roma 73, Alghero* ☎ *340/2809307* ⊘ *Closed Dec.–Feb.*

Hotels

Carlos V

$$$ | **HOTEL** | **FAMILY** | On the shore boulevard opposite the Villa Las Tronas and 15 minutes from the airport, this grand, modern hotel (pronounced "Carlos Quinto") has an array of gardens and terraces, as well as a saltwater pool with sea views and a separate children's pool. **Pros:** a true bargain in low season, when rates drop; good-size pool; wonderful vistas. **Cons:** dated in parts; sometimes falls short of five-star standards; large-hotel atmosphere. $ *Rooms from: €220* ✉ *Lungomare Valencia 24, Alghero* ☎ *079/9720600* ⊕ *www.hotelcarlosv.it* ⇆ *179 rooms* ⦿| *Free Breakfast.*

San Francesco Heritage Hotel

$$ | **B&B/INN** | Set in Alghero's central Catalan quarter, the convent that was once attached to the church of San Francesco has guest rooms grouped around a 14th-century cloister; though somewhat cramped, all accommodations have air-conditioning and private bathrooms. **Pros:** historic ambience; very tranquil; central location. **Cons:** not a good choice for kids; few facilities; little parking in the area. $ *Rooms from: €189* ✉ *Via Machin 2, Alghero* ☎ *079/980330* ⊘ *Closed mid-Nov.–Dec.* ⇆ *20 rooms.*

★ Villa Las Tronas Hotel & Spa

$$$$ | **HOTEL** | A stunning mansion dating from the 1880s has been transformed into this elegant secluded hotel that blends gold tapestries, crystal chandeliers, marble floors, canopy-draped beds, vaulted ceilings, and other Belle Époque treasures with modern amenities such as a luxury spa with a gym and an illuminated pool. **Pros:** luxury spa; promontory setting with regal sea views; incredible service. **Cons:** no meat dishes served at dinner; usually a three-night minimum stay June–Sept.; very expensive. $ *Rooms from: €359* ✉ *Lungomare Valencia 1, Alghero* ☎ *079/981818* ⊕ *www.hotelvillalastronas.it* ⇆ *24 rooms* ⦿| *Free Breakfast.*

Nightlife

Poco Loco

LIVE MUSIC | For live music, bowling, or just a slice of pizza, this long-standing establishment has been a fixture for generations of Alghero's youth. The music is mainly jazz, including big-name acts, while a range of beers and cocktails are served as well as pizza cooked in a wood oven and dispensed by the meter. Poco Loco is closed Monday from September through June. ✉ *Via Gramsci 8, Alghero* ☎ *079/983604* ⊕ *www.pocolocoalghero.com.*

Shopping

De Filippis

JEWELRY & WATCHES | On the so-called Riviera del Corallo, Alghero has long been famed for its coral products, fashioned into elegant jewelry. This shop, with three outlets within a few yards of each other in the old town, has an impressive range of bracelets, brooches, and necklaces. ✉ *Via Carlo Alberto 23, Alghero* ☎ *079/979394* ⊕ *www.defilippis.it.*

Activities

BOATING AND SAILING

Lega Navale Italiana

BOATING | This state-sponsored organization has information on the island's sailing facilities, as well as everything associated with maritime activity. ✉ *Banchina del Porto, Alghero* ☎ *079/984093* ⊕ *www.leganavale.it.*

Sassari

34 km (21 miles) northeast of Alghero, 212 km (132 miles) north of Cagliari.

With a population of about 130,000, Sassari, the island's second-largest city, is an important university town and administrative center, notable for its history of intellectualism and bohemian student culture. Look for downtown vendors of *fainè*, a pizzalike chickpea-flour pancake glistening with olive oil, which is a Genoese and Sassarese specialty. The mazelike old town is blissfully isolated from the chaotic traffic swirling though the newer neighborhoods—Sassari is the hub of several highways and secondary roads leading to various coastal resorts, among them Stintino and Castelsardo.

GETTING HERE AND AROUND

Sassari can be reached by plane, ferry, train, bus, or car. The nearest airport is Alghero-Fertilia, about 30 km (19 miles) from Sassari. Inexpensive buses can get you to the center of Sassari. The closest port is Porto Torres, about 20 km (12½ miles) away, connected by ferry to Spain, France, Genoa, and Civitavecchia (Rome). Frequent bus and train services operate between Sassari and Cagliari, Olbia, and Alghero.

VISITOR INFORMATION

CONTACT Sassari. ✉ *Via Sebastiano Satta 13* ☎ *079/2008072* ⊕ *www.turismosassari.it.*

Sights

Duomo

CHURCH | The highly ornate stone Duomo is Sassari's must-see sight. The cathedral, dedicated to St. Nicolas (of Santa Claus inspiration), took more than half a millennium to build: the foundations were laid in the 12th century, and the Spanish colonial–style facade was completed in the 18th. Of particular interest in the plainer interior are the ribbed Gothic vaults, the 14th-century painting of the Madonna del Bosco on the high altar, and the early-19th-century tomb of Placido Benedetto di Savoia, the uncle of united Italy's first king. ✉ *Piazza Duomo 3, Sassari* ☎ *079/233185* 🎫 *Free.*

Restaurants

L'Assassino

$$ | ITALIAN | Get a true taste of regional cuisine at this family-run trattoria in the old town. The menu is not for the squeamish or for vegetarians: horse, donkey, and roasted suckling pig feature prominently, as do typical Sassarese dishes such as *trippa alla parmigiana* (tripe with Parmesan), *lumaconi in rosso* (snails in a rich tomato sauce), and *cordula con piselli* (sheep's intestines with peas). 💲 *Average main: €16* ✉ *Via Pettenadu 19, Sassari* ☎ *079/233463* ⊕ *www.trattoriatipica.sassari.it* ⊗ *Closed Mon. Oct.–Apr.*

Castelsardo

32 km (20 miles) northeast of Sassari.

The seaside citadel of Castelsardo is surmounted by an impressive fortress, which now contains a museum highlighting the basketware for which the town is famous. Wandering the upper town's maze of steep alleys is a delight, as is browsing the numerous shops in the lower town. Good souvenirs include not only woven baskets but also rugs and wrought-iron items. On the road into Castelsardo from the east, note the **Roccia dell'Elefante** (Elephant Rock), which was hollowed out by primitive man to be used as a burial chamber. The local name for this type of structure is *domus de janas* (literally, "fairy house").

GETTING HERE AND AROUND
In summer, a daily bus runs between Alghero Airport and Castelsardo. Tickets can be purchased directly from the driver. Check the ARST bus timetable from Sassari, which operates a service to Castelsardo. The trip takes about an hour. The main bus stop in Castelsardo is located in the central Piazza Pianedda. There is also a stop on the seafront by the beach.

By car, access is from Alghero, heading toward Porto Torres. Follow signs for Sassari onto the SS200, merging onto the SS134. Follow signs for Santa Teresa Gallura—the route takes you along the beautiful coastline.

Santa Teresa Gallura

100 km (62 miles) northeast of Sassari, 65 km (41 miles) northwest of Olbia.

At the northern tip of Sardinia, Santa Teresa Gallura retains the relaxed, carefree air of a former fishing village. Nearby beaches rival those farther down the coast yet somehow aren't as crowded with tourists.

GETTING HERE AND AROUND
Ferry crossings from Bonifacio in Corsica operate regularly, up to four times per day. The trip lasts about 50 minutes.

By car, you can drive from Olbia following the SS125 in the direction of Arzachena-Palau. At the fork in Palau, turn left to Santa Teresa Gallura. Continue for 25 km (16 miles). From Cagliari, follow SS131 to Sassari. Before the city center, exit at Sassari Latte Dolce, heading in the direction of Platamona/Castelsardo, which leads to the scenic coastal road Porto Torres–Santa Teresa.

From Alghero, follow SS291 until Sassari. Continue toward Porto Torres until you reach the northern part of the island.

There are frequent bus connections with Olbia, but there is no train station in Santa Teresa Gallura. The nearest main-line train station is in Olbia.

Hotels

Hotel Canne al Vento
$ | B&B/INN | Family-run Canne al Vento has been a quiet, cheerful haven in town since the late 1950s. **Pros:** abundant and memorable breakfasts; clean and orderly rooms; personal, friendly service. **Cons:** few facilities; on a main road; no elevator for upper-floor rooms. ⑤ *Rooms from: €80 ⊠ Via Nazionale 23, Santa Teresa Gallura ☎ 0789/754219 ⊕ www.hotelcannealvento.com ↘ 22 rooms* ⦿| *Free Breakfast.*

Hotel Corallaro
$$$ | HOTEL | FAMILY | A brief walk from the town center, this hotel occupies a panoramic spot right by the beach and has functional rooms—most of them spacious, a few of them with balconies and sea views. **Pros:** airy rooms with plenty of storage space; welcoming management and staff; steps away from the excellent Rena Bianca beach. **Cons:** steep uphill walk to town center; rooms with sea views and balconies fill up early; attracts

groups. $ *Rooms from: €230* ✉ *Spiaggia Rena Bianca, Santa Teresa Gallura* ☎ *0789/755475* ⊕ *www.hotelcorallaro.it* ⌂ *83 rooms* ◎| *Free Breakfast* ⊘ *Closed late Oct.–early May.*

La Maddalena

45 km (20 miles) northwest of Olbia, 68 km (42 miles) northeast of Castelsardo.

From the port of Palau you can visit the archipelago of La Maddalena, seven granite islands embellished with aromatic scrub and wind-bent pines. The most significant of the handful of sites to see here is Giuseppe Garibaldi's home and tomb. Explore the lively port (also called La Maddalena), then head to one of several picture-postcard coves, the perfect spot for a picnic and to rejuvenate after your journey to the archipelago.

GETTING HERE AND AROUND

The only way to get to this small island is by boat or ferry. From Olbia, take a bus or drive to Palau, then catch the ferry to La Maddalena. During the day, car ferries make the 3-km (2-mile) trip 2–4 times an hour. The town center is right in front of the dock. Local buses are available for accessing the beaches, although the island is best explored by scooter or bike.

 Sights

★ Compendio Garibaldino

HISTORIC HOME | Pilgrims from around the world converge on the Compendio Garibaldino, a complex on Isola Caprera that contains not only the restored home of Giuseppe Garibaldi (1807–82) but also his tomb. The national hero and military leader who laid the groundwork for the first unification of Italy in 1861 lived a simple life as a farmer on the island that he eventually owned. There are guided tours in Italian, and written guides in other languages. You can also buy a

combined ticket for the Compendio and the Memoriale Giuseppe Garibaldi, 4 km (2½ miles) away, a multimedia museum that chronicles the swashbuckling career of the Italian hero. For both, take the ferry to Isola Maddalena and then the bridge to Caprera. Note that visits to the Compendio Garibaldino should always be booked ahead and take place every 15 minutes in groups of up to 15 people. ✉ *7 km (4½ miles) east of Isola Maddalena, Caprera* ☎ *0789/727162 for information, 335/7505401 for booking visits* ⊕ *www.compendiogaribaldino.it* ✉ *€7; €11 combined ticket includes Memoriale Giuseppe Garibaldi* ⊘ *Closed Sun. Nov.–mid-Oct.* ⚲ *Book ahead for Compendio Garibaldino.*

Porto Cervo

35 km (22 miles) southeast of La Maddalena, 30 km (19 miles) north of Olbia.

Sardinia's northeastern coast is fringed with low cliffs, inlets, and small bays. This has become an upscale vacationland, with glossy resorts such as Baia Sardinia and Porto Rotondo just outside the confines of the famed Costa Smeralda. Some of Italy's most expensive hotels are here, and magnificent yachts anchor in the waters of Porto Cervo. Golf courses, yacht clubs, and numerous alfresco restaurants and bars cater to those who want to see and be seen.

All along the coast, carefully tended lush vegetation surrounds vacation villages and discreet villas that have sprung up in eclectic architectural styles best described as "bogus Mediterranean." The trend has been to keep this an enclave of the very rich. Outside the peak season, however, prices dip and the majesty of the natural surroundings shines through, justifying all the hype and the Emerald Coast's fame as one of the truly romantic corners of the Mediterranean.

GETTING HERE AND AROUND

Porto Cervo is accessible by boat, car, taxi, and bus. Buses run regularly from Olbia and Palau.

Whichever airport or port of entry into Sardinia you choose, head to Olbia. By car, follow SS125 north toward Arzachena and Costa Smeralda. After 10 km (6 miles), turn right onto SP73 toward Porto Rotondo/Porto Cervo. Continue on SP94 and turn onto SP59 to Porto Cervo. The trip takes about 30 minutes.

Beaches

The beaches around the Costa Smeralda are some of the most exclusive in Europe, and they don't disappoint—with fine golden sand sheltered by red cliffs and fronting azure waters. Many can only be reached by boat, and there are regular launches from Porto Cervo. Rentals of sun beds and towels are as expensive as you'd expect.

Spiaggia del Principe

BEACH | FAMILY | Among the less developed of the Costa Smeralda's five-star beaches, the Spiaggia del Principe is tucked well away from the crowds, mainly because it is not so readily accessible as some of the others. The rewards, however, are all the greater. Edged by jagged, gold-tinted rocks, the beach has fine white sand and water ranging from emerald to a Caribbean shade of turquoise. Access from the car park is tricky—a ten-minute walk along a rough path (stout sneakers needed)—but a tuk-tuk service is sometimes on hand for a small charge. **Amenities:** food and drink; toilets; parking (fee in summer). **Best for:** swimming; people-watching; walking. ⊠ *Porto Cervo* ✛ *3km east of Cala di Volpe on Via Romazzino and Via delle Mimose.*

Restaurants

I Frati Rossi

$$$ | ITALIAN | In the hills above Porto Cervo, this soothing hideaway—where a sheltered terrace looks out onto a verdant garden—is a great place to take a break from the coast's glossy trappings. Recommended antipasti include *sa cannacca* (dried sausage with pecorino cheese) and octopus salad with potatoes; pappardelle *ai funghi porcini* (with porcini mushrooms) is a great pasta choice; and the grilled fish is an excellent main. **Known for:** terrace seating with garden views; secluded dining; tasty seafood dishes. $ *Average main: €25* ⊠ *Via Paolino Azara, off SP59, Pantogia* ☎ *0789/1876486* ⊕ *www.fratirossi.it* ⊙ *Closed Nov.–early Jan. No dinner Sun. and Mon. early Jan.–Easter. No lunch Mon.*

Hotels

★ Cala di Volpe

$$$$ | RESORT | Long a magnet for the beautiful people, this hyperglamorous Starwood hotel was designed by Jacques Couëlle to resemble an ancient Sardinian fishing village, complete with its own covered bridge; the exterior is complemented by a rustic-elegant interior with beamed ceilings, terra-cotta floors, Sardinian arts and crafts, and porticoes overlooking the Cala di Volpe Bay. There's an Olympic-size saltwater pool and boat service to a private beach. **Pros:** professional staff; stunning architecture and grounds; luxurious ambience. **Cons:** some rooms disappoint; car necessary; astronomical rates for room, additional amenities, drinks, and meals. $ *Rooms from: €1240* ⊠ *Cala di Volpe, Porto Cervo* ☎ *0789/976111* ⊕ *www.caladivolpe.com* ⊙ *Closed early Oct.–mid-May* 🛏 *121 rooms* ❍ *Free Breakfast.*

Cervo Hotel, Costa Smeralda Resort

$$$$ | HOTEL | Designed in 1962 by the architect Luigi Vietti, this Starwood property—next to the busy piazzetta in the car-free heart of Porto Cervo—features low Mediterranean buildings with Spanish tile roofs surrounding a large pool and garden and spacious, white adobe rooms, most with a terrace, that have colorfully painted wood furniture and slip-covered sofas. **Pros:** shuttle service to private beach; open year-round; prime central location. **Cons:** some rooms and bathrooms are small; no nearby beach; very expensive rates and extras. $ *Rooms from: €460* ⊠ *Waterfront, Porto Cervo* ☎ *0789/931111* ⊕ *www.hotelcervocostasmeralda.com* ⇨ *80 rooms* ⦿⃝ *Free Breakfast.*

Nibaru

$$$ | HOTEL | Amid lush gardens on a secluded inlet, this complex of pinkish-red brick buildings with tiled roofs has the feel of a small resort—albeit one with fewer amenities and lower prices than most of the Costa Smeralda's full-scale resorts. **Pros:** nice pool; courteous staff; close to good beaches. **Cons:** a car is necessary; no restaurant; no sea view. $ *Rooms from: €210* ⊠ *Località Cala di Volpe, Porto Cervo* ☎ *0789/1876628* ⊕ *www.hotelnibaru.it* ⊗ *Closed Oct.–Apr.* ⇨ *58 rooms* ⦿⃝ *Free Breakfast.*

⚙ Activities

BOATING AND SAILING

Yacht Club Costa Smeralda

SAILING | The Aga Khan IV founded this yacht club with some local associates in 1967 in order to promote nautical activities. The club provides use of its pool, restaurant, bar, and guest rooms to those with memberships at associated yacht clubs. Watch for regattas from June to September, and check out the YCCS Sailing School, which organizes courses on dinghies and cabin cruisers. ⊠ *Via della Marina, Porto Cervo* ☎ *0789/902200* ⊕ *www.yccs.it.*

GOLF

Pevero Golf Course

GOLF | Designed by Robert Trent Jones Sr. and opened in 1972, Pevero is a world-class course with some of Europe's most beautiful fairways. Stretching nearly 6½ km (4 miles) between the Gulf of Pevero and Cala di Volpe (Bay of Foxes), it provides challenging playing conditions that incorporate 70 bunkers, several rock formations, and vegetation. The dress code is formal in the upscale club house. Note that the course and club house are closed on Monday and Tuesday between November and February. ⊠ *Località Cala di Volpe 20, Porto Cervo* ☎ *0789/958046* ⊕ *www.peverogolfclub.com* ⎘ *€90–€145, depending on season; €50 for golf cart* ⛳ *18 holes, 6700 yards, par 72.*

Olbia

30 km (19 miles) south of Porto Cervo.

Amid the resorts of Sardinia's northeastern coast, Olbia, a town of about 60,000, is a lively little seaport and port of call for mainland ferries at the head of a long, wide bay.

GETTING HERE AND AROUND

The main airport, Olbia–Costa Smeralda, is only 1½ km (1 mile) from the town center. Inexpensive city buses and taxis are available outside the terminal. Trains operate between Olbia and Cagliari and take about four hours.

The Olbia–Isola Bianca harbor provides daily connections with the Italian mainland, less than 300 km (186 miles) away. Regular ferries arrive from Genoa, Piombino, Civitavecchia (Rome), and Livorno. Most ferries take 6–10 hours.

VISITOR INFORMATION

CONTACT Olbia. ⊠ *Municipio, Via Dante 1, at Corso Umberto I, Olbia* ☎ *0789/52206* ⊕ *www.helloolbia.com.*

Sights

Basilica San Simplicio

CHURCH | Olbia's little basilica, a short walk from the main Corso Umberto I, is the city's unmissable sight. The simple granite structure dates from the 11th century, part of the great Pisan church-building program, using pillars and columns recycled from Roman buildings. The basilica has a bare, somewhat somber interior; its three naves are separated by a series of Romanesque arches, and fragments of frescoes are visible behind the altar. ■TIP➔ **Recent renovations of the monument have unearthed the remains of a Greek and Roman necropolis, which is now open to the public (the entrance is in the car park beneath the piazza).** ✉ *Piazza San Simplicio, Olbia* ☏ *345/6328150* ⊕ *www. museumtempioampurias.it.*

Restaurants

Il Gambero

$$ | ITALIAN | This backstreet trattoria has a strong rustic flavor, its two rooms adorned with brass cooking pots, colorful embroideries, old photographs, and agricultural knickknacks. The menu, too, has a local focus and might include tagliolini pasta with squid ink, artichokes, and mullet roe or sliced tuna with a sesame crust and pistachios. **Known for:** informal but discreet service; simple, rustic decor; fresh, local meat and seafood dishes. ⑤ *Average main: €17* ✉ *Via Lamarmora 6, Olbia* ☏ *0789/23874* ⊕ *ristorante-il-gambero-seafood-restaurant.business.site* ⊘ *Closed Mon.*

Hotels

La Locanda del Conte Mameli

$$ | HOTEL | Housed in a remodeled palazzo built at the end of the 19th century for the count after which it is named, this hotel occupies a quiet location on a cobbled backstreet just a few steps from Corso Umberto. **Pros:** central but quiet location; small hotel with personal service; antique furnishings. **Cons:** some rooms are slightly cramped and gloomy; tricky to access by car; no parking. ⑤ *Rooms from: €139* ✉ *Via delle Terme 8, Olbia* ☏ *0789/23008* ⊕ *www.lalocandadelcontemameli.com* ⇆ *11 rooms* ⦿ *Free Breakfast.*

Petra Segreta Resort and Spa

$$$$ | HOTEL | Sea and mountain views, top-quality cuisine, and chic and spacious guest rooms are the main draws at this romantic boutique hotel outside the picturesque village of San Pantaleo. **Pros:** two good restaurants; tranquil mountainside setting with spectacular views; blend of traditional surroundings and modern amenities. **Cons:** remote and isolated; three-night minimum stay July–Aug.; not suitable for families. ⑤ *Rooms from: €378* ✉ *Via Buddeu, San Pantaleo* ☏ *0789/1876441* ⊕ *www.petrasegretaresort.com* ⇆ *25 rooms* ⦿ *Free Breakfast* ⊘ *Closed Nov.–Apr.*

Index

Photo Credits

Fodor's ESSENTIAL ITALY

Publisher: Stephen Horowitz, *General Manager*

Editorial: Douglas Stallings, *Editorial Director*; Jill Fergus, Amanda Sadlowski, Caroline Trefler, *Senior Editors*; Kayla Becker, Alexis Kelly, *Editors;* Angelique Kennedy-Chavannes, *Assistant Editor*

Design: Tina Malaney, *Director of Design and Production*; Jessica Gonzalez, *Graphic Designer*

Production: Jennifer DePrima, *Editorial Production Manager*; Elyse Rozelle, *Senior Production Editor*; Monica White, *Production Editor*

Maps: Rebecca Baer, *Senior Map Editor*; David Lindroth, Mark Stroud (Moon Street Cartography), *Cartographers*

Photography: Viviane Teles, *Senior Photo Editor*; Namrata Aggarwal, Payal Gupta, Ashok Kumar, *Photo Editors*; Rebecca Rimmer, *Photo Production Associate*; Eddie Aldrete, *Photo Production Intern*

Business and Operations: Chuck Hoover, Chief *Marketing Officer*; Robert Ames, *Group General Manager*; Devin Duckworth, *Director of Print Publishing*

Public Relations and Marketing: Joe Ewaskiw, *Senior Director of Communications & Public Relations*

Fodors.com: Jeremy Tarr, *Editorial Director*; Rachael Levitt, *Managing Editor*

Technology: Jon Atkinson, *Director of Technology*; Rudresh Teotia, *Lead Developer*; Jacob Ashpis, *Content Operations Manager*

Writers: Robert Andrews, Nick Bruno, Liz Humphreys, Laura Itzkowitz, Fergal Kavanagh, Patricia Rucidlo, Liz Shemaria

Editor: Jill Fergus

Production Editor: Monica White

4th Edition

ISBN 978-1-64097-413-5

ISSN 2476-0692

SPECIAL SALES
This book is available at special discounts for bulk purchases for sales promotions or premiums. For more information, e-mail SpecialMarkets@fodors.com.

PRINTED IN THE UNITED STATES OF AMERICA

10 9 8 7 6 5 4 3 2 1

About Our Writers

Born of Sicilian stock, **Robert Andrews** has been living and working in various parts of Italy for most of his adult life. He has written articles and guidebooks on this multifaceted peninsula, and provides travel consultancy services as well as leading individual and small-group tours in Sicily and Sardinia. For this edition, Robert updated the Sardinia chapter.

Nick Bruno is an Italy specialist and frequent Fodor's contributor. As well as authoring and updating books and features, he makes radio packages for the BBC. A lifelong interest in history and Italian language has led to a project researching his paternal Italian family during the Il Ventennio Fascista period. Nick updated the Experience, Veneto and Friuli-Venezia Giulia, Naples and Campania, and Puglia, Basilicata and Calabria chapters. Follow him on Instagram and Twitter @nickjgbruno and barbruno.com.

Liz Humphreys is a transplant to Europe from New York City, where she spent a decade in editorial positions for media companies including Condé Nast and Time Inc. Since then she's written and edited for publications including *Condé Nast Traveler*, *Michelin Green Guides*, *Time Out*, *Forbes Travel*, and *Rough Guides*. Liz updated The Dolomites, Umbria and the Marches, and Venice chapters. Follow Liz on Instagram @winederlust_wanderings.

Laura Itzkowitz is a freelance writer and editor based in Rome with an MFA in creative writing and a passion for covering travel, arts and culture, lifestyle, design, food and wine. Her writing has appeared in *Travel +*

Leisure, *Architectural Digest*, *Vogue*, *GQ*, *Departures*, *AFAR*, and others. Laura updated the Rome and Side Trips from Rome chapters. Follow her on Instagram and Twitter @lauraitzkowitz.

Fergal Kavanagh travels extensively throughout Italy with his Tune Into English Roadshow, where he teaches English through pop music (www.tuneintoenglish.com). In his twenty-five years in the country there is hardly a town square he has not passed through. He updated Travel Smart and Sicily.

Patricia Rucidlo holds master's degrees in Italian Renaissance history and art history. She is also a licensed tour guide in Florence and also works in Lucca. When she's not extolling the virtues of a Pontormo masterpiece or angrily defending the Medici, you can find her leading food and wine tours in Florence and environs. Patricia updated the chapters of Florence, Tuscany, Piedmont and the Valle D'Aosta, and the Italian Riviera chapters.

Liz Shemaria is an award-winning journalist and third-generation Northern Californian who has trekked solo in Himalaya and interviewed artists in military-ruled Burma. Liz is a founding editor at Hidden Compass and has contributed to more than a dozen publications and organizations including Human Rights Watch, BBC Travel, *AFAR*, and Roads & Kingdoms. Liz lives in Italy and updated the Milan, Lombardy, and the Lakes and Emilia-Romagna chapters. Follow her on Instagram @lizshemaria.